ARSENAL

A Complete Record   1886-1992

ARSENAL

A Complete Record   1886-1992

FRED OLLIER

BREEDON
BOOKS
SPORT

First published in Great Britain by
The Breedon Books Publishing Company Limited
44 Friar Gate, Derby, DE1 1DA.
1992

ISBN 1 873626 12 6

Printed by The Bath Press — Bath and London.
Jacket printed by BDC Printing Services Limited, Derby.

CONTENTS

Acknowledgements

In particular I would like to thank Bernard Chaplin and Leonard Evans for giving me access to their Arsenal collections, and Maurice Cooper, who constantly provides me with 'treasures' for my own collection. Roger Desouches, John Burt, Peter Emmins and Stuart Myers, Gary Chalk and Stephen McGarrigle have also been helpful when called upon, and the continued co-operation by the staffs at the Football League offices at Lytham St Annes and the British Newspaper Library at Colindale is appreciated. Again, my thanks to my wife for her continued support and considerable practical assistance with the proof-reading of the manuscript.

The Publishers also acknowledge use of information contained in Simon Inglis' book *The Football Grounds of England and Wales* (Collins-Willow).

Photographic Credits

Photographs have been supplied by Colorsport, Empics of Nottingham, Illustrated London News Picture Library, North West Counties Press and The Press Association.

Introduction

Since this work was last published two years ago, Arsenal have added yet another League Championship to their list of honours, and it affords an appropriate opportunity to bring the book up to date.

As previously mentioned, my research on Arsenal Football Club is continuous, the result of which, more information has come to light. A few additional friendly matches have been discovered, the most important of which are three games played on tour in Sweden at the end of the 1930-31 season, which I believe are not on record at the club. Much information on the births and deaths of past players has been found, and in some cases the details have kindly been provided by relatives of the players.

On this aspect, it is particularly sad to have to record the more recent passing of Joe Hulme, Cliff Bastin, and Jack Kelsey — three names synonymous with Arsenal Football Club.

The Who's Who section, therefore, has been considerably updated, and the statistics throughout are up to and including the last league match of the 1991-2 season.

In order to maintain this work as the most accurate and comprehensive available on Arsenal Football Club, the research still goes on, and I would ask anybody who can provide further information, especially with regard to births and deaths, to contact me through Breedon Books.

Fred Ollier
Crewe
May 1992

The Arsenal Story

ARSENAL Football Club, as it is known today, was originally formed as Dial Square FC at a meeting held at the Prince of Wales public house at Plumstead in October 1886. The club seems to have owed its birth to a group of Association Football enthusiasts from the north, mainly David Danskin, a Scotsman from Kirkcaldy; Fred Beardsley, who had played in goal for Nottingham Forest; Richard Pearce, from Bolton, and Elijah Watkins, who was the club's first secretary. They had all come south to work in the munitions factory and they named the club Dial Square, after the workshop in which they were employed in Woolwich Arsenal.

The first match was a 6-0 victory over Eastern Wanderers, at Millwall in December 1886. The team on that occasion was: Beardsley; Danskin, Porteous, Gregory, Bee, Wolfe, Smith, Moy, Whitehead, Morris, Duggan.

Later in December 1886, a further meeting was held, this time at the Royal Oak in Woolwich where it was decided to change the club's name to Royal Arsenal. The first match under that name took place on Plumstead Common on 8 January 1887, against Erith. The Arsenal line-up was: Beardsley; Danskin, Porteous, Gregory, Price, Wells, Smith, Moy, Whitehead, Crighton, Bee.

For their second season (1887-8), Arsenal rented the Sportsman Ground on Plumstead Marshes to play their fixtures and, entering the London Senior Cup for the first time, they were beaten by Barnes in the second round.

With increasing support the club rented the Manor Ground for the following season, during which they were beaten by Clapton in the semi-final of the London Cup.

In 1889-90, Arsenal appeared in the FA Cup for the first time and, after reaching the last of the qualifying rounds, they were beaten 5-1 at home by Swifts. In the London Senior Cup Final they lost by a single goal to Old Westminsters but the Gunners did achieve their first successes this season, winning the London Charity Cup, the Kent Senior Cup and the Kent Junior Cup.

The 1890-91 season saw Royal Arsenal operating from yet another venue, the Invicta Ground in Plumstead, which was let to the club at a modest rent. In addition to the major Cup competitions, a number of senior friendly matches were still the main ingredient of the club's fixture list. Arsenal were excused the qualifying rounds of the FA Cup this season and, in the first round proper, they were narrowly beaten at home by Derby County. Knocked out of the London Charity Cup at the semi-final stage by Old Carthusians, Arsenal were successful in winning the London Senior Cup, with a crushing 6-0 victory over St Bartholomew's Hospital at Kennington Oval.

Increased playing success prompted the club committee, at a meeting held at the Windsor Castle Music Hall in the summer, to overwhelmingly support founder-member John Humble's motion to adopt professionalism. The move shocked and offended the football authorities in the south and presented Arsenal with difficulties. Expelled from the London FA, barred from the southern cup competitions and boycotted by most of the clubs in the south, Arsenal had to arrange fixtures with the northern and midland professional clubs. This arrangement continued throughout 1891-2 and 1892-3, with Arsenal showing reasonable success against an overall better standard of opposition, although in the FA Cup they were heavily beaten in the first round proper in both of the seasons.

Woolwich Arsenal pictured in 1895. Back row (left to right): James Boyle, Joe Powell, Harry Storer, Jock Caldwell, Hollis (trainer). Middle row: Fred Davis, Caesar Jenkyns, Allen Ward. Front row: Sam Mills, Charlie Hare, Bob Buchanan, Pat O'Brien, Peter Mortimer.

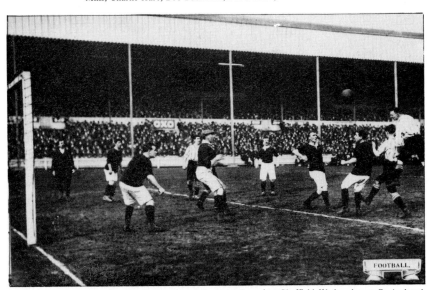

Action from Woolwich Arsenal's FA Cup semi-final match against Sheffield Wednesday at St Andrew's, Birmingham, in March 1907. Wednesday won 3-1 and went on to beat Everton in the Final at the Crystal Palace. Arsenal players (left to right) are Jimmy Sharp, Archie Gray, Jim Ashcroft, Roddy McEachrane, Tom Hynds and Jim Bigden.

9

Further advancement was necessary and the close season of 1893 was quite eventful. The club was formed into a limited company which carried the name of Woolwich Arsenal Football & Athletic Company Limited, although the Football League still referred to them as Royal Arsenal until around 1896. Faced with an increase in rent for the Invicta Ground, they went back to the Manor Ground which they purchased outright and which became their home for the next 20 years until the move to Highbury in 1913. Finally, Arsenal made a successful application for a place in the Second Division of the Football League.

They made a steady start in League football. In the first season, 1893-4, they finished in ninth place and for the first decade, results and final placing were uniformly satisfactory. One significant feature of 1896-7, apart from the fact that it was the club's lowest position (tenth) in Division Two to date, was that they lost 8-0 at Loughborough Town in December, a result which is still the club's heaviest defeat. In 1897-8, Arsenal appointed T.B.Mitchell of Blackburn Rovers as their first professional manager. He was replaced 12 months later by George Elcoat of Stockton, who in turn remained only for one season. Harry Bradshaw became the third manager in as many seasons when he joined Arsenal in 1899-1900, but he was to guide the club into the First Division within five years.

Bradshaw faced initial difficulties, but not on the field of play. The Boer War had broken out in 1899 and, apart from many men serving overseas with the army, many others were heavily engaged on munition work and there was very little time for watching football. Attendances inevitably declined and the financial position became critical. Money was raised by bazaars and even an archery tournament was held which produced £1,200 for the club. The danger was averted, at least for the time being, and Bradshaw was able to start building a successful side. The League position improved gradually each season until promotion was eventually won in 1903-04, when Arsenal finished runners-up, a point behind Preston North End.

Arsenal started in the First Division with a new manager, Phil Kelso taking over from Harry Bradshaw who surprisingly left to join Fulham. The Gunners proved worthy of Division One status and, although no great League heights were scaled, the results and final placings were creditable. In 1906 they reached the FA Cup semi-final for the first time but were beaten by Newcastle United. A year later they were semi-finalists again, this time only to be beaten by Sheffield Wednesday, who went on to win the Cup.

As soon as playing fortunes started to decline, the financial problems returned. Plumstead was not an ideal site and transport from the city was poor, whilst other London clubs had now joined the League and added to the competition for support. Manager Phil Kelso left in 1908, also for Fulham, and he was succeeded by George Morrell, whose first task was to sell a number of the star players to help the club to survive. In 1909-10, the financial situation was grave and, to make matters worse, relegation threatened.

Arsenal were kept alive by the intervention of Henry Norris, the chairman of Fulham and a very influential man who was later knighted. Norris' initial ideas were to take over Arsenal, amalgamate with Fulham and operate from Craven Cottage or, alternatively, arrange for Arsenal to share Craven Cottage with Fulham. The League opposed both proposals, the Arsenal slide continued and, in 1912-13, the Gunners were relegated with one of the worst-ever playing records in the League. Norris recognised an even greater need for a move from Plumstead and, after a long search, he found an easily accessible site at Highbury. He used his influence to overcome all objections and Woolwich Arsenal returned to Second Division football in 1913-14 with a move to a new ground.

The club made an encouraging start in their new surroundings at Highbury and,

10

Arsenal centre-forward Donald Cock lunges after the ball as Tottenham's Arthur Grimsdell challenges during the North London derby game at Highbury on the opening day of the 1925-6 season. This was the first season of the present offside rule, during which Herbert Chapman devised the 'stopper' centre-half system. It proved an immediate success for Arsenal who recovered from a poor start to finish League Championship runners-up.

A scramble around the Arsenal goalmouth during the 1930 FA Cup Final against Huddersfield Town at Wembley.

in the first two seasons, promotion just eluded them. It was during this period that 'Woolwich' was dropped from the title and the club became known as simply 'Arsenal FC'. The move to Highbury and the provision of new playing facilities, however, had been made at great expense and when League football officially closed down for World War One, the club were again in financial difficulty.

By the time regular League football started again in 1919-20, Arsenal were back in the First Division. The Football League had decided to increase Division One by two clubs and Chelsea and Tottenham Hotspur, the bottom clubs in 1914-15, were the obvious choices to take those places. But, thanks to some behind-the-scenes lobbying of the League clubs and the Management Committee by Sir Henry Norris, it was Arsenal (who had finished fifth in Division Two in the last pre-war season) and not Tottenham Hotspur, who were elected along with Chelsea.

Leslie Knighton, who had managed Huddersfield Town and Manchester City, was appointed as Arsenal's new manager but it was Norris who dictated the policies and fully controlled the club. The first six seasons after the resumption of peacetime football brought Arsenal only moderate success and, indeed, there were occasions when relegation was a danger. Norris, obviously dissatisfied with the lack of success, advertised for a new manager in the summer of 1925. It was then that Arsenal obtained the services of Herbert Chapman, who had built up a magnificent reputation with Huddersfield Town.

The arrival of Chapman marked the rebirth of the Arsenal club and its present status as a world-renowned football club dates from 1925. In Chapman's first season, Arsenal reached the quarter-final of the FA Cup and were runners-up in the First Division. Charlie Buchan, one of Chapman's first signings, was captain and Jimmy Brain broke the club's individual scoring record with 34 League goals. A year later, the Gunners — the nickname was now in general use — reached the FA Cup Final for the first time and, although defeated by Cardiff City, it was another landmark in their history. The FA Cup semi-final was reached again the following season but Arsenal lost to Blackburn Rovers at Leicester. The 1928-9 season saw the club pay the first of several record-breaking transfer fees when centre-forward David Jack came from Bolton Wanderers for £10,890.

In 1929-30, with Alex James and Cliff Bastin now in the side, Arsenal won their first major trophy, beating Huddersfield Town 2-0 in the FA Cup Final at Wembley. The triumph signalled the start of the greatest period in the Gunners' history and for the next decade they were the envy of the football world.

In the following season, not only did Arsenal take the First Division title for the first time, they were also the first southern club to win the title. In doing so they created what was then a record for the highest number of First Division points (66). It was a magnificent season and the Reserves carried off their fifth consecutive London Combination championship under Chapman and also won the London FA Challenge Cup. The 1931-2 season was also a remarkable one. Arsenal did splendidly without winning anything except the FA Charity Shield. For a long time they looked like winning the double but both honours were just out of their reach — they finished second in the League, two points behind Everton, and lost the FA Cup Final against Newcastle United to the most controversial goal in the history of the competition. The following season the winning of their second League Championship was marred only by the sensational FA Cup defeat at Third Division Walsall. One other interesting point from that 1932-3 season — the now-famous red shirts with white sleeves were worn for the first time.

In January 1934, Herbert Chapman died after a short illness. His services to the club are beyond estimation and the period 1925-1934 will always be remembered as 'the Chapman era' although, happily, the spell of success did not end with the great manager's death. Despite this sad blow and its effect on everybody at Highbury,

12

Skipper Joe Mercer receives the FA Cup from King George VI after Arsenal's victory over Liverpool in the 1950 Final.

Arsenal went on to win the Championship for the second year in succession.

George Allison, one of the club's directors, was appointed secretary-manager and in 1934-5, the League Championship was won for the third successive year.

In 1935-6, Arsenal won the FA Cup for the second time when they beat Sheffield United 1-0 at Wembley and, after a season in which no major honours were gained, Arsenal became League Champions again in 1937-8 — for the fifth time in eight seasons. Before the start of 1938-9 season, the Gunners broke the British transfer record by paying £14,000 for Bryn Jones from Wolverhampton Wanderers. Alas, the Welshman was never able to justify such a large fee and, after seven years of League football had been lost because of World War Two, his chance had gone. During the war Arsenal, competing in the 'makeshift' regional leagues, won a few trophies but by the time League football resumed, they had lost the services of such grand players as Hapgood, Crayston, Drake and Kirchen, mainly through serious injuries.

It is not surprising that Arsenal did not have a successful season in 1946-7. Indeed, at one stage relegation was a serious threat. Having seen a difficult season through, George Allison retired in the summer of 1947 and the club appointed his assistant, Tom Whittaker as manager. In Whittaker's first season Arsenal won the League Championship for the sixth time and, two seasons later, the FA Cup returned to Highbury when two brilliant goals by Reg Lewis enabled the Gunners to beat Liverpool 2-0 at Wembley. In 1951-2, Arsenal came close to winning the League and FA Cup double but, as had been the case 20 years earlier, both trophies eluded them in the end. In the League they finished third and it was Newcastle United who again denied them the FA Cup, this time after the Gunners had put up a tremendous ten-man performance after losing Barnes through injury. The following season the club again won the League Championship but only by the narrowest

13

of mathematical margins, taking the title on goal-average over Preston North End.

The 1953 title win was to prove Arsenal's last major honour for 17 years. The team was getting old and, even with unlimited resources, Whittaker found difficulty in buying the replacements he needed. Under great stress, Tom Whittaker died in October 1956. His total contribution to Arsenal was as great as that of Herbert Chapman and, in terms of material success, he had emulated both Chapman and Allison. Whittaker had been only Arsenal's third manager in 30 years but they were to have four in the course of the next decade, in an attempt to regain the glories of the past. The first two, Jack Crayston and George Swindin, both former players with the club, managed competently but without the extra degree of excellence required to produce consistently successful teams. Crayston resigned after less than two years in charge and during a four-year reign (1958-1962), Swindin was often dogged by injuries to his key players. The highest League position achieved during that period was third in 1958-9, Swindin's first season as manager, and the first team did win a trophy that season — the Southern Floodlight Challenge Cup. In 1962, Arsenal broke with tradition and for the first time in years appointed a manager from outside the club. Billy Wright, the former Wolves and England captain, had excellent qualifications as a player but his lack of managerial experience showed. Nevertheless Wright's four-year period at Highbury was not all failure and many foundations were laid for the successes to come.

The promotion of Bertie Mee, the club's physiotherapist and trainer, was similar to that of Tom Whittaker some years before and had the same effect in terms of success. Mee's strength lay in his ability to manage and motivate men and, allied to the first-class coaching of Dave Sexton and then Don Howe, he soon restored the Gunners' challenge for honours. In only their second season in the competition, Arsenal reached the Football League Cup Final at Wembley in 1968 but were beaten by a controversial goal in an untidy match against Leeds United. The following

Swindon Town's Roger Smart nets a 34th-minute goal against Arsenal in the 1969 League Cup Final. Peter Simpson is the Gunners' player on the ground. The Third Division club scored a sensational victory over their First Division opponents.

14

year the Gunners again reached the League Cup Final, but again they failed to carry off the trophy. With half of their team having gone down with a virus infection only a week before, and on a pitch badly damaged by having staged too many previous events, Arsenal were humiliated by talented Third Division Swindon Town, who deserved their surprising 3-1 victory in extra-time.

In 1969-70, Arsenal ended their 17-year wait for a major trophy by overcoming a first-leg deficit to beat Anderlecht of Belgium on a 4-3 aggregate in the European Fairs Cup Final. Twelve months later came the greatest achievement in the club's history. Bertie Mee managed to complete what both Chapman and Whittaker had gone so close to accomplishing in the past — the winning of the League and FA Cup double. The quality of the team was highlighted by the fact that Arsenal came from eight points behind to finish one point ahead of Leeds United in the First Division; and they recovered from being a goal down in extra-time to beat Liverpool in the FA Cup.

After such achievements, anything was always likely to be an anti-climax. The following season Arsenal were FA Cup Finalists again, but were beaten by Leeds United, and in 1972-3 they were runners-up in the League to Liverpool and reached the FA Cup semi-finals. The famous double team had broken up and Mee, finding increasing pressure in trying to maintain the high standards he had previously achieved, announced his retirement at the end of the 1975-6 season.

Arsenal brought Terry Neill back to Highbury as manager. He began by paying a record transfer fee — £333,333 for Malcolm Macdonald from Newcastle United — and set about putting Arsenal on the road to success again with some sweeping changes in the playing staff. By the end of his first season the Gunners had improved to eighth position in the League. However, it was not until coach Don Howe also returned to Arsenal, as partner to Neill, that the club began to mount a serious challenge for honours. In 1977-8 the Gunners were beaten by Liverpool in the League Cup semi-final but went one better in the FA Cup, reaching Wembley before a disappointing performance saw them lose 1-0 to Ipswich Town. A year later Arsenal were back at Wembley again, this time winning the FA Cup for the fifth time

Eddie Kelly scores the only goal of the Gunners' penultimate League game of 1970-71, firing the ball past Stoke's Gordon Banks before 55,000 fans at Highbury. Victory over the Potters left only Spurs barring Arsenal's path on the first leg of the double.

Frank Stapleton heads Arsenal's second goal against Manchester United in the 1979 FA Cup Final.

in their history in an exciting finish against Manchester United. The following season the Gunners reached their third successive FA Cup Final — their 11th in all — and also went through to the European Cup-winners' Cup Final. In the space of five days in May they lost both of them. Arsenal went down 1-0 unexpectedly to West Ham in the FA Cup and, after 120 minutes had failed to produce a goal in the Cup-winners' Cup Final in Brussels, the Gunners lost 5-4 on penalty kicks to Valencia of Spain. In the seasons that followed, Neill had to face the loss of some of his top-class players and his ventures into the transfer market to find replacements were not always successful. In 1982-3 the Gunners reached the semi-finals of both the League Cup and the FA Cup but lost both ties and the team did not seem to be able to fulfil the promise which they often showed. Neill came under considerable pressure and, when the Gunners were humiliatingly beaten at home in the Milk Cup by Walsall in November 1983, the manager was sacked within a month.

Don Howe was appointed 'caretaker' manager and his position as manager confirmed before the end of the season. His two seasons in charge, however, followed the pattern of the previous years — satisfactory but not outstanding. Arsenal nominated 1985-6 as the club's centenary season but it ended in managerial turmoil. Impatient for success, the directors let it be known that they would be interested in appointing Terry Venables as manager if his release from Barcelona could be obtained. It was intolerable for Don Howe to work under such circumstances and in March 1986 he asked to be released from his contract. Chief scout Steve Burtenshaw saw out the remainder of the season in charge of the team.

Arsenal's centenary celebrations continued with a new manager and it was another former player, George Graham, a success as manager of Millwall, who took up the reins. In his first season Graham brought fresh honours to Highbury in the shape of the Littlewoods Challenge Cup. His young team beat Liverpool 2-1 in the Final after being a goal down. In 1987-8 the Gunners again reached the Littlewoods Final but suffered the disappointment of losing to Luton Town. One bright spot, however, was the promising juniors who lifted the FA Youth Cup.

The winning of two minor trophies in the early part of the following season was a prelude to the momentous achievement, when, in the most dramatic finale

The unseemly brawl against Manchester United that cost Arsenal two points in 1990-91.

The Gunners with the League Championship trophy in May 1991.

in the League's history, victory over Liverpool brought the Championship back to Highbury for the first time in 18 years.

Much was expected of Arsenal, therefore, in 1989-90, but a lack of consistency throughout and a particular mid-season slump, ended with a disappointing fourth place.

The following season, with a number of staff changes, including the introduction of David Seaman and the Swedish Anders Limpar, the consistency returned and despite having two points deducted, the Gunners, in impressive style, regained the League Championship.

The promise of further success in 1991-2 was not fulfilled, however, when the return to European Cup football ended in failure to qualify for the final stages, whilst in the League, the club found the same difficulties as before in retaining the Championship and had to settle for fourth place.

Arsenal's Homes

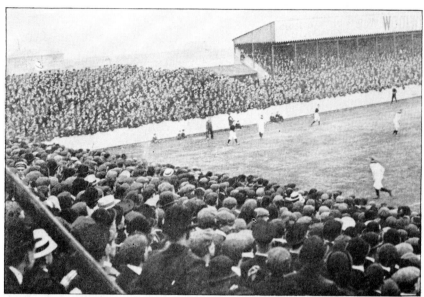

The Manor Ground, Plumstead, packed with 20,000 spectators for the opening game of the 1905-06 season. After a goalless first half, Arsenal beat Liverpool 3-1 with goals from Coleman, Satterthwaite and Blair.

IN their initial season, when the club was reorganised under the name of Royal Arsenal, the Gunners began playing their 'home' matches on Plumstead Common, which still exists today.

As the club had started so well, the members felt that a more private home was appropriate and for the 1887-8 season they chose to rent the Sportsman Ground on the edge of Plumstead Marshes, a ground which was part of the property of a local pig-breeder, Mr Walton. The pitch there had a tendancy to become waterlogged.

After one year Arsenal moved again, this time to the nearby Manor Field which they called the Manor Ground and which was owned by a Mr Cavey. The ground had to be roped off and wagons, borrowed from the nearby barracks, had to be brought in for spectators when the size of the crowd warranted it. The players changed in the Railway Tavern close by. Arsenal used this ground for two seasons.

In 1890-91 the club moved to a more substantial home a few hundred yards away at the Invicta Ground in Plumstead. It belonged to George Weaver, of the Weaver Mineral Water Company, and the main entrance was in High Street, close to Plumstead Railway Station with an entrance for carriages at Butcher's Lane. On the south side, the ground had a stand which housed about 1,500 people and on part of the west side there were concrete terraces to hold around 3,000. There are still traces of the terracing in some of the gardens in Hector Street. The playing area was 130 yards by 90 yards. Arsenal played there between 1890 and 1893, during which time the club turned professional. At first, Weaver charged a rent of £200 a year but, on learning of the club's election to the Football League in 1893, he raised the amount to an extortionate £350 plus tax. Woolwich Arsenal decided to seek alternative accommodation.

A limited company was formed in 1893 and it was decided to buy the Manor Field, where the club had played before moving to the Invicta Ground. Money was raised and 13½ acres of land was purchased from Mr Cavey for £4,000. Just over five acres were developed for the football ground, a large iron stand was erected to house 2,000 and, including the terraces, the ground accommodated 20,000. Until the banking could be raised properly, military wagons were again brought in as viewing platforms. Supporters had worked hard throughout the summer, helping to prepare the ground in time for Woolwich Arsenal's first Football League fixture in September 1893. The Manor Ground continued as the club's headquarters for 20 years until the move to Highbury in 1913. The ground was eventually taken over by the War Office.

Plumstead had not been an ideal site. Access by public transport from the city centre was difficult and support in the area was poor. The survival of Woolwich Arsenal Football Club was due to the intervention of Henry Norris, a wealthy estate agent and property developer and a director of Fulham FC. He was responsible for the move to North London, for the purchase of the site and the establishment of the club at Highbury. Objections to yet another football club in the area came from Tottenham Hotspur and Clapton Orient, Islington Borough Council and local residents. They were all overcome by the astute and influential Norris.

The new ground was situated on playing fields belonging to the St John's College of Divinity. It cost Arsenal £20,000 for only a 21-year lease, negotiated with the Ecclesiastical Commissioners on condition that the club did not to play home matches on Good Friday or Christmas Day. The site had two main advantages — it was easily accessible from the city centre and was adjacent to Gillespie Road underground station. The new stadium, which was designed by Archibald Leitch, had one main stand on the east side and three large banks of open terracing. The two-tier stand, which housed 9,000, had an unusual multi-span roof in which the individual letters of the word 'Arsenal' were painted on each gable front. The banking had to be raised considerably and the pitch itself raised 11ft at one end and lowered 5ft at the other. Construction work was delayed by bad weather and when the ground opened for the first match of the 1913-14 season, it was far from complete and the directors deferred the use of the stand until the next home game. Conditions improved by the end of the year and the Arsenal club settled into its new surroundings.

After World War One, Highbury became a sporting focal point in the capital and in March 1920 the ground staged its first international match. In March 1923 it became the first English ground to host a national team from a foreign country when Belgium were England's opponents. Around 1925 the ground was purchased outright for £64,000 and Norris also persuaded the Commissioners to drop the prohibition of games on Good Friday and Christmas Day.

The redevelopment of Highbury began in 1931 with increased banking at the North End. The following summer work began on a new West Stand. Designed by architect Claude Waterlow Ferrier, the most architecturally advanced grandstand ever seen in this country was erected on the side of the ground which had previously been uncovered banking. The double-decker stand, costing £50,000, had seats for 4,000, plus standing room for 17,000, and was opened in December 1932. Other significant changes around this time were made by manager Herbert Chapman. He persuaded London Transport to change the name of Gillespie Road underground station to 'Arsenal' and the ground's name itself was changed from Highbury to 'Arsenal Stadium'. Chapman also had a 12ft-diameter 45-minute clock erected on top of the North Bank and when the FA objected, its markings were changed to that of a standard timepiece. In 1935, when the North Bank was covered, the clock was transferred to the opposite end, thereafter referred to as the Clock End.

In 1936 work began on a new East Stand on Avenell Road. Its design was almost identical to the West Stand but it housed all the offices, players' and executive facilities and included a grand main entrance from the road.

The East Stand had five floors and seating accommodation for 4,000 on the top tier and seated a further 4,000 on the lower tier with a narrow paddock in front of the stand. It was completed at a cost of £130,000 and was opened in October 1936. Apart from a few alterations, the stadium has remained the same ever since.

During World War Two, the ground became a first-aid post and ARP Centre with a barrage balloon flown from the practice ground behind the Clock End. A bomb fell on the training pitch and incendiary bombs destroyed the North Bank roof.

There have been a number of post-war developments at Arsenal Stadium. Floodlights, mounted on the roofs of the stands, were installed in 1951 and have since been replaced by updated lamps. In 1954 the North Bank roof was rebuilt, an exact copy of the pre-war construction with money granted by the War Damages Commission. Arsenal, one of the first British clubs to try undersoil heating, installed an electric system in 1964 but this was replaced by the present heating system in 1970, at a cost of £30,000. In 1969 extra seating accommodation for 5,500 was put into the paddock in front of the West Stand at a cost of £80,000. An indoor training centre, sponsored by JVC, with an artificial playing pitch, was installed on the site of the old practice ground at the Clock End. Also at the Clock End, an experiment with a video screen installation proved unsuccessful mainly due to objections by the local planning authority.

A complete redevelopment of the Clock End, converting the area into a large commercial complex, began during the summer of 1988 and was opened in May 1989. The scheme included the building of a new stand housing 48 executive boxes, new offices, restaurants and conference facilities. The JVC training centre was replaced with a new ultra-modern sports hall.

Improvements are continuous — two electronic scoreboards have been installed, every seat in the ground has been replaced with upgraded seating. To comply with the Taylor Report, the club plans to build a two-tier stand on the North Bank and provide an all-seater stadium of 37,000 capacity by 1993-4.

An aerial view of Highbury in the 1970s.

20

ARSENAL
MANAGERS

Thomas B.Mitchell
1897-1898

VERY little is known about Arsenal's first professional manager, Mr T.B.Mitchell, other than he came from Blackburn Rovers and remained at Plumstead for less than one season.

During that time, the club, boosted by their best away record to date, rose from tenth to fifth in the League. In the FA Cup, having progressed through three qualifying rounds, they were knocked out in the first round proper at Burnley.

Among the players who joined the club this season were goalkeeper Roger Ord, full-backs McAuley and McConnell and forwards Fergus Hunt, David Hannah, White and McGeoch, although some of them, like the manager, remained only one season.

Despite the improved performances, support continued to fall away and the financial position became acute. It is probably because of these circumstances that Mitchell resigned in March 1898.

George Elcoat
1898-1899

GEORGE Elcoat succeeded T.B.Mitchell as manager, but he too remained for only one season. Elcoat, a native of Stockton-on-Tees, showed a remarkable preference for Scottish footballing talent and during his regime there was a period when no less than eight of the first team were from over the border. One of these, John Dick, proved to be an exceptionally good capture and went on to give the club excellent service as a wing-half and captain for over 12 years.

The League was increased to 18 clubs in 1898-9 and Arsenal's final position of seventh was on par with the previous season. Whilst being excused from qualifying rounds in the FA Cup, the club were heavily beaten in the first round proper at Derby.

The support for Woolwich Arsenal however, did not improve and to keep the club from sliding into bankruptcy, more players had to be released. Elcoat could face the situation no longer and left at the end of the season, to be succeeded by Harry Bradshaw.

21

Harry Bradshaw
1899-1904

HARRY Bradshaw was Arsenal's first successful manager. In the space of five years he transformed the fortunes of the club, taking them from the verge of bankruptcy and building a team which won promotion to the First Division.

Bradshaw first made his name with Burnley from 1891 to 1899. At Plumstead he was faced with waning local interest, falling attendances and the fact that the club's best players had been sold to raise money.

With little funds available, he initially brought in local talent, obtaining goalkeeper Jimmy Ashcroft from Gravesend and Archie Cross from Dartford, as well as recruiting full-backs Jackson and McNichol from Scotland. Bradshaw adopted the Scottish-style short, accurate passing game and with it came better results. Arsenal rose from seventh in the table to fourth in 1901-02, their best League position to date. There was a continued improvement in playing results, an increase in support and, with the club able to afford new players, Bradshaw acquired Roddy McEachrane and a complete forward line of Briercliffe, Coleman, Gooing, Shanks and Linward. Third position in the League was achieved in 1902-03 and the hopes of promotion were realised the following season, when Arsenal finished runners-up to Preston North End.

Bradshaw, a good administrator and a clever tactician, had put Arsenal on the football map and it was quite a sensation, therefore, when he was tempted away by a big-money offer to Fulham instead of First Division football at Plumstead. Bradshaw's two sons, William and Joseph, had been players with Woolwich Arsenal and they too followed him to Fulham.

In five years at Fulham, Bradshaw took the club from the Southern League into the Football League and to the semi-final of the FA Cup before becoming the secretary of the Southern League, a position he held until his death in 1921.

Phil Kelso
1904-1908

PHIL Kelso was appointed as Harry Bradshaw's successor and therefore became Arsenal's first manager in First Division football.

A hard and rugged Scot, Kelso had been associated for many years with Hibernian and was one of the best known men in Scottish football circles. His first priority was to consolidate Arsenal's newly acquired status and as goalscoring proved more difficult in the higher division, he strengthened the attack with the signings of Satterthwaite, Fitchie and Templeton, and later, Garbutt and Freeman. Maintaining a sound defence by the inclusion of Scottish full-backs, Gray and Sharp, Arsenal not only progressed beyond the second round of the FA Cup, but also reached the semi-final stage in Kelso's second season with the club, only to be beaten 2-0 by Newcastle · United. The 1906-07 season was the club's best so far — seventh position in Division One and FA Cup semi-finalists for a second time. Beaten this time by Sheffield Wednesday, Arsenal again failed to progress to the Final.

The following season, results began to fall away, attendances dropped and the financial position again became insecure. Kelso did not seem to possess the same qualities as Harry Bradshaw in such a situation and before the end of the season he resigned and returned to Scotland to run a hotel in Largs.

Twelve months later, he too was persuaded by Fulham to become their manager and stayed with them through World War One until 1924, when he retired. He became a publican in the area until his death in 1935, at the age of 64.

George Morrell
1908-1915

GEORGE Morrell had the misfortune to be the Arsenal manager on the only occasion that the club has been relegated. In taking over from Phil Kelso, Morrell became the fifth Arsenal manager in ten years and arrived at Plumstead at the beginning of what was to turn out to be the most critical period in the club's history.

A sturdy Scotsman, born in Glasgow circa 1873, he attached himself to football at an early age, not so much as a player but in managing the affairs of Glenure Athletic, a Glasgow junior club. He served as committee man, secretary, treasurer and president as well as being an occasional player. With junior football on the wane, he joined the staff of Glasgow Rangers who were struggling at that time, and over a period of two to three years he helped to revive the club's fortunes. He also served as a qualified referee. In 1905, Morrell was appointed out of a list of 85 applicants as secretary-manager of Greenock Morton, a club that was also heavily in debt. Morrell not only made them solvent, he also enabled them to be voted into the Scottish First Division.

Taking up his appointment at Woolwich Arsenal in February 1908, Morrell was again faced with a club experiencing poor support and therefore financial difficulties. He was forced to part with several of the club's key players and Tim Coleman, Bert Freeman, Peter Kyle, Jimmy Sharp, Jimmy Ashcroft and Billy Garbutt were all sold within months of Morrell taking over. The club reached a respectable sixth position in the League in his first season and Morrell, in an attempt to boost the support, brought in such well-known players as Leigh Roose and Alf Common. But even Common, together with the club's other big asset, Andy Ducat, eventually had to be sold as the financial crisis became worse.

Relegation inevitably came in 1912-13 and with it the worst playing record in the club's history. Arsenal moved across to North London in search of better support and Morrell became the club's first manager at Highbury. For two seasons a brave attempt was made to regain First Division status but with little change in the financial situation, Morrell was forced to resign at the end of 1914-15, as the club officially closed down because of the war.

It is worth quoting from Morrell's programme notes for the first match ever played at Highbury. "Possibly, early failures need not discourage. With the loyal support of our followers, we will win through in the end, and ere long you will, I trust, see football at Highbury well worthy of the greatest city in the world." How right he was.

Leslie Knighton
1919-1925

WHEN football was resumed after World War One, Sir Henry Norris, the Arsenal chairman, used his influence to ensure Division One status for the Gunners. His first step in his determination to make the club the most successful in the country was to appoint Leslie Knighton as manager.

Born near Burton-upon-Trent in March 1884, Knighton had his playing career cut short by an ankle injury and was appointed team manager of Castleford Town at the age of 20. He was offered the post of assistant secretary-manager of Huddersfield Town in 1909 and, almost three years later, moved to Manchester City in the summer of 1912. He earned himself a fine reputation there by building up a young and successful side before the war intervened.

Knighton joined Arsenal as manager in May 1919 and immediately came under the power of the chairman. The club was in debt, having spent a fortune on the move to Highbury, and Knighton's task was clearly defined by Norris — to build a successful team without spending on big transfer fees and preferably by developing his own players. Knighton was always fair in his dealings with players and his persuasiveness convinced both Alf Baker and Bob John that they should sign for Arsenal rather than other interested clubs. To add to these and the nucleus of pre-war players who still remained, he was able to recruit at little expense, Whittaker, Milne, Toner, Pagnam, Turnbull and later, Brain and full-backs Mackie and Kennedy.

Knighton, however, was rarely allowed to manage and with the restrictions imposed on him, his task became virtually impossible. This was reflected in the playing record. During his six seasons at Highbury, not once did the goals for exceed the goals against, the best League position achieved was ninth and relegation was narrowly avoided on two occasions. In 1924-5, Knighton displeased Norris by challenging his authority with demands to buy key players. And with the club having been knocked out of the Cup in the first round and in 20th position in the League, Norris advertised for a new manager.

Within two weeks, Knighton was appointed manager of Bournemouth FC, where he stayed for three years before joining Birmingham. At St Andrew's, he reached the summit of his career when he led the Blues to the FA Cup Final in 1931. In 1933 he became manager of Chelsea where he spent six years prior to the war. After the war he had a spell with Shrewsbury Town in the Midland League but, following a breakdown in health, he returned to Bournemouth where he became secretary of a golf club. Knighton died in hospital after a major operation in May 1959.

Herbert Chapman
1925-1934

HERBERT Chapman not only put Arsenal on top of the soccer world but his far-sighted ideas and methods were also a benefit to professional football as a whole. Yet Chapman came into football management by chance. A colleague on the playing staff at Tottenham Hotspur was offered the post of player-manager of Northampton Town and suggested to Chapman that he would be more suited to the job. His application was accepted and thus the career of one of the greatest managers the game has known, had begun.

Born at Kiveton Park, near Sheffield, in January 1878, Chapman served an apprenticeship in mining engineering and played football for several local clubs. As a hard-working forward he gained experience with several minor League clubs and Southern League Northampton Town, before joining Tottenham Hotspur in March 1905.

Taking up his duties as player-manager in April 1907, he took Northampton to the Southern League title in his second season. His success continued as manager of Leeds City until, after irregularities (in which Chapman was not involved), the club was closed down and he went back to engineering for a time. He returned to football with Huddersfield Town and, in his five years at Leeds Road, the club reached the FA Cup Final, were promoted to Division One and twice won the League Championship.

When Arsenal advertised for a manager in 1925, the challenge appealed to Chapman's imagination and ambition. On his appointment, he immediately influenced chairman Norris into reversing his policy on transfer fees and set about selecting key players to strengthen the Arsenal team. Initially he brought in Buchan, Harper, Parker, Hulme and Lambert. Arsenal quickly lifted themselves out of the relegation area to runners-up in the League and reached the Cup quarter-finals, a foretaste of the success to come. With a combination of his ability to determine the most suitable potential of players and further imports in the form of Jack, James, Hapgood and Bastin, the club won its first major honour in 1930. (A year later, Arsenal became the first southern club to win the League Championship.) In 1931-2 they narrowly failed to win the League and Cup 'double', while the following season the Championship was achieved for the second time.

Chapman always subjected himself to the utmost limits in the interests of his work and it was following a hectic spell attending matches at the beginning of 1934 that he returned home with what he thought was no more than a heavy cold. His condition worsened and he died on 6 January.

George Allison
1934-1947

UPON the death of Herbert Chapman in January 1934, the Arsenal directors were faced with the difficult task of finding a worthy successor. Until the end of the season, Joe Shaw became team manager, John Peters was the secretary and the overall management duties were taken over by George Allison.

Allison was born near Darlington in October 1883 and began a long career in journalism at Stockton-on-Tees in 1903, initially reporting on local games in which he had played as an undistinguished full-back. He became assistant to the secretary-manager of Middlesbrough FC at the age of 21 but the lure of journalism was too strong and in 1906 he moved to London, where, after years of reporting Woolwich Arsenal matches at Plumstead, he acquired a great affinity for the club. Allison became the Arsenal historian and editor of the club's programme and handbook and, in 1926, he joined the board of directors. He was the London correspondent of the *New York Herald* for over 35 years and also gained fame as the pioneer of radio broadcasting of football.

Relinquishing his position as 'manager-director', Allison became secretary-manager at Highbury on 1 June 1934. Arsenal, in the meantime, had won their third League Championship in four seasons. He maintained the strength and success of the team by signing centre-forward Ted Drake and wing-halves Crayston and Copping and a further two Championships and the FA Cup were won before the arrival of war, the intervention of which deprived Allison's record signing, Bryn Jones, the chance to prove himself. During wartime Allison practically ran Arsenal on his own for seven years.

Although he gave himself unstintingly and always had the best interests of the club at heart, Allison was a figure-head and a showman and did not possess the same football knowledge as Chapman. Whittaker and Shaw were responsible for much of the management of the players. With his journalistic and broadcasting background, Allison was equal to his predecessor in the aspect of public relations and overall he maintained the success and Arsenal as the leading club in the country.

After a difficult season for the club, Allison retired in May 1947. Ten years later he died of a heart attack at his Golders Green home, at the age of 73.

Tom Whittaker MBE
1947-1956

ALTHOUGH born in Aldershot in 1898, Tom Whittaker was brought up in the Newcastle area, where he qualified as a marine engineer. He joined Arsenal as a promising centre-forward in November 1919 but went on to serve the club at left-half and full-back. His playing career was terminated by a knee injury sustained whilst playing for the FA team on a tour of Australia in the summer of 1925. He made 64 League and six FA Cup appearances for Arsenal and won a London Combination Championship and two London FA Challenge Cup winners' medals. He was appointed assistant-trainer in 1926 and succeeded George Hardy as trainer in February 1927. Whittaker built up a reputation as the finest trainer in the game, not only to Arsenal throughout the late 1920s and the 1930s, when the club were so successful, but also to the full England international and FA touring teams with whom he travelled all over the world. Many famous personalities from other major sports often sought his advice and services.

On his demobilization in 1946, Whittaker was appointed assistant-manager to George Allison and together they rescued Arsenal from the threat of relegation with the inspired signings of Joe Mercer and Ronnie Rooke. In June 1947 he succeeded Allison and, with Roper and Macaulay added to the playing staff, the Gunners ran away with the League Championship in his first season as secretary-manager. Whittaker turned down a chance of rebuilding the Italian club, Turin, following an air disaster which destroyed their team and in 1950 he guided Arsenal to an FA Cup Final victory over Liverpool. Two years later, he again led the Gunners out at Wembley to what he considered was the club's finest performance when, due to an injury to Barnes, his ten-man team fought a gallant losing battle with Newcastle United.

In 1952-3, Arsenal, by winning the final match of the season, completed their seventh League Championship but with an ageing team breaking up and some poor results, there followed a transitional period which proved a marked contrast to the heady days of Cups and Championships.

The lack of success, compared to the previous high standards, caused Tom Whittaker great concern. He was ordered to take a complete rest, was found to be suffering from nervous exhaustion and finally entered hospital. A short while later, in October 1956, the most popular and respected of all Arsenal servants died of a heart attack.

Jack Crayston
1956-1958

AFTER the death of Tom Whittaker, Jack Crayston was appointed manager in November 1956. For the first time in over 30 years, the combined job of secretary-manager was split and the post of secretary went to Bob Wall.

Crayston was born in Grange-over-Sands, Lancashire, in October 1910 and began his League career with Barrow in 1928. After two years he joined Bradford and although he was unlucky enough to break both a wrist and a leg during his four seasons with the Yorkshire club, he developed into a top-class wing-half. Arsenal signed him in May 1934 and in five seasons (at Highbury) before the war he made over 200 first-class appearances and won every major honour in the game. A leg operation during the war ended his playing career and, after service as a flying officer, he returned to Highbury and joined the coaching staff. He became assistant-manager in 1947 and was elevated to the post of manager in 1956.

Crayston met with initial success. Arsenal, in 11th position in the League when he took over, were lifted to third place by an unbeaten run of ten games and the final position of fifth was quite satisfactory in the circumstances, as was the Gunners' appearance in sixth round of the FA Cup. The following season was quite different however. Performances became inconsistent, results fluctuated dramatically and far too many goals were conceded. Crayston was fully aware of the shortcomings of his team but the money required to recruit the players he needed was not forthcoming. Arsenal slipped to 12th place with their lowest points total since 1930 and there was another shock result in the FA Cup at Northampton. Crayston believed that money should have been made available. He became frustrated and at a board meeting in May 1958, he resigned after 24 years service at Arsenal.

He moved back to Yorkshire in July 1958 as manager and then secretary of Doncaster Rovers until March 1961, when he left football to run a newsagents and general store business in Streetly, near Birmingham, where he now lives in retirement.

George Swindin
1958-1962

ON the strength of his success at Peterborough United, former Arsenal goalkeeper George Swindin was invited to return to Highbury to take over the managerial chair in the summer of 1958.

A strong-minded Yorkshireman, born near Doncaster, Swindin was an amateur on Rotherham United's books and gained League experience with Bradford City before joining Arsenal in April 1936. He made his League debut in the following September and won a League Championship medal in 1937-8. After the war, when he was acknowledged as the best uncapped goalkeeper in the country, he was an automatic choice for Arsenal for a number of years and won a further Championship medal and both winners' and runners-up medals in the FA Cup. In February 1954 he became player-manager of Peterborough United and out of the four years he was at the club, he guided them to the championship of the Midland League on three occasions. Having turned down a number of offers from other League clubs, he was persuaded to return to Arsenal as manager in July 1958.

In Swindin's first season, the playing staff underwent a drastic overhaul. His excursions into the transfer market brought in Docherty, Henderson, McCullough and Julians, while Tapscott, Holton, Charlton and Fotheringham were among the departures. Arsenal finished in third place, after heading the table for part of the season and, but for injuries to key players at crucial times, might well have taken the title. Swindin was not to be so successful again. The following campaign was a nightmare for him — 13th in the League, an early exit in the FA Cup and another serious run of injuries (including Mel Charles, who had now joined the club). In 1960-61 there were further changes in the playing staff, including the signing of George Eastham, but again the season ended in mediocrity. Laurie Brown and John MacLeod joined Arsenal for the start of the next season but the blend was still not right and the playing position showed no improvement. In addition, neighbours and rivals Tottenham Hotspur were enjoying a highly successful period. Swindin was highly criticised and, accepting full responsibility, he resigned at the end of the season, a sad and disillusioned man.

During his four years as manager it seemed that Swindin made too many changes, not just in playing staff but in team selection from match to match. He was, however, often faced with a spate of injuries and it is difficult, therefore, to assess how many of the changes were forced on him.

From Arsenal, Swindin became manager of Norwich City and five months later moved to Cardiff City, where he stayed until April 1964. He left football to manage a garage business in Corby and later went to live in Spain.

Billy Wright CBE
1962-1966

BILLY Wright became manager at Arsenal in May 1962, having declined the position of coach at Highbury a few months earlier. He was the first post-war manager who had no previous association with the club and, indeed, had no previous managerial experience of any kind.

Wright was born at Ironbridge, Shropshire, in February 1924, and joined the groundstaff at Wolverhampton Wanderers as a centre-forward at the age of 14. He survived Major Frank Buckley's initial impression that he would not make the grade and making his senior debut at 15 ½, he came to prominence in wartime football. Making his League debut immediately after the war, Wright became one of the game's top stars, for many years captaining Wolves and England. He made close on 500 League appearances for Wolves between 1946 and 1959 and won three Championship medals and an FA Cup winners' medal. He won 105 full international caps for England and was awarded the CBE in 1959. On leaving Wolves he joined the FA coaching staff and was in charge of the England Youth and Under-23 teams.

Amid a blaze of publicity, Wright arrived as manager at Highbury and his immediate purchase of Joe Baker from Italian football was a good sign of his intentions. Although the club finished in seventh position in the League, Wright's first season was not particularly outstanding. The attack returned an adequate 86 goals but the defence conceded almost as many. The signing of centre-half Ian Ure in 1963-4 did not have the desired effect and the Gunners' final position was almost identical to the previous season. In the following campaign, despite the arrival of Don Howe and Frank McLintock, results and attendances deteriorated and Arsenal were subjected to a shock FA Cup defeat at Peterborough. The 1965-6 season was even more disappointing — 14th in the League, knocked out of the FA Cup at the first hurdle and attendances down to an all-time low of 4,554 — it was clear that time was running out for Billy Wright.

Always aware of Arsenal's tradition and lacking in managerial experience, Wright was perhaps too genial a person to ever succeed but, although he brought no honours to the club, he did bring in many fine players and develop a promising youth team which were to form the foundation of successes to come.

In the summer of 1966, the directors, impatient for success and under pressure from the supporters, had little alternative than to relieve Wright of his duties and he left football to become head of Sport and Outside Broadcasts with ATV in the Midlands.

Bertie Mee OBE
1966-1976

BERTIE Mee rose from the position of the club's physiotherapist and trainer to become Arsenal's most successful post-war manager. He took over from Billy Wright on a 'temporary' basis in June 1966 and was officially appointed manager in March 1967.

Born at Bulwell, Nottingham, in December 1918, Mee had his playing career as a winger with Derby County and Mansfield Town cut short by injury. After six years service as a sergeant in the Royal Army Medical Corps, he qualified as a physiotherapist and then spent 12 years as a rehabilitation officer to disabled servicemen. In August 1960 he became Arsenal's trainer and physiotherapist, replacing Billy Milne, who had retired.

On taking control of the playing staff for the opening of 1966-7, Mee brought Colin Addison, George Graham and Bob McNab to Highbury and, at the end of the season, the club held a respectable seventh position in the League. The following campaign, in only their second season in the competition, the Gunners reached the League Cup Final but were beaten by Leeds United.

Mee, a modest man, but thoroughly efficient and knowledgeable in the arts of man-management and motivation, gradually steered the club from strength to strength. In 1968-9 Arsenal were again unsuccessful in the League Cup Final but 12 months later, Mee and his team won the European Fairs Cup and the first major trophy in 17 years arrived at Highbury.

Then followed the greatest triumph in the club's history. With Don Howe now as coach, Mee guided the Gunners to the League and FA Cup 'double', an achievement that even the great Chapman and Whittaker had not managed. Naturally, Bertie Mee was voted 'Manager of the Year'.

In the next two seasons Mee was close to further honours — a narrow FA Cup Final defeat in 1971-2, followed by runners-up in the League and FA Cup semi-finalists in 1972-3.

From then on the Arsenal's fortunes were on the decline and, after two particularly difficult seasons with the pressures beginning to tell, Mee announced in March 1976 that he would be retiring at the end of that season.

After a break from the game, he joined Watford as general manager and, on retirement in 1986, remained a director of the club.

Terry Neill
1976-1983

TERRY Neill was another of the club's former players who became manager. He took over from Bertie Mee in July 1976 and, in just over seven years in office, he led Arsenal to three successive FA Cup Finals and a European Final.

Born in Belfast in May 1942, Neill started his playing career with Bangor City and joined Arsenal as a wing-half in December 1959. He was one of Arsenal's youngest-ever captains and made 241 League appearances at Highbury before also becoming the youngest boss in the League when he joined Second Division Hull City as player-manager in June 1970. He won his first cap for Northern Ireland in 1961 and was a permanent fixture in the side for 12 years, winning a total of 59 caps. He was also captain and manager of his country. Neill had also been chairman of the Professional Footballers' Association. After managerial experience with Hull and Northern Ireland, he succeeded Bill Nicholson as Tottenham manager in September 1974.

He became Arsenal manager in time for the start of the 1976-7 season and immediately splashed out £333,333 to sign Malcolm Macdonald from Newcastle United. Initially Neill could not handle being in charge of old playing colleagues and contemporaries and made the mistake of publicising his disagreements and criticisms of his players. In 1977-8 Don Howe returned as coach and forged a partnership with Neill which was to bring the Gunners further honours. That season ended with Arsenal as FA Cup runners-up, but they returned the following year and Neill won his first trophy in club management. In 1979-80 Neill suffered the double disappointment of losing in the FA Cup and European Cup-winners' Cup Finals. The subsequent years promised much but, despite numerous changes in the playing staff, Neill could never recover the loss of the irreplaceable Brady and Stapleton or attain the right level of consistency required to win the major honours. The semi-finals of the League Cup and FA Cup were reached in 1982-3 but both ended in defeat and, under mounting pressure from management and fans, Neill was sacked in December 1983.

Neill's Irish sense of humour often camouflaged his serious attitude and philosophical approach to the game. His reign as manager was studded with spectacular and sometimes unsuccessful raids into the transfer market but, whatever opinions may be held on his ability, he never saw the Gunners fall below tenth in the League and did bring a measure of success in the knock-out competitions.

He has concentrated on charity work since leaving the game.

Don Howe
1983-1986

ONE of the most respected coaches in Europe, Don Howe was appointed caretaker boss in December 1983, after the departure of Terry Neill, and confirmed as manager the following April.

Wolverhampton-born in October 1935, Howe had a distinguished playing career as a right-back with West Bromwich Albion, for whom he made close on 350 League appearances in nine seasons and captained the side. He won 23 full England caps and played in the 1958 World Cup Finals in Sweden. He earned a reputation as a skilful, thoughtful defender and in April 1964, Billy Wright paid £42,000 to take him to Highbury. Howe suffered a broken leg in March 1966 and had made 70 League appearances for the Gunners when he became reserve-team coach, moving up to chief coach in succession to Dave Sexton in October 1967.

Howe and manager Bertie Mee formed a partnership that brought the Fairs Cup to Highbury and the League and FA Cup 'double' a year later. After the 'double' triumph Howe left Arsenal to become manager of West Bromwich Albion and after further spells as coach with Turkish club, Galatasary, and Leeds United he returned to Highbury as chief coach in August 1977. In another successful partnership, this time with Terry Neill, Howe coached Arsenal to the 1979 FA Cup Final triumph over Manchester United and to the 1978 and 1980 FA Cup Finals, as well as the European Cup-winners' Cup Final against Valencia. He was also coach to the England 1982 World Cup team under Ron Greenwood.

Taking over from Terry Neill in mid-term 1983-4, Howe guided Arsenal to a final sixth position in the League table, just one place short of UEFA Cup qualification. Mariner, Anderson and Williams arrived at Highbury and one of the strongest squads in the country began to assemble. Although the club finished in seventh position in both the other seasons he was in charge, Howe was unable to sustain a challenge for honours and there were also some disappointing results in both the Cup competitions. Amid the usual clamourings for success and an indication that the club were interested in bringing in Terry Venables as manager, Howe asked to be released from his contract in March 1986.

He continued as coach and assistant to Bobby Robson with the England team and in 1987-8 he again showed that he is one of the best coaches in the game by helping Wimbledon to a sensational FA Cup Final victory over Liverpool before becoming coach and then manager of Queen's Park Rangers and currently Coventry City.

George Graham
1986-

ARSENAL'S 'interest' in Terry Venables as a successor to Don Howe never materialised and in May 1986 the club decided to maintain a long tradition and appoint another 'old boy', George Graham, as manager.

Born at Bargeddie, Lanark, in November 1944, Graham was a Scottish Schoolboy international and started his career in English football with Aston Villa in 1961. He moved to Chelsea in 1964 and after scoring 35 goals in 72 appearances, he was signed by Bertie Mee for Arsenal in September 1966. In his six and a half seasons at Highbury, initially as a striker and later as a midfield player, Graham scored 82 goals in close on 350 senior matches and was a member of the Fairs Cup and the League and FA Cup 'double' winning teams. Leaving Arsenal for Manchester United, he later had experience with Portsmouth. Graham represented Scotland at both Under-23 and full levels. He joined Crystal Palace in November 1976 and helped them to promotion to Division Two before retiring from playing in 1980 and taking up coaching with Palace and Queen's Park Rangers.

His first managerial appointment was with Millwall in December 1982 and he saved them from relegation to the Fourth Division that season. He led the Lions to a Football League Trophy win in 1983 and to the FA Cup quarter-finals and to promotion to the Second Division in 1985. His good work at The Den has been followed up and Millwall attained First Division status for the first time in their history, a success based on the foundations which Graham laid.

In his first season back at Highbury, Graham took the club to fourth position in the League. The Gunners, who led the table at one stage, enjoyed greater success in winning the Littlewoods Cup, when Liverpool were beaten in the Final. The following year he also experienced the disappointments of football management when the Gunners reached the Littlewoods Cup Final for a second time, this time to be beaten by Luton Town.

By leading the club to the League Championship in 1988-9, he became not only the fifth Arsenal manager to achieve the honour, but also joined the 'élite band' of footballers who have won the game's top honour both as a player and as a manager.

Following a disappointing 1989-90, the ever-ambitious Graham won his second Manager of the Year award by guiding the club to a further League Championship success.

ARSENAL
Who's Who

Playing positions shown are those with which the player was normally associated, although some players may also have appeared in other positions. The years following each player's name are those when he was on Arsenal's books. Club titles are those in use at the time. The first team is referred to as Senior and the Reserve and Youth teams as Junior. Figures are up to and including the end of the 1991-92 season. Junior football covers local junior and non-League clubs, ie any other level of football than the Football League, etc. Appearances in abandoned matches, unofficial trials, public practice matches, and 5/6 a-side tournaments are not included. Substitute appearances are shown after full appearances ie 10/2. Appearances and goalscorers in wartime football are given as a total (ie League, Cup and other matches). Only details of honours gained whilst with Arsenal and at schoolboy and youth level prior to joining Arsenal directly from that level are included. Broad references only are made to honours won whilst with other clubs, where known. Abbreviations: cs = close season, FA Cup (Q) = FA Cup Qualifying round, gl(s) = goal(s), (Res) = Reserves, (sub) = substitute, app = appearances, Fdly = Friendly, Jnr = Junior, Snr = Senior.

ADAMS, Tony Alexander   **1982-**
Central defender   6ft 3in. 13st 2lb.
Born: Romford, Essex, 10 Oct 1966.
School: Eastbrook Comprehensive, Dagenham.
Jnr football: Romford Royals, Gidea Park R, Dagenham U. Joined ARSENAL: Nov 1980 (schoolboy), Apr 1983 (apprentice), 30 Jan 1984 (professional). First app: Jnr fdly v Colchester U (a) 7 Aug 1982. First-team debut: Snr fdly v Chelsea (a) 1 Nov 1983. League debut v Sunderland (h) 5 Nov 1983.

ARSENAL record: League 248/1 (20 gls); FA Cup 18 (1 gl); Football League Cup 33/1 (2 gls); FA Charity Shield 2; European comp: 4; Other snr comp: 13 (1 gl); Football Combination 84 (10 gls); SE Counties League 21 (3 gls); FA Youth Cup 9; Other jnr comp: 11 (2 gls); Friendlies 69/6 (10 gls). Made 1 app: Arsenal/Luton on tour 1986-7.
Honours: Barking & Dagenham, Essex County and London Schoolboys. Division One champions 1988-9, 1990-91. Football League Cup winners 1986-7, runners-up 1987-8. FA Charity Shield runners-up 1989-90, medal 1991-2; Football Combination champions 1983-4. Mercantile Credit Centenary Trophy winners 1988-9. Captain of Arsenal. PFA Young Player of the Year 1987. Fiat Young Player of the Season 1986-7. Arsenal Player of the Year 1987, 1990. 18 England Youth caps (and captain); 5 Under-21 caps (1 gl) (and

captain) 1985-1987; 4 'B' caps (1 gl) 1989-90; 19 full caps (4 gls) 1987.

ADDISON, Colin   **1966-67**
Inside-forward   5ft 10in. 11st 2lb.
Born: Taunton, Somerset, 18 May 1940.
School: At Pill, nr Bristol.
Jnr football: City Schools (York), Cliftonville (York). Previous Clubs: York City (May 1957), Nottingham Forest (Jan 1961). Joined ARSENAL: 16 Sep 1966 from Nottingham Forest for £45,000. First app: League v Blackpool (h) 17 Sep 1966. Final app: League v Leeds United (a) 4 Nov 1967. Snr fdly v Portsmouth (a) 21 Nov 1967. Transferred to Sheffield United (£40,000) 30 Nov 1967.
ARSENAL record: League 27/1 (9 gls); FA Cup 2; Football League Cup 2 (1 gl); Football Combination 7 (1 gl); Friendlies 8/2 (5 gls).
Later player-manager of Hereford United and held managerial positions at Durban City (manager), Notts County (assistant), Newport County (manager), West Bromwich Albion (assistant), Derby County (manager) and Newport County (manager). Also had spells in management of Spanish clubs, Celta and Atlético Madrid. Was manager of Hereford again (1990-91).

ALLINSON, Ian James Robert   **1983-87**
Forward   5ft 10in. 11st.

Born: Stevenage, Herts, 1 Oct 1957.
School: Alleyne's Secondary.
Jnr football: Local Hertfordshire leagues.
Previous Club: Colchester United (Oct 1975). Joined ARSENAL: 15 Aug 1983 from Colchester United on free transfer. First app: Jnr fdly v Aston Villa Reserves (h) 20 Aug 1983. First-team debut: Milk Cup v Walsall (h) 29 Nov 1983. Final first-team app: League (sub) v Manchester City (a) 25 Apr 1987. Final app: Football Combination v Southampton (a) 9 May 1987. Joined Stoke City (free transfer), 20 Jun 1987.
ARSENAL record: League 60/23 (16 gls); FA Cup 7/2 (4 gls); Football League Cup 8/5 (3 gls); Football Combination 69 (40 gls); Friendlies 25/6 (16 gls).
Honours: Football Combination champions 1983-4.
Joined Luton Town, Oct 1987, then Colchester United, Dec 1988. Now player-manager of Baldock Town.

AMBLER, Charles James   **1891-94 & 1895-96**
Goalkeeper   5ft 10in. 10st 11lb.
Born: Hampshire, 1869.
Jnr football: Bostal Rovers. Joined: Royal Arsenal 1891. Woolwich Arsenal 23 Jul 1893 (professional). First app: Jnr fdly v Edmonton (a) 21 Nov 1891. Snr fdly v 2nd West Kent Regiment (a) 10 Dec 1891. First-team debut: League v Newton Heath (a) 30 Nov 1895. (only app). Transferred to Tottenham Hotspur summer 1894 and rejoined ARSENAL 22 Nov 1895 (for 1 match).
ARSENAL record: League 1; FA Cup (Q) 1; Friendlies 22.
In addition during 1891-2 and 1892-3 made 5 snr apps: and 36 reserve apps: for Royal Arsenal. Later played for West Ham United (1901-02).

AMPADU, Kwame   **1988-91**
Forward   5ft 7in. 10st 13lb.
Born: Bradford, 20 Dec 1970.
Jnr football: Sherrards United, Belvedere FC (both Dublin). Joined ARSENAL: Jul 1988. First app: Jnr fdly v Abingdon (a) 30 Jul 1988. First-team debut: Snr fdly v Shrewsbury Town (a) 13 Dec 1988 (as sub). League debut v Derby County (a) 24 Mar 1990 (as sub). Final app: Football Combination (sub) v Southampton (a) 26 Mar 1991. Transferred to West Bromwich Albion (£50,000) 5 Jun 1991.
ARSENAL record: League 0/2; Football Combination 55/10 (14 gls); SE Counties League/Cup 26 (23 gls); FA Youth Cup 4 (2 gls); Other

jnr comp: 2 (1 gl); Friendlies: 24/7 (13 gls).
Honours: Football Combination champions 1989-90.
Republic of Ireland Youth and Under-21 caps
(parentage qualification).
Was on loan to Plymouth Argyle and West
Bromwich Albion during 1990-91.

ANDERSON, Edward   **1903-04**
Outside-left.
Born: Scotland.
Joined ARSENAL: 24 Nov 1903 from St Mirren.
First app: Snr fdly v Army (h) 30 Nov 1903. League
debut: v Stockport County (a) 1 Jan 1904. Final
app: League v Blackpool (a) 2 Jan 1904.
ARSENAL record: League 2; London League 1;
London League (Res) 1 (2 gls); South Eastern
League 3 (3 gls); Friendlies 1.
Later played for Fulham and Queen's Park
Rangers.

ANDERSON, John   **1896-1903**
Full-back/half-back   5ft 10in. 12st 7lb.
Born: 1878.
Jnr football: Crook Town. Joined ARSENAL: 17
Dec 1896. First app: League v Darwen (a) 1 Jan
1897. Final first-team app: Snr fdly v Northampton
Town (a) 14 Apr 1903. Final app: Chatham Charity
Cup v Chatham (a) 27 April 1903.
ARSENAL record: League 144 (10 gls); FA Cup
9 (1 gl); United League 32 (1 gl); Southern District
Combination 12 (1 gl); London League 8; London
League (Res) 9 (3 gls); Other Snr comp: 6 (1 gl);
Kent League 23 (2 gls); Friendlies 59 (3 gls).
Honours: Chatham Charity Cup runners-up 1902-03.
Later played for Portsmouth.

ANDERSON, Terence Keith   **1959-65**
Winger   5ft 8in. 11st 4lb.
Born: Woking, Surrey, 11 Mar 1944. Died:
Yarmouth, Jan 1980.
Joined ARSENAL: Jul 1959 (groundstaff), Aug
1960 (apprentice), 9 Aug 1961 (professional). First
app: South East Counties League v West Ham
(h) 22 Aug 1959. First-team debut: League v West
Ham (a) 2 Mar 1963. Final app: League v Leeds
United (h) 13 Feb 1965. Transferred to Norwich
City (£15,000) 18 Feb 1965.
ARSENAL record: League 25 (6 gls); European
comp: 1 (1 gl); Football Combination 56 (26 gls);
London FA Challenge Cup 4 (1 gl); FA Youth
Cup 11 (7 gls); Metropolitan League 70 (19 gls);
South East Counties League 35 (35 gls); Other
jnr comp: 2 (1 gl); Friendlies 52/1 (33 gls).
Honours: Football Combination champions 1962-3.
London FA Challenge Cup winner 1962-3.
Metropolitan League champions 1960-61.
Metropolitan League Professional Cup winner
1960-61, 1961-2. Metropolitan League Cup winner
1960-61. South East Counties League Cup winner
1960-61. 2 England Youth caps 1961.
Also played for Colchester U, Scunthorpe U,
Crewe A, Bournemouth and Colchester U (again),
later becoming a publican at Caister. He was found
drowned after a training run.

ANDERSON, Vivian Alexander   **1984-87**
Full-back   6ft. 11st 1lb.
Born: Nottingham, 29 Jul 1956.
School: Fairham Comprehensive, Nottingham.
Jnr football: Manchester United (trial),
Nottingham Forest (apprentice). Previous Club:
Nottingham Forest (Aug 1974). Joined
ARSENAL: 23 Jul 1984 from Nottingham Forest
for £250,000. First app: Snr fdly v Celtic (a) 4
Aug 1984. League v Chelsea (h) 25 Aug 1984.
Final app: League v Norwich City (h) 9 May 1987.
Transferred to Manchester United (£250,000,
tribunal) 1 Jul 1987.
ARSENAL record: League 120 (9 gls); FA Cup
12 (3 gls); Football League Cup 18 (3 gls); Football

Combination 1; Friendlies 18/1 (1 gl).
Honours: Football League Cup winners 1987. 16
full England caps (2 gls).
Had short spell working as a printer before taking
up football. Won further club and international
honours with Nottingham Forest. Was the first
'black' footballer to win a full England cap. Joined
Sheffield Wednesday Jan 1991.

ANDERSON, Walter   **1901-03**
Forward   5ft 8in. 12st.
Born: c.1878. Died: Mar 1904.
Joined ARSENAL: 27 Dec 1901 from Sheffield
United. First app: League v Preston North End
(h) 11 Jan 1902. Final app: Snr fdly v Chesterfield
(h) 25 Apr 1903. Transferred to Plymouth Argyle,
summer 1903.
ARSENAL record: League 28 (10 gls); FA Cup
2 (1 gl); London League 9 (4 gls); London League
(Res) 3 (1 gl); Other snr comp: 3 (1 gl); Kent
League 4 (6 gls); Friendlies 6 (1 gl).

ARMSTRONG, George   **1961-77**
Winger   5ft 6in. 11st.
Born: Hebburn, Durham, 9 Aug 1944.
Jnr football: Hawthorn Leslie Boys Club, Grimsby
Town (trial), Newcastle United (trial). Joined
ARSENAL: Aug 1961 (amateur), 24 Aug 1961
(professional). First app: Jnr fdly v Gravesend (a)

12 Aug 1961. First-team debut: Snr fdly v
Stamford FC (a) 6 Sep 1961. League v Blackpool
(a) 24 Feb 1962. Final first-team app: v Red Star

(in Adelaide, Australia), 26 Jul 1977. Final app:
Football Combination v Hereford United (h) 10
Sep 1977. Transferred to Leicester City (£15,000)
13 Sep 1977.
ARSENAL record: League 490/10 (53 gls); FA
Cup 58/2 (10 gls); Football League Cup 35 (3
gls); European comp: 24/2 (2 gls); Other snr comp:
1 (1 gl); Football Combination 95 (27 gls); London
FA Challenge Cup 7 (2 gls); Metropolitan League
7 (2 gls); South East Counties League 2; FA Youth
Cup 3 (2 gls); Other jnr comp: 2 (1 gl); Friendlies
140/10 (40 gls).
Honours: Division One champions 1970-71. FA
Cup winners 1971, runners-up 1972. Football
League Cup runners-up 1968, 1969. Football
Combination champions 1969-70. Fairs Cup
winners 1970. Arsenal Player of the Year 1970.
3 England Youth caps 1962, 5 Under-23 caps (2
gls) 1965-6.
Fully apprenticed electrician before starting
football career. After Leicester played for
Stockport County (Sep 1978) and after 1979 had
various appointments at Aston Villa (coach),
Fulham (coach), Trowbridge Town (player),
Enderby Town (manager), Middlesbrough
(coach), Narvik in Norway and Kuwait (coach).
Currently Reserve-team coach at Arsenal.

ARNOLD, Thomas   **1905-06**
Winger   5ft 8in. 11st 6lb.
Born: Coventry, 1879.
Joined ARSENAL: 3 May 1905 from Coventry
City. First app: London League (Reserves) v
Tottenham Hotspur (a) 2 Sep 1905. First-team
debut: Snr fdly v Faversham (a) 21 Sep 1905.
League debut v Stoke (a) 23 Sep 1905. Final first-
team app: Snr fdly v Corinthians (a) 18 Oct 1905.
Final app: London League (Reserves) v Leyton
(a) 28 Apr 1906.
ARSENAL record: League 2; South Eastern
League 16 (3 gls); London League (Res) 12 (2
gls); Friendlies 11 (1 gl).
Honours: South Eastern League champions 1905-06.
Returned to Coventry City 1907. Retired 1911.
Became trainer of Coventry City and later a
director of the club.

ASHCROFT, James   **1900-08**
Goalkeeper   5ft 9½in. 11st.
Born: Liverpool, 12 Sep 1878. Died: 9 Apr 1943.
Jnr football: Wilby's United, Anfield Recreation
Club, Garston Copperworks, Everton (amateur),
Gravesend United (1899). Joined ARSENAL: 20
Jun 1900 from Gravesend United. First app:
London League (Reserves) v Millwall (a) 1 Sep
1900. First-team debut: League v Burton Swifts
(a) 15 Sept 1900. Final app: League v Sheffield
Wednesday (h) 20 Apr 1908. Scottish tour v
Kilmarnock 30 April 1908. Transferred to
Blackburn Rovers 5 May 1908.
ARSENAL record: League 273; FA Cup 30;
London League 25; London League (Res) 3; Other
snr comp: 12; Kent League 1; South Eastern
League 1; Friendlies 48.
Honours: Division Two runners-up (promotion)
1903-04. Southern Professional Charity Cup
winners 1905-06. Southern Professional Charity
Cup runners-up 1903-04. 3 full England caps 1906.
2 apps for Football League 1904-06.
Later played for Tranmere Rovers (1913).

ASTON, James   **1899-1900**
Inside-forward.
Born: Walsall, 1877. Died: Feb 1934.
Previous Club: Walsall (1896). Joined
ARSENAL: 29 May 1899 from Walsall. First app:
League v Leicester Fosse. (h) 2 Sep 1899. Final
snr app: Snr fdly v Southampton (h) 9 December
1899. Final app: Kent League v Ashford (h) 14
Apr 1900.

ARSENAL record: League 11 (3 gls); FA Cup 4 (2 gls); Southern District Combination 3; Kent League 4; Friendlies 3 (1 gl).
Later played for Small Heath (1900) and Doncaster Rovers (1902).

BACUZZI, David Reno   **1958-64**
Full-back   5ft 10in. 12st.
Born: Islington, London, 12 Oct 1940.
School: Clerkenwell and St Aloysius College, Highgate.
Jnr football: Highgate Schools Old Boys, Eastbourne United. Joined ARSENAL: from Eastbourne United Mar 1958 (amateur), 11 May 1959 (professional). First app: London Midweek League v Charlton Athletic (h) 12 Mar 1958. First-team debut: League v West Brom (a) 18 Feb 1961. Final app: League v Chelsea (h) 14 Mar 1964. Snr fdly v Watford (a) 14 Apr 1964. Transferred to Manchester City (£25,000) 24 Apr 1964.
ARSENAL record: League 46; FA Cup 2; Football Combination 93 (1 gl); London FA Challenge Cup 13; FA Youth Cup 6; Metropolitan League 55; South East Counties League 12; London Midweek League 1; Other Jnr comp: 1; Friendlies 46/1 (1 gl).
Honours: Football Combination champions 1962-3. London FA Challenge Cup winners 1961-2, 1962-3. Metropolitan League champions 1958-9, 1960-61. Played for London Grammar Schools and Middlesex Schools. 7 England Youth caps 1959.
Son of Joe Bacuzzi (Fulham & England). A qualified printer. Later played for Reading.

BAKER, Alfred   **1919-31**
Utility player   5ft 8in. 11st 9lb.
Born: Ilkeston, Derbyshire, 27 Apr 1898. Died: 1 Apr 1955.
School: Chaucer Street, Ilkeston.
Jnr football: Cossall St Catherine's (Long Eaton), Eastwood Rangers. Previous Clubs: Chesterfield, Crystal Palace, Huddersfield Town (all during World War One). Joined ARSENAL: May 1919. First app: League v Newcastle United (h) 30 Aug 1919. Final snr app: League v Huddersfield Town (h) 7 Mar 1931. Final app: London Midweek League v Fulham (a) 30 Apr 1931. Retired end of 1930-31 season.
ARSENAL record: League 310 (23 gls); FA Cup 41 (3 gls); Other snr comp: 5; Football Combination 43 (6 gls); London FA Challenge Cup 18 (2 gls); London Midweek League 5; Friendlies 29 (12 gls).
Honours: Captain of Arsenal 1924-5. FA Cup winners 1930, runners-up 1927. London FA Challenge Cup winners 1921-2, runners-up 1925-6. 1 full England cap 1927. 2 apps for Football League 1925, 1926. Played for Professionals v Amateurs (FA Charity Shield) 1924-5.
After retirement became sports club groundsman in South London and scouted for Arsenal.

BAKER, Joseph Henry   **1962-66**
Centre-forward   5ft 8in. 11st 7lb.
Born: Liverpool, 17 Jul 1940.
School: St Joseph's, Motherwell.
Jnr football: Coltness United, Armadale Thistle (Edinburgh). Previous Clubs: Chelsea (trial), Hibernian (1956), AC Torino (Italy). Joined ARSENAL: 16 Jul 1962 from AC Torino for £70,000. First app: Snr fdly v Bristol XI (a) 8 Aug 1962. League debut v Leyton Orient (a) 18 Aug 1962. Final snr app: FA Cup v Blackburn Rovers (a) 22 Jan 1966. Final app: Snr fdly v Southampton (a) 12 Feb 1966. Transferred to Nottingham Forest (£65,000) 26 February 1966.
ARSENAL record: League 144 (93 gls); FA Cup 10 (4 gls); European comp: 2 (3 gls); Other snr comp: 1 (1 gl); Friendlies 30 (22 gls).
Honours: Played for Lanarkshire and Scotland

Schoolboys. 3 full England caps (2 gls), 1 Under-23 cap.
After Nottingham Forest played for Sunderland, Hibernian and Raith Rovers (1974). Manager-coach to Albion Rovers. Became a publican at Craigneuk and now works in the building trade.

BALDWIN, Thomas   **1962-66**
Inside-forward   5ft 9¾in. 11st 6lb.
Born: Gateshead, 10 Jun 1945.
Jnr football: Wrekenton Jnrs, Gateshead. Joined ARSENAL: Sep 1962 (amateur), 14 Dec 1962 (professional). First app: South East Counties League v Chelsea (a) 29 Sept 1962. First-team debut: League v Birmingham City (h) 6 Apr 1965. Final app: Football League Cup v Gillingham (h) 28 Sep 1966. Transferred to Chelsea (£25,000 as part of George Graham deal) 30 Sep 1966.

ARSENAL record: League 17 (7 gls); Football League Cup 3 (4 gls); Other snr comp: 1 (2 gls); Football Combination 60 (41 gls); London FA Challenge Cup 7 (3 gls); FA Youth Cup 2; Metropolitan League 60 (32 gls); South East Counties League 17 (9 gls); Friendlies 39/1 (22 gls). In addition played one Metropolitan League match for Arsenal 1965-6, later removed from records.
Honours: London FA Challenge Cup runners-up 1965-6.

Won international and club honours with Chelsea. Later played for Millwall, Manchester United, Gravesend and Brentford.

BALL, Alan James   **1971-76**
Inside-forward   5ft 6in. 10st 5lb.
Born: Farnworth, Lancs, 12 May 1945.
School: St Peter's Grammar, Farnworth.
Jnr football: Wolves (amateur), Bolton Wanderers (amateur). Previous Clubs: Blackpool (Sep 1961), Everton (Aug 1966). Joined ARSENAL: 22 Dec 1971 from Everton for £220,000. First app: League v Nottingham Forest (a) 27 Dec 1971. Final snr app: League v Newcastle United (h) 4 Dec 1976. Final app: Football Combination v Norwich City (a) 26 Dec 1976. Transferred to Southampton (£60,000) 23 Dec 1976.

ARSENAL record: League 177 (45 gls); FA Cup 28 (7 gls); Football League Cup 12; Other snr comp: 1; Football Combination 2 (1 gl); Friendlies 23 (5 gls).
Honours: FA Cup runners-up 1972. Arsenal Player of the Year 1974. Captain of Arsenal and England. 19 full England caps (1 gl) 1972-5.
Won other international and club honours with Blackpool and Everton. Member of England's World Cup winning team 1966. Later played in North American Soccer League (Philadelphia Fury and Vancouver Whitecaps), Blackpool (player-manager), Southampton, Hong Kong and Bristol Rovers. Manager (May 1984-Jul 1988) then coach of Portsmouth. Stoke City manager 1989 and Exeter City (1991).

BANNISTER, William   **1902-04**
Centre-half   5ft 11½in. 12st 10lb.
Born: Burnley, 1879. Died: Leicester, 26 Mar 1942.
Jnr football: Earley (Burnley). Previous Clubs: Burnley (1899), Bolton Wanderers (Nov 1901). Joined ARSENAL: 23 Dec 1902 from Bolton Wanderers. First app: League v Stockport County (a) 1 Jan 1903. Final app: Southern Professional Charity Cup Final v Millwall (a) 28 Apr 1904. Transferred to Leicester Fosse 3 May 1904.
ARSENAL record: League 18; FA Cup 4; London League 8; London League (Res) 3 (1 gl); Other snr comp: 3; South Eastern League 4; Friendlies 2.
Honours: Southern Professional Charity Cup runners-up 1903-04.
Illness prevented him playing for much of 1903-04. Won England caps with Burnley and Bolton Wanderers, 1901-02. After Leicester, returned to Burnley (1910) and retired 1911. Became a publican in Burnley and Leicester.

BARBOUR, Humphrey   1888-93
Forward.
Born: Glasgow.
Previous Clubs: Third Lanark, Airdrie. First app:
Kent Senior Cup v Gravesend, 13 Dec 1888. Made
only one first-class app: FA Cup v Derby County
17 Jan 1891. Final app: Reserves v Luton Town
(a) 15 Apr 1893.
ARSENAL record: FA Cup 1; FA Cup(Q) 4 (4
gls). In addition, between 1888-9 and 1892-3 made
66 snr (55 gls) and 18 reserve (8 gls) apps for
Royal Arsenal.
*Honours: London Senior Cup winners 1890-91,
runners-up 1889-90. London Challenge Cup winners
1889-90. Kent Senior Cup winners 1889-90.
Played for Clapton after Arsenal.*

BARLEY, John Charles   1925-29
Wing-half/inside-forward   5ft 9in. 11st 2lb.
Born: Staveley, Derbyshire, Oct 1904.
School: Staveley Council.
Jnr football: Poolsbrook, Lowgates Jnrs, Staveley
Town. Joined ARSENAL: Oct 1925 (amateur),
21 Oct 1925 (professional). First app: Friendly
v Lincoln City (a) 14 Oct 1925. First-team debut:
Snr fdly v Clapton Orient (a) 11 Oct 1926. League
v Leeds United (h) 12 Feb 1927. Final snr app:
FA Cup v Stoke City (h) 12 Jan 1929. Final app:
London Combination v Cardiff City (h) 1 May
1929. Transferred to Reading, 6 May 1929.
ARSENAL record: League 8 (1 gl); FA Cup 2;
Football Combination 135 (14 gls); London FA
Challenge Cup 1; Friendlies 22 (6 gls).
*Honours: Played for North-East Derbyshire
Schoolboys (captain). London Combination
champions 1926-7, 1927-8, 1928-9.*
On retirement ran a shop in Reading. His son, Derek,
played for Arsenal Reserves and Jnrs 1951-2.

BARNES, Walley   1943-55
Full-back   5ft 10½in. 11st 11lb.
Born: Brecon, Wales, 16 Jan 1920. Died: London,
4 Sep 1975.

School: Clarence Road, Gosport.
Jnr football: Pink's Athletic, Portsmouth Gas
Company (Hants League). Previous Clubs:
Portsmouth (amateur), Southampton (amateur).
Joined ARSENAL: 17 Sep 1943. Re-signed Oct
1946. First app: Football League South v Brighton
(a) 25 Sep 1943. First-team debut: League v
Preston North End (a) 9 Nov 1946. Final app:
League v Portsmouth (a) 17 Sep 1955. Retired
Sep 1955.
ARSENAL record: League 267 (11 gls); FA Cup
25 (1 gl); FA Charity Shield 2; Football
Combination 10; Friendlies 46 (1 gl). In addition
made 40 apps (3 gls) during wartime.
Honours: Played for Hampshire Schoolboys.

Division One champions 1947-8. FA Cup winners
1950, runners-up 1952. FA Charity Shield winners
1948-9, 1953-4. Captain of Arsenal and Wales.
22 full Wales caps (1 gl) 1947-54 and made 2 apps
in wartime internationals.
Served as a sergeant major in the Army Physical
Training Corps during the War. Received two
serious knee injuries during his career — in 1944,
when it was thought he would never play again
and in the 1952 FA Cup Final which resulted
in him missing the whole of 1952-3 season. On
retiring in 1955, he became BBC Television
football adviser.

BARNETT, Geoffrey Colin   1969-76
Goalkeeper   6ft. 12st 7lb.
Born: Northwich, Cheshire, 16 Oct 1946.
School: Verdin Grammar, Winsford.
Previous Club: Everton (1964). Joined
ARSENAL: 1 Oct 1969 from Everton for £35,000.
First app: League v Coventry City (h) 4 Oct 1969.
Final app: League v Stoke City (a) 13 Dec 1975.
Contract cancelled Feb 1976.
ARSENAL record: League 39; FA Cup 3;
Football League Cup 5; European Competitions
2; Football Combination 183; London FA
Challenge Cup 8; Friendlies 20/16.
*Honours: FA Cup runners-up 1972. Football
Combination Cup winners 1969-70.*
Won England Schoolboy and Youth international
and club honours with Everton. Contract with
Arsenal was cancelled by mutual consent (Feb
1976) and after a short spell as a publican, went
to play for Minnesota Kicks in America,
eventually becoming coach-manager.

BARNWELL, John   1955-64
Wing-half/inside-forward   5ft 8in. 11st 6lb.
Born: High Heaton, Newcastle, 24 Dec 1938.
Jnr football: Whitley Bay, Bishop Auckland.
Joined ARSENAL: Aug 1955 (amateur), 28 Nov
1956 (professional). First app: Youth Friendly v
West German Youth (a) 22 Aug 1955. First snr
app: Southern Floodlit Challenge Cup v West
Ham United (h) 4 Dec 1956. League v Sunderland
(a) 13 Apr 1957. Final snr app: League v Fulham
(h) 18 Jan 1964. Final app: Football Combination
v Colchester (a) 29 Feb 1964. Transferred to
Nottingham Forest (£30,000) 10 Mar 1964.
ARSENAL record: League 138 (23 gls); FA Cup
10; European Competitions 3 (1 gl); Other snr
comp: 4; Football Combination 78 (19 gls);
London FA Challenge Cup 14 (3 gls); FA Youth
Cup 7 (4 gls); Metropolitan League 5; South East
Counties League 11 (1 gl); London Midweek
League 4 (1 gl); Other jnr comp: 8; Friendlies 43/
3 (20 gls).
*Honours: Played for Newcastle Schoolboys. Southern
Floodlight Challenge Cup winners 1958-9. 10
England Youth caps 1955-7, 1 Under-23 cap 1961.*
Served National Service in RASC and played
many matches for British Army. Later played for
Sheffield United (1970) and then became coach
at Hereford and Peterborough followed by spells
as manager of Peterborough, Wolves (1978), AEK
(Athens), Notts County (Jun 1987) and Walsall
(Jan 1989).

BARRON, Paul George   1978-80
Goalkeeper   6ft 2in. 13st 5lb.
Born: London, 16 Sep 1953.
School: Erith Grammar; Borough Road College,
Isleworth.
Jnr football: Slough Town. Previous Club:
Plymouth Argyle (Jul 1976). Joined ARSENAL:
5 Jul 1978 from Plymouth Argyle for £70,000.
First app: Snr fdly (sub) v Borussia Dortmund
28 Jul 1978. First snr app: League v Manchester
City (a) 22 Aug 1978. Final snr app: League v
Coventry City (a) 3 May 1980. Final app: Jnr

fdly v Luton Town Res (L Colney) 5 Aug 1980.
Transferred to Crystal Palace (£200,000) 13 Aug
1980.
ARSENAL record: League 8; Football
Combination 60; Friendlies 7/2.
Son of George Barron (Tottenham Hotspur).
Played for Kent Schoolboys and Kent Youth. Was
a PE teacher before taking up professional
football. Later played for West Brom (1982) and
Queen's Park Rangers (1984). Came out of
retirement and played for Welling 1988-9.

BASSETT, Spencer T.   1906-10
Half-back   5ft 9½in. 11st 7lb.
Born: Blackheath. Died: France, 9 Apr 1917.
Joined ARSENAL: 1906 (amateur), 3 May 1907
(professional) from Maidstone. First app: Jnr fdly
v Local District XI 29 Aug 1906. First snr app:
Snr fdly v Reading (a) 12 Sep 1906. League v
Notts County (a) 7 Oct 1909 (only app). Final
app: Snr fdly v Ilford (a) 30 Apr 1910.
ARSENAL record: League 1; Other snr comp:
1; South Eastern League 95 (6 gls); London League
(Res) 27 (2 gls); Other jnr comp: 2 (1 gl); Friendlies
24 (1 gl).
Honours: South East League champions 1907-08.
Later played for Exeter City (1910-13) and
Swansea Town. Died in France after being badly
wounded during World War One.

BASTIN, Clifford Sydney   1929-46
Outside-left/inside-forward/wing-half   5ft 8in.
10st 12lb.
Born: Exeter, 14 Mar 1912. Died: Exeter, 4 Dec
1991.

School: Ladysmith Road, Exeter.
Jnr football: St Marks (Exeter), St James (Exeter).
Previous Club: Exeter City (1926). Joined
ARSENAL: 17 May 1929 from Exeter City for
£2,000. First app: Football Combination v Luton
Town (a) 31 Aug 1929. First snr app: Snr fdly
v Nottingham Forest (h) 19 Sep 1929. League v
Everton (a) 5 Oct 1929. Final snr app: League
v Manchester United (a) 28 Sep 1946. Final app:
Football Combination v Cardiff City (h) 26 Oct
1946. Retired Jan 1947.
ARSENAL record: League 350 (150 gls); FA Cup
42 (26 gls); FA Charity Shield 4 (2 gls); Other
snr comp: 6 (4 gls); Football Combination 23 (15
gls); London FA Challenge Cup 2 (1 gl); London
Midweek League 3; Friendlies 26/1 (14 gls). In
addition played three League matches (1 gl) 1939-
40 prior to outbreak of war and made 241 apps
(70 gls) during wartime.
*Honours: Played for Exeter Schoolboys. Division
One champions 1930-31, 1932-3, 1933-4, 1934-5,
1937-8. FA Cup winners 1930, 1936, runners-up*

1932. FA Charity Shield winners 1930-31, 1931-2, 1934-5, runners-up 1935-6. Sheriff of London Shield winners 1930-31, 1932-3. Northampton Charity Shield winners 1930, 1931, 1932. London Combination champions 1929-30. Football League South Cup winners 1942-3. Football League War Cup runners-up 1940-41. England Schoolboy international. 21 full England caps (12 gls) 1931-8. Made 4 apps (4 gls) for Football League 1931-6.
Worked as electrician before professional football. Won every major honour before 19 years old. Holds record for number of goals scored by a winger — 33 in 42 matches in 1932-3. On retirement worked on Sunday newspaper and then restaurant owner in Edgware. Became a publican in Exeter and retired in Apr 1977.

BATES, Joseph Morris   **1888-91**
Half-back.
Born: 1864. Died: 6 Sep 1905.
Previously with Nottingham Forest. First app: Snr fdly v London Scottish (h) 15 Sep 1888. First first-class app: FA Cup (Q) v Lyndhurst (h) 5 Oct 1889. Final app: Res v Uxbridge (a) 19 Sep 1891.
ARSENAL record: FA Cup(Q) 3. In addition, between 1888-9 and 1891-2 made 70 Senior apps. (6 gls) and 6 reserve apps for Royal Arsenal.
Honours: London Challenge Cup winners 1889-90. Kent Senior Cup winners 1889-90. London Senior Cup runners-up 1889-90. Played for Kent County.
Captain of Royal Arsenal. Was in Royal Army Medical Corps Volunteers.

BATEUP, Edward   **1905-08 & 1910-11**
Goalkeeper   5ft 10in. 12st.
Born: Croydon, 1886.
Jnr football: Faversham FC (Kent). Joined ARSENAL: Apr 1905 (amateur), 19 May 1905 (professional) from Faversham. Rejoined 5 Jul 1910 from New Brompton. First app: Snr fdly v Sheffield United (h) 29 Apr 1905. League v Manchester City (a) 7 Apr 1906. Final snr app: League v Bristol City (h) 25 Mar 1911. Final app: South Eastern League v Luton Town (a) 22 Apr 1911. Transferred to New Brompton Summer 1908. Finally left Arsenal for Burslem Port Vale 1911.
ARSENAL record: League 34; FA Cup 2; Other snr comp: 2; London FA Challenge Cup 2; South Eastern League 72; London League (Res) 39; Friendlies 20 (1 gl).
Honours: South Eastern League champions 1905-06, 1906-07, 1907-08. London League (Res) champions 1906-07.
Was formerly in the 7th Dragoon Guards.

BATSON, Brendon Martin   **1969-74**
Defender   5ft 10in. 11st 9lb.
Born: St George's, Grenada, West Indies, 6 Feb 1953.
School: Walthamstow.
Joined ARSENAL: Feb 1969 (amateur), 1 Jul 1969 (apprentice), 25 Jan 1971 (professional). First app: Metropolitan v Romford (a) 15 Feb 1969. First snr app: League (sub) v Newcastle United (a) 11 Mar 1972. Final snr app: League (sub) v Liverpool (h) 3 Nov 1973. Snr fdly (sub) v Portsmouth (a) 5 Nov 1973. Final app: Football Combination v Luton Town (h) 19 Jan 1974. Transferred to Cambridge United (£6,000) 31 Jan 1974 .
ARSENAL record: League 6/4; Other snr comp: 1; Football Combination 106/1 (2 gls); London FA Challenge Cup 8; FA Youth Cup 4; Metropolitan League 5 (2 gls); South East Counties League 20 (4 gls); Other jnr comp: 3; Friendlies 43/4 (3 gls).
Honours: Played for Waltham Forest Schoolboys and Essex Schoolboys. Football Combination Cup winners 1969-70. FA Youth Cup winners (and

captain) 1970-71. South East Counties League Cup winners 1970-71.
Later played for West Brom (Feb 1978) with whom he won international honour. Serious injury ended his career in 1983 and is now Assistant Secretary of the Professional Footballers Association.

BEARDSLEY, Frederick W.   **1886-91**
Goalkeeper.
Born: Nottingham.
Previously with Nottingham Forest. One of the originators of Royal Arsenal FC in 1886. First app: Friendly v Eastern Wanderers (a) 11 Dec 1886. First first-class app: FA Cup (Q) v Lyndhurst (h) 5 Oct 1889. Final app: Res v Erith (h) 4 Apr 1891.
ARSENAL record: FA Cup(Q) 2. In addition, between 1886-7 and 1890-91 made 67 Senior and 19 reserve apps for Royal Arsenal.
Honours: London Challenge Cup winners 1889-90. Kent Senior Cup winners 1889-90. London Senior Cup runners-up 1889-90.
On retirement had a confectionary business in Plumstead and became a director of Woolwich Arsenal.

BEASLEY, Albert Edward 'Pat'   **1931-36**
Wing-forward   5ft 8in. 11st.
Born: Stourbridge, 27 Jul 1913. Died: Taunton, Somerset, 3 Mar 1986.
School: Amblecote; Brierley Hill.
Jnr football: Cookley (Kidderminster),

Stourbridge FC. Joined ARSENAL: 7 May 1931 from Stourbridge for £550. First app: London Combination v Reading (h) 3 Oct 1931. First snr app: League v Sunderland (a) 6 Apr 1932. Final snr app: League v Manchester United (a) 3 Oct 1936. Final app: London FA Challenge Cup v Clapton Orient (h) 5 Oct 1936. Transferred to Huddersfield Town (£750) 8 Oct 1936 .
ARSENAL record: League 79 (19 gls); FA Cup (5 gls); Other snr comp: 1 (1 gl); Football Combination 112 (73 gls); London FA Challenge Cup 12 (7 gls); London Midweek League 12 (4 gls); Friendlies 14/1 (6 gls). In addition made 18 'guest' apps (2 gls) during wartime.
Honours: Played for Birmingham Schoolboys. Division One champions 1933-4, 1934-5. London Combination champions 1933-4. Northampton Charity Shield winners 1932. London Midweek League champions 1931-2.
Worked on the Royal Mint during the war. After Huddersfield Town played for Fulham and won club and international honours with those clubs. Became player-manager of Bristol City, manager of Birmingham City and finally manager of Dover FC, retiring in 1964 to Chard, Somerset.

BEE, Edward   **1890-93**
Goalkeeper   5ft 8in. 11st.
Born: Nottingham, 1868.
Previously played for various Nottingham clubs. First app: Snr fdly v 93rd Highlanders (h) 6 Sep 1890. First first-class app: FA Cup v Derby County (h) 17 Jan 1891. Final app: Res v St Luke's (a) 29 Apr 1893.
ARSENAL record: FA Cup 2; FA Cup(Q) 2. In addition, between 1890-91 and 1892-3 made 105 Senior and 11 reserve apps for Royal Arsenal.
Honours: London Senior Cup winners 1890-91.
A bricklayer by trade. Played for Luton Town after Arsenal. Became trainer at Nottingham Forest.

BELL, Charles   **1913-14**
Centre-forward   5ft 8in. 11st 10lb.
Born: Dumfries, Scotland, 1894.
Jnr football: Dumfries Amateurs, Dumfries Wanderers, Douglas Wanderers, Carlisle City. Joined ARSENAL: 2 Sep 1913 from Carlisle City. First app: Snr fdly v Queen's Park Rangers (a) 11 September 1913. First first-class app: League v Leicester Fosse (a) 27 Dec 1913. Final app: South Eastern League v Brighton (h) 11 Apr 1914. Transferred to Chesterfield 10 Jul 1914.
ARSENAL record: League 1 (2 gls); South Eastern League (Res) 11 (4 gls); Other jnr comp: 1; Friendlies 3 (5 gls).
Scored two goals in his only first class app for Arsenal.

BELLAMY James   **1903-07**
Outside-right/wing-half   5ft 7in. 11st.
Born: Barking, 1885.
Joined ARSENAL: 2 May 1903 from Reading. First app: London League v Tottenham Hotspur (a) 1 Sep 1903. League v Everton (h) 22 Apr 1905. Final snr app: League v Blackburn Rovers (h) 30 Mar 1907. Final app: South Eastern League v Maidstone (h) 15 Apr 1907. Transferred to Portsmouth Summer 1907.
ARSENAL record: League 29 (4 gls); London League 4 (1 gl); London League (Res) 30 (7 gls); Other snr comp: 2; South Eastern League 48 (12 gls); Other jnr comp: 1 (1 gl); Friendlies 24 (4 gls).
Honours: South Eastern Counties League champions 1903-04. London League (Res) champions 1903-04. Southern Charity Cup winners 1905-06.
Later played for Norwich, Dundee, Motherwell, Burnley, Fulham, and Southend.

BENEY, Albert   **1909-10**
Inside-forward   5ft 8in. 11st 3lb.
Born: Hastings, Sussex, 1887.
Jnr football: Hastings & St Leonards. Joined ARSENAL: 3 Feb 1909 from Hastings for £225. First app: League v Manchester City (a) 13 Feb 1909. Final app: League v Sheffield Wednesday (h) 26 Mar 1910. Snr fdly v Ilford (a) 30 Apr 1910. Transferred to Carlisle Summer 1910.
ARSENAL record: League 16 (6 gls); FA Cup 1; London FA Challenge Cup 3; South Eastern League 19 (18 gls); London League (Res) 1; Friendlies 11 (13 gls).

BENSON, Robert William   **1913-16**
Full-back   5ft 10in. 12st 10lb.
Born: Swalwell, Northumberland, 9 Feb 1883.
Died: London, 19 Feb 1916.
Jnr football: Dunstan Villa, Shankhouse, Swalwell FC. Previous Clubs: Newcastle United (1903), Southampton (1904), Sheffield United (1905). Joined ARSENAL: 18 Nov 1913 from Sheffield United. First app: London League (Res) v Queen's Park Rangers (h) 27 Nov 1913. First snr app: League v Bristol City (a) 29 Nov 1913. Final snr app: League v Nottingham Forest (h)

38

24 Apr 1915. Final app: Supplementary Competition (War) v Reading (h) 19 Feb 1916. ARSENAL record: League 52 (7 gls); FA Cup 2; Other snr comp: 3; London FA Challenge Cup 4; South Eastern League 10 (5 gls); London League (Res) 5; Friendlies 2. In addition made 1 app during wartime (see below).
Honours: London FA Challenge Cup runners-up 1914-15. Norwich Cup Hospital winners 1913-14. Won international honours with Sheffield United. On 19 Feb 1916 he chose to play for Arsenal when they were a player short during wartime. He had been engaged on munitions work and had not played for almost 12 months. During the match he had to retire from the field, and died later in the dressing-room.

BIGDEN, James Henry   **1904-08**
Half-back   5ft 8in. 12st.
Born: 1880.
Jnr football: Gravesend. Previous Club: West Ham. Joined ARSENAL: 22 Jun 1904 from West Ham. First app: League v Bristol City (h) 1 September 1904. League v Newcastle United (a) 3 Sep 1904. Final app: League v Sheffield Wednesday (h) 20 Apr 1908. Transferred to Bury 27 Jun 1908.
ARSENAL record: League 75 (1 gl); FA Cup 12; Other snr comp: 4; South Eastern League 28 (2 gls); London League (Res) 10; Friendlies 17 (1 gl).
Honours: South Eastern Counties League champions 1905-06. Southern Charity Cup winners 1905-06.
Later played for Southend (1909).

BIGGS, Anthony   **1955-58**
Centre-forward   6ft 1in. 12st 7lb.
Born: Greenford, Middlesex, 17 Apr 1936.
Jnr football: Brentford (juniors), Bexleyheath, Hounslow Town. Joined ARSENAL: Jul 1955 (amateur), 2 Aug 1956 (professional). First app: Football Combination v Charlton Athletic (h) 5 Nov 1955. First snr app: Snr fdly v Eintracht (h) 15 Feb 1958. League v Wolves (a) 8 Apr 1958. Final snr app: League v Blackpool (h) 29 Nov 1958. Final app: Football Combination v Chelsea (h) 6 Dec 1958. Transferred to Leyton Orient (part of L.Julians deal) 27 Dec 1958 .
ARSENAL record: League 4 (1 gl); Football Combination 64 (44 gls); London FA Challenge Cup 8 (2 gls); Metropolitan League 2; London Midweek League 1 (1 gl); Friendlies 7/1 (4 gls).
Honours: Played for Middlesex Youth. London FA Challenge Cup winners 1957-8. Won 2 England Amateur international caps 1955-6.
Served National Service in RAF before joining Arsenal as a professional. Played cricket for Middlesex 2nd XI. Later played for Hereford United and Folkestone.

BIGGS, Arthur Gilbert   **1933-37**
Inside-forward   5ft 10in. 11st.
Born: Wootton, Bedfordshire.
Jnr football: Bedfordshire. Joined ARSENAL: 27 Oct 1933 (amateur), 16 Dec 1933 (professional). First app: London Midweek League v West Ham (a) 1 Nov 1933. First snr app: League v Stoke City (a) 29 Mar 1937. Final snr app: Snr fdly (sub) v Racing Club de Paris (a) 28 Nov 1937. Final app: London FA Challenge Cup v Millwall (a) 6 Dec 1937. Transferred to Hearts (£2,500) 9 Dec 1937.
ARSENAL record: League 3; Football Combination 106 (60 gls); London FA Challenge Cup 10 (3 gls); London Midweek League 8 (3 gls); Friendlies 15/1 (8 gls).
Honours: London Combination champions 1934-5, 1936-7. London FA Challenge Cup winners 1935-6, runners-up 1936-7.
At one time held the club's Football Combination

record for most goals in a season — 41 in 1936-7. Became coach to Vauxhall Motors FC.

BIRKETT, Ralph James Evans   **1933-35**
Outside-right   5ft 9in. 11st 4lb.
Born: Torquay, Devon, 9 Jan 1912.
School: Woodthorpe School, Ashford, Middlesex.
Jnr football: Dartmouth United (amateur). Previous Club: Torquay United (1929). Joined ARSENAL: 20 Apr 1933 from Torquay United. First app: London Combination v Portsmouth (h) 6 May 1933. First snr app: League v Sheffield Wednesday (a) 2 Sep 1933. Final snr app: League v Stoke City (h) 20 Feb 1935. Final app: London Combination v Southend (a) 9 Mar 1935. Transferred to Middlesbrough (£2,000) 15 Mar 1935.
ARSENAL record: League 19 (7 gls); FA Cup 2 (1 gl); FA Charity Shield 2 (3 gls); Football Combination 43 (27 gls); London FA Challenge Cup 2 (4 gls); London Midweek League 2 (1 gl); Friendlies 4 (1 gl).
Honours: Division One champions 1933-4. FA Charity Shield winners 1933-4, 1934-5. London Combination champions 1933-4, 1934-5. London FA Challenge Cup winners 1933-4. Played for Middlesex Schoolboys.
Won international honours with Middlesbrough. Later played for Newcastle United (1938). Retired during the war. Now lives at Paignton.

BLACK, Thomas   **1931-33**
Full-back   5ft 10in. 11st 3lb.
Born: Mossend, Glasgow.
Jnr football: Strathclyde. Joined ARSENAL: 4 Jul 1931 from Strathclyde. First app: London Combination v Coventry (a) 29 Aug 1931. First snr app: Snr fdly v Plymouth Argyle (a) 4 May 1932. Final app: FA Cup v Walsall (a) 14 Jan 1933. Transferred to Plymouth Argyle 20 Jan 1933.
ARSENAL record: FA Cup 1; Football Combination 26 (1 gl); London FA Challenge Cup 2; London Midweek League 17; Friendlies 9.
Honours: London Midweek League champions 1931-2.
Made an undistinguished app in the 'famous' Cup defeat at Walsall, 1933 and was transferred within a week afterwards. After Plymouth Argyle he played for Southend United (1939).

BLACKWOOD, John   **1900-01**
Centre-forward   5ft 8½in. 11st 4lb.
Born: Glasgow, 1877.
Previous Clubs: Partick Thistle, Glasgow Celtic. Joined ARSENAL: 9 May 1900 from Glasgow Celtic. First app: League v Gainsborough Trinity. (h) 1 Sep 1900. First snr app: Snr fdly v Nottingham Forest (h) 5 Apr 1901. Final app: London League (Res) v Brentford (h) 25 Apr 1901. Transferred to Reading May 1901.
ARSENAL record: League 17 (6 gls); FA Cup 1 (1 gl); London League (Res) 3 (4 gls); Kent League 2 (1 gl); Friendlies 11 (11 gls).

BLAIR, James   **1905-06**
Inside-forward
Born: Dumfries, Scotland, 1885. Died: Dumfries, Scotland, 24 Mar 1913.
Joined ARSENAL: 3 May 1905 from Kilmarnock. First app: League v Liverpool (h) 2 Sep 1905. Final snr app: Snr fdly v West Norwood (a) 19 Sep 1906. Final app: London League (Res) v Brentford (a) 17 Nov 1906. Transferred to Manchester City 23 Nov 1906.
ARSENAL record: League 13 (3 gls); Other snr comp: 1; South Eastern League 5 (2 gls); London League (Reserves) 8 (2 gls); Friendlies 8 (1 gl).
Later played for Bradford City (May 1910) and Stockport County (Aug 1912). Took his own life at home in Dumfries 1913.

BLOCKLEY, Jeffrey Paul   **1972-75**
Centre-half   6ft 1in. 12st 6lb.
Born: Leicester, 12 Sep 1949.
School: New Parks Secondary, Leicester.
Jnr football: Midland Athletic (Leicester). Previous Club: Coventry City (1966). Joined ARSENAL: 4 Oct 1972 from Coventry City for £200,000. First app: League v Sheffield United (a) 7 Oct 1972. Final snr app: League v Leeds United (a) 5 Oct 1974. Final app: Football Combination v Norwich City (a) 4 Jan 1975. Transferred to Leicester City (£100,000) 18 Jan 1975.
ARSENAL record: League 52 (1 gl); FA Cup 7; Football League Cup 3; Other snr comp: 1; Football Combination 16; Friendlies 7.
Honours: Played for Leicester and Leicestershire Schoolboys. 1 full England cap 1972; 4 Under-23 caps 1973.
Won other international honours with Coventry. Later played for Notts County and Enderby Town.

BLOOMFIELD, James Henry   **1954-60**
Inside-forward   5ft 9in. 10st 5lb.
Born: Kensington, London, 15 Feb 1934. Died: London, 3 Apr 1983.
School: St Clements, North Kensington.
Jnr football: Hayes (Athenian League). Previous Club: Brentford (Nov 1952). Joined ARSENAL: 16 Jul 1954 from Brentford for £10,000. First app: Football Combination v Tottenham Hotspur (a) 21 Aug 1954. First snr app: League v Everton (a) 25 Aug 1954. Final app: League v Leicester City (a) 8 Oct 1960. Snr fdly v Northampton (a) 10 Oct 1960. Transferred to Birmingham (£30,000) 19 Nov 1960.

ARSENAL record: League 210 (54 gls); FA Cup 17 (2 gls); Other snr comp: 9 (4 gls); Football Combination 21 (7 gls); London FA Challenge Cup 3 (1 gl); Friendlies 52/1 (16 gls).
Honours: Played for Middlesex Youth. 2 England Under-23 caps (1 gl) 1956-7. Made 1 app for Football League 1960.
Served National Service in the Army and played many representative matches for them. Later played for Brentford (1964), West Ham (1965) and Plymouth (1966). Became player-manager at Orient (1968), manager Leicester City (1971) and Orient (1977) resigning 1981.

BLYTH, William Naismith   **1914-29**
Inside-forward/wing-half   5ft 7in. 11st 7lb.
Born: Dalkeith, Midlothian, Scotland, 17 Jun

39

1895. Died: Worthing, 1 Jul 1968.
Jnr football: Wemyss Athletic. Previous Club:
Manchester City. Joined ARSENAL: 6 May 1914
from Manchester City. First app: South Eastern
League v Fulham (h) 5 Sep 1914. First snr app:
League v Huddersfield Town (a) 21 Nov 1914.
Final snr app: League v Aston Villa (a) 6 Apr
1929. Final fdly v Kettering (a) 3 May
1929. Transferred to Birmingham 25 May 1929.
ARSENAL record: League 314 (45 gls); FA Cup
29 (6 gls); Other snr comp: 6 (2 gls); Football
Combination 37 (6 gls); London FA Challenge
Cup 18 (1 gl); South Eastern League 19 (7 gls);
London League (Reserves) 13 (7 gls); Friendlies
38 (12 gls). In addition made 3 apps (1 gl) during
wartime.
*Honours: Played for Scotland in two junior
internationals 1912. Captain of Arsenal. FA Cup
runners-up 1927. London FA Challenge Cup
winners 1921-2, 1923-4, runners-up 1925-6.
Was also an expert golfer. Served in RASC in
France during war.*

BOOT, Michael C.   1963-67
Wing-half/inside-forward   5ft 6in. 10st 5lb.
Born: Leicester, 17 Dec 1947.
Jnr football: Enderby Town. Joined ARSENAL:
Summer 1963 (apprentice), 18 Dec 1964
(professional). First app: South East Counties
League v West Ham (h) 24 Aug 1963. First snr
app: Football League Cup v West Ham (h) 5 Oct
1966. Final snr app: Snr fdly v Cardiff City (h)
15 Nov 1966. Final app: Football Combination
v Coventry City (a) 21 Mar 1967.
ARSENAL record: League 3/1 (2 gls); Football
League Cup 1; Football Combination 50 (8 gls);
London FA Challenge Cup 3 (1 gl); FA Youth
Cup 18 (3 gls); Metropolitan League 35 (14 gls);
South East Counties League 39 (15 gls); Other
jnr comp: 10 (4 gls); Friendlies 55/3 (16 gls).
*Honours: Played for Leicestershire Schoolboys.
England Schoolboy international 1963. FA Youth
Cup winners 1965-6, runners-up 1964-5. South
East Counties League Cup winners 1963-4,
runners-up 1965-6.*
On leaving Arsenal played for Port Elizabeth FC
(South Africa). Returned to England and played
for Nuneaton Borough.

BOOTH, Charles   1892-94
Outside-left   5ft 6½in. 11st 7lb.
Born: Gainsborough, 1869. Died: Wolver-
hampton, 17 Sep 1898.
Previous Clubs: Gainsborough Trinity,
Wolverhampton Wanderers (1889). Joined
ARSENAL: Summer 1892 from Wolverhampton
Wanderers. First app: Snr fdly v Highland Light
Infantry (h) 1 Sep 1892. First first-class app: FA
Cup (Q) v Highland Light Infantry (h) 15 Oct
1892. Final app: League v Lincoln City (a) 3 Feb
1894. Transferred to Loughborough Town 1894.
ARSENAL record: League 16 (2 gls); FA Cup
2; FA Cup (Q) 8 (8 gls); Friendlies 14 (4 gls).
In addition during 1892-3 made 42 senior apps
(11 gls) for Royal Arsenal.

BOREHAM, Reginald   1921-25
Inside-left   5ft 7in. 10st 11lb.
Born: Wycombe. Died: Mar 1976.
Previous Club: Wycombe Wanderers (amateur).
Joined ARSENAL: 21 Jul 1921 from Wycombe
Wanderers (amateur). First app: London
Combination v Queen's Park Rangers (a) 1 Sep
1921. First snr app: League v Bolton Wanderers
(h) 12 Dec 1921. Final snr app: League v West
Brom (h) 15 Sep 1923. Final app: London
Combination v Brentford (a) 19 Jan 1924.
Contract with Arsenal cancelled 11 May 1925.
ARSENAL record: League 51 (18 gls); FA Cup
2; Other snr comp: 1; Football Combination 15

(5 gls); London FA Challenge Cup 1; Friendlies
5 (2 gls).
*Honours: London FA Challenge Cup winners
1921-2.*
Won England Amateur international honours
with Wycombe Wanderers. Was Secretary of
Wycombe from 1937 to 1950.

BOULD, Stephen Andrew   1988-
Defender   6ft 3in. 12st 8lb.
Born: Stoke-on-Trent, 16 Nov 1962.
Previous Clubs: Stoke City (1980), Newport
United (loan Oct/Dec 1982). Joined ARSENAL:
3 Jun 1988 from Stoke City for £390,000
(tribunal). First app: Snr fdly v Yeovil Town (a)
23 Jul 1988. League v Wimbledon (a) 27 Aug
1988.

ARSENAL record: League 107/5 (3 gls); FA Cup
12; Football League Cup 9; European comp: 0/
1; Other snr comp: 7/2 (1 gl); Football
Combination 12 (2 gls); Friendlies 22/6.
*Honours: Division One champions 1988-9, 1990-
91. Mercantile Credit Centenary Trophy winner
1988-9.*
Suffered a severe back injury in 1987 which
threatened his career but recovered following a
disc operation.

BOULTON, Frank Preece   1936-38
Goalkeeper   6ft. 12st.
Born: Chipping Sodbury, 12 Aug 1917. Died:
Swindon, Jun 1987.
Jnr football: Bristol City (trial), Bath City. Joined
ARSENAL: 8 Oct 1936 from Bath City. First app:
Jnr fdly v Oxford University (h) 12 Nov 1936.
First snr app: League v Preston North End (a)
28 Dec 1936. Final snr app: League v Sunderland
(a) 29 Jan 1938. Final app: London Combination
v Reading (a) 6 Apr 1938. Transferred to Derby
County 23 Aug 1938.
ARSENAL record: League 36; FA Cup 6;
Football Combination 12; London FA Challenge
Cup 1; Other snr comp: 1; Friendlies 9. In addition
made 11 'guest' apps during wartime.
*Honours: Division One champions 1937-8. Bath
Coronation Cup winners 1936-7.*
Later played for Swindon Town (1946), Crystal
Palace (1950) and Bedford Town.

BOWDEN, Edwin Raymond   1933-37
Inside/centre-forward   5ft 9½in. 10st 10lb.
Born: Looe, Cornwall, 13 Sep 1909.
School: Liskeard Secondary.
Jnr football: Looe. Previous Club: Plymouth Argyle
(1926). Joined ARSENAL: 14 Mar 1933 from
Plymouth Argyle for £4,500. First app: League v
Wolverhampton (h) 18 Mar 1933. Final app: League
v Middlesbrough (h) 30 Oct 1937. Transferred to
Newcastle United (£5,000) 5 Nov 1937.
ARSENAL record: League 123 (42 gls); FA Cup
13 (5 gls); FA Charity Shield 2 (1 gl); Other snr
comp: 1 (1 gl); Football Combination 14 (4 gls);

Friendlies 5 (2 gls).
*Honours: Division One champions 1933-4, 1934-5.
FA Cup winners 1936. FA Charity Shield winners
1933-4, runners-up 1934-6. 6 full England caps (1 gl)
1934-6 and made 2 apps (1 gl) for the Football
Combination 1934-5. Bath Coronation Cup winners 1936-7.*
Was a solicitor's clerk before taking up football.
Won FA and club honours with Plymouth.
Retired from football at the outbreak of war and
returned to Plymouth where he owned a sports
outfitters shop for a good number of years.

BOWEN, David Lloyd   1950-59
Left-half   5ft 10in. 11st 2lb.
Born: Nantyffyllon, nr Maesteg, S.Wales, 7 Jun 1928.
School: Maesteg Grammar.
Previous Club: Northampton Town (1947). Joined
ARSENAL: 26 Jul 1950 from Northampton Town
for £1,000. First app: Football Combination v
Bristol Rovers (h) 19 Aug 1950. First snr app:
League v Wolverhampton Wanderers (h) 24 Mar
1951. Final snr app: League v Birmingham (h) 4 May
1959. On tour v Fiorentina (Italy) 20 May 1959.
Transferred to Northampton Town as player-
manager (£5,000) 6 Jul 1959.
ARSENAL record: League 146 (2 gls); FA Cup
16; Other snr comp: 5; Football Combination 118
(8 gls); London FA Challenge Cup 13; Friendlies
51/2 (3 gls).
*Honours: Southern Floodlit Challenge Cup
winners 1958-9. Football Combination champions
1950-1. Football Combination Cup winners 1952-3.
London FA Challenge Cup winners 1953-4.
Captain of Arsenal and Wales. 19 full Wales caps
(1 gl) 1954-9.*
Played Rugby Union as a boy. Served National
Service in RAF just before joining Arsenal.
Became manager of the Welsh international team
(1964). Was secretary/general manager of
Northampton Town.

BOWEN, Edward   1926-28
Centre-forward   5ft 8in. 10st 9lb.
Born: Goldthorpe, Yorks, 1 Jul 1903.
Jnr football: Wath Athletic. Joined ARSENAL:
17 Feb 1926 from Wath Athletic for £500. First
app: London Combination v West Ham (h) 18
Feb 1926. First snr app: On tour v Rapid (Vienna)
18 May 1926. Final snr app: League v Bury (a)
4 May 1927 (only app). Final app: London
Combination v Clapton Orient (h) 30 Jan 1928.
Transferred to Northampton Town 1 Feb 1928.
ARSENAL record: League 1; Football
Combination 60 (56 gls); Friendlies 11 (21 gls).

Honours: London Combination champions 1926-7, 1927-8.
Scored 10 hat-tricks in reserve and Jnr fdly matches. Later played for Bristol City (1932) and finished leading scorer with 28 goals in his only full season.

BOYD, Henry   **1894-97**
Centre-forward
Born: Pollokshaws, Scotland, 1868.
Joined ARSENAL: 14 May 1894 from West Bromwich Albion. First app: Snr fdly v Fleetwood Rangers (h) 8 Sep 1894. League v Grimsby Town (h) 10 Sep 1894. Final app: League v Loughborough Town (a) 12 Dec 1896. Transferred to Newton Heath (£45) 18 Jan 1897.
ARSENAL record: League 40 (31 gls); FA Cup 1; United League 4 (1 gl); Kent League 2 (1 gl); Friendlies 32 (47 gls).
Suffered a broken leg in Oct of his first season with Arsenal.

BOYLAN, P.A.   **1896-97**
Half-back   5ft 7in. 10st 10lb.
Born: Greenock, Scotland, 1876.
Jnr football: Greenock Volunteers. Joined ARSENAL: Jun 1896. First app: Snr fdly v Rossendale (h) 1 Sep 1896. League v Manchester City (a) 5 Sep 1896. Final app: Snr fdly v Southampton SM (a) 29 Apr 1897.
ARSENAL record: League 11; United League 7; Kent League 10 (4 gls); Friendlies 12 (1 gl).
Honours: Kent League champions 1896-7.
Played for Greenock Morton after Arsenal.

BOYLE, James   **1893-97**
Half-back.
Joined ARSENAL: 29 Nov 1893 from Celtic. First app: Snr fdly v London Caledonians (a) 30 Nov 1893. League v Northwich Victoria (a) 9 Dec 1893. Final app: League v Manchester City (h) 28 Apr 1897.
ARSENAL record: League 61 (7 gls); FA Cup 5 (2 gls); United League 4; Kent League 26 (3 gls); Friendlies 81 (15 gls).
Honours: Kent League champions 1896-7.
Played four League games in goal in 1895-6 season. Played for Dartford after Arsenal.

BRADSHAW, Frank   **1914-23**
Inside-left/full-back   5ft 10½in. 12st 2lb.
Born: Sheffield, 31 May 1884.
Jnr football: Oxford St Sunday School (Sheffield), Sheffield Wednesday (amateur). Previous Clubs: Sheffield Wednesday (professional 1904), Northampton Town (1910), Everton (Nov 1911). Joined ARSENAL: 8 Jun 1914 from Everton. First app: National Relief Fund v Tottenham Hotspur (a) 22 Aug 1914. League v Glossop (h) 1 Sep 1914. Final snr app: League v Birmingham (a) 2 Dec 1922. Final app: London Combination v Brentford (h) 5 May 1923. Retired May 1923.
ARSENAL record: League 132 (14 gls); FA Cup 10; Other snr com 5; Football Combination 20; South Eastern League 2 (1 gl); London FA Challenge Cup 12 (1 gl); Friendlies 10 (1 gl). In addition made 129 apps (12 gls) during wartime.
Honours: Played for Sheffield Schoolboys. London Combination champions 1922-3. London FA Challenge Cup winners 1921-2, runners-up 1914-5. Southend Hospital Cup winners 1921-2.
Won club and international honours with Sheffield Wednesday. Became manager of Aberdare Athletic. Later retired and lived in Taunton.

BRADSHAW, William   **1900-04**
Forward.
Joined ARSENAL: Mar 1900 (amateur), 5 Jul

1900 (professional). First app: Jnr fdly v Bristol City (Reserves) (h) 31 Mar 1900. First snr app: London League v Queen's Park Rangers (h) 17 Feb 1902. Final snr app: League v Burslem Port Vale (h) 25 Apr 1904. Final app: South Eastern League v St Albans (h) 30 Apr 1904. Transferred to Fulham summer 1904.
ARSENAL record: League 4 (2 gls); London League 7 (2 gls); Other snr comp: 1; London League (Reserves) 66 (39 gls); Kent League 36 (19 gls); South Eastern League 16 (12 gls); Other jnr comp: 3 (2 gls); Friendlies 23 (13 gls).
Honours: West Kent League champions 1900-01, 1901-02, 1902-03. London League (Reserves) champions 1901-02, 1903-04. South Eastern League champions 1903-04. Chatham Charity Cup runners-up 1902-03.
Son of Woolwich Arsenal manager, Harry Bradshaw. His brother, Joseph, also played for Woolwich Arsenal Reserves. After Fulham played for Burton United (1905-07) and Ton Pentre (Dec 1909). Went to Canada in 1910.

BRADY, William Liam   **1971-80**
Midfield   5ft 8½in. 10st 10lb.
Born: Dublin, Ireland, 13 Feb 1956.
School: Larkhill Primary, St Aidan's Christian Brothers (Dublin).
Jnr football: St Kevin's Boys Club. Joined ARSENAL: 11 Jun 1971 (apprentice), 23 Jul 1973 (professional). First app: Jnr fdly v Hitchin (a) 3 Aug 1971. First snr app: League (sub) v Birmingham (h) 6 Oct 1973. Final app: League v Middlesbrough (a) 19 May 1980. Transferred to Juventus (Italy) (£514,000) 1 Aug 1980.
ARSENAL record: League 227/8 (43 gls); FA Cup 31/4 (2 gls); Football League Cup 23 (10 gls); European competitions 13 (4 gls); FA Charity Shield 1; Football Combination 62 (9 gls); London FA Challenge Cup 4; FA Youth Cup 14/1 (7 gls); South East Counties League 47/1 (14 gls); Other jnr comp: 0/1 (1 gl); Friendlies 73/4 (15 gls).

Honours: FA Cup winners 1979, runners-up 1978, 1980. FA Charity Shield runners-up 1979-80. European Cup-winners' Cup runners-up 1980. South East Counties League champions 1971-2, South East Counties League Cup runners-up 1971-2. PFA Player of the Year 1979. Republic of Ireland Player of the Year 1976. Arsenal Player of the Year 1976, 1978, 1979. Republic of Ireland Schoolboy international and captain. 11 Republic of Ireland Youth caps 1972-3. 27 full Republic of Ireland caps (2 gls) 1974-80.
Nickname 'Chippy'. Three of his brothers also

played for Irish & English League clubs. After Juventus he played for Sampdoria, Inter-Milan, and Ascoli before returning to England in Mar 1987 and played for West Ham. Retired at end of 1989-90 season. Became manager of Glasgow Celtic (1991).

BRAIN, James   **1923-31**
Inside/centre-forward   5ft 9in. 10st 11lb.
Born: Bristol, 11 Sep 1900.
Jnr football: Cardiff City (trial), Ton Pentre.
Joined ARSENAL: 8 Aug 1923 from Ton Pentre. First app: Friendly v Brighton (h) 6 Sep 1923. First snr app: League v Tottenham Hotspur (h) 25 Oct 1924. Final snr app: On tour v Gothenburg 19 May 1931. Final app: London Combination v Millwall (h) 5 Sep 1931. Transferred to Tottenham Hotspur 10 Sep 1931.
ARSENAL record: League 204 (125 gls); FA Cup 27 (14 gls); FA Charity Shield 1; Football Combination 93 (56 gls); London FA Challenge Cup 11 (11 gls); London Midweek League 2 (2 gls); Friendlies 27 (18 gls).
Honours: Division One champions 1930-31. FA Cup runners-up 1927. FA Charity Shield winners 1930-31. London FA Challenge Cup winners 1930-31. London Combination champions 1929-30, 1930-31. London FA Challenge Cup runners-up 1925-6. Played in England international trial 1925-6.
Was a coal-miner in his youth. At one time held the Arsenal record for League goals scored in a season — 34 in 1925-6. On retirement he had spells as manager of King's Lynn and Cheltenham, retiring in 1948.

BREMNER, Gordon Hutton   **1937-46**
Inside-forward   5ft 8in. 10st 2lb.
Born: Glasgow.
Jnr football: Cartha Athletic (Glasgow). Joined ARSENAL: 3 Mar 1937 from Cartha Athletic. First app: Jnr fdly v Islington Corinthians (h) 29 Mar 1937. First snr app: League v Leeds United (a) 9 Apr 1938 (scored only goal). Final snr app: League v Blackburn Rovers (h) 30 Aug 1939 (became void when war broke out). Final app: Football League South v Leicester City (a) 26 Jan 1946.
ARSENAL record: League 15 (4 gls); Football Combination 43 (15 gls); London FA Challenge Cup 5; Southern League 4 (3 gls); Friendlies 12 (5 gls). In addition played 1 League and 2 Reserve matches 1939-40 prior to outbreak of war and made 22 apps (6 gls) during wartime.
Honours: London Combination champions 1937-8, 1938-9.
Brother Thomas played for Motherwell. Served in Army during the war. Made two international apps for Scotland during the war. Transferred from Arsenal to Motherwell on being demobbed from the Army.

BRIERCLIFFE, Thomas   **1901-05**
Outside-right   5ft 7½in. 10st 10lb.
Jnr football: Bacup, Clitheroe, Stalybridge Rovers. Previous Clubs: Blackburn Rovers. Joined ARSENAL: 17 May 1901 from Stalybridge. First app: League v Barnsley (h) 2 Sep 1901. Final app: League v Notts County (h) 15 Apr 1905. Transferred to Blackburn Rovers Apr 1905.
ARSENAL Record: League 122 (33 gls); FA Cup 11 (1 gl); London League 25 (5 gls); Other snr comp: 2; London League (Res) 1; Friendlies 11 (5 gls).
Honours: Division Two runners-up (promotion) 1903-04.
Later played for Plymouth Argyle and Darwen.

BRIGGS, Stanley   **1893**
Centre-half.
Joined ARSENAL: 23 Oct 1893 (amateur). First

app: Snr fdly v Wolverhampton Wanderers (h) 30 Oct 1893. League v Rotherham Town (h) 13 Nov 1893. Final app: Snr fdly v Preston North End (h) 11 Dec 1893.
ARSENAL Record: League 2; Friendlies 2.
Played for Tottenham Hotspur after Arsenal and later for Millwall.

BRIGNALL, Stephen James C.   **1975-79**
Defender/midfield   5ft 7½in. 10st 8lb.
Born: Tenterden, Kent, 12 Jun 1960.
Joined ARSENAL: Summer 1975 (apprentice), 15 May 1978 (professional). First app: South Eastern Counties League v Southend (h) 16 Aug 1975. First snr app: League (sub) v Liverpool (a) 7 Apr 1979 (only app). Final app: Football Combination v Bristol Rovers (h) 1 Dec 1979. Contract cancelled Dec 1979.
ARSENAL Record: League 0/1; Football Combination 74/5 (3 gls); FA Youth Cup 6/1; South Eastern Counties League 47/2; Other jnr comp: 4; Friendlies 7/1.
Went to play in Norway 1979. Returned and played for Hastings 1980-81.

BROCK, James   **1896-98**
Outside-right.
Born: Scotland.
Joined ARSENAL: May 1896 from East Stirlingshire. First app: Snr fdly v Rossendale (h) 1 Sep 1896. League v Manchester City (a) 5 Sep 1896. Final app: United League v Bristol City (a) 9 Nov 1898. Transferred to Cowes (IOW) (£30) Nov 1898.
ARSENAL Record: League 57 (19 gls); FA Cup 6; United League 31 (10 gls); Kent League 4 (2 gls); Friendlies 28 (11 gls).
Later played for Clyde and Paisley Abercorn.

BROWN, Laurence   **1961-64**
Half-back   6ft 1in. 12st 10lb.
Born: Shildon, Durham, 22 Aug 1937.
School: Timothy Hackworth (Shildon), All Saints Secondary (Shildon).
Jnr football: Shildon Workers Juniors FC, All Saints Rovers, Shildon Town, Woking Town, Fulham (amateur) Bishop Auckland. Previous Clubs: Darlington (amateur), Northampton Town (1960). Joined ARSENAL: 18 Aug 1961 from Northampton Town for £35,000. First app: League v Burnley (h) 19 Aug 1961. Final snr app: League v Birmingham (a) 28 Dec 1963. Final app: Football Combination v Shrewsbury Town (h) 18 Feb 1964. Transferred to Tottenham Hotspur (£40,000) 21 Feb 1964.
ARSENAL Record: League 101 (2 gls); FA Cup 5; European Competitions 3; Football Combination 8 (3 gls); London FA Challenge Cup 6; Metropolitan League 2 (2 gls); Friendlies 16/2 (3 gls).
Honours: *Played for Bishop Auckland Schoolboys and Durham Schoolboys. 14 England Amateur caps including Olympic Games (Rome 1960). Toured New Zealand & Far East with FA (1961). London FA Challenge Cup winners 1961-2.*
Was apprentice cabinetmaker before taking up football. Served National Service as a PT Instructor. After Tottenham Hotspur played for Norwich City (1966) and then had spells as player-manager at Bradford (1968), King's Lynn (1970) and Altrincham. Became a publican and then returned to Durham where he had a milk business.

BRYAN, Thomas   **1892-94**
Outside-left
First appeared for Woolwich Arsenal Res v London Polytechnic (h) 4 Apr 1892. Signed for ARSENAL: 3 Jan 1894 (amateur) having played for the Ordnance Factory. First snr app: League v Rotherham Town (a) 6 Feb 1894. Final snr app: League v Burton Swifts (h) 14 Apr 1894. Final app: Jnr fdly v Old St Lukes (a) 21 Apr 1894.

ARSENAL Record: League 9 (1 gl); Friendlies 8 (3 gls). In addition made five apps (3 gls) for Woolwich Arsenal Res 1891-2 and 1892-3.
From Arsenal joined Royal Ordnance Football Combination in Jul 1894 and later played for New Brompton and Dartford.

BUCHAN, Charles Murray MM   **1909-10 & 1925-28**
Inside-forward   6ft 0¾in. 12st 3lb.
Born: Plumstead, 22 Sep 1891. Died: Monte Carlo, 25 Jun 1960.
School: Bloomfield Road (Woolwich), High Street (Plumstead).
Jnr football: Plumstead St Nicholas Church, Woolwich Polytechnic, Plumstead FC. After first Arsenal spell — Northfleet (1910) Leyton (1910). Previous Club: Sunderland (Mar 1911). Joined ARSENAL: 26 Dec 1909 (amateur). Rejoined: 3 Jul 1925 from Sunderland for £2,000 (plus £100 per goal). First app: As amateur, South Eastern League v Croydon (a) 27 Dec 1909. As professional League v Tottenham Hotspur (h) 29 Aug 1925. Final app: League v Everton (a) 5 May 1928. Retired: May 1928.

ARSENAL Record: League 102 (49 gls); FA Cup 7 (8 gls); London FA Challenge Cup 1; Friendlies 7 (5 gls). In addition made 4 apps (3 gls) in South Eastern League for Woolwich Arsenal 1909-10.
Honours: *FA Cup runners-up 1927. Captain of Arsenal. Made 1 app for Football League 1926.*
Won club, international and Football League honours with Sunderland. Served with Grenadier Guards and Sherwood Foresters in World War One and won the Military Medal. On retirement from football, he became a journalist with *Daily News/News Chronicle* 1928-56 and was a radio broadcaster. Started his own football publications 1956.

BUCHAN, James   **1904-05**
Half-back.
Born: Perth, Scotland.
Jnr football: Perth. Previous Club: Hibernian. Joined ARSENAL: 27 Apr 1904 from Hibernian. First app: League v Newcastle United (a) 3 Sep 1904. Final snr app: League v Sunderland (a) 4 Mar 1905. Final app: London League (Res) v Willesden (h) 6 Mar 1905. Transferred to Manchester City 10 Mar 1905.
ARSENAL Record: League 8; Other snr comp: 1; South Eastern League 3; London League (Res) 2; Other jnr comp: 1; Friendlies 5 (2 gls).
Later played for Motherwell (Jun 1911).

BUCHANAN, Robert   **1894-96**
Forward   5ft 9in. 12st 7lb.
Born: Johnstone (Paisley), Scotland, 1868. Died: Woolwich, Dec 1907.
Jnr football: Johnstone (Paisley), Abercorn, Sunderland Albion. Previous Club: Burnley. Joined ARSENAL: 21 Sep 1894 from Burnley. First app: Snr fdly v Renton (h) 24 Sep 1894. League v Manchester City (h) 29 Sep 1894. Final snr app: Snr fdly v Millwall (h) 11 Apr 1896. Final Appearnce: Jnr fdly v Luton Town Res. (a) 25 Apr 1896. Transferred to Southampton St Mary's summer 1896.
ARSENAL Record: League 42 (16 gls); FA Cup 2; Kent League 9 (8 gls); Friendlies 33 (21 gls). Won one Scotland cap (1 gl) 1891 whilst with Abercorn.

BUCKENHAM, William Elijah   **1909-10**
Centre-forward
Born: Woolwich.
School: Wood Street, Plumstead.
Jnr football: Plumstead Park Villa, Plumstead Melrose, Farnham, RA (Aldershot). Joined ARSENAL: 12 Nov 1909 amateur from 86th Battery RA (Aldershot). First app: South Eastern League v Hastings (h) 13 Nov 1909. First snr app: League v Bristol City (h) 20 Nov 1909. Final app: League v Bury (h) 9 Apr 1910. Transferred to Southampton summer 1910.
ARSENAL Record: League 21 (5 gls); South Eastern League 1 (1 gl); Other jnr comp: 1 (4 gls); Friendlies 1.
Was a Bombardier in the Royal Artillery.

BUCKLEY, Christopher Sebastian   **1914-21**
Centre-half   5ft 9½in. 12st 7lb.
Born: Urmston, Manchester, 9 Nov 1888.
School: Catholic Collegiate Institute, Manchester.
Jnr football: Manchester City (amateur), West Brom (trial). Previous Clubs: Brighton & Hove Albion, Aston Villa (1906). Joined ARSENAL: 16 Jul 1914 from Aston Villa. First app: National Relief Fund v Tottenham Hotspur (a) 22 Aug 1914. First snr app: League v Glossop (h) 1 Sep 1914. Final snr app: League v Blackburn Rovers (h) 13 Nov 1920. Final app: Jnr fdly v Cambridge University (h) 17 Feb 1921.
ARSENAL Record: League 56 (3 gls); FA Cup 3; Other snr comp: 1; Football Combination 2; London FA Challenge Cup 3; Friendlies 1. In addition made 33 apps (1 gl) during wartime.
Worked on the Manchester Ship Canal as a youth. Became a director and chairman of Aston Villa.

BUIST, George   **1896-97**
Full-back.
Born: Scotland.
Joined ARSENAL: 18 Sep 1896 from Greenock Morton. First app: Jnr fdly v Worthing (a) 26 Sep 1896. First snr app: United League v Wellingborough (h) 19 Oct 1896. Final app: League v Manchester City (h) 28 Apr 1897. Snr fdly v Southampton St Mary's (a) 29 Apr 1897.
ARSENAL Record: League 6; United League 6; Kent League 4; Friendlies 11.
Brother of Robert Buist (see below).

BUIST, Robert   **1891-94**
Centre-half/full-back   5ft 7in. 10st 3lb.
Born: Glasgow, 1870.
Jnr football: Fairfield, Cowlairs. Previous Club: Clyde. Joined ARSENAL: Sep 1891 from Clyde. Signed League forms 25 Jun 1893. First snr fdly v St George's (Birmingham) (h) 3 Oct 1891. First first-class app: FA Cup v Small Heath (a) 16 Jan 1892. Final snr app: Snr fdly v Millwall (h) 17 Mar 1894. Final app: Jnr fdly v Royal Scots Fusiliers (h) 7 Apr 1894.
ARSENAL Record: League 17; FA Cup 3; FA Cup(Q) 7; Friendlies 24 (1 gl). In addition made

42

93 Senior apps (3 gls) for Royal Arsenal 1891-2 and 1892-3.
Later played for Leith Athletic, Royal Ordnance FC and Gravesend.

BURDETT, George   **1910-12**
Goalkeeper   5ft 11in. 11st 10lb.
Born: Tottenham.
Joined ARSENAL: 31 Aug 1910 (amateur). First app: South Eastern League v Chelsea (a) 15 Sep 1910. First snr app: League v Everton (h) 11 Mar 1911. Final snr app: League v Aston Villa (h) 6 Jan 1912. Final app: South Eastern League v Watford (h) 20 Apr 1912.
ARSENAL Record; League 28; London FA Challenge Cup 2; Other snr comp: 2; South Eastern League 32; Friendlies 5.
Army man who played for Fusiliers. Was a musician in the Royal Artillery Band.

BURGESS, Daniel   **1919-22**
Inside-forward   5ft 7½in. 11st 6lb.
Born: Goldenhill, Staffordshire.
Early football was in the Army. Joined ARSENAL: May 1919. First app: London Combination v Millwall (a) 30 Aug 1919. First snr app: League v Liverpool (a) 1 Sep 1919. Final snr app: League v Sheffield United (a) 3 Sep 1921. Final app: London Combination v Charlton Athletic (h) 4 May 1922. Transferred to West Ham United 12 Jun 1922.
ARSENAL Record: League 13 (1 gl); Other snr comp: 1; Football Combination 78 (41 gls); London FA Challenge Cup 1; Friendlies 20 (9 gls).
Served in Royal Field Artillery in World War One.

BURNS, Anthony John   **1963-66**
Goalkeeper   6ft. 13st 7lb.
Born: Edenbridge, Kent, 27 Mar 1944.
Jnr football: Angels Club (Kent), Tonbridge United. Joined ARSENAL: 14 Mar 1963 from Tonbridge United. First app: South East Counties League v Queen's Park Rangers (h) 16 Mar 1963. First snr app: Snr fdly v Enschede (Holland) 14 Aug 1963. Final snr app: League v Sheffield Wednesday (a) 27 Dec 1965. Final app: London FA Challenge Cup Final v Queen's Park Rangers (h) 10 May 1966. Transferred to Brighton & Hove Albion 22 Jul 1966.
ARSENAL Record: League 31; FA Cup 2; Football Combination 23; London FA Challenge Cup 2; FA Youth Cup 4; Metropolitan League 57; South East Counties League 7; Friendlies 32/3. In addition played 1 Metropolitan League match 1965-6, later removed from records.
Honours: London FA Challenge Cup runners-up 1965-6.
After Brighton played for Charlton Athletic (Mar 1969) and then went to South Africa in 1970 to play for Durban United. Returned and played for Crystal Palace (Oct 1973), Brentford (Jan 1977) and Plymouth Argyle (Aug 1978) where his contract was cancelled Jan 1979. Manager of Gravesend & Northfleet (1984-5).

BURRELL, George   **1912-14**
Outside-left   5ft 6½in. 10st 6lb.
Born: Newcastle upon Tyne, 1892.
Jnr football: Shildon Athletic, South Shields, Leyton FC. Joined ARSENAL: Jun 1912 from Leyton FC. First app: South Eastern League v Tunbridge Wells (h) 7 Sep 1912. First snr app: League v Newcastle United (h) 28 Sep 1912. Final snr app: League v Bristol City (a) 29 Nov 1913. Final app: London League (Res) v Clapton Orient (h) 30 Apr 1914.
ARSENAL Record: League 23 (3 gls); FA Cup 1; Other snr comp: 1; London FA Challenge Cup 4; South Eastern League 37 (11 gls); London League (Res) 8 (2 gls); Friendlies 4 (1 gl).

Was given a free transfer summer 1914 and joined South Shields.

BURROWS, Lycurgus   **1892-95**
Full-back.
Amateur.
Joined ARSENAL: Jan 1892. Signed League forms 23 Jul 1893. First app: Jnr fdly v Gravesend (a) 16 Jan 1892. First first-class app: League v Rotherham Town (a) 6 Feb 1894. Final app: League v Notts County (a) 2 Nov 1895. Snr fdly v Royal Ordnance (h) 4 Nov 1895.
ARSENAL Record: League 10; Friendlies 29. In addition made 1 senior and 21 reserve apps for Royal Arsenal 1891-2 and 1892-3.
Also had spells as an amateur with Tottenham Hotspur.

BUSBY Walter   **1903-05**
Outside-left   5ft 5in. 11st 4lb.
Born: 1882.
Jnr football: Wellingborough Britons, Wellingborough. Previous Club: Queen's Park Rangers. Joined Arsenal: 2 May 1903 from Queen's Park Rangers. First app: London League (Res) v Tottenham Hotspur (a) 1 Sep 1903 (abandoned match). First snr app: League v Manchester United (h) 3 Oct 1903. Final snr app: London League v Queen's Park Rangers (a) 21 Mar 1904. Final app: South Eastern League v Brighton (a) 21 Apr 1905. Transferred to Leyton summer 1905.
ARSENAL Record: League 5 (2 gls); FA Cup 1; London League 3 (1 gl); Other snr comp: 2; South Eastern League 27 (21 gls); London League (Res) 25 (16 gls); Other jnr comp: 1 (3 gls); Friendlies 6 (7 gls).
Honours: South Eastern League champions 1903-04. London League (Res) champions 1903-04.

BUTLER, John Dennis   **1914-30**
Centre-half   5ft 11½in. 11st 5lb.
Born: Colombo, Ceylon, 14 Aug 1894. Died: SE London, 5 Jan 1961.
School: West London.

Jnr football: Dartford, Fulham Wednesday. Joined ARSENAL: Mar 1914 from Fulham Wednesday. First app: South Eastern League v Southampton (h) 3 Sep 1914. First snr app: PFA Charity Fund v Tottenham Hotspur (h) 29 Sep 1919. Final snr app: League v Portsmouth (h) 26 Dec 1929. Final app: London Combination v Tottenham Hotspur (a) 26 Apr 1930. Transferred to Torquay United (£1,000) 6 Jun 1930.

ARSENAL Record: League 267 (7 gls); FA Cup 29 (1 gl); Other snr comp: 2; Football Combination 62 (3 gls); London FA Challenge Cup 16 (2 gls); South Eastern League 18 (4 gls); London League (Res) 8 (2 gls); London Midweek League 1; Friendlies 35 (4 gls). In addition made 2 apps (4 gls) during wartime.
Honours: FA Cup runners-up 1927. London Combination champions 1929-30. London FA Challenge Cup winners 1921-2, runners-up 1925-6. 1 full England cap 1924.
Served in Royal Field Artillery in France in World War One. On retiring as a player in 1932 he became coach to Royal Daring FC (Brussels) and to the Belgian National XI. Was trainer-coach at Leicester City (1940-46) and then had spells as manager of Torquay United, Crystal Palace, coaching in Denmark and again in Belgium, and finally manager of Colchester United.

CAESAR, Gus Cassius   **1982-91**
Defender   6ft. 12st.
Born: Tottenham, 5 Mar 1966.
Joined ARSENAL: Aug 1982 (apprentice), 10 Feb 1984 (professional). First app: South East Counties League v Millwall (h) 28 Aug 1982. First snr app: League v Manchester United (a) 21 Dec 1985. Final snr app: Snr fdly (sub) v Tottenham Hotspur (h) 13 Oct 1990. Final app: Football Combination v Luton Town (h) 24 Apr 1991. Given free transfer by Arsenal at end of 1990-91 season and joined Cambridge United 2 June 1991.
ARSENAL Record: League 27/17; FA Cup 0/1; Football League Cup 3/2; FA Charity Shield 1; Other snr comp: 0/1; FA Youth Cup 6 (1 gl); Football Combination 137/5 (12 gls); South East Counties League 46/1 (2 gls); Other jnr comp: 9 (1 gl); Friendlies 50/15 (1 gl).
Honours: Football League Cup runners-up 1987-8. FA Charity Shield runners-up 1989-90. Football Combination champions 1989-90. 2/1 England Under-21 caps 1987.
Has already suffered a broken ankle three times in his career. Was on loan to Queen's Park Rangers during 1990-91. Moved from Cambridge United to Bristol City (1991-2) and is now with Airdrieonians.

CAIE, Alexander   **1897**
Centre-forward   5ft 9½in. 12st 7lb.
Born: Aberdeen, 1878. Died: Dec 1914.
Jnr football: Victoria United (Aberdeen). Joined ARSENAL: 6 Feb 1897 from Victoria United. First app: Snr fdly v GLasgow Celtic (h) 15 Feb 1897. League v Burton Swifts (h) 20 Feb 1897. Final app: Snr fdly v Southampton St Mary's (a) 29 Apr 1897. Transferred to Bristol South End (City) summer 1897.
ARSENAL Record: League 8 (4 gls); United League 4 (2 gls); Friendlies 9 (5 gls).
Later played for Millwall, Newcastle United and Brentford. Emigrated to Canada and was still playing when he was killed in a rail accident in Massachusetts (USA).

CALDER, Leslie A.   **1911-13**
Forward   5ft 8½in. 11st 8lb.
Born: Southampton.
Joined ARSENAL: 24 Mar 1911 (amateur), 24 Aug 1912 (professional). First app: South Eastern League v Croydon (a) 3 Apr 1911. First snr app: League v Middlesbrough (a) 9 Apr 1911 (only app). Final snr app: On Tour v Vienna Athletic 27 May 1912. Final app: South Eastern League v Clapton Orient (h) 19 Apr 1913.
ARSENAL Record: League 1; South Eastern League 48 (30 gls); Friendlies 13 (13 gls).

CALDWELL, John   **1894-98**
Full-back   5ft 8½in. 11st 3lb.
Born: Ayr.

Junior football: Newmills FC (Ayr). Previous Club: Hibernian. Joined ARSENAL: 15 Aug 1894 from Hibernian. First app: League v Lincoln City (a) 1 Sep 1894. Final app: League v Small Heath (a) 23 Apr 1898. Snr fdly v Tottenham Hotspur (h) 28 Apr 1898. Transferred to Brighton United summer 1898.
ARSENAL Record: League 93 (2 gls); FA Cup 4; United League 18; Other snr comp: 1; Kent League 3; Friendlies 72 (5 gls).
Had a short spell with Third Lanark at the beginning of 1896-7 but returned to Arsenal.

CALDWELL, James H.   **1913-14**
Goalkeeper   5ft 10½in. 12st.
Born: Carronshore, nr Falkirk, 1886.
Jnr football: Carron Thistle, Dunipace (Stirling). Previous Clubs: East Stirling, Tottenham Hotspur, Reading, Everton (1912). Joined ARSENAL: 17 Jun 1913 from Everton. First app: South Eastern League v Swindon Town (a) 3 Sep 1913. First snr app: Snr fdly v Queen's Park Rangers (a) 11 Sep 1913. Final snr app: League v Bury (h) 4 Oct 1913. Final app: London League (Res) v Clapton Orient (h) 30 Apr 1914. Transferred to Reading summer 1914.
ARSENAL Record: League 3; London FA Challenge League 2; South Eastern League 32; London League (Res) 11; Friendlies 4.

CALVERLEY, Alfred   **1947**
Outside-left   5ft 6in. 10st 6lb.
Born: Huddersfield, 24 Nov 1917.
Previous Clubs: Huddersfield Town (wartime), Mansfield Town (1946). Joined ARSENAL: 14 Mar 1947 from Mansfield Town. First app: League v Preston North End (h) 15 Mar 1947. Final app: League v Everton (h) 31 May 1947. Transferred to Preston NE 26 Jul 1947.
ARSENAL Record: League 11; Friendlies 1.
Came to prominence during wartime making apps for Sheffield Wednesday, Sheffield United, Leeds United, Yeovil Town, Bradford City and Huddersfield Town. After Preston North End later played for Doncaster Rovers (Dec 1947).

CALVERT, Frederick J.   **1911-12**
Forward   5ft 9in. 11st 9lb.
Born: Southend.
Joined ARSENAL: 2 Apr 1911 (amateur). First app: South Eastern League v Croydon (a) 3 Apr 1911. First snr app: League v Liverpool (a) 17 Apr 1911. Final snr app: League v Notts County (a) 23 Dec 1911. Final app: South Eastern League v Luton Town (a) 6 Jan 1912.
ARSENAL Record: League 2 (1 gl); South Eastern League 13 (6 gls); Friendlies 1.
A soldier from the garrison at Woolwich.

CAMPBELL, Kevin Joseph   **1985-**
Striker   6ft. 13st 1lb.
Born: Lambeth, London, 4 Feb 1970.
School: Henry Thornton, South London.
Joined ARSENAL: 1985 (schoolboy); 1988 (professional). First app: South East Counties League (sub) v Charlton Athletic (h) 24 Aug 1985. First snr app: League (sub) v Everton (a) 7 May 1988.
ARSENAL Record: League 45/24 (24 gls); FA Cup 5/2 (1 gl); Football League Cup 2/4; European comp: 4 (1 gl); FA Charity Shield 1; Football Combination 76/6 (69 gls); South East Counties League 56/9 (69 gls); FA Youth Cup 10 (12 gls); Other snr comp: 2/3 (1 gl); Other jnr comp: 7 (5 gls); Friendlies 34/11 (31 gls).
Honours: Division One champions 1990-91. Played for South London schoolboys. Football Combination champions 1989-90. FA Youth Cup winners 1987-8. 1 England 'B' cap; 4 Under-21 caps (1 gl) 1990-91.

Went on loan to Leyton Orient (Jan-Apr 1989 – 16 apps, 9 gls) and Leicester City (1989-90).

CARR, Edward Miller   **1935-40**
Centre-forward   5ft 7in. 11st 7lb.
Born: Shadforth, Durham, 3 Oct 1917.
Joined ARSENAL: 20 Feb 1935, and went to Margate (Arsenal nursery), returning to Arsenal Aug 1937. First app: Jnr fdly v Letchworth (a) 1 May 1935. First snr app: League v Manchester City (a) 16 Feb 1938. Final snr app: League v Everton (h) 10 Sep 1938. Final app: Football League South 'C' v Millwall (a) 13 May 1940. Transferred to Huddersfield Town 1945.
ARSENAL Record: League 12 (7 gls); Other snr comp: 1; Football Combination 38 (15 gls); London FA Challenge Cup 5 (4 gls); Southern League 7 (4 gls); Friendlies 5 (1 gl). In addition made 1 app (1 gl) during wartime.
Honours: London Combination champions 1937-8.
Worked as a pit boy at Wheatley Colliery before taking up football. Suffered a serious knee injury in the reserves in 1939 and it was thought he would never play again. Worked down the pit again during the war. After Huddersfield Town he played for Newport County (Oct 1946), Bradford City (Oct 1949) and Darlington (Aug 1953). Later became manager of Darlington (1960-4) and a scout for Newcastle United. Now lives at Trimdon, Durham.

CARTER, James William Charles   **1991-**
Forward   5ft 10in. 10st 8lb.
Born: Hammersmith, London, 9 Nov 1965.
School: Drayton Park, Newington Green, Clissold Park.
Previous Clubs: Crystal Palace (apprentice), Millwall, Liverpool (Jan 1991). Joined ARSENAL: 8 Oct 1991 from Liverpool for £500,000. First app: Football Combination v Charlton Athletic (h) 12 Oct 1991. First snr app: League (sub) v Nottingham Forest (a) 8 Dec 1991.
ARSENAL Record: League 5/1; FA Cup 1; Football Combination 12; Friendlies 1 (1 gl).
Played for Islington Schoolboys.

CARTWRIGHT, Sidney   **1931-46**
Half-back   5ft 7½in. 10st 6lb.
Born: Kiveton Park, Sheffield, 1910. Died: 16 Dec 1953.
Jnr football: High Moor (Sheffield). Joined ARSENAL: Apr 1931 (amateur) from High

Moor, 13 May 1931 (professional). First app: London Midweek League v West Ham (h) 20 Apr 1931. First snr app: League v Portsmouth (h) 22 Feb 1936. Final snr app: On Tour v Danish XI (Denmark) 24 May 1939. Final app: Football League South v Tottenham Hotspur (a) 16 Feb 1946.
ARSENAL Record: League 16 (2 gls); Other snr comp: 1; Football Combination 192 (2 gls); London FA Challenge Cup 21; London Midweek League 33 (1 gl); Southern League 3; Friendlies 31/2 (3 gls). In addition made 3 apps during wartime.
Honours: London Combination champions 1933-4, 1934-5, 1936-7, 1937-8, 1938-9. London FA Challenge Cup winners 1935-6, runners-up 1936-7.
Served abroad in the Army in World War Two and returned to his native Yorkshire on demobilization after the war. Player-coach with a works team in Sheffield.

CARVER, George   **1896-1900**
Full-back.
Joined ARSENAL: 27 Aug 1896. First app: Jnr fdly v 15th Co Royal Artillery (h) 3 Sep 1896. First snr app: League v Loughborough (a) 12 Dec 1896 (only app). Final snr app: United League v Kettering (h) 6 Feb 1899. Final app: Kent League v Dartford (h) 13 Jan 1900.
ARSENAL Record: League 1; United League 1; Kent League 23; Other jnr comp: 2; Friendlies 56.
Honours: Sevenoaks Charity Cup winners 1897-98.

CASSIDY, Hugh   **1897**
Full-back.
Joined ARSENAL: Feb 1897 from Army football. Signed League forms 12 Mar 1897. First app: Snr fdly v Celtic (h) 15 Feb 1897. Final app: League v Newcastle United (h) 16 Apr 1897.
ARSENAL Record: League 1; Friendlies 1.
An army man in the 15th Hussars he also represented the Army at football.

CATON, Thomas Stephen   **1983-87**
Central-defender   6ft 1½in. 12st 9lb.
Born: Kirkby, Liverpool, 6 Oct 1962.
Married (1 son).
School: St Kevins RC Comprehensive, Liverpool.
Previous Club: Manchester City (1979). Joined ARSENAL: 30 Nov 1983 from Manchester City for £500,000. First app: League v West Brom (h) 3 Dec 1983. First snr app: Snr fdly (sub) v Shamrock Rovers (a) 10 Aug 1986. Final app: Football Combination v Portsmouth (h) 24 Jan 1987. Transferred to Oxford United (£180,000) 30 Jan 1987.
ARSENAL Record: League 81 (2 gls); FA Cup 4; Football League Cup 10 (1 gl); Football Combination 36 (1 gl); Friendlies 19/4.
Honours: 4 England Under-21 caps 1984 (and captain).
England Schoolboy international and captain. Won club and other international honours with Manchester City. Currently with Charlton Athletic (Nov 1988).

CHALMERS, John   **1910-12**
Centre-forward   5ft 9in. 11st 6lb.
Born: Glasgow, c.1885.
Jnr football: Rutherglen Glencairn (Glasgow). Previous Clubs: Glasgow Rangers, Stoke (Jan 1906), Bristol Rovers, Clyde (Nov 1908). Joined ARSENAL: 6 Oct 1910 from Clyde. First app: League v Bradford City (a) 8 Oct 1910. Final snr app: FA Cup v Bolton Wanderers (a) 13 Jan 1912. Final app: Snr fdly v Tottenham Hotspur (a) 24 Feb 1912. Transferred to Greenock Morton (£500) 1 Mar 1912.
ARSENAL Record: League 48 (21 gls); FA Cup 3 (1 gl); Other snr comp: 1 (1 gl); London FA Challenge Cup 3; South Eastern League 4 (2 gls).

CHAMBERS, Brian Mark　　　　**1973-74**
Midfield　　　　5ft 9½in. 11st 3lb.
Born: Newcastle upon Tyne, 31 Oct 1949.
Previous Club: Sunderland (Aug 1967). Joined
ARSENAL: 10 May 1973 from Sunderland for
£30,000. First app: On tour v Toronto Select
(Canada) 23 May 1973. Final snr app: Snr fdly
v Barcelona (h) 12 Mar 1974. Final app: Football
Combination v Tottenham Hotspur (h) 3 May
1974. Transferred to Luton Town (£30,000) 1 Jul
1974.
ARSENAL Record: League 1; Football League
Cup 0/1; Other snr comp: 1; Football
Combination 37 (9 gls); London FA Challenge
Cup 3; Friendlies 6/1.
England Schoolboy international. Later played
for Millwall, Bournemouth and Halifax Town.

CHAPMAN, Lee Roy　　　　**1982-83**
Striker　　　　6ft 1½in. 13st.
Born: Lincoln, 5 Dec 1959.
School: In Stoke.
Previous Clubs: Stoke City, Plymouth Argyle (on
loan). Joined ARSENAL: 11 Aug 1982 from
Stoke City for £500,000 (tribunal). First app: On
tour (sub) v Alexandria (Egypt) 14 Aug 1982. Final
snr app: League (sub) v Leicester City (a) 26 Nov
1983. Final app: Football Combination v Fulham
(a) 20 Dec 1983. Transferred to Sunderland
(£100,000) 28 Dec 1983.

ARSENAL Record: League 15/8 (4 gls); FA Cup
0/1; Football League Cup 0/2; European
Competitions 2 (2 gls); Football Combination 28
(23 gls); Friendlies 9/8 (10 gls).
Son of Roy Chapman (Aston Villa and Port Vale).
Won England Under-21 cap with Stoke City 1981.
Moved from Sunderland to Sheffield Wednesday
(Aug 1984). Signed for French club Chamois
Niortaise (summer 1988) but returned to play for
Nottingham Forest (Oct 1988) and Leeds United
(Jan 1990).

CHARLES, Melvyn　　　　**1959-62**
Half-back/centre-forward　　　　6ft. 12st 8lb.
Born: Swansea, Wales, 14 May 1935.
School: Manselton Senior.
Jnr football: Local (Swansea), Leeds United
(trial). Previous Club: Swansea Town (May 1952).
Joined ARSENAL: 28 Mar 1959 from Swansea
Town for £42,750 (plus D.Dodson and P.Davies).
First app: Football Combination v Charlton
Athletic (h) 4 Apr 1959. First app: League
Floodlit Challenge Cup v West Ham (a) 6 Apr
1959. Final app: League v Birmingham (a) 10 Feb

1962. Transferred to Cardiff City (£28,500) 22 Feb
1962.
ARSENAL Record: League 60 (26 gls); FA Cup
4 (2 gls); Other snr comp: 2 (3 gls); Football
Combination 14 (5 gls); London FA Challenge
Cup 4 (2 gls); Metropolitan League 3 (1 gl);
Friendlies 16/1 (4 gls).
Honours: Played for Swansea Schoolboys.
Southern Floodlit Challenge Cup winners 1958-9.
London FA Challenge Cup winners 1961-2,
runners-up 1960-61. 6 full Wales caps (1 gl) 1961.
Brother of John Charles (Leeds United, Juventus
and Cardiff City) and father of Jeremy Charles
(Swansea City, Queen's Park Rangers and Oxford
United). Served National Service in the Army and
played many representative matches for them.
Plagued with injuries whilst with Arsenal and had
two cartilage operations 1959-60. No other
international honours with Swansea Town and
Cardiff City. Later played for Port Vale (1967)
and on retirement ran a wholesale food business
in Swansea.

CHARLTON, Stanley　　　　**1955-58**
Full-back　　　　5ft 10½in. 12st.
Born: Exeter, 28 Jun 1929.
Jnr football: Spartans Boys Club, White Horse
Old Boys, Bromley. Previous Clubs: Exeter
(amateur), Leyton Orient (1952). Joined
ARSENAL: 4 Nov 1955 from Leyton Orient
(together with V.Groves for £30,000). First app:
Football Combination v Aldershot (a) 12 Nov
1955. First snr app: Snr fdly (sub) v Glasgow
Rangers (a) 21 Nov 1955. Final snr app: League
v Burnley (a) 2 Sep 1958. Final app: Football
Combination v Fulham (a) 20 Dec 1958.
Transferred to Leyton Orient 24 Dec 1958.
ARSENAL Record: League 99; FA Cup 11 (3
gls); Other snr comp: 4; Football Combination
18; London FA Challenge Cup 2; Friendlies 20/
2 (1 gl).
Honours: FA Amateur/Professional tour to
Nigeria and Ghana, Summer 1958.
Son of Stanley Charlton (Rochdale, Exeter and
Crystal Palace). Was in Royal Horse Artillery and
played Army football in Palestine and Egypt. Won
four England Amateur caps with Bromley 1952
and played in Olympic Games (Helsinki) 1952.
Won club honours with Leyton Orient. Was
secretary-manager of Weymouth 1965-72. Works
as district manager for a major pools company.

CHARTERIS J.M.　　　　**1888-90**
Inside-forward.
Born: Kirkcaldy, Scotland.
First app: Snr fdly v London Scottish (h) 13 Oct
1888. First first-class app: FA Cup (Q) v Crusaders
(h) 16 Nov 1889. (only app). Final app: Jnr fdly
v St Barts Hospital (h) 22 Nov 1890.
ARSENAL Record: FA Cup (Q) 1. In addition,
between 1888-9 and 1890-1 made 27 Senior (24
gls) and 25 reserve (35 gls) apps for Royal Arsenal.
Honours: Kent County Junior Cup winners 1889-90.
Twice scored seven goals in a match for reserves
1889-90. A badly broken leg in Nov 1890 finished
his career.

CHENHALL, John Colin　　　　**1944-53**
Full-back　　　　5ft 10in. 12st 10lb.
Born: Bristol, 23 Jul 1927.
School: Eastville (Bristol).
Jnr football: Knowle Athletic, Colston Sports
(Bristol), Maidenhead United (amateur). Joined
ARSENAL: 25 Oct 1944 (amateur), 10 Nov 1945
(professional). First app: Friendly v Tottenham
Hotspur (a) 19 May 1945. First snr app: League
v Charlton Athletic (a) 20 Oct 1951. Final app:
On Tour v Grasshoppers (Switzerland) 27 May
1953. Transferred to Fulham 16 Jul 1953.
ARSENAL Record: League 16; Football
Combination 172 (1 gl); London FA Challenge

Cup 5; Eastern Counties League 9; Other snr
comp: 1; London Midweek League 1; Other jnr
comp: 1; Friendlies 47 (1 gl). In addition made
5 apps during wartime.
Honours: Football Combination champions 1950-51.
Football Combination Cup winners 1952-3,
runners-up 1950-51.
Was a West of England schoolboy boxing
champion. His brother Raymond was also an
amateur on Arsenal's books. Served National
Service in the Navy and played many representative matches for them. Later played for
Guildford (Jul 1958).

CHISHOLM, Norman W.　　　　**1907-10**
Full-back.
Born: Arbroath, Scotland.
Joined ARSENAL: 24 Sep 1907 (amateur), 9 Sep
1908 (professional). First app: South Eastern
League v Fulham (a) 25 Sep 1907. First snr app:
Snr fdly (tour) v Raith Rovers (a) 22 Apr 1908.
Final snr app: League v Nottingham Forest (h)
20 Mar 1909. Final app: South Eastern League
v Coventry (h) 28 Mar 1910.
ARSENAL Record: League 3; London FA
Challenge Cup 1; South Eastern League 31;
London League (Res) 7; Friendlies 7.
Was a bank clerk in the city of London.

CHRISTMAS, Arthur　　　　**1890-91**
Forward.
Born: Wolverhampton.
Joined ARSENAL: from Kidderminster. First
app: Snr fdly v Old Harrovians (h) 18 Jan 1890.
First first-class app: FA Cup v Derby County (h)
17 Jan 1891 (only app). Final app: London Charity
Cup v Old Carthusians (a) 4 Apr 1891.
ARSENAL Record: FA Cup 1; In addition made
37 Senior (18 gls) and 5 reserve (2 gls) apps for
Royal Arsenal between 1889-90 and 1890-91.
Honours: London Charity Cup winners 1889-90.
Kent Senior Cup winners 1889-90. London Senior
Cup winners 1890-91. Kent Junior Cup winners
1889-90.
Played for Cray Wanderers after Arsenal.

CLAMP, Edwin　　　　**1961-62**
Wing-half　　　　5ft 11in. 12st.
Born: Coalville, Leicestershire, 14 Sep 1934.
School: Bridge Road Secondary Modern (Coalville).
Previous Club: Wolverhampton Wanderers
(1950). Joined ARSENAL: 17 Nov 1961 from
Wolves for £34,500. First app: League v
Nottingham Forest (h) 18 Nov 1961. Final snr
app: League v Aston Villa (h) 4 Sep 1962. Final

app: Football Combination v Plymouth Argyle (h) 15 Sep 1962. Transferred to Stoke City (£14,000) 21 Sep 1962.
ARSENAL Record: League 22 (1 gl); FA Cup 2; Football Combination 1; London FA Challenge Cup 1; Friendlies 10/1.
Honours: Played for Leicestershire Schoolboys and England Schoolboys 1949. London FA Challenge Cup winners 1961-2.
Won club and international honours with Wolverhampton Wanderers and club honours with Stoke City. Later played for Peterborough (Oct 1964), Worcester City (Aug 1965) and Lower Gornal.

CLAPTON, Daniel Robert   **1953-62**
Winger   5ft 10in. 11st 1lb.
Born: Stepney, London, 22 Jul 1934. Died: London, Jun 1986.
School: Hackney.

Jnr football: Leytonstone FC (amateur). Joined ARSENAL: 11 Aug 1953 (amateur), 15 Aug 1953 (professional). First app: South Eastern Counties League v Bury Town (a) 22 Aug 1953. First snr app: Snr fdly v South Africa (h) 23 September 1953. Final snr app: On tour v Skeid (Norway), 10 May 1962. Final app: Football Combination v Plymouth Argyle (h) 15 Sep 1962. Transferred to Luton Town (£6,000) 20 Sep 1962.
ARSENAL Record: League 207 (25 gls); FA Cup 18 (2 gls); Other snr comp: 8 (3 gls); Football Combination 62 (15 gls); London FA Challenge Cup 1; Eastern Counties League 31 (6 gls); Metropolitan League 10 (3 gls); London Midweek League 10 (5 gls); Friendlies 62/4 (11 gls).
Honours: Southern Floodlit Challenge Cup winners 1958-9. Eastern Counties League champions 1954-5. Metropolitan League Cup winners 1960-61. Metropolitan League Professional Cup winners 1960-61. 1 full England cap 1958. Made 1 app for Football League 1958.
Was a porter at Smithfield and Billingsgate before taking up football. Went to Australia in 1964 and played for Corinthians (Sydney), returning to England 1970. Suffered ill health when he finished playing football and was a publican in Hackney until his death.

CLAPTON, Denis Patrick   **1957-61**
Forward   6ft. 12st 13lb.
Born: Hackney, London, 12 Oct 1939.
Jnr football: Bexleyheath. Joined ARSENAL: Aug 1957 (amateur), 1 Aug 1958 (professional).

First app: South East Counties League v Crystal Palace (a) 31 Aug 1957. First snr app: Snr fdly v Reading (a) 1 Dec 1958. Final snr app: League v Blackpool (a) 19 Nov 1960. Final app: Football Combination v Plymouth Argyle (a) 19 Aug 1961. Transferred to Northampton Town 29 Aug 1961.
ARSENAL Record: League 4; Football Combination 54 (16 gls); London FA Challenge Cup 4 (1 gl); FA Youth Cup 9 (10 gls); Metropolitan League 48 (38 gls); South East Counties League 18 (9 gls); London Midweek League 1 (1 gl); Other jnr comp: 3 (3 gls); Friendlies 21 (13 gls). In addition played 1 Metropolitan League match 1958-9, later removed from records.
Honours: Metropolitan League champions 1958-9. Metropolitan League Cup winners 1960-61. Metropolitan League Professional Cup winners 1960-61. Southern Junior Floodlight Cup runners-up 1960-61. 2 England Youth caps 1958.
Brother of Danny Clapton (see above). Later played for Leyton Orient (Sep 1962).

CLARK, Archie   **1927-28**
Half-back   5ft 10½in. 12st 6lb.
Born: Shoreham, Kent, 4 Apr 1904. Died: 14 Jan 1967.
Jnr football: Grays (Kent Lge). Previous Club: Brentford (Mar 1927). Joined ARSENAL: 13 May 1927 from Brentford. First app: London Combination v Fulham (h) 27 Aug 1927. First snr app: Snr fdly v Corinthians (h) 21 Sep 1927. League v Blackburn Rovers (a) 5 Nov 1927 (only app). Final snr app: On tour v Hälsingborg (Sweden) 25 May 1928. Final app: Jnr fdly v Oxford University (a) 28 Nov 1928. Transferred to Luton Town 29 Nov 1928.
ARSENAL Record: League 1; Football Combination 56 (13 gls); Friendlies 12 (2 gls).
Honours: London Combination champions 1927-8, 1928-9.
Had a few games at centre-forward for Arsenal. Later played for Everton (1931) and Tranmere Rovers (1936). Became manager of Gillingham (Southern League) and chief scout at Sheffield United (1958).

CLARK, James M.   **1897-1900**
Centre-half.
Joined ARSENAL: Oct 1897 from Bostal Rovers (local), 29 Oct 1897 (professional). First app: Jnr fdly v Luton Town Res (h) 2 Oct 1897. First snr app: League v Darwen (a) 12 Mar 1898. Final snr app: League v Leicester Fosse (h) 10 Sep 1898. Final app: Kent League v Maidstone (a) 16 Apr 1900.
ARSENAL Record: League 4; United League 1; Kent League 23 (5 gls); Other jnr comp: 2; Friendlies 36.
Honours: Sevenoaks Charity Cup winners 1897-8.

CLARK, John   **1923-26**
Outside-right   5ft 6½in. 9st 13lb.
Born: Bo'ness, Scotland, 1900.
Previous Club: Bo'ness (Scottish Division Two). Joined ARSENAL: 4 Mar 1923 from Bo'ness. First app: London Combination v Chelsea (a) 8 Mar 1923. First snr app: League v Aston Villa (a) 7 Apr 1923. Final snr app: League v Sunderland (h) 22 Nov 1924. Final app: Jnr fdly v Brighton (a) 17 Apr 1926. Transferred to Luton Town 6 Aug 1926.
ARSENAL Record: League 6; Football Combination 76 (14 gls); London FA Challenge Cup 2; Friendlies 14 (4 gls).
Honours: London FA Challenge Cup winners 1923-4.

CLARKE, Frederick Robert George   **1960-65**
Left-back   5ft 7in. 10st 5lb.
Born: Kilpike, County Down, N Ireland, 4 Nov 1941.
Previous Club: Glenavon. Joined ARSENAL: 3

Nov 1960 from Glenavon for £5,000. First app: Football Combination v Charlton Athletic (h) 5 Nov 1960. First snr app: League v Aston Villa (h) 31 Mar 1962. Final snr app: League v Leeds United (h) 13 Feb 1965. Final app: Metropolitan League v Metropolitan Police (h) 11 Sep 1965. Transferred to Glenavon Nov 1965.
ARSENAL Record: League 26; FA Cup 2; Football Combination 103 (1 gl); London FA Challenge Cup 7; Metropolitan League 31 (1 gl); Friendlies 25.
Honours: Football Combination Cup winners 1962-3. London FA Challenge Cup winners 1962-3, runners-up 1960-61. Metropolitan League Professional Cup winners 1960-61. Metropolitan League Cup winners 1960-61. Sheriff of London Shield winners 1964-5. 4 Northern Ireland Under-23 caps 1962-5.
Won Amateur international and Inter-League honours with Glenavon.

COAKLEY, Thomas   **1966-67**
Winger   5ft 6in. 11st.
Born: Bellshill, Lanark, Scotland, 21 May 1947.
Jnr football: Possilpark Juniors. Previous Club: Motherwell (part-time juniors). Joined ARSENAL: 12 May 1966 from Motherwell (free transfer). First app: Snr fdly v Torquay/Plymouth (a) 10 May 1966 (trial). First snr app: On tour v NEA Salamis (Cyprus) 31 May 1967. Final app: Football Combination Cup v Swindon Town (h) 12 Dec 1967. Contract Cancelled 31 Dec 1967.
ARSENAL Record: League 9 (1 gl); Football League Cup 4 (1 gl); Football Combination 41 (10 gls); London FA Challenge Cup 1; Metropolitan League 2 (1 gl); Friendlies 20/1 (3 gls).
From Arsenal went to America to play for Detroit Cougars (Jan 1968) and on return played for Morton. Later played for Chelmsford and then had spells as manager of Bishop's Stortford and Walsall (Aug 1986-Dec 1988).

COCK, Donald J.   **1925**
Centre-forward   5ft 7in. 11st 8lb.
Born: Hayle, Cornwall, 10 Jul 1896. Died: Bradmore, nr Wolverhampton, 31 Aug 1974.
Previous Clubs: Fulham, Notts County (Oct 1922). Joined ARSENAL: 5 Mar 1925 from Notts County for £4,000. First app: League v Bolton Wanderers (h) 7 Mar 1925. Final snr Appearnce: League v Tottenham Hotspur (h) 29 Aug 1925. Final app: London Combination v Millwall (h) 19 Sep 1925. Transferred to Clapton Orient (£1,500) 2 Oct 1925.
ARSENAL Record: League 3; Football Combination 4 (2 gls); London FA Challenge Cup 1 (1 gl).
Broke his leg in his second match for Arsenal. Later played for Wolverhampton Wanderers (1927).

COLE, Andrew A.   **1986-**
Striker   5ft 11in. 11st 2lb.

46

Born: Nottingham, 15 Oct 1971.
Joined ARSENAL: Oct 1985 (schoolboy), Jul 1988 from FA School of Excellence (Lilleshall), 1989 (professional). First app: Jnr fdly (sub) v Oxford University (a) 29 Oct 1986. First snr app: League (sub) v Sheffield United (h) 29 Dec 1990. ARSENAL Record: League 0/1; FA Charity Shield 0/1; Other snr app 1/1; Football Combination 53/7 (30 gls): South East Counties League 48/1 (42 gls); FA Youth Cup 9 (10 gls); Other jnr comp: 9 (5 gls); Friendlies 40/3 (16 gls).
Honours: FA Charity Shield medal 1991-2. Southern Junior Floodlight Cup runners-up 1989-90. England Schoolboy caps. England Youth caps. Had spells on loan to Fulham and Bristol City, 1991-2.

COLEMAN, Ernest 'Tim'　　　　**1932-34**
Inside/centre-forward　　　　5ft 8in. 11st 6lb.
Born: Blidworth, Notts, 4 Jan 1908. Died: Nottingham, 20 Jan 1984.
Jnr football: Church Lads Brigade (Hucknall). Previous Clubs: Nottingham Forest (trial), Halifax Town (1927), Grimsby Town (1929). Joined ARSENAL: 4 Mar 1932 from Grimsby Town for £7,500. First app: League v Leicester City (h) 5 Mar 1932. Final snr app: League v Everton (h) 3 Feb 1934. Final app: London Combination v Leicester City (a) 5 May 1934. Transferred to Middlesbrough 10 Aug 1934.
ARSENAL Record: League 45 (26 gls); FA Cup 1; FA Charity Shield 1; Other snr comp: 1 (5 gls); Football Combination 26 (14 gls); London FA Challenge Cup 2; Friendlies 3.
Honours: Division One champions 1932-3. FA Charity Shield winners 1933-4.
Scored five goals v Corinthians (Sheriff of London Shield) 1932-3. Played in international trial match 1932-3. Won club honours with Grimsby Town. After Middlesbrough played for Norwich City. Became manager of Linby Colliery (1945) and manager of Notts County (Sep 1965).

COLEMAN, John George 'Tim'　　　**1902-08**
Inside-forward　　　　5ft 8in. 10st 9lb.
Born: Kettering, 26 Oct 1881. Died: 20 Nov 1940.
Jnr football: Kettering. Previous Club: Northampton Town (1901). Joined ARSENAL: 1 May 1902 from Northampton Town (together with E.Lawrence). First app: London League v West Ham (a) 1 Sep 1902. League v Preston North End (a) 6 Sep 1902. Final app: League v Middlesbrough (h) 22 Feb 1908. Transferred to Everton (£700) 28 Feb 1908.
ARSENAL Record: League 172 (79 gls); FA Cup 24 (5 gls); London League 11 (5 gls); Other snr comp: 9 (5 gls); South Eastern League 3 (3 gls); Friendlies 21 (16 gls).
Honours: Division Two runners-up (promotion) 1903-04. Southern Professional Charity Cup winners 1905-06, runners-up 1903-04. 1 full England cap 1907. Made 2 apps (1 gl) for Football League 1906-07.
Later played for Sunderland, Fulham and Nottingham Forest. Retired during wartime but played for Tunbridge Wells Rangers in 1920. Was a coach in Holland c.1927.

COLES, Frederick Gordon　　　　**1900-04**
Half-back　　　　5ft 10in. 12st 2lb.
Born: Nottingham, 1875. Died: 22 Apr 1947.
Jnr football: Nottingham PO FC. Previous Clubs: Notts County, Nottingham Forest. Joined ARSENAL: 22 Jun 1900 from Nottingham Forest. First app: London League (Res) v Millwall (a) 1 Sep 1900. First snr app: League v Chesterfield (h) 29 Sep 1900. Final snr app: London League v Queen's Park Rangers (a) 21 Mar 1904. Final app: South Eastern League v St Albans (h) 30 Apr 1904. Transferred to Grimsby Town 25 Jun 1904.

ARSENAL Record: League 78 (2 gls); FA Cup 8; London League 22; London League (Res) 25 (1 gl); Other snr comp: 3; South Eastern League 21 (2 gls); Kent League 5; Other jnr comp: 3; Friendlies 27 (2 gls).
Honours: South Eastern League champions 1903-04. London League (Res) champions 1903-04. Chatham Charity Cup runners-up 1902-03.
Became cricket and football coach in Gothenburg (Sweden) 1906-07 and trainer of Hague in Holland 1910-11.

COLLETT, Ernest　　　　**1933-49**
Half-back/full-back　　　　5ft 10in. 10st 12lb.
Born: Sheffield, 17 Nov 1914. Died: London, 11 Apr 1980.
Jnr football: Oughtibridge Working Mens Club. Joined ARSENAL: 25 Apr 1933 from Oughtibridge. First app: Jnr fdly v Barnsley(a) 26 Apr 1933. First snr app: League v Stoke City (a) 23 Oct 1937. First snr app: League v Aston Villa (h) 18 Apr 1947. Final app: Eastern Counties League v Gillingham (a) 3 Sep 1949.
ARSENAL Record: League 20; FA Cup 1; Other snr comp: 2; Football Combination 226 (7 gls); London FA Challenge Cup 19; London Midweek League 2; Eastern Counties League 4; Friendlies 38/2 (4 gls). In addition played two reserve matches 1939-40 prior to outbreak of war and made 187 apps (1 gl) during wartime.
Honours: London Combination champions winners 1933-4, 1934-5, 1936-7, 1937-8, 1938-9. Football Combination champions winners 1946-7. London FA Challenge Cup winners 1934-5, 1935-6, runners-up 1936-7. Mayor of Colchester Cup Winner 1938-9.
Played for Brentford in War Cup Final 1941-2. On retiring from playing he joined the coaching staff at Arsenal and later became assistant chief scout. Retired 17 Nov 1979 but died in 1980 after being knocked down by a fire engine.

COMMON, Alfred　　　　**1910-12**
Inside-forward　　　　5ft 8in. 13st.
Born: Sunderland, 25 May 1880. Died: 3 Apr 1946.
Jnr football: South Hylton (Sunderland), Jarrow. Previous Clubs: Sunderland, Sheffield United (1901), Sunderland (1904), Middlesbrough (1905) — first £1,000 transfer). Joined ARSENAL: 7 Aug 1910 from Middlesbrough for £250. First app: League v Manchester United (h) 1 Sep 1910. Final snr app: League v Blackburn Rovers (h) 30 Nov 1912. Final app: South Eastern League v Swindon Town (h) 7 Dec 1912. Transferred to Preston North End 19 Dec 1912 for £250.
ARSENAL Record: League 77 (23 gls); FA Cup 3; Other snr comp: 3 (1 gl); London FA Challenge Cup 5 (4 gls); South Eastern League 3 (2 gls); Friendlies 4 (1 gl).
Won club honours with Sheffield United and Preston North End and international honours with Sheffield United and Middlesbrough. Left football around 1914 and went to live at Darlington where he was a publican for many years until retirement in 1943.

COMPTON, Denis Charles Scott CBE　**1932-50**
Outside-left　　　　5ft 10in. 11st 4lb.
Born: Hendon, Middlesex, 23 May 1918.
School: Bell Lane, Hendon.
Jnr football: Golders Green, Hampstead Town, Nunhead. Joined ARSENAL: 23 Sep 1932 (amateur), May 1935 (professional). First app: London Midweek League v Queen's Park Rangers (h) 28 Jan 1933. First snr app: Snr fdly v Glasgow Rangers (h) 3 Sep 1936. Final app: League v Portsmouth (h) 3 May 1950. Retired May 1950.
ARSENAL Record: League 54 (15 gls); FA Cup 5 (1 gl); FA Charity Shield 1; Other snr comp: 4 (1 gl); Football Combination 145 (94 gls);

London FA Challenge Cup 13 (7 gls); London Midweek League 13; Southern League 4 (5 gls); Other jnr comp: 1 (1 gl); Friendlies 15 (9 gls). In addition made 127 apps (74 gls) during wartime.
Honours: Division One champions 1947-8. FA Cup winners 1950. FA Charity Shield runners-up 1936-7. London Combination champions 1936-7, 1937-8, 1938-9. London FA Challenge Cup winners 1935-6, runners-up 1936-7. Bath Coronation Cup winners 1936-7. Lowestoft Hospital Cup winners 1938-9. Football League South Cup winners 1943. Football League War Cup runners-up 1941. England Schoolboy international. Made 12 apps (2 gls) for England in Wartime internationals.
Twice scored five goals in a match for reserves 1936-7. Brother of Leslie Compton (see below). Well-known cricketer for Middlesex and England, winning many county and Test honours. Was in the Army during the war and served in India. On retirement from playing became a cricket and football reporter with the *Sunday Express* and a television commentator. Was awarded the CBE in 1958. Is a director of an advertising agency.

COMPTON, Leslie Harry　　　　**1931-52**
Full-back/centre-half　　　6ft 1½in. 13st 2lb.
Born: Woodford, Essex, 12 Sep 1912. Died: Essex, 27 Dec 1984.
School: Bell Lane, Hendon.
Jnr football: Bell Lane Old Boys, Hampstead Town. Joined ARSENAL: 6 Aug 1930 (amateur), 22 Feb 1932 (professional), from Hampstead Town. First app: London Midweek League v Queen's Park Rangers (h) 18 Nov 1931. First snr app: League v Aston Villa (a) 25 Sep 1932. First app: Alex Wilson Benefit v All Stars (a) 29 Sep 1952. Final app: Football Combination v Plymouth Argyle (h) 15 Nov 1952. Retired Jul 1953.
ARSENAL Record: League 253 (5 gls); FA Cup 17 (1 gl); FA Charity Shield 3; Other snr comp: 6; Football Combination 227 (31 gls); London FA Challenge Cup 21 (2 gls); Southern League 10; Friendlies 50/2 (4 gls). In addition played two reserve matches 1939-40 prior to outbreak of war and made 131 apps during wartime.
Honours: Played for Middlesex Schoolboys. Division One champions 1947-8. FA Cup winners 1950. FA Charity Shield winners 1938-9, 1948-9, runners-up 1936-7. London Combination champions 1933-4, 1934-5, 1936-7, 1937-8, 1938-9. London FA Challenge Cup winners 1933-4, 1935-6, runners-up 1936-7. Northampton Charity Shield winners 1931-2. Norwich Hospital Cup winners 1934-5. Bath Coronation Cup winners 1936-7.

Mayor of Colchester Cup winners 1938-9. Football League South Cup winners 1943. Football League War Cup runners-up 1941. Captain of Arsenal. 2 full England caps 1950. Made 1 app for Football League 1948. Made 5 apps for England in wartime internationals.
Worked as a plumber's mate before taking up football. Played county cricket for Middlesex. Scored ten goals in wartime match v Clapton Orient Feb 1941. Served in Army during the war and played in BAOC touring team (Germany). On retirement from playing was a coach and scout at Arsenal 1953-6. Became a publican in North London and a representative for a wine & spirits business. Was a prominent player in North London Bowling but suffered badly from arthritis and had a foot amputated in 1982.

CONNOLLY, Peter   1888-93
Centre-forward/full-back   5ft 9½in. 12st.
Born: Kirkcaldy, Fife, Scotland, c.1867. Died: Kirkcaldy, 12 Sep 1895.
Joined ARSENAL: From Kirkcaldy Wanderers and first appeared 1888. First first-class app: FA Cup (Q) v Lyndhurst (h) 5 Oct 1889. Final first-class app: FA Cup v Small Heath (a) 16 Jan 1892. Final app: Res v St Lukes (a) 29 Apr 1893.
ARSENAL Record: FA Cup 2; FA Cup (Q) 4 (2 gls). In addition between 1887-8 and 1892-3 made 127 Senior (49 gls) and 25 Reserve (25 gls) apps for Royal Arsenal.
Honours: London Charity Cup winners 1889-90. Kent Senior Cup winners 1889-90. London Senior Cup winners 1890-91, runners-up 1889-90. Represented Kent County.
Later played for Royal Ordnance.

CONNOR, Maurice Joseph   1902
Inside-forward   5ft 6in. 11st.
Born: Lochee, Scotland, Jul 1877. Died: Scotland, Aug 1934.
School: Lochee Welfare.
Jnr football: Dundee Fereday, Queen's Gordon Highlanders. Previous Clubs: Glentoran, West Brom, Walsall, Bristol City. Joined ARSENAL: 2 May 1902 from Bristol City. First app: London League v West Ham (a) 1 Sep 1902. League v Preston North End (a) 6 Sep 1902. Final app: London League v Millwall (a) 26 Dec 1902. Transferred to Brentford end of Dec 1902.
ARSENAL Record: League 14 (2 gls); FA Cup 2 (1 gl); London League 6 (3 gls); Friendlies 1 (2 gls).

Later played for New Brompton, Fulham (1903) and Glentoran. Won Ireland caps with Brentford and Fulham.

COOPER, Joseph   1893-94
Centre-forward.
Born: Wolverhampton, 1865.
Jnr football: Milton FC. Previous Club: Wolverhampton Wanderers (Aug 1888). Joined ARSENAL: Oct 1893 from Wolverhampton Wanderers. Signed League forms 2 Nov 1893. First app: Snr fdly v Mr Roston Bourkes XI (h) 23 Oct 1893. Final snr app: League v Burton Swifts (h) 14 Apr 1894. Final app: Jnr fdly v Old St Lukes (a) 21 Apr 1894.
ARSENAL Record: League 6; FA Cup 2 (2 gls); Friendlies 18 (16 gls).

COOPLAND, Walter Ernest   1920-23
Outside-left/left-half   5ft 11in. 11st 3lb.
Born: Sheffield, c.1900.
Joined ARSENAL: 23 Jan 1920 from Birley Carr, Sheffield. First app: London Combination v Brentford (a) 24 Jan 1920. First snr app: League v Aston Villa (a) 11 Feb 1920 (only app). Final app: Jnr fdly v Northfleet (a) 17 Feb 1923. Transferred to Exeter City 23 Feb 1923.
ARSENAL Record: League 1; Football Combination 46 (11 gls); Friendlies 37 (9 gls).
Later played for Aberdare.

COPE, Horace Walter   1926-33
Left-back   5ft 9in. 13st.
Born: Treeton, nr Sheffield, 24 May 1899.
Jnr football: Treeton United. Previous Club: Notts County (1920). Joined ARSENAL: 10 Dec 1926 from Notts County for £3,125. First app: London Combination v Charlton Athletic (h) 11 Dec 1926. First snr app: League v Cardiff City (a) 27 Dec 1926. Final snr app: League v Blackpool (h) 11 Feb 1933. Final app: London Combination v Clapton Orient (h) 17 Apr 1933. Transferred to Bristol Rovers (£1,500) 3 Jul 1933.
ARSENAL Record: League 65; FA Cup 11; Football Combination 149 (10 gls); London FA Challenge Cup 12 (2 gls) Friendlies 8/1.
Honours: London Combination champions 1928-9, 1929-30, 1930-31. London FA Challenge Cup winners 1930-31. Played in England trial 1926-7.
Worked as a miner before taking up football. Won club honours and international selection (missed through injury) with Notts County. Missed Arsenal's 1927 FA Cup Final because of a knee injury. Became trainer at Norwich City (Jul 1934) Southampton (Mar 1937) and later Blackburn Rovers.

COPPING, Wilfred   1934-39
Left-half   5ft 7½in. 10st 13lb.
Born: Middlecliffe, nr Barnsley, 17 Aug 1909. Died: Southend, Jun 1980.
School: Houghton Council.
Jnr football: Dearne Valley Old Boys, Middlecliffe and Darfield Rovers, Barnsley (trial). Previous Club: Leeds United (1930). Joined ARSENAL: 2 Jun 1934 from Leeds United for £8,000. First app: League v Portsmouth (a) 25 Aug 1934. Final app: League v Preston North End (a) 25 Feb 1939. Transferred to Leeds United 3 Mar 1939.
ARSENAL Record: League 166; FA Cup 19; FA Charity Shield 4; Other snr comp: 2; Football Combination 1; London FA Challenge Cup 1; Friendlies 12. In addition made three 'guest' apps during wartime.
Honours: Division One champions 1934-5, 1937-8. FA Cup winners 1936. FA Charity Shield winners 1934-5, 1938-9, runners-up 1935-6, 1936-7. Bath Coronation Cup winners 1936-7. 13 full England caps 1934-8.
Won club and international honours with Leeds

United. Was a CSMI in the Army during the war and served in North Africa. Became coach to Royal Beerschot (Antwerp) and the Belgium national team (1945). Had spells as trainer/coach at Southend United (1946), Bristol City (1954) and Coventry City (1959). Retired from football in 1959 and moved to Prittlewell, near Southend, and took a job at Fords, Dagenham. Retired in Aug 1972.

CORK, David   1978-85
Midfield   5ft 9in. 11st 8lb.
Born: Doncaster, 28 Oct 1962.
School: Edlington Comprehensive, nr Doncaster.
Jnr football: Bentley Green Imps. Joined ARSENAL: 24 May 1978 (schoolboy), 2 Jun 1980 (professional). First app: South East Counties League v Queen's Park Rangers (h) 2 Sep 1978. First snr app: League (sub) v St Mirren (a) 15 Feb 1981. Final snr app: Snr fdly v Australia (h) 27 Nov 1984. Final app: Football Combination v Millwall (a) 30 May 1985.
ARSENAL Record: League 5/2 (1 gl); FA Cup 1; Football Combination 158/5 (15 gls); FA Youth Cup 6 (1 gl); South East Counties League 50 (4 gls); Other jnr comp: 10; Friendlies 62/12 (16 gls). In addition made three apps (2 gls) in Football Combination matches expunged from records 1981-2.
Honours: Played for Don Valley District Schoolboys and for South Yorkshire Schoolboys. Football Combination champions 1983-4. South East Counties League Cup winners 1979-80. President's Cup winners 1980-81.
Given a free transfer by Arsenal at end of 1984-5 and joined Huddersfield Town. Later played for West Bromwich Albion (1988-9), Scunthorpe United (1988-9) and Darlington (1990-91).

COTTRELL, Ernest Herbert   1898-1901
Forward   5ft 9in. 11st 11lb.
Born: 31 Jan 1877. Died: Watford, 12 Jan 1929.
Joined ARSENAL: 10 May 1898. First app: Jnr fdly v Brentford (a) 1 Sep 1898. First snr app: United League v Brighton United (h) 31 Oct 1898. Final snr app: Snr fdly v West Ham (a) 25 Apr 1901. Final app: West Kent League v Swanscombe (h) 29 Apr 1901. Transferred to Watford summer 1901.
ARSENAL Record: League 24 (12 gls); United League 7 (3 gls); Southern District Combination 1; Other snr comp: 1 (1 gl); London League (Res) 14 (7 gls); Kent League 32 (22 gls); Friendlies 27 (20 gls).
Honours: West Kent League champions 1900-01.
Later played for Fulham (Jun 1903) and Willesden Town. Continued his trade as a painter after football. During the war was a gas 'instructor' in the Army. Collapsed and died whilst watching Watford v Preston North End in 1929.

COURT, David John   1959-70
Forward/wing-half   5ft 8in. 11st 3lb.
Born: Mitcham, Surrey, 1 Mar 1944.
School: Western Road Secondary, Mitcham.
Joined ARSENAL: 14 Apr 1959 (amateur), Jul 1960 (apprentice), 8 Jan 1962 (professional). First app: South East Counties League v West Ham (h) 22 Aug 1959. First snr app: League v Aston Villa (a) 10 Sep 1962. Final snr app: League (sub) v Sunderland (h) 28 Feb 1970. Final app: Football Combination v Gillingham (h) 30 Apr 1970. Transferred to Luton Town (£35,000) 13 Jul 1970.
ARSENAL Record: League 168/7 (17 gls); FA Cup 9/1; Football League Cup 9/2 (1 gl); European Competitions 8; Football Combination 103 (44 gls); London FA Challenge Cup 8 (4 gls); FA Youth Cup 15 (10 gls); Metropolitan League 61 (32 gls); South East Counties League 43 (26 gls); Other jnr comp: 7; Friendlies 104/6 (33 gls).

48

In addition made two apps (2 gls) in South East Counties League matches, removed from records 1959-60.
Honours: Played for Surrey and London Schoolboys. Football League Cup runners-up 1969. Football Combination champions 1969-70. London FA Challenge Cup winners 1962-3. Metropolitan League champions 1960-61. Metropolitan League Professional Cup winners 1961-2. South East Counties League Cup winners 1959-60, 1960-61, 1961-2.
Later played for Brentford (Aug 1972) and Barnet. Retired from football 1974 and now runs a bakery and delicatessen in Brookmans Park.

COWNLEY, Francis Frederick   **1919-23**
Full-back   5ft 8in. 10st 13lb.
Born: Scunthorpe.
Jnr football: Scunthorpe United. Previous Club: Nottingham Forest (wartime only). Joined ARSENAL: May 1919. First app: London Combination v Millwall (a) 30 Aug 1919. First snr app: League v Oldham Athletic (h) 7 Feb 1920. Final snr app: League v Liverpool (a) 25 Feb 1922. Final app: London Combination v West Ham (a) 10 Mar 1923.
ARSENAL Record: League 15; Football Combination 64 (1 gl); London FA Challenge Cup 1; Friendlies 19 (1 gl).
Served with Royal Field Artillery in World War One. His progress was hampered by injury whilst at Arsenal.

COX, Frederick James Arthur   **1949-53**
Outside-right   5ft 7in. 10st 8lb.
Born: Reading, 1 Nov 1920. Died: Bournemouth, 7 Aug 1973.
School: Redlands Senior (Reading).
Jnr football: St George's Lads Club (Reading), Northfleet. Previous Club: Tottenham Hotspur (1938). Joined ARSENAL: 13 Sep 1949 from Tottenham Hotspur for £12,000. First app: League v West Brom (h) 14 Sep 1949. Final app: On tour v Grasshoppers (Switzerland) 27 May 1953. Transferred to West Brom (player-coach) 15 Jul 1953.
ARSENAL Record: League 79 (9 gls); FA Cup 15 (7 gls); Football Combination 48 (3 gls); London FA Challenge Cup 3; London Midweek League 1; Friendlies 12/3.
Honours: Played for Reading Schoolboys. FA Cup winners 1950, runners-up 1952. Football Combination Cup winners 1952-3.
Was a Flight Lieutenant in the RAF during the war and spent several years flying transport planes in the Far East. Played for the Combined Services in India. Was a qualified FA coach, scored valuable goals in the semi-finals of 1950 and 1952 to put Arsenal into the FA Cup Final on each occasion. After retirement from playing he became assistant manager at West Brom and then manager of Bournemouth (1956), Portsmouth (1958) and Gillingham (1962). Ran a family newsagent's business in Bournemouth. Had a further spell as manager of Bournemouth (1965) before taking up full-time management of his newsagent's business.

COX, George   **1933-36**
Centre-forward   5ft 9in. 11st 10lb.
Born: Warnham, nr Horsham, Sussex, 29 Aug 1911. Died: Burgess Hill, Sussex, 30 Mar 1985.
School: Collyers.
Jnr football: Horsham. Joined ARSENAL: Nov 1933 (amateur), 22 Dec 1933 (professional). First app: Jnr fdly v Oxford University (a) 22 Nov 1933. First snr app: League v Leicester City (a) 8 Mar 1934. Final app: League v Bolton Wanderers (a) 29 Apr 1936. Transferred to Fulham (£150) 5 May 1936.
ARSENAL Record: League 7 (1 gl); Other snr

comp: 1; Football Combination 75 (53 gls); London FA Challenge Cup 6 (5 gls); London Midweek League 2 (3 gls); Friendlies 10 (18 gls).
Honours: London Combination champions 1933-4, 1934-5. London FA Challenge Cup winners 1933-4. Norwich Hospital Cup winners 1934-5.
Son of a well-known Sussex cricketer, he also played County cricket for Sussex from 1931 to 1960. After Fulham played football for Luton Town (1937). Played cricket for Winchester (1955) and coach to Sussex (1960-64).

CRAWFORD, Gavin   **1891-98**
Outside-right/right-half   5ft 9in. 11st 4lb.
Born: Kilmarnock, c.1867. Died: 2 Mar 1955.
Jnr football: Ash Lea FC, Fairfield Rangers (Glasgow). Previous Club: Sheffield United (1890). Joined ARSENAL: Summer 1891 from Sheffield United. First app: Snr fdly v Sheffield United (h) 5 Sep 1891. First first-class app: FA Cup v Small Heath (a) 16 Jan 1892. Final app: Snr fdly v Millwall (a) 30 Apr 1898. Transferred to Millwall summer 1898.
ARSENAL Record: League 122 (14 gls); FA Cup 14 (3 gls); FA Cup (Q) 2 (1 gl); United League 21; Kent League 3 (1 gl); Friendlies 94 (19 gls). In addition between 1891-2 and 1892-3 made 83 Senior (49 gls) and 7 Reserve apps (4 gls) for Royal Arsenal.
A driller by trade. Was one of Arsenal's first professionals and captain for several years. Later played for Queen's Park Rangers. Became groundsman at Charlton Athletic, a position he held up to his 80th birthday.

CRAWFORD, Harold Sydney   **1911-13**
Goalkeeper   5ft 11½in. 11st.
Born: Dundee, Scotland.
Jnr football: Hebburn Argyle (Newcastle). Joined ARSENAL: 22 Jun 1911 from Hebburn Argyle. First app: South Eastern League v West Ham (a) 2 Sep 1911. First snr app: League v Tottenham Hotspur (a) 25 Dec 1911. Final snr app: League v Sheffield Wednesday (h) 29 Mar 1913. Final app: South Eastern League v Clapton Orient (h) 19 Apr 1913. Given free transfer by Arsenal 9 May 1913 and joined Reading 28 Jun 1913.
ARSENAL Record: League 26; FA Cup 1; Other snr comp: 1; South Eastern League 38; Other jnr comp: 1; Friendlies 14.

CRAYSTON, William John   **1934-43**
Right-half   6ft 1in. 12st 12lb.
Born: Grange-over-Sands, Lancs, 9 Oct 1910.
School: Barrow.
Jnr football: Ulverston Town. Previous Clubs: Barrow (1928), Bradford (1930). Joined ARSENAL: 19 May 1934 from Bradford for £5,250. First app: London Combination v Bristol City (h) 25 Aug 1934. First snr app: League v Liverpool (h) 1 Sep 1934. Final app: Football League South v West Ham (h) 11 Dec 1943.
ARSENAL Record: League 168 (16 gls); FA Cup 16 (1 gl); FA Charity Shield 3; Other snr comp: 4; Football Combination 7 (2 gls); Friendlies 17 (4 gls). In addition played 3 League matches 1939-40 prior to outbreak of war and made 94 apps (26 gls) during wartime.
Honours: Played for Barrow Schoolboys. Division One champions winners 1934-5, 1937-8. FA Cup winners 1936. FA Charity Shield winners 1938-9, runners-up 1935-6, 1936-7. Bath Coronation Cup winners 1936-7. Football League South Cup winners 1943. Football League War Cup runners-up 1941. 8 full England caps (1 gl) 1935-7 and made 1 international app during wartime. Played for England v Anglo-Scots 1935. Made 1 app for Football League 1935.
Despite breaking a wrist and a leg during 1933-4 was signed by Arsenal. Served as a Flight

Lieutenant in the RAF during the war. An injury in a wartime match in Dec 1943 ended his playing career. On demobilization he joined the Arsenal coaching staff and became assistant manager Jun 1947. Appointed Arsenal manager Nov 1956 on the death of Tom Whittaker and resigned 19 May 1958. Became manager of Doncaster Rovers Jul 1958 to Mar 1961. Retiring from football in 1961 he took up a newsagents and general store business in Streetly, near Birmingham, where he still lives after retiring in 1972.

CREEGAN, Walter Warden   **1921-23**
Outside-right   5ft 6in. 10st 8lb.
Born: Manchester, c.1903.
Joined ARSENAL: 25 Jan 1921 (amateur), 5 Mar 1921 (professional). First app: London Combination v Clapton Orient (a) 19 Feb 1921. First snr app: FA Cup v Queen's Park Rangers (a) 11 Jan 1922. Final snr app: On tour v Gais (Gothenburg) 16 May 1922. Final app: Jnr fdly v Wycombe Wanderers (a) 5 May 1923.
ARSENAL Record: League 5; FA Cup 1; Other snr comp: 1; Football Combination 44 (5 gls); London FA Challenge Cup 1; Friendlies 23/1 (7 gls).
Honours: Southend Hospital Cup winners 1921-2.

CROPLEY, Alexander James   **1974-76**
Inside-forward   5ft 7in. 10st.
Born: Aldershot, Hants, 16 Jan 1951.
School: Norton Park, Edinburgh.
Jnr football: Edina Hibernians, Chelsea (trial). Previous Club: Hibernian (1968). Joined ARSENAL: 4 Dec 1974 from Hibernian for £150,000. First app: League v Carlisle United (a) 7 Dec 1974. Final app: League v West Ham (a) 11 Sep 1976. Transferred to Aston Villa (£125,000) 22 Sep 1976.
ARSENAL Record: League 29/1 (5 gls); FA Cup 2; Football League Cup 2 (1 gl); Football Combination 15 (1 gl); Friendlies 14/1 (3 gls).
His father, John, played for Aldershot. Moved to Scotland when very young. Learned a trade as an electrician before taking up football. Won club and Scotland international honours (parentage qualification) whilst with Hibernian. Broke his leg after only nine apps for Arsenal. After Aston Villa played for Newcastle United (on loan Feb 1980), Toronto Blizzard (NASL) and Portsmouth (Oct 1981) before returning to Scotland in 1982. On retirement from football has been a publican and a taxi driver in Edinburgh.

CROSS, Arthur George 'Archie'   **1900-10**
Full-back   6ft. 12st 4lb.
Born: Kent, c.1881.
Jnr football: Dartford. Joined ARSENAL: 16 Apr 1900 from Dartford. First app: Jnr fdly v Deptford (h) 3 Sep 1900. First snr app: League v Blackpool (a) 6 Oct 1900. Final app: Snr fdly v Ilford (a) 30 Apr 1910. Transferred back to Dartford, summer 1910.
ARSENAL Record: League 132; FA Cup 17; London League 9; Other snr comp: 7; London FA Challenge Cup 3; South Eastern League 66; London League (Res) 52 (1 gl); Kent League 18 (1 gl); Other jnr comp: 1; Friendlies 58.
Honours: Division Two runners-up (promotion) 1903-04. Southern Charity Cup winners 1905-06, runners-up 1903-04. London League (Res) champions 1901-02. West Kent League champions 1900-01, 1901-02. South Eastern League champions 1907-08. Played in international trials 1905-06, 1906-07.
Was reinstated as an amateur in 1911. Became a director of Dartford FC in 1921 and was a publican in Dartford for over 40 years.

CROWE, Alfred 'Happy'   **1903-06**
Centre-forward.
A local, he joined ARSENAL, 21 Aug 1903 (amateur) from North Woolwich Invicta. First app: London League (Res) v Tottenham Hotspur (h) 1 Sep 1903 (abandoned match). First snr app: London League v West Ham (h) 14 Sep 1903. Final snr app: League v Birmingham (a) 28 Oct 1905. Final app: London League (Res) v Leyton (a) 28 Apr 1906.
ARSENAL Record: League 6 (4 gls); London League 4 (2 gls); South Eastern League 52 (56 gls); London League (Res) 39 (32 gls); Other jnr comp: 1 (5 gls); Friendlies 22 (17 gls).
Honours: South Eastern League champions 1903-04. London League (Res) champions 1903-04.
Scored two goals in his first League match for Arsenal 1904-05. Scored five goals in a match for the reserves 1904-05.

CROZIER, James   **1894**
Goalkeeper.
Joined ARSENAL: 14 May 1894 from Partick Thistle. First app: Jnr fdly v Pyebank Rovers (Sheffield) (h) 1 Sep 1894. First snr app: Snr fdly v Fleetwood Rangers (h) 8 Sep 1894. Final snr app: League v Grimsby Town (h) 10 Sep 1894 (only app). Final app: Jnr fdly v Sheffield & District (h) 26 Dec 1894.
ARSENAL Record: League 1; Friendlies 14.
As far as can be traced he returned to Partick Thistle (1895).

CUMNER, Reginald Horace   **1938-46**
Outside-left   5ft 8in. 10st 10lb.
Born: Aberdare, Wales, 31 Mar 1918.
Jnr football: Margate (Arsenal nursery). Previous Club: Hull City (sent by Arsenal from Margate, 29 Jan 1938). Joined ARSENAL: 9 May 1936. Returned from Margate & Hull, May 1938. First app: London Combination v Portsmouth (a) 27 Aug 1938. First snr app: Snr fdly v Glasgow Rangers (a) 29 Aug 1938. Final first-class app: FA Cup (2nd leg) v West Ham (h) 9 Jan 1946. Final app: Football League South v Brentford (h) 29 Apr 1946. Transferred to Notts County (exchange for I.McPherson) 2 Aug 1946.
ARSENAL Record: League 12 (2 gls); FA Cup 1 (1 gl); FA Charity Shield 1; Other snr comp: 1; Football Combination 13 (7 gls); Southern League 7 (2 gls); Friendlies 3 (1 gl). In addition played 2 reserve matches 1939-40 prior to outbreak of war and made 29 apps (6 gls) during wartime.
Honours: Played for Wales Schoolboys. FA Charity Shield winners 1938-9. Mayor of

---

Colchester Cup winners 1938-9. 3 full Wales caps (1 gl) 1938-9 and made 10 international apps (3 gls) during wartime.
Was in the Royal Marines during the war and received severe burns in service. After Notts County he played for Watford (Jul 1948), Scunthorpe United (Sep 1950) and Bradford City (Aug 1953). Now lives in Poole, Dorset.

CURLE, William   **1908-10**
Centre-forward/outside-left   5ft 8in.
Born: Glasgow, c.1886.
Jnr football: Rutherglen Glencairn. Joined ARSENAL: 4 May 1908. First app: League v Notts County (a) 5 Sep 1908. Final app: Snr fdly v Ilford (a) 30 Apr 1910.
ARSENAL Record: League 3; Other snr comp: 1; London FA Challenge Cup 1; South Eastern League 52 (12 gls); London League (Res) 12; Other jnr comp: 2 (1 gl); Friendlies 16 (1 gl).

CURTIS, George Frederick   **1936-47**
Inside-forward   5ft 9½in. 10st 11lb.
Born: West Thurrock, Essex, 3 Dec 1919.
Jnr football: Anglo (Purfleet), Margate (Arsenal nursery). Joined ARSENAL: 24 Dec 1936 (amateur) from Anglo, 2 Apr 1937 (professional). Returned from Margate 28 Feb 1938. First app: Jnr fdly v Margate (a) 30 Jan 1937. First snr app: Snr fdly v Southampton (a) 2 May 1938. Final snr app: League v Blackpool (h) 8 Feb 1947. Final app: Football Combination Cup Final v Swansea (Tottenham) 14 Jun 1947. (Played in public practice match 9 Aug 1947). Transferred to Southampton (£8,000) 9 Aug 1947.
ARSENAL Record: League 13; FA Cup 1; Football Combination 81 (12 gls); London FA Challenge Cup 3 (1 gl); Southern League 8 (3 gls); Friendlies 12 (2 gls). In addition, played 2 reserve matches 1939-40 prior to outbreak of war and made 48/1 apps (6 gls) during wartime.
Honours: London Combination champions 1938-9. Football Combination champions 1946-7. Football Combination Cup runners-up 1946-7.
Was a Corporal in the RAF during the war and served in India. Played for French club Valenciennes 1952 and player-coach at Chelmsford 1953. A fully qualified FA coach, he then had a variety of managerial and coaching appointments at Grays Athletic, the England Youth team, in the Sudan, at Sunderland, Brighton & Hove Albion and Stevenage Town. Was coach to the Norway national team 1972.

DAILLY, Hugh   **1898-99**
Outside-left   5ft 7in. 10st 3lb.
Born: Scotland, c.1879.
Jnr football: Dundee North End. Joined ARSENAL: 7 May 1898 from Dundee North End. First app: Kent League v Maidstone United (h) 3 Sep 1898. First snr app: United League v Reading (a) 14 Sep 1898. Final app: Chatham Charity Cup v Chatham (a) 18 Jan 1899.
ARSENAL Record: League 8 (4 gls); United League 8 (4 gls); Other snr comp: 1; Kent League 4 (3 gls); Friendlies 6 (3 gls).
Left Arsenal for Dundee, Feb 1899.

DANIEL, Raymond Wyn   **1946-53**
Centre-half   6ft 1in. 12st 2lb.
Born: Swansea, Wales, 2 Nov 1928.
School: Plasmarl, Swansea.
Jnr football: Local Youth Club. Previous Club: Swansea Town (amateur in wartime). Joined ARSENAL: 19 Aug 1946 (amateur), 19 Oct 1946 (professional). First app: Jnr fdly v Cheltenham (a) 14 Sep 1946. First snr app: League v Charlton Athletic (h) 7 May 1949. Final app: On tour v Rapid Vienna (in Bruges) 24 May 1953. Transferred to Sunderland (£27,500) 17 Jun 1953.

ARSENAL Record: League 87 (5 gls); FA Cup 12; Other snr comp: 1; Football Combination 76; London FA Challenge Cup 2; Eastern Counties League 18 (1 gl); Friendlies 43 (3 gls).
Honours: Division One champions 1952-3. FA Cup runners-up 1952. Football Combination champions 1950-51. 12 full Wales caps 1950-53.
Elder brother, Bobby, also played for Arsenal but was killed during the war. Played the 1952 FA Cup Final with a broken arm in plaster cast. Won further international honours with Sunderland. Later played for Cardiff City (1957), Swansea Town (1958), and player-manager of Hereford Town. Became a publican in Swansea and then South Wales area manager of Courvoisier Brandy Company. Lives in Sketty, Swansea.

DAVIDSON, Alexander   **1904-05**
Goalkeeper   6ft.
Born: Strathclyde, Scotland.
Joined ARSENAL: 2 Jun 1904. First app: South Eastern League v Hastings (h) 3 Sep 1904. First snr app: League v Blackburn Rovers (a) 15 Oct 1904 (only app). Final snr app: Snr fdly v Corinthians (a) 18 Feb 1905. Final app: London League (Res) v Clapton Orient (a) 25 Apr 1905.
ARSENAL Record: League 1; South Eastern League 19; London League (Res) 14; Other jnr comp: 1; Friendlies 1.
A Scotland Junior international.

DAVIDSON, Robert Trimming   **1935-37**
Inside-forward   5ft 7in. 10st 11lb.
Born: Lochgelly, Fifeshire, Scotland, 27 Apr 1913.
Jnr football: Bowhill Juniors, St Bernard. Previous Club: St Johnstone (Mar 1933). Joined ARSENAL: 1 Feb 1935 from St Johnstone. First app: League v Stoke City (h) 20 Feb 1935. Final app: League v Middlesbrough (h) 30 Oct 1937. Transferred to Coventry City (exchange for L.Jones) 4 Nov 1937.
ARSENAL Record: League 57 (13 gls); FA Cup 4 (2 gls); FA Charity Shield 2; Other snr comp: 1; Football Combination 36 (18 gls); London FA Challenge Cup 4; Friendlies 9 (4 gls).
Honours: FA Charity Shield runners-up 1935-6, 1936-7. London FA Challenge Cup winners 1935-6. Bath Coronation Cup winners 1936-7.
Played for Cowdenbeath & District Schoolboys. Won Scottish League honours with St Johnstone. Scored four goals for Arsenal at Portsmouth, Dec 1936. After Coventry he played for Hinckley, and Redditch and later became player-manager of Rugby Town (1954) and manager of Redditch.

DAVIDSON, Roger   **1964-69**
Inside-forward/wing-half   5ft 7½in. 11st 6lb.
Born: Islington, London, 27 Oct 1948.
School: Sir Philip Magnus Secondary, London.
Joined ARSENAL: Jul 1964 (apprentice), 28 Oct 1965 (professional). First app: South East Counties League v Fulham (h) 22 Aug 1964. First snr app: Snr fdly (sub) v Southampton (a) 12 Feb 1966. Final snr app: League (sub) v Wolverhampton Wanderers (h) 16 Mar 1968 (only app). Final app: Football Combination v Gillingham May 1969. Transferred to Portsmouth 27 May 1969.
ARSENAL Record: League 0/1; Football Combination 67/1 (9 gls); London FA Challenge Cup 1; FA Youth Cup 11 (6 gls); Metropolitan League 58 (28 gls); South East Counties League 30 (12 gls); Other jnr comp: 8 (3 gls); Friendlies 42/3 (21 gls). In addition made 1 Metropolitan League match 1965-6, later removed from records.
Honours: Played for Islington Schoolboys. England Schoolboy international. Football Combination Cup winners 1967-8. Football Combination champions 1968-9. South East

50

Counties League champions 1964-5, runners-up 1965-6.
Later played for Fulham, Lincoln City and Aldershot.

DAVIE George   **1891-92**
Centre-forward.
Born: c.1865.
Previous Clubs: Everton, Sunderland. Joined ARSENAL: Oct 1891 from Renton (Dumbartonshire). First app: Snr fdly v Clapton (a) 31 Oct 1891. First first-class app: FA Cup v Small Heath (a) 16 Jan 1892. Final first-class app: FA Cup (Q). v Millwall Athletic (h) 19 Nov 1892. Final app: Snr fdly v West Brom (h) 3 Dec 1892.
ARSENAL Record: FA Cup 1 (1 gl); FA Cup (Q) 3 (2 gls). In addition between 1891-2 and 1892-3 made 58 Senior apps (39 gls) for Royal Arsenal.
Took the club to court in Jan 1893 for wrongful dismissal and loss of earnings but lost the case.

DAVIES, Paul   **1968-72**
Centre-forward   5ft 11in. 11st 5lb.
Born: St Asaph, Flintshire, Wales, 10 Oct 1952.
School: Holywell High.
Joined ARSENAL: Oct 1968 (amateur), 6 Jan 1969 (apprentice), 21 Oct 1969 (professional). First app: Jnr fdly v Charterhouse (a) 23 Oct 1968. First snr app: European Cup (sub) v Strömgodset, 15 Sep 1971. Final snr app: League (sub) v Newcastle United (h) 9 Oct 1971. Final app: Football Combination v Bristol Rovers (h) 12 Aug 1972. Transferred to Charlton Athletic (£20,000 after a period on loan) 30 Nov 1972.
ARSENAL Record: League 0/1; European Competitions 0/1; Football Combination 93/4 (30 gls); London FA Challenge Cup 5 (1 gl); FA Youth Cup 10 (5 gls); Metropolitan League 13 (5 gls); South East Counties League 13 (4 gls); Other jnr comp: 3; Friendlies 46/2 (23 gls).
Honours: Played for Flintshire Schoolboys. Wales Schoolboy international. Football Combination champions 1969-70. FA Youth Cup winners 1970-71. South East Counties League Cup winners 1970-71. 5 Wales Youth caps 1971-2.
Younger brother of Welsh international, Ron Davies (Norwich City and Southampton).

DAVIS, Frederick William   **1893-99**
Wing-half   5ft 8½in. 10st.
Born: Smethwick, c.1871.
Jnr football: Soho Villa, Birmingham St Georges. Joined ARSENAL: Sep 1893 from Birmingham SG. First app: Snr fdly v New Brompton (a) 2 Sep 1893. First snr app: Snr fdly v Doncaster Rovers (h) 4 Sep 1893. Final snr app: Snr fdly v Woolwich League (h) 26 Apr 1899. Final app: Jnr fdly v Grays United (h) 29 Apr 1899.
ARSENAL Record: League 137 (8 gls); FA Cup 13 (2 gls); United League 25 (1 gl); Kent League 6; Other jnr comp: 2; Friendlies 110 (5 gls).
Later played for Nottingham Forest.

DAVIS, Paul Vincent   **1978-**
Midfield   5ft 8in. 9st 7lb.
Born: Dulwich, London, 9 Dec 1961.
School: Springfield Primary, Beaufoy Secondary (Kennington).
Joined ARSENAL: 27 Jun 1978 (apprentice), 18 Jun 1979 (professional). First app: South East Counties League v Crystal Palace (h) 25 Feb 1978. First snr app: E.Drake Testimonial (sub) v Fulham (a) 11 Sep 1979. League v Tottenham Hotspur (a) 7 Apr 1980.
ARSENAL Record: League 301/18 (29 gls); FA Cup 19/5 (3 gls); European comp: 6/1; Football League Cup 41/3 (4 gls); FA Charity Shield 2; Other snr comp: 10 (1 gl); Football Combination 123/4 (23 gls); South East Counties League 35/

1 (5 gls); FA Youth Cup 3 (1 gl); Other jnr comp: 4 (1 gl); Friendlies 95/12 (22 gls).
Honours: Played for South London Schoolboys. Division One champions 1988-9, 1990-91. Football League Cup winners 1986-7, runners-up 1987-8. FA Charity Shield medal 1991-2. Mercantile Credit Centenary Trophy winners 1988-9. South East Counties League Cup winners 1979-80. President's Cup winners 1980-81. 1 England 'B' cap (1 gl); 9/2 England Under-21 caps (2 gls). Made 1 app for Football League 1990-91.
Initial apps for Arsenal were as a schoolboy.

DEVINE, Archibald   **1913-14**
Inside-forward   5ft 9½in. 12st 4lb.
Born: Lochgelly, Fifeshire, Scotland, c.1886. Died 30 Sep 1964.
Jnr football: Lochgelly United. Previous Clubs: Hearts, Raith Rovers, Falkirk, Bradford City (Apr 1910). Joined ARSENAL: 14 Feb 1913 from Bradford City for £1,000. First app: League v Chelsea (a) 15 Feb 1913. First snr app: League v Huddersfield Town (h) 14 Feb 1914. Final app: South Eastern League v Brentford (a) 21 Mar 1914. Transferred to Bradford City summer 1914.
ARSENAL Record: League 24 (5 gls); London FA Challenge Cup 3 (2 gls); South Eastern League 10 (3 gls); London League (Res) 3; Friendlies 1 (1 gl).
Won Scotland international honours with Falkirk and club honours with Bradford City. Retired cs 1915.

DEVINE, Daniel   **1892-93**
Centre-forward/right-half   5ft 8in. 10st 7lb.
Born: Dumbarton, Scotland, c.1870.
Jnr football: Dumbarton Athletic, Renton. Joined ARSENAL: Nov 1892, 25 Jan 1893 (League forms). First app: Snr fdly v Lincoln City (h) 5 Nov 1892. First first-class app: FA Cup v Sunderland (a) 21 Jan 1893. Final app: League v Ardwick (h) 11 Nov 1893.
ARSENAL Record: League 2; FA Cup 2; Friendlies 10 (1 gl). In addition in 1892-3 made 35 Senior (2 gls) and 3 reserve (2 gls) apps for Royal Arsenal. Later played for Partick Thistle.

DEVINE, John Anthony   **1974-83**
Defender   5ft 10½in. 12st 1lb.
Born: Dublin, Ireland, 11 Nov 1958.
Jnr football: St John Bosco Juniors. Joined ARSENAL: Jan 1974 (amateur), Nov 1974 (apprentice), 11 Oct 1976 (professional). First app:

Jnr fdly v University Athletics Union (h) 15 Jan 1974. First snr app: Snr fdly v Northampton Town (a) 20 Sep 1977. League v Leeds United (a) 22 Apr 1978. Final app: Snr fdly v Gillingham (a) 17 May 1983. Transferred to Norwich City (free transfer) 13 Jun 1983.
ARSENAL Record: League 86/3; FA Cup 6; Football League Cup 8; European Competitions 8; Football Combination 158/6 (8 gls); FA Youth Cup 12; South East Counties League 40/1 (5 gls); Other jnr comp: 7; Friendlies 49/13 (6 gls).
Honours: FA Cup runners-up 1980. Republic of Ireland Schoolboy and Youth (captain) international. 7 full Republic of Ireland caps 1979-83.
A good guitarist/vocalist who has recorded. Broke his leg Mar 1976. Won further international honours with Norwich City. Later played for Stoke City where a badly broken leg ended his first-class career. At present is playing for East Bengal, India.

DEVLIN, James   **1897-98**
Centre-forward   5ft 10in.
Joined ARSENAL: 19 Dec 1897 from Sunderland for £80. Previous Clubs: Dundee, Tottenham Hotspur. First app: United League v Tottenham Hotspur (h) 25 Dec 1897. Final snr app: League v Blackpool (a) 1 Jan 1898. Final app: Jnr fdly v Woolwich & District League (h) 26 Feb 1898.
ARSENAL Record: League 1 (1 gl); United League 1; Friendlies 1.
Was ill with pleurisy soon after joining Arsenal. Moved to Airdrie in exchange for John Dick (see below).

DICK, John   **1898-12**
Half-back   5ft 7in. 10st 12lb.
Born: Eaglesham, Renfrewshire, Scotland, c.1876.
Previous Club: Airdrieonians. Joined ARSENAL: 7 Aug .898 from Airdrie (exchange for J.Devlin). First app: Snr fdly v Gravesend (h) 1 Sep 1898. League v Luton Town (a) 3 Sep 1898. Final snr app: Snr fdly v Ilford (a) 30 Apr 1910. Final app: Jnr fdly v New Brompton (a) 27 Apr 1912.
ARSENAL Record: League 262 (12 gls); FA Cup 22 (1 gl); United League 19 (1 gl); Southern District Combination 15; London League 17; Other snr comp: 8; London FA Challenge Cup 3; Kent League 3 (3 gls); London League (Res) 39 (2 gls); South Eastern League 134 (17 gls); Other jnr comp: 5 (1 gl); Friendlies 88 (6 gls).
Honours: Captain of Arsenal. Division Two runners-up (promotion) 1903-04. Southern Charity Cup runners-up 1903-04. South Eastern League champions 1906-07. London League (Res) champions 1906-07.
Was appointed coach to Prague Deutscher Club (Czechoslovakia) in Jun 1912 and, coach to Sparta, Prague cs 1922. In his latter playing years for Arsenal, he also ran a tobacco and confectionery business in Plumstead.

DICKSON, William   **1953-56**
Half-back   5ft 9in. 11st 13lb.
Born: Lurgan, Co Armagh, N.Ireland, 15 Apr 1923.
Jnr football: Sunnyside FC. Previous Clubs: Glenavon (amateur), Notts County (1945), Chelsea (Nov 1947). Joined ARSENAL: 2 Oct 1953 from Chelsea for £15,000. First app: Snr fdly v Anderlecht (Belgium) (h) 21 Oct 1953. First snr app: League v Blackpool (a) 24 Aug 1955. Final app: Football Combination v Birmingham (h) 25 Feb 1956. Transferred to Mansfield Town (free transfer) 23 Jul 1956.
ARSENAL Record: League 29 (1 gl); FA Cup 2; Football Combination 17; London FA Challenge Cup 1; Eastern Counties League 1; Friendlies 8.
Honours: 3 full Northern Ireland caps 1953-4.
Worked as a joiner before taking up football. Won other international honours with Chelsea. Had a

disastrous 1954-5 season through injury — a dislocated shoulder, appendicitis, a knee operation and, finally, a slipped disc. It was a recurring dislocated shoulder, despite several operations, which ended his career. Became Arsenal's Northern Ireland scout. Is now in the joinery trade.

DIXON, Lee Michael   **1988-**
Right-back   5ft 9in. 10st 12lb.
Born: Manchester, 17 Mar 1964.
Previous Clubs: Burnley (1982-3), Chester City (Feb 1984), Bury (Jul 1985), Stoke City (Jul 1986). Joined ARSENAL: 29 Jan 1988 from Stoke City for £350,000. First app: Football Combination v Queen's Park Rangers (h) 6 Feb 1988. First snr app: League v Luton Town (h) 13 Feb 1988.
ARSENAL Record: League 151/2 (15 gls); FA Cup 13 (1 gl); Football League Cup 16; European comp: 4; FA Charity Shield 2; Other snr comp: 12 (1 gl); Football Combination 14/1 (3 gls); Friendlies 31/1 (4 gls).
Honours: Division One champions 1988-9, 1990-91. FA Charity Shield runners-up 1989-90, medal 1991-2. Mercantile Credit Centenary Trophy winners 1988-9. 12 full England caps (1 gl) 1990. 4 'B' caps 1989-90. Made 1 app for Football League 1990-91.

DOCHERTY, Thomas Henderson   **1958-61**
Wing-half   5ft 7in. 11st 11lb.
Born: Shettleston, Glasgow, 24 Aug 1928.
School: St Marks RC, Glasgow.
Jnr football: St Pauls Boys Guild, Shettleston Rovers. Previous Clubs: Celtic (1948), Preston North End (Nov 1949). Joined ARSENAL: 23 Aug 1958 from Preston North End for £20,000. First app: League v Burnley (h) 26 Aug 1958. Final app: League v Newcastle United (a) 4 Feb 1961. Transferred to Chelsea (player-coach) in Feb 1961.
ARSENAL Record: League 83 (1 gl); FA Cup 7; Other snr comp: 4 (1 gl); Football Combination 3; London FA Challenge Cup 1; Friendlies 27/1 (2 gls).
Honours: Southern Floodlit Challenge Cup winners 1958-9. 3 full Scotland caps 1958-59.
Was a baker before taking up football. Served in the Highland Light Infantry. Won club and international honours with Preston North End. Suffered broken ankle 1959. Became manager of Chelsea (Jan 1962) and then had numerous managerial appointments including Rotherham, Queen's Park Rangers, Aston Villa, Oporto (Portugal), Hull City (assistant), Scotland national team, Manchester United, Derby County, Australian national team, Preston North End, Wolverhampton Wanderers and Altrincham.

DODGIN, William   **1952-61**
Centre-half   6ft 2in. 12st 4lb.
Born: Wardley Colliery, Co Durham, 4 Nov 1931.
School: St Mary's College, Southampton.
Previous Clubs: Southampton (amateur), Fulham (Sep 1949). Joined ARSENAL: 4 Dec 1952 from Fulham for £4,000 (plus junior player). First app: Football Combination v Birmingham (h) 13 Dec 1952. First snr app: League v Bolton Wanderers (h) 15 Apr 1953. Final snr app: On tour (sub) v RSC Anderlecht (Belgium) 14 May 1960. Final app: Football Combination v Charlton Athletic (a) 11 Mar 1961. Transferred to Fulham (£7,000) 16 Mar 1961.
ARSENAL Record: League 191; FA Cup 16 (1 gl); FA Charity Shield 1; Other snr comp: 9; Football Combination 114; London FA Challenge Cup 11; Eastern Counties League 1; Metropolitan League 1 (1 gl); Friendlies 53/1.
Honours: FA Charity Shield winners 1953-4. Southern Floodlit Challenge Cup winners 1958-9. Football Combination Cup winners 1952-3.

London FA Challenge Cup winners 1954-5, runners-up 1960-61. 1 England Under-23 cap (and captain) 1954.
Son of Bill Dodgin, Southampton, Fulham and Brentford manager. Served National Service in RAOC and played for the Army. Moved from Fulham to Millwall (1965) and became coach, later had spells as coach at Queen's Park Rangers, Fulham, Leicester and manager of Fulham, Northampton (twice) and Brentford.

DOUGALL, Peter   **1933-37**
Inside-forward   5ft 7in. 11st 3lb.
Born: Denny, Stirlingshire, Scotland, 21 Mar 1909. Died: 12 Jun 1974.
Previous Clubs: Burnley, Clyde, Southampton. Joined ARSENAL: Sep 1933 (on trial), 23 Oct 1933 (professional). First app: London Combination v Queen's Park Rangers (a) 30 Sep 1933. First snr app: Snr fdly v Racing Club de Paris (a) 19 Nov 1933. Final snr app: League v Brentford (h) 4 Apr 1936. Final app: Jnr fdly v Oxford University (h) 12 Nov 1936. Transferred to Everton Aug 1937.
ARSENAL Record: League 21 (4 gls); FA Cup 2 (1 gl); Other snr comp: 1; Football Combination 80 (14 gls); London FA Challenge Cup 7 (1 gl); Friendlies 9 (3 gls).
Honours: London Combination champions 1933-4, 1934-5. London FA Challenge Cup winners 1933-4. Norwich Hospital Cup winners 1934-5.
Injury made him miss the 1936-7 season, playing in only one junior match. Later played for Bury 1938.

DRAIN, Thomas   **1909-10**
Inside-forward   5ft 9in. 11st 7lb.
Born: Pollokshaws, Glasgow, c.1880.
Jnr football: Maybole. Previous Clubs: Bradford City (Oct 1903), Leeds City (Jun 1905), Exeter City. Joined ARSENAL: 1909 from Exeter City. First app: League v Aston Villa (a) 1 Sep 1909. Final snr app: League v Notts County (a) 7 Oct 1909. Final app: South Eastern League v Southend (a) 9 Apr 1910.
ARSENAL Record: League 2; London FA Challenge Cup 1; South Eastern League 10; Friendlies 6 (1 gl).

DRAKE, Edward Joseph   **1934-45**
Centre-forward   5ft 10in. 11st 10lb.
Born: Southampton, 16 Aug 1912.
Jnr football: Southampton Gasworks FC, Winchester City. Previous Club: Southampton (Nov 1931). Joined ARSENAL: 14 Mar 1934 from Southampton for £6,500. First app: League v Wolverhampton Wanderers (h) 24 Mar 1934. Final app: Football League South v West Ham (a) 5 May 1945.
ARSENAL Record: League 168 (124 gls); FA Cup 14 (12 gls); FA Charity Shield 2 (3 gls); Other snr comp: 2; Football Combination 4 (4 gls); Friendlies 12 (14 gls). In addition played 1 League (4 gls) and 1 reserve (1 gl) match prior to outbreak of war and made 128 apps (86 gls) during wartime.
Honours: Played for Southampton Schoolboys. Division One champions 1934-5, 1937-8. FA Cup winners 1936. FA Charity Shield winners 1934-5, 1938-9. Mayor of Colchester Cup winners 1938-9. Football League South Cup winners 1943. Football League War Cup runners-up 1941. 5 full England caps (6 gls) 1934-8.
Holds the Arsenal record for most League goals scored in a season - 42 goals in 41 apps 1934-5, Scored 7 goals in one match at Aston Villa 14 Dec 1935 (also a League Division One record). Played county cricket for Hampshire in the 1930s. Was a Flight Lieutenant in the RAF during the war. Received a spinal injury at Reading in 1945 which eventually ended his playing career. After

the war he assisted at Highbury for a while before becoming manager of Reading (Jun 1947) and then Chelsea (1952-61). Became a life assurance salesman in London (1970) and then took on scouting and other duties at Fulham, becoming a director in 1979 and is now a life president.

DRURY, George Benjamin   **1938-46**
Inside-forward   5ft 6in. 10st 8lb.
Born: Hucknall, Nottinghamshire, 22 Jan 1914. Died: 1972.
Jnr football: Heanor Town, Loughborough Town. Previous Club: Sheffield Wednesday (Sep 1934). Joined ARSENAL: 10 Mar 1938 from Sheffield Wednesday for £7,000. First app: League v Middlesbrough (a) 12 Mar 1938. Final app: League v Derby County (h) 21 Sep 1946. Final app: Football Combination v Norwich City (h) 23 Oct 1946. Transferred to West Brom 26 Oct 1946.
ARSENAL Record: League 38 (3 gls); FA Cup 2; Other snr comp: 3 (3 gls); Football Combination 22 (18 gls); London FA Challenge Cup 3 (2 gls); Southern League 1 (1 gl); Friendlies 10 (8 gls). In addition played 2 League matches (1 gl) 1939-40 prior to outbreak of war and made 22 apps (9 gls) during wartime.
Honours: London Combination champions 1938-9. Mayor of Colchester Cup winners 1938-9. Played for London Combination v Central League 1938.
Served in the RAF during the war and played football in Ireland. After West Brom he played for Watford (1948), Darlaston and Linby Colliery.

DUCAT, Andrew   **1905-12**
Centre-forward/right-half   5ft 9½in. 11st 11lb.
Born: Brixton, Surrey, 16 Feb 1886. Died: London, 23 Jul 1942.
School: Brewery Road, Compton House, London. Jnr football: Westcliffe Athletic, Southend Athletic. Joined ARSENAL: 10 Jan 1905 (amateur) from Southend Athletic, 12 Feb 1905 (professional). First app: South Eastern League v Blackburn Rovers (h) 11 Feb 1905. Final app: League v Blackburn Rovers (h) 22 Apr 1912. Transferred to Aston Villa (£1,000) 15 Jun 1912.
ARSENAL Record: League 175 (19 gls); FA Cup 13 (2 gls); Other snr comp: 5 (1 gl); London FA

Challenge Cup 6 (1 gl); South Eastern League 30 (26 gls); London League (Res) 22 (11 gls); Friendlies 22 (14 gls). In addition made 47 'guest' apps (3 gls) during wartime.
Honours: Southern Charity Cup winners 1905-06. South Eastern League champions 1906-07. London League champions 1906-07. 3 full England caps (1 gl) 1910.
Played county cricket for Surrey 1906-31 and won Test honours for England. Won club and further international honours with Aston Villa. Transferred to Fulham (May 1921) retired in 1924 and became manager of Fulham. Was reinstated as an amateur cs 1926 and played for Casuals. After football, in addition to his cricket career he was cricket coach at Eton, later a part-time journalist and later a publican. Died at Lords Cricket Ground whilst playing for the Home Guard during wartime.

DUFF, Hugh   **1895-98 & 1899-1900**
Outside-left.
Previous Club: Millwall. Joined ARSENAL: 29 Aug 1895 (amateur) from Millwall, Sep 1895 (professional). Went back to Millwall for season 1898-9 and returned to ARSENAL for 1899-1900. First app: Kent League v Sheppey United (a) 7 Sep 1895. First snr app: Snr fdly v Tottenham Hotspur (h) 16 Mar 1896. Final snr app: Southern District Combination v Bristol City (h) 30 Oct 1899. Final app: Kent League v Faversham (h) 3 Feb 1900.
ARSENAL Record: League 1 (1 gl); FA Cup 1 (1 gl); United League 1; Southern District Combination 1; Other snr comp: 1 (1 gl); Kent League 42 (22 gls); Friendlies 68/1 (35 gls).
Honours: Kent League champions 1896-7. Sevenoaks Charity Cup winners 1897-8.

DUNCAN, David   **1912-13**
Centre-forward.
Born: Co Antrim, Ireland, 1891.
Jnr football: Glasgow St Anthony, Bellshill Athletic. Joined ARSENAL: 12 Dec 1912 from Fulham. Previous Clubs: Albion Rovers (Sep 1910), Fulham (May 1911). First app: League v Tottenham Hotspur (h) 14 Dec 1912. Final snr app: League v Oldham Athletic (h) 8 Feb 1913. Final app: Jnr fdly v Woolwich & District League (h) 23 Apr 1913.
ARSENAL Record: League 3 (1 gl); FA Cup 2 (1 gl); South Eastern League 5 (1 gl); Friendlies 4.
Played for Albion Rovers again (1916) before retiring in 1921.

DUNN, Stephen   **1919-25**
Goalkeeper   5ft 8in. 11st 7lb.
Born: Darlaston, Staffordshire.
Joined ARSENAL: May 1919 from the Army. First app: London Combination v Millwall (a) 30 Aug 1919. First snr app: League v Everton (a) 11 Oct 1919. Final snr app: Snr fdly v Luton Town (h) 20 Apr 1925. Final app: London Combination v Crystal Palace (h) 25 Apr 1925.
ARSENAL Record: League 43; FA Cup 1; Other snr comp: 3; Football Combination 143; London FA Challenge Cup 2; Friendlies 44.
Honours: Southend Hospital Cup winners 1920-21. Metropolitan Hospital Cup winners 1920-21. Southend Hospital Cup runners-up 1922-3.
Served with the Gloucestershire Regiment in India and had considerable experience in Army football before joining Arsenal. Went into business in the Bristol area in 1925.

DUNNE, James   **1933-36**
Centre-forward   5ft 9½in. 11st 10lb.
Born: Dublin, Ireland, 3 Sep 1905. Died: Dublin, Dec 1949.
Previous Clubs: Shamrock Rovers, New Brighton

(1925), Sheffield United (Feb 1926). Joined ARSENAL: 30 Sep 1933 from Sheffield United for £8,250. First app: League v Middlesbrough (h) 30 Sep 1933. Final snr app: League v Middlesbrough (a) 11 Apr 1936. Final app: London Combination v Portsmouth (h) 25 Apr 1936. Transferred to Southampton (£2,000) 13 Jul 1936.
ARSENAL Record: League 28 (10 gls); FA Cup 4 (3 gls); FA Charity Shield 1; Football Combination 48 (42 gls); Friendlies 2/1 (1 gl).
Honours: Division One champions 1933-4. FA Charity Shield runners-up 1935-6. London Combination champions 1934-5. 3 full Republic of Ireland caps (1 gl) 1936.
Won other international honours with Sheffield United, Southampton and Shamrock Rovers. After one season with Southampton, he returned to Shamrock Rovers, first as a player and then as coach (Jun 1937). Joined Bohemians as coach (1942), returning to Shamrock Rovers (1947).

DUNSBEE, Charles Richard   **1899-1900**
Wing-half.
Joined ARSENAL: 8 Jun 1899 from Kidderminster. First app: Kent League v Swanscombe (a) 2 Sep 1899. First snr app: Southern District Combination v Portsmouth (h) 23 Oct 1899. Final app: League v Barnsley (a) 23 Apr 1900.
ARSENAL Record: League 8; FA Cup 3; Southern District Combination 6; Kent League 13; Friendlies 6.

DWIGHT, Frederick   **1903-05**
Full-back.
Joined ARSENAL, 5 Jun 1903 from Fulham. First app: London League (Res) v Tottenham Hotspur (h) 1 Sep 1903 (abandoned match). First snr app: London League v Brentford (a) 23 Nov 1903. Final app: Snr fdly v Sheffield United (h) 29 Apr 1905.
ARSENAL Record: League 1; London League 5; South Eastern League 41 (2 gls); London League (Res) 33 (1 gl); Other jnr comp: 1; Friendlies 11 (2 gls).
Honours: South Eastern League champions 1903-04. London League (Res) champions 1903-04.
After Arsenal he played for Nelson (Lancashire).

DYER, Frank   **1892-93**
Left-half/full-back.
Born: Bishopbriggs, Glasgow, 1870.
Jnr football: Warwick County. Previous Club: West Bromwich Albion (1890). Joined ARSENAL: Summer 1892 from West Bromwich Albion. First app: Snr fdly v Highland Light Infantry (h) 1 Sep 1892. First first-class app: FA Cup (Q) v Highland Light Infantry (h) 15 Oct 1892. Final first-class app: FA Cup v Sunderland (a) 21 Jan 1893. Final app: Snr fdly v Derby County (h) 22 Apr 1893. Transferred to Manchester City 15 Aug 1893.
ARSENAL Record: FA Cup 1; FA Cup (Q) 4. In addition in 1892-3 made 36 senior (2 gls) and 7 reserve apps for Royal Arsenal.
Retired May 1898.

EARLE, Stanley George James   **1922-24**
Inside-right   6ft 1½in. 12st 7lb.
Born: Stratford, London, 6 Sep 1897. Died: Brightlingsea, 26 Sep 1971.
School: Goodwin Road, West Ham.
Jnr football: Clapton (Amateur). Joined ARSENAL: 16 Mar 1922 (amateur). First app: League v Aston Villa (a) 18 Mar 1922. Final app: League v Huddersfield Town (h) 15 Dec 1923. Registration cancelled 4 Jul 1924.
ARSENAL Record: League 4 (3 gls); Football Combination 1.
Played for England Schoolboys and also won England Amateur and full international caps.

Won an Amateur Cup medal with Clapton. Signed professional for West Ham (Aug 1924) and later played for Clapton Orient (May 1932) before retiring cs 1933. Later had spells as coach at Walthamstow Avenue and manager of Leyton.

EASTHAM, George Edward OBE   **1960-66**
Inside-forward   5ft 7in. 9st 12lb.
Born: Blackpool, 23 Sep 1936.
School: Revoe Primary, Arnold Grammar, Blackpool.
Jnr football: Bispham Church Team, Highfield Youth Club. Previous Clubs: Ards (N.Ireland), Newcastle United (May 1956). Joined ARSENAL: 18 Nov 1960 from Newcastle United for £47,500. First app: Football Combination v Leicester City (h) 19 Nov 1960. First snr app: League v Bolton Wanderers (a) 10 Dec 1960. Final app: Snr fdly v Huddersfield Town (a) 13 Aug 1966. Transferred to Stoke City (£35,000) 18 Aug 1966.
ARSENAL Record: League 207 (41 gls); FA Cup 13; European Competitions 3; Football Combination 11 (8 gls); London FA Challenge Cup 6 (3 gls); Friendlies 40 (26 gls).

Honours: Played for Blackpool Schoolboys. London FA Challenge Cup winners 1961-2, runners-up 1960-61. 19 full England caps (2 gls) 1963-6. Made 1 app for Football League 1966.
Son of George Eastham (Bolton Wanderers, Brentford and England international). Won club and Irish League representative honours with Ards. Won Under-23 honours with Newcastle United and club and Football League honours with Stoke City. Became assistant manager and then manager of Stoke City. Now working for a sports firm in Cape Town, South Africa. Awarded the OBE in 1973.

EDGAR, John   **1901-02**
Inside-forward.
Born: Scotland.
Joined ARSENAL: 3 Oct 1901 from Parkhead FC (Glasgow). First app: League v Gainsborough Trinity (a) 12 Oct 1901. First app: Southern Professional Charity Cup v Tottenham Hotspur (a) 29 Apr 1902.
ARSENAL Record: League 10 (1 gl); FA Cup 1; London League 4; Other snr comp: 2; London League (Res) 4 (6 gls); Kent League 5 (6 gls); Friendlies 9 (3 gls).
After Arsenal he moved back to Scotland and played for Aberdeen (1904-12).

53

ELLIOTT, Arthur 1892-94
Inside-left 5ft 5in. 10st 6lb.
Born: Nottingham, c.1870.
Jnr football: Notts Rangers. Previous Clubs:
Gainsborough Trinity, Accrington. Joined
ARSENAL: Summer 1892 from Accrington. First
app: Snr fdly v Highland Light Infantry (h) 1
Sep 1892. First first-class app: FA Cup (Q) v
Highland Light Infantry (h) 15 Oct 1892. Final
app: League v Small Heath (h) 31 Mar 1894. Snr
fdly v Westerham & District (a) 12 Apr 1894.
ARSENAL Record: League 24 (11 gls); FA Cup
2 (1 gl); FA Cup (Q) 8 (8 gls); Friendlies 20 (16
gls). In addition in 1892-3 made 52 senior (29 gls)
and 1 reserve (1 gl) apps for Royal Arsenal.
Reinstated as an amateur in 1894-5 and played
for Tottenham Hotspur.

ELVEY, John Richard 1922-23
Right-back.
Born: Luton, Beds.
Jnr football: Luton Clarence. Previous Clubs:
Luton Town, Bolton Wanderers (1920). Joined
ARSENAL: 15 Sep 1922 from Bolton Wanderers.
First app: London Combination v Queen's Park
Rangers (a) 16 Sep 1922. First snr app: Southend
Hospital Cup v Southend (a) 11 Oct 1922. Final
snr app: League v Preston North End (h) 14 Apr
1923. Final app: Jnr fdly v Wycombe Wanderers
5 May 1923.
ARSENAL Record: League 1; Other snr comp:
1; Football Combination 9; Friendlies 16.
*Honours: Southend Hospital Cup runners-up
1922-3.*
Played for Millwall during wartime. Won England
international honours in South Africa 1920 when
with Luton Town.

EVANS, Dennis Joseph 1951-63
Left-back 5ft 11in. 12st 11lb.
Born: Old Swan, Liverpool, 18 May 1930.
School: St Oswald's
Jnr football: Churchdown FC, South Liverpool,
Ellesmere Port Town. Previous Club: Wolver-
hampton Wanderers (amateur). Joined
ARSENAL: 3 Jan 1951 from Ellesmere Port
Town for £1,500. First app: London Midweek
League v Queen's Park Rangers (a) 25 Jan 1951.
First snr app: On tour (sub) v Grasshoppers
(Switzerland) 27 May 1953. Final snr app: League
v Tottenham Hotspur (a) 16 Jan 1960. Final app:
Metropolitan League v Kettering Town (a) 27 Apr
1963.
ARSENAL Record: League 189 (10 gls); FA Cup
18 (2 gls); Other snr comp: 6 (1 gl); Football
Combination 106 (5 gls); London FA Challenge
Cup 13 (1 gl); Eastern Counties League 38 (6 gls);
London Midweek League 25 (1 gl); Metropolitan
League 28 (11 gls); Other jnr comp: 3; Friendlies
59/2 (2 gls).
*Honours: Football Combination Cup winners
1952-3. London FA Challenge Cup winners 1953-4,
1957-8. Metropolitan League champions 1962-3.
East Anglian Cup runners-up 1951-2.*
Served National Service in Royal Artillery and
played in Army representative games. Suffered a
fractured ankle twice, the second of which,
together with cartilage trouble, caused him to be
out of the game for 10 months from Nov 1960.
Although he played reserve matches afterwards
the ankle injuries ended his career and he became
a coach at Arsenal in 1963. Left football and
became a warehouse manager in Tottenham and
after a short spell as trainer-coach at Luton Town,
became a private hire chauffeur.

EVANS, Robert 1912-13
Full-back.
Born: North London.
Joined ARSENAL: 3 Sep 1912 (amateur). First

app: South Eastern League v Tottenham Hotspur
(h) 21 Sep 1912. First snr app: League v Newcastle
United (a) 25 Jan 1913. Final snr app: FA Cup
v Liverpool (a) 1 Feb 1913. Final app: South
Eastern League v Tunbridge Wells (a) 24 Mar
1913. Transferred to Clapton Orient 16 Aug 1913.
ARSENAL Record: League 1; FA Cup 1; South
Eastern League 9.

EVERITT, Michael Dennis 1956-61
Wing-half/inside-forward 5ft 9in. 10st 7lb.
Born: Weeley, nr Clacton-on-Sea, 16 Jan 1941.
Jnr football: Clacton Town. Joined ARSENAL:
Aug 1956 (groundstaff), 5 Feb 1958 (professional).
First app: South East Counties League v Charlton
Athletic (a) 1 Sep 1956. First snr app: Snr fdly
v Bristol XI (a) 8 May 1959. League v Fulham
(h) 15 Apr 1960. Final snr app: League v Preston
North End (a) 30 Aug 1960. Final app: Football
Combination v Leyton Orient (h) 18 Feb 1961.
Transferred to Northampton Town (£4,000) 20
Feb 1961.
ARSENAL Record: League 9 (1 gl); Football
Combination 36 (9 gls); London FA Challenge
Cup 2; FA Youth Cup 20 (5 gls); Metropolitan
League 48 (21 gls); South East Counties League
54 (16 gls); London Midweek League 9 (3 gls);
Other jnr comp: 9 (3 gls); Friendlies 24/1 (19 gls).
*Honours: Metropolitan League champions 1958-9.
Southern Junior Floodlit Cup runners-up 1957-8.*
Played for Colchester Schoolboys and Essex
Schoolboys. Played for New York Americans in
the United States League Cup (summer 1960).
After Northampton, played for Plymouth Argyle
(Mar 1967) and Brighton (1968) before becoming
player, coach, and then secretary-manager of
Wimbledon (Southern League). Became manager
of Brentford (1974) and was trainer at Leicester
City 1976-7.

FAIRCLOUGH, William Oliver 1895-97
Goalkeeper 5ft 11in.
Joined ARSENAL: 4 Dec 1895. First app: League
v Leicester Fosse (a) 25 Jan 1896. Final app:
League v Darwen (h) 19 Apr 1897.
ARSENAL Record: League 26; FA Cup 1; United
League 9; Kent League 3; Friendlies 28.
Was in the 1st Scots Guards and secured a
discharge to join Arsenal. Played for New
Brompton after Arsenal.

FARMER, George A. 1896
Outside-right 5ft 7in. 11st 10lb.
Born: 25 Nov 1874.
Jnr football: Derby Swifts, Derby Bedford
Rangers, Belper Town. Joined ARSENAL: May
1896 from the Midlands. First app: Jnr fdly v
15th Co Royal Artillery (h) 3 Sep 1896. First snr
app: United League v Rushden (h) 7 Sep 1896.
Final snr app: FA Cup v Leyton (h) 12 Dec 1896.
Final app: Kent League v Ashford (a) 19 Dec
1896.
ARSENAL Record: League 1; FA Cup 1 (1 gl);
United League 1; Kent League 4 (6 gls); Friendlies
4 (1 gl).

FARR, Andrew Martin 1937-40
Inside-forward 5ft 4¾in. 9st 8½lb.
Born: Larkhall, Scotland.
Jnr football: Yoker Athletic, Margate (Arsenal
nursery). Joined ARSENAL: 16 Dec 1937 from
Margate. First app: London Combination v
Portsmouth (h) 18 Dec 1937. First snr app: League
v Derby County (a) 29 Apr 1939. Final snr app:
League v Brentford (h) 6 May 1939. Final app:
London Combination v Brighton (a) 2 Sep 1939
(prior to outbreak of war). Transferred to
Airdrieonians 12 Aug 1940.
ARSENAL Record: League 2 (1 gl); Football
Combination 31 (15 gls); Southern League 28 (7

gls); Friendlies 4 (3 gls).
In addition played 1 reserve match 1939-40 prior
to outbreak of war.
Honours: London Combination champions 1937-8.
Captain of Arsenal's Southern League side 1938-9.
Was a munitions worker in Scotland during the
war and played for Hearts.

FARRELL, Patrick 1897-98
Half-back
Born: Belfast, 3 Apr 1872.
Previous Club: Glasgow Celtic. Joined ARSENAL:
4 May 1897 from Glasgow Celtic. First app: League
v Grimsby Town (h) 1 Sep 1897. Final snr app:
Snr fdly v Thames Iron (a) 26 Apr 1898. Final
app: Jnr fdly v Deptford (h) 30 Apr 1898.
Transferred to Brighton United summer 1898.
ARSENAL Record: League 2 (2 gls); FA Cup
(Q) 3; United League 9 (2 gls); Friendlies 9.
Moved from Brighton to Distillery (1900) where
he won 2 international caps. Returned to Brighton
(1902).

FERGUSON, James 1906-07
Outside-left 5ft 6½in. 10st 6lb.
Born: Scotland.
Jnr football: Cambuslang Hibernians (Glasgow).
Joined ARSENAL: 2 Jun 1906 from Cambuslang
Hibs. First app: London League (Res) v
Tottenham Hotspur (h) 1 Sep 1906. First snr
app: Snr fdly v Reading (a) 12 Sep 1906. Final snr
app: League v Liverpool (a) 9 Feb 1907. Final
app: South Eastern League v Sittingbourne (a)
13 Apr 1907.
ARSENAL Record: League 1; South Eastern
League 21 (5 gls); London League (Res) 13;
Friendlies 9 (1 gl).
*Honours: South Eastern League champions 1906-07.
London League (Res) champions 1906-07.*

FERRY, Gordon 1960-65
Centre-half 5ft 10in. 11st 10lb.
Born: Sunderland, 22 Dec 1943.
Jnr football: Marsden CW Juniors. Joined
ARSENAL: Feb 1960 (amateur), Jul 1960
(apprentice), 5 Jan 1961 (professional). First app:
South East Counties League v Charlton Athletic
(a) 6 Feb 1960. First snr app: Snr fdly (sub) v
Watford (a) 14 Apr 1964. Final snr app: League
v Sheffield United (a) 24 Oct 1964. Final app:
Football Combination v Portsmouth (h) 24 Apr
1965. Given free transfer by Arsenal at end of
1964-5 and joined Leyton Orient 7 May 1965.
ARSENAL Record: League 1; Other snr comp:
1; Football Combination 70; London FA
Challenge Cup 5; FA Youth Cup 11; Metropolitan
League 78; South East Counties League 27; Other
jnr comp: 3; Friendlies 44/1.
*Honours: London FA Challenge Cup winners
1962-3. Sheriff of London Shield winners 1964-5.
Metropolitan League champions 1962-3.
Metropolitan League Cup winners 1960-61.
Metropolitan League Professional Cup winners
1961-2. South East Counties League Cup winners
1960-61.*
Played for Sunderland Schoolboys. Moved from
Leyton Orient to Atlanta Braves (USA) 1966.

FIDLER, Joseph 1913-14
Full-back 5ft 10in. 12st 2lb.
Born: Sheffield.
Previous Club: Queen's Park Rangers. Joined
ARSENAL: 7 Feb 1913 from Queen's Park
Rangers. First app: League v Oldham Athletic
(h) 8 Feb 1913. Final snr app: League v
Birmingham (h) 22 Nov 1913. Final app: London
League (Res) v Clapton Orient (h) 30 Apr 1914.
ARSENAL Record: League 25; Other snr comp:
1; London FA Challenge Cup 4; South Eastern
League 12; London League (Res) 9; Friendlies.2.
Played for Port Vale after Arsenal.

FIELDS, Alfred George BEM **1936-52**
Centre-half 6ft 2in. 13st 2lb.
Born: Canning Town, London, 15 Nov 1918.
School: Pretoria Road, West Ham.
Jnr football: West Ham Youth Club, Margate
(Arsenal nursery). Joined ARSENAL: 30 Jan 1936
(amateur), 3 May 1937 (professional). First app:
Jnr fdly v London University. (a) 19 Feb 1936.
First snr app: Snr fdly v Southampton (a) 2 May
1938. Final snr app: On tour v Lausanne-Sports
(Switzerland) 22 May 1952. Final app: Eastern
Counties League v Tottenham Hotspur (h) 24 Sep
1952.
ARSENAL Record: League 19; Other snr comp:
2; Football Combination 110; London FA
Challenge Cup 7; Southern League 3; Eastern
Counties League 29; London Midweek League
4; Friendlies 38/1. In addition played 2 reserve
matches 1939-40 prior to outbreak of war and
made 7 apps during wartime.
Honours: Played for West Ham Schoolboys.
London Combination champions 1938-9. Mayor
of Colchester Cup winners 1938-9. Football
Combination champions 1946-7.
Served with the Royal Artillery in North Africa
and Italy during the war and won the BEM. His
career was hampered by a number of serious knee
injuries requiring operations and leaving him with
arthritis which ended his playing days in 1952.
He immediately became coach to the juniors at
Arsenal and took up physiotherapy. Gained an
FA trainer's certificate and became trainer of
Arsenal's junior teams in 1966. Retired 18 Nov
1983.

FISHER, George **1909**
Goalkeeper.
Joined ARSENAL: 3 Oct 1909 from Lancashire
'on trial' and after a few games was not engaged.
Moved to Manchester United 24 Nov 1909. First
app: South Eastern League v Watford (h) 4 Oct
1909. First snr app: League v Notts County (a)
7 Oct 1909. Final app: League v Nottingham
Forest (h) 9 Oct 1909.
ARSENAL Record: League 2; South Eastern
League 1.

FITCHIE, Thomas Tindal **1901-06 & 1908-09**
Inside-forward 5ft 9in. 11st 7lb.
Born: Edinburgh, 11 Dec 1881. Died: 17 Oct 1947.
Jnr football: West Norwood. Other Clubs:
Tottenham Hotspur, Queen's Park Rangers,
Fulham. Joined ARSENAL: 2 Nov 1901
(amateur). Rejoined — 19 Sep 1908 (amateur)
from Queen's Park. First app: League v
Gainsborough Trinity (h) 8 Feb 1902. Final app:
League v Manchester United (a) 27 April 1909.
Transferred to Queen's Park 5 Oct 1906 and to
Glossop summer 1909.
ARSENAL Record: League 56 (27 gls); FA Cup
7 (3 gls); London League 2; Other snr comp: 2
(1 gl); Friendlies 4 (2 gls).
Honours: 3 full Scotland caps (1 gl) 1905-06.
Represented London whilst with West Norwood
and further international honours with Queen's
Park. Remained an amateur throughout his career
and therefore, on occasion, was on the books of
more than one club at the same time. Made apps
for Brighton and Fulham (again) after Arsenal.

FLANAGAN, John **1910-17**
Inside-forward 5ft 6in. 10st 10lb.
Born: Preston, c.1891.
Jnr football: Verity's, Stourbridge. Previous Clubs:
Norwich City, Fulham. Joined ARSENAL: 30 Dec
1910 from Fulham. First app: South Eastern
League v Swindon Town (a) 31 Dec 1910. First
snr app: FA Cup v Swindon Town (a) 4 Feb 1911.
Final snr app: League v Preston North End (a)

17 Apr 1915. Final app: London Combination
(wartime) v West Ham (a) 10 Mar 1917.
ARSENAL Record: League 114 (28 gls); FA Cup
7; Other snr comp: 7 (5 gls); London FA Challenge
Cup 4; South Eastern League 16 (12 gls); London
League (Res) 4 (5 gls); Other jnr comp: 1;
Friendlies 7 (4 gls). In addition made 5 apps (3
gls) during wartime.
Honours: Norwich Hospital Cup winners 1913-14.

FLETCHER, Alfred **1914-15**
Wing-half 6ft. 12st 7lb.
Born: Ripley, Derbyshire.
Previous Club: Glossop. Joined ARSENAL: 2 Jun
1914 from Glossop. First app: South Eastern
League v Fulham (h) 5 Sep 1914. First snr app:
League v Bristol City (a) 3 Apr 1915. Final snr
app: League v Preston North End (a) 17 Apr 1915.
Final app: South Eastern League v Croydon
Common (a) 28 Apr 1915.
ARSENAL Record: League 3; London FA
Challenge Cup 1 (1 gl); South Eastern League
32 (3 gls); London League (Res) 15 (1 gl);
Friendlies 2.

FORBES, Alexander Rooney **1948-56**
Wing-half 5ft 9in. 11st 11lb.
Born: Dundee, Scotland, 21 Jan 1925.
School: Rockwell Central (Dundee).
Jnr football: Ashdale Boys Club, Dundee North End.
Previous Club: Sheffield United (Dec 1944). Joined
ARSENAL: 19 Feb 1948 from Sheffield United for
£12,500. First app: League v Wolverhampton
Wanderers (h) 6 Mar 1948. Final app: League v
Cardiff City (a) 28 Apr 1956. Transferred to
Leyton Orient (free transfer) 1 Aug 1956.
ARSENAL Record: League 217 (20 gls); FA Cup
22; FA Charity Shield 1; Other snr comp: 2;
Football Combination 22 (4 gls); London FA
Challenge Cup 1; Friendlies 59 (1) (8 gls).
Honours: Played for Scotland Schoolboys.
Division One champions 1952-3. FA Cup winners
1950, runners-up 1952. FA Charity Shield winners
1953-4. 9 full Scotland caps 1950-52.

Played ice hockey for Dundee Tigers and Scotland
at 16. Won other international honours with
Sheffield United. A serious knee injury in 1955-6
caused Arsenal to release him at the end of this
season. After Leyton Orient he played for Fulham
(1957) and Gravesend (1958) before returning to
Arsenal as coach to the juniors in Sep 1962. Went
to Johannesburg, South Africa as coach and team
manager.

FORD, George E. **1912-15**
Full-back 5ft 8in. 11st 3lb.
Born: Woolwich, London, c.1891.
Jnr football: Gravesend, Dartford. Joined
ARSENAL: Sep 1912 (amateur), 1 Nov 1912
(professional). First app: South Eastern League
v West Ham (a) 14 Sep 1912. First snr app: League
v Liverpool (h) 28 Dec 1912. Final snr app: League
v Clapton Orient (a) 13 Feb 1915. Final app: South
Eastern League v Croydon (a) 28 Apr 1915.
ARSENAL Record: League 9; FA Cup 1; London
FA Challenge Cup 1; South Eastern League 91
(1 gl); London League (Res) 24; Other jnr comp:
1; Friendlies 11.
Joined the First Footballer's Battalion, Dec 1914.

FOSTER, R. **1889**
Goalkeeper.
First app: Snr fdly v St Mark's College (a) 19
Oct 1889. First-class app: FA Cup (Q) v
Crusaders (h) 16 Nov 1889. Final app: Kent Senior
Cup v Gravesend (a) 14 Dec 1889.
ARSENAL Record: FA Cup (Q) 2. In addition
made 3 senior and 2 reserve apps for Royal Arsenal
during 1889-90.
Very little can be traced about this player other
than his playing details.

FOTHERINGHAM, James Gibb **1949-59**
Centre-half 6ft 4in. 13st 8lb.
Born: Hamilton, Lanarkshire, Scotland, 19 Dec
1933. Died: Sep 1977.
School: Samuel Lloyd School (Corby), Corby
Technical College.
Joined ARSENAL: Oct 1949 (amateur), 29 Mar
1951 (professional). First app: London Midweek
League v Leyton Orient (a) 13 Oct 1949. First
snr app: League v Bolton Wanderers (a) 6 Nov
1954. Final snr app: League v Luton Town (a)
26 Dec 1958. Final app: Football Combination
v Nottingham Forest (a) 11 Mar 1959. Transferred
to Hearts (£10,000) 27 Mar 1959.
ARSENAL Record: League 72; FA Cup 4; Other
snr comp: 4; Football Combination 150 (1 gl);
London FA Challenge Cup 15; Eastern Counties
League 33; Metropolitan League 3; London
Midweek League 7; Other jnr comp: 2; Friendlies
28/1.
Honours: Played for Uppingham Corby School-
boys and had an England Schoolboy international
trial. Played for Northamptonshire Youth.
London FA Challenge Cup winners 1953-4.
Served National Service in the Royal Engineers
and played for the Army in representative
matches. Transferred to Northampton Town from
Hearts (Aug 1959).

FOXALL, Abraham **1901-02**
Outside-left.
Born: Sheffield, 1874.
Jnr football: In Sheffield. Previous Clubs:
Gainsborough Trinity, Liverpool (1899-1900),
Queen's Park Rangers. Joined ARSENAL: 8 May
1901 from Queen's Park Rangers. First app:
League v Barnsley (a) Sep 1901. Final app:
League v Burton United (a) 19 Apr 1902. Southern
Professional Charity Cup v Tottenham Hotspur
(a) 29 Apr 1902.
ARSENAL Record: League 31 (3 gls); London
League 5; Other snr comp: 3 (1 gl); Friendlies 4.
Played again for Gainsborough Trinity (1903-06)
after Arsenal.

FREEMAN, Bertram Clewley **1905-08**
Centre/inside-forward 5ft 8in. 11st 6lb.
Born: Birmingham, Oct 1885. Died: 11 Aug 1955.
School: Gower Street, Aston.
Jnr football: Gower St Old Boys, Aston Manor.
Previous Club: Aston Villa (Apr 1904). Joined
ARSENAL: 24 Nov 1905 from Aston Villa. First

app: League v Nottingham Forest (a) 25 Nov 1905. Final snr app: League v Nottingham Forest (a) 14 Mar 1908. Final app: South Eastern League v Leyton Orient (a) 4 Apr 1908. Transferred to Everton 10 Apr 1908.
ARSENAL Record: League 44 (21 gls); FA Cup 5 (3 gls); Other snr comp: 1; South Eastern League 24 (34 gls); London League (Res) 24 (43 gls); Friendlies 16 (27 gls).
Honours: London League (Res) champions 1906-07. South Eastern League champions 1907-08.
Scored seven goals in a match for the reserves in the London League in 1907-08. Transferred from Everton to Burnley (Apr 1911) and won international honours with Everton and club and international honours with Burnley. Was the League's leading scorer in 1908-09, 1911-12 and 1912-13. Played for Wigan Borough (1921) and Kettering Town (1923), retiring cs 1924.

FURNELL, James   **1963-68**
Goalkeeper   6ft 2in. 14st 1lb.
Born: Manchester, 23 Nov 1937.
School: Clitheroe, Lancs.
Previous Clubs: Burnley (Nov 1954), Liverpool (Feb 1962). Joined ARSENAL: 22 Nov 1963 from Liverpool for £18,000. First app: League v Blackpool (h) 23 Nov 1963. Final snr app: On tour v Presidents XI (Malaya) 2 Jun 1968. Final app: Football Combination Cup v Reading (a) 28 Aug 1968. Transferred to Rotherham United (£8,000) 4 Sep 1968.
ARSENAL Record: League 141; FA Cup 13; Football League Cup 12; European Competitions 1; Football Combination 39; Metropolitan League 2; Friendlies 37/6.
Honours: Football League Cup runners-up 1968. Football Combination Cup winners 1967-8.
After Rotherham he played for Plymouth Argyle (Dec 1970), rejoining in 1976 to become assistant manager. Had a spell as chief scout at Exeter City before returning to the administrative staff at Plymouth in Jan 1979.

FYFE, James   **1898**
Full-back   5ft 10in. 12st 8lb.
Born: Scotland.
Previous Club: Alloa Athletic. Joined ARSENAL: 23 May 1898 from Alloa Athletic. First app: Snr fdly v Gravesend (h) 1 Sep 1898. League v Luton Town (a) 3 Sep 1898. Final snr app: United League v Brighton United (h) 31 Oct 1898. Final app: Jnr fdly v Southampton Reserves (a) 19 Nov 1898.
ARSENAL Record: League 7; United League 5; Friendlies 3.
Left Arsenal early Dec 1898, possibly went back to Scotland.

GARBUTT, William   **1905-08**
Outside-right   5ft 7in. 11st.
Previous Club: Reading. Joined ARSENAL: 16 Dec 1905 from Reading. First app: League v Preston North End (a) 23 Dec 1905. Final snr app: FA Cup v Hull City (a) 16 Jan 1908. Final app: South Eastern League v Queen's Park Rangers (a) 2 May 1908. Transferred to Blackburn Rovers 5 May 1908.
ARSENAL Record: League 52 (8 gls); FA Cup 13 (6 gls); Other snr comp: 3; South Eastern League 6 (2 gls) London League (Res) 2 (1 gl); Friendlies 4 (2 gls).
Won Football League honours with Blackburn Rovers. After giving up playing he held a series of coaching appointments in Italy and Spain. Firstly at Genoa (1914), then Rome (1927), Naples (1929) and Athletic Bilbao (1935). The Spanish war forced him back to Italy, where he hid out during World War Two and took up his original post at Genoa in 1946.

GARTON, John   **1899**
Full-back.
From Castle Donington, Leicestershire.
Joined ARSENAL: 4 Mar 1899 (amateur). First app: Snr fdly v Casuals (a) 9 Mar 1899. League v Loughborough (h) 13 Mar 1899. Final snr app: Snr fdly v Woolwich League (h) 26 Apr 1899. Final app: Jnr fdly v Grays United (h) 29 Apr 1899.
ARSENAL Record: League 5; United League 2; Friendlies 7.

GATTING, Stephen Paul   **1974-81**
Defender/midfield   5ft 10in. 11st 8lb.
Born: Park Royal, London, 29 May 1959.
Jnr Football: Watford (apprentice). Joined ARSENAL: Sep 1974 (amateur), Jul 1975 (apprentice), 23 Feb 1977 (professional). First app: South East Counties League Cup v Millwall (a) 28 Sep 1974. First snr app: Snr fdly (sub) v Tottenham Hotspur (h) 9 Oct 1976. Final snr app: On tour (sub) v Olympiakos (Greece) 16 Aug 1981. Final app: Football Combination v Norwich City (h) 5 Sep 1981. Transferred to Brighton & Hove Albion (£200,000) 10 Sep 1981.
ARSENAL Record: League 50/8 (5 gls); FA Cup 9/1 (1 gl); Football League Cup 3/1; European Competitions 3/1; Football Combination 144/2 (19 gls); South East Counties League 38/2 (3 gls); FA Youth Cup 8; Other jnr comp: 5; Friendlies 41/8 (5 gls). In addition made 1 Football Combination, app 1981-82, later removed from records.
Played for Brent District Schoolboys and Middlesex Schoolboys. Brother of Mike Gatting, Middlesex and England cricketer, he has also played cricket for Middlesex Second XI. Currently with Charlton Athletic.

GAUDIE, Ralph   **1899-1901**
Centre-forward
Born: Guisborough.
Previous Club: Sheffield United. Joined ARSENAL: Oct 1899 from Sheffield United. Rejoined 5 Oct 1900. First app: League v Gainsborough Trinity (h) 14 Oct 1899. Final app: League v New Brighton Tower (a) 27 Apr 1901.
ARSENAL Record: League 47 (24 gls); FA Cup 3; Southern District Combination 10 (2 gls); Friendlies 13 (3 gls).
Won club honours with Sheffield United. Retired from football for a short while because of illness and on recovering rejoined Arsenal. Later played for Manchester United.

GEMMELL, Duncan   **1892-94**
Outside/inside-right   5ft 5in. 10st 7lb.
Born: Glasgow, c.1870.
Jnr Football: Elderslee Ranger Swifts. Previous Club: Sheffield Wednesday (2 seasons). Joined ARSENAL: Summer 1892 from Sheffield Wednesday. Jnr League forms 25 Jun 1893. First app: Snr fdly v Gainsborough Town (h) 3 Sep 1892. First first-class app: FA Cup (Q) v Highland Light Infantry (h) 15 Oct 1892. Final snr app: Snr fdly v New Brompton (a) 18 Apr 1894. Final app: Jnr fdly v Old St Luke's (a) 21 Apr 1894.
ARSENAL Record: League 5; FA Cup (Q) 3; Friendlies 16 (2 gls).
In addition, during 1892-3 made 46 senior (16 gls) and 3 reserve apps (2 gls) for Royal Arsenal.

GEORGE, Frederick Charles   **1966-75**
Midfield   5ft 11in. 11st 9lb.
Born: Islington, North London, 10 Oct 1950.
School: Holloway Comprehensive, New Middleton.
Joined ARSENAL: 10 May 1966 (apprentice), 22 Feb 1968 (professional). First app: Jnr fdly v

Walton & Hersham (a) 6 Aug 1966. First snr app: On tour (sub) v Reykjavik (Iceland) 4 May 1969. Final snr app: FA Cup v Coventry City (a) 25 Jan 1975. Final app: Football Combination v Bournemouth (h) 30 Apr 1975. Transferred to Derby County (£90,000) 8 Jul 1975.
ARSENAL Record: League 113/20 (31 gls); FA Cup 21/1 (11 gls); Football League Cup 8 (2 gls); European Competitions 15/1 (5 gls); Football Combination 88/3 (60 gls); London FA Challenge Cup 3 (2 gls); FA Youth Cup 5 (2 gls); Metropolitan League 26 (12 gls); South East Counties League 20/2 (12 gls); Other jnr comp: 7 (5 gls); Friendlies 69/9 (64 gls).

Honours: Division One champions 1970-71. FA Cup winners 1971, runners-up 1972. European Fairs Cup winners 1969-70. Football Combination champions 1968-9. Football Combination Cup winners 1967-8, 1969-70. London FA Challenge Cup winners 1969-70. Southern Junior Floodlit Cup runners-up 1967-8. 5 England Under-23 caps (1 gl) 1972-3.
Played for Islington Schoolboys, Middlesex Schoolboys and London Schoolboys. Scored winning goal in 1971 Cup Final which brought Arsenal the League & Cup Double. Won international honours with Derby County. After Derby County played for Southampton (1978). Nottingham Forest, Bulova (Hong Kong), Bournemouth and Derby County (again). After retiring from football became a hotelier in Hampshire.

GILMER, William   **1895-96**
Goalkeeper
Joined ARSENAL: 24 Dec 1895 from Royal Ordnance FC. First app: Snr fdly v Cliftonville (h) 26 Dec 1895. League v Loughborough Town (h) 4 Jan 1896. Final snr app: Snr fdly v Tottenham Hotspur (h) 16 Mar 1896. Final app: Kent League v Sittingbourne (a) 18 Apr 1896.
ARSENAL Record: League 3; Kent League 9; Friendlies 10.

GLOAK, Davis H.   **1889-91**
Outside-left/centre-forward.
First app: Reserves v Ilford Reserves (a) 9 Nov 1889. First first-class app: FA Cup v Derby County (h) 17 Jan 1891 (only app). Final app:

56

London Charity Cup v Old Carthusians (a) 11 Apr 1891.
ARSENAL Record: FA Cup 1. In addition during 1889-90 and 1890-1 made 33 senior (13 gls) and 11 reserve (5 gls) apps for Royal Arsenal.
Honours: London Senior Cup winners 1890-91. Kent Junior Cup winners 1889-90.
Later played for Millwall Athletic.

GOOING, William Henry   1901-05
Centre-forward   5ft 9in. 11st.
Born: Penistone, 1874.
Jnr Football: Penistone, Wath. Previous Clubs: Sheffield Wednesday (1895), Chesterfield (1899). Joined ARSENAL: 7 Nov 1901 from Chesterfield. First app: League v Newton Heath (h) 16 Nov 1901. Final app: FA Cup v Bristol City (h) 4 Feb 1905.
ARSENAL Record: League 94 (45 gls); FA Cup 12 (3 gls); London League 12 (3 gls); Other snr comp: 5 (2 gls); Friendlies 6 (3 gls).
Honours: Division Two runners-up (promotion) 1903-04. Southern Charity Cup runners-up 1903-04.
Played for Northampton Town (1905-06) after Arsenal.

GORDON, Robert   1895-96
Centre-forward.
Born: Leith, Scotland, 1873.
Jnr Football: Leith Rangers (1889-90). Previous Clubs: Hearts (1890-91), Middlesbrough Ironopolis (1891-2), Hearts (1892-3), Aston Villa (1893-4), Leicester Fosse (1894-5). Joined ARSENAL: 1895 from Leicester Fosse. First app: League v Grimsby Town (h) 2 Sep 1895. Final app: Snr fdly v Tottenham Hotspur (a) 30 Apr 1896.
ARSENAL Record: League 20 (6 gls); Kent League 4 (2 gls); Friendlies 20 (1 gl).
Played for Reading (1896-7) after Arsenal.

GORING, Harry 'Peter'   1948-60
Centre-forward/wing-half   5ft 11in. 12st 4lb.
Born: Bishop's Cleeve, Gloucestershire, 2 Jan 1927.
Jnr Football: Bishop's Cleeve, Cheltenham Town. Joined ARSENAL: 22 Jan 1948 from Cheltenham Town for £1,000. First app: Jnr fdly v Chatham Town (a) 31 Jan 1948. First snr app: On tour v Flamengo (Brazil) 29 May 1949. Final snr app: League v Leeds United (h) 24 Feb 1959. Final app: Football Combination v Leyton Orient (a) 30 Apr 1960. Transferred to Boston (free transfer) Oct 1960.
ARSENAL Record: League 220 (51 gls); FA Cup 20 (2 gls); Other snr comp: 5; Football Combination 145 (31 gls); London FA Challenge Cup 6; Eastern Counties League 3 (9 gls); Metropolitan League 11 (1 gl); Other jnr comp: 1; Friendlies 71/3 (23 gls). In addition, made 1 jnr fdly app (1 gl) in 1945-6 (on trial).
Honours: Division One champions 1952-3. FA Cup winners 1950. Football Combination Cup runners-up 1950-1. Captain of Arsenal. Played for the FA in representative matches and toured the West Indies with an FA XI in 1955.
Was a butcher's assistant and a market gardener before taking up football. After Boston he played for Romford, and on retiring from playing he owned his own butchery and greengrocery business in Cheltenham.

GORMAN, Paul Anthony   1979-84
Midfield   5ft 10in. 11st 8lb.
Born: Dublin, Ireland, 6 Aug 1963.
School: Crumlin CBS Primary and Secondary, Dublin.
Joined ARSENAL: Jul 1979 (apprentice), 1 Sep 1980 (professional). First app: South East Counties League v Crystal Palace (a) 18 Aug 1979. First snr app: League v Manchester City (a) 6 Mar 1982. Final snr app: League v Everton (h)

19 Nov 1983. Final app: Football Combination v Swindon Town (a) 16 May 1984. Transferred to Birmingham City (free transfer) 1983-4.
ARSENAL Record: League 5/1; Football Combination 129/10 (10 gls); FA Youth Cup 8 (1 gl); South East Counties League 45 (17 gls); Other jnr comp: 11 (2 gls); Friendlies 44/9 (7 gls). In addition, made 3 apps in Football Combination 1981-2, later removed from the records.
Honours: Football Combination champions 1983-4. South East Counties League winners 1979-80. President's Cup winners 1980-81. Republic of Ireland Schoolboy international. Won over 20 Ireland Youth caps 1978 to 1982. Republic of Ireland Under-21 international.
Later played for Carlisle United and Shrewsbury Town.

GOULD, Robert Alfred   1968-70
Centre-forward   5ft 10in. 11st 5lb.
Born: Coventry, 12 Jun 1946.
School: Keresley, Walgrave (Coventry).
Jnr Football: St James' YC. Previous Club: Coventry City (1962). Joined ARSENAL: 2 Feb 1968 from Coventry City for £90,000. First app: League v Manchester City (a) 3 Feb 1968. Final snr app: League (sub) v Everton (a) 14 Feb 1970. Final app: Football Combination v Gillingham (h) 30 Apr 1970. Transferred to Wolverhampton Wanderers (£55,000) 2 Jun 1970.
ARSENAL Record: League 57/8 (16 gls); FA Cup 7 (3 gls); Football League Cup 6/3 (3 gls); European comp: 2 (1 gl); Football Combination 24 (32 gls); London FA Challenge Cup 1 (2 gls); Friendlies 15/1 (12 gls).
Honours: Played for Coventry Schoolboys. Football League Cup runners-up 1969. Football Combination champions 1969-70. London FA Challenge Cup winners 1969-70.
Won club honours with Coventry City. After Wolves played for West Brom (1971), Bristol City (1972), West Ham (1973), Wolverhampton Wanderers (1975), Bristol Rovers (1977), Hereford Town (1978) and player-coach appointments at Wimbledon, Chelsea and Aldershot without making League apps. Became manager of Coventry City (1983), Bristol Rovers (1985), Wimbledon (1987-90) and West Bromwich Albion (Feb 1991). Currently assistant manager at Coventry.

GOULDEN, Roy Leonard   1953-61
Inside-forward   5ft 8in. 9st 9lb.
Born: Ilford, Essex, 22 Sep 1937.
School: Ilford.
Joined ARSENAL: 25 May 1953 (amateur), 22 Sep 1954 (professional). First app: Eastern Counties League v West Ham (h) 30 Sep 1953. First snr app: On tour v Enschede (Holland) 13 Aug 1958. Final snr app: Snr fdly (sub) v Leyton Orient (h) 12 Mar 1960. Final app: Metropolitan League Professional Cup Final v Hastings (h) 3 May 1961. Transferred to Southend (free transfer) 13 May 1961.
ARSENAL Record: League 1; Other snr comp: 1; Football Combination 85 (22 gls); London FA Challenge Cup 7 (3 gls); FA Youth Cup 5 (2 gls); Eastern Counties League 5; Metropolitan League 35 (11 gls); London Midweek League 28 (8 gls); South East Counties League 32 (30 gls); Other jnr comp: 6 (3 gls); Friendlies 38/6 (21 gls). In addition played one Metropolitan League match 1958-9, later removed from the records.
Honours: Played for Ilford Schoolboys and London Schoolboys. England Schoolboy International. Metropolitan League champions 1960-61. Metropolitan League Professional Cup winners 1960-61. South East Counties champions 1955-6. South East Counties Cup winners 1955-6.
Son of Len Goulden (West Ham, Chelsea and

England). His apps were limited around 1956 and 1957 due to a knee operation and National Service in the RAF. Was given a free transfer by Southend and joined Ipswich Town (Jul 1962).

GOY, Peter John   1953-60
Goalkeeper   6ft. 11st 1lb.
Born: Beverley, Yorkshire, 8 Jun 1938.
School: Brumby Secondary Modern, Scunthorpe.
Jnr Football: Appleby-Frodingham Works, Frodingham Athletic (Lincs.) Joined ARSENAL: 5 Aug 1953 (amateur), 15 Jun 1955 (professional). First app: London Midweek League v West Ham (h) 7 Oct 1953. First snr app: League v Leeds United (h) 24 Feb 1959. Final snr app: Snr fdly (sub) v Leyton Orient (h) 1 Mar 1960. Final app: Football Combination v Chelsea (h) 22 Oct 1960. Transferred to Southend (£2,000) 22 Oct 1960.
ARSENAL Record: League 45; London FA Challenge Cup 2; FA Youth Cup 6; Metropolitan League 47; South East Counties League 44; London Midweek League 20; Other jnr comp: 5; Friendlies 29/1. In addition played one Metropolitan League match 1958-9, later removed from records.
Honours: Played for Lincoln and Lincolnshire Schoolboys. Metropolitan League champions 1958-9. South East Counties League champions and League Cup winners 1955-6.
Was high jump and long jump champion of both Scunthorpe and Lincolnshire in 1953. Served National Service in Royal Artillery. Transferred from Southend to Watford (Jul 1964) and to Huddersfield Town (1965). Later went to South Africa and played for Apollon FC.

GRAHAM, Alexander   1911-24
Half-back   5ft 8½in. 11st 7lb.
Born: Hurlford, Ayrshire, Scotland, 11 Jul 1890.
Died: 1943.
Jnr football: Larkhall United (Lanarkshire). Joined ARSENAL: Dec 1911 (on trial), 3 Jan 1912 (professional). First app: South Eastern League v Swindon Town (a) 26 Dec 1911 (trial under the name Allan). First snr app: Snr fdly v West Ham (h) 30 Mar 1912. Final snr app: League v Burnley (a) 28 Apr 1924. Final app: London Combination v Millwall (h) 30 Oct 1924. Transferred to Brentford 4 Dec 1924.
ARSENAL Record: League 166 (17 gls); FA Cup 13 (3 gls); Other snr comp: 6; Football Combination 47 (13 gls); London FA Challenge Cup 2 (2 gls); South Eastern League 60 (13 gls); London League (Res) 13 (2 gls); Other jnr comp: 1; Friendlies 14 (7 gls). In addition made 5 apps (1 gl) during wartime.
Honours: London FA Challenge Cup winners 1923-4, runners-up 1914-15. Norwich Hospital Cup winners 1913-14. Metropolitan Hospital Cup winners 1920-21. Southend Hospital Cup runners-up 1922-3. 1 full Scotland cap 1921.
Played in Scotland during the War. Became assistant manager of Brentford Dec 1925.

GRAHAM, George
Player 1966-72   Manager 1986-
Midfield/striker   5ft 11in. 12st 1lb.
Born: Bargeddie, Lanark, Scotland, 30 Nov 1944.
School: Coatbridge.
Jnr Football: Swinton (West of Scotland). Previous Clubs: Aston Villa (Dec 1961), Chelsea (cs 1964, £6,000). Joined ARSENAL: 30 Sep 1966 from Chelsea for £50,000 (plus T.Baldwin). First app: League v Leicester City (h) 1 Oct 1966. Final snr app: League (sub) v Coventry City (h) 4 Nov 1972. Final app: Football Combination v Leicester City (h) 19 Dec 1972. Transferred to Manchester United (£120,000) 27 Dec 1972.
ARSENAL Record: League 219/8 (59 gls); FA Cup 27 (2 gls); Football League Cup 27/2 (9 gls);

European Competitions 23/2 (7 gls); Football Combination 14 (6 gls); London FA Challenge Cup 1; Friendlies 37/3 (5 gls).
Honours: Played for Coatbridge Schoolboys and 5 Scotland Schoolboy internationals. Division One champions 1970-71. FA Cup winners 1971 (and voted Man of the Match), runners-up 1972. European Fairs Cup winners 1969-70. Football League Cup runners-up 1968, 1969. 8 full Scotland caps (1 gl) 1971-2.

Won club and Scotland Youth international honours with Aston Villa and club and Scotland Under-23 international honours with Chelsea. Moved from Manchester United to Portsmouth (Nov 1974) and to Crystal Palace (Nov 1976). Retired from playing May 1980 and became youth coach at Crystal Palace. Took up a similar position at Queen's Park Rangers and then became manager of Millwall (Dec 1982). Was appointed manager of Arsenal in May 1986 and took the club to Wembley as winners of the Littlewood's Cup in his first season.

GRAHAM, John   **1899-1900**
Full-back.
Born: Derby 1873. Died: 13 Apr 1925.
Jnr football: Cray Wanderers. Previous Club: Millwall Athletic. Joined ARSENAL: 26 Jul 1895 but returned to Millwall 20 Sep 1899. First app: Jnr fdly v Woolwich League (h) 23 Sep 1899. First snr app: League v Gainsborough Trinity (h) 14 Oct 1899. Final app: Jnr fdly v Tottenham Hotspur Res (h) 21 Apr 1900.
ARSENAL Record: League 1; Southern District Combination 4; Kent League 11; Friendlies 6.
Later played for Fulham after Arsenal.

GRAHAM, Thomas   **1891-92**
Forward   5ft 10in. 12st.
Born: Balloch, Scotland, c.1868.
Jnr football: Jamestown, Vale of Leven. Joined ARSENAL: Summer 1891 from Vale of Leven. First app: Snr fdly v Sheffield United (h) 5 Sep 1891. First first-class app: FA Cup v Small Heath (a) 16 Jan 1892 (only app). Final app: Snr fdly v Glasgow Rangers (h) 30 Apr 1892.
ARSENAL Record: FA Cup 1. In addition during 1891-2 made 55 senior (47 gls) and 2 reserve (3 gls) apps for Royal Arsenal.

GRANT, Cyril   **1946**
Centre-forward   5ft 10in. 11st 6lb.
Born: Wath upon Dearne, Yorks, 10 Jul 1920.
School: Swinton Bridge, Yorks.
Jnr football: Shipcroft United (Barnsley), Wolverhampton Wanderers (trial), Mexborough FC. Previous Club: Lincoln City (wartime). Joined ARSENAL: 15 Jul 1946 from Lincoln City. First app: Football Combination v Clapton Orient (h) 31 Aug 1946. First snr app: League v Preston North End (a) 9 Nov 1946. Final app: League v Middlesbrough (a) 7 Dec 1946. Transferred to Fulham (part of R.Rooke deal) 13 Dec 1946.
ARSENAL Record: League 2; Football Combination 9 (6 gls); London FA Challenge Cup 1 (1 gl); Friendlies 2 (3 gls).
Later played for Southend United (Mar 1948).

GRANT, George M.   **1910-19**
Half-back   5ft 11in. 12st 10lb.
Born: Plumstead, London, c.1891.
Jnr football: Woolwich Wesley Guild: Northumberland Oddfellows: Dartford Invicta FC. Joined ARSENAL: 4 Mar 1910 (amateur) from Invicta FC; 13 Sep 1911 (professional). First app: South Eastern League v Southend (h) 5 Mar 1910. First snr app: League v Aston Villa (a) 9 Sep 1911. Final snr app: League v Hull City (a) 2 Apr 1915. Final app: Jnr fdly (wartime) v Bristol City Res (a) 26 Apr 1919.
ARSENAL Record: League 54 (4 gls); FA Cup 3; Other snr comp: 5; South Eastern League 110 (5 gls); London FA Challenge Cup 4; London League (Res) 5 (1 gl); Other jnr comp: 1; Friendlies 22 (4 gls). In addition made 43 apps during wartime.
Honours: Norwich Hospital Cup winners 1913-14. London FA Challenge Cup runners-up 1914-15.
Later played for Millwall (1919) and Queen's Park Rangers (1921).

GRANT, John W.   **1912**
Centre-forward.
Previous Club: Southport Central (amateur). Joined ARSENAL: 28 Feb 1912 (amateur). First app: League v Preston North End (h) 8 Apr 1912. Final app: League v Notts County (h) 27 Apr 1912.
ARSENAL Record: League 4 (3 gls); South Eastern League 1.
Son of an ex-Arsenal director, Grant was an amateur with Southport Central, who whilst on business in Gravesend, agreed to assist Arsenal. Scored a hat-trick v Blackburn Rovers (h) Apr 1912.

GRAY, Archibald 'Baldie'   **1904-12**
Full-back   5ft 7in. 11st 7lb.
Born: Govan, Scotland, 1883.
Jnr football: Govan Columbia, Glasgow Ashfield. Previous Club: Hibernian. Joined ARSENAL: 13 May 1904. First app: Snr fdly v Bristol City (h) 1 Sep 1904. League v Newcastle United (a) 3 Sep 1904. Final snr app: League v Notts County (a) 23 Dec 1911. Final app: South Eastern League v Chelsea (a) 27 Mar 1912. Transferred to Fulham (£250) 4 Apr 1912.
ARSENAL Record: League 184; FA Cup 16; Other snr comp: 5; London FA Challenge Cup 5; South Eastern League 30; London League (Res) 1; Other jnr comp: 2; Friendlies 32/1.
Won club, Scottish League and Scotland international honours whilst with Hibernian. On retirement he became a dairyman in Glasgow.

GREENAWAY, David   **1908-21**
Outside-right   5ft 6½in. 10st 6lb.
Born: Coatdyke, Lanark, Scotland, c.1889.
Jnr football: Shettleston FC (Glasgow). Joined ARSENAL: 10 May 1908 from Scotland. First app: League v Notts County (a) 5 Sep 1908. Final

snr app: League v Bradford (h) 1 May 1920. Final app: Jnr fdly v Brighton (h) 21 Apr 1921.
ARSENAL Record: League 161 (13 gls); FA Cup 9; Other snr comp: 5; Football Combination 41 (4 gls); London FA Challenge Cup 11; South Eastern League 57 (11 gls); London League (Res) 20 (3 gls); Friendlies 29 (9 gls).
Signed by Arsenal following the club's Scottish tour at the end of 1907-08 season. Served with the Royal Field Artillery during the war. Was given a free transfer by Arsenal at the end of 1920-21 and the club lost trace of him.

GRICE, Neville Joseph   **1906**
Outside-right.
An amateur from Ealing. Joined ARSENAL: 15 Mar 1906 (amateur). First app: League v Middlesbrough (a) 21 Apr 1906 (his only Arsenal app).
ARSENAL Record: League 1.

GRIEVE, Thomas   **1900-01**
Outside-right.
Jnr football: Gravesend. Joined ARSENAL: 26 May 1900 from Gravesend. First app: Jnr fdly v Deptford (h) 3 Sep 1900. First snr app: League v Barnsley (h) 22 Sep 1900. Final snr app: League v Newton Heath (a) 16 Mar 1901. Final app: West Kent League v Dartford (h) 27 Apr 1901.
ARSENAL Record: League 6; London League (Res) 13 (3 gls); Kent League 4; Friendlies 4 (4 gls).
Honours: West Kent League champions 1900-01.
Later played for Watford (1904) and Brighton & Hove Albion.

GRIFFITHS, Arfon Trevor MBE   **1961-62**
Inside-forward   5ft 5in. 9st 3lb.
Born: Wrexham, Wales, 23 Aug 1941.
Previous Club: Wrexham (amateur). May 1957, (professional) May 1959. Joined ARSENAL: 3 Feb 1961 from Wrexham for £14,000. First app: Football Combination v Cardiff City (a) 11 Feb 1961. First snr app: League v Wolverhampton Wanderers (h) 22 Apr 1961. Final snr app: On tour v International FC (Denmark) 15 May 1962. Final app: Football Combination v Mansfield Town (a) 8 Sep 1962. Transferred to Wrexham (£10,000) 17 Sep 1962.
ARSENAL Record: League 15 (2 gls); Football Combination 24 (10 gls); Metropolitan League 2; Friendlies 17/1 (7 gls).
Honours: 2 Wales Under-23 caps 1961-2.
Was a part-time clerk with National Coal Board at Wrexham before taking up full-time football. Won club honours and Wales Youth, Under-23, and full international caps with Wrexham. Was awarded the MBE. Became manager of Wrexham (May 1977 to Jun 1981)and Crewe Alexandra (1981-2). Now has a newsagents' business in Gresford.

GRIFFITHS, William Malwyn   **1936-38**
Outside-right   5ft 8in. 10st 2lb.
Born: Merthyr, Wales, 8 Mar 1919. Died: 5 Apr 1969.
School: Queens Road, Merthyr.
Jnr football: Merthyr Thursday, Margate. Joined ARSENAL: 21 Sep 1935 (amateur), 4 May 1936 (to Margate), 27 Feb 1937 (professional). First app: Football Combination v Portsmouth (h) 27 Feb 1937. First snr app: On tour v Gothenburg (Sweden) 25 May 1937. Final snr app: Football League Jubilee final v Tottenham Hotspur (h) 20 Aug 1938. Final app: London Combination v Leicester City (£800) 20 Sep 1938.
ARSENAL Record: League 9 (5 gls); Other snr comp: 1; Football Combination 38 (18 gls); London FA Challenge Cup 3; Southern League 2; Friendlies 8 (3 gls).

58

Honours: London Combination champions 1937-8. London FA Challenge Cup runners-up 1936-7. Won club honours and Wales caps with Leicester City. Retired at end of 1955-6 and signed part-time for Burton Albion. Became a publican at Wigston, Leicester.

GROVES, Frederick William   **1912-21**
Forward   5ft 7½in. 11st 4lb.
Born: Shadwell(Stepney), 13 Jan 1891.
Previous Club: Glossop (amateur). Joined ARSENAL: 30 Aug 1912 (amateur), 11 Oct 1913 (professional). First app: South Eastern League v Tunbridge Wells (h) 7 Sep 1912. First snr app: League v Derby County (a) 7 Dec 1912. Final snr app: League v Sheffield United (h) 26 Mar 1921. Final app: Jnr fdly v Athenian League (h) 7 May 1921. Transferred to Brighton (£500) 8 Aug 1921.
ARSENAL Record: League 50 (6 gls); FA Cup 3 (1 gl); Other snr comp: 2; Football Combination 18 (2 gls); London FA Challenge Cup 2 (2 gls); South Eastern League 72 (17 gls); London League (Res) 19 (6 gls); Friendlies 18 (4 gls). In addition made 132/1 apps (31 gls) during wartime.
Later played for Charlton Athletic (Aug 1924).

GROVES, Perry   **1986-**
Striker   5ft 11in. 11st 12lb.
Born: Bow, London, 19 Apr 1965.
School: Sudbury, Suffolk.
Previous Club: Colchester United Sep 1981 (apprentice), Jun 1982 (professional). Joined ARSENAL: 4 Sep 1986 from Colchester United for £50,000. First app: Football Combination v Oxford United (h) 10 Sep 1986. First snr app: League (sub) v Luton Town (a) 13 Sep 1986.
ARSENAL Record: League 91/64 (21 gls); FA Cup 11/6 (1 gl); Football League Cup 18/8 (6 gls); European comp: 0/4; Other snr comp: 4/3 (1 gl); Football Combination 50/1 (27 gls); Friendlies 29/21 (13 gls).
Honours: Division One Champions 1988-89, 1990-91. Football League Cup winners 1986-7, runners-up 1987-8. Mercantile Credit Centenary Trophy winners 1988-9.
Played for Suffolk schoolboys. Nephew of Vic Groves (see below).

GROVES, Victor George   **1955-64**
Forward/wing-half   5ft 9in. 12st 13lb.
Born: Stepney, London, 5 Nov 1932.

Jnr football: Leytonstone (amateur), Walthamstow Avenue (amateur). Previous Clubs: Tottenham Hotspur (amateur), Leyton Orient (amateur), Oct 1954 (professional). Joined ARSENAL: 4 Nov 1955 from Leyton Orient for £30,000 (& S.Charlton). First app: League v Sheffield United (h) 12 Nov 1955. Final snr app: League v Nottingham Forest (a) 7 Mar 1964. Final app: Football Combination v Plymouth Argyle (a) 27 Mar 1964. Transferred to Canterbury City (free transfer) end of 1963-4.
ARSENAL Record: League 185 (31 gls); FA Cup 16 (6 gls); European Competitions 2; Other snr comp: 7 (1 gl); Football Combination 62 (19 gls); London FA Challenge Cup 10 (2 gls); Metropolitan League 2; Friendlies 59 (21 gls).
Honours: England Schoolboy, Youth and Amateur international. Southern Floodlit Cup winners 1958-9. London FA Challenge Cup winners 1962-3. Captain of Arsenal. 1 England Under-23 cap 1956.
Worked in a fish market in East London before taking up football. Won FA and England 'B' international honours with Leyton Orient. Suffered a series of injuries requiring operations early in his Arsenal career. Retired from playing in 1965 and became a publican in Edmonton and in Enfield. Later became a salesman and then branch manager with Hambro Insurance.

GUDMUNDSSON, Albert S.   **1946-47**
Inside-forward   6ft. 11st 8lb.
Born: Iceland, 5 Oct 1923.
Previous Club: Glasgow Rangers (wartime). Joined ARSENAL: 27 Sep 1946 (amateur). First app: Snr fdly v Sparta Prague (h) 2 Oct 1946. League v Stoke City (h) 19 Oct 1946. Final snr app: Snr fdly v Tottenham Hotspur (a) 25 Jan 1947. Final app: Football Combination Cup v Reading (a) 29 Mar 1947.
ARSENAL Record: League 2; Football Combination 14 (7 gls); London FA Challenge Cup 1 (1 gl); Friendlies 3. In addition made 5/1 apps (1 gl) as guest for Arsenal on Brazil tour, summer 1951.
Studied marine engineering in Glasgow prior to 1946 and made apps for Rangers first and reserve teams during the war. Was not allowed to become a professional in English football so joined Milan (Italy) at end of 1946-7. After Italy had spells with French clubs Nancy, Racing Club de Paris and FC Nice before returning to Iceland to play for Valur (Jul 1957). Won many Iceland international caps. Became a successful businessman and was also President of the Icelandic FA. Was appointed French Consul in Iceland and later Finance Minister in Reykjavik.

GUTHRIE, Ralph   **1952-56**
Goalkeeper   5ft 9½in. 11st 7lb.
Born: West Hartlepool, 13 Sep 1932.
Jnr football: Darlington Reserves, Tow Law Town. Joined ARSENAL: 9 Dec 1952 (amateur) from Tow Law Town, 16 May 1953 (professional). First app: London Midweek League v Southend (h) 10 Dec 1952. First snr app: League v Manchester City (a) 8 Sep 1954. Final snr app: League v Portsmouth (h) 16 Oct 1954. Final app: Jnr fdly v Rickmansworth Town (a) 18 Apr 1956. Transferred to Hartlepools United 11 Jul 1956.
ARSENAL Record: League 2; Football Combination 31; London FA Challenge Cup 1; Eastern Counties League 33; London Midweek League 20; Other jnr comp: 2; Friendlies 7.
Honours: London FA Challenge Cup winners 1953-4. Eastern Counties League champions 1954-5.
Was Arsenal's reserve goalkeeper on the prestigious trip to Moscow, Oct 1954.

HADEN, Samson   **1922-27**
Winger   5ft 6in. 9st 11lb.
Born: Royston, nr Barnsley, 1904.
School: Carlton St John's Sunday School.
Jnr football: Castleford Town. Joined ARSENAL: 11 Mar 1922 from Castleford Town (amateur), 26 Apr 1922 (professional). First app: Jnr fdly v Boscombe (a) 14 Apr 1922. First snr app: On tour v Frem (Denmark) 10 May 1923. League v West Ham United (a) 27 Aug 1923. Final snr app: Snr fdly v Corinthians (h) 21 Sep 1927. Final app: London Combination v Coventry City (a) 3 Oct 1927. Transferred to Notts County 6 Oct 1927.
ARSENAL Record: League 88 (10 gls); FA Cup 5 (1 gl); Football Combination 67 (23 gls); London FA Challenge Cup 8 (2 gls); Friendlies 41 (22 gls).
Honours: London Combination champions 1922-23. London FA Challenge Cup winners 1923-4, runners-up 1925-6.
Worked as a coal-miner before taking up professional football. Broke a leg v Burnley, Feb 1926. Later became manager of Peterborough United.

HALLIDAY, David   **1929-30**
Centre-forward   6ft. 11st 7lb.
Born: Dumfries, Scotland, 11 Dec 1897. Died: Aberdeen, Jan 1965.
Jnr football: Queen of the South Wanderers. Previous Clubs: Queen of the South (1919), St Mirren (1920), Dundee (1921), Sunderland (Apr 1925). Joined ARSENAL: 8 Nov 1929 from Sunderland for £6,500. First app: League v Birmingham (a) 9 Nov 1929. Final snr app: League v Leicester City (a) 21 Apr 1930 (scored 4 gls). Final app: London FA Challenge Cup v Crystal Palace (h) 19 Nov 1930. Transferred to Manchester City (£5,700) 20 Nov 1930.
ARSENAL Record: League 15 (8 gls); Football Combination 29 (39 gls); London FA Challenge Cup 3 (3 gls); Friendlies 1 (4 gls).
Honours: London Combination champions 1929-30.
Won club honours and Scottish League honours with Dundee. After Manchester City played for Clapton Orient (Dec 1933). Became player-manager at Yeovil (1935) and manager of Aberdeen (Dec 1937). Was manager of Leicester City (Jul 1955 — Nov 1958) and then became their scout in North-East Scotland.

HAMILTON, Thomas S.   **1898-1900**
Goalkeeper.
Joined ARSENAL: as amateur in Apr 1898 from Stockton, 3 May 1898 (professional). First app: Snr fdly v Thames Ironworks (a) 26 Apr 1898. League v New Brighton Tower (a) 10 Dec 1898. Final snr app: League v Barnsley (h) 28 Apr 1900. Final app: Jnr fdly v Woolwich & District XI (h) 30 Apr 1900. Left ARSENAL to play for Gravesend, summer 1900.
ARSENAL Record: League 7; United League 2; Southern District Combination 9; Kent League 37; Friendlies 30.

HANKIN, Raymond   **1981**
Striker   6ft 2in. 13st 12lb.
Born: Wallsend, 2 Feb 1956.
Previous Clubs: Burnley (Feb 1973), Leeds United (Sep 1976), Vancouver Whitecaps (Canada). Joined ARSENAL: As non-contract player on month's trial, Nov 1981 from Vancouver Whitecaps. First app: Football Combination v Hereford Town (a) 30 Nov 1981 (match later expunged). First snr app: Football League Cup (sub) v Liverpool (h) 1 Dec 1981. Final app: Snr fdly v Glentoran (a) 29 Dec 1981. Not engaged by Arsenal and subsequently joined Middlesbrough (Sep 1982).
ARSENAL Record: Football League Cup 0/2;

Football Combination 2 (1 gl); Friendlies 1. In addition made 1 app (1 gl) in a Football Combination match, later removed from the records.
Won England Youth and Under-23 caps with Burnley. After Middlesbrough, had spells with Peterborough United, Wolverhampton Wanderers and Guisborough Town, before becoming manager of Northallerton Town and Darlington.

HANKS, Ernest   1912-13
Centre-forward.
Joined ARSENAL: 15 Apr 1912 from Army Service Corps (amateur); 16 Nov 1912 (professional). First app: South Eastern League v Croydon (h) 15 Apr 1912. First snr app: Snr fdly v Glasgow Rangers (a) 20 Apr 1912. Final snr app: League v Middlesbrough (a) 21 Dec 1912. Final app: Jnr fdly v Woolwich & District League (h) 23 Apr 1913. Transferred to Southend United 29 Jul 1913.
ARSENAL Record: League 4 (1 gl); South Eastern League 22 (13 gls); Friendlies 4 (1 gl).

HANNAH, David   1897-99
Inside-forward   5ft 6in. 11st 3lb.
Born: Raffrey, Co Down, 28 Apr 1867.
Jnr football: Renton. Previous Clubs: Sunderland 1889, Liverpool 1894, Dundee (cs 1897). Joined ARSENAL: 20 Oct 1897 from Dundee. First app: Snr fdly v Reading (h) 1 Nov 1897. League v Walsall (a) 6 Nov 1897. Final app: United League v Tottenham Hotspur (a) 29 Apr 1899.
ARSENAL Record: League 46 (17 gls); FA Cup 4; United League 27 (7 gls); Other snr comp: 2; Kent League 3 (1 gl); Friendlies 19 (6 gls).
Won club honours with Sunderland and Liverpool.

HANNIGAN, Richard   1899
Outside-right.
Joined ARSENAL: 2 May 1899 from Notts County. First app: League v Leicester Fosse (h) 2 Sep 1899. Final snr app: FA Cup v New Brompton (at Gravesend) 14 Nov 1899. Final app: Jnr fdly v Dartford (a) 9 Dec 1899. Transferred to Burnley 13 Dec 1899.
ARSENAL Record: League 1; FA Cup 1; Southern District Combination 1; Kent League 3; Friendlies 1.

HAPGOOD, Edris Albert   1927-45
Left-back   5ft 9in. 11st.
Born: Bristol, 27 Sep 1908. Died: Royal Leamington Spa, 20 Apr 1973.
School: St Phillips, Bristol.
Jnr football: Bristol Rovers (trial); Kettering Town. Joined ARSENAL: 20 Oct 1927 from Kettering Town for £1,000. First app: London Combination v Chelsea (h) 22 Oct 1927. First snr app: League v Birmingham (a) 19 Nov 1927. Final first-class app: League v Brentford (h) 6 May 1939. Final app: Football League South v Wolves (h) 29 Dec 1945. Retired.
ARSENAL Record: League 393 (2 gls); FA Cup 41; FA Charity Shield 6; Other snr comp: 9; Football Combination 50 (3 gls); London FA Challenge Cup 1; Friendlies 41. In addition played 3 League matches 1939-40 prior to outbreak of war and during wartime made 99 apps (1 gl).
Honours: Division One champions 1930-31, 1932-3, 1933-4, 1934-5, 1937-8. FA Cup winners 1930, 1936, runners-up 1932. FA Charity Shield winners 1930-31, 1931-2, 1933-4, 1934-5, runners-up 1935-6 and 1936-7. Sheriff of London Shield winners 1930-31. Northampton Charity Shield winners 1930, 1931, 1932. Norwich Hospital Cup winners 1934-5. Bath Coronation Cup winners 1936-7. London Combination champions 1927-8, 1928-9. Football League War Cup runners-up 1940-41. Captain of Arsenal and England. 30 full

England caps 1933-9 and made a further 13 apps in wartime internationals. Made 4 apps for Football League 1931-9.
Served as Flying Officer in RAF during the war. Became manager of Blackburn Rovers (1946), player-coach at Shrewsbury Town (Midland League), manager of Watford (1948-50), manager Bath City 1950-56. Became warden of a Youth Hostel at Weymouth in 1957. Retired to Royal Leamington Spa 1970.

HARDING Edwin   1896
Full-back.
Joined ARSENAL: Nov 1896. First app: Kent League v Cray Wanderers (h) 21 Nov 1896. Final app: FA Cup (Q) v Leyton (h) 12 Dec 1896.
ARSENAL Record: FA Cup (Q) 1; Kent League 3.
A reserve-team player who played in an FA Cup Qualifying Round, when Arsenal, compelled to fulfill League and FA Cup fixtures on the same date, fielded their reserve side for the Cup match.

HARDINGE, Harold Thomas William 'Wally'   1913-21
Inside-forward   5ft 8in. 12st 4lb.
Born: Greenwich, London, 25 Feb 1886. Died: Cambridge, Kent, 8 May 1965.
School: Blackheath Road, Greenwich.
Jnr football: Eltham, Tonbridge FC, Maidstone United. Previous Clubs: Newcastle United (Sep 1905), Sheffield United (Dec 1907). Joined ARSENAL: 19 Jun 1913 from Sheffield United. First app: League v Leicester Fosse (h) 6 Sep 1913. Final snr app: League v Manchester City (a) 17 Jan 1920. London Professional Charity Fund v Tottenham Hotspur (a) 25 Oct 1920. Final app: London Combination v Brentford (a) 29 Mar 1921. Retired: cs 1921.
ARSENAL Record: League 54 (14 gls); FA Cup 1; Other snr comp: 2; Football Combination 22 (8 gls); London FA Challenge Cup 9 (6 gls); South Eastern League 4 (3 gls); London League (Res) 3; Friendlies 7 (8 gls). In addition made 70 apps (37 gls) during wartime.
Honours: London FA Challenge Cup runners-up 1914-15.
Won England international honours with Sheffield United. Served as a Chief Petty Officer in Royal Navy (Air Force) during World War One. Played county cricket for Kent (1902-33) and for England in a Test Match (therefore a 'double' international). Was manager-coach to Tottenham Hotspur reserve team (1935). Was on the staff of John Wisden Limited (sports outfitters) for many years.

HARE, Charles Boyd   1895-96
Forward   5ft 10in.
Born: Yardley, Birmingham, Jun 1871. Died: Feb 1934.
Jnr football: Birmingham United. Previous Club: Aston Villa (1891). Joined ARSENAL: 27 Feb 1895 from Aston Villa. First app: Snr Fdly v Eastbourne (a) 6 Mar 1895. League v Leicester Fosse (at Leyton) 9 Mar 1895. Final app: League v Darwen (a) 14 Mar 1896. Snr Fdly v Tottenham Hotspur (a) 30 Apr 1896. Transferred to Small Heath 6 Nov 1896.
ARSENAL Record: League 19 (7 gls); FA Cup 1; Kent League 8 (6 gls); Friendlies 38 (12 gls).
Represented Warwick County. Won club honours with Aston Villa. Also made a few apps at full-back for Arsenal. After Small Heath also played for Watford (Jun 1898), Plymouth Argyle (1903-04) and Fulham.

HARPER, William   1925-27 & 1930-31
Goalkeeper   5ft 11½in. 12st 2lb.
Born: Tarbrax, Lanarkshire, Scotland, 19 Jan 1898. Died: Apr 1989.

Jnr football: Winchburgh Thistle; Edinburgh Emmett. Previous Club: Hibernian (Sep 1921). Joined ARSENAL: 9 Nov 1925 from Hibernian for £4,000. Left Arsenal at end of 1926-7 season to play for Fall River FC in USA. Rejoined ARSENAL: 18 Sep 1930 from America. First app: League v Blackburn Rovers (a) 31 Aug 1931. Final app: London Midweek League v Thames (h) 16 Dec 1931. Transferred to Plymouth Argyle 18 Dec 1931.
ARSENAL Record: League 63; FA Cup 10; Football Combination 26; London FA Challenge Cup 3; London Midweek League 6; Other snr comp: 2; Friendlies 8.
Honours: Division One champions 1930-31. London Combination winners 1926-7. 2 full Scotland caps 1926. Northampton Charity Shield winner 1930-31. Sheriff of London Shield winner 1930-31.
Was a blacksmith by trade before taking up football. Served with the 5th Brigade Scots Guards in France during World War One. Won club, international and Scottish League honours with Hibernian. Retired from playing in 1939 and became trainer at Plymouth Argyle. Worked in the dockyard at Rosyth during World War Two. Returned to Plymouth Argyle as trainer until 1950, became groundsman until 1964 and, finally, odd-job man for a number of years.

HARTLEY, Abraham   1899
Forward   5ft 7½in. 12st.
Born: Dumbarton, Scotland, 8 Feb 1872. Died: Southampton, 9 Oct 1909.
Jnr football: Artizan Thistle (Dumbarton). Previous Clubs: Dumbarton, Everton (1892-7), Liverpool (1897-8), Southampton (1898-9). Joined ARSENAL: 15 Jul 1899 from Southampton. First app: League v Walsall (a) 23 Sep 1899. Final snr app: FA Cup (Q) v New Brompton (at Gravesend) 14 Nov 1899. Final app: Jnr fdly v Dartford (a) 9 Dec 1899. Transferred to Burnley 13 Dec 1899.
ARSENAL Record: League 5 (1 gl); FA Cup 4; Southern District Combination 4 (2 gls); Kent League 2 (2 gls); Friendlies 1.
Won club honours with Everton.

HARVEY, James   1977-80
Midfield   5ft 9½in. 11st 4lb.
Born: Lurgan, N.Ireland, 2 May 1958.
Previous Club: Glenavon. Joined ARSENAL: 6 Aug 1977 from Glenavon for £20,000. First app: Jnr fdly v Worthing (a) 10 Aug 1977. First snr app: Snr fdly v Northampton Town (a) 20 Sep 1977. League v Derby County (a) 9 May 1978. Final snr app: UEFA Cup v Leipzig (h) 13 Sep 1978. Final app: Football Combination v Ipswich Town (23 Feb 1980). Given a free transfer by Arsenal and joined Hereford Town 14 Mar 1980 (after previously on loan).
ARSENAL Record: League 2/1; European Competitions 1; Football Combination 94/4 (7 gls); Friendlies 8/3.
Ulster's 'Young Player of the Year' 1976-7. After Hereford Town played for Bristol City, Wrexham (on loan) and is currently with Tranmere Rovers.

HATFIELD, Thomas   1895-96
Goalkeeper.
Joined ARSENAL: Jan 1895 (amateur), 11 Apr 1895 (professional). First app: Jnr fdly v Old Castle Swifts (a) 12 Jan 1895. First snr app: Snr fdly v Dumbarton (h) 13 Apr 1895. League v Burton Wanderers (a) 20 Apr 1895. Final app: League v Leicester Fosse (h) 7 Dec 1895. Final app: Jnr fdly v Luton Town Reserves (a) 25 Apr 1896. Moved to Tottenham Hotspur in cs 1896.
ARSENAL Record: League 2; Kent League 11; Other jnr comp: 2; Friendlies 16.

60

HAVERTY, Joseph   **1954-61**
Outside-left   5ft 3½in. 9st 6lb.
Born: Dublin, 17 Feb 1936.
Jnr football: Home Farm (Dublin). Previous
Club: St Patrick's Athletic (Dublin). Joined
ARSENAL: 19 Jul 1954 from St Patrick's
Athletic. First app: Eastern Counties League v
March Town (a) 21 Aug 1954. First snr app:
League v Everton (a) 25 Aug 1954. Final app:
League v Fulham (a) 31 Mar 1961. On tour v
Vejle BK (Denmark) 21 May 1961. Transferred
to Blackburn Rovers (£17,500) 31 Jul 1961.

ARSENAL Record: League 114 (25 gls); FA Cup
8 (1 gl); Other snr comp: 6 (2 gls); London FA
Challenge Cup 10 (5 gls); Football Combination
86 (21 gls); Eastern Counties League 7 (1 gl);
Metropolitan League 1 (1 gl); London Midweek
League 9 (4 gls); Friendlies 44/3 (10 gls).
*Honours: Republic of Ireland Youth inter-
national. London FA Challenge Cup winners
1954-5, 1957-8, runners-up 1960-1. 15 full
Republic of Ireland caps (3 gls) 1956-61.*
Won club honours with St Patrick's Athletic. After
Blackburn Rovers he played for Millwall (Sep
1962), Celtic (1 app), Bristol Rovers (Dec 1964)
and Shelbourne (Ireland). He won further international honours with each of those clubs. Went
to America in 1967 to play for Chicago Spurs.

HAWLEY, John East   **1981-83**
Striker   6ft 0½in. 13st 8lb.
Born: Patrington, Yorks, 8 May 1954.
Previous Clubs: Hull City 1973 (amateur), Leeds
1976 (professional), Leeds United (May 1978),
Sunderland (Oct 1979). Joined ARSENAL: 8 Sep
1981 from Sunderland for £50,000. First app:
Football Combination v Leicester City (h) 19 Sep
1981. First snr app: League v Manchester United
(h) 26 Sep 1981. Final app: League (sub) v
Sunderland (h) 7 May 1983. Released by Arsenal
at end of 1982-3 and went to play in Hong Kong.
ARSENAL Record: League 14/6 (3 gls); Football
League Cup 1; Football Combination 30/1 (10
gls); Friendlies 9/2 (2 gls). In addition made 3
apps in Football Combination 1981-2, later
removed from the records.
Helped to run a family antique business in
Beverley before taking up professional football.
Had a spell on loan to Orient in 1982-3 and
returned to Highbury. Later played for Bradford
City 1983-4 and 1984-5 and Scunthorpe United
(1985-6).

HAYES, Martin   **1981-90**
Forward   6ft. 11st 8lb.
Born: Walthamstow, London, 21 Mar 1966.
Joined ARSENAL: 1981 (amateur), Jun 1982
(apprentice), 2 Nov 1983 (professional). First app:
South East Counties League (sub) v Charlton (h)
29 Aug 1981. First snr app: Snr Fdly (sub) v
Australia (h) 27 Nov 1984. League v Oxford
United (h) 16 Nov 1985. Final app: League v
Norwich City (a) 5 May 1990. Transferred to
Glasgow Celtic (£650,000) 29 May 1990.

ARSENAL Record: League 70/32 (26 gls); FA
Cup 8/1 (3 gls); Football League Cup 14/7 (5
gls); Other snr comp: 0/6; Football Combination
157/8 (69 gls); South East Counties League 59/
6 (29 gls); FA Youth Cup 9 (5 gls); Other jnr
comp: 11 (6 gls); Friendlies 68/16 (33 gls).
*Honours: Played for Waltham Forest schoolboys
and Essex schoolboys. Division One champions
1988-9. Football League Cup winners 1986-7,
runners-up 1987-8. Football Combination
champions 1983-4, 1989-90. Southern Junior
Floodlit Cup winners 1983-4. 3 England Under-
21 caps.*
On loan to Wimbledon (Feb 1992).

HAYNES, Alfred Edward   **1928-33**
Half-back   5ft 11½in. 11st 2lb.
Born: Oxford, 1910. Died: Jun 1953.
Jnr football: Oxford City. Joined ARSENAL:
May 1928 from Oxford City. First app: Jnr fdly
v Kettering Town (a) 3 May 1928. First snr app:
League v Liverpool (a) 21 Dec 1929. Final snr
app: League v Blackburn Rovers (a) 7 Oct 1933.
Final app: Jnr fdly v Cambridge University (a)
16 Nov 1933. Transferred to Crystal Palace 17
Nov 1933.
ARSENAL Record: League 29; FA Cup 1; FA
Charity Shield 1; Other snr comp: 3; Football
Combination 174 (4 gls); London FA Challenge
Cup 9; London Midweek League 8; Friendlies 26.
*Honours: FA Charity Shield winners 1931-2.
London Combination champions 1928-9, 1929-30,
1930-31. London FA Challenge Cup winners
1930-31. Sheriff of London Shield winners 1930-31,
1932-3. Northampton Charity Shield winners 1931-2.*

HAYWOOD, Adam   **1896-99**
Inside-forward   5ft 5in. 10st 6lb.
Born: Horninglow, nr Burton upon Trent, 23 Mar
1875. Died: May 1932.
Jnr football: Burton Ivanhoe; Burton Wanderers
(junior); Swadlincote (Derbyshire). Joined
ARSENAL: 17 Jan 1896 from Swadlincote. First
app: Snr fdly v Cambridge University (h) 20 Jan

1896. League v Leicester Fosse (a) 25 Jan 1896.
Final app: United League v Tottenham Hotspur
(a) 29 Apr 1899. Transferred to Glossop (£50)
summer 1899.
ARSENAL Record: League 84 (31 gls); FA Cup
7 (5 gls); United League 41 (16 gls); Kent League
3; Other jnr comp: 2; Friendlies 48 (33 gls).
Later played for Queen's Park Rangers, New
Brompton (1900-01), Wolverhampton Wanderers
(1901-05), West Bromwich Albion (1905-06),
Blackpool (Dec 1907) and Crystal Palace (1908).
Was coach at Crystal Palace (1909).

HEANEY, Neil A.   **1987-**
Winger   5ft 9in. 11st 1lb.
Born: Middlesbrough, 3 Nov 1971.
Joined ARSENAL: 1987 (schoolboy), Jul 1988
(apprentice), 1989 (professional). First app: Jnr fdly
v Staines Town (a) 9 Aug 1987. First snr app:
League (sub) v Sheffield United (a) 18 Apr 1992.
ARSENAL Record: League 0/1; Football
Combination 61/6 (18 gls); South East Counties
League 49/3 (16 gls); FA Youth Cup 9/1 (1 gl);
Other jnr comp 8 (4 gls); Friendlies 29/2 (2 gls).
*Honours: Played for Teesside Schoolboys.
Football Combination champions 1989-90. FA
Youth Cup winner 1987-8. Southern Junior
Floodlight Cup runners-up 1989-90. England
Youth caps.*
Had spells on loan to Hartlepool United (1990-
91) and Cambridge United (1991-2).

HEATH, Joseph Frederick   **1893-95 & 1896-99**
Centre-forward/half-back   5ft 9in. 12st 9lb.
Born: Bristol, c.1869.
Jnr football: Walsall Town Swifts; Wednesbury
Old Athletic. Previous Club: Wolverhampton
Wanderers. Joined ARSENAL: 25 Jun 1893
(League forms) from Wolverhampton Wanderers.
First app: Jnr fdly v Woolwich & District League
(a) 3 Apr 1893. The app: Snr fdly v Doncaster
Rovers (h) 4 Sep 1893. League v Notts County
(a) 9 Sep 1893. Final app: Jnr fdly v Leyton
(h) 12 Dec 1896. Final app: Kent League v Bromley
(h) 18 Feb 1899. Transferred to Gravesend United
Sep 1895. Rejoined ARSENAL as reserve 1896-7.
ARSENAL Record: League 10 (5 gls); FA Cup
2 (2 gls); Kent League 22 (13 gls); Other jnr comp:
5 (2 gls); Friendlies 89 (47 gls). In addition made
2 reserve apps for Royal Arsenal in 1892-3 season.
*Honours: Kent League champions 1896-7.
Sevenoaks Charity Cup winners 1897-8.*
Was Woolwich Arsenal reserve-team coach 1894-5.

HEELEY, David Mark   **1977-80**
Winger   5ft 6in. 9st.
Born: Peterborough, 8 Sep 1959.
Previous Club: Peterborough United, Nov 1976
(professional). Joined ARSENAL: 3 Oct 1977
(after a month's loan) from Peterborough United
for £50,000. First app: Football Combination v
Cardiff City (a) 7 Sep 1977. First snr app: Snr
fdly v Northampton Town (a) 20 Sep 1977. League
(sub) v Birmingham (h) 29 Oct 1977. Final snr
app: Snr fdly v Fulham (a) 1 May 1979. Final
app: Football Combination v Oxford United (h)
1 Mar 1980. Transferred to Northampton Town
(£35,000) 12 Mar 1980.
ARSENAL Record: League 9/6 (1 gl); European
Competitions 4/1; Football Combination 71/1 (19
gls); FA Youth Cup 3; Other jnr comp: 3 (2 gls);
Friendlies 8/2 (1 gl).
Played for Northampton Town until end of
1982-3 season.

HENDERSON, James   **1892-95**
Inside-forward   5ft 6½in. 10st 7lb.
Born: Thornhill (Dumfries), Scotland, c.1867.
Jnr football: 5th Kirkudbright RV. Previous Club:
Glasgow Rangers. Joined ARSENAL: Summer

1892 from Glasgow Rangers. First app: Snr fdly v Highland Light Infantry (h) 1 Sep 1892. First first-class app: FA Cup (Q) v Highland Light Infantry (h) 15 Oct 1892. Final app: League v Burton Wanderers (h) 26 Jan 1895. Released by Arsenal Mar 1895 and returned to Scotland. ARSENAL Record: League 38 (18 gls); FA Cup 5 (7 gls); FA Cup (Q) 4 (5 gls); Other jnr comp: 1 (1 gl); Friendlies 38 (25 gls). In addition made 49 senior (30 gls) and 2 reserve apps for Royal Arsenal during 1892-3.

HENDERSON, John Gillespie   1958-62
Forward   5ft 9in. 11st 10lb.
Born: Bishopbriggs, Glasgow, 17 Jan 1932.
School: Bishopbriggs Public.
Jnr football: Kirkintilloch Boys Club. Previous Clubs: Portsmouth (Jan 1949), Wolverhampton Wanderers (Mar 1958). Joined ARSENAL: 9 Oct 1958 from Wolverhampton Wanderers for £20,000. First app: League v West Bromwich Albion (h) 4 Oct 1958 (2 gls). Final snr app: League v Nottingham Forest (h) 18 Nov 1961. Snr fdly v Dinamo Kiev (h) 20 Nov 1961. Final app: Football Combination v Tottenham Hotspur (a) 23 Dec 1961. Transferred to Fulham (£14,000) 12 Jan 1962.
ARSENAL Record: League 103 (29 gls); FA Cup 8; Other snr comp: 5 (1 gl); Football Combination 13 (14 gls); London FA Challenge Cup 5 (6 gls); Friendlies 34 (23 gls).
Honours: Southern Floodlit Challenge Cup winners 1958-9. 2 full Scotland caps 1958.
Served with the Army on National Service and played many representative games for them. Won club and international honours with Portsmouth. Was given free transfer by Fulham, summer 1964 and joined Poole Town. After retirement from football, worked for a building firm in Poole, Dorset.

HENDERSON, William   1921-23
Centre-forward   5ft 9in. 11st 10lb.
Born: Carlisle, 11 Jan 1899.
Previous Club: Carlisle United. Joined ARSENAL: 5 Oct 1921 from Carlisle United for £1,000. First app: London Combination v Brentford (h) 6 Oct 1921. First snr app: League v Huddersfield Town (a) 22 Oct 1921. Final snr app: League v Birmingham (a) 2 Dec 1922. Final app: Jnr fdly v Northfleet (a) 17 Feb 1923. Transferred to Luton Town 12 Mar 1923.
ARSENAL Record: League 7; Other snr comp: 1; Football Combination 34 (13 gls); London FA Challenge Cup 4 (1 gl); Friendlies 15 (6 gls).
Honours: London Combination champions 1922-3. London FA Challenge Cup winners 1921-2.
After Luton Town, played for Southampton, Nov 1923, and Coventry City (1928). Became a tobacconist in Carlisle.

HENLEY, Leslie   1939-46
Inside-forward/half-back.
Born: Lambeth, London, 26 Sep 1922.
Joined ARSENAL: 8 May 1939 (amateur), 1941 (professional). First app: Football League South v Fulham (h) 7 Sep 1940. First snr app: FA Cup v West Ham United (a) 5 Jan 1946 (only senior app). Final app: Football Combination v Norwich City (a) 28 Dec 1946. Transferred to Reading (£250) 28 Dec 1946.
ARSENAL Record: FA Cup 1; Football Combination 4 (4 gls); London FA Challenge Cup 1; Friendlies 1. In addition, made 95 apps (17 gls) during wartime.
Played for South London Schoolboys. Won England Schoolboy cap 1937. Served in the Army during the war. Forced to retire from playing due to injury, 1952-3 season. Became coach and manager of Bohemians (Ireland). Joined

Wimbledon FC in Jul 1955, first as coach and then as team manager.

HEPPINSTALL, Frank   1909-11
Outside-left   5ft 9in. 11st 6lb.
Born: South Hiendley, nr Barnsley.
Jnr football: Denaby United. Previous Clubs: Barnsley, Swindon Town. Joined ARSENAL: May 1909 from Swindon Town. First app: League v Aston Villa (a) 1 Sep 1909. Final snr app: League v Manchester City (h) 29 Oct 1910. Final app: South Eastern League v Bristol City (h) 17 Apr 1911. Left Arsenal at end of 1910-11 season and joined Hamilton, 15 Aug 1913.
ARSENAL Record: League 23; London FA Challenge Cup 1 (1 gl); South Eastern League 30 (4 gls); Other jnr comp: 1; Friendlies 10 (1 gl).

HERD, David George   1954-61
Inside/centre-forward   5ft 11½in. 11st 13lb.
Born: Hamilton, Lanarkshire, Scotland, 15 Apr 1934.
School: Princess Road, Moss Side, Manchester.
Previous Club: Stockport County (amateur) 1949, Apr 1951 (professional). Joined ARSENAL: 24 Aug 1954 from Stockport County for £10,000. First app: Football Combination Cup v Brentford (a) 2 Sep 1954. First snr app: Snr fdly v Grasshoppers FC (h) 21 Sep 1954. League v Leicester City (h) 19 Feb 1955. Final app: League v Everton (a) 29 Apr 1961. Transferred to Manchester United (£35,000) 20 Jul 1961.
ARSENAL Record: League 166 (97 gls); FA Cup 14 (10 gls); Other snr comp: 5 (2 gls); Football Combination 75 (37 gls); London FA Challenge Cup 10 (9 gls); Metropolitan League 1 (1 gl); Friendlies 37/1 (26 gls).
Honours: London FA Challenge Cup winners 1954-5. 5 full Scotland caps (3 gls) 1958-61.
Son of Alex Herd (Manchester City & Scotland). Served with RAF Regiment during National Service. Won club honours with Manchester United. Played for Stoke City (1968-70) until injured knee terminated his playing career. Had short spell as manager of Lincoln City. Left football to run a garage business in Manchester.

HILL, Colin Frederick   1979-86
Defender   5ft 11in. 11st.
Born: Uxbridge, 12 Nov 1963.
Jnr football: Hillingdon. Joined ARSENAL: 1979 (amateur), 1980 (apprentice), 31 Jul 1981 (professional). First app: South East Counties League v Fulham (h) 8 Dec 1979. First snr app: Snr fdly v Barnet (a) 11 Oct 1982. League v Norwich City (a) 20 Apr 1983. Final snr app: League v Watford (h) 22 Dec 1984. Snr fdly (sub) v Shamrock Rovers (a) 25 Feb 1985. Final app: Football Combination v Reading (h) 7 May 1986. Given free transfer by Arsenal at end of 1985-6 and joined CS Marítimo (Funchal), Madeira.
ARSENAL Record: League 46 (1 gl); FA Cup 1; Football League Cup 4; Football Combination 145/2 (12 gls); South East Counties League 32/2 (12 gls); FA Youth Cup 6 (1 gl); Other jnr comp: 4/1 (1 gl); Friendlies 59/6 (4 gls). In addition, made 1 app (1 gl) in Football Combination 1981-2, later removed from records .
Played for Middlesex schoolboys. Was a champion sprinter and javelin thrower as a schoolboy. Returned from Madeira in 1987 and played for Colchester United before being transferred to Sheffield United.

HILL, Frank Robert 'Tiger'   1932-36
Wing-half   5ft 6in. 11st 6lb.
Born: Forfar, Scotland, 21 May 1906. Died: Luton, Jun 1970.
Previous Clubs: Forfar Athletic (1924), Aberdeen (1928). Joined ARSENAL: 19 May 1932 from Aberdeen for £3,000. First app: London

Combination v Millwall (h) 27 Aug 1932. First snr app: Snr fdly v St Johnstone (a) 26 Sep 1932. League v Blackburn Rovers (a) 15 Oct 1932. Final snr app: League v Middlesbrough (a) 11 Apr 1936. Final app: London Combination v Portsmouth (h) 25 Apr 1936. Transferred to Blackpool 9 Jun 1936.
ARSENAL Record: League 76 (4 gls); FA Cup 2; FA Charity Shield 3; Other snr comp: 2; Football Combination 53 (5 gls); London FA Challenge Cup 3 (2 gls); Friendlies 11 (2 gls).
Honours: Division One champions 1932-3, 1933-4, 1934-5. FA Charity Shield winners 1933-4, 1934-5, runners-up 1935-6. Sheriff of London Shield winners 1932-3. Norwich Hospital Cup winners 1934-5. Played for Anglo-Scots v England XI 1935.
Won international honours with Aberdeen. Won club honours with Blackpool. Transferred from Blackpool to Southampton 1937. Appointed coach and assistant trainer to Preston North End as war broke out 1939. Was Flight Lieutenant in RAF and served in India during the war. Player-manager at Crewe Alexandra (Jul 1944-Sep 1948). Manager of Burnley (Oct 1948) and Preston North End (Aug 1954). Became coach in Baghdad, Iraq (Jan 1957). Returned to become manager of Notts County (Oct 1958) and was manager of Charlton Athletic (Nov 1961-Aug 1965).

HILLIER, David   1985-
Defender/Midfield   5ft 10in. 11st 6lb.
Born: Blackheath, 18 Dec 1969.
Jnr football: Camden (Sunday League). Joined ARSENAL: 1985 (schoolboy), Jul 1986 (apprentice), 1987-8 (professional). First app: South East Counties League (sub) v Orient (h) 18 Apr 1987. First snr app: Snr fdly (sub) v Shrewsbury Town (a) 13 Dec 1988. Football League Cup v Chester City (a) 25 Sep 1990.
ARSENAL Record: League 36/7 (1 gl); FA Cup 4/1; Football League Cup 2; FA Charity Shield 1; Other snr comp: 3; Football Combination 79/11 (2 gls); South East Counties League 36/7 (7 gls); FA Youth Cup 9 (2 gls); Other jnr comp: 1/2; Friendlies 42/6 (10 gls).
Honours: Division One champions 1990-91. FA Charity Shield medal 1991-2. Football Combination champions 1989-90. FA Youth Cup winners 1987-8 (and captain). 1 England Under-21 cap 1991.

HOAR, Sidney   1924-29
Winger   5ft 8in. 10st 7lb.
Born: Leagrave, near Luton, 1896.
Jnr football: Luton Clarence. Previous Club: Luton

Town (1911). Joined ARSENAL: 25 Nov 1924 from Luton Town for £3,000. First app: League v Cardiff City (a) 29 Nov 1924. Final snr app: FA Cup v Aston Villa (a) 2 Mar 1929. Final app: Jnr Fdly v Kettering Town (a) 3 May 1929. Transferred to Clapton Orient (£1,000) 13 Sep 1929.
ARSENAL Record: League 100 (16 gls); FA Cup 17 (2 gls); Football Combination 34 (3 gls); London FA Challenge Cup 4; Friendlies 13 (2 gls).
Honours: FA Cup runners-up 1927. London Combination champions 1926-7. London FA Challenge Cup runners-up 1925-6. Played in England international trial match 1924-5.
Was a straw-hat maker before taking up football. Was a victim of German poisonous gas whilst serving in France and his future as an athlete was in doubt. Retired from football at end of 1929-30 season.

HOARE, Gordon Rahere   1907-09 & 1910-12
Forward   5ft 10in. 11st 10lb.
Born: Blackheath, 18 Apr 1884. Died: 27 Oct 1973.
Jnr football: West Norwood, Woolwich Polytechnic; Bromley. Joined ARSENAL: 18 May 1907 (amateur). Transferred to Glossop, 10 Dec 1909. Rejoined ARSENAL: 23 Dec 1910 (amateur) from Glossop. First app: London League (Res) v Crystal Palace (a) 7 Sep 1907. First snr app: League v Sheffield Wednesday (h) 20 Apr 1908. Final app: League v Bury (a) 9 Dec 1911. Transferred to Glossop 17 Feb 1912.
ARSENAL Record: League 30 (12 gls); FA Cup 4 (1 gl); Other snr comp: 1; London FA Challenge Cup 1 (1 gl); South Eastern League 16 (7 gls); London League (Res) 3 (1 gl); Friendlies 5 (2 gls).
England Amateur international. Won gold medal with England football team in Olympic Games 1912. Also played for Queen's Park (1914) and Fulham (during wartime and in 1919-20).

HODGES, Cyril L.   1944-46
Wing-forward.
Born: Hackney, London, 18 Sep 1919. Died: Sep 1979.
School: Eleanor Road, Hackney.
Joined ARSENAL: 12 Feb 1944 (amateur), Apr 1945 (professional). First app: Wartime fdly v Fulham (a) 7 Apr 1945. First snr app: League v Blackburn Rovers (h) 4 Sep 1946. Final app: League v Blackpool (a) 5 Oct 1946. Transferred to Brighton & Hove Albion 14 Oct 1946.
ARSENAL Record: League 2; Football Combination 7 (7 gls). In addition, made 9 apps (3 gls) during wartime.
Played for Hackney schoolboys. Became assistant trainer at Brighton, 1956-7.

HOLLINS, John William MBE   1979-83
Full-back/midfield   5ft 7¾in. 11st 5lb.
Born: Guildford, 16 Jul 1946.
Jnr football: Guildford Juniors. Previous Clubs: Chelsea, Jul 1963 (professional), Queen's Park Rangers (Jul 1975). Joined ARSENAL: 15 Jul 1979 from Queen's Park Rangers for £75,000. First app: On tour (sub) v München 1860 (at Duisberg) 28 Jul 1979. League (sub) v Brighton (a) 18 Aug 1979. Final app: League (sub) v Norwich City (a) 20 Apr 1983. Snr fdly v Gillingham (a) 17 May 1983. Released by Arsenal to become player-coach at Chelsea May 1983.
ARSENAL Record: League 123/4 (9 gls); FA Cup 12; FA Charity Shield 0/1; Football League Cup 19/1 (3 gls); European Competitions 10/3 (1 gl); Football Combination 22 (1 gl); Friendlies 24/4 (2 gls).
Honours: European Cup-winners' Cup runners-up 1980; FA Charity Shield runners-up 1979-80. Arsenal Player of the Year 1982.
Son of Bill Hollins (Stoke & Wolves) and brother of Dave Hollins (Newcastle & Wales). Played for Guildford schoolboys. Won domestic and

European competition honours and Youth, Under-23, 'B', and full international honours whilst at Chelsea. Awarded MBE in 1982. Was manager of Chelsea, Jul 1985 to Mar 1988.

HOLTON, Clifford Charles   1947-58
Centre-forward/wing-half   6ft. 13st 10lb.
Born: Oxford, 29 Apr 1929.
School: St Mary & St John, Cowley, Oxford.
Jnr football: Marston Minors, Oxford City. Joined ARSENAL: 22 Oct 1947 (amateur), 19 Nov 1947 (professional) from Oxford City. First app: Jnr fdly v Cambridge University (a) 23 Oct 1947. First snr app: League v Stoke City (a) 26 Dec 1950. Final app: League v Burnley (a) 2 Sep 1958. Southern Floodlit Challenge Cup v Aldershot (a) 15 Oct 1958. Transferred to Watford (£10,000) 20 Oct 1958.
ARSENAL Record: League 198 (83 gls); FA Cup 18 (5 gls); FA Charity Shield 1; Other snr comp: 4 (2 gls); Football Combination 121 (98 gls); London FA Challenge Cup 7 (8 gls); Eastern Counties League 13 (1 gl); London Midweek League 5; Friendlies 51/2 (31 gls).
Honours: Played for Oxford schoolboys. Division One champions 1952-3. FA Cup runners-up 1952. FA Charity Shield winners 1953-4. Football Combination champions 1950-51. London FA Challenge Cup winners 1954-5. Captain of Arsenal.

Was an apprentice at Morris Motors. Served National Service in the Army (1947-9) and played for the Army in representative matches. Played cricket for Oxfordshire and Middlesex Second XI. After Watford played for Northampton Town (Sep 1961), Crystal Palace (Dec 1962), Watford (May 1965), Charlton Athletic (Feb 1966) and Orient (Jul 1966). Won club honours with Watford and Crystal Palace and broke goalscoring records at Watford and Northampton. Retired from football because of a knee injury (Nov 1967). Ran his own precision engineering business in Stonebridge until 1989 before working part-time for a sports marketing firm.

HOPKINS, James   1919-23
Inside-forward   5ft 7in. 10st 3lb.
Born: Belfast, N.Ireland, 12 Jul 1901.
Jnr football: Willowfield United, Belfast United. Joined ARSENAL: Sep 1919 from Belfast. First

app: London Combination v Millwall (h) 6 Sep 1919.
First snr app: Snr fdly v Nottingham Forest (h) 5 Mar 1921. League v West Bromwich Albion (a) 29 Mar 1921. Final snr app: League v Newcastle United (a) 21 Oct 1922. Final app: London Combination v Millwall (a) 15 Jan 1923. Transferred to Brighton & Hove Albion 29 Jan 1923.
ARSENAL Record: League 21 (7 gls); FA Cup 1; Other snr comp: 2; Football Combination 47 (9 gls); London FA Challenge Cup 3; Friendlies 15 (9 gls).
Honours: Southend Hospital Cup winners 1920-21, 1921-2.
Was often troubled with illness whilst at Arsenal. Won international honours with Brighton. Later played for Aldershot.

HORNSBY, Brian Geoffrey   1970-76
Midfield   5ft 8in. 10st 7lb.
Born: Great Shelford, Cambridge, 10 Sep 1954.
School: Sir Harry Smith, Whittersley (Peterborough).
Jnr football: Had trials with Peterborough, Leicester City, Bristol C. Joined ARSENAL: 1969 (schoolboy); 27 May 1970 (apprentice); 10 Sep 1971 (professional). First app: Jnr fdly v Hounslow (a) 5 Aug 1970. First snr app: Snr fdly v Plymouth Argyle (a) 17 Oct 1972. League v Leeds United (a) 9 May 1973. Final snr app: League v Derby County (h) 8 Nov 1975. Final app: Football Combination v Oxford United (a) 26 Apr 1976. Transferred to Shrewsbury Town (£20,000) 19 May 1976.
ARSENAL Record: League 23/3 (6 gls); Other snr comp: 1 (1 gl); Football Combination 118/3 (27 gls); London FA Challenge Cup 3 (2 gls); FA Youth Cup 19 (9 gls); South East Counties League 57 (16 gls); Other jnr comp: 2; Friendlies 59/6 (16 gls).
Honours: Played for Peterborough schoolboys and Cambridgeshire schoolboys. England Schoolboy international (1969-70). FA Youth Cup winners 1970-71. South East Counties League champions 1971-2. South East Counties League Cup winners 1970-71, runners-up 1971-2. 6 England Youth caps 1973.
Later played for Sheffield Wednesday (Mar 1978), Chester (loan 1981), Carlisle United (Aug 1982), Edmonton Drillers (NASL) and Chesterfield (loan 1983-4).

HORSINGTON, Richard T.   1889-90
Outside-right.
Previous Club: Swindon Town. Joined ARSENAL: 1889 from Swindon Town. First app: Snr fdly v Vulcan (Willesden) 5 Jan 1889. First first-class app: FA Cup (Q) v Lyndhurst (h) 5 Oct 1889. Final first-class app: FA Cup (Q) v Norwich Thorpe (a) 26 Oct 1889. Final app: Reserves v Cray Wanderers (h) 4 Oct 1890.
ARSENAL Record: FA Cup (Q) 2 (1 gl). In addition made 31 senior (9 gls) and 2 reserve apps (2 gls) for Royal Arsenal between 1888-89 and 1890-91.
Honours: London Senior Cup runners-up 1889-90.

HOWARD, Patrick   1976-77
Central defender   5ft 11in. 12st.
Born: Dodworth, nr Barnsley, 7 Oct 1947
Previous Clubs: Barnsley 1962 (apprentice); 1965 (professional), Newcastle United (Sep 1971). Joined ARSENAL: 9 Sep 1976 from Newcastle United for £50,000. First app: League v West Ham United (a) 11 Sep 1976. Final app: On tour v Roros (Norway) 20 May 1977. Transferred to Birmingham (£40,000) 17 Aug 1977.
ARSENAL Record: League 15/1; Football League Cup 4; Football Combination 16 (2 gls); Friendlies 8/1.
Won club honours whilst with Barnsley and

63

Newcastle United. Transferred from Birmingham to Bury (Jul 1979). Released by Bury at end of 1981-2. Owns a sports shop in Bury.

HOWAT, David   **1889-96**
Half-back   5ft 8½in. 11st 10lb.
Born: Preston, 1 Oct 1870.
Jnr football: Fishwick Ramblers. Previous Club: Preston North End Reserves (2 seasons). Joined ARSENAL: Early 1889 as an amateur, then as professional. First app: Friendly v 2nd Rifle Brigade, 1 Apr 1889. First first-class app: FA Cup (Q) v Lyndhurst (h) 5 Oct 1889. Final snr app: League v Loughborough Town (h) 4 Jan 1896. Snr fdly v Nat Whittaker's London XI (h) 20 Apr 1896. Final app: Jnr fdly v Luton Town Res (a) 25 Apr 1896.
ARSENAL Record: League 56 (2 gls); FA Cup 8; FA Cup (Q) 8 (1 gl); Kent League 17; Friendlies 71 (4 gls). In addition made 143 senior (10 gls) and 8 reserve (3 gls) apps for Royal Arsenal between 1888-9 and 1892-3.
Honours: London Senior Cup winners 1890-91, runners-up 1889-90. London Charity Cup winners 1889-90. Kent Senior Cup winners 1889-90.
Was an engineer by trade before becoming a professional footballer. After Arsenal, played for Third Lanark Reserves (1896-7).

HOWE, Donald
Player 1964-67   **Manager 1983-86**
Full-back   5ft 11in. 10st 13lb.
Born: Wolverhampton, 12 Oct 1935.
School: St Peter's, Wolverhampton.
Previous Club: West Bromwich Albion 1951 (amateur), 1952 (professional). Joined ARSENAL: 21 Apr 1964 from West Bromwich Albion for £42,000. First app: On tour v Transvaal (South Africa) 14 May 1964. League v Liverpool (a) 22 Aug 1964. Final snr app: On tour v NEA Salamis (Cyprus) 31 May 1967. Final app: Football Combination Cup v Plymouth (a) 18 Oct 1967. Retired and became Arsenal chief coach, 27 Oct 1967.
ARSENAL Record: League 70 (1 gl); FA Cup 3; Football League Cup 1; Football Combination 41; London FA Challenge Cup 3; Metropolitan League 2; Friendlies 39/5 (6 gls).
Won England Under-23, 'B' and full international caps whilst at West Brom. Suffered a broken leg with Arsenal, Mar 1966. From chief coach at Arsenal, became assistant manager, Mar 1969. Left Arsenal to become manager of West Bromwich Albion, Jul 1971. After spells as coach at Galatasaray (Turkey) and Leeds United, rejoined Arsenal as chief coach, 9 Aug 1977. Also took on the duties of coach to the England team. Became caretaker manager at Arsenal, Dec 1983 and manager, 28 Apr 1984. Was released from his contract, Mar 1986, at his own request. Was coach at Wimbledon and Queen's Park Rangers before becoming manager of that club. Resigned his England post in Aug 1990. Now manager of Coventry City.

HUDSON, Alan Anthony   **1976-78**
Midfield   5ft 10½in. 12st 1lb.
Born: Chelsea, 21 Jun 1951.
Previous Clubs: Chelsea (schoolboy); 1966 (apprentice); Jul 1968 (professional), Stoke City (Jan 1974). Joined ARSENAL: 13 Dec 1976 from Stoke City for £200,000. First app: Football Combination v Chelsea (h) 1 Jan 1977. First snr app: League v Sunderland (h) 3 Jan 1977. Final app: League v Derby County (a) 9 May 1978. Snr fdly v Tottenham Hotspur (a) 3 May 1978. Transferred to Seattle Sounders (USA) (£120,000) 20 Oct 1978.
ARSENAL Record: League 36; FA Cup 7;

Football League Cup 3/1; Football Combination 9 (1 gl); Friendlies 10.
Honours: FA Cup runners-up 1978.
Played for London schoolboys. Won club and Under-23 honours with Chelsea. Won full international honours with Stoke City. Returned from America, 1983-4, and had further spells with Chelsea and Stoke City. Now a night-club owner in Stoke-on-Trent.

HUGHES, Joseph   **1925**
Centre-forward   5ft 9in. 11st 10lb.
Born: Manchester, 4 Jun 1902.
School: Local Secondary.
Jnr football: Gorton, New Cross (Manchester), Bolton Wanderers Reserves, Guildford United (1924-5). Previous Club: Chelsea (amateur and professional) before Guildford United. Joined ARSENAL: 10 Mar 1925 from Guildford United. First app: London Combination v Crystal Palace (a) 21 Mar 1925. First snr app: League v West Bromwich Albion (a) 13 Apr 1925 (only first-class app). Final snr app: Snr fdly v Luton Town (h) 20 Apr 1925 (scored hat-trick). Final app: London Combination v Southend (a) 25 Dec 1925.
ARSENAL Record: League 1; Football Combination 5 (2 gls); Friendlies 2 (3 gls).
Was appointed schoolmaster at St Mary's College, Hammersmith and joined Chelsea as an amateur. Received a severe knee injury playing for Arsenal reserves soon after making his League debut, which brought a premature end to his playing career.

HULME, Joseph Harold Anthony   **1926-38**
Outside-right   5ft 8½in. 10st 11lb.
Born: Stafford, 26 Aug 1904. Died: Winchmore Hill, 26 Sep 1991.

Jnr football: Stafford YMCA. Previous Clubs: York City (1923); Blackburn Rovers (Feb 1924). Joined ARSENAL: 5 Feb 1926 from Blackburn Rovers for £3,500. First app: League v Leeds United (a) 6 Feb 1926. Final app: League v Liverpool (a) 18 Dec 1937. Transferred to Huddersfield Town 6 Jan 1938.
ARSENAL Record: League 333 (107 gls); FA Cup 39 (17 gls); FA Charity Shield 2 (1 gl); Other snr comp: 4 (3 gls); Football Combination 48 (26 gls); London FA Challenge Cup 6 (2 gls); London Midweek League 4 (1 gl); Friendlies 24 (12 gls).
Honours: Division One champions 1930-31, 1932-3, 1934-5. FA Cup winners 1930, 1936, runners-up 1927, 1932. FA Charity Shield winners 1930-31, 1931-2.

Sheriff of London Shield winners 1930-31, 1932-3. Northampton Charity Shield winners 1929-30, 1930-31. 9 full England caps (4 gls) 1927-33 and, made 6 apps (3 gls) for Football League 1926-32.
Played cricket for Middlesex 1929-39. Won club honours with Huddersfield Town. Retired from playing at end of 1937-8. Was a reserve policeman during World War Two. Assistant-secretary of Tottenham Hotspur (Feb 1944) and manager (Oct 1945-May 1949). Became a journalist with *The People*. Retired 1968.

HUMPISH, Albert Edward   **1930**
Half-back   5ft 8½in. 11st 11lb.
Born: Newcastle.
Jnr football: Walker Celtic. Previous Clubs: Bury (1923-4), Wigan Borough (1925). Joined ARSENAL: 8 Jan 1930 from Wigan Borough. First app: London Combination v Cardiff City (h) 18 Jan 1930. First snr app: League v Derby County (a) 19 Feb 1930. Final snr app: League v Newcastle United (a) 5 Apr 1930. Final app: Jnr fdly v Oxford University (h) 3 Dec 1930. Transferred to Bristol City 12 Dec 1930.
ARSENAL Record: League 3; Football Combination 21; London Midweek League 2; Friendlies 1.
Honours: London Combination champions 1929-30.
Played for Bristol City 1930-32. Later became trainer at Rochdale.

HUNT, Fergus   **1897-1900 & 1902-03**
Forward   5ft 8in. 12st.
Born: 1876.
Jnr football: Mexborough. Previous Clubs: Middlesbrough Ironopolis, Darwen. Joined ARSENAL: 21 May 1897 from Darwen. Rejoined ARSENAL: 17 Oct 1902 from West Ham. First app: League v Grimsby Town (h) 1 Sep 1897. Final snr app: League v Stockport County (h) 28 Feb 1903. Final app: Chatham Charity Cup v Chatham (a) 27 Apr 1903. Transferred to West Ham United summer 1900 and to Fulham summer 1903.
ARSENAL Record: League 72 (30 gls); FA Cup 9 (5 gls); United League 28 (12 gls); Southern District Combination 7 (1 gl); Other snr comp: 1; Kent League 13 (8 gls); London League (Res) 10 (3 gls); Other jnr comp: 6 (2 gls); Friendlies 29 (10 gls).
Honours: West Kent League champions 1902-03. Chatham Charity Cup runners-up 1902-03.
Later played for Burton United (1905-07).

HUNT, George Samuel   **1937-38**
Inside/centre-forward   5ft 8½in. 10st 3lb.
Born: Barnsley, 22 Feb 1910.
School: Regent St Congregationals (Barnsley).
Jnr football: Barnsley (trial), Sheffield United (trial). Previous Clubs: Chesterfield (1929), Tottenham Hotspur (Jun 1930). Joined ARSENAL: 1 Oct 1937 from Tottenham Hotspur. First app: League v Manchester City (h) 2 Oct 1937. Final app: League v Portsmouth (a) 26 Feb 1938. Final app: London Combination v Brighton (h) 12 Mar 1938. Transferred to Bolton Wanderers 16 Mar 1938.
ARSENAL Record: League 18 (3 gls); FA Cup 3; Football Combination 12 (6 gls); Friendlies 1 (1 gl).
Honours: Division One champions 1937-8.
Won club and international honours with Tottenham Hotspur. Transferred from Bolton Wanderers to Sheffield Wednesday (Nov 1946). Was coach and trainer at Bolton Wanderers (May 1948-Sep 1968).

HUNTER, John 'Sailor'   **1904-05**
Inside-forward   5ft 6in. 10st 7lb.
Born: Johnstone, Renfrewshire, Scotland, 6 Apr 1878. Died: 12 Jan 1966.
Jnr football: Westmarch (Paisley), Abercorn.

Previous Clubs: Liverpool (1899-1902), Heart of Midlothian. Joined ARSENAL: 3 May 1904 from Hearts. First app: Snr fdly v Bristol City (h) 1 Sep 1904. League v Newcastle United (a) 3 Sep 1904. Final app: League v Everton (h) 22 Apr 1905. Snr fdly v Norwich City (a) 27 Apr 1905. Transferred to Portsmouth summer 1905. ARSENAL Record: League 22 (4 gls); Other snr comp: 1; Friendlies 7 (7 gls). After Portsmouth, played for Dundee (1907), Clyde (1910) and Motherwell. Won Scotland international honours with Dundee. Became manager of Motherwell (May 1911-May 1946) and then secretary until 1959.

HUTCHINS, Arthur Victor   1916-23
Left-back   5ft 10½in. 12st 6lb.
Born: Bishop Waltham, Southampton, 15 Sep 1890. Died: 1948.
Previous Club: Croydon Common (Southern League). Joined ARSENAL: Apr 1919 from Croydon Common for £50, having assisted Arsenal as a 'guest player' during wartime. First app: London Combination (wartime) v West Ham United (a) 2 Sep 1916. First snr app: League v Sunderland (a) 13 Sep 1919. Final snr app: League v Sunderland (h) 25 Nov 1922. Final app: London Combination v Brentford (h) 5 May 1923. Transferred to Charlton Athletic 31 Jul 1923. ARSENAL Record: League 104 (1 gl); FA Cup 4; Other snr comp: 3; Football Combination 26 (5 gls); London FA Challenge Cup 6 (1 gl); Friendlies 10 (1 gl). In addition, made 102 apps (2 gls) during wartime.
Honours: London Combination champions 1922-3. London FA Challenge Cup winners 1921-2. Southend Hospital Cup winners 1920-21, 1921-2. Metropolitan Hospital Cup winners 1920-21.
Played in England international trial 1920-21. Retired from soccer in 1926 and later became a publican in Peckham.

HYNDS, Thomas   1906-07
Centre-half   5ft 10in. 12st 8lb.
Born: Hurlford, Scotland, c.1880.
Previous Clubs: Glasgow Celtic, Manchester City (Sep 1901). Joined ARSENAL: 6 Dec 1906 from Manchester City. First app: League v Sheffield Wednesday (a) 1 Jan 1907. Final app: League v Notts County (a) 17 Apr 1907. Transferred to Leeds City 15 May 1907.
ARSENAL Record: League 13; FA Cup 4 (1 gl). Won club honours with Manchester City. Was involved in illegal payments at Manchester City and was still serving a suspension when he signed for Arsenal. After playing career ended, he became a coach in British Columbia and Italy.

JACK, David Bone Nightingale   1928-34
Inside-forward   5ft 10in. 11st 8lb.
Born: Bolton, 3 Apr 1899. Died: London, 10 Sep 1958.
School: Leigh Road (Westcliff, Southend).
Jnr football: Plymouth Presbyterians, Royal Navy. Previous Clubs: Plymouth Argyle (1919), Bolton Wanderers (Dec 1920-£3,000). Joined ARSENAL: 13 Oct 1928 from Bolton Wanderers for £10,890 (record). First app: League v Newcastle United (a) 20 Oct 1928. Final app: League v Sheffield United (h) 5 May 1934. Retired and appointed manager of Southend United, 9 May 1934.
ARSENAL Record: League 181 (113 gls); FA Cup 25 (10 gls); FA Charity Shield 2 (1 gl); Other snr comp: 4 (2 gls); Football Combination 2 (5 gls); London FA Challenge Cup 2; Friendlies 15 (11 gls).
Honours: Division One champions 1930-31, 1932-3, 1933-4. FA Cup winners 1930, runners-up 1932. FA Charity Shield winners 1930-31, 1931-2. Sheriff

of London Shield winners 1930-31, 1932-3. Northampton Charity Shield winners 1929-30, 1930-31. 5 full England caps (2 gls) 1930-32. Captain of England (first Arsenal player to do so). Made 2 apps (1 gl) for the Football League 1929-30.
Son of Robert Jack (Bolton Wanderers, Plymouth Argyle and manager of Southend United, Plymouth Argyle). Brother of Rollo Jack (Bolton Wanderers). He served with the Royal Navy during World War One. Won club, international and Football League honours with Bolton Wanderers. Scorer of the first FA Cup Final goal at Wembley. He was manager of Southend United (1934-Aug 1940), Middlesbrough (Sep 1944-Apr 1952) and Shelbourne, Dublin (Aug 1953-Apr 1955). Was employed by the Air Ministry when he died.

JACKSON, James   1899-1905
Left-back   5ft 8½in. 11st 12lb.
Born: Cambuslang, Scotland, 15 Sep 1875.
Jnr football: Emmdale Rosebud(Australia), Newton Thistles. Previous Clubs: Glasgow Rangers, Newcastle United. Joined ARSENAL: 10 May 1899 from Newcastle United. First app: League v Leicester Fosse (h) 2 Sep 1899. Final app: League v Everton (h) 22 Apr 1905. Snr fdly v Dundee (h) 24 Apr 1905. Left Arsenal, summer 1905 to become player-manager of Leyton (Southern League).
ARSENAL Record: League 183; FA Cup 21 (1 gl); Southern District Combination 12; London League 16; Other snr comp: 4; Friendlies 32.
Honours: Division Two runners-up (promotion) 1903-04. Southern Professional Charity Cup runners-up 1903-04. Captain of Arsenal.
Emigrated with his family to Australia when he was two years old. Returned to Scotland when he was 18 years old. Had a sports outfitters shop just outside the Manor Ground, Plumstead, when he was an Arsenal player. Played in an FA trial in 1901-02. He played for West Ham United (1905-06) and returned to Scotland with Glasgow Rangers (May 1906). Became a blacksmith at Greenock and played for Morton (1911). His son, Revd James Jackson was a player and captain of Liverpool.

JAQUES, G.H.   1894
Outside-left.
Born: c.1875.
Joined ARSENAL: 10 Mar 1894 from Rushden. First app: Jnr fdly v Dartford (a) 10 Mar 1894.

First snr app: League v Northwich Victoria (h) 23 Mar 1894. Final app: Snr fdly v Nottingham Forest (h) 2 Apr 1894.
ARSENAL Record: League 2 (2 gls); Friendlies 3 (1 gl).

JAMES, Alexander Wilson   1929-37
Inside-left   5ft 6in. 11st.
Born: Mossend, Lanarkshire, 14 Sep 1901. Died: London, 1 Jun 1953.
School: Bellshill Academy.
Jnr football: Brandon Amateurs, Orbiston Celtic, Ashfield (Glasgow). Previous Clubs: Motherwell (trial), Raith Rovers (1922), Preston North End (1925). Joined ARSENAL: 1 Jun 1929 from Preston North End for £8,750. First app: League v Leeds United (h) 31 Aug 1929. Final app: League v Bolton Wanderers (h) 1 May 1937. On tour v Feyenoord (Rotterdam) 6 Jun 1937. Retired Jun 1937.
ARSENAL Record: League 231 (26 gls); FA Cup 28 (1 gl); FA Charity Shield 2; Other snr comp: 3; Football Combination 7 (1 gl); Friendlies 11 (2 gls). In addition played in 2 Charity matches (1949, 1951).

Honours: Division One champions 1930-31, 1932-3, 1933-4, 1934-5. FA Cup winners 1930, 1936. FA Charity Shield winners 1931-2, 1933-4. Sheriff of London Shield winners 1930-31. Northampton Charity Shield winners 1929-30. Bath Coronation Cup winners 1936-7. Captain of Arsenal. 4 full Scotland caps (1 gl) 1929-32.
Worked as a checking clerk at a steelworks before professional football. Won international honours whilst at Preston North End. After football he became a journalist with the *News of the World*. Served in the Army during World War Two. Returned to Arsenal as coach to the juniors (Jan 1949).

JEFFREY, William Walls   1892-94
Full-back   5ft 9in. 11st 9lb.
Born: Dalderby, Lincolnshire, c.1868.
Jnr football: West Manchester. Previous Clubs: Lincoln City, Grimsby Town, Gainsborough Trinity, Burnley. Joined ARSENAL: 1891-2 season from Burnley. First app: Snr fdly v Everton (h) 26 Mar 1892. First first-class app: FA Cup (Q) v Highland Light Infantry (h) 15 Oct 1892. Final app: League v Burton Swifts (h) 14 Apr 1894. Snr fdly v Stoke (h) 28 Apr 1894. Transferred to Southampton St Mary's summer 1894.
ARSENAL Record: League 22; FA Cup 2; FA Cup (Q) 7; Friendlies 24 (1 gl). In addition, made 61 senior (2 gls) and 2 reserve apps for Royal Arsenal during 1891-2 and 1892-3.

His League and FA Cup apps for Arsenal include a number of matches played as goalkeeper. Played only one season for Southampton St Mary's (1894-5).

JENKINS, David John   **1962-68**
Midfield   5ft 8¼in. 10st 12lb.
Born: Bristol, 2 Sep 1946.
School: Wick Road, Bristol.
Joined ARSENAL: Jul 1962 (apprentice), 21 Oct 1963 (professional). First app: South East Counties League v Fulham (h) 18 Aug 1962. First snr app: Football League Cup v Gillingham (a) 21 Sep 1966. Final app: League v Coventry City (h) 12 Oct 1968. Transferred to Tottenham Hotspur (in exchange for J.Robertson) 17 Oct 1968.
ARSENAL Record: League 16/1 (3 gls); FA Cup 2 (1 gl); Football League Cup 6 (5 gls); Football Combination 79 (17 gls); London FA Challenge Cup 4 (2 gls); FA Youth Cup 14 (9 gls); Metropolitan League 91 (21 gls); South East Counties League 41 (18 gls); Other jnr comp: 9 (2 gls); Friendlies 66/7 (24 gls).
Honours: Played for Bristol schoolboys. Football League Cup runners-up 1967-8. Football Combination Cup winners 1967-8. London FA Challenge Cup runners-up 1967-8. FA Youth Cup runners-up 1964-5. Metropolitan League Challenge Cup winners 1965-6. Southern Junior Floodlit Cup winners 1963. London Minor Challenge Cup runners-up 1964-5.
Broke his leg in a pre-season practice match 1965-6. After Tottenham Hotspur he played for Brentford (1972), Hereford United (loan), Newport County, Shrewsbury Town (1974) and, after a short spell in South Africa, returned to play for Workington (Oct 1975).

JENKYNS, Caesar Augustus Llewelyn 1895-96
Centre-half   5ft 10in. 14st 6lb.
Born: Builth Wells, Wales, 24 Aug 1866. Died: Birmingham, 23 Jul 1941.
Jnr football: Builth; Small Heath St Andrew's, Unity Gas FC, Small Heath Alliance (before League entry). Previous Club: Small Heath (1888). Joined ARSENAL: 30 Apr 1895 from Small Heath. First app: League v Grimsby Town (h) 2 Sep 1895. Final app: League v Darwen (h) 18 Apr 1896. Snr fdly v Tottenham Hotspur (a) 30 Apr 1896. Transferred to Newton Heath May 1896.
ARSENAL Record: League 27 (6 gls); Kent League 1; Friendlies 27 (3 gls).
Honours: Captain of Arsenal. 1 full Wales cap 1896.
Was Arsenal's first current international player. After Newton Heath, played for Walsall and Coventry. Won further international honours with Small Heath, Newton Heath and Walsall. In retirement became a publican in Birmingham.

JENNINGS, Patrick Anthony MBE, OBE   1977-85
Goalkeeper   6ft. 13st 2lb.
Born: Newry, Co Down, 12 Jun 1945.
School: Newry.
Jnr football: Newry United, Newry Town. Previous Clubs: Watford (May 1963), Tottenham Hotspur (Jun 1964-£27,000). Joined ARSENAL: 6 Aug 1977 from Tottenham Hotspur for £45,000. First app: Snr fdly v Luton Town (a) 12 Aug 1977. League v Ipswich Town (a) 20 Aug 1977. Final snr app: Testimonial v Tottenham Hotspur (h) 8 May 1985. Final app: Football Combination v Luton Town (h) 11 May 1985. Retired Jun 1985. Rejoined Tottenham Hotspur on a non-contract basis 1986.
ARSENAL Record: League 237; FA Cup 38; FA Charity Shield 1; Football League Cup 32; European Competitions 19; Football Combination 35; Friendlies 51/2.
Honours: FA Cup winners 1979, runners-up 1978, 1980. European Cup-winners' Cup runners-up

1979-80. FA Charity Shield runners-up 1979-80. 42 full Northern Ireland caps 1977-85.
Won Youth, Under-23 and full international honours with Watford. Won domestic and European competition club honours and full international honours with Tottenham Hotspur. Footballer of the Year 1973. PFA Player of the Year 1976. Awarded the MBE in 1976 and the OBE in 1987. Held the world record for the most international caps (119) until Peter Shilton surpassed it in the 1990 World Cup finals.

JOBEY, George   **1913-14**
Half-back   5ft 8½in. 12st 2lb.
Born: Heddon-on-the-Wall, Tyneside, 1886. Died: Chaddesden, Derby, 9 May 1962.
Jnr football: Morpeth Harriers. Previous Club: Newcastle United. Joined ARSENAL: 5 May 1913 from Newcastle United. First app: League v Leicester Fosse (h) 6 Sep 1913. Final app: League v Bristol City (h) 4 Apr 1914. Friendly (wartime) v West Ham United (a) 3 May 1919 (as a guest). Transferred to Bradford 18 Jun 1914.
ARSENAL Record: League 28 (3 gls); London FA Challenge Cup 3 (1 gl); Other snr comp: 1. In addition made 6 apps during wartime as a 'guest' player.
Won club honours with Newcastle United. Was the scorer of the first goal at Highbury. After Bradford, played for Hamilton Academical (wartime) and Leicester Fosse. Became player-manager of Northampton Town (1921) and manager of Wolverhampton Wanderers (1922). Was manager of Derby County (1925-41). Had a short spell as manager of Mansfield Town (1952).

JOHN, Robert Frederick   **1922-37**
Left-half   5ft 7½in. 11st 4lb.
Born: Barry Dock, South Wales, 3 Feb 1899. Died: Barry, 17 Jul 1982.
Jnr football: Barry Town, Caerphilly Town. Joined ARSENAL: 17 Jan 1922 from Caerphilly Town. First app: London Combination v West Ham (a) 21 Jan 1922. First snr app: Snr fdly v Southampton (a) 16 Oct 1922. League v Newcastle United (h) 28 Oct 1922. Final snr app: League v Birmingham (h) 20 Mar 1937. Final app: London Combination v Southend (a) 11 Dec 1937. Retired end of 1937-8 season.
ARSENAL Record: League 421 (12 gls); FA Cup 46 (1 gl); FA Charity Shield 3; Other snr comp: 8 (2 gls); Football Combination 85 (2 gls); London

FA Challenge Cup 9; London Midweek League 1 (1 gl); Friendlies 53 (1 gl).
Honours: Division One champions 1930-31, 1932-3, 1933-4. FA Cup winners 1930, runners-up 1927, 1932. FA Charity Shield winners 1930-31, 1933-4, 1934-5. London Combination champions 1922-3, 1936-7. London FA Challenge Cup runners-up 1925-6. Southend Hospital Cup winners 1921-2. Northampton Charity Shield winners 1929-30, 1930-31, 1931-2. Sheriff of London Shield winners 1930-31, 1932-3. Norwich Hospital Cup winners 1934-5. 15 full Wales caps 1923-36.
On retiring became coach at West Ham (1938). After the war, had spells as trainer and then manager of Torquay United, trainer at Crystal Palace and coaching/scouting activities at Cardiff City.

JOHNSTON, George   **1967-69**
Inside-forward   5ft 7in. 10st 5lb.
Born: Glasgow, 21 Mar 1947.
Jnr football: St George Road Youth; Maryhill (Glasgow). Previous Club: Cardiff City (amateur), May 1964 (professional). Joined ARSENAL: 13 Mar 1967 from Cardiff City for £25,000. First app: Football Combination v Northampton Town (h) 18 Mar 1967. First snr app: Snr fdly v Apoel (Cyprus) (h) 3 May 1967. League v Stoke City (h) 19 Aug 1967. Final snr app: League (sub) v Ipswich Town (h) 18 Feb 1969. Final app: Football Combination v Gillingham (a) 29 Apr 1969. Transferred to Birmingham City 15 May 1969.
ARSENAL Record: League 17/4 (3 gls); Football League Cup 3/1; Football Combination 57 (34 gls); London FA Challenge Cup 1; Metropolitan League 1; Friendlies 14/4 (12 gls).
Honours: Football Combination champions 1968-9. Football Combination Cup winners 1967-8.
Played for Glasgow schoolboys. Won club honours with Cardiff City. After Birmingham, played for Walsall (loan), Fulham (Oct 1970), Hereford United (Aug 1972) and Newport County (Sep 1973).

JOHNSTONE, William   **1929-31**
Inside-forward   5ft 10in. 12st 7lb.
Born: Fife, Scotland, 18 May 1900.
Jnr football: Fife and Rosyth Juniors, Kings Park. Previous Clubs: Dundee United, Clyde, Reading (Sep 1926). Joined ARSENAL: 4 May 1929 from Reading. First app: London Combination v Portsmouth (a) 2 Sep 1929. First snr app: League v Sheffield Wednesday (a) 7 Sep 1929. Final snr app: League v Sunderland (a) 13 Sep 1930. Final app: London Combination v Clapton Orient (h) 1 Jan 1931. Transferred to Oldham Athletic (£2,130) 2 Jan 1931.
ARSENAL Record: League 9 (4 gls); Football Combination 40 (21 gls); London FA Challenge Cup 1 (1 gl); London Midweek League 7 (1 gl); Friendlies 4 (3 gls).
Honours: London Combination champions 1929-30, 1930-31.
Was never on the losing side in his first-team apps for Arsenal. Later played for Clyde again (1935).

JONES, Brynmor   **1938-49**
Inside-forward   5ft 6½in. 10st 7lb.
Born: Merthyr Tydfil, Wales, 14 Feb 1912. Died: North London, 18 Oct 1985.
School: Queen's Road, Merthyr.
Jnr football: Merthyr Amateurs; Aberaman (1933). Previous Clubs: Glenavon (Ireland) (1931), Wolverhampton Wanderers (Oct 1933). Joined ARSENAL: 4 Aug 1938 from Wolverhampton Wanderers for £14,000 (record). First app: Football Jubilee Fund v Tottenham Hotspur (h) 20 Aug 1938. League v Portsmouth (h) 27 Aug 1938. Final app: League v Everton (a) 16 Apr 1949. On tour v São Paulo (Brazil) 4 Jun 1949. Transferred to

orwich City as player-coach 24 Jun 1949.
RSENAL Record: League 71 (7 gls); FA Cup
FA Charity Shield 2 (1 gl); Other snr comp:
Football Combination 9 (3 gls); Friendlies 17/
(1 gl). In addition played 3 League matches
939-40 prior to outbreak of war and made 25
ops (6 gls) during wartime.
onours: FA Charity Shield winners 1938-9, 1948-
Mayor of Colchester Cup winners 1938-9. 7 England
ales caps (3 gls) 1938-48 and made 8 inter-
ational apps (1 gl) during wartime.
orked in the pit at Merthyr Tydfil before playing
ootball. Two of his brothers also played
rofessional football. Won international honours
ith Wolverhampton Wanderers. Served in Royal
rtillery in Italy and North Africa during the war.
etired from football in 1950 on doctor's advice.
an a newsagent/tobacconist business at Stoke
ewington from 1951 to retirement in 1979.

ONES, Charles   **1928-34**
utside-left/wing-half   5ft 7in. 11st 5lb.
orn: Troedyrhiw, South Wales, 12 Dec 1899.
ied: Brentwood, Apr 1966.
revious Clubs: Cardiff City (1920), Stockport
ounty (1921), Oldham Athletic (Mar 1923),
ottingham Forest (1925). Joined ARSENAL: 18
lay 1928 from Nottingham Forest. First app:
n tour v Danish FA (Denmark) 20 May 1928.
eague v Sheffield Wednesday (a) 25 Aug 1928.
inal app: League v Chelsea (a) 28 Apr 1934.
etired and became manager of Notts County
k May 1934).
RSENAL Record: League 176 (8 gls); FA Cup
7; FA Charity Shield 2; Other snr comp: 3;
ootball Combination 24 (8 gls); London FA
hallenge Cup 5 (1 gl); London Midweek League
Friendlies 12 (2 gls).
lonours: Division One champions 1930-31, 1932-3,
933-4. FA Cup runners-up 1932. FA Charity
hield winners 1931-2, 1933-4. Sheriff of London
hield winners 1930-31. Northampton Charity
hield winners 1930-31, 1931-2. Captain of
Arsenal and Wales. Won 4 Wales caps 1929-33.
Von club honours with Stockport County. Won
international honours with Nottingham Forest.
n retirement from football became a successful
usiness man in Liverpool.

ONES, Frederick John   **1923-24**
nside-forward.
orn: Greenwich, 11 Dec 1898.
oined ARSENAL: 16 Jun 1923 from Royal
lavy. First app: Jnr fdly v Guildford (a) 28 Aug
923. First snr app: League v Burnley (a) 28 Apr
924. Final app: League v Preston North End
n) 3 May 1924.
RSENAL Record: League 2; Football
ombination 27 (6 gls); Friendlies 10 (6 gls).
after Arsenal he played for Aberdare Athletic,
harlton Athletic (1925-6) and Blackpool.

ONES, Leslie Jenkin   **1937-46**
nside-forward/wing-half   5ft 7½in. 11st 6lb.
korn: Aberdare, Wales, 1 Jul 1911. Died:
'embroke, South Wales, 11 Jan 1981.
nr football: Aberdare. Previous Clubs: Cardiff
city (1929), Coventry City (Jan 1934). Joined
ARSENAL: 4 Nov 1937 from Coventry City
exchange for R.Davidson). First app: League v
?A Cup v West Ham (h) 3 Apr 1946. Final app:
nr fdly (wartime) v Yeovil (a) 13 Apr 1946. Given
ree transfer 22 May 1946 and joined Swansea
fown as player-coach.
ARSENAL Record: League 46 (3 gls); FA Cup
FA Charity Shield 1; Other snr comp: 2;
football Combination 9 (6 gls); Friendlies 8. In
addition played three League matches 1939-40

prior to outbreak of war and made 68 apps (10
gls) during wartime.
Honours: Division One champions 1937-8. FA
Charity Shield winner 1938-9. Mayor of
Colchester Cup winners 1938-9. Football League
War Cup runners-up 1940-41. 4 full Wales caps
(1 gl) 1937-8 and made 5 international apps during
wartime.
Won international honours with Cardiff City and
Coventry City. Won club honours with Coventry
City. Served in the RAF during the war. After
Swansea Town he became player-manager of Barry
Town before returning to League soccer with
Brighton & Hove Albion (Aug 1948). Continued
at Brighton as coach and scout (1949-50) and
became manager of Scunthorpe United (Jun 1950).

JONSSON, Sigurdur 'Siggi'   **1989-91**
Midfield   5ft 11in. 11st 11lb.
Born: Akranes, Iceland, 27 Sep 1966.
Previous Clubs: IA Akranes (Iceland), Sheffield
Wednesday (Feb 1985). Joined ARSENAL: 28
Jul 1989 from Sheffield Wednesday (£475,000,
tribunal). First app: Jnr fdly v Bishop's Stortford
(a) 2 Aug 1989. First snr app: League (sub) v
Manchester City (h) 14 Oct 1989. First snr app:
League v Norwich City (h) 6 Oct 1990. Snr fdly
v Watford (a) 7 Aug 1991. Final app: Football
Combination v Tottenham Hotspur (a) 26 Oct
1991. Forced to retire from football Jan 1992 due
to a back injury.
ARSENAL Record: League 2/5 (1 gl); FA Cup
0/1; Football League Cup 1; Football
Combination 31 (4 gls); Friendlies 17/4 (2 gls).
Iceland international. Had spell on loan to
Barnsley whilst with Sheffield Wednesday.

JOY, Bernard   **1935-46**
Centre-half   6ft 2in. 13st.
Born: Fulham, 29 Oct 1911. Died: Kenton, 19
Jul 1984.
Jnr football: London University, Corinthians,
Casuals. Previous Clubs: Southend 1931
(amateur), Fulham 1933 (amateur). Joined
ARSENAL: 24 May 1935 (amateur). First app:
London Combination v Leicester City (a) 31 Aug
1935. First snr app: Snr fdly v Glasgow Rangers
(a) 25 Sep 1935. League v Bolton Wanderers (h)
1 Apr 1936. Final app: League v Sheffield United
(h) 2 Nov 1946. Snr fdly v Racing Club de Paris
(a) 11 Nov 1946. Retired from League football,
Dec 1946.
ARSENAL Record: League 86; FA Cup 6; FA

Charity Shield 3; Other snr comp: 2; Football
Combination 28; Friendlies 9. In addition, played
3 League matches 1939-40 prior to outbreak of
war and made 205 apps during wartime.
Honours: Division One champions 1937-8. FA
Charity Shield winners 1938-9, runners-up 1935-6,
1936-7. Football League War Cup runners-up
1940-41. Football League South Cup winners
1942-3. 10 England Amateur caps 1934-7. Captain
of British team in Olympic Games, 1936. 1 full
England cap 1936 (last amateur to do so) and
made 1 international app during wartime.
Was a schoolmaster at Hounslow. Was FA
Amateur Cup winner with Casuals. A Flight
Lieutenant in RAF during the war. After Arsenal
played again for Corinthian Casuals (1947-8).
Became a journalist for many years with the
Evening Standard and the *Sunday Express*.
Author of *Forward Arsenal*. Retired 1976.

JULIAN, John William   **1889-92**
Wing-half   5ft 9¼in. 11st 3lb.
Born: Boston, Lincolnshire, c.1865. Died: 14 Mar
1957.
Jnr football: Boston Town. Joined ARSENAL:
summer 1889. First app: Snr fdly v London
Caledonians (h) 7 Sep 1889. First first-class app:
FA Cup (Q) v Lyndhurst (h) 5 Oct 1889. Final
first-class app: FA Cup v Derby County (h) 17 Jan
1891. Final app: Reserves v St Lukes (h) 30 Apr
1892. Transferred to Luton Town summer 1892.
ARSENAL Record: FA Cup 1; FA Cup (Q) 3.
In addition made 71 senior (3 gls) and 31 reserve
(15 gls) apps for Royal Arsenal 1889-92.
Honours: London Charity Cup winners1889-90.
London Senior Cup winners 1890-91. Kent Senior
Cup winners 1889-90. London Senior Cup
runners-up 1889-90. Captain of Arsenal.
Was a smith by trade. Later played for Tottenham
Hotspur (1894-6) and Dartford. Became a trainer
to a team in Holland (1910-11).

JULIANS, Leonard Bruce   **1958-60**
Centre/inside-forward   5ft 9in. 10st 9lb.
Born: Tottenham, 19 Jun 1933.
School: Rowland Hill, Tottenham.
Jnr football: Harris Lebus Youth, Walthamstow
Avenue; Leytonstone. Previous Clubs: Tottenham
Hotspur (amateur), Leyton Orient (Jun 1955).
Joined ARSENAL: 24 Dec 1958 from Leyton
Orient (exchange for S.Charlton & A.Biggs). First
app: League v Luton Town (a) 26 Dec 1958. Final
snr app: League v Fulham (a) 8 Apr 1960. Final
app: Football Combination v Leyton Orient (a)
30 Apr 1960. Transferred to Nottingham Forest
(£10,000) 31 May 1960.
ARSENAL Record: League 18 (7 gls); FA Cup
6 (3 gls); Other snr comp: 3 (1 gl); Football
Combination 27 (17 gls); London FA Challenge
Cup 1 (2 gls); Friendlies 7/2 (12 gls).
Played for Tottenham schoolboys. Won amateur
club honours with Walthamstow Avenue. Won
club honours with Leyton Orient. Transferred to
Millwall (Jan 1964). Appointed coach of Detroit
Cougars (America) at end of 1966-7 season.

KANE, Edward T.   **1896-97**
Centre-hal.f
Joined ARSENAL: 9 Oct 1896. First app: League
v Darwen (h) 19 Apr 1897. (His only app for
Arsenal).
ARSENAL Record: League 1.
An Army man, from the Gordon Highlanders.

KANE, Peter   **1960-63**
Inside-forward   5ft 8in. 11st.
Born: Govan, Glasgow, 4 Apr 1939.
School: St Constantine's.
Jnr football: St Constantine's Old Boys, Petershill
Juniors. Previous Clubs: Queen's Park (1958),

Northampton Town (Oct 1959). Joined ARSENAL: 22 Jul 1960 from Northampton Town for £7,000. First app: Jnr fdly v British Olympic XI (a) 6 Aug 1960. First snr app: League v Manchester City (a) 3 Sep 1960. Final snr app: League v Birmingham (a) 14 Sep 1960. Final app: Metropolitan League v St Neots (h) 23 May 1963. Transferred to Northampton Town (£3,500) Sep 1963.
ARSENAL Record: League 4 (1 gl); Football Combination 54 (37 gls); London FA Challenge Cup 5 (7 gls); Metropolitan League 36 (33 gls); Friendlies 10/1 (10 gls).
Honours: Football Combination champions 1962-3. Metropolitan League champions 1962-3. Metropolitan League Cup winners 1960-61. Metropolitan League Professional Cup winners 1960-61. Played for Glasgow schoolboys. Won Scotland Youth and Amateur caps with Queen's Park. Missed a chance to play in 1960 Olympic Games to turn professional. Served National Service (1960-62) in RAMC and played for the Army. Was also a successful boxer in his youth and in the Army. Transferred from Northampton Town to Crewe Alexandra (Mar 1964) and to St Mirren (1966).

KAY, John   **1979-84**
Full-back   5ft 10in. 11st 6lb.
Born: Great Lumley, Chester-le-Street, Durham, 29 Jan 1964.
Joined ARSENAL: 1979 (schoolboy), 1980 (apprentice), 31 Jul 1981 (professional). First app: South East Counties League v Crystal Palace (a) 18 Aug 1979. First snr app: Snr fdly (sub) v Barnet (a) 11 Oct 1982. League v West Bromwich Albion (a) 26 Feb 1983. Final app: League (sub) v Coventry City (a) 31 Mar 1984. Snr fdly v Charlton Athletic (a) 16 May 1984. Transferred to Wimbledon (£25,000) 20 Jul 1984.
ARSENAL Record: League 13/1;- Football Combination 75/5 (2 gls); FA Youth Cup 5 (1 gl); South East Counties League 50/1 (8 gls); Other jnr comp: 6 (1 gl); Friendlies 28/7 (4 gls). In addition played 1 Football Combination match 1981-2, later removed from the records.
Honours: Played for Chester-le-Street and for Durham schoolboys. Football Combination champions 1983-4. Was North of England 200 metres champion as a schoolboy. Played for Middlesbrough (on loan) 1984-5. Currently with Sunderland (Jul 1987).

KELLY, Edward Patrick   **1966-76**
Half-back   5ft 7in. 12st.
Born: Glasgow, 7 Feb 1951.
School: St Teresa, Glasgow.
Jnr football: Possilpark YMCA (Glasgow). Joined ARSENAL: 1966 (apprentice), 15 Feb 1968 (professional). First app: Jnr fdly v Walton & Hersham (a) 6 Aug 1966. First snr app: On tour v Reykjavik (Iceland) 4 May 1969. League (sub) v Sheffield Wednesday (h) 6 Sep 1969. Final snr app: League v Ipswich Town (a) 26 Dec 1975. Final app: Football Combination v Tottenham Hotspur (h) 24 Aug 1976. Transferred to Queen's Park Rangers (£60,000) 2 Sep 1976.
ARSENAL Record: League 168/7 (13 gls); FA Cup 15/2 (4 gls); Football League Cup 15; European Competitions 13/2 (2 gls); Football Combination 114 (11 gls); London FA Challenge Cup 5 (1 gl); FA Youth Cup 5; Metropolitan League 14; South East Counties League 28 (3 gls); Other jnr comp: 4; Friendlies 52/4 (11 gls).
Honours: Division One champions 1970-71. FA Cup winners 1971. European Fairs Cup winners 1969-70. Football Combination champions 1968-9, 1969-70. Football Combination Cup winners 1967-8. London FA Challenge Cup winners 1969-70. Captain of Arsenal at Youth, Reserve

and Senior levels. *5 Scotland Youth caps 1969 and 3 Under-23 caps (1 gl) 1971-4.* Transferred from Queen's Park Rangers to Leicester City (Jul 1977) and to Notts County (Jul 1980). Had a short spell with Bournemouth (1981) before returning to Leicester City. Moved into non-League football with Melton Town (1982-3) before a spell with Torquay United (1984-6). Was the first substitute to score in an FA Cup Final (1971).

KELLY, Noel   **1947-50**
Inside-forward   5ft 7in. 10st 10lb.
Born: Dublin, 28 Dec 1921.
Jnr football: Dublin Bohemians (amateur). Previous Clubs: Shamrock Rovers, Glentoran. Joined ARSENAL: 26 Sep 1947 from Glentoran for £650. First app: Jnr fdly v Bexhill Town (a) 15 Oct 1947. First snr app: Snr fdly v Nottingham Forest (a) 24 Jan 1948. League v Everton (a) 25 Feb 1950 (his only first-class app). Final app: Football Combination v Crystal Palace (a) 4 Mar 1950. Transferred to Crystal Palace (£8,000) 10 Mar 1950.
ARSENAL Record: League 1; Football Combination 74 (16 gls); London FA Challenge Cup 1; Friendlies 11 (2 gls).
Was a linotype operator before professional football. Won League of Ireland honours with Glentoran. Transferred from Crystal Palace to Nottingham Forest (Aug 1951). Won Republic of Ireland international honours with Nottingham Forest. Moved to Tranmere Rovers (Jul 1955) and later became player-manager. Was player-manager of Ellesmere Port Town (1957) and later manager of Holyhead Town.

KELSEY, Alfred John   **1949-62**
Goalkeeper   6ft. 12st 11b.
Born: Llansamlet, Swansea, 19 Nov 1929. Died: 19 Mar 1992.
School: Cwm School, Swansea.
Jnr football: Llanelly (trial), Winch Wen (Swansea). Joined ARSENAL: 29 Aug 1949 from Winch Wen. First app: Jnr fdly v March Town (a) 24 Sep 1949. First snr app: League v Charlton Athletic (h) 24 Feb 1951. Final app: League v Everton (h) 1 May 1962. Retired Nov 1962 due to injury.
ARSENAL Record: League 327; FA Cup 24; FA Charity Shield 1; Other snr comp: 4; Football

Combination 92; London FA Challenge Cup 6; Eastern Counties League 12; London Midweek League 8; Friendlies 71/3.
Honours: Division One champions 1952-3. FA Charity Shield winners 1953-4. Football Combination champions 1950-51. Football Combination Cup winners 1952-3. London FA Challenge Cup winners 1961-2. 41 full Wales caps 1954-62 (then a British record for a goalkeeper). Played for Great Britain v Rest of Europe 1955. Made 1 app for Football League 1960. Was a blacksmith by trade. Served National Service in the Army. Displaced two vertebrae at the base of his spine playing for Wales in May 1962 and was forced to retire. Testimonial match May 1963 (£8,250). Took up the post of commercial manager at Arsenal, retiring in 1989.

KEMP, Frederick   **1905-06**
Outside-left.
Joined ARSENAL: 24 Aug 1905 from Barking. First app: London League (Res) v Tottenham Hotspur (a) 2 Sep 1905. First snr app: League v Birmingham (a) 28 Oct 1905. Final snr app: League v Everton (h) 4 Nov 1905. Final app: London League (Res) v Luton (a) 28 Apr 1906. Transferred to West Ham United summer 1906.
ARSENAL Record: League 2; South Eastern League 20 (5 gls); London League (Res) 10 (6 gls); Friendlies 6 (3 gls).
Honours: South Eastern League champions 1905-06. Played for West Ham United 1906-08.

KEMPTON, Arthur Richard   **1914-21**
Goalkeeper   5ft 11in. 12st 10lb.
Born: West Thurrock, Essex, c.1893.
Jnr football: Hastings & St Leonards, Tufnell Park. Joined ARSENAL: 23 Oct 1914 (amateur), Nov 1914 (professional). First app: South Eastern League v Norwich City (h) 24 Oct 1914. First snr app: FA Cup v Merthyr Tydfil (h) 9 Jan 1915 (only senior app). Final app: Jnr fdly v Athenian League (h) 7 May 1921. Given free transfer by Arsenal at end of 1920-21 and joined Reading 3 Jun 1921.
ARSENAL Record: FA Cup 1; Football Combination 27; South Eastern League 22; London League (Res) 8; Friendlies 13. In addition made 30 apps during wartime.
Served in the RAF during World War One.

KENNEDY, Andrew Lynd   **1922-28**
Left-back   5ft 8in. 11st 3lb.
Born: Belfast, Ireland, 1 Sep 1897. Died: 21 Dec 1963.
Jnr football: Belfast Celtic Juniors. Previous Clubs: Glentoran, Crystal Palace (1920). Joined ARSENAL: 13 Aug 1922 from Crystal Palace. First app: Jnr fdly v Wealdstone (a) 2 Sep 1922. First snr app: League v Birmingham (a) 2 Dec 1922. Final snr app: League v Derby County (a) 24 Sep 1927. Final app: London Combination v Queen's Park Rangers (h) 7 Jan 1928. Transferred to Everton 12 Jan 1928.
ARSENAL Record: League 122; FA Cup 7; Other snr comp: 1; Football Combination 80; London FA Challenge Cup 3; Friendlies 17.
Honours: FA Cup runners-up 1927. London Combination champions 1926-7. 2 full Ireland caps 1923-4.
Won club honours with Crystal Palace. Transferred from Everton to Tranmere Rovers (Jun 1930). After retiring from soccer had a job connected with Liverpool schools.

KENNEDY, Raymond   **1968-74**
Striker   5ft 11in. 13st 4lb.
Born: Seaton Delaval, Northumberland, 28 Jul 1951.
School: Astley Secondary Modern.
Jnr football: New Hartley Juniors. Previous Club:

68

Port Vale (apprentice). Joined ARSENAL: 6 May 968 (apprentice) from New Hartley Juniors, 11 Nov 1968 (professional). First app: Metropolitan League v Metropolitan Police (h) 6 May 1968. First snr app: European Fairs Cup (sub) v Glentoran (a) 29 Sep 1969. Final app: League v Queen's Park Rangers (h) 30 Apr 1974. Transferred to Liverpool (£180,000) 12 Jul 1974. ARSENAL Record: League 156/2 (53 gls); FA Cup 25/2 (6 gls); Football League Cup 11 (4 gls); European Competitions 14/2 (8 gls); Other snr comp: 1; Football Combination 60/2 (32 gls); London FA Challenge Cup 4 (3 gls); FA Youth Cup 3 (4 gls); Metropolitan League 11 (3 gls); Other jnr comp: 2; Friendlies 60/3 (31 gls).
Honours: Played for South Northumberland schoolboys. Division One champions 1970-71. FA Cup winners 1971, runners-up 1972. European Fairs Cup winners 1969-70. Football Combination champions 1968-9, 1969-70. London FA Challenge Cup winners 1969-70. Southern Junior Floodlit Cup runners-up 1967-8. 6 England Under-23 caps 1972-3.
Won domestic and European club honours and full international honours with Liverpool. Later played for Swansea City (Jan 1982) and Hartlepool United (1983-4). On retiring from football became a publican in Northumberland. Now suffers from Parkinson's Disease.

KEOWN, Martin Raymond   **1981-86**
Central-defender   6ft 1in. 12st 4lb.
Born: Oxford, 24 Jul 1966.
Joined ARSENAL: 1981 (schoolboy), Jun 1982 (apprentice), 2 Feb 1984 (professional). First app: South East Counties League v Charlton Athletic (h) 29 Aug 1981. First snr app: Snr fdly (sub) v Windsor & Eton (a) 20 Mar 1984. League v West Bromwich Albion (a) 23 Nov 1985. Final app: League v Oxford United (a) 5 May 1986. Transferred to Aston Villa (£125,000) (after refusing a further contract by Arsenal) Jul 1986. ARSENAL Record: League 22; FA Cup 5; Football Combination 68/2 (2 gls); South East Counties League 45/1 (5 gls); FA Youth Cup 11; Other jnr comp: 9; Friendlies 28/1 (1 gl).
Honours: Played for Oxford and for Oxfordshire schoolboys. Football Combination champions 1983-4. Southern Junior Floodlight Cup winners 1983-4. 4 England Youth caps 1983-4.
Went on loan from Arsenal to Brighton & Hove Albion (Feb 1985-Nov 1985). Has won club and Under-21 international honours with Aston Villa. Transferred to Everton (cs 1989) and won full England caps in 1992.

KEYSER, Gerard Pieter   **1930-31**
Goalkeeper   5ft 10½in. 11st 8lbs
Born: Holland.
Jnr football: Millwall Reserves (1929-30), Margate (1929-30). Joined ARSENAL: 30 Aug 1930 (amateur) from Margate, 28 May 1931 (professional). First app: League v Blackpool (a) 30 Aug 1930. Final snr app: League v West Ham United (h) 25 Oct 1930. Final app: London Combination v Southend (h) 28 Feb 1931. Transferred to Charlton Athletic Jul 1931. ARSENAL Record: League 12; FA Charity Shield 1; Football Combination 8; London Midweek League 1.
Honours: FA Charity Shield winners 1930-31.
Later played for Queen's Park Rangers (1932-3).

KIDD, Brian   **1974-76**
Striker   6ft. 12st 9lb.
Born: Manchester, 29 May 1949.
School: St Patrick's, Collyhurst (Manchester).
Previous Club: Manchester United 1964 (apprentice), Jun 1966 (professional). Joined ARSENAL: 12 Jul 1974 from Manchester United for £110,000. First app: Snr fdly v Cardiff City

(a) 31 Jul 1974. League v Leicester City (a) 17 Aug 1974. Final app: League v Queen's Park Rangers (a) 19 Apr 1976. Transferred to Manchester City (£100,000) 1 Jul 1976. ARSENAL Record: League 77 (30 gls); FA Cup 9 (3 gls); Football League Cup 4 (1 gl); Friendlies 20 (12 gls).
England Schoolboy international. Won European Cup winners' medal and England Youth, Under-23 and full international caps with Manchester United. After Manchester City, he played for Everton (Mar 1979), Bolton Wanderers (May 1980) and Atlanta Chiefs and Fort Lauderdale (both NASL). Had a short spell as manager of Preston North End (Jan-Mar 1986). Returned to Manchester United as coach.

KING, Edward   **1912-14**
Half-back   5ft 7½in. 11st 8lb.
Born: Blyth, Northumberland, c.1890.
Jnr football: Leyton. Joined ARSENAL: 1 Aug 1912 from Leyton. First app: South Eastern League v Tunbridge Wells (h) 7 Sep 1912. First snr app: London FA Challenge Cup v Clapton Orient (a) 23 Sep 1912. League v West Bromwich Albion (a) 9 Nov 1912. Final snr app: League v Everton (a) 22 Mar 1913. Final app: London League (Reserves) v Clapton Orient (h) 30 Apr 1914. Transferred to Clapton Orient 30 Jun 1914. ARSENAL Record: League 11; FA Cup 2; Other snr comp: 1; London FA Challenge Cup 1; South Eastern League 40 (2 gls); London League (Res) 9; Other jnr comp: 1; Friendlies 1.

KING, Henry Edward   **1914-19**
Centre-forward   5ft 9½in. 11st 12lb.
Born: Evesham, 1884.
Jnr football: Worcester, Crewe Alexandra (Birmingham League) (1911). Previous Clubs: Birmingham (before Crewe Alexandra), Northampton Town. Joined ARSENAL: 27 Apr 1914 from Northampton Town. First app: Norwich Hospital Cup v Norwich City (a) 30 Apr 1914. League v Glossop (h) 1 Sep 1914. Final snr app: League v Nottingham Forest (h) 24 Apr 1915. London FA Challenge Cup v Dulwich Hamlet (h) 22 Sep 1919. Final fdly v Bristol City (h) 11 Oct 1919. Transferred to Leicester City 17 Oct 1919. ARSENAL Record: League 37 (26 gls); FA Cup 2 (3 gls); Other snr comp: 2 (5 gls); Football Combination 6 (5 gls); London FA Challenge Cup 5 (4 gls); South Eastern League 1 (1 gl); Friendlies 1 (2 gls). In addition made 37 apps (26 gls) during wartime.
Honours: London FA Challenge Cup runners-up 1914-15. Norwich Hospital Cup winners 1913-14.
Served with the Royal Garrison Artillery in Italy during the war. Lived in Worcester on retirement from football.

KINGTON, Edward   **1895-98**
Left-half
Jnr football: Charlton United. Joined ARSENAL: 1895 (amateur) from Charlton United, 24 Sep 1896 (professional). First app: Kent League v Northfleet (a) 7 Dec 1895. First snr app: United League v Wellingborough (h) 19 Oct 1896. Final snr app: FA Cup v Leyton (h) 12 Dec 1896. Final app: Sevenoaks Charity Cup Final v Swanscombe (h) 16 Apr 1898. ARSENAL Record: FA Cup 1; United League 1; Kent League 28 (2 gls); Other jnr comp: 1; Friendlies 30 (1 gl).
Honours: Kent League champions 1896-7. Sevenoaks Charity Cup winners 1897-8.

KIRCHEN, Alfred John   **1935-43**
Wing-forward   5ft 10½in. 12st 3lb.
Born: Shouldham, Norfolk, 26 Apr 1913.

School: King's Lynn.
Jnr football: Shouldham. Previous Club: Norwich City (Nov 1933). Joined ARSENAL: 1 Mar 1935 from Norwich City for £6,000. First app: League v Tottenham Hotspur (a) 6 Mar 1935. Final snr app: League v Sunderland (h) 2 Sep 1939 (later deleted from records). Final app: Football League South v West Ham United (a) 11 Sep 1943. Retired 1943 due to injury.
ARSENAL Record: League 92 (38 gls); FA Cup 7 (6 gls); FA Charity Shield 2 (1 gl); Other snr comp: 2; Football Combination 31 (25 gls); London FA Challenge Cup 3 (5 gls); Southern League 4 (5 gls); Friendlies 12 (7 gls). In addition played 3 League matches (1 gl) 1939-40 prior to outbreak of war and made 113 apps (80 gls) during wartime.

Honours: Division One champions 1937-8. FA Charity Shield winners 1938-9, runners-up 1936-7. London FA Challenge Cup winners 1935-6. Norwich Hospital Cup winners 1934-5. Football League South Cup winners 1942-3. Football League War Cup runners-up 1940-41. 3 full England caps (2 gls) 1937 and made 3 international apps during wartime.
Played for King's Lynn and for Norfolk schoolboys. Served as PTI in the RAF during the war. Received a severe knee injury during wartime football which ended his playing career. Had a short spell as trainer at Norwich City (1946) and then became a farmer in Norfolk. Became a director of Norwich City. Won honours at clay pigeon shooting (1956-8) and represented England at this sport. Also a fine bowls player. Retired from farming 1980.

KIRK, Frank V.   **1892-94**
Outside-left
Joined ARSENAL: from local football 1892 and signed League forms 28 Jul 1893. First app: Reserves v London Polytechnic (h) 4 Apr 1892. First snr app: Snr fdly v Glasgow Thistle (h) 2 Jan 1893. Final app: League v Liverpool (a) 1 Jan 1894 (only first-class app).
ARSENAL Record: League 1; Friendlies 9 (2 gls). In addition made 6 senior and 21 reserve (7 gls) apps for Royal Arsenal between 1891-2 and 1892-3.
Played for Royal Arsenal after Arsenal.
Played for Royal Ordnance after Arsenal.

KOSMINA, Alexander John   **1978-79**
Forward   5ft 10in. 11st.
Born: Adelaide, Australia, 17 Aug 1956.

Previous Club: Polonia (Adelaide), Australia. Joined ARSENAL: 14 Feb 1978 for £20,000. First app: Football Combination v Southampton (h) 11 Mar 1978. First snr app: On tour v Borussia Dortmund (Germany) 28 Jul 1978. League (sub) v Leeds United (h) 19 Aug 1978. Final snr app: UEFA Cup (sub) v Red Star Belgrade (h) 6 Dec 1978. Final app: Football Combination v Chelsea (h) 20 Mar 1979. Transferred to West Adelaide (Australia) (£25,000) 27 Mar 1979. ARSENAL Record: League 0/1; European Competitions 1/2; Football Combination 38 (13 gls); Friendlies 3/1 (1 gl). Won over 50 international caps for Australia.

KYLE, Peter 1906-08
Centre-forward
Born: Rutherglen, Scotland, Sep 1880. Died: Scotland, c.1961.
Jnr football: Larkhill, Royal Albert. Previous Clubs: Partick Thistle, Liverpool (1899-1900), Leicester Fosse, West Ham United (1901-02), Kettering Town (Southern League), Tottenham Hotspur (1905-06). Joined ARSENAL: 28 Apr 1906 from Tottenham Hotspur. First app: League v Manchester City (a) 1 Sep 1906. Final app: League v Aston Villa (h) 8 Feb 1908. Transferred to Aston Villa 3 Mar 1908.
ARSENAL Record: League 52 (21 gls); FA Cup 8 (2 gls); Other snr comp: 2; South Eastern League 1; Friendlies 10 (2 gls).
Later played for Sheffield United and Watford.

LAIDLAW, James 1901
Inside-forward
Born: Scotland, 1877.
Previous Clubs: Burnley, Leith Athletic, Newcastle United. Joined ARSENAL: Aug 1901 from Newcastle United. First app: London League (Res) v Fulham (a) 7 Sep 1901. First snr app: London League v Tottenham Hotspur (h) 16 Sep 1901. Final snr app: League v Chesterfield (h) 5 Oct 1901. Final app: London League (Res) v Clapton Orient (h) 26 Oct 1901. Returned to Scotland Nov 1901.
ARSENAL Record: League 3 (2 gls); London League 2; London League (Res) 2 (1 gl).

LAMBERT, John 1926-33
Centre/inside-forward 5ft 10in. 12st 6lb.
Born: Greasborough, nr Rotherham, 22 May 1902. Died: Enfield, 7 Dec 1940.
School: National (Rotherham).
Jnr football: Greasborough; Sheffield Wednesday (trial). Previous Clubs: Rotherham County (1922), Leeds United (Nov 1922), Doncaster Rovers (Jan 1925). Joined ARSENAL: Jun 1926 from Doncaster Rovers for £2,000. First app: London Combination v Clapton Orient (a) 28 Aug 1926. First snr app: League v Bolton Wanderers (a) 6 Sep 1926. Final snr app: League v West Bromwich Albion (a) 13 Sep 1933. Snr fdly v Glasgow Rangers (h) 27 Sep 1933. Final app: London Combination v Fulham (h) 7 Oct 1933. Transferred to Fulham (£2,500) 10 Oct 1933.
ARSENAL Record: League 143 (98 gls); FA Cup 16 (11 gls); Charity Shield 2; Other snr comp: 4 (6 gls); Football Combination 141 (110 gls); London FA Challenge Cup 6 (5 gls); London Midweek League 1; Friendlies 25/1 (33 gls).
Honours: Division One champions 1930-31. FA Cup winners 1930, runners-up 1932. FA Charity Shield winners 1930-31, 1931-2. London Combination champions 1926-7, 1927-8, 1928-9, 1929-30. Sheriff of London Shield winners 1930-31. Northampton Charity Shield winners 1929-30, 1930-31, 1931-2.
Worked as a miner before football. Held the Arsenal record for most League goals scored in a season — 38 goals in 34 apps. 1930-31 (beaten

by Drake, 1934-5). Became player-manager of Margate (Arsenal's nursery team) in Jan 1936 and coach to Arsenal 'A' team in 1938. Was tragically killed in a road accident in North London in 1940.

LAWRENCE, Everard Thomas 1902-03
Outside-left
Jnr football: Kettering (1900) Previous Club: Northampton Town (1901). Joined ARSENAL: 1 May 1902 from Northampton Town (together with J.Coleman). First app: London League v West Ham United (a) 1 Sep 1902. League v Preston North End (a) 6 Sep 1902. Final snr app: League v Blackpool (a) 7 Mar 1903. Snr fdly v Northampton Town (a) 14 Apr 1903. Final app: West Kent League v Swanscombe (h) 25 Apr 1903. Transferred to Fulham summer 1903.
ARSENAL Record: League 20 (3 gls); FA Cup 3; London League 6; London League (Res) 1; Kent League 6 (4 gls); Friendlies 4 (4 gls).
Honours: West Kent League champions 1902-03.
Later played for Glossop (1904-05).

LAWRENCE, Walter Henry 1909-10
Inside-forward
Jnr football: Summerstown (amateur). Previous Club: Crystal Palace (amateur). Joined ARSENAL: 4 May 1909 (amateur) from Crystal Palace, 13 May 1909 (professional). First app: South Eastern League v Brighton (h) 1 Sep 1909. First snr app: League v Sheffield United (h) 4 Sep 1909. Final app: League v Preston North End (h) 23 Apr 1910. Transferred to Crystal Palace summer 1910.
ARSENAL Record: League 25 (5 gls); FA Cup 1; Other snr comp: 1; South Eastern League 2; Friendlies 4 (3 gls).
Won amateur international honours with Crystal Palace. Later played for Merthyr (1913).

LAWSON, Herbert 1924-27
Outside-right 5ft 7½in. 10st 10lb.
Born: Luton, 12 Apr 1905.
Jnr football: Frickers Athletic, Luton Clarence. Joined ARSENAL: 18 Oct 1924 (amateur) from Luton Clarence, 26 Nov 1924 (professional). First app: Jnr fdly v Ipswich Town (a) 22 Oct 1924. First snr app: League v Burnley (h) 3 Feb 1926. Final snr app: League v Birmingham (h) 1 May 1926. Snr fdly v Clapton Orient (a) 11 Oct 1926. Final app: Jnr fdly v Biggleswade (a) 26 Feb 1927. Transferred to Brentford 11 Mar 1927.
ARSENAL Record: League 3 (2 gls); FA Cup 3; Football Combination 42 (5 gls); Friendlies 17 (6 gls).
Played for Bedfordshire. His father was trainer of Luton Town for over 30 years.

LAWTON, Thomas 1953-56
Centre-forward 5ft 11in. 12st 4lb.
Born: Bolton, 6 Oct 1919.
School: Tonge Moor Council; Castle Hill; Foulds Road (Bolton).
Jnr football: Hayes Athletic, Rossendale United. Previous Clubs: Burnley 1934 (amateur), Everton Dec 1936, Chelsea Nov 1945, Notts County Nov 1947, Brentford Mar 1952. Joined ARSENAL: 18 Sep 1953 from Brentford for £10,000 (plus J.Robertson). First app: League v Manchester City (h) 19 Sep 1953. Final snr app: League v Sunderland (a) 24 Sep 1955. Snr fdly v Glasgow Rangers (a) 21 Nov 1955. Final app: Football Combination v Brentford (h) 26 Dec 1955. Transferred to Kettering Town as player-manager (£1,000) 1 Feb 1956.
ARSENAL Record: League 35 (13 gls); FA Cup 2 (1 gl); FA Charity Shield 1 (1 gl); Football Combination 3 (8 gls); Friendlies 12 (4 gls).
Honours: FA Charity Shield winners 1953-4.
Played for Bolton and Lancashire schoolboys.

Served in the Army during the war. Won club honours with Everton and Notts County and England international honours with Everton, Chelsea, and Notts County. Played for Great Britain v Rest of Europe 1947. Was manager of Notts County (May 1957-Jul 1958). Became a publican at Lowdham, Notts. Now retired and lives in Nottingham.

LEATHER, John 1896-98
Goalkeeper 6ft. 11st 7lb.
Born: 1875.
Jnr football: Macclesfield Swifts (1893), Macclesfield FC. Joined ARSENAL: 31 Aug 1896 from Macclesfield. First app: Jnr fdly v 15th Co Royal Artillery (h) 3 Sep 1896. League v Rushden (h) 7 Sep 1896. First snr app: League v Manchester City (h) 28 Apr 1897. Snr fdly v Reading (h) 1 Nov 1897. Final app: Jnr fdly v Deptford (h) 30 Apr 1898. Transferred to Queen's Park Rangers summer 1898.
ARSENAL Record: League 8; FA Cup 2; United League 4; Other jnr comp: 2; Kent League 8; Friendlies 44.
Honours: Kent League champions 1896-7. Sevenoaks Charity Cup winners 1897-8.

LEE, Harold Godfrey 1905-09
Forward 5ft 8in. 11st.
Born: Erith, Kent.
Jnr football: Erith Albion, Erith Town, Cray Wanderers, Sittingbourne. Joined ARSENAL: 1 Sep 1905 from Sittingbourne. First app: South Eastern League v Leyton (a) 11 Sep 1905. First snr app: Snr fdly (sub) v Corinthians (h) 26 Dec 1905. League v Bristol City (h) 7 Sep 1907. Final app: League v Nottingham Forest (h) 9 Oct 1909. London FA Challenge Cup v West Ham United (h) 11 Oct 1909. Transferred to Bury 13 Oct 1909.
ARSENAL Record: League 44 (15 gls); Other snr comp: 1; London FA Challenge Cup 2; South Eastern League 78 (55 gls); London League (Res) 34 (16 gls); Friendlies 17/1 (12 gls).
Honours: South Eastern League champions 1905-06, 1906-07, 1907-08. London League (Res) champions 1906-07.
Later played for Dartford.

LEE, John William 1926-2?
Outside-left 5ft 10in. 12st 8lb.
Born: Blyth, Northumberland, 1904.
Jnr football: Blackhall Wesleyans (W.Hartlepool), Horden Athletic (1925-6). Previous Clubs

Hartlepools United (amateur), Luton Town (trial). Joined ARSENAL: 4 May 1926 (amateur) from Horden Athletic, 27 May 1926 (professional). First app: On tour v MTK Budapest (Hungary) 13 May 1926. League v Bolton Wanderers (a) 6 Sep 1926. Final snr app: League v Blackburn Rovers (a) 28 Apr 1927. Snr fdly v Corinthians (h) 21 Sep 1927. Final app: London Combination v Millwall (h) 5 May 1928. Transferred to Chesterfield 9 Jun 1928.
ARSENAL Record: League 7; Football Combination 52 (23 gls); Friendlies 16 (9 gls).
Honours: London Combination champions 1926-7, 1927-8.
Won club honours with Chesterfield. Later played for Aldershot (1933-4).

LE ROUX, Daniel Leow   **1957-58**
Wing-forward   5ft 10½in. 12st 10lb.
Born: Port Shepstone, Natal, South Africa, 25 Nov 1933.
School: Mansfield High School (Durban).
Previous Club: Queen's Park FC (Durban, South Africa). Joined ARSENAL: 12 Feb 1957 from South Africa. First app: Football Combination v Luton Town (h) 2 Mar 1957. First snr app: Friendly v Hendon (a) 29 Apr 1957. League v Burnley (a) 7 Dec 1957. Final snr app: League v Luton Town (a) 28 Dec 1957. Final app: Football Combination v Crystal Palace (a) 19 Apr 1958. Returned to South Africa.
ARSENAL Record: League 5; Football Combination 25 (12 gls); London FA Challenge Cup 5 (5 gls); Other jnr comp: 1; Friendlies 3 (1 gl).
Played Rugby Union and cricket at school. Was a bank clerk before soccer. Played for Natal and was a South African international. Was a member of the South African touring team to England (1953-4).

LEWIS, Charles Henry   **1907-21**
Forward   5ft 9in. 11st 3lb.
Born: Plumstead, c.1886. Died: Plumstead, 1967.
Jnr football: East Wickham, Eltham FC, Maidstone United. Joined ARSENAL: 3 May 1907 from Maidstone United. First app: South Eastern League v Tottenham Hotspur (a) 2 Sep 1907. Snr fdly v Liverpool (h) 26 Dec 1907. League v Sunderland (h) 28 Dec 1907. Final snr app: League v Aston Villa (h) 24 Jan 1920. Snr fdly v Clapton Orient (a) 27 Sep 1920. Final app: Jnr fdly v Athenian League (h) 7 May 1921. Transferred to Margate summer 1921.
ARSENAL Record: League 206 (30 gls); FA Cup 14 (4 gls); Other snr comp: 7 (2 gls); Football Combination 28 (3 gls); London FA Challenge Cup 12 (6 gls); South Eastern League 61 (28 gls); London League (Res) 18 (10 gls); Other jnr comp: 1; Friendlies 31 (14 gls). In addition, made 43 apps (8 gls) during wartime.
Honours: South Eastern League champions 1907-08. London FA Challenge Cup runners-up 1914-15. Norwich Hospital Cup winners 1913-14.
Played in every forward position for Arsenal first team. On retirement from football, he ran a shop in Plumstead for many years.

LEWIS, Daniel   **1924-31**
Goalkeeper   5ft 11in. 10st 10lb.
Born: Mardy, South Wales, 11 Dec 1902. Died: Scarborough, 17 Jul 1965.
Jnr football: Mardy (Welsh League). Previous Club: Clapton Orient. Joined ARSENAL: 30 Aug 1924 from Clapton Orient. First app: London Combination v Brentford (h) 30 Aug 1924. First snr app: League v Everton (a) 15 Nov 1924. Final snr app: League v Leicester City (a) 21 Apr 1930. Final app: Jnr fdly v Army (h) 26 Feb 1931. Transferred to Gillingham 9 May 1931.
ARSENAL Record: League 142; FA Cup 25; Football Combination 63; London FA Challenge

Cup 4; London Midweek League 1; Friendlies 25.
Honours: FA Cup runners-up 1927. London Combination champions 1926-7. 3 full Wales caps 1927-9.
Worked in the coal-mines before taking up football. Worked for Kodak at Harrow on retirement from football.

LEWIS, Reginald   **1935-53**
Centre/inside-forward   5ft 10½in. 11st 11lb.
Born: Bilston, Staffordshire, 7 Mar 1920.
School: Reary Central, London.
Jnr football: Nunhead, Dulwich Hamlet Juniors, Margate. Joined ARSENAL: 9 May 1935 (amateur), 15 Mar 1937 (professional) from Margate. First app: Jnr fdly v London University (a) 19 Feb 1936. First snr app: On tour v Copenhagen (Denmark) 28 May 1937. League v Everton (h) 1 Jan 1938. Final snr app: League v Manchester United (a) 26 Apr 1952. Snr fdly (sub) v Racing Club de Paris (a) 1 Oct 1952. Final app: Football Combination Cup v Southend (h) 9 Mar 1953. Retired at end of 1952-3.
ARSENAL Record: League 154 (103 gls); FA Cup 21 (13 gls); FA Charity Shield 1 (2 gls); Other snr comp: 2; Football Combination 85 (82 gls); London FA Challenge Cup 11 (7 gls); Friendlies 38/9 (42 gls). In addition made 2 League apps (1 gl) 1939-40 prior to outbreak of war and made 128 apps (142 gls) during wartime.
Honours: Played for South London and for London schoolboys (also at cricket). Division One champions 1947-8. FA Cup winners 1950. FA Charity Shield winners 1948-9. London Combination champions 1937-8, 1938-9. London FA Challenge Cup runners-up 1936-7. Mayor of Colchester Cup winners 1938-9. Football League South Cup winners 1942-3. 2 England 'B' caps (2 gls) 1950. Played for England v Scotland 1946 (Bolton Disaster Fund).
Scored 43 goals in 31 apps (including 6 and 5 in successive matches) in London Combination 1938-9 — a club record. Served with BAOR in Germany during the war. On retirement from football he became a publican in South London, and later went into the insurance business.

LIDDELL, Edward   **1914-20**
Centre-half   6ft. 12st.
Born: Sunderland, 27 May 1878. Died: Ilford, Essex, 22 Nov 1968.
Previous Clubs: Southampton (1905-06), Gainsborough Trinity, Clapton Orient (1907), Southend (1913). Joined ARSENAL: 1 Sep 1914 from Southend. First app: South Eastern League v Southampton (h) 3 Sep 1914. First snr app: League v Hull City (a) 2 Apr 1915. Final snr app: League v Bristol City (a) 3 Apr 1915. Final app: London Combination v Brentford (a) 1 May 1920. Left Arsenal 19 Nov 1920 and returned to Southend as manager.
ARSENAL Record: League 2; Other snr comp: 1; Football Combination 2; London FA Challenge Cup 2; South Eastern League 26 (1 gl); London League (Res) 13 (1 gl); Friendlies 4. In addition made 67 apps (1 gl) during wartime.
Worked in the shipyards and played amateur football as a youth. After Southend had spells as manager of Queen's Park Rangers, Fulham (1929-31) and later Luton Town. Served as a scout for West Ham, Chelsea, Brentford and Tottenham Hotspur (1945-65).

LIEVESLEY, Joseph   **1913-15**
Goalkeeper   5ft 9½in. 13st.
Born: Staveley, Derbyshire. Died: 18 Oct 1941.
Previous Club: Sheffield United. Joined ARSENAL: 28 Jun 1913 from Sheffield United. First app: League v Leicester Fosse (h) 6 Sep 1913.

Final app: League v Nottingham Forest (h) 24 Apr 1915.
ARSENAL Record: League 73; FA Cup 2; Other snr comp: 4; London FA Challenge Cup 6; South Eastern League 3; Friendlies 2.
Honours: London FA Challenge Cup runners-up 1914-15. Norwich Hospital Cup winners 1913-14. Won England international honours with Sheffield United.

LIMPAR, Anders Erik   **1990-**
Midfield   5ft 8in. 10st 12lb.
Born: Solna, Sweden, 24 Sep 1965.
Jnr football: Sparvagens Golf (Sweden). Previous Clubs: AIK, BP, Örgryte IS (all Sweden), BSC Young Boys (Switzerland) 1988, US Cremonese (Italy) 1989. Joined ARSENAL: 8 Jul 1990 from Cremonese for £1,000,000. First app: On tour v Västra Frölunda IF (Sweden) 24 Jul 1990. League v Wimbledon (a) 25 Aug 1990.

ARSENAL Record: League 55/8 (15 gls); FA Cup 5 (2 gls); Football League Cup 3; European comp: 3 (1 gl); Other snr app: 5 (1 gl); Football Combination 9 (3 gls); Friendlies 11 (3 gls).
Honours: Division One champions 1990-91. Made 1 app for Football League 1990-91. Under-21 and full Sweden caps.

LINIGHAN, Andrew   **1990-**
Defender   6ft 3½in. 12st 6lb.
Born: Hartlepool, 8 Jun 1962.

Previous Clubs: Hartlepool United (1980), Leeds United, Oldham Athletic, Norwich City (1988). Joined ARSENAL: 3 Jul 1990 from Norwich City for £1,200,000. First app: On tour (sub) v Varbergs BoIS (Sweden) 22 Jul 1990. League (sub) v Chelsea (h) 15 Sep 1990.
ARSENAL Record: League 22/5; FA Cup 3/1; Football League Cup 1/1; European comp: 2 (1 gl); Other snr comp: 2; Football Combination 36 (1 gl); Friendlies 15/5 (2 gls).
Won 'B' international honours with Norwich City. His father, uncle and brother have all played League football.

LINWARD, William   **1902-05**
Outside-left   5ft 7in. 10st 12lb.
Born: Hull, 1877.
Jnr football:: All Saints (Hull). Previous Clubs: Grimsby Town, Doncaster Rovers, West Ham United (1901). Joined ARSENAL: 20 Dec 1902 from West Ham United.
First app: London League (Res) v Clapton Orient (h) 25 Dec 1902. First snr app: London League v Millwall (a) 26 Dec 1902. League v Burnley (h) 27 Dec 1902. Final app: League v Wolverhampton Wanderers (a) 21 Jan 1905. Snr fdly v Sheffield United (h) 29 Apr 1905. Transferred to Norwich City summer 1905.
ARSENAL Record: League 47 (10 gls); FA Cup 3; London League 9 (2 gls); South Eastern League 18 (3 gls); London League (Res) 15 (1 gl); Other jnr comp: 1; Friendlies 12 (8 gls).
Honours: West Kent Charity Cup winners 1904-05. Played for South v North FA Trial 1903-04.
Later played for Kilmarnock (1906-07) and Maidstone (1907-08).

LISHMAN, Douglas John   **1948-56**
Inside-left   5ft 11in. 12st 4lb.
Born: Birmingham, 14 Sep 1923.
School: St Thomas RC, Erdington, Birmingham. Jnr football: Pagett Rangers (Birmingham). Previous Club: Walsall (1946-8). Joined ARSENAL: 27 May 1948 from Walsall for

£10,500. First app: Football Combination v Bristol City (h) 21 Aug 1948. First snr app: League v Sheffield United (a) 4 Sep 1948. Final snr app: League v Burnley (h) 26 Nov 1955. Final app: Football Combination v Plymouth Argyle (a) 12 Mar 1956. Transferred to Nottingham Forest (£8,000) 16 Mar 1956.
ARSENAL Record: League 226 (125 gls); FA Cup

17 (10 gls); FA Charity Shield 1 (2 gls); Other snr comp: 1; Football Combination 40 (14 gls); London FA Challenge Cup 3 (1 gl); Friendlies 54/4 (40 gls).
Honours: Division One champions 1952-3. FA Cup runners-up 1952. FA Charity Shield winners 1953-4. 1 England 'B' cap 1953 and made 1 app (2 gls) for the Football League 1953.
Joined the Royal Marine Commandos in 1939 serving in numerous overseas countries and took part in the Walcheren Island (Holland) landing. Suffered broken leg, Dec 1950. Scored eight hat-tricks in his Arsenal career, including three in consecutive home matches (1951-2). Retired from football 1957 and now manages a family furniture business in Stoke.

LLOYD, Frank   **1899-1900**
Outside-right   5ft 8½in. 12st
Born: c.1881.
Jnr football: Wednesbury Old Athletic. Joined ARSENAL: 12 May 1899 from Wednesbury. First app: Kent League v Swanscombe (a) 2 Sep 1899. First snr app: Southern District Combination v Bristol City (h) 30 Oct 1899. Final snr app: League v Barnsley (h) 28 Apr 1900. Final app: Jnr fdly v Woolwich District League (h) 30 Apr 1900. Transferred to Aston Villa 26 May 1900.
ARSENAL Record: League 18 (3 gls); FA Cup 1; Southern District Combination 8 (4 gls); Kent League 5 (2 gls); Friendlies 8 (1 gl).
Later played for Dundee (1902).

LOGAN, Harry   **1910-11**
Forward   5ft 7in. 11st.
Born: Glasgow, c.1888.
Previous Club: Sunderland. Joined ARSENAL: 5 Jul 1910 from Sunderland. First app: League v Bury (a) 3 Sep 1910. Final snr app: League v Aston Villa (h) 15 Mar 1911. Final app: Jnr fdly v New Brompton (h) 1 Apr 1911.
ARSENAL Record: League 11; London FA Challenge Cup 1; Other snr comp: 1; South Eastern League 10 (4 gls); Friendlies 1.

LOGAN, Peter 'Paddy'   **1899-1900 & 1901**
Inside/centre-forward   5ft 8in. 12st 4lb.
Born: Glasgow.
Previous Clubs: Motherwell, Notts County. Joined ARSENAL: 1 May 1899 from Notts County. Transferred to Reading summer 1900. Rejoined ARSENAL: summer 1901 from Reading. First app: League v Leicester Fosse (h) 2 Sep 1899. Final app: League v Middlesbrough (h) 19 Oct 1901. Transferred to Brentford Nov 1901.
ARSENAL Record: League 28 (7 gls); FA Cup 1; Southern District Combination 12 (5 gls); Kent League 6 (5 gls); Friendlies 6 (4 gls).

LOGIE, James Tullis   **1939-55**
Inside-forward   5ft 5in. 9st 9lb.
Born: Edinburgh, 23 Nov 1919. Died: London, 30 Apr 1984.
School: Castle Hill, Edinburgh.
Jnr football: Lochore Welfare (Fifeshire). Joined ARSENAL: 3 Jun 1939 from Lochore Welfare for £35. First app: Southern League v Worcester City (h) 26 Aug 1939 (deleted from records). First snr app: FA Cup v West Ham United (h) 9 Jan 1946. Final snr app: League v Manchester United (a) 20 Nov 1954. Final app: Football Combination v Coventry City (h) 22 Jan 1955. Transferred to Gravesend & Northfleet (£2,000) 1 Feb 1955.
ARSENAL Record: League 296 (68 gls); FA Cup 30 (8 gls); FA Charity Shield 2; Football Combination 3 (1 gl); Friendlies 55 (13 gls). In addition played 1 Southern League match 1939-40 prior to outbreak of war and made 9 apps (3 gls) during wartime.

Honours: Division One champions 1947-8, 1952-3. FA Cup winners 1950, runners-up 1952. FA Charity Shield winners 1948-9, 1953-4. Captain of Arsenal. 1 full Scotland cap 1952. Won Scotland cap (for making 5 apps for London FA).
Was a bricklayer by trade. Served in the Royal Navy during wartime. Retired from football Nov 1959. Became a publican in Dalston, then a café owner and later had a newspaper business. Died of throat cancer 1984.

LOW, Archibald B.   **1906-08**
Left-half
Born: Scotland.
Jnr football: Ashfield (Glasgow). Joined ARSENAL: 6 Jun 1906 from Ashfield. First app: London League (Res) v Tottenham Hotspur (h) 1 Sep 1906. First snr app: Snr fdly v Reading (a) 12 Sep 1906. League v Sunderland (h) 15 Sep 1906. Final app: Scottish tour v Greenock Morton 29 Apr 1908. Transferred to Partick Thistle 14 Sep 1908.
ARSENAL Record: League 3; Other snr comp: 1; South Eastern League 53 (2 gls); London League (Res) 30 (1 gl); Friendlies 21.
Honours: South Eastern League champions 1906-07, 1907-08. London League (Res) champions 1906-07.

LOW, Thomas Pollock   **1900-01**
Outside-right   5ft 6½in. 9st 6lb.
Born: Cambuslang, Lanark, Scotland, 3 Oct 1874.
Previous Clubs: Celtic, Glasgow Rangers (Res), Dundee. Joined ARSENAL: 1 May 1900 from Dundee. First app: League v Gainsborough Town (h) 1 Sep 1900. Final app: League v New Brighton Tower (a) 27 Apr 1901.
ARSENAL Record: League 24 (1 gl); FA Cup 2 (1 gl); London League (Res) 5 (1 gl); Kent League 1; Friendlies 7 (2 gls).
Won Scotland international honours with Glasgow Rangers.

LUKIC, Jovan 'John'   **1983-90**
Goalkeeper   6ft 4in. 13st 7lb.
Born: Chesterfield, Derbyshire, 11 Dec 1960.

School: Old Hall Junior, Newbold Green Secondary, Chesterfield.
Previous Club: Leeds United (1974). Joined ARSENAL: 25 Jul 1983 from Leeds United for £75,000. First app: On tour (sub) v Meppen (Germany) 31 Jul 1983. League v Stoke City (h) 7 Apr 1984. Final app: League v Norwich City

(a) 5 May 1990. Snr fdly: v South Korea (in Singapore) 9 May 1990. Transferred to Leeds United (£1,000,000) 22 May 1990.
ARSENAL Record: League 223; FA Cup 21; Football League Cup 32; Other snr comp: 7; Football Combination 40; Friendlies 52/6.
Honours: FA Charity Shield runners-up 1989-90. Football League Cup winners 1986-7, runners-up 1987-8. Football Combination champions 1983-4. Division One champions 1988-9. Mercantile Credit Centenary Trophy winners 1988-9.
Of Yugoslavian parents. Played for Chesterfield and for Derbyshire schoolboys. Won England Under-21 honours with Leeds United.

LYDERSEN, Pål   **1991-**
Defender
Born: Norway, Sep 1965.
Previous Club: IK Start (Norway). Joined

ARSENAL: Nov 1991 from IK Start for £500,000. First app: Football Combination v Oxford United (h) 23 Nov 1991. First snr app: League v Barnet (a) 29 Feb 1992. League (sub) v Wimbledon (a) 28 Mar 1992.
ARSENAL Record: League 5/2; Football Combination 14; Friendlies 3.
Honours: 11 full Norway caps.

MACAULAY, Archibald Renwick **1947-50**
Wing-half   5ft 11in. 11st 11lb.
Born: Falkirk, Scotland, 30 Jul 1915.
School: Comely Park, Falkirk.
Jnr football: Laurieston Villa, Camelon Juniors. Previous Clubs: Glasgow Rangers (Mar 1933), West Ham United (1937), Brentford (Oct 1946). Joined ARSENAL: 14 Jul 1947 from Brentford for £10,000. First app: League v Sunderland (h) 23 Aug 1947. Final app: League v Newcastle United (h) 15 Apr 1950. On tour v Swiss Select (in Zürich) 30 May 1950. Transferred to Fulham (£10,000) summer 1950.
ARSENAL Record: League 103 (1 gl); FA Cup 4; FA Charity Shield 1; Football Combination 2; Friendlies 20 (1 gl).
Honours: Division One champions 1947-8. FA Charity Shield winners 1948-9. 6 full Scotland caps 1947-8.
Won club honours with Glasgow Rangers. Served in the Army Physical Training Corps during the

war. Won wartime international honours with West Ham United and full international honours with Brentford. Played for Great Britain v Rest of Europe 1947. Became player-manager of Guildford City (1952) and trainer-coach at Dundee (Nov 1955). Was manager of Norwich City (May 1957), West Bromwich Albion (Oct 1961) and Brighton & Hove Albion (Apr 1963). Retired from football and later became a traffic warden in Brighton. Now lives in the Midlands.

McAULEY, James   **1897-98**
Right-back
Born: Scotland.
Previous Club: Greenock Morton. Joined ARSENAL: 4 May 1897 from Greenock Morton. First app: League v Grimsby Town (h) 1 Sep 1897. Final app: League v Gainsborough Trinity (a) 26 Mar 1898.
ARSENAL Record: League 23 (1 gl); FA Cup 4 (1 gl); United League 7 (1 gl); Friendlies 4.

McAVOY, Francis   **1895-98**
Outside-left   5ft 9in. 10st.
Born: Ayr, Scotland, 1876.
Jnr football: Ayr. Joined ARSENAL: 25 May 1895 from Ayr. First app: Kent League v Sheppey United (a) 7 Sep 1895. First snr app: Snr fdly v Millwall Athletic (a) 9 Sep 1895. League v Lincoln City (h) 21 Sep 1895. Final app: League v Manchester City (h) 5 Feb 1898. Was suspended by Arsenal, Mar 1898 and joined Brighton United, summer 1898.
ARSENAL Record: League 44 (8 gls); FA Cup 3 (2 gls); United League 17 (1 gl); Kent League 17 (20 gls); Friendlies 50 (35 gls).
Honours: Kent League champions 1896-7.
Later returned to Scotland to play for Ayr.

McAVOY, John   **1898-99**
Full-back   5ft 8in. 11st 7lb.
Born: Scotland, c.1878.
Previous Club: Glasgow Celtic (Res). Joined ARSENAL: 27 Oct 1898 from Celtic. First app: Kent League v Bromley (a) 5 Nov 1898. First snr app: United League v Bristol City (a) 9 Nov 1898. Final snr app: Southern District Combination v Bristol City (h) 30 Oct 1899. Final app: Kent League v Sittingbourne (a) 26 Dec 1899. Transferred to Grimsby Town 29 Dec 1899.
ARSENAL Record: League 25; FA Cup 1; United League 10; Southern District Combination 2; Kent League 13; Other jnr comp: 3; Friendlies 10.

McBEAN, John   **1889-92**
Left-back   5ft 9in. 10st 12lb.
Born: Kirkcaldy, Scotland, 1868. Died: Plumstead, Jan 1954.
Jnr football: Kirkcaldy Wanderers. Joined ARSENAL: End of 1888. First app: Snr fdly v Vulcan (at Willesden) 5 Jan 1889. First first-class app: FA Cup (Q) v Lyndhurst (h) 5 Oct 1889. Final first-class app: FA Cup v Small Heath (a) 16 Jan 1892. Final app: Reserves v St Lukes (h) 30 Apr 1892.
ARSENAL Record: FA Cup 2; FA Cup (Q) 4. In addition made 111 snr apps (1 gl) and 5 reserve apps for Royal Arsenal between 1888-89 and 1891-2.
Honours: Represented Fifeshire Juniors. London Senior Cup winners 1890-91, runners-up 1889-90. London Charity Cup winners 1889-90. Kent Senior Cup winners 1889-90. Represented both Kent County and London.
An engineer by trade, he came from Scotland in the 1880s. After Royal Arsenal he played for Royal Ordnance FC. Was employed at Woolwich Arsenal Ordnance factory for over 40 years and was foreman of the Light Gun Factory when he retired in 1932. Received a long service medal from King George V. On retirement lived in Plumstead.

McCLELLAND, John   **1960-64**
Goalkeeper   5ft 11in. 12st 2lb.
Born: Lurgan, Co Armagh, Ireland, 19 May 1940.
Died: Ireland, 15 Mar 1976.
School: Lurgan.
Previous Club: Glenavon. Joined ARSENAL: 13 Oct 1960 from Glenavon for £7,000. First app: League fdly v Norwich City (a) 19 Oct 1960. League v Tottenham Hotspur (a) 21 Jan 1961. Final snr app: League v Stoke City (h) 29 Feb 1964. Snr fdly v Watford (a) 14 Apr 1964. Final app: Metropolitan League v Chelmsford (a) 28 Nov 1964. Transferred to Fulham 26 Dec 1964.
ARSENAL Record: League 46; FA Cup 3; Football Combination 51; London FA Challenge Cup 2; Metropolitan League 15; Friendlies 26.
Honours: London FA Challenge Cup runners-up 1960-61. Metropolitan League Professional Cup winners 1961-2. 5 full Northern Ireland caps 1960-61.
Played for Mid-Ulster schoolboys. Won club honours, Ireland amateur international honours and played for the Irish League whilst with Glenavon. Won his first full international cap whilst still an Arsenal reserve. Won further international honours with Fulham. Had a spell on loan to Lincoln City (Dec 1968). Given a free transfer by Fulham in May 1969 and subsequently joined Barnet. Died from cancer, after a brief illness in 1976.

McCONNELL, Alexander   **1897-99**
Full-back   5ft 8in. 11st 10lb.
Born: Glenbuck, Scotland, c.1875.
Jnr football: Glenbuck Athletic. Previous Club: Everton. Joined ARSENAL: 19 Nov 1897 from Everton. First app: League v Blackpool (h) 27 Nov 1897. Final app: United League v Tottenham Hotspur (a) 29 Apr 1899. Transferred to Queen's Park Rangers summer 1899.
ARSENAL Record: League 37 (1 gl); FA Cup 1; United League 25; Kent League 1; Other jnr comp: 1; Friendlies 13.
Later played for Grimsby Town (1901).

McCOWIE, Andrew   **1899-1900**
Inside-forward
Born: Scotland.
Previous Club: Liverpool (1896). Joined ARSENAL: 9 May 1899 from Liverpool. First app: League v Leicester Fosse (a) 2 Sep 1899. Final app: League v Burton Swifts (a) 15 Sep 1900. Snr fdly v Aston Villa (h) 1 Oct 1900. Transferred to Middlesbrough 3 Oct 1900.
ARSENAL Record: League 28 (7 gls); FA Cup 5; Southern District Combination 9 (4 gls); Friendlies 10 (4 gls).

McCULLOUGH, William James   **1958-66**
Left-back   5ft 11in. 11st 7lb.
Born: Woodburn, N.Ireland, 27 Jul 1935.
School: St Nicholas Public Elementary, Carrick-fergus.
Jnr football: YMCA Carrickfergus, Barn United (Carrickfergus). Previous Clubs: Ballyclare Comrades, Portadown (Dec 1957). Joined ARSENAL: 12 Sep 1958 from Portadown for £5,000. First app: Football Combination v Swansea Town (h) 16 Sep 1958. Snr fdly v Southampton (a) 10 Nov 1958. League v Luton Town (h) 27 Dec 1958. Final snr app: League v Manchester United (a) 19 Mar 1966. Final app: London FA Challenge Cup Final v Queen's Park Rangers (h) 10 May 1966. Transferred to Millwall 1 Jul 1966.
ARSENAL Record: League 253 (4 gls); FA Cup 11; European comp: 4 (1 gl); Other snr comp: 5; Football Combination 46 (1 gl); London FA Challenge Cup 10 (2 gls); Friendlies 80/1 (1 gl).

Honours: Southern Floodlit Challenge Cup winners 1958-9. London FA Challenge Cup winners 1961-2, runners-up 1965-6. 1 Northern Ireland 'B' cap 1959 and 9 full international caps 1961-64 (mostly at left-half).
Was a grocer's assistant before taking up football. Played for the Irish League whilst with Portadown. Won further international honours with Millwall. Transferred from Millwall to Bedford Town (1967). Joined Cork Celtic (Republic of Ireland) as player-manager (1968) and then Derry City. On leaving football, worked as an electrical engineer at his father-in-law's factory in Woodford, Essex.

McDERMOTT, Brian James   **1977-84**
Forward   5ft 7½in. 9st 12lb.
Born: Slough, 8 Apr 1961.
School: Herschel High.
Joined ARSENAL: 1977 (apprentice), 8 Feb 1979 (professional). First app: South East Counties League v Ipswich Town (a) 1 Jan 1977. First snr app: League (sub) v Bristol City (h) 10 Mar 1979. Final snr app: League v Stoke City (a) 28 Jan 1984. Snr fdly v Windsor & Eton (a) 20 Mar 1984. Final app: Football Combination v Fulham (h) 18 Dec 1984. Transferred to Oxford United (£40,000) 31 Dec 1984.
ARSENAL Record: League 38/23 (12 gls); FA Cup 0/1; Football League Cup 3/1; European comp: 3/3 (1 gl); Football Combination 172/2 (81 gls); South East Counties League 40/1 (10 gls); FA Youth Cup 6 (1 gl); Other jnr comp: 5 (3 gls); Friendlies 51/8 (21 gls).
Honours: Played for Slough schoolboys. England Youth international 1979. Football Combination champions 1983-4.
Had spells on loan to Fulham (Mar 1983) and Norrköping, Sweden (Apr-Oct 1984). Won club honours with Oxford United. Played for Huddersfield Town (on loan-Nov 1986). Transferred from Oxford United to Cardiff City (summer 1987), Exeter City (Feb 1989) and later played for Yeovil Town..

McDONALD, Duncan   **1909-11**
Full-back   5ft 8in. 12st 7lb.
Born: Bo'ness, Scotland.
Jnr football: Bo'ness. Joined ARSENAL: 8 Apr 1909 from Bo'ness. First app: Snr fdly v Exeter (h) 9 Apr 1909. League v Manchester United (a) 30 Oct 1909. Final snr app: League v Bury (a)

3 Sep 1910. Final app: South Eastern League v Tunbridge Wells (h) 29 Apr 1911. Transferred to West Hartlepool summer 1911.
ARSENAL Record: League 26; FA Cup 1; Other snr comp: 1; South Eastern League 33 (1 gl); London League (Res) 1; Friendlies 15 (2 gls).

McDONALD, Hugh   **1906, 1908-10 &**
    Laughlan   **1912-13**
Goalkeeper   6ft 1in. 15st.
Born: Kilwinning, Ayrshire, 1884. Died: Plumstead, 27 Aug 1920.
Jnr football: Ayr Westerlea, Ayr; Maybole; Ayr Academical; Beith. Joined ARSENAL: 29 Jan 1906 from Beith. Transferred to Brighton 1906. Rejoined ARSENAL: 8 May 1908 from Brighton. Transferred to Oldham Athletic 5 Jul 1910. Rejoined ARSENAL: 23 Dec 1912 from Bradford. First app: Jnr fdly v Coventry City (a) 3 Feb 1906. First snr app: League v Blackburn Rovers (h) 17 Feb 1906. Final app: League v Tottenham Hotspur (a) 19 Apr 1913. Transferred to Fulham 7 Nov 1913.
ARSENAL Record: League 94; FA Cup 9; Other snr comp: 2; London FA Challenge Cup 4; South Eastern League 2; Friendlies 9.
Transferred from Oldham Athletic to Bradford (Nov 1911). Transferred Fulham to Bristol Rovers (Feb 1914). After retirement from football he was a publican in Plumstead until his death after a long illness in 1920.

MACDONALD, Malcolm Ian   **1976-79**
Centre-forward   5ft 8in. 13st 2lb.
Born: Fulham, 7 Jan 1950.
School: Queen's Manor Primary (Fulham); Sloane Grammar (Chelsea).

Jnr football: Knowle Juniors, Tonbridge. Previous Clubs: Fulham (Aug 1968), Luton Town (Jul 1969), Newcastle United (May 1971). Joined ARSENAL: 29 Jul 1976 from Newcastle United for £333,333. First app: On tour v Grasshoppers (Switzerland) 10 Aug 1976. League v Bristol City (h) 21 Aug 1976. Final app: League v Chelsea (a) 14 May 1979. On tour v Lyngby BK (Denmark) 15 May 1979. Retired through injury Aug 1979.
ARSENAL Record: League 84 (42 gls); FA Cup 9 (10 gls); Football League Cup 14 (5 gls); European comp: 0/1; Football Combination 13 (5 gls); Friendlies 23/1 (18 gls).
Honours: FA Cup runners-up 1978.
Won club honours with Luton Town. Won club, international and Football League honours with

Newcastle United. On retiring from playing became marketing executive at Fulham and then manager (Nov 1980). Became a publican at Worthing, Sussex (1984). Had a spell as manager of Huddersfield Town (Oct 1987-May 1988) before returning to the hotel business.

McEACHRANE, Roderick John   **1902-15**
Left-half   5ft 6½in. 10st 11lb.
Born: Inverness, Scotoland, c.1878. Died: 16 Nov 1952.
Jnr football: Inverness Thistle. Previous Club: Thames Ironworks (1898) — West Ham United. Joined ARSENAL: 1 May 1902 from West Ham United. First app: London League v West Ham United (a) 1 Sep 1902. League v Preston North End (a) 6 Sep 1902. Final snr app: League v Birmingham (h) 22 Nov 1913. Final app: South Eastern League v Croydon (a) 28 Apr 1915. Outbreak of war brought an end to his career (1915).
ARSENAL Record: League 313; FA Cup 33; London League 14; Other snr comp: 8; London FA Challenge Cup 5; Kent League 1; South Eastern League 84; London League (Res) 17; Friendlies 31.
Honours: Division Two runners-up (promotion) 1903-04. Southern Professional Charity Cup runners-up 1903-04.
Came from Scotland to Canning Town in 1898 to work at Thames Ironworks shipbuilding yard. Retired from football at end of 1914-15 season and worked in Royal Arsenal munitions factory during the war.

McFARLANE, Alexander   **1896-97**
Outside-left   5ft 8½in. 11st.
Born: Airdrie, Scotland, 1877.
Jnr football: Baillieston. Previous Club: Airdrieonians. Joined ARSENAL: 19 Nov 1896 from Airdrieonians. First app: League v Grimsby Town (h) 28 Nov 1896. Final app: League v Manchester City (h) 28 Apr 1897. Snr fdly v Southampton St Mary's (a) 29 Apr 1897. Transferred to Airdreonians summer 1897.
ARSENAL Record: League 5; Other League 2 (1 gl); Kent League 10 (9 gls); Friendlies 10 (5 gls).
Honours: Kent League champions 1896-7.
Later played for Newcastle United (Oct 1898), Dundee (Nov 1901), and Chelsea (Apr 1913). Won Scotland international honours with Dundee. Later had spells as manager of Dundee, Charlton Athletic and Blackpool.

McGEOCH, Craig Archibald   **1897-99**
Inside/centre-forward
Born: Scotland.
Jnr football: Dunblane. Joined ARSENAL: 14 May 1897 from Dunblane. First app: League v Grimsby Town (h) 1 Sep 1897. Final app: United League v Tottenham Hotspur (a) 29 Apr 1899.
ARSENAL Record: League 35 (13 gls); FA Cup 4 (1 gl); United League 23 (6 gls); Kent League 8 (5 gls); Other jnr comp: 4 (3 gls); Friendlies 29 (20 gls).
Honours: Sevenoaks Charity Cup winners 1897-8.
Later played for Dundee.

McGIBBON, Charles Edward   **1905, 1909-10**
Centre-forward   5ft 11in. 12st
Born: Portsmouth, 1880. Died: Hambledon, Hampshire, May 1954.
Jnr football: Eltham, New Brompton. Previous Clubs: Crystal Palace (1907), Southampton (1909). Joined ARSENAL: 31 Aug 1905 (amateur) from Royal Artillery, 1909 from Southampton. First app: London League (Res) v Tottenham Hotspur (a) 2 Sep 1905. First snr app: League v Chelsea (a) 28 Mar 1910. Final app: League v Preston North End (h) 23 Apr 1910. Transferred to Leyton 26 Aug 1910.

74

ARSENAL Record: League 4 (3 gls); London League (Res) 2 (1 gl).
Was a Sergeant in the Royal Artillery throughout his playing career. Served in World War One and in 1919 became chief clerk at Netley Hospital. His cousin, Douglas, also played for Southampton.

McGILL, James M.   **1965-67**
Wing-half   5ft 8in. 10st 7lb.
Born: Partick, Scotland, 27 Nov 1946.
Jnr football: Possil Park YMCA (Glasgow).
Joined ARSENAL: 28 Jun 1965 from Possil Park YMCA. First app: Jnr fdly v Walton & Hersham (a) 14 Aug 1965. First snr app: Snr fdly v Swansea Town (a) 3 May 1966. League v Leeds United (h) 5 May 1966. Final snr app: League v Southampton (a) 27 Dec 1966. Snr fdly v Romford (a) 15 May 1967. Final app: Football Combination v Gillingham (a) 6 Sep 1967. Transferred to Huddersfield Town (£10,000) 8 Sep 1967.
ARSENAL Record: League 6/4; Football League Cup 2; Football Combination 42 (7 gls); London FA Challenge Cup 2; Metropolitan League 31 (1 gl); Friendlies 18.
Honours: Metropolitan League Challenge Cup winners 1965-6.
Later played for Hull City (Oct 1971) and Halifax Town (Feb 1976). Went to play for San Diego (USA) 1976 and Melbourne (Australia) 1977. Retired Dec 1977. Returned to Frickley Colliery and worked for ICI in Huddersfield.

McKECHNIE, Ian Hector   **1958-64**
Goalkeeper   5ft 11in. 12st 11lb.
Born: Bellshill, Lanark, Scotland, 4 Oct 1941.
Jnr football: Lenzie (Dumbartonshire). Joined ARSENAL: Sep 1958 (amateur), 30 Apr 1959 (professional). First app: Metropolitan League v Windsor (a) 10 Sep 1958 (at outside left). First snr app: On tour v Staevnet (Denmark) 16 May 1961. League v Blackburn Rovers (a) 14 Oct 1961. Final snr app: Fairs Cup v Staevnet (Denmark) (h) 22 Oct 1963. Final app: Metropolitan League v Tonbridge (h) 28 Apr 1964. Given free transfer by Arsenal and joined Southend United, 4 May 1964.
ARSENAL Record: League 23; European comp: 2; Football Combination 43; London FA Challenge Cup 6; FA Youth Cup 5; Metropolitan League 51; South East Counties League 36 (3 gls); Other jnr comp: 3; Friendlies 33/3. In addition played 2 South East Counties League matches 1959-60, later removed from records.
Honours: Played for Dumbartonshire. Football Combination champions 1962-3. London FA Challenge Cup winners 1962-3. Metropolitan League champions 1960-61. Metropolitan League Challenge Cup winners 1960-61. Metropolitan League Professional Cup winners 1960-61. South East Counties League Cup winners 1959-60.
Came to Arsenal as an outside-left and his goalkeeping ability was accidently discovered during a practice game. Was not retained by Southend at end of 1965-6 and joined Hull City (Aug 1966). Later became manager of Sligo Rovers (Ireland).

McKELLAR, Matthew T.   **1909-10**
Centre-forward   5ft 7½in. 11st 10lb.
Born: Campsie, Stirlingshire, Scotland, c.1887.
Jnr football: Campsie, Kirkintilloch Harp. Joined ARSENAL: 8 Nov 1909 from Kirkintilloch Harp. First app: League v Sheffield Wednesday (a) 13 Nov 1909. Final snr app: FA Cup v Everton (a) 5 Feb 1910. Snr fdly v Millwall (a) 5 Mar 1910. Final app: South Eastern League v Brighton (a) 20 Apr 1910.
ARSENAL Record: League 3 (1 gl); FA Cup 2 (1 gl); South Eastern League 11 (2 gls); Other jnr comp: 1; Friendlies 1 (1 gl).

McKENZIE, Alexander   **1920-23**
Inside-forward   5ft 6in. 10st 12lb.
Born: Leith, Edinburgh.
Jnr football: Armiston Rangers. Joined ARSENAL: Nov 1920 (trial), 3 Jan 1921 (professional). First app: Jnr fdly v Thorneycrofts (a) 27 Nov 1920. First snr app: League v West Bromwich Albion (h) 28 Mar 1921. Final snr app: League v Preston North End (h) 14 Apr 1923. Final app: Jnr fdly v Summerstown (a) 25 Apr 1923. Transferred to Blackpool 9 May 1923.
ARSENAL Record: League 15 (2 gls); Other snr comp: 1 (1 gl); Football Combination 45 (16 gls); Friendlies 11 (4 gls).
Honours: London Combination champions 1922-3. Southend Hospital Cup winners 1921-2.

MACKIE, John Alexander   **1921-28**
Right-back   5ft 9in. 10st 9lb.
Born: Monkstown, Co Antrim, N.Ireland, 23 Feb 1903. Died: Isleworth, 9 Jun 1984.
Jnr football: Monkstown FC, Royal Irish Rifles (wartime), Forth River FC (Belfast). Joined ARSENAL: Nov 1921 (trial), 10 Feb 1922 from Forth River. First app: Jnr fdly v Brighton (h) 24 Nov 1921. First snr app: League v Birmingham (h) 9 Dec 1922. Final snr app: Snr fdly v Hibernians (h) 26 Apr 1926. Final app: Fdly v Kettering Town (a) 3 May 1928. Transferred to Portsmouth 30 Jun 1928.
ARSENAL Record: League 108; FA Cup 10 (1 gl); Other snr comp: 1; Football Combination 58 (1 gl); London FA Challenge Cup 12 (1 gl); Friendlies 33.

Honours: London FA Challenge Cup winners 1923-4, runners-up 1925-6. 1 full Northern Ireland cap 1923.
Made a remarkable recovery from a severe leg injury which threatened his career. Won club and international honours with Portsmouth. Transferred from Portsmouth to Northampton Town (Mar 1936). Played for Sittingbourne (1938). On retirement worked as a stonemason.

McKINNON, Angus   **1908-22**
Left-half   5ft 8in. 11st 7lb.
Born: Paisley, Scotland, c.1887.
Jnr football: Heart of Midlothian (trial), Petershill FC (Glasgow). Joined ARSENAL: 15 May 1908 from Petershill (after trial on Arsenal's Scottish tour, Apr 1908). First app: Scottish tour v Kilmarnock 30 Apr 1908 (trial). First snr app:

Snr fdly v Rest of Kent (a) 7 Oct 1908. League v Bradford City (a) 12 Dec 1908. Final snr app: League v Middlesbrough (a) 8 Apr 1922. Final app: London Combination v Tottenham Hotspur (a) 3 May 1922. Transferred to Charlton Athletic 11 Jul 1922.
ARSENAL Record: League 211 (4 gls); FA Cup 6; Other snr comp: 11; Football Combination 12; London FA Challenge Cup 14; South Eastern League 101 (5 gls); London League (Res) 18 (2 gls); Friendlies 32 (2 gls). In addition made 49 apps during wartime.
Honours: London FA Challenge Cup runners-up 1914-15. Norwich Hospital Cup winners 1913-14. Southend Hospital Cup winners 1920-21. Metropolitan Hospital Cup winners 1920-21.
Served as a driver in Royal Field Artillery in France during the war. Retired from playing in 1926. Became manager of Wigan Borough (1929-30) and was trainer-coach at New Brighton for over 25 years from 1935-6.

McLAUGHLAN, Joseph   **1911-13**
Centre-forward   5ft 10½in. 11st 8lb.
Born: Edinburgh, c.1891.
Jnr football: Linlithgow, Bathgate FC. Joined ARSENAL: 28 Sep 1911 from Bathgate. First app: South Eastern League v Fulham (h) 7 Oct 1911. First snr app: London PFA Charity Fund v Chelsea (h) 30 Oct 1911. League v Notts County (a) 23 Dec 1911. Final app: League v Derby County (h) 12 Apr 1913. Transferred to Watford 24 Jun 1913.
ARSENAL Record: League 16 (3 gls); Other snr comp: 2 (2 gls); London FA Challenge Cup 1; South Eastern League 32 (17 gls); Other jnr comp: 1; Friendlies 11 (20 gls).
Played a few games before joining the forces in wartime, during which he sustained shrapnel wounds.

MacLEOD, John Murdoch   **1961-64**
Winger   5ft 6in. 10st 2lb.
Born: Edinburgh, 23 Nov 1938.
Jnr football: Edinburgh Thistle (1954); Armadale (1955). Previous Club: Hibernian (1957). Joined ARSENAL: 1 Jul 1961 from Hibernian for £40,000. First app: Snr fdly v Middlesbrough (a) 5 Aug 1961. League v Burnley (h) 19 Aug 1961. Final app: League v Aston Villa (h) 29 Aug 1964. Transferred to Aston Villa (£35,000) 2 Sep 1964.
ARSENAL Record: League 101 (23 gls); FA Cup 8 (4 gls); European comp: 3 (1 gl); Football Combination 5 (2 gls); London FA Challenge Cup 5 (1 gl); Friendlies 24 (5 gls).
Honours: London FA Challenge Cup winners 1961-2.
Won Scotland Under-23, full international caps and Scottish League honours with Hibernian. Joined KV Mechelen (Belgium) from Aston Villa (Jul 1968). Moved to Raith Rovers (1971) and Newtongrange Star (1972). Retired 1975.

McLINTOCK, Francis MBE   **1964-73**
Wing-half/central defender   5ft 10in. 11st 2lb.
Born: Glasgow, 28 Dec 1939.
Jnr football: Shawfield Juniors (Glasgow). Previous Club: Leicester City (Jan 1957). Joined ARSENAL: 5 Oct 1964 from Leicester City for £80,000. First app: League v Nottingham Forest (h) 6 Oct 1964. Final app: League v Derby County (h) 31 Mar 1973. Transferred to Queen's Park Rangers (£25,000) 27 Apr 1973.
ARSENAL Record: League 312/2 (26 gls); FA Cup 36 (1 gl); Football League Cup 34 (4 gls); European comp: 19 (1 gl); Football Combination 10; London FA Challenge Cup 1; Friendlies 57 (11 gls).
Honours: Division One champions 1970-71. FA Cup winners 1971, runners-up 1972. European

Fairs Cup winners 1969-70. Football League Cup runners-up 1967-8, 1968-9. London FA Challenge Cup winners 1969-70. Captain of Arsenal. 6 full Scotland caps 1964-71. ARSENAL Player of the Year 1967. Footballer of the Year 1970-71. Won club and international honours with Leicester City. Awarded the MBE in 1972. Retired from playing May 1977. Was manager of Leicester City (Jun 1977-Apr 1978), Brentford (Feb 1984-Jan 1987) and assistant manager of Millwall.

McNAB, Robert   1966-75
Full-back   5ft 7½in. 11st 2lb.
Born: Huddersfield, 20 Jul 1943.
School: Rawthorpe CSM (Huddersfield).
Jnr football: Moldgreen Civic Youth Club. Previous Club: Huddersfield Town 1961 (amateur), Apr 1963 (professional). Joined ARSENAL: 1 Oct 1966 from Huddersfield Town for £50,000. First app: League v Leeds United (a) 15 Oct 1966. Final snr app: League v Stoke City (h) 29 Mar 1975. Final app: Football Combination v Tottenham Hotspur (a) 26 Apr 1975. Transferred to Wolverhampton Wanderers (free transfer) 10 Jul 1975.
ARSENAL Record: League 277/1 (4 gls); FA Cup

39; Football League Cup 26/1 (2 gls); European comp: 20/1; Other snr comp: 1; Football Combination 24; London FA Challenge Cup 1; Friendlies 45/1 (4 gls).
Honours: Division One champions 1970-71. FA Cup winners 1971, runners-up 1972. European Fairs Cup winners 1969-70. Football League Cup runners-up 1967-8, 1968-9. Captain of Arsenal. 4 full England caps 1968-9 and made 1 app for the Football League 1968.
After one season with Wolverhampton Wanderers he went to play for San Antonio (Texas) in the NASL. Returned to England in 1977 and played for Barnet before becoming coach to Vancouver Whitecaps (Canada). Returned again in Nov 1980 but after a short spell as a publican in Tottenham went back to live in Vancouver, Canada.

McNAB, William   1893-94
Centre-forward
Born: Scotland.
Previous Club: Burnley. Joined ARSENAL: 15 Dec 1893. First app: League v Northwich Victoria (h) 23 Mar 1894. Final app: League v Small Heath (h) 31 Mar 1894. Snr fdly v Burnley (h) 21 Apr 1894. Was reinstated as an amateur and joined Royal Ordnance FC (Maze Hill), Jul 1894.
ARSENAL Record: League 2 (1 gl); Friendlies 5 (4 gls).
Later returned to Scotland.

McNICHOL, Duncan   1899-1903
Full-back   6ft. 12st 10lb.
Born: Alexandria, Dunbartonshire, 1874.
Jnr football: St Bernards. Joined ARSENAL: 8 Jun 1899 from St Bernards. First app: League v Leicester Fosse (h) 2 Sep 1899. Final app: League v Lincoln City (a) 28 Mar 1903. Snr fdly v Chesterfield (h) 25 Apr 1903. Transferred to Aberdeen Oct 1903.
ARSENAL Record: League 101 (1 gl); FA Cup 11; Southern District Combination 11; London League 9; Other snr comp: 3; London League (Res) 3; Friendlies 24.
Was forced to retire from playing in 1905 and became a shopkeeper in Aberdeen.

McPHEE, John   1898-99
Full-back
Joined ARSENAL: 7 May 1898. First app: Snr fdly v Millwall (a) 30 Apr 1898 (trial). League v Burton Swifts (h) 22 Oct 1898. Final snr app: League v Glossop (a) 4 Feb 1899. Snr fdly v Woolwich League (h) 26 Apr 1899. Final app: Jnr fdly v Grays United (h) 29 Apr 1899.
ARSENAL Record: League 7; FA Cup 1; United League 6; Kent League 14; Other jnr comp: 1; Friendlies 23 (1 gl).
A junior international from Glasgow. Played for Glasgow and Perth.

McPHERSON, Ian Buchanan DFC[2]   1946-51
Wing-forward   5ft 10in. 11st 12lb.
Born: Glasgow, 26 Jul 1920. Died: St Albans, May 1983.
Previous Clubs: Glasgow Rangers (1939), Notts County (1945-6). Joined ARSENAL: 5 Aug 1946 from Notts County (part exchange R.Cumner.)
First app: Football League South v Chelsea (a) 16 Mar 1946 (as a guest). League v Wolverhampton Wanderers (a) 31 Aug 1946. Final app: League v Bolton Wanderers (h) 21 Apr 1951. On tour v Vasco da Gama (Brazil) 12 Jun 1951. Transferred to Notts County 31 Jul 1951.
ARSENAL Record: League 152 (19 gls); FA Cup 11 (2 gls); Football Combination 17 (6 gls); London FA Challenge Cup 2; Friendlies 35/6 (14 gls). In addition made 6 apps (2 gls) as a guest during wartime.
Honours: Division One champions 1947-8.

Football Combination Cup runners-up 1950-51.
Was a Flying Officer in the RAF during the war and won the DFC and bar. After Notts County he played for Brentford (Jul 1953) and Bedford Town (Oct 1953). Rejoined the RAF as physical fitness instructor at Leeming (1954-8) and played football for Cambridge United (1954-5). Became an area sales manager in the pharmaceutical industry in St Albans in 1959.

McQUILKIE J.   1892-93
Full-back
Born: Scotland.
Joined ARSENAL: from Renton in Oct 1892.
First app: FA Cup (Q) v Highland Light Infantry (h) 15 Oct 1892. Final first-class app: FA Cup (Q) v City Ramblers (h) 29 Oct 1892. Final apps: Reserves v Southampton St Marys (h) 4 Mar 1893.
ARSENAL Record: FA Cup (Q) 2. In addition made 10 senior and 11 reserve apps for Royal Arsenal 1892-3.

MADDEN, David John   1983-84
Midfield   6ft. 11st 3lb.
Born: London, 6 Jan 1963.
Previous Clubs: Southampton; Bournemouth (on loan). Joined ARSENAL: 4 Aug 1983 from Southampton (free transfer). First app: Snr fdly (sub) v Gillingham (a) 17 May 1983 (on trial). League v West Bromwich Albion (h) 3 Dec 1983. Final snr app: League v West Ham United (a) 10 Dec 1983. Final app: Football Combination v Charlton Athletic (h) 14 May 1984. Transferred to Charlton Athletic (free transfer) 20 Jun 1984.
ARSENAL Record: League 2; Football Combination 22/3 (3 gls); Friendlies 4/2 (2 gls).
Honours: Football Combination champions 1983-4.
Later played for Reading (1987-8), Crystal Palace (Aug 1988), Birmingham City (loan) and Maidstone United (1990-91). Forced to retire through injury (1991-2).

MAGILL, Edward James   1959-65
Full-back   5ft 10in. 12st 7lb.
Born: Lurgan, N.Ireland, 17 May 1939.
School: Carrick (Lurgan).
Jnr football: Edgarstown Boys Club (Portadown). Previous Club: Portadown (1955). Joined ARSENAL: Apr 1959 (trial), 11 May 1959 from Portadown for £5,000. First app: Snr fdly v Bath City (a) 30 Apr 1959 (on trial). League v Sheffield Wednesday (a) 19 Dec 1959. Final snr app: League v Nottingham Forest (a) 13 Mar 1965. Snr fdly v Corinthian Casuals (h) 21 Sep 1965. Final app: Football Combination v West Ham United (a) 23 Oct 1965. Transferred to Brighton & Hove Albion (£6,000) 29 Oct 1965.
ARSENAL Record: League 116; FA Cup 11; European comp: 4; Football Combination 96 (2 gls); London FA Challenge Cup 8; Metropolitan League 3; Other snr comp: 1; Friendlies 40/4.
Honours: London FA Challenge Cup runners-up 1960-61. Metropolitan League Professional Cup winners 1960-61. 1 Northern Ireland Under-23 cap 1962, 21 full Northern Ireland caps 1961-5.
Was a textile worker in Lurgan before taking up football. Won further international caps with Brighton. Later became coach to B1909 Odense (Denmark) and then manager of Frederikshavn (Denmark).

MAIN, Alexander   1899-1903
Inside-forward   5ft 10in. 12st.
Born: Scotland.
Jnr football: West Calder. Previous Club: Hibernian. Joined ARSENAL: 22 Nov 1899 from Hibernian. First app: Snr fdly v Eastbourne (a) 29 Nov 1899. League v Lincoln City (a) 25 Dec 1899. Final snr app: London League v Brentford (a) 23 Mar 1903. Final app: Chatham Charity

Cup final v Chatham (a) 27 Apr 1903. Transferred to Motherwell Oct 1903.
ARSENAL Record: League 63 (14 gls); FA Cup 6; Southern District Combination 6 (3 gls); London League 10 (1 gl); Other snr comp: 3; Kent League 12 (2 gls); London League (Res) 17 (14 gls); Other jnr comp: 2; Friendlies 19 (11 gls).
Honours: West Kent League champions 1902-03. Chatham Charity Cup finalist 1902-03.
Later played for Watford (Jun 1904). Retired at end of 1906-07 season.

MALE, Charles George   **1929-48**
Right-back   5ft 11½in. 12st 2lb.
Born: West Ham, London, 8 May 1910.
Jnr football: Clapton FC (amateur). Joined ARSENAL: 23 Nov 1929 (amateur), 8 May 1930 (professional). First app: London Combination v Southampton (h) 3 Sep 1930. First snr app: League v Blackpool (h) 27 Dec 1930. Final app: League v Grimsby Town (h) 1 May 1948. On tour v Liège Select (Belgium) 11 May 1948. Retired cs 1948.
ARSENAL Record: League 285; FA Cup 29; FA Charity Shield 4; Other snr comp: 4; Football Combination 84 (1 gl); London FA Challenge Cup 9; London Midweek League 1; Friendlies 34/1 (3 gls). In addition played 3 League matches 1939-40 prior to outbreak of war and made 181 apps (2 gls) during wartime.
Honours: Division One champions 1932-3, 1933-4, 1934-5, 1937-8. FA Cup winners 1936, runners-up 1932. FA Charity Shield winners 1933-4, 1934-5, 1938-9, runners-up 1935-6. London Combination champions 1930-31. London FA Challenge Cup winners 1930-31. Sheriff of London Shield winners 1932-3. Northampton Charity Shield winners 1931-2. Mayor of Colchester Cup winners 1938-9. Football League South Cup winners 1942-3. Played for West Ham schoolboys. Captain of Arsenal and England. 19 full England caps 1934-9 and made 2 apps for the Football League 1935-6.
Worked for Lloyd's insurance before taking up football. Served with the RAF in Palestine during the war. On retiring from playing he became coach to Arsenal juniors, chief scout, and held several other administrative positions at Arsenal before retiring in May 1975.

MANCINI, Terence John   **1974-76**
Central-defender   6ft. 12st.
Born: St Pancras, London, 4 Oct 1942.
Previous Clubs: Watford (Jul 1961), Port Elizabeth (South Africa) (1966), Orient (Nov 1967), Queen's Park Rangers (Oct 1971). Joined ARSENAL: 24 Oct 1974 from Queen's Park Rangers for £20,000. First app: League v West Ham United (h) 26 Oct 1974. Final snr app: League v Manchester City (a) 24 Apr 1976. Final app: Football Combination v Bristol City (h) 22 Sep 1976. Transferred to Aldershot (free transfer) 23 Sep 1976.
ARSENAL Record: League 52 (1 gl); FA Cup 8; Football League Cup 2; Football Combination 12; Friendlies 12/2 (1 gl).
Honours: 1 full Republic of Ireland cap 1974.
Came from a famous boxing family. Won club and international honours with Queen's Park Rangers. Contract with Aldershot cancelled Apr 1977. Had a spell with Los Angeles Aztecs (USA) and on returning to England now runs a car-hire firm.

MARDEN, Reuben John   **1950-55**
Outside-left   5ft 9in. 11st 2lb.
Born: Fulham, London, 10 Feb 1927.
School: Hampton, Middlesex.
Jnr football: A Chelmsford works team, Chelmsford City (professional). Joined ARSENAL: 31 Jan 1950 from Chelmsford City. First app: London Midweek League v Watford (h) 1 Feb 1950. First snr app: League v Manchester United

(a) 3 Mar 1951. Final snr app: League v Aston Villa (h) 12 Mar 1955. Snr fdly v Hendon (a) 2 May 1955. Final app: Football Combination v Cardiff City (h) 7 May 1955. Transferred to Watford (free transfer) 1 Jun 1955.
ARSENAL Record: League 42 (11 gls); Football Combination 120 (51 gls); London FA Challenge Cup 5 (3 gls); Other snr comp: 1; Eastern Counties League 11 (10 gls); London Midweek League 14 (9 gls); Other jnr comp: 1; Friendlies 26/2 (14 gls).
Honours: Football Combination champions 1950-51.
Served National Service in the Army. After Watford, played for Bedford Town (Mar 1957) and Romford (Jul 1959), later becoming trainer at that club.

MARINELLO, Peter   **1970-73**
Outside-right   5ft 8in. 10st 9lb.
Born: Edinburgh, 20 Feb 1950.
School: St Anthony's, Edinburgh.
Previous Club: Hibernian (1967). Joined ARSENAL: 6 Jan 1970 from Hibernian for £100,000. First app: League v Manchester United (a) 10 Jan 1970. Final app: League v Derby County (a) 25 Nov 1972. On tour v Devonshire Colts (Bermuda) 27 May 1973. Transferred to Portsmouth (£80,000) 26 Jul 1973.
ARSENAL Record: League 32/6 (3 gls); FA Cup 0/1; Football League Cup 5 (1 gl); European comp: 6/1 (1 gl); Football Combination 77 (22 gls); London FA Challenge Cup 3 (1 gl); Friendlies 14/6 (3 gls).

Honours: Football Combination Cup winners 1969-70. 1 Scotland Under-23 cap (sub) 1970.
Played for Edinburgh schoolboys. Won Under-23 honours with Hibernian. After Portsmouth, played for Motherwell (Dec 1975), Fulham (Dec 1978), Phoenix Inferno (USA) (1980) and Heart of Midlothian (Oct 1981). Became a publican in Edinburgh.

MARINER, Paul   **1984-86**
Striker   6ft 12st 2lb.
Born: Bolton, 22 May 1953.
School: Horwich County Secondary.
Jnr football: St Gregory's Boys Club, Chorley. Previous Clubs: Plymouth Argyle (May 1973), Ipswich Town (Oct 1976). Joined ARSENAL: 9 Feb 1984 from Ipswich Town for £150,000. First app: League v Aston Villa (h) 18 Feb 1984. Final

snr app: (sub) League v Nottingham Forest (h) 8 Apr 1986. Final app: Football Combination v Reading (h) 7 May 1986. Transferred to Portsmouth (free transfer) Aug 1986.
ARSENAL Record: League 52/8 (14 gls); FA Cup 5/1 (2 gls); Football League Cup 3/1 (1 gl); Football Combination 10 (6 gls); Friendlies 12 (5 gls).
Honours: 2 full England caps 1984-5.
Won Domestic and European competition club honours and international honours with Ipswich Town. Given free transfer by Portsmouth at end of 1987-8 and joined Naxxar Lions (Malta).

MARKS, George William   **1936-46**
Goalkeeper   5ft 11in. 11st 8lb.
Born: Figheldean, nr.Salisbury, Wiltshire, 9 Apr 1915.
Jnr football: Salisbury Corinthians; Margate (Arsenal nursery). Joined ARSENAL: 16 Mar 1936 (amateur) from Salisbury Corinthians, 21 May 1936 (professional). Returned to ARSENAL from Margate, May 1938. First app: London Combination v Millwall (a) 2 Mar 1936. First snr app: Mayor of Colchester Cup v Tottenham Hotspur 17 Apr 1939. League v Derby County (a) 29 Apr 1939. Final snr app: League v Sunderland (h) 2 Sep 1939 (later expunged). Football League South v Brentford (h) 29 Apr 1946. Final app: Jnr fdly (wartime) v Cheltenham Town (a) 4 May 1946. Transferred to Blackburn Rovers (£5,000) 30 Aug 1946.
ARSENAL Record: League 2; Football Combination 18; Other snr comp: 2; London FA Challenge Cup 3; Southern League 15; Friendlies 8. In addition played 3 League matches 1939-40 prior to outbreak of war and made 126 apps during wartime.
Honours: London Combination champions 1938-9. Mayor of Colchester Cup winners 1938-9. Football League South Cup winners 1942-3. Football League War Cup runners-up 1940-41. Made 8 apps for England in wartime internationals.
Served in the RAF in Northern Ireland during the war. Transferred from Blackburn Rovers to Bristol City (Aug 1948) and then to Reading (Oct 1948). Was trainer-coach at Reading 1954-5. Was reinstated as an amateur and played for Bulford United (Wiltshire) 1955-6.

MARSHALL, Dr James   **1934-35**
Inside-forward   5ft 9½in. 11st 6lb.
Born: Avonbridge, Stirlingshire, Scotland, 3 Jan 1908. Died: 27 Dec 1977.

Jnr football: Shettleston. Previous Club: Glasgow Rangers (Jun 1925). Joined ARSENAL: 24 Jul 1934 from Glasgow Rangers. First app: London Combination v Bristol City (h) 25 Aug 1934. First snr app: Snr fdly v Glasgow Rangers (h) 12 Sep 1934. League v Blackburn Rovers (a) 17 Sep 1934. Final Snr app: League v Preston North End (a) 26 Dec 1934. Final app: London Combination v Southend (a) 9 Mar 1935. Transferred to West Ham United (£2,000) 13 Mar 1935.
ARSENAL Record: League 4; FA Charity Shield 1 (1 gl); Football Combination 26 (7 gls); London FA Challenge Cup 1; Friendlies 4 (1 gl).
Honours: FA Charity Shield winners 1934-5. London Combination champions 1934-5.
Won club and Scotland international honours with Glasgow Rangers. Obtained medical degree Oct 1933. Retired from football at end of 1936-7 season and took up a post with Bermondsey Borough Council. Later went to live in Ashford, Kent.

MARWOOD, Brian　　　　　**1988-90**
Wing-forward　　　　　5ft 7in. 10st 10lb.
Born: Seaham Harbour, 5 Feb 1960.

School: Seaham Secondary.
Previous Clubs: Hull City (Feb 1978), Sheffield Wednesday (Aug 1984). Joined ARSENAL: 25 Mar 1988 from Sheffield Wednesday for £600,000. First app: League v Oxford United (a) 30 Mar 1988. Final Snr app: League v Southampton (h) 2 May 1990. Snr fdly v Wolverhampton Wanderers (a) 3 Aug 1990. Final app: Snr fdly v St Albans City (a) 13 Sep 1990. Transferred to Sheffield United (£350,000) 21 Sep 1990.
ARSENAL Record: League 52 (16 gls); FA Cup 2; FA Charity Shield 0/1; Football League Cup 6 (1 gl); Other snr comp: 5 (4 gls); Football Combination 14 (7 gls); Friendlies 25/3 (8 gls).
Honours: Division One champions 1988-9. Mercantile Credit Centenary Trophy winners 1988-9. 1 full England cap 1988. FA Charity Shield runners-up 1989-90.
Won club honours with Hull City. Currently PFA chairman.

MATTHEWS John Melvin　　　**1971-78**
Midfield　　　　　6ft. 11st 13lb.
Born: London, 1 Nov 1955.
School: Highbury Grove.
Joined ARSENAL: 27 Jul 1971 (apprentice), 28 Aug 1973 (professional). First app: Jnr fdly v Dulwich Hamlet (a) 7 Aug 1971. First snr app: Snr fdly (sub) v Kettering (a) 6 May 1974. League v Leicester City (a) 17 Aug 1974. Final app: League

v Derby County (a) 9 May 1978. On tour (sub) v PSV Eindhoven (Holland) 5 Aug 1978. Transferred to Sheffield United (£90,000) 17 Aug 1978.
ARSENAL Record: League 38/7 (2 gls); FA Cup 4/2 (1 gl); Football League Cup 6 (2 gls); Football Combination 119/4 (6 gls); London FA Challenge Cup 5; South East Counties League 70/1 (4 gls); Other jnr comp: 1; FA Youth Cup 12/1 (1 gl); Friendlies 62/14 (11 gls).
Honours: Played for Islington, Middlesex and London schoolboys. South East Counties League champions 1971-2. South East Counties League Cup runners-up 1971-2.
Suffered a broken ankle Dec 1975. After Sheffield United, played for Mansfield Town (Aug 1982), Chesterfield (Aug 1984), Plymouth Argyle (to summer 1985) and Torquay United (1989-90).

MAXWELL, James　　　　　**1908-09**
Outside-right
Born: Kilmarnock, Scotland, 1882. Died: On active service during World War One.
Previous Clubs: Kilmarnock; Sheffield Wednesday (Mar 1907). Joined ARSENAL: 13 May 1908 from Sheffield Wednesday. First app: League v Everton (h) 2 Sep 1908. Final snr app: League v Sunderland (a) 27 Mar 1909. Final app: South Eastern League v Queen's Park Rangers (a) 29 Apr 1909. Moved back to Scotland and played for Galston (1909-10).
ARSENAL Record: League 2; South Eastern League 26 (5 gls); London League (Res) 14 (1 gl); Friendlies 3.

MAXWELL, Thomas　　　　　**1921**
Forward.
Born: Dunfermline, Scotland
Joined ARSENAL: 21 Oct 1921. First app: London Combination v Crystal Palace (h) 22 Oct 1921. First snr app: League v Huddersfield Town (h) 29 Oct 1921 (only senior app). Final app: London Combination v West Ham United (h) 5 Nov 1921.
ARSENAL Record: League 1; Football Combination 2 (1 gl).
The above were his only three apps for Arsenal and nothing can be traced of his arrival at, or departure from, the club.

MAYCOCK, William Joseph　　**1928-31**
Wing-forward　　　　　5ft 7¾in. 10st 10lb.
Born: Burton upon Trent.
Jnr football: Burton Town; Gresley Rovers (Derbyshire). Joined ARSENAL: 7 Mar 1928 from Gresley Rovers. First app: London Combination v Southampton (h) 10 Mar 1928. First snr app: FA Cup v Swindon Town (h) 20 Feb 1929 (only senior app). Final app: London Combination v Reading (h) 13 Apr 1931. Retired at end of 1930-31 season due to injury.
ARSENAL Record: FA Cup 1; Football Combination 79 (27 gls); London FA Challenge Cup 1; London Midweek League 7 (3 gls); Friendlies 16 (6 gls).
Honours: London Combination champions 1928-9, 1929-30, 1930-1.

MEADE, Raphael Joseph　　　**1978-85**
Striker　　　　　5ft 10in. 11st 9lb.
Born: Islington, London, 22 Nov 1962.
School: Duncombe Junior; Tollington Park Senior.
Jnr football: Holly Park, Hemmingford. Joined ARSENAL: 1977 (schoolboy), Jun 1979 (apprentice), 2 Jun 1980 (professional). First app: South East Counties League v Fulham (a) 19 Aug 1978. First snr app: Snr fdly (sub) v Celtic (h) 25 Nov 1980. UEFA Cup (sub) v Panathinaikos (Greece) 16 Sep 1981. Final snr app: League v Stoke City (a) 30 Mar 1985. Final app: Football

Combination v Millwall (a) 30 May 1985. Transferred to Sporting Clube de Portugal summer 1985.
ARSENAL Record: League 25/16 (14 gls); FA Cup 2/1; Football League Cup 3/1 (1 gl); European comp: 2/1 (1 gl); Football Combination 130/3 (90 gls); South East Counties League 40/10 (18 gls); FA Youth Cup 8/1 (4 gls); Other jnr comp: 10/1 (7 gls); Friendlies 48/8 (44 gls). In addition 2 played Football Combination matches (1 gl) 1981-2, later removed from records.
Honours: Played for Islington schoolboys. Football Combination champions 1983-4. South East Counties League winners 1979-80. President's Cup winners 1980-81.
Returned from Portugal to Dundee United (summer 1988). Transferred to Luton Town (Aug 1989) then played for Ipswich Town, OB Odense (Denmark), Plymouth Argyle and currently Brighton & Hove Albion.

MEADE, Thomas George　　　**1893-97**
Centre-forward
Born: Plumstead, 14 May 1877.
Joined ARSENAL: Nov 1893 (amateur), 16 Oct 1894 (professional). First app: Jnr fdly v Erith (a) 4 Nov 1893. First snr app: Snr fdly v Luton Town (h) 29 Oct 1894. League v Leicester Fosse (a) 7 Jan 1895. Final snr app: League v Leicester Fosse (a) 13 Feb 1897. Final app: Jnr fdly v West Herts (a) 19 Apr 1897. Transferred to Tottenham Hotspur summer 1897.
ARSENAL Record: League 11 (5 gls); FA Cup 3 (2 gls); United League 3 (3 gls); Kent League 28 (31 gls); Other jnr comp: 1; Friendlies 76 (58 gls).
Honours: Kent League champions 1896-7. Wolverton Charity Cup runners-up 1894-5.
Moved from Tottenham Hotspur to Fulham (Dec 1900) with whom he played until 1904 and won Southern League honours.

MEGGS, James W.　　　　　**1889-91**
Inside-forward
Previously played for City Ramblers. Joined ARSENAL: Sep 1889. First app: Snr fdly v London Caledonians (h) 7 Sep 1889. First first-class app: FA Cup (Q) v Lyndhurst (h) 5 Oct 1889. Final app: FA Cup v Derby County (h) 17 Jan 1891. Snr fdly v Everton (h) 26 Jan 1891.
ARSENAL Record: FA Cup 1; FA Cup (Q) 4 (4 gls). In addition made 21 senior apps (14 gls) for Royal Arsenal 1889-90 to 1890-91.
Honours: Kent Senior Cup winners 1889-90. London Senior Cup runners-up 1889-90. Represented London v Sheffield.

MERCER, Joseph OBE　　　　**1946-54**
Left-half　　　　　5ft 9½in. 11st.
Born: Ellesmere Port, Cheshire, 9 Aug 1914. Died: Wirral, Cheshire, 9 Aug 1990.
School: St Johns Street (Ellesmere); Cambridge Road (Ellesmere).
Jnr football: Elton Green, Shell Mex, Runcorn, Ellesmere Port Town. Previous Club: Everton 1931 (amateur), Sep 1932 (professional). Joined ARSENAL: 29 Nov 1946 from Everton for £7,000. First app: League v Bolton Wanderers (h) 30 Nov 1946. Final app: League v Liverpool (h) 10 Apr 1954. Retired Apr 1954 due to injury.
ARSENAL Record: League 247 (2 gls); FA Cup 26; FA Charity Shield 2; Football Combination 2; Other snr comp: 1; Friendlies 19 (4 gls).
Honours: Division One champions 1947-8, 1952-3. FA Cup winners 1950, runners-up 1952. FA Charity Shield winners 1948-9, 1953-4. Captain of Arsenal. Made 1 app for Football League 1947. Footballer of the Year 1950.
Son of an ex-Nottingham Forest and Tranmere Rovers player. Played for Ellesmere Port and Cheshire schoolboys. Won club and international

honours with Everton. Served in the Army Physical Training Corps during the war. Was captain of England team during wartime. Suffered a broken leg, Arsenal v Liverpool in Apr 1954, which ended his playing career. Became manager of Sheffield United (Aug 1955), Aston Villa (Dec 1958) and Manchester City (Jul 1965). Awarded the OBE in 1976. Was general manager of Manchester City (Oct 1971), Coventry City (Jun 1972), England (Jul-Aug 1977) and a director of Coventry City for nine years before retiring from football in 1981.

MERSON, Paul Charles   **1982-**
Striker   5ft 10in. 11st 9lb.
Born: Harlesden, London, 20 Mar 1968.
Jnr football: Forest United, Trials with Chelsea, Queen's Park Rangers and Watford. Joined ARSENAL: 29 Apr 1982 (schoolboy), 26 Jul 1984 (apprentice), Feb 1987 (professional). First app: South East Counties League (sub) v West Ham United (h) 14 Apr 1984. First snr app: Snr fdly (sub) v Southend United (a) 15 Aug 1986. League (sub) v Manchester City (h) 22 Nov 1986.

ARSENAL Record: League 139/28 (50 gls); FA Cup 13/2 (3 gls); Football League Cup 13/2 (5 gls); European comp: 4; FA Charity Shield 2; Other snr comp: 9/2 (2 gls); Football Combination 71/5 (44 gls); South East Counties League 36/5 (16 gls); FA Youth Cup 9 (6 gls); Other jnr comp: 8 (6 gls); Friendlies 57/11 (31 gls).
Honours: Played for Brent, Ealing district and for Middlesex schoolboys. Division One champions 1988-9, 1990-91. FA Charity Shield runners-up 1989-90, medal 1991-2. Mercantile Credit Centenary Trophy winners 1988-9. South East Counties League Cup runners-up 1984-5, 1985-6. Southern Junior Floodlit Cup runners-up 1985-6. PFA Young Player of the Year 1989. 3 England Youth caps; 4 Under-21 caps; 2 'B' caps (2 gls); 1/1 full caps (1 gl).
He made 7 apps on loan to Brentford, 1986-7.

MILLS, Samuel   **1895-96**
Outside-right   5ft 8½in. 11st 7lb.
Born: Derby, 1871.
Jnr football: Alvaston FC, Derby Midland. Previous Clubs: Derby County (Jun 1891); Leicester Fosse (1893); Loughborough Town (1894). Joined ARSENAL: Jun 1895 from Loughborough Town. First app: Kent League v Sheppey United (a) 7 Sep 1895. First snr app: League v Millwall Athletic (a) 9 Sep 1895. League v Lincoln City (a) 14 Sep 1895. Final app: League v Darwen (h) 18 Apr 1896. Snr fdly v Tottenham Hotspur (a) 30 Apr 1896.
ARSENAL Record: League 24 (3 gls); FA Cup 1; Kent League 5 (3 gls); Friendlies 15 (6 gls).
After Arsenal played for Heanor Town (Nov 1896).

MILNE, John Vance   **1935-37**
Wing-forward   5ft 7in. 10st 3lb.
Born: Stirling, Scotland, 25 Mar 1911.
Jnr football: Glasgow Ashfield. Previous Club: Blackburn Rovers (Feb 1932). Joined ARSENAL: 18 Jun 1935 from Blackburn Rovers. First app: League v Sunderland (h) 31 Aug 1935. Final app: League v Preston North End (h) 11 Dec 1937. Transferred to Middlesbrough 14 Dec 1937.
ARSENAL Record: League 49 (19 gls); FA Cup 3; FA Charity Shield 2; Football Combination 21 (7 gls); London FA Challenge Cup 3 (2 gls); Friendlies 11 (6 gls).
Honours: FA Charity Shield runners-up 1935-6, 1936-7. London FA Challenge Cup winners 1935-6.
Gave up a chance to win Scotland Junior international honours to join Blackburn Rovers. Won full and wartime international honours with Middlesbrough. His playing career came to an end during wartime.

MILNE, William DCM
Player 1921-27   **Trainer 1927-60**
Wing-half   5ft 7in. 11st 3lb.
Born: Buckie, Banffshire, Scotland, 24 Nov 1895.
Died: London, 27 Jul 1975.
Jnr football: Buckie Thistle, Tottenham Hotspur (trial). Joined ARSENAL: Aug 1921 (trial); 24 Sep 1921 (professional) from Buckie Thistle. First app: Jnr fdly v Guildford United (a) 31 Aug 1921. First snr app: League v Cardiff City (a) 27 Dec 1921. Final snr app: League v Huddersfield Town (h) 2 Apr 1927. Final app: London Combination v Crystal Palace (a) 29 Oct 1927. Retired in 1927 and became assistant trainer at Arsenal.
ARSENAL Record: League 114 (1 gl); FA Cup 10 (2 gls); Other snr comp: 2; Football Combination 109 (9 gls); London FA Challenge Cup 8; Friendlies 29 (1 gl).
Honours: London Combination champions 1926-7. London FA Challenge Cup winners 1923-4. Southend Hospital Cup winners 1921-2. Metropolitan Hospital Cup runners-up 1922-3.

Trainer to the England international team on several occasions.
Learned his trade as a tailor before taking up football. Served with the Seaforth Highlanders in France in World War One and was awarded the DCM (Mar 1918). Suffered a broken leg in the FA Cup v West Ham United in Jan 1925. Became first-team trainer at Arsenal 1947. His son, William, played for Arsenal juniors. Retired from football at the end of season 1959-60 and continued to live near Highbury until his death after a long illness in 1975.

MILTON, Clement Arthur   **1945-55**
Outside-right   5ft 8½in. 10st 3lb.
Born: Bristol, 10 Mar 1928.
School: Cotham Grammar (Bristol).
Joined ARSENAL: Apr 1945 (amateur), 24 Jul 1946 (professional). First app: (sub) Jnr fdly (wartime) v Maidenhead (a) 12 May 1945. First snr app: League v Aston Villa (h) 10 Mar 1951. Final snr app: FA Cup v Wolverhampton Wanderers (a) 29 Jan 1955. Final app: Football Combination v Luton Town (h) 12 Feb 1955. Transferred to Bristol City (£4,000) 16 Feb 1955.
ARSENAL Record: League 75 (18 gls); FA Cup 9 (3 gls); Football Combination 69 (25 gls); London FA Challenge Cup 2; Eastern Counties League 10 (7 gls); London Midweek League 2; Friendlies 25/2 (13 gls). In addition made 5/1 apps (1 gl) during wartime.

Honours: Played for Bristol and for Gloucestershire schoolboys. Division One champions 1952-3. Football Combination champions 1950-51. London FA Challenge Cup winners 1953-4. 1 full England cap 1951.
Served National Service in the Royal Army Ordnance Corps (1946-8). Played cricket for Gloucestershire (1948-74) and England (six Tests, therefore a double international). Retired from football Jul 1955 to concentrate on his cricket career. Later became a postman in Bristol, retiring in 1988.

MITCHELL, Andrew   **1898-99**
Outside-left   5ft 9in. 11st.
Born: Scotland, c.1879.
Previous Club: Albion Rovers. Joined ARSENAL: 8 May 1898 from Albion Rovers. First app: Snr fdly v Gravesend United (h) 1 Sep 1898. League v Luton Town (a) 3 Sep 1898. Final

snr app: League v New Brighton Tower (h) 8 Apr 1899. Snr fdly v Woolwich League (h) 26 Apr 1899. Final app: Jnr fdly v Grays United (h) 29 Apr 1899. ARSENAL Record: League 10 (2 gls); United League 8 (2 gls); Kent League 14 (4 gls); Other jnr comp: 1; Friendlies 14 (8 gls).

MOIR, James Glegg   **1898-1900**
Wing-half   5ft 9in. 11st 7lb.
Born: Inverbervie, Kincardineshire, Scotland, 7 Jan 1874. Died: Marylebone, London, 20 Jan 1953. Jnr football: Kirkintilloch Rob Roy, Gowan Athletic. Previous Club: Sunderland. Joined ARSENAL: 17 May 1898. First app: Jnr fdly v Brentford (a) 1 Sep 1898. First snr app: League v Burslem Port Vale (a) 5 Sep 1898. Final snr app: League v New Brighton Tower (h) 7 Apr 1900. Final app: Jnr fdly v Woolwich League (h) 30 Apr 1900. Transferred to Gravesend United summer 1900. ARSENAL Record: League 41; FA Cup 4; United League 15 (1 gl); Southern District Combination 7; Kent League 9; Other jnr comp: 3; Friendlies 20 (2 gls). Later signed for Fulham (1901-02) and became assistant trainer at Chelsea (1908-12).

MONTEITH, James   **1897**
Outside-left
Previous Club: Glasgow Celtic. Joined ARSENAL: 13 May 1897 from Celtic. First app: League v Grimsby Town (h) 1 Sep 1897. Final app: League v Blackpool (h) 27 Nov 1897. ARSENAL Record: League 6 (1 gl); Friendlies 8 (2 gls). Later played for Belfast Distillery (Jan 1898).

MOODY, John   **1925-28**
Goalkeeper   5ft 8¾. 11st 3lb.
Born: Heeley, nr Sheffield, 1 Nov 1904. Jnr football: Hathersage (Sheffield Amateur League). Joined ARSENAL: 25 Aug 1925 from Hathersage. First app: London Combination v Fulham (h) 5 Sep 1925. First snr app: League v Bury (a) 4 May 1927. Final snr app: League v Sheffield United (a) 7 Jan 1928. Final app: London Combination v Millwall (h) 5 May 1928. Transferred to Bradford 17 May 1928. ARSENAL Record: League 6; Football Combination 38 (1 gl); Friendlies 16.
Honours: London Combination champions 1927-8.
Worked as a slater before taking up football. After Bradford, played for Doncaster Rovers (cs 1930), Manchester United (1931-2) and Chesterfield (Aug 1933).

MORDUE, John   **1907-08**
Wing forward   5ft 8in. 11st.
Born: Edmondsley, Co Durham, c.1887. Died: 14 Dec 1957. Jnr football: Sacriston, Spennymoor United. Previous Club: Barnsley. Joined ARSENAL: 8 Apr 1907 from Barnsley for £450. First app: League v Birmingham (h) 13 Apr 1907. Final app: League v Sheffield Wednesday (h) 25 Apr 1908. Scottish tour v Greenock Morton, 29 Apr 1908. Transferred to Sunderland 12 May 1908. ARSENAL Record: League 26 (1 gl); FA Cup 2; Other snr comp: 1; South Eastern League 12 (2 gls); London League (Res) 4 (2 gls); Friendlies 14 (7 gls).
Honours: South Eastern League champions 1907-08.
Brother-in-law of Jim Ashcroft (Arsenal goalkeeper). Won club and international honours with Sunderland. After Sunderland, played for Middlesbrough (May 1920) and Hartlepools United (cs 1922). Was player-manager of Durham City (Feb 1923-Feb 1924). Later became one of the world's finest fives players.

MORGAN, Alfred Stanley   **1938-48**
Outside-left   5ft 8in. 10st 4lb.
Born: Aber-gwynfi, South Wales, 10 Oct 1920. Jnr football: Gwynfi Welfare. Joined ARSENAL: 11 May 1938 (amateur) from Gwynfi Welfare, Dec 1941 (professional). First app: Southern League v Newport County (a) 16 Mar 1939. First snr app: Football League South v Watford (h) 8 Feb 1940 (wartime). League v Grimsby Town (a) 21 Dec 1946. Final snr app: League v Portsmouth (a) 26 Dec 1946. Final app: Football Combination championship play-off v West Ham United (a) 1 May 1948. Transferred to Walsall 7 Jun 1948. ARSENAL Record: League 2; Football Combination 76 (29 gls); London FA Challenge Cup 1; Southern League 5; Friendlies 5 (5 gls). In addition played 1 Southern League match 1939-40 prior to outbreak of war and made 9 apps (5 gls) during wartime.
Honours: Football Combination champions 1946-7. Football Combination Cup runners-up 1946-7.
Was a paratrooper in the Commandos serving abroad during the war. After Walsall, played for Millwall (Dec 1948), Leyton Orient (May 1953) and Tunbridge Wells (Aug 1956).

MORROW, Stephen J.   **1987-**
Defender   6ft. 11st 3lb.
Born: Kilclenny, nr Belfast, N.Ireland, 2 Jul 1970. Previous Clubs: Cliftonville, Bangor (Irish League) (1985). Joined ARSENAL: Jul 1987 (apprentice) from Bangor, 1988 (professional). First app: Jnr fdly v Abingdon (a) 27 Jul 1987. First snr app: Snr fdly (sub) v Barnet (a) 20 Oct 1987. League (sub) v Norwich City (a) 8 Apr 1992. ARSENAL Record: League 0/2; Football Combination 95/7; South East Counties League 13/1 (2 gls); FA Youth Cup 8; Other jnr comp: 1; Friendlies 28/6 (2 gls).
Honours: Football Combination champions 1989-90. FA Youth Cup winners 1987-8. Northern Ireland Schoolboy international. Northern Ireland Youth caps, Under-21 cap 'B' cap, 6 full caps.
Had spells on loan to Reading (Jan 1991) and to Watford and Barnet (1991-2).

MORTIMER, Peter   **1894-96**
Forward   5ft 8½in. 11st 6lb.
Born: Calton, Glasgow, 17 Aug 1875. Died: 1951. Jnr football: Elm Park (Glasgow) (1889-90), Cowlairs (1890-1), Elm Park (1891-2), Glasgow Northern (1892-3), Leith Athletic (1893-4). Joined ARSENAL: 7 Apr 1894 from Leith Athletic. First app: Snr fdly v Millwall Athletic (a) 7 Apr 1894. League v Lincoln City (a) 1 Sep 1894. Final app: League v Darwen (h) 8 Apr 1896. Snr fdly v Luton Town (a) 27 Apr 1896. Transferred to Chatham May/Jun 1896. ARSENAL Record: League 49 (23 gls); Kent League 4 (2 gls); Friendlies 62 (48 gls).

MOSS, Frank   **1931-37**
Goalkeeper   5ft 9½in. 11st 9lb.
Born: Leyland, Lancashire, 5 Nov 1909. Died: Preston, 7 Feb 1979. Jnr football: Leyland Motors, Lostock Hall. Previous Clubs: Preston North End, Feb 1928 (professional), Oldham Athletic (1929). Joined ARSENAL: 20 Nov 1931 from Oldham Athletic for £3,000. First app: League v Chelsea (a) 21 Nov 1931. First snr app: League v Blackburn Rovers (a) 8 Feb 1936. Final app: Jnr fdly v Cambridge University (a) 19 Nov 1936 (at outside left). Appointed manager of Heart of Midlothian, 1 Mar 1937. ARSENAL Record: League 143 (1 gl); FA Cup 16; FA Charity Shield 2; Other snr comp: 2; Football Combination 7; Friendlies 15 (2 gls).

Honours: Division One champions 1932-3, 1933-4, 1934-5. FA Cup runners-up 1932. FA Charity Shield winners 1933-4, 1934-5. Sheriff of London Shield winners 1932-3. Northampton Charity Shield winners 1931-2. 4 full England caps 1934 and made 2 apps for the Football League 1932-4.
Worked for Leyland Motors before joining Preston North End. Suffered a dislocated shoulder in Mar 1935 and plagued by this recurring injury was forced to retire in Mar 1937 and take up football management. Returned to Lancashire and became a publican in Chorley until his death in a Preston Hospital in 1970.

MURPHY, Joseph 'Judge'   **1898-1900**
Half-back/inside-forward   5ft 9in.
Born: Stockton-on-Tees, c.1873. Previous Clubs: Hibernian, Stoke. Joined ARSENAL: 26 Apr 1898 from Stoke. First app: Snr fdly v Thames Ironworks (a) 26 Apr 1898. United League v Rushden (h) 17 Oct 1898. Final app: League v Barnsley (a) 28 Apr 1900. Transferred to Raith Rovers summer 1900. ARSENAL Record: League 3; FA Cup 5; United League 3; Southern District Combination 9; Kent League 10 (3 gls); Friendlies 20 (4 gls).

MURRELL, Harry Robert 'Joe'   **1898-1900**
Full-back
Born: Hounslow, Middlesex, 19 Nov 1879. Died: West Wickham, Kent, 15 Aug 1952. Jnr football: St Thomas', Charlton; Plumstead Albion; Middlesex Regiment. Joined ARSENAL: Oct 1898 from Middlesex Regt. First app: Jnr fdly v 2nd Royal Scots Fusiliers (h) 1 Oct 1898. First snr app: League v Small Heath (a) 31 Mar 1900. Final app: League v Barnsley (a) 23 Apr 1900. Transferred to Clapton Orient summer 1900. ARSENAL Record: League 6; Southern District Combination 1; Kent League 23 (5 gls); Friendlies 11 (1 gl).
Often played at outside-left for Arsenal reserves. Was more prominent as a wicketkeeper in county cricket and played for Kent (1899-1905) and Middlesex (1906-26). For a good number of years afterwards he was scorer for Middlesex CCC.

NEAVE, David   **1904-12**
Outside-left   5ft 7in. 10st 10lb.
Born: Arbroath, Scotland, 1883. Previous Clubs: Forfar, Montrose, Arbroath.

Joined ARSENAL: 10 Mar 1904 from Arbroath. Transferred to Leyton May 1905. Rejoined ARSENAL: 14 Dec 1905 from Leyton. First app: London League v Queen's Park Rangers (a) 21 Mar 1904. League v Small Heath (a) 3 Dec 1904. Final snr app: League v Notts County (a) 23 Dec 1911. Final app: South Eastern League v Southend (h) 23 Mar 1912. Transferred to Merthyr Town 29 Jul 1912.
ARSENAL Record: League 154 (30 gls); FA Cup 14 (2 gls); London League 2; London League (Res) 21 (12 gls); Other snr comp: 6; London FA Challenge Cup 58 (14 gls); Other jnr comp: 1; Friendlies 25 (7 gls).
Honours: Southern Professional Charity Cup winners 1905-06, runners-up 1903-04.
His younger brother, Andrew played for Arsenal reserves.

NEIL, Andrew   **1924-26**
Inside-forward   5ft 6½in. 11st.
Born: Kilmarnock, Scotland, Nov 1896. Previous Clubs: Kilmarnock, Brighton & Hove Albion. Joined ARSENAL: 13 Mar 1924 from Brighton & Hove Albion for £3,000. First app: League v Nottingham Forest (a) 15 Mar 1924. Final snr app: League v Cardiff City (a) 27 Feb 1926. Final app: London Combination v Tottenham Hotspur (a) 6 Mar 1926. Transferred to Brighton & Hove Albion 13 Mar 1926.
ARSENAL Record: League 54 (10 gls); FA Cup 3; Football Combination 18 (3 gls); London FA Challenge Cup 4 (2 gls); Friendlies 6.
Honours: London FA Challenge Cup runners-up 1925-6.
A pastry cook by trade. Later played for Queen's Park Rangers (1928-9). Retired summer 1930.

NEILL, William John Terence
Player 1959-70   Manager 1976-83
Half-back   5ft 10½in. 12st 7lb.
Born: Belfast, N.Ireland, 8 May 1942.

School: Bangor Primary.
Previous Club: Bangor City (Irish League). Joined ARSENAL: 4 Dec 1959 from Bangor City for £2,500. First app: Metropolitan League v Hastings (h) 5 Dec 1959. First snr app: Snr fdly v Gt Britain Olympic XI (h) 25 Jan 1960. League v Sheffield Wednesday (a) 23 Dec 1960. Final snr app: FA Cup v Blackpool (a) 15 Jan 1970. Final app: Football Combination v West Ham United (h) 11 Apr 1970. Transferred to Hull City as player-manager (£40,000) 26 Jun 1970.

ARSENAL Record: League 240/1 (8 gls); FA Cup 12/1; Football League Cup 15/1 (2 gls); European comp: 5; Football Combination 75 (4 gls); FA Youth Cup 2; London FA Challenge Cup 5 (1 gl); Metropolitan League 35 (4 gls); South East Counties League 1; Friendlies 91/4 (6 gls).
Honours: Northern Ireland Schoolboy international. Football League Cup runners-up 1967-8. Football Combination champions 1962-3. Metropolitan League champions 1960-61. Captain of Arsenal. 4 Northern Ireland Under-23 caps 1962-5 and 44 full caps (1 gl) 1961-9. Captain of Northern Ireland.
Chairman of PFA (Nov 1967). Won further international honours with Hull City. Was team manager of Northern Ireland. Manager of Tottenham Hotspur (Sep 1974-Jun 1976). Arsenal manager (9 Jul 1976-16 Dec 1983). Left football and now concentrates on charity work.

NEILSON, Gordon   **1964-68**
Wing-forward   5ft 6in. 9st 12lb.
Born: Glasgow, 28 May 1947.
Jnr football: Glasgow United. Joined ARSENAL: Apr 1964 (amateur), 4 Jun 1964 (professional) from Glasgow United. First app: South East Counties League v Portsmouth (a) 11 Apr 1964. First snr app: League v Everton (h) 12 Mar 1966. Final snr app: League v Newcastle United (a) 25 Feb 1967. Snr fdly v Apoel (Cyprus) (h) 3 May 1967. Final app: Football Combination Cup v Bournemouth (a) 21 Sep 1968. Transferred to Brentford 2 Oct 1968.
ARSENAL Record: League 14 (2 gls); FA Cup 3 (1 gl); Football Combination 50 (18 gls); London FA Challenge Cup 4 (1 gl); FA Youth Cup 4; Metropolitan League 37 (10 gls); South East Counties League 21 (3 gls); Other jnr comp: 3 (1 gl); Friendlies 30/2 (8 gls).
Honours: London FA Challenge Cup runners-up 1965-6. FA Youth Cup runners-up 1965-6. South East Counties League champions 1964-5. London Minor Challenge Cup runners-up 1964-5.
A knee condition in Nov 1967 affected his playing career at Arsenal.

NELSON, David   **1936-46**
Forward/wing-half   5ft 8in. 11st 3lb.
Born: Douglas Water, Scotland, 3 Feb 1918. Died: Greenwich, Connecticut, USA, Sep 1988.
Jnr football: Douglas Water Thistle. Previous Club: St Bernards (Edinburgh). Joined ARSENAL: 27 May 1936 from St Bernards. First app: London Combination v Tottenham Hotspur (a) 7 Sep 1936. First snr app: League v Preston North End (a) 28 Dec 1936. Final snr app: League v Preston North End (a) 9 Nov 1946. Snr fdly v Racing Club de Paris (a) 11 Nov 1946. Final app: Football Combination v Charlton Athletic (h) 7 Dec 1946. Transferred to Fulham (part of R.Rooke deal) 13 Dec 1946.
ARSENAL Record: League 27 (4 gls); FA Cup 2; Other snr comp: 3; Football Combination 95 (26 gls); London FA Challenge Cup 12 (3 gls); Southern League 3 (1 gl); Friendlies 17 (12 gls). In addition played 2 London Combination matches (2 gls) 1939-40 prior to outbreak of war and made 162 apps (27 gls) during wartime.
Honours: London Combination champions 1936-7, 1937-8, 1938-9. London FA Challenge Cup runners-up 1936-7. Bath Coronation Cup winners 1936-7.
Served as a Sergeant in the Army during the war. After Fulham, played for Brentford (Aug 1947), Queen's Park Rangers (Feb 1950) and Crystal Palace (Mar 1952). Became player-manager of Ashford Town (1954). Emigrated to America in Dec 1955 to take up an appointment in the car industry in St Louis. Continued to live in America until his death in 1988.

NELSON, Samuel   **1966-81**
Left-back   5ft 10½in. 11st 9lb.
Born: Belfast, N.Ireland, 1 Apr 1949.
Jnr football: Fifteen Scouts Youth (Belfast). Joined ARSENAL: 1 Apr 1966 from Belfast. First app: South East Counties League v Watford (a) 2 Apr 1966. First snr app: On tour v Japan XI (Japan) 29 May 1968. League v Ipswich Town (h) 25 Oct 1969. Final snr app: League (sub) v Aston Villa (h) 2 May 1981. On tour (sub) v AIK (Sweden) 5 Aug 1981. Final app: Football Combination v Norwich City (h) 5 Sep 1981. Transferred to Brighton & Hove Albion (£35,000) 24 Sep 1981.
ARSENAL Record: League 245/10 (10 gls); FA Cup 33/2 (1 gl); Football League Cup 27 (1 gl); European comp: 19/2; FA Charity Shield 1; Football Combination 226/1 (15 gls); London FA Challenge Cup 12; FA Youth Cup 6 (1 gl); Metropolitan League 21 (6 gls); South East Counties League 13 (4 gls); Other jnr comp: 6; Friendlies 130/14 (10 gls). In addition played 1 Football Combination match 1981-2, later removed from records.

Honours: Northern Ireland schoolboy international. FA Cup winners 1979, runners-up 1978, 1980. European Cup-winners' Cup runners-up 1979-80. FA Charity Shield runners-up 1979-80. Football Combination champions 1968-9, 1969-70. London FA Challenge Cup winners 1969-70. FA Youth Cup winners 1965-6. Southern Junior Floodlit Cup winners 1965-6. London Youth Challenge Cup winners 1966-67. South East Counties League Cup runners-up 1965-6. 1 Northern Ireland Under-23 cap 1969 and 48 full international caps (1 gl) 1970-81.
Joined Arsenal as an outside-left. Won further international caps with Brighton. Was coach at Brighton (1983-Dec 1984).

NICHOLAS, Charles   **1983-88**
Striker   5ft 9in. 10st 8lb.
Born: Cowcaddens, Glasgow, 30 Dec 1961.
School: St Colomba of Iona RC, Maryhill, Glasgow.
Jnr football: Celtic Boys Club. Previous Clubs: Ipswich Town (trial), Wolverhampton Wanderers (trial), Celtic (Mar 1979). Joined ARSENAL: 22 Jun 1983 from Celtic for £650,000. First app: On tour v Meppen (Germany) 31 Jul 1983. League v Luton Town (h) 27 Aug 1983. Final snr app: League v Queen's Park Rangers (a) 22 Aug 1987. Snr fdly (sub) v Barnet (a) 20 Oct 1987. Final app: Football Combination v Crystal Palace (a) 16 Dec 1987. Transferred to Aberdeen (£400,000) 7 Jan 1988.
ARSENAL Record: League 145/6 (34 gls); FA

Cup 11/2 (10 gls); Football League Cup 20 (10 gls); Football Combination 23 (20 gls); Friendlies 37/4 (16 gls).
Honours: Football League Cup winners 1986-7. Arsenal Player of the Year 1984. 13 full Scotland caps (3 gls) 1983-7 and one Under-21 cap 1984.
Was a car mechanic before joining Celtic. Won club honours and Scotland Youth, Under-21 and full international caps whilst with Celtic. Returned to Celtic from Aberdeen, summer 1990.

NICHOLAS, Peter   **1981-83**
Midfield   5ft 8½in. 11st 8lb.
Born: Newport, Wales, 10 Nov 1959.
School: Gaer Junior, Newport; Duffryn High, Newport.
Previous Club: Crystal Palace 1973 (schoolboy), 1976 (professional). Joined ARSENAL: 11 Mar 1981 from Crystal Palace for £400,000. First app: Snr fdly v Orient (a) 17 Mar 1981. League v Norwich City (a) 21 Mar 1981. Final snr app: League v Aston Villa (a) 14 May 1983. On tour (sub) v VFL Bochum (Germany) 5 Aug 1983. Final app: Football Combination v Queen's Park Rangers (a) 5 Oct 1983. Transferred to Crystal Palace (£150,000, after loan spell) 18 Oct 1983.
ARSENAL Record: League 57/3 (1 gl); FA Cup 8; Football League Cup 8 (2 gls); European comp:

4; Football Combination 20; Friendlies 12/1(1 gl).
Honours: 1 Wales Under-21 (1982) and 17 full international caps (1 gl) 1981-3. Captain of Wales.
Played for Newport and for Gwent schoolboys. Wales Schoolboy and Youth international. Won club and international honours with Crystal Palace. Transferred to Luton Town (Jan 1985) and to Aberdeen (Aug 1987). Moved to Chelsea (Aug 1988) and to Watford (Mar 1991).

NORMAN, James   **1914-19**
Outside-left   5ft 6in. 11st 6lb.
Born: Hackney Wick, London, c.1893
Jnr football: Eton Mission; Walthamstow Grange (amateur). Joined ARSENAL: 2 May 1914 from Walthamstow Grange. First app: South Eastern League v Southampton (h) 3 Sep 1914. First snr app: London PFA Charity Cup v West Ham United (h) 2 Nov 1914. League v Birmingham (a) 7 Nov 1914. Final app: League v Huddersfield Town (a) 21 Nov 1914. Wartime fdly v Tottenham Hotspur (h) 24 May 1919.
ARSENAL Record: League 4; Other snr comp: 1; London FA Challenge Cup 1; South Eastern League 29 (3 gls); London League (Res) 7 (1 gl); Friendlies 4 (2 gls). In addition made 4 apps during wartime.

NORTH, Ernest John 'Joe' MM   **1919-22**
Centre-forward   5ft 9½in. 11st 2lb.
Born: Burton upon Trent, Staffs, 23 Sep 1895.
Died: Havant, Hampshire, 24 Aug 1955.
Previous Club: Sheffield United. Joined ARSENAL: 7 Nov 1919 (amateur) from Sheffield United, 17 Dec 1919 (professional). First app: London Combination v Clapton Orient (a) 22 Nov 1919. First snr app: League v Oldham Athletic (h) 7 Feb 1920. Final snr app: League v Oldham Athletic (h) 24 Dec 1921. Final app: London Combination v Tottenham Hotspur (a) 3 May 1922. Transferred to Reading 13 May 1922.
ARSENAL Record: League 23 (6 gls); Other snr comp: 1; Football Combination 57 (29 gls); London FA Challenge Cup 1; Friendlies 11 (7 gls).
Honours: Metropolitan Hospital Cup winners 1920-21.
Served as a Lieutenant in the Army during World War One and won the Military Medal. After Reading he played for Gillingham, Norwich City and Watford (1926). Became coach to Northfleet (1927). Played cricket for Middlesex 1923-7 and became a Minor Counties umpire.

NUTT, Gordon Edward   **1955-60**
Winger   5ft 7in. 10st 3lb.
Born: South Yardley, Birmingham, 8 Nov 1932.
School: Bierdton Road, Yardley.
Jnr football: Digby United, Sheldon Town.
Previous Clubs: Coventry City (May 1948), Cardiff City (Dec 1954). Joined ARSENAL: 23 Sep 1955 from Cardiff City (together with M.Tiddy). First app: League v Sunderland (a) 24 Sep 1955. Final snr app: League v Fulham (a) 18 Apr 1960. Final app: Metropolitan League v West Ham United (a) 10 Oct 1960. Transferred to Southend United (£3,000) 14 Oct 1960.
ARSENAL Record: League 49 (10 gls); FA Cup 2; Other snr comp: 4 (1 gl); Football Combination 118 (32 gls); London FA Challenge Cup 12 (1 gl); Metropolitan League 8 (11 gls); Friendlies 3 (6 gls).
Played for Birmingham County schoolboys. Was an amateur on Arsenal's books at 14 but not retained. Toured the West Indies with an FA XI, summer 1955. After Southend United played for PSV Eindhoven, Holland (1961), Hereford United (Jul 1962) Rugby Town (Dec 1963) and Bexley United (Feb 1964). Went to Australia to play for Corinthians of Sydney and still lives in Australia.

OAKES, Donald Joseph   **1945-55**
Inside-forward/wing-half   5ft 11in. 10st 8lb.
Born: Rhyl, Flintshire, N.Wales, 8 Oct 1928. Died: 1977.
Jnr football: Downend ATC Old Boys (Bristol). Joined ARSENAL: 28 Dec 1945 (amateur), 12 Jul 1946 (professional). First app: Jnr fdly (wartime) v Bedford Town (a) 30 Mar 1946. First snr app: League v Aston Villa (a) 23 Aug 1952. Final app: League v Portsmouth (a) 30 Apr 1955. Will Mather Cup v Hendon (a) 2 May 1955. Compelled to give up football due to rheumatic trouble, May 1956.
ARSENAL Record: League 11 (1 gl); Football Combination 158 (68 gls); London FA Challenge Cup 12 (5 gls); Eastern Counties League 31 (9 gls); London Midweek League 5 (1 gl); Friendlies 33/1 (15 gls). In addition made 2 apps during wartime.
Honours: Played for Gloucestershire Youth team. Football Combination champions 1950-51. Football Combination Cup winners 1952-3, runners-up 1950-51. London FA Challenge Cup winners 1953-4, 1954-5.
Served National Service in the Army (1946-8). His father, Alfred Oakes, was a professional with Birmingham and Millwall.

O'BRIEN, Patrick 'Paddy'   **1894-97**
Inside-left   5ft 5in. 9st 12lb.
Born: 1875. Died: 1951.
Jnr football: Elm Park, Glasgow Northern. Joined ARSENAL: 15 Apr 1894 from Scotland. First app: Snr fdly v Luton Town (a) 16 Apr 1894. League v Grimsby Town (h) 10 Sep 1894. Final app: League v Manchester City (h) 28 Apr 1897. Snr fdly v Southampton St Mary's (a) 29 Apr 1897. Transferred to Bristol City summer 1897.
ARSENAL Record: League 63 (27 gls); FA Cup 4 (2 gls); United League 12 (5 gls); Kent League 14 (3 gls); Friendlies 80 (53 gls).
Made an app for Swindon Town (1902). Became a tobacconist in Bedminster.

OFFER, Henry Thomas   **1889-91**
Forward.
Born: Devizes, 1871. Died: Newport, IOW, 12 Jan 1947.
Previous Club: Swindon Town (as a full-back). Joined ARSENAL: Sep 1889 from Swindon Town. First app: Snr fdly v Tottenham Hotspur (h) 21 Sep 1889. First first-class app: FA Cup (Q) v Norwich Thorpe (a) 26 Oct 1889. Final first-class app: FA Cup v Derby County (h) 17 Jan 1891. Final app: Snr fdly (sub) v Sunderland (h) 25 Apr 1891.
ARSENAL Record: FA Cup 1 (1 gl); FA Cup (Q) 3. In addition made 51/1 snr apps (16 gls) and 1 reserve app for Royal Arsenal 1889-90 to 1890-91.
Honours: London Charity Cup winners 1889-90. London Senior Cup winners 1890-91, runners-up 1889-90. Kent Senior Cup winners 1889-90. Played in an FA Trial 1890-91.
Later played for Southampton St Mary's (1894-5). Retired 1895.

O'FLANAGAN, Dr Kevin Patrick   **1945-49**
Winger   5ft 9½in. 11st 10lb.
Born: Dublin, 10 Jun 1919.
School: Christian Brothers, Synge Street, Dublin. University College, Dublin.
Jnr football: Bohemians (Dublin). Joined ARSENAL: Oct 1945 (wartime), 6 May 1946 signed League forms (amateur). First app: Football League South v Charlton Athletic (a) 27 Oct 1945. FA Cup v West Ham United (a) 5 Jan 1946. First snr app: League v Wolverhampton Wanderers (h) 28 Dec 1946. Final app: Football Combination Cup

82

v Millwall (a) 29 Jan 1949. Career with Arsenal ended 1949 due to ankle injury.
ARSENAL Record: League 14 (3 gls); FA Cup 2; Football Combination 2 (1 gl); Friendlies 1. In addition made 18 apps (11 gls) during wartime.
Honours: 3 full Republic of Ireland caps 1946-7. In addition made 2 apps for Ireland during wartime. Won club and international honours with Bohemians. An all-round sportsman he won sprint and long jump championships in Ireland. Qualified as a doctor and played for Arsenal when appointed to a hospital in Ruislip, Middlesex. Was also capped by Ireland at Rugby Union when playing for London Irish. Also made apps at soccer for Corinthian Casuals, Barnet and Brentford (1949). Returned to Ireland to concentrate on his practice as a doctor in Dublin, where he still lives. Was doctor to the Irish Olympic Games team on several occasions.

O'LEARY, David Anthony   **1973-**
Central defender   6ft 2in. 12st 6lb.
Born: Stoke Newington, London, 2 May 1958.
School: St Kevins, Glasnevin (Dublin).
Jnr football: Shelbourne Juniors, Manchester United (trial). Joined ARSENAL: 14 Jun 1973 (apprentice), 8 Jul 1975 (professional). First app: South East Counties League v Brighton (a) 25 Aug 1973. First snr app: Snr fdly (sub) v Reading (a) 2 Oct 1974. League v Burnley (h) 16 Aug 1975.
ARSENAL Record: League 517/30 (11 gls); FA Cup 65/1 (1 gl); Football League Cup 66/2 (2 gls); European Competitions 21; FA Charity Shield 3; Other snr comp: 7; Football Combination 71 (2 gls); South East Counties League 31; FA Youth Cup 5; Other jnr comp: 2; Friendlies 132/12 (5 gls).
Honours: Played for Republic of Ireland schoolboys (captain) and Youth international (captain). Division One champions 1988-9, 1990-91. FA Cup winners 1979, runners-up 1978, 1980. Football League Cup winners 1986-7. European Cup-winners' Cup runners-up 1979-80. FA Charity Shield runners-up 1979-80, 1989-90, medal 1991-2. Captain of Arsenal. 64 full Republic of Ireland caps (1 gl).

Missed 1987-8 Football League Cup Final through injury. Elder brother of Pierce O'Leary (Celtic and Republic of Ireland).

OLIVER, Harold   **1909-10**
Centre-forward
An amateur from Holloway, North London.
Jnr football: Great Eastern Rovers. Joined ARSENAL: 5 Sep 1909 from North London. First app: South Eastern League v Chelsea (a) 8 Sep 1909. First snr app: Snr fdly v Rest of Kent (a) 22 Sep 1909. League v Nottingham Forest (h) 9 Oct 1909. Final app: South Eastern League v Southend (a) 9 Apr 1910.
ARSENAL Record: League 1; South Eastern League 19 (15 gls); Other jnr comp: 1; Friendlies 12 (13 gls).

O'NEILL, Frank Simon   **1958-61**
Outside-right   5ft 8in. 10st 2lb.
Born: Dublin, 13 Apr 1940.
Jnr football: Home Park FC (Dublin). Joined ARSENAL: Dec 1958 (amateur) from Home Park, 16 Apr 1959 (professional). First app: Metropolitan League v Dartford (h) 20 Dec 1958. First snr app: Snr fdly v (sub) v Bristol XI (a) 8 May 1959. League v Nottingham Forest (a) 31 Dec 1960. Final snr app: League v Blackpool (h) 8 Apr 1961. Final app: Junior International Tournament v CDNA 3 Jun 1961. Transferred to Shamrock Rovers summer 1961.
ARSENAL Record: League 2; Football Combination 45 (15 gls); London FA Challenge Cup 5 (3 gls); Metropolitan League 44 (33 gls); Friendlies 19/1 (11 gls).
Honours: London FA Challenge Cup runners-up 1960-61. Metropolitan League champions 1960-61. Metropolitan League Challenge Cup winners 1960-61. Metropolitan League Professional Cup winners 1960-61. Republic of Ireland Youth international. Won Republic of Ireland full international honours with Shamrock Rovers. Joined Waterford United (1974).

ORD, Roger   **1897-1900**
Goalkeeper   5ft 10in. 11st 7lb.
Born: Northumberland, 1871.
Jnr football: Northumberland Juniors, Hebburn Argyle. Previous Club: Middlesbrough Ironopolis. Joined ARSENAL: 17 Jul 1897 from Hebburn Argyle. First app: League v Grimsby Town (h) 1 Sep 1897. Final snr app: League v Sheffield Wednesday (a) 17 Mar 1900. Final app: Kent League v Deptford (a) 13 Apr 1900. Transferred to Luton Town Sep 1900.
ARSENAL Record: League 89; FA Cup 10; United League 34; Southern District Combination 7; Kent League 3; Other jnr comp: 3; Friendlies 24 (1 gl).
Later played for Wellingborough (1903).

O'SHEA, Daniel Edward   **1978-84**
Midfield/defender   6ft. 12st 8lb.
Born: Kennington, London, 26 Mar 1963.
Jnr football: Staines Juniors. Joined ARSENAL: 1978 (apprentice), 22 Dec 1980 (professional). First app: South East Counties League v Fulham (a) 19 Aug 1978. First snr app: On tour v Trinidad XI (West Indies) 20 May 1982. League v Birmingham City (h) 30 Oct 1982. Final snr app: League v Manchester City (a) 8 Dec 1982. Snr fdly (sub) v Aldershot (a) 18 Oct 1983. Final app: Football Combination v Swindon Town (a) 16 May 1984. Transferred to Exeter City (free transfer) summer 1984.
ARSENAL Record: League 6; Football League Cup 3; Football Combination 103/5 (4 gls); South East Counties League 58/6 (3 gls); FA Youth Cup 6 (2 gls); Other jnr comp: 11 (2 gls); Friendlies

49/7 (9 gls). In addition played 3 Combination matches 1981-2, later removed from records.
Honours: Played for Staines & Sunbury schoolboys and for Surrey schoolboys. Captain of Arsenal Youth team. Went on loan to Charlton Athletic (Feb-Apr 1984). Transferred from Exeter City to Southend United (Aug 1985) and to Cambridge United (1989).

OWENS, Isaac   **1901-02**
Inside-forward   5ft 10½in. 12st 7lb.
Born: Darlington, 1881.
Jnr football: Bishop Auckland, Crook. Joined ARSENAL: 1 Oct 1901 from Crook. First app: League v Gainsborough Trinity (a) 12 Oct 1901. Final snr app: League v Blackpool (h) 25 Dec 1901. Final London League v Queen's Park Rangers (a) 3 Feb 1902. Final app: London League (Res) championship play-off v Queen's Park Rangers (at West Ham) 30 Apr 1902.
ARSENAL Record: League 9 (2 gls); FA Cup 2; London League 3 (1 gl); London League (Res) 7 (5 gls); Kent League 8 (5 gls); Friendlies 6 (4 gls).
Honours: London League (Res) champions 1901-02. West Kent League champions 1901-02. Later played for Plymouth Argyle (1904-06), Bristol Rovers (1907), Crystal Palace (1907), Grimsby Town (1908) and Darlington (1909).

PACK, Roy J.   **1962-66**
Full-back   5ft 8¼in. 10st 13lb.
Born: Islington, London, 20 Sep 1946.
Joined ARSENAL: Jun 1962 (apprentice), 11 Nov 1963 (professional). First app: South East Counties League v Fulham (h) 18 Aug 1962. First snr app: Snr fdly v Swansea Town (a) 3 May 1966. League v Leeds United (h) 5 May 1966 (only snr app). Final app: London FA Challenge Cup Final v Queen's Park Rangers (h) 10 May 1966. Transferred to Portsmouth (free transfer) 1 Jul 1966.
ARSENAL Record: League 1; Football Combination 23 (1 gl); London FA Challenge Cup 5; South East Counties League 55 (3 gls); Metropolitan League 54; FA Youth Cup 12; Other jnr comp: 10 (1 gl); Friendlies 50 (1 gl). In addition played 1 Metropolitan League match 1965-6, later removed from records.
Honours: London FA Challenge Cup runners-up 1965-6. FA Youth Cup runners-up 1964-5. South East Counties League Cup winners 1963-4. Southern Junior Floodlit Cup winners 1962-3. London Minor Challenge Cup runners-up 1964-5. Played for Hackney schoolboys. England schoolboy international trialist 1961-2.
After Portsmouth, played for Oxford United (May 1969) and then in South Africa.

PAGNAM, Frederick   **1919-21**
Centre-forward   5ft 9in. 12st 3lb.
Born: Poulton-le-Fylde, 4 Sep 1891. Died: 7 Mar 1962.
School: Poulton Grammar.
Jnr football: Lytham, Blackpool Wednesday. Previous Clubs: Huddersfield Town (1910), Southport Central (1912), Blackpool (1913), Liverpool (1914). Joined ARSENAL: 17 Oct 1919 from Liverpool for £1,500. First app: London Combination (wartime guest) v Clapton Orient (a) 8 Sep 1917. First snr app: League v Bradford City (h) 25 Oct 1919. Final app: League v Sunderland (a) 5 Feb 1921. Transferred to Cardiff City (£3,000) 7 Mar 1921.
ARSENAL Record: League 50 (26 gls); FA Cup 3 (1 gl); Football Combination 2; Friendlies 2. In addition made 20 apps (14 gls) as a guest player during wartime.
Later played for Watford (Dec 1921) and was manager of Watford (1926-9). Was coach to the Turkish FA (1932) and a coach in Holland. On

returning to England he retired from football and became a publican.

PARKER, Thomas Robert   1926-33
Right-back   5ft 11in. 12st 8lb.
Born: Woolston, Hampshire, 19 Nov 1897. Died: Southampton, 5 Nov 1987.
Jnr football: St Marks, Woolston; Sholing Rangers; Sholing Athletic. Previous Club: Southampton (1919). Joined ARSENAL: 2 Mar 1926 from Southampton. First app: London Combination v Charlton Athletic (a) 18 Mar 1926. First snr app: League v Blackburn Rovers (h) 3 Apr 1926. Final snr app: League v Derby County (h) 8 Oct 1932. Final app: London Midweek League v Fulham (h) 4 Feb 1933. Appointed manager of Norwich City 8 Mar 1933.
ARSENAL Record: League 258 (17 gls); FA Cup 34; FA Charity Shield 2; Other snr comp: 3; Football Combination 5; London FA Challenge Cup 4 (3 gls); London Midweek League 3; Friendlies 22 (2 gls).

Honours: Division One champions 1930-31. FA Cup winners 1930, runners-up 1927, 1932. FA Charity Shield winners 1930-31, 1931-2. Sheriff of London Shield winners 1930-31. Northampton Hospital Cup winners 1929-30, 1930-31. Captain of Arsenal.
Won club and England international honours with Southampton. An expert taker of penalties. Became manager of Southampton (Feb 1937). Worked for the Ministry of Transport during the war. Was manager of Norwich City again (1955-7). Became chief scout at Southampton.

PARKIN, Raymond   1928-36
Inside-forward/wing-half   5ft 9½in. 11st 8lb.
Born: Crook, Co Durham, 11 Feb 1911. Died: Market Bosworth, Leicestershire, 18 Jul 1971.
Jnr football: Esh Winning. Previous Club: Newcastle United (amateur). Joined ARSENAL: 28 Jan 1928 from Esh Winning. First app: Jnr fdly v Cambridge University (h) 9 Feb 1928. First snr app: On tour v Danish International XI (Denmark) 22 May 1928. League v Sunderland (a) 1 Jan 1929. Final snr app: League v Brentford (a) 2 Nov 1935. Final app: London Combination v Millwall (h) 11 Jan 1936. Transferred to Middlesbrough 13 Jan 1936.
ARSENAL Record: League 25 (11 gls); FA Cup 1; Other snr comp: 2 (1 gl); Football Combination 232 (60 gls); London FA Challenge Cup 14 (1 gl); London Midweek League 19 (10 gls); Friendlies 30 (22 gls).
Honours: London Combination champions

1928-9, 1929-30, 1930-31, 1933-4, 1934-5. London FA Challenge Cup winners 1930-31. Sheriff of London Shield winners 1932-3. Norwich Hospital Cup winners 1934-5. Played for London Combination v Diables Rouges 1935.
Played for Durham schoolboys. England Schoolboy international (1924-5). Later played for Southampton (Sep 1937).

PARLOUR, Raymond   1988-
Midfield
Born: Romford, 7 Mar 1973.
Joined ARSENAL: 1988 (schoolboy), Jul 1989 (apprentice), 1990 (professional). First app: Jnr fdly v Tonbridge (a) 3 Aug 1988. First snr app: Snr fdly (sub) v Watford (a) 7 Aug 1991. League v Liverpool (a) 29 Jan 1992.

ARSENAL Record: League 2/4 (1 gl); Football Combination 30/7 (6 gls); South East Counties League 49/7 (6 gls); FA Youth Cup 6/1; Other jnr comp: 13; Friendlies 35/7 (6 gls).
Honours: Played for Havering and London schoolboys. South East Counties League champions 1990-91. Southern Junior Floodlight Cup winners 1990-91, runners-up 1989-90.

PATERSON, Dr James A. MC   1920-26
Outside-left   5ft 7½in. 10st 12lb.
Born: London.
School: Bellahouston Academy.
Previous Clubs: Glasgow Rangers, Queen's Park (amateur). Joined ARSENAL: 27 Oct 1920 (amateur). First app: League v Derby County (h) 30 Oct 1920. Final snr app: FA Cup v Swansea Town (a) 6 Mar 1926. Final app: London Combination v Charlton Athletic (h) 22 Apr 1926.
ARSENAL Record: League 70 (1 gl); FA Cup 7 (1 gl); Other snr comp: 1; Football Combination 13; London FA Challenge Cup 2 (1 gl); Friendlies 4.
Honours: Made 1 app for the Football League 1921. Played in international trial match 1924.
Qualified as a doctor in Scotland. Was a medical officer in the London Scottish during the war and won the Military Cross for service in France. Played for Arsenal when he took up medical practise in Clapton, London. Retired from football at end of 1923-4 season to concentrate on his medical work but was persuaded by Herbert Chapman to play again for Arsenal during 1925-6 before finally retiring from football.

PATERSON, William   1928-29
Goalkeeper   6ft 2in. 14st 6lb.
Born: Dunfermline, Scotland.
Previous Club: Dundee United. Joined ARSENAL: 19 Jan 1928 from Dundee United. First app: London Combination v Charlton Athletic (a) 21 Jan 1928. First snr app: League v Derby County (h) 4 Feb 1928. Final app: League v Burnley (a) 4 May 1929. Transferred to Airdrieonians 20 Jul 1929.
ARSENAL Record: League 15; Football Combination 47; Friendlies 1.
Honours: London Combination champions 1927-8, 1928-9.
On retirement from football he went into the hotel business at Kingussie, Inverness-shire.

PATES, Colin George   1990-
Defender   5ft 11in. 11st.
Born: Mitcham, 10 Aug 1961.
Previous Clubs: Chelsea, Charlton Athletic (Oct 1988). Joined ARSENAL: 19 Jan 1990 from Charlton Athletic for £500,000. First app: Football Combination v Queen's Park Rangers (h) 3 Feb 1990. First snr app: League v Sheffield Wednesday (a) 17 Feb 1990.

ARSENAL Record: League 10/4; Football League Cup 2; European comp: 2 (1 gl); Football Combination 36 (2 gls); Friendlies 12/5.
England Youth international. Won club honours with Chelsea. Was on loan to Brighton & Hove Albion (Feb-May 1991).

PATTISON, George Charlton   1920-22
Half-back   5ft 11½in. 13st 1lb.
Born: North Shields, Tyneside, c.1898.
Jnr football: Wallsend. Joined ARSENAL: 1 May 1920 (amateur), 24 Aug 1920 (professional). First app: League v Bradford (h) 1 May 1920. Final snr app: Jnr fdly v Woolwich (a) 2 May 1922. Transferred to West Ham United 12 May 1922.
ARSENAL Record: League 9; FA Cup 1; Other snr comp: 2; Football Combination 43 (1 gl); London FA Challenge Cup 1; Friendlies 22 (1 gl).
Honours: Southend Hospital Cup winners 1920-21.

PAYNE, George Clark   **1912-13**
Forward   5ft 9in. 12st.
Born: c.1887.
Previous Clubs: Sunderland, Crystal Palace, Tottenham Hotspur (1906-08), Leyton FC. Joined ARSENAL: 27 Jun 1912 from Leyton FC. First app: South Eastern League v Tunbridge Wells (h) 7 Sep 1912. First snr app: League v Aston Villa (h) 16 Sep 1912. Final snr app: League v Bolton Wanderers (a) 4 Jan 1913. Final app: South Eastern League v Clapton Orient (h) 19 Apr 1913. ARSENAL Record: League 3; South Eastern League 16 (9 gls); Friendlies 2.

PEACHEY C.B.   **1891-92**
Outside-left
An amateur from Chiswick Park. First app: Snr fdly v 1st Lincolnshire Regiment (h) 26 Dec 1891. Final app: FA Cup v Small Heath (a) 16 Jan 1892 (only first-class app).
ARSENAL Record: FA Cup 1. In addition made 3 Senior apps (2 gls) for Royal Arsenal 1891-2.

PEART, John Charles   **1910-14 & 1919-21**
Full-back   5ft 7in. 11st 11lb.
Born: Tewkesbury, c.1887.
Joined ARSENAL: 24 Dec 1910 (amateur), 11 Jan 1911 (professional). Transferred to Croydon Common (free Transfer) summer 1914. Rejoined ARSENAL after the war (1919). First app: South Eastern League v Peterborough City (a) 24 Dec 1910. First snr app: League v Everton (h) 11 Mar 1911. Final app: League v Liverpool (h) 2 May 1921. Southend Hospital Cup v Southend (a) 9 May 1921. Joined Margate summer 1921.
ARSENAL Record: League 63; FA Cup 3; Other snr comp: 2; Football Combination 36 (2 gls); London FA Challenge Cup 4; South Eastern League 64; London League (Res) 9; Other jnr comp: 1; Friendlies 23 (1 gl).
Honours: Southend Hospital Cup winners 1920-21. Served with the RASC during World War One and played for Brentford (1916-19).

PEEL, Harold Burston   **1926-29**
Inside/outside-left   5ft 10½in. 12st 3lb.
Born: Bradford, 26 Mar 1900. Died: Jan 1976.
School: Grange Road Secondary; Great Horton School.
Jnr football: Calverley (Bradford League). Previous Club: Bradford 1921 (professional). Joined ARSENAL: 17 Dec 1926 from Bradford for £1,750. First snr fdly v Dartford (a) 18 Dec 1926. First snr app: League v Cardiff City (a) 27 Dec 1926. Final snr app: League v Manchester United (a) 26 Oct 1929. Final app: London Combination v West Ham United (h) 7 Dec 1929. Transferred to Bradford City (£1,000) 11 Dec 1929.
ARSENAL Record: League 47 (5 gls); FA Cup 5 (1 gl); Football Combination 76 (19 gls); London FA Challenge Cup 1; London Midweek League 1; Friendlies 13 (5 gls).
Honours: London Combination champions 1926-7, 1927-8, 1928-9.
Retired from football in 1936 and became a businessman in Bradford.

PETROVIĆ, Vladimir   **1983**
Midfield
Born: Belgrade, Yugoslavia, 1 Jul 1955.
Jnr football: Belgrade (amateur). Previous Club: Red Star (Belgrade), Yugoslavia (1970). Joined ARSENAL: 29 Dec 1982 from Red Star (Belgrade) £30,000. First app: League v Swansea City (h) 1 Jan 1983. Final app: League v Aston Villa (a) 14 May 1983. Released by Arsenal at end of 1982-3 and joined Antwerp (Belgium).
ARSENAL Record: League 10/3 (2 gls); FA Cup

6 (1 gl); Football League Cup 3; Football Combination 2 (1 gl).
Captain of Red Star. Won Yugoslavia Schoolboy, Under-18, Under-21 and full international caps. Yugoslavian Player of the Year 1980, 1981. Officialdom barred his transfer after he had joined Arsenal for pre-season training in 1982-3 and he was finally released to play on 31 Dec 1982.

PETTS, John William Frederick James   **1954-62**
Wing-half   5ft 8in. 10st 7lb.
Born: Edmonton, London, 2 Oct 1938.
Joined ARSENAL: Apr 1954 (apprentice), 28 May 1956 (professional). First app: South East Counties League v Fulham (a) 28 Aug 1954. First snr app: Southern Floodlit Challenge Cup v Reading (a) 3 Apr 1957. League v Bolton Wanderers (h) 18 Feb 1958. Final snr app: League v Everton (h) 1 May 1962. Final app: London FA Challenge Cup v Tottenham Hotspur (a) 1 Oct 1962. Transferred to Reading (£5,000) 10 Oct 1962.
ARSENAL Record: League 32; Other snr comp: 2; Football Combination 142 (22 gls); South East Counties League 32 (1 gl); London FA Challenge Cup 11 (1 gl); FA Youth Cup 8; Metropolitan League 14 (3 gls); London Midweek League 3; Other jnr comp: 6; Friendlies 54/1 (10 gls).
Honours: Played for Edmonton schoolboys, Middlesex schoolboys and London schoolboys. Played for Middlesex Youth. South East Counties League champions 1955-6. South East Counties League Cup winners 1955-6. London FA Challenge Cup runners-up 1960-61. Metropolitan League Challenge Cup winners 1960-61. Metropolitan League Professional Cup winners 1960-61. 7 England Youth caps 1955-7.
Served National Service in the Army (1957-9). After Reading played for Bristol Rovers (Jul 1965) and later became assistant manager (1974-5) and manager (1977-8) of Northampton Town. His son, Paul, played for Shrewsbury Town.

PLACE, Walter Jnr   **1900-02**
Half-back/inside-forward   5ft 10in. 12st 12lb.
Born: Burnley.
Previous Club: Burnley. Joined ARSENAL: 4 May 1900 from Burnley. First app: League v Gainsborough Trinity (h) 1 Sep 1900. Final app: League v Lincoln City (h) 5 Apr 1902.
ARSENAL Record: League 42 (6 gls); FA Cup 3 (1 gl); London League 7; London League (Res) 4 (1 gl); Kent League 3 (1 gl); Friendlies 9 (2 gls).

PLATT, Edward Hewitt   **1938-53**
Goalkeeper   6ft 1in. 12st 10lb.
Born: Woolstanton, Staffordshire, 26 Mar 1921.
School: Romford, Essex.
Jnr football: Charfield (Gloucestershire), Bath City; Colchester United. Joined ARSENAL: 30 Dec 1938 (amateur), 15 Jan 1939 (professional) from Colchester United. First app: Southern League v Barry Town (a) 14 Jan 1939. First snr app: Football South v Tottenham Hotspur (a) 25 Jan 1940. League v Leeds United (h) 16 Nov 1946. Final snr app: League v Derby County (a) 27 Sep 1952. Snr fdly v All Stars XI (a) 29 Sep 1952. Final app: Football Combination Cup v Brighton (h) 29 Aug 1953. Transferred to Portsmouth 1 Sep 1953.
ARSENAL Record: League 53; FA Cup 4; Football Combination 117; London FA Challenge League 1; Other jnr comp: 1; Friendlies 19/3. In addition played 1 Southern League match 1939-40 prior to outbreak of war and made 33 apps during wartime.
Honours: Football Combination League champions 1946-7. Football Combination Cup

runners-up 1946-7. Lowestoft Hospital Cup winners 1938-9.
Son of a former Bolton Wanderers player. Served with the Royal Fusiliers in North Africa and Italy during the war. After Portsmouth played for Aldershot (Jul 1955), Worcester City (Nov 1955) and Ashford (Kent). Worked as a porter in Smithfield Market (1959) and then became a publican in Bow (1962).

POWELL, Joseph   **1892-96**
Right-back   5ft 9½in. 12st.
Born: Bristol, 1870. Died: Plumstead, 29 Nov 1896.
Jnr football: Walsall, 80th Staffordshire Regiment (six seasons). Joined ARSENAL: Dec 1892 from the Army. First app: Snr fdly v Stockton (h) 26 Dec 1892. First first-class app: FA Cup v Sunderland (a) 21 Jan 1893. League v Newcastle United (h) 2 Sep 1893. Final app: United League v Kettering Town (a) 23 Nov 1896.

ARSENAL Record: League 86 (1 gl); FA Cup 6 (1 gl); United League 4; Kent League 1; Friendlies 76 (5 gls). In addition made 30 senior apps for Royal Arsenal 1892-3.
Represented the Army v Corinthians 1891. Arsenal bought him out of the Army to play professional football. Captain of Arsenal. Broke an arm in a United League match v Kettering on 23 Nov 1896 and contracted blood poisoning and tetanus. although the arm was amputated he died six days later at home in Plumstead.

POWLING, Richard Frederick   **1971-81**
Defender   5ft 7½in. 11st 6lb.
Born: Barking, Essex, 21 May 1956.
Joined ARSENAL: Aug 1971 (apprentice), 1 Jul 1973 (professional). First app: South East Counties League v Luton Town (h) 21 Aug 1971. First snr app: On tour v Toronto (Canada) 23 May 1973. League v Queen's Park Rangers (a) 27 Oct 1973. Final snr app: League v Nottingham Forest (h) 3 Sep 1977. Final app: Football Combination v Queen's Park Rangers (a) 21 Oct 1980. Forced to retire through injury, summer 1981.
ARSENAL Record: League 50/5 (3 gls); FA Cup 2; Football League Cup 2; London FA Challenge Cup 4; Football Combination 146/2 (3 gls); South East Counties League 41 (2 gls); FA Youth Cup 16 (1 gl); Other jnr comp: 1; Friendlies 76/8 (6 gls).
Honours: Played for Essex and for London schoolboys. South East Counties League

champions 1971-2. South East Counties League Cup runners-up 1971-2. 3 England Youth caps 1974. Suffered a serious knee injury which curtailed his first-class career. Later played for Barnet (1981-2) and Grays Athletic (1982-3) then became manager of Tiptree United (summer 1984) and Sudbury Town.

PRATT, Thomas Peet   **1903-04**
Centre-forward   5ft 9in. 13st 1lb.
Born: Fleetwood, Lancs, 28 Aug 1875. Died: Fleetwood, Aug 1935.
Jnr football: Fleetwood Rangers (three seasons). Previous Clubs: Grimsby Town (1895), Preston North End (1896), Tottenham Hotspur (May 1899), Preston North End (May 1900). Joined ARSENAL: 29 Aug 1903 from Preston North End. First app: Jnr fdly v Northfleet (a) 3 Sep 1903. First snr app: League v Blackpool (h) 5 Sep 1903. Final app: League v Grimsby Town (a) 16 Apr 1904. Transferred to Fulham 31 Aug 1904.
ARSENAL Record: League 8 (2 gls); FA Cup 2; London League 7 (7 gls); Other snr comp: 2 (3 gls); South Eastern League 3 (3 gls); London League (Res) 1 (1 gl); Friendlies 2 (2 gls).
Later played for Blackpool (Mar 1905).

PREEDY, Charles James Fane   **1929-33**
Goalkeeper   6ft 1in. 11st 10lb.
Born: Neemuch, India, 11 Jan 1903. Died: Norfolk, 1978.
School: Gordon School, Eltham.
Jnr football: British Motor Cab FC; Bostal Heath; Redhill. Previous Clubs: Charlton Athletic (Dec 1922); Wigan Borough (Jul 1928). Joined ARSENAL: 15 May 1929 from Wigan Borough. First app: London Combination v Luton Town (a) 31 Aug 1929. First snr app: League v Sheffield Wednesday (a) 7 Sep 1929. Final snr app: League v Blackpool (a) 1 Oct 1932. Final app: London Combination v Portsmouth (h) 6 May 1933. Transferred to Bristol Rovers (together with H.Cope in exchange for R.Green) 3 Jul 1933.
ARSENAL Record: League 37; FA Cup 2; FA Charity Shield 1; Other snr comp: 1; Football Combination 116; London FA Challenge Cup 7; London Midweek League 8; Friendlies 8.
Honours: FA Cup winners 1930. FA Charity Shield winners 1931-2. London Combination champions 1929-30, 1930-31. London FA Challenge Cup winners 1930-31. Northampton Charity Shield winners 1929-30.
Later played for Luton Town (Aug 1934) and Margate (Jul 1935). Retired from football 1936 and became a taxi driver in South London. Retired and lived in Norfolk.

PRICE, David James   **1970-81**
Midfield   5ft 11in. 12st 2lb.
Born: Caterham, Surrey, 23 Jun 1955.
School: Ashburton High, Croydon.
Joined ARSENAL: Jul 1970 (apprentice), 28 Jul 1972 (professional). First app: Jnr fdly v Hounslow (a) 5 Aug 1970. First snr app: League (sub) v Leeds United (a) 9 May 1973. Final app: League (sub) v Leicester City (a) 7 Mar 1981. Transferred to Crystal Palace (£80,000) 3 Jul 1981.
ARSENAL Record: League 116/10 (16 gls); FA Cup 26 (1 gl); Football League Cup 11; European comp: 11/1 (2 gls); FA Charity Shield 1; Other snr comp: 1; Football Combination 207/3 (29 gls); London FA Challenge Cup 5 (1 gl); South East Counties League 45 (1 gl); FA Youth Cup 16; Other jnr comp: 3; Friendlies 101/12 (8 gls).
Honours: Played for Croydon District, Surrey, Middlesex, and London schoolboys. FA Cup winners 1979, runners-up 1978, 1980. European Cup-winners' Cup runners-up 1979-80. FA Charity Shield runners-up 1979-80. FA Youth Cup winners 1970-71. South East Counties League

Cup winners 1970-71, runners-up 1971-2. England Schoolboy international and captain. 6 England Youth caps 1973-4.
Loaned to Peterborough United Jan 1975 (6 apps, 1 gl). Broke a leg, Nov 1975, and missed most of the season. Transferred from Crystal Palace to Orient (Mar 1983) and to Wealdstone (1983).

PRYDE, David   **1935-46**
Wing-half   5ft 8¾in. 10st 2lb.
Born: Newtongrange, nr Edinburgh, 10 Nov 1913.
Jnr football: Margate (Arsenal nursery). Joined ARSENAL: 9 May 1935 and went to Margate, returning to Highbury, Sep 1937. First app: Jnr fdly v Margate (a) 30 Jan 1937. First snr app: League v Sunderland (h) 4 Feb 1939. Final snr app: On tour v Danish XI (Denmark) 24 May 1939. Final app: London FA Challenge Cup v Brentford (h) 21 Oct 1946. Transferred to Torquay United 25 Oct 1946.
ARSENAL Record: League 4; Football Combination 56; London FA Challenge Cup 7; Southern League 15 (1 gl); Friendlies 4. In addition played 2 London Combination matches 1939-40 prior to outbreak of war and made 21 apps during wartime.
Honours: London Combination champions 1937-8, 1938-9.
Served with the RAF in India and Burma during the war.

PUGH, Sidney John   **1936-39**
Half-back   5ft 7in. 11st 1lb.
Born: Dartford, Kent. Died: Mar/Apr 1944 on active service.
Jnr football: Nunhead, Margate. Joined ARSENAL: 29 Apr 1936 (amateur), 9 May 1938 (professional). First app: Jnr fdly v Ashford (a) 2 May 1936. First and final snr app: League v Birmingham (a) 8 Apr 1939.
ARSENAL Record: League 1; Football Combination 11; London FA Challenge Cup 1; Southern League 21 (1 gl); Friendlies 2.
Joined ARSENAL: from school and acted as a telephonist at Highbury. Sustained a severe kidney injury in his only snr app at Birmingham in 1939 and made no further app for Arsenal. Served as a Flying Officer in the RAF during the war and was killed on active service.

QUAYLE, James A.   **1907, 1908 & 1910-11**
Full-back   5ft 10in. 12st 7lb.
Born: Charlton, London, c.1890.
Jnr football: Old Charlton, Woolwich Polytechnic, Fossdene Old Boys, Northfleet (1908-10). Joined ARSENAL: 24 Aug 1907 (amateur), 2 Jun

1908 (amateur), 19 Oct 1910 (professional). First app: London League (Res) v Crystal Palace (a) 7 Sep 1907. First snr app: League v Sheffield Wednesday (h) 12 Nov 1910. Final app: South Eastern League v Luton Town (a) 22 Apr 1911.
ARSENAL Record: League 1; South Eastern League 21; London League (Res) 5; Friendlies 6. After two spells with Arsenal he had two seasons with Northfleet before rejoining Arsenal in 1910. Was employed in the Civil Service prior to becoming a professional footballer. Was badly injured in his only snr app in Nov 1910.

QUINN, Niall John   **1983-90**
Striker   6ft 4in. 12st 4lb.
Born: Dublin, 6 Oct 1966.
Jnr football: Manortown United. Joined ARSENAL: 30 Nov 1983 from school. First app: South East Counties League v Watford (a) 10 Dec 1983. First snr app: Snr fdly v Colchester United (a) 9 Dec 1985. League v Liverpool (h) 14 Dec 1985. Final app: FA Cup v Stoke City (a) 6 Jan 1990. Snr fdly: (sub) v Southend (a) 21 Feb 1990. Final app: Football Combination v Charlton Athletic (a) 13 Mar 1990. Transferred to Manchester City (£700,000) 15 Mar 1990.
ARSENAL Record: League 59/8 (14 gls); FA Cup 8/2 (2 gls); Football League Cup 14/2 (4 gls); FA Charity Shield 0/1; Football Combination 101 (59 gls); South East Counties League 45/1 (19 gls); FA Youth Cup 4; Other jnr comp: 5/2 (2 gls); Friendlies 39/21 (21 gls).
Honours: Football League Cup winners 1986-7. FA Charity Shield runners-up 1989-90. Southern Junior Floodlit Cup winners 1983-4. South East Counties League Cup runners-up 1984-5. Republic of Ireland Youth international. 13 full Republic of Ireland caps.
Also successful at hurling and Gaelic football in Ireland before taking up professional soccer.

RADFORD, John   **1962-76**
Striker   5ft 11½in. 12st.
Born: Hemsworth, Yorkshire, 22 Feb 1947.
School: Hemsworth.
Jnr football: Hemsworth Youth Club. Joined

ARSENAL: 26 Oct 1962 (apprentice), 28 Feb 1964 (professional). First app: South East Counties League v Charlton Athletic (a) 25 Aug 1962. First snr app: League v West Ham United (a) 21 Mar 1964. Final app: League (sub) v Stoke City (h) 16 Oct 1976. Testimonial (guest) v Tottenham (a)

12 May 1978. Transferred to West Ham United (£80,000) 13 Dec 1976.
ARSENAL Record: League 375/4 (111 gls); FA Cup 42/2 (15 gls); European comp: 24 (11 gls) Football League Cup 34 (12 gls); Other snr comp: 1; Football Combination 74 (40 gls); Metropolitan League 27 (20 gls); London FA Challenge Cup 5 (4 gls); FA Youth Cup 16 (10 gls); South East Counties League 25 (30 gls); Other jnr comp: 6 (6 gls); Friendlies 104/8 (69 gls).
Honours: Division One champions 1970-71. FA Cup winners 1971, runners-up 1972. European Fairs Cup winners 1969-70. Football League Cup runners-up 1967-8, 1968-9. FA Youth Cup runners-up 1964-5. Metropolitan League Professional Cup runners-up 1962-3. 4 England Under-23 caps (1 gl) 1968-9 and 2 full caps 1969-72. Made 1 app for the Football League 1968. Arsenal Player of the Year 1968, 1973.
After West Ham United played for Blackburn Rovers (Feb 1978). Retired from League football and became a publican in Essex and also player-coach and then manager of Bishop's Stortford.

RAMSAY, James Howie   **1924-26**
Inside-forward   5ft 9in. 11st.
Born: Clydebank, Glasgow, 7 Aug 1898. Died: Kent, 26 Jan 1969.
School: Moor Park.
Jnr football: Moor Park, Arthurlie, Renfrew (1919). Previous Club: Kilmarnock (1919-20). Joined ARSENAL: 29 Feb 1924 from Kilmarnock. First app: League v Liverpool (h) 1 Mar 1924. Final app: League v Cardiff City (a) 27 Dec 1926. Transferred to Kilmarnock 30 Dec 1926.
ARSENAL Record: League 69 (11 gls); FA Cup 6; Football Combination 37 (14 gls); London FA Challenge Cup 5 (1 gl); Friendlies 12 (4 gls).
Served apprenticeship in engineering. Joined 6th Seaforth Highlanders in 1917 and served in France during the war. Had a spell as manager of Margate FC. Retired Jan 1936.

RANDALL, Charles E.   **1911-14**
Centre-forward   5ft 11in. 12st 4lb.
Born: Burnopfield, Durham, c.1887.
Jnr football: Hobson Welfare. Previous Club: Newcastle United (May 1908). Joined ARSENAL: 28 Sep 1911 from Newcastle United. First app: League v Bolton Wanderers (a) 7 Oct 1911. Final snr app: League v Leicester Fosse (a) 27 Dec 1913. Final app: London League (Res) v Clapton Orient (h) 30 Apr 1914. Transferred to North Shields summer 1914.
ARSENAL Record: League 43 (12 gls); FA Cup 1; London FA Challenge Cup 2 (1 gl); South Eastern League 30 (13 gls); London League (Res) 7 (2 gls); Friendlies 5 (1 gl).

RANKIN, Andrew   **1891-93**
Full-back   5ft 9in. 11st 12lb.
Born: Glasgow, c.1869.
Jnr football: Maryhill, Cowlairs, Airdrie, Glasgow Northern. Joined ARSENAL: Sep 1891 from Glasgow Northern. First app: Jnr fdly (Res) v Upton Park (a) 12 Sep 1891. First first-class app: FA Cup (Q) v Millwall Athletic (h) 19 Nov 1892. Final first-class app: FA Cup v Sunderland (a) 21 Jan 1893. Final app: Jnr fdly (Res) v Woolwich League (a) 3 Apr 1893.
ARSENAL Record: FA Cup 1; FA Cup (Q) 2. In addition made 74 senior (2 gls) and 13 reserve apps for Royal Arsenal 1891-2 and 1892-3.
Won Glasgow Inter City honours. A nibbler by trade, worked at Woolwich Ordnance factory.

RANSOM, Frank   **1900-05**
Left-half
Born: Ireland.
Joined ARSENAL: 7 Aug 1900 from local football

after trial in 1898. First app: Jnr fdly v Plumstead Gymnasium (h) 1 Apr 1898 (trial). First snr app: Snr fdly v Millwall Athletic (h) 1 Apr 1901. First app v Leicester Fosse (a) 26 Dec 1903 (only first-class app). Final app: Snr fdly v Sheffield United (h) 29 Apr 1905. Transferred to Southern United Jun 1905.
ARSENAL Record: League 1; London League 7; Other snr comp: 2; London League (Res) 91 (11 gls); Kent League 36 (4 gls); South Eastern League 44 (3 gls); Other jnr comp: 4 (1 gl); Friendlies 36 (2 gls).
Honours: West Kent League champions 1900-01, 1901-02, 1902-03. London League (Res) champions 1901-02, 1903-04. South Eastern League champions 1903-04. West Kent Charity Cup winners 1904-05. Chatham Charity Cup runners-up 1902-03.
Later played for Crystal Palace (1906-07).

RAYBOULD, Samuel F.   **1908-09**
Centre-forward   5ft 9in. 12st.
Born: Chesterfield, Derbyshire, 1875.
Jnr football: Chesterfield Town (1893), Ilkeston Town (Jan 1895), Poolsbrook United, Ilkeston Town (Feb 1898), Bolsover Colliery. Previous Clubs: Derby County (1894), New Brighton Tower (Oct 1899), Liverpool (Jan 1900), Sunderland (May 1907). Joined ARSENAL: 13 May 1908 from Sunderland. First app: League v Everton (h) 2 Sep 1908. Final app: League v Sheffield Wednesday (h) 12 Apr 1909.
ARSENAL Record: League 26 (6 gls); FA Cup 4 (1 gl); London FA Challenge Cup 3; Other snr comp: 1; South Eastern League 1 (2 gls); London League (Res) 1 (1 gl); Friendlies 1 (1 gl).
Won club and Football League honours with Liverpool.

REECE, George   **1895**
Centre-forward.
Jnr football: Soho Villa (Birmingham). Joined ARSENAL: 5 Jan 1895 from Soho Villa. First app: Snr fdly v Sheppey United (a) 5 Jan 1895. Final app: League v Burslem Port Vale (a) 19 Jan 1895.
ARSENAL Record: League 1; Friendlies 1.

RICE, Patrick James   **1964-80**
Right-back   5ft 9in. 12st 2lb.
Born: Belfast, 17 Mar 1949.
School: Highbury, London.
Joined ARSENAL: 21 Dec 1964 (apprentice), 25 Mar 1966 (professional). First app: South East Counties League v Ipswich Town (h) 21 Aug 1965. First snr app: Snr fdly v Charlton Athletic (a) 7 Apr 1967. League (sub) v Burnley (a) 2 Dec 1967. Final snr app: League (sub) v Liverpool (a) 25 Oct 1980. Final app: Football Combination v Leicester City (h) 11 Nov 1980. Transferred to Watford (£8,000) 17 Nov 1980.
ARSENAL Record: League 391/6 (12 gls); FA Cup 67 (1 gl); Football League Cup 36; European comp: 26/1; FA Charity Shield 2; Football Combination 127 (3 gls); London FA Challenge Cup 8; FA Youth Cup 8; Metropolitan League 17; South East Counties League 23; Other jnr comp: 7; Friendlies 100/11 (6 gls). Made 1 app (sub) jnr fdly 1986-7.
Honours: Division One champions 1970-71. FA Cup winners 1971, 1979, runners-up 1972, 1978, 1980. European Cup-winners' Cup runners-up 1979-80. FA Charity Shield runners-up 1979-80. Football Combination champions 1968-9, 1969-70. Football Combination Cup winners 1967-8. London FA Challenge Cup winners 1969-70. FA Youth Cup winners 1965-6. Southern Junior Floodlit Cup winners 1965-6. South East Counties League Cup runners-up 1965-6. Captain of Arsenal. Arsenal Player of the Year 1972. 2

Northern Ireland Under-23 caps 1968-9 and 49 full caps 1968-79.
Won club honours with Watford. Became youth-team coach at Arsenal (Jul 1984).

RICHARDSON, Kevin   **1987-90**
Midfield   5ft 7in. 10st 2lb.
Born: Newcastle upon Tyne, 4 Dec 1962.
Previous Clubs: Everton (1979 from school); Watford (Sep 1986). Joined ARSENAL: 26 Aug 1987 from Watford for £200,000. First app: League (sub) v Portsmouth (h) 29 Aug 1987. Final app: League v Southampton (h) 2 May 1990. Transferred to Real Sociedad (Spain) (£750,000) May 1990.

ARSENAL Record: League 88/8 (5 gls); FA Cup 9 (1 gl); Football League Cup 13/3 (2 gls); FA Charity Shield 1; Other snr comp: 4/1; Football Combination 9/1; Friendlies 14/4 (4 gls).
Honours: Division One champions 1988-9. FA Charity Shield runners-up 1989-90. Football League Cup runners-up 1987-8.
Won domestic and European club honours with Everton. Returned to England to play for Aston Villa (cs 1991).

RIMMER, John James   **1974-77**
Goalkeeper   5ft 11in. 11st 12lb.
Born: Southport, Lancs, 10 Feb 1948.
Previous Clubs: Manchester United (1963 from school), Swansea City (loan). Joined ARSENAL: 23 Feb 1974 (temporary), 2 Apr 1974 from Manchester United for £40,000. First app: Football Combination v Southampton (h) 23 Feb 1974. First snr app: League v Liverpool (a) 24 Apr 1974. Final app: League v Manchester United (a) 14 May 1977. Snr fdly v Aldershot (a) 8 Aug 1977. Transferred to Aston Villa (£70,000) 11 Aug 1977.
ARSENAL Record: League 124; FA Cup 12; Football League Cup 10; Football Combination 6; Friendlies 33/2.
Honours: Arsenal Player of the Year 1975. 1 full England cap 1976.
Won European club honours with Manchester United. Won domestic and European club honours with Aston Villa. Transferred from Aston Villa to Swansea City (Aug 1983). Retired 1986. Now runs a golf shop in Swansea.

RIPPON, Willis   **1910-11**
Inside-forward   5ft 8½in. 12st 9lb.
Born: Beighton, nr Sheffield, 15 May 1886. Died: 1956.
Jnr football: Hackenthorpe, Rawmarsh Albion, Sandhill Rovers, Kilnhurst Town. Previous Club: Bristol City (1907). Joined ARSENAL: 9 Jul 1910 from Bristol City. First app: League v Manchester United (h) 1 Sep 1910. Final snr app: League v Blackburn Rovers (a) 18 Feb 1911. Final app: South Eastern League v Brighton (a) 14 Oct 1911. Transferred to Brentford 26 Oct 1911.
ARSENAL Record: League 9 (2 gls); London FA Challenge Cup 2 (2 gls); Other snr comp: 1 (1 gl); South Eastern League 23 (9 gls); Friendlies 4 (6 gls).
Later played for Hamilton Academical (1912), Grimsby Town (1913) and Rotherham Town (1914).

RIX, Graham   **1974-88**
Midfield   5ft 9¾in. 11st.
Born: Askern, Doncaster, Yorks, 23 Oct 1957.
School: Camps Mount, Doncaster.
Jnr football: Askern Juniors, Leeds United (trials).

Joined ARSENAL: Jun 1974 (apprentice), 13 Jan 1975 (professional). First app: Jnr fdly (sub) v Enfield Town (a) 13 Aug 1974. First snr app: Snr fdly (sub) v Charlton Athletic (a) 28 Oct 1975. League v Leicester City (h) 2 Apr 1977. Final app: League (sub) v Everton (a) 7 May 1988. Snr fdly v Millwall (a) 11 May 1988. Transferred to SM Caen of France (free transfer) 22 Jun 1988.

ARSENAL Record: League 338/13 (41 gls); FA Cup 42/2 (7 gls); Football League Cup 45/2 (2 gls); European comp: 21 (1 gl); FA Charity Shield 1; Football Combination 120/4 (10 gls); South East Counties League 20 (2 gls); FA Youth Cup 7 (4 gls); Other jnr comp: 6; Friendlies 115/9 (10 gls).
Honours: Played for Doncaster and for Yorkshire schoolboys. Played for Yorkshire Youth. FA Cup winners 1979, runners-up 1978, 1980. European Cup-winners' Cup runners-up 1979-80. FA Charity Shield runners-up 1979-80. 7 England Under-21 caps 1977-80, 3 'B' caps 1979-81 and 17 full caps 1980-84. Captain of Arsenal.
Suffered a recurring Achilles tendon injury in Nov 1983 which resulted in long spells out of action. Was on a month's loan to Brentford (Dec 1987) making 6 League apps. Moved from Caen to Le Havre (1991-2).

ROBERTS, Herbert   **1926-37**
Centre-half   6ft 1in. 12st 5lb.
Born: Oswestry, Shropshire, 19 Feb 1905. Died: 19 Jun 1944.
Jnr football: Oswestry Town (1922). Joined ARSENAL: 10 Dec 1926 from Oswestry Town for £200. First app: Jnr fdly v Dartford (a) 18 Dec 1926. First snr app: League v Aston Villa (a) 18 Apr 1927. Final app: League v Middlesbrough (h) 30 Oct 1937. Forced to retire through injury (1938).
ARSENAL Record: League 297 (4 gls); FA Cup 36 (1 gl); FA Charity Shield 2; Other snr comp: 2; Football Combination 63; London FA Challenge Cup 5; Friendlies 20/1.
Honours: Division One champions 1930-31, 1932-3, 1933-4, 1934-5. FA Cup winners 1936, runners-up 1932. FA Charity Shield winners 1930-31, 1931-2. London Combination champions 1927-8. Northampton Charity Shield winners 1930-31. Norwich Hospital Cup winners 1934-5. 1 full England cap 1931.

Learned his trade as a gunsmith in Oswestry before taking up football. Missed the 1930 FA Cup Final due to injury. Suffered a badly injured knee in Oct 1937 which ended his playing career. Became trainer of Arsenal's Southern League team 1938-9. Served as a Lieutenant in the Royal Fusiliers during the war. Died suddenly from erysipelas in 1944.

ROBERTS, John Griffith   **1969-72**
Half-back   6ft. 13st.
Born: Abercynon, South Wales, 11 Sep 1946.
Jnr football: Abercynon Athletic. Previous Clubs: Swansea Town (Jul 1964), Northampton Town (Nov 1967). Joined ARSENAL: 30 Apr 1969 from Northampton Town for £35,000. First app: Snr fdly (sub) v Watford (a) 8 May 1969. League v Coventry City (h) 4 Oct 1969. Final app: Football League Cup v Rotherham United (h) 3 Oct 1972. Transferred to Birmingham City (£150,000) 11 Oct 1972.

ARSENAL Record: League 56/3 (4 gls); Football League Cup 12 (1 gl); European comp: 9/1; Football Combination 57 (1 gl); London FA Challenge Cup 3; Friendlies 15/9 (3 gls).
Honours: Division One champions 1970-71. Football Combination champions 1969-70. London FA Challenge Cup winners 1969-70. 1 Wales Under-23 cap 1969 and 7 full caps 1971-2.
Worked as a railway fireman before taking up football. Won Under-23 honours with Swansea Town and Northampton Town and full international honours with Birmingham City. After Birmingham played for Wrexham (Jul 1976) and Hull City (Aug 1980). Won club and Under-21 honours with Wrexham. Now runs his own driving school in Cheshire.

ROBERTSON, Alexander   **1891-92**
Right-half.
Previous Club: Preston North End. Joined ARSENAL: Oct 1891. First app: Snr fdly v Birmingham St George (h) 3 Oct 1891. First first-class app: FA Cup v Small Heath (a) 16 Jan 1892 (only first-class app). Final app: Snr fdly v Grimsby Town (h) 23 Jan 1892.
ARSENAL Record: FA Cup 1. In addition made 29 senior apps (1 gl) for Royal Arsenal 1891-2.

ROBERTSON, Hope S.   **1889-90**
Inside-left.
Born: Glasgow.
Jnr football: Westburn. Joined ARSENAL: Sep 1889. First app: Snr fdly v Casuals (h) 14 Sep 1889. First first-class app: FA Cup (Q) v Lyndhurst (h) 5 Oct 1889. Final first-class app: FA Cup (Q) v Swifts (h) 7 Dec 1889. Final app: Snr fdly v London Caledonians/Clapton XI (h) 3 May 1890.
ARSENAL Record: FA Cup (Q) 4 (4 gls). In addition made 27 senior (24 gls) and 1 reserve (3 gls) app for Royal Arsenal 1889-90.
Honours: London Charity Cup winners 1889-90. Kent Senior Cup winners 1889-90. London Senior Cup runners-up 1889-90.
Later played for Walsall.

ROBERTSON, James Gillen   **1968-70**
Wing-forward   5ft 8in. 10st.
Born: Cardonald, Glasgow, 17 Dec 1944.
School: Lourdes Secondary, Glasgow.
Previous Clubs: Middlesbrough (trials), Cowdenbeath, St Mirren, Tottenham Hotspur (Mar 1964). Joined ARSENAL: 18 Oct 1968 from Tottenham Hotspur (exchange for David Jenkins). First app: League v West Ham United (h) 26 Oct 1968. Final

snr app: FA Cup v Blackpool (a) 15 Jan 1970.
Final app: Football Combination v Fulham (a)
7 Mar 1970. Transferred to Ipswich Town
(£50,000) 13 Mar 1970.
ARSENAL Record: League 45/1 (7 gls); FA Cup
4 (1 gl); Football League Cup 4; European comp:
5; Football Combination 12 (5 gls); Friendlies 7
(3 gls).
Scotland Youth and Amateur international. Won
Under-23 honours with St Mirren. Won club,
Under-23 and full international honours with
Tottenham Hotspur. After Ipswich Town played
for Stoke City (Jun 1972), Walsall (Sep 1977) and
Crewe Alexandra (Sep 1978). On retirement from
football became a director of a computer insurance
company in the Stoke area.

ROBERTSON, James Wright   **1948-53**
Outside-left   5ft 6in. 9st 11lb.
Born: Falkirk, Scotland, 20 Feb 1929.
Jnr football: Dunipace Thistle (Stirlingshire).
Joined ARSENAL: 5 Jun 1948 from Dunipace
Thistle. First app: Eastern Counties League v
Chelmsford (a) 21 Aug 1948. First snr app: Snr
fdly v Bexhill Town (a) 29 Sep 1948. League v
West Bromwich Albion (a) 21 Apr 1952 (only first-
class app). Final app: Football Combination Cup
v Crystal Palace (h) 15 Sep 1953. Transferred to
Brentford (part of T.Lawton deal) 18 Sep 1953.
ARSENAL Record: League 1; Football
Combination 105 (23 gls); London FA Challenge
Cup 3; Eastern Counties League 19 (4 gls); London
Midweek League 1; Friendlies 9.
Served National Service in the Royal Artillery and
played for the Army in representative matches.
Later played for Gravesend.

ROBSON, John Hardy   **1921-26**
Goalkeeper   5ft 8½in. 11st 2lb.
Born: Innerleithen, Scotland, c.1898.
Jnr football: Innerleithen. Joined ARSENAL:
Nov 1921 from Innerleithen for £5. First app: Jnr
fdly v Tunbridge Wells Rangers (a) 5 Nov 1921.
First snr app: League v Bolton Wanderers (h) 26
Dec 1922. Final snr app: League v Manchester
City (a) 7 Nov 1925. Final app: London Combina-
tion v Charlton Athletic (h) 22 Apr 1926. Trans-
ferred to Bournemouth & Boscombe Athletic 27
Aug 1926.
ARSENAL Record: League 97; FA Cup 4; Other
snr comp: 1; Football Combination 34; London
FA Challenge Cup 9; Friendlies 27.
*Honours: London FA Challenge Cup winners 1923-
4. London FA Challenge Cup runners-up 1925-
6. Metropolitan Hospital Cup runners-up 1922-3.*
Served with the 6th Seaforth Highlanders in
France during World War One. On retiring from
football went to live in Peeblesshire, Scotland.

ROBSON, Stewart Ian   **1980-87**
Midfield   5ft 11¾in. 11st 12lb.
Born: Billericay, Essex, 6 Nov 1964.
School: Stanford-le-Hope Primary; Alleyne Court
Prep.; Brentwood Public.
Joined ARSENAL: 1978 (schoolboy), 24 Apr 1981
(apprentice), 9 Nov 1981 (professional). First app:
South East Counties League v Fulham (h) 16 Aug
1980. First snr app: League v West Ham United
(a) 5 Dec 1981. Final snr app: League v Tottenham
Hotspur (h) 6 Sep 1986. Final app: Football
Combination v West Ham United (a) 8 Nov 1986.
Transferred to West Ham United (£700,000) 7 Jan
1987.
ARSENAL Record: League 150/1 (16 gls); FA
Cup 13 (1 gl); Football League Cup 20 (3 gls);
European comp: 2 (1 gl); Football Combination
32 (4 gls); South East Counties League 18 (6 gls);
Other jnr comp: 6; FA Youth Cup 5 (2 gls);
Friendlies 51/2 (5 gls). In addition played 2

Football Combination matches 1981-2, later
removed from records.
*Honours: Played for England Public Schools. 18
England Youth caps (and captain) 1981-3 and 6
Under-21 caps (2 gls) 1984-6. Arsenal Player of
the Year 1985.*
Also an excellent cricketer, has played for Essex
Second XI. Won further Under-21 honours with
West Ham United. Joined Coventry City, 1990-91.

ROCASTLE, David   **1982-**
Midfield   5ft 9in. 11st 1lb.
Born: Lewisham, London, 2 May 1967.
School: Roger Manwoods Boys.
Joined ARSENAL: May 1982 (schoolboy), 4 Aug
1983 (apprentice), 31 Dec 1984 (professional).
First app: Jnr fdly v Colchester (a) 7 Aug 1982.
First snr app: League v Newcastle United (h) 28
Sep 1985.
ARSENAL Record: League 204/13 (24 gls); FA
Cup 18/2 (4 gls); Football League Cup 32/1 (6
gls); European comp: 4; FA Charity Shield 2; Other

snr comp: 12/1 (1 gl); Football Combination 64/
7 (11 gls); South East Counties League 53/4 (15
gls); FA Youth Cup 8 (2 gls); Other jnr comp:
9 (3 gls); Friendlies 72/16 (15 gls).
*Honours: Played for South London schoolboys.
Division One champions 1988-9, 1990-91.
Football League Cup winners 1986-7, runners-up
1987-8. FA Charity Shield runners-up 1988-9,
medal 1991-2. Mercantile Credit Centenary
Trophy winners 1988-9. Southern Junior Floodlit
Cup winners 1983-4. South East Counties League
Cup runners-up 1984-5. Arsenal Player of the Year
1986. Barclays Young Eagle of the Year 1988-
9. 14 England Under-21 caps (2 gls); 2 'B' caps;
13 full caps.*

RODGER, James   **1907-08**
Outside-left.
Born: Scotland.
Previous Clubs: Paisley St Mirren, Renton. Joined
ARSENAL: 14 Jun 1907 from Renton. First app:
South Eastern League v Hitchen (h) 20 Apr 1907.
First snr app: League v Preston North End (h)
25 Jan 1908 (only Senior app). Final app: South
Eastern League v Queen's Park Rangers (a) 25
Apr 1908.
ARSENAL Record: League 1; South Eastern
League 21 (1 gl); London League (Res) 11 (1 gl);
Friendlies 1 (1 gl).
Honours: South Eastern League champions 1907-08.

ROE, Archibald   **1922-23**
Centre-forward   5ft 6in. 11st 2lb.
Born: Hull.
Jnr football: Castleford Town. Joined ARSENAL:
4 Aug 1922 from Castleford Town. First app:
London Combination v West Ham United (h) 26
Aug 1922. First snr app: League v Newcastle United
(a) 21 Oct 1922. Final snr app: League v Everton
(h) 11 Nov 1922. Final app: London Combination
v Crystal Palace (h) 22 Sep 1923. Transferred to
Lincoln City 1 Nov 1923.
ARSENAL Record: League 4 (1 gl); Football
Combination 37 (23 gls); London FA Challenge
Cup 2 (1 gl); Friendlies 7 (7 gls).
*Honours: London Combination champions 1922-3.
Transferred from Lincoln City to Rotherham
United (Dec 1924).*

ROE, Arthur   **1925**
Left-half.
Previous Club: Luton Town (1919). Joined
ARSENAL: 1 May 1925. First app: League v Bury
(a) 2 May 1925 (his only app for Arsenal). Contract
cancelled 11 May 1925.
ARSENAL Record: League 1.
Played for Luton Town 1924-5 and as the season
ended was not retained by them. Signed for
Arsenal and played in the final League game of
the season. Contrary to expectation was not
offered further terms.

ROGERS, Ehud 'Tim'   **1935-36**
Outside-right   5ft 7in. 10st 2lb.
Born: Chirk, Wales, 15 Oct 1909
Jnr football: Weston Rhyn, Llanerch Celts, Chirk,
Oswestry Town (1933-4). Previous Club:
Wrexham (1934-5). Joined ARSENAL: 12 Jan
1935 from Wrexham for £3,000. First app: London
Combination v Fulham (h) 26 Jan 1935. First snr
app: League v Middlesbrough (h) 19 Apr 1935.
Final snr app: League v West Bromwich Albion
(a) 13 Apr 1936. Final app: London FA Challenge
Cup Final v Brentford (at Fulham) 4 May 1936.
Transferred to Newcastle United 9 Jun 1936.
ARSENAL Record: League 16 (5 gls); Football
Combination 27 (9 gls); London FA Challenge
Cup 3; Friendlies 7 (6 gls).
*Honours: London FA Challenge Cup winners
1935-6.*

89

Welsh amateur international 1934. Moved from Newcastle United to Swansea Town (May 1939) and made 2 apps for Wales in wartime internationals. Served with the RAF in the Middle East during the war. Returned to Wrexham (Dec 1945), retiring 1946-7. Owned a newsagent and tobacconist shop in Chirk.

ROOKE, Ronald Leslie   **1946-49**
Centre-forward   5ft 9½in. 12st 4lb.
Born: Guildford, Surrey, 7 Dec 1911. Died: Jul 1985.
School: Stoke School (Guildford).
Jnr football: Stoke Recreation, Guildford Pinks, Woking (amateur), Guildford City. Previous Clubs: Stoke City (trial), Crystal Palace (1933), Fulham (Nov 1936). Joined ARSENAL: 12 Dec 1946 from Fulham (in exchange for D.Nelson, C.Grant and £1,000). First app: League v Charlton Athletic (h) 14 Dec 1946. Final app: League v Everton (a) 16 Apr 1949. On tour (sub) v Flamengo (Brazil) 29 May 1949. Transferred to Crystal Palace as player-manager 20 Jun 1949.
ARSENAL Record: League 88 (68 gls); FA Cup 5 (1 gl); FA Charity Shield 1 (1 gl); Football Combination 4 (4 gls); Friendlies 12/3 (22 gls). In addition made 1 app (1 gl) as a guest during wartime.
Honours: Division One champions 1947-8. FA Charity Shield winners 1948-9.
Played for Guildford schoolboys. Served as a PT Instructor in the RAF during the war. Won England international honours with Fulham. Was the League's top scorer in 1947-8 with 33 goals. Was player-manager of Bedford Town (1951-61). Retired from football and became a businessman in London and later worked as a porter at Luton Airport. Retired and moved back to Bedford. Died of lung cancer in 1985.

ROOSE, Dr Leigh Richmond 'Dick'   **1911-12**
Goalkeeper   6ft 1in. 13st 6lb.
Born: Holt, nr Wrexham, 27 Nov 1877. Died: In action in France, 7 Oct 1916.
Jnr football: Aberystwyth, London Welsh. Previous Clubs: Stoke, Everton, Stoke, Sunderland, Huddersfield Town, Aston Villa (Sep 1911). Joined ARSENAL: 11 Dec 1911 (amateur) from Aston Villa. First app: League v Middlesbrough (h) Dec 1911. Final app: League v Notts County (h) 27 Apr 1912.
ARSENAL Record: League 13.
A doctor in bacteriology by profession, he therefore maintained his amateur status throughout his football career. Won Wales international honours with Stoke, Everton and Sunderland.

ROPER, Donald George Beaumont   **1947-57**
Forward   5ft 10⅝in. 12st 6lb.
Born: Botley, Hampshire, 14 Dec 1922.
School: Hedge End Senior.
Jnr football: Hedge End Lads, Bitterne Nomads. Previous Club: Southampton (1940). Joined ARSENAL: 11 Aug 1947 from Southampton for £11,000 plus T.Rudkin. First app: League v Sunderland (h) 23 Aug 1947. First snr app: League v Preston North End (h) 4 Sep 1956. Final app: Football Combination v Aldershot (h) 29 Dec 1956. Transferred to Southampton 8 Jan 1957.
ARSENAL Record: League 297 (88 gls); FA Cup 22 (7 gls); FA Charity Shield 2; London FA Challenge Cup 1; Other snr comp: 1; Football Combination 33 (21 gls); Friendlies 71/3 (49 gls).
Honours: Division One champions 1947-8, 1952-3. FA Cup runners-up 1952. FA Charity Shield winners 1948-9, 1953-4. 1 England 'B' cap 1953. Made 1 app for the Football League 1953.
Played for Eastleigh & District schoolboys. Worked as a fitter for Vickers Armstrong and

played initially as a part-timer for Southampton. Played county cricket for Hampshire in 1947. Scored 5 goals for Arsenal v Hibernian (Floodlit friendly, Oct 1952). After Southampton played for Weymouth (1959) and Dorchester Town (1960). On retirement from football, he returned to his trade in engineering in Southampton.

ROSS, Trevor William   **1972-77**
Midfield   5ft 9in. 11st 7lb.
Born: Ashton-under-Lyne, Lancs, 16 Jan 1957.
School: Hartshead.
Joined ARSENAL: 1970 (schoolboy), 29 May 1972 (apprentice), 15 Jun 1974 (professional). First app: Jnr fdly v Coventry City (h) 24 Jul 1972. First snr app: Snr fdly (sub) v Reading (a) 2 Oct 1974. League (sub) v Liverpool (h) 1 Feb 1975. Final app: League v Birmingham (h) 29 Oct 1977. Transferred to Everton (£170,000) 2 Nov 1977.
ARSENAL Record: League 57/1 (5 gls); FA Cup 3 (1 gl); Football League Cup 6 (3 gls). Football Combination 64/4 (14 gls); South East Counties League 31 (8 gls); FA Youth Cup 7 (1 gl); Other jnr comp: 1; Friendlies 46/5 (15 gls).
Honours: Played for Lancashire schoolboys. 8 England schoolboy caps. 1 Scotland Under-21 cap (parentage qualification).
Son of William Ross (Third Lanark, Arbroath, Bradford City). Had spells on loan to Portsmouth and Sheffield United whilst an Everton player. Transferred Everton to AEK Athens (Greece) in 1983. Returned 1984 to play for Sheffield United, Bury and later Altrincham.

ROSTRON, John Wilfred   **1972-77**
Winger   5ft 7in. 11st 11lb.
Born: Sunderland, 29 Sep 1956.
School: St Thomas Aquinas (Sunderland).
Joined ARSENAL: 1972 (amateur, apprentice), 4 Oct 1973 (professional). First app: Jnr fdly v Coventry City (h) 24 Jul 1972. First snr app: Snr fdly (sub) v Reading (a) 2 Oct 1974. League (sub) v Newcastle United (h) 18 Mar 1975. Final app: League (sub) v Aston Villa (h) 25 Apr 1977. On tour v Roros (Norway) 20 May 1977. Transferred: 8 Jul 1977 to Sunderland for £40,000.
ARSENAL Record: League 12/5 (2 gls); FA Cup 1; Football League Cup 1; Football Combination 124/4 (25 gls); London FA Challenge Cup 2; South East Counties League 39/1 (15 gls); FA Youth Cup 14 (4 gls); Other jnr comp: 1; Friendlies 49/7 (13 gls).
Honours: England Schoolboy international.
Transferred from Sunderland to Watford (Oct 1979). Converted to full-back at Watford with whom he won club honours. Moved to Sheffield Wednesday (Jan 1989) and Sheffield United (1989-90). Became assistant manager of Brentford (Jan 1991).

RUDKIN, Thomas William   **1947**
Outside-left   5ft 8in. 10st 7lb.
Born: Worksop, Notts, 17 Jun 1919.
Jnr football: Peterborough United. Previous Club: Lincoln City (pre-war). Joined ARSENAL: Jan 1947 from Peterborough United. First app: Football Combination v Plymouth Argyle (h) 4 Jan 1947. First snr app: League v Aston Villa (h) 18 Jan 1947. Final snr app: League v Chelsea (h) 1 Mar 1947. Final app: Football Combination Cup Final v Swansea Town (at Tottenham) 14 Jun 1947. Transferred to Southampton (part of D.Roper deal) 13 Aug 1947.
ARSENAL Record: League 5 (2 gls); Football Combination 9; Friendlies 2.
Honours: Football Combination Cup runners-up 1946-7.
Served in the RAF during wartime. Later played for Bristol City (May 1949).

RUSSELL, Albert Edward   **1895-96**
Goalkeeper.
A local man from the Woolwich area.
Previously played for White Hart, Dartford, New Brompton, Luton, Bostal Rovers. Joined ARSENAL: 26 Dec 1895. First app: Snr fdly v Darlington (h) 28 Dec 1895. Final app: FA Cup v Burnley (a) 1 Feb 1896 (his only first-class app).
ARSENAL Record: FA Cup 1; Friendlies 2.

RUSSELL, John   **1896-97**
Outside-left   5ft 5in. 10st 2lb.
Born: Carstairs, Lanarkshire, 29 Dec 1872. Died: Glasgow, Aug 1905.
Jnr football: Glasgow Thistle, Leith Athletic. Previous Club: St Mirren (two seasons). Joined ARSENAL: Jun 1896 from St Mirren. First app: Jnr fdly v Royal Ordnance (h) 5 Sep 1896. First snr app: League v Burton Wanderers (h) 12 Oct 1896. Final app: League v Manchester City (h) 28 Apr 1897. Snr fdly v Southampton St Mary's (a) 29 Apr 1897. Transferred to Bristol South End (Bristol City) summer 1897.
ARSENAL Record: League 23 (4 gls); FA Cup 2; United League 9 (5 gls); Friendlies 19 (14 gls).
Later played for Blackburn Rovers (summer 1900).

RUTHERFORD, John 'Jock'   **1913-26**
Outside-right   5ft 8½in. 11st 6lb.
Born: Percy Main, Northumberland, 12 Oct 1884. Died: 21 Apr 1963.
School: Percy Main.
Jnr football: Willington Athletic. Previous Club: Newcastle United (Jan 1902). Joined ARSENAL: 27 Oct 1913 from Newcastle United for £800. Re-signed 4 Sep 1923 from Stoke. First app: League v Nottingham Forest (h) 1 Nov 1913. Final snr app: League v Manchester City (h) 20 Mar 1926. Final app: London Combination v Clapton Orient (h) 27 Mar 1926. Transferred to Clapton Orient 17 Aug 1926.

ARSENAL Record: League 222 (25 gls): FA Cup 10 (2 gls); Other snr comp: 5 (2 gls); London FA Challenge Cup 11; Football Combination 16 (2 gls); South Eastern League 1; Friendlies 14 (2 gls). In addition made 91 apps (29 gls) during wartime.
Honours: London FA Challenge Cup winners 1923-4, runners-up 1914-15. Southend Hospital Cup winners 1920-21. Metropolitan Hospital Cup winners 1920-21.
On leaving school worked in the shipbuilding industry before taking up football. Won club, England international and Football League

honours with Newcastle United. Joined Stoke as manager (Apr 1923) but resigned in Aug 1923 and returned to Arsenal as a player (Sep 1923). Retired cs 1925 but again re-signed (Jan 1926) and made a few further appearances. His eldest son also played for Arsenal (see J.J.Rutherford). Finally retired from football at end of 1926-7 season and ran an off-licence in Neasden.

RUTHERFORD, John James   1924-27
Outside-right   5ft 11½in. 11st 8lb.
Born: South Shields, Durham, 4 Mar 1907.
School: Old Stationers.
Jnr football: Ilford (amateur). Joined ARSENAL: 22 Apr 1924 (amateur), 18 Jan 1927 (professional). First app: London Combination v Crystal Palace (h) 13 Sep 1924. First snr app: League v Bury (h) 14 Nov 1925 (only snr app). Final app: Jnr fdly v Columbia (a) 28 Apr 1927. Transferred to West Ham United (free transfer) 23 Jun 1927. ARSENAL Record: League 1; Football Combination 14 (3 gls); Friendlies 2 (2 gls). Eldest son of 'Jock' Rutherford. Played for the Secondary Schools of London. Represented the Isthmian League and also the FA v Army and v Cambridge University.

SAMMELS, Jonathan Charles   1961-71
Inside-forward   5ft 9½in. 11st 4lb.
Born: Ipswich, 23 Jul 1945.
School: Farlingaye, Woodbridge (Suffolk).
Joined ARSENAL: Jul 1960 (trial), 5 Jan 1961 (apprentice), 30 Jul 1962 (professional). First app: South East Counties League v Watford (a) 11 Feb 1961. First snr app: League v Blackpool (a) 27 Apr 1963. Final snr app: League (sub) v West Bromwich Albion (a) 24 Apr 1971. Final app: Football Combination v Swindon Town (a) 4 May 1971. Transferred to Leicester City (£100,000) 22 Jul 1971.

ARSENAL Record: League 212/3 (39 gls); FA Cup 20/1 (3 gls); Football League Cup 19 (3 gls); European comp: 15 (7 gls); Football Combination 78 (31 gls); London FA Challenge Cup 5; FA Youth Cup 7 (4 gls); Metropolitan League 40 (14 gls); South East Counties League 25 (10 gls); Other jnr comp: 8 (5 gls). Friendlies 81/2 (39 gls).
Honours: Played for Suffolk schoolboys and Suffolk Youth. Division One champions 1970-71. Football League Cup runners-up 1967-8, 1968-9. European Fairs Cup winner 1969-70. Football

Combination champions 1962-3. Football Combination Cup winners 1969-70. London FA Challenge Cup runners-up 1965-6. Metropolitan League Professional Challenge Cup winners 1961-2. Metropolitan League Challenge Cup winners 1965-6. South East Counties League Cup winners 1960-61, 1961-2. Southern Junior Floodlit Cup winners 1962-3. London Minor Challenge Cup runners-up 1961-2. 7 England Youth caps (2 gls) 1963 and 9 Under-23 caps (1 gl) 1966-8. Made 1 app (1 gl) for the Football League 1967.
Later played for Vancouver Whitecaps (Canada) and then became player-coach of Nuneaton. Now a driving instructor in Leicester.

SANDERS, Moses   1899-1900
Wing-half/inside-forward   5ft 10in. 12st 7lb.
Born: 26 Sep 1873. Died: 29 Apr 1941.
Previous Clubs: Preston North End, Crewe Alexandra, Accrington Stanley. Joined ARSENAL: 16 May 1899 from Preston North End. First app: League v Leicester Fosse (h) 2 Sep 1899. First snr app: Southern District Combination v Bristol City (h) 30 Oct 1899. Final app: Jnr fdly v Tottenham Hotspur (Res) (a) 6 Jan 1900.
ARSENAL Record: League 4 (1 gl); Southern District Combination 3; Kent League 7 (1 gl); Friendlies 5 (1 gl).
Later played for Dartford.

SANDS, Percy Robert   1902-19
Centre-half   5ft 10½in. 13st.
Born: Norwood, London, 1881. Died: Dec 1965.
School: Purrett Road Boarding School.
Jnr football: Maze Hill Wanderers, St Paul's Training College (Cheltenham), Cheltenham Town. Joined ARSENAL: 27 Dec 1902 (amateur), 31 Aug 1906 (professional). First app: West Kent League v Cray Wanderers (h) Jan 1903. First snr app: League v Blackpool (h) 5 Sep 1903. Final snr app: League v Nottingham Forest (h) 24 Apr 1915. Final app: Jnr wartime fdly v Bristol City (Res) (a) 26 Apr 1919. Transferred to Southend United summer 1919.
ARSENAL Record: League 327 (10 gls); FA Cup 23 (2 gls); London League 1; London FA Challenge Cup 1; Other snr comp: 2 (2 gls); London League (Res) 1; Kent League 3; South Eastern League 19; Other jnr comp: 1; Friendlies 10. In addition made 19 apps during wartime.
Honours: Division Two runner-up (promotion) 1903-04. Southern Professional Charity Cup winners 1905-06. Chatham Charity Cup runners-up 1902-03. Captain of Arsenal. Made 1 app for the Football League 1905. Played in England Trial matches 1903-04, 1904-05.
Was a schoolmaster in Plumstead which he continued to combine with his professional football career. Served as a sergeant in the RAMC in France during the war.

SANSOM, Kenneth Graham   1980-88
Left-back   5ft 6in. 11st 7lb.
Born: Camberwell, London, 26 Sep 1958.
School: Beaufoy.
Jnr football: Leeds United (trials). Previous Club: Crystal Palace (1975). Joined ARSENAL: 13 Aug 1980 from Crystal Palace (exchange for C.Allen in deal worth £1,250,000). First app: League v West Bromwich Albion (a) 16 Aug 1980. Final snr app: League v Everton (a) 7 May 1988. Snr fdly v Shrewsbury Town (a) 13 Dec 1988. Final app: Football Combination v Watford (a) 17 Dec 1988. Transferred to Newcastle United (£300,000) 23 Dec 1988.
ARSENAL Record: League 314 (6 gls); FA Cup 26; Football League Cup 48; European comp: 6; Football Combination 16; Friendlies 58 (2 gls).
Honours: Football League Cup winners 1986-7,

runners-up 1987-8. Captain of Arsenal. Arsenal Player of the Year 1981. 77 full England caps (1 gl) 1980-88.
Played for South London and for Surrey schoolboys. England Schoolboys international. Won club honours with Crystal Palace. Won England Youth (and captain), Under-21, 'B' and full international honours with Crystal Palace. Arsenal's most 'capped' player (77 caps). Moved from Newcastle United to Queen's Park Rangers (May 1989) and to Coventry City (Mar 1991).

SATTERTHWAITE, Charles Oliver   1904-10
Forward   5ft 11in. 12st 7lb.
Born: Cockermouth, Cumberland, 1877. Died: 25 May 1948.
Jnr football: Black Diamond, Workington, New Brompton (1902). Previous Clubs: Bury, Burton Swifts (1897), Liverpool (1899-1902), West Ham United (1903-04). Joined ARSENAL: 27 Apr 1904 from West Ham United. First app: Snr fdly v Bristol City (h) 1 Sep 1904. League v Newcastle United (a) 3 Sep 1904. Final snr app: League v Bradford City (h) 6 Nov 1909. Snr fdly v Millwall Athletic (a) 5 Mar 1910. Final app: South Eastern League v Tottenham Hotspur (h) 16 Apr 1910.
ARSENAL Record: League 129 (45 gls); FA Cup 12 (3 gls); London FA Challenge Cup 4 (1 gl); Other snr comp: 6 (1 gl); South Eastern League 35 (32 gls); London League (Res) 10 (8 gls); Other jnr comp: 2; Friendlies 39 (30 gls).
Honours: Southern Professional Charity Cup winners 1905-06. Played in England Trial match 1904-05.
Won club honours with Liverpool. Scorer of Arsenal's first goal in First Division football. On retirement from football became a publican in Workington.

SATTERTHWAITE, Joseph Norman   1906-08
Inside-forward   5ft 8½in. 11st.
Born: Cockermouth, Cumberland, 1885.
Jnr football: Workington. Joined ARSENAL: 1 Dec 1906. Previous Club: Brighton (a) 1 Dec 1906. First snr app: Snr fdly v Cambridge Univesity (a) 3 Dec 1906. League v Manchester United (h) 21 Mar 1908. Final snr app: Scottish tour v Heart of Midlothian 21 Apr 1908. Final app: South Eastern League v Maidstone (a) 7 Nov 1908. Transferred to Grimsby Town 12 Nov 1908.
ARSENAL Record: League 5 (1 gl); South

Eastern League 44 (24 gls); London League (Res) 30 (35 gls); Friendlies 8 (9 gls).
Honours: South Eastern League champions 1906-07, 1907-08. London League (Res) champions 1906-07.
Younger brother of Charles Satterthwaite.

SCOTT, Lawrence   **1937-51**
Full-back   5ft 7½in. 11st 6lb.
Born: Sheffield, 23 Apr 1917.
School: Attercliffe C of E.
Jnr football: Edgar Allen's (Sheffield). Previous Club: Bradford City 1931 (amateur), 1934 (professional). Joined ARSENAL: 12 Feb 1937 from Bradford City (part exchange for E.Tuckett). First app: Jnr fdly v London University (a) 17 Feb 1937. First snr app: On tour v Copenhagen (Denmark) 4 May 1937. FA Cup v West Ham United (a) 5 Jan 1946. Final app: League v Chelsea (h) 29 Aug 1951. Transferred to Crystal Palace as player-manager 18 Oct 1951.
ARSENAL Record: League 115; FA Cup 11; Other snr comp: 1; Football Combination 88; London FA Challenge Cup 9; Southern League 7; Other jnr comp: 1; Friendlies 34. In addition played 2 London Combination matches 1939-40 prior to outbreak of war and made 188/1 apps during wartime.
Honours: Division One champions 1947-8. FA Cup winners 1950. London Combination champions 1937-8, 1938-9. Lowestoft Hospital Cup winners 1938-9. Football League South Cup winners 1942-3. Football League War Cup runners-up 1940-41. Captain of Arsenal. 17 full England caps 1946-48 and 4 'B' caps (and captain) 1950. Made a further 16 apps in wartime internationals. Made 5 apps for the Football League 1947-50.
Played for Sheffield Schoolboys. Was a PT Instructor in RAF during wartime. Had two cartilage operations in 1949 which affected his playing career. Was sacked as manager of Crystal Palace in Sep 1954 and later became a sales representative for a hardware firm before retiring to live in Sheffield.

SCOTT, W.   **1888-90**
Outside-left
Previous Club: Forfar Athletic. Joined ARSENAL: Sep 1888. First app: Snr fdly v London Scottish (h) 15 Sep 1888. First first-class app: FA Cup (Q) v Lyndhurst (h) 5 Oct 1889. Final first-class app: FA Cup (Q) v Crusaders (h) 16 Nov 1889. Final app: Jnr fdly v Old St Marks Reserves (h) 18 Oct 1890.
ARSENAL Record: FA Cup (Q) 3 (4 gls). In addition made 39 senior (14 gls) and 10 reserves (5 gls) apps for Royal Arsenal 1888-89 to 1890-1.

SEAMAN, David Andrew   **1990-**
Goalkeeper   6ft 3in. 13st.
Born: Rotherham, 19 Sep 1963.
School: Kimberworth Comprehensive(Rotherham).
Previous Clubs: Leeds United (apprentice), Peterborough United (1982), Birmingham City (Sep 1984), Queen's Park Rangers (Aug 1986). Joined ARSENAL: 16 May 1990 from Queen's Park Rangers for £1,300,000 (British record for a goalkeeper). First app: On tour v Varbergs BoIS (Sweden) 22 Jul 1990. League v Wimbledon (a) 25 Aug 1990.
ARSENAL Record: League 80; FA Cup 9; Football League Cup 7; European comp: 4; FA Charity Shield 1; Other snr comp: 5; Friendlies 14.
Honours: Division One champions 1990-91. FA Charity Shield medal 1991-2. England 'B' caps, 5 full caps. Made 1 app for Football League 1990-91.

Played for Rotherham Schoolboys. Won international honours with Birmingham City and Queen's Park Rangers.

SEDDON, William Charles   **1924-32**
Half-back   5ft 10½in. 11st 4lb.
Born: Clapton, London, 28 Jul 1901.
Jnr football: Villa Athletic (NW London), Gillingham (amateur), Aston Villa (trials). Joined ARSENAL: Dec 1924. First app: Jnr fdly v Littlehampton (a) 10 Dec 1924. First snr app: Snr fdly v Luton Town (h) 20 Apr 1925. League v Sunderland (a) 10 Apr 1926. Final snr app: League v Sheffield United (h) 26 Dec 1931. Final app: London Combination v West Ham United (h) 27 Feb 1932. Transferred to Grimsby Town (£2,500) 8 Mar 1932.
ARSENAL Record: League 69; FA Cup 6; Charity Shield 1; Other snr comp: 1; Football Combination 201 (2 gls); London FA Challenge Cup 5; London Midweek League 2; Friendlies 34 (7 gls).
Honours: Division One champions 1930-31. FA Cup winners 1930. FA Charity Shield winners 1930-31. London Combination champions 1926-7, 1927-8, 1928-9, 1929-30, 1930-31. Northampton Charity Shield winners 1929-30. London FA Challenge Cup winners 1930-31.
Was captain of the London Combination team which won the championship five consecutive years. After Grimsby Town, played for Luton Town (1933-4). Became trainer at Notts County (summer 1934) and trainer-coach to Romford (Feb 1937). Served in the Army in West Africa during the war. Was groundsman at Romford until retirement in Aug 1966.

SHANKS, Thomas   **1903-04**
Inside-left   5ft 9½in. 11st.
Born: Wexford, Ireland, 1880.
Jnr football: Wexford, Derby West End. Previous Clubs: Derby County (Apr 1898), Brentford (Oct 1901). Joined ARSENAL: 2 Jan 1903 from Brentford. First app: League v Burslem Port Vale (a) 10 Jan 1903. Final app: League v Preston North End (h) 9 Apr 1904. London League v Fulham (a) 30 Apr 1904. Transferred to Brentford May 1904.
ARSENAL Record: League 44 (28 gls); FA Cup

4 (1 gl); London League 10 (7 gls); Other snr comp: 2; Friendlies 4 (2 gls).
Honours: Division Two runners-up (promotion) 1903-04. Southern Professional Charity Cup runners-up 1903-04. 2 full Ireland caps 1903-04.
Won further international honours with Brentford. Later played for Leicester Fosse (Oct 1906), Leyton (cs 1909) and Clapton Orient (1911).

SHARP, James   **1905-08**
Full-back   5ft 8in. 13st 7lb.
Born: Alyth, Perthshire, Scotland, 11 Oct 1880.
Died: 18 Nov 1949.
Jnr football: East Craigie. Previous Clubs: Dundee (1899), Fulham (1904). Joined ARSENAL: 8 Jun 1905 from Fulham. First app: League v Liverpool (h) 2 Sep 1905. Final app: League v Sheffield Wednesday (h) 20 Apr 1908. Transferred to Glasgow Rangers (£400) 22 Apr 1908.
ARSENAL Record: League 103 (4 gls); FA Cup 13 (1 gl); Other snr comp: 6 (1 gl); Friendlies 7.
Honours: Southern Professional Charity Cup winners 1905-06. 3 full Scotland caps 1907-08.
Won Scotland international and Scottish League honours with Dundee. Rejoined Fulham (Jan 1909) and won a further international cap. Went to United States (Nov 1912) but returned within months and joined Chelsea. Became trainer at Fulham (1919), Walsall (1926) and Cliftonville (1929). On retirement from football he worked in the building industry in the London area.

SHARPE, William Henry   **1894-95**
Outside-left
Previous Club: Loughborough Town. Joined ARSENAL: 2 May 1894 from Loughborough Town. First app: League v Lincoln City (a) 1 Sep 1894. First app: League v Crewe Alexandra (a) 23 Mar 1895. Snr fdly v Grimsby Town (h) 29 Apr 1895. Transferred to Glossop North End Aug 1895.
ARSENAL Record: League 13 (4 gls); FA Cup 1; Other jnr comp: 2; Friendlies 22 (6 gls).
Honours:Wolverton Charity Cup runners-up 1894-5.

SHAW, Arthur   **1948-55**
Wing-half   6ft. 11st 6lb.
Born: Limehouse, London, 9 Apr 1924.
School: Thomas Road.
Jnr football: Hounslow Town, Queen's Park Rangers (amateur), Southall, Hayes. Previous Club: Brentford (May 1946). Joined ARSENAL: 12 Apr 1948 from Brentford. First app: Football Combination v Leicester City (h) 14 Apr 1948. First snr app: Snr fdly v Bexhill Town (a) 29 Sep 1948. League v Chelsea (h) 31 Aug 1949. Final snr app: League v Newcastle United (h) 21 Aug 1954. Snr fdly v Grasshoppers (Switzerland) (h) 21 Sep 1954. Final app: Football Combination v Bristol City (a) 30 Apr 1955. Transferred to Watford 13 Jun 1955.
ARSENAL Record: League 57; FA Cup 4; Football Combination 125 (10 gls); London FA Challenge Cup 9; Eastern Counties League 3; London Midweek League 4; Friendlies 25/5.
Honours: Division One champions 1952-3. Football Combination Cup runners-up 1950-51. London FA Challenge Cup winners 1954-5. Played for FA v Army 1949-50.
Played for East London schoolboys. After Watford played for Gravesend.

SHAW, Bernard   **1891-92**
Forward   5ft 10½in. 11st 6lb.
Born: Sheffield, c.1866.
Previous Clubs: Sheffield Wednesday, Wolverhampton Wanderers (1887), Sheffield United. Joined ARSENAL: Sep 1891 from Sheffield United. First app: Jnr fdly v Upton Park (a) 12 Sep 1891. First first-class app: FA Cup v Small

Heath (a) 16 Jan 1892. (only first-class app). Final app: Snr fdly v Glasgow Rangers (h) 30 Apr 1892. ARSENAL Record: FA Cup 1. In addition made 42 senior (23 gls) and 6 reserve (5 gls) apps for Royal Arsenal 1891-2.

SHAW, Herbert   **1898-1900**
Forward
Joined ARSENAL: 15 Dec 1898 from Haverton Hill, Durham. First app: Kent League v Ashford United (h) 24 Dec 1898. First snr app: United League v Millwall Athletic (h) 26 Dec 1898. League v Luton Town (h) 31 Dec 1898. Final snr app: Southern District Combination v Tottenham Hotspur (h) 24 Apr 1900. Final app: Jnr fdly v Woolwich District League (h) 30 Apr 1900.
ARSENAL Record: League 26 (9 gls); FA Cup 4; United League 6 (3 gls); Southern District Combination 4; Kent League 12 (5 gls); Other jnr comp: 2; Friendlies 14.

SHAW, James   **1926-30**
Inside-forward   5ft 7½in. 10st 8lb.
Born: Goldenhill, Staffordshire, 1904.
Jnr football: Goldenhill Juniors, Goldenhill Wanderers, Frickley Athletic (1925). Previous Club: Bolton Wanderers (was injured and not re-engaged). Joined ARSENAL: 20 Apr 1926 from Frickley Athletic. First app: London Combination v Chelsea (a) 29 Apr 1926. First snr app: Snr fdly v Clapton Orient (a) 11 Oct 1926. League v West Ham United (a) 7 Mar 1927. Final snr app: League v Everton (a) 5 May 1928. On tour v Danish FA (Denmark) 30 May 1928. Final app: London Combination v Brighton (a) 1 May 1930. Transferred to Brentford 16 May 1930.
ARSENAL Record: League 11 (4 gls); Football Combination 92 (57 gls); London FA Challenge Cup 1; London Midweek League 8 (5 gls); Friendlies 24 (17 gls).

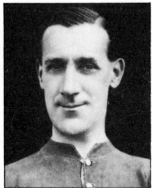

Honours: London Combination champions 1926-7, 1927-8, 1928-9.
A miner by trade.

SHAW, Joseph E.   **1907-23**
Full-back   5ft 9in. 11st 10lb.
Born: Bury, Lancashire, 1883. Died: Sep 1963.
Jnr football: Bury Athenaeum, Accrington Stanley (Lancs League). Joined ARSENAL: 3 May 1907 from Accrington Stanley. First app: South Eastern League v Tottenham Hotspur (a) 2 Sep 1907. First snr app: League v Preston North End (a) 28 Sep 1907. Final app: League v Manchester United (a) 11 Mar 1922. On tour v SFK Lyn (Norway) 23 May 1923. Retired and became manager of the reserve team.
ARSENAL Record: League 309; FA Cup 17;

Other snr comp: 14; Football Combination 21 (1 gl); London FA Challenge Cup 18; South Eastern League 36 (1 gl); London League (Res) 16; Friendlies 26 (1 gl). In addition made 68 apps during wartime.
Honours: South Eastern League champions 1907-08. London FA Challenge Cup runners-up 1914-15. Norwich Hospital Cup winners 1913-14. Metropolitan Hospital Cup winners 1920-21. Captain of Arsenal. Played for London v Birmingham.
Was a member of the Players' Union. Was Arsenal's acting manager for a short spell on the death of Herbert Chapman. Became general assistant at Arsenal 1947-8, retiring at the end of 1955-6 season.

SHAW, Walter James   **1893-95**
Forward   5ft 6½in. 10st 6lb.
Born: Small Heath, Birmingham, c.1870.
Jnr football: Coventry, Unity Gas, Small Heath St Georges. Joined ARSENAL: Jan 1893 from Birmingham. Signed League forms 25 Jun 1893. First app: Snr fdly v Oxford University (a) 25 Jan 1893. League v Newcastle United (h) 2 Sep 1893. First snr app: League v Rotherham Town (h) 9 Feb 1895. Final app: Wolverton Charity Cup Final v Wolverton (a) 27 Apr 1895. Released by Arsenal at end of 1894-5 season and returned to Birmingham.
ARSENAL Record: League 19 (11 gls); FA Cup 2; FA Cup (Q) 3 (1 gl); Other jnr comp: 3 (2 gls); Friendlies 41 (39 gls). In addition made 23 senior (16 gls) and 1 reserve app (1 gl) for Royal Arsenal 1892-3.
Honours: Wolverton Charity Cup runners-up 1894-5.

SHORTT, Matthew   **1910**
Inside-forward   5ft 9in. 10st 7lb.
Born: Dumfries, Scotland, 5 Feb 1889. Died: Kilmarnock, 7 Jun 1974.
Joined ARSENAL: 12 Nov 1910 from Dumfries, Scotland. First app: South Eastern League v Fulham (h) 19 Nov 1910. First snr app: League v Newcastle United (h) 26 Nov 1910. Final snr app: League v Preston North End (a) 17 Dec 1910. Final app: South Eastern League v Watford (h) 26 Dec 1910. Transferred to Kilmarnock 9 Jan 1911.
ARSENAL Record: League 4; South Eastern League 4 (1 gl).
Gave excellent service as a centre-half with Kilmarnock until retirement in 1924. Later played in America.

SHREWSBURY, Thomas P.   **1896-1900**
Half-back
Previous Club: Darwen. Joined ARSENAL: summer 1896 from Darwen. First app: Jnr fdly v 15th Co Royal Artillery (h) 3 Sep 1896. First snr app: League v Notts County (h) 26 Sep 1896. Final Snr app: League v Darwen (a) 12 Mar 1898. Southern District Combination v Queen's Park Rangers (a) 9 Apr 1900. Final app: Jnr fdly v Woolwich League (h) 30 Apr 1900.
ARSENAL Record: League 3; FA Cup 3; United League 6; Southern District Combination 1; Kent League 47; Other jnr comp: 2; Friendlies 60/1 (1 gl).
Honours: Kent League champions 1896-7. Sevenoaks Charity Cup winners 1897-8.

SIDEY, Norman William   **1929-39**
Centre-half   5ft 11½in. 11st.
Born: London.
Jnr football: Nunhead (Isthmian Lge). Joined ARSENAL: 8 Mar 1929 (amateur) from Nunhead, 26 Feb 1931 (professional) First app: London Midweek League v Brentford (a) 9 Oct 1929. First snr app: On tour v Stockholm XI (Sweden) 22 May 1931. League v Leeds United

(a) 27 Dec 1932. Final snr app: League v Grimsby Town (h) 19 Mar 1938. On tour v Staevnet (Denmark) 24 May 1939. Final app: Senior friendly (wartime) v Reading (a) 30 Sep 1939.
ARSENAL Record: League 40; FA Cup 3; FA Charity Shield 2; Football Combination 228 (22 gls); London FA Challenge Cup 20; London Midweek League 13 (7 gls); Southern League 3; Other jnr comp: 1; Friendlies 31 (1 gl). In addition made one app during wartime.
Honours: FA Charity Shield winners 1933-4, 1934-5. London Combination champions 1933-4, 1934-5, 1936-7, 1937-8. London FA Challenge Cup winners 1933-4, 1935-6, runners-up 1936-7. Lowestoft Hospital Cup winners 1938-9. Played for London Combination v Central League 1936, 1937.
Served as a Pilot Officer in the RAF Regiment in World War Two. After soccer he ran a boarding house in Jersey.

SIMPSON, Peter Frederick   **1960-78**
Defender   5ft 11in. 11st 10lb.
Born: Gorleston, Norfolk, 13 Jan 1945.
School: Alderman Leach Secondary, Gorleston. Jnr football: Gorleston Town; Crystal Palace (trial). Joined ARSENAL: May 1960 (ground staff), 4 Oct 1961 (apprentice), 13 Apr 1962 (professional). First app: South East Counties League v West Ham United (h) 27 Aug 1960. First snr app: League v Chelsea (h) 14 Mar 1964. Final app: League (sub) v Ipswich Town (h) 2 Jan 1978. Final app: Football Combination v Swindon Town (h) 27 Mar 1978. Released by Arsenal, Apr 1978.

ARSENAL Record: League 353/17 (10 gls); FA Cup 53 (1 gl); Football League Cup 32/1 (3 gls); European comp: 20/1 (1 gl); Other snr comp: 1; Football Combination 127 (11 gls); London FA Challenge Cup 9 (1 gl); Metropolitan League 91 (10 gls); South East Counties League 37 (10 gls); FA Youth Cup 15 (2 gls); Other jnr comp: 11 (2 gls); Friendlies 116/6 (3 gls).
Honours: Division One champions 1970-71. FA Cup winners 1971, runners-up 1972. Football League Cup runners-up 1967-8, 1968-9. European Fairs Cup winners 1969-70. Football Combination winners 1969-70. Metropolitan League champions 1962-3. Metropolitan League Professional Cup winners 1961-2, runners-up 1962-3. Metropolitan League Challenge Cup winners 1965-6. South East

Counties League Cup winners 1960-61, 1961-2.
Southern Junior Floodlit Cup winners 1962-3.
London Minor Challenge Cup runners-up 1960-61.
Arsenal Player of the Year 1969.
Played for Yarmouth and for Norfolk Schoolboys.
Was a member of England's initial squad for the
World Cup 1966 but failed to make the final 22.
Testimonial match, Mar 1976. On leaving Arsenal
played for New England Teamen in USA.
Returned and played for Hendon (Mar 1980). On
retiring from football he worked for a soft drinks
firm and now runs a car servicing business in
Hertfordshire.

SINCLAIR, Finlay   **1896-97**
Full-back   5ft 6½in. 11st.
Born: Glasgow, 18 Jun 1871.
Jnr football: Clutha Swifts, Elderslie, Linthouse.
Previous Club: Glasgow Rangers. Joined
ARSENAL: Jun 1896 from Glasgow Rangers.
First app: Snr fdly v Rossendale (h) 1 Sep 1896.
League v Manchester City (a) 5 Sep 1896. Final
app: League v Manchester City (h) 28 Apr 1897.
Snr fdly v Southampton St Mary's (a) 29 Apr
1897. Transferred to Bristol City summer 1897.
ARSENAL Record: League 26; FA Cup 2; United
League 11; Friendlies 16.

SKIRTON, Alan Frederick Graham   **1959-66**
Winger   5ft 11in. 12st 7lb.
Born: Bath, 23 Jan 1939.
School: South Twerton Junior, Bath; Bath
Technical College.
Jnr football: West Twerton YC, Bristol City
(amateur), Bath City. Joined ARSENAL: 20 Jan
1959 from Bath City for £5,000. First app:
Football Combination v Leyton Orient (h) 24 Jan
1959. First snr app: League v Burnley (a) 20 Aug
1960. Final app: League v West Ham United (h)
23 Aug 1966. Transferred 12 to Blackpool
(£65,000) Sep 1966.
ARSENAL Record: League 144/1 (53 gls); FA
Cup 8; European comp: 1 (1 gl); Football
Combination 47 (18 gls); London FA Challenge
Cup 13 (5 gls); Metropolitan League 8 (6 gls);
Friendlies 57/2 (48 gls).
Honours: London FA Challenge Cup winners
1961-2. Metropolitan League Challenge Cup
winners 1965-6.
Played for Somerset Youth. After a month at
Arsenal he contracted pneumonia and pleurisy
and was convalescent for 12 months, missing the
1959-60 season. After Blackpool, played for
Bristol City (Nov 1968), Torquay United (Jul
1971), Durban City (South Africa) and
Weymouth. On finishing playing (1975) he became
assistant commercial manager at Weymouth and
commercial manager at Bath City. Commercial
manager at Yeovil Town (1981).

SLADE, Donald   **1913-14**
Centre-forward   5ft 9in. 11st 2lb.
Born: Southampton, 26 Nov 1888. Died: Westend,
Southampton, 24 Mar 1980.
School: Boundary Lane, Southampton.
Jnr football: Southampton Ramblers. Previous
Clubs: Southampton (1910), Lincoln City (1912).
Joined ARSENAL: 5 Dec 1913 from Lincoln City
for £1,000. First app: London League (Res) v West
Ham United (h) 11 Dec 1913. First snr app: League
v Clapton Orient (a) 13 Dec 1913. Final snr app:
League v Glossop (a) 25 Apr 1914. Final app:
London League (Res) v Clapton Orient (h) 30
Apr 1914. Transferred to Fulham 2 May 1914.
ARSENAL Record: League 12 (4 gls); South
Eastern League 8 (5 gls); London League (Res)
8 (2 gls); Friendlies 1 (1 gl).
Later played for Ayr United and Dundee United
(1920). After football became a publican in
Scotland and Reading.

SLOAN, Joshua Walter 'Paddy'   **1946-48**
Inside-forward/wing-half   5ft 9in. 11st 6lb.
Born: Lurgan, N.Ireland, 30 Apr 1920.
Previous Clubs: Glenavon, Manchester United
(1937); Tranmere Rovers (1939). Joined
ARSENAL: 23 May 1946 from Tranmere Rovers.
First app: League v Wolverhampton Wanderers
(a) 31 Aug 1946. Final snr app: League v
Portsmouth (h) 4 Oct 1947. Snr fdly v Racing
Club de Paris (a) 11 Nov 1947. Final app: Football
Combination Cup v Crystal Palace (h) 21 Feb
1948. Transferred to Sheffield United 23 Feb 1948.
ARSENAL Record: League 33 (1 gl); FA Cup
3; Football Combination 18 (9 gls); London FA
Challenge Cup 2; Friendlies 9 (4 gls).
Honours: 2 full Republic of Ireland caps (1 gl)
1946 and 1 full Northern Ireland cap 1947.
Served in the Army in Germany during the war.
Won wartime international honours with
Tranmere Rovers. Transferred to Milan (Italy),
summer 1948 and also played for Turin, Udinese,
and Brescia before returning to England to play
for Norwich City (Dec 1951) and then Peter-
borough United. Became coach to Rabat FC
(Malta) in 1954. Player-manager of Lockheed
Leamington (Jan 1956) and coach at Bath City
(May 1956). Went to Australia in 1963 to coach
Juventus FC (Melbourne) and later became
chairman of National Soccer Coaches Association.

SMITH, Alan   **1946**
Outside-left
Born: Newcastle, 15 Oct 1921.
Joined ARSENAL: 4 May 1946 (amateur), 11
May 1946 (professional). First app: Football
League South (wartime) v West Ham United (h)
4 May 1946. First snr app: League v Sunderland
(h) 7 Sep 1946. Final snr app: League v Sheffield
United (h) 2 Nov 1946. Final app: Football
Combination v Crystal Palace (h) 23 Nov 1946.
Transferred to Brentford 17 Dec 1946.
ARSENAL Record: League 3; Football
Combination 14 (3 gls); London FA Challenge
Cup 2, Friendlies 2 (1 gl). In addition made 2
apps (1 gl) during wartime.
Later played for Leyton Orient (Jul 1949) and
Ashford United.

SMITH, Alan Martin   **1987-**
Striker   6ft 3in. 12st 3lb.

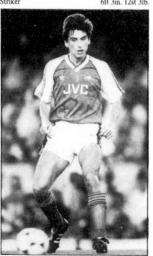

Born: Hollywood, Birmingham, 21 Nov 1962.
School: Kings Norton Grammar.
Jnr football: West Hills Athletic: Alvechurch FC.
Previous Club: Leicester City (1982). Joined
ARSENAL: 26 Mar 1987 from Leicester City for
£750,000. First app: Senior friendly v Gloucester
City (a) 21 Jul 1987. League v Liverpool (h) 15
Aug 1987.
ARSENAL Record: League 177/12 (78 gls); FA
Cup 16 (4 gls); Football League Cup 22/1 (12
gls); European comp: 4 (4 gls); FA Charity Shield
2; Other snr comp: 11 (3 gls); Football
Combination 4 (2 gls); Friendlies 36/2 (25 gls).
In addition played for Arsenal/Luton Town XI
on tour v Select XI (Cyprus) on 14 May 1987,
which was his first app in 'Arsenal colours'.
Honours: Division One champions 1988-9, 1990-
91. Football League Cup runners-up 1987-8. FA
Charity Shield runners-up 1989-90, medal 1991-
2. Mercantile Credit Centenary Trophy winners
1988-9. 4 England 'B' caps (4 gls); 10 full caps
(2 gls). Arsenal Player of the Year 1989.
Played for Birmingham and for West Midlands
schoolboys. Following his transfer to Arsenal was
loaned back to Leicester City for the remainder
of the season. Was Division One leading
goalscorer 1988-9 and 1990-91.

SMITH, James   **1920-21**
Outside-right   5ft 7½in. 10st 10lb.
Born: Preston, c.1886.
Jnr football: Stalybridge Rovers (1906),
Accrington Stanley, Chorley (Sep 1908). Previous
Clubs: Bury (1903-06), Fulham (Mar 1909). Joined
ARSENAL: 10 Jun 1920 from Fulham. First app:
League v Aston Villa (a) 28 Aug 1920. Final app:
League v Huddersfield Town (h) 27 Nov 1920.
Snr fdly v Wigan (a) 4 May 1921. Given free
transfer 5 Aug 1921.
ARSENAL Record: League 10 (1 gl); Football
Combination 15 (2 gls); Friendlies 3.

SMITH, Lionel   **1939-54**
Left-back   6ft 1in. 12st.
Born: Mexborough, Yorkshire, 23 Aug 1920.
Died: Stoke Newington, London, 8 Nov 1980.
School: Dolcliffe Road, Mexborough.
Jnr football: Mexborough Albion Juniors,

Yorkshire Tar Distillers, Denaby United. Joined
ARSENAL: Apr 1939 (amateur) from Denaby
United, 9 Aug 1939 (professional). First app:

Southern League v Aldershot (a) 26 Apr 1939. First snr app: League v Grimsby Town (h) 1 May 1948. Final app: League v Manchester United (h) 27 Mar 1954. On tour v Grasshoppers (Switzerland) 5 May 1954. Transferred to Watford 8 Jun 1954. ARSENAL Record: League 162; FA Cup 18; FA Charity Shield 1; Football Combination 64; London FA Challenge Cup 5; Southern League 2; Friendlies 37/1. In addition made 17 apps during wartime.
Honours: Division One champions 1952-3. FA Cup runners-up 1952. FA Charity Shield winners 1948-9. Football Combination Cup runners-up 1946-7. 6 full England caps 1950-53. Made 3 apps for the Football League 1951-3.
Served in the Army during the war. After Watford, became player-manager of Gravesend & Northfleet (Jun 1955). Resigned Apr 1960 and became a publican in Stoke Newington.

SMITHSON, Rodney George   **1959-64**
Wing-half   5ft 11in. 11st 8lb.
Born: Leicester, 9 Oct 1943.
School: Linwood Secondary Modern.
Joined ARSENAL: Jun 1959 (groundstaff), Jul 1960 (apprentice), 16 Oct 1960 (professional). First app: South East Counties League v Bexleyheath (a) 27 Aug 1959. First snr app: League v Fulham (a) 15 Sep 1962. First snr fdly v Bolton Wanderers (a) 29 Sep 1962. Snr fdly v Watford (a) 14 Apr 1964. Final app: Metropolitan League v Tonbridge (h) 28 Apr 1964. Transferred to Oxford United (free transfer) 1 Jul 1964.
ARSENAL Record: League 2; Football Combination 63 (2 gls); London FA Challenge Cup 6; Metropolitan League 81 (14 gls); South East Counties League 41 (3 gls); FA Youth Cup 11 (1 gl); Other jnr comp: 4 (1 gl); Friendlies 34/1 (4 gls). In addition played 2 South East Counties League matches 1959-60, later removed from records.
Honours: Played for Leicester schoolboys. England Schoolboys international. Football Combination champions 1962-3. London FA Challenge Cup winner 1962-3. Metropolitan League champions 1960-61, 1962-3. Metropolitan League Challenge Cup winners 1960-61. Metropolitan League Professional Cup winners 1960-61, 1961-2. South East Counties League Cup winners 1959-60, 1961-2. 3 England Youth caps 1962.
Later became player-manager of Whitney Town.

SNEDDEN, John Duncan   **1958-65**
Half-back   6ft. 12st 3lb.
Born: Bonnybridge, Stirlingshire, Scotland, 3 Feb 1942.
Jnr football: Bonnyvale Star Juniors. Joined ARSENAL: 3 Oct 1958 (amateur) from Bonnyvale Star Juniors, 3 Feb 1959 (professional). First app: South East Counties League v Portsmouth (a) 4 Oct 1958. First snr app: Snr fdly v Grasshoppers (Switzerland) (h) 13 Oct 1959. League v Tottenham Hotspur (a) 16 Jan 1960. Final snr app: League v Manchester United (h) 28 Nov 1964. Final app: Football Combination v Northampton Town (h) 27 Feb 1965. Transferred to Charlton Athletic (£15,000) 6 Mar 1965.
ARSENAL Record: League 83; FA Cup 10; European comp: 1; Football Combination 73; London FA Challenge Cup 4; Metropolitan League 22; South East Counties League 14; FA Youth Cup 10 (1 gl); Other jnr comp: 1; Friendlies 52/1 (1 gl).
Honours: Scotland Schoolboy International. London FA Challenge Cup winner 1961-2-3. South East Counties League Cup winners 1959-60.
Troubled with injuries at Arsenal — a broken ankle (Dec 1960) and a knee operation (Apr 1963). After Charlton Athletic, played for Orient (Jul

1966) and Halifax Town (Nov 1967). On retiring from football went to work in West Germany.

SPARROW, Brian Edward   **1977-84**
Forward   5ft 7in. 10st 2lb.
Born: East London, 24 Jun 1962.
Joined ARSENAL: May 1977 (schoolboy), 27 Jun 1978 (apprentice), 31 Jan 1980 (professional). First app: South East Counties League v Gillingham (h) 20 Aug 1977. First snr app: On tour v ASL Club (Trinidad) 18 May 1982. League v Coventry City (a) 31 Mar 1984. Final snr app: League v Stoke City (h) 7 Apr 1984. Final app: Football Combination v Swindon Town (a) 16 May 1984. Transferred to Crystal Palace (free transfer) summer 1984.
ARSENAL Record: League 2; Football Combination 147/2 (2 gls); South East Counties League 63/4 (27 gls); FA Youth Cup 5; Other jnr comp: 6 (4 gls); Friendlies 53/2 (4 gls). In addition played 3 Football Combination matches 1981-2, later removed from records.
Honours: Football Combination champions 1983-4. South East Counties League Cup winners 1979-80. President's Cup winners 1980-81.
Brother of John Sparrow (Chelsea). As an Arsenal player had spells on loan to Wimbledon 1982-3 (17 apps, 1 gl and won club honours), Millwall 1983-4 (5 apps, 2 goals) and Gillingham 1983-84 (5 apps, 1 gl). After Crystal Palace played for Enfield (1987). Was manager of Crawley Town and is now in charge of the Reserves at Wimbledon.

SPICER, Thomas Ashley   **1900-01**
Goalkeeper   5ft 11¾in. 12st 10lb.
Jnr football: Sheppey United, Brighton United.
Joined ARSENAL: 2 Apr 1900 from Brighton United. First app: Senior friendly v Burnley (h) 13 Apr 1900. League v Grimsby Town (a) 14 Apr 1900. Final snr app: League v Walsall 6h) 8 Sep 1900. Final app: West Kent League v Swanscombe (h) 29 Apr 1901.
ARSENAL Record: League 4; London League (Res) 18; Kent League 9; Friendlies 12.
Honours: West Kent League champions 1900-01.
Later played for Leyton and Brentford.

SPITTLE, William Arthur   **1912-19**
Inside-forward   5ft 6½in. 10st 9lb.
Born: Southfields, London, 1893.
Jnr football: Southfields Juniors. Joined ARSENAL: 30 August 1912 (amateur), 7 Sep 1912 (professional). First app: South Eastern League v Watford (h) 9 Sep 1912. First snr app: League v Manchester City (h) 2 Nov 1912. Final snr app: League v Lincoln City (a) 21 Feb 1914. Norwich Hospital Cup v Norwich City (a) 30 Apr 1914. Final app: London Combination v Millwall (a) 30 Aug 1919. Transferred to Leicester City 17 Oct 1919.
ARSENAL Record: League 7; Other snr comp: 1; Football Combination 1; London FA Challenge Cup 1 (1 gl); South Eastern League 70 (32 gls); London League (Res) 18 (2 gls); Other jnr comp: 1; Friendlies 7 (6 gls). In addition made 27 apps (7 gls) during wartime.
Honours: Norwich Hospital Cup winners 1913-14.
Served as a Lance-Corporal in the 17th Middlesex Regiment during the war and was wounded in France.

STANDEN, James Alfred   **1952-60**
Goalkeeper   6ft. 11st 3lb.
Born: Edmonton, London, 30 May 1935.
Jnr football: Chalfont Youth Club, Rickmansworth Town. Joined ARSENAL: 15 Oct 1952 (amateur), 20 Apr 1953 (professional). First app: London Midweek League v Portsmouth (h) 15 Oct 1952. First snr app: Southern Floodlight Challenge Cup v Brentford (a) 30 Oct 1957; League v Burnley (a) 7 Dec 1957. Final app: League v

Blackburn Rovers (a) 22 Oct 1960. Transferred to Luton Town (£8,000) 28 Oct 1960.
ARSENAL Record: League 35; FA Cup 3; Other snr comp: 3; Football Combination 67; London FA Challenge Cup 11; Eastern Counties League 16; Metropolitan League 3; London Midweek League 14; Friendlies 23/1.
Honours: Played for Hertfordshire Youth. London FA Challenge Cup winners 1957-8.
Was a plumber before taking up professional football. Served National Service in RAOC (1953-5). Whilst at Arsenal had a spell on loan to Kettering Town (Mar 1956). Played county cricket for Worcestershire and Hertfordshire. After Luton Town, played for West Ham United (Nov 1962 — won domestic and European club honours), Millwall (Oct 1968) and Portsmouth (Jul 1970). Went to America as coach to Detroit Cougars.

STAPLETON, Francis Anthony   **1972-81**
Striker   5ft 11in. 12st 8lb.
Born: Dublin, 10 Jul 1956.
Jnr football: St Martins (Dublin), Bolton Athletic (Dublin), Manchester United (trial), Wolverhampton Wanderers (trial). Joined ARSENAL: 26 Jun 1972 (apprentice), 24 Sep 1973 (professional). First app: Jnr fdly v Coventry City (h) 24 Jul 1972. First snr app: League v Stoke City (h) 29 Mar 1975. Final app: League v Aston Villa (h) 2 May 1981. On tour v Eastern AA (Hong Kong) 9 May 1981. Transferred to Manchester United (£900,000, tribunal) 21 Aug 1981.

ARSENAL Record: League 223/2 (75 gls); FA Cup 32 (15 gls); Football Combination 48 (14 gls); European comp: 15 (4 gls); FA Charity Shield 1; Football Combination 71/1 (31 gls); London FA Challenge Cup 3; South East Counties League 51 (48 gls); FA Youth Cup 12 (9 gls); Other jnr comp: 2 (1 gl); Friendlies 89/6 (48 gls).
Honours: Republic of Ireland Schoolboy international. FA Cup winners 1979, runners-up 1978, 1980. European Cup-winners' Cup runners-up 1979-80. FA Charity Shield winners 1979. Arsenal Player of the Year 1977, 1980. 5 Republic of Ireland Youth caps 1973 and 24 full caps (5 gls) 1977-81.
Won club honours with Manchester United. Later played for Ajax, Holland (Jul 1987), Derby

County (loan, Mar 1988) and with Le Havre, France. Won further international honours. Later played for Blackburn Rovers (1989-91) and currently is player-manager of Bradford City.

STEAD, Kevin 1977-79
Defender 5ft 10in. 11st.
Born: West Ham, London, 2 Oct 1958.
School: Plaistow Grammar.
Previous Club: Tottenham Hotspur Apr 1976 (professional). Joined ARSENAL: 1 Jul 1977 on free transfer from Tottenham Hotspur. First app: Jnr fdly v Hitchen Town (a) 6 Aug 1977. First snr app: Snr fdly (sub) v Northampton Town (a) 20 Sep 1977. League (sub) v Wolverhampton Wanderers (a) 14 Oct 1978. Final snr app: League v Southampton (h) 21 Oct 1978. Final app: Football Combination v West Ham United (h) 8 Sep 1979.
ARSENAL Record: League 1/1; Football Combination 79/1 (11 gls); Friendlies 5/2.
Played for Newham, for Essex and for London schoolboys. Toured Australia with England Schoolboys (1974). Played for Oxford City after Arsenal.

STEVEN, Andrew 1897
Inside-right
Born: Scotland.
Jnr football: Bathgate FC. Joined ARSENAL: 5 May 1897 from Bathgate. First app: League v Grimsby Town (h) 1 Sep 1897. Final snr app: FA Cup v St Albans (h) 30 Oct 1897. Final app: Jnr fdly v Wandsworth (h) 11 Dec 1897. Transferred to Dartford Jan 1898.
ARSENAL Record: League 5 (1 gl); FA Cup 1 (1 gl); Friendlies 8 (3 gls).

STEVENS, Robert C. 1909-10
Forward 5ft 8½in. 10st 10lb.
Born: Maryhill, Glasgow, c.1886.
Previous Club: Glasgow Rangers. Joined ARSENAL: 12 Nov 1909 from Glasgow Rangers. First app: League v Sheffield Wednesday (a) 13 Nov 1909. Final app: League v Blackburn Rovers (h) 12 Feb 1910. Snr fdly v Ilford (a) 30 Apr 1910.
ARSENAL Record: League 7 (1 gl); South Eastern League 12 (2 gls); Other jnr comp: 1; Friendlies 5.

STEVENSON, Robert 1894-95
Half-back.
Born: Barrhead, nr Glasgow, c.1869.
Previous Club: Third Lanark. Joined ARSENAL: 17 May 1894 from Third Lanark. First app: League v Lincoln City (a) 1 Sep 1894. Final app: League v Newton Heath (a) 13 Oct 1894. Snr fdly v Luton Town (a) 11 Feb 1895. Released by Arsenal 2 Mar 1895 and joined Thames Ironworks (and captain).
ARSENAL Record: League 7; Friendlies 19 (4 gls). Captain of Woolwich Arsenal.

STEWART, William 1889-93
Centre-half 5ft 7½in. 11st.
Born: Dundee, c.1867.
Jnr football: Ettrick (Edinburgh), Taybank (Dundee), Our Boys (Dundee), Dundee Wanderers, Kidderminster Harriers. Joined ARSENAL: Oct 1889. First app: Jnr fdly v Northumberland Fusiliers (h) 26 Oct 1889. First first-class app: FA Cup (Q) v Swifts (h) 7 Dec 1889. Final first-class app: FA Cup v Derby County (h) 17 Jan 1891. Final app: Jnr fdly v St Lukes (a) 29 Apr 1893.
ARSENAL Record: FA Cup 1; FA Cup (Q) 1. In addition made 58 senior (2 gls) and 33 reserve (5 gls) apps for Royal Arsenal 1889-90 to 1892-93.
Honours: London Senior Cup winners 1890-91.
Worked at the Royal Ordnance factory as a machinist. Later player for Royal Ordnance FC.

STOCKILL, Reginald Robert 1931-34
Inside-forward 5ft 8in. 11st 7lb.
Born: York, 24 Nov 1913.
Jnr football: Scarborough. Previous Club: York City (1929). Joined ARSENAL: 7 May 1931 from Scarborough. First app: London Combination v Luton Town (a) 12 Sep 1931. First snr app: League v Huddersfield Town (a) 27 Apr 1932. Final snr app: League v Blackburn Rovers (h) 25 Feb 1933. Final app: London Combination v Coventry City (h) 8 Sep 1934. Transferred to Derby County (£2,000) 11 Sep 1934.
ARSENAL Record: League 7 (4 gls); Other snr comp: 1; Football Combination 89 (56 gls); FA Challenge Cup 7 (6 gls); London Midweek League 17 (13 gls); Friendlies 11 (16 gls).
Honours: London Combination champions 1933-4. London FA Challenge Cup winners 1933-4. Northampton Charity Shield winners 1931-2.
England Schoolboy international. Later played for Luton Town (Aug 1939).

STONLEY, Stephen 1913-14
Centre-forward 5ft 8½in. 11st 10lb.
Born: Sunderland, c.1891.
Jnr football: Newcastle City (North Eastern League). Joined ARSENAL: 7 Feb 1913 from Newcastle City. First app: League v Oldham Athletic (h) 8 Feb 1913. Final snr app: League v Glossop (a) 25 Apr 1914. Final app: League (Res) v Clapton Orient (h) 30 Apr 1914. Transferred to Brentford 30 Jun 1914.
ARSENAL Record: League 38 (14 gls); FA Cup 1; London FA Challenge Cup 2; Other snr comp: 1 (1 gl); South Eastern League 7 (11 gls); London League (Res) 3 (2 gls); Friendlies 2 (6 gls).

STORER, Harry 1894-95
Goalkeeper 5ft 8½in. 12st.
Born: Ripley, Derbyshire, 24 Jul 1870. Died: Holloway, Derbyshire, 25 Apr 1908.

Jnr football: Ripley Town, Derby Midland (1888). Previous Clubs: Derby County (1891), Gainsborough Trinity (1892-3), Loughborough Town (1893-4). Joined ARSENAL: 2 May 1894 from Loughborough Town. First app: League v Lincoln City (a) 1 Sep 1894. Final app: League v Liverpool (h) 16 Nov 1895. Snr fdly v Barnsley St Peters (h) 23 Nov 1895. Transferred to Liverpool (£75) 23 Dec 1895.
ARSENAL Record: League 40; FA Cup 1; Kent League 1; Other jnr comp: 1; Friendlies 35.
Honours: 1 app for the Football League 1895.
Was the first Arsenal player to gain representative honours. Played county cricket for Derbyshire. Was suspended by Arsenal for four weeks in Nov 1895 for breach of discipline and was eventually transferred to Liverpool with whom he won club honours.

STOREY, Peter Edwin 1961-77
Full-back/midfield 5ft 9½in. 12st 3lb.
Born: Farnham, Surrey, 7 Sep 1945.
Joined ARSENAL: 31 May 1961 (apprentice), 28 Sep 1962 (professional). Counties League v Tottenham Hotspur (h) 19 Aug 1961. First snr app: On tour v Leicester (Italy) 9 May 1965. League v Leicester City (a) 30 Oct 1965. Final snr app: FA Cup (sub) v Coventry City (h) 29 Jan 1977. Final app: Football Combination v Chelsea (a) 3 Feb 1977. Transferred to Fulham (£11,000) 2 Mar 1977.
ARSENAL Record: League 387/4 (9 gls); FA Cup 49/2 (4 gls); Football League Cup 36/1 (2 gls); European comp: 22 (2 gls); Football Combination 57 (1 gl); London FA Challenge Cup 4; Metropolitan League 96 (2 gls); South East Counties League 30 (1 gl); FA Youth Cup 8; Other jnr comp: 9; Friendlies 115/5 (3 gls).

Honours: Played for Aldershot schoolboys. England Schoolboy international 1961. Division One champions 1970-71. FA Cup winners 1971, runners-up 1972. Football League Cup runners-up 1967-8, 1968-9. European Fairs Cup winners 1969-70. Metropolitan League champions 1962-3. South East Counties League winners 1963-4. Southern Junior Floodlit Cup winners 1962-3. London Minor Challenge Cup runners-up 1961-2. 19 full England caps 1971-73. Made 2 apps for the Football League 1971-4.
Retired from football, Nov 1977. Became a publican in Islington and now runs a market stall in London's West End.

STORRS, J.A. 1893-95
Left-back
Joined ARSENAL: 9 Aug 1893 from the Lincolnshire Regiment. First app: Snr fdly v Middlesbrough (h) 23 Sep 1893. League v Grimsby Town (h) 25 Sep 1893. Final snr app: League v Lincoln City (a) 3 Feb 1894. Snr fdly v Royal Ordnance (a) 25 Apr 1895. Final app: Wolverton Charity Cup Final v Wolverton (a) 27 Apr 1895.
ARSENAL Record: League 12; FA Cup (Q) 4; Other jnr comp: 3; Friendlies 53 (2 gls).
A soldier with the Lincolnshire Regiment. Appointed trainer to Dewsbury 1896-7.

STRONG, Geoffrey Hugh 1957-64
Inside-forward 5ft 11in. 11st 4lb.
Born: Kirkheaton, Northumberland, 19 Sep 1937.
Jnr football: Throckley Juniors, Stanley United 1957). Joined ARSENAL: Nov 1957 (amateur) from Stanley United for £100, 14 Apr 1958 (professional). First app: Football Combination v Southampton (h) 11 Mar 1958. First snr app: League v Newcastle United (h) 17 Sep 1960. Final snr app: League v Tottenham Hotspur (a) 10 Oct 1964. Snr fdly v Corinthian Casuals (a) 14 Oct 1964. Final app: Football Combination v Northampton Town (a) 31 Oct 1964. Transferred to Liverpool (£40,000) 7 Nov 1964.
ARSENAL Record: League 125 (69 gls); FA Cup 8 (5 gls); European comp: 4 (3 gls); Football Combination 42 (33 gls); London FA Challenge Cup 1 (2 gls); Metropolitan League 46 (55 gls); Friendlies 39/2 (28 gls).
Honours: Metropolitan League champions 1958-9.
Played for Northumberland schoolboys. A machine-tool fitter by trade. Served National Service in the RAOC (1959-61) and played for the Army in representative matches. After Liverpool he played for Coventry City (Aug 1970). Now runs a hotel interior furnishing company on Merseyside.

STUART, James 1897
Centre-forward
Previous Club: Blackburn Rovers. Joined ARSENAL: Sep 1897 from Blackburn Rovers. First app: Jnr fdly v Luton Town (Res) (h) 2 Oct 1897. First snr app: League v Luton Town (h) 9 Oct 1897. Final snr app: League v Newcastle United (h) 16 Oct 1897. Final app: Jnr fdly v Grays United (a) 13 Nov 1897. Released by Arsenal and joined New Brompton at end of 1897.
ARSENAL Record: League 2 (1 gl); United League 1; Friendlies 4 (4 gls).

SULLIVAN, Cornelius Henry 1954-58
Goalkeeper 6ft 1in. 12st 7lb.
Born: Bristol, 22 Aug 1928.
Jnr football: Horfield Old Boys, Bristol. Previous Club: Bristol City (May 1949). Joined ARSENAL: 3 Feb 1954 from Bristol City. First app: Football Combination v Bournemouth (h) 6 Feb 1954. First snr app: Snr fdly v Hull City (a) 23 Mar 1954. League v Newcastle United (a) 17 Apr 1954. Final snr app: League v Birmingham (h) 19 Oct 1957. Southern Floodlight Challenge Cup v Aldershot (a) 15 Oct 1958. Final app: Football Combination v Chelsea (a) 18 Oct 1958. Retired at end of 1958-9 season with a back injury sustained during training.
ARSENAL Record: League 28; FA Cup 4; Other snr comp: 4; Football Combination 100; London FA Challenge Cup 10; London Midweek League 2; Friendlies 20/1.
Honours: London FA Challenge Cup winners 1954-5.
Played for Gloucestershire Youth. On leaving Arsenal, returned to Bristol and became a permit player for Robertson Athletic (1960).

SUNDERLAND, Alan 1977-84
Striker 5ft 9in. 11st 6lb.
Born: Conisborough, Yorkshire, 1 Jul 1953.
School: Mexborough.
Jnr football: Wath Wanderers. Previous Club: Wolverhampton Wanderers Sep 1969 (apprentice). Joined ARSENAL: 2 Nov 1977 from Wolverhampton Wanderers for £220,000. First app: League v Manchester United (a) 5 Nov 1977. Final snr app: Football League Cup v Walsall (h) 29 Nov 1983. Final app: Football Combination v Queen's Park Rangers (h) 11 Feb 1984. Transferred to Ipswich Town (free transfer) summer 1984.
ARSENAL Record: League 204/2 (55 gls); FA Cup 34 (16 gls); Football League Cup 26 (13 gls); European comp: 13/1 (7 gls); FA Charity Shield 1 (1 gl); Football Combination 6 (3 gls); Friendlies 42/1 (14 gls).
Honours: FA Cup winners 1979, runners-up 1978, 1980. European Cup-winners' Cup runners-up 1979-80. FA Charity Shield runners-up 1979-80. 7 England 'B' caps (1 gl) 1978-81 and 1 full cap 1980.

Played for Yorkshire schoolboys. Won club, Under-21 and Under-23 honours with Wolves. Went on loan to Ipswich Town, Feb-May 1984 (15 apps, 3 gls). Played for Derry City (Ireland) 1986.

SWALLOW, Raymond 1952-58
Inside-forward 5ft 8in. 10st 10lb.
Born: Southwark, London, 15 Jun 1935.
Jnr football: Tooting and Mitcham. Joined ARSENAL: Mar 1952 (amateur), 8 Sep 1952 (groundstaff), 15 Dec 1952 (professional). First app: London Midweek League v West Ham United (a) 3 Mar 1952. First snr app: League v Cardiff City (h) 8 Apr 1955. First snr app: League v Sheffield Wednesday (a) 23 Nov 1957. Will Mather Cup v Hendon (a) 30 Apr 1958. Final app: Football Combination v Ipswich Town (a) 6 Sep 1958. Transferred to Derby County (£3,600) 12 Sep 1958.
ARSENAL Record: League 13 (4 gls); Other snr comp: 1; Football Combination 98 (67 gls); London FA Challenge Cup 8 (4 gls); Eastern Counties League 54 (19 gls); Metropolitan League 1; London Midweek League 13 (6 gls); Other jnr comp: 2 (1 gl); Friendlies 3 (4 gls).
Honours: Played for Surrey schoolboys (and captain) and for Surrey Youth. London FA Challenge Cup winners 1957-8. Eastern Counties League champions 1954-5.
Served National Service in the RAOC. Played

first-class cricket for MCC and Derbyshire. After Derby County played for Poole Town (Aug 1964).

SWAN, Andrew 1901
Centre-forward 5ft 8in. 11st 12lb.
Born: Dalbeattie, Scotland, 1878.
Previous Clubs: Lincoln City, New Brompton, Barnsley (1899-1900). Joined ARSENAL: 4 May 1901 from Barnsley. First app: League v Barnsley (h) 2 Sep 1901. Final app: League v Doncaster Rovers (h) 30 Nov 1901. Transferred to Stockport County 6 Dec 1901.
ARSENAL Record: League 7 (2 gls); London League 1; London League (Res) 2 (2 gls); Kent League 1 (1 gl); Friendlies 1.
Represented Southern Counties of Scotland. Later played for Mexborough United and Tottenham Hotspur (Nov 1904).

SWINDIN, George Hedley
Player 1936-54 Manager 1958-62
Goalkeeper 5ft 10½in. 11st 6lb.
Born: Campsall, nr Doncaster, 4 Dec 1914.
Jnr football: Rotherham YMCA, New Stubbin Colliery. Previous Clubs: Rotherham United (amateur), Bradford City (1934). Joined ARSENAL: 14 Apr 1936 from Bradford City for £4,000. First app: London Combination v Coventry City (a) 29 Aug 1936. First snr app: League v Brentford (a) 3 Sep 1936. Final snr app: League v Sunderland (a) 12 Sep 1953. Final app: Football Combination v Reading (a) 23 Jan 1954. Granted a free transfer, 3 Feb 1954, to become player-manager of Peterborough United (Midland League).
ARSENAL Record: League 271; FA Cup 23; FA Charity Shield 3; Other snr comp: 2; Football Combination 87; London FA Challenge Cup 5; Southern League 4; Friendlies 50. In addition played 2 London Combination matches 1939-40 prior to outbreak of war and made 44 apps during wartime.
Honours: Division One champions 1937-8, 1947-8, 1952-3. FA Cup winners 1950, runners-up 1952. FA Charity Shield winners 1938-9, 1948-9, runners-up 1936-7. London Combination champions 1936-7, 1937-8.
Played in England Schoolboy international trials. Served as a PT Instructor in the Army in Germany during the war. Was a member of the PFA union. Manager of Arsenal (21 Jul 1958 — resigned Apr 1962). Became manager of Norwich City (May 1962) and Cardiff City (Oct 1962-Apr 1964). On retirement from football he managed a garage business in Corby and later went to live in Spain.

TALBOT, Arthur 1896-97
Goalkeeper
Joined ARSENAL: 20 Nov 1896 from Hednesford Town (Staffordshire). First app: Snr fdly v Millwall Athletic (a) 21 Nov 1896. League v Lincoln City (a) 5 Dec 1896. Final snr app: League v Gainsborough Trinity (a) 26 Dec 1896. Snr fdly v Norfolk County (a) 20 Apr 1897. Final app: Jnr fdly v Old St Stephens (h) 24 Apr 1897.
ARSENAL Record: League 5; United League 1; Kent League 5; Friendlies 7.

TALBOT, Brian Ernest 1979-85
Midfield 5ft 10in. 11st 9lb.
Born: Ipswich, 21 Jul 1953.
Schools: Bramford Road Junior and Secondary, Ipswich.
Previous Club: Ipswich Town Jul 1968 (apprentice), Aug 1972 (professional). Joined ARSENAL: 11 Jan 1979 from Ipswich Town for £450,000. First app: League v Nottingham Forest (h) 13 Jan 1979. First snr app: League v West Bromwich Albion (a) 11 May 1985. Transferred to Watford (£150,000) 10 Jun 1985.
ARSENAL Record: League 245/9 (40 gls); FA

97

Cup 29/1 (7 gls); Football League Cup 26/1 (1 gl); European comp: 15 (1 gl); FA Charity Shield 1; Football Combination 5 (2 gls); Friendlies 28/1 (12 gls).
Honours: FA Cup winners 1979, runners-up 1980. European Cup-winners' Cup runners-up 1979-80. FA Charity Shield runners-up 1979-80. 2 England 'B' caps 1979-80 and 1 full cap 1980.
Played for Ipswich and for Suffolk schoolboys. Had a two-year spell on loan to Toronto Metros when a junior with Ipswich Town. Won club honours and Under-21 'B' and full international honours with Ipswich Town. Was chairman of PFA (1984). After Watford played for Stoke City (Oct 1986) and West Bromwich Albion (Jan 1988) becoming manager in 1988-9. Had a short spell with Fulham before joining Aldershot as player-manager (Apr 1991).

TAPSCOTT, Derek Robert   **1953-58**
Forward   5ft 9in. 10st 12lb.
Born: Barry, South Wales, 30 Jun 1932.
School: High Street, Barry.
Jnr football: Barry Town 1951 (amateur), 1953 (professional). Joined ARSENAL: 1 Oct 1953 from Barry Town for £2,750. First app: Football Combination Cup v Park Rangers (a) 3 Oct 1953. First snr app: League v Liverpool (h) 10 Apr 1954. Final snr app: League v Bolton Wanderers (h) 18 Feb 1958. Final app: Football Combination v Swansea Town (h) 16 Sep 1958. Transferred to Cardiff City (£10,000) 19 Sep 1958. ARSENAL Record: League 119 (62 gls); FA Cup 13 (6 gls); Other snr comp: 2 (2 gls); Football Combination 35 (30 gls); London FA Challenge Cup 9 (5 gls); Eastern Counties League 2; London Midweek League 1; Friendlies 24/1 (35 gls).
Honours: London FA Challenge Cup winners 1953-4, 1957-8. 12 full Wales caps (2 gls) 1954-7.
Played in Wales Amateur international trial 1953. Won further international honours with Cardiff City. After Cardiff City played for Newport County (Jul 1965) and then non-League football with Cinderford, Haverfordwest and Carmarthen Town before retiring in 1970. Became a representative for Gola sports equipment in South Wales and the Midlands.

TAWSE, Brian   **1963-65**
Winger   5ft 5in. 9st 12lb.
Born: Ellon, Aberdeenshire, Scotland, 30 Jul 1945.
Jnr football: King Street 'A'. Joined ARSENAL:

Mar 1963 (amateur), 8 Apr 1963 (professional). First app: South East Counties League v Queen's Park Rangers (h) 16 Mar 1963. First snr app: League v West Bromwich Albion (a) 21 Nov 1964. Final snr app: League v West Ham United (a) 27 Mar 1965. Snr fdly v Corinthian Casuals (h) 21 Sep 1965. Final app: Football Combination v Southampton (a) 22 Dec 1965. Transferred to Brighton & Hove Albion 27 Dec 1965.
ARSENAL Record: League 5; Football Combination 49 (12 gls); London FA Challenge Cup 6 (2 gls); Metropolitan League 52 (16 gls); South East Counties League 10 (1 gl); FA Youth Cup 4; Other jnr comp: 1; Friendlies 28/1 (6 gls).
Honours: Southern Junior Floodlit Cup winners 1962-3.
Later played for Brentford (Feb 1970).

TEMPLETON, Robert Bryson   **1904-06**
Outside-left   5ft 9¾in. 11st 3lb.
Born: Coylton, Ayr, Scotland, 22 Jun 1879. Died: 2 Nov 1919.
Jnr football: Neilston Victoria. Previous Clubs: Kilmarnock (1896), Hibernian, Aston Villa (1899), Newcastle United (Feb 1903). Joined ARSENAL: 8 Dec 1904 from Newcastle United for £375. First app: League v Notts County (a) 17 Dec 1904. Final app: Southern Professional Charity Cup semi-final v Tottenham Hotspur (a) 9 Apr 1906. Transferred to Glasgow Celtic (£250) 18 May 1906.
ARSENAL Record: League 33 (1 gl); FA Cup 8; Other snr comp: 2; Friendlies 8.
Honours: 1 full Scotland cap 1905.
Played for the Scottish League whilst with Kilmarnock and won further international honours with Aston Villa, Newcastle United and Kilmarnock. Won club honours with Celtic. After Celtic played for Kilmarnock (Oct 1907), Fulham (Jun 1913) and Kilmarnock again (Apr 1915).

TENNANT, James   **1899-1901**
Outside-left   5ft 6½in. 11st 4lb.
Born: Parkhead, Scotland, 1878.
Jnr football: Linton Villa, Parkhead, St Bernards. Joined ARSENAL: 18 May 1899 from St Bernards. First app: League v Leicester Fosse (h) 2 Sep 1899. Final app: League v New Brighton Tower (a) 27 Apr 1901. Transferred to Middlesbrough (together with P.Turner for £180) 1 May 1901.
ARSENAL Record: League 51 (8 gls); FA Cup 3 (2 gls); Southern District Combination 12 (5 gls); London League (Res) 3 (2 gls); Kent League 3 (3 gls); Friendlies 16 (7 gls).
Later played for Watford (Jun 1902) for 3 seasons.

THEOBALD, W. Stephen   **1900-09**
Centre-half
Born: Plumstead, London.
Jnr football: St Andrews (Woolwich), Woolwich Polytechnic. Joined ARSENAL: 31 Oct 1900 from St Andrews. First app: Jnr fdly v Luton Town (Res) (a) 3 Nov 1900. First snr app: League v Queen's Park Rangers (h) 17 Feb 1902. League v Burton United (a) 25 Dec 1902. Final snr app: League v Newcastle United (a) 9 Jan 1909. London FA Challenge Cup semi-final v Leyton (at Tottenham) 22 Feb 1909. Final app: South Eastern League v Fulham (h) 11 Sep 1909.
ARSENAL Record: League 24; London League 5; Other snr comp: 8; London FA Challenge Cup 3; South Eastern League 108 (6 gls); London League (Res) 100 (5 gls); Kent League 18 (1 gl); Other jnr comp: 2; Friendlies 48 (3 gls).
Honours: Southern Professional Charity Cup winners 1905-06. South Eastern League champions 1903-04, 1905-06, 1906-07, 1907-08. London League (Res) champions 1901-02, 1903-04, 1906-07. West Kent League champions 1901-02, 1902-03. West Kent Charity Cup winners 1904-05.

THOMAS, Michael Lauriston   **1982-91**
Midfield   5ft 10in. 12st 4lb.
Born: Lambeth, London, 24 Aug 1967.
School: Henry Thornton.
Joined ARSENAL: Sep 1982 (schoolboy), 18 Aug 1983 (apprentice), Jan 1987 (professional). First app: South East Counties League v Norwich City (a) 4 Sep 1982. First snr app: Snr fdly (sub) v Colchester United (a) 9 Dec 1985. League v Sheffield Wednesday (a) 14 Feb 1987. Final snr app: League v West Ham United (h) 2 Nov 1991. Final app: Football Combination v Queen's Park Rangers (h) 7 Dec 1991. Transferred to Liverpool (£1,500,000) 12 Dec 1991.
ARSENAL Record: League 149/14 (24 gls); FA Cup 14/3 (1 gl); Football League Cup 22/2 (5 gls); European comp: 1/1; FA Charity Shield 1/1; Other snr comp: 9/3 (1 gl); Football Combination 104/1 (11 gls); South East Counties League 44 (3 gls); FA Youth Cup 16 (1 gl); Other jnr comp: 14; Friendlies 76/9 (6 gls). Made 1 app (1 gl) for Combined Arsenal/Luton Town on tour in Cyprus 1986-7.

Honours: Played for South London schoolboys. Won England Schoolboy cap (and captain) and England Youth caps (and captain) 1984-6. Division One champions 1988-9 and 1990-91. Football League Cup winners 1986-7, runners-up 1987-8. FA Charity Shield runners-up 1989-90, medal 1991-2. Mercantile Credit Centenary Trophy winners 1988-9. Caltex Cup winners 1990-91. Football Combination champions 1983-4. Southern Junior Floodlit Cup winners 1983-4. South East Counties League winners 1984-5. Arsenal Player of the Year 1988. 12 England Under-21 caps (3 gls), 4 'B' caps and 2 full caps. Captain of England Under-21. 1 app for Football League 1990-91.
Went on a month's loan to Portsmouth (Jan 1987) making 3 League apps.

THOMPSON, Leonard   **1928-33**
Inside-left   5ft 8in. 10st 10lb.
Born: Sheffield, 18 Feb 1901.
Previous Clubs: Barnsley (amateur 1917), Birmingham (1918), Swansea Town (1922). Joined ARSENAL: 17 Mar 1928 from Swansea Town for £4,000. First app: London Combination v

outhend United (h) 24 Mar 1928. First snr app:
league v Portsmouth (h) 28 Mar 1928. Final snr
op: League v Bolton Wanderers (a) 2 Mar 1932.
inal app: London Combination v Leicester City
a) 29 Apr 1933. Transferred to Crystal Palace
Jun 1933.
RSENAL Record: League 26 (6 gls); FA Cup
  Football Combination 160 (86 gls); London
Midweek League 6; London FA Challenge Cup
) (4 gls); Friendlies 14 (8 gls).
Honours: London Combination champions
928-9, 1929-30, 1930-31. London FA Challenge
up winners 1930-31.
layed for Sheffield Schoolboys. England
choolboy international (1914-15). Won club
onours with Swansea Town. An expert penalty-
aker. Plagued with a knee injury at Arsenal
equiring operation. Retired from League football
t end of 1933-4 season. Was later reinstated as
a amateur and assisted Islington Corinthians and
also had a spell in charge of Tottenham Hotspur
reserves. On retirement from football had a
usiness in North London and was a scout for
rsenal.

HOMSON, Matthew   **1908-14**
alf-back   5ft 9in. 11st 6lb.
orn: Maryhill, Glasgow, c.1887.
nr football: Maryhill FC. Joined ARSENAL:
Jun 1908 after having played on trial during
rsenal's Scottish tour. First app: Scottish tour
Dundee 25 Apr 1908 (trial). League v Middles-
rough (h) 17 Mar 1909. First snr app: League
Fulham (a) 8 Nov 1913. Final app: South Eastern
eague v Clapton Orient (a) 18 Apr 1914.
ransferred to Swindon Town 29 May 1914.
RSENAL Record: League 89 (1 gl); FA Cup
London FA Challenge Cup 8; Other snr comp:
(1 gl); South Eastern League 83; London League
Res) 16 (1 gl); Other jnr comp: 1; Friendlies 29
gls).

HORPE, Harold Cheetham   **1903-04**
eft-back   5ft 8½in. 11st 2lb.
orn: Barrow Hill, Derbyshire, 1880. Died:
eicester, 9 Sep 1908.
nr football: Poolsbrook United. Previous Club:
hesterfield (1900). Joined ARSENAL: 25 Apr
903 from Chesterfield. First app: London League
Tottenham Hotspur (a) 1 Sep 1903. League v
lackpool (h) 5 Sep 1903. Final snr app: South
Burnley (a) 2 Apr 1904. Final app: South Eastern
eague v St Albans (h) 30 Apr 1904. Transferred
Fulham summer 1904.
RSENAL Record: League 10; London League
Other snr comp: 2; South Eastern League 5;
ondon League (Res) 1; Friendlies 2.
ater played for Leicester Fosse (1907). Died from
lung infection, Sep 1908.

IDDY, Michael Douglas   **1955-58**
/inger   5ft 9in. 10st 7lb.
orn: Helston, Cornwall, 4 Apr 1929.
nr football: Helston. Previous Clubs: Torquay
nited (Nov 1946), Cardiff City (Nov 1950).
oined ARSENAL: 23 Sep 1955 from Cardiff City
ogether with G.Nutt, rated at £10,000 each). First
pp: League v Sunderland (a) 24 Sep 1955. First
nr app: League v Preston North End (a) 26 Apr
958. Final app: London FA Challenge Cup v
rystal Palace (h) 20 Oct 1958. Transferred to
righton & Hove Albion 23 Oct 1958.
RSENAL Record: League 48 (8 gls); FA Cup
Other snr comp: 2 (1 gl); Football Combination
(9 gls); London FA Challenge Cup 7 (2 gls);
riendlies 11 (2 gls).
onours: London FA Challenge Cup winners
957-8.
layed for Brighton until the end of 1961-2 season.
eturned to Cornwall and played for Falmouth,

Penzance (player-manager) and Helston. Retiring
from football he became the village postmaster
at Lizard.

TILLEY, Peter   **1952-53**
Inside-forward   6ft. 12st 8lb.
Born: Lurgan, Co Armagh, N.Ireland, 13 Jan 1930.
Jnr football: Mossley; Witton Albion (Cheshire
League). Joined ARSENAL: 30 May 1952 from
Witton Albion for £2,000. First app: Football
Combination v Norwich City (h) 23 Aug 1952.
First snr app: League v Chelsea (h) 8 Sep 1953
(only snr app). Final app: Football Combination
v Norwich City (h) 7 Nov 1953. Transferred to
Bury (£4,000) 13 Nov 1953.
ARSENAL Record: League 1; Football
Combination 54 (12 gls); London FA Challenge
Cup 6 (2 gls); Friendlies 2 (2 gls).
Honours: Football Combination Cup winners
1952-3. Played for Ireland v British Army 1952.
From Bury played for Halifax Town (Jul
1958-63). On retirement from football worked as
a senior clerk in the Manchester area. Became
a top-class crown bowls player in the North-West
of England.

TONER, Joseph   **1919-26**
Outside-left   5ft 7in. 10st 4lb.
Born: Castlewellan, Co Down, 30 Mar 1894. Died:
Castlewellan, Nov 1954.
Jnr football: Belfast United. Joined ARSENAL:
Aug 1919 from Belfast United. First app: London
Combination v Queen's Park Rangers (a) 4 Sep
1919. First snr app: League v Everton (a) 11 Oct
1919. Final snr app: League v Leicester City (h)
31 Aug 1925. Final app: London Combination
v Southend United (h) 2 Jan 1926. Transferred
to St Johnstone 8 Jan 1926.
ARSENAL Record: League 89 (6 gls); FA Cup
11; London FA Challenge Cup 9; Other snr comp:
3 (2 gls); Football Combination 89 (7 gls);
Friendlies 20 (1 gl).
Honours: London Combination champions
1922-3. Southend Hospital Cup winners 1920-21.
Metropolitan Hospital Cup winners 1920-21. 6 full
Northern Ireland caps 1922-5.
Won further international caps with St Johnstone.
Suffered a broken leg which hastened the end of
his career. Gave up the game but after one year
came out of retirement and played for a short
while for Coleraine, Northern Ireland. After
retirement returned to live in Castlewellan.

TOWNROW, Frank Albert   **1921-26**
Forward   5ft 9in. 11st 5lb.
Born: West Ham, London, c.1903.
Joined ARSENAL: Mar 1921 (amateur), 20 Apr
1921 (professional). First app: London
Combination v Millwall (a) 5 Mar 1921. First snr
app: On tour v Gothenburg (Sweden) 14 May
1922. League v Sheffield United (a) 2 Oct 1922.
Final snr app: League v Blackburn Rovers (h)
1 Dec 1923. On tour v Düsseldorf (Germany) 10
May 1924. Final app: London Combination v
Southend United (a) 1 May 1926. Transferred to
Dundee summer 1926.
ARSENAL Record: League 8 (2 gls); FA Cup
1; London FA Challenge Cup 3; Football
Combination 115 (34 gls); Friendlies 47 (25 gls).
Honours: London Combination champions 1922-
3. England Schoolboy international.
Brother of John Townrow (Clapton Orient,
Chelsea & England). Transferred from Dundee
to Bristol City (summer 1930). Moved to Bristol
Rovers (1931).

TRICKER, Reginald William   **1927-29**
Inside-forward   5ft 11in. 11st 7lb.
Born: Karachi, India, 5 Oct 1904.
Jnr football: Beccles Town (Suffolk). Previous
Clubs: Luton Town 1924 (amateur), Charlton
Athletic 1925 (amateur), 1927 (professional).
Joined ARSENAL: 15 Mar 1927 from Charlton
Athletic. First app: League v Everton (h) 19 Mar
1927. Final snr app: League v Manchester City
(a) 22 Sep 1928. Final app: London Combination
v Charlton Athletic (a) 2 Feb 1929. Transferred
to Clapton Orient 9 Feb 1929.
ARSENAL Record: League 12 (5 gls); Football
Combination 40 (10 gls); Friendlies 4 (3 gls).
Honours: London Combination champions 1927-8.
Returned to Suffolk from India at the age of four.
As an athlete, was the Norfolk & Suffolk 120
yards hurdles champion for two years. Studied
at Borough Road Training College, Isleworth, to
become a schoolmaster and took up an
appointment at Crouch Hill.

TRIM, Reginald Frederick   **1933-37**
Left-back   5ft 9in. 10st 12lb.
Born: Portsmouth, 1 Oct 1913.
School: Winton and Moordown (Bournemouth).
Previous Club: Bournemouth & Boscombe United
(Apr 1931). Joined ARSENAL: 13 Apr 1933 from
Bournemouth. First app: London Combination
v Swansea Town (h) 18 Apr 1933. First snr app:
League v Derby County (h) 4 May 1935 (only
snr app). Final app: London FA Challenge Cup
Final v Tottenham Hotspur (a) 3 May 1937.
Transferred to Nottingham Forest 24 Jul 1937.
ARSENAL Record: League 1; Football
Combination 155; London FA Challenge Cup 12;
Friendlies 15.
Honours: London Combination champions
1933-4, 1934-5, 1936-7. London FA Challenge
Cup winners 1933-4, runners-up 1936-7.
Captained England Schoolboys in 1928. Later
played for Derby County (wartime) and Swindon
Town (1946-7). Was trainer of Leyton Orient
(1948-9).

TUCKETT, Ernest William   **1932-37**
Inside-forward   5ft 10¾in. 11st 11lb.
Born: Lingdale, nr Guisborough 1914. Died: On
active service, World War Two.
Jnr football: Scarborough. Joined ARSENAL: 1
Jul 1932 (amateur) from Scarborough, went to
Margate (amateur nursery) 1934, returned to
Highbury 17 Mar 1936 (professional). First app:
Jnr fdly v Bournemouth (a) 3 Sep 1932. First snr
app: League v Wolverhampton Wanderers (a) 28
Mar 1936. Final app: League v Leeds United
(h) 2 May 1936. Final app: London Combination

v Southend United (h) 3 Feb 1937. Transferred to Bradford City (in exchange for L.Scott) 12 Feb 1937. ARSENAL Record: League 2; Football Combination 40 (11 gls); London FA Challenge Cup 1; London Midweek League 24 (16 gls); Friendlies 10/1 (2 gls).
Honours: London Combination champions 1936-7.
Scored six goals in a London Midweek League match, Feb 1933. Played mainly at centre or inside-forward although both his first-team apps for Arsenal were at centre-half. Transferred from Bradford City to Fulham (Oct 1938) with whom he played during wartime football until his death on active service.

TURNBULL, Robert Hamilton   1921-24
Full-back/centre-forward   5ft 8in. 12st 3lb.
Born: Dumbarton, Scotland, 22 Jun 1894. Died: 1946.
School: Albion Road (Paisley).
Jnr football: Signal Corps of Royal Engineers, Scotland. Joined ARSENAL: 22 Jan 1921 (amateur) from Army football, 30 Sep 1921 (professional). First app: Jnr fdly v Cambridge University (h) 17 Feb 1921. First snr app: London FA Challenge Cup v Queen's Park Rangers (a) 31 Oct 1921. League v Cardiff City (a) 27 Dec 1921. Final snr app: League v Aston Villa (h) 18 Oct 1924. Final app: Jnr fdly v Northfleet (a) 1 Nov 1924. Transferred to Charlton Athletic 8 Nov 1924.
ARSENAL Record: League 59 (26 gls); FA Cup 7 (2 gls); London FA Challenge Cup 5; Other snr comp: 2; Football Combination 56 (20 gls); Friendlies 26 (28 gls).
Honours: London FA Challenge Cup winners 1921-2.
Successfully converted from full-back to centre-forward in a crisis, he became Arsenal's leading goalscorer in 1922-3 with 20 goals. After Charlton Athletic played for Chelsea (1925), Clapton Orient (1927) and Southend United before finishing his playing career in 1932 with Crystal Palace. Became trainer at Crystal Palace for a number of years.

TURNER, Peter   1900-01
Inside-left   5ft 8in. 11st 4lb.
Born: Scotland.
Jnr football: Parkhead; St Bernards. Joined ARSENAL: 1 May 1900 from St Bernards. First app: League v Gainsborough Trinity (h) 1 Sep 1900. Final app: League v New Brighton Tower (a) 27 Apr 1901. Transferred to Middlesbrough (together with J.Tennant for £180) 1 May 1901.
ARSENAL Record: League 33 (5 gls); FA Cup 3; Friendlies 9 (2 gls).
Later played for Luton Town, Watford (May 1904), Clyde and, briefly, Leyton and Doncaster Rovers. Had a laundry business in Watford..

TYRER, Alan   1965-67
Forward   5ft 8in. 10st 3lb.
Born: Liverpool, 8 Dec 1942.
Previous Clubs: Everton (Dec 1959), Mansfield Town (Jul 1963). Joined ARSENAL: 20 Aug 1965 on a free transfer from Mansfield Town. First app: Jnr fdly v Queen's Park Rangers (a) 7 Aug 1965 (trial). First snr app: Snr fdly v Valencia (Spain) (a) 9 Mar 1966. Football League Cup v Gillingham (h) 13 Sep 1966. Final snr app: Football League Cup (sub) v Gillingham (a) 21 Sep 1966. Final app: Football Combination v Northampton Town (h) 18 Mar 1967. Transferred to Bury 28 Aug 1967.
ARSENAL Record: Football League Cup 1/1 (1 gl); Football Combination 47 (17 gls); London FA Challenge Cup 6 (2 gls); Metropolitan League 4 (2 gls); Friendlies 9/1 (1 gl).
Honours: London FA Challenge Cup runners-up 1965-6. Metropolitan League Challenge Cup winners 1965-6.
After Bury played for Workington (Jul 1968-74).

URE, John Francombe 'Ian'   1963-69
Centre-half   6ft 1in. 12st 9lb.
Born: Ayr, Scotland, 7 Dec 1939.
School: Ayr Academy.
Jnr football: Ayr Albion, Dalry Thistle. Previous Club: Dundee (Aug 1958). Joined ARSENAL: 22 Aug 1963 from Dundee for £62,500. First app: League v Wolverhampton Wanderers (h) 24 Aug 1963. Final app: League v Leeds United (h) 19 Aug 1969. Transferred to Manchester United (£80,000) 21 Aug 1969.

ARSENAL Record: League 168 (2 gls); FA Cup 16; Football League Cup 14; European comp: 4; Football Combination 29 (2 gls); London FA Challenge Cup 4; Friendlies 40/4.
Honours: Football League Cup runners-up 1967-8, 1968-9. 3 full Scotland caps 1963-7.
Played for Scottish National Association of Boys' clubs. Won club, Scotland Under-23, full international and Scottish League honours with Dundee. A knee operation and a twice-broken jaw hampered his career at Arsenal. From Manchester United he played for St Mirren until Mar 1973. Was coach to Cumnock and manager of East Stirling (1974) before becoming a social worker in Kilmarnock.

VAESSEN, Paul Leon   1977-82
Striker   5ft 11in.
Born: Bermondsey, London, 16 Oct 1961.
Joined ARSENAL: 1977 (apprentice), 14 Jul 1979 (professional). First app: Jnr fdly v Hitchen Town (a) 6 Aug 1977. First snr app: League v Chelsea (a) 14 May 1979. Final snr app: League v Swansea City (h) 27 Feb 1982. Final app: Football Combination (sub) v Brighton (a) 21 Sep 1982. Retired due to injury 1982-3.
ARSENAL Record: League 23/9 (6 gls); Football League Cup 1/1 (2 gls); European comp: 3/4 (1 gl); Football Combination 89/6 (28 gls); South East Counties League 24 (6 gls); FA Youth Cup 3 (1 gl); Other jnr comp: 4/2 (4 gls); Friendlies 30/7 (11 gls). In addition played 2 Football Combination matches (1 gl) 1981-2, later removed from records.
Son of Leon Vaessen (Millwall & Gillingham). Was forced to give up the game in 1982-3 season after a two-year battle to regain fitness following a severe knee injury.

VALLANCE, Thomas Henshall Wilson 1946-53
Outside-left   5ft 11in. 11st 4lb.
Born: Stoke-on-Trent, 28 Mar 1924. Died: Sutton, 6 Jul 1980.
Previous Clubs: Stoke City (amateur), Torquay United (amateur/wartime). Joined ARSENAL: 18 Nov 1946 (amateur), 31 Jul 1947 (professional). First app: Jnr fdly v Worcester City (a) 23 Nov 1946. First snr app: League v Sheffield United (a) 4 Sep 1948. Final snr app: League v Burnley (h) 20 Aug 1949. Final app: Eastern Counties League v Harwich & Parkston (a) 29 Apr 1953. Given a free transfer at end of 1952-3 season.
ARSENAL Record: League 15 (2 gls); Football Combination 63 (21 gls); London FA Challenge Cup 1; Other jnr comp: 6 (3 gls); Eastern Counties League 49 (31 gls); London Midweek League 12 (2 gls); Friendlies 23 (18 gls).
Son of Jimmy Vallance (Stoke City player and trainer). Was an RAF pilot in Transport Command flying to and from India. Suffered a double fracture of the leg, Nov 1949 and on recovery played mainly for the Reserves and 'A' team.

VAUGHAN, John William   1900-0?
Outside-left
Joined ARSENAL: Nov 1900 from local football. Signed League forms 18 Dec 1900. First app: Jnr fdly v Luton Town Reserves (a) 3 Nov 1900. First snr app: Snr fdly v Millwall Athletic (h) 1 Apr 1901. FA Cup v Luton Town (h) 14 Dec 1901 (only first-class app). Final snr app: Southern Professional Charity Cup v Millwall Athletic (h) 9 Feb 1903. Final app: Chatham Charity Cup Final v Chatham (a) 27 Apr 1903.
ARSENAL Record: FA Cup 1; London League 2 (1 gl); Other snr comp: 1; London League (Res) 48 (17 gls); Kent League 31 (13 gls); Other jnr comp: 3; Friendlies 17 (9 gls).
Honours: West Kent League champions 1900-01 1901-02, 1902-03. London League (Res) champions 1901-02. Chatham Charity Cup runners-up 1902-03.
Later played for Millwall.

VOYSEY, Clement Ross   1919-2?
Half-back   5ft 8in. 10st 2lb.
Born: New Cross, London, Jan 1899. Died: Jan 1989.
School: New Cross.
Jnr football: RAF, Selby, Yorks; Royal Navy Air Service. Joined ARSENAL: Mar 1919 (amateur), Apr 1919 (professional). First app: London Combination (wartime) v West Ham United (h) 22 Mar 1919. League v Newcastle United (h) 30 Aug 1919. Final snr app: League v Leeds United (a) 6 Feb 1926. Final app: Football Combination v Crystal Palace (h) 2 Apr 1926.
ARSENAL Record: League 35 (6 gls); FA Cup 2; London FA Challenge Cup 2 (1 gl); Other snr comp: 2; Football Combination 91 (13 gls); Friendlies 29/1 (5 gls). In addition made 9 app during wartime.
Honours: Southend Hospital Cup winners 1921-2. Was reserve for England v Belgium 1924.
Was a craftsman attached to the Royal Naval Air Service of the RAF during the war and joined Arsenal immediately the war ended. Suffered severe knee injury after only a handful of game in 1919-20 season and was out of football for over a year.

WADE, Joseph Samuel   1944-5?
Full-back   5ft 10½in. 11st 4lb.
Born: Shoreditch, London, 7 Jul 1921.
Jnr football: Hoxton Manor Boy's Club. Joined ARSENAL: 25 May 1944 (amateur), 18 Aug 1944 (professional). First app: Football League South v Reading (h) 31 Mar 1945. First snr app: F.

up v West Ham United (a) 5 Jan 1946. Final
ar app: League v Newcastle United (a) 18 Dec
954. On tour v München 1860 (Germany) 19 May
955. Final app: Will Mather Cup v Hendon (a)
) Apr 1956. Transferred to Hereford Town as
layer-manager 19 Aug 1956.
ARSENAL Record: League 86; FA Cup 7;
Football Combination 276 (3 gls); London FA
Challenge Cup 11; Eastern Counties League 2;
other snr comp: 1; London Midweek League 1;
riendlies 49/3 (1 gl). In addition made 25 apps
uring wartime.
*Honours: Division One champions 1952-3.
Football Combination champions 1946-7, 1950-51.
London FA Challenge Cup winners 1953-4.
Football Combination Cup runners-up 1946-7,
950-51. Captain of Arsenal. Made 1 app for the
Football League 1953.*
Was a London Boys Club junior boxing
champion. Served as a fitter/armourer in the RAF
during the war. Was manager of Hereford Town
until 1962. Now runs sports equipment shops in
Hereford and Leominster.

WALDEN, Harold A.   **1920-21**
Centre-forward   5ft 10½in. 12st 3lb.
Born: Manchester, c.1890.
Previous Clubs: Halifax Town, Bradford City
(Dec 1911). Joined ARSENAL: 11 Oct 1920 from
Bradford City. First app: London Combination
Crystal Palace (h) 16 Oct 1920. First snr app:
League v Oldham Athletic (a) 12 Feb 1921. Final
snr app: League v Oldham Athletic (h) 19 Feb
1921. Final app: London Combination v Brent-
ford (a) 29 Mar 1921. Transferred to Bradford
summer 1921.
ARSENAL Record: League 2 (1 gl); Other snr
comp: 1; Football Combination 2; Friendlies 3
(2 gls).
Was a member of the British team which won
the Olympic football tournament 1912.

WALFORD, Stephen Joseph   **1977-81**
Defender   6ft 1in. 11st 7lb.
Born: Highgate, London, 5 Jan 1958.
School: Holloway, London.

Previous Club: Tottenham Hotspur Apr 1974
(apprentice), Apr 1975 (professional). Joined
ARSENAL: 1 Aug 1977 from Tottenham Hotspur
for £25,000. First app: Jnr fdly v Hitchen Town
(a) 6 Aug 1977. First snr app: Snr fdly v
Northampton Town (a) 20 Sep 1977. League (sub)
v Norwich City (a) 24 Sep 1977. Final snr app:
League v Middlesbrough (h) 28 Feb 1981. Final

app: Football Combination v Southampton (h)
7 Mar 1981. Transferred to Norwich City
(£175,000) 12 Mar 1981.
ARSENAL Record: League 64/13 (3 gls); FA Cup
5/5; Football League Cup 5 (1 gl); European
comp: 3/2; FA Charity Shield 1; Football
Combination 59 (11 gls); Friendlies 13/7.
*Honours: FA Cup winners 1979. FA Charity
Shield runners-up 1979-80. Played for Islington
Schoolboys.*
Won England Youth honours with Tottenham
Hotspur. Moved from Norwich City to West Ham
United (1983). Had spells on loan to Huddersfield
Town (1987-8), Gillingham (1988-9) and West
Bromwich Albion (1988-9).

WALLER, Henry   **1937-47**
Wing-half   5ft 10in. 11st 7lb.
Born: Ashington, Northumberland, 20 Aug 1917.
Jnr football: Ashington. Joined ARSENAL: 28
Oct 1937 from Ashington. Went to Margate
(nursery), returned May 1938. First app: Jnr fdly
v Cambridge University (a) 18 Nov 1937. First
snr app: London War Cup v Millwall (a) 24 May
1941. FA Cup v West Ham United (h) 9 Jan 1946.
Final snr app: League v Aston Villa (h) 18 Jan
1947. Final app: Football Combination Cup Final
v Swansea Town (at Tottenham) 14 Jun 1947.
Transferred to Leyton Orient 16 Jul 1947.
ARSENAL Record: League 8; FA Cup 1;
Football Combination 24; Southern League 36;
Friendlies 5. In addition played 1 Southern League
match 1939-40 prior to outbreak of war and made
11 apps during wartime.
*Honours: Football Combination champions
1946-7. Football Combination Cup runners-up
1946-7.*
Served in the Army in Sicily and Italy during
the war. Returned to the North-East from Leyton
Orient and played for Ashington and Consett.

WALLEY, John Thomas   **1964-67**
Wing-half   5ft 10in. 11st 4lb.
Born: Caernarfon, N.Wales, 27 Feb 1945.
School: Sgonsem, Caernarfon.
Jnr football: Caernarfon Town. Joined
ARSENAL: 9 Dec 1964 (amateur) from
Caernarfon Town, 23 Dec 1964 (professional).
First app: Jnr fdly v London University (a) 9 Dec
1964. First snr app: Snr fdly v Corinthian Casuals
(h) 21 Sep 1965. League (sub) v West Ham United
(h) 20 Nov 1965. Final snr app: League (sub) v
Blackpool (a) 21 Jan 1967. Final app: Football
Combination v Fulham (h) 25 Feb 1967.
Transferred to Watford (£9,000) 14 Mar 1967.
ARSENAL Record: League 10/4 (1 gl); FA Cup
1; Football League Cup 3; Football Combination
42 (7 gls); London FA Challenge Cup 5;
Metropolitan League 7 (1 gl); Friendlies 15/3 (1 gl).
*Honours: London FA Challenge Cup runners-up
1965-6. Metropolitan League Challenge Cup
winners 1965-6. 2 Wales Under-23 caps 1966-7.*
Won club and further international honours with
Watford. Transferred from Watford to Leyton
Orient (Dec 1971) and back to Watford (Jun 1976).
Became coach to Watford and later to Millwall
juniors.

WALLINGTON, Edward E.   **1923-24**
Outside-right.
Jnr football: Rickmansworth. Previous Club:
Watford 1914 (amateur), 1920 (professional).
Joined ARSENAL: Aug 1923 on a free transfer
from Watford. First app: London Combination
v Millwall (a) 25 Aug 1923. First snr app: League
v Newcastle United (a) 1 Sep 1923 (only snr app).
Final app: Jnr fdly v Slough (a) 18 Apr 1924.
ARSENAL Record: League 1; Football
Combination 2; Friendlies 6/1 (1 gl).
Was later reinstated as an amateur and played
for Watford Old Boys.

WALSH, John Brian   **1949-55**
Winger   5ft 8in. 10st 2lb.
Born: Aldershot, 26 Mar 1932.
Jnr football: Chase of Chertsey. Joined
ARSENAL: 13 Mar 1949 (amateur) from Chase
of Chertsey, 1 Aug 1949 (professional). From
Eastern Counties League v Clacton Town (a) 9
Apr 1949. First snr app: League v Cardiff City
(a) 26 Sep 1953. Final snr app: League v Tottenham
Hotspur (a) 10 Sep 1955. Final app: Football
Combination v Tottenham Hotspur (a) 21 Sep 1955.
Transferred to Cardiff City 23 Sep 1955.
ARSENAL Record: League 17; Football
Combination 81 (19 gls); London FA Challenge
Cup 9 (5 gls); Eastern Counties League 30 (6 gls);
London Midweek League 18 (4 gls); Other jnr
comp: 2 (1 gl); Friendlies 22/1 (6 gls).
*Honours: Football Combination Cup winners
1952-3. London FA Challenge Cup winners 1954-5.*
Was prominent in the 440 yards junior AAA
championships at White City 1949. National
Service in the Army (1950-52). Moved from
Cardiff City to Newport County (Nov 1961).

WALSH, Charles Henry   **1930-33**
Centre-forward   5ft 11in. 11st 8lb.
Born: London, 1910.
Jnr football: Hampstead Town. Joined
ARSENAL: 6 Aug 1930 (amateur) from Hamp-
stead Town, 16 May 1931 (professional). First app:
London Midweek League v West Ham United
(a) 6 Oct 1930. First snr app: FA Cup v Walsall
(a) 14 Jan 1933 (only snr app). Final app: London
Combination v Southampton (a) 21 Jan 1933.
Transferred to Brentford 27 Jan 1933.
ARSENAL Record: FA Cup 1; Football
Combination 32 (18 gls); London FA Challenge
Cup 2 (2 gls); London Midweek League 19 (9
gls); Friendlies 9 (13 gls).

WALSH, Wilfred   **1935-39**
Outside-right   5ft 5in. 9st 7lb.
Born: Pontlottyn, South Wales, 29 Jul 1917. Died:
1977.
Joined ARSENAL: 9 May 1935 (amateur), 4 May
1936 (professional). Went to Margate (nursery).
Returned to Highbury Aug 1938. First app: Jnr
fdly v Oxford University (a) 14 Nov 1935. First
snr app: League v Preston North End (h) 22 Oct
1938. Final app: League v Leeds United (h) 5 Nov
1938. On tour v Danish XI (Denmark) 24 May
1939. Transferred to Derby County (£2,000) 26
Jun 1939.
ARSENAL Record: League 3; Football
Combination 16 (4 gls); London FA Challenge
Cup 4 (3 gls); Southern League 24 (9 gls);
Friendlies 3.
Honours: London Combination champions 1938-9.
Transferred from Derby County to Walsall (Mar
1947). From Walsall had spells with Hednesford
Town (1948), player-manager Redditch Town
(1949) and Hednesford Town again (1952) and
on retiring from playing continued as manager.

WARD, Allen   **1895**
Half-back   5ft 10in. 13st 7lb.
Born: Parkgate, Barnsley 1872.
Jnr football: Barnsley St Peters. Previous Clubs:
Sheffield Wednesday (1893-4), Burton Wanderers
(1894-5). Joined ARSENAL: May 1895. First app:
League v Grimsby Town (h) 2 Sep 1895. Final
snr app: League v Burton Wanderers (h) 12 Oct
1895. Snr fdly v Everton (h) 14 Oct 1895. Final
app: Jnr fdly v 1st Scots Guards (a) 16 Nov 1895.
ARSENAL Record: League 7; Friendlies 5.
Was suspended for a breach of discipline by
Arsenal in Nov 1895 for the remainder of the
season and left Woolwich.

WARD, Gerald   **1952-63**
Outside-left/wing-half   5ft 8in. 10st 12lb.
Born: Stepney, London, 5 Oct 1936.
School: Leyton.
Joined ARSENAL: 17 Jun 1952 (amateur), 5 Oct 1953 (professional). First app: East Anglian Cup v Chelmsford (a) 28 Aug 1952. First snr app: League v Huddersfield Town (h) 22 Aug 1953. Final snr app: League v Bolton Wanderers (a) 29 Sep 1962. Final app: Metropolitan League v St Neots (h) 23 May 1963. Transferred to Leyton Orient (£8,000) 12 Jul 1963.
ARSENAL Record: League 81 (10 gls); FA Cup 3; Other snr comp: 5; Football Combination 170 (43 gls); London FA Challenge Cup 22 (7 gls); Eastern Counties League 7; FA Youth Cup 2; South East Counties League 6 (5 gls); Metropolitan League 9 (2 gls); Other jnr comp: 4 (4 gls); Friendlies 46/2 (12 gls).

Honours: Played for London, Leytonstone and for Essex schoolboys. England Schoolboy and Youth international. Football Combination champions 1962-3. Football Combination Cup winners 1952-3. London FA Challenge Cup winners 1953-4, 1961-2, 1962-3, runners-up 1960-61. Eastern Counties League champions 1954-5. Won England Amateur cap 1953. Played for FA XI 1958.
Was the youngest player ever to appear for Arsenal when he made his League debut in Aug 1953 at the age of 16. National Service in the Army (1955-7). After Leyton Orient played for Cambridge City (1965) before going into banking. Became a part-time player and then manager of Barnet until 1972. Went to live in Sheffield where he worked for Midland Bank.

WARNES, William Henry   **1925-33**
Winger   5ft 7½in. 11st.
Born: Rotherhithe, London, 14 Nov 1907.
Jnr football: Nunhead, Woking. Joined ARSENAL: May 1925 (amateur), 29 Jun 1929 (professional). First app: Jnr fdly v Luton Town (Res) (h) 2 May 1925. First snr app: FA Cup v Walsall (a) 14 Jan 1933 (only snr app). Final app: London Combination v Leicester City (a) 29 Apr 1933. Transferred to Norwich City 12 May 1933.
ARSENAL Record: FA Cup 1; Football Combination 89 (37 gls); London FA Challenge Cup 7; London Midweek League 3 (3 gls); Friendlies 9 (6 gls).

Honours: London Combination champions 1928-9. London FA Challenge Cup winners 1930-31. England Amateur international.
Son of Rube Warnes, a former amateur boxing champion. On retiring from football had a tobacconist and confectionary business.

WATSON, Robert   **1903-05**
Inside-forward   5ft 9in. 12st.
Born: Middlesbrough, c.1883.
Jnr football: South Bank. Previous Club: Middlesbrough (Sep 1902). Joined ARSENAL: 1 Jun 1903 from Middlesbrough. First app: Jnr fdly v Sittingbourne (a) 17 Oct 1903. First snr app: Snr fdly v Army (h) 30 Nov 1903. League v Bolton Wanderers (h) 26 Mar 1904. Final app: League v Blackburn Rovers (h) 11 Feb 1905. Snr fdly v Sheffield United (h) 29 Apr 1905. Transferred to Leeds City Jul 1905.
ARSENAL Record: League 9 (1 gl); FA Cup 1; London League 7 (1 gl); Other snr comp: 2; South Eastern League 24 (15 gls); London League (Res) 21 (15 gls); Friendlies 11 (9 gls).
Honours: Southern Professional Charity Cup runners-up 1903-04. South Eastern League champions 1903-04. London League (Res) champions 1903-04.
Scored seven goals for Woolwich Arsenal v Paris XI at Plumstead, Dec 1904. After Leeds City played for Exeter City (1908) and Stalybridge Celtic.

WEBSTER, Malcolm Walter   **1966-70**
Goalkeeper   5ft 10½in. 12st 6lb.
Born: Rossington, Yorkshire, 12 Nov 1950.
Joined ARSENAL: May 1966 (apprentice), 22 Jan 1968 (professional). First app: South East Counties League v Chelsea (h) 27 Aug 1966. First snr app: On tour (sub) v Reykjavik (Iceland) 4 May 1969; League v Tottenham Hotspur (h) 16 Sep 1969. Final snr app: Football League Cup v Everton (a) 1 Oct 1969. Final app: Football Combination Cup v Bristol Rovers (h) 2 Dec 1969. Transferred to Fulham (£10,000, after having been on loan from Dec 1969) 6 Jun 1970.
ARSENAL Record: League 3; Football League Cup 2; European comp: 1; Football Combination 34; London FA Challenge Cup 1; Metropolitan League 37; South East Counties League 20; FA Youth Cup 5; Other jnr comp: 7; Friendlies 43/5.
Honours: Played for Doncaster schoolboys. England Schoolboy international. Football Combination champions 1968-9. London Youth Challenge Cup winners 1966-7. Southern Junior Floodlit Cup runners-up 1967-8. England Youth international 1969.
Transferred from Fulham to Southend United (Jan 1974) and to Cambridge United (Sep 1976). Won club honours with Fulham and Cambridge United. Retired in 1984 and became youth-team coach at Cambridge United and assistant manager in 1986.

WESTCOTT, Ronald   **1935-36**
Centre-forward   5ft 11in. 11st 4lb.
Born: Wallasey, Cheshire, c.1913.
Jnr football: Banbury Spencer. Joined ARSENAL: 17 Jul 1935 (amateur) from Banbury Spencer, 6 Nov 1935 (professional). First app: Jnr fdly v King's Lynn (a) 16 Oct 1935. First snr app: League v Wolverhampton Wanderers (a) 28 Mar 1936. Final app: League v Bolton Wanderers (h) 1 Apr 1936.
ARSENAL Record: League 2 (1 gl); Football Combination 17 (9 gls); London FA Challenge Cup 1 (1 gl); Friendlies 2 (3 gls).
Suffered a severe knee injury in only his second League match v Bolton Wanderers in Apr 1936 and was forced to retire from football. Became a golf professional. Brother of Dennis Westcott (Wolverhampton Wanderers).

WHITE, Henry Albert   **1919-2**
Inside/centre-forward   5ft 8in. 11st 3lb
Born: Watford, 17 Apr 1892. Died: Barrow Gurney, Somerset, 27 Nov 1972.
Previous Club: Brentford (amateur, wartime) Joined ARSENAL: Jul 1919 from Brentford. First app: League v Newcastle United (h) 30 Aug 1919 Final snr app: League v Everton (a) 4 Nov 1922 Final app: Jnr fdly v Athenian League XI (a) 2 Feb 1923. Transferred to Blackpool 2 Mar 1923.
ARSENAL Record: League 101 (40 gls); FA Cup 8 (5 gls); London FA Challenge Cup 7 (4 gls Football Combination 18 (8 gls); Other snr comp 6 (4 gls); Friendlies 17 (18 gls).
Honours: London FA Challenge Cup winner 1921-2. Southend Hospital Cup winners 1920-2, 1921-2. Metropolitan Hospital Cup winners 1920-2,
Served in the Royal Fusiliers during wartime Played in an England Trial match (1919) whils with Brentford. Played county cricket fo Warwickshire 1923. After Blackpool played fo Fulham (1925), Walsall (Feb 1926), Nelson (Ma 1927) and Thames Association (1929). Wa groundsman at Brentwood school (1953).

WHITE, William   **1897-9**
Inside-forward
Previous Club: Heart of Midlothian. Joine ARSENAL: 5 May 1897 from Heart o Midlothian. First app: League v Grimsby Tow (h) 1 Sep 1897. Final snr app: League v Sma Heath (a) 4 Mar 1899. Final app: FA Cup v Cray Wanderers (a) 11 Mar 1899. Transferre to New Brompton 22 Mar 1899.
ARSENAL Record: League 39 (16 gls); FA Cu 3; United League 22 (11 gls); Kent League 4 (gls); Other jnr comp: 1 (1 gl); Friendlies 10 (5 gls). Later played for Queen's Park Rangers an Liverpool (1901-02).

WHITFIELD, Job   **1896-9**
Right-back
Joined ARSENAL: 5 Dec 1896 from Houghton le-Ware. First app: League v Blackpool (h) 1 Dec 1896. Final app: League v Darwen (a) 1 Ja 1897 (his only 2 apps for Arsenal).
ARSENAL Record: League 2.

WHITTAKER, Thomas James MBE
Player 1919-25   **Manager 1947-5**
Wing-half   5ft 9½in. 12st 2lb
Born: Aldershot, 21 Jul 1898. Died: London, 2 Oct 1956.
School: St Lawrence's, Newcastle upon Tyne.
Jnr football: Newcastle United Swifts, Arm football. Joined ARSENAL: 29 Nov 1919 fror Army football. First app: London Combinatio v Crystal Palace (a) 20 Dec 1919. First snr app League v West Bromwich Albion (a) 6 Apr 192 Final snr app: League v West Ham United (h 23 Mar 1925. Final app: London Combinatio v Chelsea (a) 2 Apr 1925.
ARSENAL Record: League 64 (2 gls); FA Cu 6; London FA Challenge Cup 10; Other snr comp 2; Football Combination 117 (19 gls); Friendlie 44 (4 gls).
Honours: London Combination champions 1922-3 London FA Challenge Cup winners 1921-2, 1923-4 Southend Hospital Cup winners 1920-21. Metro politan Hospital Cup winners 1920-21. Membe of FA touring team to Australia 1925. Traine to the England international and FA Repre sentative teams.
From school he served an apprenticeship with Hawthorn Leslie and qualified as a marin engineer. Served as an ordnance engineer in th Army in World War One. Also played at centre forward and full-back for Arsenal. His footba playing career was terminated prematurely whe he sustained a severe injury (cracked knee socket

at Woolongong, Australia, on 8 Jun 1925. Studied physiotherapy and became assistant trainer at Arsenal (1926) and chief trainer (Feb 1927). During World War Two was a Squadron Leader in the RAF on secret operational work for which he was awarded the MBE in 1947. Became assistant manager of Arsenal (1946) and secretary-manager (Jun 1947), guiding the club to win the League championship in his first season. Died of a heart attack in a London hospital in Oct 1956.

WHYTE, Christopher Anderson 1977-86
Defender   6ft 1in. 11st 10lb.
Born: Islington, London, 2 Sep 1961.
School: Highbury Grove.
Joined ARSENAL: 1977 (schoolboy), 22 Sep 1978 (professional). First app: South East Counties League v Gillingham (h) 20 Aug 1977. First snr app: Snr fdly v Celtic (h) 25 Nov 1980. League v Manchester City (h) 17 Oct 1981. Final snr app: League (sub) v West Bromwich Albion (a) 23 Nov 1985. Final app: Football Combination v Reading (h) 7 May 1986. Given free transfer by Arsenal at end of 1985-6.
ARSENAL Record: League 86/4 (8 gls); FA Cup 5; Football League Cup 14; European comp: 3/1; Football Combination 162/1 (15 gls); South East Counties League 65 (3 gls); FA Youth Cup 2/1; Other jnr comp: 6 (1 gl); Friendlies 71/4 (2 gls). In addition played 1 Football Combination match 1981-2, later removed from records.
Honours: Played for Islington and for Inner London schoolboys. Football Combination champions 1983-4. South East Counties League Cup winners 1979-80. President's Cup winners 1980-81. 4 England Under-21 caps 1982.
Went on loan to Crystal Palace (Aug-Nov 1984 — 13 apps). Went to play indoor football in America 1986. Returned 1988 and played for West Bromwich Albion. Transferred to Leeds United (cs 1990).

WILKINSON, John 1953-56
Centre-forward   6ft. 12st 1lb.
Born: Middlewich, Cheshire, 17 Sep 1931.
Jnr football: Witton Albion. Joined ARSENAL: 23 Oct 1953 from Witton Albion. First app: London Midweek League v Charlton Athletic (a) 11 Nov 1953. First snr app: League v Leicester City (h) 19 Feb 1955 (only first-class app). Final snr app: Snr fdly (sub) v Clyde (h) 20 Sep 1955. Final app: Football Combination v Southampton (a) 18 Feb 1956. Transferred to Sheffield United (£5,000) Feb 1956.
ARSENAL Record: League 1; Football Combination 69 (39 gls); London FA Challenge Cup 8 (8 gls); Eastern Counties League 16 (6 gls); London Midweek League 4 (1 gl); Friendlies 3/2 (5 gls).
Honours: London FA Challenge Cup winners 1954-5.
After Sheffield United played for Port Vale (1957), Exeter City (1959), Wellington Town and Witton Albion (1963). Became player-coach to Winsford United.

WILLIAMS, Charles Albert 1891-94
Goalkeeper   5ft 10½in. 12st.
Born: Welling, Kent, c.1875. Died: South America, 1952.
Jnr football: Phoenix; Erith. Joined ARSENAL: Nov 1891. Signed League forms 25 Jun 1893. First app: Jnr fdly v Woodville (h) 7 Nov 1891. First snr app: Snr fdly v Nottingham Forest (h) 17 Dec 1892. FA Cup v Sunderland (a) 21 Jan 1893. Final app: League v Burton Swifts (h) 14 Apr 1894. Last jnr app: FA Cup v Erith (a) 28 Apr 1894. Transferred to Manchester City 5 Jun 1894.
ARSENAL Record: League 19; FA Cup 2; FA Cup (Q) 2; Friendlies 32. In addition made 29

senior and 3 reserve apps for Royal Arsenal 1891-2 and 1892-3.
Won club and Football League honours with Manchester City. Later played for Tottenham Hotspur (1902-05), Norwich City and Brentford and, was manager of French club, Lille.

WILLIAMS, E. 1889-90
Outside-left
First app: Jnr fdly v Ilford Reserves (a) 9 Nov (h) 7 Dec 1889 (only first-class app). Final app: Snr fdly v Millwall Athletic (a) 10 May 1890.
ARSENAL Record: FA Cup (Q) 1. In addition made 6 senior (4 gls) and 9 reserve (4 gls) apps for Royal Arsenal 1889-90.

WILLIAMS, Joseph Joshua 1929-32
Winger   5ft 6in. 10st 4lb.
Born: Rotherham, Jun 1902.
Previous Clubs: Rotherham County, Huddersfield Town (cs 1924), Stoke City. Joined ARSENAL: 13 Sep 1929 from Stoke City. First app: League Combination v Cardiff City (a) 14 Sep 1929. First snr app: League v Aston Villa (a) 25 Sep 1929. Final snr app: League v Sheffield United (h) 26 Dec 1931. Final app: London Combination v Queen's Park Rangers (a) 5 Mar 1932. Transferred to Middlesbrough 10 Mar 1932.
ARSENAL Record: League 22 (5 gls); FA Cup 4; Football Combination 65 (21 gls); London FA Challenge Cup 3; London Midweek League 4 (2 gls); Friendlies 10 (2 gls).
Honours: London Combination champions 1929-30, 1930-31. London FA Challenge Cup winners 1930-31. Played for Professionals v Amateurs (Charity Shield) 1929.
Won club honours with Huddersfield Town and club and England (South Africa tour) honours with Stoke City. Missed the 1930 FA Cup Final for Arsenal due to injury. Later played for Carlisle United (1935-6).

WILLIAMS, Steven Charles 1984-88
Midfield   5ft 10½in. 11st 8lb.
Born: Hammersmith, London, 12 Jul 1958.
School: St Edward's, Chadwell Heath.
Previous Club: Southampton (1976). Joined

ARSENAL: 31 Dec 1984 from Southampton for £550,000. First app: League (sub) v Tottenham Hotspur (h) 1 Jan 1985. Final snr app: League v Southampton (a) 7 May 1988. Final app: Football Combination v Tottenham Hotspur (h) 30 Apr 1988. Transferred to Luton Town (£300,000) 23 Jul 1988.
ARSENAL Record: League 93/2 (4 gls); FA Cup 11; Football League Cup 15 (1 gl); Football Combination 24 (2 gls); Friendlies 17/5.

Honours: Football League Cup winners 1986-7.
Won club honours, England Under-21, 'B' and full international honours with Southampton.

WILLIAMS, Walter 1893-95
Forward
Jnr football: Bostal Rovers. Joined ARSENAL: Nov 1893 (amateur), Nov 1894 (professional). First app: Jnr fdly v Erith (a) 4 Nov 1893. First snr app: Snr fdly v Blackpool (h) 29 Jan 1894. League v Crewe Alexandra (h) 10 Feb 1894 (only first-class app). Final app: Kent League v Sittingbourne (h) 11 Jan 1896.
ARSENAL Record: League 1; Kent League 10 (7 gls); Other jnr comp: 3 (2 gls); Friendlies 49 (19 gls).
Honours: Wolverton Charity Cup runners-up 1894-5.

WILLIAMSON, Ernest Clark 1919-23
Goalkeeper   5ft 9in. 12st 4lb.
Born: Murton, Co Durham, 24 May 1890. Died: Norwich, 30 Apr 1964.
Jnr football: Murton Red Star, Wingate Albion, Croydon Common (Jun 1913). Joined ARSENAL: Apr 1919 from Croydon Common for £150. First app: London Combination (wartime) v West Ham United (a) 2 Sep 1916 (as a guest player). First snr app: League v Newcastle United (h) 30 Aug 1919. Final snr app: League v Cardiff City (a) 9 Sep 1922. Final app: London Combination v Brentford (h) 5 May 1923. Transferred to Norwich City 29 Jun 1923.
ARSENAL Record: League 105; FA Cup 8; London FA Challenge Cup 10; Other snr comp: 3; Football Combination 26; Friendlies 23. In addition made 122 apps during wartime as a guest player.

Honours: London Combination champions 1922-3. London FA Challenge Cup winners 1921-2. Southend Hospital Cup winners 1921-2. 2 full England caps 1923 and made 1 app for England in a Victory international 1920.
Served in the RASC during the war. First appeared for Arsenal as a guest player and was signed as the war ended. Retired from football in 1926 and became a publican in Norwich.

WILLS, Leonard Edward 1949-62
Full-back   5ft 10in. 11st.
Born: Hackney, London, 8 Nov 1927.
Jnr football: Eton Manor FC, Crystal Palace (amateur). Joined ARSENAL: Mar 1949

(amateur), 24 Oct 1949 (professional). First app: Eastern Counties League v Ipswich Town (a) 5 Sep 1949. First snr app: Snr fdly (sub) v Queen's Park Rangers (a) 5 Oct 1953. League v Tottenham Hotspur (a) 10 Oct 1953. Final snr app: League v Cardiff City (h) 11 Feb 1961. Final app: Football Combination v Luton Town (a) 24 Apr 1962. Retired at end of 1961-2 season.
ARSENAL Record: League 195 (4 gls); FA Cup 13; FA Charity Shield 1; Other snr comp: 8 (1 gl); Football Combination 251 (12 gls); London FA Challenge Cup 11; Eastern Counties League 8; London Midweek League 1; Metropolitan League 1; Friendlies 73/2 (5 gls).
Honours: FA Charity Shield winners 1953-4. Southern Floodlit Challenge Cup winners 1958-9. Football Combination champions 1950-51. Football Combination Cup winners 1952-3, runners-up 1950-51.
First signed for Arsenal 19 Jan 1946 as an amateur from Eton Manor but shortly after served National Service in the RAF for two years. Re-signed for Arsenal 1949. Played for Romford 1962. On retiring from football he first ran a sports shop in Southgate before moving into the hardware and DIY business with shops in Dagenham and then Ilford.

WILMOT, Rhys James   **1977-89**
Goalkeeper   6ft 1in. 12st.
Born: Newport, Gwent, 21 Feb 1962.
School: Chepstow Junior.
Jnr football: Rogiet Juniors. Joined ARSENAL: 1977 (schoolboy), 5 Jul 1978 (apprentice), 31 Jan 1980 (professional). First app: South East Counties League (a) 19 Nov 1977. First snr app: Snr fdly v Kent FA (at Gillingham) 8 Apr 1981. Milk Cup v Aston Villa (a) 22 Jan 1986. Final snr app: League v Norwich City (h) 9 May 1987. On tour (sub) v Bermuda 27 Jan 1989. Final app: Football Combination v West Ham United (h) 11 Feb 1989. Transferred to Plymouth Argyle (£100,000) 14 Jul 1989.
ARSENAL Record: League 8; Football League Cup 1; Football Combination 179; South East Counties League 5/1; FA Youth Cup 5; Other jnr comp: 5; Friendlies 68/18. In addition played 2 Football Combination matches 1981-2, later removed from records and made 1 app for combined Arsenal/Luton Town on tour, Cyprus 1986-7.
Honours: Wales Schoolboy and Youth international. Football Combination champions

1983-4. South East Counties League Cup winners 1979-80. President's Cup winners 1980-81. 6 Wales Under-21 caps 1981-3.
Had spells on loan from Arsenal to Hereford United (Mar-May 1983 — 9 apps), Orient (1984-5 — 46 apps), Swansea City (Aug-Nov 1988) and Plymouth Argyle (Feb-May 1989).

WILSON, Alexander   **1933-41**
Goalkeeper   5ft 10½in. 11st 2lb.
Born: Wishaw, Lanark, Scotland, 1909. Died: Boston, America, Apr 1971.
Jnr football: Overton Athletic. Previous Club: Greenock Morton (1927-8). Joined ARSENAL: 27 May 1933 from Greenock Morton. First app: London Combination v Swansea Town (a) 26 Aug 1933. First snr app: FA Cup v Crystal Palace (h) 27 Jan 1934. Final app: League v Birmingham (a) 8 Apr 1939. South Regional League (wartime) v Crystal Palace (h) 30 Nov 1940. Transferred to St Mirren 14 Jan 1941.
ARSENAL Record: League 82; FA Cup 7; FA Charity Shield 1; Other snr comp: 1; Football Combination 139; London FA Challenge Cup 14; Southern League 2; London Midweek League 2; Friendlies 11. In addition made 9 apps during wartime.
Honours: FA Cup winners 1936. FA Charity Shield runners-up 1935-6. London Combination champions 1933-4, 1934-5, 1936-7, 1937-8, 1938-9. London FA Challenge Cup winners 1933-4, 1935-6, runners-up 1936-7. Norwich Hospital Cup winners 1934-5.
Worked as a lathe operator in a factory before taking up football. Won club honours with Greenock Morton. On retiring from playing qualified as a physiotherapist and took up an appointment with Kent County Cricket Club (Mar 1939). Had spells as trainer/physio with both Brighton & Hove Albion, Worthing, Birmingham, Sunderland and Blackpool (1956-64). Went to America in 1967 as trainer/physiotherapist to Boston Beacons (NASL) and when the Soccer League folded, stayed on in Boston as a physiotherapist until his death in 1971.

WILSON Jack   **1896-97**
Left-back/outside-right
First app: Jnr fdly v 15th Co Royal Artillery (h) 3 Sep 1896. First first-class app: FA Cup v Leyton (h) 12 Dec 1896 (only first-class app). Final app: Jnr fdly v Old St Stephens (h) 24 Apr 1897.
ARSENAL Record: FA Cup 1; Kent League 9 (3 gls); Friendlies 6 (3 gls).
Honours: Kent League champions 1896-7.
Later played for Watford and became Watford trainer.

WILSON, Oliver   **1912-13**
Goalkeeper
Jnr football: Leyton. Joined ARSENAL: 13 Sep 1912 from Leyton. First app: South Eastern League v West Ham United (a) 14 Sep 1912. First snr app: London FA Challenge Cup v Clapton Orient (a) 23 Sep 1912. Final app: League v Middlesbrough (h) 26 Apr 1913 (only League app). ARSENAL Record: League 1; London FA Challenge Cup 1; South Eastern League 21; Friendlies 2.

WILSON, Robert Primrose   **1963-74**
Goalkeeper   6ft. 12st 12lb.
Born: Chesterfield, 30 Oct 1941.
School: Old Hall Primary; Tapton House Grammar; Chesterfield Grammar.
Jnr football: Loughborough College. Previous Club: Wolverhampton Wanderers (amateur). Joined ARSENAL: 16 Jul 1963 (amateur) from Wolverhampton Wanderers (£5,500), 31 Mar 1964 (professional). First app: On tour (sub) v Enschede

(Holland) 14 Aug 1963. League v Nottingham Forest (h) 26 Oct 1963. Final app: League v Queen's Park Rangers (h) 30 Apr 1974. Retired at end of 1973-4 season. Re-signed for 1977-8 to help in an injury crisis. (Final app: Football Combination v Fulham (h) 4 Apr 1978).
ARSENAL Record: League 234; FA Cup 32; Football League Cup 18; European comp: 24; Other snr comp: 1; Football Combination 103; London FA Challenge Cup 9; Metropolitan League 36; Friendlies 67/8. In addition made 4 Football Combination apps 1977-8 when called out of retirement.
Honours: Played for Chesterfield and for Derbyshire schoolboys. England Schoolboy international. Division One champions 1970-71. FA Cup winners 1971. Football League runners-up 1968-9. European Fairs Cup winners 1969-70. Metropolitan League Challenge Cup winners 1965-6. Arsenal Player of the Year 1971. 2 full Scotland caps 1971 (parentage qualification).
Trained as a PE Teacher at Loughborough College. At the start of his football career he also had appointments as a teacher at Rutherford school, Paddington and Holloway Comprehensive school. Missed the 1972 FA Cup Final for Arsenal due to injury. On retirement in 1974 became a TV commentator and presenter with the BBC.

WINSHIP, Thomas   **1910-13 & 1913-15**
Outside-left   5ft 4in. 10st 4lb.
Born: Byker, Newcastle upon Tyne, c.1890.
Jnr football: Wallsend Park Villa. Joined ARSENAL: 30 Nov 1910 from Wallsend Park Villa. First app: South Eastern League v Coventry City (h) 3 Dec 1910. First snr app: League v Manchester United (a) 26 Dec 1910. Final snr app: League v Bristol City (a) 3 Apr 1915. Final app: League (Res) v Crystal Palace (h) 22 Apr 1915. Transferred to Fulham 14 Mar 1913. Re-signed 30 Aug 1913 from Fulham.
ARSENAL Record: League 55 (7 gls); FA Cup 1; London FA Challenge Cup 3 (2 gls); Other snr comp: 2; South Eastern League 52 (8 gls); London League (Res) 9 (1 gl); Other jnr comp: 1; Friendlies 10 (13 gls).
Honours: Norwich Hospital Cup winners 1913-14.
Arsenal lost all contact with the player during the war, he having returned to the North-East, where he played for Darlington 1919-26 and won club honours with them.

WINTERBURN, Nigel 1987-
Left-back 5ft 10in. 10st 7lb.
Born: Nuneaton, 11 Dec 1963.
Previous Clubs: Birmingham City (1981), Oxford United (1983), Wimbledon (Aug 1983). Joined ARSENAL: 26 May 1987 from Wimbledon for £350,000. First app: Jnr fdly v Letchworth (a) 21 Jul 1987. First snr app: Snr fdly (sub) v Morton (a) 25 Jul 1987. League (sub) v Southampton (h) 21 Nov 1987.
ARSENAL Record: League 169/1 (4 gls); FA Cup 17; Football League Cup 19 (2 gls); European comp: 4; FA Charity Shield 2; Other snr comp: 13 (1 gl); Football Combination 16; Friendlies 32/6 (2 gls).
Honours: Division One champions 1988-9, 1990-91. Football League Cup runners-up 1987-8. FA Charity Shield runners-up 1989-90, medal 1991-2. Mercantile Credit Centenary Trophy winners 1988-9. 3 England 'B' caps 1990, 1 full cap 1990.
Played for Nuneaton Schoolboys. Won club, Youth and Under-21 honours with Wimbledon.

WOLFE, George 1900-03
Centre-half 5ft 11in. 12st.
Born: East London.
School: Hull Street, Plumstead.
Jnr football: Northfleet, Folkestone. Joined ARSENAL: 30 Mar 1900 from Folkestone. First app: Jnr fdly v Bristol City (Res) (h) 31 Mar 1900. First snr app: Snr fdly v Aston Villa (h) 1 Oct 1900. League v Burslem Port Vale (h) 8 Dec 1900. Final snr app: League v Burnley (h) 27 Dec 1902. Southern Professional Charity Cup v Millwall Athletic (h) 9 Feb 1903. Final app: Chatham Charity Cup v Sheppey United (h) 15 Apr 1903.
ARSENAL Record: League 5; London League 6; Other snr comp: 1; Kent League 32 (3 gls); London League (Res) 45 (2 gls); Other jnr comp: 2; Friendlies 25 (5 gls).
Honours: West Kent League champions 1900-01, 1901-02, 1902-03. London League (Res) champions 1901-02. Captain of Arsenal Reserves.
Later played for Swindon Town (1903) and Nottingham Forest (1905).

WOOD, George 1980-83
Goalkeeper 6ft 3in. 14st.
Born: Douglas, Lanarkshire, 26 Sep 1952.
Previous Clubs: East Stirlingshire (1970), Blackpool (Jan 1972), Everton (Aug 1977). Joined ARSENAL: 14 Aug 1980 from Everton for £150,000. First app: Football Combination v Leicester City (a) 20 Aug 1980. First snr app: League v Middlesbrough (a) 20 Sep 1980. Final app: League v Norwich City (a) 20 Apr 1983. Snr fdly (sub) v Gillingham (a) 17 May 1983. Transferred to Crystal Palace (free transfer) 20 May 1983.
ARSENAL Record: League 60; FA Cup 1; Football League Cup 7; European comp: 2; Football Combination 53; Friendlies 6/4. In addition played 1 Football Combination match 1981-2, later removed from records.
Honours: 1 full Scotland cap 1982.
Was an apprentice stonemason before taking up football. Won international honours with Everton. A keen ornithologist. After Crystal Palace played for Cardiff City (Jan 1988), Blackpool (loan) and Hereford United.

WOOD 1892
Goalkeeper
First app: Snr fdly v Preston North End (h) 22 Mar 1892. First first-class app: FA Cup (Q) v City Ramblers (h) 29 Oct 1892 (only first-class app). Final app: Snr fdly v Sunderland (h) 14 Nov 1892.
ARSENAL Record: FA Cup (Q) 1. In addition

made 5 senior apps for Royal Arsenal during 1891-2 and 1892-3.
A Corporal in the 2nd Scots Guards.

WOODCOCK, Anthony Stewart 1982-86
Striker 5ft 10in. 11st.
Born: Eastwood, Nottingham, 6 Dec 1955.
Jnr football: Priory Celtic (Eastwood). Previous Club: Nottingham Forest (Aug 1972-apprentice), 1.FC Cologne (Nov 1979). Joined ARSENAL: 8 Jun 1982 from 1.FC Cologne for £500,000. First app: On tour v Feyenoord (Holland) 6 Aug 1982. League v Stoke City (a) 28 Aug 1982. Final app: League v Oxford United (a) 5 May 1986. Transferred to 1.FC Cologne (£140,000) Jul 1986.
ARSENAL Record: League 129/2 (56 gls); FA Cup 13/1 (7 gls); Football League Cup 20/2 (5 gls); European comp: 2; Football Combination 8 (9 gls); Friendlies 22/3 (6 gls).

Honours: Arsenal Player of the Year 1983. 18 full England caps (9 gls) 1982-6.
Had spells on loan to Lincoln City (1975-6) and Doncaster Rovers (1976-7) whilst a Nottingham Forest player. Won domestic and European club, Under-21 and full international honours with Nottingham Forest. Won 'B' and full international honours with Cologne. Scored five goals for Arsenal at Aston Villa, Oct 1983. Moved from Cologne to Fortuna (Jun 1988).

WOODS, Henry 1923-26
Centre-forward 5ft 9in. 11st 6lb.
Born: St Helens, Lancashire.
School: Holy Trinity, St Helens.
Jnr football: Local. Previous Clubs: Norwich City (1912-13); South Shields Athletic (1919); Newcastle United (Jan 1923). Joined ARSENAL: 3 Jul 1923 from Newcastle United. First app: League v Newcastle United (h) 25 Aug 1923. Final snr app: FA Cup v Wolverhampton Wanderers (h) 13 Jan 1926. Final app: London Combination v Chelsea (a) 29 Apr 1926. Transferred to Luton Town 6 Aug 1926.
ARSENAL Record: League 70 (21 gls); FA Cup 5 (1 gl); London FA Challenge Cup 8 (4 gls); Football Combination 34 (8 gls); Friendlies 10 (3 gls).
Honours: London FA Challenge Cup winners 1923-4, runners-up 1925-6.
A glass worker by trade. Served in the Tank Corps in France during the war. Transferred from Luton Town to North Shields (1930-31).

WOODWARD, John 1966-71
Half-back 5ft 10in. 10st 2lb.
Born: Glasgow, 10 Jan 1949.
Jnr football: Possilpark YMCA (Glasgow). Joined ARSENAL: 10 Jan 1966 from Possilpark. First app: Southern Junior Floodlit Cup v Charlton Athletic (h) 11 Jan 1966. First snr app: Football League Cup v West Ham United (h) 5 Oct 1966. Final snr app: League v Sheffield Wednesday (a) 13 May 1967. On tour (sub) v Japan XI (Japan) 29 May 1968. Final app: Football Combination v West Ham United (a) 7 May 1971. Transferred to York City (free transfer) 1 Jul 1971.
ARSENAL Record: League 2/1; Football League Cup 1; Football Combination 147/1 (13 gls); London FA Challenge Cup 10; Metropolitan League 17 (1 gl); South East Counties League 9; FA Youth Cup 10 (1 gl); Other jnr comp: 8 (1 gl); Friendlies 51/2 (2 gls).
Honours: Football Combination champions 1968-9, 1969-70. Football Combination Cup winners 1967-8, 1969-70. FA Youth Cup winners 1965-6. Southern Junior Floodlit Cup winners 1965-6. South East Counties League Cup runners-up 1965-6. 2 Scotland Youth caps 1967.
Member of Scotland tour party (summer 1967) to the Far East, Australasia and Canada. Was given a free transfer by Arsenal in May 1970 but was taken on again in Aug 1970 and played one more season.

WORRALL, Arthur 1894
Centre-forward
Previous Clubs: Wolverhampton Wanderers; Burton Swifts. Joined ARSENAL: 9 Jan 1894 from Burton Swifts. First app: Snr fdly v Accrington (h) 13 Jan 1894. League v Lincoln City (a) 3 Feb 1894. Final app: League v Burton Swifts (h) 14 Apr 1894. Snr fdly v Stoke (h) 28 Apr 1894. Transferred: summer 1894 to Nelson.
ARSENAL Record: League 4 (1 gl); Friendlies 18 (13 gls).

WRIGHT, Ian Edward 1991-
Striker 5ft 11in. 11st 6lb.
Born: Woolwich, South London, 3 Nov 1963.
Jnr football: Ten-Em-Bee (Sunday League), Greenwich Borough. Previous Club: Crystal Palace (Aug 1985). Joined ARSENAL: 23 Sep 1991 from Crystal Palace for £2,500,000 (Arsenal

105

record). First app: Football League Cup v Leicester City (a) 25 Sep 1991.
ARSENAL Record: League 30 (24 gls); Football League Cup 3 (2 gls); Football Combination 3 (5 gls); Friendlies 2 (1 gl).
Honours: 1 England 'B' cap 1992.
Was a labourer and plasterer before becoming a footballer. Won domestic and international honours with Crystal Palace. Was Division One leading goalscorer 1991-2.

YOUNG, Allan Robert   **1956-61**
Centre-half   6ft. 11st 2lb.
Born: Edmonton, London, 20 Jan 1941.
Jnr football: Barnet Juniors. Joined ARSENAL: Nov 1956 (amateur), 11 Apr 1959 (professional). First app: London Minor Challenge Cup v Bexleyheath (a) 24 Nov 1956. First snr app: League v Sheffield Wednesday (h) 26 Dec 1960. Final snr app: League v Cardiff City (h) 11 Feb 1961. Final app: Football Combination v Bristol Rovers (a) 4 Nov 1961. Transferred to Chelsea (£6,000) 10 Nov 1961.
ARSENAL Record: League 4; Football Combination 35; South East Counties League 27; Metropolitan League 66 (2 gls); FA Youth Cup 13; Other jnr comp: 5; Friendlies 20.
Honours: Metropolitan League champions 1958-9, 1960-61. Southern Junior Floodlit Cup runners-up 1957-8.
Moved from Chelsea to Torquay United (Jan 1969).

YOUNG, Andrew   **1922-27**
Centre-forward/half-back   5ft 7½in. 10st 10lb.
Born: Darlington, Sep 1896.
Jnr football: Blyth Spartans. Previous Club: Aston Villa (1919). Joined ARSENAL: 16 Mar 1922 from Aston Villa. First app: League v Liverpool (h) 22 Mar 1922. Final snr app: League v Newcastle United (a) 6 Apr 1927. Final app: London Combination v Brentford (h) 7 May 1927. Transferred to Bournemouth & Boscombe Athletic 15 Jun 1927.
ARSENAL Record: League 68 (9 gls); FA Cup 3; London FA Challenge Cup 7 (7 gls); Other snr comp: 1; Football Combination 102 (13 gls); Friendlies 26 (6 gls).
Honours: London Combination champions 1922-3, 1926-7. London FA Challenge Cup winners 1923-4.
Converted to half-back in 1923 and played mainly in that position for the remainder of his career at Arsenal.

YOUNG, William David   **1977-81**
Central-defender   6ft 3in. 13st 12lb.
Born: Edinburgh, 25 Nov 1951.
School: Pencaitland Primary, Edinburgh; Tranent Secondary, Edinburgh.
Jnr football: Seton Athletic. Previous Clubs: Aberdeen (1969), Tottenham Hotspur (Sep 1975). Joined ARSENAL: 2 Mar 1977 from Tottenham Hotspur for £80,000. First app: League v Ipswich Town (h) 5 Mar 1977. Final snr app: Football League Cup v Sheffield United (h) 27 Oct 1981. Final app: Football Combination v West Ham United (h) 5 Dec 1981. Transferred to Nottingham Forest (£175,000) 9 Dec 1981.
ARSENAL Record: League 170 (11 gls); FA Cup 28 (3 gls); Football League Cup 20 (1 gl); FA Charity Shield 0/1; European comp: 18 (4 gls);

Football Combination 10(2 gls); Friendlies 30/1 (1 gl).
Honours: FA Cup winners 1979, runners-up 1978, 1980. European Cup-winners' Cup runners-up 1979-80. FA Charity Shield runners-up 1979-80.
Won Under-23 honours with Aberdeen. After Nottingham Forest played for Norwich City (Aug 1983), Brighton & Hove Albion (loan) and Darlington (1984-5). Left football Nov 1984 to run an equestrian centre at Newark.

Arsenal's 1936 FA Cup-winning team. Back row (left to right): Copping, Male, Crayston, Wilson, Roberts, Drake, Hapgood. Front row: George Allison (manager), Hulme, Bowden, James, Bastin, Tom Whittaker (trainer).

George Eastham in action on his debut for Arsenal, against Leicester City in November 1960.

Matches to Remember....

Match to Remember 1   2 September 1893

Woolwich Arsenal 2   Newcastle United 2

ARSENAL'S first appearance as a League club took place at the Manor Ground, Plumstead. Woolwich Arsenal and their opponents that day, Newcastle United, were both newly-elected members of a Second Division which had increased its membership from 12 to 15 that season. Newcastle fielded a strong team, whereas the home side depended on the side which had done duty the previous year under the name of Royal Arsenal.

On a bright afternoon Joe Powell, captaining the Gunners for the first time, won the toss and Arsenal had to wait only ten minutes for their first goal in League football. After a brisk opening, a neat piece of passing by Elliott and Booth set up a chance for Shaw who shot Arsenal ahead.

Undaunted, the Tynesiders pressed forward and as half-time approached, the Reds were on the defensive. Powell, Buist and Howat put in some sterling work and Williams made two good saves to deny Newcastle the equaliser they probably deserved.

Barely three minutes into the second half, Booth made a brilliant run down the wing and centred for Elliott to score Arsenal's second goal with an unstoppable shot which went in off the underside of the crossbar.

Arsenal, with their substantial lead, relaxed a little and play became scrappy before Newcastle settled down and began to force their way back. With less than 15 minutes remaining, Crate pulled a goal back for the Tynesiders and five minutes later, an Arsenal defender handled near his own goal and from the resultant free-kick Sorley headed an equaliser. That left both teams battling for the winner but the draw was considered a fair result.

Woolwich Arsenal: Williams; Powell, Jeffrey, Devine, Buist, Howat, Gemmell, Henderson, Shaw, Elliott, Booth.
Newcastle United: Ramsay; Jeffrey, Miller, Crielly, Graham, McKane, Bowman, Crate, Thompson, Sorley, Wallace.

Attendance: 10,000   *Referee: T.Stevenson (Birmingham)*

In addition to the London Football Combination, Arsenal Reserves have also competed in the Kent League, West Kent League, London League and the South Eastern League. The Juniors have competed in the London Mid-week League, Southern League, Eastern Counties League, Metropolitan League and the South East Counties League.

Arsenal's first set of red shirts were presented to the club by Nottingham Forest, for whom two or three founder members had previously played. In 1895 Arsenal briefly adopted club colours of red and light blue vertically striped shirts, but the idea was not pursued. (See Jenkyns and Storer — Arsenal Who's Who).

Long-serving Woolwich Arsenal half-back John Dick won his only major honour with the club when they were promoted to the First Division in 1904. Dick missed only one game during Arsenal's first season in the top flight.

Match to Remember 2   3 September 1904

Newcastle United 3   Woolwich Arsenal 0

FOR their first-ever game in Division One, Arsenal were again matched against Newcastle United, this time at St James' Park. The Gunners, who had won promotion one point behind Second Division champions, Preston, faced a Newcastle side already First Division veterans. The Tynesiders had taken their place in the top flight in 1898.

Newcastle introduced Irish international full-back Bill McCracken, who later became famous for his manipulation of the offside trap. Rutherford and Templeton, the Magpies' wingers, were both to serve Arsenal later, although not at the same time. The Gunners, under new manager Phil Kelso, had added Gray, Buchan, Bigden, Hunter and Satterthwaite to their promotion-winning side.

Although Newcastle won the match by the comfortable margin of three goals, Arsenal played well in the first half and for some time the result looked like being much closer. Indeed, if the Gunners had capitalised on their opportunities in the opening stages, then United would have been looking to draw level rather than extend their lead.

Alas, the Londoners seemed to have exhausted themselves by their vigorous start and in the end, Newcastle were distinctly their superiors, playing surprisingly good football for the opening match of the season.

The Tynesiders' first success came direct from a corner by Jackie Rutherford and they led at half-time by that single goal. In the second half, Ronald Orr scored after a free-kick by Templeton and it was Orr who grabbed Newcastle's third. United did not over-exert themselves in the second half but still ran out easy winners.

For Arsenal it was a season of consolidation in the top flight and they finished in tenth position. Newcastle United, meanwhile, went on to become League Champions for the first time in their history.

Newcastle United: Watts; McCracken, McCombie, Gardner, Aitken, Carr, Rutherford, Howie, Appleyard, Orr, Templeton.
Woolwich Arsenal: Ashcroft; Gray, Jackson, Dick, Buchan, Bigden, Briercliffe, Coleman, Gooing, Hunter, Satterthwaite.

Attendance: 25,000   *Referee: J.H.Brodie*

Woolwich Arsenal 2   Leicester Fosse 1

WOOLWICH Arsenal began their second spell in Division Two at a new ground and Leicester Fosse had the distinction of being the first League visitors to Highbury. The Gunners had dropped out of Division One after finishing bottom, five points adrift of also relegated Notts County. Leicester had ended the previous season 15th in Division Two.

The Arsenal playing staff which had served the club at Plumstead was supplemented by the signings of Lievesley and Hardinge from Sheffield United and Jobey from Newcastle United as the Gunners set about trying to regain their First Division place.

Despite Arsenal's relegation and the move across London, a large crowd submitted cheerfully to the discomforts of a Highbury ground which was still incomplete. The Gunners rewarded their supporters with a 2-1 win, although the victory was marred by an injury to George Jobey.

Arsenal's new centre-forward had scored the equalising goal but, midway through the second half, he received a kick in the middle of the back. The injury looked serious and Jobey was carried off on a stretcher and attended by ambulance men and a doctor. Apparently the facilities were so poor in those days that Jobey was transported to his nearby lodgings on a cart borrowed from a local milkman. The injury was certainly bad enough for him to miss the next four matches.

The game itself was a spirited, well-contested affair and although they did most of the early attacking, Arsenal were perhaps a trifle lucky to be on level terms at the end of the first half. The Fosse, showing better 'combination play', scored after 20 minutes, Benfield beating Lievesley with an excellent shot following a move by Douglas and Mills. The equaliser came on the stroke of half-time, Jobey heading home from a well-directed corner-kick by Winship.

In the second half, with the left-wing coming more into the picture, Arsenal played much better football and held their opponents, even when they were down to ten men. The winner came with about 12 minutes to go. There seemed no danger when a Fosse defender handled just inside his penalty area and Devine, to the delight of the crowd, made no mistake with the spot kick.

Arsenal maintained that form for much of the season and almost returned to Division One at the first attempt. Ultimately the issue was decided on goal-average and the Gunners had to be content with third place, four points behind champions Notts County and on the same number of points as runners-up Bradford.

Woolwich Arsenal: Lievesley; Shaw, Fidler, Grant, Sands, McKinnon, Greenaway, Hardinge, Jobey, Devine, Winship.
Leicester Fosse: R.G.Brebner; Clay, Currie, D.S.McWhirter, Harrold, Burton, Douglas, Mills, Sparrow, Benfield, Waterall.

Attendance: 20,000   *Referee: J.H.Pearson*

Woolwich Arsenal's new signing George Jobey scored Arsenal's first League goal at Highbury and was then carried off injured and went home in a milkcart. Jobey later made his name as manager of Derby County's fine team of the 1930s. During World War Two he was found guilty of making illegal payments to players and was suspended sine die. The suspension was lifted in 1945 and Jobey managed Mansfield Town for a spell from 1952 before being sacked for 'lack of interest'. He died in Derby in May 1962, aged 76.

Goalmouth action at Wembley in 1927 when Arsenal's first FA Cup Final ended in defeat.

Match to Remember 4   23 April 1927

Arsenal 0   Cardiff City 1

THIS was Arsenal's first FA Cup Final appearance but for their opponents it was the second Final in three years. Indeed, Cardiff City were enjoying the most successful period in their history and three years earlier had been League Championship runners-up on goal-average. In contrast, Arsenal were just beginning to reap the benefits of Herbert Chapman's management and were aiming for their first major honour.

In truth, the Welsh side gained little advantage from their previous Wembley appearance because only four of their 1925 Cup Final team were on duty two years later. Arsenal were forced to make a late change in their normal line-up, Andy Kennedy replacing the injured Horace Cope at left-back.

Although the 1927 Final contained a galaxy of international players — Cardiff fielded eight whilst Arsenal boasted five — the game did not produce the exhibition of classical football which one would expect from such a talented array of players.

Joe Hulme, with his lightning dashes along the wing, and Charlie Buchan, the Gunners' skipper, formed an enterprising partnership for Arsenal, whilst City's main strength was their half-back line, ably led by Fred Keenor. Nevertheless it was defences which dominated and there seemed little chance of a goal being scored — until the unexpected happened 15 minutes from time.

Collecting the ball from a throw-in, Ferguson tried a long, low, diagonal shot which Danny Lewis in the Arsenal goal appeared to take comfortably. Lewis, however, had his eyes on the onrushing Cardiff forwards and allowed the ball to spin through his arms and into the net. It was a real tragedy for Lewis, who would be forever remembered for this one unfortunate slip which presented Cardiff with the Cup. It also proved a particularly historic goal, for this was the first and only time that the FA Cup had been won by a team from outside England.

Arsenal: Lewis; Parker, Kennedy, Baker, Butler, John, Hulme, Buchan, Brain, Blyth, Hoar.
Cardiff City: Farquharson; Nelson, Watson, Keenor, Sloan, Hardy, Curtis, Irving, Ferguson, L.Davies, McLachlan.

Attendance: 91,206   *Referee: W.F.Bunnell (Lancashire)*

Leicester City 6   Arsenal 6

ARSENAL and Leicester City created a record for the highest scoring draw in any English first-class game — it has been equalled once since — in an amazing League match at Filbert Street on Easter Monday 1930.

Arsenal, looking towards the FA Cup Final five days later, took the opportunity to rest some first-teamers over this busy holiday programme, although David Jack and Alex James returned to the side, having both missed the previous match.

There was no suggestion of holding something in reserve for the Cup Final, however. The game started at a brisk pace and inside two minutes, Jack got the ball into the net, only to be ruled offside. The Gunners' forwards played some dazzling football and the home defence had an exceptionally busy time. After 21 minutes, Halliday gave Arsenal the lead from a corner but soon it was Leicester's turn to show their paces and they took a 3-1 lead before half-time.

Two of their goals could have been prevented. The first came in 27 minutes when a shot from Adcock was knocked into the air by Lewis. Parker appeared to clear off the line but a goal was awarded. Two minutes later, Lochhead put City in front and three minutes from the interval Adcock scored again, the ball going through Lewis' hands.

Two minutes into the second half, Bastin reduced the lead with a header and in the 58th minute, Halliday scored the first of a five-minute hat-trick, all the goals resulting from brilliant work by Hulme on the wing. Leicester replied with a goal from Hine after 66 minutes but 11 minutes later, Bastin took a pass by Jack and dribbled through to restore Gunners' two-goal lead.

Not to be outdone, City scored again in the 79th minute through Barry, following a centre from the opposite wing and, after 81 minutes, Lochhead completed the scoring after good work by Adcock and Barry. Before the end Wright saved brilliantly from Halliday and James had a shot cleared with the goalkeeper beaten.

Despite his four goals, there was no place for Halliday in the Cup Final side five days later when Arsenal beat Huddersfield Town 2-0 to win the trophy for the first time in their history.

Leicester City: Wright; Black, Brown, Duncan, Harrison, Watson, Adcock, Hine, Chandler, Lochhead, Barry.
Arsenal: Lewis; Parker, Cope, Baker, Haynes, John, Hulme, Jack, Halliday, James, Bastin.
Attendance: 27,241   *Referee: A.Button (Wednesbury)*

An Arsenal team from 1929-30. Back row (left to right): Baker, James, Lewis, Roberts, John. Front row: Hulme, Jack, Halliday, Parker, Jones, Hapgood.

Newcastle United's Allen heads home Richardson's cross for what proved to be the most controversial goal ever scored in an FA Cup Final at Wembley.

Match to Remember 6   23 April 1932
Arsenal 1   Newcastle United 2

ANOTHER of Arsenal's FA Cup Final appearances to be settled by a controversial issue was this great North v South battle. It was a game which produced one of the most famous goals ever scored at Wembley and gave rise to the legend of the 'over the line Final'.

Arsenal's line-up was not finalised until the day of the game. There were fitness doubts about the injured Hulme and James and, whereas Hulme subsequently passed a fitness test, James unfortunately broke down and missed the Wembley showpiece. Bastin moved to inside-left with the versatile Bob John as his wing partner whilst George Male came in at left-half for his first-ever Cup tie.

Arsenal dominated the opening stages as the speedy Hulme proved his fitness. From one of his many crosses, McInroy in the Newcastle goal saved brilliantly from Bastin. Arsenal took the lead after 13 minutes and again Hulme played a prominent part. Receiving the ball from Bastin, his centre this time evaded McInroy and John, closing in from the opposite wing, headed home. Arsenal might have scored again on two occasions before United equalised in the 38th minute with that controversial goal.

A long pass out to the right wing was hooked back into the centre by Richardson for Allen to head home. Afterwards, newspaper photographs seemed to indicate quite clearly that the ball had gone out for a goal-kick before Richardson clipped it back into play.

To a man the Arsenal defence stopped, awaiting the referee's whistle, but Newcastle kept going and the goal was allowed to stand. It was the turning point of the game and the goal spurred Newcastle back into action. Now looking much more dangerous, they deserved to be on level terms.

In the second half Moss was brought more into action and made some brilliant saves. The Arsenal attack, on the other hand, was now less effective and after 72 minutes Newcastle went ahead. Allen took advantage of a slip by Roberts and beat Moss with a fine shot. Arsenal switched their forwards and fought hard for an equaliser. They might have got it but Jack missed a simple chance five minutes from time.

The final whistle came with Newcastle still displaying the better team-work and, although they had obtained a fortunate equaliser, overall the Tynesiders were worthy winners.

Arsenal: Moss; Parker, Hapgood, C.Jones, Roberts, Male, Hulme, Jack, Lambert, Bastin, John.
Newcastle United: McInroy; Nelson, Fairhurst, McKenzie, Davison, Weaver, Boyd, Richardson, Allen, McMenemy, Lang.
Attendance: 92,298   *Referee: W.P.Harper (Stourbridge)*

113

Match to Remember 7   14 January 1933
Walsall 2   Arsenal 0

IN what is still considered to be the greatest giant-killing act in the history of the FA Cup competition, Third Division South club Walsall accomplished a thoroughly deserved victory over Arsenal. who at that time were top of Division One.

Arsenal did have a number of selection problems but this by no means excused the overall performance of a side which still contained five internationals. Hapgood and Hulme were injured and John, Lambert and Coleman were victims of a flu epidemic. Perhaps, for once, Herbert Chapman made a mistake in his choice of replacements: Tommy Black, Charlie Walsh and Billy Warnes had no previous first-team experience and Norman Sidey had made only one senior appearance.

Aided by a narrow ground and muddy pitch, Walsall, lacking the polish of their illustrious opponents, fully held their own almost from start to finish. Arsenal, on the other hand, appeared unable to cope with the Third Division club's physical 'first-time' approach. In the first half Walsall were more dangerous in front of goal and Moss saved well from Alsop and Lee.

Early in the second half it appeared that Arsenal might gain the upper hand. Bastin and Walsh went close and Jack was robbed in front of an open goal when Walsh got in his way. Walsall replied with some adventurous attacking football and after 60 minutes they took a shock lead when Alsop headed in a centre by Lee. Five minutes later Black flagrantly fouled Alsop in the penalty-area and Sheppard converted the spot-kick. The Gunners could do nothing to retrieve the situation in the remaining 25 minutes and the crowd chaired the Walsall heroes off the field at the final whistle.

Retribution by a disappointed Chapman was swift: Black was transferred to Plymouth Argyle within a week, Walsh was sold to Brentford at the end of the month and Warnes moved to Norwich City in the summer. Arsenal, though, recovered from the shock and went on to complete the first of three consecutive League Championships.

Walsall: Cunningham; Bennett, Bird, Reed, Leslie, Salt, Coward, Ball, Alsop, Sheppard, Lee.

Arsenal: Moss, Male, Black, Hill, Roberts, Sidey, Warnes, Jack, Walsh, James, Bastin.

Attendance: 11,150   *Referee: A. Taylor (Lancashire)*

Arsenal group showing six of the team humiliated by Walsall. Back row (left to right): Parker, Jones, Moss, Roberts, John, Black. Front row: Herbert Chapman (manager), Hulme, Jack, Lambert, James, Bastin, Tom Whittaker (trainer).

114

Arsenal's 1935 playing staff. Back row (left to right): Male, Roberts, Crayston, Compton. Second row: George Allison (manager), Bowden, Dunne, Moss, Wilson, Sidey, Kirchen, Tom Whittaker (trainer). Seated: Dougall, Hulme, John, Bastin, James, Hapgood, Hill, Copping, Drake. On ground: Davidson, Rogers, Trim, Beasley.

Match to Remember 8   14 December 1935

Aston Villa 1   Arsenal 7

THIS was the day that Ted Drake set a First Division record with a brilliant display of finishing. Eight shots yielded seven goals for the Arsenal centre-forward and left Aston Villa to contemplate their worst-ever home League defeat.

A capacity crowd had gathered at Villa Park to see another encounter between two of the game's most famous clubs, although at the time both sides were in a strangely quiet period of their history. Arsenal, for once, were not in contention for League honours and Villa were surprisingly languishing at the foot of the table, despite an expensively acquired team which contained six internationals.

For the first half hour, Villa were the better team and yet by half-time they were 3-0 down, thanks to Drake's remarkable finishing powers. His first goal came from a through ball by Beasley after 15 minutes. The second, after 28 minutes, was the masterpiece of the afternoon. Drake took a long pass from Bastin and strode down the centre with both Griffiths and Cummings in pursuit before shooting past Morton from the edge of the penalty-area. Drake completed his hat-trick in the 34th minute with a close range effort after Beasley's shot had rebounded to him.

A minute after the resumption, Drake chased a ball that seemed to be going out of play and surprised everyone by squeezing his shot home between Morton and the post. Four minutes later, Bowden crossed for Drake to score again and after 58 minutes he netted his sixth when the ball rebounded to him off a Villa defender. Villa managed a consolation goal in the 61st minute, through Palethorpe, but in the dying moments Drake scored again, this time from a cross-field pass by Bastin.

It was an astonishing performance, for Drake's seven goals had come from only eight shots at goal — the other hit the woodwork.

Aston Villa: Morton; Blair, Cummings, Massie, Griffiths, Wood, Williams, Astley, Palethorpe, Dix, Houghton.
Arsenal: Wilson; Male, Hapgood, Crayston, Roberts, Copping, Rogers, Bowden, Drake, Bastin, Beasley.

Attendance: 58,469   *Referee: J.M. Wiltshire (Sherborne)*

Newcastle United 1   Arsenal 0

WEMBLEY Stadium has seldom seen a more heroic display than Arsenal's brave fight in the 1952 FA Cup Final. Reduced to ten men after 20 minutes, following an injury to Walley Barnes, the Gunners gave a defiant performance against formidable opponents and only the narrowest of margins separated the sides at the end.

Arsenal were challenging for the League and Cup double right up to the last Saturday of the season and they were denied only by a fixture congestion and a spate of injuries. The Championship eluded them after two defeats in the last two games, leaving the FA Cup as the only possible reward for a most enterprising season.

Never have Arsenal undertaken so important a match under so many difficulties. No fewer than seven first-teamers were injured in the weeks leading up to the end of the season and on Cup Final day itself, the Gunners took the field with Ray Daniel carrying a light plastic covering on a broken forearm; Jimmy Logie had been confined to hospital with blood poisoning until three days before the match and his thigh was heavily strapped; and Doug Lishman had also been in hospital and was barely fit.

Yet Arsenal took charge from the start, pacing the game to their liking. After three minutes, Lishman went close with an overhead shot and shortly afterwards Logie shot wide when clean through. After 20 minutes, however, the injury jinx struck again when Barnes badly twisted his knee as his studs stuck in the turf. After attempting to continue, he left the field for good and Roper switched to right-back.

Inspired by skipper Joe Mercer, the Gunners drew on tremendous resources of energy to perform one of the greatest rearguard actions ever seen at Wembley. Although Lionel Smith had to head off the goal-line with Swindin beaten, Arsenal generally contained Newcastle and never allowed them to gain the initiative. The depleted team did not settle just for survival and with 11 minutes to go, Cox swung over a corner and Lishman beat Simpson with a header which ran along the crossbar and over the top.

Five minutes later their gallant stand was over. With Roper lying injured on the ground, play continued and Mitchell crossed the ball for George Robledo to send in a header which struck the inside of a post and rolled over the line. That proved too much for Arsenal's aching limbs and there could be no fight-back in the dying minutes.

Newcastle United: Simpson; Cowell, McMichael, Harvey, Brennan, E.Robledo, Walker, Foulkes, Milburn, G.Robledo, Mitchell.

Arsenal: Swindin; Barnes, L.Smith, Forbes, Daniel, Mercer, Cox, Logie, Holton, Lishman, Roper.

Attendance: 100,000   *Referee: A.E.Ellis (Halifax)*

George Robledo's header strikes the inside of an Arsenal post and rolls over the line.

Goalmouth action from the 1952 FA Cup Final. Above: George Swindin guards his net as the ball goes just over the bar. Below: Newcastle's Jackie Milburn is beaten in the air.

Match to Remember 10   25 December 1952

Bolton Wanderers 4   Arsenal 6

BACK in the 1950s, Bolton Wanderers could count themselves as one of the leading sides in the country. Led by the incomparable Nat Lofthouse, they maintained a healthy First Division place and on Christmas Day 1952 the Trotters and Arsenal provided a large crowd at Burnden Park with a real festive treat.

After only two minutes, Bolton took the lead with an opportunist goal scored by Moir. Their advantage was shortlived, however, and Milton soon put Arsenal back on level terms. Wanderers still enjoyed territorial advantage but four minutes from half-time the Gunners took an unexpected lead when Holton converted a fine centre from Roper.

Within five minutes of the restart, Arsenal had forged further ahead. After 47 minutes Logie made it 3-1 and three minutes later, Roper increased the Gunners' lead to three goals. Arsenal looked set for a comfortable victory but back came the home side and Moir reduced the arrears. Arsenal regained their three-goal advantage from a penalty kick converted by Daniel and the issue again seemed settled in the 82nd minute when Holton made it 6-2 with another fine goal.

Bolton were still not out of the reckoning and two goals in five minutes, both scored by Lofthouse, put them back in the game. Even then the excitement was not over and two minutes from the end, Bolton were awarded a penalty. Langton took the kick but Kelsey made a great save to bring a highly entertaining game to a close.

Arsenal went on to win the League Championship that season whilst Bolton reached Wembley where they lost the FA Cup to Blackpool in the so-called 'Matthews Final'.

Bolton Wanderers: Hanson; Ball, Higgins, Wheeler, Barrass, Neill, Holden, Moir, Lofthouse, Webster, Langton.
Arsenal: Kelsey; Wade, L.Smith, Shaw, Daniel, Mercer, Milton, Logie, Holton, Lishman, Roper.

Attendance: 47,344   *Referee: T.W.Glendenning (Sunderland)*

Arsenal 3   Burnley 2

OVER 51,000 spectators poured into Highbury on the eve of the 1953 FA Cup Final, knowing that only victory for Arsenal would be enough to bring the Football League Championship back to North London.

During the final weeks of the season, the Gunners had battled it out with Preston North End and on the penultimate Saturday of the campaign, Preston beat Arsenal 2-0 at Deepdale, then won their final game to top the table. The Lancashire club embarked on an end-of-season tour on the Continent, leaving the Gunners needing victory in their last match to win the title.

Burnley, in the top six in Division One, started in determined fashion and after only eight minutes they took a shock lead when a shot by Stephenson was deflected past Swindin. The crowd had little time to dwell on Arsenal's misfortune, however, and a minute later Alex Forbes levelled the scores with a tremendous shot.

With a delightful display of attacking football, Arsenal now took command and in the 13th minute they went ahead. Lishman, dashing into an open space to meet a cross by Roper, shot past Thompson. In the 26th minute, Jimmy Logie was on hand to round off a glorious move and Arsenal went in at half-time with a 3-1 lead.

They held that lead until the 74th minute when Elliott pulled a goal back for Burnley and threw the game wide open again. In a tense and exciting final 15 minutes, Burnley laid seige to the Arsenal goal in a desperate search for an equaliser. The Gunners, though, remained calm and with the aid of some fine goalkeeping by Swindin held out to become Champions for a record seventh time.

The issue was so close. Arsenal's goal-average was 1.516 against Preston's 1.417 — the Championship had been won by 0.099 of a goal.

Arsenal: Swindin; Wade, L.Smith, Forbes, Daniel, Mercer, Roper, Logie, Goring, Lishman, Marden.
Burnley: Thompson; Aird, Winton, Adamson, Cummings, Brown, Stephenson, McIlroy, Holden, Shannon, Elliott.

Attendance: 51,586   *Referee: R.F.Leafe (Nottingham)*

George Swindin gave a great display of goal-keeping in the closing stages.

119

СОСТАВЫ КОМАНД

«АРСЕНАЛ» (Англия)

Тренер команды — Т. Уиттекер.

Капитан команды — Д. Лоджи.

```
                    1
                 Д. Келси

           2                3
        У. Бернс         Д. Вейд
    4              5               6
Г. Горинг       У. Диксон      А. Форбс
        Д. Лоджи      Д. Лишмен
    7           8          9    10      11
Д. Тэпскотт     Т. Лаутон       Д. Роупер


В. Рыжкин      А. Мамедов      В. Шабров
    11            10         9      8       7
        С. Сальников      В. Ильин
        В. Савдунин      Е. Байков
            6                5
Б. Кузнецов    К. Крижевский    А. Родионов
    4              3                2

                    Л. Яшин
                      1
```

Капитан команды — К. Крижевский.
Тренер команды — М. Якушин.

«ДИНАМО» (Москва)

Состязание судит судья международной категории М. Мацко (Чехословакия).
Судьи на линии: судья международной категории Ю. Алхо (Финляндия) и судья международной категории И. Карас (Чехословакия).
О возможных изменениях в составах команд слушайте по радио.

Центральный Стадион „Динамо"

ФУТБОЛ

5 октября
„АРСЕНАЛ" — „ДИНАМО"
(ЛОНДОН)   (МОСКВА)
НАЧАЛО ИГРЫ в 19 час.

Физкультура и Спорт 1954

Dinamo Moscow 5　Arsenal 0

ARSENAL became the first Football League club to play in Russia when they accepted on invitation for a mid-season friendly match in Moscow. It was an arrangement which did not flatter the Gunners who were soundly beaten by a superior and much faster side.

After fulfilling a League game at Leicester on the Saturday, Arsenal endured an arduous journey by air and, after taking on the best team in the Soviet Union, they had to return immediately for another League match the following Saturday. The game in Russia, however, was of great interest and showed a vast difference in the styles of play between the two teams.

On a heavy pitch Arsenal held their own for the first half-hour but the Russians gradually took command and after 44 minutes they went ahead. Over came a harmless looking centre and Ilyin pivoted and beat Kelsey from 15 yards.

In the second half Dinamo displayed their superior skills and Arsenal, showing signs of tiredness from their long journey, were overrun. After 50 minutes Ilyin scored again with a header from a free kick and ten minutes later the home side could have been 3-0 ahead but Savdunien hit the crossbar with a penalty.

A third goal was inevitable, however, and it came from Ryshkin in the 75th minute. Two minutes later another Russian move ended in an easy goal for Mamedov. The final goal, a minute from the end, summed up Arsenal's miserable trip. Kelsey had a shot from Shabrov covered but a deflection off Dickson took the ball into the opposite corner of the net.

Alhough clearly the inferior team, Arsenal did not enjoy much luck. Most of the referee's decisions went against them and many cases of obstruction by the Russians were ignored.

The week ended on a happy note, though, and the Gunners gained their first away win of the season, at Hillsborough.

Dinamo Moscow: Yashin; Radionov, Kuznetsov, Baikov, Krijievsky, Savdunien, Shabrov, Ilyin, Mamedov, Salnikov, Ryshkin.
Arsenal: Kelsey; Barnes, Wade, Goring, Dickson, Forbes, Tapscott, Logie, Lawton, Lishman, Roper.

Attendance: 90,000　　　　　　　　　*Referee: Martin Matsko (Czechoslovakia)*

Arsenal left-back Joe Wade was a member of the Gunners' defence which found no answer to the Russian threat. Opposite page shows the programme for the historic visit to Moscow.

Match to Remember 13   1 February 1958
Arsenal 4   Manchester United 5

NOT only was this one of the greatest matches ever seen at Highbury, it was also Manchester United's last appearance in England before their magnificent team was destroyed by the Munich air disaster.

This brilliant United side, known as the 'Busby Babes', still showed all the qualities which had clinched the League Championship in each of the two previous seasons. Arsenal, meanwhile, were trying to regain the glories of the early post-war years.

United gave a marvellous first-half performance before a packed stadium and at half-time they led 3-0. Duncan Edwards opened the scoring after ten minutes with a drive from the edge of the penalty-area and, after Harry Gregg had made a fantastic save from a header by Groves in the 33rd minute, Albert Scanlon outpaced the Arsenal defence and crossed for Bobby Charlton to score with the kind of explosive shot which became his trademark. Two minutes before half-time Tommy Taylor slotted home a third.

If United felt that victory was assured with that seemingly invincible lead, Arsenal had other ideas and in a breathtaking second-half spell, lasting less than three minutes, they drew level. In the 58th minute David Herd volleyed home a lob from Bowen; less than two minutes later Groves headed down a cross by Gordon Nutt for Jimmy Bloomfield to score the second; and one minute after that, a low, hard cross by Nutt found Bloomfield who dived full length to head past Gregg.

As the Gunners continued to press forward, United showed their class and responded with two more goals. In the 65th minute, a move by Charlton and Scanlon provided Viollet with an opening which he gratefully accepted; seven minutes later, Tommy Taylor beat Kelsey from an almost impossible angle.

Arsenal were still not finished and in the 77th minute, Tapscott scored their fourth goal. United had to defend desperately for the remainder of the match, but the Gunners could not break through again.

Manchester United had claimed both points, but the honours were shared by all 22 players who had given one of the finest exhibitions of football ever seen at Highbury.

Arsenal: Kelsey; S.Charlton, Evans, Ward, Fotheringham, Bowen, Groves, Tapscott, Herd, Bloomfield, Nutt.
Manchester United: Gregg; Foulkes, Byrne, Colman, Jones, Edwards, Morgans, R.Charlton, Taylor, Viollet, Scanlon.

Attendance: 63,578   *Referee: G.W.Pullen (Bristol)*

Arsenal goalkeeper Jack Kelsey (left) watches the ball go to safety following a clearance by Stan Charlton (on ground). United's Bobby Charlton (right) stares in disbelief as the ball narrowly misses the Gunners' upright.

Vic Groves could have added to his solitary goal but three times he saw his shots hit the Everton woodwork.

Match to Remember 14   6 September 1958

Everton 1   Arsenal 6

GEORGE Swindin's first season as Arsenal manager saw the Gunners make one of their best-ever starts to a League campaign. Despite losing the opening match, at Preston, they headed the First Division after seven games, following a high-scoring spree which brought no less than 25 goals.

Included in that run was a remarkable performance at Goodison Park where a lively Arsenal forward line netted six times and could easily have doubled that score. Twice they had the ball in the Everton net, only for the effort to be ruled offside, Ward had a shot stopped on the goal-line and three times Vic Groves saw his shots strike the crossbar.

Arsenal took the lead after only one minute when Groves scored following a delightful exchange with Clapton and Bloomfield. It was an accurate cross from Clapton which provided David Herd with the Gunners' second goal after 20 minutes.

Everton fought hard but Arsenal's superiority was such that the result never looked in doubt and, just after half-time, Bloomfield put the Gunners 3-0 in front. A few minutes later Herd converted a cross from Nutt and barely ten minutes had elapsed before Herd, taking a pass from Docherty, ran through to complete his hat-trick with an accurate shot just inside the far post. After 70 minutes, Herd scored again, this time from a through-ball by Clapton. Careless defending allowed Temple to score a consolation goal for Everton ten minutes from time.

Arsenal followed up three days later with another 6-1 victory, at home to Bolton, but some mediocre results around December caused the Gunners to lose their lead in Division One and they finished the season in third place behind Wolves and Manchester United.

Everton: O'Neill; Sanders, Griffiths, B.Harris, Jones, Meagan, J.Harris, Temple, Hickson, Fielding, O'Hare.
Arsenal: Kelsey; Wills, Evans, Ward, Dodgin, Docherty, Clapton, Groves, Herd, Bloomfield, Nutt.

Attendance: 40,557   *Referee: G.McCabe (Sheffield)*

123

Match to Remember 15   28 April 1970

Arsenal 3   RSC Anderlecht 0

THE first leg of this European Fairs Cup Final — Arsenal's first European Final — saw the Belgian club, Anderlecht, take a 3-0 lead in Brussels before substitute Ray Kennedy's headed goal in the dying minutes gave the Gunners hope for the return at Highbury.

When two goals from Mulder and one from Devrindt gave the Belgians that almost unassailable lead, even the most die-hard Arsenal fan must have felt that the Gunners' chances of lifting their first European trophy had evaporated. But Kennedy's goal was vital because, on the ruling that away goals would count double in the event of a draw on aggregate, a 2-0 win at Highbury would be enough to give Arsenal overall victory. A goal by the Belgians would, of course, upset those calculations.

For the first 20 minutes at Highbury the Gunners applied the pressure, although Anderlecht caused some heart-stopping moments with menacing counter-attacks. After 26 minutes, Eddie Kelly collected a loose ball on the edge of the penalty-area and fired past the Anderlecht 'keeper to give the Gunners a crucial first goal. One goal from Anderlecht could still alter the whole course of the tie, but half-time arrived with the score still 1-0.

Without taking any chances at the back, Arsenal pushed forward with Radford causing problems in the air and Armstrong prominent on the wing. After 71 minutes Radford headed Arsenal 2-0 ahead on the night following an overlap and centre by McNab on the left. Two minutes later Charlie George sent over a dipping pass and Jon Sammels came racing in to shoot home a third goal. Arsenal did not need technicalities to win the trophy.

Arsenal: Wilson; Storey, McNab, Kelly, McLintock, Simpson, Armstrong, Sammels, Radford, George, Graham.

Anderlecht: Trappeniers; Heylens, Maartens, Nordahl, Velkeneers, Kialunda, Desanghere, Devrindt, Mulder, Van Himst, Puis.

Attendance: 51,612   *Referee: G.Kunze (East Germany)*

Anderlecht goalkeeper Trappeniers punches clear from Eddie Kelly in the European Fairs Cup Final second leg at Highbury.

124

Skipper Frank McLintock (right) and George Armstrong make sure that the drinks are on Arsenal's 19-year-old goalscorer Ray Kennedy after his header clinched the League Championship and the first leg of the double.

Match to Remember 16   3 May 1971

Tottenham Hotspur 0   Arsenal 1

AS THE 1970-71 season drew to a close, Arsenal were still in contention for the League Championship and FA Cup double, a feat last achieved by their North London rivals, Tottenham Hotspur, ten years earlier.

In the First Division, the Gunners were locked at the head of the table with Leeds United and their situation was similar to that which had preceded their last League Championship success in 1952-3. This time, with a marvellous sense of occasion, the final match was against Spurs at White Hart Lane, five days before the Cup Final.

Leeds had completed their programme and, again, mathematical permutations surrounded the issue. Arsenal needed at least a goalless draw to take the title, whilst a Gunners' defeat or a scoring draw at Tottenham would conclude matters in favour of Leeds. Arsenal's first priority, therefore, was to keep their goal intact.

A crowd of over 50,000 packed the ground and the gates were locked more than an hour before the kick-off with an estimated 100,000 left outside.

The match was played in a tremendous atmosphere throughout. Jennings saved brilliantly from George in the opening minute, McLintock saw his shot bounce clear off a defender's body, Radford and Kennedy were always a menace and Graham went close with a header. At the other end, Peters almost scored with a header, Chivers and Neighbour worried the Arsenal defence and Gilzean just failed to connect as the ball flashed across the goalmouth.

Despite all the attacking play, there were very few clear cut chances and a goalless draw seemed the most likely result. In the 87th minute, however, Jennings beat out an effort from Radford and Armstrong returned the ball into the centre for Kennedy to place a header just under the bar.

The goal was a great boost for Arsenal but they still needed to prevent Tottenham from scoring. Spurs threw everything into attack and the final three minutes seemed like a lifetime to the Arsenal fans. But the Gunners held on and at the final whistle, thousands invaded the pitch to congratulate their Arsenal heroes.

Tottenham Hotspur: Jennings; Kinnear, Knowles, Mullery, Collins, Beal, Gilzean(Pearce), Perryman, Chivers, Peters, Neighbour.

Arsenal: Wilson; Rice, McNab, Kelly, McLintock, Simpson, Armstrong, Graham, Radford, Kennedy, George.

Attendance: 51,992   *Referee: K.Howley (Teesside)*

Arsenal 2   Liverpool 1
(after extra-time)

ARSENAL, who had clinched the League Championship five days earlier, now faced Liverpool in the FA Cup Final for the 'second leg' of the coveted double.

The Gunners took a slight gamble with the fitness of Peter Storey in order to field the same team which had seen them through to Wembley. Liverpool were at full strength.

The first 90 minutes of the 1971 FA Cup Final were a highly technical affair with both sides adopting a cautious approach and scoring opportunities few. Kennedy and Armstrong both had chances which might have been put away and Graham went close with two headers, one striking the bar and the other being cleared off the line. Liverpool's best effort came from full-back Lindsay, whose low shot was well saved by Wilson. Both sides used their substitutes — Kelly for Storey midway through the second half and Thompson for Evans a few minutes later. The changes did not alter the pattern of play, however, and extra-time became inevitable.

After only two minutes of the first extra period, Heighway broke away on the left and scored with a shot just inside Wilson's near post. The Arsenal goalkeeper should have got to it but he redeemed himself minutes later with a point-blank save from Hall which kept Arsenal in the game. With four minutes of the first period of extra-time remaining, Arsenal grabbed an unexpected equaliser. Radford hooked the ball over his shoulder into the Liverpool penalty-area and, as it fell, Kelly touched it past Clemence. Graham followed the ball over the line and, although Kelly was credited with the goal, some sources still show Graham as the scorer.

A replay looked likely but with nine minutes remaining, Arsenal scored the historic goal which gave them the double. Radford was again the prime mover, laying the ball off for Charlie George to give Clemence no earthly chance with a tremendous right-foot shot from 20 yards. McLintock received the Cup and a momentous season was over.

Arsenal: Wilson; Rice, McNab, Storey(Kelly), McLintock, Simpson, Armstrong, George, Radford, Kennedy, Graham.

Liverpool: Clemence; Lawler, Lindsay, Smith, Lloyd, Hughes, Callaghan, Evans(Thompson), Toshack, Hall, Heighway.

Attendance: 100,000   *Referee: N.C.H.Burtenshaw (Great Yarmouth)*

The action is blurred but there is no mistaking Charlie George as he hammers home the winning goal in the 1971 FA Cup Final to give Arsenal the double.

126

Brian Talbot scores the Gunners' first goal in the 1979 FA Cup Final.

Match to Remember 18   12 May 1979

Arsenal 3   Manchester United 2

ARSENAL won the FA Cup in 1979 by beating Manchester United in a Final which only really came to life in the last five minutes. United were contesting their third Final at Wembley in four years and the Gunners, suffering the disappointment of having lost to Ipswich Town in the previous FA Cup Final, were determined to make amends.

Arsenal made a promising start and after 12 minutes, following a move by Stapleton and Brady, David Price broke clear on the right and drove in a low cross. Talbot and Sunderland arrived together but it was Talbot who was adjudged to have made contact and put Arsenal ahead. United had more of the play for a time but the Gunners' quick tackling forced them back and Arsenal were always dangerous with counter-attacks. Two minutes before half-time, Brady on the right, slipped past two lunging tackles and sent in a measured cross for Stapleton to pick his spot with a free header.

In the second half, United's possession came to nothing and the Gunners maintained their overall control of the match. Walford was given a taste of the Wembley atmosphere when he replaced Price and it seemed that Arsenal had the Cup securely in their grasp. With four minutes remaining, however, the game was completely transformed. Arsenal failed to clear a free-kick and, following a scramble around their penalty area, McQueen swung a boot and United were back in the match. Two minutes later, McIlroy cut in, rode first one challenge then another and rolled the ball past Jennings for the equaliser.

United were buoyant — they had clawed their way back into the game and with extra-time now imminent and Arsenal a jaded side, they looked the stronger team. But the final act had yet to be played. From the kick-off, Brady kept possession and took the ball deep into United's half before releasing a perfect pass to Rix out on the left. Rix crossed long to the far post where Sunderland was racing in. He stabbed the ball home, Wembley erupted and Arsenal had the Cup — but only just.

Arsenal: Jennings; Rice, Nelson, Talbot, O'Leary, Young, Brady, Sunderland, Stapleton, Price(Walford), Rix.

Manchester United: Bailey; Nicholl, Albiston, McIlroy, McQueen, Buchan, Coppell, J.Greenhoff, Jordan, Macari, Thomas.

Attendance: 100,000   *Referee: R.C.Challis (Tonbridge)*

Arsenal 7   Leeds United 0

WHEN Arsenal hammered Leeds United 7-0 at Highbury it gave them their biggest-ever win in the League Cup with one of their best displays for years. This season, the second round of the competition was played on a two-legged basis for the first time and, a week earlier, the teams had drawn 1-1 at Elland Road.

Arsenal struck form right from the start. Brady, Rix and Nelson wove magic patterns on the left, Sunderland and Stapleton turned the Leeds defence inside out and John Hollins, who had joined the Gunners that summer from Queen's Park Rangers, gave an inspired performance in midfield. Pat Jennings could rarely have had so little to do.

The scene was set after only three minutes. Sunderland shot home following a corner by Hollins. Eleven minutes later, a sweeping move the length of the field was started by Rix and carried on by Talbot and Stapleton. It ended with a lethal finish from Sunderland. Nelson raced forward to blast in a third goal after 23 minutes and, although there were no more goals before half-time, Arsenal were far from satisfied.

Six minutes into the second half, Sunderland completed his hat-trick by prodding in the fourth goal. The Leeds defence, now totally outplayed, became desperate and conceded penalties in the 56th and 82nd minutes. Liam Brady's deadly left foot converted both and, in between, Stapleton netted a sixth goal.

Arsenal advanced comfortably into the next round of the competition on an 8-1 aggregate which provided some sweet revenge for the fans who remembered two Cup Final defeats inflicted by Leeds United.

Arsenal: Jennings; Rice, Nelson, Talbot, O'Leary, Young, Brady, Sunderland, Stapleton, Hollins, Rix.
Leeds United: Harvey; Hird, Hampton, Flynn, Hart, Stevenson, Hankin, Cherry, Greenhoff(Harris), Curtis, Graham.

Attendance: 35,133   *Referee: P.G.Reeves (Leicester)*

Liam Brady, seen here getting the better of Leeds United's Brian Flynn, netted two penalties as the Gunners routed their visitors.

Dino Zoff collects as Alan Sunderland (second left) hopes for a mistake from the Juventus goalkeeper.

Match to Remember 20   23 April 1980
Juventus 0   Arsenal 1

ARSENAL produced one of the outstanding results in European football history to reach their second European Final with this victory over Juventus in Turin. Nineteen-year-old Paul Vaessen was the hero of the European Cup-winners' Cup semi-final second leg and it proved the greatest moment of a career which was to be so sadly curtailed by a serious knee injury.

In the first leg at Highbury, the Italians had held Arsenal to a 1-1 draw. In the 11th minute Bettega pounced on a weak back-pass and was brought down by Talbot. Jennings parried the penalty but Cabrini followed up to score. Juventus protected that lead with a mixture of skilful but often brutal defence. Tardelli was sent-off and others were lucky not to follow him, particularly Bettega after his horrific tackle which put David O'Leary out of the match. Justice of a kind was done, however, when four minutes from the end, a persistent Stapleton forced Bettega to put through his own goal for an equaliser.

The Gunners' chances of reaching the Final were still slim, however. Juventus held the advantage of an away goal and a goalless draw — a result their type of football excelled in producing — in the return leg would be sufficient to see them through.

In front of a large crowd the Italian team opened in uncertain fashion, unsure whether to press forward in an attempt to extend their advantage or whether to settle for a goalless draw. In the end, they were so aware of the importance of not conceding a goal that they rarely came forward at all. These tactics helped Arsenal and, prompted by Brady, the Gunners came more and more into the game in search of the vital goal. In the 76th minute Vaessen replaced Price and, as the remaining minutes ticked away, there was still no score.

With one minute to go Rix, out on the left, sent over another curling cross. Goalkeeper Dino Zoff, an Italian defender and Vaessen all jumped for the ball. Vaessen got there first and knocked it down over the line and into the net. The Italians were staggered and Arsenal held on for a minute or so of injury time to complete a famous victory.

Arsenal, in qualifying for the Final, became the first British club to triumph on the Turin ground in a competitive match and it was also the first time in ten years that Juventus had lost at home in European competition. In the Final, the Gunners lost to Valencia of Spain in a penalty shoot-out.

Juventus: Zoff; Gentile, Cabrini, Furino, Brio, Scirea, Causio, Tardelli, Bettega, Prandelli, Fanna.

Arsenal: Jennings; Rice, Devine, Talbot(Hollins), O'Leary, Young, Brady, Sunderland, Stapleton, Price(Vaessen), Rix.

Attendance: 66,386   *Referee: C.G.R.Corver (Holland)*

Liverpool 0   Arsenal 2

IT is doubtful whether the League Championship will ever be decided in a more dramatic manner than in the 1988-9 season. The final match of that campaign, as if scripted by a thriller writer, brought together the two leading teams, Liverpool and Arsenal, in an 'all or nothing' situation. The fixture, originally scheduled for 22 April, had been postponed due to the Hillsborough tragedy.

Having led the table from Boxing Day, Arsenal, due to some 'unexpected' results on their part and a 24-match unbeaten run by Liverpool, had allowed a 19-point margin between the clubs to be eroded. Liverpool (already FA Cup winners) had convincingly won their penultimate League match three days before, leaving Arsenal needing to win by two clear goals to take the Championship.

The fact that Liverpool had not lost at home by such a margin for three years and that Arsenal had not won at Anfield for 15 years only increased the odds heavily stacked against the Gunners.

To add to the tension, the kick-off had to be delayed by ten minutes to allow visiting fans to enter the ground, but once the game was underway, Arsenal made the early running. In the ninth minute a goal-bound header from Bould was cleared off the line by Nicol and Smith mistimed a header from a cross by Dixon. Aldridge shot over the bar, a Whelan 30-yard drive brought a good save from Lukic and Liverpool continued to improve as Beardsley replaced Rush in the 33rd minute. A few further chances were created by both sides but the first half ended goalless.

Smith's (above) 52nd-minute header gave Arsenal hope and Thomas' dramatic last-ditch effort brought the Championship to Highbury.

Thomas (white shirt) calmly stabs the ball past Grobbelaar for Arsenal's winner.

Arsenal continued where they left off, never allowing the home side to get into top gear. In the 52nd minute, Whelan was pulled up for an over-zealous tackle and from Winterburn's free-kick, Alan Smith stole behind a line of defenders to score with a fine glancing header.

Another good Arsenal move saw Richardson put Thomas through with only Grobbelaar to beat, but he finished with a tame shot straight at the goalkeeper. In an all-out effort for a further goal, the Gunners brought on Hayes for Merson in the 68th minute and in the 76th minute Groves replaced Bould.

Then, with the game entering injury time, Dixon received the ball from his goalkeeper and sent a long pass to Smith, who in turn played superbly through to Michael Thomas on the break. This time, with Grobbelaar committed, Thomas calmly stabbed the ball into the net.

Seconds later the referee blew the final whistle and Arsenal had won the League Championship by the narrowest of margins.

Liverpool: Grobbelaar; Ablett, Staunton, Nicol, Whelan, Hansen, Houghton, Aldridge, Rush(Beardsley), Barnes, McMahon.
Arsenal: Lukic; Dixon, Winterburn, Thomas, O'Leary, Adams, Rocastle, Richardson, Smith, Bould(Groves), Merson(Hayes).
Att: 41,783   *Referee: D.Hutchinson (Abingdon).*

131

Match to Remember 22   11 May 1991

Arsenal 6   Coventry City 1

ARSENAL had already won the League Championship, having lost only one match during a memorable season in which they had overcome the handicap of two points deducted and the loss of their captain for two months, to finish seven points clear of their nearest rivals.

For the last match of the season, therefore, there was a carnival atmosphere at Highbury, and the Gunners completed the campaign in the style of champions.

Coventry, however, had other ideas, and for a long period it looked as if they might just 'dampen' the celebrations a little by depriving Arsenal of the convincing victory they eventually achieved.

It was in the 14th minute that the first goal arrived — Peake, attempting to prevent a cross from Merson reaching Campbell, sent a diving header past his own goalkeeper. Taking advantage of a hesitant defence, Anders Limpar nipped in to increase the lead after 32 minutes. Three minutes later, however, the Sky Blues had reduced the arrears, when the usually reliable Arsenal defence failed to clear a corner from the left, and Gallacher turned the ball into the net.

With a resolute defence and quick on the break, Coventry were still well in contention, but with some 20 minutes to go, Arsenal began to make chances, and in the 77th minute, Hillier sent Alan Smith clear to score from 18 yards. Another two minutes and Campbell had pulled the ball back for Limpar to fire home, and in the 86th minute the Swedish winger demonstrated his brilliant skills with a hip-wiggling run and rounded Ogrizovic to complete his hat-trick.

As if saving the best to the last, the Gunners were rampant now, and in the 87th minute, Perry Groves, who had come on as substitute some five minutes earlier, completed the scoring with a volley from a cross by Winterburn.

The customary lap of honour and parade of trophies followed, as the players and fans celebrated another Championship success.

Arsenal: Seaman; Dixon, Winterburn, Hillier, Bould, Adams, Campbell(Groves), Davis, Smith, Merson(Linighan), Limpar.
Coventry City: Ogrizovic; Burrows, Sansom(Edwards), Emerson, Pearce, Peake, Woods, Gynn, Regis, Gallacher, D.Smith.

Attendance: 41,039   *Referee: J.Martin (Alton, Hants)*

Opposite page: Tony Adams lifts the League Championship trophy.

Arsenal in the Football League 1893-94 to 1991-92

Equal

	P	W	HOME D	L	F	A	W	AWAY D	L	F	A	Pts	Pos
DIVISION TWO													
1893-94	28	9	1	4	33	19	3	3	8	19	36	28	9th
1894-95	30	11	3	1	54	20	3	3	9	21	38	34	8th
1895-96	30	11	1	3	42	11	3	3	9	16	31	32	7th
1896-97	30	10	1	4	42	20	3	3	9	26	50	30	10th
1897-98	30	10	4	1	41	14	6	1	8	28	35	37	5th
1898-99	34	14	2	1	55	10	4	3	10	17	31	41	7th
1899-1900	34	13	1	3	47	12	3	3	11	14	31	36	8th
1900-01	34	13	3	1	30	11	2	3	12	9	24	36	7th
1901-02	34	13	2	2	35	9	5	4	8	15	17	42	4th
1902-03	34	14	2	1	46	9	6	6	5	20	21	48	3rd
1903-04	34	15	2	0	67	5	6	5	6	24	17	49	2nd
DIVISION ONE													
1904-05	34	9	5	3	19	12	3	4	10	17	28	33	10th
1905-06	38	12	4	3	43	21	3	3	13	19	43	37	12th
1906-07	38	15	1	3	38	15	5	3	11	28	44	44	7th
1907-08	38	9	8	2	32	18	3	4	12	19	45	36	*14th
1908-09	38	9	3	7	24	18	5	7	7	28	31	38	6th
1909-10	38	6	5	8	17	19	5	4	10	20	48	31	18th
1910-11	38	9	6	4	24	14	4	6	9	17	35	38	10th
1911-12	38	12	3	4	38	19	3	5	11	17	40	38	10th
1912-13	38	1	8	10	11	31	2	4	13	15	43	18	20th
DIVISION TWO													
1913-14	38	14	3	2	34	10	6	6	7	20	28	49	3rd
1914-15	38	15	1	3	52	13	4	4	11	17	28	43	5th
DIVISION ONE													
1919-20	42	11	5	5	32	21	4	7	10	24	37	42	10th
1920-21	42	9	8	4	31	25	6	6	9	28	38	44	9th
1921-22	42	10	6	5	27	19	5	1	15	20	37	37	17th
1922-23	42	13	4	4	38	16	3	6	12	23	46	42	11th
1923-24	42	8	5	8	25	24	4	4	13	15	39	33	19th
1924-25	42	12	3	6	33	17	2	2	17	13	41	33	20th
1925-26	42	16	2	3	57	19	6	6	9	30	44	52	2nd
1926-27	42	12	5	4	47	30	5	4	12	30	56	43	11th
1927-28	42	10	6	5	49	33	3	9	9	33	53	41	10th
1928-29	42	11	6	4	43	25	5	7	9	34	47	45	9th
1929-30	42	10	2	9	49	26	4	9	8	29	40	39	14th
1930-31	42	14	5	2	67	27	14	5	2	60	32	66	1st
1931-32	42	14	5	2	52	16	8	5	8	38	32	54	2nd
1932-33	42	14	3	4	70	27	11	5	5	48	34	58	1st
1933-34	42	15	4	2	45	19	10	5	6	30	28	59	1st
1934-35	42	15	4	2	74	17	8	8	5	41	29	58	1st
1935-36	42	9	9	3	44	22	6	6	9	34	26	45	6th
1936-37	42	10	10	1	43	20	8	6	7	37	29	52	3rd
1937-38	42	15	4	2	52	16	6	6	9	25	28	52	1st
1938-39	42	14	3	4	34	14	5	6	10	21	27	47	5th
1946-47	42	9	5	7	43	33	7	4	11	29	37	41	13th
1947-48	42	15	3	3	56	15	8	10	3	25	17	59	1st

134

		HOME						AWAY					
	P	W	D	L	F	A	W	D	L	F	A	Pts	Pos
1948-49	42	13	5	3	51	18	5	8	8	23	26	49	5th
1949-50	42	12	4	5	48	24	7	7	7	31	31	49	6th
1950-51	42	11	5	5	47	28	8	4	9	26	28	47	5th
1951-52	42	13	7	1	54	30	8	4	9	26	31	53	3rd
1952-53	42	15	3	3	60	30	6	9	6	37	34	54	1st
1953-54	42	8	8	5	42	37	7	5	9	33	36	43	12th
1954-55	42	12	3	6	44	25	5	6	10	25	38	43	9th
1955-56	42	13	4	4	38	22	5	6	10	22	39	46	5th
1956-57	42	12	5	4	45	21	9	3	9	40	48	50	5th
1957-58	42	10	4	7	48	39	6	3	12	25	46	39	12th
1958-59	42	14	3	4	53	29	7	5	9	35	39	50	3rd
1959-60	42	9	5	7	39	38	6	4	11	29	42	39	13th
1960-61	42	12	3	6	44	35	3	8	10	33	50	41	11th
1961-62	42	9	6	6	39	31	7	5	9	32	41	43	10th
1962-63	42	11	4	6	44	33	7	6	8	42	44	46	7th
1963-64	42	10	7	4	56	37	7	4	10	34	45	45	8th
1964-65	42	11	5	5	42	31	6	2	13	27	44	41	13th
1965-66	42	8	8	5	36	31	4	5	12	26	44	37	14th
1966-67	42	11	6	4	32	20	5	8	8	26	27	46	7th
1967-68	42	12	6	3	37	23	5	4	12	23	33	44	9th
1968-69	42	12	6	3	31	12	10	6	5	25	15	56	4th
1969-70	42	7	10	4	29	23	5	8	8	22	26	42	12th
1970-71	42	18	3	0	41	6	11	4	6	30	23	65	1st
1971-72	42	15	2	4	36	13	7	6	8	22	27	52	5th
1972-73	42	14	5	2	31	14	9	6	6	26	29	57	2nd
1973-74	42	9	7	5	23	16	5	7	9	26	35	42	10th
1974-75	42	10	6	5	31	16	3	5	13	16	33	37	16th
1975-76	42	11	4	6	33	19	2	6	13	14	34	36	17th
1976-77	42	11	6	4	37	20	5	5	11	27	39	43	8th
1977-78	42	14	5	2	38	12	7	5	9	22	25	52	5th
1978-79	42	11	8	2	37	18	6	9	9	24	30	48	7th
1979-80	42	8	10	3	24	12	10	6	5	28	24	52	4th
1980-81	42	13	8	0	36	17	6	7	8	25	28	53	3rd
1981-82	42	13	5	3	27	15	7	6	8	21	22	71	5th
1982-83	42	11	6	4	36	19	5	4	12	22	37	58	10th
1983-84	42	10	5	6	41	29	8	4	9	33	31	63	6th
1984-85	42	14	5	2	37	14	5	4	12	24	35	66	7th
1985-86	42	13	5	3	29	15	7	4	10	20	32	69	7th
1986-87	42	12	5	4	31	12	8	5	8	27	23	70	4th
1987-88	40	11	4	5	35	16	7	8	5	23	23	66	6th
1988-89	38	10	6	3	35	19	12	4	3	38	17	76	1st
1989-90	38	14	3	2	38	11	4	5	10	16	27	62	4th
1990-91	38	15	4	0	51	10	9	9	1	23	8	†83	1st
1991-92	42	12	7	2	51	22	7	8	6	30	24	72	4th

† *Two points deducted*

135

1893-94

Manager: None

1	Sep	2	(h)	Newcastle U	D 2-2	Shaw, Elliott	10,000
2		9	(a)	Notts C	L 2-3	Elliott, Shaw	7,000
3		11	(h)	Walsall TS	W 4-0	Heath 3, Crawford	4,000
4		25	(h)	Grimsby T	W 3-1	Elliott, Heath, Booth	2,000
5		30	(a)	Newcastle U	L 0-6		2,000
6	Oct	21	(a)	Small Heath	L 1-4	Henderson	3,000
7		28	(h)	Liverpool	L 0-5		9,000
8	Nov	11	(h)	Ardwick	W 1-0	Henderson	4,500
9		13	(h)	Rotherham T	W 3-0	Shaw 2, Elliott	3,000
10		18	(a)	Burton S	L 2-6	Elliott, Shaw	2,000
11	Dec	9	(a)	Northwich V	D 2-2	Shaw, Boyle	Fair
12		25	(h)	Burslem P.Vale	W 4-1	Shaw, Henderson, Booth, Crawford	10,000
13		26	(a)	Grimsby T	L 1-3	Buist (pen)	3,000
14		30	(a)	Ardwick	W 1-0	Crawford	4,000
15	Jan	1	(a)	Liverpool	L 0-2		5,000
16		6	(a)	Burslem P.Vale	L 1-2	Elliott	900
17	Feb	3	(a)	Lincoln C	L 0-3		2,000
18		6	(a)	Rotherham T	D 1-1	Worrall	2,000
19		10	(h)	Crewe A	W 3-2	Henderson 3	4,000
20		12	(a)	Walsall TS	W 2-1	Henderson, Elliott	2,000
21		17	(h)	Lincoln C	W 4-0	Elliott 2, Bryan, Stothart (og)	3,000
22		24	(a)	Middlesbrough I	W 6-3	Shaw 3, Henderson 2, Davis	500
23	Mar	3	(a)	Crewe A	D 0-0		2,000
24		10	(h)	Middlesbrough I	W 1-0	Shaw	5,000
25		23	(h)	Northwich V	W 6-0	Jaques 2, Henderson 2, Elliott, Howat	5,000
26		24	(h)	Notts C	L 1-2	Crawford	13,000
27		31	(h)	Small Heath	L 1-4	McNab	6,000
28	Apr	14	(h)	Burton S	L 0-2		2,000

FINAL LEAGUE POSITION: 9th in Division Two

Appearances
Goals

FA Cup

1Q	Oct	14	(h)	Ashford U	W 12-0	Elliott 3, Booth 2, Henderson 3, Crawford, Heath 2, Powell	3,000
2Q	Nov	4	(h)	Clapton O	W 6-2	Henderson 2, Cooper 2, Shaw, Elliott	2,500
3Q		25	(h)	Millwall A	W 2-0	Davis, Booth	20,000
4Q	Dec	16	(a)	2nd Scots Guards	W 2-1*	Henderson 2	9,000
1	Jan	27	(h)	Sheffield W	L 1-2	Elliott	15,000

*After extra-time

Appearances
Goals

136

Williams CA	Powell J	Jeffrey WW	Devine D	Buist R	Howat D	Gemmell D	Henderson J	Shaw W	Elliott A	Booth C	Davis FW	Heath J	Crawford G	Storrs JA	Cooper J	Briggs S	Boyle J	Kirk FV	Worrall A	Bryan T	Williams W	Burrows L	McNab W	Jaques GH	
1	2	3	4	5	6	7	8	9	10	11															1
1	2	3		5	6	7	8		10	11	4	9													2
1	2	3		5	6	7	8			11	4	9	10												3
1	2			5	6	7	8		10	11	4	9		3											4
1	2			5	6	7	8		10	11	4	9		3											5
1	2			5	6		8		10	11	4	9	7	3											6
1	2			5	6		8	7		10	11	9	4	3											7
	2	1	4		6		8		10	11	5		7	3	9										8
	2	1			6		8	9	10	11	4		7	3			5								9
	2	1			6		8	9	10	11	4		7	3			5								10
	2	1		5	6		8		10	11	4		7	3	9										11
	2	1		5	6		8	9	10	11	4		7	3											12
	2	1		5	6		8		10	11	4	9	7	3											13
1	2	3		5	8		7			10	11	4			6	9									14
1	2	3		5	6		7			10	4	9			8			11							15
1	2	3		5	6		7	9	10	11	4				8										16
	2	1		5	6		8		10	11	4		7	3	9										17
	2	1		5	6		8				4		7		10		9	11	3						18
	2	1		5	6		8	9			4		7					11	10	3					19
1	2				6		8	9		10	4		7				5		3	11					20
1	2				6		8	9		10	4		7				5		3	11					21
1		2			6		8	9		10	4		7				5		3	11					22
1		2			6		8	9		10	4		7				5		3	11					23
1	2	3			6		8	9		10	4		7				5			11					24
1	2	3			6		8			10	4		7				5				9	11			25
1	2	3			6		8			10	4		7				5		9			11			26
1	2	3			6		8			10	4		7				5			11		9			27
1	2	3			6		8				4		7		10		5		9	11					28
19	26	22	2	17	27	5	23	17	24	16	26	8	21	12	6	2	10	1	4	9	1	6	2	2	
	1	1					11	11	10	2	1	4	4		1		1	1				1	2		

I own-goal

Williams CA	Powell J	Jeffrey WW	Devine D	Buist R	Howat D	Gemmell D	Henderson J	Shaw W	Elliott A	Booth C	Davis FW	Heath J	Crawford G	Storrs JA	Cooper J	Briggs S	Boyle J	Kirk FV	Worrall A	Bryan T	Williams W	Burrows L	McNab W	Jaques GH	
1	2			4	5		8		10	11	6	9	7	3											1Q
1		2			5		8	11	10	6	4		7	3			9								2Q
	2	1		5	6		8	9	10	11	4		7	3											3Q
	2	1		5	6		8	9	10	11	4		7	3											4Q
1	2	3		5	6			9	10	11	4		7		8										1
3	4	4	1	4	4		4	4	5	5	5	1	5	4	2										
1							7	1	5	3	1	2	1		2										

1894-95

Manager: None

1	Sep	1	(a)	Lincoln C	L 2-5 Heath, Mortimer	2,000
2		10	(h)	Grimsby T	L 1-3 Boyd	4,000
3		15	(a)	Burton S	L 0-3	3,000
4		22	(h)	Bury	W 4-2 Boyd 2, Henderson, O'Brien	8,000
5		29	(h)	Manchester C	W 4-2 Boyd 3, Mortimer	5,000
6	Oct	6	(h)	Lincoln C	W 5-2 Boyd 2, Mortimer 2, O'Brien	8,000
7		13	(a)	Newton Heath	D 3-3 Mortimer 2, Boyd	4,000
8		20	(a)	Rotherham T	W 2-1 Boyle, Henderson	2,000
9		27	(a)	Notts C	D 2-2 Howat, Caldwell	2,000
10	Nov	3	(h)	Notts C	W 2-1 Henderson, O'Brien	11,000
11		10	(a)	Walsall TS	L 1-4 Boyle	3,000
12		24	(a)	Newcastle U	W 4-2 Sharpe, Crawford, Buchanan, O'Brien	3,000
13	Dec	8	(h)	Darwen	W 4-0 Mortimer, O'Brien, Henderson, Davis	8,000
14		15	(a)	Manchester C	L 1-4 Buchanan	5,000
15		25	(h)	Burslem P.Vale	W 7-0 O'Brien 3, Davis, Buchanan, Sharpe, Henderson	8,000
16		26	(a)	Grimsby T	L 2-4 Henderson, O'Brien	5,000
17	Jan	1	(a)	Darwen	L 1-3 Crawford	6,000
18		7	(a)	Leicester F	L 1-3 Mortimer	3,000
19		12	(h)	Newcastle U	W 3-2 Buchanan, Meade, Crawford	5,000
20		19	(a)	Burslem P.Vale	W 1-0 Crawford	700
21		26	(h)	Burton W	D 1-1 Henderson	7,000
22	Feb	9	(h)	Rotherham T	D 1-1 Sharpe	3,000
23		23	(h*)	Burton S	W 3-0 Mortimer 2, Buchanan	5,000
24	Mar	2	(a)	Bury	L 0-2	4,000
25		9	(h*)	Leicester F	D 3-3 O'Brien, Sharpe, Mortimer	4,000
26		23	(a)	Crewe A	D 0-0	1,000
27		30	(h)	Newton Heath	W 3-2 Mortimer, Buchanan, Crawford	6,000
28	Apr	6	(h)	Crewe A	W 7-0 Buchanan 2, Davis, Boyle, O'Brien, Crawford, Hare	4,000
29		12	(h)	Walsall TS	W 6-1 Hare 2, Mortimer 2, Buchanan, Crawford	6,000
30		20	(a)	Burton W	L 1-2 Hare	3,000

FINAL LEAGUE POSITION: 8th in Division Two.   *Following incidents against the referee on 26 January, the Arsenal ground was closed for five weeks and therefore Match 23 was played at New Brompton and Match 25 was played at Leyton.

Appearances
Goals

FA Cup

1	Feb	2	(a)	Bolton W	L 0-1	7,000

Appearances
Goals

138

Storer H	Burrows L	Caldwell J	Davis FW	Boyle J	Stevenson R	Crawford G	Henderson J	Heath J	Mortimer P	Sharpe WH	Crozier J	Howat D	Boyd H	O'Brien P	Shaw W	Powell J	Buchanan R	Meade TG	Reece G	Hare CB	Hatfield T	No.
1	2	3	4	5	6	7	8	9	10	11												1
	2	3	4		5	7	8		11		1	6	9	10								2
1	2	3	4		5	7	8			11		6	9	10								3
1		3		5	4	7	8			11		6	9	10		2						4
1		3		5	4	7				11		6	9	10		2	8					5
1		3		5	4	7				11		6	9	10		2	8					6
1		3		5	4	7				11		6	9	10		2	8					7
1		3	4	5		7	8		11			6		10		2	9					8
1		3	4	5		7	8		11			6		10		2	9					9
1		3	4	5		7	8		11			6		10		2	9					10
1		3	4	5		7	8			11		6		10		2	9					11
1		3	4	5		7	8			11		6		10		2	9					12
1		3	4	5		7	8		11			6		10		2	9					13
1		3	4	5		7	8		11			6		10		2	9					14
1		3	4	5		7	8			11		6		10		2	9					15
1		3	4	5		7	8			11		6		10		2	9					16
1		3	4	5		7	8		11			6		10		2	9					17
1		3	6	4		7		5	10	11				10		2	9	8				18
1		3	4	5		7				11		6		10		2	9	8				19
1		3	4	5		7			10	11		6				2		8	9			20
1		3	4	5		7	8		11			6		10		2	9					21
1		3	4	5		7			11			6		10	8	2	9					22
1		3	4	5		7			11			6		10		2	9			8		23
1		3	4	5		7			11			6		10		2	9			8		24
1		3	4	5		7			11			6		10		2	9			8		25
1		3	4	5		8			11			6		10		2	9			7		26
1		3	4	5		7			11			6		10		2	9			8		27
1		3	4	5		7			11			6		10		2	9			8		28
1		3	4	5		7			11			6		10		2	9			8		29
		3	4	5		7			11			6		10		2	9			8	1	30
28	3	30	26	28	7	29	15	2	22	13	1	28	6	27	2	27	25	3	1	6	1	
	1	3	3		7	7	1		14	4		1	9	11		9	1			4		

Storer H	Burrows L	Caldwell J	Davis FW	Boyle J	Stevenson R	Crawford G	Henderson J	Heath J	Mortimer P	Sharpe WH	Crozier J	Howat D	Boyd H	O'Brien P	Shaw W	Powell J	Buchanan R	Meade TG	Reece G	Hare CB	Hatfield T	No.
1		3	4	5		7			11			6		10	8	2	9					1
1		1	1	1		1			1			1		1	1	1	1					

1895-96

1	Sep	2	(h)	Grimsby T	W 3-1	Jenkyns, O'Brien, Gordon	6,000
2		7	(h)	Manchester C	L 0-1		6,000
3		14	(a)	Lincoln C	D 1-1	Buchanan	1,200
4		21	(h)	Lincoln C	W 4-0	Jenkyns, Mills, Gordon, Buchanan	6,000
5		28	(a)	Manchester C	L 0-1		9,000
6	Oct	5	(h)	Rotherham T	W 5-0	Gordon, Mortimer, Mills, Jenkyns, Buchanan	6,000
7		12	(h)	Burton W	W 3-0	McAvoy, Gordon, Mortimer	8,000
8		19	(h)	Burton S	W 5-0	Mortimer 2, Mills, Buchanan, Boyd	8,000
9		26	(a)	Rotherham T	L 0-3		2,000
10	Nov	2	(a)	Notts C	W 4-3	Hare, Gordon 2, Boyd	8,000
11		9	(h)	Newton Heath	W 2-1	Boyle, Hare	9,000
12		16	(h)	Liverpool	L 0-2		10,000
13		30	(a)	Newton Heath	L 1-5	Hare	6,000
14	Dec	7	(h)	Leicester F	D 1-1	Boyd	5,000
15		14	(a)	Burton W	L 1-4	Boyd	5,000
16		21	(a)	Burton S	L 2-3	Buchanan, Boyd	2,000
17		23	(a)	Crewe A	W 1-0	Boyd	3,000
18		25	(h)	Burslem P.Vale	W 2-1	Buchanan, Mortimer	2,000
19	Jan	4	(h)	Loughborough T	W 5-0	Boyd 2, Jenkyns, Powell, Buchanan	4,000
20		11	(a)	Liverpool	L 0-3		7,000
21		18	(a)	Newcastle U	L 1-3	Jenkyns (pen)	8,000
22		25	(a)	Leicester F	L 0-1		6,000
23	Feb	15	(a)	Burslem P.Vale	W 2-0	Boyd, Haywood	1,000
24		29	(a)	Loughborough T	L 1-2	Boyd	2,000
25	Mar	7	(h)	Notts C	W 2-0	Jenkyns, Haywood	6,000
26		14	(a)	Darwen	D 1-1	Crawford	3,000
27		21	(h)	Crewe A	W 7-0	Boyd 2 (1 pen), Mortimer 3, Haywood, Brocks (og)	5,000
28	Apr	4	(a)	Grimsby T	D 1-1	Boyd	5,000
29		6	(h)	Newcastle U	W 2-1	Mortimer, O'Brien	14,000
30		18	(h)	Darwen	L 1-3	Haywood	4,000

FINAL LEAGUE POSITION: 7th in Division Two

Appearances
Goals

FA Cup

1	Feb	1	(a)	Burnley	L 1-6	O'Brien	6,000

Appearances
Goals

Storer H	Powell J	Caldwell J	Davis FW	Jenkyns CAL	Ward A	Crawford G	Hare CB	Gordon R	Buchanan R	O'Brien P	Mortimer P	Mills S	McAvoy F	Boyd H	Burrows L	Boyle J	Ambler CA	Hatfield T	Gilmer W	Howat D	Fairclough W	Haywood A	Russell A	
1	2	3	4	5	6	7	8	9	10	11														1
1	2	3	4	5	6	7	8	9	10		11													2
1	2	3		5	6	4	8	9	10		11	7												3
1	2	3		5	6	4	8	9	10			7	11											4
1	2	3		5	6	4		9	10		8	7	11											5
1	2	3		5	6	4		9	10		8	7	11											6
1	2	3		5	6	4		9	10		8	7	11											7
1	2	3	6	5		4		9	11		8	7		10										8
1	2	3	6	5		4		9	8		11	7		10										9
1		3	6	5		4	8	9			11	7		10	2									10
1		3	2	5		4	8	9			11	7		10		6								11
1		3	2	5		4	8	9			11	7		10		6								12
	2	3	6			4	8	10			11	7		9		5	1							13
	2	3	6			4		11	10		8	7		9		5		1						14
	2	3	6	5		4		11	10		8	7		9		1								15
	2	3	6	5		4			10		8	7	11	9		1								16
	2	3	6	5		4			10		8	7	11	9		1								17
	2	3	6	5		4			10		8	7	11	9		1								18
	2		6	5		4			10		8	7	11	9					1	3				19
	2	3	6	5		4			10		8	7	11	9					1					20
	2	3	6	5		4			10		8	7	11	9					1					21
	2	3	6	5		4	7			10			11	9							1	8		22
		3	6	5		4	2	7		10	11			9							1	8		23
		3		5			2	6		10	11	7		9		4					1	8		24
	2	3	6	5		4	7			10	11			9							1	8		25
	2	3	6	5		4	7			10	11			9							1	8		26
	2	3	6			4				10	11	7		9		5					1	8		27
	2	3	6	5				4		10	11	7		9							1	8		28
	2	3	6	5				4		10	11	7		9							1	8		29
	2	3	6	5		4		9		10	11	7									1	8		30
12	25	29	24	27	7	27	13	20	17	10	27	24	11	22	1	10	1	1	3	1	9	9		
	1			6		1	3	6	7	2	9	3	1	13		1						4		

1 own-goal

		3	6			4	2		8	10		7	11	9		5							1	1
		1	1			1	1		1	1		1	1	1		1							1	
										1														

1896-97

Manager: None

#	Month	Date		Opponent	Res	Score	Scorers	Att
1	Sep	5	(a)	Manchester C	D	1-1	Haywood	8,000
2		12	(h)	Walsall	D	1-1	Boyd	6,000
3		14	(a)	Burton W	W	3-0	O'Brien, Brock, Boyd	4,000
4		19	(h)	Loughborough T	W	2-0	O'Brien, McAvoy	8,000
5		26	(h)	Notts C	L	2-3	Meade, McAvoy	9,000
6	Oct	12	(h)	Burton W	W	3-0	Haywood, Boyd 2	700
7		17	(a)	Walsall	L	3-5	Meade, Boyd (pen), Haywood	4,000
8		24	(a)	Gainsborough T	W	6-1	Boyd 2, Brock 2, Haywood, Russell	5,500
9	Nov	7	(a)	Notts C	L	4-7	Brock, Haywood, O'Brien, Boyd	3,000
10		14	(a)	Small Heath	L	2-5	McAvoy, Brock	3,000
11		28	(h)	Grimsby T	W	4-2	O'Brien 2, Boyd, Brock	6,500
12	Dec	5	(a)	Lincoln C	W	3-2	O'Brien 2, Boyd	2,000
13		12*	(a)	Loughborough T	L	0-8		500
14		19	(h)	Blackpool	W	4-2	Crawford 2, Haywood 2	6,000
15		25	(h)	Lincoln C	W	6-2	O'Brien 2, Boyd 2, Boyle, Meade 2, Russell	9,000
16		26	(a)	Gainsborough T	L	1-4	Brock	3,000
17	Jan	1	(a)	Darwen	L	1-4	Russell	5,000
18		4	(a)	Blackpool	D	1-1	Brock	1,000
19		23	(a)	Newcastle U	L	0-2		6,000
20	Feb	13	(a)	Leicester F	L	3-6	O'Brien 2, Haywood	6,000
21		20	(h)	Burton S	W	3-0	Haywood 2, Caie	5,000
22	Mar	13	(a)	Burton S	W	2-1	Caie 2	1,000
23		22	(a)	Newton Heath	D	1-1	Brock	3,000
24		29	(h)	Small Heath	L	2-3	Haywood, McAvoy	2,500
25	Apr	3	(h)	Newton Heath	L	0-2		6,000
26		8	(a)	Grimsby T	L	1-3	Hardie (og)	1,000
27		16	(h)	Newcastle U	W	5-1	Brock, Boyle, O'Brien 2, Caldwell	7,000
28		17	(h)	Leicester F	W	2-1	Caie, Brock	5,000
29		19	(h)	Darwen	W	1-0	O'Brien	8,000
30		28	(h)	Manchester C	L	1-2	Russell	2,000

FINAL LEAGUE POSITION: 10th in Division Two

Appearances
Goals

FA Cup

					Res	Score	Scorers	Att
4Q	Dec	12*	(h)	Leyton	W	5-0	Meade, McAvoy 2, Duff, Farmer	3,000
5Q	Jan	2	(h)	Chatham	W	4-0	Haywood 2, Boyle, Meade	4,500
Sup		16	(a)	Millwall	L	2-4	Boyle, O'Brien	14,000

*As Arsenal were compelled to fulfill a League fixture at Loughborough on this date, they fielded a reserve team in the FA Cup. It is ironic that whereas the reserves won handsomely the seniors suffered Arsenal's record League defeat.

Appearances
Goals

142

Appearance / line-up grid (shirt numbers by match). Columns are players; rows are matches.

Fairclough W	Powell J	Sinclair F	Crawford G	Boylan PA	Davis FW	Brock J	Haywood A	Boyd H	O'Brien P	McAvoy F	Farmer GA	Meade TG	Leather J	Shrewsbury TP	Russell J	Buist G	Boyle J	McFarlane A	Talbot A	Carver G	Whitfield J	Caldwell J	Anderson J	Caie A	Cassidy H	Kane ET	Harding E	Wilson J	Kington E	Heath J	Duff H	No.
1	2	3	4	5	6	7	8	9	10	11																						1
1	2	3	4	5	6	7		9	10	11	8																					2
1	2	3	4	5	6	7		9	10	11		8																				3
1	2	3	4	5	6	7	8	9	10	11																						4
	2	3		5	6	7	8		10	11			9	I	4																	5
1	2	3	4	5	6	7	10	9			8				11																	6
1	2	3	4	5	6	7	10	9			8				11																	7
1		3	4	5	6	7	8	9	10						11	2																8
1		3	4	5	6	7	8	9	10						11	2																9
1	2	3	4	5	6	7		9	10	8					11																	10
		3	4		6	7	8	9	10			1			11	2	5															11
		3	4		6	7	8	9	10						11	2	5					1										12
			4	5	6	7	8	9	10						11	2						1	3									13
			4	8	6	7		9	10			1			11		5					2	3									14
		3	4		6	7		9	10			8			11		5					1	2									15
		3	4		6	7		9	10			8			11		5					1	2									16
			4			7	8	9	10			1			11	6						2	3	5								17
		3	4		6	7	8	9	10			1			11	2	5															18
		3	4			7	8	9	10			1			11	6						2	5									19
	2		4		6	7	8	9	10			1			11							3	5									20
1			4		6	7	8		10						11		5					3	2	9								21
		3	4		6	7	8		10			1			11	2	5							9								22
1	2		4			7	8		10						11		5					3	6	9								23
1	2		4			7	8	9							11		5	10				3	6									24
1	2		4		6	7	8		10						11		5					3		9								25
1	2		4		6	7		9	10						11		5					3	8									26
1					6	7	8		10						11		5					3	4	9	2							27
1	2		4		6	7	8		10						11		5					3		9								28
1	2				6	7	8		10						11							3	4	9			5					29
		3	4		6		8		10			1			11	2	5	7						9								30
17	8	26	26	11	20	29	26	12	26	18	1	8	8	2	23	6	13	5	5	1	2	15	12	8	1	1						
	2				11	11	10	14	4			4			4	2						1	4									

I own-goal

Cup appearances:

Fairclough W	Powell J	Sinclair F	Crawford G	Boylan PA	Davis FW	Brock J	Haywood A	Boyd H	O'Brien P	McAvoy F	Farmer GA	Meade TG	Leather J	Shrewsbury TP	Russell J	Buist G	Boyle J	McFarlane A	Talbot A	Carver G	Whitfield J	Caldwell J	Anderson J	Caie A	Cassidy H	Kane ET	Harding E	Wilson J	Kington E	Heath J	Duff H	
1								8	7		9		4		5									2	3	6	10	11				4Q
		3	4		6	7	8		10			9	1	2	11		5															5Q
		3	4		6	7	8		10			9	1	2	11		5															Sup
1		2	2		2	2	2		2	1	1	3	2	3	2		3							1	1	1	1	1				
					2		1	2	1	2			2														1					

143

1897-98

1	Sep	1	(h)	Grimsby T	W 4-1	Monteith, Steven, Farrell, White	6,000
2		4	(a)	Newcastle U	L 1-4	McGeoch	10,000
3		6	(a)	Burnley	L 0-5		3,000
4		11	(h)	Lincoln C	D 2-2	Farrell, McAvoy	8,000
5		18	(h)	Gainsborough T	W 4-0	McGeoch 3, McAvoy	8,000
6		25	(a)	Manchester C	L 1-4	Brock	7,000
7	Oct	2	(a)	Luton T	W 2-0	McAvoy, Davis	5,000
8		9	(h)	Luton T	W 3-0	Stuart, Brock, Davis	14,000
9		16	(h)	Newcastle U	D 0-0		12,000
10		23	(h)	Leicester F	L 0-3		7,000
11	Nov	6	(a)	Walsall	L 2-3	Hannah, Hunt	3,000
12		13	(h)	Walsall	W 4-0	McGeoch 3, White	2,000
13		27	(h)	Blackpool	W 2-1	Hannah, Davis	6,500
14	Dec	4	(a)	Leicester F	L 1-2	Duff	8,000
15		18	(a)	Loughborough T	W 3-1	Brock, Hannah, White	2,000
16		27	(a)	Lincoln C	W 3-2	Hunt 2, Brock	4,000
17	Jan	1	(a)	Blackpool	D 3-3	Devlin, Cardwell (2 og)	1,500
18		8	(h)	Newton Heath	W 5-1	Hunt, Anderson, White, Brock, Hannah	8,000
19		15	(a)	Burton S	W 2-1	Haywood, Hannah	2,000
20	Feb	5	(h)	Manchester C	D 2-2	Davis, Brock	8,000
21		12	(a)	Grimsby T	W 4-1	Hunt 2 (1 pen), Hannah 2	3,500
22		26	(a)	Newton Heath	L 1-5	Hunt	8,000
23	Mar	5	(h)	Small Heath	W 4-2	Hannah 3 (1 pen), White	8,000
24		12	(a)	Darwen	W 4-1	White, Hunt, Brock, McGeoch	2,000
25		19	(h)	Loughborough T	W 4-0	Hunt 2, Haywood, McAuley	5,000
26		26	(a)	Gainsborough T	L 0-1		2,000
27	Apr	2	(h)	Burnley	D 1-1	Hunt	12,000
28		9	(h)	Darwen	W 3-1	Brock 2, Haywood	5,000
29		11	(h)	Burton S	W 3-0	Hannah 2, Haywood	6,000
30		23	(a)	Small Heath	L 1-2	Hunt	3,000

FINAL LEAGUE POSITION: 5th in Division Two

Appearances
Goals

FA Cup

3Q	Oct	30	(h)	St Albans	W 9-0	Hunt 3, Brock, Haywood, Steven, McGeoch, Davis, Farrell	3,000
4Q	Nov	20	(h)	Sheppey U	W 3-0	Crawford, Haywood, Brock	6,000
5Q	Dec	11	(h)	New Brompton	W 4-2	Haywood, McAuley, Crawford, Janes (og)	5,500
1	Jan	29	(a)	Burnley	L 1-3	Brock	6,000

Appearances
Goals

Player squad-number / appearance grid (each row = one match, numbers are shirt numbers 1–11).

Ord R	McAuley J	Caldwell J	Crawford G	Farrell P	McAvoy F	Hunt F	Steven A	McGeoch A	White W	Monteith J	Anderson J	Haywood A	Brock J	Davis FW	Stuart J	Hannah D	McConnell A	Duff H	Devlin J	Shrewsbury TP	Clark JM	#
1	2	3	4	5	6	7	8	9	10	11												1
1	2	3	4	5	6	7	8	9	10	11												2
1	2	3	4	5		7	8		10	11	6	9										3
1	2		4	5	6		8		10	11	3	9	7									4
1	2	3	4		6	7	8	9	10	11	5											5
1	2	3	4	5	6	8		9	10				11	7								6
1	2	3	8	5	9				10		4	11	7		6							7
1	2	3	8	5					10		4	11	7		6	9						8
1	2	3	8	5					10		4	11	7		6	9						9
1	2	3	10	5	9	8					4	11	7		6							10
1	2	3		5		8	9				4	11	7	6	10							11
1	2	3		5				9		11	4	8	7	6	10							12
1	2		4	5				9		11	8	7	6	10	3							13
1	2		4	5	6			9			8	7	10	3			11					14
1	2	3	4	5				9		11	8	7	6	10								15
1	2		4					9		11	5	8	7	6	10	3						16
1	2		4	7						11	5	8		6	10	3		9				17
1	2		4					9		11	5	8	7	6	10	3						18
1	2		4					9		11	5	8	7	6	10	3						19
1	2		4	5				9		11	8	7	6	10	3							20
1	2			5				9		11	4	8	7	6	10	3						21
1	2			5				9		11	4	8	7	6	10	3						22
1	2			5				9		11	4	8	7	6	10	3						23
1	2						8	9		11		7	6		10	3			4	5		24
1	2		4					9		11		8	7	6	10	3				5		25
1	2							9		11	4	8	7	6	10	3				5		26
1		2	4					9		11	5	8	7	6	10	3						27
1		2	4					9		11	5	8	7	6	10	3						28
1		2		4				9		11	5	8	7	6	10	3						29
1		2	4					9		11	5	8	7	6	10	3						30
30	23	19	19	15	22	5	9	23	6	21	26	25	23	2	20	17	1	1	1	3		
	1		2	3	12	1	8	6	1	1	4	9	4	1	12	1	1					

2 own-goals

Ord R	McAuley J	Caldwell J	Crawford G	Farrell P	McAvoy F	Hunt F	Steven A	McGeoch A	White W	Monteith J	Anderson J	Haywood A	Brock J	Davis FW	Stuart J	Hannah D	McConnell A	Duff H	Devlin J	Shrewsbury TP	Clark JM	#
1	2		4	5			8	9	10		3	11	7		6							3Q
1	2	3	4	5				9		11	8	7	6		10							4Q
1	2	3	4	5	6			9		11	8	7			10							5Q
1	2		4					9		11	5	8	7	6	10	3						1
4	4	2	4	3	1		2	1	3	3	2	4	4	3	3	1						
	1		2	1			3	1	1		3	3	1									

1 own-goal

145

1898-99

Manager: G.Elcoat

1	Sep	3	(a)	Luton T	W	1-0	Mitchell	5,000
2		5	(a)	Burslem P.Vale	L	0-3		5,000
3		10	(h)	Leicester F	W	4-0	White 2, Hunt 2	6,000
4		17	(a)	Darwen	W	4-1	Hunt, Dailly, White, Anderson	3,000
5		24	(h)	Gainsborough T	W	5-1	Dailly 2, McGeoch 2, Hunt	7,000
6	Oct	1	(a)	Manchester C	L	1-3	White	6,000
7		15	(a)	Walsall	L	1-4	Haywood	4,000
8		22	(h)	Burton S	W	2-1	McGeoch, Hunt (pen)	4,000
9	Nov	5	(h)	Small Heath	W	2-0	White, Hunt	7,000
10		12	(a)	Loughborough T	D	0-0		2,500
11		26	(a)	Grimsby T	L	0-1		2,000
12	Dec	3	(h)	Newton Heath	W	5-1	White 3, Hannah 2	7,000
13		10	(a)	New Brighton T	L	1-3	White	Good
14		17	(h)	Lincoln C	W	4-2	Mitchell, Dailly, McConnell, Hunt	3,000
15		24	(a)	Barnsley	L	1-2	Hunt	2,000
16		31	(h)	Luton T	W	6-2	Haywood 3, Hunt 3	4,000
17	Jan	7	(a)	Leicester F	L	1-2	Haywood	10,000
18		14	(h)	Darwen	W	6-0	Haywood, Hannah 2, Shaw, White, Hunt	3,000
19		21	(a)	Gainsborough T	W	1-0	Haywood	2,000
20	Feb	4	(a)	Glossop NE	L	0-2		2,000
21		11	(h)	Walsall	D	0-0		3,000
22		13	(h)	Glossop NE	W	3-0	Anderson, Hunt, McGeoch	2,000
23		18	(a)	Burton S	W	2-1	Shaw 2	Large
24		25	(h)	Burslem P.Vale	W	1-0	Shaw	6,000
25	Mar	4	(h)	Small Heath	L	1-4	Haywood	3,000
26		13	(h)	Loughborough T	W	3-1	Cottrell, Shaw, McGeoch	2,000
27		18	(h)	Blackpool	W	6-0	Cottrell 3, Hunt, Haywood 2	4,000
28		22	(a)	Blackpool	D	1-1	Cottrell	2,000
29		25	(h)	Grimsby T	D	1-1	Hannah	3,500
30	Apr	1	(a)	Newton Heath	D	2-2	Cottrell, Haywood	5,000
31		3	(h)	Manchester C	L	0-1		5,000
32		8	(h)	New Brighton T	W	4-0	Hunt, Cottrell 2, Haywood	3,000
33		15	(a)	Lincoln C	L	0-2		2,000
34		22	(h)	Barnsley	W	3-0	Shaw 2, Cottrell	4,000

FINAL LEAGUE POSITION: 7th in Division Two

Appearances
Goals

FA Cup

1	Jan	28	(h)	Derby C	L	0-6		20,000

Appearances
Goals

146

Ord R	Fyfe J	McConnell A	Anderson J	Dick J	Davis FW	Brock J	White W	McGeoch A	Hannah D	Mitchell A	Moir JG	Clark JM	Hunt F	Dailly H	Haywood A	McPhee J	Cottrell EH	McAvoy J	Hamilton TS	Shaw H	J.Garton	#
1	2	3	4	5	6	7	8	9	10	11												1
1	2	3	4	5		7	8	9	10	11	6											2
1	2	3		5			8	9	10	11	4	6	7									3
1	2	3		5	6		8	9	10		4		7	11								4
1	2	3		5	6		8	9	10		4		7	11								5
1	2	3		5	6		8	9	10		4		7	11								6
1	2	3		5	6	7		9	10	11	4				8							7
1		3		5	6		8	9	10	11	4		7		2							8
1		3		5	6		8		10				9	11	4	2	7					9
1		3		5	6		8		10				9	11	4		7	2				10
1		3		5	6			8	10				9	11	4		7	2				11
1		3			5	6		8		10	11	4	9				7	2				12
		3			5	6		8		10	11	4	9				7	2	1			13
1		3			5	6		8			11	4	9	10			7	2				14
1		3			5	6		8		10		4	9	11			7	2				15
1				5	6			9	10		4		7		8	2	3	11				16
1				5	6			9	10		4		7		8	2	3	11				17
1				5	6		9		10		4		7		8	2	3	11				18
1				5	6			9	10		4		7		8	2	3	11				19
1		6		5				9	10		4		7		8		2	11				20
1		3		5	6			9	10		4		7		8		2	11				21
1		3		5	6			9			4		7		10		8	2	11			22
1		3		5	6			9			4		7		10		8	2	11			23
1		3		5	6		8	9			4		7		10		2	11				24
1	3			5	6		8	9			4		7		10		2	11				25
1				5				9	6		4		7		10		8	3	11		2	26
1				5				9	6		4		7		10		8	3	11		2	27
1				5	6			9	6	11	4		7		10		8	3			2	28
1			5	6						10		4	7		9		8	3	11		2	29
1		4		5				9	6		4		7		10		8	3	11		2	30
1	2		6	5				9	11		4		7		10		8	3				31
1	2		6	5				9		11	4		7		10		8	3				32
1	2		6	5				9			4		7		10		8	3	11			33
1	2		6	5				9			4		7		10		8	3	11			34
33	7	20	21	30	18	3	16	26	26	10	29	1	31	8	23	7	18	25	1	16	5	
	1	2			10	5	5	2			15		4		12		9			7		

Ord R	Fyfe J	McConnell A	Anderson J	Dick J	Davis FW	Brock J	White W	McGeoch A	Hannah D	Mitchell A	Moir JG	Clark JM	Hunt F	Dailly H	Haywood A	McPhee J	Cottrell EH	McAvoy J	Hamilton TS	Shaw H	J.Garton	#
1				5	6			9	10		4		7		8	2		3	11			1
1		1	1		1	1		1		1		1	1		1		1					

147

1899-1900

Manager: H.Bradshaw

1	Sep	2	(h)	Leicester F	L	0-2	10,000
2		9	(a)	Luton T	W	2-1 Logan, Tennant	3,000
3		16	(h)	Burslem P.Vale	W	1-0 Sanders	6,000
4		23	(a)	Walsall	L	0-2	3,000
5		30	(h)	Middlesbrough	W	3-0 Shaw 2, McCowie	6,000
6	Oct	7	(a)	Chesterfield	L	1-3 Aston	4,000
7		14	(h)	Gainsborough T	W	2-1 Hartley, Hunt (pen)	6,000
8		21	(a)	Bolton W	L	0-1	5,000
9	Nov	4	(a)	Newton Heath	L	0-2	5,000
10		11	(h)	Sheffield W	L	1-2 McCowie	7,000
11		25	(h)	Small Heath	W	3-0 Aston 2, Dick	4,000
12	Dec	2	(a)	New Brighton T	W	2-0 McCowie 2	4,000
13		16	(h)	Burton S	D	1-1 Gaudie	3,000
14		25	(a)	Lincoln C	L	0-5	6,000
15		30	(a)	Leicester F	D	0-0	8,500
16	Jan	6	(h)	Luton T	W	3-1 Gaudie 2, Logan	2,500
17		13	(a)	Burslem P.Vale	D	1-1 Gaudie	2,000
18		20	(h)	Walsall	W	3-1 Logan 2, Gaudie	3,000
19	Feb	3	(a)	Middlesbrough	L	0-1	6,000
20		10	(h)	Chesterfield	W	2-0 Dick, McCowie	3,000
21		17	(a)	Gainsborough T	D	1-1 McCowie	1,000
22		24	(h)	Bolton W	L	0-1	5,500
23	Mar	3	(a)	Loughborough T	W	3-2 Logan, Gaudie, Tennant	800
24		10	(h)	Newton Heath	W	2-1 Hunt, Dick	4,000
25		12	(h)	Loughborough T*	W	12-0 Gaudie 3, Cottrell 2, Dick 2, Main 2, Tennant 2, Anderson	600
26		17	(a)	Sheffield W	L	1-3 McNichol	3,000
27		24	(h)	Lincoln C	W	2-1 McCowie, Gaudie	2,500
28		31	(a)	Small Heath	L	1-3 Gaudie	3,000
29	Apr	7	(h)	New Brighton T	W	5-0 Main, Anderson, Gaudie 2, Logan	2,000
30		14	(a)	Grimsby T	L	0-1	2,000
31		16	(h)	Grimsby T	W	2-0 Tennant 2	5,000
32		21	(a)	Burton S	L	0-2	2,000
33		23	(a)	Barnsley‡	L	2-3 Anderson, Lloyd	500
34		28	(h)	Barnsley	W	5-1 Lloyd 2, Gaudie 2, Dick	3,000

FINAL LEAGUE POSITION: 8th in Division Two.   *After abandoned match (75 mins) on 26 December — Arsenal 4
Loughborough 0. ‡After abandoned match (60 mins) on 1 January — Barnsley 1 Arsenal 1.

Appearances
Goals

FA Cup

3Q	Oct	28	(h)	New Brompton	D	1-1 Hunt	5,500
R	Nov	1	(a)	New Brompton	D	0-0	2,000
2R		6	(n†)	New Brompton	D	2-2 Aston, Hunt	2,000
3R		8	(n§)	New Brompton	D	1-1 Aston	2,000
4R	Nov	14	(n#)	New Brompton	L	0-1	3,000

†Played at Millwall. §Played at Tottenham. #Played at Gravesend.

Appearances
Goals

148

Ord R	McNichol D	Jackson J	Murphy J	Sanders M	Dick J	Hannigan R	McCowie A	Logan P	Aston J	Tennant J	Hunt F	Hartley A	Moir JG	Shaw H	Graham J	Gaudie R	Dunsbee CR	Anderson J	Lloyd F	Main A	Cottrell EH	Hamilton TS	Murrell HR	Spicer TA	
1	2	3	4	5	6	7	8	9	10	11															1
1	2	3	4	5	6		10	9	8	11	7														2
1	2	3	4	5	6		10	9	8	11	7														3
1	2	3	4	5	6		10		8	11	7	9													4
1	2	3	5		6		10	8			7	9	4	11											5
1	2	3	5		6		10		8		7	9	4	11											6
1		3	5		6				8		7	9	4	11	2	10									7
1	2	3	5		6		10		8		7		4	11		9									8
1	2	3	5		6		10		8		7		4	11		9									9
1	2	3	5		6		10		8		7	9				11	4								10
1	2	3	5		6		10		8		7			11		9	4								11
1	2	3	4		5		10		8	11						9		6	7						12
1	2	3	4		5		10				8			11		9		6	7						13
1	2	3	4		5		8			11						9		6	7	10					14
1	2	3	4		5		10	8		11						9		6	7						15
1	2	3	4		5		10	8		11						9		6	7						16
1	2	3	4		5		10	8		11						9		6	7						17
1	2	3	4		5		10	8		11						9		6	7						18
1	2	3	4		5			8		11						9		6	7	10					19
1	2	3	4		5		10	8		11	7					9		6							20
1	2	3	4		5		10	8		11						9		6	7						21
1	2	3	4		5		10	8		11						9		6	7						22
1	2	3			5		10	8		11	7		4			9		6							23
1	2	3			5		10	8		11	7		4			9		6							24
1	2	3			5					11	7		4			10		6		9	8				25
1	2				5		10	8		11			4				6	3	7	9					26
	2	3			5		10	8		11			4			9		6	7			1			27
		3			5		10	8		11			4			9	6		7			1	2		28
					5			8		11			4	7		9	6	2		10		1	3		29
			2		5			8		11						9	6	4	7	10			3	1	30
	2		4		5			8		11						10		6	7	9			3	1	31
	2		4		5			8		10				11			6	9	7			1	3		32
	2		4					9		10	7			8			6	5	11			1	3		33
	2	3	4		5			8		11						9		6	7	10		1			34
26	30	28	27	4	33	1	25	23	11	26	16	5	12	10	1	25	8	22	18	8	1	6	6	2	
	1			1	6		7	6	3	6	2	1		2		15		3	3	3	2				

1	2	3	5		6		10		8		7	9	4	11											3Q
1	2	3	5		6		10	9			8		4	11					7						R
1	2	3	11		5		10		8		7	9	4				6								2R
1	2	3	5		6		10		8		7	9		11			4								3R
1	2	3	5		6	7	10		8		9	11					4								4R
5	5	5	5		5	1	5	1	4		5	4	3	3			3		1						
									2		2														

1900-01

Manager: H.Bradshaw

1	Sep	1	(h)	Gainsborough T	W	2-1	Turner, Blackwood	8,000
2		8	(h)	Walsall	D	1-1	Anderson	7,000
3		15	(a)	Burton S	L	0-1		1,300
4		22	(h)	Barnsley	L	1-2	Main	700
5		29	(h)	Chesterfield	W	1-0	Main	5,500
6	Oct	6	(a)	Blackpool	D	1-1	Blackwood	3,000
7		13	(h)	Stockport C	W	2-0	Dick, Place	5,000
8		20	(a)	Small Heath	L	1-2	Coles	8,000
9		27	(h)	Grimsby T	D	1-1	Turner	7,000
10	Nov	3	(h)	Leicester F	W	2-1	Blackwood, Gaudie	7,000
11		10	(h)	Newton Heath	W	2-1	Anderson, Turner	8,000
12		17	(a)	Glossop	W	1-0	Place	3,000
13		24	(h)	Middlesbrough	W	1-0	Blackwood	8,000
14	Dec	1	(a)	Burnley	L	0-3		4,000
15		8	(h)	Burslem P.Vale	W	3-0	Blackwood, Place 2	7,000
16		15	(a)	Leicester F	L	0-1		10,000
17		22	(h)	New Brighton	W	2-1	Main, Gaudie	6,000
18		24	(a)	Walsall	L	0-1		4,000
19		29	(a)	Gainsborough T	L	0-1		2,000
20	Jan	12	(h)	Burton S	W	3-1	Blackwood, Main, Turner	5,000
21		19	(a)	Barnsley	L	0-3		3,000
22		26	(a)	Lincoln C	D	3-3	Gaudie 2, Main	3,000
23	Feb	16	(a)	Stockport C	L	1-3	Turner	3,000
24		19	(a)	Chesterfield	W	1-0	Gaudie	2,000
25	Mar	2	(a)	Grimsby T	L	0-1		2,500
26		9	(h)	Lincoln C	D	0-0		3,000
27		16	(a)	Newton Heath	L	0-1		5,000
28		23	(h)	Glossop	W	2-0	Place, Tennant	3,000
29		30	(a)	Middlesbrough	D	1-1	Main	6,000
30	Apr	6	(h)	Burnley	W	3-1	Gaudie 2, Coles	7,000
31		8	(h)	Blackpool	W	3-1	Gaudie, Low, Tennant	5,000
32		13	(a)	Burslem P.Vale	L	0-1		1,000
33		22	(h)	Small Heath	W	1-0	Cottrell	3,500
34		27	(a)	New Brighton	L	0-1		2,000

FINAL LEAGUE POSITION: 7th in Division Two

Appearances
Goals

FA Cup

Sup	Jan	5	(a)	Darwen	W	2-0	Blackwood, Tennant	5,000
1	Feb	9	(h)	Blackburn R	W	2-0	Tennant, Low	11,000
2		23	(h)	West Brom A	L	0-1		20,000

Appearances
Goals

Spicer TA	McNichol D	Jackson J	Anderson J	Dick J	Place W	Low TP	McCowie A	Blackwood J	Turner P	Tennant J	Ashcroft J	Grieve T	Main A	Coles FG	Cottrell EH	Cross AG	Gaudie R	Wolfe G	#
1	2	3	4	5	6	7	8	9	10	11									1
1	2	3	4	5	6	7	8	9	10	11									2
	2	3	4	5	6	7	8	9	10	11	1								3
	2	3	4	5	6	7			10	11	1	8	9						4
	2	3	6	5	10	7				11	1		9	4	8				5
		3	6	5	10	7		9		11	1			4	8	2			6
	2	3	6	5	10	7		9		11	1			4	8				7
	2	3	6	5	10	7		9	8	11	1			4					8
	2	3	6	5	10	7		9		11	1			4		8			9
	2	3	6	5	10	7		9		11	1			4		8			10
	2	3	6	5				9	10	11	1	7		4	8				11
	2	3	6	5	10			9		11	1	7		4	8				12
	2	3	6	5				9	10	11	1		8	4			7		13
	2	3	6	5	10			9	8	11	1			4			7		14
	2	3		6	10	7		9		11	1			4	8		5		15
	2	3		6	10	7		9		11	1			4	8		5		16
	2	3	6	5	10	7				11	1		9	4	8				17
	3	2	6		10	7				11	1		9	4	8		5		18
	2	3	4	5	6				10	11	1		9	7	8				19
	2	3	4	5	6			9	10	11	1		8				7		20
	2	3	4	5	6			9	10	11	1		8				7		21
	2	3	6	5		7			10	11	1		8	4			9		22
	2	3	6	5		7			10	11	1		8	4			9		23
	2		3	5	6				10	11	1	7	8	4			9		24
	2	3	6	5	9				10	11	1	7	8	4					25
	2	3	6	5		7		9	10	11	1		8	4					26
	2	3	4	5	6				10	11	1	7	9		8				27
	2	3	6	5	9	7			10	11	1		8	4					28
	2		3	5	6	7			10	11	1		8	4			9		29
		3	6	5		7			10	11	1		8	4		2	9		30
		3	6	5		7			10	11	1		8	4		2	9		31
	2	3	6	5		7			10	11	1		8	4			9		32
	2	3	6	5		7			10	11	1			4	8		9		33
	2	3		5	6	7			10	11	1		8	4			9		34
2	30	32	32	33	25	24	3	17	33	25	32	6	20	27	5	3	22	3	
		2	1	5	1		6	5	2		6	2	1		8				

Spicer TA	McNichol D	Jackson J	Anderson J	Dick J	Place W	Low TP	McCowie A	Blackwood J	Turner P	Tennant J	Ashcroft J	Grieve T	Main A	Coles FG	Cottrell EH	Cross AG	Gaudie R	Wolfe G	
	2	3	6	5				9	10	11	1		8	4			7		Sup
	2	3	6	5		7			10	11	1		8	4			9		1
	2	3	6	5		7			10	11	1		8	4			9		2
	3	3	3	3		2		1	3	3	3		3	3			3		
						1			1		2								

151

1901-02

Manager: H.Bradshaw

1	Sep	2	(h)	Barnsley	W 2-1	Foxall, Swann	6,000
2		7	(h)	Leicester F	W 2-0	J.Anderson, Briercliffe	10,000
3		14	(a)	Preston NE	L 0-2		6,000
4		21	(h)	Burnley	W 4-0	Briercliffe 2, Laidlaw, Foxall	10,000
5		28	(a)	Burslem P.Vale	L 0-1		3,000
6	Oct	5	(h)	Chesterfield	W 3-2	Laidlaw, J.Anderson (pen), Logan	8,000
7		12	(a)	Gainsborough T	D 2-2	Main, Owens	Fair
8		19	(h)	Middlesbrough	L 0-3		8,000
9		26	(a)	Bristol C	W 3-0	Briercliffe 2, Place	10,500
10	Nov	9	(a)	Stockport C	D 0-0		3,000
11		16	(h)	Newton Heath	W 2-0	Owens, Briercliffe	5,000
12		23	(a)	Glossop	W 1-0	Foxall	3,000
13		30	(h)	Doncaster R	W 1-0	Swann	10,000
14	Dec	7	(a)	Lincoln C	D 0-0		4,000
15		21	(h)	Burton U	L 0-1		4,000
16		25	(h)	Blackpool	D 0-0		3,500
17		26	(h)	Burslem P.Vale	W 3-1	Briercliffe, Gooing, Main	5,500
18		28	(a)	Barnsley	L 0-2		3,000
19	Jan	4	(a)	Leicester F	L 1-2	Gooing	7,000
20		11	(h)	Preston NE	D 0-0		8,000
21		18	(a)	Burnley	D 0-0		4,000
22	Feb	1	(a)	Chesterfield	W 3-1	Main, Dick, W.Anderson	2,000
23		8	(h)	Gainsborough T	W 5-0	Fitchie 2, Briercliffe 2, Gooing	7,000
24		15	(a)	Middlesbrough	L 0-1		8,500
25		22	(h)	Bristol C	W 2-0	Gooing 2	10,000
26	Mar	1	(a)	Blackpool	W 3-1	W.Anderson, Dick, Edgar	3,000
27		8	(h)	Stockport C	W 3-0	Gooing, W.Anderson 2	6,000
28		15	(a)	Newton Heath	W 1-0	W.Anderson	4,000
29		22	(h)	Glossop	W 4-0	Dick, Gooing 2, Briercliffe	6,000
30		29	(a)	Doncaster R	L 0-1		3,000
31		31	(h)	West Brom A	W 2-1	Gooing, Main	10,000
32	Apr	5	(h)	Lincoln C	W 2-0	Briercliffe, Fitchie	6,000
33		12	(a)	West Brom A	L 1-2	Main	8,878
34		19	(a)	Burton U	L 0-2		3,000

FINAL LEAGUE POSITION: 4th in Division Two

Appearances
Goals

FA Cup

Sup	Dec	14	(h)	Luton T	D 1-1	Jackson	10,000
R		18	(a)	Luton T	W 2-0	Gooing, Place	3,000
1	Jan	25	(h)	Newcastle U	L 0-2		15,000

Appearances
Goals

152

Player appearance and goals grid.

Ashcroft J	Cross AG	Jackson J	Coles FG	Dick J	Anderson J	Briercliffe T	Logan P	Swann A	Place W	Foxall A	Main A	Laidlaw J	Edgar J	Owens I	McNichol D	Gooing WH	Anderson W	Fitchie TT	Vaughan JW	
1	2	3	4	5	6	7	8	9	10	11										1
1	2	3	4	5	6	7		9	10	11	8									2
1	2	3	4	5	6	7		9	10	11	8									3
1	2	3	4		5	7	9	10	6	11			8							4
1	2	3	4		5	7	9	10	6	11			8							5
1	2	3	4		5	7	9	10	6	11			8							6
1	2	3	4		5	7			6	11	9		8		10					7
1		3	4		5	7	9		6	11	8		10			2				8
1	3		4		5	7			6	11	9		8		10	2				9
1	2	3	4	5	6	7				11	9		8		10					10
1		3	4	5	6	7				11	8				10	2	9			11
1		3	4	5		7			6	11	8				10	2	9			12
1		3	4	5	6	7		11			8				10	2	9			13
1	2	3	4	5		7			6	11	8				10	2	9			14
1	2	3	4	5		7			6	11	8				10	2	9			15
1	2	3	4	5		7			6	11	8				10	2	9			16
1	2	3		5	4	7			6	11	8		10			2	9			17
1	2	3	4	5		7			6	11	8		10			2	9			18
1	2	3	4	5		7			6	11	8		10			2	9			19
1		3	4	5	6	7				11	8				2	9	10			20
1		3	4	5	6	7				11	8				2	9	10			21
1		3	4	5	6	7				11	8				2	9	10			22
1		3	4	5	6	7				11	8				2	9		10		23
1		3	4	5	6	7				11	8				2	9	10			24
1		3	4	5	6	7					8	11			2	9		10		25
1		3	4	5	6	7					8	11			2	9	10			26
1		3	4	5	6	7				11		8			2	9	10			27
1		3	4	5	6	7				11	8				2	9	10			28
1		3	4	5	6	7				11	8				2	9	10			29
1		3	4	5	6	7				11	8				2	9	10			30
1		3	4	5	6	7				11	8				2	9	10			31
1		3		5	6	7		4		11					2	9	8	10		32
1		3	4	5	6	7				11	8				2	9	10			33
1		3	4	5	6	7				11	8				2	9	10			34
34	15	33	32	28	28	34	5	7	17	31	28	3	10	9	20	24	13	3		
		3	2	11	1	2	1	3	5	2	1	2			9	5	3			

Ashcroft J	Cross AG	Jackson J	Coles FG	Dick J	Anderson J	Briercliffe T	Logan P	Swann A	Place W	Foxall A	Main A	Laidlaw J	Edgar J	Owens I	McNichol D	Gooing WH	Anderson W	Fitchie TT	Vaughan JW	
1	2	3	4	5		7			6		8		10		9			11		Sup
1	2	3	4	5	6	7				11	8		10			9				R
1		3	4	5	6					11	8	7			2	9	10			1
3	2	3	3	3	2	2		3		3		1	2	1	3	1		1		
	1								1							1				

153

1902-03

Manager: H.Bradshaw

1	Sep	6	(a)	Preston NE	D	2-2	Connor, McMahon (og)	9,000
2		13	(h)	Burslem P.Vale	W	3-0	Briercliffe, Dick, Coleman	12,000
3		20	(a)	Barnsley	D	1-1	Coleman	5,000
4		27	(h)	Gainsborough T	W	6-1	Gooing 3, Connor, Coleman, Lawrence	10,000
5	Oct	4	(a)	Bristol C	L	0-1		12,024
6		11	(h)	Bristol C	W	2-1	Gooing, Hunt (pen)	16,000
7		18	(a)	Glossop	W	2-1	Coleman 2	1,000
8		25	(h)	Manchester U	L	0-1		12,000
9	Nov	1	(h)	Manchester C	W	1-0	Gooing	12,000
10		8	(h)	Blackpool	W	2-1	Bradshaw, Lawrence	8,000
11		15	(a)	Burnley	W	3-0	W.Anderson, Gooing, Briercliffe	2,500
12		22	(a)	Doncaster R	W	1-0	Gooing	5,000
13		29	(h)	Lincoln C	W	2-1	Coleman, Briercliffe	14,000
14	Dec	6	(a)	Small Heath	L	0-2		10,000
15		20	(a)	Manchester C	L	1-4	Gooing	25,000
16		25	(a)	Burton U	L	1-2	Briercliffe	4,000
17		27	(h)	Burnley	W	5-1	Coleman 3, Briercliffe, W.Anderson	13,000
18	Jan	1	(a)	Stockport C	W	1-0	Gooing	2,000
19		3	(h)	Preston NE	W	3-1	Gooing, W.Anderson, Linward	12,000
20		10	(a)	Burslem P.Vale	D	1-1	Briercliffe	4,000
21		17	(h)	Barnsley	W	4-0	Shanks 2, W.Anderson, Briercliffe	10,000
22		24	(a)	Gainsborough T	W	1-0	W.Anderson	3,000
23		31	(h)	Burton U	W	3-0	Gooing, Shanks, Coleman	12,000
24	Feb	14	(h)	Glossop	D	0-0		10,000
25		28	(h)	Stockport C	W	3-1	Lawrence, Coleman, Shanks	8,000
26	Mar	7	(a)	Blackpool	D	0-0		3,000
27		9	(a)	Manchester U	L	0-3		5,000
28		14	(a)	Chesterfield	D	2-2	Coleman 2	5,000
29		21	(h)	Doncaster R	W	3-0	Linward, Coleman, Langton (og)	10,000
30		28	(a)	Lincoln C	D	2-2	Gooing, Linward	3,000
31	Apr	4	(h)	Small Heath	W	6-1	Coleman 2, Linward 2, Gooing 2	15,000
32		10	(h)	Chesterfield	W	3-0	Briercliffe, Gooing, Thorpe (og)	14,000
33		11	(a)	Leicester F	W	2-0	Coleman, Gooing	10,000
34		13	(h)	Leicester F	D	0-0		12,000

FINAL LEAGUE POSITION: 3rd in Division Two

Appearances
Goals

FA Cup

Sup	Dec	13	(a)	Brentford	D	1-1	Gooing	7,500
R		17	(h)	Brentford	W	5-0	Coleman 2, Connor, Gooing, J.Anderson	3,000
1	Feb	7	(h)	Sheffield U	L	1-3	W.Anderson	24,000

Appearances
Goals

154

No.	Ashcroft J	McNichol D	Cross AG	Coles FG	Dick J	McEachrane RJ	Briercliffe T	Connor MJ	Gooing WH	Coleman JG	Lawrence ET	Jackson J	Anderson J	Hunt F	Main A	Anderson W	Bradshaw W	Wolfe G	Theobald WS	Linward W	Bannister W	Shanks T	Fitchie TT
1	1	2	3	4	5	6	7	8	9	10	11												
2	1	2	3	4	5	6	7	8	9	10	11												
3	1	2	3	4	5	6	7	8	9	10	11												
4	1	2	3	4	5	6	7	8	9	10	11												
5	1	2		4	5	6	7	8	9	10	11	3											
6	1	2		4		6	7		9	10	11	3	5	8									
7	1	2		4		6	7	8		10	11	3	5		9								
8	1	2			5	6	7	8		10	11	3	4		9								
9	1		2	4		6	7		9	10	11	3		8	5								
10	1		2	4		7	8	9			11	3	6		5	10							
11	1	2		4		7	8	9			11	3	6		5	10							
12	1		2	4		7	8	9			11	3	6		5	10							
13	1		2	4		7	8	9	10	11	3	6			5								
14	1			4		6	7	8	9	10	11	3	2		5								
15	1	2		4		6	7	8	9	10	11	3			5								
16	1		2	4		6	7	8	9	10	11						3	5					
17	1		2	4		6	7		9	10					8		3	5	11				
18	1	2		4		6	7		9	10		3			8				11	5			
19	1	2		4		6	7		9	10		3			8				11	5			
20	1	2		4		6	7			10		3			9				11	5	8		
21	1		2	4		6	7			10		3			9				11	5	8		
22	1		2	4		6	7		9		11	3			10					5	8		
23	1	2		4		6	7		9	10	11	3								5	8		
24	1	2		4		6	7			10		3			9				11	5	8		
25	1	2		4		6				10	11	3		7	9					5	8		
26	1	2		4		6	7		9	10	11	3								5	8		
27	1	2		4		6	7		9	10		3							11	5	8		
28	1	2		4		6	7			10		3			9				11	5	8		
29	1	2		4		6	7	8				3			10				11	5		9	
30	1	2		4		6	7	9	8			3							11	5	10		
31	1		2	4		6	7	9	8			3							11	5	10		
32	1		2	4		6	7	9	8			3							11	5	10		
33	1		2	4		6	7	9	8			3							11	5	10		
34	1		2	5	4	6	7	8				3			9				11		10		
Apps	34	21	14	18	26	28	33	14	25	30	20	28	8	3	7	15	1	2	2	14	16	14	1
Goals				1		8	2	16	17	3			1		5	1				5	4		

3 own-goals

	Ashcroft J	McNichol D	Cross AG	Coles FG	Dick J	McEachrane RJ	Briercliffe T	Connor MJ	Gooing WH	Coleman JG	Lawrence ET	Jackson J	Anderson J	Hunt F	Main A	Anderson W	Bradshaw W	Wolfe G	Theobald WS	Linward W	Bannister W	Shanks T	Fitchie TT
Sup	1	2		4	5			8	9	10	11	3	6	7									
R	1	2		4	5		7	8	9	10	11	3	6										
I	1		2	4		6	7		9	10	11	3			8					5			
	3	2	1	2	3	1	2	2	3	3	3	3	2	1	1					1			
								1	2	2		1			1								

155

1903-04

Manager: H.Bradshaw

1	Sep	5	(h)	Blackpool	W 3-0	Gooing 2, Coleman	10,000
2		12	(a)	Gainsborough T	W 2-0	Coleman 2	3,000
3		19	(h)	Burton U	W 8-0	Briercliffe 3, Coleman 2, Gooing, Shanks, Linward	12,000
4		26	(a)	Bristol C	W 4-0	Gooing 2, Coleman, Linward	14,000
5	Oct	3	(h)	Manchester U	W 4-0	Shanks, Coleman, Busby, Briercliffe	20,000
6		10	(a)	Glossop	W 3-1	Gooing 2, Coleman	1,000
7		24	(a)	Burslem P.Vale	W 3-2	Briercliffe, Shanks, Gooing	3,000
8		26	(h)	Leicester F	W 8-0	Shanks 3, Pratt 2, Gooing, Briercliffe, Busby	5,000
9		31	(a)	Barnsley	L 1-2	Briercliffe	6,000
10	Nov	7	(h)	Lincoln C	W 4-0	Shanks 3, Coleman	16,000
11		21	(h)	Chesterfield	W 6-0	Briercliffe, Shanks 2, Coleman, Linward, Gooing	10,000
12		28	(a)	Bolton W	L 1-2	Gooing	6,000
13	Dec	19	(h)	Grimsby T	W 5-1	Shanks 4, Coleman	14,000
14		25	(h)	Bradford C	W 4-1	Shanks, Sands, Coleman 2	18,000
15		26	(a)	Leicester F	D 0-0		14,000
16	Jan	1	(a)	Stockport C	D 0-0		4,000
17		2	(a)	Blackpool	D 2-2	Shanks, Sands	4,000
18		9	(h)	Gainsborough T	W 6-0	Sands, Briercliffe, Gooing 2, Shanks, Coleman	10,000
19		16	(a)	Burton U	L 1-3	Briercliffe	2,000
20		30	(a)	Manchester U	L 0-1		40,000
21	Feb	27	(h)	Barnsley	W 3-0	Gooing, Shanks, Coleman	12,000
22		29	(h)	Burnley	W 4-0	Shanks 3, Gooing	4,000
23	Mar	5	(a)	Lincoln C	W 2-0	Dick, Shanks	5,000
24		12	(h)	Stockport C	W 5-2	Coleman 2, Gooing, Linward 2	10,000
25		14	(h)	Bristol C	W 2-0	Coleman 2	10,000
26		19	(a)	Chesterfield	L 0-1		9,000
27		26	(h)	Bolton W	W 3-0	Gooing 2, Coleman	18,000
28	Apr	1	(a)	Preston NE	D 0-0		12,000
29		2	(a)	Burnley	L 0-1		5,000
30		4	(h)	Glossop	W 2-1	Coleman, Shanks (pen)	17,000
31		9	(h)	Preston NE	D 0-0		28,000
32		16	(a)	Grimsby T	D 2-2	Gooing, Coleman	6,000
33		19	(a)	Bradford C	W 3-0	Coleman, Bradshaw, Watson	12,000
34		25	(h)	Burslem P.Vale	D 0-0		20,000

FINAL LEAGUE POSITION: 2nd in Division Two

Appearances
Goals

FA Cup

Sup	Dec	12	(a)	Bristol R	D 1-1	Dick	14,000
R		15	(h)	Bristol R	D 1-1	Tait (og)	12,000
2R		21	(n*)	Bristol R	W 1-0	Briercliffe	10,000
1	Feb	6	(h)	Fulham	W 1-0	Shanks	15,000
2		20	(h)	Manchester C	L 0-2		30,000

*Played at Tottenham

Appearances
Goals

156

Ashcroft J	Thorpe H	Jackson J	Dick J	Sands PR	McEachrane RJ	Briercliffe T	Coleman JG	Gooing WH	Pratt TP	Linward W	Shanks T	Busby W	Cross AG	Bannister W	Ransom F	Anderson E	Coles FG	Watson R	Bradshaw W	No.
1	2	3	4	5	6	7	8	9	10	11										1
1	2	3	4	5	6	7	8	9		11	10									2
1	2	3	4	5	6	7	8	9		11	10									3
1	2	3	4	5	6	7	8	9		11	10									4
1	2	3	4	5	6	7	8	9			10	11								5
1	2	3	4	5	6	7	8	9		11	10									6
1		3	4	5	6	7	8	9	10	11			2							7
1		3	4		6	7	9	8	10	11			2	5						8
1		3	4	5	6	7	8	9		11	10		2							9
1	2	3	4		6	7	8	9		11	10			5						10
1		3	4	5	6	7	8	9		11	10		2							11
1		3	4	5	6	7	8	9		11	10		2							12
1		3	4	5	6	7	8	9		11	10		2							13
1		3	4	5	6	7	8	9		11	10		2							14
1		3	4	5		7	8	9		11	10		2		6					15
1		3	4	5	6	7	8	9			10	11	2							16
1		3	4	5	6	7		9	8		10	11	2							17
1		3	4	5	6	7	8	9		11	10		2							18
1	3			5	6	7	9	8	10	11			2				4			19
1		3	4	5	6	7	8	9		11	10		2							20
1		3	4	5	6	7	8	9		11	10		2							21
1		3	4	5	6	7		9	8	11	10		2							22
1		3	4	5	6	7		9	8	11	10		2							23
1		3	4	5	6	7	8	9		11	10		2							24
1		3	4	5	6	7	8	9		11	10		2							25
1		3	4	5	6	7	8	9		11	10		2							26
1		3	4	5	6		8	9		11	10		2						7	27
1	2	3	4	5	6	7		9	8	11	10									28
1	2	3	4	5	6		8	9		11	10							7		29
1		3	4	5	6		8	9		11	10		2					7		30
1		3	4	5	6		8	9		11	10		2					7		31
1		3	4	5	6		8	9	10	11			2					7		32
1		3	4	5	6		8	9		11			2			10		7		33
1		3	4	5	6		8	9		11			2			10		7		34
34	10	33	33	32	33	27	28	34	8	27	30	5	25	2	1	2	1	6	3	
		1	3			10	23	19	2	5	24	2				1	1			

Ashcroft J	Thorpe H	Jackson J	Dick J	Sands PR	McEachrane RJ	Briercliffe T	Coleman JG	Gooing WH	Pratt TP	Linward W	Shanks T	Busby W	Cross AG	Bannister W	Ransom F	Anderson E	Coles FG	Watson R	Bradshaw W	
1		3	4		6	7	8	9	10		11		2	5						Sup
1		3	4		6	7	8	9	10			11	2	5						R
1		3	4		6	7	8	9		11	10		2	5						2R
1		3	4	5	6	7	8	9		11	10		2							1
1		3	4	5	6	7	8	9		11	10		2							2
5		5	5	2	5	5	5	5	2	3	4	1	5	3						
			1		1			1												

1 own-goal

1904-05

Manager: P.Kelso

1	Sep	3	(a)	Newcastle U	L	0-3		25,000
2		10	(h)	Preston NE	D	0-0		25,000
3		17	(a)	Middlesbrough	L	0-1		15,000
4		24	(h)	Wolves	W	2-0	Satterthwaite, Coleman	20,000
5	Oct	1	(a)	Bury	D	1-1	Briercliffe	8,000
6		8	(h)	Aston Villa	W	1-0	Gooing	32,850
7		15	(a)	Blackburn R	D	1-1	Satterthwaite	10,000
8		22	(h)	Nottingham F	L	0-3		20,000
9		29	(a)	Sheffield W	W	3-0	Crowe 2, Coleman	15,000
10	Nov	5	(h)	Sunderland	D	0-0		30,000
11		12	(h)	Stoke	W	2-1	Crowe, Hunter	20,000
12		19	(a)	Derby C	D	0-0		12,000
13	Dec	3	(a)	Small Heath	L	1-2	Hunter	20,000
14		10	(h)	Manchester C	W	1-0	Satterthwaite	16,000
15		17	(a)	Notts C	W	5-1	Fitchie 3, Satterthwaite 2	15,000
16		24	(h)	Sheffield U	W	1-0	Fitchie	20,000
17		26	(a)	Aston Villa	L	1-3	Satterthwaite	40,000
18		27	(a)	Nottingham F	W	3-0	Hunter, Briercliffe, Satterthwaite	16,000
19		28	(a)	Sheffield U	L	0-4		30,000
20		31	(h)	Newcastle U	L	0-2		30,000
21	Jan	7	(a)	Preston NE	L	0-3		13,000
22		14	(h)	Middlesbrough	D	1-1	Fitchie	15,000
23		21	(a)	Wolves	L	1-4	Briercliffe	8,500
24		28	(h)	Bury	W	2-1	Satterthwaite 2	20,000
25	Feb	11	(h)	Blackburn R	W	2-0	Fitchie, Briercliffe	15,000
26		25	(h)	Sheffield W	W	3-0	Satterthwaite, Coleman 2	20,000
27	Mar	4	(a)	Sunderland	D	1-1	Coleman	14,000
28		11	(a)	Stoke	L	0-2		4,000
29		18	(h)	Derby C	D	0-0		15,000
30	Apr	1	(h)	Small Heath	D	1-1	Hunter	20,000
31		5	(a)	Everton	L	0-1		12,000
32		8	(a)	Manchester C	L	0-1		18,000
33		15	(h)	Notts C	L	1-2	Templeton	12,000
34		22	(h)	Everton	W	2-1	Satterthwaite, Ducat	25,000

FINAL LEAGUE POSITION: 10th in Division One

Appearances
Goals

FA Cup

1	Feb	4	(h)	Bristol C	D	0-0		25,000
R		8	(a)	Bristol C	L	0-1		10,000

Appearances
Goals

158

Football season appearance/line-up grid (shirt numbers by player and match).

Ashcroft J	Gray A	Jackson J	Dick J	Buchan J	Bigden JH	Briercliffe T	Coleman JG	Gooing WH	Hunter J	Satterthwaite CO	Sands PR	McEachrane RJ	Davidson A	Cross AG	Crowe A	Linward W	Neave D	Fitchie TT	Templeton RB	Watson R	Dwight F	Ducat A	Bellamy JT	#
1	2	3	4	5	6	7	8	9	10	11														1
1	2	3	4		6	7	8	9	10	11	5													2
1	2	3	4		6	7	8	9	10	11	5													3
1	2	3	4		6	7	8	9	10	11	5													4
1	2	3	4		6	7	8	9	10	11	5													5
1	2	3	4			7	8	9	10	11	5	6												6
		3	4			7	8	9	10	11	5	6		1	2									7
1		3	4			7	8	9	10	11	5	6		2										8
1	2	3	4				8		7	10	5	6				9	11							9
1	2	3	4				8		7	10	5	6				9	11							10
1	2	3	4				8		7	10	5	6				9	11							11
1		3	4				8		7	10	5	6		2		9	11							12
1	2	3	4				8	9	7	10	5	6				11								13
1	2	3	4			7	8	9		10	5	6				11								14
1	2	3	4			7		8	9		5	6						10	11					15
1	2	3	4			7		8	9		5	6						10	11					16
1	2	3	4	5		7		8	9			6						10	11					17
1	2		4			7		8	9		5	6		3				10	11					18
1	2		4			7		10	8		5	6		3					11	9				19
1	2		4			7			9		5	6		3				11	10	8				20
1	2		4		11	7	8		10	9	5	6							3					21
1	2	3	4			7	8		9		5	6						11	10					22
1	2	3	4			7	8		9		5	6						11	10					23
1	2		4			7	8	9	10		5	6		3					11					24
1	2	3	4			7					5	6						10	11	8		9		25
1	2	3	4			7	8		10		5	6							11			9		26
1	2	3	4		6	7	8		10		5								11			9		27
1	2	3	4		6	7	8				5							10	11			9		28
1	2	3	4		6	7	8		10		5								11			9		29
1		3	4			7	8		10		5	6		2					11			9		30
1		3	4	5		7	8		10			6		2					11			9		31
1		3	4			7	8		10		5	6		2					11			9		32
1		3	4		6	7	8		10		5			2					11			9		33
1		3	4		6		8		10		5			2					11			9	7	34
33	26	29	33	8	7	28	26	11	22	30	31	24	1	12	4	6	3	9	16	3	1	10	1	
						4	5	1	4	11				3				6	1			1		

Ashcroft J	Gray A	Jackson J	Dick J	Buchan J	Bigden JH	Briercliffe T	Coleman JG	Gooing WH	Hunter J	Satterthwaite CO	Sands PR	McEachrane RJ	Davidson A	Cross AG	Crowe A	Linward W	Neave D	Fitchie TT	Templeton RB	Watson R	Dwight F	Ducat A	Bellamy JT	#
1	2	3	4			7	8	9	10	5	6								11					1
1	2	3	4			7	8		10	5	6								11	9				R
2	2	2	2			2	2	1	2	2	2								2	1				

159

1905-06

Manager: P.Kelso

#	Month	Date	H/A	Opponent	Result	Score	Scorers	Attendance
1	Sep	2	(h)	Liverpool	W	3-1	Coleman, Satterthwaite, Blair	20,000
2		9	(a)	Sheffield U	L	1-3	Blair	16,000
3		16	(h)	Notts C	D	1-1	Fitchie	16,000
4		18	(h)	Preston NE	D	2-2	Fitchie 2	12,000
5		23	(a)	Stoke	L	1-2	Fitchie	15,000
6		30	(h)	Bolton W	D	0-0		20,000
7	Oct	7	(a)	Wolves	W	2-0	Coleman 2	9,000
8		14	(a)	Blackburn R	L	0-2		10,000
9		21	(h)	Sunderland	W	2-0	Blair, Bellamy (pen)	13,000
10		28	(a)	Birmingham	L	1-2	Crowe	16,000
11	Nov	4	(h)	Everton	L	1-2	Coleman	18,000
12		11	(a)	Derby C	L	1-5	Satterthwaite	6,000
13		18	(h)	Sheffield W	L	0-2		20,000
14		25	(a)	Nottingham F	L	1-3	Freeman	8,000
15	Dec	2	(h)	Manchester C	W	2-0	Freeman 2	16,000
16		9	(a)	Bury	L	0-2		8,000
17		16	(h)	Middlesbrough	D	2-2	Bellamy, Freeman	12,000
18		23	(a)	Preston NE	D	2-2	Neave 2	6,000
19		25	(h)	Newcastle U	W	4-3	Ducat 2, Fitchie 2	20,000
20		27	(a)	Aston Villa	L	1-2	Fitchie	30,000
21		30	(a)	Liverpool	L	0-3		15,000
22	Jan	1	(a)	Bolton W	L	1-6	Satterthwaite	30,000
23		6	(h)	Sheffield U	W	5-1	Coleman 2, Fitchie, Garbutt, Ducat	10,000
24		20	(a)	Notts C	L	0-1		5,000
25		27	(h)	Stoke	L	1-2	Neave	10,000
26	Feb	10	(h)	Wolves	W	2-1	Freeman 2	10,000
27		17	(h)	Blackburn R	W	3-2	Coleman 2, Bellamy (pen)	8,000
28	Mar	3	(h)	Birmingham	W	5-0	Satterthwaite 2, Coleman, Sharp, Freeman	25,000
29		17	(h)	Derby C	W	1-0	Neave	20,000
30		21	(a)	Everton	W	1-0	Garbutt	8,000
31		24	(a)	Sheffield W	L	2-4	Sharp (pen), Fitchie	15,000
32	Apr	2	(h)	Nottingham F	W	3-1	Neave 2, Freeman	10,000
33		7	(a)	Manchester C	W	2-1	Satterthwaite 2	12,000
34		13	(h)	Aston Villa	W	2-1	Coleman, Freeman	30,000
35		14	(h)	Bury	W	4-0	Ducat, Coleman, Satterthwaite 2	20,000
36		16	(a)	Newcastle U	D	1-1	Garbutt	25,000
37		21	(a)	Middlesbrough	L	0-2		12,000
38		25	(a)	Sunderland	D	2-2	Satterthwaite, Coleman	8,000

FINAL LEAGUE POSITION: 12th in Division One

Appearances
Goals

FA Cup

#	Month	Date	H/A	Opponent	Result	Score	Scorers	Attendance
1	Jan	13	(h)	West Ham U	D	1-1	Sharp (pen)	18,000
R		18	(a)	West Ham U	W	3-2	Ducat, Satterthwaite, Garbutt	12,000
2	Feb	3	(h)	Watford	W	3-0	Freeman, Coleman, Fitchie	11,000
3		24	(h)	Sunderland	W	5-0	Garbutt 2, Fitchie, Sands, Coleman	30,000
4	Mar	10	(a)	Manchester U	W	3-2	Freeman 2, Coleman	26,500
SF		31	(n*)	Newcastle U	L	0-2		19,964

*Played at the Victoria Ground, Stoke-on-Trent.

Appearances
Goals

160

Football club appearance record — shirt numbers by player and match.

Ashcroft J	Gray A	Sharp J	Dick J	Sands PR	McEachrane RJ	Bellamy JT	Coleman JG	Satterthwaite CO	Blair J	Templeton RB	Fitchie TT	Ducat A	Theobald WS	Arnold T	Crowe A	Cross AG	Kemp F	Bigden JH	Freeman BC	Garbutt W	Neave D	McDonald HL	Bateup E	Grice NJ	
1	2	3	4	5	6	7	8	9	10	11															1
1	2	3	4	5	6	7		9	10	11	8														2
1	2	3	4	5	6	7			10	11	8	9													3
1	2	3	4		6	7			10	11	8	9	5												4
1	2	3	4	5	6				10	11	8	9		7											5
1	2	3	4	5	6				10	11	8			7	9										6
1	2	3	4	5	6	7		9	10	11	8														7
1	2	3	4		6	7		9	10	11	8		5												8
1	2	3	4	5	6	7		9	10	11	8														9
1	2		4	5	6	7			10		8			9	3	11									10
1		3	4	5	6	7		9	10		8				2	11									11
1		3	4	5	6	7		9	10	11	8				2										12
1	2	3	4	5	6	7		9	10	11	8														13
1	2	3	4		6	7		9		11	8							5	10						14
1	2	3			6	7	8	11	10							5		4	9						15
1	2	3			6	7	8	11	10							5		4	9						16
1	2	3			6	7	8	11	10							5		4	9						17
1		3		5			8	10	6							2		4	9	7	11				18
1	2	3		5	6		8	10	9									4		7	11				19
1	2	3		5			8	11	10	9	6							4		7					20
1	5	3			10		8	6								2		4	9	7	11				21
1	5	3			8	9	10	6								2		4		7	11				22
1		3		5			8	10	9	6						2		4		7	11				23
1	2	3		5	6		8	10	11							9		4		7					24
1	2			5	6		8	10	9							3		4		7	11				25
1		3		5	6		8	11	10							2		4	9	7					26
		3		5	6	7	8	10								2		4	9		11	1			27
1		3		5	6		8		10							2		4	9	7	11				28
1		3		5	6		8		10							2		4	9	7	11				29
1	2				6		8		10				5			3		4	9	7	11				30
		3		5	6		8		10							2		4	9	7	11	1			31
1	2	3		5	6		8		10									4	9	7	11				32
	2	3			6		8		10				5					4	9	7	11			1	33
1	2	3		5	6		8		10									4	9	7	11				34
1	2	3		5	6		8		10							9		4		7	11				35
1	2	3			6		8		10							9	5	4		7	11				36
1	2	3		5	6		8		10									4	9	11			7		37
1		3			6		8		10				5			2		4	9	7	11				38
35	28	35	16	26	31	17	28	18	12	17	22	15	14	2	2	15	2	25	17	19	18	2	1	1	
	2			3	12	10	3	9	4		1								9	3	6				

Ashcroft J	Gray A	Sharp J	Dick J	Sands PR	McEachrane RJ	Bellamy JT	Coleman JG	Satterthwaite CO	Blair J	Templeton RB	Fitchie TT	Ducat A	Theobald WS	Arnold T	Crowe A	Cross AG	Kemp F	Bigden JH	Freeman BC	Garbutt W	Neave D	McDonald HL	Bateup E	Grice NJ	
1		3		5	6		8	11	10	9						2		4		7					1
1		3		5	6		8	10	11							9		2	4	7					R
1	2			5	6		8	11	10							3		4	9	7					2
1		3		5	6		8	11	10							2		4	9	7					3
1		3		5	6		8	11	10							2		4	9	7					4
1		3		5	6		8	11	10							2		4	9	7					SF
6	1	5		6	6		6	6	5	2						6		6	4	6					
	1			1			3	1								2			3	3					

161

1906-07

Manager: P.Kelso

1	Sep	1	(a)	Manchester C	W	4-1 Kyle 2, Coleman, Satterthwaite	18,000
2		3	(a)	Bury	L	1-4 Kyle	9,000
3		8	(h)	Middlesbrough	W	2-0 Satterthwaite 2	20,000
4		15	(a)	Preston NE	W	3-0 Satterthwaite 2, Bellamy	12,000
5		22	(h)	Newcastle U	W	2-0 Kyle 2	30,000
6		29	(a)	Aston Villa	D	2-2 Satterthwaite, Coleman	45,000
7	Oct	6	(h)	Liverpool	W	2-1 Neave 2	30,000
8		13	(a)	Bristol C	W	3-1 Bigden, Ducat, Neave	22,000
9		20	(h)	Notts C	W	1-0 Coleman	25,000
10		27	(a)	Sheffield U	L	2-4 Kyle, Satterthwaite	18,816
11	Nov	3	(h)	Bolton W	D	2-2 Satterthwaite 2	20,000
12		10	(a)	Manchester U	L	0-1	25,000
13		17	(h)	Stoke	W	2-1 Kyle, Coleman	10,000
14		24	(a)	Blackburn R	W	3-2 Freeman 2, Coleman	12,000
15	Dec	1	(h)	Sunderland	L	0-1	20,000
16		8	(a)	Birmingham	L	1-5 Sands	19,000
17		15	(h)	Everton	W	3-1 Satterthwaite, Kyle, Coleman	12,000
18		22	(a)	Derby C	D	0-0	7,000
19		26	(h)	Bury	W	3-1 Kyle 2, Satterthwaite	8,000
20		29	(h)	Manchester C	W	4-1 Coleman 2, Garbutt, Kyle	15,000
21	Jan	1	(a)	Sheffield W	D	1-1 Kyle	16,000
22		5	(a)	Middlesbrough	L	3-5 Coleman, Sharp, Neave	15,000
23		19	(h)	Preston NE	W	1-0 Coleman	12,000
24		26	(a)	Newcastle U	L	0-1	35,000
25	Feb	9	(a)	Liverpool	L	0-4	20,000
26		16	(h)	Bristol C	L	1-2 Satterthwaite	18,000
27	Mar	2	(h)	Sheffield U	L	0-1	12,000
28		16	(h)	Manchester U	W	4-0 Satterthwaite 2, Kyle, Coleman	6,000
29		27	(a)	Bolton W	L	0-3	5,000
30		29	(h)	Sheffield W	W	1-0 Satterthwaite	25,000
31		30	(h)	Blackburn R	W	2-0 Sands, Coleman	20,000
32	Apr	1	(h)	Aston Villa	W	3-1 Garbutt, Satterthwaite, Freeman	20,000
33		6	(a)	Sunderland	W	3-2 Freeman 2, Sands	12,000
34		10	(a)	Everton	L	1-2 Satterthwaite	12,000
35		13	(h)	Birmingham	W	2-1 Freeman, Coleman	18,000
36		15	(a)	Stoke	L	0-2	3,000
37		17	(a)	Notts C	L	1-4 Freeman	3,000
38		27	(h)	Derby C	W	3-2 Coleman, Garbutt, Freeman	2,000

FINAL LEAGUE POSITION: 7th in Division One

Appearances
Goals

FA Cup

1	Jan	12	(a)	Grimsby T	D	1-1 Garbutt	10,000
R		16	(h)	Grimsby T	W	3-0 Satterthwaite, Sands, Garbutt	13,269
2	Feb	2	(h)	Bristol C	W	2-1 Hynds, Kyle	31,300
3		23	(h)	Bristol R	W	1-0 Neave	22,000
4	Mar	9	(a)	Barnsley	W	2-1 Satterthwaite, Neave	13,871
SF		23	(n*)	Sheffield W	L	1-3 Garbutt	36,000

*Played at St Andrews, Birmingham.

Appearances
Goals

162

Appearance and scoring grid (positions 1–11 per match).

Ashcroft J	Cross AG	Sharp J	Bigden JH	Sands PR	McEachrane RJ	Garbutt W	Coleman JG	Kyle P	Satterthwaite CO	Neave D	Gray A	Theobald WS	Blair J	Bellamy JT	Ducat A	Freeman BC	Low AB	Bateup E	Hynds T	Ferguson J	Dick J	Mordue J	#
1	2	3	4	5	6	7	8	9	10	11													1
1		3	4		6		8	9	7	11	2	5	10										2
1	2	3	4	5	6		8	9	10	11				7									3
1		3	4	5	6		8	9	10	11	2			7									4
1		3	4	5	6		8	9	10	11	2			7									5
1		3		5	6	7	8	9	10	11	2			4									6
1		3	4	5	6		8	9	10	11	2			7									7
1		3	4		6			9	10	11	2	5		7	8								8
1		3	4	5	6		8	9	10	11	2			7									9
1		3	4	5	6	7	8	9	10	11	2												10
1		3	4	5	6	7	8	9	10	11	2												11
1		3	4	5	6	7	8	9	10	11	2												12
1		3	4	5	6		8	9	10	11	2			7									13
1		3	4	5	6		8	9	7	11	2					10							14
1		3	4	5				9	7	11	2				8	10	6						15
1		3	4	5	6	7	8	9	10	11	2												16
1		3	4	5	6	7	8	9	10	11	2												17
1		3	4	5	6	7	8	9	10	11	2												18
		3	4	5	6	7	8	9	10	11	2							1					19
1		3	4	5	6	7	8	9	10	11	2												20
		3	4		6	7	8	9	10	11	2							1	5				21
	2	3	4		6	7	8	9	10	11								1	5				22
1		3	4		6	7	8	9	10	11	2								5				23
1	2	3	4		6	7	8	9	10	11									5				24
1	2	3	4		6	7	8		10							9			5	11			25
1		3	4		6	7			10	11	2				8	9			5				26
1		3	4		6			9	10	11	2			7	8				5				27
1	2	3	4	5			8	9	10	11				7					6				28
1	2	3	4		6	7	8	9	10	11									5				29
1		3	4	5	6	7	8	9	10		2					11							30
1	2	3	4	5	6		8	9	10	11				7									31
1	2	3	4	5	6	7	8		10	11						9							32
1	2		4	5	6	7	8		10	11						9			3				33
1	2	3			6	7	8		10	11						9			5		4		34
1	2	3	4	5	6	7	8		11							9						10	35
1	2	3	4			7	8		11							9	6		5			10	36
1	2	3	4			7	8		11							9	6		5			10	37
1	2	3	4	5	6	7	8		10	11						9							38
35	16	36	37	24	34	25	34	29	38	33	23	2	1	11	4	12	3	3	13	1	1	3	
	1	1	3		3	14	13	17	4					1		1			8				

Ashcroft J	Cross AG	Sharp J	Bigden JH	Sands PR	McEachrane RJ	Garbutt W	Coleman JG	Kyle P	Satterthwaite CO	Neave D	Gray A	Theobald WS	Blair J	Bellamy JT	Ducat A	Freeman BC	Low AB	Bateup E	Hynds T	Ferguson J	Dick J	Mordue J	Round
1		3	4	5	6	7	8	9	10	11	2												1
1		3	4	5	6	7	8	9	10	11	2												R
1	2	3	4		6	7	8	9	10	11									5				2
1		3	4		6	7	8	9	10	11	2								5				3
1		3	4		6	7	8	9	10	11	2								5				4
1		3	4		6	7	8	9	10	11	2								5				SF
6	1	6	6	2	6	6	6	6	6	6	5								4				
			1			3	1	2	2										1				

1907-08

Manager: P.Kelso

1	Sep	2	(h)	Notts C	D 1-1	Garbutt	10,000
2		7	(h)	Bristol C	L 0-4		14,000
3		9	(a)	Bury	L 2-3	Neave, Kyle	10,000
4		14	(a)	Notts C	L 0-2		10,000
5		21	(h)	Manchester C	W 2-1	Sharp, Coleman	12,000
6		28	(a)	Preston NE	L 0-3		12,000
7	Oct	5	(h)	Bury	D 0-0		14,000
8		12	(a)	Aston Villa	W 1-0	Neave	25,000
9		19	(h)	Liverpool	W 2-1	Lee 2	15,000
10		26	(a)	Middlesbrough	D 0-0		18,000
11	Nov	2	(h)	Sheffield U	W 5-1	Kyle 2, Coleman, Neave, C.Satterthwaite	15,000
12		9	(a)	Chelsea	L 1-2	C.Satterthwaite	65,000
13		16	(h)	Nottingham F	W 3-1	Kyle 2, Coleman	8,000
14		23	(a)	Manchester U	L 2-4	Kyle, Garbutt	15,000
15		30	(h)	Blackburn R	W 2-0	C.Satterthwaite, Sands	7,500
16	Dec	7	(a)	Bolton W	L 1-3	Coleman	10,000
17		14	(h)	Birmingham	D 1-1	Coleman	3,000
18		21	(a)	Everton	D 1-1	Coleman	10,000
19		25	(h)	Newcastle U	D 2-2	Kyle, Freeman	25,000
20		28	(h)	Sunderland	W 4-0	Lewis 2, Neave 2	6,000
21		31	(a)	Sheffield W	L 0-6		9,000
22	Jan	1	(a)	Sunderland	L 2-5	Kyle, Neave	20,000
23		4	(a)	Bristol C	W 2-1	Freeman, Coleman	15,000
24		18	(a)	Manchester C	L 0-4		25,000
25		25	(h)	Preston NE	D 1-1	Sands	6,000
26	Feb	8	(h)	Aston Villa	L 0-1		12,000
27		15	(a)	Liverpool	L 1-4	Coleman	18,000
28		22	(h)	Middlesbrough	W 4-1	Lewis 2, Lee, Freeman	7,000
29		29	(a)	Sheffield U	D 2-2	Freeman, Lewis	8,000
30	Mar	7	(h)	Chelsea	D 0-0		30,000
31		14	(a)	Nottingham F	L 0-1		14,000
32		21	(h)	Manchester U	W 1-0	Lee	18,000
33		28	(a)	Blackburn R	D 1-1	Ducat	12,000
34	Apr	4	(h)	Bolton W	D 1-1	J.Satterthwaite	10,000
35		11	(a)	Birmingham	W 2-1	Lewis, Lee	15,000
36		17	(a)	Newcastle U	L 1-2	Neave	30,000
37		18	(h)	Everton	W 2-1	Mordue, Lewis	15,000
38		20	(h)	Sheffield W	D 1-1	Lewis	16,000

FINAL LEAGUE POSITION: 14th (Equal) in Division One

Appearances
Goals

FA Cup

1	Jan	11	(h)	Hull C	D 0-0		15,000
R		16	(a)	Hull C	L 1-4	Kyle	17,000

Appearances
Goals

164

Player appearance and goals grid (shirt numbers by match).

Ashcroft J	Gray A	Sharp J	Bigden JH	Sands PR	McEachrane RJ	Garbutt W	Coleman JG	Freeman BC	Satterthwaite CO	Neave D	Lee HG	Mordue J	Cross AG	Theobald WS	Kyle P	Bateup E	Dick J	Shaw J	Ducat A	Lewis CH	Rodger J	Satterthwaite JN	Hoare GR	#
1	2	3	4	5	6	7	8	9	10	11														1
1	2	3	4	5	6		8	9		11	7	10												2
1		3	4		6		8			11	7	10	2	5	9									3
1		3		5	6		8			11	7	10	2	4	9									4
		3		5	6		8			11	7	10	2		9	1	4							5
1		2		6			8			11	7	10	5		9	4	3							6
1		3		5	6	7	8		10	11			2		9		4							7
1	2	3		5	6	7	8		10	11					9		4							8
1	2	3		5	6		8		10	11	7				9		4							9
1	2	3		5	6		8		10		7	11			9		4							10
1	2	3		5	6	7	8		10	11					9		4							11
1	2	3		5	6	7	8		10	11					9		4							12
1	2	3		5	6	7	8		10				11		9				4					13
1	2	3		5	6	7	8		10	11					9		4							14
1	2	3		5	6	7	8		10	11					9		4							15
1		3		5	6		8		10	11	7	2			9		4							16
1		3		5	6		8		10	11	7	2			9		4							17
1	2	3		5	6		8	9		11	7				10				4					18
1	2	3		5	6		8	9		11	7				10				4					19
1		3		5	6	10	9			11	7	2							4	8				20
1		3			6		8	9		11	7	2			10		5		4					21
1		3			6			9	10	11	7	2			8		5		4					22
1	2	3		5	6		8	9		11	7				10		5		4					23
1	2	3		5	6		8	9		11	7				10				4					24
1		3		5	6		9				7	2			10				4	8	11			25
1	2			5	6		8		10	11	7	3			9				4					26
1	2	3		5	6		8	9	10	11	7								4					27
1	2	3		5	6	10	9			11	7								4	8				28
	2	3		5	6		9	10		11	7					1			4	8				29
1	2	3		5	6		9	10		11	7								4	8				30
1	2	3		5	6		9	10		11	7								4	8				31
1	2	3		5	6		9			11	7								4	8		10		32
1	2	3		5	6					11	7						4		9	8		10		33
1	2			5	6		9			11	7							3	4	8		10		34
1	2	3	4	5	6					11	9	7								8		10		35
1	2	3	4	5	6					11	9	7								8		10		36
1	2	3		5	6				10	11	9	7							4	8				37
1	2	3	4	5	6					11	9	7								8			10	38
36	30	32	6	34	38	8	26	15	21	35	18	23	11	3	23	2	17	2	18	13	1	5	1	
	1		2		2	8	4	3	7	5	1				8				1	8		1		

Ashcroft J	Gray A	Sharp J	Bigden JH	Sands PR	McEachrane RJ	Garbutt W	Coleman JG	Freeman BC	Satterthwaite CO	Neave D	Lee HG	Mordue J	Cross AG	Theobald WS	Kyle P	Bateup E	Dick J	Shaw J	Ducat A	Lewis CH	Rodger J	Satterthwaite JN	Hoare GR	#
1	2	3		5	6		8	9		11	7				10				4					1
1	2	3		5	6	7	8			11		10			9				4					R
2	2	2		2	2	1	2	1		2	2				2				2					
															1									

1908-09

Manager: G.Morrell

1	Sep	2	(h)	Everton	L	0-4	10,000
2		5	(a)	Notts C	L	1-2 Neave	13,000
3		7	(a)	Everton	W	3-0 Neave, Lee, Raybould	10,000
4		12	(h)	Newcastle U	L	1-2 Greenaway	18,000
5		19	(a)	Bristol C	L	1-2 Greenaway	16,000
6		26	(h)	Preston NE	W	1-0 Fitchie	12,000
7	Oct	3	(a)	Middlesbrough	D	1-1 Sands	20,000
8		10	(h)	Manchester C	W	3-0 Raybould 2, Lee	12,000
9		17	(a)	Liverpool	D	2-2 Satterthwaite, Neave	20,000
10		24	(h)	Bury	W	4-0 Raybould 3, Satterthwaite	9,500
11		31	(a)	Sheffield U	D	1-1 Lee	15,000
12	Nov	7	(h)	Aston Villa	L	0-1	20,000
13		14	(a)	Nottingham F	W	1-0 Hoare	10,000
14		21	(h)	Sunderland	L	0-4	12,000
15		28	(a)	Chelsea	W	2-1 Greenaway, Lewis	50,000
16	Dec	5	(h)	Blackburn R	L	0-1	12,000
17		12	(a)	Bradford C	L	1-4 Fitchie	24,000
18		19	(h)	Manchester U	L	0-1	10,000
19		25	(a)	Leicester F	D	1-1 Satterthwaite	16,000
20		26	(h)	Leicester F	W	2-1 Fitchie 2	20,000
21		28	(a)	Sheffield W	L	2-6 Fitchie, Hoare	12,000
22	Jan	2	(h)	Notts C	W	1-0 Hoare	15,000
23		9	(a)	Newcastle U	L	1-3 Fitchie	27,500
24		23	(h)	Bristol C	D	1-1 Hoare	10,000
25		30	(a)	Preston NE	D	0-0	8,000
26	Feb	13	(a)	Manchester C	D	2-2 Lewis, Ducat	20,000
27		20	(h)	Liverpool	W	5-0 Beney 3, Satterthwaite (pen), Lewis	15,000
28		27	(a)	Bury	D	1-1 Lewis	12,000
29	Mar	13	(a)	Aston Villa	L	1-2 Fitchie	20,000
30		17	(h)	Middlesbrough	D	1-1 Hoare	8,000
31		20	(h)	Nottingham F	L	1-2 Neave	10,000
32		27	(a)	Sunderland	L	0-1	7,500
33	Apr	1	(h)	Sheffield U	W	1-0 Fitchie	6,000
34		3	(h)	Chelsea	D	0-0	20,000
35		10	(a)	Blackburn R	W	3-1 Lee, Neave, Lewis	5,000
36		12	(h)	Sheffield W	W	2-0 Lee, Bartlett (og)	12,000
37		17	(h)	Bradford C	W	1-0 Lee	14,000
38		27	(a)	Manchester U	W	4-1 Lee 2, Fitchie, Lewis	30,000

FINAL LEAGUE POSITION: 6th in Division One

Appearances
Goals

FA Cup

1	Jan	16	(a*)	Croydon C	D	1-1 Fitchie	16,578
R		20	(h)	Croydon C	W	2-0 Raybould, Ducat	15,000
2	Feb	6	(h)	Millwall	D	1-1 Lewis	32,000
R		10	(a)	Millwall	L	0-1	16,285

*Played at the Crystal Palace, London.

Appearances
Goals

166

McDonald HL	Gray A	Shaw J	Ducat A	Sands PR	McEachrane RJ	Maxwell JM	Lewis CH	Raybould S	Satterthwaite CO	Neave D	Greenaway D	Curle W	Cross AG	Theobald WS	Lee HG	Dick J	Fitchie TT	Chisholm NW	Hoare GR	McKinnon A	Beney A	Thomson M	
1	2	3	4	5	6	7	8	9	10	11													1
1	2	3	4	5	6		9	10		11	7	8											2
1	2		4		6		8	10		11	7			3	5		9						3
1	2		4		6		8	10		11	7			3	5		9						4
1	2			5	6		8	10		11	7			3	9	4							5
1	2			5	6			9		11	7			3	8	4	10						6
1	3			5	6			9		11	7				8	4	10			2			7
1	3			5	6			9		11	7				8	4	10			2			8
1	2	3	4	5	6		9	10		11	7		8										9
1	2	3	4	5	6		9	10		11	7		8										10
1	2	3	4	5	6		9	10		11	7		8										11
1	2	3	4	5	6		9	10		11	7		8										12
1	3	2	4	5	6		8			11	7				9		10						13
1	2	3	4	5	6		9			11	7		8				10						14
1	3	2	4	5	6		8	9		11	7						10						15
1	3	2	4	5	6		8	9		11	7						10						16
1	3	2	4	5			8			11	7				9		10	6					17
1	3	2	4	5	6		8			11	7				9		10						18
1	3	2	4	5	6		8	9	10	11	7												19
1	2		4	5	6		8			11	7		3				10		9				20
1	2			5	6		8				7		3		11	4	10		9				21
1	2		4	5	6		8			11	7		3				10		9				22
1	3	2	4		6		8			11	7				5		10		9				23
1	3	2	4	5	6		8			11	7						10		9				24
1	3	2	4	5	6		8		10	11	7						9						25
1	3		4	5	6		8	10		11	7		2								9		26
1	3		4	5	6		8			11	7		2				10				9		27
1	3		4	5			8			11	7		2				10	6			9		28
1	3		4	5	6		8			11	7		2				10				9		29
1	3		4		6		8			11	7		2		5		10				9		30
1	2		4	5	6		8			11	7		3				10				9		31
1	3	2	4	5	6	7	8		10	11											9		32
1	3	2	4		6		8			11	7				5		10				9		33
1	3	2	4	5	6		8			11	7						10		9				34
1	3	2	4	5	6		8	10		11	7								9				35
1	3	2	4	5	6		8	10		11	7								9				36
1	3	2	4	5	6		8			11	7						10		9				37
1	3	2	4		6		8			11	7				5		10		9				38
38	33	28	33	32	36	2	23	26	18	25	36	3	12	3	17	5	21	3	11	2	8	3	
		1	1				6	6	4	5	3				8		9		5		3		

1 own-goal

McDonald HL	Gray A	Shaw J	Ducat A	Sands PR	McEachrane RJ	Maxwell JM	Lewis CH	Raybould S	Satterthwaite CO	Neave D	Greenaway D	Curle W	Cross AG	Theobald WS	Lee HG	Dick J	Fitchie TT	Chisholm NW	Hoare GR	McKinnon A	Beney A	Thomson M	
1	3	2	4	5	6		8			11	7						10		9				1
1	3	2	4	5	6		8		10	11	7								9				R
1	3	2	4	5	6		8	9		11	7						10						2
1	3	2	4	5	6		8	9	10	11	7												R
4	4	4	4	4	4		4	2	3	3	4						2		2				
		1						1	1										1				

1909-10

Manager: G.Morrell

1	Sep	1	(a)	Aston Villa	L	1-5	Lewis	12,000
2		4	(h)	Sheffield U	D	0-0		10,000
3		11	(a)	Middlesbrough	L	2-5	Beney 2	12,000
4		18	(a)	Bolton W	L	0-3		20,000
5		25	(h)	Chelsea	W	3-2	Lee 2, Greenaway	15,000
6	Oct	2	(a)	Blackburn R	L	0-7		10,000
7		7	(a)	Notts C	L	1-5	Neave	10,000
8		9	(h)	Nottingham F	L	0-1		9,500
9		16	(a)	Sunderland	L	2-6	Greenaway, Lawrence	10,000
10		23	(h)	Everton	W	1-0	Thomson	10,000
11		30	(a)	Manchester U	L	0-1		20,000
12	Nov	6	(h)	Bradford C	L	0-1		10,000
13		13	(a)	Sheffield W	D	1-1	Lawrence	10,000
14		20	(h)	Bristol C	D	2-2	Buckenham, Greenaway	8,000
15		27	(a)	Bury	W	2-1	Greenaway, Steven	7,000
16	Dec	4	(h)	Tottenham H	W	1-0	Lawrence	18,000
17		11	(a)	Preston NE	W	4-3	Buckenham 2, Neave 2	6,000
18		18	(h)	Notts C	L	1-2	Lewis	10,000
19		25	(h)	Newcastle U	L	0-3		20,000
20		27	(h)	Liverpool	D	1-1	McKellar	15,000
21	Jan	1	(a)	Liverpool	L	1-5	Neave	25,000
22		8	(a)	Sheffield U	L	0-2		17,000
23		22	(h)	Middlesbrough	W	3-0	Buckenham, Neave, Lawrence	8,000
24		29	(h)	Bolton W	W	2-0	Greenaway, Ducat	7,000
25	Feb	12	(h)	Blackburn R	L	0-1		7,500
26		26	(h)	Sunderland	L	1-2	Ducat	8,000
27	Mar	2	(a)	Nottingham F	D	1-1	Buckenham	5,000
28		7	(a)	Everton	L	0-1		6,000
29		12	(h)	Manchester U	D	0-0		5,000
30		19	(a)	Bradford C	W	1-0	Beney	14,000
31		25	(a)	Newcastle U	D	1-1	Lewis	20,000
32		26	(h)	Sheffield W	L	0-1		8,000
33		28	(a)	Chelsea	W	1-0	McGibbon	40,000
34	Apr	2	(a)	Bristol C	W	1-0	Lawrence	8,000
35		9	(h)	Bury	D	0-0		10,000
36		11	(h)	Aston Villa*	W	1-0	McGibbon	8,000
37		16	(a)	Tottenham H	D	1-1	McGibbon	39,800
38		23	(h)	Preston NE	L	1-3	Ducat	10,000

FINAL LEAGUE POSITION: 18th in Division One.
*After abandoned match (80 minutes) on 6 September.

Appearances
Goals

FA Cup

1	Jan	15	(h)	Watford	W	3-0	McKellar, Lewis 2	8,668
2	Feb	5	(a)	Everton	L	0-5		30,000

Appearances
Goals

Appearance and scoring grid (position numbers 1–11 shown per player per match).

Match	McDonald HL	Shaw J	Gray A	Ducat A	Thomson M	McEachrane RJ	Greenaway D	Lewis CH	Lee HG	Drain T	Heppinstall F	Cross AG	Dick J	Sands PR	Lawrence WH	Beney A	Satterthwaite CO	Neave D	Fisher G	Bassett S	McKinnon A	Oliver H	McDonald D	Steven R	McKellar MT	Buckenham WE	Hoare GR	McGibbon CE
1	1	2	3	4	5	6	7	8	9	10	11																	
2	1	2				6	7	8	9		11	3	4	5	10													
3	1	2				6	7	8			11	3	4	5	10	9												
4	1	2			5	6	7					3	4		10	9	8	11										
5	1		2			6	7	8	9			3	4	5			10	11										
6	1		2			6	7	8	9			3	4	5			10	11										
7		2			5	6	7		9	8		3			10			11	1	4								
8		2	3	4			7	8	10						5			11	1		6	9						
9	1	2	3	4	9		7								5	10	8	11			6							
10	1	2	3	4	9	6	7	8							5	10		11										
11	1	2			9	6	7	8						4	5	10		11					3					
12	1	2	3	4	9	6	7	8							5	10		11										
13	1		3	4		6	7					5			10			11					2	8	9			
14	1		3	4		6	7				11				5	10							2	8		9		
15	1		3	4	5	6	7				11				10								2	8		9		
16	1		3	4		6	7					5			10			11					2	8		9		
17	1		3	4	5	6	7	8							10			11					2			9		
18	1		3	4	5	6	7	8							10			11					2			9		
19	1		3	4	5	6	7								10			11					2	8		9		
20	1		3	4	5	6	7	8							10			11					2			9		
21	1	2	3	4	5	6	7	8							10			11								9		
22	1	2		4	5	6	7	8				3			10			11								9		
23	1			4	5	6	7	8				3			10			11					2			9		
24	1			4	5	6	7	8				3			10			11					2			9		
25	1		3		5	6	7							4	10			11					2	8		9		
26	1		3	4	5		7	8			11				10						6		2			9		
27	1		3	4	5		7	8			11				10						6		2			9		
28	1		3	4	5		7	8			11				10						6		2			9		
29	1		3	4	5	6	7				11				10						8		2			9		
30	1		3	4	5	6	7								10			11			8		2			9		
31	1		3	4	5	6	7								10			11			8		2			9		
32	1		3	4	5	6	7	8							10			11					2			9		
33	1		3	4	5			8			11				10						6		2	7		9		
34	1		3		5	6	7	8			11			4	10								2			9		
35	1		3	4	5	6	7	8			11				10								2					9
36	1		3	4	5	6	7	8			11				10								2					9
37	1		3	4	5	6	7	8			11				10								2					9
38	1		3	4	5	6	7	8			11				10								2					9
Apps	36	29	13	29	30	32	36	28	6	2	18	9	7	12	25	8	4	21	2	1	8	1	25	7	3	21	1	4
Gls			3	1		5	3	2							5	3		5					1	1	5			3

Supplementary (cup) appearances:

Match	McDonald HL	Shaw J	Gray A	Ducat A	Thomson M	McEachrane RJ	Greenaway D	Lewis CH	Lee HG	Drain T	Heppinstall F	Cross AG	Dick J	Sands PR	Lawrence WH	Beney A	Satterthwaite CO	Neave D	Fisher G	Bassett S	McKinnon A	Oliver H	McDonald D	Steven R	McKellar MT	Buckenham WE	Hoare GR	McGibbon CE
1	1	2		4	5	6	7	8				3			10			11								9		
2	1			4	5	6	7	8				3				10		11					2			9		
Apps	2	1		2	2	2	2	2				2			1	1		2					1			2		
Gls																		1										

169

1910-11

1	Sep	1	(h)	Manchester U	L 1-2	Rippon	15,000
2		3	(a)	Bury	D 1-1	Rippon	10,000
3		10	(h)	Sheffield U	D 0-0		14,000
4		17	(a)	Aston Villa	L 0-3		20,000
5		24	(h)	Sunderland	D 0-0		15,000
6	Oct	1	(h)	Oldham A	D 0-0		12,000
7		8	(a)	Bradford C	L 0-3		26,000
8		15	(h)	Blackburn R	W 4-1	Neave 2, Lewis, Chalmers	11,500
9		22	(a)	Nottingham F	W 3-2	Chalmers 2, Greenaway	10,000
10		29	(h)	Manchester C	L 0-1		10,000
11	Nov	5	(a)	Everton	L 0-2		15,000
12		12	(h)	Sheffield W	W 1-0	Chalmers	10,000
13		19	(a)	Bristol C	W 1-0	Chalmers	8,000
14		26	(h)	Newcastle U	L 1-2	Chalmers	14,000
15	Dec	3	(a)	Tottenham H	L 1-3	Chalmers	16,000
16		10	(h)	Middlesbrough	L 0-2		10,000
17		17	(a)	Preston NE	L 1-4	Common	6,000
18		24	(h)	Notts C	W 2-1	Chalmers, Hoare	8,000
19		26	(a)	Manchester U	L 0-5		35,000
20		31	(h)	Bury	W 3-2	Ducat, Hoare, Chalmers	7,000
21	Jan	7	(a)	Sheffield U	L 2-3	Hoare, McGuire (og)	12,000
22		28	(a)	Sunderland	D 2-2	Ducat (pen), Lewis	10,000
23	Feb	11	(h)	Bradford C	D 0-0		10,000
24		18	(a)	Blackburn R	L 0-1		20,000
25		25	(h)	Nottingham F	W 3-2	Ducat, Chalmers, Hoare	10,000
26	Mar	4	(a)	Manchester C	D 1-1	Greenaway	20,000
27		6	(a)	Oldham A	L 0-3		7,000
28		11	(h)	Everton	W 1-0	Chalmers	10,000
29		15	(h)	Aston Villa*	D 1-1	Hoare	6,000
30		18	(a)	Sheffield W	D 0-0		7,000
31		25	(h)	Bristol C	W 3-0	Common 2, Flanagan	10,977
32	Apr	1	(a)	Newcastle U	W 1-0	Chalmers	18,000
33		8	(h)	Tottenham H	W 2-0	Chalmers, Common	24,583
34		14	(h)	Liverpool	D 0-0		20,277
35		15	(a)	Middlesbrough	D 1-1	Neave	14,000
36		17	(a)	Liverpool	D 1-1	Chalmers	20,000
37		22	(h)	Preston NE	W 2-0	Hoare, Chalmers	9,092
38		29	(a)	Notts C	W 2-0	Common 2	6,500

FINAL LEAGUE POSITION: 10th in Division One.

Appearances

*After abandoned match (80 minutes) on 21 January.

Goals

FA Cup

1	Jan	16	(a)	Clapton O†	W 2-1	Chalmers, Hoare	9,519
2	Feb	4	(a)	Swindon T	L 0-1		14,861

†After abandoned match (45 minutes) on 14 January.

Appearances

Goals

Bateup E	Gray A	Shaw J	Ducat A	Sands PR	McEachrane RJ	Greenaway D	Common A	Rippon W	Lewis CH	Heppinstall F	McDonald D	Logan H	Thomson M	Neave D	Chalmers J	Quayle JA	Shortt M	McKinnon A	Hoare GR	Winship T	Flanagan J	Burdett G	Peart JC	Calder L	Calvert F	#
1	2	3	4	5	6	7	8	9	10	11																1
1		3	4	5	6	7	8	9		11	2	10														2
1		3	2	5	6	7	8	9		11		10	4													3
1		3	2	5	6	7	8	9		11		10	4													4
1		3	2	5	6	7	8	9	10				4	11												5
1		3	2	5	6		8	9	7			10	4	11												6
1	2	3	4	5	6		8	10	7					11	9											7
1	2	3	4	5	6	7	10		8					11	9											8
1	2	3	4	5	6	7	10		8					11	9											9
1	2	3	4	5	6	7	10		8	11					9											10
1	2	3	4	5	6	7	10		8					11	9											11
1	2		4	8	6	7	10						5	11	9	3										12
1	2	3	4		6		10	8	7				5	11	9											13
1	2	3	4		6		10		7				5	11	9				8							14
1	2	3	4		6		8		7				5	11	9				10							15
1	2	3	4		6		8		7				5	11	9				10							16
1	2	3			6		8		7				5	11	9				10	4						17
1	2	3	4		6		8		7				5	11	9				10							18
1	2	3	4				10		7			8	5		9				6	11						19
1	3	2	5		8				7				4		9		6		10	11						20
1	3	2	4	5	8				7						9		6		10	11						21
1	3	2	4	5	8				7						9		6		10	11						22
1	3	2	4	5	6	7	8	9							11				10							23
1	3	2	4	5	6	9	7		8						11				10							24
1	3	2	4	5	6	7			11			8			9				10							25
1	3	2	4	5	6	7			11			8			9				10							26
1	3	2		5	6	7			11			8	4		9				10							27
	2		4	5	6	7	8		11						9				10			1	3			28
	2		4	5	6	7			11			8			9				10			1	3			29
		2	5		6	7			11				4		9			8	10			1	3			30
1		2	4	5	6	7	10		11			8			9								3			31
	3	2	4	5	6	7			11						9			8	10			1				32
	3	2	4	5	6	7	8		11						9				10			1				33
	3	2	4	5	6	7	8		11						9				10			1				34
	2		4	5	8	7									11		6		10			1	3	9		35
	2		5		6	7							4		9				10	11		1	3		8	36
		2	5			7	8						4		9			6	10	11		1	3			37
	3	2	5			7	8						4		9			6	10	11		1				38
28	**26**	**35**	**33**	**31**	**30**	**22**	**29**	**9**	**34**	**5**	**1**	**11**	**17**	**15**	**29**	**1**	**4**	**10**	**14**	**6**	**9**	**10**	**7**	**1**	**1**	
	3		2	6	2	2						3	15						6	1						

I own-goal

Bateup E	Gray A	Shaw J	Ducat A	Sands PR	McEachrane RJ	Greenaway D	Common A	Rippon W	Lewis CH	Heppinstall F	McDonald D	Logan H	Thomson M	Neave D	Chalmers J	Quayle JA	Shortt M	McKinnon A	Hoare GR	Winship T	Flanagan J	Burdett G	Peart JC	Calder L	Calvert F	#
1	3	2	4	5	6		8		7					11	9				10							1
1	3	2	4	5	6		8		7						9				10	11						2
2	2	2	2	2	2		2		2					1	2				2	1						
														1	2				2	1						

1911-12

Manager: G.Morrell

1	Sep	2	(h)	Liverpool	D 2-2 Flanagan, Chalmers	12,000
2		9	(a)	Aston Villa	L 1-4 Common	24,000
3		16	(h)	Newcastle U	W 2-0 Flanagan, Common	17,000
4		23	(a)	Sheffield U	L 1-2 Common	9,000
5		30	(h)	Oldham A	D 1-1 Lewis	11,000
6	Oct	7	(a)	Bolton W	D 2-2 Chalmers 2	20,000
7		14	(h)	Bradford C	W 2-0 Common, Ducat	11,873
8		21	(a)	Preston NE	W 1-0 Common	6,000
9		28	(a)	Manchester C	D 3-3 Ducat, Randall, Common	25,000
10	Nov	4	(h)	Everton	L 0-1	15,000
11		11	(a)	West Brom A	D 1-1 Hoare	13,900
12		18	(h)	Sunderland	W 3-0 Randall 3	3,000
13		25	(a)	Blackburn R	L 0-4	15,000
14	Dec	2	(h)	Sheffield W	L 0-2	8,000
15		9	(a)	Bury	L 1-3 Chalmers	10,000
16		16	(h)	Middlesbrough	W 3-1 Chalmers 2, Randall	11,000
17		23	(a)	Notts C	L 1-3 Calvert	6,000
18		25	(a)	Tottenham H	L 0-5	47,100
19		26	(h)	Tottenham H	W 3-1 Lewis, Randall, Winship	22,000
20		30	(a)	Liverpool	L 1-4 Flanagan	16,000
21	Jan	1	(a)	Manchester U	L 0-2	20,000
22		6	(h)	Aston Villa	D 2-2 Winship, Common	6,000
23		20	(a)	Newcastle U	W 2-1 Common, Flanagan	18,000
24		27	(h)	Sheffield U	W 3-1 Common 2, Greenaway	10,299
25	Feb	10	(h)	Bolton W	W 3-0 Flanagan, Common, Lewis	14,000
26		17	(a)	Bradford C	D 1-1 Randall	10,000
27		24	(a)	Middlesbrough	W 2-0 Common, Ducat (pen)	13,000
28	Mar	2	(h)	Manchester C	W 2-0 Common, Randall	12,000
29		9	(a)	Oldham A	D 0-0	8,000
30		16	(h)	West Brom A	L 0-2	15,000
31		23	(a)	Sunderland	L 0-1	5,000
32		27	(a)	Everton	L 0-1	10,000
33	Apr	5	(h)	Manchester U	W 2-1 Common 2	15,507
34		6	(a)	Sheffield W	L 0-3	5,000
35		8	(h)	Preston NE	W 4-1 Ducat, Greenaway, Common 2	10,066
36		13	(h)	Bury	W 1-0 Ducat (pen)	8,000
37		22	(h)	Blackburn R	W 5-1 J.W.Grant 3, Flanagan 2	7,000
38		27	(h)	Notts C	L 0-3	10,000

FINAL LEAGUE POSITION: 10th in Division One

Appearances
Goals

FA Cup

1	Jan	13	(a)	Bolton W	L 0-1	24,635

Appearances
Goals

Burdett G	Shaw J	Gray A	Ducat A	Sands PR	McEachrane RJ	Greenaway D	Common A	Chalmers J	Flanagan J	Lewis CH	Grant GM	Neave D	Peart JC	McKinnon A	Winship T	Thomson M	Randall CE	Hoare GR	Roose LR	Calvert F	McLaughlan J	Crawford HS	Grant JW	No.
1	2	3	4	5	6	7	8	9	10	11														1
1	2	3	4		6	7	8	9	10		5	11												2
1	2		4	5	6		8	9	10	7		11	3											3
1	2			5	6		8	9	10	7			3	4	11									4
1	2	3		5	6		8	9	10	7				4	11									5
1	2	3		5	6		8	9	11	7				4			10							6
1	2		4	5	6		8	9	11	7			3				10							7
1	2		4	5	6		8	9	11	7			3				10							8
1	2		4	5	6		8	9	11	7			3				10							9
1	2		4	5	6		8	9	11	7			3				10							10
1	2		4	5	6	7	8		11				3				10	9						11
1	2		4	5	6	7	8	9	11				3				10							12
1	2		4	5	6	7	8	9	11				3				10							13
1	2		4	5	6	7	8		11				3			9	10							14
1	2		4	5		7	8	9	11				3	6			10							15
	2		4	5			8	9		7			3	6	11		10		1					16
		2	4	5	6		8	9	10	7		11	3						1					17
	2		4	5			8	9		7			3	6	11		10		1					18
	2		4	5	6		8	9		7			3		11		10		1					19
1	2		4	5			8	9		7			3	6	11		10							20
1	2			5	6		8			7		11	3	4			10	9						21
1	2		4	5	6		8	9		7			3		11		10							22
	2		4			7	8	9	11				3	6		5	10		1					23
	2		4			7	8	9	11				3	6		5	10		1					24
	2		4	5		7	8	9	11				3	6			10		1					25
	2		4	5		7	8	9	11				3	6			10		1					26
	2		4	5		7	8	9	11				3	6			10		1					27
	2		4	5		7	8	9	11				3	6			10		1					28
	2		4	5		7	8	9					3	6	11		10		1					29
	2		4	5		7	8	9					3	6	11		10		1					30
	2		4	5		7	8		11				3	6			10		1	9				31
	2		4			7	8	9	11				3	6		5	10				1			32
	2		4	5		7	8	9	11				3	6			10				1			33
	2			5		7	8	9	11				3	6		4	10				1			34
	2		4	5		7	8		10	11			3	6								9	1	35
	2		4	5		7	8		10	11			3	6								9	1	36
	2		4	5		7	8		10	11			3	6								9	1	37
	2			5		7	8		10	11			3	6		4						9	1	38
18	36	5	33	34	18	23	36	19	33	29	1	4	34	22	8	7	27	3	13	1	3	7	4	
	5			2	17	6	7	3				2		8	1		1					3		

Burdett G	Shaw J	Gray A	Ducat A	Sands PR	McEachrane RJ	Greenaway D	Common A	Chalmers J	Flanagan J	Lewis CH	Grant GM	Neave D	Peart JC	McKinnon A	Winship T	Thomson M	Randall CE	Hoare GR	Roose LR	Calvert F	McLaughlan J	Crawford HS	Grant JW	No.
	2		4	5	6		8	9		7			3		11		10		1					1
	1		1	1	1		1	1		1			1		1		1		1					

173

1912-13

Manager: G.Morrell

1	Sep	2	(h)	Manchester U	D	0-0		10,000
2		7	(a)	Liverpool	L	0-3		30,000
3		14	(h)	Bolton W	L	1-2	Winship	13,000
4		16	(h)	Aston Villa	L	0-3		6,805
5		21	(a)	Sheffield U	W	3-1	Randall 2, McLaughlan	20,000
6		28	(h)	Newcastle U	D	1-1	McLaughlan	18,000
7	Oct	5	(a)	Oldham A	D	0-0		7,500
8		12	(h)	Chelsea	L	0-1		20,000
9		19	(h)	Sunderland	L	1-3	McLaughlan	10,000
10		26	(a)	Bradford C	L	1-3	Hanks	7,000
11	Nov	2	(h)	Manchester C	L	0-4		8,000
12		9	(a)	West Brom A	L	1-2	Greenaway	15,980
13		16	(h)	Everton	D	0-0		10,000
14		23	(a)	Sheffield W	L	0-2		14,000
15		30	(h)	Blackburn R	L	0-1		9,000
16	Dec	7	(a)	Derby C	L	1-4	Flanagan	10,000
17		14	(h)	Tottenham H	L	0-3		13,000
18		21	(a)	Middlesbrough	L	0-2		10,000
19		25	(h)	Notts C	D	0-0		7,000
20		26	(a)	Notts C	L	1-2	Graham	12,000
21		28	(h)	Liverpool	D	1-1	Graham (pen)	9,070
22	Jan	1	(a)	Sunderland	L	1-4	Lewis	22,000
23		4	(a)	Bolton W	L	1-5	Flanagan	10,000
24		18	(h)	Sheffield U	L	1-3	Randall	6,000
25		25	(a)	Newcastle U	L	1-3	Duncan	20,000
26	Feb	8	(h)	Oldham A	D	0-0		9,000
27		15	(a)	Chelsea	D	1-1	Burrell	15,000
28	Mar	1	(h)	Bradford C	D	1-1	Burrell	10,000
29		8	(a)	Manchester C	W	1-0	Lewis	15,000
30		15	(h)	West Brom A	W	1-0	Sands	8,000
31		21	(a)	Manchester U	L	0-2		20,000
32		22	(a)	Everton	L	0-3		10,000
33		24	(a)	Aston Villa	L	1-4	Randall	30,000
34		29	(h)	Sheffield W	L	2-5	Devine, Grant	5,000
35	Apr	5	(a)	Blackburn R	D	1-1	Devine	6,000
36		12	(h)	Derby C	L	1-2	Lewis	4,000
37		19	(a)	Tottenham H	D	1-1	Grant	20,000
38		26	(h)	Middlesbrough	D	1-1	Stonley	3,000

FINAL LEAGUE POSITION: 20th in Division One

Appearances
Goals

FA Cup

1	Jan	11	(a)	Croydon C	D	0-0		8,000
R		15	(h)	Croydon C	W	2-1	Duncan, Graham	9,000
2	Feb	1	(h)	Liverpool	L	1-4	Lewis	8,653

Appearances
Goals

174

Crawford HS	Shaw J	Peart JC	Thomson M	Sands PR	McKinnon A	Greenaway D	Common A	McLaughlan J	Flanagan J	Winship T	Payne GC	Randall CE	Burrell G	Lewis CH	McEachrane RJ	Hanks E	Spittle WA	King E	Groves FW	Duncan D	McDonald HL	Graham A	Grant GM	Ford GE	Evans R	Fidler J	Stonley SJ	Devine A	Wilson O	
1	2	3	4	5	6	7	8	9	10	11																				1
1	2	3	4	5	6	7	8	9	10	11																				2
1	2	3	4	5	6	7	8	9	10	11																				3
1	2	3	4	5	6	7	9		8	11	10																			4
1	2	3	4	5	6	7	8	9		11		10																		5
1	2	3	4	5	6	7	8	9	å0					11																6
1	2	3	4	5	6	7	8	9				10		11																7
1	2	3	4	5	6	7	8	9		11		10																		8
1	2	3	4	5				9	8	11		10			7	6														9
1	2	3	4	5	6	7			8	11		10					9													10
1	2	3	4	5	6	7			8					11			9	10												11
1		3	5	2	6	7	8		10	11							9	4												12
1		3	5	2	6	7	8	9		11		10						4												13
1		3	5	2	6		8	9				10		11	7			4												14
1		3	5	2	6		9	8				10		11	7			4												15
1		3	9	5	2	6	8							11			10	4	7											16
1	2	3		5			8							11	6		10	4	7	9										17
	2	3	5		4		8							11	10	6		9		7	1									18
	2	3		5			8							11	10	7	6	4			1	9								19
	2			5	6		8							11	10	7		4			1	9	3							20
	2			5	4	7	8							11	6	10					1	9	3							21
	2			5	4	7	8				10			11	6						1	9	3							22
	2			5	4	7	8				10			11	6						1	9	3							23
	2	3		5	6	7	8							11	10			4			1	9								24
3			6	5		7						10		11				4			9		1		8	2				25
	2			5		7								11	8		10				1	6	4		3	9				26
	2			5		7								11	8						1	6	4		3	9	10			27
	2			5	6	7								11	8						1		4		3	9	10			28
	2			5	6	7								11	8						1		4		3	9	10			29
	2			5	6	7								11	8						1		4		3	9	10			30
	2			5	6	7								11	8						1		4		3	9	10			31
	2			5	6	7								11	8			4			1				3	9	10			32
1	2			5		7		9				10		11	8							6	4		3					33
1	2			5	6	7								11	8								4		3	9	10			34
	2					7		9					5	11	8						1	6	4		3		10			35
	2				6			9	8				5	11	7						1		4		3		10			36
	2			5										11	7		8				1	6	4		3	9	10			37
	2			5	6									11	7		8				1		4		3	9	10		1	38
19	38	16	25	28	29	27	12	13	22	14	3	15	17	24	7	4	6	11	3	3	18	12	13	3	1	13	10	11	1	
							1		1			3	2	1	4	2	3			1		1				2	2	1	2	

Crawford HS	Shaw J	Peart JC	Thomson M	Sands PR	McKinnon A	Greenaway D	Common A	McLaughlan J	Flanagan J	Winship T	Payne GC	Randall CE	Burrell G	Lewis CH	McEachrane RJ	Hanks E	Spittle WA	King E	Groves FW	Duncan D	McDonald HL	Graham A	Grant GM	Ford GE	Evans R	Fidler J	Stonley SJ	Devine A	Wilson O	
	2	3		5		7			8					11	6						4	9	1	10						1
	2	3		5	4	7			8					11	6						9	1	10							R
3			6	5		7						10		11	8			4			1	9	2							2
3	2	3	1	1	3	3			1			3	2	2	2			1			3	3	1							
														1							1	1								

1913-14

Manager: G.Morrell

1	Sep	6	(h)	Leicester F	W	2-1	Jobey, Devine (pen)	20,000
2		13	(a)	Wolves	W	2-1	Winship, Stonley (pen)	15,000
3		15	(h)	Notts C	W	3-0	Stonley 2, Grant	20,000
4		20	(h)	Hull C	D	0-0		25,000
5		27	(a)	Barnsley	L	0-1		11,000
6	Oct	4	(h)	Bury	L	0-1		30,000
7		11	(a)	Huddersfield T	W	2-1	Stonley, Burrell	8,000
8		18	(h)	Lincoln C	W	3-0	Flanagan, Stonley 2	25,000
9		25	(a)	Blackpool	D	1-1	Jobey	18,000
10	Nov	1	(h)	Nottingham F	W	3-2	Rutherford 2, Flanagan	25,000
11		8	(a)	Fulham	L	1-6	Stonley	35,000
12		15	(a)	Grimsby T	D	1-1	Devine (pen)	8,000
13		22	(h)	Birmingham	W	1-0	Flanagan	25,000
14		29	(a)	Bristol C	D	1-1	Hardinge	15,000
15	Dec	6	(h)	Leeds C	W	1-0	Benson (pen)	18,000
16		13	(a)	Clapton O	L	0-1		27,000
17		20	(h)	Glossop	W	2-0	Stonley, Devine	14,500
18		25	(a)	Bradford	W	3-2	Stonley 3	22,000
19		26	(h)	Bradford	W	2-0	Flanagan, Hardinge	30,000
20		27	(a)	Leicester F	W	2-1	Bell 2	10,000
21	Jan	1	(a)	Notts C	L	0-1		7,000
22		3	(h)	Wolves	W	3-1	Rutherford 2, Hardinge	20,000
23		17	(a)	Hull C	W	2-1	Flanagan 2	10,000
24		24	(h)	Barnsley	W	1-0	Rutherford	19,000
25	Feb	7	(a)	Bury	D	1-1	Stonley	10,000
26		14	(h)	Huddersfield T	L	0-1		25,000
27		21	(a)	Lincoln C	L	2-5	Slade, Hardinge	9,000
28		28	(h)	Blackpool	W	2-1	Jobey, Slade	20,000
29	Mar	7	(a)	Nottingham F	D	0-0		10,000
30		14	(h)	Fulham	W	2-0	Flanagan, Slade	30,000
31		28	(a)	Birmingham	L	0-2		18,000
32	Apr	4	(h)	Bristol C	D	1-1	Winship	12,000
33		10	(a)	Stockport C	L	0-2		15,000
34		11	(a)	Leeds C	D	0-0		22,000
35		13	(h)	Stockport C	W	4-0	Flanagan 2, Benson, Rutherford	18,000
36		18	(h)	Clapton O	D	2-2	Flanagan 2	35,000
37		23	(h)	Grimsby T	W	2-0	Stonley, Flanagan	25,000
38		25	(a)	Glossop	W	2-0	Slade, W.Stapley (og)	4,000

FINAL LEAGUE POSITION: 3rd in Division Two

Appearances
Goals

FA Cup

1	Jan	10	(a)	Bradford C	L	0-2		18,000

Appearances
Goals

Football appearances and goals grid (shirt numbers by player and match).

Lievesley J	Shaw J	Fidler J	Grant GM	Sands PR	McKinnon A	Greenaway D	Hardinge HTW	Jobey G	Devine A	Winship T	Stonley SJ	Thomson M	Burrell G	Caldwell JH	Graham A	Lewis CH	Flanagan J	Rutherford J	McEachrane RJ	Benson RW	Slade D	Randall CE	Bell C	Groves FW	Spittle WA	#
1	2	3	4	5	6	7	8	9	10	11																1
1	2	3	4	5	6	7	8		10	11	9															2
1	2		4	3	6	7	8		10	11	9	5														3
	2	3	4	5	6	7	8		10		9			11	1											4
	2	3	4	5	6	7	8		10	11	9					1										5
		3		2	6	7	8	5	10				4	11	1	9										6
1		3		2	6				10	5			9	4		11	7	8								7
1	2	3			6				10	5			9	4		11	7	8								8
1	2	3			6				10	5			9	4		11	7	8								9
1	2	3			6				10	5			11		9	4	8	7								10
1	2	3			6				10	5			11		9	4	8	7								11
1	2	3		5			8	4	10	11	9							7	6							12
1	2	3		5				10	4	11	9					8	7	6								13
1	2			5	6			10	4		9					11	8	7		3						14
1	2			5			8	4	10		9				6	11		7		3						15
1	2			5				4	10						6	11	8	7		3	9					16
1	2			5		7	8	4	10		9				6	11				3						17
1	2			5					10	4	9				6	11	8	7		3						18
1	2			5					10	4	9				6	11	8	7		3						19
1	2			5					10	4					6	11		7		3		8	9			20
1	2			5	6				10	4	9					11		7		3				8		21
1	2		5						10	4	9				6	11	8	7		3						22
1	2			5	6				4	10	9					11	8	7		3						23
1	2			5	6				4	10	9					11	8	7		3						24
1	2			5	6			10	4		9					11	8	7		3						25
1	2			5	6				4	10	9					11		7		3				8		26
1	2			5	6			10	4							11				3	9			7	8	27
1	2			5	6			10	4							11	8	7		3	9					28
1	2			5	6			10	4	11							7	8		3	9					29
1	2			5	6			10	4	11							7	8		3	9					30
1	2			5	6			10	4							11	8	7		3	9					31
1	2			5	6				4	11	9					10	8	7		3						32
1	2		4	5	6	7	8		11						10					3	9					33
1	2		4	5			8		11	9					6	7				3	10					34
1	2		4	5					9						6	11	8	7		3	10					35
1	2		4	5					9						6	11	8	7		3	10					36
1	2		4	5					11	9					6	7	8			3	10					37
1	2		4	5					11	9					6	7	8			3	10					38
35	36	12	12	33	24	8	29	28	13	15	28	7	6	3	13	26	24	21	2	25	12	1	1	3	1	
		1			4	3	3	2	13		1					12	6			2	4		2			

1 own-goal

Lievesley J	Shaw J	Fidler J	Grant GM	Sands PR	McKinnon A	Greenaway D	Hardinge HTW	Jobey G	Devine A	Winship T	Stonley SJ	Thomson M	Burrell G	Caldwell JH	Graham A	Lewis CH	Flanagan J	Rutherford J	McEachrane RJ	Benson RW	Slade D	Randall CE	Bell C	Groves FW	Spittle WA	#
1	2		4	5					10		9				6	11	8			3				7		1
1	1		1	1					1		1				1	1	1			1				1		

177

1914-15

Manager: G.Morrell

1	Sep	1	(h)	Glossop	W 3-0	King 2, Bradshaw	7,000
2		5	(a)	Wolves	L 0-1		8,000
3		8	(a)	Glossop	W 4-0	King 2, Flanagan, Bradshaw	7,000
4		12	(h)	Fulham	W 3-0	King 2, Rutherford	10,000
5		19	(a)	Stockport C	D 1-1	King	6,000
6		26	(h)	Hull C	W 2-1	Hardinge 2	20,000
7	Oct	3	(a)	Leeds C	D 2-2	Bradshaw, Hardinge	12,000
8		10	(h)	Clapton O	W 2-1	King, Bradshaw	30,000
9		17	(h)	Blackpool	W 2-0	King 2	17,000
10		24	(a)	Derby C	L 0-4		8,000
11		31	(h)	Lincoln C	D 1-1	Hardinge	15,000
12	Nov	7	(a)	Birmingham	L 0-3		15,000
13		14	(h)	Grimsby T	W 6-0	King 3, Bradshaw, Benson (pen), McKinnon	15,000
14		18	(a)	Nottingham F	D 1-1	Benson (pen)	3,000
15		21	(a)	Huddersfield T	L 0-3		9,000
16		28	(h)	Bristol C	W 3-0	Hardinge 2, King	7,000
17	Dec	5	(a)	Bury	L 1-3	Bradshaw	5,000
18		12	(h)	Preston NE	L 1-2	Hardinge	10,000
19		25	(a)	Leicester F	W 4-1	Grant, King, Benson, Blyth	13,000
20		26	(h)	Leicester F	W 6-0	Lewis 3, McKinnon, King, Flanagan	6,000
21	Jan	1	(a)	Barnsley	L 0-1		5,000
22		2	(h)	Wolves	W 5-1	King 4, Buckley	9,000
23		16	(a)	Fulham	W 1-0	Bradshaw	10,000
24		23	(h)	Stockport C	W 3-1	Flanagan 2, Bradshaw	6,000
25	Feb	6	(h)	Leeds C	W 2-0	Rutherford, Bradshaw	10,000
26		13	(a)	Clapton O	L 0-1		4,000
27		20	(a)	Blackpool	W 2-0	Winship, King	6,000
28		27	(h)	Derby C	L 1-2	King (pen)	18,000
29	Mar	6	(a)	Lincoln C	L 0-1		6,000
30		13	(h)	Birmingham	W 1-0	Bradshaw	19,000
31		20	(a)	Grimsby T	L 0-1		5,000
32		27	(h)	Huddersfield T	L 0-3		14,000
33	Apr	2	(a)	Hull C	L 0-1		8,000
34		3	(a)	Bristol C	D 1-1	Winship	7,000
35		5	(h)	Barnsley	W 1-0	Lewis	15,000
36		10	(h)	Bury	W 3-1	Flanagan 2, Blyth	12,000
37		17	(a)	Preston NE	L 0-3		14,000
38		24	(h)	Nottingham F	W 7-0	Benson 2, King 4, Rutherford	10,000

FINAL LEAGUE POSITION: 5th in Division Two

Appearances
Goals

FA Cup

1	Jan	9	(h*)	Merthyr T	W 3-0	King 3	9,000
2		30	(a)	Chelsea	L 0-1		40,372

*Played at home by arrangement.

Appearances
Goals

178

Lievesley J	Shaw J	Benson RW	Grant GM	Buckley CS	Graham A	Rutherford J	Flanagan J	King HE	Bradshaw F	Lewis CH	Winship T	Hardinge HTW	Sands PR	Groves FW	Norman J	McKinnon A	Blyth WN	Ford GE	Greenaway D	Liddell E	Fletcher A	Kempton AR	
1	2	3	4	5	6	7	8	9	10	11													1
1	2	3	4	5	6	7	8	9	10	11													2
1	2	3	4	5	6	7	8	9	10		11												3
1	2	3	4	5	6	7	8	9	10		11												4
1	2	3	4	5	6	7		9	10		11	8											5
1	2	3	4	5	6	7		9	10		11	8											6
1	2	3	4	5	6	7		9	10		11	8											7
1	2	3	4	5	6	7		9	10		11	8											8
1	2	3	4	5	6	7		9	10		11	8											9
1	2	3	4		6	7	8	9	10			11	5										10
1	2	3	4	5	6	7	8		10		11	9											11
1	2	3	4	5	6		8	9	10					7	11								12
1	2	3	4	5				9	10	7		8			11	6							13
1	2	3	4	5				9	10	7		8			11	6							14
1	2	3	4	5				9	10	7					11	6	8						15
1	2	3	4	5		7		9	10	11		8				6							16
1	2		4	3	5	7		9	10	11		8				6							17
1	2	3	4		5	7		9	10	11		8				6							18
1	2	3	4	5		7	8	9		11						6	10						19
1	2	3	4	5		7	8	9		11						6	10						20
1	2		4	5			8	9	7	11						6	10	3					21
1	2		4	5			8	9	10	11				7		6		3					22
1	2		4	5		7	8	9	10	11						6		3					23
1	2		4	5		7	8	9	10	11						6		3					24
1	2		4	5		7	8	9	10	11						6		3					25
1	2		4	5		7	8	9	10	11						6		3					26
1	3			5	4		8	9			11		2			6	10		7				27
1	3			5	4	7	8	9			11		2			6	10						28
1	3		5		4	7	8	9	10		11		2			6							29
1	2	3			4		8	9	10	11			5			6			7				30
1	2	3			4		8	9	10	11			5			6			7				31
1	2	3		5	4	7	8	9	10	11						6							32
1	2	3	4		6	7	8	9		11							10			5			33
1	3			5	6		8	9			11						10		7	2	4		34
1	2	3			4		8	9		11			5			6	10		7				35
1	2	3			6	7	8	9		11			5				10				4		36
1	2	3			6		8	9		11			5				10		7		4		37
1	3	9		5	4	7		8	6	11			2				10						38
38	38	27	28	29	26	26	26	37	29	24	12	12	10	2	4	21	12	6	6	2	3		
		5	1	1		3	6	26	10	4	2	7				2	2						

Lievesley J	Shaw J	Benson RW	Grant GM	Buckley CS	Graham A	Rutherford J	Flanagan J	King HE	Bradshaw F	Lewis CH	Winship T	Hardinge HTW	Sands PR	Groves FW	Norman J	McKinnon A	Blyth WN	Ford GE	Greenaway D	Liddell E	Fletcher A	Kempton AR	
	2		4	5		7	8	9	10	11						6		3				1	1
1	2	3	4	5		7	8	9	10	11						6							2
1	2	1	2	2		2	2	2	2	2						2		1				1	
								3															

1919-20

Manager: L.Knighton

1	Aug	30	(h)	Newcastle U	L	0-1		40,000
2	Sep	1	(a)	Liverpool	W	3-2	White 2, Blyth	15,000
3		6	(a)	Newcastle U	L	1-3	Groves	45,000
4		8	(h)	Liverpool	W	1-0	Rutherford	20,000
5		13	(a)	Sunderland	D	1-1	White	30,000
6		20	(h)	Sunderland	W	3-2	White 3	42,000
7		27	(a)	Blackburn R	D	2-2	White, Burgess	5,000
8	Oct	4	(h)	Blackburn R	L	0-1		30,000
9		11	(a)	Everton	W	3-2	White 2, Blyth	35,000
10		18	(h)	Everton	D	1-1	Groves	30,000
11		25	(h)	Bradford C	L	1-2	Graham (pen)	35,000
12	Nov	1	(a)	Bradford C	D	1-1	White	16,000
13		8	(h)	Bolton W	D	2-2	Pagnam, Rutherford	30,000
14		15	(a)	Bolton W	D	2-2	Hardinge, Pagnam	20,000
15		22	(h)	Notts C	W	3-1	Pagnam 2, Toner	25,000
16		29	(a)	Notts C	D	2-2	Buckley, Pagnam	6,000
17	Dec	6	(h)	Chelsea	D	1-1	White	50,000
18		13	(a)	Chelsea	L	1-3	White	60,000
19		20	(h)	Sheffield W	W	3-1	Hardinge, Pagnam, Butler	30,000
20		25	(a)	Derby C	L	1-2	Pagnam (pen)	14,000
21		26	(h)	Derby C	W	1-0	Groves	25,000
22		27	(a)	Sheffield W	W	2-1	Hardinge, White	23,000
23	Jan	3	(h)	Manchester C	D	2-2	White, Lewis	32,000
24		17	(a)	Manchester C	L	1-4	Graham (pen)	25,000
25		24	(h)	Aston Villa	L	0-1		55,000
26	Feb	7	(h)	Oldham A	W	3-2	North, Graham, Blyth	32,000
27		11	(a)	Aston Villa	L	1-2	Graham (pen)	20,000
28		14	(a)	Oldham A	L	0-3		14,000
29		21	(h)	Manchester U	L	0-3		25,000
30		28	(a)	Manchester U	W	1-0	Rutherford	30,000
31	Mar	6	(a)	Sheffield U	L	0-2		25,000
32		13	(h)	Sheffield U	W	3-0	Graham, Pagnam 2	35,000
33		20	(a)	Middlesbrough	L	0-1		22,000
34		27	(h)	Middlesbrough	W	2-1	Blyth, Groves	25,000
35	Apr	3	(a)	Burnley	L	1-2	Pagnam	20,000
36		5	(h)	West Brom A	W	1-0	Blyth	40,000
37		6	(a)	West Brom A	L	0-1		40,000
38		10	(h)	Burnley	W	2-0	Bradshaw, Pagnam	20,000
39		17	(a)	Preston NE	D	1-1	White	13,000
40		24	(h)	Preston NE	D	0-0		35,000
41		28	(a)	Bradford	D	0-0		7,000
42	May	1	(h)	Bradford	W	3-0	Groves, Pagnam, Bradshaw	30,000

FINAL LEAGUE POSITION: 10th in Division One

Appearances
Goals

FA Cup

1	Jan	10	(h*)	Rochdale	W	4-2	Rutherford, Groves, Graham, Pagnam	26,596
2		31	(a)	Bristol C	L	0-1		25,900

*At home by arrangement.

Appearances
Goals

180

Team line-up grid (players as columns, matches as numbered rows 1–42):

Williamson EC	Shaw J	Bradshaw F	Graham A	Voysey CR	McKinnon A	Rutherford J	Groves FW	White HA	Blyth WN	Baker A	Burgess D	Hutchins AV	Buckley CS	Dunn S	Toner J	Pagnam F	Hardinge HTW	Butler JD	Lewis CH	Cownley FF	Coopland WE	North EJ	Peart JC	Greenaway D	Whittaker TJ	Pattison GC	#
1	2	3	4	5	6	7	8	9	10	11																	1
1	2	3	4	5	6	7	11	9	10		8																2
1	2	3	4	5	6	7	11	9	10		8																3
1	2	3	4	5	6	7	11	9	10		8																4
1	2		4	5	6	7	11	9	10		8	3															5
1	2		4		6	7	11	9	10		8	3	5														6
1	2	3	4		6		7	9	10	11	8		5														7
1	2	3	4		6	7	11	9	10		8		5														8
	2	3	4		6	7	8	9	10				5	1		11											9
1	2		4		6	7	8	9	10			3	5			11											10
1	2		4		6	7		8	10			3	5			11	9										11
1	2	3	5		6	7	4	8								11	9	10									12
1	2	3	5		6	7	4	8								11	9	10									13
1	2	3			6	7		8					5			11	9	10	4								14
1	2	3			6	7		8					5			11	9	10	4								15
1	2				6	7		8				3	5			11	9	10	4								16
1	2	3			6	7		8					5			11	9	10	4								17
1	2	3			6	7		8					5			11	9	10	4								18
1	2	3			6	7	8						5			11	9	10	4								19
1	2	3			6	7	8		11				5				9	10	4								20
1	2	3			6	7	8		4				5				9	10		11							21
1	2	3			6	7	8	9	4				5					10		11							22
1	2	3			6	7	8	9	4				5					10		11							23
	2	3	4		6		7	8						1			9	10	5	11							24
	2	3	4		6		8	9	10					1			7		5	11							25
		3	4		6	7	8		10				5	1	11						2	9					26
		3	4			7	8		10	6			5	1							2	11	9				27
		3	4		6	7	8		10					1	11			5			2						28
		3	4		6	7		9	10				5	1	11			8			2						29
	2	8	10		6	7			11			3	5	1			9	4									30
	2	8			6	7			11			3	5	1			9	4			10						31
		8	10		6	7	8		11	4		3		1			9	5			2						32
		10			6	7	8		11	4		3		1			9	5			2						33
		10			6	7	8		11	4		3	5	1			9				2						34
	2	10			6	7	8		11	4		3		1			9	5									35
	2	10			6	7	8		11	4		3		1			9	5									36
		10			6		8		11			3	5	1	4						2	7	9				37
	2	10			6	7	8		11	4		3		1			9	5									38
1	2				6	7	8	10	11	4		3					9	5									39
1	2				6	7	8	10	11	4		3					9	5									40
1					6		8	10	11	4		3					9	5			2	7					41
1	2	10			6		8		11	4		3					9						7		5		42
26	33	33	22	5	41	36	29	29	29	17	7	18	23	16	15	25	13	21	5	4	1	4	5	3	1	1	
	2	5			3	5	15	5		1		1		1		12	3	1	1			1					

Williamson EC	Shaw J	Bradshaw F	Graham A	Voysey CR	McKinnon A	Rutherford J	Groves FW	White HA	Blyth WN	Baker A	Burgess D	Hutchins AV	Buckley CS	Dunn S	Toner J	Pagnam F	Hardinge HTW	Butler JD	Lewis CH	Cownley FF	Coopland WE	North EJ	Peart JC	Greenaway D	Whittaker TJ	Pattison GC	#
1	2	3	4		6	7	8	9								10			5	11							1
	2	3	4		6	7	8		10					5	1	11	9										2
1	2	2	2		2	2	2	1	1					1	1	1	2		1	1							
			1			1	1									1											

1920-21

1	Aug	28	(a)	Aston Villa	L 0-5		50,000
2		30	(h)	Manchester U	W 2-0	Pagnam, Smith	25,000
3	Sep	4	(h)	Aston Villa	L 0-1		45,000
4		6	(a)	Manchester U	D 1-1	White	30,000
5		11	(h)	Manchester C	W 2-1	Pagnam, Groves	42,000
6		18	(a)	Manchester C	L 1-3	Blyth	30,000
7		25	(h)	Middlesbrough	D 2-2	Graham (pen), Pagnam	40,000
8	Oct	2	(a)	Middlesbrough	L 1-2	White	25,000
9		9	(h)	Bolton W	D 0-0		38,000
10		16	(a)	Bolton W	D 1-1	White	35,000
11		23	(a)	Derby C	D 1-1	White	18,000
12		30	(h)	Derby C	W 2-0	Pagnam, White	45,000
13	Nov	6	(a)	Blackburn R	D 2-2	McKinnon, Buckley	20,000
14		13	(h)	Blackburn R	W 2-0	White, Pagnam	40,000
15		20	(a)	Huddersfield T	W 4-0	Pagnam 2, Blyth, Graham (pen)	19,000
16		27	(h)	Huddersfield T	W 2-0	Pagnam 2	35,000
17	Dec	4	(a)	Chelsea	W 2-1	Pagnam 2	60,000
18		11	(h)	Chelsea	D 1-1	Blyth	50,000
19		18	(a)	Bradford C	L 1-3	Blyth	20,000
20		25	(a)	Everton	W 4-2	White, Toner, Blyth, Pagnam	35,000
21		27	(h)	Everton	D 1-1	Pagnam	40,000
22	Jan	1	(h)	Bradford C	L 1-2	Graham (pen)	20,000
23		15	(a)	Tottenham H	L 1-2	Rutherford	39,221
24		22	(h)	Tottenham H	W 3-2	Rutherford 2, White	60,600
25		29	(h)	Sunderland	L 1-2	Pagnam	40,000
26	Feb	5	(a)	Sunderland	L 1-5	Blyth	30,000
27		12	(a)	Oldham A	D 1-1	Graham (pen)	18,313
28		19	(h)	Oldham A	D 2-2	Rutherford, Walden	40,000
29		26	(a)	Preston NE	W 1-0	White	25,000
30	Mar	12	(a)	Burnley	L 0-1		30,000
31		19	(h)	Burnley	D 1-1	Baker (pen)	45,000
32		26	(h)	Sheffield U	L 2-6	White, Baker	30,000
33		28	(h)	West Brom A	W 2-1	Graham (pen), Blyth	20,000
34		29	(a)	West Brom A	W 4-3	North 2, Hopkins, McKenzie	23,650
35	Apr	2	(a)	Sheffield U	D 1-1	Rutherford	35,000
36		9	(h)	Bradford	W 2-1	Toner, Rutherford	30,000
37		16	(a)	Bradford	W 1-0	Toner	14,000
38		23	(h)	Newcastle U	D 1-1	Rutherford	20,000
39		25	(h)	Preston NE	W 2-1	Hopkins, McKinnon	12,000
40		30	(a)	Newcastle U	L 0-1		35,000
41	May	2	(h)	Liverpool	D 0-0		17,000
42		7	(a)	Liverpool	L 0-3		20,000

FINAL LEAGUE POSITION: 9th in Division One

Appearances

Goals

FA Cup

1	Jan	8	(a)	Queen's Park R	L 0-2		18,000

Appearances

Goals

182

Player appearance and position grid (positions 1–11 by match; match number in final column).

Williamson EC	Shaw J	Hutchins AV	Baker A	Buckley CS	McKinnon A	Smith J	Groves FW	Pagnam F	Bradshaw F	Blyth WN	Graham A	White HA	Rutherford J	Paterson Dr JA	Butler JD	Toner J	Dunn S	North EJ	Cownley FF	Walden HA	Burgess D	Pattison GC	Whittaker TJ	McKenzie A	Hopkins J	Peart JC	Voysey CR	
1	2	3	4	5	6	7	8	9	10	11																		1
1	2	3	4	5	6	7	8	9	10	11																		2
1	2	3	4		6	7	8	9	10	11	5																	3
1	2	3	4		6	7	10	9		11	5	8																4
1	2	3	4		6	7	10	9		11	5	8																5
1	2	3	4		6	7	10	9		11	5	8																6
1	2	3	4		6	7	10	9		11	5	8																7
1	2	3	4		6		10	9		11	5	8	7															8
1	2	3	4		6			9	10	11	5	8	7															9
1	2	3	4		6			9	10	11	5	8	7															10
1	2	3	4		6			9	10	11	5	8	7															11
1		3	4		6			9	2	10	5	8	7	11														12
1	2		4	5	6			9	3	10		8	7	11														13
1	2	3	4	5	6	7		9		10		8		11														14
1	2	3	4		6	7		9		10	5	8		11														15
1	2	3	4			7		9		10	5	8		11	6													16
1	2	3	4		6			9		10	5	8	7	11														17
1	2	3	4		6			9		10	5	8	7	11														18
1	2	3	4		6			9		10	5	8	7			11												19
1		3	4		6			9	2	10		8	7		5	11												20
1	2	3	4		6			9		10		8	7	11	5													21
1	2	3	4		6			9		10	5	8	7			11												22
1		3	4		6			9	2	10		8	7	11	5													23
		3	4		6				2	10		8	7	11	5		1	9										24
1		3	4		6			9	2	10	5	8	7	11														25
1			4		6		8	9	3	10	5		7	11				2										26
1		3	4				8		2	10	5		7	11	6					9								27
1		3	4		6		8		2	10	5		7	11						9								28
1		3	4		6		8		2	10		9	7	11	5													29
1		3	4		6				2	10	5	9	7			11							8					30
1		3	4		6				2	10		9	7	11									8	5				31
1		3	4		6		8		2	10	5	9	7	11														32
1	2	3	4							10	5		7	11					9			6	8		10			33
1	2	3	4								5		7	11				9				6	8		10			34
	2	3									5		7	11			1	9			4	6	8		10			35
	2		4		6				3	10	5		7			11	1	9					8					36
	2	3	4		6							8	5				1	9							10			37
	2	3	4		6							8	5				1	9							10			38
		3			6				2			8	5				1	9				4			10			39
	2	3			6					9	5		7	11			1				4		8		10			40
		3			6					9			7	11			1					8	5	4	10	2		41
	2	3			6					9			7	11			1					8	5	4	10			42
33	28	39	37	4	37	10	13	25	21	40	30	26	32	20	6	12	9	8	1	2	4	6	5	5	8	1		
	2		1		2	1	1	14		7	5	10	7			3		2		1					1	2		

| 1 | 2 | 3 | | | 6 | | | 9 | | 10 | | 8 | 7 | 4 | 11 | | | | | | | | | | 5 | | | 1 |
| 1 | 1 | 1 | | | 1 | | | 1 | | 1 | | 1 | 1 | 1 | 1 | | | | | | | | | | 1 | | | |

183

1921-22

Manager: L.Knighton

1	Aug	27	(h)	Sheffield U	L 1-2 White	40,000
2		29	(a)	Preston NE	L 2-3 White 2	25,000
3	Sep	3	(a)	Sheffield U	L 1-4 White	25,000
4		5	(h)	Preston NE	W 1-0 White	20,000
5		10	(a)	Manchester C	L 0-2	25,000
6		17	(h)	Manchester C	L 0-1	25,000
7		24	(a)	Everton	D 1-1 Bradshaw	30,000
8	Oct	1	(h)	Everton	W 1-0 White	35,000
9		8	(a)	Sunderland	L 0-1	30,000
10		15	(h)	Sunderland	L 1-2 Bradshaw	40,000
11		22	(a)	Huddersfield T	L 0-2	12,000
12		29	(h)	Huddersfield T	L 1-3 North	30,000
13	Nov	5	(a)	Birmingham	W 1-0 North	30,000
14		12	(h)	Birmingham	W 5-2 Whittaker, Baker, Hopkins 2, North	30,000
15		19	(a)	Bolton W	L 0-1	20,000
16	Dec	3	(a)	Blackburn R	W 1-0 Baker	25,000
17		10	(h)	Blackburn R	D 1-1 Hopkins	35,000
18		12	(h)	Bolton W*	D 1-1 Butler	10,000
19		17	(a)	Oldham A	L 1-2 Boreham	10,517
20		24	(h)	Oldham A	L 0-1	20,000
21		26	(h)	Cardiff C	D 0-0	35,000
22		27	(a)	Cardiff C	L 3-4 White, Boreham 2	37,000
23		31	(a)	Chelsea	W 2-0 White, Boreham	40,000
24	Jan	14	(h)	Chelsea	W 1-0 Boreham	40,000
25		21	(h)	Burnley	D 0-0	23,000
26	Feb	4	(h)	Newcastle U	W 2-1 Boreham, Toner	30,000
27		11	(a)	Newcastle U	L 1-3 Rutherford	30,000
28		20	(a)	Burnley	L 0-1	15,000
29		25	(a)	Liverpool	L 0-4	30,000
30	Mar	11	(a)	Manchester U	L 0-1	25,000
31		18	(a)	Aston Villa	L 0-2	30,000
32		22	(h)	Liverpool	W 1-0 Baker	12,000
33		25	(h)	Aston Villa	W 2-0 White, Boreham	40,000
34	Apr	1	(h)	Middlesbrough	D 2-2 White, Boreham	30,000
35		5	(h)	Manchester U	W 3-1 White, Butler, Boreham	25,000
36		8	(a)	Middlesbrough	L 2-4 Baker, White	20,000
37		15	(a)	Tottenham H	L 0-2	40,394
38		17	(a)	West Brom A	W 3-0 Boreham, Young, Graham	24,000
39		18	(h)	West Brom A	D 2-2 White, Graham (pen)	22,000
40		22	(h)	Tottenham H	W 1-0 Graham (pen)	42,000
41		29	(a)	Bradford C	W 2-0 White, Young	35,000
42	May	6	(h)	Bradford C	W 1-0 Blyth	32,000

FINAL LEAGUE POSITION: 17th in Division One
*After abandoned match (38 mins) on Nov 26 — Arsenal 0 Bolton 0 team as per Match 15 — Att: 15,000

Appearances
Goals

FA Cup

1	Jan	7	(h)	Queen's Park R	D 0-0	31,000
R		11	(a)	Queen's Park R	W 2-1 Graham (pen), Milne	15,000
2		28	(a)	Bradford	W 3-2 White 2, Blyth	10,400
3	Feb	18	(h)	Leicester C	W 3-0 Rutherford, White 2	39,421
4	Mar	4	(h)	Preston NE	D 1-1 White	37,517
R		8	(a)	Preston NE	L 1-2† Blyth	30,000

†After extra-time

Appearances
Goals

184

Player appearance / line-up grid (shirt numbers by match).

Williamson EC	Shaw J	Hutchins AV	Baker A	Graham A	McKinnon A	Rutherford J	Blyth WN	White HA	North EJ	Voysey CR	Whittaker TJ	Butler JD	Burgess D	Hopkins J	Cownley FF	McKenzie A	Bradshaw F	Paterson Dr JA	Henderson W	Maxwell T	Toner J	Boreham R	Turnbull R	Pattison GC	Creegan WW	Milne W	Dunn S	Earle SGJ	Young A	No.
1	2	3	4	5	6	7	8	9	10	11																				1
1	2	3			6	7		9	10		4	5	8	11	2															2
1		3			6	7		9	10		4	5	8	11	2															3
1		3			6	7		9	10		4	5		11	2	8														4
1		3			6	7		9	10		4	5		11	2	8														5
1		3	4	10	6	7	11	9				5			2	8														6
1		3	9		6	7	11	8			4	5			2		10													7
1		3	9		6	7	11	8			4	5			2		10													8
1		3	9		6	7	11	8			4	5			2		10													9
1		3	9		6	7		8			4	5			2		10		11											10
1	2	3	4		6	7	11	8				5					10		9											11
1	2	3	4		6	7		10		9		5						11		8										12
1		3	4			7	8	9			6	5			10		2				11									13
1		3	4			7	8	9			6	5			10		2				11									14
1		3	4			7	8				6	5			10	9	2				11									15
1		3	4			7	8				6	5			10	9	2				11									16
1		3	4			7	8				6	5			10	9	2				11									17
1		3	4			7	8	9			6	5					2				11	10								18
1		3			6	7	8	9			4	5					2				11	10								19
1		3			6	7	8	9			4	5					2				11	10								20
1		3		5	6	7	8				4	9			10		2				11									21
1	2					7		8			4			11					9			10	3	5	6					22
1		3		5		7	8	9			6						2				11	10			4					23
1		3	4	5			8	9			6						2				11	10				7				24
1		3	10	5		7	8	9			6						2				11				4					25
			4	5		7	8	9			6						2				11	10	3				1			26
1			4	5		7	8	9			6						2				11	10	3							27
1								10	9		6	8			3		2				11		5	7	4					28
1			4	5		7		9			6	8					2				11	10	3							29
1	2	3	4			7	8	9			6	5									11	10								30
1		3	4	5		7		9			6						2				11	10							8	31
1		3	4	5			8				6						2				11	10				7			9	32
1		3	4	5			8				6						2				11	10				7			9	33
1		3	4	5		11	8				6						2					10				7			9	34
1		3	4	5	6	7	8	9									2				11	10								35
1		3	4	5	6	7	8	9									2				11	10								36
1		3	4	5		7		8			6						2				11	10							9	37
1		3	4	5		7		8			6						2				11	10							9	38
1		3	4	5		7	11	8			6						2					10							9	39
1		3	4	5		7	11	8			6						2					10							9	40
1		3	4	5		7	11	8			6						2					10							9	41
1		3	4	5		7	11				6						2					10	9						8	42
41	6	37	32	21	17	36	25	35	11	1	36	25	2	11	10	3	32	2	5	1	24	22	5	2	5	4	1	1	9	
				4	3			1	1		14	3		1	2		3				2	1	10						2	

Williamson EC	Shaw J	Hutchins AV	Baker A	Graham A	McKinnon A	Rutherford J	Blyth WN	White HA	North EJ	Voysey CR	Whittaker TJ	Butler JD	Burgess D	Hopkins J	Cownley FF	McKenzie A	Bradshaw F	Paterson Dr JA	Henderson W	Maxwell T	Toner J	Boreham R	Turnbull R	Pattison GC	Creegan WW	Milne W	Dunn S	Earle SGJ	Young A	No.
1		3	8					9			6				7		10				11	2	5		4					1
1		3	10	5			8	9			6						2				11		7		4					R
1		3	10	5		7	8	9			6						2				11				4					2
1			4	5		7	10	9			6	8					2				11		3							3
1			4	5		7	10	9			6	8					2				11		3							4
1			4	5		7	10	9			6	8					2				11		3							R
6		3	6	5		4	5	6			6	3			1		6				6	4	1	1	3					
			1			1	2	5									1													

1922-23

Manager: L.Knighton

1	Aug	26	(a)	Liverpool	L 2-5	Boreham, Young	43,000
2		28	(h)	Burnley	D 1-1	Young	25,000
3	Sep	2	(h)	Liverpool	W 1-0	Hutchins	35,000
4		4	(a)	Burnley	L 1-4	Hopkins	20,000
5		9	(a)	Cardiff C	L 1-4	Whittaker	30,000
6		16	(h)	Cardiff C	W 2-1	Young, Boreham	40,000
7		23	(a)	Tottenham H	W 2-1	Boreham 2	40,582
8		30	(h)	Tottenham H	L 0-2		55,000
9	Oct	2	(a)	Sheffield U	L 1-2	Boreham	15,000
10		7	(h)	West Brom A	W 3-1	White, Voysey, Boreham	30,000
11		14	(a)	West Brom A	L 0-7		21,730
12		21	(a)	Newcastle U	D 1-1	Hopkins	30,000
13		28	(h)	Newcastle U	L 1-2	Roe	35,000
14	Nov	4	(a)	Everton	L 0-1		30,000
15		11	(h)	Everton	L 1-2	Blyth	30,000
16		18	(a)	Sunderland	D 3-3	Voysey 2, Turnbull	15,000
17		25	(h)	Sunderland	L 2-3	Turnbull 2	30,000
18	Dec	2	(a)	Birmingham	L 2-3	Voysey, Turnbull	30,000
19		9	(h)	Birmingham	W 1-0	Graham (pen)	30,000
20		16	(h)	Huddersfield T	D 1-1	Rutherford	25,000
21		23	(a)	Huddersfield T	L 0-4		10,000
22		25	(a)	Bolton W	L 1-4	Turnbull	32,000
23		26	(h)	Bolton W	W 5-0	Turnbull 4, Blyth	35,000
24		30	(h)	Stoke	W 3-0	Blyth, Boreham, Turnbull	25,000
25	Jan	1	(a)	Blackburn R	W 5-0	Turnbull 4, Baker	20,000
26		6	(a)	Stoke	L 0-1		15,000
27		20	(h)	Manchester C	W 1-0	Turnbull	25,000
28		27	(a)	Manchester C	D 0-0		30,000
29	Feb	3	(a)	Nottingham F	L 1-2	Baker	15,000
30		10	(h)	Nottingham F	W 2-0	Baker 2	20,000
31		17	(a)	Chelsea	D 0-0		50,000
32		24	(h)	Chelsea	W 3-1	Blyth 2, Baker	30,000
33	Mar	3	(a)	Middlesbrough	L 0-2		20,000
34		10	(h)	Middlesbrough	W 3-0	Turnbull 3	25,000
35		17	(h)	Oldham A	W 2-0	Blyth, Freeman (og)	30,000
36		24	(a)	Oldham A	D 0-0		13,724
37		31	(h)	Aston Villa	W 2-0	Baker, Blyth	45,000
38	Apr	2	(h)	Blackburn R	D 1-1	McKenzie	32,000
39		7	(a)	Aston Villa	D 1-1	Blyth	18,000
40		14	(h)	Preston NE	D 1-1	Boreham	23,000
41		21	(a)	Preston NE	W 2-1	Earle, Turnbull	15,000
42		28	(h)	Sheffield U	W 2-0	Turnbull, Blyth	25,000

FINAL LEAGUE POSITION: 11th in Division One

Appearances
Goals

FA Cup

1	Jan	13	(a)	Liverpool	D 0-0		37,000
R		17	(h)	Liverpool	L 1-4	Turnbull	39,000

Appearances
Goals

186

Appearance / shirt-number grid (league table). Column headers (left → right):

1 Williamson EC · 2 Bradshaw F · 3 Hutchins AV · 4 Butler JD · 5 Voysey CR · 6 Whittaker TJ · 7 Rutherford J · 8 White HA · 9 Young A · 10 Boreham R · 11 Blyth WN · 12 Turnbull R · 13 Baker A · 14 Hopkins J · 15 Dunn S · 16 Paterson Dr JA · 17 Graham A · 18 Townrow FA · 19 Milne W · 20 Roe, Archibald · 21 John RF · 22 Henderson W · 23 Toner J · 24 Kennedy AL · 25 Mackie JA · 26 Robson JH · 27 McKenzie A · 28 Clark J · 29 Elvey JR · 30 Earle SGJ

Willi	Brad	Hutc	Butl	Voys	Whit	Ruth	Whit(HA)	Youn	Bore	Blyt	Turn	Bake	Hopk	Dunn	Pate	Grah	Town	Miln	Roe	John	Hend	Tone	Kenn	Mack	Robs	McKe	Clar	Elve	Earl	#
1	2	3	4	5	6	7	8	9	10	11																				1
1	2			5	6	7	8	9	10	11	3	4																		2
1	2	3		5	6	7	8	9	10	11		4																		3
1	2	3		5	6	7	8	9		11		4	10																	4
1	2			5	6	7	8	9	10	11	3	4																		5
	2	3		5	6	7	8	9	10			4		1	11															6
	2	3		5		7	8	9	10	11		4		1		6														7
	2	3		5		7	8	9	10	11		4		1		6														8
	2	3		5		7		9	10	11		4		1		6	8													9
		3		5		7	8	9	10		2	4		1	11	6														10
	2			5		7	8	9	10		3	4		1	11	6														11
	2				6	7			10		3		8	1	11			5	9											12
	2								10		3		8	1	11	5		4	9	6	7									13
	2				6		8		10		3			1		7		5	9				4							14
	2				6	7			10		3		8	1	11	5		4	9											15
	2	3	5	8	6	7			10					1		4						11								16
	2	3	5	8	6	7			10					1	11			4												17
	2			8					10					1	9			5		4			6	7	11	3				18
				8		7			10					1	9			5		4			6			3	2			19
				8		7			10					1	9			5		4			6			3	2			20
				8	7				10					1	9			5		4			6		11	3	2		21
				8					10	5	9	7		1				4		6			11	3	2					22
			5						10	8	9	7			11			4		6			3	2	1					23
			5						10	8	9	7			11			4		6			3	2	1					24
			5							8	9	7			11			4		6			3	2	1	10				25
									10	8	9	7			11	5		4		6			3	2	1					26
										8	9	7			11	5		4		6			3	2	1	10				27
										8	9	7			11	5		4		6			3	2	1	10				28
										8	9	7			11	5		4		6			3	2	1	10				29
			5			7				8	9	10			11			4		6			3	2	1					30
			5			7				8	9	10			11			4		6			3	2	1					31
			5			7				8	9	10			11			4		6			3	2	1					32
			5			7				8	9	10						4		6		11	3	2	1					33
			5			7				8	9	10			11			4		6			3	2	1					34
			5		6	7				8	9	10			11			4					3	2	1					35
			5			7				8	9	10			11			4		6			3	2	1					36
			5			7				8	9	10			11			4		6			3	2	1					37
			5							8	9				11			4		6			3	2	1	10				38
			5							8	9							4		6		11	3	2	1	10	7			39
			5						6	10	8	9	3			11		4					1	7	2					40
									5	10	11	9	7					4		6			3	2	1			8		41
			5							10	8	9			11			4		6			3	2	1		7			42
5	17	10	18	18	13	26	11	13	27	31	35	29	2	17	26	17	1	31	4	24	2	7	24	23	20	7	2	1	1	
	1		4	1	1	1	3	8	9	20	6	2			1			1					1			1		1		

1 own-goal

Cup appearances (rounds 1 and R):

Butl	Bore	Blyt	Turn	Bake	Pate	Roe	Miln	Kenn	Robs	McKe	Clar	Earl	
5	10	8	9	7	11	4	6	3	2	1			1
5	10	9	7	11	8	4	6	3	2	1			R
1 1	2 1 2	2	2	1 2	2	2 2 2							
		1											

1923-24

Manager: L.Knighton

1	Aug	25	(h)	Newcastle U	L	1-4	Turnbull	45,000
2		27	(a)	West Ham U	L	0-1		22,000
3	Sep	1	(a)	Newcastle U	L	0-1		40,000
4		8	(a)	West Brom A	L	0-4		25,000
5		10	(h)	West Ham U	W	4-1	Earle 2, Woods, Graham	36,000
6		15	(h)	West Brom A	W	1-0	Voysey	36,004
7		22	(a)	Birmingham	W	2-0	Turnbull, Voysey	20,000
8		29	(h)	Birmingham	D	0-0		35,000
9	Oct	6	(a)	Manchester C	L	0-1		23,477
10		13	(h)	Manchester C	L	1-2	Turnbull	32,000
11		20	(a)	Bolton W	W	2-1	Woods, Rutherford	20,000
12		27	(h)	Bolton W	D	0-0		30,000
13	Nov	3	(h)	Middlesbrough	W	2-1	Townrow, Woods	25,000
14		10	(a)	Middlesbrough	D	0-0		12,000
15		17	(h)	Tottenham H	D	1-1	Townrow	50,000
16		24	(a)	Tottenham H	L	0-3		31,624
17	Dec	1	(h)	Blackburn R	D	2-2	Young, McIntyre (og)	20,000
18		8	(a)	Blackburn R	L	0-2		20,000
19		15	(h)	Huddersfield T	L	1-3	Young	25,000
20		22	(a)	Huddersfield T	L	1-6	Baker	15,000
21		26	(a)	Notts C	W	2-1	Woods, Blyth	25,000
22		27	(h)	Notts C	D	0-0		16,000
23		29	(h)	Chelsea	W	1-0	Turnbull	38,000
24	Jan	5	(a)	Chelsea	D	0-0		38,000
25		19	(h)	Cardiff C	L	1-2	Turnbull	30,000
26		26	(a)	Cardiff C	L	0-4		20,000
27	Feb	9	(a)	Sheffield U	L	1-3	Blyth	10,000
28		16	(h)	Aston Villa	L	0-1		35,000
29		25	(h)	Sheffield U	L	1-3	Milne	15,000
30	Mar	1	(h)	Liverpool	W	3-1	Woods 2, Rutherford	35,000
31		12	(a)	Aston Villa	L	1-2	Blyth	10,000
32		15	(a)	Nottingham F	L	1-2	Ramsay	14,000
33		22	(h)	Nottingham F	W	1-0	Neil	20,000
34	Apr	2	(a)	Liverpool	D	0-0		30,000
35		5	(h)	Burnley	W	2-0	Ramsay, Neil	30,000
36		12	(h)	Sunderland	W	2-0	Woods, Haden	18,000
37		18	(a)	Everton	L	1-3	Haden	30,000
38		19	(a)	Sunderland	D	1-1	Woods	20,000
39		21	(h)	Everton	L	0-1		25,000
40		26	(a)	Preston NE	W	2-0	Haden, Ramsay	12,000
41		28	(a)	Burnley	L	1-4	Woods	9,000
42	May	3	(h)	Preston NE	L	1-2	Turnbull	25,000

FINAL LEAGUE POSITION: 19th in Division One

Appearances
Goals

FA Cup

1	Jan	12	(h)	Luton T	W	4-1	Blyth, Woods, Turnbull, Milne	37,500
2	Feb	2	(a)	Cardiff C	L	0-1		35,000

Appearances
Goals

Robson JH	Mackie JA	Kennedy AL	Milne W	Butler JD	John RF	Baker A	Woods H	Turnbull R	Young A	Toner J	Voysey CR	Boreham R	Haden S	Wallington EE	Rutherford J	Graham A	Earle SGJ	Whittaker TJ	Blyth WN	Paterson Dr JA	Townrow FA	Clark J	Ramsay JH	Neil A	Jones FJ	
1	2	3	4	5	6	7	8	9	10	11																1
1	2	3	4	5	6		8	9			7	10	11													2
1	2	3	4	5	6			10	9		8		11	7												3
1	2	3	4	5	6			10	9		8		11		7											4
1	2	3	4		6			10	9				11		7	5	8									5
1	2	3	4		6				9		8	10	11		7	5										6
1		3	4		6				9		8		11		7	5			2	10						7
1	2	3	4		6				9		8		11		7	5				10						8
1	2		4		6		8	9					11		7	5		3	10							9
1	2	3	4			6	8	9							7	5			10	11						10
1	2	3	4	5				10	9						7	6				11	8					11
1	2	3	4	5				10	9						7	6				11	8					12
1	2	3		5				10	9				11			4		6	7	8						13
1	2			5				10	9	11	7					4		3	6		8					14
1	2			5				10	9		7					4		3	6	11	8					15
1	2			5			10		9							7	4	3	6	11	8					16
1	2		4					10	9						7	5		3	6	11	8					17
1	2		4					10	9		8		11		7	5		3	6							18
1	2			5				10	9						7	4	8	3	6	11						19
1	2	3		5			10	8	9				11		7	4			6							20
1	2		4				3	10	9	6					11	7	5		8							21
1	2		4				3	10	9	6					11		5		8	7						22
1	2		4				3	10	9	6					11		5		8	7						23
1	2		4				3	10	9						11		5		6	8	7					24
1	2		4				3	10	9	6					11		5		8	7						25
1	2		4				3	10	9	6		5			11				8		7					26
1		3	4	9			6	2	10							7	5		8	11						27
1		3	4	9	6		2								10	7	5		8	11						28
1	2	3	4	5	6		10	9		11									8	7						29
1	2	3	4			6		9							11	7	5		8			10				30
1		3	4			6	2	9							11	7	5		8			10				31
1		3	4			6	2	9							11	7	5					10	8			32
1		3	4	5			2	9							11				7			10	8			33
1		3	4	5			2	9							11				7			10	8			34
1		3	4	5			2	9							11				7			10	8			35
1		3	4	5			2	9							11				7			10	8			36
1	2	3	4	5				9							11				7			10	8			37
1	2	3	4	5				9							11				7			10	8			38
1	2	3	4	5	6			9							11	7						10	8			39
1		3	4	5			2	9							11				7			10	8			40
1	2	3	4					9							11		5				7		8	10		41
1		3	4	5			2	9							11				7				8	10		42
42	31	29	36	24	15	21	36	18	25	3	10	2	31	1	22	25	2	8	27	21	7	2	11	11	2	
		1				1	9	6	2			2			2	3			2	1	2			3	2	

I own-goal

Robson JH	Mackie JA	Kennedy AL	Milne W	Butler JD	John RF	Baker A	Woods H	Turnbull R	Young A	Toner J	Voysey CR	Boreham R	Haden S	Wallington EE	Rutherford J	Graham A	Earle SGJ	Whittaker TJ	Blyth WN	Paterson Dr JA	Townrow FA	Clark J	Ramsay JH	Neil A	Jones FJ	
1	2		4				3	10	9	6					11		5			8	7					1
1	2	3	4	9			10			6					11		5			8	7					2
2	2	1	2	1			2	1	1	2					2		2			2	2					
		1					1	1									1									

1924-25

1	Aug	30	(a)	Nottingham F	W	2-0	Ramsay, Woods	20,000
2	Sep	1	(h)	Manchester C	W	1-0	Neil	25,000
3		6	(h)	Liverpool	W	2-0	Woods 2	45,000
4		13	(a)	Newcastle U	D	2-2	Rutherford, Woods	30,000
5		17	(a)	Manchester C	L	0-2		34,000
6		20	(h)	Sheffield U	W	2-0	Butler, Rutherford	40,000
7		27	(a)	West Ham U	L	0-1		31,000
8	Oct	4	(h)	Blackburn R	W	1-0	Neil	40,000
9		11	(a)	Huddersfield T	L	0-4		15,000
10		13	(h)	Bury	L	0-1		20,000
11		18	(h)	Aston Villa	D	1-1	Butler	40,000
12		25	(h)	Tottenham H	W	1-0	Brain	51,000
13	Nov	1	(a)	Bolton W	L	1-4	Brain	18,000
14		8	(h)	Notts C	L	0-1		35,000
15		15	(a)	Everton	W	3-2	Ramsay 2, Young	20,000
16		22	(h)	Sunderland	D	0-0		35,000
17		29	(a)	Cardiff C	D	1-1	Young	20,000
18	Dec	6	(h)	Preston NE	W	4-0	Woods 3, Toner	30,000
19		13	(a)	Burnley	L	0-1		6,000
20		20	(h)	Leeds U	W	6-1	Brain 4, Woods, Ramsay	30,000
21		25	(a)	Birmingham	L	1-2	Woods	36,000
22		26	(h)	Birmingham	L	0-1		40,000
23		27	(h)	Nottingham F	W	2-1	Butler, Ramsay	12,000
24	Jan	3	(a)	Liverpool	L	1-2	Hoar	24,000
25		17	(h)	Newcastle U	L	0-2		30,000
26		24	(a)	Sheffield U	L	1-2	Ramsay	12,000
27	Feb	7	(a)	Blackburn R	L	0-1		20,000
28		14	(h)	Huddersfield T	L	0-5		25,000
29		28	(a)	Tottenham H	L	0-2		29,457
30	Mar	7	(h)	Bolton W	W	1-0	Blyth	35,000
31		14	(a)	Notts C	L	1-2	Brain	12,000
32		21	(h)	Everton	W	3-1	Woods 2, Baker	20,000
33		23	(h)	West Ham U	L	1-2	Baker	10,000
34		28	(a)	Sunderland	L	0-2		18,000
35	Apr	1	(a)	Aston Villa	L	0-4		10,000
36		4	(h)	Cardiff C	D	1-1	Brain	35,000
37		11	(a)	Preston NE	L	0-2		12,000
38		13	(a)	West Brom A	L	0-2		24,000
39		14	(h)	West Brom A	W	2-0	Brain, John	21,000
40		18	(h)	Burnley	W	5-0	Brain 3, Haden, Woods	25,000
41		25	(a)	Leeds U	L	0-1		20,000
42	May	2	(a)	Bury	L	0-2		15,000

FINAL LEAGUE POSITION: 20th in Division One

Appearances
Goals

FA Cup

1	Jan	14	(a)	West Ham U	D	0-0		26,000
R		21	(h)	West Ham U	D	2-2‡	Brain 2	34,160
2R		26	(n*)	West Ham U	L	0-1		36,955

*Played at Stamford Bridge, London.   ‡After extra-time.

Appearances
Goals

190

Player appearance / goals grid (columns = players; final column = match number).

Robson JH	Baker A	Kennedy AL	Milne W	Butler JD	John RF	Rutherford J	Neil A	Woods H	Ramsay JH	Toner J	Clark J	Blyth WN	Mackie JA	Haden S	Turnbull R	Brain J	Lewis D	Young A	Hoar S	Cock D	Whittaker TJ	Hughes J	Roe, Arthur	No.
1	2	3	4	5	6	7	8	9	10	11														1
1	2	3	4	5	6	7	8	9	10	11														2
1	2	3	4	5	6	7	8	9	10	11														3
1	2	3	4	5	6	7	8	9	10	11														4
1	2	3	4	5	6	7	8	9	10	11														5
1	2	3	4	5	6	7	8	9	10	11														6
1	2	3	4	5	6		8	9	10		7	11												7
1	2	3	4	5	6	7	8	9	10	11														8
1		3	4	5	6		8	9	10			7	2	11										9
1	2	3	4	5	6	7	8	9	10	11														10
1		3	4	5	6	7	8		10	11			2		9									11
1		3	4	5	6	7		9	10	11			2			8								12
1		3	4	5	6	7		9	10	11			2			8								13
1	2	3	4	5	6	7		9	10	11						8								14
	2	3	4	5	6	7	8		10	11							1	9						15
	2	3	4	5	6		8		10	11	7						1	9						16
	2	3	4	5	6				10	11						8	1	9	7					17
	2	3	4	5	6	7		9	10	11						8	1							18
	2	3	4	5	6	7		9	10	11						8	1							19
	2	3	4	5	6	7		9	10	11						8	1							20
	2	3	4	5	6			9	10	11						8	1		7					21
	2	3	4	5		7		9	10	11						8	1	6						22
	2	3	4	5	6			8	10	11						9	1		7					23
		3	4	5	6			8	10	11			2			9	1		7					24
	2	3	4	5	6			8	10	11						9	1		7					25
		3			6			9	10	11		5	2			8	1	4	7					26
	2			5	6			9	10	11			3			8	1	4	7					27
	2				6			9	10	11		5	3			8	1	4	7					28
1	4	3		5	6			8				10	2	11		9			7					29
1	4	3		5	6							10	2	11		8			7	9				30
1	4	3		5	6							10	2	11		8			7	9				31
1	4	3		5	6			9				10	2	11		8			7					32
1	5	3			6			9				10	2	11		8			7		4			33
1	4	3		5	6			9				10	2	11		8			7					34
1	4	3		5	6			9				10	2	11		8			7					35
1	2	3	4	5	6			9				10		11		8			7					36
1	2	3	4	5	6			9				10		11		8			7					37
1	2	3	4	5	6		8					10		11					7			9		38
1		3	4	5	6	7						10	2	11		8		9						39
1		3	4	5		7		8	6			10	2	11		9								40
		3	4	5	6		8					10	2	11		9	1		7					41
		3	4	5		7	8		10				2	11		9	1						6	42
26	**32**	**40**	**32**	**39**	**39**	**20**	**16**	**32**	**30**	**26**	**2**	**17**	**19**	**15**	**1**	**28**	**16**	**8**	**19**	**2**	**1**	**1**	**1**	
2		3	1	2	2	12	6	1			1		1			12		2	1					

Cup (Round 1, Replay, 2nd Replay):

Robson JH	Baker A	Kennedy AL	Milne W	Butler JD	John RF	Rutherford J	Neil A	Woods H	Ramsay JH	Toner J	Clark J	Blyth WN	Mackie JA	Haden S	Turnbull R	Brain J	Lewis D	Young A	Hoar S	Cock D	Whittaker TJ	Hughes J	Roe, Arthur	Rd
	2	3	4	5	6			8	10	11						9	1		7					1
	2	3	4	5	6			9	10	11						8	1		7					R
	2	3		5	6			9	10	11						8	1	4	7					2R
	3	**3**	**2**	**3**	**3**			**3**	**3**	**3**						**3**	**3**	**1**	**3**					
																2								

191

1925-26

Manager: H.Chapman

1	Aug	29	(h)	Tottenham H	L 0-1	53,183
2		31	(h)	Leicester C	D 2-2 Neil, Brain	23,823
3	Sep	5	(a)	Manchester U	W 1-0 Brain	32,288
4		7	(a)	Leicester C	W 1-0 Brain	25,401
5		12	(h)	Liverpool	D 1-1 Buchan	32,553
6		19	(a)	Burnley	D 2-2 Haden, Baker	12,334
7		21	(h)	West Ham U	W 3-2 Buchan 2, Neil	24,800
8		26	(h)	Leeds U	W 4-1 Brain 2, Buchan, Neil	32,531
9	Oct	3	(a)	Newcastle U	L 0-7	40,683
10		5	(a)	West Ham U	W 4-0 Buchan 2, Brain 2	18,769
11		10	(h)	Bolton W	L 2-3 Buchan, Baker	41,076
12		17	(h)	Cardiff C	W 5-0 Brain 3, Neil, Blyth	38,130
13		24	(a)	Sheffield U	L 0-4	27,555
14		31	(h)	Everton	W 4-1 Brain 3, Hoar	24,926
15	Nov	7	(a)	Manchester C	W 5-2 Brain 2, Buchan, Hoar, Haden	11,384
16		14	(h)	Bury	W 6-1 Brain 3, Buchan 2, Baker	22,566
17		21	(a)	Blackburn R	W 3-2 Buchan, Brain, Rollo (og)	11,386
18		28	(h)	Sunderland	W 2-0 Buchan, Brain	44,870
19	Dec	5	(a)	Huddersfield T	D 2-2 Neil, Buchan	22,115
20		12	(h)	West Brom A	W 1-0 Blyth	34,178
21		19	(a)	Birmingham	L 0-1	26,843
22		25	(h)	Notts C	W 3-0 Neil, Buchan, Hoar	33,398
23		26	(a)	Notts C	L 1-4 Baker	32,045
24	Jan	2	(a)	Tottenham H	D 1-1 Baker	43,221
25		16	(h)	Manchester U	W 3-2 Brain 2, Buchan	25,252
26		23	(a)	Liverpool	L 0-3	38,232
27	Feb	3	(h)	Burnley	L 1-2 Buchan	14,800
28		6	(a)	Leeds U	L 2-4 Brain, Johnson (og)	26,239
29		13	(h)	Newcastle U	W 3-0 Buchan, Blyth, Paterson	48,346
30		27	(a)	Cardiff C	D 0-0	21,684
31	Mar	13	(a)	Everton	W 3-2 Brain 3	30,515
32		17	(h)	Sheffield U	W 4-0 Brain 2, Buchan, Blyth	15,609
33		20	(h)	Manchester C	W 1-0 Blyth	34,974
34		27	(a)	Bury	D 2-2 Brain, Hulme	18,078
35	Apr	2	(a)	Aston Villa	L 0-3	26,177
36		3	(h)	Blackburn R	W 4-2 Baker, Blyth, Lawson, Buchan	31,031
37		5	(h)	Aston Villa	W 2-0 Brain 2	25,990
38		10	(a)	Sunderland	L 1-2 Brain	20,990
39		17	(h)	Huddersfield T	W 3-1 Lawson, Hulme, Parker (pen)	34,110
40		24	(a)	West Brom A	L 1-2 Blyth	14,226
41		28	(a)	Bolton W	D 1-1 Parker	22,198
42	May	1	(h)	Birmingham	W 3-0 Brain 2, Parker (pen)	22,240

FINAL LEAGUE POSITION: 2nd in Division One

Appearances
Goals

FA Cup

3	Jan	9	(a)	Wolves	D 1-1 Brain	42,083
R		13	(h)	Wolves	W 1-0 Baker	42,823
4		30	(h)	Blackburn R	W 3-1 Haden, Brain, Hope (og)	44,836
5	Feb	20	(a)	Aston Villa	D 1-1 Buchan	55,400
R		24	(h)	Aston Villa	W 2-0 Paterson, Brain	71,446
6	Mar	6	(a)	Swansea T	L 1-2 Mackie	25,198

Appearances
Goals

192

Robson JH	Mackie JA	Kennedy AL	Milne W	Butler JD	John RF	Hoar S	Buchan CM	Cock DJ	Ramsay JH	Toner J	Brain J	Neil A	Blyth WN	Haden S	Baker A	Lewis D	Rutherford JJ	Harper W	Woods H	Young A	Rutherford J	Lawson H	Hulme JHA	Voysey CR	Paterson Dr JA	Parker TR	Seddon WC	Match
1	2	3	4	5	6	7	8	9	10	11																		1
1	2	3	4	5	6	7	8			11	9	10																2
1	2	3	4	5		7	8				9	10	6	11														3
1	2	3	4	5		7	8				9	10	6	11														4
1	2	3	4	5		7	8				9	10	6	11														5
1	2	3		5		7	8				9	10	6	11	4													6
1	2	3		5		7	8				9	10	6	11	4													7
	2	3		5		7	8				9	10	6	11	4	1												8
	2	3		5		7	8				9	10	6	11	4	1												9
	2	3		5		7	8				9	10	6	11	4	1												10
	2	3		5		7	8				9	10	6	11	4	1												11
	2	3		5		7	8				9	10	6	11	4	1												12
	2	3		5	6	7	8				9	10	4	11		1												13
1	2			5	3	7	8				9	10	6	11	4													14
1	2			5	3	7	8				9	10	6	11	4													15
	2			5	3		8				9	10	6	11	4		7	1										16
	2			5	3		8				9	10	6	11	4			1	7									17
	2			5	3	7	8				9	10	6	11	4			1										18
	2			5	3	7	8				9	10	6	11	4			1										19
	2			5	3	7	8				9	10	6	11	4			1										20
	2			5	3	7	8				9	10	6	11	4			1										21
	2			5	3	7	8				9	10	6	11	4			1										22
	2			5	3		8				9	10	6	11	4			1	7	8								23
	2			5	3	7	8				9	10	6	11	4			1										24
	2			5	3		8				9	10	6	11	4			1		7								25
	2			5	3		8				9	10	6	11	4			1		7								26
	2			5	3		8				9	10	6	11	4			1				7						27
	2			5	3		8		10		9		6		4			1					7	11				28
	2				3		8		10		9		6		4			1	5				7		11			29
	2			5	3		8		10		9	8	6		4			1			11		7					30
	2			5	3		8		10		9		6		4			1			11		7					31
	2			5	3		8		10		9		6		4			1			11		7					32
	2			5	3		8		10		9		6		4			1				11	7					33
	2			5	3		8		10		9		6		4			1				11	7					34
	2			5	3		8		10		9		6		4	1				8		11	7					35
		3		5			8		10		9		6		4	1						7	11			2		36
		3		5			8		10		9		6		4	1						7	11			2		37
		3		5			8		10		9		6			1						7	11			2	4	38
				5	3		8		10		9		6			1				4		7	11			2		39
				5	3		8		10		9		6			1				4		7	11			2		40
				5	3		8		10		9		6			1				4		7	11			2		41
				5	3		8		10		9		6			1				4		7	11			2		42
9	35	16	5	41	29	21	39	1	16	2	41	27	40	25	31	14	1	19	2	7	3	13	15	1	1	7	1	
				3	19						34	6	7	2	6							2	2			1	3	

2 own-goals

Robson JH	Mackie JA	Kennedy AL	Milne W	Butler JD	John RF	Hoar S	Buchan CM	Cock DJ	Ramsay JH	Toner J	Brain J	Neil A	Blyth WN	Haden S	Baker A	Lewis D	Rutherford JJ	Harper W	Woods H	Young A	Rutherford J	Lawson H	Hulme JHA	Voysey CR	Paterson Dr JA	Parker TR	Seddon WC	Match
	2			5	3	7	8				9	10	6	11	4			1										3
	2			5	3		8				9	10	6	11	4			1	7									R
	2			5	3		8				9	10	6	11	4			1		7								4
	2			5	3		8		10		9		6		4			1				7	11					5
	2			5	3		8		10		9		6		4			1				7	11					R
	2			5	3		8		10		9		6		4			1				7	11					6
	6			6	6	1	6		3		6	3	6	3	6			6	1	1		3	3					
	1				1						3		1	1								1						

1 own-goal

1926-27

Manager: H.Chapman

1	Aug	28	(h)	Derby C	W 2-1	Parker (pen), Buchan	32,990
2	Sep	1	(h)	Bolton W	W 2-1	Hulme 2	23,002
3		4	(a)	Sheffield U	L 0-4		21,942
4		6	(a)	Bolton W	D 2-2	Brain, Hulme	19,717
5		11	(h)	Leicester C	D 2-2	Brain, Hulme	30,800
6		15	(a)	Manchester U	D 2-2	Brain 2	15,259
7		18	(h)	Liverpool	W 2-0	Brain, Hoar	35,497
8		25	(a)	Leeds U	L 1-4	Buchan	20,544
9	Oct	2	(h)	Newcastle U	D 2-2	Buchan, Parker (pen)	38,842
10		9	(a)	Burnley	L 0-2		12,709
11		16	(h)	West Ham U	D 2-2	Lambert, Brain	35,534
12		23	(h)	Sheffield W	W 6-2	Brain 4, Haden 2	27,846
13		30	(a)	Everton	L 1-3	Brain	34,153
14	Nov	6	(h)	Blackburn R	D 2-2	Buchan, Brain	29,439
15		13	(a)	Huddersfield T	D 3-3	Blyth, Haden, Ramsay	16,219
16		20	(h)	Sunderland	L 2-3	Buchan, Ramsay	20,087
17		27	(a)	West Brom A	W 3-1	Hulme, Haden, Brain	20,815
18	Dec	4	(h)	Bury	W 1-0	Brain	30,375
19		11	(a)	Birmingham	D 0-0		22,982
20		18	(h)	Tottenham H	L 2-4	Butler, Brain	49,429
21		27	(a)	Cardiff C	L 0-2		25,386
22		28	(h)	Manchester U	W 1-0	Blyth	30,111
23	Jan	1	(h)	Cardiff C	W 3-2	Brain 3	30,000
24		15	(a)	Derby C	W 2-0	Buchan, Parker	21,899
25		22	(h)	Sheffield U	D 1-1	Buchan	16,831
26	Feb	5	(a)	Liverpool	L 0-3		30,618
27		10	(a)	Leicester C	L 1-2	Brain	16,736
28		12	(h)	Leeds U	W 1-0	Buchan	25,961
29		26	(h)	Burnley	W 6-2	Brain 4, Buchan, Hoar	29,070
30	Mar	7	(a)	West Ham U	L 0-7		11,764
31		12	(a)	Sheffield W	L 2-4	Buchan, Brain	21,252
32		19	(h)	Everton	L 1-2	Buchan	33,788
33	Apr	2	(h)	Huddersfield T	L 0-2		24,409
34		6	(a)	Newcastle U	L 1-6	Buchan	33,635
35		9	(a)	Sunderland	L 1-5	Shaw	23,163
36		15	(a)	Aston Villa	W 2-1	Brain 2	38,096
37		16	(h)	West Brom A	W 4-1	Brain, Parker (pen), Buchan 2	24,506
38		18	(a)	Aston Villa	W 3-2	John 2, Barley	22,542
39		28	(a)	Blackburn R	W 2-1	Hulme, Brain	13,833
40		30	(h)	Birmingham	W 3-0	Brain, Tricker,John	22,619
41	May	4	(a)	Bury	L 2-3	Hulme 2	8,513
42		7	(a)	Tottenham H	W 4-0	Brain 2, Tricker 2	29,555

FINAL LEAGUE POSITION: 11th in Division One

Appearances
Goals

FA Cup

3	Jan	8	(a)	Sheffield U	W 3-2	Brain, Buchan, Hulme	28,137
4		29	(a)	Port Vale	D 2-2	Buchan, Brain	18,000
R	Feb	2	(h)	Port Vale	W 1-0	Buchan	35,781
5		19	(h)	Liverpool	W 2-0	Brain, Buchan	43,000
6	Mar	5	(h)	Wolves	W 2-1	Blyth Butler	52,821
SF		26	(n*)	Southampton	W 2-1	Hulme, Buchan	52,133
F	Apr	23	(n†)	Cardiff C	L 0-1		91,206

*Played at Stamford Bridge, London. †Played at Wembley Stadium.

Appearances
Goals

194

Team line-up / appearances grid (numbers indicate the shirt number worn by each player in each match; the final column is the match number).

Harper W	Parker TR	John RF	Baker A	Butler JD	Blyth WN	Hulme JHA	Buchan CM	Brain J	Ramsay JH	Haden S	Lambert J	Lee JW	Kennedy AL	Hoar S	Young A	Seddon WC	Lewis D	Cope HW	Peel HB	Milne W	Barley JC	Shaw J	Tricker RW	Roberts H	Moody J	Bowen E	
1	2	3	4	5	6	7	8	9	10	11																	1
1	2	3	4	5	6	7	8	9	10	11																	2
1	2	3	4	5	6	7	8	9	10	11																	3
1	2	3	4	5	6	7		9	10			8	11														4
1	2	3	4	5	6	7	8	9				10	11														5
1	2	6	4	5		7		9	10			8	11	3													6
1	2	6	4	5		7		10	9			8	3	11													7
1	2	6	4	5		7		10	9			8	11	3													8
1	2	3	4	5	6	7	8	9				10	11														9
1	2	3		5	6	7	8	9	10	11				4													10
1	2	3		5	6	7	8	9	11	10				4													11
1	2	3		5	6	7	8	9	11	10				4													12
1	2	3		5	6	7		9	10	11	8			4													13
1	2	3		5	6	7	8	9	10	11				4													14
1	2	3		5	6	7	9	8	10	11				4													15
1	2	3		5	6	7	9	8	10	11				4													16
1	2	3		5	6	7	9	8	11	10				4													17
1	2	3			6	7	9	8		11	10		5	4													18
1	2	3		5	6	7		9		10	8	11		4													19
1	2	3		5	6	7	9	8	10	11				4													20
	2	6		5		7	9	8	10					4		1	3	11									21
	2	6		5	10	7	8	9						11		1	3	4									22
	2	6		5	10	7	8	9						11		1	3	4									23
	2	6		5	10	7	8	9						11		1	3	4									24
	2	6		5	10	7	8	9						11		1	3	4									25
	2	6	4	5	10	7		9			8					1	3										26
	2	6	4	5		7	8	9								1	3	10									27
1	2			5	10	7	8	9						11		3	4	6									28
	2	6	4		10	7	8	9						11	5	1	3										29
	2	3		5	10			9		11			7	4	1					6	8						30
	2	6	4	5	10	7	8	9					3	11		1											31
1	2	6	4		10	7		9						11	5		3					8					32
	2	6		5	10		8	9	7					11		1	3	4									33
	2	6	3		10	7	8						11	4	5	1						9					34
	2	6	3	4		7	8						11		5	1		10				9					35
	2	6	4		10		8	9				3	7		5	1		11									36
	2	6	4				8	9				7	3		5	1		10			11						37
	2	11		5							8	3				1		10			6	7	9	4			38
	2	6	4		10	7		9				8	11	3	5	1											39
1	2	6	4	5		7		9			11			3				10				8					40
	2	6	4			7	8		10					3	5			11						1	9		41
	2	6		5	8	7			10					3				11				9	4	1			42
23	**42**	**41**	**23**	**31**	**33**	**37**	**33**	**37**	**12**	**17**	**16**	**7**	**11**	**16**	**6**	**17**	**17**	**11**	**9**	**6**	**3**	**5**	**4**	**2**	**2**	**1**	
4	3		1	2	8	14	31	2	4	1		2										1	1	3			

Cup matches:

Harper W	Parker TR	John RF	Baker A	Butler JD	Blyth WN	Hulme JHA	Buchan CM	Brain J	Ramsay JH	Haden S	Lambert J	Lee JW	Kennedy AL	Hoar S	Young A	Seddon WC	Lewis D	Cope HW	Peel HB	Milne W	Barley JC	Shaw J	Tricker RW	Roberts H	Moody J	Bowen E	
	2	6		5	10	7	8	9						11		1	3	4									3
	2	6	4	5	10	7	8	9						11		1	3										4
	2	6	4	5	10	7	8	9						11		1	3										R
1	2	6	4	5	10	7	8	9						11			3										5
	2	3	4	5	10	7	8	9						11		1		6									6
	2	6	4	5	10	7	8	9						11		1	3										SF
	2	6	4	5	10	7	8	9					3	11		1											F
1	7	7	6	7	7	7	7	7					1	7		6	5	1	1								
			1	1	2	5	3																				

195

1927-28

Manager: H.Chapman

1	Aug	27	(a)	Bury	L	1-5	Brain	17,614
2		31	(h)	Burnley	W	4-1	Buchan, Brain 2, Blyth	19,910
3	Sep	3	(h)	Sheffield U	W	6-1	Hulme, Blyth, Buchan 2, Brain, Parker	30,910
4		5	(a)	Burnley	W	2-1	Blyth, Brain	14,668
5		10	(a)	Aston Villa	D	2-2	Blyth 2	42,136
6		17	(h)	Sunderland	W	2-1	Baker, Brain	45,501
7		24	(a)	Derby C	L	0-4		16,539
8	Oct	1	(h)	West Ham U	D	2-2	Brain 2	34,931
9		8	(a)	Portsmouth	W	3-2	Blyth, Hulme, Brain	27,261
10		15	(h)	Leicester C	D	2-2	Brain, Hoar	36,640
11		22	(a)	Sheffield W	D	1-1	Buchan	12,698
12		29	(h)	Bolton W	L	1-2	Buchan	35,787
13	Nov	5	(a)	Blackburn R	L	1-4	Parker (pen)	9,656
14		12	(h)	Middlesbrough	W	3-1	Buchan 2, Hulme	25,921
15		19	(a)	Birmingham	D	1-1	Hoar	10,030
16	Dec	3	(a)	Huddersfield T	L	1-2	Brain	15,140
17		10	(h)	Newcastle U	W	4-1	Hulme, Brain, Parker, Hoar	42,630
18		17	(a)	Manchester U	L	1-4	Wilson (og)	18,120
19		24	(h)	Everton	W	3-2	Hulme, Buchan, Blyth	27,995
20		27	(a)	Liverpool	W	2-0	Hoar, Brain	41,024
21		31	(h)	Bury	W	3-1	Lambert, John, Parker (pen)	20,742
22	Jan	2	(h)	Tottenham H	D	1-1	Hoar	13,518
23		7	(a)	Sheffield U	L	4-6	Hoar 2, Brain 2	18,158
24		21	(h)	Aston Villa	L	0-3		32,505
25	Feb	4	(h)	Derby C	L	3-4	Brain 3	21,405
26		11	(a)	West Ham U	D	2-2	Brain 2	28,086
27		25	(a)	Leicester C	L	2-3	Hoar, Buchan	25,835
28	Mar	7	(h)	Liverpool	W	6-3	Brain 3, Hulme, Buchan, Lambert	14,037
29		10	(a)	Bolton W	D	1-1	Buchan	15,546
30		14	(a)	Sunderland	L	1-5	Lambert	9,478
31		17	(h)	Blackburn R	W	3-2	Buchan 2, Hoar	33,446
32		28	(h)	Portsmouth	L	0-2		15,416
33		31	(h)	Birmingham	D	2-2	Buchan 2	13,990
34	Apr	6	(h)	Cardiff C	W	3-0	Hulme, Buchan, Brain	36,828
35		7	(a)	Tottenham H	L	0-2		39,193
36		9	(a)	Cardiff C	D	2-2	Tricker 2	17,699
37		14	(h)	Huddersfield T	D	0-0		38,707
38		18	(a)	Middlesbrough	D	2-2	Baker, Hulme	16,731
39		21	(a)	Newcastle U	D	1-1	Shaw	22,819
40		28	(h)	Manchester U	L	0-1		22,452
41	May	2	(h)	Sheffield W	D	1-1	Brain	15,818
42		5	(a)	Everton	D	3-3	Shaw 2, O'Donnell (og)	48,715

FINAL LEAGUE POSITION: 10th in Division One

Appearances
Goals

FA Cup

3	Jan	14	(h)	West Brom A	W	2-0	Brain, Hulme	43,322
4		28	(h)	Everton	W	4-3	Hulme 2, Brain, Buchan	44,328
5	Feb	18	(h)	Aston Villa	W	4-1	Brain 2, Lambert, Hulme	58,505
6	Mar	3	(h)	Stoke C	W	4-1	Blyth 2, Hoar 2	41,974
SF	Mar	24	(n*)	Blackburn R	L	0-1		25,633

*Played at Filbert Street, Leicester.

Appearances
Goals

196

Appearance and scoring grid (player columns across the top; match numbers down the right-hand side). Shirt numbers are shown in each cell.

Lewis D	Parker TR	Kennedy AL	Baker A	Butler JD	John RF	Hulme JHA	Buchan CM	Brain J	Blyth WN	Peel HB	Cope HW	Hoar S	Lambert J	Moody J	Seddon WC	Clark A	Tricker RW	Roberts H	Hapgood EA	Barley JC	Paterson W	Thompson L	Shaw J	No.
1	2	3	4	5	6	7	8	9	10	11														1
1	2		4	5	6	7	8	9	10		3	11												2
1	2		4	5	6	7	8	9	10		3	11												3
1	2		4	5	6	7	9	8			3	11	10											4
1	2		4	5	6	7	8	9	10		3	11												5
1	2		4	5	6	7	8	9	10		3	11												6
	2	3	4	5	6	7	8	9	10			11		1										7
	2		4	5	6	7	8	9	10		3	11		1										8
1	2		4	5	6	7	8	9	10		3	11												9
1	2		4	5	6	7	8	9	10		3	11												10
1	2		5			8	9	6	11		3	7	10		4									11
1	2			5	6	7	8	9	10		3	11			4									12
1	2				6	7	9		8		3	11			5	4	10							13
1	2			5	6	7		9	10		3	11					8	4						14
1	2		4	5	6	7		9	10		3	11					8	3						15
1	2		4	5	6	7		9	10		3	11					8							16
1	2		4	5	6	7	8	9	10		3	11												17
1	2		4	5	6	7		9	10		3	11					8							18
1	2		4	5	6	7	8	9	10		3	11												19
1	2		4	5	6			9	10	11	3	7	8											20
1	2		4	5	6			9	10	11	3	7	8											21
	2		4	5	6	7	8	9	10			11		1				3						22
	2		4		6	7		9				11	8	1	5			3				10		23
1	2		4	5	6	7	9	8			3	11	10											24
	2		4	5		7	8	9	10		3	11	6								1			25
1	2			5	6	7	8	9	4		3	11	10											26
1	2		5		6	7	8	9	4		3	11	10											27
1	2		4	5	3	7	8	9	6			11	10											28
	2		4	5	3		8	9	6			11	7							10	1			29
1	2		4	5	3	7	8		6			11	9							10				30
	2		4	5	3	7	8	9	6			11								10	1			31
1	2		4	5				9	6	11	3	7	8										10	32
1	2		4	5	11		8	9	6		3	7	10											33
1	2		4	5	3	7	8	9	6			11	10											34
1	2		4		3	7		9	6			11	10		5								8	35
	2		4	5	3	7	8	9	6			11	10								1			36
1	2		4	5	3	7	8	9	6			11	10											37
1	2		4	5		7		9	6	10		11							3				8	38
1	2		4	5		7		9	6	10		11							3				8	39
1	2		4	5		7		9	6	10		11							3				8	40
1	2		4	5	3	7		9	6			11	10										8	41
	2		4	5	3	7	8	10	6			11	9								1			42
33	42	2	37	38	39	36	30	39	39	13	24	38	16	4	4	1	7	3	3	2	5	1	6	—
	4		2		1	8	16	25	7			9	3				2						3	

2 own-goals

Lewis D	Parker TR	Kennedy AL	Baker A	Butler JD	John RF	Hulme JHA	Buchan CM	Brain J	Blyth WN	Peel HB	Cope HW	Hoar S	Lambert J	Moody J	Seddon WC	Clark A	Tricker RW	Roberts H	Hapgood EA	Barley JC	Paterson W	Thompson L	Shaw J	No.
1	2		4	5	6	7	8	9	10		3	11												3
1	2		4	5	6	7	8	9	10		3	11												4
1	2			5	6	7	8	9	4		3	11	10											5
1	2		4	5	6	7	8	9	10		3	11												6
1	2		4	5	6	7	8	9	10		3	11												SF
5	5		4	5	5	5	5	5	5		5	5	1											
				4	1	4	2					2	1											

1928-29

Manager: H.Chapman

1	Aug	25	(a)	Sheffield W	L	2-3	Jones, Brain	23,684
2		29	(h)	Derby C	L	1-3	Blyth	20,064
3	Sep	1	(h)	Bolton W	W	2-0	Peel, Brain	35,124
4		8	(a)	Portsmouth	L	0-2		24,846
5		15	(h)	Birmingham	D	0-0		30,118
6		22	(a)	Manchester C	L	1-4	Brain	36,223
7		26	(a)	Derby C	D	0-0		16,754
8		29	(h)	Huddersfield T	W	2-0	Lambert, John	39,938
9	Oct	6	(a)	Everton	L	2-4	Brain, Jones	37,846
10		13	(h)	West Ham U	L	2-3	Jones 2	43,327
11		20	(a)	Newcastle U	W	3-0	Thompson 2 (1 pen), Brain	30,121
12		27	(h)	Liverpool	D	4-4	Thompson 2 (pen), Brain, Davidson (og)	33,782
13	Nov	3	(a)	Cardiff C	D	1-1	Jones	18,757
14		10	(h)	Sheffield U	W	2-0	Hulme, Jack	28,560
15		17	(a)	Bury	L	0-1		10,957
16		24	(h)	Aston Villa	L	2-5	Jack 2	30,491
17	Dec	1	(a)	Leicester C	D	1-1	Brain	26,851
18		8	(h)	Manchester U	W	3-1	Jack 2, Brain	18,923
19		15	(a)	Leeds U	D	1-1	Brain	20,293
20		22	(h)	Burnley	W	3-1	Hulme, Peel, Brain	14,990
21		25	(a)	Blackburn R	L	2-5	Jack, Brain	30,828
22		26	(h)	Sunderland	D	1-1	Peel	15,747
23		29	(h)	Sheffield W	D	2-2	Brain, Hulme	39,255
24	Jan	1	(a)	Sunderland	L	1-5	Parkin	32,843
25		5	(a)	Bolton W	W	2-1	Jack 2	17,597
26		19	(h)	Portsmouth	W	4-0	Jack 2, Peel, Brain	32,224
27	Feb	2	(h)	Manchester C	D	0-0		13,764
28		9	(a)	Huddersfield T	W	1-0	Jack	14,697
29		23	(a)	West Ham U	W	4-3	Brain, Jack, Hoar, Hulme	28,931
30	Mar	9	(a)	Liverpool	W	4-2	Hulme 2, Brain, Jones	26,195
31		13	(a)	Birmingham	D	1-1	Jack	11,001
32		16	(h)	Cardiff C	W	2-1	Brain, Jack	28,393
33		23	(a)	Sheffield U	D	2-2	Parker (pen), Jack	20,266
34		29	(h)	Blackburn R	W	1-0	Brain	39,038
35		30	(h)	Bury	W	7-1	Jack 4, Parkin 2, Thompson	22,577
36	Apr	2	(h)	Newcastle U	L	1-2	Jack	21,699
37		6	(a)	Aston Villa	L	2-4	Brain, Jack	26,664
38		13	(h)	Leicester C	D	1-1	Parker (pen)	19,139
39		20	(a)	Manchester U	L	1-4	Jack	22,858
40		22	(h)	Everton	W	2-0	Jack, Parker (pen)	11,696
41		27	(h)	Leeds U	W	1-0	Peel	21,465
42	May	4	(a)	Burnley	D	3-3	Jack 2, Brain	7,400

FINAL LEAGUE POSITION: 9th in Division One

Appearances
Goals

FA Cup

3	Jan	12	(h)	Stoke C	W	2-1	Brain, Hulme	30,762
4		26	(h)	Mansfield T	W	2-0	Jack, Peel	44,493
5	Feb	16	(a)	Swindon T	D	0-0		16,692
R		20	(h)	Swindon T	W	1-0	Brain	44,582
6	Mar	2	(a)	Aston Villa	L	0-1		73,700

Appearances
Goals

Football appearance and goalscoring grid (league season). Columns are players; rows are matches (match number at far right). Cell values are the shirt number worn.

Lewis D	Parker TR	Cope HW	Baker A	Butler JD	John RF	Hulme JHA	Blyth WN	Brain J	Thompson L	Jones C	Paterson W	Peel HB	Hoar S	Lambert J	Tricker RW	Roberts H	Jack DBN	Barley JC	Parkin R	Hapgood EA	Maycock WJ	#
1	2	3	4	5	6	7	8	9	10	11												1
1	2	3	4	5	6	7	8	9	10	11												2
	2	3	4	5	6	7		9		10	1	8	11									3
	2	3	4	5	6	7	8	9		10	1		11									4
	2		4	5	3	7	6	9		8	1	11		10								5
	2		4	5	3	7	6	9	10	11	1	8										6
1	2	3	4		6	7	8	9	10	11						5						7
1	2	3	4		6	7	8	9	10	11						5						8
1	2	3	4		6	7	8	9	10	11						5						9
1	2	3	4		6	7	8	9	10	11						5						10
1	2	3	4		6	7		9	10	11		8				5						11
1	2	3	4		6	7		9	10	11						5	8					12
1	2	3		5	6	7	4	9	10	11							8					13
1	2	3		5		7	4	9	10	11			6				8					14
1	2	3		5			4	9	10	11			6		7		8					15
1	2	3		5	6	7	4		10	11		9					8					16
1	2	3		5	6	7	4	9	10	11							8					17
1	2	3		5	6	7	4	9	10	11							8					18
1	2	3		5	6	7	4	9	10	11							8					19
1	2	3		5	6	7	4	9	10	11							8					20
1	2	3	4		6	7		9	10	11						5	8					21
1	2	3	4	5	6	7		9	10	11							8					22
1	2	3	4	5	6	7		9	10	11							8					23
1	2	3		5	6	7	4	9	10	11							8					24
1	2	3	4			7		9	10	11		6				5	8					25
1	2		4	5	6	7		9	10	11							8			3		26
1	2		4		6	7		9	10	11						5	8			3		27
1	2		4		6	7		9	10	11						5	8			3		28
	2		4		6	7	8	9	10	11	1					5				3		29
1	2		4		6	7		9	10	11						5	8			3		30
1	2		4		6	7		9	10	11						5	8			3		31
1	2		4		6	7		9	10	11						5	8			3		32
1	2		4		6	7		9	10	11						5	8			3		33
1	2				6	7	4	9	10	11						5	8			3		34
1	2		4		6	7		9	10	11						5	8			3		35
1	2		4		6	7		9	10	11						5	8			3		36
1	2		4		6	7		9	10	11						5	8			3		37
	2		4		6	7		9	10	11	1					5	8			3		38
	2		4	5	6	7		9	10	11	1						8			3		39
	2		4	5	6	7		9	10	11	1						8			3		40
	2		4	5	6	7		9	10	11	1						8			3		41
	2		4	5	6	7		9	10	11	1						8			3		42
32	**42**	**23**	**31**	**22**	**34**	**41**	**21**	**37**	**17**	**39**	**10**	**24**	**6**	**6**	**1**	**20**	**31**	**3**	**5**	**17**		
3			1	6	1	19	5	6		5	1	1				25	3					

I own-goal

Lewis D	Parker TR	Cope HW	Baker A	Butler JD	John RF	Hulme JHA	Blyth WN	Brain J	Thompson L	Jones C	Paterson W	Peel HB	Hoar S	Lambert J	Tricker RW	Roberts H	Jack DBN	Barley JC	Parkin R	Hapgood EA	Maycock WJ	#
1	2	3	4		7		9		11	10						5	8		6			3
1	2		4	5	7	6	9		11	10							8			3		4
1	2		4		6	7	9		11	10						5	8			3		5
1	2		4		6	7	9		10							5	8		3		11	R
1	2		4		6	7	8		10	11						5	9			3		6
5	**5**	**1**	**5**	**1**	**3**	**5**	**1**	**5**	**3**	**5**	**1**	**4**	**5**	**1**		**4**	**1**					
					1		2						1				1					

199

1929-30

Manager: H.Chapman

1	Aug	31	(h)	Leeds U	W	4-0	Jack 2, Hulme, Parker (pen)	41,885
2	Sep	4	(a)	Manchester C	L	1-3	Jack	38,458
3		7	(a)	Sheffield W	W	2-0	Jack, Hulme	31,735
4		11	(h)	Manchester C	W	3-2	Jack 2, Johnstone	23,057
5		14	(h)	Burnley	W	6-1	Lambert 2, Hulme, Jack, James, Waterfield (og)	38,556
6		21	(a)	Sunderland	W	1-0	Lambert	34,804
7		25	(a)	Aston Villa	L	2-5	James, Thompson	33,850
8		28	(h)	Bolton W	L	1-2	Jones	42,723
9	Oct	5	(a)	Everton	D	1-1	Hulme	45,015
10		12	(h)	Derby C	D	1-1	Parker (pen)	42,448
11		19	(h)	Grimsby T	W	4-1	Lambert 3, Hulme	43,794
12		26	(a)	Manchester U	L	0-1		12,662
13	Nov	2	(h)	West Ham U	L	0-1		44,828
14		9	(a)	Birmingham	W	3-2	Hulme 2, Jack	33,904
15		23	(a)	Blackburn R	D	1-1	Halliday	25,591
16		27	(h)	Middlesbrough*	L	1-2	Jack	28,326
17		30	(h)	Newcastle U	L	0-1		40,365
18	Dec	14	(h)	Huddersfield T	W	2-0	Hulme, Jack	34,097
19		16	(a)	Sheffield U	L	1-4	Halliday	16,134
20		21	(a)	Liverpool	L	0-1		32,819
21		25	(a)	Portsmouth	W	1-0	James	27,475
22		26	(h)	Portsmouth	L	1-2	Hulme	49,433
23		28	(a)	Leeds U	L	0-2		29,167
24	Jan	4	(h)	Sheffield W	L	2-3	Bastin, Parker	40,766
25		18	(a)	Burnley	D	2-2	Bastin, Jack	22,566
26	Feb	1	(a)	Bolton W	D	0-0		27,336
27		8	(h)	Everton	W	4-0	Lambert 3, Williams	27,302
28		19	(a)	Derby C	L	1-4	Halliday	11,136
29		22	(a)	Grimsby T	D	1-1	Lambert	17,151
30	Mar	8	(a)	West Ham U	L	2-3	Jack 2	31,268
31		12	(h)	Manchester U	W	4-2	Bastin, Williams, Lambert, Hulme	18,082
32		15	(h)	Birmingham	W	1-0	James	32,174
33		29	(h)	Blackburn R	W	4-0	Williams, Hulme, Lambert 2	40,459
34	Apr	2	(h)	Liverpool	L	0-1		18,824
35		5	(a)	Newcastle U	D	1-1	Halliday	36,309
36		9	(a)	Middlesbrough	D	1-1	Hulme	9,287
37		12	(h)	Sheffield U	W	8-1	Lambert 3, Johnstone 2, Hulme, Bastin, James	24,217
38		18	(h)	Leicester C	D	1-1	James	46,663
39		19	(a)	Huddersfield T	D	2-2	Bastin, Hulme	11,988
40		21	(a)	Leicester C	D	6-6	Halliday 4, Bastin 2	27,241
41		28	(h)	Sunderland	L	0-1		31,250
42	May	3	(h)	Aston Villa	L	2-4	Lambert 2	37,020

FINAL LEAGUE POSITION: 14th in Division One Appearances
*After abandoned match (55 minutes) on November 16 Goals

FA Cup

3	Jan	11	(h)	Chelsea	W	2-0	Lambert, Bastin	55,579
4		25	(h)	Birmingham	D	2-2	Bastin, Jack	43,274
R		29	(a)	Birmingham	W	1-0	Baker (pen)	47,521
5	Feb	15	(a)	Middlesbrough	W	2-0	Lambert, Bastin	42,073
6	Mar	1	(a)	West Ham U	W	3-0	Lambert 2, Baker	40,797
SF		22	(n†)	Hull C	D	2-2	Jack, Bastin	47,549
R		26	(n‡)	Hull C	W	1-0	Jack	46,200
F	Apr	26	(n§)	Huddersfield T	W	2-0	Lambert, James	92,486

†Played at Elland Road, Leeds. ‡Played at Villa Park, Birmingham. §Played at Wembley Stadium. Appearances
Goals

200

Lewis D	Parker TR	Hapgood EA	Baker A	Roberts H	John RF	Hulme JHA	Brain J	Jack DBN	James A	Jones C	Preedy CJF	Seddon WC	Johnstone W	Thompson L	Lambert J	Williams JJ	Bastin CS	Peel HB	Halliday D	Haynes AE	Butler JD	Humpish AE	Cope HW	
1	2	3	4	5	6	7	8	9	10	11														1
1	2	3	4	5	6	7	8	9	10	11														2
	2	3		5	6	7		8		11	1	4	9	10										3
	2	3		5	6	7		8		11	1	4	9	10										4
	2	3		5	6	7		8	10	11	1	4			9									5
	2	3		5		7		8	10	11	1	4		6	9									6
	2	3		5		7		8	10		1	4		6	9	11								7
1	2	3	6	5		7	9	8	10	11		4												8
1	2	3		5	6	7		9	10	11		4					8							9
1	2	3		5	6	7		9	10	11		4					8							10
1	2	3		5	6	7		8	10	11		4			9									11
1	2	3	6	5		7		8				4			9	11		10						12
1	2	3	4	5	6	7	8		10	11					9									13
1	2	3	4	5	6	7		8	10	11									9					14
1	2	3	4	5	6	7		8	10	11									9					15
	2	3	4	5	6	7		8	10	11	1								9					16
1	2	3	4	5	6	7		8	10	11									9					17
1	2	3		5	6	7		8	10	11		4							9					18
1	2	3		5	6	7		8		11		4		10					9					19
1	2	3		5	6	7		8	10	11									9	4				20
1	2	3			6	7		8	10	11									9	4	5			21
1	2	3			6	7		8	10								11		9	4	5			22
1		3	2		6	7	8	4		10							11		9	5				23
1	2	3	4	5		7		9	8	10							11			6				24
1	2	3		5	6	7		8							9		11		10	4				25
1	2	3		5	6			8	10						9	7	11			4				26
1	2	3	4	5	6			8	10						9	7	11							27
1	2	3		5	6		8			10						7	11		9			4		28
1	2	3						8		6		5	10		9	7	11					4		29
1	2	3	4	5				8	10	6					9	7	11							30
1	2		4		3	7			10	6		5			9	11	8							31
1	2	3	4			7		8	10	6		5			9	11								32
1	2	3			6	7			10			5			9	11	8			4				33
1	2	3			6	7				10		5			9	11	8			4				34
1	2				3	7				6		5	10			11	8		9			4		35
	2				3	7			10	6	1	5	8				11		9	4				36
	2	3			6	7			10		1	5	8		9		11			4				37
	2	3	4		6	7		8	10	11	1	5			9									38
	2	3	4		6	7				11	1	5	10		9		8							39
1	2		4		6	7		8	10								11		9	5			3	40
	2	3	4		6	7		8	10		1	5			9		11							41
	2	3			6	7		8	10		1	5			9		11			4				42
30	41	38	19	26	34	37	6	33	31	31	12	24	7	5	20	12	21	1	15	13	2	3	1	
	3					14		13	6	1			3	1	18	3	7		8					

1 own-goal

1	2	3		5	6	7		8						10	9		11			4				3
	2	3	4	5	6	7		8		10	1				9		11							4
1	2	3	4	5	6			8	10						9	7	11							R
1	2	3	4	5	6			8	10						9	7	11							5
1	2	3	4	5				8	10	6					9	7	11							6
1	2	3	4			7		8	10	6		5			9		11							SF
1	2	3	4					8	10	6		5			9	7	11							R
	2	3	4		6	7		8	10		1	5			9		11							F
6	8	8	7	5	5	4		8	6	4	2	3		1	8	4	8			1				
			2					3	1						5		4							

1930-31

Manager: H.Chapman

1	Aug	30	(a)	Blackpool	W 4-1 Bastin 2 (1 pen), Jack 2	28,723
2	Sep	1	(a)	Bolton W	W 4-1 Lambert 3, Hulme	20,684
3		6	(h)	Leeds U	W 3-1 Lambert 2, Jack	40,828
4		10	(h)	Blackburn R	W 3-2 Bastin 2, Johnstone	20,863
5		13	(a)	Sunderland	W 4-1 Lambert 3, Hulme	26,525
6		15	(a)	Blackburn R	D 2-2 Hulme, Lambert	25,572
7		20	(h)	Leicester C	W 4-1 Hulme, Lambert 2, Bastin	37,851
8		27	(a)	Birmingham	W 4-2 Lambert 3, Bastin	31,693
9	Oct	4	(h)	Sheffield U	D 1-1 Lambert	47,113
10		11	(a)	Derby C	L 2-4 Bastin, Roberts	29,783
11		18	(a)	Manchester U	W 2-1 Williams, Lambert	23,406
12		25	(h)	West Ham U	D 1-1 Bastin	51,918
13	Nov	1	(a)	Huddersfield T	D 1-1 Jack	25,772
14		8	(h)	Aston Villa	W 5-2 Bastin 2, Jack 2, Lambert	56,417
15		15	(a)	Sheffield W	W 2-1 Lambert 2	43,671
16		22	(h)	Middlesbrough	W 5-3 Lambert 3, Bastin 2 (1 pen)	32,517
17		29	(a)	Chelsea	W 5-1 Jack 3, Lambert, Williams	74,667
18	Dec	13	(a)	Liverpool	D 1-1 Jack	44,342
19		20	(h)	Newcastle U	L 1-2 Jack	32,212
20		25	(a)	Manchester C	W 4-1 Bastin, Jack, Lambert, Hulme	56,750
21		26	(h)	Manchester C	W 3-1 Hulme, Bastin, John	17,624
22		27	(h)	Blackpool	W 7-1 Jack 3, Brain 3, Bastin	35,113
23	Jan	17	(h)	Sunderland	L 1-3 James	35,975
24		28	(h)	Grimsby T*	W 9-1 Jack 4, Lambert 3, Bastin, Hulme	15,751
25		31	(h)	Birmingham	D 1-1 Lambert	30,913
26	Feb	5	(a)	Leicester C	W 7-2 Lambert 3, Bastin 2, Jack, Hulme	17,416
27		7	(a)	Sheffield U	D 1-1 Hulme	49,602
28		14	(h)	Derby C	W 6-3 Bastin 3 (1 pen), James, Hulme, Jack	34,785
29		21	(h)	Manchester U	W 4-1 Hulme, Jack, Brain, Bastin	41,510
30		28	(a)	West Ham U	W 4-2 John, Jack 2, Bastin	30,361
31	Mar	7	(h)	Huddersfield T	D 0-0	31,058
32		11	(a)	Leeds U	W 2-1 Bastin, James	12,212
33		14	(a)	Aston Villa	L 1-5 Jack	60,997
34		21	(h)	Sheffield W	W 2-0 Jack, Bastin	47,872
35		28	(a)	Middlesbrough	W 5-2 Lambert 3, Jack 2	23,476
36	Apr	3	(a)	Portsmouth	D 1-1 Bastin	31,398
37		4	(h)	Chelsea	W 2-1 Hulme, Bastin	53,867
38		6	(h)	Portsmouth	D 1-1 James	40,490
39		11	(a)	Grimsby T	W 1-0 Lambert	22,394
40		18	(h)	Liverpool	W 3-1 Lambert, Bastin, Jack	39,143
41		25	(a)	Newcastle U	W 3-1 Jones, Hulme 2	21,747
42	May	2	(h)	Bolton W	W 5-0 Lambert 2, Jack 2, James	35,406

FINAL LEAGUE POSITION: 1st in Division One

Appearances

*After abandoned match (63 minutes) on December 6

Goals

FA Cup

3	Jan	10	(h)	Aston Villa	D 2-2 Lambert, Jack	40,864
R		14	(a)	Aston Villa	W 3-1 Hulme 2, Jack	73,668
4		24	(a)	Chelsea	L 1-2 Bastin	62,945

Appearances

Goals

202

Keyser GP	Parker TR	Hapgood EA	Jones C	Roberts H	John RF	Hulme JHA	Jack DBN	Lambert J	James A	Bastin CS	Johnstone W	Seddon WC	Brain J	Williams JJ	Harper W	Preedy CJF	Male CG	Cope HW	Baker A	Thompson L	Haynes AE	No.
1	2	3	4	5	6	7	8	9	10	11												1
1	2	3	4	5	6	7	8	9	10	11												2
1	2	3	4	5	6	7	8	9	10	11												3
1	2	3	4	5	6	7	8	9		11	10											4
1	2	3		5	6	7	8	9		11	10	4										5
1	2	3		5	6	7		9	10	11		4	8									6
1	2	3		5	6	7		9	10	11		4	8									7
1	2	3		5	6	7		9	10	11		4	8									8
1	2	3		5	6	7		9	10	11		4	8									9
1	2	3		5	6	7	8	9	10	11		4										10
1	2	3		5	6			9	10	11		4	8	7								11
1	2	3		5	6			9	10	11		4	8	7								12
	2	3		5	6		8	9	10	11		4		7	1							13
	2	3		5	6		8	9	10	11		4		7	1							14
	2	3		5	6		8	9	10	11		4		7	1							15
	2	3		5	6		8	9	10	11		4		7	1							16
	2	3		5	6		8	9	10	11		4		7	1							17
	2	3		5	6		8	9	10	11		4		7	1							18
	2	3		5	6		8	9	10	11		4		7	1							19
	2	3		5	6	7	8	9	10	11		4			1							20
	2	3	4	5	6	7	8	9	10	11					1							21
	2		4	5	3	7		9	10	11			8		1		6					22
	2	3		5	6	7		9	10	11		4	8		1							23
	2	3	4	5	6	7	8	9	10	11					1							24
	2	3	4	5	6	7	8	9	10	11					1							25
	2	3		5	6	7	8	9	10	11		4			1							26
	2	3	4	5	6	7		9	10	11			8		1							27
		3	4	5	6	7		9	10	11			8		1		2					28
	2	3	4	5	6	7		9	10	11			8		1							29
	2	3	4	5	6	7		9	10	11			8		1							30
	2		4	5		7		9	10	11			8		1		6	3				31
	2		4	5		7		9	10	11			8			1			6		3	32
	2		4	5	3	7		9	10	11			8			1					6	33
	2	3	4	5	6	7		9	10	11			8			1						34
	2	3	4		6	7	8	9	10	11						1				5		35
	2	3	4	5	6	7	8	9	10	11						1						36
	2	3	4	5	6	7	8	9	10	11						1						37
	2	3	4	5	6	7	8	9	10	11						1						38
	2	3	4		6	7	8	9	10	11						1				5		39
	2	3	4	5	6	7	8	9	10	11						1						40
	2	3	4	5	6	7	8	9	10	11						1						41
	2	3	4	5	6	7	8	9	10	11						1						42
12	41	38	24	40	40	32	35	34	40	42	2	18	16	9	19	11	3	1	1	2	2	
			1	1	2	14	31	38	5	28	1		4	2								

Keyser GP	Parker TR	Hapgood EA	Jones C	Roberts H	John RF	Hulme JHA	Jack DBN	Lambert J	James A	Bastin CS	Johnstone W	Seddon WC	Brain J	Williams JJ	Harper W	Preedy CJF	Male CG	Cope HW	Baker A	Thompson L	Haynes AE	No.
	2	3		5	6	7	8	9	10	11		4			1							3
	2	3		5	6	7		9	10	11		4	8		1							R
	2	3		5	6	7	8	9	10	11		4			1							4
	3	3		3	3	3	2	3	3	3		3	1		3							
						2	2	1	1													

203

1931-32

Manager: H.Chapman

1	Aug	29	(h)	West Brom A	L 0-1		52,478
2		31	(a)	Blackburn R	D 1-1	Hulme	22,138
3	Sep	5	(a)	Birmingham	D 2-2	Lambert, Hulme	26,810
4		9	(h)	Portsmouth	D 3-3	Lambert 2, Bastin	25,403
5		12	(h)	Sunderland	W 2-0	Hulme 2	22,926
6		16	(a)	Portsmouth	W 3-0	Bastin 2, Parkin	22,977
7		19	(a)	Manchester C	W 3-1	Jack 2, Lambert	46,756
8		26	(h)	Everton	W 3-2	Hulme, Jack, Lambert	47,637
9	Oct	3	(a)	Grimsby T	L 1-3	Lambert	17,840
10		10	(a)	Blackpool	W 5-1	Bastin 3 (1 pen), Hulme, Lambert	29,516
11		17	(h)	Bolton W	D 1-1	Hulme	42,141
12		24	(a)	Leicester C	W 2-1	Jack, Osborne (og)	26,233
13		31	(h)	Aston Villa	D 1-1	Jack	54,951
14	Nov	7	(a)	Newcastle U	L 2-3	Lambert, Jack	28,949
15		14	(h)	West Ham U	W 4-1	Jack 3, Hulme	41,028
16		21	(a)	Chelsea	L 1-2	Jack	64,427
17		28	(h)	Liverpool	W 6-0	Jack 2, Lambert 3, Hulme	29,220
18	Dec	5	(a)	Sheffield W	W 3-1	Jack 2, Bastin	27,265
19		12	(h)	Huddersfield T	D 1-1	Jack	39,748
20		19	(a)	Middlesbrough	W 5-2	Jack 2, Bastin 2, Lambert	17,083
21		25	(a)	Sheffield U	L 1-4	Hulme	49,737
22		26	(h)	Sheffield U	L 0-2		55,207
23	Jan	2	(a)	West Brom A	L 0-1		25,823
24		16	(h)	Birmingham	W 3-0	Hulme, Bastin, Booton (og)	37,843
25		30	(h)	Manchester C	W 4-0	Parkin 3, James	39,834
26	Feb	6	(a)	Everton	W 3-1	Bastin, Hulme, John	56,698
27		17	(h)	Grimsby T	W 4-0	Bastin, Jack, Parkin, James	20,980
28		20	(h)	Blackpool	W 2-0	Jack, Parkin	39,045
29	Mar	2	(a)	Bolton W	L 0-1		20,922
30		5	(h)	Leicester C	W 2-1	Bastin (pen), Hulme	53,920
31		19	(h)	Newcastle U	W 1-0	Hulme	57,516
32		25	(h)	Derby C	W 2-1	Lambert 2	56,435
33		26	(a)	West Ham U	D 1-1	Lambert	34,852
34		28	(a)	Derby C	D 1-1	Jack	25,790
35	Apr	2	(h)	Chelsea	D 1-1	Lambert	56,124
36		6	(a)	Sunderland	L 0-2		30,443
37		9	(a)	Liverpool	L 1-2	Lambert	30,100
38		16	(h)	Sheffield W	W 3-1	John 2, Jack	25,220
39		25	(a)	Aston Villa	D 1-1	Parkin	25,959
40		27	(a)	Huddersfield T	W 2-1	Coleman, Lambert	13,370
41		30	(h)	Middlesbrough	W 5-0	Bastin 2, Lambert 2, Webster (og)	30,714
42	May	7	(h)	Blackburn R	W 4-0	Lambert 2, Stockill, Hutton (og)	23,127

FINAL LEAGUE POSITION: 2nd in Division One

Appearances
Goals

FA Cup

3	Jan	9	(h)	Darwen	W 11-1	Bastin 4, Jack 3, Lambert 2, Hulme 2	37,486
4		23	(h)	Plymouth A	W 4-2	Lambert 2, Hulme, Roberts (og)	65,386
5	Feb	13	(a)	Portsmouth	W 2-0	Bastin, Hulme	38,918
6		27	(a)	Huddersfield T	W 1-0	Roberts	67,037
SF	Mar	12	(n*)	Manchester C	W 1-0	Bastin	50,337
F	Apr	23	(n†)	Newcastle U	L 1-2	John	92,298

*Played at Villa Park, Birmingham. †Played at Wembley Stadium.

Appearances
Goals

204

Arsenal Football Club — League appearances and goals grid

Harper W	Parker TR	Hapgood EA	Jones C	Roberts H	John RF	Hulme JHA	Jack DBN	Lambert J	James A	Bastin CS	Preedy CJF	Parkin R	Seddon WC	Haynes AE	Male CG	Moss F	Cope HW	Williams JJ	Thompson L	Coleman E	Beasley AE	Compton LH	Stockill R	No.
1	2	3	4	5	6	7	8	9	10	11														1
1	2	3	4	5	6	7	8	9	10	11														2
	2	3	4	5	6	7	8	9	10	11	1													3
	2	3	4	5	6	7	8	9	10	11	1													4
	2	3	4	5	6	7		9	10	11	1	8												5
	2	3	4	5	6	7		9	10	11	1	8												6
	2	3	4	5	6	7	11	9	10		1	8												7
	2	3	4	5	6	7	8	9	10	11	1													8
	2	3	4	5	6	7	8	9	10	11	1													9
	2	3	4	5	6	7	8	9	10	11	1													10
	2	3	4	5	6	7	8	9	10	11	1													11
	2	3	4	5	6	7	8	9	10	11	1													12
	2	3		5	6	7	8	9	10	11	1		4											13
	2	3	4	5	6	7	11	9	10		1	8												14
	2	3	4			7	8	9	10	11	1		5	6										15
	2	3	4		6	7	8	9	10	11			5			1								16
	2	3	4	5	6	7	8	9	10	11						1								17
	2	3	4	5	6	7	8	9	10	11						1								18
	2	3	4	5	6	7	8	9	10	11						1								19
	2	3		5	6	7	8	9	10	11			4			1								20
	2	3		5	6	7	8	9	10	11			4			1								21
	2			5	6	7	8		10			9			4	1					11	3		22
	2	3	4	5	6	7	8	9	10	11						1								23
	2	3		5	6	7	8	9	10	11					4	1								24
	2	3	4	5	6	7	8		10	11		9				1								25
	2	3	4	5	6	7	8		10	11		9				1								26
	2	3	4	5	6	7	8		10	11		9				1								27
	2	3	4	5	6	7	8		10	11		9				1								28
	2	3	4			7	8	9		11			5	6		1				10				29
	2	3	4	5	6	7	8		10	11						1							9	30
	2	3	4	5	6	7		9	10	11						1				8				31
	2	3	4	5	6	7	8	9	10	11						1								32
	2	3	4	5	6	7		9	10	11						1				8				33
	2	3	4	5	6	7	10	8		11						1							9	34
	2	3	4	5	6	7	8	9	10	11						1								35
	2	3	4	5	6	7	8	9	10							1					11			36
	2	3	4	5			8	9	10					6		1				11	7			37
	2	3	4	5	11	7	8	9		10					6	1								38
		3	4			7		9	10					6	2	1				8	11	5		39
		3	4		6	7		9	10	11					2	1				8		5		40
		3	4		6	7		9	10	11					2	1				8		5		41
		3	4		6	7		9	10	11					2	1				8		5		42
2	38	41	37	35	38	40	34	36	32	40	13	9	5	7	9	27	1	1	1	6	3	4	3	
					3	14	21	22	2	15		7								1			1	

4 own-goals

Parker TR	Hapgood EA	Jones C	Roberts H	John RF	Hulme JHA	Jack DBN	Lambert J	James A	Bastin CS	Parkin R	Seddon WC	Male CG	Moss F	Cope HW	Coleman E	Stockill R	Rd
2	3	4	5	6	7	8	9	10	11				1				3
2	3	4	5	6	7	8	9	10	11				1				4
2	3	4	5	6	7	8		10	11	9			1				5
2	3	4	5	6	7	8	9	10	11				1				6
2	3	4	5	6	7	8	9	10	11				1				SF
2	3	4	5	11	7	8	9		10			6	1				F
6	6	6	6	6	6	6	5	5	6	1		1	6				
		1		1	1	4	6	3	4								

1 own-goal

205

1932-33

Manager: H.Chapman

					Result	Scorers	Attendance
1	Aug	27	(a)	Birmingham	W 1-0	Stockill	31,592
2		31	(h)	West Brom A	L 1-2	Stockill	37,748
3	Sep	3	(h)	Sunderland	W 6-1	Hulme 3, Coleman, Jack, Bastin	28,896
4		10	(a)	Manchester C	W 3-2	Jack, Coleman 2	36,542
5		14	(a)	West Brom A	D 1-1	Jack	45,038
6		17	(h)	Bolton W	W 3-2	Hulme, Coleman, Bastin	42,395
7		24	(h)	Everton	W 2-1	Jack, Coleman	51,182
8	Oct	1	(a)	Blackpool	W 2-1	Bastin, Coleman	30,218
9		8	(h)	Derby C	D 3-3	Coleman 2, Hulme	32,055
10		15	(a)	Blackburn R	W 3-2	Bastin, Jack, Coleman	28,799
11		22	(a)	Liverpool	W 3-2	Bastin 2, Coleman	38,548
12		29	(h)	Leicester C	W 8-2	Hulme 3, Bastin 2, Coleman 2, Jack	36,714
13	Nov	5	(a)	Wolves	W 7-1	Jack 3, Bastin 2, Lambert 2	43,570
14		12	(h)	Newcastle U	W 1-0	Hulme	56,498
15		19	(a)	Aston Villa	L 3-5	Jack, Lambert, Bastin	58,066
16		26	(h)	Middlesbrough	W 4-2	Coleman 2, Hulme, Jack	34,640
17	Dec	3	(a)	Portsmouth	W 3-1	Bastin 2, Jack	31,401
18		10	(h)	Chelsea	W 4-1	Bastin 2, Coleman, Hulme	53,206
19		17	(a)	Huddersfield T	W 1-0	Coleman	23,198
20		24	(h)	Sheffield U	W 9-2	Lambert 5, Bastin 3, Jack	41,520
21		26	(h)	Leeds U	L 1-2	Hulme	55,876
22		27	(a)	Leeds U	D 0-0		56,776
23		31	(h)	Birmingham	W 3-0	Jack, James, Bastin	37,800
24	Jan	2	(a)	Sheffield W	L 2-3	Jack, Bastin (pen)	64,492
25		7	(a)	Sunderland	L 2-3	Lambert 2	36,707
26		21	(h)	Manchester C	W 2-1	Bastin 2	32,456
27	Feb	1	(a)	Bolton W	W 4-0	Coleman 3, Bastin	13,401
28		4	(a)	Everton	D 1-1	Coleman	55,463
29		11	(h)	Blackpool	D 1-1	Coleman	35,180
30		22	(a)	Derby C	D 2-2	Jack, Bastin	23,148
31		25	(h)	Blackburn R	W 8-0	Coleman 3, Hulme 2, Bastin 2, Stockill	27,576
32	Mar	4	(h)	Liverpool	L 0-1		42,868
33		11	(a)	Leicester C	D 1-1	James	32,228
34		18	(h)	Wolves	L 1-2	Bowden	44,711
35		25	(a)	Newcastle U	L 1-2	Hulme	51,215
36	Apr	1	(h)	Aston Villa	W 5-0	Lambert 2, Jack, Bowden, James	54,265
37		8	(a)	Middlesbrough	W 4-3	Hulme 3, Bastin	22,137
38		14	(h)	Sheffield W	W 4-2	Hulme 2, Lambert, Bastin	61,945
39		15	(h)	Portsmouth	W 2-0	Lambert, Bastin	42,809
40		22	(a)	Chelsea	W 3-1	Bastin 2, Jack	72,260
41		29	(h)	Huddersfield T	D 2-2	Bastin 2	30,779
42	May	6	(a)	Sheffield U	L 1-3	Hill	18,620

FINAL LEAGUE POSITION: 1st in Division One

Appearances
Goals

FA Cup

					Result		Attendance
3	Jan	14	(a)	Walsall	L 0-2		11,150

Appearances
Goals

Moss F	Compton LH	Hapgood EA	Male CG	Roberts H	John RF	Hulme JHA	Jack DBN	Stockill R	James A	Bastin CS	Jones C	Coleman E	Haynes AE	Parker TR	Preedy CJF	Hill FR	Lambert J	Sidey NW	Cope HW	Parkin R	Bowden ER	Black T	Warnes WH	Walsh CH	#
1	2	3	4	5	6	7	8	9	10	11															1
1	2	3	4	5	6	7	8	9	10	11															2
1	2	3			6	7	8		10	11	4	9	5												3
1	2	3			6	7	8		10	11	4	9	5												4
1		3			6	7	8		10	11	4	9	5	2											5
1		3			6	7	8		10	11	4	9	5	2											6
1		3		5	6	7	8		10	11	4	9		2											7
		3		5	6	7	8		10	11	4	9		2	1										8
1		3		5	6	7	8		10	11	4	9		2											9
1		3	2	5	6	7	8		10	11		9				4									10
1		3	2		6	7	8		10	11		9	5			4									11
1		3	2	5	6	7	8		10	11		9				4									12
1		3	2	5	6	7	8		10	11						4	9								13
1		3	2	5	6	7	8		10	11		9				4									14
1		3	2	5	6	7	8		10	11						4	9								15
1		3	2	5	6	7	8			11		9				4				10					16
1		3	2	5	6	7	8		10	11		9				4									17
1		3	2	5	6	7	8		10	11		9				4									18
1		3	2	5	6	7	8		10	11		9				4									19
1		3	2	5	6	7	8		10	11						4	9								20
1		3	2	5	6	7	8		10	11						4	9								21
1		3	2		6	7	9	8	10	11			5					4							22
1		3	2	5	6	7	8		10	11		9				4									23
1		3	2	5	6	7	8		10	11		9				4									24
1		3	2	5	6	7	8		10	11						4	9								25
1			2	5		7	8		10	11		9				4		6	3						26
1			2	5	6	7			10	11		9				4			3	8					27
1			2	5	6	7	8		10	11		9							3	4					28
1			2	5	6	7	8		10	11		9							3	4					29
1		3	2	5	6	7	8		10	11		9								4					30
1		3	2	5	6	7	8		10	11	4	9													31
1		3	2	5	6	7	8		10	11	4	9													32
1		3	2	5	6	7	8		10	11	4	9													33
1		3	2	5	6	7			10	11	4	9									8				34
1		3	2	5		7	8		10	11	4	9				6									35
1		3	2	5	6	7			10	11						4	9				8				36
1		3	2	5	6	7			10	11						4	9				8				37
1		3	2	5	6	7			10	11						4	9				8				38
1		3	2	5		7			10	11	6					4	9				8				39
1		3	2	5		7			10	11	6					4	9				8				40
1		3	2	5		7			10	11	6					4	9				8				41
1		3	2	5			10	7		11	6					4	9				8				42
41	4	38	35	36	37	40	34	4	40	42	16	27	6	5	1	26	12	2	4	5	7				
						20	18	3	3	33		24				1	14				2				

Moss F	Compton LH	Hapgood EA	Male CG	Roberts H	John RF	Hulme JHA	Jack DBN	Stockill R	James A	Bastin CS	Jones C	Coleman E	Haynes AE	Parker TR	Preedy CJF	Hill FR	Lambert J	Sidey NW	Cope HW	Parkin R	Bowden ER	Black T	Warnes WH	Walsh CH	#
1			2	5			8		10	11						4		6			3	7	9		3
1			1	1			1		1	1						1		1			1	1	1		

207

1933-34

Manager: H.Chapman/J.Shaw

1	Aug	26	(h)	Birmingham	D	1-1	Jack	44,662
2	Sep	2	(a)	Sheffield W	W	2-1	Bastin, Jack	23,186
3		6	(h)	West Brom A	W	3-1	Bastin 2 (1 pen), Lambert	34,688
4		9	(h)	Manchester C	D	1-1	Coleman	43,412
5		13	(a)	West Brom A	L	0-1		29,429
6		16	(a)	Tottenham H	D	1-1	Bowden	56,612
7		23	(a)	Everton	L	1-3	Bowden	53,792
8		30	(h)	Middlesbrough	W	6-0	Birkett 2, Jack 2, Bastin, Bowden	28,293
9	Oct	7	(a)	Blackburn R	D	2-2	Bastin, Bowden	31,636
10		14	(h)	Newcastle U	W	3-0	Birkett, Bowden, Fairhurst (og)	32,821
11		21	(h)	Leicester C	W	2-0	Dunne 2	44,014
12		28	(a)	Aston Villa	W	3-2	Dunne 2, Bastin	54,323
13	Nov	4	(h)	Portsmouth	D	1-1	Bastin	51,765
14		11	(a)	Wolves	W	1-0	Bowden	37,210
15		18	(h)	Stoke C	W	3-0	Hulme, Dunne, John	32,972
16		25	(a)	Huddersfield T	W	1-0	Dunne	29,407
17	Dec	2	(h)	Liverpool	W	2-1	Hulme, Dunne	38,362
18		9	(a)	Sunderland	L	0-3		35,166
19		16	(h)	Chelsea	W	2-1	Beasley 2	43,897
20		23	(a)	Sheffield U	W	3-1	Beasley 2, Bowden	31,453
21		25	(a)	Leeds U	W	1-0	Bastin	33,193
22		26	(h)	Leeds U	W	2-0	Bowden, Dunne	22,817
23		30	(a)	Birmingham	D	0-0		34,771
24	Jan	6	(h)	Sheffield W	D	1-1	Dunne	45,156
25		20	(a)	Manchester C	L	1-2	Beasley	60,401
26		31	(h)	Tottenham H	L	1-3	Bastin	68,828
27	Feb	3	(h)	Everton	L	1-2	Birkett	24,025
28		10	(a)	Middlesbrough	W	2-0	Birkett, Bowden	15,894
29		21	(h)	Blackburn R	W	2-1	Bastin, Beasley	29,886
30		24	(a)	Newcastle U	W	1-0	Beasley	40,065
31	Mar	8	(a)	Leicester C	L	1-4	Bowden	23,976
32		10	(h)	Aston Villa	W	3-2	Jack, Roberts, Hulme	41,169
33		24	(h)	Wolves	W	3-2	Drake, James, Bastin	41,143
34		30	(h)	Derby C	W	1-0	James	69,070
35		31	(a)	Stoke C	D	1-1	Bastin	43,163
36	Apr	2	(a)	Derby C	W	4-2	Drake 2, Bowden 2	32,180
37		7	(h)	Huddersfield T	W	3-1	Beasley, Bowden, Drake	55,930
38		14	(a)	Liverpool	W	3-2	Beasley, Hulme 2	43,027
39		18	(a)	Portsmouth	L	0-1		28,442
40		21	(h)	Sunderland	W	2-1	Drake, Beasley	37,783
41		28	(a)	Chelsea	D	2-2	James, Bastin	65,344
42	May	5	(h)	Sheffield U	W	2-0	Drake 2	25,265

FINAL LEAGUE POSITION: 1st in Division One

Appearances

Goals

FA Cup

3	Jan	13	(a)	Luton T	W	1-0	Dunne	18,641
4		27	(h)	Crystal P	W	7-0	Dunne 2, Bastin 2, Beasley 2, Birkett	56,177
5	Feb	17	(h)	Derby C	W	1-0	Jack	66,905
6	Mar	3	(h)	Aston Villa	L	1-2	Dougall	67,366

Appearances

Goals

Player appearance and goals grid.

Moss F	Male CG	Hapgood EA	Hill FR	Roberts H	John RF	Hulme JHA	Jack DBN	Coleman E	James A	Bastin CS	Birkett RJ	Bowden ER	Lambert J	Jones C	Parkin R	Sidey NW	Dunne J	Beasley AE	Dougall P	Cox G	Wilson A	Drake EJ	Haynes AE	
1	2	3	4	5	6	7	8	9	10	11														1
1	2	3	4	5	6		8	9		11	7	10												2
1	2	3	4	5	6		8	7		11	10	9												3
1	2	3	4	5	6		8	7		11	10	9												4
1	2	3	6	5		7			10	11	8	9		4										5
1	2	3	4	5	6		8		10	11	9	7												6
1	2	3	4	5	6		8		10	11	9	7												7
1	2	3			6				10	11	7	8		4		5	9							8
1	2	3			6				10	11	7	8		4		5	9							9
1	2	3	6				8			11	7	10		4		5	9							10
1	2	3			6				10	11	7	8		4		5	9							11
1	2	3			6	7			10	11		8		4		5	9							12
1	2	3			6	7			10	11		8		4		5	9							13
1	2	3			6	7	8			11		10		4		5	9							14
1	2	3			6	7	8			11		10		4		5	9							15
1	2	3			6	7			10	11		8		4		5	9							16
1	2	3			6	7	8			11		10		4		5	9							17
1	2	3			6	7	8			11		10		4		5	9							18
1	2	3		5	6				10	8	7	9		4				11						19
1	2	3		5	6				10	8	7			4			9	11						20
1	2	3		5	6				10	8	7			4			9	11						21
1	2	3		5	6				10	8	7			4			9	11						22
1	2	3		5	6				10	8	7			4			9	11						23
1	2	3		5	6					8	7	10		4			9	11						24
1	2	3		5	6				10	8	7			4			9	11						25
1	2	3		5	6				10	8	7			4			9	11						26
1	2	3	4	5	6					8	7	10					9	11						27
1	2	3		5	6					8	7	10		4			9	11						28
1	2	3		5	6					8				4			9	11	10	7				29
1	2	3			6					8				4		5	9	11	10	7				30
1	2	3		5	6					8				4				11	10	7		9		31
	2	3		5	6					8	7	10		4				11			1	9		32
1	2	3		5	6					8	7	10		4				11				9		33
	2	3		5	6					8		10		4				11		7	1	9		34
	2	3		5	6					8				4				11	10	7	1	9		35
	2	3	4	5	6					8		10						11		7	1	9		36
1	2	3	4	5	6					8		10						11		7		9		37
	2	3		5	6					8		10		4				11		7	1	9		38
1	2	3		5	6					8		10		4				11		7		9		39
1	2	3		5	6					8	7	10		4				11				9		40
1	2	3		5	6					8		10		4				11		7		9		41
1	2	3	4	5	6					8		10						11		7		9		42
37	42	40	25	30	31	8	14	12	22	38	15	32	3	29	5	12	21	23	5	2	5	10	1	
				1	1	5	5	1	3	13	5	13	1				9	10				7		

1 own-goal

Moss F	Male CG	Hapgood EA	Hill FR	Roberts H	John RF	Hulme JHA	Jack DBN	Coleman E	James A	Bastin CS	Birkett RJ	Bowden ER	Lambert J	Jones C	Parkin R	Sidey NW	Dunne J	Beasley AE	Dougall P	Cox G	Wilson A	Drake EJ	Haynes AE	
1	2	3		5	6					8	7	10		4			9	11						3
	2	3		5	6					8	7	10		4			9	11			1			4
1	2	3		5	6					8		11		4			9		10	7				5
1	2	3		5	6					8		11		4			9		10	7				6
3	4	4		4	4					2	1	4		4			4	4	2	2	1			
										1		2		1			3	2		1				

1934-35

Manager: G.Allison

1	Aug	25	(a)	Portsmouth	D	3-3	Bowden, Drake, Bastin	39,710
2	Sep	1	(h)	Liverpool	W	8-1	Drake 3, Bowden 3, Bastin, Crayston	54,062
3		5	(h)	Blackburn R	W	4-0	Drake 2, Bowden, Bastin	39,654
4		8	(a)	Leeds U	D	1-1	Drake	29,447
5		15	(h)	West Brom A	W	4-3	Bowden, James, Bastin, Drake	40,016
6		17	(a)	Blackburn R	L	0-2		25,472
7		22	(a)	Sheffield W	D	0-0		24,751
8		29	(h)	Birmingham	W	5-1	Drake 4, Bastin	47,868
9	Oct	6	(a)	Stoke C	D	2-2	Bastin 2	45,348
10		13	(h)	Manchester C	W	3-0	Bowden 2, Bastin	68,145
11		20	(h)	Tottenham H	W	5-1	Drake 3, Beasley, Evans T (og)	70,544
12		27	(a)	Sunderland	L	1-2	Drake	43,744
13	Nov	3	(h)	Everton	W	2-0	Bastin 2	50,350
14		10	(a)	Grimsby T	D	2-2	Drake, Hulme	26,288
15		17	(h)	Aston Villa	L	1-2	Bastin (pen)	54,226
16		24	(a)	Chelsea	W	5-2	Drake 4, Hulme	43,419
17	Dec	1	(h)	Wolves	W	7-0	Drake 4, Birkett 2, Bowden	39,532
18		8	(a)	Huddersfield T	D	1-1	Roughton (og)	36,113
19		15	(h)	Leicester C	W	8-0	Drake 3, Hulme 3, Bastin 2	23,689
20		22	(a)	Derby C	L	1-3	Bowden	26,091
21		25	(h)	Preston NE	W	5-3	Hulme 2, Bowden, Bastin, Hough (og)	40,201
22		26	(a)	Preston NE	L	1-2	Hill	39,411
23		29	(h)	Portsmouth	D	1-1	Drake	36,054
24	Jan	5	(a)	Liverpool	W	2-0	Drake, Hapgood	55,794
25		19	(h)	Leeds U	W	3-0	Bowden 2, Bastin	37,026
26		30	(a)	West Brom A	W	3-0	Drake, Bastin, Hulme	30,713
27	Feb	2	(h)	Sheffield W	W	4-1	James 3, Bastin	57,922
28		9	(a)	Birmingham	L	0-3		50,188
29		20	(h)	Stoke C	W	2-0	Davidson, Hill	27,067
30		23	(a)	Manchester C	D	1-1	Bowden	79,491
31	Mar	6	(a)	Tottenham H	W	6-0	Kirchen 2, Drake 2, Dougall, Bastin (pen)	47,714
32		9	(h)	Sunderland	D	0-0		73,295
33		16	(a)	Everton	W	2-0	Moss, Drake	50,389
34		23	(h)	Grimsby T	D	1-1	Drake	33,591
35		30	(a)	Aston Villa	W	3-1	Beasley, Drake, Bastin (pen)	59,572
36	Apr	6	(h)	Chelsea	D	2-2	Drake, Compton (pen)	54,020
37		13	(a)	Wolves	D	1-1	Hill	40,888
38		19	(h)	Middlesbrough	W	8-0	Drake 4, Rogers 2, Bastin, Beasley	45,719
39		20	(h)	Huddersfield T	W	1-0	Beasley	41,892
40		22	(a)	Middlesbrough	W	1-0	Drake	29,171
41		27	(a)	Leicester C	W	5-3	Beasley 2, Crayston 2, Davidson	26,958
42	May	4	(h)	Derby C	L	0-1		36,421

FINAL LEAGUE POSITION: 1st in Division One

Appearances
Goals

FA Cup

3	Jan	12	(a)	Brighton & HA	W	2-0	Hulme, Drake	22,343
4		26	(a)	Leicester C	W	1-0	Hulme	39,494
5	Feb	16	(a)	Reading	W	1-0	Bastin	30,621
6	Mar	2	(a)	Sheffield W	L	1-2	Catlin (og)	66,945

Appearances
Goals

210

Moss F	Male CG	John RF	Hill FR	Roberts H	Copping W	Hulme JHA	Bowden ER	Drake EJ	James A	Bastin CS	Hapgood EA	Crayston WJ	Beasley AE	Sidey NW	Marshall Dr J	Birkett RJ	Compton LH	Dougall P	Dunne J	Davidson RT	Kirchen AJ	Wilson A	Rogers E	Trim RF	
1	2	3	4	5	6	7	8	9	10	11															1
1	2			5	6		8	9	10	11	3	4	7												2
1	2			5	6		8	9	10	11	3	4	7												3
1	2			5	6		8	9	10	11	3	4	7												4
1	2			5	6		8	9	10	11	3	4	7												5
1	2	6					8	9		11	3	4	7	5	10										6
1	2			5	6	7	8	9	10	11	3	4													7
1	2	3		5	6	7		9	10	11		4			8										8
1	2			5	6	7	8	9	10	11	3	4													9
1	2			5	6		8	9	10	11	3	4	7												10
1	2	6		5			8	9	10	11	3	4	7												11
1	2			5	6		8	9	10	11	3	4	7												12
1	2			5	6		8		10	11	3	4	7						9						13
1	2			5	6	7	8	9	10	11	3	4													14
1	2			5	6	7		9	10	11	3	4			8										15
1	2		4	5	6	7	8	9	10	11	3														16
1	2			5	6		8	9	10	11	3	4				7									17
1	2			5	6		8	9	10	11	3	4				7									18
1	2			5	6	7	8	9	10	11	3	4													19
1	2			5	6		8	9	10	11	3	4				7									20
1				5	6	7	8	9	10	11	3	4					2								21
1	2	11			6	7		9		10	3	4		5	8										22
1	2	10	4	5	6	7	8	9			11	3													23
1	2			5	6	7	8	9		11	3	4													24
1	2			5	6	7	8	9		11	3	4						10							25
1			4		6	7		9		8	3		11	5			2	10							26
1	2			5	6	7		9	10	8	3	4	11												27
1	2			5	6	7		9	10	8	3	4	11												28
1	2	11			6			9			3	4		5		7		10		8					29
1	2	3		5	6	7		9		11		4						10		8					30
1	2				6			9		11		4		5			3	10		8	7				31
1	2			5	6			9	10	11	3	4								8	7				32
1	2			5	6			9		11	3	4						10		8	7				33
	2			5	6			9		11	3	4						10		8	7	1			34
	2			5	6			9	10		3	4	11							8	7	1			35
		3		5	6			9	10			4	11				2			8	7	1			36
	2			5	6			9	10	8		4	11				3				7	1			37
	2			5	6			9			3	4	11					10				1	7		38
	2			5	6			9			3	4	11					10		8		1	7		39
	2	3			6		8	9	10			4	11	5								1	7		40
	2			5	6			9	10		3	4	11							8		1	7		41
	2	6	4	5				9	10	11										8		1	7	3	42
33	39	9	15	36	31	16	24	41	30	36	34	37	20	6	4	4	5	8	1	11	7	9	5	1	
1		3				8	14	42	4	20	1	3	6		2	1	1			2	2		2		

3 own-goals

Moss F	Male CG	John RF	Hill FR	Roberts H	Copping W	Hulme JHA	Bowden ER	Drake EJ	James A	Bastin CS	Hapgood EA	Crayston WJ	Beasley AE	Sidey NW	Marshall Dr J	Birkett RJ	Compton LH	Dougall P	Dunne J	Davidson RT	Kirchen AJ	Wilson A	Rogers E	Trim RF	
1	2	10		5	6	7	8	9		11	3	4													3
1	2		4	5	6	7	8	9	10	11	3														4
1	2			5	6			9	10	8	3	4	11			7									5
1	2	3		5	6			9	10	11		4	7					8							6
4	4	2	1	4	4	2	2	4	3	4	3	3	2			1		1							
								2	1	1															

1 own-goal

1935-36

Manager: G.Allison

1	Aug	31	(h)	Sunderland	W	3-1	Drake 2, Bastin	66,428
2	Sep	3	(a)	Grimsby T	L	0-1		25,978
3		7	(a)	Birmingham	D	1-1	Drake	42,804
4		11	(h)	Grimsby T	W	6-0	Milne 3, Beasley, Bowden, Drake	33,633
5		14	(h)	Sheffield W	D	2-2	Drake, Milne	59,492
6		18	(a)	Leeds U	D	1-1	Drake	24,283
7		21	(h)	Manchester C	L	2-3	Bastin (pen), James	61,290
8		28	(a)	Stoke C	W	3-0	Bastin 2, Crayston	45,570
9	Oct	5	(h)	Blackburn R	W	5-1	Bowden 3, Bastin, Milne	45,981
10		12	(a)	Chelsea	D	1-1	Crayston	82,905
11		19	(a)	Portsmouth	L	1-2	Milne	34,165
12		26	(h)	Preston NE	W	2-1	Drake, Bastin	42,126
13	Nov	2	(a)	Brentford	L	1-2	Parkin	26,330
14		9	(h)	Derby C	D	1-1	Drake	54,027
15		16	(a)	Everton	W	2-0	Drake, Bastin	46,990
16		23	(h)	Wolves	W	4-0	Rogers, Drake 2, Hulme	39,860
17		30	(a)	Huddersfield T	D	0-0		35,816
18	Dec	9	(h)	Middlesbrough	W	2-0	Rogers 2	23,365
19		14	(a)	Aston Villa	W	7-1	Drake 7	58,469
20		25	(a)	Liverpool	W	1-0	Hulme	45,899
21		26	(h)	Liverpool	L	1-2	Hulme	57,035
22		28	(a)	Sunderland	L	4-5	Bowden, Drake, Bastin (pen), Clarke (og)	58,773
23	Jan	4	(h)	Birmingham	D	1-1	Drake	44,534
24		18	(a)	Sheffield W	L	2-3	Drake, Roberts	35,576
25	Feb	1	(h)	Stoke C	W	1-0	Drake	49,347
26		8	(a)	Blackburn R	W	1-0	Crayston	24,998
27		22	(h)	Portsmouth	L	2-3	Compton, Dougall	21,728
28	Mar	4	(a)	Derby C	W	4-0	Dougall, Kirchen, Cox, Crayston	17,930
29		7	(h)	Huddersfield T	D	1-1	Bastin	43,930
30		11	(a)	Manchester C	L	0-1		32,750
31		14	(a)	Preston NE	L	0-1		30,039
32		25	(h)	Everton	D	1-1	Hulme	18,593
33		28	(a)	Wolves	D	2-2	Beasley, Kirchen	32,330
34	Apr	1	(h)	Bolton W	D	1-1	Westcott	10,485
35		4	(h)	Brentford	D	1-1	Dougall	28,303
36		10	(h)	West Brom A	W	4-0	Crayston, Dunne, Hulme, James	59,245
37		11	(a)	Middlesbrough	D	2-2	Bowden, Bastin (pen)	31,006
38		13	(a)	West Brom A	L	0-1		42,286
39		18	(h)	Aston Villa	W	1-0	Drake	55,431
40		27	(h)	Chelsea	D	1-1	Drake	40,402
41		29	(a)	Bolton W	L	1-2	Hulme	29,479
42	May	2	(h)	Leeds U	D	2-2	Bastin, Kirchen	25,920

FINAL LEAGUE POSITION: 6th in Division One

Appearances
Goals

FA Cup

3	Jan	11	(a)	Bristol R	W	5-1	Bastin 2, Drake 2, Bowden	24,234
4		25	(a)	Liverpool	W	2-0	Bowden, Hulme	53,720
5	Feb	15	(a)	Newcastle U	D	3-3	Bowden 2, Hulme	65,484
R		19	(h)	Newcastle U	W	3-0	Bastin 2 (pens), Beasley	62,391
6		29	(h)	Barnsley	W	4-1	Beasley 2, Bowden, Bastin (pen)	60,420
SF	Mar	21	(n*)	Grimsby T	W	1-0	Bastin	63,210
F	Apr	25	(n†)	Sheffield U	W	1-0	Drake	93,384

*Played at Leeds Road, Huddersfield. †Played at Wembley Stadium.

Appearances
Goals

212

Wilson A	Male CG	Hapgood EA	Crayston WJ	Roberts H	Copping W	Milne JV	Davidson RT	Drake EJ	James A	Bastin CS	Compton LH	Beasley AE	Bowden ER	Hill FR	Dunne J	John RF	Hulme JHA	Parkin R	Rogers E	Sidey NW	Moss F	Dougall P	Cartwright S	Kirchen AJ	Cox G	Tuckett EW	Westcott R	Joy B	
1	2	3	4	5	6	7	8	9	10	11																			1
1	2		4	5	6	7	8	9	10	11	3																		2
1	2		4	5	6	7	8	9		10	3	11																	3
1	2		4	5	6	11	10	9			3	7	8																4
1	2	3	4	5	6	11	10	9				7	8																5
1	2	3	4	5	6	11	10	9		8		7																	6
1	2	3	4	5		7	8	9	10	11			6																7
1	2	3	4	5		7			10	11		8	6	9															8
1	2	3	4	5		7		9	10	11		8	6																9
1	2	3	4	5		7		9	10	11		8	6																10
1			4	5	6	7	8	9	10	11	2			3															11
1	2	3	4	5	6			9	10	11		8					7												12
1	2	3	4	5	6			9	10	11							7	8											13
1	2	3	4	5	6	11		9	10			8					7												14
1	2	3	4	5	6			9	10			8					7		11										15
1	2	3	4	5	6			9	10			8					7		11										16
1	2	3	4	5	6			9	10		11	8					7												17
1	2	3	4	5	6			9	10		11	8					7												18
1	2	3	4	5	6			9	10		11	8					7												19
1	2	3	4		6			9	10		11	8					7			5									20
1	2	3	4		6			9	10	8	11						7			5									21
	2	3	4	5	6			9	10		11	8					7				1								22
	2	3	4	5	6			9	10		11	8					7				1								23
	2	3	4	5	6			9	10	8	11						7				1								24
	2	3	4		6			9	10	11		8					7			5	1								25
	2		4		6		8				3	11		9			7			5	1	10							26
1		3			6		8				2	11		9			7			5		10	4						27
1	2	3	4				8					11								5		10	6	7	9				28
1	2		5	6			8					11					7					10	4		9				29
1		3			6						2	11	8							5		10	4	7	9				30
1	2		3		5		11	10					9	6	7		8					4							31
1	2	5		6			8	3				4	11		7				10			9							32
1		3	4								2	11	8	6					10				5		9				33
1			6				10				2	11		4	3		7	8						9	5				34
1			6								2	11		4	9	3	7	8				10					5		35
1	2	3	4	5	6			10	8		11			9			7												36
1	2	3	4						10		11	8	6	9			7			5									37
1			4	5	6		10				2	11	9		3		8					7							38
1	2	3	4		6			9	10	8	11						7			5									39
1	2	3	4		6			9	10		11	8					7			5									40
1	2	3	4		6	11	8		10								7			5				9					41
1	2	3	4					10	8		11	9			6							7	5						42
37	35	33	36	26	33	14	13	26	17	31	12	26	22	10	6	6	21	1	11	11	5	8	5	6	5	2	2	2	
			5	1		6		24	2	11	1	2	6		1		6	1	3			3		3	1		1		

1 own-goal

Wilson A	Male CG	Hapgood EA	Crayston WJ	Roberts H	Copping W	Milne JV	Davidson RT	Drake EJ	James A	Bastin CS	Compton LH	Beasley AE	Bowden ER	Hill FR	Dunne J	John RF	Hulme JHA	Parkin R	Rogers E	Sidey NW	Moss F	Dougall P	Cartwright S	Kirchen AJ	Cox G	Tuckett EW	Westcott R	Joy B	
	2	3	4	5	6		10	9		11			8				7				1								3
	2	3	4		6			9	10	11			8				7			5	1								4
1	2	3	4		6				10	8		9	11				7			5									5
1	2	3	4	5	6				10	8		9	11				7												R
1	2	3	4	5	6				10	8		9	11				7												6
1	2	3	4	5	6				10	8		9	11				7												SF
1	2	3	4	5	6			9	10	11			8				7												F
5	7	7	7	5	7		1	3	6	7		4	7				7			2	2								
								3		6		3	5				2												

1936-37

Manager: G.Allison

1	Aug	29	(h)	Everton	W	3-2	Hapgood, Bowden, James	50,321
2	Sep	3	(a)	Brentford	L	0-2		31,056
3		5	(a)	Huddersfield T	D	0-0		32,013
4		9	(h)	Brentford	D	1-1	Drake	44,010
5		12	(h)	Sunderland	W	4-1	Crayston, Beasley, Bastin, Roberts	56,820
6		19	(a)	Wolves	L	0-2		53,097
7		26	(h)	Derby C	D	2-2	D.Compton, Drake	61,390
8	Oct	3	(a)	Manchester U	L	0-2		55,884
9		10	(h)	Sheffield W	D	1-1	Drake	46,421
10		17	(a)	Charlton A	W	2-0	Davidson, D.Compton	68,160
11		24	(h)	Grimsby T	D	0-0		51,202
12		31	(a)	Liverpool	L	1-2	Kirchen	39,251
13	Nov	7	(h)	Leeds U	W	4-1	Kirchen, Drake, Milne, Davidson	32,535
14		14	(a)	Birmingham	W	3-1	Drake 2, Kirchen	39,940
15		21	(h)	Middlesbrough	W	5-3	Milne 2, Drake, Bastin, Bowden	44,829
16		28	(a)	West Brom A	W	4-2	Drake 2, Milne 2	27,609
17	Dec	5	(h)	Manchester C	L	1-3	Drake	41,783
18		12	(a)	Portsmouth	W	5-1	Davidson 4, Drake	32,184
19		19	(h)	Chelsea	W	4-1	Kirchen 2, Drake, Davidson	49,917
20		25	(h)	Preston NE	W	4-1	Drake 2, Kirchen, Milne	42,781
21		26	(a)	Everton	D	1-1	Kirchen	59,440
22		28	(a)	Preston NE	W	3-1	Kirchen, Nelson, Milne	25,787
23	Jan	1	(a)	Bolton W	W	5-0	Drake 4, Milne	42,171
24		2	(h)	Huddersfield T	D	1-1	Kirchen	44,224
25		9	(a)	Sunderland	D	1-1	Milne	54,694
26		23	(h)	Wolves	W	3-0	Bastin (pen), Drake, Bowden	33,896
27	Feb	3	(a)	Derby C	L	4-5	Drake, Bastin (pen), Kirchen, Howe (og)	22,064
28		6	(h)	Manchester U	D	1-1	Davidson	37,236
29		13	(a)	Sheffield W	D	0-0		35,813
30		24	(h)	Charlton A	D	1-1	Kirchen	60,568
31		27	(a)	Grimsby T	W	3-1	Kirchen 3	18,216
32	Mar	10	(h)	Liverpool	W	1-0	Kirchen	16,145
33		13	(a)	Leeds U	W	4-3	Kirchen 2, Bastin (pen), Bowden	25,148
34		20	(h)	Birmingham	D	1-1	Bowden	46,086
35		26	(h)	Stoke C	D	0-0		59,495
36		27	(a)	Middlesbrough	D	1-1	Bowden	44,523
37		29	(a)	Stoke C	D	0-0		51,480
38	Apr	3	(h)	West Brom A	W	2-0	Davidson, Nelson	38,773
39		10	(a)	Manchester C	L	0-2		74,918
40		17	(h)	Portsmouth	W	4-0	D.Compton 2, Nelson, Kirchen	29,098
41		24	(a)	Chelsea	L	0-2		53,325
42	May	1	(h)	Bolton W	D	0-0		22,875

FINAL LEAGUE POSITION: 3rd in Division One

Appearances
Goals

FA Cup

3	Jan	16	(a)	Chesterfield	W	5-1	Drake 2, Kirchen 2, Davidson	21,786
4		30	(h)	Manchester U	W	5-0	Bastin, Davidson, Drake, Kirchen, Brown (og)	45,637
5	Feb	20	(a)	Burnley	W	7-1	Drake 4, Crayston, Bastin, Kirchen	54,445
6	Mar	6	(a)	West Brom A	L	1-3	Bastin	64,815

Appearances
Goals

214

Wilson A	Male CG	Hapgood EA	Crayston WJ	Roberts H	Copping W	Hulme JHA	Bowden ER	Drake EJ	James A	Bastin CS	Swindin GH	Davidson RT	Beasley AE	Cartwright S	John RF	Kirchen AJ	Sidey NW	Milne JV	Compton DCS	Compton LH	Boulton FP	Joy B	Nelson D	Biggs AG	
1	2	3	4	5	6	7	8	9	10	11															1
	2	3	4	5	6	7		9		8	1	10	11												2
	2	3		5		7			10	8	1		11	4	6	9									3
	2	3	4		6			9	10	8	1	11			5	7									4
	2	3	4	5	6		8	9	10	11	1					7									5
	2	3	4		6		8	9	10	11	1					7	5								6
	2	3	4	5	6		8	9		10	1					7			11						7
	2	3	4	5	6		8	9		10	1					7			11						8
	2	3	4	5	6		8	9		10	1					7			11						9
	2	3	4	5	6			9		10	1	8				7			11						10
	2	3	4	5	6			9	10	11	1	8				7									11
	2	3		5	6			9		8	1	10		4		7			11						12
	2	3		5	6		8	9		4	1	10				7			11						13
	2	3	6	5			8	9		4	1	10				7			11						14
	2	3		5	6		8	9		4	1	10				7			11						15
	2	3	4	5	6		8	9			1	10				7			11						16
1		3	4	5	6		8	9		10						7			11	2					17
	2			5	6			9	8	4	1	10				7			11	3					18
	2		4	5	6			9	8		1	10				7			11	3					19
	2		4	5	6			9	8		1	10				7			11	3					20
	2		4	5	6			9	8		1	10				7			11	3					21
		3	4		6		10		8							9			11	2	1	5	7		22
	2		4		6		9	10	8							7		5	11	3	1				23
	2		4		6		9	10	8							7		5	11	3	1				24
	2			5	6			9	8	4						7			11	3	1		10		25
	2			5	6		8	9		4		10				7			11	3	1				26
	2			5	6		8	9		4		10				7			11	3	1				27
	2			5	6			9	8	4		10				7			11	3	1				28
		3	4		6		9		8			10				7			11	2	1	5			29
	2	3	4	5	6		8	9		11		10				7					1				30
	2	3	4		6		8								10	9		7	11		1	5			31
	2	3		5	4			9		10		8			6	7			11		1				32
	2	3		5			8	9		4		10			6	7			11		1				33
	2	3	4	5				9		10		8			6	7			11		1				34
	2	3	4	5	6		8	9	10							7			11		1				35
	2	3	4		6		9					8			10	7			11		1	5			36
		3		5	6		8			4		10							11	2	1		7	9	37
	2	3	4	5	6		9			10		8				7			11		1				38
	2	3	4		6		9			10		8				7			11		1	5			39
		3	4		6		8					10				9			11	2	1	5	7		40
	2	3	4		6		9			10		8						5	11		1		7		41
	2	3	4		6		8			11		10				9					1	5	7		42
2	37	32	30	30	38	3	28	26	19	33	19	28	7	2	5	33	6	19	14	15	21	6	8	1	
		1	1	1			6	20	1	5		9	1			18		9	4			3			

1 own-goal

Wilson A	Male CG	Hapgood EA	Crayston WJ	Roberts H	Copping W	Hulme JHA	Bowden ER	Drake EJ	James A	Bastin CS	Swindin GH	Davidson RT	Beasley AE	Cartwright S	John RF	Kirchen AJ	Sidey NW	Milne JV	Compton DCS	Compton LH	Boulton FP	Joy B	Nelson D	Biggs AG	
	2			5	6			9	8	4		10				7			11	3	1				3
	2			5	6			9	8	4		10				7			11	3	1				4
	2	3	4	5	6		8	9	10	11						7					1				5
	2	3	4	5	6		8		10	11						9					1		7		6
	4	2	2	4	4		2	3	4	4		2				4			4	3	2		4		
		1						7		3		2				4									

1 own-goal

1937-38

Manager: G.Allison

1	Aug	28	(a)	Everton	W	4-1	Drake 3, Bastin	53,856
2	Sep	1	(h)	Huddersfield T	W	3-1	Drake, Crayston, Bastin	32,758
3		4	(h)	Wolves	W	5-0	Drake 2, Crayston, Hulme, Bastin (pen)	67,311
4		8	(a)	Huddersfield T	L	1-2	Bowden	28,405
5		11	(a)	Leicester C	D	1-1	Drake	39,106
6		15	(a)	Bolton A	L	0-1		39,750
7		18	(h)	Sunderland	W	4-1	Milne, Drake, Hulme, Davidson	65,635
8		25	(a)	Derby C	L	0-2		33,101
9	Oct	2	(h)	Manchester C	W	2-1	Milne, Kirchen	68,353
10		9	(a)	Chelsea	D	2-2	Kirchen 2	75,952
11		16	(h)	Portsmouth	D	1-1	Hunt	45,150
12		23	(a)	Stoke C	D	1-1	Davideson	35,684
13		30	(h)	Middlesbrough	L	1-2	Milne	39,066
14	Nov	6	(a)	Grimsby T	L	1-2	L.Jones	20,244
15		13	(h)	West Brom A	D	1-1	L.Compton	34,324
16		20	(a)	Charlton A	W	3-0	Bastin, Drake, Ford (og)	55,078
17		27	(h)	Leeds U	W	4-1	Drake 2, Bastin (pen), Kirchen	34,350
18	Dec	4	(a)	Birmingham	W	2-1	Kirchen, Cartwright	18,440
19		11	(h)	Preston NE	W	2-0	Bastin Milne	35,679
20		18	(a)	Liverpool	L	0-2		32,093
21		25	(a)	Blackpool	L	1-2	Bastin (pen)	23,229
22		27	(h)	Blackpool	W	2-1	Bastin, Cartwright	54,163
23	Jan	1	(h)	Everton	W	2-1	Lewis, Hunt	36,953
24		15	(a)	Wolves	L	1-3	Drake	39,383
25		29	(a)	Sunderland	D	1-1	Hunt	42,638
26	Feb	2	(h)	Leicester C	W	3-1	Drake, Bastin, L.Jones	23,839
27		5	(h)	Derby C	W	3-0	Crayston 2, Lewis	47,263
28		16	(a)	Manchester C	W	2-1	Drake, D.Compton	34,299
29		19	(h)	Chelsea	W	2-0	Griffiths, Drake	49,573
30		26	(a)	Portsmouth	D	0-0		43,991
31	Mar	5	(h)	Stoke C	W	4-0	Carr, Griffiths 2, Drake	35,296
32		12	(a)	Middlesbrough	L	1-2	Bastin	46,747
33		19	(h)	Grimsby T	W	5-1	Bastin 2 (1 pen), Griffiths 2, L.Jones	40,701
34		26	(a)	West Brom A	D	0-0		33,954
35	Apr	2	(a)	Charlton A	D	2-2	Drake, Carr	52,858
36		9	(a)	Leeds U	W	1-0	Bremner	29,365
37		15	(h)	Brentford	L	0-2		51,299
38		16	(h)	Birmingham	D	0-0		35,161
39		18	(h)	Brentford	L	0-3		34,601
40		23	(a)	Preston NE	W	3-1	Carr 2, Bastin	42,684
41		30	(h)	Liverpool	W	1-0	Carr	34,703
42	May	7	(h)	Bolton W	W	5-0	Bastin 2 , Carr 2, Kirchen	40,500

FINAL LEAGUE POSITION: 1st in Division One

Appearances
Goals

FA Cup

3	Jan	8	(h)	Bolton W	W	3-1	Bastin 2, Kirchen	64,016
4		22	(a)	Wolves	W	2-1	Kirchen, Drake	61,267
5	Feb	12	(h)	Preston NE	L	0-1		72,121

Appearances
Goals

Wilson A	Male CG	Hapgood EA	Crayston WJ	Roberts H	Copping W	Kirchen AJ	Bowden ER	Drake EJ	Bastin CS	Milne JV	Hulme JHA	Boulton FP	Compton DCS	Compton LH	Biggs AG	Davidson RT	Hunt GS	Collett E	Joy B	Jones LJ	Cartwright S	Sidey NW	Lewis R	Swindin GH	Griffiths WM	Carr EM	Drury GB	Bremner GH	#
1	2	3	4	5	6	7	8	9	10	11																			1
1	2	3	4	5	6		8	9	10	11	7																		2
1	2	3	4	5	6		8	9	10	11	7																		3
1	2	3	4	5	6		8	9	10	11	7																		4
	2	3	4	5	6		8	9	10	7		1	11																5
		3	4	5	6		8	9	10	7		1	2	11															6
	2	3	4	5	6		9	8	11	7	1			10															7
1	2	3	4	5	6		9	8	11	7				10															8
1		3	4	5	6	7		8	11				2	10	9														9
		3	4	5	6	7		8	10	11		1	2		9														10
		3	4	5	6	7		8	10	11		1	2		9														11
1		3		5		7	8	4	11				2	10	9	6													12
1		3	4	5	6		9	8	11	7			2	10															13
1		3	4		6			10	7				11	2			9		5	8									14
1		3	4		6			9		7			11	2			8		5	10									15
	2	3	4		6	7		9	11			1					8		5	10									16
	2	3	4		6	7		9	11			1					8		5	10									17
	2	3				7		9	11			1			6	4	8		5	10									18
	2	3			6			9	11	7		1				4	8		5	10									19
	2	3			6			9	11	7		1				4	8		5	10									20
	2	3	4		6	7		9	11			1					8		5	10									21
	2	3			6	7		9	11			1				4	8		5	10									22
	2	3			6	7			11			1					8			10	4	5	9						23
	2	3	4		6	7		9				1	11				8		5	10									24
	2	3	4		6	7			11			1					8		5	10		9							25
	2	3	4		6			9	11								8		5	10				1		7			26
	2	3	4		6				11								8		5	10			9	1		7			27
	2	3	4		6	7		9	11										5	8				1			10		28
	2	3	4		6			9	11										5	8				1		7	10		29
	2	3	4		6			9	11					10					5	8				1		7			30
	2	3	4					9	11									6	5	8				1		7	10		31
	2	3	4		6			9	11										5					1	9	7	10		32
	2	3	4		6			9	11								8		5					1		7	10		33
	2	3	4		6			9	11									4	5	8				1			10		34
	2	3			6			9	11									4	5	8				1		7	10		35
	2		4										11	3				6	5	8				1	9	10	7		36
	2	3			6			9	11									4	5	8				1		7	10		37
	2	3			6	7			11									4	5				9	1		8	10		38
	2	3			6	7		9	10				11					4	5					1		8			39
	2	3	4		6	7			11										5	8				1	9		10		40
	2	3	4		6	7			11										5	8				1	9		10		41
	2	3			6	7			11									4	5					1	9		10	8	42
10	34	41	31	13	38	19	10	27	38	16	7	15	7	9	2	5	18	5	26	28	6	3	4	17	9	11	11	2	
			4			6	1	17	15	4	2		1	1		2	3		3	2			2			5	7	1	

I own-goal

Wilson A	Male CG	Hapgood EA	Crayston WJ	Roberts H	Copping W	Kirchen AJ	Bowden ER	Drake EJ	Bastin CS	Milne JV	Hulme JHA	Boulton FP	Compton DCS	Compton LH	Biggs AG	Davidson RT	Hunt GS	Collett E	Joy B	Jones LJ	Cartwright S	Sidey NW	Lewis R	Swindin GH	Griffiths WM	Carr EM	Drury GB	Bremner GH	#
	2	3	4		6	7		9	11			1					8		5	10									3
	2	3	4		6	7		9	11			1					8		5	10									4
	2	3	4		6	7		9	11								8		5	10				1					5
	3	3	3		3	3		3	3			2					3		3	3				1					
								2									1		2										

1938-39

Manager: G.Allison

1	Aug	27	(h)	Portsmouth	W 2-0 B.Jones, Rochford (og)	54,940
2	Sep	3	(a)	Huddersfield T	D 1-1 B.Jones	26,126
3		8	(a)	Brentford	L 0-1	38,535
4		10	(h)	Everton	L 1-2 B.Jones	64,555
5		14	(h)	Derby C	L 1-2 Drake	25,756
6		17	(a)	Wolves	W 1-0 Cumner	45,364
7		24	(h)	Aston Villa	D 0-0	66,456
8	Oct	1	(a)	Sunderland	D 0-0	51,042
9		8	(h)	Grimsby T	W 2-0 Bremner, Kirchen	39,174
10		15	(a)	Chelsea	L 2-4 Cumner, Kirchen	65,443
11		22	(h)	Preston NE	W 1-0 A.Beattie (og)	40,296
12		29	(a)	Bolton W	D 1-1 B.Jones	46,611
13	Nov	5	(h)	Leeds U	L 2-3 Bastin, Drake	39,092
14		12	(a)	Liverpool	D 2-2 Drake, Kirchen	42,540
15		19	(h)	Leicester C	D 0-0	36,407
16		26	(a)	Middlesbrough	D 1-1 Drury	29,147
17	Dec	3	(h)	Birmingham	W 3-1 Drake, Crayston, Nelson	33,710
18		10	(a)	Manchester U	L 0-1	42,008
19		17	(h)	Stoke C	W 4-1 Lewis 2, Bastin, Drury	30,006
20		24	(a)	Portsmouth	D 0-0	21,344
21		27	(a)	Charlton A	L 0-1	51,479
22		31	(h)	Huddersfield T	W 1-0 Drake	34,146
23	Jan	14	(a)	Everton	L 0-2	47,178
24		21	(h)	Charlton A	W 2-0 Crayston, Lewis	39,702
25		28	(a)	Aston Villa	W 3-1 Lewis 2, Kirchen	57,453
26	Feb	1	(h)	Wolves	D 0-0	33,103
27		4	(h)	Sunderland	W 2-0 Bastin, Lewis	45,875
28		18	(h)	Chelsea	W 1-0 Bremner	54,510
29		21	(a)	Grimsby T	L 1-2 Kirchen	10,845
30		25	(a)	Preston NE	L 1-2 Lewis	29,678
31	Mar	4	(h)	Bolton W	W 3-1 Drake 2, Winter (og)	29,814
32		11	(a)	Leeds U	L 2-4 Drake, L.Compton (pen)	22,160
33		18	(h)	Liverpool	W 2-0 Kirchen, Drake	31,495
34		25	(a)	Leicester C	W 2-0 Kirchen, Drake	22,565
35	Apr	1	(h)	Middlesbrough	L 1-2 Bremner	34,669
36		7	(a)	Blackpool	L 0-1	31,497
37		8	(a)	Birmingham	W 2-1 Kirchen, Drury	33,250
38		10	(h)	Blackpool	W 2-1 Drake, L.Compton (pen)	30,760
39		15	(h)	Manchester U	W 2-1 Drake, Crayston	25,741
40		22	(a)	Stoke C	L 0-1	26,039
41		29	(a)	Derby C	W 2-1 Farr, Drake	10,186
42	May	6	(h)	Brentford	W 2-0 Kirchen, Drake	30,928

FINAL LEAGUE POSITION: 5th in Division One

Appearances
Goals

FA Cup

3	Jan	7	(a)	Chelsea	L 1-2 Bastin	58,095

Appearances
Goals

218

Swindin GH	Male CG	Hapgood EA	Crayston WJ	Joy B	Copping W	Kirchen AJ	Jones LJ	Drake EJ	Jones B	Bastin CS	Nelson D	Carr EM	Bremner GH	Cumner RH	Compton LH	Collett E	Walsh W	Drury GB	Wilson A	Lewis R	Pryde D	Fields AG	Cartwright S	Pugh SJ	Curtis GF	Marks GW	Farr AM	Compton DCS	
1	2	3	4	5	6	7	8	9	10	11																			1
1	2	3	4	5	6	7	8	9	10	11																			2
1	2	3	4	5	6	7	8	9	10	11																			3
1	2	3	4	5	6		8		10	11	7	9																	4
1	2	3		5	6		4	9	10	11	7		8																5
1	2	3	4	5	6			9	10		7		8		11														6
1	2	3	4	5	6	7		9	10				8		11														7
1	2	3	4	5	6		8	9	10		7				11														8
1	2	3		5	6	7	4	9	10				8		11														9
1	2	3	4	5	6	7		9	10				8		11														10
1	2		4	5				9		11			8		3	6		7		10									11
1	2	3		5			4	9		11			8			6		7		10									12
1	2			5	6		4	9		11			8		3			7		10									13
1	2	3	4	5	6	7		9	10				8		11														14
1	2	3	4	5	6	7		9	10				8		11														15
1		3	4	5	6	7	8	9		11					2			10											16
1		3	4	5	6		8	9		11	7				2			10											17
1		3	4	5	6		8	9					7		11	2		10											18
		3	4	5	6		8			11	7				2			10	1	9									19
		3	4	5	6		8			11	7				2			10	1	9									20
		3	4	5	6		8			11	7				2			10	1	9									21
	2	3	4	5	6						7		8		11			10	1	9									22
	2	3	4	5	6	7							8		11			10	1	9									23
	2	3	4	5	6								8	7	11			10	1	9									24
	2	3	4	5	6								8	7	11			10	1	9									25
	2	3	4	5									8	7	11	6		10	1	9									26
	2	3		5		7							8		11	6		10	1	9			4						27
	2	3		5	6								8	7	11			10	1	9			4						28
	2	3		5	6								8	7	11			10	1	9			4						29
	2	3		5	6								8	7	11			10	1	9			4						30
		3	4	5		7		9	10	11					2	6		8	1										31
		3	4	5		7		9	10	11					2	6		8	1										32
		3	4	5		7		9	10	11					2	6		8	1										33
		3	4	5		7		9	10	11			8		2	6			1										34
		3	4	5		7		9	10	11			8		2	6			1										35
		3	4			7		9	10	11			8		2				1					5	6				36
	2	3	4			7				11			8					10	1	9				5	6				37
1	2		4			7				11			8		3			10		9				5	6				38
1	2		4	5		7				11			8		3			10		9					6				39
1	2	3	4	5		7	8								11	6		10		9									40
		3	4	5		7									2	6		10		9					8	1	11		41
		3	4	5		7									2	6		10		9					8	1		11	42
21	28	38	34	39	26	27	18	38	30	23	9	1	13	12	18	9	3	23	19	15	4	3	3	1	2	2	2	1	
			3			9		14	4	3	1		3	2	2			3		7					1				

3 own-goals

Swindin GH	Male CG	Hapgood EA	Crayston WJ	Joy B	Copping W	Kirchen AJ	Jones LJ	Drake EJ	Jones B	Bastin CS	Nelson D	Carr EM	Bremner GH	Cumner RH	Compton LH	Collett E	Walsh W	Drury GB	Wilson A	Lewis R	Pryde D	Fields AG	Cartwright S	Pugh SJ	Curtis GF	Marks GW	Farr AM	Compton DCS	
	2	3	4	5	6		7	8		11								10	1	9									3
	1	1	1	1	1		1	1		1								1	1	1									
										1																			

1946-47

Manager: G.Allison

1	Aug	31	(a)	Wolves	L 1-6	Lewis	50,845
2	Sep	4	(h)	Blackburn R	L 1-3	Lewis	28,700
3		7	(h)	Sunderland	D 2-2	Lewis 2	60,000
4		11	(a)	Everton	L 2-3	Lewis 2	40,000
5		14	(a)	Aston Villa	W 2-0	Lewis, O'Flanagan	40,000
6		17	(a)	Blackburn R	W 2-1	Lewis 2	28,000
7		21	(h)	Derby C	L 0-1		63,000
8		28	(a)	Manchester U	L 2-5	Lewis, McPherson	62,718
9	Oct	5	(a)	Blackpool	L 1-2	Logie	24,039
10		12	(h)	Brentford	D 2-2	Lewis, Logie	45,000
11		19	(h)	Stoke C	W 1-0	O'Flanagan	62,000
12		26	(a)	Chelsea	L 1-2	Lewis	56,568
13	Nov	2	(h)	Sheffield U	L 2-3	Lewis, Logie	45,000
14		9	(a)	Preston NE	L 0-2		29,971
15		16	(h)	Leeds U	W 4-2	Lewis 2 (1 pen), Logie, McPherson	40,000
16		23	(a)	Liverpool	L 2-4	Lewis, Logie	51,435
17		30	(h)	Bolton W	D 2-2	Lewis (pen), O'Flanagan	47,000
18	Dec	7	(a)	Middlesbrough	L 0-2		35,000
19		14	(h)	Charlton A	W 1-0	Rooke	45,000
20		21	(a)	Grimsby T	D 0-0		17,000
21		25	(h)	Portsmouth	W 2-1	Rooke, Logie	38,000
22		26	(a)	Portsmouth	W 2-0	Rooke 2	38,000
23		28	(h)	Wolves	D 1-1	Rooke	63,000
24	Jan	4	(a)	Sunderland	W 4-1	Rooke 2, Lewis 2	36,812
25		18	(h)	Aston Villa	L 0-2		61,000
26	Feb	1	(h)	Manchester U	W 6-2	Rooke 3, Rudkin, Logie, McPherson	38,000
27		8	(h)	Blackpool	D 1-1	Rooke	36,000
28		22	(a)	Stoke C	L 1-3	Rooke	30,000
29	Mar	1	(h)	Chelsea	L 1-2	Rudkin	57,000
30		15	(h)	Preston NE	W 4-1	Lewis 3, Rooke	50,000
31		22	(a)	Leeds U	D 1-1	Lewis	32,000
32	Apr	4	(h)	Huddersfield T	L 1-2	B.Jones	50,000
33		5	(a)	Bolton W	W 3-1	Rooke 2, Lewis	34,398
34		7	(a)	Huddersfield T	D 0-0		33,381
35		12	(h)	Middlesbrough	W 4-0	Rooke 4 (1 pen)	50,000
36		19	(a)	Charlton A	D 2-2	McPherson, Logie	55,000
37		26	(h)	Grimsby T	W 5-3	Lewis 4, D.Compton	50,000
38	May	10	(a)	Derby C	W 1-0	Rooke	19,153
39		24	(h)	Liverpool	L 1-2	McPherson	48,000
40		26	(a)	Brentford	W 1-0	Sloan	17,599
41		31	(h)	Everton	W 2-1	Rooke, Lewis	30,000
42	Jun	7	(a)	Sheffield U	L 1-2	McPherson	20,000

FINAL LEAGUE POSITION: 13th in Division One

Appearances
Goals

FA Cup

3	Jan	11	(a)	Chelsea	D 1-1	McPherson	70,195
R		15	(h)	Chelsea	D 1-1‡	Rooke	53,350
2R		20	(n*)	Chelsea	L 0-2		59,590

*Played at White Hart Lane, London.   ‡After extra-time.

Appearances
Goals

Player appearance grid (shirt numbers shown per match; column = player, row = match).

Swindin GH	Scott L	Male CG	Nelson D	Joy B	Curtis GF	McPherson IB	Sloan WJ	Lewis R	Logie JT	Bastin CS	Compton LH	Waller H	O'Flanagan Dr KP	Drury GB	Hodges CL	Smith A	Jones B	Collett E	Gudmundsson A	Barnes W	Grant C	Platt EH	Wade JS	Mercer J	Rooke RL	Morgan AS	Fields AG	Rudkin TW	Calverley A	Compton DCS	Mt
1	2	3	4	5	6	7	8	9	10	11																					1
1	2		4	3		8		9			5	6	7	10	11																2
1	2		4	3		8		9	10		5	6	7			11															3
1	2		7	3		8		9	10	4	5	6				11															4
1	2			3	10	7		9	6	4	5					11	8														5
1	2	11		3		7		9	6	4	5					8				10											6
1	2	11		3		7			6	4	5		9	8						10											7
1		2	11	3		7	8	9	6	4	5									10											8
1	2	4	7	3	10		9		8		5					11	6														9
1			2	10	7		9	8		5	4	11					6	3													10
1	2	4		3	10	7		9			5	6	11										8								11
1	2			7	3	10		9			5	4	11			6	8														12
1	2	4		3		7		9	8		5	6				11	10														13
1	2	4	11			10	7		8		5									6		3	9								14
	2					10	7	4	9	8	5		11							6		1		3							15
	2					10	7	4	9	8	5		11							6		1		3							16
	2					7	4	9	8		5		11				10			3		1		6							17
	2					7			8		5		11				10	6		3	9	1		4							18
1		2				7	4	8			5		11				10			3				6	9						19
1		2				7	4	8			5						10			3				6	9	11					20
1		2				7	4	8			5		11				10			3				6	9						21
1						10		4		8	2						7			3				6	9	11	5				22
1	2					7	4	8			5		11				10			3				6	9						23
1						7	4	8	11		2						10			3				6	9		5				24
1						7	4	8	10		2	6								3					9		5		11		25
1	2					7	4	8			5						10			3				6	9				11		26
1	2					10	7	4	8		5									3				6	9				11		27
1	2					7	4	8			5						10			3				6	9				11		28
1	2					7	4	8			5						10			3				6	9				11		29
1	2					7	4	9			5						10			3				6	8				11		30
1	2					7	4	9			5						10			3				6	8				11		31
1	2					7	4	9			5						10			3				6	8				11		32
1	2					7	4	9	8		5									3				6	10				11		33
1	2						4	9	8		5						7			3				6	10				11		34
1		2					4	9	8		5						7			3				6	10				11		35
1	2					7	4	8			5						10			3				6	9				11		36
1	2					7	4	9	8		5									3				6	10					11	37
1	2					7	4	9	8											3				6	10		5		11		38
1		2				7	4	9	8											3				6	10		5		11		39
1		2				7	4	8									10			3				6	9		5		11		40
1	2					7	4	9	8								11			3				6	10		5				41
1	2					7	4	9	8								11			3				6	10		5				42
38	**28**	**15**	**10**	**13**	**11**	**37**	**30**	**28**	**35**	**6**	**36**	**8**	**14**	**4**	**2**	**3**	**26**	**6**	**2**	**26**	**2**	**4**	**2**	**25**	**24**	**2**	**8**	**5**	**11**	**1**	—
						6	1	29	8		3						1								21	2				1	—

FA Cup:

Swindin GH	Scott L	Male CG	Nelson D	Joy B	Curtis GF	McPherson IB	Sloan WJ	Lewis R	Logie JT	Bastin CS	Compton LH	Waller H	O'Flanagan Dr KP	Drury GB	Hodges CL	Smith A	Jones B	Collett E	Gudmundsson A	Barnes W	Grant C	Platt EH	Wade JS	Mercer J	Rooke RL	Morgan AS	Fields AG	Rudkin TW	Calverley A	Compton DCS	Mt
1	2					7	4	8	11		5						10			3				6	9						3
1		2			11	7	4	8	10		5									3				6	9						R
1		2				7	4	8	11		5						10			3				6	9						2R
3	**1**	**2**			**1**	**3**	**3**	**3**	**3**		**3**						**2**			**3**				**3**	**3**						—
								1																	1						—

1947-48

Manager: T.Whittaker

1	Aug	23	(h)	Sunderland	W 3-1	McPherson, Logie, Rooke	60,000
2		27	(a)	Charlton A	W 4-2	McPherson, Roper, Lewis, Logie	60,000
3		30	(a)	Sheffield U	W 2-1	Rooke, Roper	39,130
4	Sep	3	(h)	Charlton A	W 6-0	Lewis 4, Rooke 2	58,000
5		6	(h)	Manchester U	W 2-1	Rooke, Lewis	62,000
6		10	(h)	Bolton W	W 2-0	McPherson, Rooke (pen)	50,000
7		13	(a)	Preston NE	D 0-0		40,061
8		20	(h)	Stoke C	W 3-0	Logie, McPherson 2	62,000
9		27	(a)	Burnley	W 1-0	Lewis	47,258
10	Oct	4	(h)	Portsmouth	D 0-0		62,000
11		11	(h)	Aston Villa	W 1-0	Rooke	61,000
12		18	(a)	Wolves	D 1-1	Rooke (pen)	55,998
13		25	(h)	Everton	D 1-1	Lewis	59,000
14	Nov	1	(a)	Chelsea	D 0-0		67,277
15		8	(h)	Blackpool	W 2-1	Rooke (pen), Roper	62,000
16		15	(a)	Blackburn R	W 1-0	Rooke	37,423
17		22	(h)	Huddersfield T	W 2-0	Rooke, Logie	50,000
18		29	(a)	Derby C	L 0-1		35,605
19	Dec	6	(h)	Manchester C	D 1-1	Rooke (pen)	43,000
20		13	(a)	Grimsby T	W 4-0	Rooke 2, Logie, Roper	20,000
21		20	(a)	Sunderland	D 1-1	B.Jones	58,391
22		25	(a)	Liverpool	W 3-1	Rooke 2, Roper	53,604
23		27	(h)	Liverpool	L 1-2	Lewis	59,000
24	Jan	1	(a)	Bolton W	W 1-0	Lewis	30,028
25		3	(h)	Sheffield U	W 3-2	Rooke 2, Lewis	50,000
26		17	(a)	Manchester U	D 1-1	Lewis	81,962
27		31	(h)	Preston NE	W 3-0	Lewis 2, Rooke	62,000
28	Feb	7	(a)	Stoke C	D 0-0		41,000
29		14	(h)	Burnley	W 3-0	Rooke 2, Roper	62,000
30		28	(a)	Aston Villa	L 2-4	Rooke, Moss (og)	65,690
31	Mar	6	(h)	Wolves	W 5-2	Rooke 2, Forbes, Roper, Logie	58,000
32		13	(a)	Everton	W 2-0	D.Compton 2	64,059
33		20	(h)	Chelsea	L 0-2		59,000
34		26	(h)	Middlesbrough	W 7-0	Rooke 3, D.Compton 2, Roper, Robinson (og)	60,000
35		27	(a)	Blackpool	L 0-3		32,678
36		29	(a)	Middlesbrough	D 1-1	Rooke	38,469
37	Apr	3	(h)	Blackburn R	W 2-0	Logie, Rooke	48,000
38		10	(a)	Huddersfield T	D 1-1	Roper	38,110
39		17	(h)	Derby C	L 1-2	Roper	52,000
40		21	(a)	Portsmouth	D 0-0		42,813
41		24	(a)	Manchester C	D 0-0		20,782
42	May	1	(h)	Grimsby T	W 8-0	Rooke 4, D.Compton 2, Forbes, Logie (pen)	35,000

FINAL LEAGUE POSITION: 1st in Division One

Appearances
Goals

FA Cup

3	Jan	10	(h)	Bradford	L 0-1		47,738

Appearances
Goals

222

Swindin GH	Scott L	Barnes W	Macaulay AR	Fields AG	Mercer J	Roper DGB	Logie JT	Lewis R	Rooke RL	McPherson IB	Compton LH	Sloan WJ	Male CG	Jones B	Wade JS	Compton DCS	Forbes AR	Smith L	No.
1	2	3	4	5	6	7	8	9	10	11									1
1	2	3	4	5	6	7	8	9	10	11									2
1	2	3	4	5	6	7	8	9	10	11									3
1	2	3	4	5	6	7	8	9	10	11									4
1	2	3	4	5	6	7	8	9	10	11									5
1	2	3	4	5	6	7	8	9	10	11									6
1	2	3	4		6	7	8		10	11	5	9							7
1		3	4		6	7	8		9	11	5		2	10					8
1	2	3	4			7	8	9	10	11	5	6							9
1	2	3				7	8	9	10	11	5	6	4						10
1	2	3	4		6	7	8		9	11	5			10					11
1			4		6	7	8	9	10	11	5		2		3				12
1	2	3	4		6	7	8	9	10	11	5								13
1	2	3	4		6	7	8	9	10	11	5								14
1	2	3	4		6	7	10	8	9	11	5								15
1	2	3	4		6	7	10	8	9	11	5								16
1	2	3	4		6	7	10	8	9	11	5								17
1	2	3	4		6	7	10	8	9	11	5								18
1	2	3	4		6	7	10	8	9	11	5								19
1	2	3	4		6	7	8		9	11	5			10					20
1	2	3	4		6	7	8		9	11	5			10					21
1	2		4		6	7	8	9	10	11	5				3				22
1	2		4		6	7	8	9	10	11	5				3				23
1		3	4		6	7	8	9	10	11	5		2						24
1		3	4		6	7	8	9	10	11	5		2						25
1	2	3	4		6	7	10	8	9	11	5								26
1	2	3	4		6	7	8	10	9	11	5								27
1	2	3	4		6	7	8	10	9	11	5								28
1	2	3	4		6	7	8		9		5			10		11			29
1	2	3	4		6	7		8	9		5			10		11			30
1	2	3	4		6	7	8		9		5					11	10		31
1	2	3	4		6		8	7	9		5					11	10		32
1	2	3	4		6	7	8		9		5					11	10		33
1	2	3	4		6	7	8		9		5					11	10		34
1	2	3	4		6	8	10	9	7		5					11			35
1	2	3	4		6	7	8		9		5					11	10		36
1	2	3	4		6	7	8		9		5					11	10		37
1		3			6	7	8	10	9		5		2			11	4		38
1	2	3	4		6	7	8		9		5					11	10		39
1	2	3	4		6	7			9		5		8			11	10		40
1		3	4		6	7	8		9		5		2			11	10		41
1		3	4		6	7	8		9				2			11	10	5	42
42	**39**	**35**	**40**	**6**	**40**	**40**	**39**	**28**	**42**	**29**	**35**	**3**	**8**	**7**	**3**	**14**	**11**	**1**	
						10	8	14	33	5				1		6	2		

2 own-goals

Swindin GH	Scott L	Barnes W	Macaulay AR	Fields AG	Mercer J	Roper DGB	Logie JT	Lewis R	Rooke RL	McPherson IB	Compton LH	Sloan WJ	Male CG	Jones B	Wade JS	Compton DCS	Forbes AR	Smith L	No.
1		3	4		6	7	8	9	10	11	5		2						3
1	1	1	1		1	1	1	1	1	1	1		1						

1948-49

Manager: T.Whittaker

1	Aug	21	(a)	Huddersfield T	D	1-1	Rooke	30,620
2		25	(h)	Stoke C	W	3-0	Logie, Forbes, Roper	47,000
3		28	(h)	Manchester U	L	0-1		62,000
4		30	(a)	Stoke C	L	0-1		39,534
5	Sep	4	(a)	Sheffield U	D	1-1	Cox (og)	38,111
6		8	(h)	Liverpool	D	1-1	Rooke	48,000
7		11	(h)	Aston Villa	W	3-1	Rooke 2 (pens), Roper	58,000
8		15	(a)	Liverpool	W	1-0	Lewis	46,714
9		18	(a)	Sunderland	D	1-1	B.Jones	64,436
10		25	(h)	Wolves	W	3-1	Lewis 2, D.Compton	59,000
11	Oct	2	(a)	Bolton W	L	0-1		43,110
12		9	(h)	Burnley	W	3-1	Lewis 2, Logie	57,000
13		16	(a)	Preston NE	D	1-1	Rooke	31,443
14		23	(h)	Everton	W	5-0	Rooke 2, Logie 2, Forbes	53,000
15		30	(a)	Chelsea	W	1-0	Rooke (pen)	56,476
16	Nov	6	(h)	Birmingham C	W	2-0	Forbes, Lewis	62,000
17		13	(a)	Middlesbrough	W	1-0	Lewis	35,727
18		20	(h)	Newcastle U	L	0-1		62,000
19		27	(a)	Portsmouth	L	1-4	Lewis (pen)	42,687
20	Dec	4	(h)	Manchester C	D	1-1	Rooke	45,000
21		11	(a)	Charlton A	L	3-4	Roper, McPherson, Lewis	52,549
22		18	(h)	Huddersfield T	W	3-0	Rooke 3	40,000
23		25	(h)	Derby C	D	3-3	Logie, Rooke, McPherson	43,000
24		27	(a)	Derby C	L	1-2	Lewis	33,378
25	Jan	1	(a)	Manchester U	L	0-2		61,288
26		15	(h)	Sheffield U	W	5-3	Logie 2, Lishman, Rooke, McPherson	45,000
27		22	(a)	Aston Villa	L	0-1		65,000
28	Feb	5	(h)	Sunderland	W	5-0	Lewis, Macaulay, Lishman, Vallance, McPherson	55,000
29		19	(a)	Wolves	W	3-1	Lewis 2, Logie	54,536
30		26	(h)	Bolton W	W	5-0	Logie 2, Lewis, Vallance, McPherson	53,000
31	Mar	5	(a)	Burnley	D	1-1	Lishman	20,303
32		12	(h)	Preston NE	D	0-0		59,000
33		19	(a)	Newcastle U	L	2-3	Lewis, Forbes (pen)	60,000
34	Apr	2	(a)	Birmingham C	D	1-1	Lishman	38,503
35		9	(h)	Middlesbrough	D	1-1	Lishman	55,000
36		15	(a)	Blackpool	D	1-1	Lewis	28,718
37		16	(a)	Everton	D	0-0		56,987
38		18	(h)	Blackpool	W	2-0	Lishman 2	47,000
39		23	(h)	Chelsea	L	1-2	D.Compton	58,000
40		27	(a)	Manchester C	W	3-0	Lishman 2, Roper	27,955
41	May	4	(h)	Portsmouth	W	3-2	Lishman 2, Logie	60,000
42		7	(h)	Charlton A	W	2-0	Roper, Lishman	50,000

FINAL LEAGUE POSITION: 5th in Division One

Appearances
Goals

FA Cup

3	Jan	8	(h)	Tottenham H	W	3-0	McPherson, Roper, Lishman	47,314
4		29	(a)	Derby C	L	0-1		31,073

Appearances
Goals

224

Appearances and goals grid (figures in cells are shirt numbers worn)

Swindin GH	Barnes W	Smith L	Macaulay AR	Fields AG	Mercer J	Roper DGB	Logie JT	Rooke RL	Forbes AR	McPherson IB	Compton LH	Lishman DJ	Vallance THW	Scott L	Jones B	Compton DCS	Lewis R	Platt EH	Daniel RW	Match
1	2	3	4	5	6	7	8	9	10	11										1
1	2	3	4		6	7	8	9	10	11	5									2
1	2	3	4		6	7	8	9	10	11	5									3
1	2	3	4		6	7	8	9	10	11	5									4
1	2	3	4		6	7	8	9			5	10	11							5
1	2	3	4		6	7	8	9			5	10	11							6
1	3		4		6	7		9			5	10		2	8	11				7
1	3		4			7		9			5	10		2	6	11	8			8
1	3		4		6	7					5	10		2	8	11	9			9
1	2	3	8		6	7			4		5	10				11	9			10
1	3		8		6	11			4	7	5			2	10		9			11
1	2	3	4		6	7	8		10		5				11	9				12
1	3		4		6	7	8	9	10		5			2	11					13
1	3		4		6	7	8	9	10	11	5			2						14
1	3		4		6	7	8	9	10	11	5			2						15
1	3		4		6	7	8		10	11	5			2		9				16
1	2	3	4		6	7	8		10	11	5					9				17
1	2	3	4		6	7	8	11	10		5					9				18
1	2	3	4		6	7	8		10	11	5					9				19
1	2	3	4		6	7	8	9	10	11	5									20
	2	3	4		6	7	8	9		11	5	10						1		21
1	2	3	4		6	7	8	9		11	5	10								22
1	2	3	4		6	7	8	9		11	5	10								23
1	2	3	4		6	7	8	9		11	5	10								24
1	2	3	4		6	7		9		11	5	10			8					25
1	2	3	4		6	7	8	9		11	5	10								26
1	2	3	4		6	7	8	9		11	5	10								27
	2	3	4		6		8	7			5	10	11			9		1		28
	2	3	4		6		8	7			5	10	11			9		1		29
	2	3	4			8	6	7			5	10	11			9		1		30
	2	3	4			8	6	7			5	10	11			9		1		31
	3		4		6		8	7			5	10	11	2		9		1		32
	3		4			8	6	7			5	10	11	2		9		1		33
	3		4			8	6	7			5	10	11	2		9		1		34
	3		4			8	6	7			5	10	11	2		9		1		35
	2	3	4			8	6	7			5	10	11			9		1		36
1	2	3	4				11	9	6	7	5	10			8					37
1	2	3	4			8	6	7			5	10	11			9				38
1	2	3	4			8	6	7			5	10	11			9				39
1	2	3	4		6	9	8	7			5	10	11							40
1	2	3	4				9	8	6	7	5	10	11							41
1	2	3	4				9	8	6	7		10	11						5	42
32	40	32	39	1	33	31	35	22	25	33	40	23	14	12	8	6	25	10	1	
			1		5	11	14	4	5		12	2			1	2	16			

1 own-goal

Swindin GH	Barnes W	Smith L	Macaulay AR	Fields AG	Mercer J	Roper DGB	Logie JT	Rooke RL	Forbes AR	McPherson IB	Compton LH	Lishman DJ	Vallance THW	Scott L	Jones B	Compton DCS	Lewis R	Platt EH	Daniel RW	Match
1	2	3	4		6	7	8	9		11	5	10								3
1	2	3	4	5		7	8		6	11		10				9				4
2	2	2	2	1	2	2	2	1	1	2	1	2				1				
						1	1					1								

1949-50

Manager: T.Whittaker

					Result	Scorers	Attendance
1	Aug	20	(h)	Burnley	L 0-1		50,000
2		24	(a)	Chelsea	W 2-1	Lishman, Goring	63,124
3		27	(a)	Sunderland	L 2-4	Logie, Hudgell (og)	56,500
4		31	(h)	Chelsea	L 2-3	Goring 2	56,000
5	Sep	3	(h)	Liverpool	L 1-2	Lishman	56,000
6		7	(a)	West Brom A	W 2-1	Lewis, Barnes (pen)	43,000
7		10	(a)	Huddersfield T	D 2-2	Lewis, Goring	20,882
8		14	(h)	West Brom A	W 4-1	Lewis, Goring, Roper, Barnes (pen)	44,000
9		17	(a)	Bolton W	D 2-2	Lewis, Barnes (pen)	35,000
10		24	(h)	Birmingham C	W 4-2	Goring 2, Logie, Lewis	53,000
11	Oct	1	(a)	Derby C	W 2-1	Lewis 2	29,000
12		8	(h)	Everton	W 5-2	Goring 2, Lewis 2, Roper	56,000
13		15	(a)	Middlesbrough	D 1-1	Roper	43,000
14		22	(h)	Blackpool	W 1-0	Lewis	65,000
15		29	(a)	Newcastle U	W 3-0	Roper 3	55,000
16	Nov	5	(h)	Fulham	W 2-1	McPherson, Barnes (pen)	43,000
17		12	(a)	Manchester C	W 2-0	Logie, Cox	28,288
18		19	(h)	Charlton A	L 2-3	Logie, Lewis	60,000
19		26	(a)	Aston Villa	D 1-1	Lewis	45,000
20	Dec	3	(h)	Wolves	D 1-1	Roper	60,000
21		10	(a)	Portsmouth	L 1-2	Goring	39,537
22		17	(a)	Burnley	D 0-0		25,661
23		24	(h)	Sunderland	W 5-0	Lewis, Forbes, Goring, Logie, McPherson	45,000
24		26	(a)	Manchester U	L 0-2		53,928
25		27	(h)	Manchester U	D 0-0		65,000
26		31	(a)	Liverpool	L 0-2		55,020
27	Jan	14	(h)	Huddersfield T	W 1-0	Lewis	50,000
28		21	(h)	Bolton W	D 1-1	Lewis	49,000
29	Feb	4	(a)	Birmingham C	L 1-2	Goring	35,000
30		18	(h)	Derby C	W 1-0	Logie	67,000
31		25	(a)	Everton	W 1-0	Cox	43,632
32	Mar	8	(h)	Middlesbrough	D 1-1	Forbes (pen)	37,000
33		11	(a)	Charlton A	D 1-1	D.Compton	52,000
34		25	(a)	Fulham	D 2-2	Logie, Cox	40,000
35		29	(h)	Aston Villa	L 1-3	Lishman	27,000
36	Apr	1	(h)	Manchester C	W 4-1	Lewis 2, Lishman, Goring	42,000
37		8	(a)	Blackpool	L 1-2	Goring	32,000
38		10	(h)	Stoke C	W 6-0	Goring 2, Lishman 2, Barnes (pen), Franklin (og)	30,000
39		15	(h)	Newcastle U	W 4-2	Goring 3, Lewis	54,000
40		22	(a)	Wolves	L 0-3		53,082
41	May	3	(h)	Portsmouth	W 2-0	Goring 2	65,000
42		6	(a)	Stoke C	W 5-2	Lishman 3, Lewis, McPherson	18,000

FINAL LEAGUE POSITION: 6th in Division One

Appearances

Goals

FA Cup

					Result	Scorers	Attendance
3	Jan	7	(h)	Sheffield W	W 1-0	Lewis	54,193
4		28	(h)	Swansea T	W 2-1	Logie, Barnes (pen)	57,305
5	Feb	11	(h)	Burnley	W 2-0	Lewis, D.Compton	55,458
6	Mar	4	(h)	Leeds U	W 1-0	Lewis	62,573
SF		18	(n*)	Chelsea	D 2-2	Cox, L.Compton	67,752
R		22	(n*)	Chelsea	W 1-0†	Cox	66,482
F	Apr	29	(n‡)	Liverpool	W 2-0	Lewis 2	100,000

*Played at White Hart Lane, London. †After extra-time. ‡Played at Wembley Stadium.

Appearances

Goals

226

Swindin GH	Barnes W	Smith L	Mercer J	Daniel RW	Forbes AR	McPherson IB	Macaulay AR	Roper DGB	Lishman DJ	Vallance THW	Logie JT	Goring H	Scott L	Compton LH	Shaw A	Lewis R	Platt EH	Cox FJA	Wade JS	Compton DCS	Kelly N	
1	2	3	4	5	6	7	8	9	10	11												1
1	2	3		5	6	7	4	11	10		8	9										2
1	2	3		5	6	7	4	11	10		8	9										3
1		3	4			7		11	10		8	9	2	5	6							4
1		3	4		6	7		11	10		8	9	2	5								5
1	2	3	6			7		11			4	9		5	10	8						6
1	2	3	6			7		11			4	9		5	10	8						7
	2	3	6				4	11			10	9		5		8	1	7				8
	2	3	6			11	4				10	9		5		8	1	7				9
	2	3	6				4	11			10	9		5		8	1	7				10
	2	3	6				4	11			8	9		5		10	1	7				11
	2	3	6				4	11			8	9		5		10	1	7				12
		3	6			11	4	9			8			5		10	1	7	2			13
	2	3	6			11	4	9			8			5		10	1	7				14
	2	3	6	5		11	4	9			8					10	1	7				15
	2	3	6			11	4	9			8			5		10	1	7				16
	2	3	6			11	4	9			8			5		10	1	7				17
	2	3	6			11	4	9			8			5		10	1	7				18
	2	3	6		4	11		9			8			5		10	1	7				19
	2	3	6		4	11		9			8			5		10	1	7				20
	2	3	6		4			11			8	9		5		10	1	7				21
	2	3	6		4			11			8	9		5		10	1	7				22
	2	3	6		4	11					8	9		5		10	1	7				23
	2	3	6		4	11					8	9		5		10	1	7				24
1		3			6	11	4				8	9	2	5		10		7				25
1		3			6		4	11	10		8	9	2	5				7				26
1		3			6		4	11			8	9	2	5		10		7				27
1		3			6		4				8	9	2	5		10		7		11		28
1		3		5	6		4	11			8	9	2			10		7				29
1		3			6		4		7		8	9	2	5		10				11		30
1		3			6		4	9	10		8		2	5				7		11		31
1		3			6	7	4	9	10		8		2	5						11		32
1		3	6	5			4		10			9	2			8		7		11		33
1		3	6			11	4	9	10		8		2	5				7				34
	2	3	6			7	4		10		8			5			1	9		11		35
1	2	3	4						10			9		5	6	8		7		11		36
1	2	3	6				4		10			9		5		8		7		11		37
	2	3				7	4	11	10		8	9		5	6		1					38
1	2	3	6				4				8	9		5		10		7		11		39
1		3			6		4				8	9	2	5		10		7		11		40
1		3			6		4				8	9	2	5		10		7		11		41
1		3	6	5			4	11	10			9	2			8		7				42
23	38	31	35	6	23	27	24	27	14	1	34	29	15	35	5	31	19	32	1	11	1	
	5		2	3		7	9				7	21				19		3		1		

2 own-goals

Swindin GH	Barnes W	Smith L	Mercer J	Daniel RW	Forbes AR	McPherson IB	Macaulay AR	Roper DGB	Lishman DJ	Vallance THW	Logie JT	Goring H	Scott L	Compton LH	Shaw A	Lewis R	Platt EH	Cox FJA	Wade JS	Compton DCS	Kelly N	
1		3			6		4	11			8	9	2	5		10		7				3
1		3			6		4	11			8	9	2	5		10		7				4
1		3			6		4				8	9	2	5		10		7		11		5
1		3			6		4	9			8		2	5		10		7		11		6
1		3			6		4	11			8	9	2	5		10		7				SF
1		3			6		4				8	9	2	5		10		7		11		R
1		3			6		4				8	9	2	5		10		7		11		F
7	7				7		6	2	1	1	7	6	7	7		7		7		5		
	1								1			1		5		2		1				

227

1950-51

Manager: T.Whittaker

1	Aug	19	(a)	Burnley	W	1-0	Roper	32,957
2		23	(h)	Chelsea	D	0-0		63,000
3		26	(h)	Tottenham H	D	2-2	Roper, Barnes (pen)	64,500
4		30	(a)	Chelsea	W	1-0	Cox	48,792
5	Sep	2	(h)	Sheffield W	W	3-0	Logie 2, Lishman	48,300
6		6	(h)	Everton	W	2-1	Cox, Barnes (pen)	40,000
7		9	(a)	Middlesbrough	L	1-2	Lishman	45,000
8		13	(a)	Everton	D	1-1	Goring	47,518
9		16	(h)	Huddersfield T	W	6-2	Goring 3, Logie 2, Lishman	54,200
10		23	(a)	Newcastle U	L	1-2	Logie	65,000
11		30	(h)	West Brom A	W	3-0	Lishman 2, Logie	53,700
12	Oct	7	(a)	Charlton A	W	3-1	Goring, Forbes, Roper	64,000
13		14	(h)	Manchester U	W	3-0	Lishman, Goring, Cockburn (og)	66,150
14		21	(a)	Aston Villa	D	1-1	Logie	45,000
15		28	(h)	Derby C	W	3-1	Logie, Forbes, Goring	64,750
16	Nov	4	(a)	Wolves	W	1-0	Lishman	55,548
17		11	(h)	Sunderland	W	5-1	Lishman 4, Roper	66,250
18		18	(a)	Liverpool	W	3-1	Lishman, Logie, Roper	44,193
19		25	(h)	Fulham	W	5-1	Lishman 3, Goring, Forbes	45,450
20	Dec	2	(a)	Bolton W	L	0-3		40,489
21		9	(h)	Blackpool	D	4-4	Lishman, Forbes, Goring, Barnes (pen)	57,445
22		16	(h)	Burnley	L	0-1		35,300
23		23	(a)	Tottenham H	L	0-1		54,898
24		25	(h)	Stoke C	L	0-3		38,800
25		26	(a)	Stoke C	L	0-1		45,000
26		30	(a)	Sheffield W	W	2-0	Goring 2	39,583
27	Jan	13	(h)	Middlesbrough	W	3-1	Lewis 2, Goring	65,038
28		20	(a)	Huddersfield T	D	2-2	Lewis 2	37,175
29	Feb	3	(h)	Newcastle U	D	0-0		55,073
30		17	(a)	West Brom A	L	0-2		38,000
31		24	(h)	Charlton A	L	2-5	Goring 2	58,137
32	Mar	3	(a)	Manchester U	L	1-3	Holton	46,202
33		10	(h)	Aston Villa	W	2-1	Lewis 2	43,747
34		17	(a)	Derby C	L	2-4	Lewis, Goring	22,168
35		23	(h)	Portsmouth	L	0-1		52,051
36		24	(h)	Wolves	W	2-1	Holton 2	54,213
37		26	(a)	Portsmouth	D	1-1	Marden	39,189
38		31	(a)	Sunderland	W	2-0	Marden, Roper	31,515
39	Apr	7	(h)	Liverpool	L	1-2	Holton	42,000
40		14	(a)	Fulham	L	2-3	Holton, Lewis	35,000
41		21	(h)	Bolton W	D	1-1	Lishman	45,040
42	May	2	(a)	Blackpool	W	1-0	Roper	25,000

FINAL LEAGUE POSITION: 5th in Division One

Appearances
Goals

FA Cup

3	Jan	6	(h)	Carlisle U	D	0-0		57,932
R		11	(a)	Carlisle U	W	4-1	Lewis 2, Logie, Goring	21,215
4		27	(h)	Northampton T	W	3-2	Lewis 2, Roper	72,408
5	Feb	10	(a)	Manchester U	L	0-1		55,058

Appearances
Goals

228

Swindin GH	Barnes W	Smith L	Forbes AR	Fields AG	Mercer J	Cox FJA	Logie JT	Goring H	Lishman DJ	Roper DGB	Compton LH	Shaw A	McPherson IB	Platt EH	Scott L	Holton CC	Lewis R	Daniel RW	Kelsey AJ	Marden RJ	Milton CA	Bowen DL	
1	2	3	4	5	6	7	8	9	10	11													1
1	2	3	4		6	7	8	9	10	11	5												2
1	2	3			6	7	8	9	10	11	5	4											3
1	2	3			6	7	8	9	10		5	4	11										4
		3			6	7	8	9	10		5	4	11	1	2								5
		3	4		6	7	8	9	10		5		11	1	2								6
		3	4		6	7	8	9	10	11	5			1	2								7
1	2	3	4		6		8	9	10	11	5		7										8
1	2	3			6		8	9	10	11	5	4	7										9
1	2	3			6		8	9	10	11	5	4	7										10
1	2	3	4		6		8	9	10	11	5		7										11
1	2	3	4		6		8	9	10	11	5		7										12
1	2	3	4		6		8	9	10	11	5		7										13
1		3			6		8	9	10	11	5	4	7			2							14
	2	3	4		6		8	9	10	11	5		7	1									15
	2	3	4		6		8	9	10	11	5		7	1									16
	2	3	4		6		8	9	10	11	5		7	1									17
	2	3	4		6		8	9	10	11	5		7	1									18
	2	3	4		6		8	9	10	11	5		7	1									19
	2	3	4		6		8	9	10	11	5		7	1									20
1	2	3	4		6		8	9	10	11	5		7										21
1		3	4		6		8	9	10	11	5		7			2							22
1		3	4		6	11	8	9	10		5		7			2							23
1		3			6	11	8	9	10		5	4	7			2							24
	2	3			6	7	8			11	5	4				9	10						25
		3	4		6	7	8	9		11				1	2	10	5						26
	2	3			6		8	9		11	5	4	7	1		10							27
	2	3			6		8	9		11	5	4	7	1		10							28
	2	3	4		6		8	9		11	5		7	1		10							29
	2	3			6	7	8	9		11	5	4		1		10							30
	2	3			6		8	9		11	5	4	7	1		10							31
		3	6		4		8	10			5		7			2		9	1	11			32
	2	3			6		8				4			1		9	10	5		11	7		33
	2	3			6	7	8	9			4			1		10	5			11			34
		3	4				8	9	7		5	6				2	10		1	11			35
		3	10		4		8		7		5					2		9	1	11		6	36
1		3	10				8		7		4					2	5	9		11		6	37
1		3	4				8		7		5					2	10	9		11		6	38
1		3	4				8		7		5					2	10	9		11		6	39
1		3	4				8		7		5					2	10	9		11		6	40
1		3	4				8		10		5		7			2		9		11		6	41
1		3	4				8		10		5		7			2		9		11		6	42
21	35	32	32	1	31	13	39	34	26	34	36	16	26	17	17	10	14	5	4	11	1	7	
		3	4			2	9	15	17	7						5	8			2			

I own-goal

Swindin GH	Barnes W	Smith L	Forbes AR	Fields AG	Mercer J	Cox FJA	Logie JT	Goring H	Lishman DJ	Roper DGB	Compton LH	Shaw A	McPherson IB	Platt EH	Scott L	Holton CC	Lewis R	Daniel RW	Kelsey AJ	Marden RJ	Milton CA	Bowen DL	
	2	3	4		6	7	8	9		11				1		10	5						3
	2	3			6		8	9		11	5	4	7	1		10							R
	2	3	4		6		8	9		11	5		7	1		10							4
	2	3	4		6		8	9		11	5		7	1		10							5
	4	4	4		3	1	4	4		4	3	1	3	4		4	1						
							1	1		1						4							

1951-52

Manager: T.Whittaker

1	Aug	18	(h)	Huddersfield T	D	2-2 Marden, Holton	54,072
2		22	(a)	Chelsea	W	3-1 Holton, Marden, Roper	59,143
3		25	(a)	Wolves	L	1-2 Holton	40,000
4		29	(h)	Chelsea	W	2-1 Holton, Lishman	48,768
5	Sep	1	(h)	Sunderland	W	3-0 Lishman 3	66,137
6		5	(h)	Liverpool	D	0-0	50,483
7		8	(a)	Aston Villa	L	0-1	60,000
8		12	(a)	Liverpool	D	0-0	39,853
9		15	(h)	Derby C	W	3-1 Holton 2, Lishman	50,181
10		22	(a)	Manchester C	W	2-0 Holton, Lishman	48,367
11		29	(h)	Tottenham H	D	1-1 Holton	68,164
12	Oct	6	(a)	Preston NE	L	0-2	39,000
13		13	(h)	Burnley	W	1-0 Lewis	48,531
14		20	(a)	Charlton A	W	3-1 Holton 2, Milton	57,000
15		27	(h)	Fulham	W	4-3 Lishman 3, Holton	54,178
16	Nov	3	(a)	Middlesbrough	W	3-0 Holton, Lishman, Milton	36,000
17		10	(h)	West Brom A	W	6-3 Lishman 3, Holton 2, Logie	53,432
18		17	(a)	Newcastle U	L	0-2	61,192
19		24	(h)	Bolton W	W	4-2 Lishman 3, Roper	53,790
20	Dec	1	(a)	Stoke C	L	1-2 Lewis	26,000
21		8	(h)	Manchester U	L	1-3 Logie	55,451
22		15	(a)	Huddersfield T	W	3-2 Roper 2, Lewis	22,427
23		22	(h)	Wolves	D	2-2 Lewis 2	45,644
24		25	(h)	Portsmouth	W	4-1 Cox, Goring, Lewis, Logie	54,241
25		26	(a)	Portsmouth	D	1-1 Cox	41,305
26		29	(a)	Sunderland	L	1-4 Goring	47,045
27	Jan	5	(h)	Aston Villa	W	2-1 Roper 2	53,540
28		19	(a)	Derby C	W	2-1 Logie, Roper	28,791
29		26	(h)	Manchester C	D	2-2 Lishman 2	54,527
30	Feb	9	(a)	Tottenham H	W	2-1 Roper, Forbes	66,438
31		16	(h)	Preston NE	D	3-3 Lewis 2, Roper	61,849
32	Mar	1	(a)	Burnley	W	1-0 Milton	41,000
33		13	(h)	Charlton A	W	2-1 Goring 2	37,985
34		15	(a)	Fulham	D	0-0	46,000
35		22	(h)	Middlesbrough	W	3-1 Holton, Lishman, Milton	52,000
36	Apr	11	(a)	Blackpool	D	0-0	32,186
37		12	(a)	Bolton W	L	1-2 Forbes	44,722
38		14	(h)	Blackpool	W	4-1 Lishman 2, Barnes (pen), Crosland (og)	50,445
39		16	(h)	Newcastle U	D	1-1 Milton	53,203
40		19	(h)	Stoke C	W	4-1 Holton 2, Barnes (pen), Lishman	47,962
41		21	(a)	West Brom A	L	1-3 Lishman	29,700
42		26	(a)	Manchester U	L	1-6 Cox	53,651

FINAL LEAGUE POSITION: 3rd in Division One

Appearances
Goals

FA Cup

3	Jan	12	(a)	Norwich C	W	5-0 Lishman 2, Logie, Goring, Roper	38,964
4	Feb	2	(h)	Barnsley	W	4-0 Lewis 3, Lishman	69,466
5		23	(a)	Leyton O	W	3-0 Lishman 2, Lewis	30,000
6	Mar	8	(a)	Luton T	W	3-2 Cox 2, Milton	28,433
SF	Apr	5	(n*)	Chelsea	D	1-1 Cox	68,084
R		7	(n*)	Chelsea	W	3-0 Cox 2, Lishman	57,450
F	May	3	(n†)	Newcastle U	L	0-1	100,000

*Played at White Hart Lane, London. †Played at Wembley Stadium.

Appearances
Goals

230

Player appearance and scoring grid (shirt numbers worn per match).

Swindin GH	Scott L	Barnes W	Forbes AR	Daniel RW	Bowen DL	Roper DGB	Logie JT	Holton CC	Lishman DJ	Marden RJ	Mercer J	Smith L	Cox FJA	Milton CA	Lewis R	Chenhall JC	Wade JS	Compton LH	Goring H	Shaw A	Robertson JW	No.
1	2	3	4	5	6	7	8	9	10	11												1
1	2	3	4	5		7	8	9	10	11	6											2
1	2	3	4	5		7	8	9	10	11	6											3
1	2	3	4	5		7	8	9	10	11	6											4
1		2	4	5		7	8	9	10		6	3	11									5
1		2	4	5		7	8	9	10		6	3	11									6
1		2	4	5	6	7	8	9	10			3	11									7
1		2	4	5			8	9	10		6	3	11	7								8
1		2	4	5			8	9	10		6	3	11	7								9
1		2	4	5			8	9	10		6	3	11	7								10
1		2	4	5			8	9	10		6	3	11	7								11
1		2	4	5			8	9	10		6	3	11	7								12
1		2	4	5		11	7	9	10		6	3			8							13
1			4			11	8	9	10		6			7	2	3	5					14
1		2	4	5		11	8	9	10		6	3		7								15
1		2	4	5		11	8	9	10		6	3		7								16
1		2	4	5		11	8	9	10		6			7			3					17
1		2	4	5		11	8	9	10		6			7			3					18
1		3	4	5		11	8	9	10		6			7		2						19
1		3	4	5		11	8	9			6			7	10	2						20
1		2	4	5		11	8	9	10		6	3		7								21
1		2	4	5	6	11		10				3		7	8				9			22
1		2	4	5	6	11		10				3		7	8				9			23
1		2	4	5				8	11		6	3	7						9	10		24
1		2		5	6			10	11				7				8	3	9	4		25
1		2	4					8	10	11	6	3	7				5		9			26
1		2	4	5		11	8		10		6	3	7						9			27
1		2	4	5		11	8		10		6	3	7						9			28
1		2	4	5		11	8		10		6	3	7						9			29
1		2	4	5		11	8		10		6	3	7					9				30
1		2	4	5		11	8		10		6	3	7					9				31
1		2		5				8	10		6	3	11	7					9	4		32
1		2		5		11		9	10		6	3	7						8	4		33
1		2		5				9	10		6	3	11	7					8	4		34
1		2	4	5				8	9	10	6	3	11	7								35
1		2	4	5		11	8		10		6	3	7						9			36
1		2	4			11	8				6	3	7				5	9		10		37
1		2	4			11	8	9	10		6		7				3		5			38
1		2	4		6	11	8		10		5		7				3		9			39
1		2	8		6	11		9	10		4		7				3		5			40
1		2	4		6			9	10				7					3	8	5	11	41
1		2	4			11		9			6	3	7		10				8	5		42
42	4	41	38	34	8	30	34	28	38	7	36	28	25	20	9	3	8	4	16	8	1	
	2	2				9	4	17	23		2	3	5	8					4			

1 own-goal

Swindin GH	Scott L	Barnes W	Forbes AR	Daniel RW	Bowen DL	Roper DGB	Logie JT	Holton CC	Lishman DJ	Marden RJ	Mercer J	Smith L	Cox FJA	Milton CA	Lewis R	Chenhall JC	Wade JS	Compton LH	Goring H	Shaw A	Robertson JW	Round
1		2	4	5		11	8		10		6	3	7						9			3
1		2	4	5		11	8		10		6	3	7		9							4
1		2		5		11	8		10		6	3	7						9	4		5
1		2		5		11			10		6	3	7	8					9	4		6
1		2	4	5		11	8		10		6	3	7		9							SF
1		2	4	5		11	8		10		6	3	7		9							R
1		2	4	5		11	8	9	10		6	3	7									F
7		7	5	7		7	6	1	7		7	7	7	1	3				3	2		
		1	1				6		5			1	4						1			

1952-53

Manager: T.Whittaker

1	Aug	23	(a)	Aston Villa	W 2-1	Lishman, Oakes	55,000
2		27	(h)	Manchester U	W 2-1	Cox, Goring	58,831
3		30	(h)	Sunderland	L 1-2	Lishman	57,873
4	Sep	3	(a)	Manchester U	D 0-0		37,367
5		6	(a)	Wolves	D 1-1	Roper	43,371
6		10	(h)	Portsmouth	W 3-1	Goring, Milton, Roper	40,743
7		13	(h)	Charlton A	L 3-4	Milton, Goring, Daniel	61,102
8		17	(a)	Portsmouth	D 2-2	Holton 2	37,256
9		20	(a)	Tottenham H	W 3-1	Goring, Milton, Logie	69,220
10		27	(a)	Derby C	L 0-2		24,582
11	Oct	4	(h)	Blackpool	W 3-1	Roper 2, Logie	66,682
12		11	(h)	Sheffield W	D 2-2	Roper, Logie	55,678
13		25	(h)	Newcastle U	W 3-0	Roper 2, Lishman	63,744
14	Nov	1	(a)	West Brom A	L 0-2		41,000
15		8	(h)	Middlesbrough	W 2-1	Milton, Holton	49,564
16		15	(a)	Liverpool	W 5-1	Holton 3, Marden 2	45,010
17		22	(h)	Manchester C	W 3-1	Logie 2, Lishman	39,161
18		29	(a)	Stoke C	D 1-1	Holton	24,033
19	Dec	13	(a)	Burnley	D 1-1	Milton	32,840
20		20	(h)	Aston Villa	W 3-1	Lishman, Holton, Roper	32,064
21		25	(a)	Bolton W	W 6-4	Holton 2, Milton, Logie, Roper, Daniel	47,344
22	Jan	3	(a)	Sunderland	L 1-3	Lishman	54,912
23		17	(h)	Wolves	W 5-3	Lishman 2, Daniel, Logie, Milton	58,983
24		24	(a)	Charlton A	D 2-2	Lishman, Roper	66,426
25	Feb	7	(h)	Tottenham H	W 4-0	Holton 2, Lishman, Logie	69,051
26		18	(h)	Derby C	W 6-2	Daniel 2, Holton 2, Lishman 2	32,681
27		21	(a)	Blackpool	L 2-3	Mercer, Goring	27,000
28	Mar	2	(a)	Sheffield W	W 4-1	Holton 4	30,452
29		7	(h)	Cardiff C	L 0-1		59,580
30		14	(a)	Newcastle U	D 2-2	Lishman 2	51,560
31		19	(h)	Preston NE	D 1-1	Mercer	33,697
32		21	(h)	West Brom A	D 2-2	Holton, Roper	50,078
33		28	(a)	Middlesbrough	L 0-2		35,000
34	Apr	3	(a)	Chelsea	D 1-1	Goring	72,614
35		4	(h)	Liverpool	W 5-3	Roper 2, Lishman, Goring, Hughes (og)	39,570
36		6	(h)	Chelsea	W 2-0	Lishman, Marden	40,536
37		11	(a)	Manchester C	W 4-2	Goring 2, Logie, Roper	53,418
38		15	(h)	Bolton W	W 4-1	Lishman 2, Goring, Marden	35,006
39		18	(h)	Stoke C	W 3-1	Lishman 3	47,376
40		22	(a)	Cardiff C	D 0-0		57,800
41		25	(a)	Preston NE	L 0-2		40,000
42	May	1	(h)	Burnley	W 3-2	Forbes, Lishman, Logie	51,586

FINAL LEAGUE POSITION: 1st in Division One

Appearances
Goals

FA Cup

3	Jan	10	(h)	Doncaster R	W 4-0	Lishman, Holton, Logie, Roper	57,443
4		31	(h)	Bury	W 6-2	Holton, Lishman, Logie, Milton, Roper, T.Daniel (og)	45,071
5	Feb	14	(a)	Burnley	W 2-0	Holton, Lishman	52,122
6		28	(h)	Blackpool	L 1-2	Logie	69,158

Appearances
Goals

Appearance grid (First Division, 42 matches)

Swindin GH	Wade JS	Smith L	Shaw A	Daniel RW	Mercer J	Forbes AR	Oakes DJ	Goring H	Lishman DJ	Roper DGB	Cox FJA	Chenhall JC	Holton CC	Bowen DL	Milton CA	Logie JT	Platt EH	Kelsey AJ	Marden RJ	Dodgin W	№
1	2	3	4	5	6	7	8	9	10	11											1
1	2	3	4	5	6		8	9	10	11	7										2
1	3		4	5	6		8		10	11	7	2	9								3
1	3		4	5			8		10	11	7	2	9	6							4
1	2	3	4	5	6		8		10	11			9								5
1	2	3	10	5	6	4		9		11					7	8					6
1	2	3	10	5	6	4		9		11					7	8					7
	3	4	5				8		10	11		2	9	6	7		1				8
	3	4	5		6			9	10	11		2			7	8	1				9
3		4	5		6			9	10	11		2			7	8	1				10
3		4	5		6			9	10	11		2			7	8		1			11
3		4	5		6			9	10	11		2			7	8		1			12
	2	3		5	6	4		9	10	11					7	8		1			13
	2	3		5	6	4		9	10	11					7	8		1			14
	2	3	4	5	6				10	11			9		7	8		1			15
3			5	6	4				10			2	9		7	8		1	11		16
	2	3		5	6	4			10	11			9		7	8		1			17
3			5	6	4				10	11		2	9		7	8		1			18
	2	3		5	6	4			10	11			9		7	8		1			19
	2	3	4	5	6				10	11			9		7	8		1			20
	2	3	4	5	6				10	11			9		7	8		1			21
	2	3		5	6	4			10	11			9		7	8		1			22
	2	3	6	5		4			10	11			9		7	8		1			23
	2	3		5	6	4			10	11			9		7	8		1			24
	2	3		5	6	4			10	11			9		7	8		1			25
	2	3	6	5		4	8		10	11			9		7			1			26
	2			5	6	4	8		10	11	3	9			7			1			27
	2		4	5	6		8		10	11	7	3	9					1			28
	2	3	4	5	6				10	11	7		9			8		1			29
	2	3	4	5	6			9	10	11					7	8		1			30
	2	3		5	6	4		9	10	11					7	8		1			31
	2	3	4	5	6		8		10	11	7		9					1			32
	2	3		5	6	4	8		10	11	7		9					1			33
	2	3	4	5				6	10	11	7					8		1			34
	2	3	4	5				6	9	10	11				7	8		1			35
1	2	3		5	6	4		9	10	7						8			11		36
1	2	3		5	6	4		9	10	7						8			11		37
1	2			6	4			9	10	7	3					8			11	5	38
1	2			5	6	4		9	10	7	3					8			11		39
1	2	3	6	5		4		9	10	7						8			11		40
1	2	3	6	5		4		9	10	7						8			11		41
1	2	3		5	6	4		9	10	7						8			11		42
14	40	31	25	41	28	33	2	29	39	41	9	13	21	2	25	32	3	25	8	1	
		5	2	1	1	10	22	14	1		19		7	10				4			

1 own-goal

Swindin GH	Wade JS	Smith L	Shaw A	Daniel RW	Mercer J	Forbes AR	Oakes DJ	Goring H	Lishman DJ	Roper DGB	Cox FJA	Chenhall JC	Holton CC	Bowen DL	Milton CA	Logie JT	Platt EH	Kelsey AJ	Marden RJ	Dodgin W	№
	2	3	4	5		6			10	11			9		7	8		1			3
	2	3		5	6	4			10	11			9		7	8		1			4
	2	3		5	6	4			10	11			9		7	8		1			5
	2	3		5	6	4			10	11			9		7	8		1			6
	4	4	1	4	3	4			4	4			4		4	4		4			
									3	2			3		1	3					

1 own-goal

1953-54

Manager: T.Whittaker

1	Aug	19	(a)	West Brom A	L	0-2	39,710
2		22	(h)	Huddersfield T	D	0-0	54,847
3		24	(a)	Sheffield U	L	0-1	51,070
4		29	(a)	Aston Villa	L	1-2 Forbes	40,000
5	Sep	1	(h)	Sheffield U	D	1-1 Shaw (og)	43,077
6		5	(h)	Wolves	L	2-3 Roper, Holton	60,460
7		8	(h)	Chelsea	L	1-2 Holton	55,086
8		12	(a)	Sunderland	L	1-7 Lishman	59,808
9		15	(a)	Chelsea	W	2-0 Lishman 2	60,652
10		19	(h)	Manchester C	D	2-2 Lishman 2	65,869
11		26	(a)	Cardiff C	W	3-0 Lishman 2, Mansell (og)	55,000
12	Oct	3	(h)	Preston NE	W	3-2 Roper 2, Barnes (pen)	61,807
13		10	(a)	Tottenham H	W	4-1 Logie 2, Milton, Forbes	69,821
14		17	(h)	Burnley	L	2-5 Forbes, Roper	47,373
15		24	(a)	Charlton A	W	5-1 Marden 3, Holton, Roper	60,245
16		31	(h)	Sheffield W	W	4-1 Holton 2, Logie 2	52,543
17	Nov	7	(a)	Manchester U	D	2-2 Holton, Roper	28,141
18		14	(h)	Bolton W	W	4-3 Holton 3, Lishman	52,319
19		21	(a)	Liverpool	W	2-1 Logie, Lishman	47,814
20		28	(h)	Newcastle U	W	2-1 Holton, Forbes	62,456
21	Dec	5	(a)	Middlesbrough	L	0-2	35,000
22		12	(h)	West Brom A	D	2-2 Lishman 2	55,264
23		19	(a)	Huddersfield T	D	2-2 Milton, Lishman	34,018
24		26	(a)	Blackpool	D	2-2 Lishman, Roper	29,347
25		28	(h)	Blackpool	D	1-1 Roper	62,900
26	Jan	16	(a)	Wolves	W	2-0 Logie, Lishman	45,974
27		23	(h)	Sunderland	L	1-4 Holton	60,218
28	Feb	6	(a)	Manchester C	D	0-0	39,026
29		13	(h)	Cardiff C	D	1-1 Lishman	45,497
30		24	(a)	Preston NE	W	1-0 Lishman	23,000
31		27	(h)	Tottenham H	L	0-3	64,211
32	Mar	6	(a)	Burnley	L	1-2 Holton	22,726
33		13	(h)	Charlton A	D	3-3 Holton, Lishman, Dickson	41,256
24		20	(a)	Sheffield W	L	1-2 Holton	42,072
35		27	(h)	Manchester U	W	3-1 Logie 2, Holton	42,735
36	Apr	3	(a)	Bolton W	L	1-3 Holton	30,473
37		6	(a)	Aston Villa*	D	1-1 Lawton	14,519
38		10	(h)	Liverpool	W	3-0 Tapscott 2, Roper	33,178
39		16	(h)	Portsmouth	W	3-0 Tapscott 2, Roper	44,948
40		17	(a)	Newcastle U	L	2-5 Milton, Holton	48,540
41		19	(a)	Portsmouth	D	1-1 Roper	30,958
42		24	(h)	Middlesbrough	W	3-1 Roper, Lishman, Tapscott	35,196

FINAL LEAGUE POSITION: 12th in Division One   Appearances

*After abandoned match (23 minutes) on January 2   Goals

FA Cup

3	Jan	9	(h)	Aston Villa	W	5-1 Roper 2, Holton, Logie, Milton	50,990
4		30	(h)	Norwich C	L	1-2 Logie	55,767

Appearances

Goals

234

Kelsey AJ	Wade JS	Smith L	Forbes AR	Dodgin W	Mercer J	Roper DGB	Logie JT	Holton CC	Lishman DJ	Marden RJ	Evans DJ	Ward G	Bowen DL	Goring H	Milton CA	Tilley P	Swindin GH	Barnes W	Shaw A	Walsh JB	Dickson W	Wills LE	Lawton T	Tapscott DR	Sullivan CH	
1	2	3	4	5	6	7	8	9	10	11																1
1	2		4	5	6	7	8	9	10			3	11													2
1	2		4	5		7	8		10			3	11	6	9											3
1	2		4	5	6	7	8		10			3	11		9											4
1	2			5	6	7	8	9	10	11	3			4												5
1	2		4	5		7	8	9	10	11	3			6												6
		3	4	5			11	8	9				6		7	10	1	2								7
			4	5	6	11	8	9	10		3				7		1	2								8
1	2		7	5			11	8	9	10				6	4			3								9
1	2		7	5			11	8		10				6	4			3				9				10
1	2		4	5	6	11	8	9	10		3				7											11
1	2		4	5	6	11	8	9	10		3				7											12
1			4	5	6			8	10	11				3	7							2	9			13
1			4	5	6			8	10	11					7			3				2	9			14
1				5	6	7	8	9	10	11								3			4	2				15
1				5	6	7	8	9	10	11								3			4	2				16
1			6	5		7	8	9	10	11								3			4	2				17
1			6	5		7	8	9	10	11								3			4	2				18
1			6	5			11	8	9	10					7			3			4	2				19
1			6	5			11	8	9	10					7			3			4	2				20
1	3		6	5			11	8	9	10					7						4	2				21
1	3			5	6	7	8	9	10	11											4	2				22
1	3			5	6	11	8	9	10						7						4	2				23
1	3			5	6	11	8	9	10						7						4	2				24
1				5	6	11	8	9	10					3	7						4	2				25
1	3		6	5			11	8	9	10					7						4	2				26
1	3		6	5			11	9		10					7						4	2	8			27
1			4	5	6			8	10	11				3						7		2	9			28
1			4	5	6			8	10					3						7		2	9			29
1			4	5		11								3	8					7	6	2				30
1			4	5	6	11	8	9	10					3						7		2				31
1			4	5			8	9	10	11	3		6					7				2				32
1			4	5			8	9	10		3		11					7			6	2				33
1			4	5			8	9	10		3		11					7			6	2				34
1	3		6	5			11	8	9				10					7			4	2				35
1			6	5			11	8	9				10	3				7			4	2				36
1	3			5	6			11	9	10					7						4	2	8			37
1	3				6	11			10		4				7						5	2	9	8		38
1	3					11			10		6		4		7						5	2	9	8		39
	3					11			10		6		4		7						5	2		8	1	40
1	3			5			11			10			4		7						6	2		8		41
1	3			5			11	8		10			4		7						6	2		9		42
39	18	7	30	39	19	39	35	32	39	9	10	3	10	9	21	1	2	19	2	10	24	30	9	5	1	
			4			12	8	17	18	3					3			1			1		1	5		

2 own-goals

Kelsey AJ	Wade JS	Smith L	Forbes AR	Dodgin W	Mercer J	Roper DGB	Logie JT	Holton CC	Lishman DJ	Marden RJ	Evans DJ	Ward G	Bowen DL	Goring H	Milton CA	Tilley P	Swindin GH	Barnes W	Shaw A	Walsh JB	Dickson W	Wills LE	Lawton T	Tapscott DR	Sullivan CH	
1	3		6	5			11	8	9	10					7						4	2				3
1		3	6	5			11	8	9	10					7						4	2				4
2	1	1	2	2			2	2	2	2					2						2	2				
				2	2	1									1											

1954-55

Manager: T.Whittaker

1	Aug	21	(h)	Newcastle U	L 1-3	Lishman	65,334
2		25	(a)	Everton	L 0-1		69,134
3		28	(a)	West Brom A	L 1-3	Lishman	50,000
4		31	(h)	Everton	W 2-0	Lishman, Roper	42,146
5	Sep	4	(h)	Tottenham H	W 2-0	Logie, Lishman	53,977
6		8	(a)	Manchester C	L 1-2	Lishman	38,146
7		11	(h)	Sheffield U	W 4-0	Forbes, Lishman, Tapscott, Roper	41,679
8		14	(h)	Manchester C	L 2-3	Tapscott, Lishman	33,898
9		18	(a)	Preston NE	L 1-3	Logie	36,000
10		25	(h)	Burnley	W 4-0	Lawton 2, Lishman, Roper	46,190
11	Oct	2	(a)	Leicester C	D 3-3	Lawton 2, Logie	42,486
12		9	(a)	Sheffield W	W 2-1	Roper, Bloomfield	38,167
13		16	(h)	Portsmouth	L 0-1		44,866
14		23	(a)	Aston Villa	L 1-2	Roper	40,000
15		30	(h)	Sunderland	L 1-3	Roper	65,424
16	Nov	6	(a)	Bolton W	D 2-2	Goring, Lishman	31,222
17		13	(h)	Huddersfield T	L 3-5	Milton 2, Lishman	42,950
18		20	(a)	Manchester U	L 1-2	Tapscott	33,373
19		27	(h)	Wolves	D 1-1	Roper	55,055
20	Dec	4	(a)	Blackpool	D 2-2	Tapscott, Roper	16,348
21		11	(h)	Charlton A	W 3-1	Roper 2, Milton	40,498
22		18	(a)	Newcastle U	L 1-5	Wills (pen)	35,060
23		25	(h)	Chelsea	W 1-0	Lawton	47,178
24		27	(a)	Chelsea	D 1-1	Tapscott	66,922
25	Jan	1	(h)	West Brom A	D 2-2	Tapscott, Lishman	40,246
26		15	(a)	Tottenham H	W 1-0	Lawton	36,263
27	Feb	5	(h)	Preston NE	W 2-0	Tapscott, Roper	41,228
28		12	(a)	Burnley	L 0-3		24,940
29		19	(h)	Leicester C	D 1-1	Roper	27,384
30		26	(h)	Sheffield W	W 3-2	Tapscott 3	26,910
31	Mar	5	(a)	Charlton A	D 1-1	Bloomfield	42,064
32		12	(h)	Aston Villa	W 2-0	Tapscott, Roper	30,136
33		19	(a)	Sunderland	W 1-0	Bloomfield	40,279
34		26	(h)	Bolton W	W 3-0	Lishman 2, Roper	33,852
35	Apr	2	(a)	Huddersfield T	W 1-0	Roper	22,853
36		8	(h)	Cardiff C	W 2-0	Tapscott 2	39,052
37		9	(h)	Blackpool	W 3-0	Lishman 2, Roper	60,741
38		11	(a)	Cardiff C	W 2-1	Bloomfield Lishman	38,000
39		16	(a)	Wolves	L 1-3	Lishman	34,985
40		18	(h)	Sheffield U	D 1-1	Roper	21,380
41		23	(h)	Manchester U	L 2-3	Lishman 2	42,754
42		30	(a)	Portsmouth	L 1-2	Herd	28,156

FINAL LEAGUE POSITION: 9th in Division One

Appearances

Goals

FA Cup

3	Jan	8	(h)	Cardiff C	W 1-0	Lawton	51,298
4		29	(a)	Wolves	L 0-1		52,857

Appearances

Goals

236

Appearance grid (numbers indicate playing position). Player columns left→right; final column is the match number.

Kelsey AJ	Wills LE	Wade JS	Forbes AR	Dickson W	Shaw A	Walsh JB	Logie JT	Holton CC	Lishman DJ	Roper DGB	Evans DJ	Goring H	Bloomfield JH	Tapscott DR	Haverty J	Bowen DL	Lawton T	Barnes W	Guthrie R	Dodgin W	Milton CA	Fotheringham JG	Marden RJ	Clapton DR	Herd DG	Wilkinson J	Sullivan CH	Oakes DJ	Swallow R	#
1	2	3	4	5	6	7	8	9	10	11																				1
1	2		4	5			8	9				3	6	7	10	11														2
1	2			5		7			10			4		8	11	6	9	3												3
1	2			5			8		10	11		4		7		6	9	3												4
1	2			5			8		10	11		4		7		6	9	3												5
	2			5			8		10	11		4		7		6	9	3	1											6
1	2			5			8		10	11		4		7		6	9	3												7
1	2			5			8	9	10	11		4		7		6		3												8
1	2			5			8		10	11		4		7		6	9	3												9
1		3	4	5			8		10	11		6		7			9	2												10
1		3		5			8		10	11		4		7		6	9	2												11
1		3	6	5		7				11		4	10	8			9	2												12
	2	3	6			7	8	9		11		4	10						1	5										13
1		3	6			7	8			11		4	10				9	2		5										14
1		3	6					9		11		4	10	8				2		5	7									15
1		3	6						10	11		4		8			9	2			7	5								16
1		3	6						10	9		4		8				2			7	5	11							17
1	2	3					8		10	11		4		9		6					7	5								18
1	2	3	6						10	9		4		8							7	5	11							19
1	2	3							10	9		4		8		6					7	5	11							20
1	2	3							10	9		4		8		6					7	5	11							21
1	2	3				7			10	9		4		8		6						5	11							22
1									10		3	4		8	11	6	9	2				5		7						23
1									10		3	4		8	11	6	9	2				5		7						24
1									10		3	4		8	11	6	9	2				5		7						25
1									10	11	3	4		8		6	9	2				5		7						26
1								11	10	7	3	4		8		6	9	2				5								27
1								11	10	7	3	4		8		6	9	2				5								28
1									10	11	3	4			7	6		2				5					8	9		29
1										11	3	4	10	8		6	9	2				5		7						30
1					6			9		11	3	4	10	8				2				5		7						31
1								9		11	3	4	10	8		6		2				5		7						32
1			6							11	3	4	10	8			9	2				5		7						33
	2								8	11	3	4	10	9								5		7			1	6		34
1	2								8	11	3	4	10	9								5		7				6		35
1	2								8		3	4	10	9								5		7				6	11	36
1	2								8	11	3	4	10	9								5		7				6		37
1	2								8	11	3	4	10	9								5		7				6		38
1	2								8	11	3	4	10	9								5		7				6		39
	2								8	11	3	4	10	9								5		7			1	6		40
1	2									11	3	4	10	9								5		7	8			6		41
1	2									11	3	4	10	9								5		7	8			6		42
38	24	14	20	4	1	6	13	8	32	35	21	41	19	37	6	21	18	25	2	3	8	27	7	16	3	1	2	9	1	
1		1			3				19	17	1		4	13				6				3				1				

Kelsey AJ	Wills LE	Wade JS	Forbes AR	Dickson W	Shaw A	Walsh JB	Logie JT	Holton CC	Lishman DJ	Roper DGB	Evans DJ	Goring H	Bloomfield JH	Tapscott DR	Haverty J	Bowen DL	Lawton T	Barnes W	Guthrie R	Dodgin W	Milton CA	Fotheringham JG	Marden RJ	Clapton DR	Herd DG	Wilkinson J	Sullivan CH	Oakes DJ	Swallow R	#
1											3	4	10	8	11	6	9	2				5		7						3
1										11	3	4	10	8		6	9	2				5		7						4
2										1	2	2	2	2	1	2	2	2				2		2						
																	1													

1955-56

Manager: T.Whittaker

1	Aug	20	(a)	Blackpool	L	1-3	Tapscott	30,928
2		23	(h)	Cardiff C	W	3-1	Lawton 3	31,352
3		27	(h)	Chelsea	D	1-1	Lawton	55,011
4		31	(a)	Manchester C	D	2-2	Roper, Lawton	36,955
5	Sep	3	(a)	Bolton W	L	1-4	Lawton	22,690
6		6	(h)	Manchester C	D	0-0		30,864
7		10	(a)	Tottenham H	L	1-3	Roper	51,029
8		17	(h)	Portsmouth	L	1-3	Lishman	48,816
9		24	(a)	Sunderland	L	1-3	Lishman	55,397
10	Oct	1	(h)	Aston Villa	W	1-0	Nutt	43,824
11		8	(a)	Everton	D	1-1	Lishman	47,794
12		15	(h)	Newcastle U	W	1-0	Roper	46,093
13		22	(a)	Luton T	D	0-0		23,997
14		29	(h)	Charlton A	L	2-4	Lishman, Clapton	47,038
15	Nov	5	(a)	Manchester U	D	1-1	Lishman	41,586
16		12	(h)	Sheffield U	W	2-1	Groves, Roper	46,647
17		19	(a)	Preston NE	W	1-0	Holton	23,000
18		26	(h)	Burnley	L	0-1		37,583
19	Dec	3	(a)	Birmingham C	L	0-4		35,765
20		10	(h)	West Brom A	W	2-0	Tapscott, Williams (og)	33,217
21		17	(h)	Blackpool	W	4-1	Groves, Holton, Tapscott, Bloomfield	45,086
22		24	(a)	Chelsea	L	0-2		43,022
23		26	(a)	Wolves	D	3-3	Groves 2, Bloomfield	43,738
24		27	(h)	Wolves	D	2-2	Tapscott 2	61,814
25		31	(h)	Bolton W	W	3-1	Tapscott 2, Groves	42,677
26	Jan	14	(h)	Tottenham H	L	0-1		59,603
27		21	(a)	Portsmouth	L	2-5	Tapscott 2	30,513
28	Feb	4	(h)	Sunderland	W	3-1	Herd 2, Bloomfield	38,780
29		11	(a)	Aston Villa	D	1-1	Groves	28,000
30		21	(h)	Everton	W	3-2	Tapscott 2, Groves	16,039
31		25	(a)	Newcastle U	L	0-2		50,800
32	Mar	6	(h)	Preston NE	W	3-2	Tapscott 2, Groves	34,672
33		10	(a)	Charlton A	L	0-2		39,553
34		17	(h)	Manchester U	D	1-1	Holton	50,758
35		24	(a)	Sheffield U	W	2-0	Holton, Tapscott	26,556
36		31	(h)	Luton T	W	3-0	Holton 2, Haverty	45,968
37	Apr	2	(h)	Huddersfield T	W	2-0	Haverty, Holton	30,836
38		3	(a)	Huddersfield T	W	1-0	Clapton	24,469
39		7	(a)	Burnley	W	1-0	Swallow	24,403
40		14	(h)	Birmingham C	W	1-0	Tapscott	31,733
41		21	(a)	West Brom A	L	1-2	Tapscott	22,400
42		28	(a)	Cardiff C	W	2-1	Holton, Tapscott	20,000

FINAL LEAGUE POSITION: 5th in Division One

Appearances
Goals

FA Cup

3	Jan	7	(h)	Bedford T	D	2-2	Tapscott, Groves	55,178
R		12	(a)	Bedford T	W	2-1	Groves, Tapscott	15,306
4		28	(h)	Aston Villa	W	4-1	Tapscott 2, Groves, Charlton	43,052
5	Feb	18	(a)	Charlton A	W	2-0	Groves, Bloomfield	71,758
6	Mar	3	(h)	Birmingham C	L	1-3	Charlton	67,872

Appearances
Goals

238

Appearance / line-up chart (shirt numbers worn per match). Row numbers appear in the right-hand column.

Kelsey AJ	Barnes W	Evans DJ	Goring H	Dickson W	Bowen DL	Clapton DR	Tapscott DR	Holton CC	Lishman DJ	Bloomfield JH	Fotheringham JG	Lawton T	Roper DGB	Herd DG	Walsh JB	Tiddy MD	Nutt GE	Wills LE	Sullivan CH	Groves VG	Charlton S	Forbes AR	Dodgin W	Haverty J	Swallow R	
1	2	3	4	5	6	7	8	9	10	11																1
1	2	3	4		6	7	8		10	11	5	9														2
1	2	3	4		6	7	8		10		5	9	11													3
1	2	3	4		6	7	8		10		5	9	11													4
1	2	3	4		6	7	11		10		5	9		8												5
1	2	3	4		6	7	8			11	5	9	10													6
1	2	3	4		6	7	8				5	9	10		11											7
1	2	3	4		6	7	8		10		5	9	11													8
1		3	4		6				10		5	9	8		7	11	2									9
1		3	4		6		5	10	8		9		7	11	2											10
1		3	4			6	10	8	5		9		7	11	2											11
1		3	4		11	6	10	8	5		9		7		2											12
		3	4		7		6	10	8	5	9		11	2	1											13
1		3	4		7		6	10	8	5	9		11	2												14
1		3	4		7	8	6	10		5	9		11	2												15
1		3	4		7		6	10		5	8		11	2		9										16
1		3	4		7	8	6		5	10			11	2		9										17
1		3	4		7	8	6	10		5	9		11	2												18
1		3	4		7	8	6		10	5	9		11	2												19
		3	4		7	8	6		10	5			11	2	1	9										20
		3	4		7	8	6		10	5			11	2	1	9										21
		3	4		7	8	6		10	5			11		2	1	9									22
		3	4		7	8	6		10	5			11		2	1	9									23
		3	4		7	8	6		10	5			11		2	1	9									24
		3	4		7	8	6		10	5			11		2	1	9									25
1		3			7	8	6		10	5				11	2		9		4							26
		3			7	8	6		10	5				11	2	1	9		4							27
1		3	4		6	7			10				8	11			9	2		5						28
1		3	4		6	7			10				8	11			9	2		5						29
		3	4		6	7	8		10					11		1	9	2		5						30
		3			6	7		4	10					11		1	9	2		5						31
1		3			6	7	8	4	10					11			9	2		5						32
1		3			6	7	9	4	10				8	11				2		5						33
1		3	4		6	7	8	9	10									2		5	11					34
1		3	4		6	7	8	9	10									2		5	11					35
1		3	4		6	7	8	9	10									2		5	11					36
1		3	4		6	7	8	9	10									2		5	11					37
1		3	4		6	7	8	9	10									2		5	11					38
1		3	4		6	7		9	8									2		5	11	10				39
1		3	4			7	8	9	10									2	6	5	11					40
1		3	4			7	8	9	10									2	6	5						41
1		3	4			7	8	9	10				11					2	6	5						42
32	8	42	37	1	22	39	31	31	15	32	25	8	16	5	1	21	8	15	10	15	19	5	15	8	1	
		2			17	8	5	3		6	4	2				1		8				2	1			

1 own-goal

Kelsey AJ	Barnes W	Evans DJ	Goring H	Dickson W	Bowen DL	Clapton DR	Tapscott DR	Holton CC	Lishman DJ	Bloomfield JH	Fotheringham JG	Lawton T	Roper DGB	Herd DG	Walsh JB	Tiddy MD	Nutt GE	Wills LE	Sullivan CH	Groves VG	Charlton S	Forbes AR	Dodgin W	Haverty J	Swallow R	
		3	4		7	8	6		10	5			11			1	9	2								3
1		3	4			8	6		10	5		9	11			7	2									R
1		3	4		7	8	6		10				11			9	2		5							4
1		3	4		6	7	8		10				11			9	2		5							5
1		3	4		6	7	8		10					11		9	2		5							6
4		5	5		2	4	5	3		5	2		1			4	1		1	5	5	3					
					4			1								4	2									

239

1956-57

Manager: T.Whittaker/J.Crayston

1	Aug	18	(h)	Cardiff C	D 0-0		51,069
2		21	(h)	Burnley	W 2-0	Tiddy, Bloomfield	38,321
3		25	(a)	Birmingham C	L 2-4	Holton, Roper	37,200
4		28	(a)	Burnley	L 1-3	Tiddy	18,829
5	Sep	1	(h)	West Brom A	W 4-1	Roper 2, Tiddy, Tapscott	39,973
6		4	(h)	Preston NE	L 1-2	Bloomfield	40,470
7		8	(a)	Portsmouth	W 3-2	Bloomfield, Tiddy, Holton	30,768
8		10	(a)	Preston NE	L 0-3		35,450
9		15	(h)	Newcastle U	L 0-1		46,318
10		22	(a)	Sheffield W	W 4-2	Bloomfield 2, Tapscott, Tiddy	40,629
11		29	(h)	Manchester U	L 1-2	Evans (pen)	62,429
12	Oct	6	(h)	Manchester C	W 7-3	Holton 4, Evans (pen), Bloomfield, Haverty	33,651
13		13	(a)	Charlton A	W 3-1	Tapscott 2, Clapton	40,051
14		20	(h)	Tottenham H	W 3-1	Herd 2, Haverty	60,580
15		27	(a)	Everton	L 0-4		52,074
16	Nov	3	(h)	Aston Villa	W 2-1	Groves 2	40,045
17		10	(a)	Wolves	L 2-5	Tapscott, Haverty	34,019
18		17	(h)	Bolton W	W 3-0	Tapscott 2, Haverty	33,377
19		24	(a)	Leeds U	D 3-3	Tapscott 2, Holton	39,000
20	Dec	1	(h)	Sunderland	D 1-1	Tapscott	36,442
21		8	(a)	Luton T	W 2-1	Haverty, Tapscott	22,000
22		15	(a)	Cardiff C	W 3-2	Herd 2, Haverty	15,000
23		22	(h)	Birmingham C	W 4-0	Evans (pen), Holton, Bloomfield, Watts (og)	28,644
24		25	(a)	Chelsea	D 1-1	Bloomfield	32,094
25		26	(h)	Chelsea	W 2-0	Clapton, Tapscott	22,526
26		29	(a)	West Brom A	W 2-0	Haverty, Tapscott	25,000
27	Jan	12	(h)	Portsmouth	D 1-1	Herd	48,949
28		19	(a)	Newcastle U	L 1-3	Evans (pen)	45,990
29	Feb	2	(h)	Sheffield W	W 6-3	Herd 3, Tapscott 2, Bloomfield	40,217
30		9	(a)	Manchester U	L 2-6	Herd 2	60,384
31		23	(h)	Everton	W 2-0	Holton, Tapscott	30,562
32	Mar	9	(h)	Luton T	L 1-3	Tapscott	41,288
33		13	(a)	Tottenham H	W 3-1	Bowen 2, Tapscott	65,455
34		16	(a)	Aston Villa	D 0-0		40,000
35		20	(a)	Manchester C	W 3-2	Tiddy, Bloomfield, Tapscott	27,974
36		23	(h)	Wolves	D 0-0		51,021
37		30	(a)	Bolton W	L 1-2	Tapscott	23,879
38	Apr	6	(h)	Leeds U	W 1-0	Herd	40,388
39		13	(a)	Sunderland	L 0-1		34,749
40		19	(h)	Blackpool	D 1-1	Tapscott	50,270
41		20	(h)	Charlton A	W 3-1	Tapscott 2, Holton	26,364
42		22	(a)	Blackpool	W 4-2	Tapscott 2, Herd, Haverty	24,118

FINAL LEAGUE POSITION: 5th in Division One

Appearances
Goals

FA Cup

3	Jan	5	(h)	Stoke C	W 4-2	Herd 2, Tapscott, Haverty	56,173
4		26	(a)	Newport C	W 2-0	Tapscott, Herd	22,450
5	Feb	16	(a)	Preston NE	D 3-3	Clapton, Herd, Dunn (og)	39,608
R		19	(h)	Preston NE	W 2-1	Dodgin, Herd	61,501
6	Mar	2	(a)	West Brom A	D 2-2	Herd, Charlton	58,000
R		5	(h)	West Brom A	L 1-2	Holton	58,757

Appearances
Goals

Kelsey AJ	Charlton S	Evans DJ	Goring H	Dodgin W	Bowen DL	Clapton DR	Tapscott DR	Holton CC	Bloomfield JH	Tiddy MD	Wills LE	Roper DGB	Swallow R	Groves VG	Haverty J	Sullivan CH	Herd DG	Nutt GE	Barnwell J	
1	2	3	4	5	6	7	8	9	10	11										1
1	2	3	6	5		7	8	9	10	11	4									2
1	2	3		5		7	8	6	10	11	4	9								3
1	2	3		5		7	8	6	10	11	4	9								4
1	2	3		5		7	8	6	10	11	4	9								5
1	2	3		5		7	8	6	10	11	4	9								6
1	2	3	6	5		7		9	8	11	4		10							7
1	2	3	6	5		7		9	8	11	4		10							8
1	2	3	6	5		7	9		8	11	4		10							9
1	2	3	6			7	8	5	10	11	4			9						10
1	2	3	4	5	6	7	8		10	11				9						11
1	2	3	4	5	6	7	8	9	10						11					12
1	2	3	4	5	6	7	8	9	10						11					13
	2	3		5		7	8	6	10		4				11	1	9			14
1	2	3		5		7	8	6	10		4				11		9			15
1	2	3		5	6		8	9	10		4			7	11					16
1	2	3		5	6	7	8	9	10		4				11					17
	2	3		5	6	7	8	9	10		4				11	1				18
	2	3	4	5	6	7	8	9	10	11						1				19
	2	3	4	5	6	7	8	9	10						11	1				20
	2	3	4	5	6	7	8		10						11	1	9			21
	2	3		5	6	7	8	4	10						11	1	9			22
	2	3		5	6	7	8	4	10						11	1	9			23
	2	3		5	6	7	8	4	10						11	1	9			24
1	2	3		5	6	7	8	4	10						11		9			25
1	2	3		5	6	7	8	4	10						11		9			26
	2	3		5	6	7	8	4	10						11	1	9			27
	2	3		5	6	7	8	4	10						11	1	9			28
	2	3		5	6	7	8	4	10						11	1	9			29
	2	3		5	6	7		4	10				8		11	1	9			30
1	2			5	6	7	8	4	10		3			9	11					31
1	2	3		5	6	7	8	4	10						11		9			32
1		3		5	6	7	8	4	10		2				11		9			33
1		3		5	6	7	8	4	10		2						9	11		34
1	2	3	6	5		7	8	4	10	11							9			35
1	2	3		5	6	7	8	4	10						11		9			36
1	2	3		5	6	7	8	4	10						11		9			37
1	2	3		5	6	7	8	4	10						11		9			38
1	2	3		5	6	7		4	10						11		9		8	39
1	2	3		5	6	7	8	4	10						11		9			40
1	2	3		5	6		8	4	10	7				9	11					41
1	2			5	6		8	4	10	7	3				11		9			42
30	40	40	13	41	30	39	38	39	42	15	18	4	4	5	28	12	22	1	1	
		4			2	2	25	10	10	6		3		2	8		12			

1 own-goal

	2	3		5	6	7	8	4	10						11	1	9			3
	2	3		5	6	7	8	4	10						11	1	9			4
	2	3		5	6	7	8	4	10						11	1	9			5
1	2	3		5	6	7	8	4	10						11		9			R
1	2			5	6	7	8	4	10		3			11			9			6
1	2			5	6	7	8	4	10		3			11			9			R
3	6	4		6	6	6	6	6	6		2			2	4	3	6			
	1			1		1	2	1							1		6			

1 own-goal

1957-58

Manager: J.Crayston

1	Aug	24	(a)	Sunderland	W	1-0	Groves	56,493
2		27	(h)	West Brom A	D	2-2	Herd 2	45,988
3		31	(h)	Luton T	W	2-0	Groves, Holton	50,111
4	Sep	4	(a)	West Brom A	W	2-1	Bloomfield, Swallow	25,600
5		7	(a)	Blackpool	L	0-1		31,486
6		10	(h)	Everton	L	2-3	Groves 2	42,010
7		14	(h)	Leicester C	W	3-1	Groves 2, Herd	45,321
8		21	(a)	Manchester U	L	2-4	Tiddy, Herd	47,142
9		28	(h)	Leeds U	W	2-1	Herd 2	39,347
10	Oct	2	(h)	Aston Villa	W	4-0	Swallow, Tiddy, Bloomfield, Herd	18,472
11		5	(a)	Bolton W	W	1-0	Herd	20,212
12		12	(a)	Tottenham H	L	1-3	Holton	60,671
13		16	(a)	Everton	D	2-2	Bloomfield, Herd	54,345
14		19	(h)	Birmingham C	L	1-3	Swallow	39,006
15		26	(a)	Chelsea	D	0-0		66,007
16	Nov	2	(h)	Manchester C	W	2-1	Tapscott, Bloomfield	43,664
17		9	(a)	Nottingham F	L	0-4		34,216
18		16	(h)	Portsmouth	W	3-2	Herd 2, Clapton	40,528
19		23	(a)	Sheffield W	L	0-2		25,200
20		30	(h)	Newcastle U	L	2-3	Holton, Clapton	41,694
21	Dec	7	(a)	Burnley	L	1-2	Holton	18,530
22		14	(h)	Preston NE	W	4-2	Nutt, Herd, Bloomfield, Dunn (og)	31,830
23		21	(h)	Sunderland	W	3-0	Herd 2, Groves	28,105
24		26	(a)	Aston Villa	L	0-3		41,000
25		28	(a)	Luton T	L	0-4		27,291
26	Jan	11	(h)	Blackpool	L	2-3	Herd 2	38,667
27		18	(a)	Leicester C	W	1-0	Groves	31,778
28	Feb	1	(h)	Manchester U	L	4-5	Bloomfield 2, Herd, Tapscott	63,578
29		18	(h)	Bolton W	L	1-2	Bloomfield	28,420
30		22	(h)	Tottenham H	D	4-4	Clapton, Herd, Nutt, Henry (og)	59,116
31	Mar	1	(a)	Birmingham C	L	1-4	Bloomfield	26,824
32		8	(h)	Chelsea	W	5-4	Herd 3, Clapton, Bloomfield	41,570
33		15	(a)	Manchester C	W	4-2	Bloomfield 3, Herd	31,645
34		19	(a)	Leeds U	L	0-2		26,000
35		22	(h)	Sheffield W	W	1-0	Herd	28,074
36		29	(a)	Portsmouth	L	4-5	Bloomfield, Clapton, Nutt, Gunter (og)	23,000
37	Apr	7	(h)	Wolves	L	0-2		51,318
38		8	(a)	Wolves	W	2-1	Groves, Wills (pen)	47,501
39		12	(a)	Newcastle U	D	3-3	Herd, Groves, Bloomfield	42,700
40		19	(h)	Burnley	D	0-0		31,440
41		21	(h)	Nottingham F	D	1-1	Bloomfield	23,217
42		26	(a)	Preston NE	L	0-3		21,528

FINAL LEAGUE POSITION: 12th in Division One

Appearances
Goals

FA Cup

3	Jan	4	(a)	Northampton T	L	1-3	Clapton	21,344

Appearances
Goals

242

Appearances grid (players as columns, match numbers 1–42 as rows):

Kelsey AJ	Charlton S	Evans DJ	Holton CC	Fotheringham JG	Bowen DL	Clapton DR	Herd DG	Groves VG	Bloomfield JH	Haverty J	Wills LE	Dodgin W	Swallow R	Sullivan CH	Tiddy MD	Tapscott DR	Nutt GE	Goring H	Le Roux DL	Ward G	Standen JA	Petts JWFJ	Biggs A	No.
1	2	3	4	5	6	7	8	9	10	11														1
1	2	3	4	5	6	7	8	9	10	11														2
1	2		4	5	6	7	8	9	10	11	3													3
1	2	3	4		6	7	9		8	11		5				10								4
1	2	3	4		6	7	8	9	10	11		5												5
1	2	3	4		6	7	8	9	10	11		5												6
1	2	3	4		6	7	8	9	10	11		5												7
	2	3	4		6	7	8	9	10			5		1			11							8
		3	4		6	7	9		10		2	5	8	1			11							9
1		3	4		6	7	9		10		2	5	8				11							10
1		3	4		6	7	9		10		2	5	8				11							11
1	2	3	4		6		9	8	10			5					11	7						12
1	2	3	4		6		9		10			5	8				11	7						13
	2	3	4				9		10			5	8	1			11	7	6					14
1	2	3	9			7			10	11	6	5				8				4				15
1	2	3	4		6	7	9		10	11		5				8								16
1	2	3	4			7	9		10	11		5				8			6					17
1	2	3	4		6	7	9	8	10	11		5												18
1	2	3	4		6	7	9		10	11		5	8											19
1	2	3	9		6	7	8		10		4	5					11							20
	2	3	9		6			8	10			5					11		4	7	1			21
1	2	3	4		6		8	9	10			5					11	7						22
1	2	3	4		6		8	9	10			5					11	7						23
1	2	3	4		6		8	9	10			5					11	7						24
1	2	3	4				8	9	10			5					11	6	7					25
1		3			6	7	9		10		2	5				8	11		4					26
1	2	3		5	6	7	9		10							8	11			4				27
1	2	3		5	6		9	7	10							8	11			4				28
1	2	3		5			9	7	10							8	11		6	4				29
1	2	3		5		7	9	8	10								11		6	4				30
1	2	3		5		7	9	8	10								11		6	4				31
1	2			5		7	9	8	10		3						11		6	4				32
1	2			5		7	9	8	10		3						11		6	4				33
1	2		6	5		7	9	8	10		3						11			4				34
1	2			5		7	9	8	10		3						11		6	4				35
1	2			5	4	7	9	8	10		3						11		6					36
1	2			5	4	7	9	8	10		3						11		6					37
1	2			5	6	7	8		10	11	3									4			9	38
1	2			5	6		9	8	10		3				7		11			4				39
1		3		5	6		9	8	10		2				7		11			4				40
1	2			5			8		10	11	3				7				6	4			9	41
1		3		5	6		9	8	10	11	2				7					4				42
38	36	32	26	19	30	28	39	30	40	15	18	23	7	3	12	8	21	10	5	10	1	9	2	
			4		5		24	10	16	1			3		2	2	3							

3 own-goals

Kelsey AJ	Charlton S	Evans DJ	Holton CC	Fotheringham JG	Bowen DL	Clapton DR	Herd DG	Groves VG	Bloomfield JH	Haverty J	Wills LE	Dodgin W	Swallow R	Sullivan CH	Tiddy MD	Tapscott DR	Nutt GE	Goring H	Le Roux DL	Ward G	Standen JA	Petts JWFJ	Biggs A	No.
1		3	4		6	7	8	9	10		2	5					11							3
1		1	1		1	1	1	1	1		1	1					1							
									1															

1958-59

Manager: G.Swindin

1	Aug	23	(a)	Preston NE	L 1-2	Bloomfield	30,578
2		26	(h)	Burnley	W 3-0	Bloomfield, Holton, Docherty	41,305
3		30	(h)	Leicester C	W 5-1	Holton 2, Evans, Clapton, Nutt	35,411
4	Sep	2	(a)	Burnley	L 1-3	Groves	28,240
5		6	(a)	Everton	W 6-1	Groves, Herd 4, Bloomfield	40,557
6		9	(h)	Bolton W	W 6-1	Herd, Nutt 2, Bloomfield, Clapton, Evans (pen)	45,255
7		13	(h)	Tottenham H	W 3-1	Nutt, Herd 2	65,565
8		17	(a)	Bolton W	L 1-2	Bloomfield	42,391
9		20	(h)	Manchester C	W 4-1	Herd 2, Evans (pen), Bloomfield	47,878
10		27	(a)	Leeds U	L 1-2	Herd	34,000
11	Oct	4	(h)	West Brom A	W 4-3	Henderson 2, Herd, Barlow (og)	57,770
12		11	(a)	Manchester U	D 1-1	Ward	55,909
13		18	(h)	Wolves	D 1-1	Biggs	49,393
14		22	(a)	Aston Villa	W 2-1	Ward, Nutt	30,000
15		25	(a)	Blackburn R	L 2-4	Evans (pen), Ward	37,600
16	Nov	1	(h)	Newcastle U	W 3-2	Groves, Henderson 2	62,801
17		8	(a)	West Ham U	D 0-0		38,250
18		15	(h)	Nottingham F	W 3-1	Herd, Henderson, McKinlay (og)	49,106
19		22	(a)	Chelsea	W 3-0	Henderson, Clapton, Barnwell	57,910
20		29	(h)	Blackpool	L 1-4	Clapton	54,792
21	Dec	6	(a)	Portsmouth	W 1-0	Nutt	33,321
22		13	(h)	Aston Villa	L 1-2	Henderson	32,170
23		20	(h)	Preston NE	L 1-2	Henderson	32,860
24		26	(a)	Luton T	L 3-6	Julians, Evans (pen), Bloomfield	21,870
25		27	(h)	Luton T	W 1-0	Bloomfield	56,501
26	Jan	3	(a)	Leicester C	W 3-2	Julians 2, Bloomfield	33,979
27		17	(h)	Everton	W 3-1	Groves 2, Bloomfield	39,474
28		31	(a)	Tottenham H	W 4-1	Groves, Herd, Henderson 2	60,241
29	Feb	7	(a)	Manchester C	D 0-0		31,819
30		21	(a)	West Brom A	D 1-1	Julians	32,700
31		24	(h)	Leeds U	W 1-0	Herd	30,244
32		28	(h)	Manchester U	W 3-2	Barnwell 2, Herd	67,386
33	Mar	7	(a)	Wolves	L 1-6	Haverty	40,080
34		14	(h)	Blackburn R	D 1-1	Wills (pen)	40,155
35		21	(a)	Newcastle U	L 0-1		32,620
36		28	(h)	West Ham U	L 1-2	Henderson	52,452
37	Apr	4	(a)	Nottingham F	D 1-1	Haverty	32,558
38		11	(h)	Chelsea	D 1-1	Ward	40,900
39		14	(a)	Birmingham C	L 1-4	Clapton	25,791
40		18	(a)	Blackpool	W 2-1	Haverty, Julians	17,118
41		25	(h)	Portsmouth	W 5-2	Groves 3, Henderson, Gunter (og)	24,569
42	May	4	(h)	Birmingham C	W 2-1	Clapton, Groves	26,129

FINAL LEAGUE POSITION: 3rd in Division One

Appearances
Goals

FA Cup

3	Jan	10	(a)	Bury	W 1-0	Herd	29,880
4		24	(a)	Colchester U	D 2-2	Groves 2	16,000
R		28	(h)	Colchester U	W 4-0	Herd 2, Julians, Evans (pen)	62,686
5	Feb	14	(h)	Sheffield U	D 2-2	Evans (pen), Julians	55,407
R		18	(a)	Sheffield U	L 0-3		48,763

Appearances
Goals

244

Player appearance and scoring grid (shirt numbers worn each match; right-hand column = match number):

Kelsey AJ	Charlton S	Evans DJ	Ward G	Dodgin W	Bowen DL	Clapton DR	Groves VG	Herd DG	Bloomfield JH	Haverty J	Docherty TH	Holton CC	Nutt GE	Wills LE	Henderson JG	Standen JA	Petts JWFJ	Biggs A	Barnwell J	Goring H	Fotheringham JG	Julians LB	McCullough WJ	Goy PJ	Goulden RL	
1	2	3	4	5	6	7	8	9	10	11																1
1	2	3	4	5		7	8		10		6	9	11													2
1	2	3	4	5		7	8		10		6	9	11													3
1	2	3	4	5		7	8		10		6	9	11													4
1		3	4	5		7	8	9	10		6		11	2												5
1		3	4	5		7	8	9	10		6		11	2												6
1		3	4	5		7	8	9	10		6		11	2												7
1		3	4	5		7	8	9	10		6		11	2												8
1		3	4	5		7	8	9	10		6		11	2												9
1		3	4	5		7	8	9	10		6		11	2												10
1		3	4	5		7	8	9	10		6			2	11											11
1		3	4	5		7	8	9	10		6			2	11											12
		3	4	5		7	8		10				11	2		1	6			9						13
1		3	4	5		7	8	9	10		6		11	2												14
1		3	4	5		7	8	9	10		6		11	2												15
1		3	4	5		7	8	9	10		6			2	11											16
1		3	4	5		7	8	9	10		6			2	11											17
1		3	4	5		7	8	9	10		6			2	11											18
1		3		5	6	7			10	11	4			2	9				8							19
1		3		5		7			10	11	4			2			6		9	8						20
1		3	4	5		7			10		6		11	2	9				8							21
1		3	8	5		7			10		6		11	2	9				4							22
1		3	4	5		7	8		10		6			2	11				9							23
1		3	4			7	8		10		6			2	11			5				9				24
1				5		7	8		10		4			2	11				6			9	3			25
1				5	6	7		9	10		4			2	11				8				3			26
		3	4		6	7	8	9	10		5			2	11	1										27
1		3	4	5	6	7	8	9						2	11							10				28
1		3	4	5	6	7	8	9						2	11				10							29
		3		5	6	7		9			4			2	11	1			10	8						30
		3		5		7				11	4			2					10	9		8		1		31
		3	8	5	6	7		9		11	4			2		1			10							32
		3	8	5	6	7		9		11	4			2		1			10							33
				5	6	7		9		11	4			2		1			8			10	3			34
				5	6	7	8	9			4		11	2		1			10				3			35
	2		4	5		7	8				6				11	1		9				10	3			36
	2			5	6	7	8	9					11			1			4			10	3			37
	2		4	5	6		8			11	7					1			10			9	3			38
	2		4	5		7	8	9							11	1			10				3			39
	2		4	5		7	8			11	6					1			10			9	3			40
				5	6	7	8		10		4			2	11	1						9	3			41
		3	4		6	7		9	10		5								8						1	42
27	4	37	31	39	16	39	33	26	29	10	38	3	16	33	21	13	3	2	16	2	1	10	10	2	1	
		5	4			6	10	15	10	3	1	3	6	1	12			1	3			5				

3 own-goals

Kelsey AJ	Charlton S	Evans DJ	Ward G	Dodgin W	Bowen DL	Clapton DR	Groves VG	Herd DG	Bloomfield JH	Haverty J	Docherty TH	Holton CC	Nutt GE	Wills LE	Henderson JG	Standen JA	Petts JWFJ	Biggs A	Barnwell J	Goring H	Fotheringham JG	Julians LB	McCullough WJ	Goy PJ	Goulden RL	
1				5	6	7		9	10		4			2	11				8				3			3
1		3	4		6	7	8	9	10		5			2	11							10				4
1		3	4	5	6	7	8	9			5			2								10				R
1		3	4	5	6	7	8	9		11				2								10				5
1		3		5	6	7	8	9			4			2	11							10				R
5		4	3	3	5	5	4	5	2	1	4			5	4							4	1			
		2				2	3								2											

1959-60

Manager: G.Swindin

1	Aug	22	(h)	Sheffield W	L	0-1		47,585
2		26	(a)	Nottingham F	W	3-0	Clapton 3	32,386
3		29	(a)	Wolves	D	3-3	Clapton, Herd 2	45,885
4	Sep	1	(h)	Nottingham F	D	1-1	Herd	41,585
5		5	(h)	Tottenham H	D	1-1	Barnwell	61,011
6		9	(a)	Bolton W	W	1-0	Herd	32,571
7		12	(h)	Manchester C	W	3-1	Clapton, Barnwell, Haverty	38,392
8		15	(h)	Bolton W	W	2-1	Herd, Clapton	38,795
9		19	(a)	Blackburn R	D	1-1	Herd	31,800
10		26	(h)	Blackpool	W	2-1	Barnwell, Herd	47,473
11	Oct	3	(a)	Everton	L	1-3	Barnwell	40,587
12		10	(a)	Manchester U	L	2-4	Henderson, Herd	51,872
13		17	(h)	Preston NE	L	0-3		44,073
14		24	(a)	Leicester C	D	2-2	Barnwell, Bloomfield	29,152
15		31	(h)	Birmingham C	W	3-0	Herd, Barnwell, Henderson	34,605
16	Nov	7	(a)	Leeds U	L	2-3	Herd, Henderson	21,500
17		14	(h)	West Ham U	L	1-3	Bloomfield	49,760
18		21	(a)	Chelsea	W	3-1	Haverty 2, Bloomfield	52,748
19		28	(h)	West Brom A	L	2-4	Groves, Bloomfield	41,157
20	Dec	5	(a)	Newcastle U	L	1-4	Haverty	39,940
21		12	(h)	Burnley	L	2-4	Haverty, Bloomfield	26,249
22		19	(a)	Sheffield W	L	1-5	Julians	25,135
23		26	(h)	Luton T	L	0-3		31,466
24		28	(a)	Luton T	W	1-0	Julians	27,055
25	Jan	2	(h)	Wolves	D	4-4	Evans, Haverty, Charles, Wills (pen)	47,854
26		16	(a)	Tottenham H	L	0-3		58,962
27		23	(a)	Manchester C	W	2-1	Charles, Barnes (og)	28,441
28	Feb	6	(h)	Blackburn R	W	5-2	Charles 3, Haverty, Herd	35,633
29		13	(a)	Blackpool	L	1-2	Charles	14,868
30		20	(h)	Everton	W	2-1	Charles 2	28,872
31		27	(h)	Newcastle U	W	1-0	Barnwell	47,657
32	Mar	5	(a)	Preston NE	W	3-0	Haverty, Henderson, Bloomfield	23,635
33		15	(h)	Leicester C	D	1-1	Herd	27,838
34		19	(a)	Burnley	L	2-3	Henderson 2	20,166
35		26	(h)	Leeds U	D	1-1	Herd	19,735
36	Apr	2	(a)	West Ham U	D	0-0		29,000
37		9	(h)	Chelsea	L	1-4	Bloomfield	40,700
38		15	(h)	Fulham	W	2-0	Henderson, Herd	37,873
39		16	(a)	Birmingham C	L	0-3		27,216
40		18	(a)	Fulham	L	0-3		31,058
41		23	(h)	Manchester U	W	5-2	Bloomfield 3, Clapton, Ward	41,057
42		30	(a)	West Brom A	L	0-1		25,600

FINAL LEAGUE POSITION: 13th in Division One

Appearances
Goals

FA Cup

3	Jan	9	(a)	Rotherham U	D	2-2	Julians, Williams (og)	24,750
R		13	(h)	Rotherham U	D	1-1	Bloomfield	57,598
2R		18	(n*)	Rotherham U	L	0-2		56,290

*Played at Hillsborough, Sheffield.

Appearances
Goals

Standen JA	Wills LE	Evans DJ	Docherty TH	Charles M	Ward G	Clapton DR	Groves VG	Herd DG	Bloomfield JH	Henderson JG	Dodgin W	Barnwell J	Haverty J	McCullough WJ	Julians LB	Kelsey AJ	Petts JWFJ	Magill EJ	Nutt GE	Snedden JD	Clapton DP	Everitt MD	
1	2	3	4	5	6	7	8	9	10	11													1
1	2	3		4		7	6	9	10		5	8	11										2
1	2	3		4		7	6	9		10	5	8	11										3
1	2			4		7	6	9	10		5	8	11	3									4
1	2	6	4			7		9	10		5	8	11	3									5
1	2	6	4			7		9		10	5	8	11	3									6
1	2	6	4			7		9	10		5	8	11	3									7
1	2	6		4	7			9	10	11	5	8		3									8
1	2	6			7	4		9	10	11	5	8		3									9
1	2	6			7	4		9	10		5	8	11	3									10
1	2	6			7	4		9	10		5	8	11	3									11
1	2	4			7	6	9	8	10		5		11	3									12
1	2	4					6	10	8	7	5		11	3	9								13
	2		6		4	7	8	11	5	10				3	9	1							14
	2				4			9	10	7	5	8	11	3		1	6						15
1	2				4			9	10	7	5	8	11	3			6						16
	2		4			7	9	8	10		5		11	3		1	6						17
	2				7	4		10	9		5	8	11	3		1	6						18
	2					7	9	10	8		5	4	11	3		1	6						19
	2	5				7	9	10	8			4	11	3		1	6						20
	2		6		7	4		10	9		5	8	11	3		1							21
1		3			7	4			10	8	5	6	11		9			2					22
1		3	4	11		7			10		5	8			9		6	2					23
1	4	3						8	10		5	6	11		9		7	2					24
1	6	3		9			8	10		7	5	4	11					2					25
1	4	3				7		8	10			6	11		9			2		5			26
	6	5	9	4	7		8		10				11	3		1		2					27
	6	5	9	4			8		10	7			11	3		1		2					28
	6	5	9				8		10	7		4	11	3		1		2					29
	6	9	4						10	7	5	8	11	3		1		2					30
	6	9	4						10	7	5	8	11	3		1		2					31
	6	9	4				8		10	7	5		11	3		1		2					32
1	6	9	4					10	8	7	5		11	3				2					33
			4			6		8		7	5	10	11	3		1		2			9		34
			4		6		9	10		7	5	8	11	3		1		2					35
		5	4		6		8		10	7			11	3	9	1		2					36
			4		6		9	10		7	5	8	11	3		1		2					37
	2	5	4				8		10	7			11	3		1			9	6			38
	3	5			6		8		10	7			11	3		1	2	11	9	4			39
	2	5	9	6					10	7				3	8	1	11				4		40
	2	5		4	7			9	10	8			11	3		1						6	41
	2	5		4	7			9	10	8			11	3		1						6	42
20	33	7	24	20	15	23	30	31	36	31	30	28	35	33	8	22	7	17	3	1	3	5	
	1	1		8	1	7	1	14	10	7		7	8		2								

1 own-goal

Standen JA	Wills LE	Evans DJ	Docherty TH	Charles M	Ward G	Clapton DR	Groves VG	Herd DG	Bloomfield JH	Henderson JG	Dodgin W	Barnwell J	Haverty J	McCullough WJ	Julians LB	Kelsey AJ	Petts JWFJ	Magill EJ	Nutt GE	Snedden JD	Clapton DP	Everitt MD	
1	6	3	4						10	7	5	8	11		9			2					3
1	4	3	5		7		9	10	8		6	11						2					R
1	3		4	9		7			10	11		6			8			2	5				2R
3	3	2	3	1		2		1	3	3	1	3	2		2			3		1			
								1							1								

1 own-goal

247

1960-61

Manager: G.Swindin

1	Aug	20	(a)	Burnley	L 2-3	Herd, Bloomfield	23,653
2		23	(h)	Preston NE	W 1-0	Everitt	31,612
3		27	(h)	Nottingham F	W 3-0	Henderson, Skirton 2	28,878
4		30	(a)	Preston NE	L 0-2		20,105
5	Sep	3	(a)	Manchester C	D 0-0		36,656
6		6	(h)	Birmingham C	W 2-0	Herd, Kane	20,285
7		10	(h)	Tottenham H	L 2-3	Herd, Ward	60,088
8		14	(a)	Birmingham C	L 0-2		22,904
9		17	(h)	Newcastle U	W 5-0	Herd 3, Strong, Clapton	34,885
10		24	(a)	Cardiff C	L 0-1		35,000
11	Oct	1	(h)	West Brom A	W 1-0	Herd	27,176
12		8	(a)	Leicester C	L 1-2	Henderson	22,501
13		15	(h)	Aston Villa	W 2-1	Herd, Strong	34,048
14		22	(a)	Blackburn R	W 4-2	Strong 2, Charles, Herd	21,500
15		29	(h)	Manchester U	W 2-1	Barnwell, Herd	45,715
16	Nov	5	(a)	West Ham U	L 0-6		29,375
17		12	(h)	Chelsea	L 1-4	Charles	38,886
18		19	(a)	Blackpool	D 1-1	Herd	15,417
19		26	(h)	Everton	W 3-2	Herd 3	36,709
20	Dec	3	(a)	Wolves	L 3-5	Herd 2, Barnwell	25,658
21		10	(h)	Bolton W	W 5-1	Barnwell, Strong 2, Eastham 2	30,818
22		17	(h)	Burnley	L 2-5	Strong, Herd	37,209
23		23	(a)	Sheffield W	D 1-1	Neill	29,311
24		26	(h)	Sheffield W	D 1-1	Eastham	43,555
25		31	(a)	Nottingham F	W 5-3	Herd 3, Eastham, Henderson	30,735
26	Jan	14	(h)	Manchester C	W 5-4	Herd 3, Henderson, Clapton	36,440
27		21	(a)	Tottenham H	L 2-4	Henderson, Haverty	65,251
28	Feb	4	(a)	Newcastle U	D 3-3	Strong 2, Eastham	34,780
29		11	(h)	Cardiff C	L 2-3	Herd 2	33,754
30		18	(a)	West Brom A	W 3-2	Haverty 2, Skirton	21,500
31		25	(h)	Leicester C	L 1-3	Henderson	31,721
32	Mar	4	(a)	Aston Villa	D 2-2	Haverty, Barnwell	35,000
33		11	(h)	Blackburn R	D 0-0		34,250
34		18	(a)	Manchester U	D 1-1	Charles	29,732
35		25	(h)	West Ham U	D 0-0		27,665
36		31	(a)	Fulham	D 2-2	Herd 2	35,476
37	Apr	1	(a)	Bolton W	D 1-1	Henderson	18,618
38		3	(h)	Fulham	W 4-2	Henderson 2, Barnwell 2	20,142
39		8	(h)	Blackpool	W 1-0	Herd	36,301
40		15	(a)	Chelsea	L 1-3	Strong	38,233
41		22	(h)	Wolves	L 1-5	Henderson	34,429
42		29	(a)	Everton	L 1-4	Herd	39,810

FINAL LEAGUE POSITION: 11th in Division One

Appearances
Goals

FA Cup

3	Jan	7	(a)	Sunderland	L 1-2	Herd	58,575

Appearances
Goals

248

Kelsey AJ	Wills LE	McCullough WJ	Everitt MD	Snedden JD	Docherty TH	Skirton AFG	Barnwell J	Herd DG	Bloomfield JH	Henderson JG	Ward G	Kane P	Clapton DR	Groves VG	Strong GH	Charles M	Standen JA	Haverty J	Clapton DP	Eastham GE	Magill EJ	Neill WJT	Young AR	O'Neill FS	McClelland J	Bacuzzi DR	Petts JWFJ	Griffiths AT	
1	2	3	4	5	6	7	8	9	10	11																			1
1	2	3	6		5	7	8	9	10	11	4																		2
1	2	3	4	5	6	7	8	9	10	11																			3
1	2	3	4	5	6	7	8	9	10	11																			4
1	2	3		5	6	7		9	8	11	4	10																	5
1	2	3		5	6			9	8	11	4	10	7																6
1	2	3		5	6			9	8	11	4	10	7																7
1	2	3		5	6	7		9	8	11	4	10																	8
1	2	3		5				8	10	11	4		7	6	9														9
1	2	3		5				8	10	11	4		7	6	9														10
1	2	3		5	4			8	10	11			7	6	9														11
1	2	3		5	4			8	10	11			7	6	9														12
1	2	3		5	4		8	10		11			7	6	9														13
	2	3		5	4		8	10		11				6	7	9	1												14
1	2	3		5	4		8	10		11				6	7	9													15
1	2	3		5	4		8	10						6	7	9		11											16
1	2	3		5	4		8	10		11				6	7	9													17
1	2	3		5			8	10		11			7	6	9				4										18
1	2	3		5	4		8	10		11			7	6	9														19
1	2	3		5	4		8	10		11			7	6	9														20
1	2	3		5	4		8			11			7	6	9					10									21
1	2	3		5	4			10		11			7	6	9					8									22
1		3		5		11		9		10			7	6						8	2	4							23
1		3				7	8	9		11				6						10	2	4	5						24
1		3					8	9		11				6		5				10	2	4		7					25
1		3						9		10			7	6		5		11		8	2	4							26
		3			6			9		10			7					11		8	2	4	5		1				27
	2	3			4	7				10				6	9			11		8			5		1				28
	2	3				7		9						6	8	4		11		10			5		1				29
		3				7	8	9						6		5		11		10		4			1	2			30
1		3				7		9		10				6		5		11		8		4				2			31
1		3					8	9		7	4			6		5		11		10						2			32
1		3					8	9		7	4			6		5		11		10						2			33
1		3		5			10	9		7				6		4		11		8						2			34
1		3					10	9		7				6		4		11		8		5				2			35
1		3						9		10			7	6		4		11		8		5				2			36
1						11	8	9		10			7	6		4					3	5				2			37
1		3				11	8	9		10			7	6								5				2	4		38
1		3				11	8	9		10				6		4						5		7		2			39
1		3					8	9		11				6	7	4				10		5				2			40
1		3					6	9		11					7	4				10		5				2		8	41
1		3				7	4	10		11				6	9	5				8						2			42
37	24	41	4	23	21	16	26	40	12	39	9	4	18	32	19	19	1	12	1	19	6	14	4	2	4	13	1	1	
			1			3	6	29	1	10	1	1	2		10	3		4		5		1							

1		3					7	8		11				6	9	5				10	2	4							3
1		1					1	1		1				1	1	1				1	1	1							
								1																					

1961-62

Manager: G.Swindin

1	Aug	19	(h)	Burnley	D	2-2 Charles 2	42,856
2		23	(a)	Leicester C	W	1-0 Eastham	29,396
3		26	(a)	Tottenham H	L	3-4 Charles 2, Skirton	59,371
4		29	(h)	Leicester C	D	4-4 MacLeod, Eastham, Skirton, Charles	35,055
5	Sep	2	(a)	Bolton W	L	1-2 Charles	18,414
6		9	(h)	Manchester C	W	3-0 Griffiths, Skirton, Sears (og)	41,478
7		16	(a)	West Brom A	L	0-4	20,560
8		20	(a)	Sheffield W	D	1-1 Charles	35,903
9		23	(h)	Birmingham C	D	1-1 Skirton	31,749
10		30	(a)	Everton	L	1-4 Charles	43,289
11	Oct	7	(h)	Blackpool	W	3-0 Charles 2, Ward	41,166
12		14	(a)	Blackburn R	D	0-0	14,000
13		21	(h)	Manchester U	W	5-1 Skirton 2, Eastham, Barnwell, Ward	54,099
14		28	(a)	Cardiff C	D	1-1 Charles	25,400
15	Nov	4	(h)	Chelsea	L	0-3	37,590
16		11	(a)	Aston Villa	L	1-3 Skirton	24,200
17		14	(h)	Sheffield W	W	1-0 Strong	19,331
18		18	(h)	Nottingham F	W	2-1 Strong, MacLeod	34,217
19		25	(a)	Wolves	W	3-2 Ward 2, Skirton	28,882
20	Dec	2	(h)	West Ham U	D	2-2 Strong, Skirton	47,206
21		9	(a)	Sheffield U	L	1-2 Strong	19,213
22		16	(a)	Burnley	W	2-0 Skirton, Charles	22,887
23		23	(h)	Tottenham H	W	2-1 Charles, Skirton	63,440
24		26	(h)	Fulham	W	1-0 Charles	32,969
25	Jan	13	(h)	Bolton W	L	1-2 Charles	33,351
26		20	(a)	Manchester C	L	2-3 Skirton 2	20,414
27	Feb	3	(h)	West Brom A	L	0-1	29,597
28		10	(a)	Birmingham C	L	0-1	27,797
29		24	(a)	Blackpool	W	1-0 Strong	13,728
30	Mar	3	(h)	Blackburn R	D	0-0	25,744
31		17	(h)	Cardiff C	D	1-1 Strong	25,059
32		24	(a)	Chelsea	W	3-2 Skirton, Barnwell, MacLeod	31,016
33		31	(h)	Aston Villa	L	4-5 Skirton 2, Strong 2	20,107
34	Apr	7	(a)	Nottingham F	W	1-0 Strong	21,129
35		11	(a)	Fulham	L	2-5 Skirton, MacLeod	26,517
36		14	(h)	Wolves	W	3-1 Skirton, Strong 2	24,367
37		16	(a)	Manchester U	W	3-2 Eastham, Skirton, Cantwell (og)	24,788
38		20	(a)	Ipswich T	D	2-2 MacLeod, Eastham	30,649
39		21	(a)	West Ham U	D	3-3 Clapton, Strong, MacLeod	31,912
40		23	(h)	Ipswich T	L	0-3	44,694
41		28	(h)	Sheffield U	W	2-0 Barnwell, Eastham	18,761
42	May	1	(h)	Everton	L	2-3 Griffiths, Armstrong	20,034

FINAL LEAGUE POSITION: 10th in Division One

Appearances

Goals

FA Cup

3	Jan	6	(h)	Bradford C	W	3-0 Charles 2, Lawlor (og)	40,232
4		31	(a)	Manchester U	L	0-1	54,082

Appearances

Goals

250

Kelsey AJ	Magill EJ	McCullough WJ	Brown L	Snedden JD	Neill WJT	MacLeod JM	Eastham GE	Charles M	Henderson JG	Skirton AFG	McClelland J	Petts JWFJ	Griffiths AT	Groves VG	Bacuzzi DR	Ward G	McKechnie IH	Strong GH	Barnwell J	Clamp E	Armstrong G	Clapton DR	Clarke FRG	
1	2	3	4	5	6	7	8	9	10	11														1
	2	3	4	5	6	7	8	9	10	11	1													2
	2	3	4	5	6	7	8	9	10	11	1													3
	2	3	4	5	6	7	8	9	10	11	1													4
	2	3	4		5	7	8	9	10	11	1	6												5
1	2	3	4	5	6	7	10		9	11				8										6
1	2	3	4	5	6	7	10	9		11				8										7
1	2	3	4	5	6	7	8	9	10	11														8
1	2	3	4	5	6	7	8	9	10	11														9
1	2	3	4	5	6	7	8	9		11				10										10
1		3		5		11	8	9	10	7				6	2	4								11
		3		5		7	8			11				6	2	4	1	9	10					12
1		3		5		7		10	9	11				6	2	4		8						13
1		3		5		7		10	9	11				6	2	4		8						14
1	2	3		5		7		10	9	11				6		4		8						15
1		3		5		7	8	9	10	11				6	2	4								16
		3		5		7	8		10	11				6	2	4	1	9						17
1		3		5		7	10			11				6	2			9		4				18
1		3		5		7	10			11				6	2	8		9		4				19
1		3		5		7	10			11				6	2	8		9		4				20
1		3		5	6	7	10			11					2	8		9		4				21
1		3		5	6	7	10	9		11					2	8				4				22
1		3		5	6	7	10	9		11					2			8		4				23
1		3		5	6	7	10	9		11					2			8		4				24
1		3		5	6	7	10	9		11		8			2					4				25
1		3		5	6		11	10	9	7					2			8		4				26
1		3		5			11		9	7		6	10		2	8				4				27
1		3		5			11		8	7		6			2			9	10	4				28
1		3		5	4		10			11		6		9	2			8			7			29
1		3		5	4		10			7		6		9	2			8				11		30
1		3		5			10			11				6	2			9	8	4	7			31
1		3		5		7	10			11				6	2			9	8	4				32
1				5		7				11		8	6		2			9	10	4			3	33
1	2	3	4	5		7	10			11		8						9	6					34
	2	3		5		7	10			11		6		8			1	9		4				35
1	2	3	4	5		7				11		8						9	10	6				36
1	2	3	4	5		7	10			11		6	8					9						37
1	2	3	4	5		7	10			11		6	8					9						38
1	2	3	4	5		11	10					6	8					9			7			39
1	2	3		5		11	10					6	8					9		4		7		40
1	2	3	4	5			10					6	8					9			11	7		41
1	2	3	4	5			10					6	8					9			11	7		42
35	21	40	41	15	20	37	38	21	12	38	4	12	14	16	22	11	3	20	14	18	4	5	1	
						6	6	15		19				2		4		12	3		1	1		

2 own-goal

Kelsey AJ	Magill EJ	McCullough WJ	Brown L	Snedden JD	Neill WJT	MacLeod JM	Eastham GE	Charles M	Henderson JG	Skirton AFG	McClelland J	Petts JWFJ	Griffiths AT	Groves VG	Bacuzzi DR	Ward G	McKechnie IH	Strong GH	Barnwell J	Clamp E	Armstrong G	Clapton DR	Clarke FRG	
1		3		5	6	7	10	9		11					2			8		4				3
1		3		5	4		11	10	9	7					2			8		6				4
2		2		2	2	2	2	2		2					2			2		2				
								2																

1 own-goal

1962-63

Manager: W.Wright

1	Aug	18	(a)	Leyton O	W	2-1	Strong, Baker	26,300
2		21	(h)	Birmingham C	W	2-0	Baker, McCullough	34,004
3		25	(h)	Manchester U	L	1-3	Clamp	62,308
4		29	(a)	Birmingham C	D	2-2	Strong 2	27,135
5	Sep	1	(a)	Burnley	L	1-2	Skirton	26,231
6		4	(h)	Aston Villa	L	1-2	Skirton	33,861
7		8	(h)	Sheffield W	L	1-2	Baker	31,115
8		10	(a)	Aston Villa	L	1-3	Baker	36,705
9		15	(a)	Fulham	W	3-1	Skirton, MacLeod, Baker	31,442
10		22	(h)	Leicester C	D	1-1	Baker	31,291
11		29	(a)	Bolton W	L	0-3		16,572
12	Oct	6	(a)	Tottenham H	D	4-4	Court 2, MacLeod, Strong	61,749
13		13	(h)	West Ham U	D	1-1	Baker	49,597
14		27	(h)	Wolves	W	5-4	Baker 3, Eastham 2	43,002
15	Nov	3	(a)	Blackburn R	D	5-5	Baker 2, Skirton 2, Eastham	15,400
16		10	(h)	Sheffield U	W	1-0	Strong	25,503
17		14	(a)	Liverpool	L	1-2	Strong	38,452
18		17	(a)	Nottingham F	L	0-3		24,804
19		24	(h)	Ipswich T	W	3-1	Baker, Armstrong, Barnwell	25,056
20	Dec	1	(a)	Manchester C	W	4-2	MacLeod 2, Baker, Strong	25,454
21		8	(h)	Blackpool	W	2-0	Strong, Martin (og)	23,767
22		15	(h)	Leyton O	W	2-0	Baker 2	29,075
23	Feb	9	(a)	Leicester C	L	0-2		26,320
24		16	(h)	Bolton W	W	3-2	MacLeod, Brown, Armstrong	25,204
25		23	(h)	Tottenham H	L	2-3	Strong, Baker	59,980
26	Mar	2	(a)	West Ham U	W	4-0	Baker 2, McCullough, Strong	31,467
27		9	(h)	Liverpool	D	2-2	MacLeod, McCullough	30,496
28		23	(h)	Blackburn R	W	3-1	Strong 2, MacLeod	21,467
29		26	(h)	Everton	W	4-3	Strong, Baker, MacLeod, Skirton	38,061
30		30	(a)	Ipswich T	D	1-1	Thrower (og)	16,686
31	Apr	6	(h)	Nottingham F	D	0-0		25,134
32		8	(a)	Wolves	L	0-1		18,593
33		12	(h)	West Brom A	W	3-2	Strong 2, Skirton	28,219
34		13	(a)	Sheffield U	D	3-3	Baker, Anderson, Barnwell	21,487
35		15	(a)	West Brom A	W	2-1	Baker 2	16,600
36		20	(h)	Manchester C	L	2-3	MacLeod, Strong	20,539
37		24	(a)	Everton	D	1-1	Strong	56,034
38		27	(a)	Blackpool	L	2-3	Sammels, Skirton	13,864
39	May	6	(a)	Manchester U*	W	3-2	Baker, Strong, Skirton	36,000
40		11	(h)	Burnley	L	2-3	Skirton, Baker	23,256
41		14	(h)	Fulham	W	3-0	Baker 3	17,389
42		18	(a)	Sheffield W	W	3-2	Baker, Eastham, Court	20,514

FINAL LEAGUE POSITION: 7th in Division One   Appearances

*After abandoned match (57 minutes) on December 22   Goals

FA Cup

3	Jan	30	(h)	Oxford U	W	5-1	Baker 2, Strong 2, MacLeod	14,649
4	Mar	12	(h)	Sheffield W	W	2-0	MacLeod, Strong	40,367
5		16	(h)	Liverpool	L	1-2	MacLeod	55,245

Appearances

Goals

McKechnie IH	Magill EJ	McCullough WJ	Brown L	Neill WJT	Snedden JD	Armstrong G	Strong GH	Baker JH	Barnwell J	Skirton AFG	Clamp E	Eatham GE	Bacuzzi DR	McClelland J	Court DJ	Smithson RG	Ward G	MacLeod JM	Groves VG	Anderson TK	Clarke FRG	Sammels JC	No.
1	2	3	4	5	6	7	8	9	10	11													1
1	2	3	4	5	6	7	8	9	10	11													2
1	2	3	5		6	7	9		10	11	4	8											3
1	2	3	5		6	7	8	9	10	11	4												4
1		3	5		6	7	8	9	10	11	4		2										5
	3	5			6	7	9	8		11	4	10	2	1									6
	2	3	4	5	6	7		9	10	11		8		1									7
1	2	3	4	5	6	7		9	10	11					8								8
1	2	3	5		6		9			11		8	4	10				7					9
1	2	3	4	5	6		8	9	10	11								7					10
1	2	3	5				8	9	10	11			4		6			7					11
	2	3	5	4			8			11		10		1	9			7	6				12
	2	3	5	4	6		8	9		11		10		1				7					13
	2	3	5	4	6		8	9		11		10		1				7					14
	2	3	5	4			8	9		11		10		1				7	6				15
	2	3	5	4			8	9		11		10		1				7	6				16
	2	3	5	4			8	9		11		10		1				7	6				17
	2	3	5	4		11	8	9				10		1				7	6				18
	2	3	5		6	11		9	4			10		1	8			7					19
	2	3	5		6	11	8	9	4			10		1				7					20
	2	3	5		6	11	8	9	4			10		1				7					21
	2	3	5		6	11	8	9	4			10		1				7					22
	2	3	5		6		8	9	4			10		1	7			11					23
	2	3	5		6	11	8	9	4			10		1				7					24
	2	3	5		6	11	8	9	4			10		1				7					25
	2	3	5		6		8	9	4			10		1				7	11				26
	2	3	5		6		8	9	4			10		1				7	11				27
	2	3	5		6		8	9	4	11		10		1				7					28
	2	3	5		6		8	9	4	11		10		1				7					29
	2	3	5		6		8	9	4	11		10		1				7					30
		3	5		6		8	9	4	11		10	2	1				7					31
		3	5		6		8	9	4	11		10	2	1				7					32
		3	5		6		8	9	4	11		10	2	1				7					33
	2	11	5		6		8	9	4			10	3	1					7				34
		3	5				8	9	4			10		1				7	6	11	2		35
	2	3	5				8	9	4			10		1				7	6	11			36
	2	6	5				8	9	4	11		10		1				7			3		37
	2	6	5					9	4	11		10		1				7			3	8	38
	2	6	5				8	9	4	11				1				7			3	10	39
	2	6	5				8	9	4	11		10		1				7			3		40
	2	3	5			11	8	9	4			10		1				7	6				41
	2	3	5					9	4	11		10		1	8			7	6				42
9	36	42	38	17	27	16	36	39	34	28	4	33	6	33	6	2	2	33	9	5	5	2	
			3	1		2	18	29	2	10	1	4			3			9		1		1	

2 own-goals

McKechnie IH	Magill EJ	McCullough WJ	Brown L	Neill WJT	Snedden JD	Armstrong G	Strong GH	Baker JH	Barnwell J	Skirton AFG	Clamp E	Eatham GE	Bacuzzi DR	McClelland J	Court DJ	Smithson RG	Ward G	MacLeod JM	Groves VG	Anderson TK	Clarke FRG	Sammels JC	No.
	2	3	5		6		8	9	4			10		1	7			11					3
	2	3	5		6		8	9	4	11		10		1				7					4
	2	3	5		6		8	9	4	11		10		1				7					5
	3	3	3		3		3	3	3	2		3		3	1			3					
							3	2										3					

1963-64

1	Aug	24	(h)	Wolves	L	1-3	Strong	50,302
2		27	(h)	West Brom A	W	3-2	Baker 2, Strong	31,381
3		31	(a)	Leicester C	L	2-7	Barnwell (pen), MacLeod	29,620
4	Sep	4	(a)	West Brom A	L	0-4		24,500
5		7	(h)	Bolton W	W	4-3	Skirton 2, Baker, Ure	26,016
6		10	(h)	Aston Villa	W	3-0	Baker 3	29,189
7		14	(a)	Fulham	W	4-1	Strong 2, Baker, MacLeod	34,910
8		21	(h)	Manchester U	W	2-1	Eastham, Baker	56,776
9		28	(a)	Burnley	W	3-0	Strong 2, Eastham	20,618
10	Oct	2	(a)	Everton	L	1-2	Strong	51,829
11		5	(h)	Ipswich T	W	6-0	Strong 3, Baker 2, MacLeod	31,803
12		9	(a)	Stoke C	W	2-1	Baker 2	31,014
13		15	(h)	Tottenham H	D	4-4	Eastham 2, Baker, Strong	67,986
14		19	(a)	Aston Villa	L	1-2	MacLeod	22,981
15		26	(h)	Nottingham F	W	4-2	Strong 2, Anderson, McKinlay (og)	41,124
16	Nov	2	(a)	Sheffield U	D	2-2	Baker, Strong	33,908
17		5	(h)	Birmingham C	W	4-1	Baker 3, Strong	23,499
18		9	(h)	West Ham U	D	3-3	MacLeod, Eastham, Anderson	52,742
19		16	(a)	Chelsea	L	1-3	Eastham	47,050
20		23	(h)	Blackpool	W	5-3	Strong 2, Barnwell, Brown, Eastham	33,847
21		30	(a)	Blackburn R	L	1-4	Baker	21,000
22	Dec	7	(h)	Liverpool	D	1-1	Baker	40,551
23		10	(h)	Everton	W	6-0	Baker 2, Eastham 2, Armstrong, Strong	33,644
24		14	(a)	Wolves	D	2-2	Strong 2	18,952
25		21	(h)	Leicester C	L	0-1		28,019
26		28	(a)	Birmingham C	W	4-1	MacLeod 2, Baker, Armstrong	23,329
27	Jan	11	(a)	Bolton W	D	1-1	Baker	14,651
28		18	(h)	Fulham	D	2-2	Baker, Strong	35,895
29	Feb	1	(a)	Manchester U	L	1-3	McCullough	48,340
30		8	(h)	Burnley	W	3-2	Strong, Armstrong, Anderson	30,863
31		18	(a)	Ipswich T	W	2-1	Eastham, Strong	17,486
32		22	(a)	Tottenham H	L	1-3	Strong	57,358
33		29	(h)	Stoke C	D	1-1	Baker	26,208
34	Mar	7	(a)	Nottingham F	L	0-2		18,416
35		14	(h)	Chelsea	L	2-4	Neill, Baker	25,513
36		21	(a)	West Ham U	D	1-1	Skirton	28,170
37		24	(h)	Sheffield W	D	1-1	Strong	18,221
38		28	(h)	Sheffield U	L	1-3	Strong	21,001
39		30	(a)	Sheffield W	W	4-0	Skirton 3, Court	26,433
40	Apr	4	(a)	Blackpool	W	1-0	Skirton	14,067
41		11	(h)	Blackburn R	D	0-0		26,164
42		18	(a)	Liverpool	L	0-5		48,623

FINAL LEAGUE POSITION: 8th in Division One

Appearances

Goals

FA Cup

3	Jan	4	(h)	Wolves	W	2-1	Strong, Baker	40,803
4		25	(a)	West Brom A	D	3-3	MacLeod, Armstrong, Baker	39,597
R		29	(h)	West Brom A	W	2-0	Armstrong, Strong	57,698
5	Feb	15	(h)	Liverpool	L	0-1		61,295

Appearances

Goals

254

McClelland J	Magill EJ	McCullough WJ	Barnwell J	Ure IF	Brown L	Skirton AFG	Strong GH	Baker JH	Eastham GE	Armstrong G	MacLeod JM	McKechnie IH	Neill WJT	Bacuzzi DR	Groves VG	Court DJ	Wilson RP	Anderson TK	Clarke FRG	Furnell J	Snedden JD	Simpson PF	Radford J	
1	2	3	4	5	6	7	8	9	10	11														1
1	2	3	4	5	6	11	8	9	10		7													2
1	2	3	4	5	6	11	8	9	10		7													3
	2	3	6	5		11	8	9	10		7	1	4											4
		3		6	5	11	8	9	10		7	1	4	2										5
	2	3		5	4	11	8	9	10		7	1			6									6
	2	3		5	4	11	8	9	10		7	1			6									7
	2	3		5	4		8	9	10	11	7	1			6									8
	2	3		5	4		8	9	10	11	7	1			6									9
	2	3		5	4		8	9	10	11	7	1			6									10
	2	3		5	4		8	9	10	11	7	1			6									11
	2	3	10	5	4			9		11	7	1			6	8								12
	2	3		5	4		8	9	10	11	7	1			6									13
	2	3	10	5	4		8	9		11	7	1			6									14
	2	3	6	5	4		8	9	10		7						1	11						15
	2	3	6	5	4		8	9	10		7						1	11						16
	2		6		4		8	9	10		7		5				1	11	3					17
	2	3	6	5	4		8	9	10		7						1	11						18
	2	3	6	5	4		8	9	10		7						1	11						19
		3	6	5	4		8	9	10		7							11	2	1				20
	2	3	6	5	4	11	8	9	10							7				1				21
	2	3	4	5			8	9	10	11	7									1	6			22
	2	3	4	5			8	9	10	11	7									1	6			23
	2	3	4	5			8	9	10	11	7									1	6			24
	2	3		5	4		8	9	10	11	7									1	6			25
	2	3	10	5	4		8	9		11	7									1	6			26
	2	3	4	5			8	9	10	11	7									1	6			27
		3	4	5			8	9	10	11	7			2						1	6			28
	2	3		5		7	8	9	10	11					4					1	6			29
	2	3		5			8	9	10	7					4			11		1	6			30
	2			5		7	8	9	10	11					4				3	1	6			31
1		3		5			8	9	10	11	7				4				2		6			32
1		3		5			8	9	10	11	7			2	4						6			33
		3		5			8	9	10	11	7			2	4					1	6			34
		3		5			8	9	10	11	7		4	2						1		6		35
	2	3		5		7			10				4			8		11		1		6	9	36
	2	3		5			8		10	7			4			9		11		1		6		37
	2	3		5			8		10	7			4			9		11		1		6		38
	2	3		5		11		9	10	7			4			8				1		6		39
	2	3		5		7		9	10	11			4			8				1		6		40
	2	6		5		7	8	9		11			4			10			3	1				41
	2	3		5		7	8	9	10	11			4							1	6			42
5	35	40	19	41	22	15	38	39	38	28	30	11	11	5	15	8	5	10	5	21	14	6	1	
		1	2	1	1	7	26	26	10	3	7		1			1		3						

1 own-goal

	2	3	4	5			8	9	10	11	7									1	6			3
	2	3		5			8	9	10	11	7				4					1	6			4
	2	3		5		7	8	9	10	11					4					1	6			R
	2	3		5			8	9	10	11	7				4					1	6			5
	4	4	1	4		1	4	4	4	4	3				3					4	4			
							2	2		2	1													

1964-65

1	Aug	22	(a)	Liverpool	L	2-3	Baker, Strong	47,620
2		25	(h)	Sheffield W	D	1-1	Simpson	35,590
3		29	(h)	Aston Villa	W	3-1	Armstrong, MacLeod, Strong	28,732
4	Sep	2	(a)	Sheffield W	L	1-2	Baker	22,555
5		5	(a)	Wolves	W	1-0	Skirton	23,000
6		8	(h)	Blackburn R	D	1-1	Baker	29,510
7		12	(h)	Sunderland	W	3-1	Eastham 2, Strong	34,291
8		16	(a)	Blackburn R	W	2-1	Armstrong, Baker	17,675
9		19	(a)	Leicester C	W	3-2	Baker, Court, Eastham	21,364
10		26	(h)	Chelsea	L	1-3	Court	54,936
11	Oct	6	(h)	Nottingham F	L	0-3		35,041
12		10	(a)	Tottenham H	L	1-3	Baker	55,959
13		17	(h)	Burnley	W	3-2	Baker, Simpson, Sammels	24,962
14		24	(a)	Sheffield U	L	0-4		16,906
15		31	(h)	Everton	W	3-1	Baker 2, Anderson	33,561
16	Nov	7	(a)	Birmingham C	W	3-2	Baker, Eastham, Sammels	20,210
17		11	(a)	Leeds U	L	1-3	Sammels	38,620
18		14	(h)	West Ham U	L	0-3		36,026
19		21	(a)	West Brom A	D	0-0		18,000
20		28	(h)	Manchester U	L	2-3	Anderson, Eastham	59,637
21	Dec	5	(a)	Fulham	W	4-3	Baker 2, Skirton, Armstrong	13,764
22		12	(h)	Liverpool	D	0-0		25,171
23		19	(a)	Aston Villa	L	1-3	Baker	16,000
24		26	(h)	Stoke C	W	3-2	Baker, Sammels, McLintock	27,663
25		28	(a)	Stoke C	L	1-4	Sammels	20,491
26	Jan	2	(h)	Wolves	W	4-1	Radford 3, Baker	25,561
27		16	(a)	Sunderland	W	2-0	Radford, Baker	42,158
28		23	(h)	Leicester C	W	4-3	Baker 2, Eastham, Armstrong	31,063
29	Feb	6	(a)	Chelsea	L	1-2	Radford	46,798
30		13	(h)	Leeds U	L	1-2	Eastham	32,132
31		20	(h)	Fulham	W	2-0	Radford, Baker	22,101
32		23	(h)	Tottenham H	W	3-1	Baker 2, Radford	48,367
33		27	(a)	Burnley	L	1-2	Court	12,841
34	Mar	6	(h)	Sheffield U	D	1-1	Ure	22,001
35		13	(a)	Nottingham F	L	0-3		24,497
36		27	(a)	West Ham U	L	1-2	Baker	24,665
37	Apr	3	(h)	West Brom A	D	1-1	Eastham	18,797
38		6	(h)	Birmingham C	W	3-0	Baker, Skirton, McLintock	16,048
39		16	(a)	Blackpool	D	1-1	Eastham	18,620
40		19	(h)	Blackpool	W	3-1	Baker 2, Neill	17,063
41		24	(a)	Everton	L	0-1		32,643
42		26	(a)	Manchester U	L	1-3	Eastham	51,625

FINAL LEAGUE POSITION: 13th in Division One

Appearances
Goals

FA Cup

3	Jan	9	(a)	Darlington	W	2-0	Radford, Armstrong	19,717
4		30	(a)	Peterborough U	L	1-2	Radford	32,000

Appearances
Goals

Furnell J	Howe D	McCullough WJ	Snedden JD	Ure IF	Simpson PF	Armstrong G	Strong GH	Baker JH	Eastham GE	Anderson TK	Clarke FRG	MacLeod JM	Ferry G	Skirton AFG	Court DJ	Neill WJT	McLintock F	Burns AJ	Sammels JC	Radford J	Tawse B	Magill EJ	Baldwin T	#
1	2	3	4	5	6	7	8	9	10	11														1
1	2	3	4	5	6	7	8	9	10	11														2
1	2	6		5	4	11	8	9	10		3	7												3
1	2	6				11	4	9	10		3			5	7	8								4
1	2	3				11	4	9	10					5	7	8	6							5
1	2	3				11	4	9	10					5	7	8	6							6
1	2					11	4	9	10		3			5	7	8	6							7
1	2					11	4	9	10		3			5	7	8	6							8
1	2					11	4	9	10		3			5	7	8	6							9
1	2					11	4	9	10		3			5	7	8	6							10
1		3				11	8	9	10	2				5	7	6	4							11
1	2				6	11	8	9	10	7	3			5			4							12
	2				6	11		9	10	7	3			5			4	1	8					13
	2				6	11		9	10	7	3			5			4	1	8					14
	2	3				11		9	10	7					6	5	4	1	8					15
	2	3				11		9	10	7					6	5	4	1	8					16
	2	3				11		9	10	7					6	5	4	1	8					17
	2	3				11		9	10					7	6	5	4	1	8					18
	2	3				11		9	10						6	5	4	1	8	7				19
	2	3	4			11		9	10	7					6	5	8	1						20
	2	3				11		9	10					7	6	5	4	1	8					21
	2	3				11		9	10					7	6	5	4	1	8					22
	2	3		5		11		9	10						7	6	4	1	8					23
	2	3		5		11		9	10						7	6	4	1	8					24
	2	3				11		9	10					7	6	5	4	1	8					25
	2			5		11		9	10		3				7	6	4	1	8					26
	2			5		11		9	10		3				7	6	4	1	8					27
	2			5		11		9	10		3				7	6	4	1	8					28
	2			5		11		9	10		3				7	6	4	1	8					29
	2			5		11		9	10	7	3				6		4	1	8					30
	2	3		5		11		9	10						6		4	1	8	7				31
	2	3		5		11		9	10						6		4	1	8	7				32
	2	3		5		11		9	10						7	6	4	1	8					33
	2	3		5			7	9	11						6		4	1	10	8				34
		3		5				9	8						7	6	4	1	10	11	2			35
	2	3		5		11		9	10						6		4	1	8	7				36
1	2	3		5		11		9	10						7	6	4		8					37
1	2	3		5				9	10					11	6		4		8	7				38
1	2	3		5		11		9	10					8	4	6				7				39
1	2	3		5		11		9	10					8	4	6				7				40
1	2	3		5		11		9	10					8	4	6				7				41
1	2	3		5		11		9	10					8	4	6				7				42
18	**40**	**30**	**3**	**22**	**6**	**40**	**12**	**42**	**42**	**10**	**15**	**1**	**11**	**22**	**33**	**29**	**25**	**24**	**17**	**13**	**5**	**1**	**1**	
	1		2	4	3	25	10	2		1			3		3	1	2		5	7				

Lower sub-table:

Furnell J	Howe D	McCullough WJ	Snedden JD	Ure IF	Simpson PF	Armstrong G	Strong GH	Baker JH	Eastham GE	Anderson TK	Clarke FRG	MacLeod JM	Ferry G	Skirton AFG	Court DJ	Neill WJT	McLintock F	Burns AJ	Sammels JC	Radford J	Tawse B	Magill EJ	Baldwin T	#
	2			5		11		9	10		3			7	6		4	1		8				3
	2			5		11		9	10		3			7	6		4	1		8				4
	2			2		2		2	2		2			2	2		2	2		2				
				1															2					

257

1965-66

Manager: W.Wright

1	Aug	21	(h)	Stoke C	W	2-1	Baker 2	30,107
2		25	(a)	Northampton T	D	1-1	Baldwin	17,352
3		28	(a)	Burnley	D	2-2	Eastham, Baker	16,737
4	Sep	4	(h)	Chelsea	L	1-3	Baker	45,456
5		7	(a)	Nottingham F	W	1-0	Sammels	30,431
6		11	(a)	Tottenham H	D	2-2	Baker, L.Brown (og)	53,962
7		14	(h)	Nottingham F	W	1-0	Eastham	34,542
8		18	(a)	Everton	L	1-3	Baker	38,935
9		25	(h)	Manchester U	W	4-2	Baker, Radford, Armstrong, Eastham	56,757
10		28	(h)	Northampton T	D	1-1	Radford	33,240
11	Oct	2	(a)	Newcastle U	W	1-0	McLintock	42,790
12		9	(h)	Fulham	W	2-1	Sammels, Baker	32,318
13		16	(a)	Blackpool	L	3-5	Armstrong, Radford, Armfield (og)	19,533
14		23	(h)	Blackburn R	D	2-2	McLintock, Baker	27,703
15		30	(a)	Leicester C	L	1-3	Armstrong	22,528
16	Nov	6	(h)	Sheffield U	W	6-2	Baker 2, Skirton 2, Armstrong 2	28,541
17		13	(a)	Leeds U	L	0-2		36,383
18		20	(h)	West Ham U	W	3-2	Skirton 2, Baker	35,855
19	Dec	4	(h)	Aston Villa	D	3-3	Skirton 2, Eastham	25,880
20		11	(a)	Liverpool	l	2-4	Radford, Baldwin	43,727
21		27	(a)	Sheffield W	L	0-4		33,101
22		28	(h)	Sheffield W	W	5-2	Eastham 2, Skirton, Sammels, Baker	21,035
23	Jan	1	(a)	Fulham	L	0-1		25,801
24		8	(h)	Liverpool	L	0-1		43,917
25		15	(a)	Blackburn R	L	1-2	Radford	12,532
26		29	(a)	Stoke C	W	3-1	Radford 2, Howe	21,883
27	Feb	5	(h)	Burnley	D	1-1	Sammels	28,652
28		19	(a)	Chelsea	D	0-0		48,641
29	Mar	5	(h)	Blackpool	D	0-0		21,881
30		8	(h)	Tottenham H	D	1-1	Court	51,805
31		12	(h)	Everton	L	0-1		24,821
32		19	(a)	Manchester U	L	1-2	Walley	47,246
33		26	(h)	Newcastle U	L	1-3	Noble (og)	13,979
34	Apr	5	(h)	West Brom A	D	1-1	Skirton	8,738
35		11	(a)	West Brom A	D	4-4	Baldwin 2, Radford, Armstrong	20,000
36		16	(a)	West Ham U	L	1-2	Baldwin	26,022
37		20	(a)	Sunderland	W	2-0	Skirton, Sammels	32,349
38		23	(h)	Sunderland	D	1-1	Sammels	25,699
39		25	(a)	Sheffield U	L	0-3		15,045
40		30	(a)	Aston Villa	L	0-3		18,866
41	May	5	(h)	Leeds U	L	0-3		4,554
42		7	(h)	Leicester C	W	1-0	Rodrigues (og)	16,435

FINAL LEAGUE POSITION: 14th in Division One

Appearances
Sub Appearances
Goals

FA Cup

3	Jan	22	(a)	Blackburn R	L	0-3		22,951

Appearances
Goals

Furnell J	Howe D	McCullough WJ	McLintock F	Ure IF	Neill WJT	Baldwin T	Eastham GE	Baker JH	Court DJ	Armstrong G	Wilson RP	Radford J	Simpson PF	Skirton AFG	Burns AJ	Storey PE	Walley JT	Sammels JC	Neilson G	Pack RJ	McGill JM	No.
1	2	3	4	5	6	7	8	9	10	11												1
	2	3	6	5	4	7	8	9	10	11	1											2
	2	3	6	5	4		8	9	10	11	1							7				3
1	2	3	6	5	4		8	9	10	11								7				4
1	2	3	6		5		11	9	4	7		8						10				5
1	2	3	4		5		11	9	6	7		8						10				6
1	2	3	4		5		11	9	6	7		8						10				7
1	2	3	4		5		11	9		7		8	6					10				8
1	2	3	4		5		11	9	6	7		8						10				9
1	2	3	4		5		11	9	6	7		8		12				10*				10
1	2	3	4	5			11	9*	6	7		8		12				10				11
1	2	3	4		5		11	9	6	7		8						10				12
1	2	3	4		5		11	9	6	7		8						10				13
	2	3	4		5		11	9	6	7		8			1			10				14
1	2		4		5		11	9	6	7		8				3		10				15
	2		4		5		10	9	6	11				7	1	3		8				16
	2		4		5		10	9	6	11				7	1	3		8				17
	2		4		5		10	9	6	11				7	1	3	12	8*				18
	2		4		5		10	9	6	11		8		7	1	3						19
	2		4		5	9	10		6	11		8		7	1	3						20
	2		4*		5		10	9		11		6		7	1	3	12	8				21
	2	5	4				11	9			1	8		7		3	6	10				22
	2	6	5		4		10	9		11	1			7		3		8				23
1	2		4		5		11	9	6			10		7		3		8				24
1	2		4		5		10	9	6	11		8		7		3						25
1	2		4	6	5		10			11		9		7		3		8				26
1	2		4		5	8			6	11		9		7		3	12	10*				27
1	2		4	6	5		10			11		9		7		3		8				28
1	2*		4	6	5		10			11		9	12	7		3		8				29
1		3	5		4		10		6	11		9		7		2		8				30
1		3	4		5	6	8		10	11		9				2			7			31
1		3*	4	6	5		10			7		9	12			2		8		11		32
1		6			5		10		4	11		9	3	7		2		8				33
1			4		5	6	10		2	11		9		7		3		8				34
1			4		5	6	10		2	11		9		7		3		8				35
1			4		5	6	10		2	11		9		7		3		8				36
1			4		5	6	10		2			9		7		3		8			11	37
1			4		5		10		2	11		9		7		3	6	8				38
1			4		5		10		2	11		9		7		3	6	8				39
1					5		10		2	11		9	4	7		3	6	8				40
1		9		5	8		10	6	7	11						3			2		4	41
1					5		10		2	11		9		7		3	6	8			4	42
31	29	17	36	21	39	8	37	24	38	39	4	32	5	23	7	28	7	32	2	1	2	
													3	1			3					
	1	2			5	6	13	1	6			8		9				1	6			

4 own-goals

Furnell J	Howe D	McCullough WJ	McLintock F	Ure IF	Neill WJT	Baldwin T	Eastham GE	Baker JH	Court DJ	Armstrong G	Wilson RP	Radford J	Simpson PF	Skirton AFG	Burns AJ	Storey PE	Walley JT	Sammels JC	Neilson G	Pack RJ	McGill JM	No.
1	2		4		5		10	9		11				7		3	6	8				3
1	1		1		1		1	1		1				1		1	1	1				

1966-67

Manager: B.Mee

1	Aug	20	(a)	Sunderland	W	3-1	Skirton 2, Armstrong	33,3
2		23	(h)	West Ham U	W	2-1	Radford, Baldwin	40,6
3		27	(h)	Aston Villa	W	1-0	Baldwin	26,7
4		29	(a)	West Ham U	D	2-2	McLintock, Sammels	34,9
5	Sep	3	(a)	Tottenham H	L	1-3	Sammels	56,2
6		6	(h)	Sheffield W	D	1-1	Sammels	28,8
7		10	(a)	Manchester C	D	1-1	Sammels	27,9
8		17	(h)	Blackpool	D	1-1	Coakley	28,9
9		24	(a)	Chelsea	L	1-3	Addison	48,0
10	Oct	1	(h)	Leicester C	L	2-4	Addison, Graham	33,9
11		8	(h)	Newcastle U	W	2-0	Boot, Clark (og)	24,5
12		15	(a)	Leeds U	L	1-3	Boot	31,4
13		22	(h)	West Brom A	L	2-3	Armstrong 2	31,6
14		29	(a)	Manchester U	L	0-1		45,3
15	Nov	5	(h)	Leeds U	L	0-1		24,2
16		12	(a)	Everton	D	0-0		45,7
17		19	(h)	Fulham	W	1-0	McLintock	25,7
18		26	(a)	Nottingham F	L	1-2	Neilson	20,4
19	Dec	3	(h)	Burnley	D	0-0		23,2
20		10	(a)	Sheffield U	D	1-1	Graham	15,4
21		17	(h)	Sunderland	W	2-0	McLintock, Sammels	20,4
22		26	(h)	Southampton	W	4-1	Radford 2, Armstrong 2	29,5
23		27	(a)	Southampton	L	1-2	Addison	27,7
24		31	(a)	Aston Villa	W	1-0	McLintock	19,4
25	Jan	7	(h)	Tottenham H	L	0-2		49,8
26		14	(h)	Manchester C	W	1-0	McLintock	22,3
27		21	(a)	Blackpool	W	3-0	Sammels 2, Neilson	12,0
28	Feb	4	(h)	Chelsea	W	2-1	Graham, Armstrong	52,4
29		11	(a)	Leicester C	L	1-2	Graham	24,5
30		25	(a)	Newcastle U	L	1-2	Graham	27,4
31	Mar	3	(h)	Manchester U	D	1-1	Sammels	63,5
32		18	(a)	West Brom A	W	1-0	McLintock	16,5
33		25	(h)	Sheffield U	W	2-0	Sammels, McLintock	23,0
34		27	(a)	Liverpool	D	0-0		46,1
35		28	(h)	Liverpool	D	1-1	Graham	35,8
36	Apr	1	(a)	Stoke C	D	2-2	Graham 2	14,6
37		19	(a)	Fulham	D	0-0		27,6
38		22	(h)	Nottingham F	D	1-1	Storey	36,1
39		25	(h)	Everton	W	3-1	Sammels, Graham, McLintock	20,5
40		29	(a)	Burnley	W	4-1	Addison, Graham, Armstrong, Simpson	10,9
41	May	6	(h)	Stoke C	W	3-1	Radford, McLintock, Allen (og)	24,6
42		13	(a)	Sheffield W	D	1-1	Graham	23,2

FINAL LEAGUE POSITION: 7th in Division One

Appearances
Sub Appeara
Goals

FA Cup

3	Jan	28	(a)	Bristol R	W	3-0	Graham, Neilson, Armstrong	35,4
4	Feb	18	(a)	Bolton W	D	0-0		31,8
R		22	(h)	Bolton W	W	3-0	Radford 3	47,0
5	Mar	11	(a)	Birmingham C	L	0-1		40,6

Appearances
Sub Appeara
Goals

League Cup

2	Sep	13	(h)	Gillingham	D	1-1	Baldwin	13,02
R		22	(a)	Gillingham	D	1-1	Baldwin	20,56
2R		28	(h)	Gillingham	W	5-0	Baldwin 2, McLintock 2, Coakley	18,40
3	Oct	5	(h)	West Ham U	L	1-3	Jenkins	33,64

Appearances
Sub Appearar
Goals

260

Furnell J	Court DJ	Storey PE	McLintock F	Ure IF	Neill WJT	Skirton AFG	Baldwin T	Radford J	Sammels JC	Armstrong G	McGill JM	Simpson PF	Coakley T	Howe D	Addison C	Walley JT	Graham G	Boot MC	Woodward J	McNab R	Neilson G	Tyrer A	Jenkins DJ	
1	2*	3	4	5	6	7	8	9	10	11	12													1
1	2	3	4	5	6	7*	8	9	10	11		12												2
1	2	3	4	5	6		8	9	10	11			7											3
1		3	4	5	6		9		10	11	8	2	7											4
1	2		4	5	6		8	9	10	11		3	7											5
1	2		4	5	6		8	9	10	11	12	3*	7											6
1			4	5	6		8	9	10	11	3		7	2										7
1		3	4	5	6			9*	10	11	12	2	7		8									8
1		3	4	5			9		10		6	2	7		8	11								9
1		3	4	5	6*				10	11	12	2	7		8		9							10
1		3	8	5					10	11		2	7				9	4	6					11
1		3	8	5					10	11		6				7	9	4		2				12
1		3	4	5				9	10	11		6					8	7		2				13
1		3	4		5			10	7	11		6			8		9			2				14
1		2	4		5			8	7*	11		6			10	3	9	12						15
1		3	4	5	6			7	8			10			11		9			2				16
1		3	4	6	5				10	11					8		9			2	7			17
1		3	4	6	5				10	11					8		9			2	7			18
1		3	4	6	5			8	10	11		12					9			2*	7			19
1		3	4	6	5			8	10*	11		2					9		12		7			20
1		3	4	5	6			8	10	11					7		9			2				21
1		3	4	6				8	10	11		5					9			2	7			22
1		3		5				8	10	11	4	6			7		9			2				23
1		3	4	6					10	11		5			8		9			2	7			24
1		3	4	6				8	10	11		5					9			2	7			25
1		3	4	6	5			8	10	11		2					9				7			26
1		3	4	5	6			8*	10	11		2				12	9				7			27
1		3	4	5	6				10	11		2			8*		9			12	7			28
1		3	4	5	6				10	11		2			8		9				7			29
1	12	3	4		5			8	10*	11		6					9			2	7			30
1	12	3	4*		5			8	10	11		6			7		9			2				31
1	7	3	4		5			8	10	11		6					9			2				32
1	7		4	5	6			8	10	11		3					9			2				33
1	7		4	5	6			8	10	11		3					9			2				34
1	7		4	5	6			8	10	11		3					9			2				35
1	7		4	5	6			8	10	11		3					9			2				36
1		3	4	6	5			8	10	11		7					9			2				37
1		3	4	6	5			8	10	11		7					9			2				38
1		3	4	6	5				10	11		7			8		9			2				39
1	12	3	4	6	5				10	11		7			8*		9			2				40
1		3	4	6	5			8	10	11		7					9			2				41
1				6	5			4	10	11		7			8		9		3	2				42
42	10	34	40	37	34	2	8	30	42	40	4	34	9	1	17	3	33	3	2	25	12			
	3										4	2				1		1	1	1				
		1	9			2	2	4	10	7		1	1		4		11	2			2			

2 own-goals

Furnell J	Court DJ	Storey PE	McLintock F	Ure IF	Neill WJT	Skirton AFG	Baldwin T	Radford J	Sammels JC	Armstrong G	McGill JM	Simpson PF	Coakley T	Howe D	Addison C	Walley JT	Graham G	Boot MC	Woodward J	McNab R	Neilson G	Tyrer A	Jenkins DJ	
1		3	4	6	5				10	11		2			8		9				7			3
1		3	4	6	5			8	10	11		2					9				7			4
1		3	4	6	5			8	10	11		2					9				7			R
1	4	3			5			8	10	11		6			7		9			2				5
4	1	4	3	3	4			3	4	4		4			2		4			1	3			
								3		1							1				1			

Furnell J	Court DJ	Storey PE	McLintock F	Ure IF	Neill WJT	Skirton AFG	Baldwin T	Radford J	Sammels JC	Armstrong G	McGill JM	Simpson PF	Coakley T	Howe D	Addison C	Walley JT	Graham G	Boot MC	Woodward J	McNab R	Neilson G	Tyrer A	Jenkins DJ	
1			4	5	6		9		10	11			7	2		3						8		2
1		3		4	5		9	8	10		2		7			6						12	11*	R
1		3	4	5	6		8		10	11	2	9	7											2R
1		3		5					10	11		2	7			9		4	6				8	3
4		3	2	4	3		3	1	4	3	2	2	4	1		3		1	1			1	2	
																						1		
			2				4						1										1	

1967-68

Manager: B.Mee

1	Aug	19	(h)	Stoke C	W	2-0	Graham, Sammels	27,048
2		22	(a)	Liverpool	L	0-2		52,033
3		26	(a)	Nottingham F	L	0-2		33,991
4		28	(h)	Liverpool	W	2-0	Sammels, Hateley (og)	33,420
5	Sep	2	(h)	Coventry C	D	1-1	Graham	30,404
6		6	(a)	West Brom A	W	3-1	Armstrong, Sammels, Addison	19,232
7		9	(a)	Sheffield U	W	4-2	Addison, Graham 2, McLintock	14,939
8		16	(h)	Tottenham H	W	4-0	Radford, Neill (pen), Graham, Addison	62,836
9		23	(h)	Manchester C	W	1-0	Radford	41,466
10		30	(a)	Newcastle U	L	1-2	Graham	33,350
11	Oct	7	(a)	Manchester U	L	0-1		60,197
12		14	(h)	Sunderland	W	2-1	Radford, Graham	30,864
13		23	(a)	Wolves	L	2-3	Graham, Armstrong	36,664
14		28	(h)	Fulham	W	5-3	Radford 3, Addison 2	29,974
15	Nov	4	(a)	Leeds U	L	1-3	McLintock	31,632
16		11	(h)	Everton	D	2-2	Johnston, Sammels	36,371
17		18	(a)	Leicester C	D	2-2	Radford, Johnston	28,150
18		25	(h)	West Ham U	D	0-0		42,029
19	Dec	2	(a)	Burnley	L	0-1		15,381
20		16	(a)	Stoke C	W	1-0	Graham	16,119
21		23	(h)	Nottingham F	W	3-0	Graham 2, Armstrong	32,512
22		26	(a)	Chelsea	L	1-2	Neill (pen)	51,672
23		30	(h)	Chelsea	D	1-1	Radford	47,157
24	Jan	6	(a)	Coventry C	D	1-1	Graham	32,839
25		13	(h)	Sheffield U	D	1-1	Graham	27,447
26		20	(a)	Tottenham H	L	0-1		57,885
27	Feb	3	(a)	Manchester C	D	1-1	Graham	42,392
28		10	(h)	Newcastle U	D	0-0		36,996
29		24	(h)	Manchester U	L	0-2		46,417
30	Mar	16	(h)	Wolves	L	0-2		25,983
31		23	(a)	Fulham	W	3-1	Graham, Gould, Court	20,612
32		29	(a)	West Ham U	D	1-1	Armstrong	33,986
33	Apr	6	(a)	Everton	L	0-2		40,029
34		10	(a)	Southampton	L	0-2		23,247
35		13	(h)	Leicester C	W	2-1	Gould, Graham	19,108
36		15	(h)	Southampton	L	0-3		23,165
37		20	(a)	Sunderland	L	0-2		31,255
38		27	(h)	Burnley	W	2-0	Court, Armstrong	15,278
39		30	(h)	Sheffield W*	W	3-2	Court, Radford, Gould	11,262
40	May	4	(a)	Sheffield W	W	2-1	Radford, Gould	25,066
41		7	(h)	Leeds U	W	4-3	Gould, McLintock, Johnston, Madeley (og)	25,043
42		11	(h)	West Brom A	W	2-1	Gould, McLintock	24,896

FINAL LEAGUE POSITION: 9th in Division One

*After abandoned match (47 minutes) on December 9

Appearances
Sub Appearance
Goals

FA Cup

3	Jan	27	(a)	Shrewsbury T	D	1-1	Radford	18,280
R		30	(h)	Shrewsbury T	W	2-0	Sammels, Jenkins	41,958
4	Feb	17	(a)	Swansea T	W	1-0	Gould	31,919
5	Mar	9	(h)	Birmingham C	D	1-1	Radford	45,515
R		12	(a)	Birmingham C	L	1-2	Gould	51,586

Appearances
Sub Appearance
Goals

League Cup

2	Sep	12	(a)	Coventry C	W	2-1	Sammels, Graham	22,605
3	Oct	11	(h)	Reading	W	1-0	Simpson	27,866
4	Nov	1	(h)	Blackburn R	W	2-1	Graham, Addison	20,044
5		29	(a)	Burnley	D	3-3	Graham 2, McLintock	16,033
R	Dec	5	(h)	Burnley	W	2-1	Radford, Neill	36,570
SF	Jan	17	(h)	Huddersfield T	W	3-2	Graham, Radford, McNab	39,986
	Feb	6	(a)	Huddersfield T	W	3-1	Sammels, Jenkins, McLintock	27,312
F	Mar	2	(n*)	Leeds U	L	0-1		97,887

*Played at Wembley Stadium

Appearances
Sub Appearance
Goals

Furnell J	Court DJ	Storey PE	McLintock F	Neill WJT	Simpson PF	Johnston G	Radford J	Graham G	Sammels JC	Armstrong G	McNab R	Ure IF	Addison C	Jenkins DJ	Rice PJ	Gould RA	Wilson RP	Davidson R	
1	2	3	4	5	6	7	8	9	10	11									1
1	9	3	4	5	6	7	8		10	11	2								2
1	2	3	4	5	6	7	8	9	10	11									3
1		3	4	5	2	12	8*	9	10	11			6	7					4
1	12	2	4	5	6	7		9	10	11	3*		8						5
1		2	4	5	3	7		9	10	11		6	8						6
1		2	4	5	3		7	9	10	11		6	8						7
1		2	4	5	3		7	9	10	11		6	8						8
1		2	4	5	3		7	9	10	11		6	8						9
1		2	4	5	3		7	9	10	11		6	8						10
1		2	4	5	8		7	9	10	11	3	6							11
1		2	4	5	8*		7	9	10	11	3	6	12						12
1		2	4	5			7	9	10	11	3	6	8						13
1		2	4	5			7	9	10	11	3	6	8						14
1		2	4	5	6		7	9	10	11	3		8						15
1		2	4	5	6	8	7	9	10	11	3								16
1		2	4	5	6	8	7	9	10	11	3								17
1		2	4	5	6	8	7	9*	10	11	3			12					18
1		2	4	5	6	8	7	9*	10	11	3			12					19
1		2	4*		6	8	7	9	10	11	3	5		12					20
1		2	4	5	10	8	7	9		11	3	6							21
1		2	4	5	10	8	7	9		11	3	6							22
1		2	4	5	10		7	9	8	11	3	6							23
1		2		5	4	8	7	9	10	11	3	6							24
1			5	4	8	7		9	10	11	3	6		2					25
1		4	5	2			7	9	10	11	3	6	8*	12					26
1		3	4	5	2		7	9	10	11		6				8			27
1		3	4	5	2		7	9	10	11		6				8			28
1		3	4	5	6			9	10	11	2		7			8			29
		3	4	6	5*		7	9	10	11					2	8	1	12	30
	10	3	4	5	6		7	9		11					2	8	1		31
	8	2	4	5	6		7	9		11	3					10	1		32
	8	2	4		6		7	9		11	3	5				10	1		33
	8	3	4		6		7	9		11	2	5				10	1		34
	8	2	4	5	6		7	9		11	3					10	1		35
	8	2	4*	5	6		7	9	12	11	3					10	1		36
8*		2	4	5	6		7	9	10	11	3					12	1		37
	4	3		5	6		7	9	8	11	2					10	1		38
	4	3		5	6		7	9*	8	11	2				12	10	1		39
	6	2	4		5	8	7		10	11	3					9	1		40
	4	3	2	5	6	8	7		9	11						10	1		41
	4		3	5	6	8	7		9	11	2					10	1		42
29	15	39	38	38	40	17	39	38	34	42	30	21	10	2	2	15	13		
	1				1			1				1	1	4	1		1		
	3		4	2			3	10	16	4	5		5			6			

2 own-goals

Furnell J	Court DJ	Storey PE	McLintock F	Neill WJT	Simpson PF	Johnston G	Radford J	Graham G	Sammels JC	Armstrong G	McNab R	Ure IF	Addison C	Jenkins DJ	Rice PJ	Gould RA	Wilson RP	Davidson R	
1		2	4	12	5		7*	9	10	11	3	6		8					3
1	12	3	4	5	2		7	9	10	11		6	8*						R
1		2	4	5	3		7	9	10	11		6		8					4
1		2	4	6	5		7	9	10	11	3			8					5
		2	4	6	5		7	9	10	11	3			8			1		R
4		5	5	4	5		5	5	5	5	5	3	3		2		3	1	
	1			1															
					2			1					1			2			

Furnell J	Court DJ	Storey PE	McLintock F	Neill WJT	Simpson PF	Johnston G	Radford J	Graham G	Sammels JC	Armstrong G	McNab R	Ure IF	Addison C	Jenkins DJ	Rice PJ	Gould RA	Wilson RP	Davidson R	
1		2	4	5	3		7	9	10	11		6	8						2
1		2	4	5	8		7	9	10	11	3	6							3
1		2	4	5	6	12	7*	9	10	11	3		8						4
1		2	4	5	6	8	7	9	10	11	3								5
1		2	4	5	6	8	7	9	10	11				3					R
1			4	5	2	8	7	9	10	11	3	6							SF
1		3	4	5	2		7	9	10	11		6	8						SF
1		2	4	12	5		7	9	10	11	3	6	8*						F
8		7	8	7	8	3	8	8	8	8	5	5	2	2		1			
			1		1														
		2	1	1		2	5	2		1		1	1						

1968-69

Manager: B.Mee

1	Aug	10	(a)	Tottenham H	W 2-1	Radford, Beal (og)	56,280
2		13	(h)	Leicester C	W 3-0	Court, Gould 2	32,164
3		17	(h)	Liverpool	D 1-1	Radford	43,535
4		21	(a)	Wolves	D 0-0		36,006
5		24	(a)	Ipswich T	W 2-1	Radford, Jenkins	25,825
6		27	(h)	Manchester C	W 4-1	Jenkins 2, Sammels, Radford	40,776
7		31	(h)	Queen's Park R	W 2-1	McLintock, Neill (pen)	44,407
8	Sep	7	(a)	Southampton	W 2-1	Radford 2	25,126
9		14	(h)	Stoke C	W 1-0	Neill	28,275
10		21	(a)	Leeds U	L 0-2		39,946
11		28	(h)	Sunderland	D 0-0		35,277
12	Oct	5	(a)	Manchester U	D 0-0		61,843
13		9	(a)	Manchester C	D 1-1	Radford	33,830
14		12	(h)	Coventry C	W 2-1	Court, Radford	35,240
15		19	(a)	West Brom A	L 0-1		29,324
16		26	(h)	West Ham U	D 0-0		59,533
17	Nov	9	(h)	Newcastle U	D 0-0		34,277
18		16	(a)	Nottingham F	W 2-0	Armstrong, Radford	24,550
19		23	(h)	Chelsea	L 0-1		45,588
20		30	(a)	Burnley	W 1-0	Robertson	16,264
21	Dec	7	(h)	Everton	W 3-1	Radford, Court, Graham	40,108
22		14	(a)	Coventry C	W 1-0	Gould	27,332
23		21	(h)	West Brom A	W 2-0	Gould, Fraser (og)	30,765
24		26	(h)	Manchester U	W 3-0	Armstrong, Court, Radford	62,300
25	Jan	11	(h)	Sheffield W	W 2-0	Gould, Radford	39,008
26		18	(a)	Newcastle U	L 1-2	Gould	34,227
27	Feb	1	(h)	Nottingham F	D 1-1	Gould	35,585
28		15	(h)	Burnley	W 2-0	Gould 2	27,614
29		18	(h)	Ipswich T	L 0-2		23,891
30	Mar	1	(a)	Sheffield W	W 5-0	Radford 3, Sammels, Gould	21,436
31		22	(a)	Queen's Park R	W 1-0	Armstrong	23,076
32		24	(h)	Tottenham H	W 1-0	Sammels	43,972
33		29	(h)	Southampton	D 0-0		28,990
34		31	(a)	Liverpool	D 1-1	Robertson	44,843
35	Apr	5	(a)	Sunderland	D 0-0		23,214
36		7	(h)	Wolves	W 3-1	Robertson, Armstrong, Graham	31,011
37		8	(a)	Leicester C	D 0-0		35,573
38		12	(h)	Leeds U	L 1-2	Graham	44,715
39		14	(a)	Chelsea	L 1-2	Court	38,905
40		19	(a)	Stoke C	W 3-1	Armstrong, Court, Stevenson (og)	14,996
41		21	(a)	West Ham U	W 2-1	Sammels, Graham	34,941
42		29	(a)	Everton	L 0-1		39,689

FINAL LEAGUE POSITION: 4th in Division One

Appearances
Sub Appearances
Goals

FA Cup

3	Jan	4	(a)	Cardiff C	D 0-0		55,316
R		7	(h)	Cardiff C	W 2-0	Armstrong, Gould	52,681
4		25	(h)	Charlton A	W 2-0	Sammels, Robertson	55,760
5	Feb	12	(a)	West Brom A	L 0-1		46,000

Appearances
Sub Appearances
Goals

League Cup

2	Sep	4	(h)	Sunderland	W 1-0	Neill	28,460
3		25	(a)	Scunthorpe U	W 6-1	Jenkins 3, Gould, Sammels, Court	17,450
4	Oct	15	(h)	Liverpool	W 2-1	Simpson, Radford	39,299
5		29	(h)	Blackpool	W 5-1	Armstrong 2, Radford, Gould, Simpson	32,321
SF	Nov	20	(h)	Tottenham H	W 1-0	Radford	55,237
SF	Dec	4	(a)	Tottenham H	D 1-1	Radford	55,923
F	Mar	15	(n*)	Swindon T	L 1-3†	Gould	98,189

*Played at Wembley Stadium. †After extra-time.

Appearances
Sub Appearances
Goals

Wilson RP	Storey PE	McNab R	McLintock F	Neill WJT	Simpson PF	Radford J	Sammels JC	Graham G	Court DJ	Jenkins DJ	Gould RA	Johnston G	Armstrong G	Ure IF	Robertson JG	No
1	2	3	4	5	6	7	8	9	10	11						1
1	2	3	4	5	6	7	8	9*	10	11	12					2
1	2	3	4	5	6	7	8		10	11	9					3
1	2	3	4	5	6	7	8		10	11	9					4
1	2	3	4	5	6	7	8		10	11	9					5
1	2	3	4	5	6	7	8		10	11	9					6
1	2	3	4	5	6	7	8		10	11	9					7
1	2	3	4	5	6	7	8		10	11•	9	12				8
1	2	3	4	5	6	7*	8		10	11	9	12				9
1	2	3	4	5	6		8		10	11•	9	12	7			10
1	2	3	4	5	6	7	8		10	11	9					11
1	2	3	4	5	6	7	8		10	11	9					12
1	2	3	4	5	6	7	8*		10	11	9	12				13
1	2	3		5	6	7		12	10	11•	9		8	4		14
1	2	3	4	5	8	7		9*	10		12		11	6		15
1	2	3	4	5	10	8		9					11	6	7	16
1	2	3		5		8	10	9	4		12		11	6	7*	17
1	2	3	8	5	6	7	9	10	4				11			18
1	2	3	4		6	7	9	10*	8		12		11	5		19
1	2	3	4		6		9		8		10		11	5	7	20
1	2	3	4		6	7	9*	12	8		10		5	11		21
1	2	3	4		6	7		11	9		10		5	8		22
1	2	3	4		6	7		11	9		10		5	8		23
1	2	3	4		6	7		8	9		10		11	5		24
1	2	3	4	5	6	7	8		9		10		11			25
1	2	3	4		6	7	8	9*		10			11	5	12	26
1	2	3	4		6	7	8		9*		10		12	5	11	27
1	2	3			6		8	4	9		10		11	5	7	28
1	2	3			6		8	4	9		10	12	11	5	7*	29
1	2	3			6	7	8	4	9		10		11	5		30
1	2	3	4		6	7	8		9		10		11	5		31
1	2*	3	4		6	7	8	12	9		10		11	5		32
1	2	3	4		6	7	8		9		10		11	5		33
1	2	3	4			8	6	9			10		11	5	7	34
1	2	3	4		12	8	6	9			10*		11	5	7	35
1	2	3	4			8	6	9			10		11	5	7	36
1	2	3	4			8	6	9			10		11	5	7	37
1	2	3	4		12	8	6	9			10*		11	5	7	38
1	2	3	4	12	5	10	8	6*	9				11		7	39
1	2	3	4	5		8	6	9			10		11		7	40
1	2	3	4		5*	10	8	6	9		12		11		7	41
1	2	3	4	5		12	8*	6	9		10		11		7	42
42	42	42	37	21	34	31	36	23	40	14	33		26	23	18	
				1		3		3			5	3	3		1	
	1	2		15	4	4	6	3	10		5		3			

3 own-goals

Wilson RP	Storey PE	McNab R	McLintock F	Neill WJT	Simpson PF	Radford J	Sammels JC	Graham G	Court DJ	Jenkins DJ	Gould RA	Johnston G	Armstrong G	Ure IF	Robertson JG	No
1	2	3	4		6	7		11	9		10		8	5		3
1	2	3	4		6	7	8		9		10		11	5		R
1	2	3	4		6	7	8		9		10		5	11		4
1	2	3	4		6	7	8*		9		10		12	5	11	5
4	4	4	4		4	4	3	1	4		4		2	4	2	
									1							
						1					1	1			1	

Wilson RP	Storey PE	McNab R	McLintock F	Neill WJT	Simpson PF	Radford J	Sammels JC	Graham G	Court DJ	Jenkins DJ	Gould RA	Johnston G	Armstrong G	Ure IF	Robertson JG	No
1	2	3	4	5	6	7	8		10	11	9					2
1	2	3	4	5	6		8		10	11	9		7			3
1	2	3	4	5	8*	7		9	10		12		11	6		4
1	2	3	4*	5	10	7		9	12		8		11	6		5
1	2	3	4		6	7	9	10*	8		12		11	5		SF
1	2	3*	4		6	7	9	12	8		10		11	5		SF
1	2	3	4		6*	7	8	12	9		10		11	5		F
7	7	7	7	4	7	6	5	3	6	2	5		6	5		
								2	1		2					
	1	2	4	1		1	3	3			2					

265

1969-70

1	Aug	9	(h)	Everton	L	0-1		44,364
2		13	(a)	Leeds U	D	0-0		37,164
3		16	(a)	West Brom A	W	1-0	George	32,215
4		19	(h)	Leeds U	D	1-1	Rice	44,923
5		23	(h)	Nottingham F	W	2-1	McNab, Graham	30,290
6		25	(a)	West Ham U	D	1-1	Lampard (og)	39,590
7		30	(a)	Newcastle U	L	1-3	Robertson	47,208
8	Sep	6	(h)	Sheffield W	D	0-0		28,605
9		13	(a)	Burnley	W	1-0	Graham	14,721
10		16	(h)	Tottenham H	L	2-3	Robertson, Radford	55,280
11		20	(h)	Manchester U	D	2-2	Graham, Sammels	59,489
12		27	(a)	Chelsea	L	0-3		46,370
13	Oct	4	(h)	Coventry C	L	0-1		28,877
14		7	(h)	West Brom A	D	1-1	Radford	21,165
15		11	(a)	Stoke C	D	0-0		25,801
16		18	(a)	Sunderland	D	1-1	Sammels	17,864
17		25	(h)	Ipswich T	D	0-0		22,458
18	Nov	1	(a)	Crystal P	W	5-1	Radford 3, Armstrong, Graham	34,894
19		8	(h)	Derby C	W	4-0	Sammels 2, George, Armstrong	49,763
20		15	(a)	Wolves	L	0-2		26,796
21		22	(h)	Manchester C	D	1-1	Neill (pen)	42,923
22		29	(a)	Liverpool	W	1-0	Robertson	40,295
23	Dec	6	(h)	Southampton	D	2-2	Sammels, Radford	24,509
24		13	(h)	Burnley	W	3-2	Robertson, Radford, Armstrong	21,404
25		20	(a)	Sheffield W	D	1-1	Sammels	17,101
26		26	(a)	Nottingham F	D	1-1	McNab	38,915
27		27	(h)	Newcastle U	D	0-0		39,637
28	Jan	10	(a)	Manchester U	L	1-2	Marinello	41,055
29		17	(h)	Chelsea	L	0-3		53,793
30		31	(a)	Coventry C	L	0-2		31,661
31	Feb	7	(h)	Stoke C	D	0-0		26,601
32		14	(a)	Everton	D	2-2	George, Radford	48,564
33		18	(a)	Manchester C	D	1-1	Graham	25,508
34		21	(a)	Derby C	L	2-3	Radford, Roberts	35,284
35		28	(h)	Sunderland	W	3-1	Storey (pen), Kennedy, Kelly	21,826
36	Mar	14	(h)	Liverpool	W	2-1	Sammels, Radford	32,295
37		21	(a)	Southampton	W	2-0	Sammels, George	23,902
38		28	(h)	Wolves	D	2-2	Graham 2	32,353
39		30	(h)	Crystal P	W	2-0	Radford, George	34,144
40		31	(a)	Ipswich T	L	1-2	George	25,713
41	Apr	4	(h)	West Ham U	W	2-1	Kelly, Radford	36,212
42	May	2	(a)	Tottenham H	L	0-1		46,969

FINAL LEAGUE POSITION: 12th in Division One

Appearances
Sub Appearances
Goals

FA Cup

3	Jan	3	(h)	Blackpool	D	1-1	Radford	32,210
R		15	(a)	Blackpool	L	2-3	Sammels, Radford	24,801

Appearances
Sub Appearances
Goals

League Cup

2	Sep	2	(a)	Southampton	D	1-1	McNab	21,111
R		4	(h)	Southampton	W	2-0	Graham 2	26,362
3		24	(h)	Everton	D	0-0		36,102
R	Oct	1	(a)	Everton	L	0-1		41,140

Appearances
Sub Appearances
Goals

Wilson RP	Rice PJ	McNab R	McLintock F	Neill WJT	Simpson PF	Robertson JG	George FC	Gould RA	Graham G	Radford J	Court DJ	Ure IF	Storey PE	Sammels JC	Kelly EP	Armstrong G	Webster MW	Barnett GC	Roberts JG	Kennedy R	Nelson S	Marinello P	
1	2	3	4	5	6	7	8	9	10	11													1
1	2*	3	4		6	7		9	10	11	12	5	8										2
1	2	3			6	7	8		10	11	4	5	9										3
1	2	3			6	7	8		10	11	4	5	9										4
1	2	3	4	5	6	7	8*	12	10	11				9									5
1		3	4	5	6	7	8		10	11			9	2									6
1		3	4	5	6	7	8		10	11			9	2									7
1	2	3		5	6	7		8	10	9*			4	12	11								8
1		3	4	5	6	7	9*		10	12			2	8	11								9
		3	4	5	6	7	8		10	9			2	11			1						10
		3	4		6	7			10	9	5		2	11	8		1						11
		3		5	6	7		11	10	9	4		2	8			1						12
		3	4		6	7	12	11	10	9*			2	8				1	5				13
		3	4		6	7			10	9	11		2	8				1	5				14
		3	4		6	7		9	10	11			2	8				1	5				15
		3*	4	5	6	7			10	9	11		2	8				1	12				16
			4	5	6	7	12	9*	10	11			2	8				1	3				17
		3		5	6	7			10	9	4		2	8	11			1					18
		3		5*	6	7	12		10	9	4		2	8	11			1					19
		3		5	6	7	12		10*	9	4		2	8	11			1					20
		3		5	6	7	12		10	9	4		2	8	11*			1					21
		3	5		6	7			10	9	4		2	8	11			1					22
			5		6	7			10	9	4		2	8	11			1	3				23
1		3	5*		6	7			10	9	4		2	8	12	11							24
1		3*		5	6	7	12			9	4		2	8	10	11							25
1		3		5	6	7				9	4		2	8	10	11							26
1		3		5	6	7	4			9			2	8	10	11							27
1				5	6		8			9	4		2	10		11			3			7	28
1		3	4		6		12			9			2	8	10*			5	11			7	29
1		3	4		6				10	9			2	8		11		5				7	30
1		3	4		6				10	9			2	8		11		5				7	31
1		3	4		6*		11	12	10	9			2	8				5				7	32
1		3	4		8				11	9			2	10	6			5				7	33
1		3	4		8				11	9			2	10	6			5				7	34
1		3	4						11	9	12		2	8*	6			5	10			7	35
1		3	5		6				10	11	9		2	8	4							7	36
1		3	5		6				10	11	9		2	8	4							7	37
1		3	5		6				10	11	9		2	8	4							7	38
1			5		6				10	11	9		2	8	4				3			7	39
1		3	5		6				10	11	9		2	8	4							7	40
1		3	5		6				10	11	9		2	8	4							7	41
1		3			6				10	11	9		2	8	4*	7			5	12			42
28	7	37	30	17	39	27	21	9	36	39	18	3	39	36	14	17	3	11	11	2	4	14	
						7	2				3				2					2			
	1	2		1			4	6			7	12		1	8	2	3		1	1		1	

I own-goal

Wilson RP	Rice PJ	McNab R	McLintock F	Neill WJT	Simpson PF	Robertson JG	George FC	Gould RA	Graham G	Radford J	Court DJ	Ure IF	Storey PE	Sammels JC	Kelly EP	Armstrong G	Webster MW	Barnett GC	Roberts JG	Kennedy R	Nelson S	Marinello P	
1			5	6	7				10	9	4		2	8		11			3				3
1		3	5	6	7	4			10	9			2	8		11							R
2		1	2	2	2	1			2	2	1		2	2		2			1				
									2					1									

Wilson RP	Rice PJ	McNab R	McLintock F	Neill WJT	Simpson PF	Robertson JG	George FC	Gould RA	Graham G	Radford J	Court DJ	Ure IF	Storey PE	Sammels JC	Kelly EP	Armstrong G	Webster MW	Barnett GC	Roberts JG	Kennedy R	Nelson S	Marinello P	
1		3	4		6	7	8		10	11	9		2					5					2
1		3	4		6	7	8	12	10	11	9		2					5*					R
		3	5		6	7			10	9	4		2	8		11	1						3
2	3	4*	5	6	7		9	10		12	11	8				1							R
2	1	4	4	1	4	4	2	1	4	3	3	4	2	1		2	2	2					
		1								1		1											
		1							2														

267

1970-71

Manager: B.Mee

1	Aug	15	(a)	Everton	D	2-2	George, Graham	49,684
2		17	(a)	West Ham U	D	0-0		39,904
3		22	(h)	Manchester U	W	4-0	Radford 3, Graham	54,117
4		25	(h)	Huddersfield T	W	1-0	Kennedy	34,848
5		29	(a)	Chelsea	L	1-2	Kelly	53,722
6	Sep	1	(h)	Leeds U	D	0-0		47,749
7		5	(h)	Tottenham H	W	2-0	Armstrong 2	48,713
8		12	(a)	Burnley	W	2-1	Kennedy, Radford	12,675
9		19	(h)	West Brom A	W	6-2	Kennedy 2, Graham 2, Armstrong, Cantello (og)	33,326
10		26	(a)	Stoke C	L	0-5		18,153
11	Oct	3	(h)	Nottingham F	W	4-0	Kennedy 3, Armstrong	32,053
12		10	(a)	Newcastle U	D	1-1	Graham	38,024
13		17	(h)	Everton	W	4-0	Kennedy 2, Kelly, Storey (pen)	50,012
14		24	(a)	Coventry C	W	3-1	Kennedy, Radford, Graham	30,017
15		31	(h)	Derby C	W	2-0	Kelly Radford	43,013
16	Nov	7	(a)	Blackpool	W	1-0	Radford	17,115
17		14	(h)	Crystal P	D	1-1	Radford	34,503
18		21	(a)	Ipswich T	W	1-0	Armstrong	22,856
19		28	(h)	Liverpool	W	2-0	Graham, Radford	45,097
20	Dec	5	(a)	Manchester C	W	2-0	Armstrong, Radford	33,027
21		12	(h)	Wolves	W	2-1	Radford, Graham	38,816
22		19	(a)	Manchester U	W	3-1	McLintock, Graham, Kennedy	33,182
23		26	(h)	Southampton	D	0-0		34,169
24	Jan	9	(h)	West Ham U	W	2-0	Graham, Kennedy	49,007
25		16	(a)	Huddersfield T	L	1-2	Kennedy	30,455
26		30	(a)	Liverpool	L	0-2		43,847
27	Feb	6	(h)	Manchester C	W	1-0	Radford	46,122
28		20	(h)	Ipswich T	W	3-2	George, Radford, McLintock	39,822
29		27	(a)	Derby C	L	0-2		35,875
30	Mar	2	(a)	Wolves	W	3-0	Armstrong, Kennedy, Radford	33,644
31		13	(a)	Crystal P	W	2-0	Graham, Sammels	35,022
32		20	(h)	Blackpool	W	1-0	Storey	37,372
33	Apr	3	(h)	Chelsea	W	2-0	Kennedy 2	62,087
34		6	(h)	Coventry C	W	1-0	Kennedy	37,029
35		10	(a)	Southampton	W	2-1	Radford, McLintock	30,231
36		13	(a)	Nottingham F	W	3-0	McLintock, Kennedy, George	40,727
37		17	(h)	Newcastle U	W	1-0	George	48,106
38		20	(h)	Burnley	W	1-0	George (pen)	47,484
39		24	(a)	West Brom A	D	2-2	McLintock, Hartford (og)	36,858
40		26	(a)	Leeds U	L	0-1		48,350
41	May	1	(h)	Stoke C	W	1-0	Kelly	55,011
42		3	(a)	Tottenham H	W	1-0	Kennedy	51,992

FINAL LEAGUE POSITION: 1st in Division One

Appearances
Sub Appearances
Goals

Wilson RP	Rice PJ	McNab R	Kelly EP	McLintock F	Roberts JG	Armstrong G	Storey PE	Radford J	George FC	Graham G	Marinello P	Kennedy R	Nelson S	Simpson PF	Sammels JC	
1	2	3	4	5	6	7	8	9	10*	11	12					1
1		3	4	5	6	7	2	9		11	10	8				2
1	2	3	4	5	6	7	8	9*		11	12	10				3
1	2	3	4	5	6	7	8	9*		11		10	12			4
1	2	3	4	5	6	7	8			11		10	9			5
1	2	3	4	5	6	7	8	9		11		10				6
1	2	3	4	5*	6	7	8	9		11		10	12			7
1	2	3	4	5	6	7	8	9		11		10				8
1	2	3	4	5	6	7	8	9		11		10				9
1	2	3	4	5	6	7	8	9		11		10				10
1	2	3	4	5	6	7	8	9		11		10				11
1	2	3	4	5	6	7	8	9		11		10				12
1	2	3	4	5	6	7	8	9		11		10				13
1	2	3	4	5	6	7	8	9		11		10				14
1	2	3	4	5	6	7	8	9		11		10				15
1	2	3	4	5	6	7	8	9		11		10				16
1	2	3	4	5	6	7	8	9		11		10				17
1	2	3	4	5		7	8	9				10		6	11	18
1	2	3	4*	5		7	8	9	12			10		6	11	19
1	2	3		5		7	8	9	4			10		6	11	20
1	2	3		5		7	4	9		11		10		6	8	21
1	2	3		5		7	4	9		11		10		6	8	22
1	2	3		5		7	4	9		11		10		6	8	23
1	2			5		7	4	9		11		10	3	6	8	24
1	2	3		5		7	4	9		11		10		6	8	25
1	2	3		5		7	4	9		11		10		6	8	26
1	2	3		5		7	4	9	11			10		6	8	27
1	2	3		5		7	4	9	11			10		6	8	28
1	2*	3		5		7	4	9	11	12		10		6	8	29
1	2	3		5		7	4	9	11			10		6	8	30
1	2	3		5		7	4	9	11*	8		10		6	12	31
1	2	3		5		7	4	9	11	8		10		6		32
1	2	3	12	5		7*	4	9	11	8		10		6		33
1	2	3		5		7	4	9	11	8		10		6		34
1	2	3		5		7	4	9	11	8		10		6		35
1	2	3		5		7	4	9	11	8		10		6		36
1	2	3		5		7	4	9	11	8		10		6		37
1	2		4	5	3	7		9	11	8		10		6		38
1	2*	3		5		7	4	9	11	8		10		6	12	39
1	2	3		5		7	4	9	11	8		10		6		40
1	2	3	12	5		7	4*	9	11	8		10		6		41
1	2	3	4	5		7		9	11	8		10		6		42
42	41	40	21	42	18	42	40	41	17	36	1	41	2	25	13	—
			2						2	2		2			2	—
		4	5			7	2	15	5	11		19			1	—

2 own-goals

1970-71 (continued)

FA Cup

3	Jan	6	(a) Yeovil T	W	3-0	Radford 2, Kennedy	4,374
4		23	(a) Portsmouth	D	1-1	Storey (pen)	39,659
R	Feb	1	(h) Portsmouth	W	3-2	George, Simpson, Storey (pen)	47,865
5		17	(a) Manchester C	W	2-1	George 2	45,105
6	Mar	6	(a) Leicester C	D	0-0		42,000
R	Mar	15	(h) Leicester C	W	1-0	George	57,443
SF		27	(n*) Stoke C	D	2-2	Storey 2 (1 pen)	53,436
R		31	(n†) Stoke C	W	2-0	Graham, Kennedy	62,500
F	May	8	(n‡) Liverpool	W	2-1§	Kelly, George	100,000

*Played at Hillsborough, Sheffield. †Played at Villa Park, Birmingham. ‡Played at Wembley Stadium. §After extra-time.

Appearances

Sub Appearances

Goals

League Cup

2	Sep	8	(a) Ipswich T	D	0-0		21,564
R		28	(h) Ipswich T	W	4-0	Kennedy 2, Radford, Roberts	26,379
3	Oct	6	(a) Luton T	W	1-0	Graham	27,023
4		28	(a) Crystal P	D	0-0		40,451
R	Nov	9	(h) Crystal P	L	0-2		45,026

Appearances

Sub Appearances

Goals

Charlie George and John Radford celebrate after Radford's winning goal against Manchester City at Highbury on 6 February 1971. The unhappy City goalkeeper is Joe Corrigan.

270

Wilson RP	Rice PJ	McNab R	Kelly EP	McLintock F	Roberts JG	Armstrong G	Storey PE	Radford J	George FC	Graham G	Marinello P	Kennedy R	Nelson S	Simpson PF	Sammels JC	
1	2	3*	12	5		7	4	9		11		10		6	8	3
1	2*	3		5		7	4	9	12	11		10		6	8	4
1	2	3		5		7	4	9		11		10		6	8	R
1	2	3		5		7	4	9		11		10		6	8	5
1	2	3		5		7	4	9		11		10		6	8	6
1	2	3		5		7	4	9		11	8	10		6		R
1	2	3		5		7	4	9		11*	8	10		6	12	SF
1	2	3		5		7	4	9		11	8	10		6		R
1	2	3	12	5		7	4*	9		11	8	10		6		F
9	9	9		9		9	9	9		9	4	9		9	5	
			2						1						1	
		1				4	2	5	1			2		1		

Wilson RP	Rice PJ	McNab R	Kelly EP	McLintock F	Roberts JG	Armstrong G	Storey PE	Radford J	George FC	Graham G	Marinello P	Kennedy R	Nelson S	Simpson PF	Sammels JC	
1	2	3	4	5	6	7	8			11		10	9			2
1	2	3	4	5	6	7	8	9		11		10				R
1	2	3	4	5	6	7	8	9		11		10				3
1	2	3	4	5	6	7	8	9		11		10				4
1	2	3	4	5	6	7	8	9		11		10				R
5	5	5	5	5	5	5	5	4		5		5	1			
			1					1		1		2				

Ray Kennedy and Ipswich Town's Mick Mills in action at Highbury on 20 February 1971.

1971-72

Manager: B.Mee

1	Aug	14	(h)	Chelsea	W 3-0 McLintock, Kennedy, Radford	49,174
2		17	(a)	Huddersfield T	W 1-0 Kennedy	21,279
3		20	(a*)	Manchester U	L 1-3 McLintock	27,649
4		24	(h)	Sheffield U	L 0-1	45,395
5		28	(h)	Stoke C	L 0-1	37,637
6	Sep	4	(a)	West Brom A	W 1-0 Roberts	29,922
7		11	(h)	Leeds U	W 2-0 Graham, Storey (pen)	51,196
8		18	(a)	Everton	L 1-2 Kennedy	39,710
9		25	(h)	Leicester C	W 3-0 Radford 2, Rice	40,201
10	Oct	2	(a)	Southampton	W 1-0 Simpson	23,738
11		9	(h)	Newcastle U	W 4-2 Graham, Kennedy, Armstrong, Kelly	40,509
12		16	(a)	Chelsea	W 2-1 Kennedy 2	52,338
13		23	(a)	Derby C	L 1-2 Graham	36,480
14		30	(h)	Ipswich T	W 2-1 George, Sivell (og)	39,065
15	Nov	6	(a)	Liverpool	L 2-3 Kennedy, Smith (og)	46,929
16		13	(h)	Manchester C	L 1-2 Nelson	47,443
17		20	(a)	Wolves	L 1-5 Kennedy	28,851
18		24	(a)	Tottenham H	D 1-1 Kennedy	52,884
19		27	(h)	Crystal P	W 2-1 Kelly, Radford	32,461
20	Dec	4	(a)	West Ham U	D 0-0	35,155
21		11	(h)	Coventry C	W 2-0 Radford 2	28,599
22		18	(h)	West Brom A	W 2-0 Roberts 2	28,177
23		27	(a)	Nottingham F	D 1-1 Graham	42,750
24	Jan	1	(h)	Everton	D 1-1 Simpson	47,031
25		8	(a)	Stoke C	D 0-0	18,965
26		22	(h)	Huddersfield T	W 1-0 Armstrong	36,670
27		29	(a)	Sheffield U	W 5-0 George 2, Graham, Simpson, Kennedy	30,778
28	Feb	12	(h)	Derby C	W 2-0 George 2 (1 pen)	52,055
29		19	(a)	Ipswich T	W 1-0 George	28,657
30	Mar	4	(a)	Manchester C	L 0-2	44,213
31		11	(a)	Newcastle U	L 0-2	31,920
32		25	(a)	Leeds U	L 0-3	45,055
33		28	(h)	Southampton	W 1-0 Marinello	27,172
34	Apr	1	(h)	Nottingham F	W 3-0 Kennedy, George (pen), Graham	33,895
35		4	(a)	Leicester C	D 0-0	27,431
36		8	(h)	Wolves	W 2-1 Graham 2	38,189
37		11	(a)	Crystal P	D 2-2 Radford, Ball	34,384
38		22	(h)	West Ham U	W 2-1 Ball 2	45,251
39		25	(h)	Manchester U	W 3-0 Radford, Kennedy, Simpson	49,125
40	May	2	(a)	Coventry C	W 1-0 McLintock	23,509
41		8	(h)	Liverpool	D 0-0	39,285
42		11	(h)	Tottenham H	L 0-2	42,038

FINAL LEAGUE POSITION: 5th in Division One

*Played at Anfield, Liverpool — Manchester United ground closed.

Appearances
Sub Appearances
Goals

272

Wilson RP	Rice PJ	McNab R	Storey PE	McLintock F	Simpson PF	Armstrong G	Kelly EP	Radford J	Kennedy R	Graham G	Roberts JG	Nelson S	George FC	Davies P	Marinello P	Ball AJ	Batson BM	Barnett GC	#
1	2	3	4	5	6	7	8	9	10	11									1
1	2	3	4	5	6	7	8	9	10	11									2
1	2	3	4	5	6	7	8	9	10	11									3
1	2	3	4	5	6	7	8	9	10	11									4
1	2*	3	4	5	6	7	8	9	10	11	12								5
1	2	3	4	5		7	8	9	10	11	6								6
1	2	3	4	5	8	7		9	10	11	6								7
1	2	3	4	5*	8	7	12	9	10	11	6								8
1	2	4*		5		7	8	9	10	11	6	3	12						9
1	2	4		5		7	8	9	10	11	6	3							10
1	2	4		5		7	8	9*	10	11	3	6	12						11
1	2	4		12		7	8*	9	10	11	5	3	6						12
1	2	5		12		7	4*	9	10	11	6	3	8						13
1	2	4	6			7		9	10	11	5	3	8						14
1	2	4	6			7		9	10	11	5	3	8						15
1	2	4	6			7		9	10	11	5	3	8						16
1	2	4	6			7		9	10	11	5	3	8						17
1	2	3	4		6	7	8	9	10	11	5								18
1	2	3	4		6	7	8	9	10	11	5								19
1	2	3	4	5	6	7	8	9	10	11									20
1	2	3	4	5	6*	7	8	9	10	11					12				21
1	2	3	4	5		7	8	9	10	11	6								22
1	2	3		5	6	7	4	9	10	11						8			23
1	2	3			6	7*	4	9	10	11	5				12	8			24
1	2	3		5	6	7	4	9	10	11						8			25
1	2			5	6	7	4	9	10	11			3		12	8*			26
1	2			5	6	7			10	11	4	3	9			8			27
1	2			5	6	7	4		10	11		3	9			8			28
1	2			5	6	7	4		10	11		3	9			8			29
1	2	4		5	6	7		10		11		3	9			8			30
1	2	4		5		7	11		10		6	3	9*		12	8			31
1	2	4		5	6	7			10	11*			3	9	12	8			32
1	2	4		5	6	7			10				3	9	11	8			33
1	2	4			6	7		10*	12		5		3	9	11	8			34
1	2	4		5	6	7			10				3	9	11	8			35
1	2	4		5	6	12		10	11				3	9	7*	8			36
1	2	4			6	7		9		11	5		3	10		8			37
	2	3	4	5*	6	7		9	10	11						8	12	1	38
	2	3		5	6	7		9	10	11*	4					8	12	1	39
	2	3	4	5	6	7		9	10	11						8		1	40
	2*		4	5	6	7		9	10	11	12	3				8		1	41
	2	3	5	8*		7		9	10	11	6	4			12			1	42
37	42	20	29	37	32	41	22	34	37	39	21	24	20		4	18		5	
			2	1	1			1	2			3	1	4		2			
	1		1	3	4	2	2	8	12	8	3	1	7		1	3			

2 own-goals

1971-72 (continued)

FA Cup

3	Jan	15	(a)	Swindon T	W 2-0	Armstrong, Ball		32,000
4	Feb	5	(a)	Reading	W 2-1	Rice, Morgan (og)		25,756
5		26	(a)	Derby C	D 2-2	George 2		39,622
R		29	(h)	Derby C	D 0-0†			63,077
2R	Mar	13	(n‡)	Derby C	W 1-0	Kennedy		36,534
6		18	(a)	Orient	W 1-0	Ball		31,768
SF	Apr	15	(n§)	Stoke C	D 1-1	Armstrong		56,576
R		19	(n¹)	Stoke C	W 2-1	George, Radford		38,970
F	May	6	(n²)	Leeds U	L 0-1			100,000

†After extra-time. ‡Played at Filbert Street, Leicester. §Played at Villa Park, Birmingham. ¹Played at Goodison Park, Liverpool. ²Played at Wembley Stadium.

When goalkeeper Wilson was injured in semi-final on April 15 Radford went in goal and Kennedy substituted outfield.

Appearances
Sub Appearances
Goals

League Cup

2	Sep	8	(h)	Barnsley	W 1-0	Kennedy		27,294
3	Oct	6	(h)	Newcastle U	W 4-0	Radford 2, Kennedy, Graham		34,071
4		26	(h)	Sheffield U	D 0-0			44,061
R	Nov	8	(a)	Sheffield U	L 0-2			35,461

Appearances
Sub Appearances
Goals

David Serella of Nottingham Forest challenges Ray Kennedy in the match at Highbury on 1 April 1972.

Wilson RP	Rice PJ	McNab R	Storey PE	McLintock F	Simpson PF	Armstrong G	Kelly EP	Radford J	Kennedy R	Graham G	Roberts JG	Nelson S	George FC	Davies P	Marinello P	Ball AJ	Batson BM	Barnett GC	
1	2			5	6	7	4	9	10	11		3				8			3
1	2			5	6	7	4		10	11		3	9			8			4
1	2		12	5	6	7	4*		10	11		3	9			8			5
1	2			4	5	6	7		12	10*	11		3	9		8			R
1	2			4	5	6	7		10	11		3	9			8			2R
1	2			4	5	6	7		10	11		3	9			8			6
1*	2	3	4	5	6	7			10	12	11			9		8			SF
	2	3	4	5	6	7		9		11		10				8	1		R
	2	3	4	5	6	7		10*	12	11			9			8	1		F
7	9	3	6	9	9	9	3	4	6	9		6	8			9	2		
			1					1	2										
1					2		1	1		3			2						

1 own-goal

Wilson RP	Rice PJ	McNab R	Storey PE	McLintock F	Simpson PF	Armstrong G	Kelly EP	Radford J	Kennedy R	Graham G	Roberts JG	Nelson S	George FC	Davies P	Marinello P	Ball AJ	Batson BM	Barnett GC	
1	2	3	4	5			8	9	10	11	6			7					2
1	2			4	5	7	8	9	10	11	6	3				7			3
	2		4	6		7		9	10	11	5	3	8		1				4
1	2	12		6*		7	4	9	10	11	5	3	8						R
3	4	1	2	4	1	3	3	4	4	4	4	3	2		1	1			
			1																
								2	2	1									

Bob Wilson (left) was an ever-present until he was injured in the FA Cup semi-final and missed the remainder of the season. Ray Kennedy (right) netted 12 goals in 37 League games

1972-73

Manager: B.Mee

1	Aug	12	(a)	Leicester C	W	1-0	Ball (pen)	28,009
2		15	(h)	Wolves	W	5-2	Radford 2, Kennedy, Simpson, McNab	38,524
3		19	(h)	Stoke C	W	2-0	Kennedy 2	42,146
4		22	(a)	Coventry C	D	1-1	Rice	24,670
5		26	(a)	Manchester U	D	0-0		48,108
6		29	(h)	West Ham U	W	1-0	Ball (pen)	43,802
7	Sep	2	(h)	Chelsea	D	1-1	Webb (og)	46,675
8		9	(a)	Newcastle U	L	1-2	Kennedy	23,849
9		16	(h)	Liverpool	D	0-0		47,597
10		23	(a)	Norwich C	L	2-3	Storey, Radford	32,273
11		26	(h)	Birmingham C	W	2-0	Storey, George	30,003
12		30	(h)	Southampton	W	1-0	Graham	34,694
13	Oct	7	(a)	Sheffield U	L	0-1		24,478
14		14	(h)	Ipswich T	W	1-0	Graham	34,196
15		21	(a)	Crystal P	W	3-2	George (pen), Radford, Rice	35,865
16		28	(h)	Manchester C	D	0-0		45,536
17	Nov	4	(h)	Coventry C	L	0-2		33,699
18		11	(a)	Wolves	W	3-1	Radford 2, Marinello	25,988
19		18	(h)	Everton	W	1-0	Radford	35,728
20		25	(a)	Derby C	L	0-5		31,034
21	Dec	2	(h)	Leeds U	W	2-1	Ball (pen), Radford	39,108
22		9	(a)	Tottenham H	W	2-1	Storey, Radford	47,505
23		16	(h)	West Brom A	W	2-1	Radford, Nisbet (og)	27,119
24		23	(a)	Birmingham C	D	1-1	Kelly	32,721
25		26	(h)	Norwich C	W	2-0	Radford, Ball	39,038
26		30	(a)	Stoke C	D	0-0		24,586
27	Jan	6	(h)	Manchester U	W	3-1	Kennedy, Armstrong, Ball	56,194
28		20	(a)	Chelsea	W	1-0	Kennedy	36,292
29		27	(h)	Newcastle U	D	2-2	Kennedy, Ball	37,906
30	Feb	10	(a)	Liverpool	W	2-0	Ball (pen), Radford	49,898
31		17	(h)	Leicester C	W	1-0	Manley (og)	42,047
32		28	(a)	West Brom A	L	0-1		23,515
33	Mar	3	(h)	Sheffield U	W	3-2	George 2, Ball	33,346
34		10	(a)	Ipswich T	W	2-1	Radford, Ball (pen)	34,636
35		24	(a)	Manchester C	W	2-1	George, Kennedy	32,031
36		26	(h)	Crystal P	W	1-0	Ball	41,879
37		31	(h)	Derby C	L	0-1		45,217
38	Apr	14	(h)	Tottenham H	D	1-1	Storey	50,863
39		21	(a)	Everton	D	0-0		42,888
40		23	(a)	Southampton	D	2-2	George, Radford	23,919
41		28	(a)	West Ham U	W	2-1	Kennedy, Radford	37,366
42	May	9	(a)	Leeds U	L	1-6	Armstrong	25,088

FINAL LEAGUE POSITION: 2nd in Division One

Appearances
Sub Appearances
Goals

276

Barnett GC	Rice PJ	McNab R	Storey PE	McLintock F	Simpson PF	Armstrong G	Ball AJ	Radford J	Kennedy R	Graham G	Roberts JG	George FC	Marinello P	Blockley JP	Kelly EP	Nelson S	Wilson RP	Batson BM	Hornsby BG	Price DJ	
1	2	3	4	5	6	7	8	9	10	11											1
1	2	3	4	5	6*	7	8	9	10	11	12										2
1	2	3	4	5		7	8	9	10	11	6										3
1	2	3	4	5	6	7	8	9	10	11											4
1	2	3	4	5	6	7	8		10	11		9									5
1	2	3	4	5	6	7*	8	9	10	11		12									6
1	2	3	4	5	6	7*	8	9	10	11		12									7
1	2	3	4	5			8	9	10	11	6		7								8
1	2	3	4	5			8	9	10	11	6		7								9
1	2	3	4	5			8	9	10	11	6		7								10
1	2	3	4	5			8	9	10		6	11	7								11
1	2	3	4	5			8	9	10*	12	6	11	7								12
1	2	3	4	5			8	9	10			11	7	6							13
1	2	3	4	5			8	9	10			11	7	6							14
1	2	3	4	5				9	10			11	7	6	8*	12					15
1	2	3	4	5				9	11			10	7	6	8						16
1	2	3	4	5			8	9	12			10	7	6	11*						17
1	2	3	4	5			8	9	10				7	6	11						18
1	2	3	4	5			8	9	10				7	6	11						19
	2	3	4	5	6	12	8	9	10				7*		11		1				20
	2	3	4		6	7	8	9	10					5	11		1				21
	2	3	4	12	6*	7	8	9	10					5	11		1				22
1	2*	3	4	5	6	7	8	9	10			12	11								23
		3	4		6	7	8	9	10					5	11	2	1				24
		3	4		6	7	8	9	10			12		5	11	2	1				25
	2	3	4		6	7	8	9	10					5	11		1				26
	2	3	4		6	7	8	9	10					5	11		1				27
	2	3	4	12	6	7	8	9	10					5	11*		1				28
	2	3	4		6	7*	8	9	10			12		5	11		1				29
	2	3	4		6	7	8	9*	10			12		5	11		1				30
	2	3	4		6	7	8	9	10			12		5*	11		1				31
	2	3		5		7	8	9	10			6			11		1	4			32
	2	3		5		7	8	9	10			4	12		11		1	6*			33
	2	3	4	5	6	7	8	9	10						11		1				34
	2	3	4	5	6	7	8	9	10			11*					1		12		35
	2	3	4	5	6	7	8	9	10			11					1				36
	2	3	4	5*	6	7	8	9	10			11			12		1				37
	2	3	4		6	7	8	9	10			12		5	11*		1				38
	2	3	4		6	7	8	9	10			12		5*	11		1				39
	2	3	4		6	7	8	9	11			10		5			1				40
	2	3	4		6	7	8	9	10			11		5			1				41
		3	4		6	7	8	9	10					5	11*		1	2	12		42
20	39	42	40	27	27	29	40	38	34	14	6	18	13	20	27	2	22	3	1		
			2		1				2	1			9		4			1			
	2	1	4	1	2		10	15	9	2		6	1		1						

3 own-goals

1972-73 (continued)

FA Cup

3	Jan	13	(h)	Leicester C	D	2-2 Kennedy, Armstrong	36,433
R		17	(a)	Leicester C	W	2-1 Radford, Kelly	32,973
4	Feb	3	(h)	Bradford C	W	2-0 Ball, George	40,407
5		24	(a)	Carlisle U	W	2-1 Ball, McLintock	23,922
6	Mar	17	(a)	Chelsea	D	2-2 Ball, George	37,685
R		20	(h)	Chelsea	W	2-1 Ball (pen), Kennedy	62,746
SF	Apr	7	(n*)	Sunderland	L	1-2 George	53,301

*Played at Hillsborough, Sheffield.

Appearances
Sub Appearances
Goals

FA Cup — Third place play-off (played at beginning of 1973-4 season)

PO	Aug	18	(h)	Wolves	L	1-3 Hornsby	21,038

Appearances
Sub Appearances
Goals

League Cup

2	Sep	5	(h)	Everton	W	1-0 Storey	35,230
3	Oct	3	(h)	Rotherham U	W	5-0 Radford 2, George, Storey, Marinello	25,241
4		31	(a)	Sheffield U	W	2-1 Radford, George	20,128
5	Nov	21	(h)	Norwich C	L	0-3	37,671

Appearances
Sub Appearances
Goals

Action from two games at Highbury during November 1972. Left: Charlie George gets the best of the aerial action against Everton. Terry Darracott (8) and John Hurst are the Blues' players. Right: Coventry City goalkeeper Bill Glazier punches clear from Peter Storey. The other Coventry players are Willie Carr and Mick Coop.

Barnett GC	Rice PJ	McNab R	Storey PE	McLintock F	Simpson PF	Armstrong G	Ball AJ	Radford J	Kennedy R	Graham G	Roberts JG	George FC	Marinello P	Blockley JP	Kelly EP	Nelson S	Wilson RP	Batson BM	Hornsby BG	Price DJ	Chambers BM	
	2	3	4		6	7	8	9	10					5	11		1					3
	2	3	4		6	7	8	9	10					5	11		1					R
	2	3	4		6	7	8		10			9*	12	5	11		1					4
1	2	3	4*	5	6	7	8	9	10						11	12						5
	2	3	4	5	6	7	8		10			9			11		1					6
	2	3	4	5	6	7	8		10			9			11		1					R
	2	3	4		6	7	8	12	10			9		5*	11		1					SF
1	7	7	7	3	7	7	7	3	7			4		4	7		6					
											1		1			1						
		1			1	4	1	2				3			1							

Barnett GC	Rice PJ	McNab R	Storey PE	McLintock F	Simpson PF	Armstrong G	Ball AJ	Radford J	Kennedy R	Graham G	Roberts JG	George FC	Marinello P	Blockley JP	Kelly EP	Nelson S	Wilson RP	Batson BM	Hornsby BG	Price DJ	Chambers BM	
		3			6		8	9	10					5			1	2	11	4	7	PO
		1			1		1	1	1					1			1	1	1	1	1	
																	1					

Barnett GC	Rice PJ	McNab R	Storey PE	McLintock F	Simpson PF	Armstrong G	Ball AJ	Radford J	Kennedy R	Graham G	Roberts JG	George FC	Marinello P	Blockley JP	Kelly EP	Nelson S	Wilson RP	Batson BM	Hornsby BG	Price DJ	Chambers BM	
1	2	3	4	5	6		8	9	10	11		7										2
1	2		4	5			8	9		10	6	11		7								3
1	2	3	4	5	6			9		10	11	7		8								4
1	2	3	4	5	6		8	9		10	7			11								5
4	4	3	4	4	3		3	4	1	3	1	3	4		2	1						
		2						3			2	1										

Eddie Kelly (left) scored one goal during 1972-3 and it earned Arsenal a draw at Birmingham, in the Gunners' unbeaten sequence of 11 games. John Radford (right) scored 15 goals in 38 League games as the Gunners finished runners-up in the First Division.

1973-74

Manager: B.Mee

1	Aug	25	(h)	Manchester U	W 3-0	Kennedy, Radford, Ball	51,501
2		28	(h)	Leeds U	L 1-2	Blockley	47,429
3	Sep	1	(a)	Newcastle U	D 1-1	George	28,697
4		4	(a)	Sheffield U	L 0-5		27,839
5		8	(h)	Leicester C	L 0-2		28,558
6		11	(h)	Sheffield U	W 1-0	Kennedy	29,434
7		15	(a)	Norwich C	W 4-0	George, McNab, Ball (pen), Kennedy	29,278
8		22	(h)	Stoke C	W 2-1	Radford, Ball	30,578
9		29	(a)	Everton	L 0-1		31,359
10	Oct	6	(h)	Birmingham C	W 1-0	Kennedy	23,915
11		13	(a)	Tottenham H	L 0-2		41,855
12		20	(h)	Ipswich T	D 1-1	Simpson	28,344
13		27	(a)	Queen's Park R	L 0-2		29,115
14	Nov	3	(h)	Liverpool	L 0-2		39,837
15		10	(a)	Manchester C	W 2-1	Kelly, Hornsby	31,041
16		17	(h)	Chelsea	D 0-0		38,677
17		24	(a)	West Ham U	W 3-1	George, Ball 2	28,287
18	Dec	1	(h)	Coventry C	D 2-2	Hornsby, Nelson	22,340
19		4	(h)	Wolves	D 2-2	George, Hornsby	13,482
20		8	(a)	Derby C	D 1-1	Newton (og)	25,161
21		15	(a)	Burnley	L 1-2	Radford	13,200
22		22	(h)	Everton	W 1-0	Ball	19,886
23		26	(a)	Southampton	D 1-1	Ball	24,133
24		29	(a)	Leicester C	L 0-2		25,860
25	Jan	1	(h)	Newcastle U	L 0-1		29,258
26		12	(h)	Norwich C	W 2-0	Ball 2	22,084
27		19	(a)	Manchester U	D 1-1	Kennedy	38,589
28	Feb	2	(h)	Burnley	D 1-1	Ball	20,789
29		5	(a)	Leeds U	L 1-3	Ball	26,778
30		16	(h)	Tottenham H	L 0-1		38,804
31		23	(a)	Birmingham C	L 1-3	Kennedy	29,822
32	Mar	2	(h)	Southampton	W 1-0	Ball	19,210
33		16	(a)	Ipswich T	D 2-2	Kennedy, Simpson	22,297
34		23	(h)	Manchester C	W 2-0	Radford 2	25,319
25		30	(a)	Stoke C	D 0-0		18,532
36	Apr	6	(h)	West Ham U	D 0-0		37,868
37		13	(a)	Chelsea	W 3-1	Kennedy 2, Radford	29,152
38		15	(a)	Wolves	L 1-3	Kennedy	25,881
39		20	(h)	Derby C	W 2-0	Ball (pen), George	26,017
40		24	(a)	Liverpool	W 1-0	Kennedy	47,997
41		27	(a)	Coventry C	D 3-3	Rice, Kennedy, Radford	19,945
42		30	(h)	Queen's Park	D 1-1	Brady	40,396

FINAL LEAGUE POSITION: 10th in Division One

Appearances
Sub Appearances
Goals

FA Cup

3	Jan	5	(a)	Norwich C	W 1-0	Kelly	21,500
4		26	(h)	Aston Villa	D 1-1	Kennedy	41,682
R		30	(a)	Aston Villa	L 0-2		47,821

Appearances
Sub Appearances
Goals

League Cup

2	Oct	2	(h)	Tranmere R	L 0-1		20,337

Appearances
Sub Appearances
Goals

Wilson RP	Rice PJ	McNab R	Price DJ	Blockley JP	Simpson PF	Armstrong G	Ball AJ	Radford J	Kennedy R	George FC	Hornsby BG	Storey PE	Kelly EP	Batson BM	Brady WL	Chambers BM	Powling RF	Nelson S	Rimmer JJ	Match
1	2	3	4	5	6	7	8	9*	10	11	12									1
1	2	3	12	5	6*	7	8	9	10	11		4								2
1	2	3	4	5		7	8		10	11			6	9						3
1	2	3		5		7	8		10	11			6	9	4					4
1	2	3		5	6	12	8	9	10	11		4	7*							5
1	2	3		5	6	7	8	9	10			4	11							6
1	2	3		5		7	8	9	10	6		4	11							7
1	2	3		5	6	7	8	9	10	11*		4	12							8
1	2	3		5	6	7	8	9	10	11*		4	12							9
1	2	3	5*	6	7		9		10			4	11			12	8			10
1	2	3			5	7		9*	10	8		4	6	12	11					11
1	2	3	11		5	7			10	8		4	6	9						12
1	2	3			5	7			10	8		4	6	9	11					13
1	2	3			5	7		9	10	8		4	6	11*	12					14
1	2	3			5	11	7		10	8	9	4	6							15
1	2	3			5	11	7		10	8	9	4	6							16
1	2	3			5	11	7		10	8	9	4	6							17
1	2	3			5	11	7		10	8	9	4	6*		12					18
1	2	3			5	11	7	9	10	8*	12	4	6							19
1	2	3	8		5	11	7	9	10			4	6							20
1	2		8		5	11	7	9	10			4	6					3		21
1	2	3			5	6	7	8	10	9		4	11							22
1	2				5	6	7	8	9	10	12	4	11*					3		23
1	2				5	6	7	8	9	10	11	4						3		24
1	2				5	6	7	8	9	10		4	11					3		25
1	2				5	6	7	8	9	10		3	4		11					26
1	2	3			5	6	7	8	9	10		4	11							27
1	2				5	6	7	8	9	10		3	4		11					28
1	2				5	6	7	8	9	10		4	11					3		29
1	2				5		7	8	9	10		4	6		11			3		30
1	2				5		8	9	10	7		4	6		11			3		31
1	2				5	11	8	9	10	7		4	6					3		32
1		2			5	11		9	10	7		4	6				8	3		33
1	2				5	11	8	9	10	7		4	6*		12			3		34
1	2			5	12	7	8	9	10	11		4	6*					3		35
1	2				5		7	8	9	10	11	4	6					3		36
1	2				5	12	7	8	9	10	11	4	6*					3		37
1	2				5	6	7	8	9*	10	11	4			12			3		38
1	2				5	12	7	8		10	9*	4	6		11			3		39
	2			5*	12	7	8	9	10			4	6		11			3	1	40
1	2				5		7	8	9	10	11	4	6					3		41
1	2				5		7	8*	9	10	11	4	6		12					42
41	41	23	3	26	34	40	36	32	42	28	6	41	35	3	9	1	2	18	1	
		1			4	1			3		2	2	4		1					
	1	1		1	2		13	7	12	5	3		1		1			1		

1 own-goal

Wilson RP	Rice PJ	McNab R	Price DJ	Blockley JP	Simpson PF	Armstrong G	Ball AJ	Radford J	Kennedy R	George FC	Hornsby BG	Storey PE	Kelly EP	Batson BM	Brady WL	Chambers BM	Powling RF	Nelson S	Rimmer JJ	
1	2	3		5	6	11	8	9	10			4	7							3
1	2	3		5	6	7	8	9	10			4	11							4
1	2	3*		5	6	7	8	9	10			4	11		12					R
3	3	3		3	3	3	3	3	3			3	3		1					
															1					
											1		1							

Wilson RP	Rice PJ	McNab R	Price DJ	Blockley JP	Simpson PF	Armstrong G	Ball AJ	Radford J	Kennedy R	George FC	Hornsby BG	Storey PE	Kelly EP	Batson BM	Brady WL	Chambers BM	Powling RF	Nelson S	Rimmer JJ	
1	2	3		5	6	7	8*	9	10			4	11		12					2
1	1	1		1	1	1	1	1	1			1	1		1					
																1				

1974-75

Manager: B.Mee

1	Aug	17	(a)	Leicester C	W 1-0 Kidd	26,448
2		20	(h)	Ipswich T	L 0-1	31,027
3		24	(h)	Manchester C	W 4-0 Kidd 2, Radford 2	27,143
4		27	(a)	Ipswich T	L 0-3	28,036
5		31	(a)	Everton	L 1-2 Kidd	42,438
6	Sep	7	(h)	Burnley	L 0-1	23,586
7		14	(a)	Chelsea	D 0-0	34,596
8		21	(h)	Luton T	D 2-2 Kidd 2	21,629
9		28	(a)	Birmingham C	L 1-3 George	25,584
10	Oct	5	(a)	Leeds U	L 0-2	32,784
11		12	(h)	Queen's Park R	D 2-2 Kidd, Radford	29,690
12		16	(a)	Manchester C	L 1-2 Radford	26,658
13		19	(a)	Tottenham H	L 0-2	36,194
14		26	(h)	West Ham U	W 3-0 Radford, Brady, Kidd	41,004
15	Nov	2	(h)	Wolves	D 0-0	27,572
16		9	(a)	Liverpool	W 3-1 Ball 2, Brady	43,850
17		16	(h)	Derby C	W 3-1 Ball 2 (1 pen) Kidd	32,286
18		23	(a)	Coventry C	L 0-3	15,669
19		30	(h)	Middlesbrough	W 2-0 Brady, Ball (pen)	25,283
20	Dec	7	(a)	Carlisle U	L 1-2 Kidd	12,926
21		14	(h)	Leicester C	D 0-0	20,849
22		21	(a)	Stoke C	W 2-0 Kidd 2	23,292
23		26	(h)	Chelsea	L 1-2 Ball (pen)	33,784
24		28	(a)	Sheffield U	D 1-1 George	19,967
25	Jan	11	(h)	Carlisle U	W 2-1 Radford, Cropley	21,538
26		18	(a)	Middlesbrough	D 0-0	27,996
27	Feb	1	(h)	Liverpool	W 2-0 Ball 2 (1 pen)	43,028
28		8	(a)	Wolves	L 0-1	19,807
29		22	(a)	Derby C	L 1-2 Radford	24,002
30	Mar	1	(h)	Everton	L 0-2	32,216
31		15	(h)	Birmingham C	D 1-1 Kidd	17,845
32		18	(h)	Newcastle U	W 3-0 Kidd, Ball (pen), Rostron	16,540
33		22	(a)	Burnley	D 3-3 Rostron, Hornsby 2	17,539
34		25	(a)	Luton T	L 0-2	22,101
35		29	(h)	Stoke C	D 1-1 Kelly	26,852
36		31	(h)	Sheffield U	W 1-0 Kidd	24,338
37	Apr	8	(h)	Coventry C	W 2-0 Kidd 2	17,291
38		12	(h)	Leeds U	L 1-2 Kidd	36,619
39		19	(a)	Queen's Park R	D 0-0	24,362
40		23	(a)	Newcastle U	L 1-3 Hornsby	21,895
41		26	(h)	Tottenham H	W 1-0 Kidd	43,752
42		28	(a)	West Ham U	L 0-1	30,195

FINAL LEAGUE POSITION: 16th in Division One

Appearances
Sub Appearances
Goals

FA Cup

3	Jan	4	(h)	York C	D 1-1 Kelly	27,029
R		7	(a)	York C	W 3-1* Kidd 3	15,362
4		25	(a)	Coventry C	D 1-1 Ball	31,165
R		29	(h)	Coventry C	W 3-0 Armstrong 2, Matthews	30,867
5	Feb	15	(h)	Leicester C	D 0-0	43,841
R		19	(a)	Leicester C	D 1-1* Radford	35,009
2R		24	(a)	Leicester C	W 1-0* Radford	39,025
6	Mar	8	(h)	West Ham U	L 0-2	56,742

*After extra-time

Appearances
Sub Appearances
Goals

League Cup

2	Sep	10	(h)	Leicester C	D 1-1 Kidd	20,788
R		18	(a)	Leicester C	L 1-2 Brady	17,303

Appearances
Sub Appearances
Goals

282

Rimmer JJ	Matthews JM	Nelson S	Storey PE	Simpson PF	Kelly EP	Armstrong G	Brady WL	Radford J	George FC	Kidd B	Price DJ	Hornsby BG	Rice PJ	Powling RF	Blockley JP	Ball AJ	McNab R	Mancini TJ	Cropley AJ	Ross TW	Rostron JW	Stapleton FA	Barnett GC	
1	2	3	4	5	6*	7	8	9	10	11	12													1
1	6	3	2	5	4	7	11	9		10		8												2
1	7	3	6	5*	4	12	11	9	8	10			2											3
1	6	3	11	5	4		7	9	8	10			2											4
1		3	4	5	6*		8	9	10	11			2	12	7									5
1	6	3	4	12		7	8	9	10	11			2*		5									6
1	6		4	3	2	7	11	9	8	10					5									7
1	6	3	4	2	8	7	11	9		10					5									8
1	6		2	3	4		11	9	7	10					5	8								9
1	6		2	3	4	7	11	9		10				12	5*	8								10
1	6		2	3	4	7	11	9		10				5		8								11
1		4	2	3	6	11	8	9		10				5		7								12
1		3	2	6	4	7	10	9		11				5		8								13
1			2	6	4	12	10	9		11			7*			8	3	5						14
1			2	6	4		10	9		11			7			8	3	5						15
1			7	6	4		11	9		10			2			8	3	5						16
1			7	6	4		11	9		10			2			8	3	5						17
1				5	4	7	11*	9	12	10			2	6		8	3							18
1				5	4		11	9	7	10			2	6		8	3							19
1			7	5	4			9		10			2			8	3	6	11					20
1			7	6	4			9		10			2			8	3	5	11					21
1			7	6	4			9		10			2			8	3	5	11					22
1			7	6	4			9		10			2			8	3	5	11					23
1			7	6	4*	12			9	10			2			8	3	5	11					24
1				6	4	7		9		10			2			8	3	5	11					25
1			9	6	4	7				10			2			8	3	5	11					26
1	4		11	6		7	9			10			2			8*	3	5		12				27
1			11	6		7	8	9		10			2				3	5		4				28
1			4	6		7	11	9		10			2			8	3	5						29
1			4	6		7	11	9		10			2			8	3	5						30
1	7	3	4	6			11	9		10			2			8		5						31
1	7	3		6			11			10		9	2			8		5			4			32
1	4*	3		6			11			10		9	2	12		8		5			7			33
1		3	4	6			11	9				10	2			8		5			7			34
1	7		4	6	5		12					11	2			8	3				10	9*		35
1	7	3	4	6	8	11				10		9	2					5						36
1	7	3	4	6	8	11				10		9	2					5						37
1	7	3*	4	6	8	11	12			10		9	2					5						38
1		3	4	6	8	11				10		9	2			7		5						39
1	3	12	4		8*		6			10		9	2			7		5			11			40
		3	4	6		11	8			10		9	2			7		5					1	41
	6	3	2		4		8			10		9				7		5			11		1	42
40	20	19	37	39	32	21	30	29	9	40		12	32	5	6	30	18	26	7	1	6	1	2	
		1		1		3	2		1		1			3						1				
					1		3	7	2	19		3				9			1		2			

Rimmer JJ	Matthews JM	Nelson S	Storey PE	Simpson PF	Kelly EP	Armstrong G	Brady WL	Radford J	George FC	Kidd B	Price DJ	Hornsby BG	Rice PJ	Powling RF	Blockley JP	Ball AJ	McNab R	Mancini TJ	Cropley AJ	Ross TW	Rostron JW	Stapleton FA	Barnett GC	
1			7		4	9				10			2	6		8	3	5	11					3
1				5	4	7		9		10			2			8	3	6	11					R
1	12		4	6		7		9	11*	10			2			8	3	5						4
1	4		11	6		7	12	9*		10			2			8	3	5						R
1			4	6		7	11	9		10			2			8	3	5						5
1	11*		4	6		7	12	9		10			2			8	3	5						R
1	11*		4	6		7	12	9		10			2			8	3	5						2R
1	7		4	6		12	11	9*		10			2			8	3	5						6
8	4		7	7	2	7	2	7	1	8			8	1		8	8	8	2					
	1					1	3																	
	1				1	2		2		3						1								

Rimmer JJ	Matthews JM	Nelson S	Storey PE	Simpson PF	Kelly EP	Armstrong G	Brady WL	Radford J	George FC	Kidd B	Price DJ	Hornsby BG	Rice PJ	Powling RF	Blockley JP	Ball AJ	McNab R	Mancini TJ	Cropley AJ	Ross TW	Rostron JW	Stapleton FA	Barnett GC	
1	6		4	3	2	7	11	9	8	10					5									2
1	6	3	4	2	8	7	11	9		10					5									R
2	2	1	2	2	2	2	2	2	1	2					2									
							1			1														

1975-76

Manager: B.Mee

1	Aug	16	(a)	Burnley	D	0-0		18,603
2		19	(a)	Sheffield U	W	3-1	Brady, Rice, Kidd	23,344
3		23	(h)	Stoke C	L	0-1		28,025
4		26	(h)	Norwich C	W	2-1	Ball (pen), Kelly	22,613
5		30	(a)	Wolves	D	0-0		18,144
6	Sep	6	(h)	Leicester C	D	1-1	Stapleton	22,005
7		13	(a)	Aston Villa	L	0-2		34,474
8		20	(h)	Everton	D	2-2	Kidd, Stapleton	24,864
9		27	(a)	Tottenham H	D	0-0		37,092
10	Oct	4	(h)	Manchester C	L	2-3	Ball, Cropley	24,928
11		11	(h)	Coventry C	W	5-0	Cropley 2, Ball, Kidd 2	19,234
12		18	(a)	Manchester U	L	1-3	Kelly	52,958
13		25	(h)	Middlesbrough	W	2-1	Stapleton, Cropley	23,591
14	Nov	1	(a)	Newcastle U	L	0-2		32,824
15		8	(h)	Derby C	L	0-1		32,012
16		15	(a)	Birmingham C	L	1-3	Ball	21,652
17		22	(h)	Manchester U	W	3-1	Ball, Armstrong, Greenhoff (og)	40,102
18		29	(a)	West Ham U	L	0-1		31,012
19	Dec	2	(a)	Liverpool	D	2-2	Ball (pen), Kidd	27,447
20		6	(h)	Leeds U	L	1-2	Brady	36,003
21		13	(a)	Stoke C	L	1-2	Armstrong	18,628
22		20	(h)	Burnley	W	1-0	Radford	16,459
23		26	(a)	Ipswich T	L	0-2		28,457
24		27	(h)	Queen's Park R	W	2-0	Ball, Kidd	39,021
25	Jan	10	(h)	Aston Villa	D	0-0		24,501
26		17	(a)	Leicester C	L	1-2	Ross	21,331
27		31	(h)	Sheffield U	W	1-0	Brady	14,477
28	Feb	7	(a)	Norwich C	L	1-3	Kidd	23,038
29		18	(a)	Derby C	L	0-2		24,875
30		21	(h)	Birmingham C	W	1-0	Brady	20,907
31		24	(h)	Liverpool	W	1-0	Radford	36,127
32		28	(a)	Middlesbrough	W	1-0	Radford	20,000
33	Mar	13	(a)	Coventry C	D	1-1	Powling	13,938
34		16	(h)	Newcastle U	D	0-0		18,424
35		20	(h)	West Ham U	W	6-1	Kidd 3, Ball 2, (1 pen), Armstrong	34,011
36		27	(a)	Leeds U	L	0-3		26,657
37	Apr	3	(h)	Tottenham H	L	0-2		42,134
38		10	(a)	Everton	D	0-0		20,774
39		13	(h)	Wolves	W	2-1	Brady, Mancini	19,518
40		17	(h)	Ipswich T	L	1-2	Stapleton	26,973
41		19	(a)	Queen's Park R	L	1-2	Kidd	30,362
42		24	(a)	Manchester C	L	1-3	Armstrong	31,003

FINAL LEAGUE POSITION: 17th in Division One

Appearances
Sub Appearances
Goals

FA Cup

3	Jan	3	(a)	Wolves	L	0-3		22,215

Appearances
Sub Appearances
Goals

League Cup

2	Sep	9	(a)	Everton	D	2-2	Cropley, Stapleton	17,174
R		23	(h)	Everton	L	0-1		21,813

Appearances
Sub Appearances
Goals

Rimmer JJ	Rice PJ	Nelson S	Kelly EP	Mancini TJ	O'Leary DA	Armstrong G	Cropley AJ	Hornsby BG	Kidd B	Brady WL	Storey PE	Ball AJ	Radford J	Stapleton FA	Rostron JW	Simpson PF	Powling RF	Matthews JM	Barnett GC	Ross TW	
1	2	3	4	5	6	7	8	9	10	11											1
1	2	3	4	5	6	7	8	9	10	11											2
1	2	3	4	5	6	7	8	9	10	11											3
1	2		4	5	6	7	8		10	11	3	9									4
1	2	3	4	5	6		8		10	11		7	9								5
1	2	3	4	5	6		8		10	11		7		9							6
1	2	3	4	5	6		8		10	11		7		9							7
1	2	3	4	5	6		8		10	11		7		9							8
1	2	3	4	5	6		8		10	12		7		9	11*						9
1	2	3	4*		6		8		10	11		7		9	12	5					10
1	2	3			6		8*		10	11		7		9	12	5	4				11
1	2	3	4		5		8		10	11		7		9		6					12
1	2	3	4*		5		8		10	11		7		9		6	12				13
1	2	3	4		5				10	11		7		9		6	8				14
1	2		4		5		8	10		11	3	7		9			6				15
1	2		4		5		8*		10	11	3	7		9			6	12			16
1	2	4			5	8			10	11	3	7		9			6				17
1	2	3			5	8			10	11	4	7		9			6				18
1	2	4			5	8			10	11	3	7		9			6				19
1	2	3			5	7			10	11	4	8		9			6				20
	2	3*			5	7			10	11	4	8		9		12	6		1		21
1	2		4	5		7			10	11*		8	9	12		3	6				22
1	2		3		5	7			10	11	4	8	9				6				23
1	2	3			5	7			10	11	4	8		9			6				24
1	2	3		6	5	7			10	11		8		9			4				25
1	2	3		6	5	7			10	11		8		9						4	26
1	2	3*		5		7			10	11		8		9	12		6			4	27
1	2			5		7			10	11	3	8		9		6				4	28
1	2	3		5		7			10	11		8	9				6			4	29
1	2	3		5		7			10	11*		8	9			12	6			4	30
1	2	3		5		7			10	11		8	9				6			4	31
1	2	3		5		7			10	11		8	9				6			4	32
1	2	3		5		7			10	11		8	9				6			4	33
1	2	3		5		7			10	11		8	9				6			4	34
1	2*	3		5		7			10	11		8	9	12			6			4	35
1	2	3		5		7			10	11		8	9				6			4	36
1	2	3		5		7			10	11		8	9				6			4	37
1	2	3		5		7	10			11		8	9				6			4	38
1	2	3		5		7	10			11		8	9				6			4	39
1	2	3			5		10			11		8		9	7		6			4	40
1	2	3			5	12	10		7	11		8	9*				6			4	41
1	2	3		5		7	10			11		8		9			6			4	42
41	42	36	17	26	27	28	20	4	37	41	11	39	15	23	2	7	28		1	17	
						1				1				2	3	2	1	1			
	1		2	1		4	4		11	5		9	3	4			1			1	

1 own-goal

Rimmer JJ	Rice PJ	Nelson S	Kelly EP	Mancini TJ	O'Leary DA	Armstrong G	Cropley AJ	Hornsby BG	Kidd B	Brady WL	Storey PE	Ball AJ	Radford J	Stapleton FA	Rostron JW	Simpson PF	Powling RF	Matthews JM	Barnett GC	Ross TW	
1	2	3			5	7			10	11	4	8		9			6				3
1	1	1			1	1			1	1	1	1		1			1				

Rimmer JJ	Rice PJ	Nelson S	Kelly EP	Mancini TJ	O'Leary DA	Armstrong G	Cropley AJ	Hornsby BG	Kidd B	Brady WL	Storey PE	Ball AJ	Radford J	Stapleton FA	Rostron JW	Simpson PF	Powling RF	Matthews JM	Barnett GC	Ross TW	
1	2	3	4	5*	6		8		10	11		7	9	12							2
1	2	3	4	5	6		8		10			7		9	11						R
2	2	2	2	2	2		2		2	1		2	1	1	1						
														1							
							1							1							

1976-77

Manager: T.Neill

1	Aug	21	(h)	Bristol C	L	0-1	41,082
2		25	(a)	Norwich C	W	3-1 Nelson, Macdonald, Stapleton	26,769
3		28	(a)	Sunderland	D	2-2 Ross, Macdonald	41,211
4	Sep	4	(h)	Manchester C	D	0-0	35,132
5		11	(a)	West Ham U	W	2-0 Ross, Stapleton	32,415
6		18	(h)	Everton	W	3-1 Brady, Stapleton, Macdonald	34,076
7		25	(a)	Ipswich T	L	1-3 Hunter (og)	25,505
8	Oct	2	(h)	Queen's Park R	W	3-2 Rice, Brady, Stapleton	39,442
9		16	(h)	Stoke C	W	2-0 Rice, Macdonald	28,745
10		20	(a)	Aston Villa	L	1-5 Ball	33,860
11		23	(a)	Leicester C	L	1-4 Stapleton	19,351
12		30	(a)	Leeds U	L	1-2 Matthews	33,556
13	Nov	6	(h)	Birmingham C	W	4-0 Stapleton, Nelson, Macdonald (pen), Ross	23,063
14		20	(h)	Liverpool	D	1-1 Armstrong	45,016
15		27	(a)	Coventry C	W	2-1 Macdonald, Stapleton	18,313
16	Dec	4	(h)	Newcastle U	W	5-3 Macdonald 3, Ross, Stapleton	34,053
17		15	(a)	Derby C	D	0-0	24,016
18		18	(h)	Manchester U	W	3-1 Macdonald 2, Brady	39,572
19		27	(a)	Tottenham H	D	2-2 Macdonald 2	47,751
20	Jan	3	(h)	Leeds U	D	1-1 Macdonald	44,090
21		15	(h)	Norwich C	W	1-0 Rice	30,537
22		18	(a)	Birmingham C	D	3-3 Macdonald 3	23,247
23		27	(a)	Bristol C	L	0-2	26,282
24	Feb	5	(h)	Sunderland	D	0-0	30,925
25		12	(a)	Manchester C	L	0-1	45,368
26		15	(a)	Middlesbrough	L	0-3	26,083
27		19	(h)	West Ham U	L	2-3 Brady, Stapleton	38,221
28	Mar	1	(a)	Everton	L	1-2 Macdonald	29,802
29		5	(h)	Ipswich T	L	1-4 Macdonald (pen)	34,688
30		8	(h)	West Brom A	L	1-2 Macdonald	19,517
31		12	(a)	Queen's Park R	L	1-2 Young	26,191
32		23	(a)	Stoke C	D	1-1 Price	13,951
33	Apr	2	(h)	Leicester C	W	3-0 Rix, O'Leary 2	23,013
34		9	(a)	West Brom A	W	2-0 Stapleton, Macdonald	24,275
35		11	(h)	Tottenham	W	1-0 Macdonald	47,432
36		16	(a)	Liverpool	L	0-2	48,174
37		23	(h)	Coventry C	W	2-0 Stapleton, Macdonald	22,790
38		25	(h)	Aston Villa	W	3-0 Macdonald, Armstrong, Nelson	24,011
39		30	(a)	Newcastle U	W	2-0 Macdonald, Matthews	44,763
40	May	3	(h)	Derby C	D	0-0	26,659
41		7	(h)	Middlesbrough	D	1-1 Stapleton	23,911
42		14	(a)	Manchester U	L	2-3 Brady, Stapleton	53,232

FINAL LEAGUE POSITION: 8th in Division One

Appearances
Sub Appearances
Goals

FA Cup

3	Jan	8	(a)	Notts C	W	1-0 Ross	17,328
4		29	(h)	Coventry C	W	3-1 Macdonald 2, Stapleton	41,078
5	Feb	26	(a)	Middlesbrough	L	1-4 Macdonald	35,208

Appearances
Sub Appearances
Goals

League Cup

2	Aug	31	(h)	Carlisle U	W	3-2 Ross 2, Macdonald	21,550
3	Sep	21	(a)	Blackpool	D	1-1 Armstrong	18,983
R		28	(h)	Blackpool	D	0-0	27,195
2R	Oct	5	(h)	Blackpool	W	2-0 Stapleton, O'Leary	26,791
4		26	(h)	Chelsea	W	2-1 Ross, Stapleton	52,285
5	Dec	1	(a)	Queen's Park R	L	1-2 Stapleton	27,621

Appearances
Sub Appearances
Goals

286

Rimmer JJ	Rice PJ	Nelson S	Ross TW	O'Leary DA	Simpson PF	Ball AJ	Armstrong G	Macdonald MI	Radford J	Cropley AJ	Storey PE	Stapleton FA	Brady WL	Howard P	Powling RF	Matthews JM	Rostron JW	Hudson AA	Young WD	Price DJ	Rix G	
1	2	3	4	5	6	7	8	9	10	11*	12											1
1	2	3	4	5	6	7	8	9				10	11									2
1	2	3	4	5	6	7	8	9				10	11									3
1	2	3	4	5	6	7	11	9		12		10*	8									4
1	2	3	4	5*		7	11			9	12	10	8	6								5
1	2	3	4			7	11	9				10	8	5	6							6
1	2	3	4	5		7	11	9				10	8	6								7
1	2	3*	4	5		7	11	9			12	10	8	6								8
1	2		4	5		7	11	9	12		3	10*	8	6								9
1	2		4	5		7	11	9			3	10	8	6								10
1	2		4			7	11	9			3	10	8	6		5						11
1	2	3	4		5		11	9				10	8	6		7						12
1	2	3	4	5*	6		11	9			12	10	8			7						13
1	2	3	4	5	6	7	11	9				10	8									14
1	2	3	4	5	6	7	11	9				10	8									15
1	2*	3	4	5		7	11	9				10	8	6		12						16
1	2	3	4	5	6		11	9			7	10	8									17
1	2		4	5	6		11	9			7	10*	8		3		12					18
1	2		4	5	6			9			7	10	8		3		11					19
1	2		4	5	6		11	9				10	8		3			7				20
1	2	3	4	5	6		11	9				10	8					7				21
1	2	3	4	5	6		11	9				10	8					7				22
1	2	3		5	6			9			4	10	8				11	7				23
1	2	3	4	5	6			9				10	8				11	7				24
1	2	3	4	5*	6			9				10	8	11		12		7				25
1	2	3	4		6			9				10		5*	12	7	11	8				26
1	2	3	4		6		11	9				10	8		5			7				27
1	2	3	4				11	9				10	7	5	6			8				28
1	2	12	4				11	9				10	7	5	6	8*			3			29
1	2	3					11	9				10	7	6	8				5	4		30
1	2	3					11	9				10	7	6	4			8*	5	12		31
1	2	3		6			11	9					7		4			8	5	10		32
1	2	3		5			11	9				10			4*	12			6	8	7	33
1	2			5			11	9				10				3		7	6	4	8	34
1	2			5			11	9				10	12			3		8	6	4	7*	35
1	2			5			11	9				10	8			3		7	6	4		36
1	2		4*	5			11	9				10	7			3		8	6		12	37
1	2	3		5			11	9				10	7*			4	12	8	6			38
1	2	3		5*			11	9				10	7	12		4		8	6			39
1	2	3		5			11	9				10	7			4		8	6*		12	40
1	2	3		5			11	9				10	7			4*			6	12	8	41
1	2	3		5			11	9				10	7			4		8	6*		12	42
42	42	31	29	33	19	14	37	41	1	2	7	40	37	15	11	14	4	19	14	6	4	
		1							1	1	4		1	1	1	3	2			2	3	
	3	3	4	2		1	2	25				13	5			2			1	1	1	

1 own-goal

1	2	3	4	5	6		11	9				10	8					7				3
1	2	3	4	5	6			9*			12	10	8				11	7				4
1	2	3	4	5*	6		11	9				10	7			12		8				5
3	3	3	3	3	3		2	3				3	3				1	3				
											1					1						
			1					3				1										

1	2	3	4	5	6	7	11	9				10	8									2
1	2	3	4			7	11	9				10	8	6	5							3
1	2	3*	4	5		7	11	9			12	10	8	6								R
1	2			5		7	11	9			3	10	8	6		4						2R
1	2	3	4		5	7	11	9				10	8	6								4
1	2	3	4	5	6	7	11	9				10	8									5
6	6	5	5	4	3	6	6	6			1	6	6	4	1	1						
											1											
			3	1			1	1				3										

1977-78

Manager: T.Neill

1	Aug	20	(a)	Ipswich T	L	0-1		30,384
2		23	(h)	Everton	W	1-0	Powling	32,924
3		27	(a)	Wolves	D	1-1	Powling	22,909
4	Sep	3	(h)	Nottingham F	W	3-0	Stapleton 2, Brady (pen)	40,810
5		10	(a)	Aston Villa	L	0-1		36,929
6		17	(h)	Leicester C	W	2-1	Stapleton, Macdonald	27,371
7		24	(a)	Norwich C	L	0-1		19,312
8	Oct	1	(h)	West Ham U	W	3-0	Stapleton, Rice, Brady (pen)	41,245
9		4	(h)	Liverpool	D	0-0		47,110
10		8	(a)	Manchester C	L	1-2	Macdonald	43,177
11		15	(h)	Queen's Park R	W	1-0	Macdonald	36,290
12		22	(a)	Bristol C	W	2-0	Rix, Macdonald	25,497
13		29	(h)	Birmingham C	D	1-1	Rice	31,355
14	Nov	5	(a)	Manchester U	W	2-1	Macdonald, Stapleton	53,055
15		12	(h)	Coventry C	D	1-1	Coop (og)	31,653
16		19	(a)	Newcastle U	W	2-1	Stapleton, Sunderland	22,880
17		26	(h)	Derby C	L	1-3	Nelson	31,989
18	Dec	3	(a)	Middlesbrough	W	1-0	Cooper (og)	17,422
19		10	(h)	Leeds U	D	1-1	Young	40,162
20		17	(a)	Coventry C	W	2-1	Stapleton 2	20,993
21		26	(h)	Chelsea	W	3-0	Price, Rix, O'Leary	46,074
22		27	(a)	West Brom A	W	3-1	Sunderland, Macdonald, Brady (pen)	27,723
23		31	(a)	Everton	L	0-2		47,039
24	Jan	2	(h)	Ipswich T	W	1-0	Price	43,705
25		14	(h)	Wolves	W	3-1	Brady, Macdonald, Stapleton	34,784
26		21	(a)	Nottingham F	L	0-2		35,743
27	Feb	4	(h)	Aston Villa	L	0-1		30,127
28		11	(a)	Leicester C	D	1-1	Brady (pen)	15,780
29		25	(a)	West Ham U	D	2-2	Macdonald 2	31,675
30		28	(h)	Norwich C	D	0-0		23,506
31	Mar	4	(h)	Manchester C	W	3-0	Sunderland, Young, Price	34,003
32		18	(h)	Bristol C	W	4-1	Stapleton 2, Sunderland, Price	28,463
33		21	(a)	Birmingham C	D	1-1	Brady (pen)	22,087
34		25	(h)	West Brom A	W	4-0	Macdonald 3, Young	36,763
35		27	(a)	Chelsea	D	0-0		40,764
36	Apr	1	(h)	Manchester U	W	3-1	Macdonald 2, Brady	40,739
37		11	(a)	Queen's Park R	L	1-2	Brady (pen)	25,683
38		15	(h)	Newcastle U	W	2-1	Brady, Price	33,353
39		22	(a)	Leeds U	W	3-1	Stapleton, Macdonald, Hart (og)	33,263
40		25	(a)	Liverpool	L	0-1		38,318
41		29	(h)	Middlesbrough	W	1-0	Stapleton	32,138
42	May	9	(a)	Derby C	L	0-3		21,189

FINAL LEAGUE POSITION: 5th in Division One

Appearances
Sub Appearances
Goals

FA Cup

3	Jan	7	(a)	Sheffield U	W	5-0	Macdonald 2, Stapleton 2, O'Leary	32,156
4		28	(h)	Wolves	W	2-1	Sunderland, Macdonald	49,373
5	Feb	18	(h)	Walsall	W	4-1	Stapleton 2, Macdonald, Sunderland	43,789
6	Mar	11	(a)	Wrexham	W	3-2	Macdonald, Sunderland, Young	25,547
SF	Apr	8	(n*)	Orient	W	3-0	Macdonald 2, Rix	49,698
F	May	6	(n†)	Ipswich T	L	0-1		100,000

*Played at Stamford Bridge, London. †Played at Wembley Stadium.

Appearances
Sub Appearances
Goals

League Cup

2	Aug	30	(h)	Manchester U	W	3-2	Macdonald 2, Brady	36,171
3	Oct	25	(h)	Southampton	W	2-0	Brady (pen), Stapleton	40,749
4	Nov	29	(h)	Hull C	W	5-1	Matthews 2, Brady, Macdonald, Stapleton	25,922
5	Jan	18	(a)	Manchester C	D	0-0		42,435
R		24	(h)	Manchester C	W	1-0	Brady	57,960
SF	Feb	7	(a)	Liverpool	L	1-2	Macdonald	44,764
		14	(h)	Liverpool	D	0-0		49,561

Appearances
Sub Appearances
Goals

Jennings PA	Rice PJ	Nelson S	Ross TW	Young WD	OLeary DA	Powling RF	Brady WL	Macdonald MI	Stapleton FA	Rix G	Price DJ	Hudson AA	Simpson PF	Matthews JM	Walford SJ	Heeley MD	Sunderland A	Devine JA	Harvey J	No.
1	2	3	4	5	6	7	8*	9	10	11	12									1
1	2	3	8	5	6	4	7	9	10	11										2
1	2	3	7	5	6	4	8	9		11	10									3
1	2	3	8	6	5	4	7	9	10	11										4
1	2	3	8	6	5		7	9	10	11		4								5
1	2	3	8	6	5		7	9	10	11		4								6
1	2	3	8	5				9	10	11		4	6	7*	12					7
1	2	3	8				7	9	10	11		4	6							8
1	2	3	8*	5			7	9	10	11		4	6	12						9
1	2	3					7	9	10	11		4	6	8						10
1	2	3		6	5		7	9	10	11		4					8			11
1	2	3		5			7	9	10	11		4	8	6						12
1	2	3	8				7	9	10	11		4*	6		12					13
1	2	3		6	5		7	9	10	11		4					8			14
1	2	3		6	5		7	9	10	11		4					8			15
1	2	3		6	5		7		10	11		4	9				8			16
1	2	3		6	5		7	9	10	11		4					8			17
1	2	3		6	5		7	9	10	11		4					8			18
1	2	3		6	5		7	9	10	11		4					8			19
1	2	3		6	5		7	9	10	11		4					8			20
1	2	3		6	5		7	9	10*	11		4	12				8			21
1	2	3		6	5		7	9	10	11		4					8			22
1	2	3		6	5		7	9*	10	11		4	12				8			23
1	2	3		6	5		7	9		11		4	12	10*			8			24
1	2	3		6	5		7	9	10	11		4					8			25
1	2	3		6	5		7	9	10	11		4					8			26
1	2	3		6	5		7	9		11		4	10				8			27
1	2	3		6	5		7	9	10	11		4					8			28
1	2	3		6	5		7	9	10	11*		4		12			8			29
1	2	3		6	5		7	9*	10			4	11		12		8			30
1	2	3		6	5		7		10			4*	9		12	11	8			31
1	2	3		6	5		7	9	10	12		4	11				8*			32
1	2	3		6	5		7	9	10			4	11				8			33
1	2	3		6	5		7	9	10	12		4	11				8*			34
1	2	3		6	5		7	9	10	8		4	11							35
1	2	3		6	5		7	9	10	8		4	11							36
1	2	3		6*	5		7	9	10	11		4	8	12						37
1	2	3			5		7	9	10	8		4	11				6			38
1		3		6	5		7	9	10	8		4			11			2		39
1		3		6	5		7*	9	10	8		4	11	12				2		40
1		3		6	5			9	10	11		4	8			7		2		41
1				5				10	8	2	11		3	6	7	9			4	42
42	38	41	10	35	41	4	39	39	39	37	38	17	6	4	2	3	23	3	1	
												2	1		3	3	3	2		
	2	1		3	1	2	9	15	13	2	5						4			

3 own-goals

1	2	3		6	5		7	9	10	11		4					8			3
1	2	3		6	5		7	9		11		4	10				8			4
1	2	3		6	5		7	9	10	11		4					8			5
1	2	3		6	5		7	9	10			4	11				8			6
1	2	3		6	5		7	9	10	8		4	11							SF
1	2	3		6	5		7*	9	10	12		4	11				8			F
6	6	6		6	6		6	6	5	4		6	4				5			
									1											
		1	1				7	4	1								3			

1	2	3	8	6	5	4	7	9	10	11										2
1	2	3		5			7	9	10	11		4	8	6						3
1	2	3		6	5*		7	9	10	11		4	12	8						4
1	2	3		6	5		7	9	10	11		4					8			5
1	2	3		6	5		7	9	10	11		4	12	8*						R
1	2	3		6	5		7	9	10	11		4	8							SF
7	7	7	1	7	6	1	7	7	7	7		6	3	1			3			
												1	1							
								4	4	2				2						

1978-79

Manager: T.Neill

1	Aug	19	(h)	Leeds U	D 2-2	Brady 2 (1 pen)	42,057
2		22	(a)	Manchester C	D 1-1	Macdonald	39,506
3		26	(a)	Everton	L 0-1		41,179
4	Sep	2	(h)	Queen's Park R	W 5-1	Rix 2, Brady, Stapleton 2	33,883
5		9	(a)	Nottingham F	L 1-2	Brady	28,124
6		16	(h)	Bolton W	W 1-0	Stapleton	31,120
7		23	(h)	Manchester U	D 1-1	Price	45,393
8		30	(a)	Middlesbrough	W 3-2	O'Leary, Price, Walford	14,404
9	Oct	7	(h)	Aston Villa	D 1-1	Sunderland	34,537
10		14	(a)	Wolves	L 0-1		19,664
11		21	(h)	Southampton	W 1-0	Brady	33,074
12		28	(a)	Bristol C	W 3-1	Brady 2 (1 pen), Stapleton	27,016
13	Nov	4	(h)	Ipswich T	W 4-1	Stapleton 3, Nelson	35,083
14		11	(a)	Leeds U	W 1-0	Gatting	33,961
15		18	(h)	Everton	D 2-2	Brady 2 (1 pen)	39,801
16		25	(a)	Coventry C	D 1-1	Stapleton	26,786
17	Dec	2	(h)	Liverpool	W 1-0	Price	51,902
18		9	(a)	Norwich C	D 0-0		20,165
19		16	(h)	Derby C	W 2-0	Price, Stapleton	26,943
20		23	(a)	Tottenham H	W 5-0	Sunderland 3, Stapleton, Brady	42,273
21		26	(h)	West Brom A	L 1-2	Brady (pen)	40,055
22		30	(h)	Birmingham C	W 3-1	Stapleton, Rice, Sunderland	27,877
23	Jan	13	(h)	Nottingham F	W 2-1	Price, Stapleton	52,158
24	Feb	3	(a)	Manchester U	W 2-0	Sunderland 2	45,460
25		10	(h)	Middlesbrough	D 0-0		28,371
26		13	(a)	Queen's Park R	W 2-1	Price, Brady	21,125
27		24	(h)	Wolves	L 0-1		32,215
28	Mar	3	(a)	Southampton	L 0-2		25,052
29		10	(h)	Bristol C	W 2-0	Rix, Stapleton	24,288
30		17	(a)	Ipswich T	L 0-2		26,407
31		24	(h)	Manchester C	D 1-1	Sunderland	35,014
32		26	(a)	Bolton W	L 2-4	Price, Heeley	20,704
33	Apr	3	(h)	Coventry C	D 1-1	Nelson	30,091
34		7	(a)	Liverpool	L 0-3		47,297
35		10	(h)	Tottenham H	W 1-0	Stapleton	53,896
36		14	(a)	West Brom A	D 1-1	Brady	28,353
37		16	(h)	Chelsea	W 5-2	Stapleton 2, O'Leary, Sunderland, Price	37,232
38		21	(a)	Derby C	L 0-2		18,674
39		25	(a)	Aston Villa	L 1-5	Stapleton	26,168
40		28	(h)	Norwich C	D 1-1	Walford	28,885
41	May	5	(a)	Birmingham C	D 0-0		14,015
42		14	(a)	Chelsea	D 1-1	Macdonald	30,705

FINAL LEAGUE POSITION: 7th in Division One

Appearances
Sub Appearances
Goals

FA Cup

3	Jan	6	(a)	Sheffield W	D 1-1	Sunderland	33,635
R		9	(h)	Sheffield W	D 1-1§	Brady	37,987
2R		15	(n*)	Sheffield W	D 2-2§	Brady, Sunderland	25,011
3R		17	(n*)	Sheffield W	D 3-3§	Stapleton 2, Young	17,088
4R		22	(n*)	Sheffield W	W 2-0	Gatting, Stapleton	30,275
4	Jan	27	(h)	Notts C	W 2-0	Young, Talbot	39,195
5	Feb	26	(a)	Nottingham F	W 1-0	Stapleton	35,906
6	Mar	19	(a)	Southampton	D 1-1	Price	24,536
R		21	(h)	Southampton	W 2-0	Sunderland 2	44,820
SF		31	(n†)	Wolves	W 2-0	Stapleton, Sunderland	46,244
F	May	12	(n‡)	Manchester U	W 3-2	Talbot, Stapleton, Sunderland	100,000

*Played at Filbert Street, Leicester. §After extra-time. †Played at Villa Park, Birmingham. ‡Played at Wembley Stadium.

Appearances
Sub Appearances
Goals

League Cup

2	Aug	29	(a)	Rotherham U	L 1-3	Stapleton	10,481

Appearances
Sub Appearances
Goals

290

Player appearance grid (columns left to right): Jennings PA, Devine JA, Nelson S, Price DJ, O'Leary DA, Young WD, Brady WL, Sunderland A, Macdonald MI, Stapleton FA, Harvey J, Kosmina AJ, Rice PJ, Walford SJ, Barron PG, Rix G, Heeley MD, Stead K, Gatting SP, Talbot BE, McDermott BJ, Brignall SJC, Vaessen PL.

Jen PA	Dev JA	Nel S	Pri DJ	OL DA	You WD	Bra WL	Sun A	Mac MI	Sta FA	Har J	Kos AJ	Ric PJ	Wal SJ	Bar PG	Rix G	Hee MD	Ste K	Gat SP	Tal BE	McD BJ	Bri SJC	Vae PL	Match
1	2	3	4*	5	6	7	8	9	10	11	12												1
	7	3	4	5	6		8	9	10			2	11	1									2
	11*	3	4	5	6	7	8	9	10			2	12	1									3
1		3	4	5	6	7	8		10			2	9		11								4
1		3	4	5*	6	7	8		10	12		2	9		11								5
1		3	4		6	7	8		9			2	5		11	10							6
1		3	4	5	6	7	8		9			2	10*		11	12							7
1	10*	3	4	5	6	7	8		9			2	12		11								8
1		3	4	5	6	7	8		9			2	10		11								9
1		3	4	5	6	7	8*		9			2	10		11	12							10
1		3			6	7			9			2	10		11	8	4	5					11
1		3	4	5*	6	7			9			2	12		11	10		8					12
1		3	4	5	6	7	8		9			2			11			10					13
1		3	4	5	6	7	8		9			2			11			10					14
1		3	4	5	6	7	8		9			2			11			10					15
1		3	4*	5	6	7	8		9			2	10		11	12							16
1		3	4	5	6	7	8		9			2			11			10					17
1		3*	4	5	6	7	8		9			2	12		11			10					18
1			4	5	6	7	8		9			2	3		11			10					19
1			4	5	6	7	8		9			2	3		11			10					20
1			4	5	6	7	8		9			2	3		11			10					21
1			4	5	6	7	8		9			2	3		11			10					22
1		3	10	5	6	7	8		9			2			11				4				23
1		3	10	5	6	7	8		9			2			11				4				24
1		3	10	5	6	7	8		9			2			11				4				25
1		3	10	5	6*	7	8		9			2	12		11				4				26
1			10	5		7	8		9			2	6		11		3	4					27
1		3	10	5		7			9			2	6		11	12	8*	4					28
1		3	10	5		7			9			2	6		11	8*		4	12				29
1		3	10*	5		7	8		9			2	6		11			12	4				30
1		3	10	5	6*		8		9			2			11	7		4	12				31
1		3	10	5			8		9			2	6		11	12		7	4*				32
1		3		5	6		8		9			2	12		11	10*		7	4				33
1			10	5	6		8		9*			2	3		11			7	4	12			34
1			10	5	6	7	8		9			2	3		11				4				35
1		3	10	5		7	8		9			2	6		11*			12	4				36
1		3	10	5		7	8		9			2	6		11				4				37
1			10		6	7	8		9			2	3		11			5	4				38
1	6		10			7	8		9			2	3		11			5	4				39
1	2	3	10			7	8		9				6		11			5	4				40
		3	10	5	6		8		9			2	12	1*	11				4				41
1	10	3		5	6	7		9				2			11				4		8		42
39	7	33	39	37	33	37	37	4	41	1		39	26	3	39	6	1	19	20		1		
									1	1			7			4	1	2		2	1		
		2	8	2			13	9	2	17			1	2		3	1		1				

*In match 41, when Barron was injured, Price went in goal and Walford substituted outfield.

Jen PA	Dev JA	Nel S	Pri DJ	OL DA	You WD	Bra WL	Sun A	Mac MI	Sta FA	Har J	Kos AJ	Ric PJ	Wal SJ	Bar PG	Rix G	Hee MD	Ste K	Gat SP	Tal BE	McD BJ	Bri SJC	Vae PL	Rd
1			4	5	6	7	8		9			2	3		11			10					3
1		3	4	5	6	7	8		9			2			11			10					R
1		3	4	5	6	7	8		9			2			11			10					2R
1		3	4	5	6	7	8		9			2			11			10					3R
1		3*	4	5	6	7	8		9			2	12		11			10					4R
1		3	10	5	6	7	8		9			2			11				4				4
1		3	10	5		7	8		9			2	6		11				4				5
1		3	10*	5	6	7	8		9			2	12		11				4				6
1		3	10	5	6	7*	8		9			2	12		11			7	4				R
1		3	10	5	6		8		9			2			11			7	4				SF
1		3	10*	5	6	7	8		9			2	12		11				4				F
11		10	11	11	10	10	11		11			11	2		11			6	6				
													4										
	1		2	2	6		6						1	2									

Jen PA	Dev JA	Nel S	Pri DJ	OL DA	You WD	Bra WL	Sun A	Mac MI	Sta FA	Har J	Kos AJ	Ric PJ	Wal SJ	Bar PG	Rix G	Hee MD	Ste K	Gat SP	Tal BE	McD BJ	Bri SJC	Vae PL	Rd
1		3	4	5	6	7	8	9	10			2			11								2
1		1	1	1	1	1	1	1	1			1			1								
					1																			

1979-80

Manager: T.Neill

#	Month	Date		Opponent	Result		Scorers	Attendance
1	Aug	18	(a)	Brighton & HA	W	4-0	Sunderland 2, Stapleton, Brady (pen)	28,604
2		21	(h)	Ipswich T	L	0-2		33,255
3		25	(h)	Manchester U	D	0-0		44,380
4	Sep	1	(a)	Leeds U	D	1-1	Nelson	23,245
5		8	(a)	Derby C	L	2-3	Sunderland, Stapleton	16,429
6		15	(h)	Middlesbrough	W	2-0	Sunderland, Stapleton	30,341
7		22	(a)	Aston Villa	D	0-0		27,277
8		29	(h)	Wolves	L	2-3	Stapleton, Hollins	41,844
9	Oct	6	(h)	Manchester C	D	0-0		34,688
10		9	(a)	Ipswich T	W	2-1	Sunderland, Rix	21,527
11		13	(a)	Bolton W	D	0-0		17,032
12		20	(h)	Stoke C	D	0-0		31,591
13		27	(a)	Bristol C	W	1-0	Sunderland	23,029
14	Nov	3	(h)	Brighton & HA	W	3-0	Rix, Brady (pen), Sunderland	34,400
15		10	(a)	Crystal P	L	0-1		42,887
16		17	(h)	Everton	W	2-0	Stapleton 2	33,450
17		24	(h)	Liverpool	D	0-0		55,546
18	Dec	1	(a)	Nottingham F	D	1-1	Stapleton	27,925
19		8	(h)	Coventry C	W	3-1	Stapleton, Sunderland, O'Leary	27,563
20		15	(a)	West Brom A	D	2-2	Nelson, Stapleton	18,280
21		21	(h)	Norwich C	D	1-1	Stapleton	18,869
22		26	(h)	Tottenham H	W	1-0	Sunderland	44,560
23		29	(a)	Manchester U	L	0-3		54,295
24	Jan	1	(a)	Southampton	W	1-0	Young	22,473
25		12	(h)	Leeds U	L	0-1		35,945
26		19	(h)	Derby C	W	2-0	Brady (pen), Young	22,091
27	Feb	9	(h)	Aston Villa	W	3-1	Sunderland 2, Rix	33,816
28		23	(h)	Bolton W	W	2-0	Young, Stapleton	24,383
29	Mar	1	(a)	Stoke C	W	3-2	Sunderland, Price, Brady	19,752
30		11	(h)	Bristol C	D	0-0		21,559
31		15	(a)	Manchester C	W	3-0	Brady 2 (1 pen), Stapleton	33,792
32		22	(h)	Crystal P	D	1-1	Brady	37,606
33		28	(a)	Everton	W	1-0	Gatting	28,184
34	Apr	2	(a)	Norwich C	L	1-2	Rix	16,923
35		5	(h)	Southampton	D	1-1	Sunderland	34,593
36		7	(a)	Tottenham H	W	2-1	Vaessen, Sunderland	41,369
37		19	(a)	Liverpool	D	1-1	Talbot	46,878
38		26	(h)	West Brom A	D	1-1	Stapleton	30,027
39	May	3	(a)	Coventry C	W	1-0	Vaessen	16,817
40		5	(h)	Nottingham F	D	0-0		34,632
41		16	(a)	Wolves	W	2-1	Walford, Stapleton	23,619
42		19	(a)	Middlesbrough	L	0-5		15,603

FINAL LEAGUE POSITION: 4th in Division One

Appearances

Sub Appearance

Goals

Jennings PA	Rice PJ	Nelson S	Talbot BE	O'Leary DA	Young WD	Brady WL	Sunderland A	Stapleton FA	Price DJ	Rix G	Hollins JW	Gatting SP	McDermott BJ	Barron PG	Walford SJ	Devine JA	Vaessen PL	Davis PV	#
1	2	3	4	5	6	7*	8	9	10	11	12								1
1	2	3	4	5	6	7	8	9	10*	11	12								2
1	2	3	4	5	6		8	9		11	10	7*		12					3
1	2	3	4	5	6		8	9		11	10	7							4
1	2	3	4	5	6	7	8	9		11	10								5
1	2	3	4	5	6	7	8	9		11	10								6
	2	3	4	5	6	7	8	8		11	10		1						7
1	2	3	4*		6	7	8	9	12	11	10			5					8
1	2	3	4	5	6	7	8	9		11	10								9
1		3	4	5	6	7	8	9		11	10	2							10
1	2	3	4	5	6	7	8	9		11	10								11
1	2	3	4	5	6	7	8	9		11	10								12
1	2	3	4	5	6	7	8	9		11	10								13
1		3	4	5	6	7	8*	9		11	10	12				2			14
1		3	4	5	6	7		9	10	11		8			12	2*			15
1		3	4	5	6	7*		9	10	11		12				2	8		16
1		3	4	5	6		8	9	10	11		7				2			17
1		3	4	5			8	9	10	11		7			6	2			18
1		3*	4	5		7	8	9		11	10	12			6	2			19
1		3	4	5		7	8	9		11	10				6	2			20
1		3*	4	5		7	8	9		11	10	12			6	2			21
1		3	4	5	6	7	8	9		11	10					2			22
1		3	4	5*	6	7	8	9		11	10				12	2			23
1	2		4		6		8	9		11	10	7			5	3			24
1	2	3	4		6	7	8	9		11	10				5				25
1	2	3	4		6	7	8	9	10	11					5				26
1	2	3	4	5	6	7	8	9	10	11									27
1	2*	3	4	5	6	7	8	9	10	11					12				28
1		3	4	5	6	7	8	9	10	11						2			29
1		3	4	5	6	7		9	10	11						2	8		30
1		3	4	5	6	7		9*	10	11		12				2	8		31
1		3	4	5	6	7	8	9	10	11						2			32
	2	3	4	5	6		8		10	11		7		1		9			33
1		3*	4	5	6	7	8	9	10	11		2			12				34
1			4	5	6	7	8	9	10*	11				3	2	12			35
	2		4	5	6	7*	12			10				1	3	8	9	11	36
1	2		4	5	6		8	9*	10	11		7			3	12			37
	2		4		6*	7	8	9		10	12			1	5	3	11		38
	2	3	4		6		8		10*	11		7		1	5	9	12		39
1		3	4	5	6	7		9*	10	11	12					2	8		40
1	2	3	4		6	7	8	9	10*	11					5	12			41
1	2	3	4		6	7	8	9	10	11					5*	12			42
37	26	35	42	34	38	34	36	39	21	38	23	9		5	16	20	8	1	
						1		1		3	5	1		3		6	1		
		2	1	1	3	7	14	14	1	4	1	1		1		2			

293

1979-80 (continued)

FA Cup

3	Jan	5	(a)	Cardiff C	D	0-0	21,972
R		8	(h)	Cardiff C	W	2-1 Sunderland 2	36,155
4		26	(h)	Brighton & HA	W	2-0 Nelson, Talbot	43,202
5	Feb	16	(a)	Bolton W	D	1-1 Stapleton	23,530
R		19	(h)	Bolton W	W	3-0 Sunderland 2, Stapleton	40,564
6	Mar	8	(a)	Watford	W	2-1 Stapleton 2	27,975
SF	Apr	12	(n*)	Liverpool	D	0-0	50,174
R		16	(n†)	Liverpool	D	1-1§ Sunderland	40,679
2R		28	(n†)	Liverpool	D	1-1§ Sunderland	42,975
3R	May	1	(n‡)	Liverpool	W	1-0 Talbot	35,335
F		10	(n¹)	West Ham U	L	0-1	100,000

*Played at Hillsborough, Sheffield. †Played at Villa Park, Birmingham. §After extra-time. ‡Played at Highfield Road, Coventry. ¹Played at Wembley Stadium.

Appearances
Sub Appearances
Goals

League Cup

2	Aug	29	(a)	Leeds U	D	1-1 Stapleton	23,421
2	Sep	4	(h)	Leeds U	W	7-0 Sunderland 3, Brady 2 (pens), Nelson, Stapleton	35,133
3		25	(h)	Southampton	W	2-1 Stapleton, Brady	37,348
4	Oct	30	(a)	Brighton & HA	D	0-0	25,231
R	Nov	13	(h)	Brighton & HA	W	4-0 Stapleton 2, Vaessen 2	30,351
QF	Dec	4	(h)	Swindon T	D	1-1 Sunderland (pen)	38,024
R		11	(a)	Swindon T	L	3-4§ Brady 2, Talbot	21,795

§After extra-time

Appearances
Sub Appearances
Goals

Frank Stapleton tries a spectacular overhead kick against Aston Villa at Highbury on 9 February 1980. The Villa players are Allan Evans (4) and Ken McNaught (5).

294

Jennings PA	Rice PJ	Nelson S	Talbot BE	O'Leary DA	Young WD	Brady WL	Sunderland A	Stapleton FA	Price DJ	Rix G	Hollins JW	Gatting SP	McDermott BJ	Barron PG	Walford SJ	Devine JA	Vaessen PL	Davis PV	
1	2		4		6		8	9		11	10	7			5	3			3
1	2	3	4		6		8	9		11	10	7			5				R
1	2	3	4	5	6	7	8	9	10	11									4
1	2	3	4	5	6	7	8	9	10	11									5
1	2	3	4	5	6	7	8	9	10	11									R
1		3	4	5	6	7	8*	9	10	11		12			2				6
1	2	3*	4	5	6	7	8	9	10	11		12							SF
1	2		4	5	6	7	8	9	10	11		3							R
1	2		4	5	6	7	8	9	10	11			3						2R
1	2		4	5	6	7	8	9	10	11			3						3R
1	2	12	4	5	6	7	8	9	10	11			3*						F
11	10	6	11	9	11	9	11	11	9	11	2	2			3	5			
	1											1		1					
		1	2				6	4											

Jennings PA	Rice PJ	Nelson S	Talbot BE	O'Leary DA	Young WD	Brady WL	Sunderland A	Stapleton FA	Price DJ	Rix G	Hollins JW	Gatting SP	McDermott BJ	Barron PG	Walford SJ	Devine JA	Vaessen PL	Davis PV	
1	2	3	4	5	6	7	8	9		11	10								2
1	2	3	4	5	6	7	8	9		11	10								2
1	2	3	4		6	7	8	9		11	10			5					3
1	2*	3	4	5	6	7	8	9		11	10	12							4
1		3	4	5	6	7		9	10	11					2	8			R
1		3	4	5			8	9	10*	11	12	7		6	2				QF
1			4	5	6	7	8	9		11	10			3	2				R
7	4	6	7	6	6	6	6	7	2	7	5	1			3	3	1		
												1	1						
	1	1			5	4	5				2								

Bolton defender Mike Walsh wards off Arsenal's Stapleton in the game at Highbury on 23 February 1980.

1980-81

Manager: T.Neill

1	Aug	16	(a)	West Brom A	W	1-0	Stapleton	22,364
2		19	(h)	Southampton	D	1-1	Stapleton	43,050
3		23	(a)	Coventry C	L	1-3	Stapleton	15,399
4		30	(h)	Tottenham H	W	2-0	Price, Stapleton	54,045
5	Sep	6	(a)	Manchester C	D	1-1	Young	32,233
6		13	(h)	Stoke C	W	2-0	Hollins, Sansom	27,183
7		20	(a)	Middlesbrough	L	1-2	Rix	14,680
8		27	(h)	Nottingham F	W	1-0	Rix	37,582
9	Oct	4	(h)	Leicester C	W	1-0	Stapleton	28,490
10		7	(a)	Birmingham C	L	1-3	Sunderland	15,511
11		11	(a)	Manchester U	D	0-0		49,036
12		18	(h)	Sunderland	D	2-2	Gatting, Young	32,135
13		21	(h)	Norwich C	W	3-1	Talbot, McDermott, Sansom	21,839
14		25	(a)	Liverpool	D	1-1	Sunderland	40,310
15	Nov	1	(h)	Brighton & HA	W	2-0	Rix, McDermott	28,569
16		8	(a)	Leeds U	W	5-0	Hollins 2, Gatting, Talbot, Sunderland	20,855
17		11	(a)	Southampton	L	1-3	Rix	21,244
18		15	(h)	West Brom A	D	2-2	Sunderland, Batson (og)	25,858
19		22	(h)	Everton	W	2-1	McDermott, Stapleton	30,911
20		29	(a)	Aston Villa	D	1-1	Talbot	30,140
21	Dec	6	(h)	Wolves	D	1-1	Stapleton	26,050
22		13	(a)	Sunderland	L	0-2		21,595
23		20	(h)	Manchester U	W	2-1	Rix, Vaessen	33,730
24		26	(a)	Crystal P	D	2-2	Stapleton, McDermott	29,850
25		27	(h)	Ipswich T	D	1-1	Sunderland	42,818
26	Jan	10	(a)	Everton	W	2-1	Gatting, Vaessen	29,362
27		17	(a)	Tottenham H	L	0-2		32,994
28		31	(h)	Coventry C	D	2-2	Talbot, Stapleton	24,876
29	Feb	7	(a)	Stoke C	D	1-1	Stapleton	14,428
30		21	(a)	Nottingham F	L	1-3	Stapleton	25,357
31		24	(h)	Manchester C	W	2-0	Talbot, Sunderland	24,790
32		28	(h)	Middlesbrough	D	2-2	Stapleton, Hollins (pen)	24,504
33	Mar	7	(a)	Leicester C	L	0-1		20,198
34		21	(a)	Norwich C	D	1-1	Talbot	19,569
35		28	(h)	Liverpool	W	1-0	Sunderland	47,058
36		31	(h)	Birmingham C	W	2-1	Stapleton, O'Leary	17,431
37	Apr	4	(a)	Brighton & HA	W	1-0	Hollins	21,015
38		11	(h)	Leeds U	D	0-0		29,339
39		18	(a)	Ipswich T	W	2-0	Sansom, Nicholas	30,935
40		20	(h)	Crystal P	W	3-2	Talbot, Davis, Young	24,346
41		25	(a)	Wolves	W	2-1	Stapleton, Berry (og)	15,160
42	May	2	(h)	Aston Villa	W	2-0	Young, McDermott	57,472

FINAL LEAGUE POSITION: 3rd in Division One

Appearances
Sub Appearances
Goals

FA Cup

3	Jan	3	(a)	Everton	L	0-2	34,236

Appearances
Sub Appearances
Goals

League Cup

2	Aug	26	(a)	Swansea C	D	1-1	Stapleton	17,036
	Sep	2	(h)	Swansea C	W	3-1	Hollins (pen), Sunderland, Walford	26,399
3		22	(a)	Stockport C	W	3-1	Hollins, Sunderland, Stapleton	11,635
4	Nov	4	(a)	Tottenham H	L	0-1		42,511

Appearances
Sub Appearances
Goals

296

Player appearance / goalscoring grid (shirt numbers per match; right-hand column = match number).

Jennings PA	Devine JA	Sansom KG	Talbot BE	O'Leary DA	Young WD	Vaessen PL	Price DJ	Stapleton FA	Hollins JW	Rix G	McDermott BJ	Sunderland A	Rice PJ	Wood G	Gatting SP	Walford SJ	Davis PV	Nicholas P	Nelson S	No.
1	2	3	4	5	6	7	8	9	10	11										1
1	2	3	4*	5	6		8	10	9	7	11	12								2
1	2	3	4	5	6			10*	9	7	11	8	12							3
1	2	3	4	5	6			10	9	7	11	8								4
1	2	3	4	5	6			10	9	7	11	8								5
1	2	3	4	5	6			10	9	7	11	8								6
	2	3	4	5	6			10	9	7	11	8		1						7
	2	3	4	5	6			9	7	11		8		1	10					8
	2	3	4		6			9	7	11		8		1	10	5				9
	2	3	4		6			9	7	11		8		1	10	5				10
	2	3	4		6			9	7	11		8		1	10	5				11
	2	3	4*		6			9	7	11	12	8		1	10	5				12
	2	3	4		6			9	7*	11	12	8		1	10	5				13
	2	3	4		6			10*	9	7	11	8	12	1		5				14
	2	3	4		6			9	7	11	10	8		1		5				15
	2	3	4		6				7	11	10	8		1	9	5				16
	2	3	4		6			12	7	11	9	8		1	10*	5				17
1	2	3	4	5	6			9	7	11		8				10				18
1	2	3*	4	5				9	7	11	10	8			12	6				19
1	2	3	4	5				9	7	11		8			10	6				20
1	2	3	4		6		12	9	7*	11		8			10	5				21
1	2	3	4		6		12	7	9			8			10*	5		11		22
1	2	3	4		6	7		9		11		8			10	5				23
1	2	3	4		6		8	9	7	11					10	5				24
1	2	3	4		6			9	7	11		8			10	5				25
1	2	3			6		8	12	9	7*	11	10				5	4			26
1	2	3			6			9	7	11	4	8			10	5				27
1		3	4		6			9	2	11	7	8			10	5				28
1		3	4	5	6			9	2	11	7	8			10					29
1	12	3	4	5	6			9	2	11	7	8			10*					30
1	2	3	4	5	6			9	7	11		8			10					31
1	2	3	4	5				9	7	11	12	8*			10	6				32
1	2	3	4	5	6		12	9	7*	11		8			10					33
1	2	3	4	5	6			9		11		10			8		7			34
1	2	3	4	5	6			9	7*	11					12	10				35
1	2*	3	4	5	6			9		11	12	8			7	10				36
1	2	3	4	5	6			9	10	11		8				7				37
1	2	3	4	5	6			9	7*		12	8				11	10			38
1	2	3	4	5	6			9	7			8				11	10			39
1	2	3	4	5	6			9	7		12	8*				11	10			40
1	2	3	4	5	6			9	7			8				11	10			41
1		3	4*	5	6			9	2		7	8				11	10	12		42
31	38	42	40	24	40	5	9	40	38	35	16	34		11	22	20	9	8		
1						2	3				7		2		1		1		1	
	3	7	1	4	2	1	14	5	5	5	7			3	1	1				

2 own-goals

Jennings PA	Devine JA	Sansom KG	Talbot BE	O'Leary DA	Young WD	Vaessen PL	Price DJ	Stapleton FA	Hollins JW	Rix G	McDermott BJ	Sunderland A	Rice PJ	Wood G	Gatting SP	Walford SJ	Davis PV	Nicholas P	Nelson S	No.
1	2	3	4*	5	6			9	7	11	12	8			10					3
1	1	1	1	1	1			1	1	1	1	1			1					
										1										

Jennings PA	Devine JA	Sansom KG	Talbot BE	O'Leary DA	Young WD	Vaessen PL	Price DJ	Stapleton FA	Hollins JW	Rix G	McDermott BJ	Sunderland A	Rice PJ	Wood G	Gatting SP	Walford SJ	Davis PV	Nicholas P	Nelson S	No.
1	2	3	4	5	6			10	9	7	11	8								2
1	2	3	4		6			10	9	7	11	8				5				
	2	3	4	5	6			9	7	11		8		1	10					3
	2	3	4		6			9	7*	11	12	8		1	10	5				4
2	4	4	4	2	4			4	4	4	2	4		2	2	2				
								1												
								2	2			2			1					

297

1981-82

Manager: T.Neill

1	Aug	29	(h)	Stoke C	L	0-1	28,012
2	Sep	2	(a)	West Brom A	W	2-0 Talbot, Sunderland	17,104
3		5	(a)	Liverpool	L	0-2	35,269
4		12	(h)	Sunderland	D	1-1 Sunderland	26,527
5		19	(a)	Leeds U	D	0-0	21,410
6		22	(h)	Birmingham C	W	1-0 Talbot	19,588
7		26	(h)	Manchester U	D	0-0	39,797
8	Oct	3	(a)	Notts C	L	1-2 Hawley	10,840
9		10	(a)	Swansea C	L	0-2	20,591
10		17	(h)	Manchester C	W	1-0 Meade	25,466
11		24	(a)	Ipswich T	L	1-2 Sunderland	24,362
12		31	(h)	Coventry C	W	1-0 Thomas (og)*	23,102
13	Nov	7	(a)	Aston Villa	W	2-0 Talbot, Rix	27,316
14		21	(a)	Nottingham F	W	2-1 Talbot, Sunderland	20,912
15		28	(h)	Everton	W	1-0 McDermott	25,860
16	Dec	5	(a)	West Ham U	W	2-1 Hollins (pen), Whyte	33,833
17	Jan	20	(a)	Stoke C	W	1-0 Sunderland	9,625
18		23	(a)	Southampton	L	1-3 O'Leary	22,263
19		26	(h)	Brighton & HA	D	0-0	17,922
20		30	(h)	Leeds U	W	1-0 Vaessen	22,408
21	Feb	2	(h)	Wolves	W	2-1 Rix, Vaessen	15,163
22		6	(a)	Sunderland	D	0-0	16,345
23		13	(h)	Notts C	W	1-0 Meade	18,229
24		16	(h)	Middlesbrough	W	1-0 Rix	13,738
25		20	(a)	Manchester U	D	0-0	43,833
26		27	(h)	Swansea C	L	0-2	29,724
27	Mar	6	(a)	Manchester C	D	0-0	30,288
28		13	(h)	Ipswich T	W	1-0 Robson	25,977
29		16	(h)	West Brom A	D	2-2 Meade, Sunderland	15,799
30		20	(a)	Coventry C	L	0-1	11,965
31		27	(h)	Aston Villa	W	4-3 Sunderland, Rix 2, Meade	24,756
32		29	(a)	Tottenham H	D	2-2 Sunderland 2	40,940
33	Apr	3	(a)	Wolves	D	1-1 Davis	11,532
34		10	(a)	Brighton & HA	L	1-2 Talbot	21,019
35		12	(h)	Tottenham H	L	1-3 Hawley	48,897
36		17	(h)	Nottingham F	W	2-0 Talbot, Rix	21,986
37		24	(a)	Everton	L	1-2 Rix	19,136
38	May	1	(h)	West Ham U	W	2-0 Rix, Sunderland	34,977
39		4	(a)	Birmingham C	W	1-0 Whyte	13,133
40		8	(a)	Middlesbrough	W	3-1 Talbot, Davis, Rix	9,565
41		11	(h)	Liverpool	D	1-1 Sunderland	30,932
42		15	(h)	Southampton	W	4-1 Davis 2, Robson, Hawley	28,534

FINAL LEAGUE POSITION: 5th in Division One

Appearances
Sub Appearances
Goals

*Most sources give goalscorer as Thomas (og). Although Arsenal later credited the goal to Rix their records do not always reflect this.

FA Cup

3	Jan	2	(a)	Tottenham H	L	0-1	38,421

Appearances
Sub Appearances
Goals

League Cup

2	Oct	6	(a)	Sheffield U	L	0-1	19,101
		27	(h)	Sheffield U	W	2-0 Sunderland, Young	22,301
3	Nov	10	(h)	Norwich C	W	1-0 Nicholas	19,899
4	Dec	1	(h)	Liverpool	D	0-0	37,917
R		8	(a)	Liverpool	L	0-3	21,375

Appearances
Sub Appearances
Goals

298

Jennings PA	Devine JA	Sansom KG	Talbot BE	O'Leary DA	Young WD	Davis PV	Sunderland A	McDermott BJ	Nicholas P	Rix G	Vaessen PL	Hollins JW	Hawley JE	Whyte CA	Meade RJ	Robson SI	Wood G	Gorman PA	Hankin R	
1	2*	3	4	5	6	7	8	9	10	11	12									1
1	2	3	4	5	6	7	8	9	10	11										2
1	2	3	4	5	6	12	8	9	10*	11		7								3
1		3	4	5	6	7	8	9	10	11		2								4
1	12	3	4	5	6	7	8	9	10*	11		2								5
1	2	3	4	5	6	7	8	9		11		10								6
1	2	3	4	5	6	11	8		10			7	9*							7
1		3	4	5	6	7	8	12	10	11		2	9*							8
1	2	3	4	5	6	7	8		10			11	9							9
1		3	4	5			8	7	10	11		2		6	9					10
1		3	4	5	6	7	8		10	11		2		9						11
1		3	4	5				7	10	11	8	2	9	6						12
1	2	3	4	5		9			10	11	8	7		6						13
1	2	3	4	5		9	8		10	11		7		6						14
1	2*	3	4	5		9	8	12	10	11		7		6						15
1		3	4	5		9	8		10	11		7		6		2				16
		3	4	5		9	8		10	11		7		6		2	1			17
		3	4	5*		9	8	12	10	11		7		6		2	1			18
		3	4			9*	8	7	10	11	5	6	12			2	1			19
		3	4	5		9	8		10	11	7	2		6			1			20
		3	4	5		9	8*		10	11	7	2	12	6			1			21
		3	4	5		9	8		10	11	7	2		6			1			22
		3	4	5		9	8		10*	11	7	2		6	12		1			23
		3	4	5		9	8		10*	11	7	2		6	12		1			24
		3	4	5		9	8		10	11	7*	2		6	12		1			25
		3	4	5		9	8		10	11	7*	2		6	12		1			26
		3	4	5		9	8			11		2		6		10	1	7		27
		3	4	5		9	8			11		2		6		10	1	7		28
		3	4	5		9	8			11		2		6	12	10	1	7*		29
	5	3	4			9	8			11		2		6	12	10	1	7*		30
		3	4	5		9	8			11		2		6	7	10	1			31
		3	4	5		9*	8		12	11		2		6	7	10	1			32
		3	4	5		9	8			11		2	12	6	7*	10	1			33
		3	4	5		9	8			11		2		6	7	10	1			34
		3	4	5			12	9		11		2	8	6	7	10*	1			35
		3	4	5		9	8			11		2	8	6	7	10	1			36
		3	4	5		9	8	12		11		2*	7	6		10	1			37
		3	4	5		9	8			11		2	7	6		10	1			38
		3	4	5		9	8			11		2	7	6		10	1			39
		3	4	5		9*	8	12		11		2	7	6		10	1			40
		3	4	5			8	7		11		2	9*	6	12	10	1			41
		3	4	5			7	8		11		2	9	6		10	1			42
16	10	42	42	40	10	37	38	9	28	39	9	40	12	32	8	20	26	4		
1				1			4	3		1		2		8						
		7	1		4	11	1		9	2	1	3	2	4	2					

I own-goal

Jennings PA	Devine JA	Sansom KG	Talbot BE	O'Leary DA	Young WD	Davis PV	Sunderland A	McDermott BJ	Nicholas P	Rix G	Vaessen PL	Hollins JW	Hawley JE	Whyte CA	Meade RJ	Robson SI	Wood G	Gorman PA	Hankin R	
1*		3	4	5		11	8		10	9		7		6	12	2				3
1		1	1	1		1	1		1	1		1		1	1	1				
												1								

*When Jennings was injured Nicholas went in goal and Meade substituted outfield.

Jennings PA	Devine JA	Sansom KG	Talbot BE	O'Leary DA	Young WD	Davis PV	Sunderland A	McDermott BJ	Nicholas P	Rix G	Vaessen PL	Hollins JW	Hawley JE	Whyte CA	Meade RJ	Robson SI	Wood G	Gorman PA	Hankin R	
1	2	3	4	5	6	11	8		10			7	9							2
1		3	4	5	6		8	7	10	11	12	2			9*					
1		3	4	5		9	8*	7	10	11		2		6	12					3
1		3	4	5		9	8	7*	10	11		2		6			12			4
		3	4	5		9	8		10*	11		7		6		2	1		12	R
4	1	5	5	5	2	4	5	3	5	4		5	1	3	1	1	1			
										1				1				2		
			1			1	1													

1982-83

Manager: T.Neill

1	Aug	28	(a)	Stoke C	L	1-2	Sunderland	15,532
2		31	(h)	Norwich C	D	1-1	Woodcock	22,652
3	Sep	4	(h)	Liverpool	L	0-2		36,429
4		7	(a)	Brighton & HA	L	0-1		13,507
5		11	(a)	Coventry C	W	2-0	Chapman, Woodcock	10,246
6		18	(h)	Notts C	W	2-0	Rix, Hollins (pen)	20,556
7		25	(a)	Manchester U	D	0-0		43,198
8	Oct	2	(h)	West Ham U	L	2-3	Talbot, Davis	30,484
9		9	(a)	Ipswich T	W	1-0	Woodcock	20,792
10		16	(h)	West Brom A	W	2-0	Sunderland, Woodcock	21,666
11		23	(a)	Nottingham F	L	0-3		17,161
12		30	(h)	Birmingham C	D	0-0		20,699
13	Nov	6	(a)	Luton T	D	2-2	Rix, Talbot	16,597
14		13	(h)	Everton	D	1-1	McDermott	23,067
15		20	(a)	Swansea C	W	2-1	Woodcock, Chapman	12,389
16		27	(h)	Watford	L	2-4	Robson, Talbot	34,287
17	Dec	4	(a)	Manchester C	L	1-2	McDermott	23,057
18		7	(h)	Aston Villa	W	2-1	Whyte, Woodcock	17,384
19		18	(a)	Sunderland	L	0-3		11,753
20		27	(h)	Tottenham H	W	2-0	Sunderland, Woodcock	51,497
21		28	(a)	Southampton	D	2-2	Woodcock, Chapman	22,025
22	Jan	1	(h)	Swansea C	W	2-1	Sunderland, Woodcock	25,237
23		3	(a)	Liverpool	L	1-3	Talbot	37,713
24		15	(h)	Stoke C	W	3-0	Rix, Petrovic, Hollins (pen)	19,428
25		22	(a)	Notts C	L	0-1		9,731
26	Feb	5	(h)	Brighton & HA	W	3-1	Meade 2, Rix	17,972
27		26	(a)	West Brom A	D	0-0		13,923
28	Mar	5	(h)	Nottingham F	D	0-0		21,698
29		15	(a)	Birmingham C	L	1-2	Sunderland	11,276
30		19	(h)	Luton T	W	4-1	Woodcock 3, Davis	23,987
31		22	(h)	Ipswich T	D	2-2	Rix, Whyte	17,639
32		26	(a)	Everton	W	3-2	Sunderland, Robson, Woodcock	16,318
33	Apr	2	(h)	Southampton	D	0-0		24,911
34		4	(a)	Tottenham H	L	0-5		43,642
35		9	(h)	Coventry C	W	2-1	Rix, Woodcock	19,152
36		20	(a)	Norwich C	L	1-3	Davis	16,858
37		23	(h)	Manchester C	W	3-0	Talbot 3	16,810
38		30	(a)	Watford	L	1-2	McDermott	20,043
39	May	2	(h)	Manchester U	W	3-0	O'Leary, Talbot 2	23,602
40		7	(h)	Sunderland	L	0-1		18,053
41		10	(a)	West Ham U	W	3-1	Whyte, Petrovic, McDermott	28,930
42		14	(a)	Aston Villa	L	1-2	Davis	24,647

FINAL LEAGUE POSITION: 10th in Division One

Appearances
Sub Appearances
Goals

300

Appearance / team-sheet grid (player columns left → right; match number on the far right).

Wood G	Hollins JW	Sansom KG	Talbot BE	O'Leary DA	Whyte CA	Robson SI	Sunderland A	Chapman LR	Woodcock AS	Rix G	Davis PV	Devine JA	Hawley JE	O'Shea DE	Jennings PA	McDermott BJ	Nicholas P	Petrovic V	Meade RJ	Kay J	Hill CF	Match
1	2	3	4	5	6	7	8*	9	10	11	12											1
1	2	3*	4		6	7	8	9	10	11	5	12										2
1	2		4	5	6	7		9	10	11	8	3										3
1	2		4*	5	6	7		9	10	11	8	3	12									4
1	2	3	4	5	6	8		9	10	11	7											5
1	2	3	4	5	6	8		9	10	11	7											6
1	2	3	4	5	6	8		9	10	11	7											7
1	2	3	4	5	6		8	9	10	11	7											8
1	2*	3	4	5	6	9	8		10	11	7		12									9
1		3	4	5	6	9	8		10	11	7	2										10
1	2	3	4	5	6	9*	8	12	10	11	7											11
1		3	4	5	6	9	8	12	10*	11	7			2								12
1		3	4	5	6	9	8		10	11	7			2								13
		3	4	5*	6	9		8	10	11	7			2	1	12						14
1		3	4	5	6	9	8	12	10*	11	7			2								15
1		3	4	5	6	9	8		10	11	7			2								16
1		3	4	5	6	10	8	9		11	7			2*	12							17
1	2	3	4	5	6	9	8		10	11	7											18
	2	3	4	5	6	9	8	12	10	11	7*				1							19
	2	3	4	5	6		8		10	11	7				1	9						20
	2	3	4	5	6		8	12	10*	11	7				1	9						21
	2	3	4	5	6		8*	12	10	11	7				1			9				22
	2	3	4	5	6		8		10	11					1		7	9				23
	2	3	12	5*	4		8		10	11	7				1		6	9				24
	2	3	12	5	4		8		10	11	7*				1		6	9				25
	2	3	7	5	4				10	11					1		6	9	8			26
		3	12	5	4		8		10	11*	7				1		6	9	2			27
	2	3	7	5	4	9*			10	11	8				1		6	12				28
	2	3	12	5	4	9			10	11	8				1		6	7*				29
		3	7	2*	5	9			10	11	8				1		6	12				30
1	2	3	7	5		9	8		10	11	4						6					31
1		3	7	5	4	9	8		10	11	2						6					32
1		3	7	5	4	9	8		10	11							6		2			33
1		3	7	5	4*	9	8		10	11	2						6	12				34
1		3	7		4		8	12	10	11	2			6*			9	5				35
1	12	3	4	5	6				10	11*	9						7			2	8	36
		3	7	5	4		10*		8		12				1	9	6			2	11	37
		3	7	5	4		8		10*						1	9	6	12		2	11	38
		3	7	5	4		8		10*		2				1	9	6	12			11	39
		3	7	5	4		8		10		2*	12			1	9	6				11	40
		3	7	5	4		8		10						1	9	6		2		11	41
		3	7	5	4		8		10		2				1	9	6				11	42
23	22	40	38	36	36	31	25	12	34	36	40	8	2	6	19	7	21	10	2	7	7	
1		4				7					1	1	4			2		3	2			
	2	9	1	3	2	6	3	14	6	4				4		2	2					

301

1982-83 (continued)

FA Cup

3	Jan	8	(h)	Bolton W	W	2-1	Davis, Rix	22,576
4		29	(h)	Leeds U	D	1-1	Sunderland	33,930
R	Feb	2	(a)	Leeds U	D	1-1§	Rix	24,410
2R		9	(h)	Leeds U	W	2-1	Woodcock, Rix	26,802
5	Feb	19	(a)	Middlesbrough	D	1-1	Rix	20,580
R		28	(h)	Middlesbrough	W	3-2	Talbot, Woodcock, Davis	28,689
6	Mar	12	(h)	Aston Villa	W	2-0	Woodcock, Petrovic	41,774
SF	Apr	16	(n*)	Manchester U	L	1-2	Woodcock	46,535

§After extra-time. *Played at Villa Park, Birmingham.

Appearances
Sub Appearances
Goals

League Cup

2	Oct	5	(h)	Cardiff C	W	2-1	Hollins, Davis	15,115
		26	(a)	Cardiff C	W	3-1	Sunderland, Woodcock, Davis	11,632
3	Nov	9	(a)	Everton	D	1-1	Robson	13,089
R		23	(h)	Everton	W	3-0	Sunderland 3	19,547
4		30	(h)	Huddersfield T	W	1-0	Sunderland (pen)	17,742
5	Jan	18	(h)	Sheffield W	W	1-0	Woodcock	30,937
SF	Feb	15	(h)	Manchester U	L	2-4	Nicholas, Woodcock	43,136
		23	(a)	Manchester U	L	1-2	Meade	56,635

Appearances
Sub Appearances
Goals

FA Cup

Wood G	Hollins JW	Sansom KG	Talbot BE	O'Leary DA	Whyte CA	Robson SI	Sunderland A	Chapman LR	Woodcock AS	Rix G	Davis PV	Devine JA	Hawley JE	O'Shea DE	Jennings PA	McDermott BJ	Nicholas P	Petrovic V	Meade RJ	
	2	3	4	5		6	8		10	11	7				1			9		3
	2	3	7	5		4	8		10	11					1		6	9		4
	2	3	7	5		4	8*		10	11	12				1		6	9		R
	2	3	7	5		4			10	11					1		6	9	8	2R
	2	3	7		5	4			10	11	8				1		6	9		5
	2	3	7		5	4	9		10	11	8				1		6			R
	2	3			5	4	9		10	11	8				1		6	7		6
1	6	3	7	5	4	2*		12	10	11	8						9			SF
1	8	8	7	5	4	8	5		8	8	5				7		7	6	1	
								1			1									
			1			1			4	4	2						1			

League Cup

Wood G	Hollins JW	Sansom KG	Talbot BE	O'Leary DA	Whyte CA	Robson SI	Sunderland A	Chapman LR	Woodcock AS	Rix G	Davis PV	Devine JA	Hawley JE	O'Shea DE	Jennings PA	McDermott BJ	Nicholas P	Petrovic V	Meade RJ	
1	2	3	4	5	6	9	8		10	11	7									2
1	2	3	4	5	6	9	8		10	11	7									
		3	4	5	6	9	8*	12	10	11	7	2			1					3
1		3	4	5	6	9	8	12	10*	11	7	2								R
1		3	4	5	6	9	8		10	11	7	2								4
	2	3		5		6	8		10	11	7				1		4	9		5
	2	3	7	5*		4			10	11	12				1		6	9	8	SF
	2*	3	7		5	4			10	11	12				1		6	9	8	
4	5	8	7	7	6	8	6		8	8	6	3			4		3	3	2	
								2			2									
		1				1	5		3		2						1	1		

Arsenal's David O'Leary made 36 League appearances when Arsenal finished tenth in Division One. Apart from injury, O'Leary had been a regular member of the Gunners' defence for some years and by 1990 he was the longest-serving player currently on the club's books.

1983-84

Manager: T.Neill/D.Howe

1	Aug	27	(h)	Luton T	W	2-1	Woodcock, McDermott	39,348
2		29	(a)	Wolves	W	2-1	Nicholas 2 (1 pen)	18,571
3	Sep	3	(a)	Southampton	L	0-1		19,377
4		6	(h)	Manchester U	L	2-3	Woodcock, Talbot	42,704
5		10	(h)	Liverpool	L	0-2		41,896
6		17	(a)	Notts C	W	4-0	Rix, Woodcock, Talbot, Hunt (og)	10,217
7		24	(h)	Norwich C	W	3-0	Chapman, Sunderland 2	24,438
8	Oct	1	(a)	Queen's Park R	L	0-2		26,293
9		15	(h)	Coventry C	L	0-1		20,290
10		22	(h)	Nottingham F	W	4-1	Woodcock 2, Hill, Sunderland	22,870
11		29	(a)	Aston Villa	W	6-2	Woodcock 5, McDermott	23,678
12	Nov	5	(h)	Sunderland	L	1-2	Woodcock	26,064
13		12	(a)	Ipswich T	L	0-1		21,652
14		19	(h)	Everton	W	2-1	Sunderland, Robson	24,330
15		26	(a)	Leicester C	L	0-3		14,777
16	Dec	3	(h)	West Brom A	L	0-1		22,271
17		10	(a)	West Ham U	L	1-3	Whyte	25,118
18		17	(h)	Watford	W	3-1	Meade 3	25,104
19		26	(a)	Tottenham H	W	4-2	Nicholas 2, Meade 2	38,756
20		27	(h)	Birmingham C	D	1-1	Nicholas (pen)	25,642
21		31	(h)	Southampton	D	2-2	Cork, Nicholas (pen)	27,596
22	Jan	2	(a)	Norwich C	D	1-1	Woodcock	20,482
23		14	(a)	Luton T	W	2-1	Sansom, Woodcock	16,320
24		21	(h)	Notts C	D	1-1	Nicholas	20,110
25		28	(a)	Stoke C	L	0-1		12,840
26	Feb	4	(h)	Queen's Park R	L	0-2		31,014
27		11	(a)	Liverpool	L	1-2	Rix	34,642
28		18	(h)	Aston Villa	D	1-1	Rix	26,640
29		25	(a)	Nottingham F	W	1-0	Mariner	20,045
30	Mar	3	(a)	Sunderland	D	2-2	Nicholas (pen), Woodcock	15,370
31		10	(h)	Ipswich T	W	4-1	Mariner 2, Talbot, Woodcock	24,000
32		17	(a)	Manchester U	L	0-4		48,942
33		24	(h)	Wolves	W	4-1	Robson, Woodcock, Nicholas (pen), Rix	18,612
34		31	(a)	Coventry C	W	4-1	Talbot, Whyte, Robson, Mariner	10,550
35	Apr	7	(h)	Stoke C	W	3-1	Nicholas, Mariner, Woodcock	21,211
36		9	(a)	Everton	D	0-0		21,174
37		21	(h)	Tottenham H	W	3-2	Robson, Nicholas, Woodcock	48,831
38		23	(a)	Birmingham C	D	1-1	Woodcock	11,164
39		28	(h)	Leicester C	W	2-1	Woodcock, Davis	24,143
40	May	5	(a)	West Brom A	W	3-1	Talbot, Mariner, Robson	13,566
41		7	(h)	West Ham U	D	3-3	Talbot, Woodcock, Mariner	33,347
42		12	(a)	Watford	L	1-2	Robson	22,007

FINAL LEAGUE POSITION: 6th in Division One

Appearances

Sub Appearances

Goals

FA Cup

3	Jan	7	(a)	Middlesbrough	L	2-3	Woodcock, Nicholas	17,813

Appearances

Sub Appearances

Goals

League Cup

2	Oct	4	(a)	Plymouth A	D	1-1	Rix	20,983
		25	(h)	Plymouth A	W	1-0	Sunderland	22,640
3	Nov	9	(a)	Tottenham H	W	2-1	Nicholas, Woodcock	48,200
4		29	(h)	Walsall	L	1-2	Robson	22,406

Appearances

Sub Appearances

Goals

Jennings PA	Robson SI	Sansom KG	Talbot BE	O'Leary DA	Hill CF	McDermott BJ	Davis PV	Woodcock AS	Nicholas C	Rix G	Whyte CA	Sunderland A	Chapman LR	Adams TA	Gorman PA	Meade RJ	Kay J	Caton TS	Madden DJ	Allinson IJR	Cork D	Mariner P	Sparrow BE	Lukic J	
1	2	3	4	5	6	7	8	9	10	11															1
1	2	3	4	5	6	7	8	9	10	11															2
1	2	3	4	5	6	7*	8	9	10	11	12														3
1	2	3	4	5	6	7*	8	9	10	11		12													4
1	2	3	4	5	6		8	9	10	11		7													5
1	2	3	12	5	6		8	9	10*	11	4	7													6
1	2	3		5	6	12	8		10*	11	4	7	9												7
1	2	3		5	6		8		10	11	4	7	9												8
1	2	3		5	6	12	8		10	11	4*	7	9												9
1	2	3		5	6	12	8	9	10*	11	4	7													10
1	2*	3		5	6	12	8	9	10	11	4	7													11
1	2	3	8		6	12		9	10	11	4	7*		5											12
1	2	3		5	6		8	9	10	11	4	7*			12										13
1	2	3		5	6	9			10	11	4	7*			8	12									14
1	2	3		5			8	9	10	11*	4	7	12			6									15
1	2	3*			6		8	9	10					5	12	4	7			11					16
1		3			2*		8	9	10					5		4	6	7		11					17
1		3			2		8	9	10					5		7		6		11	4				18
1	4*	3		5	2		8	9	10							7		6		11	12				19
1		3			2	12	8	9	10					5		7		6*		11	4				20
1		3		5	2		8	9	10							7		6		11	4				21
1		3		5	2		8	9	10							7		6		11	4				22
1		3	4	5			8	9	10	11						7	2	6							23
1		3	4		12		8	9	10	11				5*		7	2	6							24
1		3	4	5	7		8	9	10	11							2	6							25
1		3	4	5			8	9	10	11						7*	2	6	12						26
1		3	4	5	2		8	9	10	11								6	12	7*					27
1		3	4	5	2			7	10	8		11						6				9			28
1		3	4	5	2			7	10	8		11						6				9			29
1		3	4	5	2			7	10	8		11						6				9			30
1		3	4	5	2			7	10	8		11*						6				9			31
1	7	3	4	5	2				10	8		11						6				9			32
1	7	3	4	5	2				10	8		11						6				9			33
1*	7		4	5	2				10	8		11						6	12			9	3		34
	7		4	5	2				10	8*		11						6	12			9	3	1	35
	7	3	4	5	2				10	8		11						6				9		1	36
	7	3	4	5	2	12			10	8		11*						6				9		1	37
	7	3	4	5	2	11			10	8								6				9		1	38
1	7	3	4*	5	2	12			10	8		11						6				9			39
1	7*	3	4	5	2	12			10	8		11						6				9			40
1	7	3	4	5	2	12			10	8		11*						6				9			41
1	7	3	4	5	2			8	10	11								6				9			42
38	28	40	26	36	37	6	31	37	41	34	14	11	3	3	1	9	6	26	2	7	5	15	2	4	
			1					7	4			1	1	1		1	4	1		2	2				
6	1	6		1	2		1	21	11	4	2	4	1			5				1		7			

I own-goal

Jennings PA	Robson SI	Sansom KG	Talbot BE	O'Leary DA	Hill CF	McDermott BJ	Davis PV	Woodcock AS	Nicholas C	Rix G	Whyte CA	Sunderland A	Chapman LR	Adams TA	Gorman PA	Meade RJ	Kay J	Caton TS	Madden DJ	Allinson IJR	Cork D	Mariner P	Sparrow BE	Lukic J	
1		3	12	5	2		8	9	10	11						7		6		4*					3
1		1	1	1	1		1	1	1	1						1		1		1					
		1																							
								1	1																

Jennings PA	Robson SI	Sansom KG	Talbot BE	O'Leary DA	Hill CF	McDermott BJ	Davis PV	Woodcock AS	Nicholas C	Rix G	Whyte CA	Sunderland A	Chapman LR	Adams TA	Gorman PA	Meade RJ	Kay J	Caton TS	Madden DJ	Allinson IJR	Cork D	Mariner P	Sparrow BE	Lukic J	
1	2	3	12	5	6		8	9*	10	11	4	7													2
1	2	3		5	6		8	9	10	11	4	7													
1	2	3		5	6		8	9	10	11	4	7													3
1	2	3		5	6		8	9	10		4	7							11						4
4	4	4		4	4		4	4	4	3	4	4							1						
		1																							
	1							1	1	1															

305

1984-85

Manager: D.Howe

1	Aug	25	(h)	Chelsea	D 1-1	Mariner	45,329
2		29	(a)	Nottingham F	L 0-2		17,972
3	Sep	1	(a)	Watford	W 4-3	Nicholas 2, Talbot, Woodcock	21,320
4		4	(h)	Newcastle U	W 2-0	Talbot, Anderson	37,078
5		8	(h)	Liverpool	W 3-1	Talbot 2, Woodcock	50,006
6		15	(a)	Ipswich T	L 1-2	Nicholas	24,508
7		22	(h)	Stoke C	W 4-0	Woodcock 2, (1 pen), Mariner, Sansom	26,758
8		29	(a)	Coventry C	W 2-1	Woodcock, Mariner	14,394
9	Oct	6	(h)	Everton	W 1-0	Nicholas (pen)	37,049
10		13	(a)	Leicester C	W 4-1	Talbot 2 (1 pen), Anderson, Rix	19,944
11		20	(h)	Sunderland	W 3-2	Caton, Allinson, Talbot	36,944
12		27	(a)	West Ham U	L 1-3	Allinson	33,218
13	Nov	2	(a)	Manchester U	L 2-4	Allinson, Woodcock	32,379
14		10	(h)	Aston Villa	D 1-1	Mariner	33,193
15		17	(h)	Queen's Park R	W 1-0	Woodcock	34,953
16		25	(a)	Sheffield W	L 1-2	Woodcock	25,575
17	Dec	1	(h)	Luton T	W 3-1	Allinson, Woodcock, Anderson	26,366
18		8	(a)	Southampton	L 0-1		20,243
19		15	(h)	West Brom A	W 4-0	Allinson 2, Talbot, Davis (pen)	23,728
20		22	(h)	Watford	D 1-1	Allinson	31,302
21		26	(a)	Norwich C	L 0-1		17,702
22		29	(a)	Newcastle U	W 3-1	Nicholas 2, Talbot	27,349
23	Jan	1	(h)	Tottenham H	L 1-2	Woodcock	48,714
24		19	(a)	Chelsea	D 1-1	Mariner	34,752
25	Feb	2	(h)	Coventry C	W 2-1	Meade, Allinson	21,791
26		12	(a)	Liverpool	L 0-3		28,645
27		23	(h)	Manchester U	L 0-1		48,612
28	Mar	2	(h)	West Ham U	W 2-1	Mariner, Robson	25,818
29		9	(a)	Sunderland	D 0-0		27,694
30		13	(a)	Aston Villa	D 0-0		15,487
31		16	(h)	Leicester C	W 2-0	Williams, Meade	20,663
32		19	(h)	Ipswich T	D 1-1	Meade	18,365
33		23	(a)	Everton	L 0-2		36,387
34		30	(a)	Stoke C	L 0-2		7,371
35	Apr	6	(h)	Norwich C	W 2-0	Nicholas, Robson	19,597
36		13	(h)	Nottingham F	D 1-1	Allinson	24,152
37		17	(a)	Tottenham H	W 2-0	Nicholas, Talbot	40,399
38		20	(a)	Queen's Park R	L 0-1		20,189
39		27	(h)	Sheffield W	W 1-0	Mariner	23,803
40	May	4	(a)	Luton T	L 1-3	Nicholas (pen)	12,251
41		6	(h)	Southampton	W 1-0	Rix	21,214
42		11	(a)	West Brom A	D 2-2	Allinson, Robertson (og)	13,485

FINAL LEAGUE POSITION: 7th in Division One
Appearances
Sub Appearances
Goals

FA Cup

3	Jan	5	(a)	Hereford U	D 1-1	Woodcock	15,777
R		22	(h)	Hereford U	W 7-2	Mariner 2, Talbot 2, Nicholas, Anderson, Woodcock	26,023
4		26	(a)	York C	L 0-1		10,840

Appearances
Sub Appearances
Goals

League Cup

2	Sep	25	(h)	Bristol R	W 4-0	Woodcock, Anderson, Nicholas 2	23,871
	Oct	9	(a)	Bristol R	D 1-1	Caton	10,408
3		31	(a)	Oxford U	L 2-3	Rix, Allinson	14,393

Appearances
Sub Appearances
Goals

Jennings PA	Anderson VA	Sansom KG	Talbot BE	O'Leary DA	Caton TS	Robson SI	Davis PV	Mariner P	Woodcock AS	Allinson IJR	Nicholas C	Rix G	Hill CF	Lukic J	Adams TA	Meade RJ	Williams SC	
1	2	3	4	5	6	7	8	9	10	11								1
1	2	3	4*	5	6	7	11	9	10	12	8							2
1	2	3	4	5	6	7	8	9	10		11							3
1	2	3	4	5	6	7	8	9	10		11							4
1	2	3	4	5	6	7	8	9	10		11							5
1	2	3	4	5	6	7		9	10		11	8						6
1	2	3	4	5	6	7		9	10		11	8						7
1	2	3	4*	5	6	7	12	9	10		11	8						8
1	2	3	4	5	6	7		9	10		11	8						9
1	2	3	4	5	6	7		10	9		11	8						10
1	2	3	4	5	6	7	12	10*	9		11	8						11
1	2	3	4	5		7	10		9		11	8	6					12
	2	3	4	5	6	7		10	9		11	8*		1	12			13
1	2	3	4	5	6*	7	8	9	10	12	11							14
1	2	3	4	5		7	8	10	9		11		6					15
1	2	3	4	5*		7	8	9	10	12	11		6					16
	2	3	4		6	7	8	9	10		11			1	5			17
	2	3	4	5		7	8	9	10		11*			1	6	12		18
	2	3	4		6	7	8	9	10		11			1	5			19
			4	2	6	7		9	10	11	8	3		1	5			20
	2	3	4	5	8	7		9	10		11*	12		1	6			21
	2		4	5	3	7		9	10		11	8		1	6			22
	2		4	5	3	7		9	10	8	11*			1	6	12		23
	2	3	4	5	6	7		9	10		11	8		1				24
	2	3	4	5	6*	7		9			11	12		1		10	8	25
	2	3	4	5		7		9			11*	12		1	6	10	8	26
	2	3	12	5	6	7	8*	9	10		11			1	4			27
	2	3		5	6	7	8	9	10		11			1	4			28
	2	3	4	5	6	7	8	9	10		11			1				29
	2	3	4	5	6	7	8	9	10*		11			1	12			30
	2	3	12		6	7	8	9			11*			1	5	10	4	31
	2	3	12		6	7	8*	9			11			1	5	10	4	32
	2	3	12	5	6	7*		9			11	8		1		10	4	33
	2	3	7	5	6			9	12		11	8		1		10*	4	34
	2	3	10	5	6	7		9*	12		11	8		1			4	35
	2	3	10	5	6	7		9			11	8		1			4	36
	2	3	10	5*	6	7	12	9			11	8		1			4	37
	2	3	10		6	7	12	9			11	8		1	5*		4	38
	2	3	10	5	6	7*		9	12		11	8		1			4	39
	2	3	4	5	6*	7	12	9	10		11	8		1				40
	2	3	4		6	7		9	10		11	8		1	5			41
	2	3	4	5		7		10	9	12	11*	8		1	6			42
15	41	39	37	36	35	40	21	34	27	20	35	18	2	27	15	6	14	
			4				3	2		7	3				1	2	1	
	3	1	10		1	2	1	7	10	10	9	2			3		1	

1 own-goal

Jennings PA	Anderson VA	Sansom KG	Talbot BE	O'Leary DA	Caton TS	Robson SI	Davis PV	Mariner P	Woodcock AS	Allinson IJR	Nicholas C	Rix G	Hill CF	Lukic J	Adams TA	Meade RJ	Williams SC	
	2		4	5	3	7		9	10	12	11*			1	6		8	3
	2	3	4	5	6	7		9	10		11			1			8	R
	2	3	4	5	6	7		9	10	12	11*			1			8	4
	3	2	3	3	3	3		3	3		3			3	1		3	
									2									
	1		2					2	2						1			

Jennings PA	Anderson VA	Sansom KG	Talbot BE	O'Leary DA	Caton TS	Robson SI	Davis PV	Mariner P	Woodcock AS	Allinson IJR	Nicholas C	Rix G	Hill CF	Lukic J	Adams TA	Meade RJ	Williams SC	
1	2	3	4	5	6	7		9	10		11	8						2
1	2	3	4	5	6	7		9	10		11	8						
1	2	3	4	5	6	7*		10	9		11	8			12			3
3	3	3	3	3	3	3		2	3		3	3			1			
															1			
	1			1			1	1	2	1								

1985-86

Manager: D.Howe/S.Burtenshaw

1	Aug	17	(a)	Liverpool	L	0-2		38,261
2		20	(h)	Southampton	W	3-2	Caton, Robson, Woodcock	21,895
3		24	(h)	Manchester U	L	1-2	Allinson (pen)	37,145
4		27	(a)	Luton T	D	2-2	Woodcock, Donaghy (og)	10,012
5		31	(h)	Leicester C	W	1-0	Woodcock	18,207
6	Sep	3	(a)	Queen's Park R	W	1-0	Allinson	15,993
7		7	(a)	Coventry C	W	2-0	Woodcock, Nicholas	12,189
8		14	(h)	Sheffield W	W	1-0	Allinson (pen)	23,108
9		21	(a)	Chelsea	L	1-2	Nicholas	33,241
10		28	(h)	Newcastle U	D	0-0		24,104
11	Oct	5	(h)	Aston Villa	W	3-2	Woodcock, Anderson, Whyte	18,881
12		12	(a)	West Ham U	D	0-0		24,057
13		19	(h)	Ipswich T	W	1-0	Davis	19,523
14		26	(a)	Nottingham F	L	2-3	Rix, Davis	17,756
15	Nov	2	(h)	Manchester C	W	1-0	Davis	22,264
16		9	(a)	Everton	L	1-6	Nicholas	28,620
17		16	(h)	Oxford U	W	2-1	Davis, Woodcock	19,632
18		23	(a)	West Brom A	D	0-0		9,165
19		30	(h)	Birmingham C	D	0-0		16,673
20	Dec	7	(a)	Southampton	L	0-3		15,052
21		14	(h)	Liverpool	W	2-0	Nicholas, Quinn	35,048
22		21	(a)	Manchester U	W	1-0	Nicholas	44,386
23		28	(h)	Queen's Park R	W	3-1	Rix, Nicholas, Woodock	25,770
24	Jan	1	(h)	Tottenham H	D	0-0		45,109
25		18	(a)	Leicester C	D	2-2	Robson, Nicholas	11,246
26	Feb	1	(h)	Luton T	W	2-1	Allinson (pen), Rix	22,473
27	Mar	1	(a)	Newcastle U	L	0-1		21,860
28		8	(a)	Aston Villa	W	4-1	Nicholas, Hayes, Rocastle, Elliott (og)	10,584
29		11	(a)	Ipswich T	W	2-1	Nicholas, Woodcock	13,967
30		15	(h)	West Ham U	W	1-0	Woodcock	31,240
31		22	(h)	Coventry C	W	3-0	Woodcock, Hayes, McInally (og)	17,189
32		29	(a)	Tottenham H	L	0-1		33,427
33		31	(h)	Watford	L	0-2		19,599
34	Apr	1	(a)	Watford	L	0-3		18,635
35		5	(a)	Manchester C	W	1-0	Robson	19,590
36		8	(h)	Nottingham F	D	1-1	Allinson (pen)	15,098
37		12	(h)	Everton	L	0-1		28,251
38		16	(a)	Sheffield W	L	0-2		16,344
39		26	(h)	West Brom A	D	2-2	Robson, Allinson (pen)	14,843
40		29	(h)	Chelsea	W	2-0	Anderson, Nicholas	24,025
41	May	3	(a)	Birmingham C	W	1-0	Woodcock	6,234
42		5	(h)	Oxford U	L	0-3		13,651

FINAL LEAGUE POSITION: 7th in Division One

Appearances
Sub Appearances
Goals

FA Cup

3	Jan	4	(a)	Grimsby T	W	4-3	Rix, Nicholas 3	12,829
4		25	(h)	Rotherham U	W	5-1	Rix, Nicholas, Allinson 2 (1 pen), Robson	28,490
5	Feb	15	(a)	Luton T	D	2-2	Allinson, Rocastle	15,799
R	Mar	3	(h)	Luton T	D	0-0§		26,547
2R		5	(a)	Luton T	L	0-3		13,251

§After extra-time

Appearances
Sub Appearances
Goals

League Cup

2	Sep	25	(a)	Hereford U	D	0-0		6,049
	Oct	8	(h)	Hereford U	W	2-1§	Anderson, Nicholas	15,789
3		30	(a)	Manchester C	W	2-1	Nicholas, Allinson	18,279
4	Nov	19	(h)	Southampton	D	0-0		18,244
R		26	(a)	Southampton	W	3-1	Hayes, Nicholas, Robson	14,010
5	Jan	22	(a)	Aston Villa	D	1-1	Nicholas	26,093
R	Feb	4	(h)	Aston Villa	L	1-2	Mariner	33,091

§After extra-time

Appearances
Sub Appearances
Goals

308

Lukic J	Anderson VA	Sansom KG	Williams SC	O'Leary DA	Caton TS	Allinson IJR	Robson SI	Nicholas C	Woodcock AS	Rix G	Davis PV	Mariner P	Rocastle D	Whyte CA	Hayes M	Keown MR	Quinn NJ	Caesar GC	Wilmot RJ	Adams TA	
1	2	3	4	5	6	7	8	9	10	11											1
1	2	3	4	5	6	8	7	9	10	11											2
1	2	3	4*	5	6	8	7	9	10	11	12										3
1	2	3		5*	6	8	7	9	10	11	4	12									4
1	2	3			6	8	7	9	10	11	4	5									5
1	2	3		5	6	8	7	9	10	11	4										6
1	2	3		5	6	8	7	9	10	11	4										7
1	2	3		5	6	8	7	9	10	11	4										8
1	2	3		5	6	8	7	9	10	11	4										9
1	2	3		5	6	8*		9	10	11	4		7	12							10
1	2	3		5	6	8		9	10	11	4		7								11
1	2	3		5*	6	8		9	10	11	4	12	7								12
1	2	3		5	6	8		9*	10	11	4	12	7								13
1	2	3		5	6	8*		9	10	11	4	12	7								14
1	2	3	7	5	6	8*		9	10	11	4	12									15
1	2	3	7	5	6	8		9	10	11	4										16
1	2	3	7	5	6	12	8	9	10*		4				11						17
1	2	3	7		6	8		9	10		4		12		11*		5				18
1	2	3	7*	5	6	12	8	9	10		4				11						19
1	2	3	7	5	6	12	8	9	10		4				11*						20
1	2	3		5		7	8	9		11	4				10	6					21
1		3		5		7	8	9		11	4				10	6		2			22
1		3		5		7	8*	9		11	4		12		10	6		2			23
1	2	3		5		7	8	9	10*	11	4		12			6					24
1	2	3		5		7	8	9		11	4				10	6					25
1	2	3		5		7	8	9		11	4				10	6					26
1	2	3	4	5		7	8	9	10*	11			12			6					27
	2	3	4	5			8	9	10	11			7			6			1		28
	2	3	4	5*			8	9	10	11			7			6			1	12	29
1	2	3	4	5			8	9	10	11			7			6					30
1		3	4	5			8	9	10	11			7			6	2				31
1	2	3	4	5			8	9	10*	11			7			6				12	32
1	2	3	4	5			8	9	10	11			7*			6				12	33
1	2	3	4*			7	8	9	10	11		12				6				5	34
1	2	3				7	8	9		11	4	12			10*	6				5	35
1	2	3	4			7	8*	9		11		12			10	6				5	36
1	2	3	4			7	8	9		11					10	6				5	37
1	2	3	4			7	8	9	10	11						6				5	38
1	2	3		5		7	8	9	10*	11	4					6	12				39
1	2	3		5		7	8	9	10	11*	4					6	12				40
1	2	3		5		7	8	9	10	11	4					6					41
1	2	3		5*		7	8	9	10	11	4					6	12				42
40	39	42	17	35	20	28	26	41	31	38	28	3	13	4	11	22	10	2	2	10	—
					5	1				2		1	6	3	3		2				—
	2			1	6	4	10	11	3	4	1		1		1	2				1	—

3 own-goals

Lukic J	Anderson VA	Sansom KG	Williams SC	O'Leary DA	Caton TS	Allinson IJR	Robson SI	Nicholas C	Woodcock AS	Rix G	Davis PV	Mariner P	Rocastle D	Whyte CA	Hayes M	Keown MR	Quinn NJ	Caesar GC	Wilmot RJ	Adams TA	
1	2	3		5		7		9		11	4				8	6	10				3
1	2	3		5		7	8*	9	12	11	4					6	10				4
1	2	3	4	5		7	8	9*	10	11			12			6					5
1	2	3	4	5		7	8	9	10	11						6					R
1	2	3	4	5		7	8	9	10	11*			12			6					2R
5	5	5	3	5		5	1	5	1	4	1		2		5	1	5			2	—
								1					1			1					—
			3	1		4			2				1								—

Lukic J	Anderson VA	Sansom KG	Williams SC	O'Leary DA	Caton TS	Allinson IJR	Robson SI	Nicholas C	Woodcock AS	Rix G	Davis PV	Mariner P	Rocastle D	Whyte CA	Hayes M	Keown MR	Quinn NJ	Caesar GC	Wilmot RJ	Adams TA	
1	2	3		5	6	8	7*	9	10	11	4	12									2
1	2	3		5	6	8		9	10	11	4*	12	7								
1	2	3	7	5	6	8		9	10	11	4										3
1	2	3	7	5	6	12	8	9	10		4					11*					4
1	2	3	7	5	6		8	9	10		4					11					R
	2	3		5	6	7	8*	9	12	11	4					10		1			5
1	2	3		5	6	7*		9	12	11	8	4					10				R
6	7	7	3	7	7	5	4	7	5	5	5	1	2	1	2	2	1				—
								1													—
	1							2			1	1									—
	1					1	1	4		2	1		1								—

309

1986-87

Manager: G.Graham

1	Aug	23	(h)	Manchester U	W	1-0	Nicholas	41,382
2		26	(a)	Coventry C	L	1-2	Anderson	11,182
3		30	(a)	Liverpool	L	1-2	Adams	38,637
4	Sep	2	(h)	Sheffield W	W	2-0	Adams, Quinn	20,101
5		6	(h)	Tottenham H	D	0-0		44,707
6		13	(a)	Luton T	D	0-0		9,876
7		20	(h)	Oxford U	D	0-0		20,676
8		27	(a)	Nottingham F	L	0-1		25,371
9	Oct	4	(a)	Everton	W	1-0	Williams	30,007
10		11	(h)	Watford	W	3-1	Groves, Hayes (pen), Quinn	24,076
11		18	(a)	Newcastle U	W	2-1	Anderson, Williams	22,368
12		25	(h)	Chelsea	W	3-1	Rocastle, Hayes 2 (1 pen)	32,990
13	Nov	1	(a)	Charlton A	W	2-0	Adams, Hayes	19,614
14		8	(h)	West Ham U	D	0-0		36,084
15		15	(a)	Southampton	W	4-0	Hayes (pen), Quinn, Groves, Anderson	18,728
16		22	(h)	Manchester C	W	3-0	Quinn, Anderson, Adams	29,000
17		29	(a)	Aston Villa	W	4-0	Hayes, Rocastle, Groves, Keown (og)	21,658
18	Dec	6	(h)	Queen's Park R	W	3-1	Hayes 2, Quinn	34,049
19		13	(a)	Norwich C	D	1-1	Hayes (pen)	21,409
20		20	(h)	Luton T	W	3-0	Quinn, Adams, Hayes	28,217
21		26	(a)	Leicester C	D	1-1	Hayes (pen)	19,205
22		27	(h)	Southampton	W	1-0	Quinn	38,138
23	Jan	1	(h)	Wimbledon	W	3-1	Nicholas 2, Hayes (pen)	36,144
24		4	(a)	Tottenham H	W	2-1	Adams, Davis	37,723
25		18	(h)	Coventry C	D	0-0		17,561
26		24	(a)	Manchester U	L	0-2		51,367
27	Feb	14	(a)	Sheffield W	D	1-1	Quinn	24,792
28		25	(a)	Oxford U	D	0-0		13,296
29	Mar	7	(a)	Chelsea	L	0-1		29,301
30		10	(h)	Liverpool	L	0-1		47,777
31		17	(h)	Nottingham F	D	0-0		18,352
32		21	(a)	Watford	L	0-2		18,172
33		28	(h)	Everton	L	0-1		36,218
34	Apr	8	(a)	West Ham U	L	1-3	Hayes (pen)	26,174
35		11	(h)	Charlton A	W	2-1	Davis, Hayes	26,111
36		14	(h)	Newcastle U	L	0-1		17,353
37		18	(a)	Wimbledon	W	2-1	Davis, Merson	8,515
38		20	(h)	Leicester C	W	4-1	Davis, Hayes 2 (1 pen), Nicholas	18,767
39		25	(a)	Manchester C	L	0-3		18,072
40	May	2	(h)	Aston Villa	W	2-1	Hayes 2 (1 pen)	18,463
41		4	(a)	Queen's Park R	W	4-1	Rix 2, Merson, Hayes	13,387
42		9	(h)	Norwich C	L	1-2	Merson	24,001

FINAL LEAGUE POSITION: 4th in Division One

Appearances
Sub Appearances
Goals

FA Cup

3	Jan	10	(a)	Reading	W	3-1	Nicholas 2, Hayes (pen)	16,822
4		31	(h)	Plymouth A	W	6-1	Nicholas, Davis, Quinn, Rocastle, Anderson 2	39,029
5	Feb	21	(h)	Barnsley	W	2-0	Hayes (pen), Nicholas	28,302
6	Mar	14	(h)	Watford	L	1-3	Allinson	43,276

Appearances
Sub Appearances
Goals

League Cup

2	Sep	23	(h)	Huddersfield T	W	2-0	Davis, Quinn	15,194
	Oct	7	(a)	Huddersfield T	D	1-1	Haynes	8,713
3		28	(h)	Manchester C	W	3-1	Rocastle, Hayes (pen), Davis	21,604
4	Nov	18	(a)	Charlton A	W	2-0	Quinn, Curbishley (og)	28,301
5	Jan	21	(h)	Nottingham F	W	2-0	Nicholas, Hayes	38,617
SF	Feb	8	(h)	Tottenham H	L	0-1		41,306
	Mar	1	(a)	Tottenham H	W	2-1§	Anderson, Quinn	37,099
R		4	(a)	Tottenham H	W	2-1	Allinson, Rocastle	41,055
F	Apr	5	(n*)	Liverpool	W	2-1	Nicholas 2	96,000

§After extra-time. *Played at Wembley Stadium.

Appearances
Sub Appearances
Goals

Appearances, substitute appearances and goals grid.

Football League Division One

Lukic J	Anderson VA	Sansom KG	Robson SI	O'Leary DA	Adams TA	Rocastle D	Davis PV	Quinn NJ	Nicholas C	Rix G	Hayes M	Williams SC	Groves P	Allinson IJR	Caesar GC	Merson PC	Thomas ML	Wilmot RJ	
1	2	3	4	5	6	7*	8	9	10	11	12								1
1	2	3	4	5	6	7	8	9	10	11*	12								2
1	2	3	4*	5	6	7	8	9	10	11		12							3
1	2	3	4	5	6	7*	8	9	10	11	12								4
1	2	3	4	5	6	7*	8	9	10	11	12								5
1	2	3		5	6	7	8	9*	10	11		4	12						6
1	2	3		5	6	7	8	9	10	11*		4	12						7
1	2	3		5	6	7	8	9	10*			4	11	12					8
1	2	3		5	6	7	8	9				4	11*	10	12				9
1	2	3		5*	6	7	8	9			11	4	10	12					10
1	2	3		5	6	7	8	9*			11	4	10		12				11
1	2	3		5	6	7	8	9*			11	4	10	12					12
1	2	3		5	6	7	8	9			11	4	10*		12				13
1	2	3		5	6	7	8	9			11	4	10						14
1	2	3		5	6	7*	8	9			11	4	10	12					15
1	2	3		5	6	7	8	9*			11	4		10	12				16
1	2	3		5	6	7	8	9			11	4	10						17
1	2	3		5	6	7	8	9		12	11	4	10*						18
1	2	3		5	6	7*	8	9			11	4	10		12				19
1	2	3		5	6	7	8	9		12	11	4	10*						20
1	2	3		5	6	7	8	9			11	4	10*		12				21
1	2	3		5	6	7	8	9	10	11*		4	12						22
1	2	3		5	6	7*	8	9	10	11		4	12						23
1	2	3		5	6	7	8	9*	10	12	11	4							24
1	2	3		5	6	7	8	9	10	12	11*	4							25
1	2	3		5	6	7	8	9	10*	11		4	12						26
1		3		5	6		8	9	10	11		4*	7	12		2			27
1	2	3		5	6	7	8	9	12	11	10*	4							28
1	2	3		5	6	7		9		11*	10	8	12	4					29
1	2	3		5	6	7		9	10			8	12	11					30
					6	7		9	10			4	8*	12	5	11			31
1		3		5	6		8	9*	10	12	11		7	2		4			32
1	2	3		5	6	7	8	9	10	11*		4	12						33
	2			5	6	7	8		10	12	11*	4	9				3	1	34
1	2	3		5	6	7	8	9*	10	11		4	12						35
1	2			5	6	7*	8		10	12	11	4	9				3		36
1				5	6	7*	8		10	11		4	12	3	9				37
	2	3		5*	6		8		10	11	7	4		12	9			1	38
	2				6		8		10	11	7	4	12	5	9*	3		1	39
	2			5	6	7	8	9*	10		11	4	12				3	1	40
	2				6		8		10	11	7	4		5	9	3		1	41
	2*			5	6		8		10	11	7	4	12		9	3		1	42
36	40	35	5	39	42	36	39	35	25	13	31	33	19	5	6	5	12	6	
								3	5	4	1	6	9	9	2				
	4			6	2	4	8	4	2	19	2	3					3		

1 own-goal

FA Cup

Lukic J	Anderson VA	Sansom KG	Robson SI	O'Leary DA	Adams TA	Rocastle D	Davis PV	Quinn NJ	Nicholas C	Rix G	Hayes M	Williams SC	Groves P	Allinson IJR	Caesar GC	Merson PC	Thomas ML	Wilmot RJ	
1	2	3		5	6	7	8	9	10		11	4							3
1	2	3		5	6	7	8	9	10		11*	4	12*	14					4
1	2	3		5	6	7	8	9*	12		11	10	4*	14					5
1	2	3		5	6	7		9	12		11*	4	8	10*					6
4	4	4		4	4	4	3	4	2		4	3	2	2					
									2			1		1		2			
							1	1	1	4		2		1					

1 own-goal

Littlewoods Cup

Lukic J	Anderson VA	Sansom KG	Robson SI	O'Leary DA	Adams TA	Rocastle D	Davis PV	Quinn NJ	Nicholas C	Rix G	Hayes M	Williams SC	Groves P	Allinson IJR	Caesar GC	Merson PC	Thomas ML	Wilmot RJ	
1	2	3		5	6	7	8	9*	10	11		4	12						2
1	2	3		5	6	7	8	9		12	4	11	10*						
1	2	3		5	6	7	8	9*			11	4	10	12					3
1	2	3		5	6	7	8	9			11	4	10*	12					4
1	2	3		5	6	7	8	9*	10	12	11	4							5
1		3		5	6		8	9	10*	12	11	4	7		2*		14		SF
1	2	3		5	6	7	8	9	10	11*			12		4				
1	2	3		5	6	7	8	9	10*	11			12		4				R
1	2	3		5	6	7	8	9*	10	11*	4	12			14				F
9	8	9		9	9	8	9	9	6	1	7	7	4	1	1		2		
									2	1		2	4		2				
	1					2	2	3	3		3		1						

1 own-goal

1987-88

Manager: G.Graham

1	Aug	15	(h)	Liverpool	L 1-2	Davis	54,703
2		19	(a)	Manchester U	D 0-0		42,890
3		22	(a)	Queen's Park R	L 0-2		18,981
4		29	(h)	Portsmouth	W 6-0	Smith 3, Adams, Rocastle, Davis	30,865
5		31	(a)	Luton T	D 1-1	Davis	8,745
6	Sep	12	(a)	Nottingham F	W 1-0	Smith	18,490
7		19	(h)	Wimbledon	W 3-0	Rocastle, Smith, Thomas (pen)	27,752
8		26	(h)	West Ham U	W 1-0	Sansom	40,127
9	Oct	3	(a)	Charlton A	W 3-0	Thomas, Adams, Groves	15,326
10		10	(h)	Oxford U	W 2-0	Davis, Williams	25,244
11		18	(a)	Tottenham H	W 2-1	Rocastle, Thomas	36,680
12		24	(h)	Derby C	W 2-1	Richardson, Thomas (pen)	32,374
13		31	(a)	Newcastle U	W 1-0	Smith	23,622
14	Nov	3	(h)	Chelsea	W 3-1	Richardson 2, Wegerle (og)	40,230
15		14	(a)	Norwich C	W 4-2	Rocastle 2, Thomas, Groves	20,558
16		21	(h)	Southampton	L 0-1		32,477
17		28	(a)	Watford	L 0-2		19,598
18	Dec	5	(h)	Sheffield W	W 3-1	Groves, Richardson, Merson	23,670
19		13	(a)	Coventry C	D 0-0		17,557
20		19	(h)	Everton	D 1-1	Rocastle	34,857
21		26	(h)	Nottingham F	L 0-2		31,211
22		28	(a)	Wimbledon	L 1-3	Quinn	12,473
23	Jan	1	(a)	Portsmouth	D 1-1	Smith	17,366
24		2	(h)	Queen's Park R	D 0-0		28,271
25		16	(a)	Liverpool	L 0-2		44,294
26		24	(h)	Manchester U	L 1-2	Quinn	29,392
27	Feb	13	(h)	Luton T	W 2-1	Thomas, Rocastle	22,615
28		27	(h)	Charlton A	W 4-0	Merson 2, Thomas, Smith	25,394
29	Mar	6	(h)	Tottenham H	W 2-1	Smith, Groves	37,143
30		19	(h)	Newcastle U	D 1-1	Groves	25,889
31		26	(a)	Derby C	D 0-0		18,382
32		30	(a)	Oxford U	D 0-0		9,088
33	Apr	2	(a)	Chelsea	D 1-1	McLaughlin (og)	26,084
34		4	(h)	Norwich C	W 2-0	Smith, Groves	19,341
35		9	(a)	Southampton	L 2-4	Davis, Bond (og)	14,521
36		12	(a)	West Ham U	W 1-0	Thomas	26,746
37		15	(h)	Watford	L 0-1		19,541
38		30	(a)	Sheffield W	D 3-3	Merson 2, Smith	16,681
39	May	2	(h)	Coventry C	D 1-1	Marwood (pen)	16,963
40		7	(a)	Everton	W 2-1	Thomas, Hayes	22,445

FINAL LEAGUE POSITION: 6th in Division One

Appearances
Sub Appearances
Goals

FA Cup

3	Jan	9	(h)	Millwall	W 2-0	Hayes, Rocastle	42,083
4		30	(a)	Brighton & HA	W 2-1	Richardson, Groves	26,467
5	Feb	20	(h)	Manchester U	W 2-1	Smith, Duxbury (og)	54,161
6	Mar	12	(h)	Nottingham F	L 1-2	Rocastle	50,157

Appearances
Sub Appearances
Goals

League Cup

2	Sep	23	(a)	Doncaster R	W 3-0	Groves, Smith, Williams	5,469
	Oct	6	(h)	Doncaster R	W 1-0	Rocastle	18,321
3		27	(h)	Bournemouth	W 3-0	Richardson, Smith, Thomas (pen)	26,050
4	Nov	17	(h)	Stoke C	W 3-0	O'Leary, Rocastle, Richardson	30,058
5	Jan	20	(a)	Sheffield W	W 1-0	Winterburn	34,535
SF	Feb	7	(a)	Everton	W 1-0	Groves	25,476
		24	(h)	Everton	W 3-1	Thomas, Rocastle, Smith	51,148
F	Apr	24	(n*)	Luton T	L 2-3	Hayes, Smith	95,732

*Played at Wembley Stadium

Appearances
Sub Appearances
Goals

312

Football appearance and goal record table (player columns with match-by-match shirt numbers).

Lukic J	Thomas ML	Sansom KG	Williams SC	O'Leary DA	Adams TA	Rocastle D	Davis PV	Smith AM	Nicholas C	Hayes M	Groves P	Rix G	Merson PC	Richardson K	Caesar GC	Quinn NJ	Winterburn N	Dixon LM	Marwood B	Campbell K	
1	2	3	4	5	6	7*	8	9	10	11	12										1
1	2	3	4	5	6	7	8	9	10*	11	12										2
1	2	3	4	5	6	7*	8	9	10	11			12								3
1	2	3	4	5	6	7	8	9			10*	11†	12	14							4
1	2	3	4	5	6	7	8	9			10	11									5
1	2	3	4	5	6	7*	8	9			12	10	11								6
1	2	3	4†	5	6	7	8	9			10*	11	12	14							7
1	2	3	4	5	6	7*	8	9			12	10	11								8
1	2	3	4	5	6	7*	8	9			12	10	11								9
1	2	3	4	5	6	7*	8	9†			12	10		11	14						10
1	2	3	4	5	6	7	8	9			12	10*		11							11
1	2	3	4	5	6	7	8	9			10*		12	11							12
1	2	3	4*	5	6†	7	8	9			12	10		11	14						13
1	2	3	4	5	6	7	8	9			10		11								14
1	2	3	4	5	6†	7	8	9			10		11	14							15
1	2	3	4	5	6	7	8	9			10*		11	12†	14						16
1	2	3	4	5	6	7	8	9			12	10	11*								17
1	2	3	4	5	6	7	8*	9			10	12	11								18
1	2	3	4	5	6	7		9	8*	10	12	11									19
1	2	3	4	5	6	7	8	9			10	12	11*								20
1	2	3	4	5*	6	7		14			10	8†	11	12	9						21
1	2	3	4		6	7		12	8*	10	11	5	9								22
1	2		4		6	7		12	8	10†	14	11	5	9*	3						23
1		3	4		6	7		9	8	12	10*	11	5		2						24
1	12	3	4		6	7†		9	8	14	11	5*	10	2							25
1	2		4	5	6	7		9	12	8*	11	10	3								26
1	4			5	6†	7		9	8	10	11	14	3	2							27
1	4	3			6	7	14	9	8	10*	11†	5	12	2							28
1	4	3			6	7		9	8	10	11	5	2								29
1	4			6	7	8	9†	11	10		5	14	3	2							30
1	4		6	7*	8	9†	11	10	12		5	14	3	2							31
1	4	3		6	7†	8	9	10	12		5	14	2	11*							32
1		4		6	7	8	11	10			5	9	3	2							33
1		3	4	6	7	8	9	11	10		5		2								34
1	6	3	4	7	8	9	11	10*			12	5	2								35
1	4	3	6	7	8	9		12	10	11*	5	2									36
1	4	3	6	7	8	9	12		10	11*	5	2									37
1	4	3	6	7	8*	9	14		10	12	5	2†	11								38
1	4	3	6	7	9	12	14	10*	8†	5	2	11									39
1	4	3	6	7	9	10†	12	8	5*	2	11	14									40
40	36	34	29	23	39	40	28	36	3	17	28	7	7	24	17	6	16	6	4		
1					1	3		10	6	3	8	5	5	5	1		1				
9	1	1		2	7	5	11		1	6		5	4		2		1				

3 own-goals

Lukic J	Thomas ML	Sansom KG	Williams SC	O'Leary DA	Adams TA	Rocastle D	Davis PV	Smith AM	Nicholas C	Hayes M	Groves P	Rix G	Merson PC	Richardson K	Caesar GC	Quinn NJ	Winterburn N	Dixon LM	Marwood B	Campbell K	
1		3	4	5	6	7		9		8	12	10*	11		2						3
1		3	4	5	6	7			12	9	8*	11		10	2						4
1	4	3	5†	6	7		9	8	10	14		11			2						5
1	4	3	5*	6	7	12	9	8†	10			11		14	2						6
4	2	4	2	4	4	4		3	3	3	1	1	4		1	4					
	1				1	1	1			1											
2		1	1	1	1		1														

1 own-goal

Lukic J	Thomas ML	Sansom KG	Williams SC	O'Leary DA	Adams TA	Rocastle D	Davis PV	Smith AM	Nicholas C	Hayes M	Groves P	Rix G	Merson PC	Richardson K	Caesar GC	Quinn NJ	Winterburn N	Dixon LM	Marwood B	Campbell K	
1	2	3	4	5	6	7	8	9			10*	11†		14		12					2
1	2	3	4		6	7	8	9	11	10			5								
1	2	3	4	5	6	7	8	9			10*	12	11								3
1	2	3	4	5	6	7	8	9			12	10*	11								4
1		3	4	5	6	7		9			12	8	11	10*	2						5
1	4	3		5	6	7†	9*		8	10		11	14	12	2						SF
1	4	3	5†	6	7		14	9	8	10		11			2						
1	4	3	6	7	8	9		14	10†		11		5		2						F
8	7	8	5	6	8	8	5	8	3	7		6	2	1	4						
	1								2	1		1	1	1	2						
2		1	1		3		4		1	2		2		1							

313

1988-89

Manager: G.Graham

1	Aug	27	(a)	Wimbledon	W	5-1	Smith 3, Marwood, Merson		15,710
2	Sep	3	(h)	Aston Villa	L	2-3	Marwood, Smith		37,417
3		10	(a)	Tottenham H	W	3-2	Winterburn, Marwood, Smith		32,621
4		17	(h)	Southampton	D	2-2	Marwood (pen), Smith		31,384
5		24	(a)	Sheffield W	L	1-2	Smith		17,830
6	Oct	1	(a)	West Ham U	W	4-1	Smith 2, Thomas, Rocastle		27,658
7		22	(h)	Queen's Park R	W	2-1	Adams, Smith		33,202
8		25	(a)	Luton T	D	1-1	Smith		10,548
9		29	(h)	Coventry C	W	2-0	Thomas, Adams		31,273
10	Nov	6	(a)	Nottingham F	W	4-1	Smith, Bould, Adams, Marwood		19,038
11		12	(a)	Newcastle U	W	1-0	Bould		24,003
12		19	(h)	Middlesbrough	W	3-0	Merson 2, Rocastle		32,294
13		26	(a)	Derby C	L	1-2	Thomas		21,209
14	Dec	4	(h)	Liverpool	D	1-1	Smith		31,863
15		10	(a)	Norwich C	D	0-0			23,069
16		17	(h)	Manchester U	W	2-1	Thomas, Merson		37,422
17		26	(a)	Charlton A	W	3-2	Marwood 2 (1 pen), Merson		18,439
18		31	(a)	Aston Villa	W	3-0	Smith, Rocastle, Groves		32,486
19	Jan	2	(h)	Tottenham H	W	2-0	Merson, Thomas		45,129
20		14	(a)	Everton	W	3-1	Merson, Smith, Richardson		34,825
21		21	(h)	Sheffield W	D	1-1	Merson		33,490
22	Feb	4	(h)	West Ham U	W	2-1	Groves, Smith		40,139
23		11	(a)	Millwall	W	2-1	Marwood, Smith		21,854
24		18	(a)	Queen's Park R	D	0-0			20,543
25		21	(a)	Coventry C	L	0-1			21,390
26		25	(h)	Luton T	W	2-0	Groves, Smith		31,012
27		28	(h)	Millwall	D	0-0			37,524
28	Mar	11	(h)	Nottingham F	L	1-3	Smith		39,639
29		21	(h)	Charlton A	D	2-2	Rocastle, Davis		30,259
30		25	(a)	Southampton	W	3-1	Groves, Rocastle, Merson		19,202
31	Apr	2	(a)	Manchester U	D	1-1	Adams		37,977
32		8	(h)	Everton	W	2-0	Dixon, Quinn		37,608
33		15	(h)	Newcastle U	W	1-0	Marwood		38,023
34	May	1	(h)	Norwich C	W	5-0	Winterburn, Smith 2, Rocastle, Thomas		28,449
35		6	(a)	Middlesbrough	W	1-0	Hayes		21,803
36		13	(h)	Derby C	L	1-2	Smith		41,008
37		17	(h)	Wimbledon	D	2-2	Winterburn, Merson		39,132
38		26	(a)	Liverpool	W	2-0	Smith, Thomas		41,728

FINAL LEAGUE POSITION: 1st in Division One

Appearances
Sub Appearances
Goals

FA Cup

3	Jan	8	(a)	West Ham U	D	2-2	Merson 2		22,017
R		11	(h)	West Ham U	L	0-1			44,124

Appearances
Sub Appearances
Goals

League Cup

2	Sep	28	(a)	Hull C	W	2-1	Winterburn, Marwood		11,450
	Oct	12	(h)	Hull C	W	3-0	Merson, Smith 2		17,885
3	Nov	2	(a)	Liverpool	D	1-1	Rocastle		31,951
R		9	(h)	Liverpool	D	0-0*			54,029
2R	Nov	23	(n†)	Liverpool	L	1-2	Merson		21,708

†Played at Villa Park.   *After extra-time.

Appearances
Sub Appearances
Goals

314

Main table

Lukic J	Dixon LM	Winterburn N	Thomas ML	Bould SA	Adams TA	Rocastle D	Davis PV	Smith AM	Merson PC	Marwood B	O'Leary DA	Groves P	Richardson K	Hayes M	Caesar GC	Quinn NJ	#
1	2	3	4	5	6	7	8	9	10	11							1
1	2	3	4		6	7*	8	9	10	11	5	12					2
1	2	3	4		6	7*	8	9	10	11†	5	14	12				3
1	2	3	4		6	7	8*	9	10†	11	5		12	14			4
1	2	3	4		6	7	8	9	10*	11	5	12					5
1	2	3	4	5	6	7	8	9		11	10*		12				6
1	2	3	4	5	6	7		9	10*	11	12	8					7
1	2	3	4	5	6	7		9	10	11		8					8
1	2	3	4	5	6	7*		9	10†	11		14	8	12			9
1	2	3	4	5	6	7		9	10*	11		8	12				10
1	2	3	4	5	6	7*		9	12	11		8	10				11
1	2	3	4	5	6	7		9	10	11*		8	12				12
1	2	3	4	5	6	7		9	10		12	8*	11				13
1	2	3	4	5	6	7		9	10	11*		8	12				14
1	2	3	4	5	6	7		9	10*	11		8	12				15
1	2	3	4	5	6	7		9	10	11		8					16
1		3	4	5	6	7		9	10	11	2		8				17
1		3	4	5	6	7		9	10*	11	2	12	8				18
1		3	4	5	6	7	12	9	10	11†	2	14	8*				19
1	2	3	14		7	4	9	10*	11†	5	12	8			6		20
1	2	3	12		7†	4	9	10	11	5	14	8			6*		21
1	2	3	4	12	6	7		9	10†		5*	11	8	14			22
1	2	3	4	12	6	7		9	10	11	5*		8				23
1	2*	3	4	12	6	7		9	10†	11	5		8	14			24
1		3	4	2	6	7		9	10	11*	5		8	12			25
1		3	4	2	6	7*		9	12	11	5	10	8				26
1	14	3	4	2	6	7*		9	12	11	5	10	8†				27
1	12	3	4	2*	6	7		9	14	11	5	10†	8				28
1	2	3	12		6	7	4	9	10†	11	5	14	8*				29
1	2	3			6	7	4	9	12	11	5	10*	8				30
1	2	3	12	10	6	7	4*	9	14	11†	5		8				31
1	2	3	4	10	6	7			12	11*	5		8			9	32
1	2	3	4	10	6	7†			12	11	5*	14	8			9	33
1	2	3	4	10	6	7	9*	11†		5		8	14	12			34
1	2	3	4	10	6	7		9	11*		5		8	12			35
1	2	3	4	10*	6	7		9	11†		5	14	8	12			36
1	2	3	4	14	6	7		9	11†		5	12	8	10*			37
1	2	3	4	10*	6	7		9	11†		5	12	8	14			38
38	31	38	33	26	36	38	11	36	29	31	26	6	32	3	2	2	
2		4	4			1		8			15	2	14			1	
	1	3	7	2	4	6	1	23	10	9		4	1	1		1	

Second table

Lukic J	Dixon LM	Winterburn N	Thomas ML	Bould SA	Adams TA	Rocastle D	Davis PV	Smith AM	Merson PC	Marwood B	O'Leary DA	Groves P	Richardson K	Hayes M	Caesar GC	Quinn NJ	#
1		3	4	5*	6	7	12	9	10	11†	2	14	8				3
1	2	3	4		6	7*	12	9	10	11†	5	14	8				R
2	1	2	2	1	2	2		2	2	2	2		2				
							2				2						
											2						

Third table

Lukic J	Dixon LM	Winterburn N	Thomas ML	Bould SA	Adams TA	Rocastle D	Davis PV	Smith AM	Merson PC	Marwood B	O'Leary DA	Groves P	Richardson K	Hayes M	Caesar GC	Quinn NJ	#
1	2	3	4*	5	6	7†	8	9		11		10	12	14			2
1	2	3	4	5	6	7	8*	9	10†	11		12	14				3
1	2	3	4	5	6	7		9	10*	11	12	8					R
1	2	3	4	5	6	7		9	10*	11		8	12				R
1	2	3	4	5	6	7		9	10	11*		8	12				2R
5	5	5	5	5	5	2	5	4	5		1	3					
											1	2	4				
	1				1	2	2	1									

1989-90

Manager: G.Graham

1	Aug	19	(a)	Manchester U	L	1-4 Rocastle	47,245
2		22	(h)	Coventry C	W	2-0 Thomas, Marwood	33,886
3		26	(h)	Wimbledon	D	0-0	32,279
4	Sep	9	(h)	Sheffield W	W	5-0 Merson, Smith, Thomas, Adams, Marwood	30,058
5		16	(a)	Nottingham F	W	2-1 Marwood, Merson	22,216
6		23	(h)	Charlton A	W	1-0 Marwood (pen)	34,583
7		30	(a)	Chelsea	D	0-0	31,833
8	Oct	14	(h)	Manchester C	W	4-0 Groves 2, Merson, Thomas	40,414
9		18	(a)	Tottenham H	L	1-2 Thomas	33,944
10		21	(a)	Everton	L	0-3	32,917
11		28	(h)	Derby C	D	1-1 Smith	33,189
12	Nov	4	(h)	Norwich C	W	4-3 Quinn, O'Leary, Dixon 2 (1 pen)	35,338
13		11	(a)	Millwall	W	2-1 Quinn, Thomas	17,265
14		18	(h)	Queen's Park R	W	3-0 Dixon (pen), Smith, Jonsson	38,236
15		26	(a)	Liverpool	L	1-2 Smith	35,983
16	Dec	3	(h)	Manchester U	W	1-0 Groves	34,484
17		9	(a)	Coventry C	W	1-0 Merson	16,255
18		16	(h)	Luton T	W	3-2 Smith, Marwood, Merson	28,761
19		26	(a)	Southampton	L	0-1	20,229
20		30	(a)	Aston Villa	L	1-2 Adams	40,665
21	Jan	1	(h)	Crystal P	W	4-1 Smith 2, Dixon, Adams	38,711
22		13	(a)	Wimbledon	L	0-1	13,793
23		20	(h)	Tottenham H	W	1-0 Adams	46,132
24	Feb	17	(a)	Sheffield W	L	0-1	20,640
25		27	(a)	Charlton A	D	0-0	17,504
26	Mar	3	(a)	Queen's Park R	L	0-2	18,067
27		7	(h)	Nottingham F	W	3-0 Groves, Adams, Campbell	31,879
28		10	(a)	Manchester C	D	1-1 Marwood	29,087
29		17	(h)	Chelsea	L	0-1	33,805
30		24	(a)	Derby C	W	3-1 Hayes 2, Campbell	17,514
31		31	(h)	Everton	W	1-0 Smith	35,223
32	Apr	11	(h)	Aston Villa	L	0-1	30,060
33		14	(a)	Crystal P	D	1-1 Hayes	28,094
34		18	(h)	Liverpool	D	1-1 Merson	33,395
35		21	(a)	Luton T	L	0-2	11,595
36		28	(h)	Millwall	W	2-0 Davis, Merson	25,607
37	May	2	(h)	Southampton	W	2-1 Dixon (pen), Rocastle	23,732
38		5	(a)	Norwich C	D	2-2 Smith 2	19,256

FINAL LEAGUE POSITION: 4th in Division One

Appearances
Sub Appearances
Goals

FA Cup

3	Jan	6	(a)	Stoke C	W	1-0 Quinn	23,827
4		27	(h)	Queen's Park R	D	0-0	43,483
R		31	(a)	Queen's Park R	L	0-2	21,547

Appearances
Sub Appearances
Goals

League Cup

2	Sep	19	(h)	Plymouth A	W	2-0 Smith, Brimacombe (og)	26,865
	Oct	3	(a)	Plymouth A	W	6-1 Thomas 3, Smith, Groves, Byrne (og)	17,360
3		25	(h)	Liverpool	W	1-0 Smith	40,814
4	Nov	22	(a)	Oldham A	L	1-3 Quinn	14,924

Appearances
Sub Appearances
Goals

Lukic J	Dixon LM	Winterburn N	Thomas ML	O'Leary DA	Adams TA	Rocastle D	Richardson K	Smith AM	Merson PC	Marwood B	Caesar GC	Groves P	Hayes M	Jonsson S	Quinn NJ	Campbell KJ	Davis PV	Bould SA	Pates CG	Ampadu K	
1	2	3	4	5	6*	7	8	9	10†	11	12	14									1
1	2	3	4	5	6	7*	8	9	10	11		12									2
1	2	3	4	5	6	7	8	9	10*	11		12									3
1	2	3	4	5	6	7	8	9	10	11											4
1	2	3	4	5	6	7	8	9	10*	11		12									5
1	2	3	4	5	6	7*	8	9	10	11		12									6
1	2	3	4	5	6	7*	8	9	12			10	11								7
1	2	3	4	5	6	7	8*	9	14	11†		10		12							8
1	2	3	4	5	6	7	8†	9*	12			10	11	14							9
1	2	3	4	5	6	7	8	12	10				11*		9						10
1	2	3†	4	5	6	7	8	9	11					14	10*	12					11
1	2	3	4	5	6	7	8	9	11*			12			10						12
1	2	3	4	5	6	7	8	9		11		12			10*						13
1	2	3	4	5	6	7*	8	9		11†		12		14	10						14
1	2	3	4	5†	6	7	8	9				11	12	14	10*						15
1	2	3	4	5	6	7	8	9	12	11*		10									16
1	2	3	4	5	6	7	8	9	12	11*		10									17
1	2	3	4	5	6	7	8	9*	12	11		10									18
1	2	3	4	5	6	7	8	9	10†	11*		14					12				19
1	2	3	4	5	6	12	8	9	11			7						10*			20
1	2	3†	4	5	6	12	8	9*	11			7					14	10			21
1	2	3		5*	6	14	8	9†	11		12	7					4	10			22
1	2		4	5	6	7	8	9				11					3	10			23
1	2			5	6	7†	8	9	11		12					14	4	10	3*		24
1	2	3	4		6	7	8	9	10	11*						12		5			25
1	2	3	4*	12	6	7	8	9†	10			11				14		5			26
1	2	3	4	14	6	7	8	9	10*			11†				12		5			27
1	2	3	4		6	7*	8	9		11			12			10		5			28
1	2	3	4	14	6	7*	8	9				11	12			10†		5			29
1	2	3	4	12	6		8	9				11	7			10†		5*		14	30
1	2	3	4	12	6		8*	9				11	7			10†		5		14	31
1	2	3	4	8	6			9	12			11	7*			10		5			32
1	2	3	4	8	6			9	12			11	7			10*	14	5†			33
1	2	3	4	8	6			9	10			11*				12	7	5†	14		34
1	2	3	4	8*	6	14		9	10†				12			11	7	5			35
1	2	3	4†		6	7	14	9	10	11*						12	8	5			36
1	2	3	4		6	12	7*	9	10	11†		14					8	5			37
1	2	3	14	12	6	7		9				11	4			10	8†	5*			38
38	38	36	35	28	38	28	32	37	21	17		20	8		6	8	8	19	1		
			1	6		5	1	1	8		3	10	4	5		7	3		1	2	
	5		5	1	5	2		10	7	6		4	3	1	2	2	1				

1	2		4*	5	6	14	8		11†			7		12	9		3	10			3
1	2	3	12	5	6	7	8	9	14			11					4*	10†			4
1	2	3	4	5	6	7	8	9	12			11*						10			R
3	3	2	2	3	3	2	3	2	1			3			1		2	3			
			1			1			2					1							
															1						

1	2	3	4	5	6	7	8	9	10*	11		12									2
1	2*	3	4	5	6	7	8	9	14		12	10†	11								
1	2	3	4	5	6	7	8	12	10				11*		9						3
1	2	3	4	5	6	7	8	9				12		11*	10						4
4	4	4	4	4	4	4	4	3	2	1		1	2	1	2						
								1	1		1	2									
			3					3				1			1						

2 own-goals

1990-91

Manager: G.Graham

1	Aug	25	(a)	Wimbledon	W 3-0	Merson, Smith, Groves	13,733
2		29	(h)	Luton T	W 2-1	Merson, Thomas	32,723
3	Sep	1	(h)	Tottenham H	D 0-0		40.009
4		8	(a)	Everton	D 1-1	Groves	29,919
5		15	(h)	Chelsea	W 4-1	Limpar, Dixon (pen), Merson, Rocastle	40,475
6		22	(a)	Nottingham F	W 2-0	Rocastle, Limpar	26,013
7		29	(a)	Leeds U	D 2-2	Limpar 2	30,085
8	Oct	6	(h)	Norwich C	W 2-0	Davis 2	36,737
9		20	(a)	Manchester U	W 1-0	Limpar	47,232
10		27	(h)	Sunderland	W 1-0	Dixon (pen)	38,485
11	Nov	3	(a)	Coventry C	W 2-0	Limpar 2	15,336
12		10	(a)	Crystal P	D 0-0		28,282
13		17	(h)	Southampton	W 4-0	Smith 2, Merson, Limpar	36,229
14		24	(a)	Queen's Park R	W 3-1	Merson, Smith, Campbell	18,555
15	Dec	2	(h)	Liverpool	W 3-0	Merson, Dixon (pen), Smith	40,419
16		8	(a)	Luton T	D 1-1	Smith	12,506
17		15	(h)	Wimbledon	D 2-2	Merson, Adams	30,164
18		23	(a)	Aston Villa	D 0-0		22,687
19		26	(h)	Derby C	W 3-0	Smith 2, Merson	25,558
20		29	(h)	Sheffield U	W 4-1	Dixon (pen), Smith 2, Thomas	37,810
21	Jan	1	(a)	Manchester C	W 1-0	Smith	30,579
22		12	(a)	Tottenham H	D 0-0		34,753
23		19	(h)	Everton	W 1-0	Merson	35,349
24	Feb	2	(a)	Chelsea	L 1-2	Smith	29,094
25		23	(h)	Crystal P	W 4-0	O'Leary, Merson, Smith, Campbell	42,162
26	Mar	3	(a)	Liverpool	W 1-0	Merson	37,221
27		17	(h)	Leeds U	W 2-0	Campbell 2	26,218
28		20	(h)	Nottingham F	D 1-1	Campbell	34,152
29		23	(a)	Norwich C	D 0-0		20,131
30		30	(a)	Derby C	W 2-0	Smith 2	18,397
31	Apr	3	(h)	Aston Villa	W 5-0	Campbell 2, Smith 2, Davis	41,868
32		6	(a)	Sheffield U	W 2-0	Campbell, Smith	26,920
33		9	(a)	Southampton	D 1-1	M.Adams (og)	21,200
34		17	(h)	Manchester C	D 2-2	Campbell, Merson	38,412
35		23	(h)	Queen's Park R	W 2-0	Dixon (pen), Merson	42,393
36	May	4	(a)	Sunderland	D 0-0		22,606
37		6	(h)	Manchester U	W 3-1	Smith 3 (1 pen)	40,229
38		11	(h)	Coventry C	W 6-1	Limpar 3, Smith, Groves, Peake (og)	41,039

FINAL LEAGUE POSITION: 1st in Division One

Appearances
Sub Appearances
Goals

FA Cup

3	Jan	5	(h)	Sunderland	W 2-1	Smith, Limpar	35,128
4		27	(h)	Leeds U	D 0-0		30,905
R		30	(a)	Leeds U	D 1-1†	Limpar	27,763
2R	Feb	13	(h)	Leeds U	D 0-0†		30,433
3R		16	(a)	Leeds U	W 2-1	Merson, Dixon	27,190
5		27	(a)	Shrewsbury T	W 1-0	Thomas	12,536
6	Mar	9	(h)	Cambridge U	W 2-1	Campbell, Adams	42,960
SF	Apr	14	(n*)	Tottenham H	L 1-3	Smith	77,893

†After extra time. *Played at Wembley Stadium.

Appearances
Sub Appearances
Goals

League Cup

2	Sep	25	(a)	Chester C	W 1-0	Merson	4,135
	Oct	9	(h)	Chester C	W 5-0	Groves 2, Adams, Smith, Merson	22,890
3		30	(a)	Manchester C	W 2-1	Groves, Adams	26,825
4	Nov	28	(h)	Manchester U	L 2-6	Smith 2	40,884

Appearances
Sub Appearances
Goals

318

Seaman DA	Dixon LM	Winterburn N	Thomas ML	Bould SA	Adams TA	Rocastle D	Davis PV	Smith AM	Merson PC	Limpar AE	Groves P	Campbell KJ	Linighan A	Hillier D	Jonsson S	O'Leary DA	Cole AA	Pates CG	
1	2	3	4	5	6	7	8	9	10	11*	12								1
1	2	3	4	5	6	7	8	9	10	11*	12								2
1	2	3	4	5	6	7	8	9	10*	11	12								3
1	2	3	4	5	6	7	8	9*	10	11	12								4
1	2	3	4	5†	6	7	8		10	11	9*	12	14						5
1	2	3	4	5	6	7*	8	12	10	11	9								6
1	2	3*		5	6	7	8	9	10†	11		14	12	4					7
1	2	3		5	6	7	8	9	10*	11†	12	14		4					8
1	2	3	4	5	6	7*	8	9	10	11	12								9
1	2	3	4	5	6	7*	8	9	10	11	12								10
1	2	3	4	5	6		8	9*	10	11	7†	12	14						11
1	2	3	4	5	6		8	14	10*	11†	12	9		7					12
1	2*	3	4	5	6		8	9	10	11	7†	14	12						13
1	2	3	4	5	6†		8	9	10	11	7*	12		14					14
1	2	3	4	5	6		8	9	10	11				7					15
1	2	3	4	5	6		8	9	10	11*	12			7					16
1	2	3*	4	5	6		8	9	10	11	7	12							17
1	2	3	4	5	12		8	9	10	11*	7	6		7					18
1	2	3	4	5		7*	8	9	10	11†	12		6	14					19
1	2	3†	4	5			8	9	10	11	7*	6	14	12					20
1	2	3	4	5			8	9	10	11†	14	6	12	7*					21
1	2	3	4	5			8*	9	10†	11	14	6	12	7					22
1	2	3	4	5†			8	9	10	11*	6	12	14	7					23
1	2	3	4	5*			8	9	10	11†	7	14	6	12					24
1	2	3	4	5	14		8	9	10†	11	6*			7		12			25
1	2	3	4	5	6†	12	14	9	10	11*	8			7					26
1	2	3	4	5	6			9	10	11	8			7					27
1	2	3	4	5	6		8*	9	10†	14	12	11		7					28
1	2	3		5	6	4†	8	9	10	11*	12		14	7					29
1	2	3		5	6	7†	8	9	10	11*	12	4		14					30
1	2	3	12	5	6		8	9	10†	11	14	7		4*					31
1	2	3	14	5	6		8	9	10*	11†	12	7		4					32
1	2	3	12	5	6		8	9	14	11†	10	7		4*					33
1	2†	3	4	5	6		8	9	10*	11	12	7		14					34
1	2	3		5	6		8	9	10*	11†	14	7	4	12					35
1	2	3		5	6		8	9	10	11*	7	4		12					36
1	2	3	12	5	6		8	9	10	11†	7	4*		14					37
1	2	3		5	6		8	9	10*	11	14	7†	12	4					38
38	38	38	27	38	30	13	36	35	36	32	13	15	7	9	2	11			
			4		3	1	2	1	2	19	7	3	7			10	1	1	
	5		2		1	2	3	22	13	11	3	9				1			

2 own-goals

Seaman DA	Dixon LM	Winterburn N	Thomas ML	Bould SA	Adams TA	Rocastle D	Davis PV	Smith AM	Merson PC	Limpar AE	Groves P	Campbell KJ	Linighan A	Hillier D	Jonsson S	O'Leary DA	Cole AA	Pates CG	
1	2	3	4	5			8	9	10	11*	7		6			12			3
1	2	3	4	5			8	9	10	11†	6	14		12		7*			4
1¹	2	3	4	5			8	9	10	11			6	7					R
1	2	3	4	5			8	9	10	11†	6*	12	14	7					2R
1	2	3	4	5			8	9	10		11	6		7					3R
1	2	3	4	5	6	12		9	10*	11		8		7					5
1	2	3	4	5	6		12	9	10	11	8*			7					6
1	2	3	4	5	6		8	9	10	11*	12	7							SF
8	8	8	8	8	3		6	8	8	5	3	4	3	3		5			
					1	1		1	2	1	1			1					
	1		1		1		2	1	2		1								

Seaman DA	Dixon LM	Winterburn N	Thomas ML	Bould SA	Adams TA	Rocastle D	Davis PV	Smith AM	Merson PC	Limpar AE	Groves P	Campbell KJ	Linighan A	Hillier D	Jonsson S	O'Leary DA	Cole AA	Pates CG	
1	2	3		5	6	7*	8	9	10		11	12	4						2
1	2	3		5†	6	7*	8	9	10		11	12	4	14					
1	2	3	4	5	6		8	9	10	11*	7	12							3
1	2	3	4	5	6		8	9	10	11*	7	12							4
4	4	4	2	4	4	2	4	4	4	2	4		2						
													4			1			
		2			3	2		3											

1991-92

Manager: G.Graham

1	Aug	17	(h)	Queen's Park R	D	1-1	Merson	38,099
2		20	(a)	Everton	L	1-3	Winterburn	31,200
3		24	(a)	Aston Villa	L	1-3	Smith	29,684
4		27	(h)	Luton T	W	2-0	Smith, Merson	25,898
5		31	(h)	Manchester C	W	2-1	Smith, Limpar	35,009
6	Sep	3	(a)	Leeds U	D	2-2	Smith 2	29,396
7		7	(h)	Coventry C	L	1-2	Adams	28,142
8		14	(a)	Crystal P	W	4-1	Campbell 2, Smith, Thomas	24,228
9		21	(h)	Sheffield U	W	5-2	Dixon (pen), Campbell, Rocastle, Smith, Groves	30,244
10		28	(a)	Southampton	W	4-0	Wright 3, Rocastle	18,050
11	Oct	5	(h)	Chelsea	W	3-2	Dixon (pen), Wright, Campbell	42,074
12		19	(a)	Manchester U	D	1-1	Rocastle	46,594
13		26	(h)	Notts C	W	2-0	Wright, Smith	30,011
14	Nov	2	(h)	West Ham U	L	0-1		33,539
15		16	(a)	Oldham A	D	1-1	Wright	15,681
16		23	(a)	Sheffield W	D	1-1	Bould	32,174
17	Dec	1	(h)	Tottenham H	W	2-0	Wright, Campbell	38,892
18		8	(a)	Nottingham F	L	2-3	Smith, Merson	22,095
19		21	(h)	Everton	W	4-2	Wright 4	29,684
20		26	(a)	Luton T	L	0-1		12,665
21		28	(a)	Manchester C	L	0-1		32,325
22	Jan	1	(h)	Wimbledon	D	1-1	Merson	26,339
23		11	(h)	Aston Villa	D	0-0		31,413
24		18	(a)	Queen's Park R	D	0-0		20,497
25		29	(a)	Liverpool	L	0-2		33,753
26	Feb	1	(h)	Manchester U	D	1-1	Rocastle	41,703
27		8	(a)	Notts C	W	1-0	Smith	11,221
28		11	(h)	Norwich C	D	1-1	Merson	22,352
29		15	(h)	Sheffield W	W	7-1	Campbell 2, Limpar 2, Smith, Wright, Merson	26,805
30		22	(a)	Tottenham H	D	1-1	Wright	33,124
31	Mar	10	(h)	Oldham A	W	2-1	Merson, Wright	22,096
32		14	(a)	West Ham U	W	2-0	Wright 2	22,640
33		22	(h)	Leeds U	D	1-1	Merson	27,844
34		28	(a)	Wimbledon	W	3-1	Parlour, Wright, Campbell	11,299
35		31	(h)	Nottingham F	D	3-3	Dixon (pen), Merson, Adams	27,036
36	Apr	4	(a)	Coventry C	W	1-0	Campbell	14,133
37		8	(a)	Norwich C	W	3-1	Wright 2 (1 pen), Campbell	12,971
38		11	(h)	Crystal P	W	4-1	Merson 3, Campbell	36,016
39		18	(a)	Sheffield W	D	1-1	Campbell	25,034
40		20	(h)	Liverpool	W	4-0	Wright 2, Hillier, Limpar	38,517
41		25	(a)	Chelsea	D	1-1	Dixon	26,003
42	May	2	(h)	Southampton	W	5-1	Wright 3 (1 pen), Campbell, Smith	37,702

FINAL LEAGUE POSITION: 4th in Division One

Appearances
Sub Appearances
Goals

FA Cup

3	Jan	4	(a)	Wrexham	L	1-2	Smith	13,343

Appearances
Sub Appearances
Goals

League Cup

2	Sep	25	(a)	Leicester C	D	1-1	Wright	20,679
	Oct	8	(h)	Leicester C	W	2-0	Merson, Wright	28,580
3		30	(a)	Coventry C	L	0-1		15,337

Appearances
Sub Appearances
Goals

Player appearance grid (shirt numbers worn per match; * and † denote substitute appearances).

#	Seaman DA	Dixon LM	Winterburn N	Hillier D	O'Leary DA	Adams TA	Campbell KJ	Davis PV	Smith AM	Merson PC	Limpar AE	Rocastle D	Groves P	Linighan A	Thomas ML	Pates CG	Wright IE	Bould SA	Carter JC	Parlour R	Lydersen P	Morrow SJ	Heaney NA
1	1	2	3	4	5*	6	7†	8	9	10	11	12	14										
2	1	2	3	4†	5	6		8	9	10	11*	7	12	14									
3	1	2	3		5*	6		8	9	10	11	7†	12	4	14								
4	1	2	3			6		8	9	10	11	7		5	4								
5	1	2	3			6	12	8	9	10	11†	7*		5	4	14							
6	1	2	3		7	6	11	8	9	10		12		5	4*								
7	1	2	3	12	6	4	8†	9	10	11*	7			5	14								
8	1	2	3	4†	14	6	11		9	10	7	8*	5	12									
9	1	2	3*	12	6	4	8		9	10	7	11†	5	14									
10	1	2	3		6	12		9	10*	11	7	5	4	8									
11	1	2	3	14	10	9	12	11*	7	5	4	6	8†										
12	1	2	3	6	11	4		9	10	7		5			8								
13	1	2	3	6	11*	4		9	10	12	7	5			8								
14	1	2	3		9	10	11	7	12	6	4*	5			8								
15	1	2	3	4	12	9	10	7	14	5	11†	8	6*										
16	1	2	3	4*	12	9	10	7	6	11		8	5										
17	1	2	3	4	14	11	9	10	12	7†	6	8*	5										
18	1	2	3	4	14	8	9	10	11*	7	6	5†	12										
19	1	2	3	4	12	6	14	9	10†	11	7*	8	5										
20	1	2	3	4	6	12	9	10	11*	7	8	5											
21	1	2	3	4†	6	11	9	10	7	14	12	8	5*										
22	1	2	3	4	6	12	9	10	7		8*		11										
23	1	2	3	4	5	6	8	9	10*	7	12	11											
24	1	2	3	5	6	4	9	10	7		8		11										
25	1	2	3	5*	6	9	10	7	14	8	12	11	4†										
26	1	2	3	4	6	9	10	14	7*	12	8	5	11†										
27	1	2	3*	4	6	14	9	10	11†	7		8	5	12									
28	1	2	3†	4	6	12	9	10	11*	7		8	5	14									
29	1	2	3	4	6	12	9*	10	11	7		8	5										
30	1	2	3	4*	12	11	9	10	14	7†	6	8	5										
31	1	2	3	4	12	6	9	10	11*	7		8	5										
32	1	2	3	4	14	6	12	9*	10	7	11†	8	5										
33	1	2	3	4*	9	6	11	10	14	7†		8	5	12									
34	1	2	3	4	6	9	10†	12	11*		8	5	7	14									
35	1	2	3	4	6	9	14	10	11	7*	8†	5	12										
36	1	2	3*	4	6	9	14	10	11†	12	8	5	7										
37	1		4	2*	6	9	14	10	11†	7	8	5	3	12									
38	1	3†	4	6	9	12	10	11*	7	8	5	2	14										
39	1	3	4	6	8	9	10	11*	7	5	2	12											
40	1	3	4	12	6	9	10	11	7	8	5	2*											
41	1	2	3	4	14	6	9	12	10†	11*	7	8	5										
42	1	2	3	4	6	9	12	10†	11*	7	8	5	14										
Apps	42	38	41	27	11	35	22	12	33	41	23	36	5	15	6	9	30	24	5	2	5		
Sub				14			9		6	1	6	3	8	2	4	2		1	1	4	2	2	1
Gls		4	1	1		2	13		12	12	4	4	1		1		24	1		1			

	Seaman DA	Dixon LM	Winterburn N	Hillier D	O'Leary DA	Adams TA	Campbell KJ	Davis PV	Smith AM	Merson PC	Limpar AE	Rocastle D	Groves P	Linighan A	Thomas ML	Pates CG	Wright IE	Bould SA	Carter JC	Parlour R	Lydersen P	Morrow SJ	Heaney NA	#
	1	2	3	4	5	6	8*		9	10		7	12				11							3
Apps	1	1	1	1	1	1	1		1	1		1					1							
Sub													1											
Gls													1											

	Seaman DA	Dixon LM	Winterburn N	Hillier D	O'Leary DA	Adams TA	Campbell KJ	Davis PV	Smith AM	Merson PC	Limpar AE	Rocastle D	Groves P	Linighan A	Thomas ML	Pates CG	Wright IE	Bould SA	Carter JC	Parlour R	Lydersen P	Morrow SJ	Heaney NA	#
	1	2		12	6	4	8		10		7	11	5*	3		9								2
	1	2	3	6	11		9	10		7	12		4	5	8*									3
	1	2	3	6		4	9	10	11*	7	12	14	5†	8										3
Apps	3	3	2	3	2	2	2	3	1	3	1	1	2	2	3									
Sub					1								2	1										
Gls					1										2									

Arsenal in Wartime - 1915-1919

WHEN World War One began in August 1914, the FA and Football League decided to continue competitive football. Not without difficulty, the 1914-15 season was completed amid adverse public opinion and hostile criticism from certain sections of the Press who believed that all footballers should be fighting for their country. In December 1914, a Footballers' Battalion was formed, in which members were allowed leave on Saturdays to play for their clubs. Arsenal players Bill Spittle, George Ford, Jack Butler, Bob Houston and Tom Ratcliffe (trainer) were amongst those who joined. As the war progressed and it was realized just how many footballers had joined up, the ill feeling against football petered out.

In 1915-16 all the Football League clubs divided into two regional groups except in the South, where the League clubs of London combined with some Southern League teams to form a London Combination, in which Arsenal competed for the next four seasons.

By the time the first season was underway, practically all the Arsenal staff were doing something towards the country's welfare, many of them serving in the forces, and the remainder were heavily engaged in the war effort of some nature. Arsenal, therefore, like many other clubs, often found difficulty in fielding a full team — exemplified by the tragic fatality of Bob Benson (see *Arsenal Who's Who*) — and the use of 'guest' players was essential to the continuation of competitive football. On a number of occasions, Arsenal fielded men from the forces who were not attached to any professional club and whose names and identity were not always clear.

So far as the playing record was concerned, although they did not win any honours, Arsenal performed creditably throughout. Their best performance was in the final season, 1918-19, when they finished runners-up to Brentford and of the other seasons they were 3rd in 1915-16 and 5th in both 1916-17 and 1917-18.

Arsenal guest players in 1915-19 included:-
R.H.Beale (Manchester United), W.Blackmore (Southampton), J.Caddick (Bristol Rovers), J.Chipperfield (Luton Clarence), J.Cook (Middlesbrough), J.Cooper (Barnsley), A.Dominy (Southampton), G.H.Douglas (Leicester Fosse), A.Ducat (Aston Villa), V.Gregory (Watford), W.Hibbert (Newcastle United), F.Knowles (Manchester City), J.Lees (Barnsley), J.Moore (Glossop), F.Pagnam (Liverpool), R.Pearson (Southampton), W.J.Stapley (Glossop), A.A.Thompson (Glossop), C.Wallace (Aston Villa), D.Williams (Notts County), E.C.Williamson (Croydon Common).

 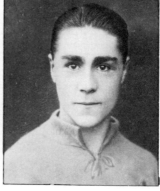

Two Arsenal 'guests'. Far left: Ernie William-son of Croydon Com-mon who later played for the Gunners and won an England cap. Left: George Douglas of Leicester Fosse was an England amateur inter-national in his days with Ilford. Douglas later played for Burnley, Oldham Athletic and Bristol Rovers.

Telegraphic Address—"GUNNERITIC, FINSPARK, LONDON."   Registered Office—AVENELL ROAD, GILLESPIE ROAD.

THE ARSENAL FOOTBALL CLUB, LTD.,

Secretary (*Pro Tem.*)   卐   **Colours :**
H. J. PETERS.   RED SHIRTS, WHITE KNICKS.

DIRECTORS : H. G. NORRIS, ESQ., J.P. (CHAIRMAN).

C. D. CRISP, ESQ., G. E. DAVIS, ESQ.,W. HALL, ESQ., J. W. HUMBLE, ESQ., W. E. MIDDLETON, ESQ.

Vol. III. No. 1]   SATURDAY, SEPTEMBER 4, 1915.   [Price ONE PENNY.

SOME RANDOM NOTES.
THE PAST, THE PRESENT, AND THE FUTURE.

BY "THE GUNNERS' MATE."

Out of the uncertainty of the last few months has come a concrete scheme, which enables us to extend a welcome once again to our patrons. We are no longer in the happy position of speculating upon what are our prospects of securing promotion during the coming season, nor have we an absorbing story to tell of the men who have been secured to help us to attain that much-to-be-desired object. The professional player is no longer in England for reasons which need not be enumerated here. To-day, all the men taking part in our match with Tottenham Hotspur are playing as amateurs for the love of the game.

Some of them are serving the King as soldiers; others are "doing their bit at home," and materially helping to provide the goods for the complete subjection of the thrice-accursed Hun. Practically every man, so far as I can gather, is doing something in his country's welfare, and so far as The Arsenal men are concerned a perusal of the following details will, or should if their minds are open to reason, provide food for the serious consideration of those who have been so ready to revile the great game of football.

While Lievesley and Mitchell are away in business of some sort, the nature of which is not known to me, Kempton is doing Government work, Shaw and Benson are in the Royal Arsenal at Plumstead, and both George Ford and J. Houston, the reserve backs, are in the Football Battalion. Percy Sands is still teaching the young idea, George Grant and Angus McKinnon are in the Royal Arsenal, as is A. Fletcher and "Roddy" MacEachrane. Alec. Graham is doing motor work and Liddell is on Government duty. In the absence of his

brother Frank, Chris. Buckley is looking after his farm in the Midlands and hopes to be able to help us on occasions.

Hardinge on Foreign Service.

Young Blyth has joined the Army in Scotland, Winship is shipbuilding on the Tyne, and Walter Hardinge is now on Foreign Service with the Royal Naval Air Service. Groves is engaged with a Government contractor, and both Rutherford and Flanagan are in the Royal Arsenal. Thompson is a schoolmaster, and Bradshaw is employed in important motor works in London. Spittle and Assistant Trainer Ratcliffe are in the Football Battalion, and I have heard that Butler has joined the Army, but of that I have no definite knowledge at the moment. I believe King is doing some sort of munition work, and both "Punch" McEwan and Financial Secretary Peters have been engaged on Government work for some months. I understand that Lewis is in business at Plumstead, and Norman's present whereabouts is unknown to me.

With the exception of Lievesley, Blyth, Hardinge and Winship, every man with the club last year has promised to assist us when circumstances permit, but, of course, everything will depend upon when they can get free to take the recreation they all love so well.

We have to acknowledge with keen pleasure the promise of assistance we have received from that famous goalkeeper Beale, of Manchester United. Beale is doing important work in the South, and has intimated that he will be pleased to guard the fort whenever possible. He will be a decided acquisition.

It is not my intention to speculate upon what

Front page of an Arsenal programme for a wartime game against Spurs.

1915-16

1	Sep	4	(h)	Tottenham H	W 2-0	Thompson, Lewis	14,819
2		11	(a)	Crystal P	L 1-3	Bradshaw	4,000
3		18	(h)	Queen's Park R	W 2-1	King, Hardinge	4,000
4		25	(a)	Fulham	L 3-4	Lewis, Hardinge, Chipperfield	9,000
5	Oct	2	(h)	Clapton O	W 2-0	King, Wallace	6,000
6		9	(a)	Watford	L 0-1		2,500
7		16	(h)	Millwall A	D 1-1	King	12,000
8		23	(a)	Croydon C	W 4-1	Thompson 2, King, Moore	3,000
9		30	(a)	Chelsea	L 1-3	Moore	12,500
10	Nov	6	(h)	Brentford	W 3-1	F.W.Groves 2, Chipperfield	7,500
11		13	(a)	Tottenham H	D 3-3	King 3	7,000
12		20	(h)	Crystal P	D 2-2	King, Chipperfield	5,000
13		27	(a)	Queen's Park R	D 1-1	F.W.Groves	2,500
14	Dec	4	(h)	Fulham	W 2-1	King, Buckley	3,000
15		11	(a)	Clapton O	W 2-0	Chipperfield, King	3,000
16		18	(h)	Watford	W 3-1	King 2, Tyler	5,000
17		25	(a)	West Ham U	L 2-8	Tyler, King	5,500
18		27	(h)	West Ham U	W 3-2	King, Rutherford, Chipperfield	8,869
19	Jan	1	(a)	Millwall A	L 0-3		5,000
20		8	(h)	Croydon C	W 4-2	King 3, Chester (og)	4,500
21		15	(h)	Chelsea	L 0-6		15,000
22		22	(a)	Brentford	D 2-2	Legge, King	2,500

	P	W	D	L	F	A	W	D	L	F	A	Pts	Pos	
	22	8	2	1	24	17	2	3	6	19	29	25	3rd	Appearances
														Goals

23	Feb	5	(h)	Watford	D 1-1	King	5,000
24		12	(a)	Brentford	L 1-2	Newsham	3,000
25		19	(h)	Reading	W 4-1	Thompson 2, Lewis, Rutherford	5,500
26		26	(a)	Clapton O	D 1-1	Caddick	6,000
27	Mar	4	(h)	Tottenham H	L 0-3		10,000
28		11	(a)	Millwall A	L 0-2		4,000
29		18	(h)	Brentford	W 5-2	Thompson 2, Lees 2, F.W.Groves	6,000
30		25	(a)	Reading	D 1-1	F.W.Groves	1,500
31	Apr	1	(h)	Clapton O	W 2-1	Chipperfield, Elkington	8,500
32		8	(a)	Tottenham H	L 2-3	Lees, Chipperfield	8,000
33		15	(h)	Millwall A	D 0-0		9,000
34		21	(a)	Chelsea	L 0-9		25,000
35		24	(h)	Chelsea	L 1-3	F.W.Groves	13,000
36		29	(a)	Watford	L 1-2	Chipperfield	1,000

	P	W	D	L	F	A	W	D	L	F	A	Pts	Pos	
	14	3	2	2	13	11	0	2	5	6	20	10	11th	Appearances
														Goals

Beale RH	Shaw J	Liddell E	Fordham JA	Buckley CS	Graham A	Rutherford J	Groves FW	Thompson AA	Bradshaw F	Lewis CH	Sands PR	Wallace C	King HE	Hardinge HTW	Ducat A	Grant GM	Chipperfield J	Norman J	Kempton AR	Tyler FA	Moore J	Madge W	McKinnon A	Fletcher A	Flanagan J	Cooper J	Foreman S	Emms J	Lege S	Horton HH	Dawson H	Mason	Cockle E	Lees J	Elkington J	Bourne HS	Broderick MA	Morris CE	
1	2	3	4	5	6	7	8	9	10	11																													1
1	2	3	6	5	4	7	8	9	10	11																													2
1	2			5	4		8			6	11	3	7	9	10																								3
1		3		5	6		8				11		7	9	2	4	10																						4
1	2			5			8					3	7	9	4	6	10	11																					5
		3	4	5			8			6		2	7	9					11	1	10																		6
		3		5						6	11	2	7	9	8	4				1	10																		7
2				5						6	8	3	7	9	4	11				1	10																		8
		3		5			8			6	11	2	7	9	4					1	10																		9
2				5			8					3	11	7	9	6	4	10		1																			10
		3		5			8	11		6		2	7	9	4	10				1																			11
2				5			8	11		3			7	9	6	4	10			1																			12
2					4	10	3	11					7	9	5	6				1	8																		13
2		4		5			8					3	7	9	10	6	11			1																			14
		3		5				9				2	7	8	4	6				1	10		11																15
		3			4		8					7	9	6	2	5	11			1	10																		16
2							8	11				3	7	9	5	4				1	10						6												17
				5			8	4	11			3	7	9	2	10				1							6												18
						7	8	11							2	4			5	1	9						6	3											19
2				5			8					3	11	4	7	9	6			1										10									20
		3		5						11		8	10		2	7	9	4	6	1																			21
		3	5			7	4			11			9													6					1	2	8	10					22
5	18	4	3	18	4	8	17	12	14	10	12	18	19	10	9	10	12	3	16	6	3	2	3	1	1	1	1	1	1										
	1			1	3	3	1	2		1	18	2		5		2	2				1																		

1 own-goal

Beale RH	Shaw J	Liddell E	Fordham JA	Buckley CS	Graham A	Rutherford J	Groves FW	Thompson AA	Bradshaw F	Lewis CH	Sands PR	Wallace C	King HE	Hardinge HTW	Ducat A	Grant GM	Chipperfield J	Norman J	Kempton AR	Tyler FA	Moore J	Madge W	McKinnon A	Fletcher A	Flanagan J	Cooper J	Foreman S	Emms J	Lege S	Horton HH	Dawson H	Mason	Cockle E	Lees J	Elkington J	Bourne HS	Broderick MA	Morris CE	
				5		7	4		3		11	9			2	1	10										6		8										23
				5			4	10	3		7	8			1							2	6																24
				5		7	6	8	2	11		9			1	10	4																						25
			3	5						11	7	2			1	10	4																6						26
2				5							7	3	11		9	1	8										6						4	10					27
				5				10	3			2	7	8	4	1													9										28
				5		7	8	9	3	2					6	4	1																10	11					29
				5		7	10		3						6		1					4								9			11	2		8			30
2							8	9		5					10		1					4	6										11	3		7			31
				5						11		2			9		1						6									8	10	3		7	4		32
			6	5						8		2			9		1															10	11	3		7	4		33
				5								2	7		9		1						6									10	11	3		8	4		34
3				5							7	8	6	2		4	9									1						10	11						35
				5				9				8	2		10		1					4					6					11	3						36
	4		3	11		7	9	6	13	4	3	4	5	4	7	11	5		7	4		1	3			1	2	2	4	5		7	6	5		3			
			1	3			4	1	1			3			2	2	3						1																

E. Roe played number 9 in Match 24; F. Newsham played number 11 in Match 24 and scored once; R.W. Benson played number 3 in Match 25; J. Caddick played number 8 in Match 26 and scored once; S. Whittaker played number 9 in Match 26; J. Small played number 6 in Match 28; Ellerby played number 11 in Match 28; H.G. Groves played number 7 in Match 36.

1916-17

London Combination

1	Sep	2	(a)	West Ham U	L	1-2	Weaver	3,000
2		9	(h)	Tottenham H	D	1-1	King	10,000
3		16	(a)	Crystal P	L	0-1		3,000
4		23	(h)	Brentford	D	0-0		6,000
5		30	(a)	Chelsea	L	0-3		12,000
6	Oct	7	(h)	Southampton	D	3-3	King 2, Chipperfield	7,000
7		14	(h)	Luton T	W	2-1	King 2	5,000
8		21	(a)	Portsmouth	L	0-1		5,000
9		28	(h)	Millwall A	W	1-0	Chipperfield	8,000
10	Nov	4	(a)	Watford	W	4-2	Williams 2, Weaver, Chipperfield	2,500
11		11	(h)	Clapton O	W	4-0	Chipperfield 2, Ducat, Hardinge	7,000
12		18	(a)	Fulham	L	0-2		1,500
13		25	(h)	West Ham U	L	0-2		8,000
14	Dec	2	(a*)	Tottenham H	L	1-4	Williams	8,000
15		9	(h)	Crystal P	L	1-2	King	3,000
16		23	(h)	Chelsea	W	2-1	Hardinge, Chipperfield	4,000
17		25	(a)	Queen's Park R	W	3-2	Chipperfield 2, Rutherford	3,000
18		26	(h)	Queen's Park R	D	0-0		4,500
19		30	(a)	Southampton	W	1-0	Allman	3,000
20	Jan	6	(a)	Luton T	W	4-1	Allman, Rutherford, Williams (pen), Hutchins (pen)	3,000
21		13	(h)	Portsmouth	W	1-0	Allman	2,500
22		20	(a)	Millwall A	L	0-1		10,000
23		27	(h)	Watford	D	1-1	Rutherford	2,300
24	Feb	3	(a)	Clapton O	D	2-2	Rutherford, H.G.Groves	
25		10	(h)	Fulham	W	3-2	Rutherford, Chipperfield 2	4,800
26		17	(h)	Chelsea	W	3-0	Hardinge, F.W.Groves, Rutherford	7,500
27		24	(a)	Southampton	W	2-0	H.G.Groves, Allman	3,000
28	Mar	3	(h)	Clapton O	W	3-1	Hardinge 2, Flanagan	4,500
29		10	(a)	West Ham U	W	3-2	Flanagan 2, Hardinge	6,500
30		17	(a)	Crystal P	L	0-1		2,000
31		24	(h)	Portsmouth	W	2-1	Spittle, F.W.Groves	4,500
32		31	(a)	Chelsea	L	0-2		6,000
33	Apr	6	(a†)	Tottenham H	D	0-0		9,000
34		7	(h)	Southampton	D	2-2	Hutchins, Hardinge	6,500
35		9	(h)	Tottenham H	W	3-2	Cockerill, Wilkins, Sanderson	12,000
36		14	(a)	Clapton O	W	3-1	Chipperfield 2, F.W.Groves	3,000
37		21	(h)	West Ham U	W	2-1	Spittle, Hardinge	7,000
38		26	(a)	Brentford	D	0-0		1,000
39		28	(h)	Crystal P	W	4-0	F.W.Groves 3, Hardinge	4,500
40	May	5	(a)	Portsmouth	D	0-0		3,000

P	W	D	L	F	A	W	D	L	F	A	Pts	Pos	
36	11	3	4	52	26	9	2	7	33	30	45	2nd	Goals

Appearances

*Played at Highbury.   †Played at Homerton.

Williamson EC	Elkington J	Hutchins AV	Allman P	Stapley WJ	Madge W	Rutherford J	Groves FW	Weaver J	Chipperfield J	Tyler FA	Shaw J	Bradshaw F	Knowles F	King HE	Ducat A	Williams D	Cockle E	Hardinge HWT	Little J	Groves HG	O'Neill	Baker WJ	Broderick MA	Liddell E	Blyth WN	Hibbert W	Buckley CS	Silto E	McKinnon A	Grant GM	Pearson RC	Blackmore W	Melville	Wilkins W	Spittle WA	Thomas J	Flanagan J	Cockerill H	
1	2	3	4	5	6	7	8	9	10	11																													1
1	11		4	5		7		9	10		2	3	6	8																									2
1	11	3	6			7				10	2		5		4	8	9																						3
1	11	3	4	5		7		8	10			2	6	9																									4
1	11	3	4	5		7						2	6	9		8		10																					5
1			4	5		7			11			3	6	9		10			2	8																			6
1				5		7			4		2	3	6	8		10					9	11																	7
1	9	3	4	5					11			6		8		10			2				7																8
1				6				7	4		2	3		8		9		10				11		5															9
1		3	6		4			7	11			10				8		9	2					5															10
1	11	3		6				7	10			2			4	8		9						5															11
1		3		6				7	10		2	4				8		9				11		5															12
1				5	4	7		11			2	3		9		8		6							10														13
1		3		6				7				2		9		10		4				11		5		8													14
1		3		4			8	7	11			2		9		10											5	6											15
1	11	3	4			7	8		10			2						9						5					6										16
1	2	3			9	7	8		10											11				5					6	4									17
1	2	5	4			7	8		10			3						9		11									6										18
1		3	10		4		2		6											9			7	5							8	11							19
1		3	10			7	8		6		2					9													4	5			11						20
1		3	10			7	8		4			2				9													6	5				11					21
1		3				7	8		11			2				9		10						5					6	4									22
1	11					7	8		10		3	2				9								5					6	4									23
1		3	10	5	9	7	2													8									6	4				11					24
1		3		6		7	8		10			2												5						4				11	9				25
1		3				7	8		6			2						10									5			4				11	9				26
1		3	10				6		5											8														11		2			27
1		3		5		7	8					2						9											6	4				11			10		28
1		3				7	8		4			2						9											6	5				11			10		29
1		3		5		7	8		10			2								9									6	4				11					30
1		3		5			7		10			2						9											6	4				11	8				31
1		3		5			7		4			2						9		8									6					11	10				32
1	9	3	10	5		7	8				2																		6					11				4	33
1		9		5		7	8				2	3						10											6					11				4	34
1		3		5		7	8				2							10											6					11				4	35
1			8	5			7		10			3							2										6					11	9			4	36
1						7	8		4		2	3						9						5										11	10			6	37
1	10	3				7	8					2						9											5					11				6	38
1		3		5		7	8					2						9											6					11	10			4	39
1		3	9			7	8		10			2												5					6					11				4	40
40	13	32	18	24	6	28	27	10	29	2	12	31	6	10	2	16	1	20	4	8	1	4	2	13	1	1	2	1	20	12	1	1	1	18	7	1	2	8	
		2	4			6	6	2	12					6	1	4		9		2														1	2		3	1	

C.W.Wright played number 4 in Match 27; D.Slade played number 7 in Match 27; J.Johnson played number 9 in Match 27; V.Sanderson played number 9 in Match 35 and scored once; J.Bailey played number 4 in Match 38.

1917-18

London Combination

1	Sep	1	(h)	Queen's Park R	W 2-0 F.W.Groves, Lewis	6,000
2		8	(a)	Clapton O	W 5-0 Pagnam 3, Rutherford 2	3,500
3		15	(h)	Millwall A	W 4-0 F.W.Groves, Chipperfield, Pagnam 2	11,000
4		22	(a*)	Tottenham H	W 2-1 Rutherford, Pagnam	10,000
5		29	(h)	Chelsea	L 0-1	16,000
6	Oct	6	(a)	Brentford	D 2-2 Pagnam, F.W.Groves	4,000
7		13	(a)	Crystal P	L 0-2	7,000
8		20	(h)	West Ham U	D 2-2 Chipperfield, F.W.Groves	6,000
9		27	(a)	Queen's Park R	L 0-2	4,500
10	Nov	3	(h)	Clapton O	W 3-1 F.W.Groves, Chipperfield, Pagnam	3,000
11		10	(a)	Millwall	D 2-2 Chipperfield, Pagnam	6,000
12		17	(h)	Tottenham H	L 0-1	9,000
13		24	(a)	Chelsea	L 3-4 Bradshaw (pen), Rutherford, F.W.Groves	5,000
14	Dec	1	(h)	Brentford	W 4-1 Rayner 2, F.W.Groves, Rutherford	4,000
15		8	(h)	Crystal P	L 0-2	3,500
16		15	(a)	West Ham U	L 2-3 Cook, Rutherford	5,000
17		22	(h)	Queen's Park R	W 3-0 Bradshaw, Grant, Chipperfield	3,000
18		25	(a)	Fulham	D 1-1 Chipperfield	7,000
19		26	(h)	Fulham	D 1-1 Liddell	7,000
20		29	(a)	Clapton O	W 2-1 Rooney 2	2,000
21	Jan	5	(h)	Millwall	W 1-0 Rayner	4,000
22		12	(a*)	Tottenham H	L 1-4 Tyler	9,000
23		19	(h)	Chelsea	W 4-1 Hardinge, Rutherford, F.W.Groves, Lewis	7,000
24		26	(a)	Brentford	L 2-3 Douglas, Rayner	3,000
25	Feb	2	(a)	Crystal P	W 4-1 Lewis 2, Douglas, Rutherford	3,500
26		9	(h)	Fulham	L 0-3	8,000
27		16	(a)	Queen's Park R	W 3-0 Hardinge 2, Rutherford	3,500
28		23	(h)	Clapton O	W 7-1 Pagnam 5, F.W.Groves, Douglas (pen)	4,000
29	Mar	2	(a)	Millwall A	W 3-0 Rutherford 2, Hardinge	3,000
30		9	(h)	Tottenham H	W 4-1 Hardinge, Chipperfield, Rutherford, Ralston (og)	16,000
31		16	(a)	Chelsea	L 2-4 Chipperfield, Douglas	4,000
32		23	(h)	Brentford	L 1-3 Cook	6,000
33		29	(a)	West Ham U	L 1-4 Bradshaw	10,500
34		30	(h)	Crystal P	W 3-0 F.W.Groves, Rutherford, Bradshaw	800
35	Apr	1	(h)	West Ham U	L 1-3 Lewis	7,000
36		6	(a)	Fulham	L 1-2 Chipperfield	2,000

P	W	D	L	F	A	W	D	L	F	A	Pts	Pos	
36	10	2	6	40	21	6	3	9	36	36	37	5th	Appearances
													Goals

*Played at Highbury.

Supplementary Competition (National War Fund)

37	Apr	13	(h)	Millwall A	W 4-3 Bradshaw 2, F.W.Groves, Chipperfield	3,500
38		20	(a)	Millwall A	W 1-0 F.W.Groves	3,500
39		27	(h)	Brentford	W 3-1 Bradshaw 2, F.W.Groves	3,000
40	May	4	(a)	Brentford	D 1-1 Bradshaw	1,500

Appearances
Goals

Williamson EC	Bradshaw F	Hutchins AV	Gregory V	Stapley WJ	Cockerill H	Rutherford J	Groves FW	Chipperfield J	Simmons AW	Lewis CH	McKinnon A	Pagnam F	Grant GM	Plumb DJ	Liddell E	Tyler FA	Broderick MA	Hunt J	Eyles J	Shaw J	Ducat A	Sanders	Johnson	Blyth WN	Ison J	Rayner W	Brien W	Reid W	Cook J	Groves HG	Rooney	Gisling	Webber A	Relfe A	Hardinge HTW	Baker	Douglas GH	Emery A	
1	2	3	4	5	6	7	8	9	10	11																													1
1	2	3	4	5		7	8			11	6	9	10																										2
1	2	3	4	5	6	7	8	10		11		9																											3
1	2	3				7	8	6		11	4	9	10	5																									4
1	2	3				7	8	10		11	6	9	4		5																								5
1	2	3				7	8	4		11		9		5	6	10																							6
1	2	3	6	5		7	8			11	4	9				10																							7
1	2	3		4			8	6		11		9		5		10	7																						8
1	2	3				7	8	6	10	11		9		5				4																					9
1	2	3					8	6		11		9		5			7	4	10																				10
1	2			6			7	8		11		9			5					3	4	10																	11
1	2	3					8	6		11		9	5			10	7						4																12
1	2			5	3	7	8	6				9	4											10	11														13
1	2	3				7	8	10					6		5	11					4					9													14
1	2	3				7	8	6					4		5	11											9	10											15
1	2	3				7	8	6				9	4		5	11													10										16
1	2	3		5	6		7	10					4			11										9				8									17
1	2	3		5	11		7	10				9	4		6															8									18
1	2	3				7	8			11		9			5						4										6	10							19
1	2	3		5	4	7	8	10					6																	11	9								20
1		3		5		7	2	6		11			4													9				8	10								21
1		3				7	2	6		11					5	8										9							4	10					22
1	2	3			6	7	8			11					5						4														9	10			23
	2	3				7	8	6		11			4		5											10					1						10		24
1	2	3				7		6		11					5											8									9		10	4	25
1	2	3					7	10		11		8	6		5																				9			4	26
1	2			5		7		6		11		9								3															10		8	4	27
1	3			5		7	8	6				9	4							2															10		11		28
1	2	3				7	8	6				9	4		5																				10		11		29
1		3		5		7	8	10		11	6									2	4														9				30
1	2	3		6		7	8	10		11					5						4																9		31
1	3			5	6		8	4		11		9								2									10								7		32
1	9	3					8	10					4		5	11		6		2										7									33
1	9	3				7	8	11					4		5					2						10												6	34
1		3		5		7	8	10		11										2	4					9												6	35
1	9	3		5		7	8	11							6					2										10								4	36
35	32	31	4	18	8	27	34	32	2	24	5	20	18	5	18	10	3	3	1	9	7	1	1	1	1	8	1	1	2	6	4	1	1	1	7	1	7	6	
	4					13	10	9		5		14	1		1	1										4			2		2				5		4		

1 own-goal

Williamson EC	Bradshaw F	Hutchins AV	Gregory V	Stapley WJ	Cockerill H	Rutherford J	Groves FW	Chipperfield J	Simmons AW	Lewis CH	McKinnon A	Pagnam F	Grant GM	Plumb DJ	Liddell E	Tyler FA	Broderick MA	Hunt J	Eyles J	Shaw J	Ducat A	Sanders	Johnson	Blyth WN	Ison J	Rayner W	Brien W	Reid W	Cook J	Groves HG	Rooney	Gisling	Webber A	Relfe A	Hardinge HTW	Baker	Douglas GH	Emery A	
1	9	3		5		7	8	11							10					2	4																	6	37
1	9	3		5		7	8	6		11										2						4				10									38
1	9	3		5		7	8													2						4				11								6	39
1	9	3					7	11					8							2																			40
4	4	4		3		3	4	3		1			1		1					4	1					2				2								2	
	5						3	1																															

H.Wood played number 10 in Matches 39 & 40; G.Brown played number 4 in Match 40; A.Robinson played number 5 in Match 40; E.Cooper played number 6 in Match 40.

1918-19

London Combination

							Att.
1	Sep	7	(a)	Queen's Park R	W	3-2 Thompson 2, Carville	7,000
2		14	(h)	Millwall	W	4-0 Carville, F.W.Groves 2, Dominy	5,000
3		21	(a)	Fulham	W	2-1 Hardinge, Carville	6,000
4		28	(h)	Brentford	D	1-1 Dominy	8,000
5	Oct	5	(a)	West Ham U	W	4-1 Hardinge 3, Spittle	6,500
6		12	(h)	Tottenham H	W	3-0 Hardinge 2 (1 pen), F.W.Groves	30,000
7		19	(a)	Chelsea	L	1-4 Spittle	25,000
8		26	(a)	Crystal P	L	1-2 F.W.Groves	5,000
9	Nov	2	(h)	Queen's Park R	W	1-0 Bradshaw	6,000
10		9	(a)	Millwall	D	3-3 Dominy 3	4,000
11		16	(h)	Fulham	L	1-3 Rutherford	8,000
12		23	(a)	Brentford	L	1-4 Thompson	5,000
13		30	(h)	West Ham U	L	0-2	7,000
14	Dec	7	(a*)	Tottenham H	L	0-1	12,000
15		14	(h)	Chelsea	W	3-0 Chipperfield, Dominy, Thompson	8,000
16		21	(h)	Crystal P	D	3-3 Chipperfield 3	8,500
17		25	(a)	Clapton O	L	2-3 Plumb, F.W.Groves	7,500
18		26	(h)	Clapton O	W	9-2 Butler 4, Chipperfield 3, Rutherford, Spittle	6,000
19		28	(a)	Queen's Park R	W	2-0 Chipperfield, Spittle	4,000
20	Jan	4	(h)	Millwall	W	4-1 Hardinge 2, Chipperfield 2	8,000
21		11	(a)	Fulham	L	1-3 Blyth	8,000
22		18	(h)	Brentford	D	3-3 Chipperfield, Ducat, Miller	30,000
23		25	(a)	West Ham U	W	2-1 Hardinge, Miller	18,000
24	Feb	1	(h)	Tottenham H	L	2-3 Miller, Hardinge	18,000
25		8	(a)	Chelsea	W	2-1 Hardinge, Chipperfield	12,000
26		15	(h)	Clapton O	W	4-0 Miller, Ducat, Chipperfield, Robson	16,000
27		22	(h)	Queen's Park R	L	1-3 Chipperfield	13,000
28	Mar	1	(a)	Millwall	W	3-0 Hardinge, Spittle, Miller	14,000
29		8	(h)	Fulham	W	5-0 Hardinge 2, Chipperfield, Robson 2	22,000
30		15	(a)	Brentford	L	0-2	20,000
31		22	(h)	West Ham U	W	3-2 Hughes, Hardinge, Robson	20,000
32		29	(a*)	Tottenham H	W	1-0 Hardinge	33,000
33	Apr	5	(h)	Chelsea	W	2-1 Hardinge, Rutherford	35,000
34		12	(a)	Clapton O	D	2-2 Chipperfield 2	10,000
35		18	(a†)	Crystal P	W	3-0 Rutherford 2, Hughes	20,000
36		21	(h)	Crystal P	W	3-2 Rutherford, Hardinge, Chipperfield	10,000

	P	W	D	L	F	A	W	D	L	F	A	Pts	Pos	
	36	11	3	4	52	26	9	2	7	33	30	45	2nd	Appearances
														Goals

*Played at Highbury.†Played at Millwall.

London Victory Cup

							Att.
37	Jan	1	(a)	Millwall	W	1-0 Miller	6,000
38	Mar	31	(h)	Fulham	L	1-4 Graham (pen)	20,000

		Appearances
		Goals

Player appearance and goalscoring grid. Column headers (left to right): Williamson FC, Liddell E, Hutchins AV, Gregory V, Carville J, Chipperfield J, Groves FW, Spittle WA, Thompson AA, Wood H, Tyler AF, Bradshaw F, Dominy A, Ducat A, Rutherford J, Hardinge HTW, Shaw J, Cockerill H, Linnett, Kempton AR, Jones J, Wallace C, Plumb DJ, Williams W, Weaver J, Hughes J, Butler JD, Miller W, Groves HG, Blyth WN, Wilkins W, McKinnon A, Robson D, Voysey CR, Lewis CH, Jobey G, Sands PR, Buckley CS, King HE.

Match	Williamson FC	Liddell E	Hutchins AV	Gregory V	Carville J	Chipperfield J	Groves FW	Spittle WA	Thompson AA	Wood H	Tyler AF	Bradshaw F	Dominy A	Ducat A	Rutherford J	Hardinge HTW	Shaw J	Cockerill H	Linnett	Kempton AR	Jones J	Wallace C	Plumb DJ	Williams W	Weaver J	Hughes J	Butler JD	Miller W	Groves HG	Blyth WN	Wilkins W	McKinnon A	Robson D	Voysey CR	Lewis CH	Jobey G	Sands PR	Buckley CS	King HE
1	1	2	3	4	5	6	7	8	9	10	11																												
2	1	4	3	6	5	11	7	10	9			2	8																										
3	1		3	6	5	11	10					2	8	4	7	9																							
4	1	4	3	5		7	11					10	8	6		9	2																						
5	1		3	5	10	11	8	7						4		9	2	6																					
6	1	6	3	5		7	11	8				10	4			9	2																						
7	1	6	3	5	11	7	8					10	4			9	2																						
8	1	5	3		9	11	6					2	8		7	10				4																			
9	1	4	3	5		7	8	11				10				9	2	6																					
10	1	6	3		5	8	10	11				2	9	4	7																								
11	1	6		5	11	8						2	9	4	7	10	3																						
12			6	7	11	9						2		4		10	3				1	5	8																
13	1	6		10	7	8	11					3		4		9	2						5																
14	1	5	3	6	11	7	10						8	4		9	2																						
15	1	5	3		11	7		9				10	8	4			2									6													
16	1		3	6	11	7		9				10	8	4			2						5																
17	1		3	6	11	7	10					2		4									5						8	9									
18	1	2	3		11	6	8						4	7	10								5					9											
19	1	6	3		11	7	10					2	8	4									5					9											
20	1	6	3		11	7						2		4		10							5					9	8										
21	1	6	3		11	7						8		4		10	2						5					9											
22	1	6	3		11	7						2	8	4		10							5					9											
23	1	6	3	5	11	7	10						4		8	2							9																
24	1		3	6		7						2	8	4		10							5					9			11								
25	1	5			11	7						2		4		10	3											9				6	8						
26	1	5	3		11	7						4		10			2											9				6	8						
27	1	5	3		11	4	9					2		7		10																6	8						
28	1		3		4	8						2		7		10							5					9	11			6							
29	1	6	3		11	4						2		7		10							5					9				8							
30	1	6	3		11	4						2		7		10							5					9				8							
31	1		3	6		11						2		7		10										9						4	8	5					
32	1											3		4	7	10	2									9						6	8	5	11				
33	1	2	3		11		10							7	9						5											6	8		4				
34	1		3		10		7								8	5	11	4			2					6							9		5	11	4	2	6	9
35	1		3		11		2	8					10		9			6					5			7							4						
36	1		3		11	8						2		7		10										9						6	5	4					
Apps	35	24	31	13	6	26	33	19	11	1	1	28	12	23	15	28	16	2	1	1	1	1	13	1	1	4	1	11	2	1	1	9	9	5	3	4	1	1	1
Goals		3	18	5	5	4						1	6	2	6	18							1					2				4	5	1		4			

Match	Williamson FC	Liddell E	Hutchins AV	Gregory V	Carville J	Chipperfield J	Groves FW	Spittle WA	Thompson AA	Wood H	Tyler AF	Bradshaw F	Dominy A	Ducat A	Rutherford J	Hardinge HTW	Shaw J	Cockerill H	Linnett	Kempton AR	Jones J	Wallace C	Plumb DJ	Williams W	Weaver J	Hughes J	Butler JD	Miller W	Groves HG	Blyth WN	Wilkins W	McKinnon A	Robson D	Voysey CR	Lewis CH	Jobey G	Sands PR	Buckley CS	King HE
37	1	2	3		11	4		7				8	6			10							5					9											
38	1			4	11		7					3				10	2											9				6	8						
Apps	2	1	1	1		2	1	1	1			1	1	1		2	1		1				1					2				1	1						
Goals																1																							

A.Graham played number 5 in Match 38 and scored once.

331

Arsenal in Wartime - 1939-1946

UNLIKE World War One, regular League and FA Cup football was abandoned immediately upon the outbreak of World War Two and, after three fixtures had been completed, the programme was terminated. At first a number of friendly matches were played until the Football League organized competitive football on a regional basis, commencing in October 1939.

The Arsenal Stadium was closed to football and converted into a major ARP centre and throughout the war Arsenal played their 'home' games at neighbouring White Hart Lane, coincidental for the fact that Tottenham had played some of their 'home' fixtures at Highbury during World War One.

Initially, Arsenal were able to call on most of their own regular players but gradually the staff began to drift away to join the forces and the permitted use of guest players became more necessary. Such famous names as Stanley Matthews, Stan Mortensen and Bill Shankly were among many well-known professionals who donned the Gunners' red shirt.

In this second war period, Arsenal were more successful and a number of honours came their way. Competing in the first season (1939-40) in both League South 'A' and 'C', Arsenal were champions of the former, and in the Football League War Cup were beaten in the third round by Birmingham. The following season the club were placed third in the League South but qualified to meet Preston North End in the League War Cup Final at Wembley, where Leslie Compton missed a penalty in a 1-1 draw and the Gunners lost 2-1 in the replay at Blackburn.

In 1941-2 the London clubs formed a breakaway London League in which Arsenal finished champions, scoring 108 goals in 30 matches and in the London War Cup won their qualifying group to reach the semi-finals, only to be beaten by Brentford after a replay, in which they again failed to convert a penalty. Back in the Football League South in 1942-3, Arsenal carried off both the League championship and the League South Cup, again scoring over 100 goals in 28 League games and turning in a tremendous performance in the Cup Final at Wembley to overwhelm Charlton Athletic 7-1, Reg Lewis netting four times. In the next two seasons in the League South the Gunners finished fourth and eighth while in the League South Cup they failed to reach the semi-finals in 1943-4 and, qualifying in 1944-5, the usual missed-penalty habit was doubled this time (both Mortensen and Hall failed from the spot) as Arsenal surprisingly lost 1-0 to Millwall.

In 1945-6, the final wartime season, as players slowly returned to their clubs, Arsenal struggled to 11th position in the League South. The FA Cup returned to its official status, although it was run for the first and only time on a two-legged basis up to the semi-final stage, Arsenal losing 6-1 on aggregate to West Ham United in the third round. A significant feature of this season was the prestigious friendly match in November, when an 'Arsenal' team containing six guests faced a Moscow Dynamo touring side in a farcical encounter played in thick fog and in which a Russian referee controlling the game 'allowed' the visitors to win 4-3.

Fixtures at international level continued throughout the war and Arsenal players D.Compton, L.Compton, J.Crayston, E.Hapgood, B.Joy, A.Kirchen, G.Marks, L.Scott (England), G.Bremner (Scotland), W.Barnes, R.Cumner, B.Jones, L.Jones (Wales) and K.O'Flanagan (Ireland) all represented their countries in wartime internationals.

Many Arsenal players were engaged in active service with the forces and among those who gave their lives to the cause were Henry Cook, Bobby Daniel (elder brother of Ray Daniel), Bill Dean, Hugh Glass, Leslie Lack, Bill Parr, Sidney Pugh and Cyril Tooze.

Leslie Compton beats Charlton Athletic goalkeeper Sam Bartram from the penalty-spot in Arsenal's opening wartime League game on 21 October 1939. Compton scored four goals, including another penalty, in this League South 'A' Division match at White Hart Lane, whilst his brother Denis netted two goals. The near-9,000 crowd were treated to 12 goals, with the Gunners emerging 8-4 winners.

Arsenal guest players in 1939-46 included:-
E.Alsford (Tottenham Hotspur), A.E.Beasley (Fulham), A.Beattie (Preston North End), F.P.Boulton (Derby County), J.Bowden (Oldham Athletic), G.Bradley (Newcastle United), J.E.R.Briscoe (Hearts), B.Bryant (Clapton Orient), P.Cabrelli (Raith Rovers), W.Copping (Leeds United), A.Cross (Queen's Park), J.Crozier (Brentford), A.G.Dawes (Crystal Palace), G.H.Dingwall (St Bernard's), H.P.Duke (Luton Town), M.Edelston (Reading), H.Ferrier (Barnsley), F.Fisher (Grimsby Town), W.Flack (Norwich City), R.Flavell (Airdrie), L.Gallimore (Watford), M.Gillies (Bolton Wanderers), L.Goldberg (Leeds United), L.A.Goulden (West Ham United), W.R.Griffiths (Cardiff City), F.Hall (Blackburn Rovers), R.L.Halton (Bury), W.Hamilton (St Bernard's), C.Harris (Shamrock Rovers), S.G.Hobbins (Charlton Athletic), P.G.Hooper (Tottenham Hotspur), L.Horsman (Bradford), W.Hughes (Huddersfield Town), D.Johnston (Hearts), E.Jones (West Bromwich Albion), J.T.Jones (Northampton Town), T.Jones (Watford), P.Joslin (Torquay United), P.Kelly (Aberdeen), A.Little (Glasgow Rangers), S.Matthews (Stoke City), D.L.McFarlane (Crystal Palace), T.B.McKillop (Glasgow Rangers), J.McLennan (Hearts), I.B.McPherson (Notts County), F.Mennie (Kilmarnock), S.Mercer (Leicester City), N.Miller (Arbroath), G.R.Mills (Chelsea), F.R.Mitchell (Birmingham), K.Moody (Grimsby Town), F.Morrad (Notts County), S.H.Mortensen (Blackpool), B.Nieuwenhuys (Liverpool), T.Orr (Greenock Morton), J.Paton (Glasgow Celtic), G.Patterson (Glasgow Celtic), B.Ratcliffe (Oldham Athletic), T.Rigg (Middlesbrough), F.Roberts (Bury), G.Scaife (Leeds United), W.Shankly (Preston North End), J.Southam (West Bromwich Albion), F.C.Steele (Stoke City), L.Stevens (Tottenham Hotspur), W.Strauss (Aberdeen), E.Taylor (Luton Town), R.A.Thomas (Brentford), G.J.Tweedy (Grimsby Town), R.A.Ward (Tottenham Hotspur), D.Winter (Bolton Wanderers), W.Wrigglesworth (Manchester United).

1939-40

League South 'A' Division

Manager: G.Allison

1	Oct	21	(h)	Charlton A	W 8-4	L.Compton 4, Crayston, D.Compton 2, Lewis	8,934
2		28	(a)	Clapton O	W 6-1	D.Compton 3, Kirchen, Nelson, L.Compton	8,000
3	Nov	4	(h)	Crystal P	W 5-0	D.Compton 2, Lewis, L.Compton, Crayston	7,306
4		11	(a)	Norwich C	D 1-1	Bastin	12,000
5		18	(h)	Tottenham H	W 2-1	D.Compton, Nelson	15,000
6		25	(a)	Millwall	D 3-3	Kirchen, L.Compton 2	15,000
7	Dec	2	(h)	West Ham U	W 3-0	Lewis, D.Compton, Crayston	10,000
8		9	(a)	Watford	W 3-1	L.Compton, Kirchen 2	12,000
9		16	(h)	Southend	W 5-1	Crayston, L.Jones, L.Compton 2, Kirchen	3,396
10		25	(h)	Clapton O	W 3-0	Lewis, Kirchen, Crayston	4,000
11		26	(a)	Crystal P	W 3-0	Lewis 3	10,400
12		30	(h)	Norwich C	D 2-2	Nelson, Lewis	3,000
13	Jan	1	(a)	Charlton A*	W 6-2	Kirchen 2, L.Compton 2, Lewis 2	2,000
14		13	(h)	Millwall	W 4-1	Crayston, Kirchen 2, L.Compton	8,013
15		20	(a)	West Ham U	L 0-3		8,000
16		25	(a)	Tottenham H	W 1-0	Bastin	9,054
17	Feb	8	(h)	Watford	D 2-2	L.Compton, Morgan	1,000
18	Apr	3	(a)	Southend	W 5-0	Lewis 2, Bastin, Hapgood, L.Compton	3,048

P	W	D	L	F	A	W	D	L	F	A	Pts	Pos	
18	7	2	0	34	11	6	2	1	28	11	30	1st	Appearances
													Goals

*After abandoned match (57 minutes) on December 23 — Charlton 0 Arsenal 0 team as per Match 10

League South 'C' Division

19	Feb	10	(h)	Brentford	W 3-1	L.Compton 2, Lewis	5,000
20		24	(h)	Millwall	W 4-1	L.Compton 3 (1 pen), Crayston	9,954
21	Mar	2	(a)	Fulham	D 1-1	Lewis	8,600
22		9	(a)	Southampton	L 2-3	Logie, Lewis	8,000
23		16	(h)	West Ham U	L 2-3	Bastin, L.Compton	10,731
24		22	(a)	Charlton A	W 2-1	L.Compton, B.Jones	14,757
25		23	(h)	Chelsea	W 3-0	D.Compton, L.Compton, Weaver (og)	15,000
26		25	(h)	Charlton A	D 1-1	Kirchen	10,642
27		30	(a)	Tottenham H	D 1-1	Nelson	15,000
28	Apr	6	(a)	Brentford	W 4-2	L.Compton 3 (1 pen), Lewis	8,000
29		8	(a)	West Ham U	L 1-2	Lewis	8,000
30		13	(h)	Portsmouth	W 3-2	Bastin, Crayston, Drake	7,000
31		17	(a)	Chelsea	D 2-2	Lewis 2	8,500
32		24	(h)	Tottenham H	L 2-4	Drake, Bastin	4,432
33	May	13	(a)	Millwall	W 2-0	L.Compton, Carr	8,100
34		22	(h)	Fulham	W 2-1	Drake, Curtis	6,000
35		25	(a)	Portsmouth	D 1-1	Drake	4,000
36	Jun	1	(h)	Southampton	W 5-0	Kirchen, L.Jones 2, Drake, Crayston	2,800

P	W	D	L	F	A	W	D	L	F	A	Pts	Pos	
18	6	1	2	25	13	3	4	2	16	13	23	3rd	Appearances
													Goals

Football League War Cup

1	Apr	20	(h)	Notts C	W 4-0	L.Compton 3, L.Jones	11,521
1		27	(a)	Notts C	W 5-1	Lewis 2, L.Compton 2, Kirchen	14,755
2	May	4	(h)	Crystal P	W 3-1	L.Compton 2, Drake	15,500
2		11	(a)	Crystal P	W 2-0	Kirchen 2	21,406
3	May	18	(h)	Birmingham	L 1-2	Kirchen	11,259

Appearances
Goals

Appearances and goals grid (player shirt numbers by match):

Marks GW	Male CG	Hapgood EA	Crayston WJ	Joy B	Jones LJ	Kirchen AJ	Nelson D	Compton LH	Lewis R	Compton DCS	Collett E	Bastin CS	Scott L	Pryde D	Platt EH	Bremner GH	Curtis GF	Smith EF	Morgan AS	Parr WW	Logie JT	Swindin GH	Jones B	Drake EJ	Wilson A	Carr EM	Holmes E	
1	2	3	4	5	6	7	8	9	10	11																		1
1	2	3	4	5		7	8	9		11	6	10																2
1	2	3	4	5		7	8	9	10	11	6																	3
1	2			5		7	8		9	11	6	10	3	4														4
1	2	3	4	5	6	7	8	9	10	11																		5
1	2		4	5	6	7	8	9	10		11	3																6
1	2		4	5	10		7	9	8	11	6		3															7
1	2	3	4	5	6	7	8	9		11		10																8
1	2	3	4	5	10	7	11	9	8		6																	9
1	2	3	4	5		7	10	9	8	11	6																	10
1	2		4	5		7	10	9	8	11	6		3															11
1	2	3	4	5		7	10	9	8	11	6																	12
1		3	4	5	10	7		9	8	11	6		2															13
1	2	3	4	5		7	10	9	8	11	6																	14
1	2			5	10	7		9	8		6	11	3	4														15
	2	3		5	4		9		11	6	7			1	8	10												16
	2	3		5	6		9	8			7	1		10	4	11												17
1	2	3		5	6		9	8		11		4		10		7												18
16	17	13	13	18	11	14	13	17	15	13	11	8	6	4	2	1	3	1	1	1								
	1	6		1	10	3	16	12	9		3					1												

Marks GW	Male CG	Hapgood EA	Crayston WJ	Joy B	Jones LJ	Kirchen AJ	Nelson D	Compton LH	Lewis R	Compton DCS	Collett E	Bastin CS	Scott L	Pryde D	Platt EH	Bremner GH	Curtis GF	Smith EF	Morgan AS	Parr WW	Logie JT	Swindin GH	Jones B	Drake EJ	Wilson A	Carr EM	Holmes E	
1	2			5		6	7	11	9	8			3	4			10											19
1	2	3	4	5	6	7		9	8	11		10																20
	2	3		5	6		7	9	8	11		4			1		10											21
	2	3		5	6			9	8			4			11	1	7		10									22
1	2			5	6		8	3	9			11		4		7	10											23
	2	3		5	6			9	8	11				4		7				1	10							24
	2	3	4	5	6	7		9	8	11										1	10							25
	2	3	4	5	6	7		9				11			1	8					10							26
	2			5	6		7	3	9	11		4				8				1	10							27
	2	3		5	6	7		9	8	11		4					10			1								28
	2	3		5	6			9	8	11		4			1						10	7						29
	2		4	5			11	8	9			6	3				10				1		7					30
	2	3	4	5	6			9	8			11					10						7	1				31
	2	3		5	6			9	8			11		4			10						7	1				32
	2	3		5	6			9	8			11		4			10							1	7			33
	2	3	4	5	6			9				11					8				10		7	1				34
	2	3			10			8	9			6	4		1		11						7		5			35
		3	4	5	10	7		9				6	11	2								8	1					36
3	17	14	8	16	17	7	6	18	13	7	2	15	3	6	5	5	10			1	5	6	7	5	1	1		
		3		2	2	1		12	7	1		3					1			1		1	5		1			

1 own-goal

Marks GW	Male CG	Hapgood EA	Crayston WJ	Joy B	Jones LJ	Kirchen AJ	Nelson D	Compton LH	Lewis R	Compton DCS	Collett E	Bastin CS	Scott L	Pryde D	Platt EH	Bremner GH	Curtis GF	Smith EF	Morgan AS	Parr WW	Logie JT	Swindin GH	Jones B	Drake EJ	Wilson A	Carr EM	Holmes E	
	2	3		5	6	7	10	9	8	11		4											1					1
1	2	3	4	5	6	7		9	8			11									10							1
1	2	3	4	5	6			9	8			11									10	7						2
1	2			5	6	7	8	9		11		4	3								10							2
	2	3	4	5	6	7		9				11					10					8	1					3
3	5	4	3	5	5	4	2	5	3	2		5	1				1				3	2	2					
				1	4		7	2				1																

1940-41

South Regional League   Manager: G.Allison

1	Aug	31	(a)	Southend U	W	7-1	L.Compton 5, Drake 2	1,542
2	Sep	7	(h)	Fulham	W	5-0	Nelson, Drake 2, Bastin, Kirchen	3,000
3		14	(a)	Fulham	W	1-0	Drake	1,000
4		21	(h)	Brentford	W	3-1	Fisher 2, Bastin	1,700
5		28	(a)	Queen's Park R	L	2-3	Kirchen, D.Compton	2,500
6	Oct	5	(h)	Southend U	W	7-0	L.Compson 2, Kirchen 2, Bastin, Lewis, Turton (og)	1,410
7		12	(a)	Tottenham H	W	3-2	Kirchen 2, L.Compton	4,568
8		19	(h)	Northampton T	W	5-4	Drake, Kirchen 3, D.Compton	2,191
9		26	(a)	Brentford	D	3-3	Kirchen 2, Fisher	1,200
10	Nov	2	(h)	Charlton A	D	2-2	L.Compton, Green (og)	1,477
11		16	(h)	Tottenham H	D	1-1	Drake	4,000
12		23	(a)	Northampton T	W	8-1	Bastin 2, Kirchen 2, L.Compton 2, Jobson, Mills	7,000
13		30	(h)	Crystal P	D	2-2	Drake 2	761
14	Dec	7	(a)	Charlton A	L	0-5		1,000
15		14	(h)	Queen's Park R	W	3-2	D.Compton, Bastin, L.Compton	1,300
16		21	(a)	Crystal P	D	3-3	Henley, L.Compton, Crayston	4,000
17		25	(a)	West Ham U	L	2-4	Curtis, Kirchen	8,000
18		28	(h)	Luton T	W	8-1	L.Compton 2, Kirchen 2, D.Compton, L.Jones, Bastin, Gager (og)	8,000
19	Apr	14	(a)	Chelsea	L	1-3	Nelson	4,000

	P	W	D	L	F	A	W	D	L	F	A	Ave	Pos	Appearances
	19	6	3	0	36	13	4	2	4	30	25	1.736	4th*	Goals

*League position determined on goal average. Fixtures v Brighton (a) on November 9 and West Ham (h) on December 26 were not played.

London War Cup

20	Jan	4	(a)	Reading	L	0-2		6,158
21		11	(h)	Reading	L	0-1		3,069
22		25	(a)	West Ham U	W	3-1	Drake, Curtis, Bastin	5,000
23	Feb	1	(a)	Clapton O	D	3-3	L.Compton, Bastin, Kirchen	1,200
24		8	(h)	Clapton O	W	15-2	L.Compton 10, Bastin 2, D.Compton 2, L.Jones	2,780
25	Mar	22	(a‡)	Millwall	W	6-1	L.Compton 3, Nelson, Crayston, Henley	5,500
26	May	3	(a)	Tottenham H	D	3-3	Kirchen, L.Compton 2	9,651
27		17	(h)	West Ham U	W	3-0	Drake 2, L.Compton (pen)	7,365
28		21	(h)	Tottenham H	L	0-3		6,673
29		24	(a‡)	Millwall	W	5-2	Drake 3, Blakeney, Henley	5,000

	P	W	D	L	F	A	W	D	L	F	A	Pts	Pos	Appearances
	10	2	0	2	18	6	3	2	1	20	12	12	4th†	Goals

†Arsenal finished 4th in Group 'B' of the Qualifying Competition but did not qualify for the semi-finals. ‡Both fixtures played at Millwall.

Football League War Cup

1	Feb	15	(a)	Brighton & HA	W	4-1	Kirchen 2, D.Compton, L.Compton	11,000
1		22	(h)	Brighton & HA	W	3-1	Drake, Kirchen, D.Compton	3,846
2	Mar	1	(a)	Watford	W	4-0	L.Compton 2, Kirchen 2	10,884
2		8	(h)	Watford	W	5-0	L.Compton 3, Kirchen 2	4,427
3		15	(a)	West Ham U	W	1-0	L.Compton	14,000
3		29	(h)	West Ham U	W	2-1	Kirchen, L.Compton	12,835
4	Apr	5	(h)	Tottenham H	W	2-1	Nelson, Bastin	22,107
4		12	(a)	Tottenham H	D	1-1	L.Compton	25,258
SF		19	(h)	Leicester C	W	1-0	Crayston	9,240
SF		26	(a)	Leicester C	W	2-1	L.Compton, Crayston	26,500
F	May	10	(n*)	Preston NE	D	1-1	D.Compton	60,000
R		31	(n†)	Preston NE	L	1-2	Gallimore (og)	45,000

*Played at Wembley Stadium. †Played at Ewood Park, Blackburn.   Appearances
                                                                                  Goals

Appearances and goals grid (shirt number shown in each player's column per match; final two rows of each block are appearance totals and goals).

Matches 1–19

Platt EH	Scott L	Hapgood EA	Pryde D	Joy B	Collett E	Drake EJ	Bastin CS	Compton LH	Curtis GF	Compton DCS	Marks GW	Kirchen AJ	Nelson D	Henley L	Scaife G	Male CG	Jones LJ	Fisher AN	Beasley AE	Dean WB	Lewis R	Wilson A	Crayston WJ	Rigg T	Jobson TH	Mills GR	Dobson JR	Smith EF	Boulton FP	Waller H	Beattie A	Alsford E	Smith L	Blakeney J	#
1	2	3	4	5	6	7	8	9	10	11																									1
	2	3	4	5	6	9	11				1	7	8	10																					2
	2		4	5	6	7	8	9		11	1			10		3																			3
	3				5	6	7	11	9			1		8		2	4	10																	4
	3				5	8	6	9		11		1	7	4		2				10															5
	3				5	6			9	11			7	4		2				10		8	1												6
	3				5	6	4	9	8	11			7			2				10			1												7
	3				5	8	6	9		11			7	4		2				10			1												8
	3				5	8	6	9		11			7	4		2				10		1													9
	3				5	6		9		11	1	7		4		2				10		8													10
	3				5	6	7	10	9	11	1			8		2							4												11
	3					6	11	9				7		4		2				10			1	5	8										12
	3					6	9	4	2				7			11						8	1	5	10										13
3	2					6	9	11	3	10			7	8									5		1	4									14
	3				5	6	10	9		11		8	2			7							4	1											15
	2	3	4	5	6		11	9			1	7				10							8												16
	2	3			5	9	4		10	11		7	8	6									1												17
	2	3			5	6	10	9		11		7		4						8			1												18
	2	3				6	9	10	5			7	11	4						8									1						19
1	18	7	4	9	19	12	19	17	4	12	7	13	5	14	1	10	3	5	4	3	5	2	3	4	3	2	1	1	1						
					9	7	15	1	4	16	2	1				1	3				1		1		1	1									

3 own-goals

Matches 20–29

Platt EH	Scott L	Hapgood EA	Pryde D	Joy B	Collett E	Drake EJ	Bastin CS	Compton LH	Curtis GF	Compton DCS	Marks GW	Kirchen AJ	Nelson D	Henley L	Scaife G	Male CG	Jones LJ	Fisher AN	Beasley AE	Dean WB	Lewis R	Wilson A	Crayston WJ	Rigg T	Jobson TH	Mills GR	Dobson JR	Smith EF	Boulton FP	Waller H	Beattie A	Alsford E	Smith L	Blakeney J	#
	3				5	6	7	10	9	11	1			4		2	8																		20
	3				5	6	8	4	9	10		7				2			11				1												21
	3				5	6	9	8		10	11	1	7	4		2																			22
					5	6	9	8	3	10	11		7	4		2											1								23
	3				5		8	9		11			7	4		2	6	10									1								24
	2	3			5	6	10	9		11		7	8							4							1								25
	3				5	6	2		9			7	11	4						10		8					1								26
		4	5	3	9	10	2	8		11			6							7							1								27
	3	4	5	6	9	10	2		11				8							7							1								28
	6	9	10					11	8																				1	2	3	4	5	7	29
6	2	2	8	10	8	9	8	4	6	2	4	5	9	5	2	5	1	1	1	7	1	1	1	1	1				7	1	1	1	1	1	
					6	4	17	1	2	2		1	2			1				1														1	

Cup matches

Platt EH	Scott L	Hapgood EA	Pryde D	Joy B	Collett E	Drake EJ	Bastin CS	Compton LH	Curtis GF	Compton DCS	Marks GW	Kirchen AJ	Nelson D	Henley L	Scaife G	Male CG	Jones LJ	Fisher AN	Beasley AE	Dean WB	Lewis R	Wilson A	Crayston WJ	Rigg T	Jobson TH	Mills GR	Dobson JR	Smith EF	Boulton FP	Waller H	Beattie A	Alsford E	Smith L	Blakeney J	#
	3				5	6		8	9	10	11	1	7			4				2															1
	3				5	6	8	10	9		11		7							2	4						1								1
	3				5	6		8	9	10	11		7			4				2							1								2
	3					6	7	10	9			1	11	8		4				2													5		2
	2	3			5	6	7	11	9	10	1									8			4												3
	2	3			5	6		10	9			1	7	11	8								4												3
	2	3			5	6		10	9			1	7	11	4								8												4
	3	1			5	6		10	9			11		7		8	2						4												4
	2	3			5	6		10	9			11	1	7		8							4												SF
	2	3			5	6			9	11	1	7	10			8							4												SF
	2	3			5	6		10	9	11	1	7				8							4												F
	2	3			5	6	9	10		11	1	7				8							4												R
12	8	11	12	4	11	11	3	8	9	11	4	7	5	4	2	7							2		7				2			1			
				1	1	10		3		8		1				2							2												

1 own-goal

1941-42

Manager: G.Allison

1	Aug	30	(a)	Brentford	L	1-4	Nelson	12,000
2	Sep	6	(h)	Crystal P	W	7-2	Lewis 5, Bastin 2	6,027
3		13	(a)	Fulham	W	5-2	Lewis 3, Henley, Kirchen	10,473
4		20	(h)	Tottenham H	W	4-0	Cumner 2, Lewis 2	17,446
5		27	(a)	Portsmouth	W	5-1	Bastin 2, Lewis 2, Henley	16,000
6	Oct	4	(h)	Chelsea	W	3-0	Lewis, Crayston, Weaver (og)	7,747
7		11	(a)	Charlton A	W	3-1	Lewis, Bastin, Crayston	15,000
8		18	(h)	West Ham U	W	4-1	Lewis 2, D.Compton, Kirchen	13,419
9		25	(a)	Watford	L	1-3	Beasley	6,000
10	Nov	1	(h)	Aldershot	W	3-2	D.Compton, Miller, Lewis	8,884
11		8	(a)	Millwall	D	2-2	Miller, Male	15,000
12		15	(h)	Clapton O	W	5-2	L.Compton 2, Lewis 3	7,036
13		22	(h)	Queen's Park R	W	4-1	Miller 2, D.Compton 2	7,377
14		29	(h)	Reading	W	3-1	Lewis 2, Miller	8,198
15	Dec	6	(a)	Brighton & HA	W	3-2	Bastin (pen), Drake, Miller	10,000
16		13	(h)	Brentford	L	1-3	Crayston	9,739
17		25	(h)	Fulham	W	2-0	Lewis, Kirchen	10,578
18		27	(a)	Tottenham H	W	2-1	Drake, D.Compton	16,777
19	Jan	3	(h)	Portsmouth	W	6-1	Lewis 3, Kirchen 2, Flewin (og)	10,160
20		10	(a)	Chelsea	W	5-1	L.Compton 2, Miller, Kirchen 2	12,260
21		17	(h)	Charlton A	W	3-2	Kirchen 3	3,958
22		24	(a)	West Ham U	L	0-3		20,000
23		31	(h)	Watford	W	11-0	Lewis 5, Kirchen 2, D.Compton 2, Bastin 2	4,761
24	Feb	7	(a)	Aldershot	L	0-1		10,000
25		14	(h)	Millwall	W	10-0	Lewis 4, Nelson 3, Bastin 2, Henley	7,520
26		21	(a)	Clapton O	W	3-1	Lewis 2, Kirchen	6,000
27		28	(a)	Queen's Park R	W	1-0	Drake	8,932
28	Mar	7	(a)	Reading	W	4-1	Lewis 2, Nelson, D.Compton	10,000
29		14	(h)	Brighton & HA	W	4-2	Drake 4	6,206
30	May	9	(a)	Crystal P	D	3-3	Lewis 3	10,024

P	W	D	L	F	A	W	D	L	F	A	Pts	Pos		
30	14	0	1	70	17	9	2	4	38	26	48	1st	Appearances	
													Goals	

London War Cup

31	Mar	21	(h)	Clapton O	W	4-1	Drake 2, Nelson, D.Compton	6,790
32		28	(a)	West Ham U	W	4-0	Drake, Nelson, Bastin, Kirchen	19,000
33	Apr	4	(a)	Clapton O	W	2-1	Lewis, Henley	6,000
34		6	(h)	West Ham U	L	1-4	D.Compton	18,405
35		11	(a)	Brighton & HA	W	3-0	D.Compton 2, Drake	12,000
36		18	(h)	Brighton & HA	W	5-1	Lewis 2, Bastin, D.Compton, Ford (og)	8,362
SF	May	2	(n*)	Brentford	D	0-0		41,154
R		16	(n†)	Brentford	L	1-2	Poyser (og)	37,600

P	W	D	L	F	A	W	D	L	F	A	Pts	Pos		
6	2	0	1	10	6	3	0	0	9	1	10	1st‡	Appearances	
													Goals	

‡Arsenal finished 1st in Group 1 of the Qualifying Competition. *Played at Stamford Bridge, London. †Played at White Hart Lane, London.

338

Appearance/scorer grid (players as columns, match numbers as rows). Shirt numbers worn are recorded in each cell.

Platt EH	Scott L	Hapgood EA	Jones LJ	Joy B	Collett E	Kirchen AJ	Nelson D	Lewis R	Bastin CS	Cumner RH	Curtis GF	Crayston WJ	Henley L	Male CG	Compton LH	Drake EJ	Compton DCS	Smith L	Beasley AE	Blakeney J	Marks GW	Miller N	Goldberg L	Waller H	Young AE	Hooper PG	Hobbins SG	Tweedy GJ	Pryde D	Drury GB	No.
1	2	3	4	5	6	7	8	9	10	11																					1
1	2	3		5	6	7	8	9	11		10	4																			2
1	2	3		5	6	7	8	9	11			4	10																		3
1		3		5	6	7	8	9	4	11	10				2																4
1	2	3		5	6	7	8	9	11					10	4																5
1	2			5	6	8	10	9	11			4			3	7															6
1	2	3		5	6	7		10				4	8		9	11															7
1	2	3		5	6	7	8	9				4			10	11															8
1	2				6	7						4	10		3	9		5	8	11											9
		6		5				9	10	7		4			2	3	11				1	8									10
1		10			6		7	9	11						4	3					8	2	5								11
	2	3			6			9	10			4			5	8	7	11			1										12
1					6			9	4	7					5	3	10	11				8	2								13
1	2				6	7		9	11			4			5	10						8			3						14
1	2	3					7		6	11	10	4					9	5				8									15
1		3		5	6			9	11			4			2	10	7					8									16
1	2	3		5	6	7		9	10						4	8		11													17
1		3		5	6	7		9	10						4	2	8	11													18
1	2	3		5	6	7		9	8				4			10	11														19
		3		5	6	7			11			4	10		2	9					1	8									20
1		3		5	6	7	10		11			4			2	9	8														21
1	2	3			6	7		9	11			4			5	10	8														22
1	2	3		5	6	7	8	9	10						4	11															23
1	2	3		5	6	7	8		10						4	9	11														24
	2			5	6	7	10	9	11			4	8		3									1							25
	2	3		5	6	7		9	10			4	8			11							1								26
	2	3			6		8		10			4			5	9	7	11			1										27
1	2	3		5	6	7		9	10			8			4		11														28
	2			5	6		8		11						10	4	3	9										1	7		29
				5	3		8	9	10						4	2	7	11	6									1			30
22	23	19	3	21	29	20	17	23	30	5	4	15	9	19	20	12	14	2	2	1	4	7	2	1	1	1	1	2	1		
									13	5		42	10	2		3	3	1	4	7	8	1									7

2 own-goals

Platt EH	Scott L	Hapgood EA	Jones LJ	Joy B	Collett E	Kirchen AJ	Nelson D	Lewis R	Bastin CS	Cumner RH	Curtis GF	Crayston WJ	Henley L	Male CG	Compton LH	Drake EJ	Compton DCS	Smith L	Beasley AE	Blakeney J	Marks GW	Miller N	Goldberg L	Waller H	Young AE	Hooper PG	Hobbins SG	Tweedy GJ	Pryde D	Drury GB	No.
	3			5	6		8		10						4	2	9	11			1							7			31
	2	3		5	6	7	8								4	9	11				1										32
	2			5	6		8	9	11				10		4	3	7				1										33
	2	3		5	6		8	9	10						4		7	11			1										34
	2	3	8	5		7	6						10		4		9	11			1										35
1	2			5				10	9	6			8		4	3	7	11													36
	3			5	6	7	8	9	10						4	2		11			1										SF
1	2	3		5	6			9	10						4		7	11									8				R
2	7	5	1	8	6	2	7	5	8	1	2	1	8	3	7	7	2	4			4				1	1					
												1	2	3	2		1		4	5											

2 own-goals

1942-43

Football League — South   Manager: G.Allison

1	Aug	29	(a)	Charlton A	W 6-2	B.Jones 3, Drake 2, Kirchen	15,000
2	Sep	5	(h)	Southampton	W 6-1	Kirchen 3, Lewis, Cumner, Drake	9,153
3		12	(a)	Millwall	W 2-1	Bastin, Drake	12,500
4		19	(h)	Luton T	W 2-0	L.Compton, Chew (og)	8,994
5		26	(a)	Portsmouth	D 2-2	Drake, Kirchen	14,000
6	Oct	3	(a)	Fulham	W 4-3	Lewis 2, Kirchen, Drake	11,000
7		10	(a)	Clapton O	W 4-1	Drake 2, Lewis 2	4,000
8		17	(h)	Brentford	L 0-2		16,700
9		24	(h)	Reading	W 4-1	D.Compton 2, Lewis, Drake	9,007
10		31	(a)	Crystal P	W 7-1	Lewis 5, D.Compton 2	12,900
11	Nov	7	(a)	Tottenham H	L 0-1		21,551
12		14	(h)	Queen's Park R	W 3-0	Kirchen 2, Reay (og)	14,646
13		21	(a)	Aldershot	W 7-4	Lewis 3, D.Compton 2, Bastin 2	10,000
14		28	(h)	Charlton A	W 3-0	D.Compton, Henley, Bastin	9,129
15	Dec	5	(a)	Southampton	W 3-1	Lewis 2, Morgan	9,000
16		12	(h)	Millwall	W 6-0	Crayston 2, Lewis 2, Drake, Kirchen	10,200
17		19	(a)	Luton T	W 4-0	Bastin 2, Crayston, D.Compton	3,000
18		25	(a)	Chelsea	L 2-5	Lewis, Colley	17,000
19		26	(h)	Chelsea	L 1-5	Bastin	18,253
20	Jan	2	(h)	Portsmouth	W 5-0	Kirchen 2, Bastin, Lewis 2	9,778
21		9	(h)	Fulham	W 7-2	Lewis 3, B.Jones, Male, D.Compton, Kirchen	8,332
22		16	(h)	Clapton O	W 6-0	Lewis 3, Kirchen 2, Bastin	8,387
23		23	(a)	Brentford	W 1-0	D.Compton	23,180
24		30	(a)	Reading	W 5-4	Henley 3, Lewis, Nelson	8,000
25	Feb	6	(h)	Crystal P	W 9-0	Lewis 3, Drake 3, Nelson, Crayston, D.Compton	7,926
26		13	(h)	Tottenham H	W 1-0	Kirchen	30,690
27		20	(a)	Queen's Park R	L 2-3	Lewis 2	13,495
28		27	(h)	Aldershot	L 0-1		6,848

P	W	D	L	F	A	W	D	L	F	A	Pts	Pos	
28	11	0	3	53	12	10	1	3	49	23	43	1st	Appearances
													Goals

Football League Cup — South

29	Mar	6	(a)	Brighton & HA	W 5-1	Lewis 3, D.Compton 2	10,000
30		13	(h)	Watford	W 4-1	D.Compton 2, (1 pen), Drake, Brown (og)	7,521
31		20	(a)	West Ham U	W 3-1	Lewis 2, Kirchen	22,000
32		27	(h)	Brighton & HA	W 5-0	Lewis 3, Crayston, L.Compton	7,991
33	Apr	3	(a)	Watford	D 1-1	Lewis	8,726
34		10	(h)	West Ham U	W 3-1	Bastin, D.Compton, Briscoe	31,016
SF		24	(n†)	Queen's Park R	W 4-1	D.Compton, Bastin, Lewis, Briscoe	50,048
F	May	1	(n‡)	Charlton A	W 7-1	Lewis 4, Drake 2, D.Compton	75,000

P	W	D	L	F	A	W	D	L	F	A	Pts	Pos	
6	3	0	0	12	2	2	2	1	0	9	3	11	1st*	Appearances
													Goals

*Arsenal finished 1st in Group 1 of the Qualifying Competition. †Played at Stamford Bridge, London. ‡Played at Wembley Stadium.

Comrades-in-arms, from the left, Reg Lewis, Bryn Jones and Les Compton.

340

Compton LH	Male CG	Collett E	Crayston WJ	Joy B	Bastin CS	Kirchen AJ	Nelson D	Drake EJ	Jones B	Cumner RH	Marks GW	McKillop T	Hapgood EA	Henley L	Lewis R	Swindin GH	Scott L	Compton DCS	Strauss W	Shankly W	Colley H	Young AE	Jones LJ	Kelly P	Johnston D	Fields AG	Morgan AS	Watson-Smith N	Pryde D	Tweedy GJ	Winter D	Joslin P	Copping W	Crozier J	Briscoe J	
1	2	3	4	5	6	7	8	9	10	11																										1
	6		5			7		9	10	11	1	2	3	4	8																					2
3	2	6	4	5	11	7	8	9	10			1																								3
2		6	4	5	11	7	8	9	10				3			1																				4
3		5			6	7	10	8					4	9	1	2	11																			5
3		4	5			10	7	11		8			1	6	9	2																				6
3	5				6		8	7	10				4	9	1	2		11																		7
	6	4	5		8	7	11		10				3	9	1	2																				8
	2		5			10	7	8					6	9	1	3	11		4																	9
	6		5			10	7	8					1	3	4	9	2	11																		10
	6		5			10	7	8					1	3	4	9	2	11																		11
	6		4	5				11					9	10	1				2		7	3	8													12
	5		4						10					7					2	11		3	6	1												13
2	6		5				10	7						8				9		11	4	3	1													14
	6				8			7										9	2	11		3		1	4	5	10									15
	6	8	5				10	11						7	1	3		9	2			4														16
3	6	8	5				10							7				9	2	11		4														17
	5	6					10	8		11							3	9	2		7								1	4						18
	5						10	8		11			6					9	2		7	3							1	4						19
	6		5		8			11	7				10		1		3		4			9	2													20
	6		5		8			7					10				4	9	2	11											1	3				21
	5	6			8			11	7				10				4	9	2												3	1				22
3	2	6	5		8			7					9	10						11											1		4			23
	5	6	4				10	7	11								8	9				3									1	2				24
2	3	4	5				7	10					8		1				11																	25
3	2	6	5				10	7					8	9	1				11														4			26
3	6		5		8			11	7				10		1			9	2														4			27
3	6		5		8		10	11		7								9	2							4							1			28
10	25	9	14	20	25	22	18	17	12	4	12	1	10	13	22	5	19	12	1	5	3	6	2	3	1	1	1	2	2	4	3	1	3			
1	1		4		9	15	2	13	4				4	33		11				1											1					

2 own-goals

Compton LH	Male CG	Collett E	Crayston WJ	Joy B	Bastin CS	Kirchen AJ	Nelson D	Drake EJ	Jones B	Cumner RH	Marks GW	McKillop T	Hapgood EA	Henley L	Lewis R	Swindin GH	Scott L	Compton DCS	Strauss W	Shankly W	Colley H	Young AE	Jones LJ	Kelly P	Johnston D	Fields AG	Morgan AS	Watson-Smith N	Pryde D	Tweedy GJ	Winter D	Joslin P	Copping W	Crozier J	Briscoe J	
	2	6	5				10		8					3				9								11		4						1	7	29
	2	6		5	10	7		8		1								9	3	11				4												30
3	6		8	5	10	7			1									9	2	11				4												31
3	6		8	5		7			1				10					9	2					4												32
3	6		8	5	10	7	11		1									9	2					4												33
3	6		4	5	10		8		1									9	2	11														7		34
3	6		4	5	10		1											9	2	11				8										7		SF
3	6		4	5	10	7		8	1									9	2	11																F
6	8	2	7	7	7	5	3	2	7	1	1		8		7	7		6																	1	3	
1			1		2	1		3					14			7																			2		

1 own-goal

341

1943-44

1	Aug	28	(a)	Charlton A	L 0-1		13,500
2	Sep	4	(h)	Southampton	W 4-1	Curtis 2, Bastin 2	11,525
3		11	(a)	West Ham U	D 2-2	Briscoe, Kirchen	15,000
4		18	(h)	Portsmouth	L 1-2	Crayston	12,738
5		25	(a)	Brighton & HA	D 1-1	Bastin (pen)	7,000
6	Oct	2	(a)	Fulham	W 4-3	D.Compton 3, Bastin	17,994
7		9	(a)	Clapton O	D 1-1	D.Compton	7,500
8		16	(h)	Brentford	D 3-3	Briscoe, Bastin, Lewis	17,658
9		23	(h)	Watford	W 4-2	Lewis 3, Drake	8,033
10		30	(a)	Crystal P	D 1-1	Lewis	14,000
11	Nov	6	(h)	Chelsea	W 6-0	Lewis 2, Bastin 2, D.Compton 2	16,007
12		13	(h)	Queen's Park R	W 5-0	Lewis 3, D.Compton, Bastin	20,014
13		27	(h)	Charlton A	W 6-2	Lewis 2, Briscoe, D.Compton, Bastin, Crayston	7,275
14	Dec	4	(a)	Southampton	W 2-1	Lewis 2 (1 pen)	12,000
15		11	(h)	West Ham U	D 1-1	Flavell	22,497
16		18	(a)	Tottenham H	L 1-2	Briscoe	22,683
17		25	(a)	Millwall	W 5-1	Lewis 2, Drake, D.Compton, Flavell	10,000
18		27	(h)	Millwall	D 1-1	Lewis	16,454
19	Jan	1	(a)	Portsmouth	L 1-2	Thomas	16,000
20		8	(a)	Chelsea	L 0-2		19,310
21		22	(h)	Fulham	D 1-1	Nelson	8,116
22		29	(h)	Clapton O	W 1-0	Drake	8,971
23	Feb	5	(a)	Brentford	L 1-4	D.Compton	20,270
24		12	(a)	Watford	W 2-0	Briscoe, Nelson	7,887
25	Apr	1	(a)	Aldershot*	W 3-0	Flavell, Lewis, Nelson	8,000
26		8	(h)	Crystal P	W 5-2	Lewis 2, Barnes 2, Bastin	11,563
27		10	(h)	Brighton & HA	W 3-1	Briscoe, Drake, Bastin	8,369
28		22	(h)	Tottenham H	D 3-3	Drake, Alexander, Bastin	26,330
29		29	(a)	Queen's Park R	D 1-1	Lewis	10,000
30	May	6	(h)	Aldershot	W 3-1	Lewis 2, Drake	6,335

P	W	D	L	F	A	W	D	L	F	A	Pts	Pos	
30	9	5	1	47	20	5	5	5	25	22	38	4th	Appearances
													Goals

*After abandoned match (67 minutes) on November 20 — Aldershot 3 Arsenal 2 (Drake, D.Compton) — Att: 10,000.

Football League Cup — South

31	Feb	19	(h)	Luton T	W 7-1	Drake 4, D.Compton 3	4,954
32		26	(a)	Queen's Park R	D 1-1	Barnes	15,000
33	Mar	4	(h)	Reading	L 2-3	Lewis, Flavell	12,582
34		11	(a)	Luton T	D 1-1	Drake	10,000
35		18	(h)	Queen's Park R	L 1-4	Drake	17,367
36		25	(a)	Reading	L 1-5	Drake	19,722

P	W	D	L	F	A	W	D	L	F	A	Pts	Pos	
6	1	0	2	10	8	0	2	1	3	7	4	4th‡	Appearances
													Goals

‡Arsenal finished 4th in Group 'D' of the Qualifying Competition and did not qualify for the semi-finals.

No.	Marks GW	Scott L	Male CG	Henley L	Joy B	Collett E	Kirchen AJ	Nelson D	Compton LH	Bastin CS	Compton DCS	Crayston WJ	Curtis GF	Crozier J	Edington J	Cabrelli P	Briscoe J	Jones JT	Hamilton W	Drake EJ	Lewis R	Barnes W	Jones A	Goulden LA	Swindin GH	Flavell R	Stroud RW	Hooper PG	Thomas RA	McLennan J	Duke HP	Jones E	Young AE	Hughes W	Farquhar D	Alexander T	Jones A(Frickley)	Cumner RH	Gillies M	No.
1	1	2	3	4	5	6	7	8	9	10	11																													1
2	1	3	2		5	6	9	7	10	11	4	8																												2
3		2		5		9	11		10		4	8	1	3	6	7																								3
4		3	2		5		8		11	4			10		1	6	7	9																						4
5	1		2		5	6		10		4			7			8	9	3	11																					5
6	1	2	6		5		10	11	4	8			7			9	3																							6
7	1	3	2	8	5		10	11	4				6	7		9																								7
8	1			5	3		11		6		4			7		8	9	2		10																				8
9	1	2	4		5	6		8	10	11				7		9	3																							9
10	1	2	4		5	6		8	10	11				7		9	3																							10
11		2		5	6		10	11	4	8			7			9	3		1																					11
12	1	2	4		5	6		10	11			8		7		9	3																							12
13	1	2		5	6		10	11	4				7		8	9	3																							13
14	1	2	4		5	6		8	10			11		7		9	3																							14
15	1	2	4		5	6		10	11	8			7				3		9																					15
16	1	2	4		5	6		10	11				7			9	3		8																					16
17	1	3	2		5	6		4	11				8	9		10	7																							17
18		2	4		5	6		10	11				8	9	3	7	1																							18
19	1		2		5	4		11		6		7		8	9	3		10																						19
20	1	3	2		5	4		10	11		6			7		8	9																							20
21	1		2		5	4	11	10			6		7			3		8																						21
22	1	2	5		4		10	11		6			7	9	3	8																								22
23	1	2		5	6		11			7		9	4	10		8																								23
24		2		5	4	8		6	7	9	3	10	1	11																										24
25	1		2	4	5		10			11	6	9	8	7		3																								25
26		2		5		10		7	6	9	11	8	3	1																										26
27	2		5		10		11	6	7	9	1	8	3	4																										27
28	1	3	2		5	8	10		6	9	11	4	7																											28
29	1		2		5	11	10		6	9	8	4	7	3																										29
30			5	2	11	8	6	7	9	1	4	3																												30
	22	19	25	3	27	24	3	12	1	24	18	10	7	1	6	3	19	1	7	17	22	20	1	1	1	8	3	1	1	4	1	1	3	2	4	2	2			
							1	3			12	10	2	2		6				6	23	2				3				1					1					

No.	Marks GW	Scott L	Male CG	Henley L	Joy B	Collett E	Kirchen AJ	Nelson D	Compton LH	Bastin CS	Compton DCS	Crayston WJ	Curtis GF	Crozier J	Edington J	Cabrelli P	Briscoe J	Jones JT	Hamilton W	Drake EJ	Lewis R	Barnes W	Jones A	Goulden LA	Swindin GH	Flavell R	Stroud RW	Hooper PG	Thomas RA	McLennan J	Duke HP	Jones E	Young AE	Hughes W	Farquhar D	Alexander T	Jones A(Frickley)	Cumner RH	Gillies M	No.
31		2		5	4		8	3	10	11						9													1				1	11					7	31
32		2	4		6		7	3								9			10			8							1	11			1	7				5		32
33		2		5	6		4									10	9	3				8							1	7					11					33
34	1	2	4		5		10						6			11	7	9	3			8																		34
35	1	2	4		6	11	10			7			9			3																			5					35
36	1	3	2		5	4	10		6			7				9	8	11																						36
	3	5	5		4	5	3	2	5	1			2			2	1	6	3	5			3				3	2							2	2				
								3									7	1	1			1																		

B.Bryant played number 9 in Match 21; L.Delaney played number 3 in Match 23; G.Dingwall played number 4 in Match 26; C.Smith played number 10 in Match 30; W.Flack played number 6 in Match 31; M.Buckby played number 8 in Match 35.

1944-45

Football League — South   Manager: G.Allison

1	Aug	26	(a)	Luton T	D	2-2	Horsman, Briscoe	7,500
2	Sep	2	(a)	Tottenham H	L	0-4		13,624
3		9	(h)	Aldershot	W	1-0	Horsman	11,760
4		16	(a)	Southampton	W	2-0	Drake, Farquhar	18,000
5		23	(h)	Queen's Park R	W	2-0	Drake, Wrigglesworth	15,336
6		30	(a)	Millwall	W	4-1	Mortensen 2, Bastin, Horsman	12,403
7	Oct	7	(h)	Brighton & HA	W	6-3	Farquhar 2, Mortensen 2, Drake, Wrigglesworth	10,281
8		14	(a)	Fulham	D	4-4	Drake, Mortensen 2, Nelson	16,000
9		21	(h)	West Ham U	L	0-3		27,800
10		28	(a)	Crystal P	L	3-4	Bastin, Drake, Farquhar	15,000
11	Nov	4	(a)	Reading	L	1-3	Bastin	15,000
12		11	(h)	Charlton A	W	4-3	Nelson 2, Bastin, Smith (og)	11,945
13		18	(h)	Watford	W	4-0	Farquhar 2, Mortensen, Shaw (og)	7,910
14		25	(a)	Chelsea	L	1-2	Steele	37,753
15	Dec	2	(h)	Luton T	W	9-3	Mortensen 3, Wrigglesworth 2, Bastin 2, Drake, Steele	7,664
16		9	(h)	Tottenham H	L	2-3	Drake, Farquhar	29,432
17		16	(a)	Aldershot	W	3-2	Mortensen 2, Drake	8,000
18		23	(h)	Brentford	W	5-2	Wrigglesworth 2, Mortensen 2, Steele	18,527
19		30	(h)	Southampton	L	2-4	Drake 2	9,975
20	Jan	6	(a)	Queen's Park R	L	2-3	Steele 2	10,000
21		13	(h)	Millwall	W	4-1	Drake 2, Matthews, Bastin	21,081
22		20	(a)	Brighton & HA	L	0-3		10,000
23		27	(h)	Fulham	W	8-3	Mortensen 4, Wrigglesworth, Drake 2, Steele	5,246
24	Mar	24	(h)	Crystal P	W	1-0	Holland	9,619
25		31	(h)	Reading	L	0-2		11,039
26	Apr	2	(a)	Brentford*	L	1-3	Beasley	12,700
27		14	(a)	Charlton A	L	0-5		12,000
28		21	(a)	Watford	L	2-3	Gallimore 2	5,980
29		28	(h)	Chelsea	W	3-0	Drake, Farquhar, Bastin	10,349
30	May	5	(a)	West Ham U	D	1-1	Drake	9,000

P	W	D	L	F	A	W	D	L	F	A	Pts	Pos	Appearances
30	11	0	4	51	27	3	3	9	26	40	31	8th	Goals

*After abandoned match (28 minutes) on December 25 — Brentford 1 Arsenal 1 (Wrigglesworth) team as per Match 18 except Marks played number 1, Nelson 8 and Steele 9 — Att: 7,000.

Football League Cup — South

31	Feb	3	(a)	Reading	W	3-1	Drake, Wrigglesworth, Bowden	10,067
32		10	(h)	Clapton O	W	5-0	Mortensen 3, Drake, Wrigglesworth	10,753
33		17	(a)	Portsmouth	W	4-2	Farquhar 2, Drake, Mortensen	28,000
34		24	(h)	Reading	W	3-0	Drake, Paton, Mortensen	15,085
35	Mar	3	(a)	Clapton O	W	3-1	Mortensen 2, Drake	7,000
36		10	(h)	Portsmouth	L	2-4	Drake 2	13,552
SF		17	(n†)	Millwall	L	0-1		49,513

P	W	D	L	F	A	W	D	L	F	A	Pts	Pos	Appearances
6	2	0	1	10	4	3	0	0	10	4	10	1st‡	Goals

‡Arsenal finished 1st in Group 1 of the Qualifying Competition and qualified for the semi-finals. †Played at Stamford Bridge, London.

344

Duke HP	Scott L	Barnes W	Hamilton W	Joy B	Collett E	Briscoe J	Henley L	Horsman L	Bastin CS	Smith C	Swindin GH	Jones A	Ferrier H	Bradley G	Nelson D	Male CG	Farquhar D	Cumner RH	Drake EJ	Wrigglesworth W	Mortensen SH	Marks GW	Orr T	Morrad F	Mennie F	Tunnicliffe G	Steele FC	McFarlane D	Matthews S	Bowden NH	Moody K	Hall F	Holland E	Griffiths WR	Wade JS	Mitchell FR	Harris C	Taylor V	
1	2	3	4	5	6	7	8	9	10	11																													1
					6		4	7	8	9	10	1	2	3	5	11																							2
		3			5		6	9	10			1		4	8	2	7	11																					3
			2		5		6		8		10	1		3	4		7		9	11																			4
			3		5		6		8		10	1			4	2	7		9	11																			5
1	2	3			6			9	10						4	5	7			11	8																		6
1	2	3			5		6		10						4		7		9	11	8																		7
	2		4		6				10			1		3	5	7			9	11	8																		8
	2	3			5		6	4	10			1					7		9	11	8																		9
	2	3		6			5	4	10			1			8		7		9	11																			10
	2				5		6	4	8	10				3			7		9	11			1																11
	2				5		3		6						4	8	7		9	11	10	1																	12
		3			5		6		4			1				2	7		11		9					8	10												13
					6				4	8		1				2	7		11					10	3	5	9												14
		3			5		6		4			1				2	7		9	11	10						8												15
					5		6		4			1			10	2	7		8	11						3	9												16
					5		3		6			1			4	2	7		9	11	10						8												17
	2				5		3		6			1			4		7		9	11	10						8												18
	2				5		3		6			1			4		7		9	11	10						8												19
					5		3	2	6						4		7		9	11	10	1					8												20
	2				5		3		6						10		4		8	11												1	7	9					21
		10			6				8			1					4			11						5						2							22
	2	3			5				6						4		7		9	11	10	1					8												23
					6				8	10				3	4		7		9			1										2		5	11				24
			3		4												7		9								8					2		11	1	5	6		25
					6				8						4		7		9													2		5	11	1			26
					6				4	10				3			7			11							8										2		27
	2				6				10					3	4					11									5										28
	2	3			6					10					4		7		9			1											5			8	11		29
		3			6					10					4		7		9			1											5		2	8	11		30
3	12	13	14	17	20	2	18	5	28	4	15	5	3	5	14	10	26	1	21	20	12	7	1	2	2	3	10	1	1	1	4	4	3	2	3	1	2	2	
									1					3	8		3		16	7	18						6					1		1					

2 own-goals

Duke HP	Scott L	Barnes W	Hamilton W	Joy B	Collett E	Briscoe J	Henley L	Horsman L	Bastin CS	Smith C	Swindin GH	Jones A	Ferrier H	Bradley G	Nelson D	Male CG	Farquhar D	Cumner RH	Drake EJ	Wrigglesworth W	Mortensen SH	Marks GW	Orr T	Morrad F	Mennie F	Tunnicliffe G	Steele FC	McFarlane D	Matthews S	Bowden NH	Moody K	Hall F	Holland E	Griffiths WR	Wade JS	Mitchell FR	Harris C	Taylor V	
		3			5		6		8						4		7		9	11		1										10	2						31
		3			6		5	4	8								7		9	11	10	1										2							32
		3			6		5	4	8								7		9	11	10	1																	33
	2				5		3		6						4		7		9		10	1																	34
		3			4			6									7		9	11	10	1					8					2		5					35
		6							10						4		7		9	11		1										2		5					36
		3		6					4								7		9	11	10	1										2		5					SF
5	1	3	4	5		1		6							4	6	7	7	5	7		1					1					5	3						
		2							7							2	7					1																	

E.Taylor played number 3 in Match 22; A.Dawes played number 7 in Match 22; S.Davies played number 9 in Match 22; L.Stevens played number 10 in Match 25; R.A.Ward played number 3 in Match 26; A.E.Beasley played number 10 in Match 26 and scored once; P.Kelly played number 1 in Match 27; B.Ratcliffe played number 5 in Match 27; C.L.Hodges played number 9 in Match 27; C.C.Griggs played number 1 in Match 28; T.Jones played number 7 in Match 28; E.Stanley played number 8 in Match 28; L.Gallimore played number 9 in Match 28 and scored twice; J.Southam played number 2 in Match 33; J.Bowden played number 8 in Match 34; J.Paton played number 11 in match 34 and scored once; J.Barr played number 3 in Match 36; G.H.Bremner played number 8 in Match 36; M.Edelston played number 8 in the semi-final.

345

1945-46

Football League — South

1	Aug	25	(a)	Coventry C	L	0-2	20,943
2		27	(a)	West Ham U	D	1-1 Mercer	22,256
3	Sep	1	(h)	Coventry C	D	0-0	20,303
4		3	(a)	Wolves	D	1-1 Wilson	29,152
5		8	(h)	Luton T	L	0-2	13,365
6		15	(a)	Luton T	W	2-1 Morgan 2	13,939
7		22	(h)	Aston Villa	L	2-4 Bowden, Bremner	32,605
8		29	(a)	Aston Villa	L	1-5 L.Jones	44,159
9	Oct	6	(h)	Swansea T	W	4-1 Horsfield 2, Nelson, Farquhar	20,606
10		13	(a)	Swansea T	L	2-3 Young, Holland	25,570
11		20	(h)	Charlton A	L	1-2 Drury	30,582
12		27	(a)	Charlton A	L	2-6 O'Flanagan, Drury	38,450
13	Nov	3	(a)	Fulham	L	2-5 Drury, O'Flanagan	32,374
14		10	(h)	Fulham	W	2-0 Drury, Wallbanks (og)	19,000
15		17	(h)	Plymouth A	W	3-0 O'Flanagan, Cumner, Drury	14,479
16		24	(a)	Plymouth A	W	4-0 Hodges 3, Bremner	26,419
17	Dec	1	(a)	Portsmouth	D	1-1 Drury	26,639
18		8	(h)	Portsmouth	W	4-3 Bremner, O'Flanagan, Drury, Bushby (og)	18,480
19		15	(h)	Nottingham F	D	2-2 Drury 2	17,500
20		22	(a)	Nottingham F	L	2-3 Bastin (pen), O'Flanagan	20,202
21		25	(a)	Newport C	W	2-1 Cumner, Henley	13,003
22		26	(h)	Newport C	W	7-0 Farquhar 3, Bastin, O'Flanagan 2, Henley	16,536
23		29	(h)	Wolves	W	3-2 Henley 2, O'Flanagan	37,970
24	Jan	12	(h)	West Brom A	W	2-0 Bremner, Henley	22,334
25		19	(a)	West Brom A	W	1-0 Bremner	18,748
26		26	(a)	Leicester C	W	5-4 Barnard 2, L.Jones 2, Bremner	14,723
27	Feb	2	(h)	Birmingham C	L	0-3	29,921
28		9	(h)	Tottenham H	D	1-1 Bastin	38,927
29		16	(a)	Tottenham H	L	0-2	44,510
30		23	(a)	Brentford	L	3-6 D.Compton, Bastin, O'Flanagan	21,030
31	Mar	9	(h)	Chelsea	L	1-2 D.Compton	30,554
32		13	(a)	Birmingham C	W	1-0 D.Compton	14,240
33		16	(a)	Chelsea	W	2-1 D.Compton 2	45,000
34		23	(a)	Millwall	D	1-1 O'Flanagan	30,000
35		30	(h)	Millwall	W	4-0 McPherson, Bastin, D.Compton, O'Flanagan	29,444
36	Apr	6	(h)	Southampton	D	1-1 Roffi	21,248
37		13	(a)	Southampton	D	1-1 Morgan	16,000
38		19	(a)	Derby C	D	1-1 McPherson	28,156
39		20	(h)	Leicester C	L	1-2 Roffi	20,000
40		22	(h)	Derby C	L	0-1	27,540
41		29	(h)	Brentford	D	1-1 Nelson	5,250
42	May	4	(h)	West Ham U	W	2-1 Farquhar, Lewis	29,189

P	W	D	L	F	A	W	D	L	F	A	Pts	Pos	
42	9	5	7	41	28	7	6	8	35	45	43	11th	Appearances
													Goals

FA Cup

3	Jan	5	(a)	West Ham U	L	0-6	35,000
3		9	(h)	West Ham U	W	1-0 Cumner	21,733

Appearances

Goals

Griffiths WR	Scott L	Wade JS	Farquhar D	Joy B	Collett E	Nelson D	Henley L	Holland EJ	Horsfield A	Wrigglesworth W	Moody K	Smith L	Marks GW	Bremner GH	Morgan AS	Jones LJ	Compton LH	Chenhall JC	Drury GB	Bastin CS	Beasley AE	O'Flanagan KP	Cumner RH	Hodges CL	Hapgood EA	Griggs C	Swindin GH	Male CG	Waller H	Patterson G	Barnard C	Cartwright S	Compton DCS	McPherson IB	Roffi G	Curtis GF	Logie JT	Lewis R	
1	2	3	4	5	6	8	10	11																														1
	2	3	7	5	6	8		10	4	11																												2
1	2	6	7					10	4	11	3	5																										3
	2	6	7			8	4			11		5	1																									4
	2	6	7			10	8	11			3	5	1																									5
1		3	6			7	10		4		2	5		8	11																							6
1	2	3				10			4					8	11																							7
1	2					11			4		3					8																						8
1	2	3	11			7	4		9					8		10	5																					9
1	2	6	7		9			11						8		10	5																					10
1		2				7	4		9			5						3	8	10	11																	11
1	2	5	6			11								9				3	8	4	10	7																12
1	2	3			6	7						5		8					10	4		9	11															13
1	2	3			6	7						5		8					10	4	11	9																14
1	2	3			6	7						5		8					10	4		9	11															15
1	2	3			6	7						5		8					10	4	11			9														16
1	2	3			6	7						5		8					10	4	11			9														17
1	2	6			5									8					10	4		9	11	7	3													18
1	2				5	10													8	4		9	11	7	3													19
	2			5	6	7	8													10	4		9		11	3	1												20
	2		7		6	4	8									10			9				11			1												21
	2		7	5	6	4	8												10	11		9			3	1												22
	2			5	6	4	8												10	11		7			3	1											9	23
					3	4	8						7						11						1	2	5	6	9								24
					3	4								7		8				10			11				1		5	6		2							25
	3					10								7		8	5			11						1	2	4	6	9								26
	3	6				7										8	5			10			11				1	2	4		9								27
	2				3	8											5			10			11				1	4		6	9	7							28
					3	4										8				10			7				1	2	5		9	6	11						29
	2			5	3	8														10		9					1	4		6	7		11						30
	3			5		7										8				10		9					1	2	4	6			11						31
	3			5	6	7	8													10							1	2	4		9		11						32
	2			5	3	4														10		7					1		6		9		11	8					33
	2			5	3	4	8													10		7					1		6		9		11						34
	2			5	3	4														10		7					1	6					11	8	9				35
				5	3	4							1		11					6		7												8	9	10			36
						4						5			11			3		8		7					1	2							9	10	6		37
	3			5		4							1							6		9	7					2					11	8		10			38
	2			5		4																	7				1						11	8	9	10	6		39
	3			5		4													8			7					1	2			9		11			10	6		40
	3			5		4							1							10			7					2					11	9		8	6		41
	2	3	7	5		4														6							1									8	10	9	42
16	35	19	12	17	24	39	13	5	7	3	4	11	5	14	4	9	5	3	14	29	5	18	12	5	5	4	16	13	9	6	10	3	11	6	4	7	5	2	
			5			2	5	1	2					6	3	3			9	5		11	2	3							2		6	2	2			1	

2 own-goals

	2	3		5	6	4	8												10	11		7					1											9	3
	2	3		5		7										8						9	11				1	4	6								10		3
	2	2		2	1	2	1									1			1	1		2	1				2	1	1								1	1	
																							1																

F.Roberts played number 7 in Match 1; J.Hitchen played number 9 in Match 1; P.Joslin played number 1 in Match 2; S.Mercer played number 9 in Match 2 and scored once; W.Barnes played number 8 in Match 3; S.H.Mortensen played number 9 in Match 3 and number 10 in Match 4; F.Fisher played number 3 in Match 4; J.Wilson played number 9 in Match 4 and number 4 in Match 5 and scored once; P.Mackenzie played number 9 in Matches 5 & 6; A.G.Fields played number 5 in Match 7; Dr A.Little played number 6 in Matches 7 & 8; B.Nieuwenhuys played number 7 in Matches 7 & 8; N.H.Bowden played number 9 in Matches 7 & 8 and scored once; F.Hall played number 5 in Match 8; B.Jones played number 10 in Match 8; W.Hamilton played number 6 in Match 9 and number 4 in Match 10; A.E.Young played number 3 in Match 10 and scored once; R.Halton played number 6 in Match 11; Dr A.Cross played number 6 in Match 19; S.Jones played number 3 in Match 21; D.Lillie played number 5 in Match 21; D.Russell played number 10 in Match 24; E.Stanley played number 9 in Match 25; J.Ollerenshaw played number 2 in Match 36; L.Delaney played number 3 in Match 39; A.Smith played number 11 in Match 42.

Other Wartime Matches
1915-1919

1915-16
Jan 29 v Fulham (h) 2-0 (Footballer's Battalion Charity Fund)
Rutherford, Groves
Cooper; Shaw, Bradshaw, Liddell, Buckley, McKinnon, Rutherford, Flanagan, King, Legge, F.Groves.
Att: 6,500
May 6 v Rest of London Combination (h) 2-2 (R.Benson's Widow Benefit Match)
H.Groves, Bradshaw
Kempton; Sands, Shaw, Liddell, Bradshaw, Bourne, Rutherford, H.Groves, F.Groves, Tyler, Elkington.
Att: 5,000

1918-19
Friendlies
Apr 19 v Clapton O (a) 3-1
Thompson 2, Robson
Williamson; Sands, Liddell, A.Brown, Grant, McKinnon, H.Groves, Hughes, Robson, Thompson, F.Groves.
Apr 26 v Brentford (a) 3-3
Chipperfield, Hardinge, Sutcliffe
Williamson; Bradshaw, Hutchins, Jobey, Voysey, McKinnon, F.Groves, Hughes, Sutcliffe, Hardinge, Chipperfield.
Att: 3,000

May 3 v West Ham United (a) 0-1
Williamson; Bradshaw, Hutchins, Jobey, Voysey, McKinnon, F.Groves, Robson, Sutcliffe, J.Jones, Chipperfield.
May 10 v West Ham United (h) 3-2
King, Hardinge, Rutherford
Williamson; Shaw, Bradshaw, Brown, Voysey, McKinnon, Rutherford, Robson, King, Hardinge, Chipperfield(F.Groves)
Att: 8,000
May 17 v Chelsea (h) 1-2
Hardinge
Williamson; Shaw, Hutchins, Brown, Voysey, McKinnon, Lewis, Robson, Butler, Hardinge, F.Groves.
Att: 5,000
May 24 v Tottenham Hotspur (h) 0-0
Williamson; Bradshaw, A.Smith, Hughes, Plumb, McKinnon, F.Groves, Robson, W.Williams, Norman, Rose.
Att: 6,000

1939-1946

1939-40
Sep 13 v Cardiff City (a) 4-3
Crayston 2, Cumner, Daniel
Marks; Male, Hapgood, Crayston, Fields, Daniel, Scott, L.Jones, Young, B.Jones, Cumner.
Sep 16 v Chelmsford (a) 4-0
L.Compton 3, B.Jones
Marks; Male, Hapgood, Crayston, Fields, L.Jones, Cumner, Curtis, L.Compton, B.Jones, D.Compton.
Sep 23 v Brentford (a) 0-3
Marks; Male, Hapgood, Crayston, Fields, L.Jones, Nelson, Bastin, Drake (Scott), B.Jones (Curtis), Cumner.
Att: 6,969
Sep 30 v Reading (a) 3-1
Bastin 2, L.Compton
Marks; Male, Hapgood, Crayston, Joy, L.Jones, Kirchen, Nelson, L.Compton, Sidey, Bastin.
Att: 8,000
Oct 7 v Chelsea (a) 3-0
L.Compton 2, Kirchen
Marks; Scott, Hapgood, Crayston, Joy, L.Jones, Kirchen, Nelson, L.Compton, Bastin, D.Compton.
Att: 10,036
Oct 14 v Swindon Town (a) 7-0
Kirchen 3, L.Compton 3, D.Compton
Marks; Male, Hapgood, Crayston, Joy, Collett, Kirchen, Nelson, L.Compton, Lewis, D.Compton.
Att: 8,000
Dec 13 v Army XI (at Aldershot) 1-0
Crayston
Marks; Male, Hapgood, Crayston, Joy, L.Jones, Kirchen, Nelson, L.Compton, Lewis, Bastin.
Att: 3,000

1941-42
Aug 2 v Heart of Midlothian (a) 1-0 (Scottish War Memorial Fund)
Kirchen
Marks; Scott, Hapgood, Crayston, Joy, Collett, Kirchen, L.Jones, Mills (of Aberdeen), Bastin, D.Compton.
Att: 20,817
Apr 25 v Millwall (a) 2-2
D.Compton, Henley
Tweedy; Scott, Delaney, Pryde, Joy, Collett, Beasley, Henley, Drake, Bastin, D.Compton.
May 23 v RAF XI (h) 1-1
Kirchen
Boulton; Scott, Hapgood, Crayston, Joy, Male, Kirchen, Bastin, Drake, Curtis, L.Jones.
Att: 11,978

1942-43
Apr 17 v Luton Town (a) 4-1
Stroud, Briscoe, Collett, Bastin
Marks; Scott, Hapgood Crayston, Joy, Hamilton, R.Stroud, Collett, Drake, Bastin, Briscoe.
Att: 3,000
May 8 v Tottenham Hotspur (a) 2-1
Kirchen, Bastin (pen)
Marks; Male, Delaney, Collett, Joy, Hamilton, Briscoe, Henley, C.Vaughan, Bastin, Kirchen.
Att: 8,560
May 15 v Blackpool (at Stamford Bridge) 2-4 (North v South Cup Winner's Play-off)
Lewis, D.Compton
Marks; Scott, L.Compton, Crayston, Joy, Male, Kirchen, Drake, Lewis, Bastin, D.Compton.
Att: 55,195

1944-45
Apr 7 v Fulham (a) 3-0
Drake, Nelson, Wilson
Griffiths; Wade, Hamilton, Farquhar, Hall, Henley,
Nelson, Wilson(of Brighton), Drake, Bremner, Hodges.
May 19 v Tottenham Hotspur (a) 0-4
Marks; Collett, Chenhall, E.Woodford, Wade, Farquhar,
Nelson, J.Whent, Harris, E.Stanley, Taylor.
Att: 10,450

1945-46
**Aug 12 v Combined Services (at Düsseldorf, Germany)
6-1**
Wrigglesworth 3, Lewis 2, Mortensen
Swindin; Scott, Hapgood, Henley, L.Compton, Collett,
Farquhar, Nelson, Lewis, Mortensen, Wrigglesworth.

Nov 21 v Dynamo Moscow (h) 3-4 (tour match)
Mortensen 2, Rooke
Griffiths(Brown); Scott, Bacuzzi, Bastin, Joy, Halton,
Matthews, Drury, Rooke, Mortensen, Cumner.
Att: 54,640
Mar 2 v Fulham (a) 1-2
Barnard
Swindin; Ollerenshaw, Scott, L.Jones, Fields, Collett,
Nelson, C.A.Milton, Barnard, Bastin, D.Compton.
Att: 10,000

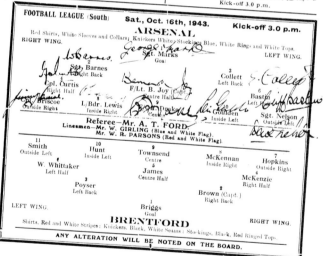

349

Football League 1939-40
(Abandoned after three games and deleted from the records)

Aug 26 v Wolverhampton Wanderers (a) 2-2
Kirchen, Lewis
Marks; Male, Hapgood, Crayston, B.Joy, L.Jones,
Kirchen, Drury, Lewis, B.Jones, Bastin.
Att: 41,199

Aug 30 v Blackburn Rovers (h) 1-0
Bastin (pen)
Marks; Male, Hapgood, Crayston, B.Joy, L.Jones,
Kirchen, Bremner, Lewis, B.Jones, Bastin.
Att: 17,137

Sep 2 v Sunderland (h) 5-2
Drake 4, Drury
Marks; Male, Hapgood, Crayston, B.Joy, L.Jones,
Kirchen, Drury, Drake, B.Jones, Bastin.
Att: 17,141

Abandoned League and FA Cup Matches
(All League except where stated)

1899-1900
Dec 26 v Loughborough T (h) 4-0
(Abandoned after 75 minutes – fog)
Dick, Logan, McCowie, Gaudie
Ord; McNichol, Jackson, Murphy, Dick, Anderson,
Lloyd, Logan, Gaudie, McCowie, Tennant.
Att: 3,000

Jan 1 v Barnsley (a) 1-1
(Abandoned after 60 minutes – fog)
Lloyd
Ord; McNichol, Jackson, Murphy, Dick, Anderson,
Lloyd, Logan, Gaudie, McCowie, Tennant.
Att: 1,000

1903-04
Dec 5 v Burnley (h) 1-0
(Abandoned after 63 minutes – fog)
Linward
Ashcroft; Cross, Jackson, Dick, Sands, McEachrane,
Briercliffe, Coleman, Gooing, Shanks, Linward.
Att: 7,000

Feb 13 v Bradford City (a) 0-1
(Abandoned after 45 minutes – rain)
Ashcroft; Cross, Jackson, Dick, Sands, McEachrane,
Briercliffe, Coleman, Gooing, Watson, Linward.
Att: 10,000

1904-05
Nov 26 v Everton (h) 1-3
(Abandoned after 76 minutes – fog)
Coleman
Ashcroft; Cross, Jackson, Dick, Sands, McEachrane,
Hunter, Coleman, Gooing, Satterthwaite, Linward.
Att: 13,000

1908-09
Mar 6 v Sheffield United (h) 3-0
(Abandoned after 71 minutes – ground waterlogged)
Lewis, Beney, Parker (og)
McDonald; Cross, Gray, Ducat, Sands, McEachrane,
Greenaway, Lewis, Beney, Fitchie, Satterthwaite.
Att: 2,500

1909-10
Sep 6 v Aston Villa (h) 3-1
(Abandoned after 80 minutes – bad light)
McEachrane, Lawrence, Lyons (og)
McDonald; Shaw, Cross, Dick, Sands, McEachrane,
Greenaway, Lewis, Beney, Lawrence, Heppinstall.
Att: 7,000

1910-11
FA Cup
Round 1
Jan 14 v Clapton Orient (a) 1-0
(Abandoned after 45 minutes – fog)
McEachrane
Bateup; Shaw, Gray, Ducat, Sands, McEachrane,
Lewis, Common, Chalmers, G.Hoare, Neave.
Att: 13,416

Jan 21 v Aston Villa (h) 2-1
(Abandoned after 80 minutes – bad light)
Ducat 2
Bateup; Shaw, Gray, Ducat, Sands, McKinnon, Lewis,
Logan, Chalmers, Flanagan, Winship.
Att: 11,709

1921-22
Nov 26 v Bolton Wanderers (h) 0-0
(Abandoned after 38 minutes – fog)
Williamson; Bradshaw, Hutchins, Baker, Butler,
Whittaker, Rutherford, Blyth, Henderson, Hopkins,
Toner.
Att: 15,000

1929-30
Nov 16 v Middlesbrough (h) 1-0
(Abandoned after 55 minutes – fog)
C.Jones
Lewis; Parker, Hapgood, Baker, Roberts, John, Hulme,
Jack, Halliday, James, C.Jones.
Att: 10,743

1930-31
Dec 6 v Grimsby Town (h) 1-0
(Abandoned after 63 minutes – fog)
James
Harper; Parker, Hapgood, Seddon, Roberts, John,
Williams, Jack, Lambert, James, Bastin.
Att: 27,087

1953-54
Jan 2 v Aston Villa (h) 3-0
(Abandoned after 23 minutes – fog)
Holton 2, Lawton
Kelsey; Wills, Wade, Dickson, Dodgin, Forbes, Milton,
Lawton, Holton, Lishman, Roper.
Att: 30,000

1962-63
Dec 22 v Manchester United (a) 1-0
(Abandoned after 57 minutes – fog)
Barnwell
McClelland; Magill, McCullough, Barnwell, Neill,
Snedden, MacLeod, Strong, Baker, Eastham,
Armstrong.
Att: 22,559

1967-68
Dec 9 v Sheffield Wednesday (h) 1-0
(Abandoned after 47 minutes – snowstorm)
McLintock
Wilson; Storey, McNab, McLintock, Neill, Simpson,
Radford, Johnston, Graham, Sammels, Armstrong.
Att: 25,842

Arsenal in Europe
Inter-Cities Fairs Cup

1963-64
Round 1 (1st leg)
Sep 25 v Staevnet (Denmark) (a) 7-1
Strong 3, Baker 3, MacLeod
McKechnie; Magill, McCullough, Brown, Ure, Groves, MacLeod, Strong, Baker, Eastham, Armstrong.
Att: 15,000
Round 1 (2nd leg)
Oct 22 v Staevnet (h) 2-3 (agg 9-4)
Skirton, Barnwell
McKechnie; Magill, McCullough, Brown, Ure, Groves, Skirton, Strong, Court, Barnwell, Armstrong.
Att: 13,569

Round 2 (1st leg)
Nov 13 v Standard Liège (Belgium) (h) 1-1
Anderson
R.Wilson; Magill, McCullough, Brown, Ure, Barnwell, MacLeod, Strong, Baker, Eastham, Anderson.
Att: 22,003
Round 2 (2nd leg)
Dec 18 v Standard Liège (a) 1-3 (agg 2-4)
McCullough
Furnell; Magill, McCullough, Barnwell, Ure, Snedden, MacLeod, Strong, Court, Eastham, Armstrong.
Att: 10,000

European Fairs Cup

1969-70
Round 1 (1st leg)
Sep 9 v Glentoran (Northern Ireland) (h) 3-0
Graham 2, Gould
Wilson; Storey, McNab(Nelson), McLintock, Simpson, Graham, Robertson, Court(Kelly), Gould, Sammels, Armstrong.
Att: 24,292
Round 1 (2nd leg)
Sep 29 v Glentoran (a) 0-1 (agg 3-1)
Webster; Rice, McNab, Court, Neill, Simpson, Robertson, Sammels, Radford(Kennedy), Gould, George.
Att: 13,000
Round 2 (1st leg)
Oct 20 v Sporting Clube de Portugal(Portugal)(a) 0-0
Barnett; Storey, McNab, Court, Neill, Simpson, Robertson, Sammels, Radford, Graham, Armstrong.
Att: 32,000
Round 2 (2nd leg)
Nov 26 v Sporting Clube de Portugal(h) 3-0(agg 3-0)
Graham 2, Radford
Barnett; Storey, McNab, Court, Neill, Simpson, Robertson, Sammels, Radford, Graham, Armstrong.
Att: 35,253
Round 3 (1st leg)
Dec 17 v FC Rouen (France) (a) 0-0
Wilson; Storey, McNab, Court, Neill, Simpson, Robertson, Sammels, Radford, Graham(Kelly), Armstrong.
Att: 12,093
Round 3 (2nd leg)
Jan 13 v FC Rouen (h) 1-0 (agg 1-0)
Sammels
Wilson; Storey, Nelson, Court(Graham), Neill, Simpson, Marinello, Sammels, Radford, George, Armstrong.
Att: 38,018
Round 4 (1st leg)
Mar 11 v Dinamo Bacău (Romania) (a) 2-0
Sammels, Radford
Wilson; Storey, McNab, Kelly, McLintock, Simpson, Marinello, Sammels, Radford, George, Graham.
Att: 20,000

Round 4 (2nd leg)
Mar 18 v Dinamo Bacău (h) 7-1 (agg 9-1)
Radford 2, George 2, Sammels 2, Graham
Wilson; Storey, McNab, Kelly, McLintock, Simpson, Marinello, Sammels, Radford, George, Graham (Armstrong).
Att: 35,342
Semi-final (1st leg)
Apr 8 v Ajax Amsterdam (Holland) (h) 3-0
George 2, Sammels
Wilson; Storey, McNab, Kelly, McLintock, Simpson, Marinello(Armstrong), Sammels, Radford, George, Graham.
Att: 46,271
Semi-final (2nd leg)
Apr 15 v Ajax Amsterdam (a) 0-1 (agg 3-1)
Wilson; Storey, McNab, Kelly, McLintock, Simpson, Armstrong, Sammels, Radford, George, Graham.
Att: 32,000
Final (1st leg)
Apr 22 v RSC Anderlecht (Belgium) (a) 1-3
Kennedy
Wilson; Storey, McNab, Kelly, McLintock, Simpson, Armstrong, Sammels, Radford, George(Kennedy), Graham.
Att: 37,000
Final (2nd leg)
Apr 28 v RSC Anderlecht (h) 3-0 (agg 4-3)
Kelly, Radford, Sammels
Wilson; Storey, McNab, Kelly, McLintock, Simpson, Armstrong, Sammels, Radford, George, Graham.
Att: 51,612

1970-71
Round 1 (1st leg)
Sep 16 v Lazio (Italy) (a) 2-2
Radford 2
Wilson; Rice, McNab, Kelly, McLintock, Roberts, Armstrong, Storey, Radford, Kennedy, Graham.
Att: 60,000

351

John Radford (far left) rushes past the goal-post after heading Arsenal's second goal against Anderlecht in the 1970 Fairs' Cup Final second leg at Highbury. Also in the picture are the Belgians' goalkeeper, Trappeniers, and Arsenal players Charlie George (10) and George Armstrong.

Round 1 (2nd leg)
Sep 23 v Lazio (h) 2-0 (agg 4-2)
Radford, Armstrong
Wilson; Rice, McNab, Kelly, McLintock, Roberts, Armstrong, Storey, Radford, Kennedy, Graham (Nelson).
Att: 53,013
Round 2 (1st leg)
Oct 21 v SK Sturm Graz (Austria) (a) 0-1
Wilson; Rice, McNab, Kelly, McLintock, Roberts, Armstrong, Storey, Radford, Kennedy, Graham.
Att: 13,000
Round 2 (2nd leg)
Nov 4 v SK Sturm Graz (h) 2-0 (agg 2-1)
Kennedy, Storey (pen)
Wilson; Rice, McNab, Kelly, McLintock, Roberts, Armstrong, Storey, Radford, Kennedy, Graham.
Att: 37,667
Round 3 (1st leg)
Dec 2 v SK Beveren-Waas (Belgium) (h) 4-0
Kennedy 2, Sammels, Graham
Wilson; Rice, McNab, Sammels, McLintock, Simpson, Armstrong, Storey, Radford, Kennedy, Graham.
Att: 33,444

Round 3 (2nd leg)
Dec 16 v SK Beveren-Waas (a) 0-0 (agg 4-0)
Wilson; Rice, McNab, Storey, Roberts, Simpson, Armstrong(Marinello), Sammels, Radford (George), Kennedy, Graham.
Att: 16,000
Round 4 (1st leg)
Mar 9 v 1.FC Köln (West Germany) (h) 2-1
McLintock, Storey
Wilson; Rice, McNab, Storey, McLintock, Simpson, Armstrong, Sammels(Graham), Radford, Kennedy, George.
Att: 40,007
Round 4 (2nd leg)
Mar 23 v 1.FC Köln (a) 0-1 (agg 2-2; lost on away goals rule)
Wilson; Rice, McNab, Storey, McLintock, Simpson, Armstrong, Graham, Radford, Kennedy, George.
Att: 50,000

European Cup

1971-72
Round 1 (1st leg)
Sep 15 v Strømgodset IF (Norway) (a) 3-1
Simpson, Marinello, Kelly
Wilson; Rice, Simpson, McLintock, McNab, Roberts, Kelly, Marinello(P.Davies), Graham, Radford, Kennedy.
Att: 23,000
Round 1 (2nd leg)
Sep 29 v Strømgodset IF (h) 4-0 (agg 7-1)
Radford 2, Kennedy, Armstrong
Wilson; Rice, Nelson, Kelly, Simpson, Roberts, Armstrong, George, Radford, Kennedy, Graham.
Att: 27,176

Round 2 (1st leg)
Oct 20 v Grasshopper Zürich (Switzerland) (a) 2-0
Kennedy, Graham
Wilson; Rice, Nelson, McLintock, Roberts, George, Armstrong, Kelly, Radford, Kennedy, Graham.
Att: 23,000
Round 2 (2nd leg)
Nov 3 v Grasshopper Zürich (h) 3-0 (agg 5-0)
Kennedy, George, Radford
Wilson; Rice, Nelson, Storey, Roberts(Simpson), McLintock(McNab), Armstrong, George, Radford, Kennedy, Graham.
Att: 31,105

Arsenal's Ray Kennedy gets his head to a high ball during the Gunners' European Cup first round second leg match against Norwegian champions Strømgodset at Highbury in September 1971. Arsenal won the game 4-0 to take the tie 7-1 on aggregate.

Round 3 (1st leg)
Mar 8 v Ajax Amsterdam (Holland) (a) 1-2
Kennedy
Wilson; Rice, Nelson, Storey, McLintock, Simpson, Armstrong, George, Radford, Kennedy, Graham.
Att: 63,000
Round 3 (2nd leg)
Mar 22 v Ajax Amsterdam (h) 0-1 (agg 1-3)
Wilson; Rice, Nelson(Roberts), Storey, McLintock, Simpson, Armstrong, George, Marinello, Kennedy, Graham.
Att: 56,155

1991-92
Round 1 (1st leg)
Sep 18 v FK Austria Memphis (Austria) (h) 6-1
Smith 4, Linighan, Limpar
Seaman; Dixon, Winterburn, Campbell, Linighan, Adams, Rocastle, Davis, Smith, Merson, Limpar (Groves).
Att: 24,124

Round 1 (2nd leg)
Oct 2 v FK Austria Memphis (a) 0-1 (agg 6-2)
Seaman; Dixon, Winterburn, Thomas, Linighan, Adams, Rocastle, Campbell, Smith, Merson(Groves), O'Leary.
Att: 11,000
Round 2 (1st leg)
Oct 23 v Benfica (Portugal) (a) 1-1
Campbell
Seaman; Dixon, Winterburn, Davis, Pates, Adams, Rocastle, Campbell(Groves), Smith, Merson, Limpar (Thomas).
Att: 80,000
Round 2 (2nd leg)
Nov 6 v Benfica (h) 1-3 aet (agg 2-4)
Pates
Seaman; Dixon, Winterburn, Davis, Pates(Bould), Adams, Rocastle, Campbell, Smith, Merson, Limpar (Groves).
Att: 35,815

Paul Merson in action for Arsenal against two 1991 European Cup opponents. Top picture he rounds two FK Austria players in the 6-1 win and below he heads after the ball in the 1-1 draw against Benfica in Lisbon.

UEFA Cup

1978-79

Round 1 (1st leg)
Sep 13 v 1.FC Lokomotive Leipzig(E Germany)(h) 3-0
Stapleton 2, Sunderland
Jennings; Rice, Nelson, Price, Walford, Young, Brady(Gatting), Sunderland, Stapleton, Harvey (Heeley), Rix.
Att: 34,183

Round 1 (2nd leg)
Sep 27 v 1.FC Lokomotive Leipzig(a) 4-1 (agg 7-1)
Stapleton 2, Brady, Sunderland
Jennings; Rice, Nelson, Price(Vaessen), O'Leary, Young(Walford), Brady, Sunderland, Stapleton, Devine, Rix.
Att: 22,000

Round 2 (1st leg)
Oct 19 v Hajduk Split (Yugoslavia) (a) 1-2
Brady
Jennings; Rice, Nelson, Price, O'Leary, Young, Brady,
Heeley, Stapleton, Kosmina, Rix.
Att: 25,000
Round 2 (2nd leg)
Nov 1 v Hajduk Split (h) 1-0 (agg 2-2; won on away-
goals rule)
Young
Jennings; Rice, Nelson, Price, O'Leary, Young, Brady,
Gatting, Stapleton, Heeley(Kosmina [Vaessen]), Rix.
Att: 41,812
Round 3 (1st leg)
Nov 22 v Red Star, Belgrade (Yugoslavia) (a) 0-1
Jennings; Rice, Nelson, Price, O'Leary, Young, Heeley,
Walford, Stapleton, Sunderland, Rix.
Att: 51,000
Round 3 (2nd leg)
Dec 6 v Red Star, Belgrade (h) 1-1 (agg 1-2)
Sunderland
Jennings; Rice, Nelson, Price, O'Leary, Young,
Heeley(Kosmina), Sunderland, Stapleton, Gatting,
Rix(Macdonald).
Att: 41,452

1981-82
Round 1 (1st leg)
Sep 16 v Panathinaikos (Greece) (a) 2-0
McDermott, Meade
Jennings; Hollins, Sansom, Talbot, O'Leary, Young,
Davis, Vaessen(Meade), McDermott, Nicholas, Rix.
Att: 20,000

Round 1 (2nd leg)
Sep 30 v Panathinaikos (h) 1-0 (agg 3-0)
Talbot
Jennings; Devine, Sansom, Talbot, O'Leary(Whyte),
Young, Hollins, Sunderland, McDermott, Nicholas, Rix.
Att: 23,513
Round 2 (1st leg)
Oct 20 v KFC Winterslag (Belgium) (a) 0-1
Jennings; Devine, Sansom, Talbot, O'Leary, Young,
Hollins, Sunderland, Meade(McDermott), Nicholas, Rix.
Att: 10,000
Round 2 (2nd leg)
Nov 3 v KFC Winterslag (h) 2-1 (agg 2-2; lost on
away-goals rule)
Hollins, Rix
Jennings; Hollins, Sansom, Talbot, O'Leary, Whyte,
McDermott, Vaessen(Davis), Meade, Nicholas, Rix.
Att: 22,930

1982-83
Round 1 (1st leg)
Sep 14 v Spartak Moscow (Soviet Union) (a) 2-3
Robson, Chapman
Wood; Hollins, Sansom, Talbot, O'Leary, Whyte,
Davis, Robson, Chapman, Woodcock, Rix.
Att: 68,500
Round 1 (2nd leg)
Sep 29 v Spartak Moscow (h) 2-5 (agg 4-8)
Chapman, Dasaev (og)
Wood; Hollins(Sunderland), Sansom, Talbot,
O'Leary, Whyte, Davis(McDermott), Robson,
Chapman, Woodcock, Rix.
Att: 28,445

European Cup-winners' Cup

1979-80
Round 1 (1st leg)
Sep 19 v Fenerbahçe (Turkey) (h) 2-0
Sunderland, Young
Jennings; Rice, Nelson, Talbot, O'Leary, Young,
Brady, Sunderland, Stapleton, Hollins, Rix.
Att: 34,973
Round 1 (2nd leg)
Oct 3 v Fenerbahçe (a) 0-0 (agg 2-0)
Jennings; Rice, Nelson, Talbot, O'Leary, Young,
Brady, Sunderland, Stapleton, Hollins, Rix.
Att: 30,000
Round 2 (1st leg)
Oct 24 v 1.FC Magdeburg (East Germany) (h) 2-1
Young, Sunderland
Jennings; Rice, Nelson, Talbot, O'Leary, Young,
Brady, Sunderland, Stapleton, Hollins, Rix.
Att: 34,575
Round 2 (2nd leg)
Nov 7 v 1.FC Magdeburg (a) 2-2 (agg 4-3)
Price, Brady
Jennings; Devine, Nelson(Walford), Talbot, O'Leary,
Young, Brady, Gatting, Stapleton, Hollins (Price), Rix.
Att: 22,000
Round 3 (1st leg)
Mar 5 v IFK Gothenburg (Sweden) (h) 5-1
Sunderland 2, Price, Brady, Young
Jennings; Devine, Nelson, Talbot, O'Leary, Young,
Brady(Hollins), Sunderland(McDermott), Stapleton,
Price, Rix.
Att: 36,323

Round 3 (2nd leg)
Mar 19 v IFK Gothenburg (a) 0-0 (agg 5-1)
Jennings; Devine, Nelson, Talbot, O'Leary, Young,
Brady, Vaessen, Stapleton, Price, Rix.
Att: 40,044
Semi-final (1st leg)
Apr 9 v Juventus (Italy) (h) 1-1
Bettega (og)
Jennings; Devine(Vaessen), Walford, Talbot, O'Leary
(Rice), Young, Brady, Sunderland, Stapleton, Price, Rix.
Att: 51,998
Semi-final (2nd leg)
Apr 23 v Juventus (a) 1-0 (agg 2-1)
Vaessen
Jennings; Rice, Devine, Talbot(Hollins), O'Leary,
Young, Brady, Sunderland, Stapleton, Price (Vaessen),
Rix.
Att: 66,386
Final
May 14 v Valencia (Spain) (at Brussels) 0-0 (agg 4-5
on penalties)
Jennings; Rice, Nelson, Talbot, O'Leary, Young,
Brady, Sunderland, Stapleton, Price(Hollins),
Rix.
Att: 40,000

355

Arsenal players and officials pictured in 1931 with some of the trophies the club won that year, including the Football League Championship trophy (third from left) and the FA Charity Shield (second from right) which they collected for the first time after beating FA Cup winners, Sheffield Wednesday, 2-1 at Stamford Bridge.

FA Charity Shield

1930-31
Oct 8 v Sheffield Wednesday (at Stamford Bridge) 2-1
Hulme, Jack
G.P.Keyser; Parker, Hapgood, Seddon, Roberts, John, Hulme, Brain, Lambert, Jack, Bastin.
Att: 25,000

1931-32
Oct 7 v West Bromwich Albion (at Villa Park) 1-0
Bastin
Preedy; Parker, Hapgood, C.Jones, Roberts, Haynes, Hulme, Jack, Lambert, James, Bastin.
Att: 21,276

1933-34
Oct 18 v Everton (a) 3-0
Birkett 2, Bowden
Moss; Male, Hapgood, C.Jones, Sidey, John, Birkett, Coleman, Bowden, James, Hill.
Att: 30,000

1934-35
Nov 28 v Manchester City (h) 4-0
Birkett, Bastin, Drake, Marshall
Moss; Male, Hapgood, Hill, Sidey, Copping, Birkett, Marshall, Drake, John, Bastin.
Att: 10,888

1935-36
Oct 23 v Sheffield Wednesday (h) 0-1
Wilson; Male, Hapgood, Hill, B.Joy, Copping, Milne, Crayston, Dunne, Davidson, Bastin.
Att: 30,000

1936-37
Oct 28 v Sunderland (a) 1-2
Kirchen
Swindin; L.Compton, Hapgood, Crayston, B.Joy, Copping, Milne, Bowden, Kirchen, Davidson, D.Compton.
Att: 30,000

1938-39
Sep 26 v Preston North End (h) 2-1
Drake 2
Swindin; Male, L.Compton, Crayston, B.Joy, Copping, Kirchen, L.Jones, Drake, B.Jones, Cumner.
Att: 35,000

1948-49
Oct 6 v Manchester United (h) 4-3
Lewis 2, Rooke, B.Jones
Swindin; Barnes, L.Smith, Macaulay, L.Compton, Mercer, Roper, Logie, Lewis, Rooke, B.Jones.
Att: 31,000

1953-54
Oct 12 v Blackpool (h) 3-1
Lishman 2, Lawton
Kelsey; Wills, Barnes, Forbes, Dodgin, Mercer, Holton, Logie, Lawton, Lishman, Roper.
Att: 39,853

1979-80
Aug 11 v Liverpool (at Wembley) 1-3
Sunderland
Jennings; Rice, Nelson(Young), Talbot, O'Leary, Walford, Brady, Sunderland, Stapleton, Price (Hollins), Rix.
Att: 92,000

1989-90
Aug 12 v Liverpool (at Wembley) 0-1
Lukic; Dixon, Winterburn, Thomas, O'Leary, Adams, Rocastle, Richardson, Smith(Quinn), Caesar (Marwood), Merson.
Att: 63,149

1991-92
Aug 10 v Tottenham Hotspur (at Wembley) 0-0
Seaman; Dixon, Winterburn, Hillier, O'Leary, Adams, Rocastle(Thomas), Davis, Smith, Merson, Campbell (Cole).
Att: 65,483

356

FA Cup Record 1889-1893

1889-90
Qualifying Competition
Round 1
Oct 5 v Lyndhurst (h) 11-0
Barbour 3, Scott 3, Meggs 2, Robertson 2, Horsington
F.W.Beardsley; P.Connolly, J.McBean, D.Howat,
J.M.Bates, J.W.Julian, R.T.Horsington, J.W.Meggs,
H.Barbour, H.S.Robertson, W.Scott.
Att: 2,500
Round 2
Oct 26 v Thorpe (Norwich) (a) 2-2 (aet)*
Barbour, Connolly
F.W.Beardsley; P.Connolly, J.McBean, D.Howat,
J.M.Bates, H.Offer, R.T.Horsington, J.W.Meggs,
H.Barbour, H.S.Robertson, W.Scott.
Att: 1,000
*Thorpe scratched after this game.
Round 3
Nov 16 v Crusaders (h) 5-2 (aet 90 mins 2-2)
Robertson 2, Scott, Connolly, Meggs
R.Foster; P.Connolly, J.McBean, D.Howat,
J.M.Bates, J.W.Julian, J.W.Meggs, J.M.Charteris,
H.Barbour, H.S.Robertson, W.Scott.
Att: 4,500
Round 4
Dec 7 v Swifts (h) 1-5
Meggs
R.Foster; P.Connolly, J.McBean, H.Offer, D.Howat,
J.W.Julian, J.W.Meggs, W.Stewart, H.Barbour,
H.S.Robertson, E.Williams.
Att: 6,000

1890-91
Competition Proper (Excused Qualifying Rounds)
Round 1
Jan 17 v Derby County (h) 1-2
Offer
E.Bee; P.Connolly, J.McBean, D.Howat,
W.S.Stewart, J.W.Julian, J.W.Meggs, A.Christmas,
H.Barbour, H.Offer, D.Gloak.
Att: 8,000

1891-92
Competition Proper (Excused qualifying Rounds)
Round 1
Jan 16 v Small Heath (a) 1-5
Davie
Bee; Connolly, McBean, Howat, Buist, Robertson,
Shaw, Crawford, Davie, Graham, C.B.Peachey.
Att: 4,000

1892-93
Qualifying Competition
Round 1
Oct 15 v Highland Light Infantry (h) 3-0
Elliott, Davie, Booth
Bee; J.McQuilkie, Jeffrey, Howat, Buist, Dyer,
Gemmell, Henderson, Davie, Elliott, Booth.
Att: 5,000
Round 2
Oct 29 v City Ramblers (h) 10-1
Henderson 3, Booth 3, Elliott 3, Davie
Wood; J.McQuilkie, Jeffrey, Howat, Buist, Dyer,
Crawford, Henderson, Davie, Elliott, Booth.
Att: 4,000
Round 3
Nov 19 v Millwall Athletic (h) 3-2
Howat, Henderson, Caygill (og)
Bee; Rankin, Jeffrey, Howat, Buist, Dyer, Gemmell,
Henderson, Davie, Elliott, Booth.
Att: 12,000
Round 4
**Dec 10 v Clapton (h) 3-0 (Clapton drawn at home
but waived the right)**
Henderson, Booth, Crawford
Ambler; Rankin, Jeffrey, Howat, Buist, Dyer,
Gemmell, Crawford, Henderson, Elliott, Booth.
Att: 4,000
Competition Proper
Round 1
Jan 21 v Sunderland (a) 0-6
Williams; Powell Jeffrey, Rankin, Buist, Dyer, Howat,
Henderson, Devine, Elliott, Booth.
Att: 4,500

Before they joined the Football League, Arsenal relied heavily upon friendly games to make up their fixture list. This photograph shows the team which beat Accrington 3-1 on 1 April 1893. The following season Arsenal were elected to the League. Accrington, however, who finished next to bottom in Division One in 1892-3, were not re-elected to Division Two.

Royal Arsenal 1886-1893

1886-87

Friendlies   (Home matches played on Plumstead Common)

P10 W7 D1 L2 F36 A8

Dec 11 (a)	Eastern Wanderers		W	6-0	Feb 5 (a)	Millwall Rovers	L	0-4
Jan 8 (h)	Erith		W	6-1	12 (a)	Alexandria United	W	6-0
15 (h)	Alexandria United		W	11-0	26 (h)	2nd Rifle Brigade	D	0-0
22 (h)	Eastern Wanderers		W	1-0	Mar 12 (h)	Millwall Rovers	W	3-0
29 (a)	Erith		W	3-2	26 (a)	2nd Rifle Brigade	L	0-1

1887-88

Friendlies

P22* W12 D4 L4 F62 A27   *Two matches untraced

Oct 1 (h)	Alexandria United		W	5-1	Jan 14 (a)	Iona Deptford	W	3-2
15 (h)	Clapton Pilgrims		D	2-2	28 (h)	Champion Hill	W	6-0
22 (?)	St Lukes	Not traced			Feb 4 (h)	Tottenham H	W	6-2
Nov 5 (h)	Grange Institute		W	4-0	11 (h)	Millwall Rovers	D	3-3
12 (h)	Iona Deptford		D	1-1	18 (h)	Erith	W	2-1
19 (a)	Tottenham H*		L	1-2	25 (h)	Forest Gate Alliance	D	1-1
26 (a)	Millwall Rovers		L	0-3	Mar 3 (h)	Grange Institute	W	2-1
Dec 3 (h)	Grange Park	Not traced			10 (a)	Brixton Rangers	W	9-3
10 (h)	Brixton Rangers		L	1-2	17 (h)	Ascham	W	5-0
17 (a)	Shrewsbury Park		W	4-0	30 (h)	Millwall Rovers	W	3-0
31 (a)	Forest Gate Alliance		L	1-2	Apr 7 (a)	Alexandria United	W	3-1

*Only 75 minutes played — bad light.

London Senior Cup

Oct 8 Grove House (h) 3-1
Potter; J.Crighton, Morris
Beardsley; Brown, Danskin, Banks, Price, Wells,
Potter, R.Crighton, J.Crighton, Morris, J.Bee.
Att: 600

Oct 29 (h) Barnes 0-4
Beardsley; Brown, Danskin, Price, Banks, Wells,
Morris, Bates, Ridgewell, J.Crighton, J.Bee.
Att: 500

Arsenal fielded a junior XI for the first time this season, as follows:

Nov 19 (h)	Woolwich Pupils & Teachers	W	1-0
26 (a)	Erith	L	0-1
Feb 25 (a)	Thistle	L	1-2

1888-89

Friendlies

P24 W10 D5 L9 F50 A29   (plus two matches untraced)

Sep 15 (h)	London Scottish		D	3-3	Feb 16 (?)	Millwall Rovers	Not traced	
22 (h)	Tottenham H		L	0-1	23 (a)	Ilford	L	0-1
29 (h)	Old St Pauls		W	7-3	Mar 2 (h)	London Caledonians	L	1-2
Oct 6 (h)	Grove House		W	2-0	9 (a)	Tottenham H	W	1-0
13 (h)	London Scottish		W	4-0	16 (h)	South Eastern Rangers	L	1-2
20 (h)	2nd Rifle Brigade		L	1-2	23 (h)	2nd Rifle Brigade	W	2-0
27 (a)	Brixton Rangers		L	1-3	Apr 1 (?)	2nd Rifle Brigade	W	6-1
Nov 17 (a)	St Lukes		D	1-1	6 (a)	Old St Pauls	W	1-0
Dec 1 (a)	Phoenix		D	0-0	13 (?)	Millwall Rovers	W	3-0
Jan 5 (a)	Vulcan*		D	1-1	19 (?)	Boston Town	L	1-4
12 (h)	Unity		D	0-0	20 (h)	Spartan Rovers	W	6-0
26 (a)	St Lukes	Not traced			23 (?)	Scots Guards	W	7-2
Feb 2 (h)	Ilford		L	1-2	27 (h)	London Caledonians	L	0-1

*Abandoned after 60 minutes — fog.

London Association Cup

Nov 3 v Phoenix (h) 3-0
Connolly 2, Scott
Beardsley; Brown, J.Crighton, Danskin, Bates, Wells,
Morris, Hill, Connolly, Charteris, Scott.
Nov 24 v Dulwich (h) 4-2
Connolly 3, Charteris
Beardsley; Brown, J.Crighton, Danskin, Bates, Wells,
Morris, Hill, Connolly, Charteris, Scott.
Att: 1,000

Dec 8 v Old St Pauls (h) 3-1
Connolly 2, R.Crighton
Beardsley; Brown, J.Crighton, Danskin, Bates, Wells,
Morris, R.Crighton, Connolly, Charteris, Scott.
Att: 1,200
Semi-final
Jan 19 v Clapton (at Leyton) 0-2
Beardsley; J.Crighton, McBean, Brown, Bates, Danskin,
Morris, R.Crighton, Connolly, Charteris, Scott.
Att: 2,000

Kent County Challenge Cup

Nov 10 v Horton Kirby (a) W 6-2
Charteris 2, Connolly, Scott, Wells, Morris
Dec 29 v Iona (a) W 5-1
Connolly 4, R.Crighton

Feb 9 v Gravesend (a) D 3-3
Bates, Charteris, Connolly
Att: 800
(Arsenal were disqualified for refusing to play extra-time).

1889-90

Friendlies

P24 W17 D4 L3 F81 A30

Sep 7 (h)	London Caledonians	D	2-2	Jan 25 (h)	Foxes		W	7-2
14 (h)	Casuals	W	6-0	Feb 8 (h)	Chiswick Park		D	1-1
21 (h)	Tottenham H	W	10-1	Mar 1 (h)	Birmingham St Georges		L	1-4
28 (h)	Unity	W	8-0	15 (a)	Ilford		W	4-1
Oct 19 (a)	St Marks College	W	2-1	29 (a)	Clapton		L	0-2
Nov 30 (a)	Great Marlow	L	0-2	31 (h)	Mr W.H.Loraines XI		W	3-1
Dec 21 (a)	Ilford	W	2-0	Apr 7 (h)	1st Lincolnshire Regiment		W	2-1
25 (h)	Preston Hornets	W	5-0	12 (h)	Great Marlow		W	3-1
26 (a)	Chatham	D	2-2	19 (h)	Chatham		W	1-0
27 (h)	Reading Town	W	5-1	26 (h)	Clapton		W	6-1
Jan 4 (h)	Windsor Phoenix	W	3-1	May 3 (h)	Ldn Caled'ns/Clapton'ns XI		W	3-2
18 (h)	Old Harrovians	W	2-1	10 (a)	Millwall Athletic		D	3-3

FA Cup (See *FA Cup Record – 1889-1893*)

Oct 5 v Lyndhurst   (h) W 11-0
Oct 26 v Thorpe (Norwich) (a) D 2-2
(Thorpe later scratched)

Nov 16 v Crusadrers   (h) W 5-2
Dec 7 v Swifts   (h) L 1-5

Kent Senior Cup

Round 1
Oct 12 5th Northumberland Fusiliers (h) 6-1
Meggs 2, Scott, Bates, Barbour, Cunningham (og)
Beardsley; Connolly, McBean, Howat, Bates, Offer,
Horsington, Meggs, Barbour, Robertson, Scott.
Round 2
Nov 9 West Kent (h) 10-1
Barbour 5, Robertson 3, Hill, Scott
Thomas; Connolly, McBean, Offer, Bates, Julian,
Horsington, Hill, Barbour, Robertson, Scott.
Att: 1,000
Round 3
Dec 14 Gravesend (a) 7-2
Robertson 3, Barbour 2, Williams, Horsington
Foster; Connolly, McBean, Offer, Stewart, Julian,
Horsington, Meggs, Barbour, Robertson, Williams.
Att: 800

Semi-final
Feb 15 v Chatham (a) 5-0
Meggs 3, Robertson, Offer
Beardsley; Connolly, McBean, Howat, Bates, Julian,
Horsington, Meggs, Barbour, Robertson, Offer.
Att: 3,000
Final
Mar 21 Thanet Wanderers (at Chatham) 3-0
Barbour 2, Offer
Beardsley; Connolly, McBean, Howat, Bates, Julian,
Christmas, Meggs, Barbour, Robertson, Offer.
Att: 5,000

London Senior Cup

Round 1
Bye
Round 2
Nov 2 v Unity (h) 4-1
Meggs, Barbour, Charteris 2
Beardsley; Connolly, McBean, Howat, Bates, Julian,
Horsington, Meggs, Barbour, Charteris, Scott.
Att: 2,000
Round 3
Nov 23 v Foxes (h) 4-1
Connolly 2, Charteris, Meggs
Beardsley; Connolly, McBean, Howat, Bates, Julian,
Horsington, Meggs, Barbour, Charteris, Scott.

Round 4
Dec 14 v St Martins Athletic (h) 6-0
Campbell 2, Tomas, Morris, Charteris, Opp og
Beardsley; Wilson, Brown, Howat, Bates, Walton,
Morris, Tomas, Campbell, Charteris, Leath.
Semi-final
Jan 11 v London Caledonians (at Leyton) 3-1
Robertson 2, Horsington
Beardsley; Connolly, McBean, Howat, Bates, Offer,
Horsington, Meggs, Barbour, Julian, Robertson.
Final
Mar 8 v Old Westminsters (at Kennington Oval) 0-1
Beardsley; Connolly, McBean, Howat, Bates, Julian,
Horsington, Meggs, Barbour, Robertson, Offer.
Att: 5,000

London Charity Cup

Round 1
Feb 1 v Great Marlow (h) 4-1
Robertson 2, Barbour, Horsington
Beardsley; Connolly, McBean, Howat, Bates, Julian,
Horsington, Meggs, Barbour, Robertson, Offer.
Semi-final
Feb 22 v 2nd Battalion Scots Guards * (h) 3-0
Robertson, Scott, Barbour
Beardsley; Connolly, McBean, Howat, Bates, Julian,
Horsington, Meggs, Barbour, Robertson, Scott.
Att: 3,000
*Originally drawn against London Caledonians who
scratched

Final
Apr 5 v Old Westminsters (at Leyton) 3-1
Offer, Christmas, Fry
F.W.Beardsley; P.Connolly, J.McBean, D.Howat,
J.M.Bates, J.W.Julian, A.Christmas, H.Offer,
H.Barbour, H.S.Robertson, W.E.Fry (also sometimes
described as J.C.Edwards).
Att: 10,000

Also this season, Arsenal Juniors (Reserves) won the Kent Junior Cup. The club also entered a six-a-side
competition run by the National Physical Recreation Society at Agricultural Hall on May 31 and beat
London Caledonians 15-7.

1890-91

Friendlies

P27 W17 D5 L5 F72 A41

Sep	6 (h)	93rd Highlanders	D	1-1	Jan 24 (a)	Millwall Athletic	W	1-0
	13 (h)	Casuals	W	5-4	26 (h)	Everton	L	0-5
	20 (h)	Ilford	W	6-0	Feb 7 (h)	St Bartholomews Hospital	W	5-4
	27 (h)	London Caledonians	W	3-1	Mar 14 (h)	Old Harrovians	W	5-1
Oct	4 (a)	Chiswick Park	W	4-0	21 (h)	Sheffield United	D	1-1
	11 (h)	93rd Highlanders	W	4-1	27 (h)	71st Highland Light Infantry	W	3-1
	18 (a)	Old St Marks	W	4-0	28 (h)	Old Harrovians	W	5-0
	25 (h)	St Bartholomews Hospital	W	1-0	30 (h)	Heart of Midlothian	L	1-5
Nov	1 (h)	South Shore (Blackpool)	D	2-2	31 (h)	Nottingham Forest	L	0-5
	8 (a)	Ilford	W	3-0	Apr 18 (h)	Clapton	W	3-1
	15 (h)	Clapton	L	1-2	25 (h)	Sunderland	L	1-3
	22 (h)	Gainsborough Trinity	W	2-1	30 (h)	London Caledonians	D	1-1
Dec	1 (h)	Cambridge University	W	5-1	May 2 (h)	1st Highland Light Infantry	W	5-1
	6 (h)	Casuals	D	0-0				

Fixtures on November 29 v Boston (h) and January 3 v London Caledonians were postponed due to bad
weather.

FA Cup   (See *FA Cup Record - 1889-1893*)

Round 1
Jan 17 v Derby County   (h) L   1-2

360

London Senior Cup

Round 1
Dec 13 Old Westminsters (at Leyton) 4-1*
Offer 3, Campbell
Bee; Connolly, McBean, Howat, Stewart, Julian,
Christmas, W.C.Campbell, Barbour, Offer, Fry.
Att: 5,500
Replay
Jan 31 Old Westminsters (at Kennington Oval) 4-5
(after extra time, 90 mins 3-3)
Barbour 2, Fry, Christmas
Bee; Connolly, McBean, Howat, Stewart, Julian,
Christmas, Barbour, Gloak, Offer, Fry.
* A protest by Old Westminsters was upheld and the
match ordered to be replayed. Attempts on December
20 at Kennington Oval and on January 10 at Leyton
were postponed due to bad weather and the fixture
was eventually replayed on January 31. There followed
a protest, this time by Arsenal, on the ineligibility of
a player and the match was again ordered to be
replayed, but Old Westminsters scratched from the
competition.

Round 2
Feb 21 Casuals (h) 3-2
Gloak 2, Barbour
Bee; Connolly, McBean, Howat, Stewart, Julian,
Christmas, Offer, Barbour, Gloak, Fry.
Att: 9,000
Semi-final
Feb 28 Clapton (at Kennington Oval) 3-2
Barbour, Connolly, Christmas
Bee; Connolly, McBean, Howat, Stewart, Julian,
Christmas, Offer, Barbour, Gloak, Fry.
Final
Mar 7 St Bartholomews Hospital (at Kennington Oval)
6-0
Barbour 2, Offer, Fry, Connolly, Gloak
Bee; Connolly, McBean, Howat, Stewart, Julian,
Christmas, Offer, Barbour, Gloak, Fry.
Att: 6,000

London Charity Cup

Round 1
Feb 14 Crusaders (h) 1-0
Christmas
Bee; Connolly, McBean, Howat, J.Campbell, Julian,
Christmas, Mills, Barbour, Gloak, Fry.
Att: 7,000
Semi-final
Apr 4 Old Carthusians (at Leyton) 1-1
Barbour
Bee; Connolly, McBean, Howat, Stewart, Julian,
Christmas, Offer, Barbour, Wood, Gloak.
Att: 6,000

Replay
Apr 7 Old Carthusians (at Leyton) 2-2
Connolly, Fry
Bee; Connolly, McBean, Collins, Stewart, Julian,
Croxen, Offer, Barbour, Gloak, Fry.
Att: 3,000
Second Replay
Apr 11 v Old Carthusians (at Leyton) 1-2
Connolly
Bee; Connolly, McBean, McHardy, Stewart, Julian,
Croxen, Mills, Barbour, Wood, Gloak.
Att: 6,000

1891-92

Friendlies

P57 W33 D8 L16 F181 A102

Sep 5 (h)	Sheffield United	L	0-2	12 (h)	Chiswick Park	W	5-1
12 (h)	Casuals	W	2-1	19 (h)	Preston North End	L	0-3
19 (h)	Gainsborough Trinity	L	1-4	25 (a)	Sheffield United	D	3-3
26 (h)	West Bromwich Albion	D	1-1	26 (h)	1st Lincolnshire Regiment	W	6-0
Oct 3 (h)	Birmingham St Georges	L	1-5	Jan 2 (h)	Cowlairs (Glasgow)	L	1-2
8 (h)	Royal Engineers	W	8-0	7 (h)	City Ramblers	W	3-0
10 (h)	Crusaders	W	4-1	9 (h)	Crusaders	W	4-1
17 (a)	Bootle	D	2-2	21 (h)	Windsor Phoenix	W	3-1
19 (h)	Sheffield Wednesday	L	1-8	23 (h)	Grimsby Town	W	4-1
24 (h)	Long Eaton Rangers	W	3-1	30 (h)	Burton Wanderers	W	3-1
29 (h)	Royal Artillery	W	10-0	Feb 4 (h)	Sheffield United	L	1-4
31 (a)	Clapton	W	7-0	6 (h)	Cambridge University	W	2-1
Nov 5 (h)	Notts County	L	3-4	13 (a)	Chatham	W	3-2
7 (a)	London Caledonians	W	4-3	20 (h)	Burton Swifts	W	3-1
12 (h)	Erith	W	7-0	25 (a)	Windsor Phoenix	W	5-0
14 (h)	Cambridge University	W	5-1	27 (h)	Derby County	L	3-4
19 (h)	Woolwich District League	W	6-1	Mar 3 (h)	Borough Road College	W	4-1
21 (h)	St Bartholomews Hospital	W	9-0	5 (h)	Wolverhampton Wanderers	L	1-4
23 (h)	2nd Scots Guards	W	6-0	10 (h)	Casuals	W	3-1
28 (h)	Canadians	D	1-1	12 (a)	Great Marlow	W	5-2
30 (a)	Sheffield Wednesday	L	1-5	14 (h)	3rd Lanark Rovers	L	0-1
Dec 3 (h)	Canadians	W	4-0	19 (h)	71st Highland Light Infantry	W	3-2
5 (h)	Lincoln City	W	3-1	22 (h)	Preston North End	D	3-3
10 (h)	2nd Royal West Kent Regt.	L	1-2	26 (h)	Everton	D	2-2

361

Mar 31 (h)	Notts County	L	2-4		18 (h)	Bootle	D	1-1
Apr 2 (h)	Chatham	W	5-3		23 (h)	Clapton	W	4-1
9 (h)	South Shore (Blackpool)	D	1-1		26 (h)	Bolton Wanderers	W	3-2
15 (h)	Small Heath	L	1-2		30 (h)	Glasgow Rangers	L	2-3
16 (h)	Crewe Alexandra	W	2-1					

FA Cup   (See *FA Cup Record – 1889-1893*)

Round 1
Jan 16 v Small Heath   (a) L   1-5

1892-93

Friendlies

P56 W33 D4 L19 F144 A80

Sep 1 (h)	Highland Light Infantry	W	8-0		Jan 7 (h)	Middlesbrough Ironopolis	L	0-2
3 (h)	Gainsborough Trinity	W	4-2		11 (a)	Sussex Martlets	W	2-0
8 (h)	2nd Scots Guards	W	5-1		14 (h)	Wolverhampton Wanderers	L	1-3
10 (h)	Casuals	L	2-4		25 (a)	Oxford University	L	0-1
12 (a)	Sheffield United	L	0-1		28 (a)	Chatham	L	1-3
17 (h)	Darlington	W	3-2		30 (a)	1st Batt. Sherwood Foresters	W	3-0
24 (h)	Crusaders	W	4-0		Feb 4 (a)	Casuals	W	4-2
Oct 1 (h)	Marlow	W	4-0		6 (h)	Royal Lancaster Regiment	W	2-0
6 (h)	2nd Royal West Kent Regt.	W	3-0		9 (a)	Cambridge University	L	2-4
8 (h)	Clapton	W	4-1		11 (h)	Small Heath Alliance	W	3-1
20 (h)	Sheffield United	W	1-0		13 (h)	3rd Lanark	W	2-1
22 (h)	Staffordshire Regiment	W	1-0		18 (h)	Millwall Athletic	W	5-0
27 (h)	Oxford University	L	0-4		25 (h)	Walsall Town Swifts	W	2-0
Nov 5 (h)	Lincoln City	W	4-0		27 (h)	Notts Greenhalgh	L	1-3
7 (h)	Fleetwood Rangers	L	1-2		Mar 4 (a)	Middlesbrough	L	0-2
12 (h)	Cambridge University	D	6-6		11 (h)	Dumbarton	W	3-1
14 (h)	Sunderland	L	0-4		13 (h)	Aston Villa	L	0-1
23 (a)	Ipswich Town	W	5-0		18 (h)	Middlesbrough Ironopolis	W	3-0
24 (a)	Norfolk County	W	4-1		25 (a)	Millwall Athletic	W	1-0
26 (a)	Clapton	W	5-0		31 (h)	Middlesbrough	W	4-1
Dec 3 (h)	West Bromwich Albion	L	2-4		Apr 1 (h)	Accrington Stanley	W	3-1
12 (h)	Mr F.G.Armitages XI	W	3-1		3 (h)	Grimsby Town	L	3-5
17 (h)	Nottingham Forest	L	2-3		8 (a)	Crusaders	W	2-0
24 (h)	Burslem Port Vale	L	1-3		15 (h)	Casuals	W	3-0
26 (h)	Stockton	W	4-3		22 (h)	Derby County	D	0-0
27 (h)	Blackpool	D	1-1		24 (h)	London Welsh	W	4-2
31 (h)	Leith Athletic	D	1-1		26 (a)	Sevenoaks	W	11-0
Jan 2 (h)	Glasgow Thistle	L	1-2		29 (h)	Stoke	L	0-1

Appearances: C.Ambler 4, H.Barbour 1, E.Bee 20, C.Booth 42, R.Buist 51, L.Burrows 1, G.Crawford 31, G.Davie 12, D.Devine 35, F.Dyer 36, H.Earle 3, A.Elliott 52, D.Gemmell 45, W.George 1, J.Henderson 49, D.Howat 50, J.Hyslop 2, W.Jeffrey 51, F.V.Kirk 6, A.McKenzie 1, J.McQuilkie 10, J.Powell 30, A.Rankin 26, W.J.Shaw 23, Spencer 1, W.Stewart 1, C.A.Williams 29, Wood 3.

Goalscorers: Elliott 30, Henderson 30, Crawford 18, Gemmell 16, Shaw 16, Booth 11, Davie 5, Howat 5, Devine 3, Buist 2, Jeffrey 2, Dyer 2, Rankin 1, Spencer 1, Opponents 2.

FA Cup   (See *FA Cup Record – 1889-1893*)

Qualifying round 1
Oct 15 v Highland Light Infantry   (h) W   3-0
Qualifying round 2
Oct 29 v City Ramblers   (h) W   10-1
Qualifying round 3
Nov 19 v Millwall Athletic   (h) W   3-2

Qualifying round 4
De 10 v Clapton   (h) W   3-0
Round 1
Jan 21 v Sunderland   (a) L   0-6

During the Woolwich period, in addition to playing in the Football League, Arsenal also played in the following league competitions.

United League

1896-97
P14 W6 D3 L5 F28 A34 Pts15 Pos 3rd
Sep 7 v Rushden (h) 3-2
O'Brien 2, Johnson
Leather; Powell, Sinclair, Crawford, Boylan, Davis, Farmer, Haywood, Johnson, O'Brien, McAvoy.
Att: 'Good'
Oct 3 v Luton Town (h) 2-2
Meade 2
Fairclough; Powell, Sinclair, Shrewsbury, Boylan, Davis, Brock, Haywood, Meade, O'Brien, McAvoy.
Att: 8,000
Oct 5 v Rushden (a) 3-5
Brock 2, Haywood
Fairclough; Powell, Sinclair, Shrewsbury, Boylan, Davis, Brock, Haywood, Meade, O'Brien, McAvoy.
Att: 1,500
Oct 19 v Wellingborough (h) 2-1
Russell, O'Brien
Fairclough; Buist, Sinclair, Crawford, Boylan, Kington, Brock, Haywood, Johnson, O'Brien, Russell.
Att: 1,500
Nov 2 v Kettering Town (h) 1-1
McAvoy
Fairclough; Buist, Sinclair, Crawford, Boylan, Davis, Brock, McAvoy, Boyd, O'Brien, Duff.
Att: 1,000
Nov 9 v Tottenham Hotspur (h) 2-1
Russell 2
Fairclough; Buist, Sinclair, Crawford, Steel, Davis, Brodie, Haywood, Boyd, McAvoy, Russell.
Att: 2,000
Nov 23 v Kettering Town (a) 1-0
Boyd
Fairclough; Powell, Buist, Shrewsbury, Boyle, Boylan, Brock, Haywood, Boyd, McAvoy, Russell.
Att: 2,000
Nov 30 v Wellingborough (a) 1-4
McFarlane
Talbot; Boyd, Sinclair, Crawford, Boyle, Boylan, Brock, Haywood, McAvoy, O'Brien, McFarlane.
Att: 2,000
Jan 9 v Loughborough Town (h) 5-3
Haywood 2, Russell 2, Meade
Leather; Shrewsbury, Sinclair, Crawford, Boyle, Davis, Brock, Haywood, Meade, O'Brien, Russell.
Att: 2,500
Feb 25 v Tottenham Hotspur (a) 2-2
Haywood, Brock
Fairclough; Anderson, Caldwell, McAvoy, Crawford, Davis, Brock, Haywood, Caie, O'Brien, Russell.
Att: 2,000
Feb 27 v Millwall Athletic (h) 3-1
O'Brien 2, Brock
Fairclough; Anderson, Caldwell, McAvoy, Crawford, Davis, Brock, Haywood, Caie, O'Brien, Russell.
Att: 15,000
Mar 20 v Luton Town (a) 2-5
Haywood, Caie
Leather; Sinclair, Caldwell, Crawford, Anderson, McAvoy, Brock, Haywood, Caie, O'Brien, Russell.
Att: 'Record'

Apr 7 v Loughborough Town (a) 0-4
Fairclough; Sinclair, Caldwell, Crawford, Anderson, McAvoy, Brock, McFarland, Haywood, O'Brien, Russell.
Att: 1,000
Apr 24 v Millwall Athletic (a) 1-3
Caie
Leather; Sinclair, Anderson, Crawford, Boyle, McAvoy, Brock, Haywood, Caie, O'Brien, Russell.
Att: 8,000
1897-98
P16 W8 D5 L3 F35 A24 Pts21 Pos 3rd
Sep 22 v Loughborough Town (a) 3-1*
White, McAuley, Farrell
Ord; McAuley, Caldwell, Crawford, Anderson, Davis, Brock, Hunt, McGeoch, White, McAvoy(Farrell).
Att: 1,500
*Abandoned after 8½ minutes with the score at 2-1. The remaining 8½ minutes were completed following the Football League match between the two clubs on 18 December when Arsenal increased the score to 3-1.
Oct 4 v Kettering Town (h) 4-0
Farrell, Davis, Brock, White
Ord; McAuley, Caldwell, Anderson, Farrell, Davis, Brock, Crawford, McAvoy, White, Haywood.
Att: 1,000
Oct 11 v Wellingborough (a) 3-2
Haywood, Brock, Farrell
Ord; McAuley, Caldwell, Anderson, Farrell, Davis, Brock, Crawford, Stuart, McAvoy, Haywood.
Att: 1,200
Dec 13 v Rushden (h) 3-1
Hannah, White 2
Ord; McConnell, Caldwell, Crawford, Farrell, Anderson, Hunt, Haywood, McGeoch, Hannah, White.
Att: 1,000
Dec 20 v Southampton (h) 1-1
Brock
Ord; McAuley, Caldwell, Crawford, Farrell, Davis, Brock, Haywood, Hunt, Hannah, White.
Att: 2,000
Dec 25 v Tottenham Hotspur (h) 2-3
Brock 2
Ord; McAuley, Caldwell, Crawford, Farrell, Davis, Brock, Haywood, Devlin, Hannah, White.
Att: 5,000
Jan 10 v Wellingborough (h) 3-1
White 2, Haywood
Ord; McConnell, Caldwell, Davis, Anderson, McAvoy, Brock, Haywood, McGeoch, Hunt, White.
Att: 1,000
Jan 22 v Millwall Athletic (a) 2-2
White, Haywood
Ord; McConnell, Caldwell, Crawford, McAvoy, Davis, Brock, Haywood, Hunt, Hannah, White.
Att: 8,000
Feb 19 v Millwall Athletic (h) 2-2
Haywood, White
Ord; McAuley, McConnell, Anderson, Farrell, Davis, Brock, Haywood, Hunt, Hannah, White.
Att: 12,000

Feb 21 v Luton Town (h) 2-2 (After abandoned match, 0-0 on 17 January)
McGeoch, Hannah
Ord; McAuley, McConnell, Haywood, Farrell, Anderson, Brock, McGeoch, Hunt, Hannah, White.
Att: 3,000
Mar 28 v Rushden (a) 3-2
Brock, McGeoch 2
Ord; McConnell, Caldwell, Shrewsbury, Anderson, Davis, Brock, Haywood, McGeoch, Hannah, White.
Att: 800
Apr 1 v Loughborough Town (h) 4-1
Hannah 2 (1 pen), McGeoch, Haywood
Ord; McConnell, Caldwell, Crawford, Clark, Anderson, Brock, Haywood, McGeoch, Hannah, White.
Att: 3,000
Apr 4 v Kettering Town (a) 2-1
Haywood, White
Ord; Caldwell, McConnell, Crawford, Anderson, Shrewsbury, Brock, Haywood, McGeoch, Hannah, White.
Att: 1,000
Apr 8 v Tottenham Hotspur (a) 0-0
Ord; Caldwell, McConnell, Crawford, Anderson, Davis, Brock, Haywood, Hunt, Hannah, White.
Att: 14,500
Apr 13 v Southampton (a) 0-3
Ord; Caldwell, McConnell, Anderson, Farrell, Davis, Brock, Haywood, Hunt, Hannah, White.
Att: 3,000
Apr 16 v Luton Town (a) 1-2
Hunt
Ord; Caldwell, McConnell, Farrell, Anderson, Davis, Brock, Haywood, Hunt, Hannah, White.
Att: 'Large'
1898-99
P20 W10 D4 L6 F40 A30 Pts24 Pos 4th
Sep 14 v Reading (a) 1-1
Anderson (pen)
Ord; Fyfe, McConnell, Moir, Anderson, Gilmour, Brock, Hunt, McGeoch, Hannah, Dailly.
Att: 1,200
Oct 3 v Reading (h) 2-0
Haywood 2 (1 pen)
Hamilton; Fyfe, McConnell, Moir, Dick, Gilmour, Brock, Haywood, McGeoch, Dailly, Mitchell.
Att: 1,000
Oct 8 v Millwall Athletic (a) 1-1
White
Ord; Fyfe, McConnell, Moir, Dick, Anderson, Hunt, White, McGeoch, Dailly, Mitchell.
Att: 12,000
Oct 10 v Luton Town (h) 3-2
Hunt, Hannah, Mitchell
Ord; Fyfe, McConnell, Moir, Dick, Anderson, Brock, White, Hunt, Hannah, Mitchell.
Att: 1,500
Oct 17 v Rushden (h) 2-0
Haywood, Hunt
Ord; Gilmour, McConnell, Moir, Anderson, Dick, Hunt, Haywood, McGeoch, Murphy, Mitchell.
Att: 1,000
Oct 24 v Kettering Town (a) 1-2
Mitchell
Ord; McPhee, McConnell, Moir, Anderson, Dick, Hunt, White, McGeoch, Hannah, Mitchell.
Att: 2,000

Oct 29 v Southampton (a) 1-5
White
Ord; McPhee, McConnell, Moir, Anderson, Dick, Hunt, White, McGeoch, Hannah, Mitchell.
Att: 3,000
Oct 31 v Brighton United (h) 5-2
Hunt 2, Dailly 2, Hendry (og)
Ord; McPhee, Fyfe, Haywood, Anderson, Dick, Cottrell, White, Hunt, Hannah, Dailly.
Att: 2,000
Nov 9 v Bristol City (a) 2-1
Hunt, Dailly
Ord; McAvoy, McConnell, Haywood, Anderson, Dick, Brock, White, Hunt, Hannah, Dailly.
Att: 3,000
Nov 14 v Wellingborough (a) 0-3
Ord; McAvoy, McConnell, Moir, Anderson, Dick, Cottrell, McGeoch, Hunt, Murphy, Mitchell.
Att: 'Good'
Nov 19 v Southampton (h) 2-1
Hunt 2
Ord; McAvoy, McConnell, Haywood, Anderson, Dick, Cottrell, White, Hunt, Hannah, Dailly.
Att: 8,000
Nov 21 v Rushden (a) 6-0
Hannah 2, Hunt 3, Bailey (og)
Ord; McAvoy, McConnell, Haywood, Dick, Davis, Cottrell, McGeoch, Hunt, Hannah, Dailly.
Att: 'Small'
Dec 12 v Bristol City (h) 1-3
Dailly
Hamilton; McAvoy, McConnell, Moir, Dick, Gilmour, McGeoch, Haywood, Hunt, Murphy, Dailly.
Att: 3,000
Dec 26 v Millwall Athletic (h) 0-1
Ord; McPhee, McAvoy, Moir, Dick, Davis, McGeoch, Haywood, Hunt, Hannah, Shaw.
Att: 14,000
Dec 27 v Luton Town (a) 1-1
Shaw
Ord; Anderson, McPhee, Moir, Dick, Davis, McGeoch, Haywood, Hunt, Hannah, Shaw.
Att: 'Large'
Jan 4 v Brighton United (a) 1-1
McGeoch
Ord; McAvoy, McPhee, Moir, Dick, Davis, Hunt, Haywood, McGeoch, Hannah, Shaw.
Att: 1,500
Feb 6 v Kettering Town (h) 4-2
Shaw 2, Dick, Moir
Ord; McAvoy, Carver, Moir, Dick, Anderson, Hunt, Haywood, McGeoch, Hannah, Shaw.
Att: 600
Mar 11 v Tottenham Hotspur (h) 2-1
Haywood 2
Ord; J.Garton, McAvoy, Moir, Dick, Hannah, Hunt, Cottrell, McGeoch, Haywood, Shaw.
Att: 6,000
Mar 31 v Wellingborough (h) 3-0
Cottrell 2, McGeoch
Ord; Garton, McConnell, Moir, Dick, Davis, Anderson, Cottrell, McGeoch, Hannah, Mitchell.
Att: 3,000
Apr 29 v Tottenham Hotspur (a) 2-3
Hunt, Cottrell
Ord; McConnell, McAvoy, Hannah, Dick, Anderson, Hunt, Cottrell, McGeoch, Haywood, Shaw.
Att: 7,000

Southern District Combination

1899-1900
P15 W7 D1 L7 F25 A21 Pts15 Pos 4th*

Sep 11 v Millwall Athletic (a) 0-1
Ord; McNichol, Jackson, Murphy, Sanders, Dick, Hunt, Aston, Logan, McCowie, Tennant.
Att: 5,000

Sep 27 v Reading (a) 3-0
Hartley, Hunt, McCowie
Ord; McNichol, Jackson, Moir, Murphy, Dick, Hunt, Logan, Hartley, McCowie, Shaw.
Att: 1,500

Oct 11 v Southampton (a) 0-3
Ord; Anderson, Jackson, Moir, Murphy, Dick, Hunt, Aston, Logan, Hartley, Shaw.
Att: 'Large'

Oct 23 v Portsmouth (h) 0-2
Hamilton; Jackson, McAvoy, Dunsbee, Sanders, Dick, Aston, Hannigan, Gaudie, Hartley, Shaw.
Att: 'Small'

Oct 30 v Bristol City (h) 3-0
Lloyd 2, Hartley
Hamilton; Graham, McAvoy, Anderson, Sanders, Dunsbee, Lloyd, Hartley, Gaudie, Groves, Duff.
Att: 1,200

Jan 10 v Bristol City (a) 3-1
Logan, McCowie, Tennant (pen)
Ord; McNichol, Anderson, Murphy, Dick, Dunsbee, Lloyd, Logan, Gaudie, McCowie, Tennant.
Att: 'Small'

Jan 29 v Chatham (h) 4-0
Logan 3, Tennant
Ord; McNichol, Jackson, Murphy, Dick, Anderson, Hunt, Gaudie, Logan, Main, Tennant.
Att: 500

Feb 7 v Portsmouth (a) 1-3
Lloyd
Hamilton; McNichol, Jackson, Murphy, Dick, Anderson, Lloyd, Logan, Gaudie, Main, Tennant.
Att: 1,700

Feb 26 v Chatham (a) 2-1
Main 2
Ord; McNichol, Jackson, Moir, Dick, Anderson, Hunt, Logan, Main, McCowie, Tennant.
Att: 500

Mar 5 v Southampton (h) 1-0
Gaudie
Ord; McNichol, Jackson, Moir, Dick, Anderson, Hunt, Cottrell, Gaudie, McCowie, Tennant.
Att: 2,000

Mar 19 v Queen's Park Rangers (h) 5-1
Main, Lloyd, Anderson (pen), McCowie, Tennant
Hamilton; McNichol, Anderson, Moir, Dick, Dunsbee, Lloyd, Logan, Main, McCowie, Tennant.
Att: 600

Mar 26 v Reading (h) 1-1
McCowie
Hamilton; McNichol, Jackson, Moir, Dick, Anderson, Lloyd, McCowie, Main, Gaudie, Tennant.
Att: 1,200

Apr 2 v Millwall Athletic (h) 0-1
Hamilton; Murrell, Jackson, Moir, Dick, Dunsbee, Lloyd, Logan, Gaudie, McCowie, Tennant.
Att: 2,000

Apr 9 v Queen's Park Rangers (a) 0-3
Hamilton; Murphy, Anderson, Shrewsbury, Dick, Dunsbee, Lloyd, Logan, Ayling, Gaudie, Tennant.
Att: 'Good'

Apr 17 v Tottenham Hotspur (a) 2-4
Gaudie, Tennant
Hamilton; McNichol, Jackson, Murphy, Dick, Anderson, Lloyd, Logan, Main, Gaudie, Tennant.
Att: 4,500

Apr 24 v Tottenham Hotspur (h) 2-1* (Abandoned after 65 minutes)
Logan, Tennant
Hamilton; McNichol, Jackson, Murphy, Dick, Anderson, Hunt, McCowie, Logan, Shaw, Tennant.
Att: Unknown

*This match was abandoned due to abusive language from the crowd. Following a League enquiry, the club were censured, ordered to post notices, and the referee was also highly criticised. As it was the end of the season, the match was not replayed and it is not clear whether the result was allowed to stand, most final League tables excluded the unfinished match.

London League - Premier Division

1901-02
P8 W2 D2 L4 F9 A13 Pts6 Pos 5th

Sep 16 v Tottenham Hotspur (h) 0-2
Ashcroft; Cross, Jackson, Coles, Wolfe, J.Anderson, Briercliffe, Laidlaw, Swann, Place, Foxall.
Att: 6,000

Sep 30 v Millwall (h) 1-1
Childs
Ashcroft; Wright, Jackson, Coles, Wolfe, Place, Briercliffe, Main, Childs, Laidlaw, Foxall.
Att: 3,000

Oct 21 v West Ham United (h) 0-1
Ashcroft; McNichol, Cross, Coles, Jackson, Place, Briercliffe, Edgar, Childs, Owens, Foxall.
Att: 2,000

Nov 4 v Tottenham Hotspur (a) 0-5
Ashcroft; J.Anderson, Cross, Coles, Dick, Place, Briercliffe, Edgar, Main, Owens, Foxall.
Att: 3,833

Feb 3 v Queen's Park Rangers (a) 2-2
Gooing, Owens
Ashcroft; McNichol, Jackson, Coles, Dick, J.Anderson, Briercliffe, Main, Gooing, W.Anderson, Owens.
Att: 600

Feb 17 v Queen's Park Rangers (h) 3-0
Briercliffe, Bradshaw 2
Ashcroft; McNichol, Jackson, Coles, Theobald, Place, Briercliffe, Edgar, Gooing, Bradshaw, Vaughan.
Att: 1,000

365

Feb 24 v Millwall (a) 1-2
W.Anderson
Ashcroft; McNichol, J.Anderson, Coles, Dick, Place, Briercliffe, Main, Gooing, W.Anderson, Edgar.
Att: 3,000
Mar 28 v West Ham United (a) 2-0
W.Anderson 2
Ashcroft; McNichol, Jackson, Coles, Dick, Place, Briercliffe, Main, Gooing, W.Anderson, Foxall.
Att: 10,000

1902-03
P10 W6 D0 L4 F14 A10 Pts12 Pos 3rd
Sep 1 v West Ham United (a) 3-1
Gooing, Connor, Coleman
Ashcroft; McNichol, Jackson, Coles, Dick, McEachrane, Briercliffe, Connor, Gooing, Coleman, Lawrence.
Att: 3,000
Sep 15 v Queen's Park Rangers (h) 3-1
Coleman, Briercliffe, Connor
Ashcroft; McNichol, J.Anderson, Coles, Dick, McEachrane, Briercliffe, Connor, Gooing, Coleman, Lawrence.
Att: 1,500
Oct 27 v Queen's Park Rangers (a) 2-0
W.Anderson, Coleman
Ashcroft; Wolfe, Cross, Coles, Main, McEachrane, Briercliffe, Bradshaw, W.Anderson, Coleman, Lawrence.
Att: 1,000
Nov 10 v Brentford (h) 3-0
Vaughan, Connor, Main
Ashcroft; Wolfe, Jackson, Coles, Theobald, Ransom, Briercliffe, Main, Connor, Bradshaw, Vaughan.
Att: 700
Nov 17 v Tottenham Hotspur (h) 2-1
Gooing, Briercliffe
Wilcox; Cross, Jackson, Coles, Main, J.Anderson, Briercliffe, Connor, Gooing, W.Anderson, Lawrence.
Att: 4,000
Dec 1 v Tottenham Hotspur (a) 0-1
Ashcroft; J.Anderson, Wolfe, Coles, Main, Ransom, Briercliffe, Connor, Gooing, W.Anderson, Lawrence.
Att: 6,000
Dec 26 v Millwall (a) 0-3
Ashcroft; Coles, Wolfe, Dick, Theobald, Ransom, Briercliffe, Connor, W.Anderson, Coleman, Linward.
Att: 1,000
Feb 21 v West Ham United (h) 0-1
Ashcroft; McNichol, Jackson, Dick, Bannister, McEachrane, Briercliffe, Shanks, Keena, W.Anderson, Linward.
Att: 6,000
Mar 23 v Brentford (a) 1-0
Shanks
Ashcroft; Coles, J.Anderson, Dick, Main, McEachrane, Briercliffe, Coleman, Lawrence, Shanks, Linward.
Att: 2,000
Apr 18 v Millwall (h) 0-2
Ashcroft; McNichol, Jackson, Dick, Coles, McEachrane, Briercliffe, Bradshaw, W.Anderson, Shanks, Linward.
Att: 4,000

1903-04
P12 W6 D2 L4 F24 A19 Pts14 Pos 3rd
Sep 1 v Tottenham Hotspur (a) 1-0
Coleman
Ashcroft; Thorpe, Jackson, Dick, Theobald, McEachrane, Briercliffe, Coleman, Gooing, Bellamy, Linward.
Att: 7,000
Sep 7 v Fulham (h) 2-0
Bellamy, Linward
Ashcroft; Thorpe, Jackson, Dick, Pratt, McEachrane, Briercliffe, Coleman, Gooing, Bellamy, Linward.
Att: 3,000
Sep 14 v West Ham United (h) 4-1
Shanks 2, Crowe, Linward
Ashcroft; Thorpe, Jackson, Dick, Pratt, McEachrane, Briercliffe, Coleman, Crowe, Shanks, Linward.
Att: 3,000
Nov 14 v Tottenham Hotspur (h) 1-1
Briercliffe
Ashcroft; Cross, Jackson, Dick, Sands, McEachrane, Briercliffe, Coleman, Gooing, Shanks, Linward.
Att: 16,000
Nov 23 v Brentford (a) 1-1
Coleman
Ashcroft; Cross, Dwight, Dick, Bannister, McEachrane, Briercliffe, Coleman, Pratt, Shanks, Linward.
Att: 4,000
Dec 7 v Millwall (h) 1-3
Pratt
Eggett; Coles, Cross, Bellamy, Bannister, Ransom, Tomlinson, Watson, Crowe, Pratt, E.Anderson.
Att: 'Moderate'
Jan 11 v Queen's Park Rangers (h) 6-2
Busby, Pratt 2, Briercliffe, Shanks 2
Ashcroft; Dwight, Thorpe, Coles, Bannister, McEachrane, Briercliffe, Pratt, Watson, Shanks, Busby.
Att: 3,000
Feb 8 v Brentford (h) 3-2
Pratt 2, Watson
Ashcroft; Dwight, Thorpe, Dick, Bannister, McEachrane, Briercliffe, Coleman, Pratt, Watson, Shanks.
Att: 'Unknown'
Feb 22 v West Ham United (a) 4-2
Shanks 2, Pratt 2
Eggett; Dwight, Thorpe, Coles, Bannister, Ransom, Bradshaw, Watson, Pratt, Fitchie, Shanks.
Att: 2,000
Mar 7 v Millwall (a) 0-3
Eggett; Thorpe, Coles, Bellamy, Bannister, Ransom, Bradshaw, Watson, Crowe, Fitchie, Busby.
Att: 1,500
Mar 21 v Queen's Park Rangers (a) 1-3
Crowe
Eggett; Thorpe, Dwight, Coles, Bannister, Ransom, Bradshaw, Watson, Crowe, Busby, Neave.
Att: 1,000
Apr 30 v Fulham (a) 0-1
Ashcroft; Cross, Jackson, Dick, Theobald, McEachrane, Tomlinson, Watson, Gooing, Shanks, Neave.
Att: 8,000

Woolwich Arsenal pictured in 1910-11. Back row (left to right): Hardy (trainer), Dick, Thomson, Bateup, Common, Rippon, Hedley. Middle row: Gray, Ducat, Grant, McDonald, Rogers, Sands. Front row: Lewis, McKinnon, Greenaway, Heppinstall, G.Morrell (secretary), Logan, Neave, Shaw, McEachrane.

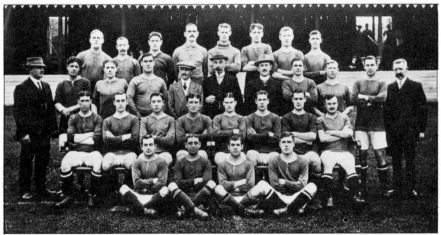

The Woolwich club pose for the camera in 1912-13. Back row (left to right): A.Common, R.J.McEachrane, W.Madge, G.Burdett, H.S.Crawford, J.McLaughlan, G.Grant, E.Pendergast. Standing: G.Hardy (trainer), P.R.Sands, L.A.Calder, C.Randall, A.Keard (financial secretary), J.W.Humble (director), G.Morrell (secretary-manager), G.Rogers, E.King, G.Payne, A.Rae (groundsman and assistant trainer). Seated: C.Lewis, A.McKinnon, A.Graham, J.Peart, G.Burrell, M.Thomson, J.Shaw, E.Hanks. On ground: T.Winship, J.Flanagan, D.Greenaway, T.Anthony.

367

London FA Challenge Cup

This competition was inaugurated in the 1908-09 season on a knock-out basis for the London clubs and leading amateur teams. For some years the club's first teams were used, but from around 1931 onwards mainly reserve XIs were fielded. From 1925 attendances were not always reported and in most cases have been omitted.

1908-09
Round 1
Sep 28 v Fulham (a) 1-0
Satterthwaite
McDonald; Chisholm, Gray, Dick, Theobald, McKinnon, Greenaway, Lee, Raybould, Satterthwaite, Curle.
Att: 5,000
Round 2
Nov 9 v Crystal Palace (h) 2-1
Lewis, Hoare
McDonald; Gray, Shaw, Ducat, Theobald, McEachrane, Greenaway, Lewis, Raybould, G.Hoare, Satterthwaite.
Att: 4,000
Semi-final
Feb 22 v Leyton (at Tottenham) 1-2
Lewis
McDonald; Cross, Gray, Ducat, Theobald, McEachrane, Greenaway, Lewis, Beney, Raybould, Satterthwaite.
Att: 4,000

1909-10
Round 1
Sep 20 v Bromley (h) 4-0
Lewis 3, Heppinstall
McDonald; Cross, Shaw, Dick, Thomson, McEachrane, Greenaway, Lewis, Beney, Satterthwaite, Heppinstall.
Att: 'Small'
Round 2
Oct 11 v West Ham United (h) 0-1
Cannon; Cross, Shaw, Ducat, Thomson, Dick, Greenaway, Beney, Lee, Drain, Neave.
Att: 5,500

1910-11
Round 1
Sep 19 v Queen's Park Rangers (h) 3-0
Rippon 2, Cannon
Bateup; Rogers, Shaw, Ducat, Thomson, McEachrane, Lewis, Common, Rippon, Logan, Neave.
Att: 1,800
Round 2
Oct 10 v Millwall (a) 0-1
Bateup; Gray, Shaw, Ducat, Thomson, McEachrane, Lewis, Common, Chalmers, Rippon, Neave.
Att: 3,000

1911-12
Round 1
Sep 18 v Queen's Park Rangers (a) 2-0
Lewis, Common
Burdett; Shaw, Gray, Peart, Grant, McKinnon, Lewis, Common, Chalmers, Winship, Greenaway.
Att: 3,500
Round 2
Oct 16 v Chelsea (h) 2-3
Common, Ducat (pen)
Burdett; Shaw, Peart, Ducat, Sands, McKinnon, Lewis, Common, Chalmers, Randall, Flanagan.
Att: 3,574

1912-13
Round 1
Sep 23 v Clapton Orient (a) 2-4
Common, Randall
Wilson; Shaw, Peart, King, Grant, McKinnon, Greenaway, Common, McLaughlan, Randall, Burrell.

1913-14
Round 1
Sep 22 v Queen's Park Rangers (h) 1-1
Devine (pen)
Caldwell; Shaw, Fidler, Graham, Thomson, McKinnon, Greenaway, Hardinge, Stonley, Devine, Burrell.
Att: 6,000
Replay
Sep 29 v Queen's Park Rangers (a) 3-2
Jobey, Winship, Spittle
Caldwell; G.Ford, Fidler, Thomson, Jobey, McKinnon, Greenaway, Lewis, Spittle, Devine, Winship.
Att: 6,000
Round 2
Oct 20 v Chelsea (a) 1-0
Hardinge (pen)
Lievesley; Shaw, Fidler, Thomson, Jobey, McKinnon, Lewis, Flanagan, Stonley, Hardinge, Burrell.
Att: 12,000
Semi-final
Nov 10 v Tottenham Hotspur (at Chelsea) 1-2
Devine
Lievesley; Shaw, Fidler, Jobey, Thomson, Graham, Lewis, Flanagan, Devine, Hardinge, Burrell.
Att: 8,000

1914-15
Round 1
Sep 21 v Tufnell Park (h) 6-0
Hardinge 2, Bradshaw, King, Winship, Groves
Lievesley; Shaw, Benson, Grant, Liddell, Graham, Groves, Hardinge, King, Bradshaw, Winship.
Att: 1,200
Round 2
Oct 19 v Queen's Park Rangers (h) 2-1
King, Hardinge
Lievesley; Shaw, Benson, McKinnon, Liddell, Graham, Rutherford, Flanagan, King, Bradshaw, Hardinge.
Att: 4,000
Semi-final
Nov 9 v Crystal Palace (at Tottenham) 2-0
Fletcher, King
Lievesley; Shaw, Benson, Fletcher, Buckley, McKinnon, Lewis, Hardinge, King, Bradshaw, Norman.
Att: 2,400
Dec 7 v Millwall (at New Cross) 1-2
King
Lievesley; Shaw, Benson, Grant, Graham, McKinnon, Rutherford, Hardinge, King, Bradshaw, Lewis.
Att: 2,000

1919-20
Round 1
Sep 22 v Dulwich Hamlet (h) 2-0
Hardinge, Groves
Williamson; Shaw, Hutchins, Butler, Plumb, Cockerill, Greenaway, Groves, King, Hardinge, Baker.
Att: 2,000
Round 2
Oct 6 v Fulham (a) 0-0
Williamson; Shaw, Bradshaw, Graham, Butler, McKinnon, Rutherford, Burgess, White, Blyth, Toner.
Att: 5,500
Replay
Oct 20 v Fulham (h) 1-3
Hardinge
Williamson; Bradshaw, Hutchins, Graham, Buckley, McKinnon, Rutherford, Blyth, White, Hardinge, Toner.
Att: 10,000

1920-21
Round 1
Oct 11 v Brentford (h) 3-0
Pagnam 3
Williamson; Shaw, Hutchins, Baker, Graham, McKinnon, Rutherford, White, Pagnam, Bradshaw, Blyth.
Att: 6,500
Round 2
Nov 1 v Tottenham Hotspur (a) 1-3
White
Williamson; Buckley, Peart, Baker, Pattison, Whittaker, Greenaway, White, Pagnam, Blyth, Toner.
Att: 14,500

1921-22
Round 1
Oct 17 v Barking (a) 5-2
White 2, Baker 2, Butler
Williamson; Cownley, Hutchins, Whittaker, Butler, McKinnon, Rutherford, White, Baker, Bradshaw, Blyth.
Att: 4,500
Round 2
Oct 31 v Queen's Park Rangers (a) 2-0
Blyth, White
Williamson; Bradshaw, Turnbull, Baker, Butler, Whittaker, White, Blyth, North, Hopkins, Paterson.
Att: 5,000
Semi-final
Nov 14 v Tottenham Hotspur (at Chelsea) 0-0 (abandoned after 5 minutes of extra-time)
Williamson; Bradshaw, Hutchins, Baker, Butler, Whittaker, Creegan, Blyth, Henderson, Hopkins, Toner.
Att: 12,000
Replay
Nov 21 v Tottenham Hotspur (at Clapton Orient) 2-1 (after extra-time)
Henderson, Butler
Williamson; Bradshaw, Turnbull, Baker, Butler, Milne, Rutherford, Blyth, Henderson, Hopkins, Toner.
Att: 9,029
Final
May 8 v Crystal Palace (at Millwall) 1-0
Hutchins (pen)
Williamson; Bradshaw, Hutchins, Baker, Butler, Whittaker, Henderson, White, Turnbull, Boreham, Blyth.
Att: 12,000

1922-23
Round 1
Oct 23 v Tottenham Hotspur (h) 3-2
Paterson, Roe, Graham (pen)
Dunn; Mackie, Turnbull, Milne, Graham, John, Rutherford, Young, Roe, Baker, Paterson.
Att: 11,207
Round 2
Oct 30 v Crystal Palace (a) 0-1
Dunn; Mackie, Turnbull, Milne, Graham, Whittaker, Henderson, Young, Roe, Baker, Blyth.
Att: 2,500

1923-24
Round 1
Oct 22 v Tufnell Park (h) 4-0
Young 3, Woods
Robson; Mackie, Kennedy, Milne, Butler, Blyth, Rutherford, Townrow, Young, Woods, Haden.
Att: 4,000
Round 2
Nov 5 v Brentford (h) 3-2
Woods, Young, Voysey
Robson; Mackie, Whittaker, Graham, Butler, Blyth, Voysey, Townrow, Young, Woods, Toner.
Att: 2,500
Semi-final
Dec 3 v Millwall (at Clapton Orient) 2-1 (after extra-time)*
Graham, Young
Robson; Mackie, Whittaker, Milne, Graham, Blyth, Clark, Townrow, Young, Woods, Haden.
Att: 3,000
*Followed a match abandoned after 70 minutes (fog) on November 26, score 2-0.
Final
Dec 10 v Charlton Athletic (at West Ham) 3-1
Young 2, Haden
Robson; Mackie, Whittaker, Milne, Graham, Irving, Rutherford, Blyth, Young, Woods, Haden.
Att: 4,000

1924-25
Round 1
Oct 27 v Chelsea (h) 2-0
Woods, Brain
Robson; Mackie, Kennedy, Milne, Butler, John, Rutherford, Brain, Woods, Ramsay, Toner.
Att: 5,582
Round 2
Nov 10 v West Ham United (a) 1-4
Mackie (pen)
Robson; Mackie, Collin, Milne, Butler, John, Haden, Neil, Whittaker, Ramsay, Toner.
Att: 10,000

1925-26
Round 1
Sep 14 v London Caledonians (h) 3-2
Neil, Cock, Brain
Robson; Mackie, Kennedy, Baker, Butler, Ramsay, Hoar, Cock, Brain, Neil, Toner.
Att: 5,000
Round 2
Oct 12 v Fulham (h) 4-0
Brain 3, Haden
Lewis; Mackie, John, Baker, Young, Voysey, Clark, Woods, Brain, Ramsay, Haden.

369

Semi-final
Oct 26 v Millwall (at Tottenham) 3-1
Woods, Neil, Brain
Robson; Mackie, John, Baker, Butler, Blyth, Hoar,
Woods, Brain, Neil, Haden.
Final
Nov 9 v West Ham United (at Clapton Orient) 1-2
Brain
Robson; Mackie, John, Baker, Butler, Blyth, Hoar,
Woods, Brain, Neil, Haden.
Att: 6,000

1926-27
Round 1
Sep 27 v Charlton Athletic (h) 1-4
Ramsay
Harper; Parker, John, Baker, Butler, Blyth, Hulme,
Lambert, Brain, Ramsay, Haden.

1927-28
Round 1
Oct 17 v Clapton Orient (a) 1-2
Parker (pen)
Lewis; Roberts, Parker, Baker, Butler, Barley, Hoar,
Buchan, Brain, Lambert, Peel.

1928-29
Round 1
Oct 15 v Queen's Park Rangers (a) 1-5
Parker
Lewis; Parker, Cope, Blyth, Roberts, John, Hulme,
Parkin, Shaw, Thompson, C.Jones.

1929-30
Round 1
Oct 14 v Brentford (a) 1-2
Parker (pen)
Lewis; Parker, Hapgood, Baker, Roberts, Brain,
Hulme, Jack, Lambert, Thompson, C.Jones.

1930-31
Round 1
Oct 13 v Clapton Orient (h) 3-0
Halliday, Jones, Johnstone
Harper; Robinson, Cope, Parkin, Haynes, Male,
Williams, Johnstone, Halliday, Thompson, C.Jones.
Round 2
Oct 27 v Crystal Palace (a) 2-2
Hulme, Thompson
Harper; Robinson, Cope, Parkin, Haynes, Male,
Hulme, Jack, Halliday, Thompson, C.Jones.
Replay
Nov 19 v Crystal Palace (h) 5-0
Thompson 2, Halliday 2, Brain
Preedy; Baker, Cope, Parkin, Haynes, Male,
W.Warnes, Brain, Halliday, Thompson, C.Jones.
Semi-final
Mar 25 v Millwall (at West Ham) 0-0
Preedy; Robinson, Cope, Diaper, Seddon, Male,
W.Warnes, H.Lewis, Parkin, Thompson, Maycock.
Replay
Apr 15 v Millwall (at Tottenham) 3-2
Brain 2, Thompson
Preedy; Robinson, Cope, Seddon, Haynes, Male,
W.Warnes, Brain, Parkin, Thompson, H.Lewis.
Att: 4,000
Final
May 4 v Tottenham Hotspur (a) 2-1
Cope, Brain
Preedy; Robinson, Cope, Seddon, Haynes, Male,
W.Warnes, Brain, Parkin, Thompson, Williams.
Att: 10,160

1931-32
Round 1
Oct 12 v Leyton (h) 8-1
Stockill 6, Lewis 2
Solly; Male, Cope, Seddon, Haynes, Sidey, Beasley,
Parkin, Stockill, Thompson, H.Lewis.
Round 2
Oct 26 v Crystal Palace (a) 1-2
Beasley
Solly; Male, Cope, Seddon, Haynes, Sidey, Williams,
H.Lewis, Stockill, Thompson, Beasley.

1932-33
Round 1
Oct 10 v Barnet (h) 5-1
Lambert 3, Cope, Parkin
Preedy; Cope, Black, Haynes, Sidey, Male, W.Warnes,
Parkin, Lambert, Bastin, Beasley.
Round 2
Oct 24 v Brentford (h) 7-2
Beasley 2, Walsh 2, Lambert 2
Preedy; Cope, Black, Parkin, Sidey, Cartwright,
W.Warnes, Walsh, Lambert, Stockill, Beasley.
Semi-final
Nov 14 v Queen's Park Rangers (a) 0-1
Preedy; L.Compton, Cope, Parkin, Sidey, Cartwright,
W.Warnes, Walsh, Lambert, Stockill, Beasley.

1933-34
Round 1
Oct 9 v Finchley (a) 3-0
Beasley, Green, Dougall
Wilson; L.Compton, Cartwright, Walker, Sidey,
Collett, Green, Stockill, J.Carr, Dougall, Beasley.
Round 2
Oct 25 v Kingstonian (a) 3-2
Hill 2, Beasley
Wilson; L.Compton, Trim, Cartwright, Roberts,
Haynes, Hill, Coleman, Stockill, Dougall, Beasley.
Semi-final
Nov 13 v Chelsea (h) 3-2
Birkett 3
Wilson; L.Compton, Cartwright, Hill, Roberts,
Collett, Birkett, Coleman, Green, Dougall, Beasley.
Final
May 7 v Tottenham Hotspur (h) 4-0
Green 2, Cox, Birkett
Wilson; L.Compton, Trim, Walker, Sidey, Collett,
Birkett, Stockill, Cox, Dougall, Green.

1934-35
Round 1
Oct 8 v Clapton Orient (h) 3-1
Cox 2, Biggs
Wilson; L.Compton, Trim, Cartwright, Sidey, Collett,
Beasley, Parkin, Cox, Biggs, Green.
Round 2
Oct 22 v West Ham United (a) 0-1
Wilson; L.Compton, Trim, Hill, Sidey, Collett, Hulme,
Marshall, Cox, Dougall, Green.

1935-36
Round 1
Oct 7 v Charlton Athletic (h) 2-1
L.Compton, Cox
Watson; L.Compton, Trim, Parkin, Sidey, Copping,
Rogers, Biggs, Cox, Dougall, Beasley.
Round 2
Oct 21 v Nunhead (h) 2-0
Cox, Clark
Watson, L.Compton, Trim, Parkin, Cartwright,
Collett, Rogers, Clark, Cox, Dougall, D.Compton.

370

Semi-final
Nov 25 v Tottenham Hotspur (a) 2-1
Beasley, Westcott
Bradshaw; L.Compton, Trim, Cartwright, Sidey, Collett, Beasley, Davidson, Westcott, Cox, D.Compton.
Final
May 4 v Brentford (at Fulham) 4-2
Kirchen 3, Milne
Wilson; L.Compton, Collett, Biggs, Sidey, Cartwright, Milne, Rogers, Kirchen, Davidson, D.Compton.

1936-37
Round 1
Oct 5 v Clapton Orient (h) 1-1
Kirchen
Wilson; L.Compton, Trim, Cartwright, Sidey, Collett, Kirchen, Nelson, Biggs, Davidson, Beasley.
Replay
Oct 12 v Clapton Orient (a) 1-0 (after extra-time)
Milne
Wilson; L.Compton, Trim, Cartwright, Sidey, Collett, Nelson, Davidson, Biggs, MacFarlane, Milne.
Round 2
Oct 19 v Brentford (h) 3-0
Compton (pen), Kirchen, MacFarlane
Wilson; L.Compton, Trim, Cartwright, Sidey, Collett, Nelson, Biggs, Kirchen, MacFarlane, Milne.
Semi-final
Nov 16 v Walthamstow Avenue (a) 3-0
D.Compton, Nelson, Hulme
Wilson; L.Compton, Trim, Cartwright, Tuckett, Collett, Hulme, Nelson, Biggs, MacFarlane, D.Compton.
Final
May 3 v Tottenham Hotspur (a) 0-1
Wilson; L.Compton, Trim, Cartwright, Sidey, Collett, Griffiths, Nelson, R.Lewis, Biggs, D.Compton.

1937-38
Round 1
Oct 4 v Hayes (h) 1-1
D.Compton
Swindin; Scott, Cartwright, Pryde, Sidey, Collett, Griffiths, Bremner, Lewis, Carr, D.Compton.
Replay
Oct 20 v Hayes (h) 12-0
Lewis 4, D.Compton 3, Biggs 2, Carr 2, Nelson
Swindin; Scott, Cartwright, Atter, Sidey, Pryde, Nelson, Biggs, Lewis, Carr, D.Compton.
Round 2
Oct 25 v Tottenham Hotspur (a) 2-1
Carr 2
Boulton; Scott, Cartwright, Pryde, Sidey, Collett, Griffiths, Nelson, Lewis, Carr, D.Compton.
Semi-final
Dec 6 v Millwall (a) 1-3
D.Compton
Swindin; Scott, L.Compton, Pryde, Sidey, John, Nelson, Biggs, Lewis, Carr, D.Compton.

1938-39
Round 1
Oct 3 v Crystal Palace (a) 2-2
Lewis, D.Compton
Wilson; Scott, L.Compton, Cartwright, Fields, Collett, Walsh, Bremner, Lewis, Drury, D.Compton.
Replay
Oct 10 v Crystal Palace (h) 5-1
Drury 2, Walsh 2, Lewis
Marks; Scott, L.Compton, Cartwright, Fields, Collett, Walsh, Carr, Lewis, Drury, D.Compton.

Round 2
Oct 17 v Fulham (h) 4-0
Lewis, Curtis, L.Compton (pen), Nelson
Marks; Scott, L.Compton, Cartwright, Fields, Collett, Walsh, Bremner, Lewis, Curtis, Nelson.
Semi-final
Nov 7 v Queen's Park Rangers (h) 0-0
Wilson; Scott, L.Compton, Cartwright, Fields, Collett, Nelson, Bremner, Lewis, Curtis, D.Compton.
Replay
Mar 6 v Queen's Park Rangers (a) 1-3
Walsh
Marks; Scott, Tooze, Pryde, Fields, Pugh, Walsh, Bremner, Lewis, Curtis, Nelson.

1946-47
Round 1
Oct 14 v Brentford (a) 1-1
Gudmundsson
Platt; S.Jones, Wade, Pryde, Fields, Farquhar, Nelson, Gudmundsson, Sloan, Drury, A.Smith.
Replay
Oct 21 v Brentford (h) 2-3
Grant, Bastin
Newman; Delaney, Wade, Pryde, L.Smith, Henley, Farquhar, Sloan, Grant, Bastin, A.Smith.

1947-48
Round 1
Oct 13 v Millwall (a) 0-2
Newman; Delaney, Chenhall, Horsfield, L.Smith, Farquhar, Clelland, Vallance, Bowden, Morgan, Holland.

1948-49
Round 1
Oct 11 v Millwall (a) 1-0
Duffy
Dunkley; Wade, L.Smith, N.Smith, Fields, Shaw, McPherson, Lishman, Duffy, Forbes, Robertson.
Round 2
Oct 25 v Chelsea (a) 1-4
Lishman
Dunkley; Wade, Chenhall, N.Smith, L.Smith, Horsfield, Dubois, Kelly, Goring, Lishman, Robertson.

1949-50
Round 1
Oct 10 v Millwall (h) 2-3
Duffy 2
Swindin; Wade, Chenhall, Shaw, Daniel, Horsfield, McPherson, Milton, Duffy, Lishman, D.Compton.

1950-51
Round 1
Oct 9 v Crystal Palace (a) 0-1
Platt; Chenhall, Wade, Wills, Daniel, N.Smith, Cox, Oakes, Holton, Shaw, Bowen.

1951-52
Round 1
Oct 8 v Hendon (h) 0-1
Kelsey; Roper, Wade, Wills, Healey, Chenhall, Ryan, Grimshaw, Lewis, Shaw, Robertson.

1952-53
Round 1
Oct 6 v Walthamstow Avenue (h) 2-2
Holton 2
Dunkley; Wills, Healey, Smailes, Dove, Bowen, F.Cox, Oakes, Holton, P.Tilley, Bennett.

Replay
Oct 13 v Walthamstow Avenue (h) 8-3
Holton 3, Marden 2, Oakes 2, P.Tilley
Dunkley; Wills, Healey, Smailes, Dove, Bowen, F.Cox,
Oakes, Holton, P.Tilley, Marden.
Round 2
Oct 20 v Charlton Athletic (a) 1-2
Marden
Dunkley; Wills, Evans, N.Smith, Dove, Bowen,
Bennett, Oakes, Walsh, P.Tilley, Marden.

1953-54
Round 1
Oct 6 v Leytonstone (h) 4-3
Walsh 2, Carson, Ward
Amos; Bennett, Doughty, Johnson, Fotheringham,
Bowen, Clapton, Walsh, Tilley, Carson, Ward.
Round 2
Oct 14 v Brentford (h) 4-3
Walsh, Oakes, Tilley, Holton
Dunkley; Bennett, Evans, Shaw, Fotheringham,
Bowen, Walsh, Oakes, Holton, Tilley, Marden.
Semi-final
Nov 2 v Wealdstone (h) 4-1
Davis 3, Walsh
Amos; Bennett, L.Smith, Shaw, Fotheringham,
Bowen, Walsh, Oakes, Davis, Tilley, Ward.
Final
Dec 7 v Chelsea (a) 1-1
Ward
Swindin; Bennett, Evans, Shaw, Fotheringham,
Bowen, Walsh, Tapscott, Davis, Goring, Ward.
Replay
Mar 29 v Chelsea (h) 3-2
Oakes 2, Ward
Guthrie; Wade, Evans, Batsford, Fotheringham,
Bowen, Milton, Oakes, Tapscott, Ward, Marden.

1954-55
Round 1
Oct 4 v Brentford (a) 2-0
Wilkinson, Opponent (og)
T.Dove; Bennett, Evans, Oakes, Dodgin, Doughty,
Walsh, Wilkinson, Brasted, Bloomfield, Ward.
Round 2
Oct 18 v Hounslow Town (a) 5-2
Wilkinson 2, Holton 2, Herd
Sullivan; H.Dove, Evans, Oakes, Fotheringham,
Doughty, Clapton, Herd, Holton, Wilkinson, Marden.
Semi-final
Nov 1 v Chelsea (h) 4-1
Wilkinson, Walsh, Haverty, Opponent (og)
Sullivan; Wills, Evans, Oakes, Fotheringham, Bowen,
Walsh, Herd, Wilkinson, Ward, Haverty.
Final
Dec 6 v West Ham United (h) 1-1
Wilkinson
Sullivan; Bennett, Evans, Oakes, Dodgin, Shaw,
Walsh, Herd, Wilkinson, Bloomfield, Haverty.
Att: 5,000
Replay
Mar 7 v West Ham United (a) 2-1
Haverty, Herd
Sullivan; Dodgin, Doughty, Oakes, Smailes, Shaw,
Walsh, Herd, Holton, Wilkinson, Haverty.

1955-56
Round 1
Oct 3 v Leyton Orient (h) 4-1
Tapscott 2, Wilkinson, Goulden
Sullivan; Bennett, Wade, Vernon, Fotheringham,
Cook, Clapton, Tapscott, Wilkinson, Goulden,
D.Flanagan.

Round 2
Oct 17 v Fulham (a) 3-1
Haverty 2, Wilkinson
Standen; Nicholas, Wade, Smailes, Dodgin, Doughty,
Saxby, Herd, Wilkinson, Goulden, Haverty.
Semi-final
Nov 1 v Queen's Park Rangers (h) 1-2
Wilkinson
Sullivan; Bennett, Wade, Smailes, Dodgin, Dickson,
Tapscott, Herd, Wilkinson, Swallow, Haverty.

1956-57
Round 1
Oct 8 v Wembley (h) 5-1
Swallow 3, Herd 2
Sullivan; D.Bennett, Doughty, Wills, Fotheringham,
Petts, Nutt, Herd, Biggs, Swallow, D.Dodson.
Round 2
Oct 15 v Queen's Park Rangers (h) 2-2
Herd 2
Sullivan; Wills, Doughty, Crouch, Fotheringham,
Petts, Nutt, Herd, Vernon, Swallow, Tiddy.
Replay
Oct 22 v Queen's Park Rangers (a) 3-1
Swallow 2, Tiddy
Standen; Nicholas, Doughty, Crouch, H.Dove, Ward,
Nutt, J.Barnwell, Biggs, Swallow, Tiddy.
Semi-final
Oct 29 v Millwall (a) 0-1
Sullivan; H.Dove, Doughty, Ward, Fotheringham,
Bowen, Nutt, Herd, Biggs, Swallow, D.Dodson.

1957-58
Round 1
Oct 7 v Millwall (h) 5-0
Tapscott 2, Le Roux, Barnwell, Groves
Sullivan; D.Bennett, Doughty, Ward, Cox, Goring, Le
Roux, Tapscott, Groves, Barnwell, D.M.Bennett.
Round 2
Nov 4 v Brentford (h) 3-3
Swallow 2, Le Roux
Standen; Wills, D.Bennett, Ward, Fotheringham,
Petts, Nutt, Barnwell, Le Roux, Swallow, Tiddy.
Replay
Nov 19 v Brentford (a) 3-3
Le Roux, Tiddy Biggs
Standen; Wills, D.Bennett, Smailes, H.Dove, Goring,
Le Roux, Tapscott, Biggs, Swallow, Tiddy.
Second Replay
Nov 25 v Brentford (h) 3-0
Barnwell, Nutt, Le Roux
Standen; D.Bennett, Doughty, Goring, H.Dove, Petts,
Le Roux, Tapscott, Biggs, Barnwell, Nutt.
Semi-final
Dec 9 v Leyton Orient (h) 2-0*
Le Roux, Groves
Standen; D.Bennett, Doughty, Fotheringham, Goring,
Le Roux, Tapscott, Groves, Barnwell, Nutt.
*Followed a match abandoned after 36 minutes on
December 2, score 2-0.
Final
Mar 17 v West Ham United (a) 3-1
Swallow 2, Tapscott
Standen; D.Bennett, Evans, Davies, Dodgin, Holton,
Tiddy, Tapscott, Biggs, Swallow, Haverty.
Att: 8,000

1958-59
Round 1
Oct 4 v Wimbledon (h) 5-2
Herd 3, Bloomfield, Evans
Kelsey; Wills, Evans, Docherty, Dodgin, Bowen,
Tiddy, Groves, Herd, Bloomfield, Nutt.

Round 2
Oct 20 v Crystal Palace (h) 3-2
Dodson, Petts, Opponent (og)
Standen; Charlton, McCullough, Everitt, Fotheringham, Petts, Tiddy, Goulden, Biggs, Dodson, Nutt.
Semi-final
Nov 3 v West Ham United (a) 3-4
Goulden 2, Biggs
Standen; Charlton, McCullough, P.Davies, Fotheringham, Bowen, Nutt, Barnwell, Biggs, Goulden, Haverty.

1959-60
Round 1
Oct 5 v Charlton Athletic (h) 7-2
Henderson 4, Julians 2, O'Neill
Goy; Magill, Meldrum, Ward, Snedden, Petts, O'Neill, Goulden, Julians, Henderson, Nutt.
Round 2
Oct 15 v Chelsea (h) 1-2
D.P.Clapton
Goy; Magill, Bacuzzi, Ward, Snedden, Petts, O'Neill, Goulden, D.P.Clapton, Barnwell, Nutt.

1960-61
Round 1
Oct 3 v Wimbledon (a) 4-1
Kane 3, Haverty
Standen; Magill, Evans, Everitt, Dodgin, Petts, Skirton, Barnwell, D.P.Clapton, Kane, Haverty.
Round 2
Oct 17 v Tottenham Hotspur (h) 1-0
Charles
Standen; Magill, Evans, D.P.Clapton, Dodgin, Petts, O'Neill, Scurr, Charles, Kane, Haverty.
Semi-final
Nov 15 v Brentford (a) 5-3
Kane 3, O'Neill, Skirton
McKechnie; Magill, Evans, Ward, Dodgin, D.P.Clapton, D.R.Clapton, Goulden, O'Neill, Kane, Skirton.
Final
Dec 5 v Chelsea (a) 1-3
O'Neill
McClelland; Magill, Clarke, Ward, Dodgin, Petts, O'Neill, Scurr, Charles, Eastham, Haverty.

1961-62
Round 1
Oct 2 v Barnet (h) 4-1
Strong 2, Skirton, Henderson
Kelsey; Bacuzzi, McCullough, Charles, Brown, Groves, MacLeod, Eastham, Strong, Henderson, Skirton.
Round 2
Oct 16 v Brentford (a) 3-3
MacLeod, Henderson, Ward
McKechnie; Bacuzzi, McCullough, Ward, Brown, Groves, MacLeod, Eastham, Henderson, Barnwell, Skirton.
Replay
Oct 23 v Brentford (h) 5-1
Skirton 2, McCullough, Eastham, Neill
Kelsey; Bacuzzi, McCullough, Ward, Brown, Neill, MacLeod, Barnwell, Henderson, Eastham, Skirton.
Semi-final
Oct 30 v Tottenham Hotspur (h) 3-2
McCullough, Skirton, Eastham
Kelsey; Bacuzzi, McCullough, Ward, Brown, Groves, MacLeod, Barnwell, Henderson, Eastham, Skirton.

Final
Dec 4 v Millwall (h) 3-1
Eastham, Charles, Opponent (og)
Kelsey; Bacuzzi, McCullough, Clamp, Brown, Snedden, MacLeod, Ward, Charles, Eastham, Skirton.

1962-63
Round 1
Oct 1 v Tottenham Hotspur (a) 2-1
Kane, Armstrong
McClelland; Bacuzzi, Clarke, Petts, Ferry, Groves, Armstrong, Sammels, Kane, Bloomfield, Whittaker.
Round 2
Oct 15 v Enfield (h) 2-1
Court, Barnwell
McKechnie; Bacuzzi, Clarke, Smithson, Brown, Groves, Armstrong, Barnwell, Court, Ward, Whittaker.
Semi-final
Oct 29 v Wealdstone (a) 1-1
Court
McKechnie; Bacuzzi, Clarke, Smithson, Ferry, Groves, Kinsella, Ward, Court, Kane, Armstrong.
Replay
Nov 12 v Wealdstone (h) 3-1
Whittaker, Ward, Armstrong
McKechnie; Bacuzzi, Clarke, Barnwell, Ferry, Smithson, Armstrong, Sammels, Court, Ward, Whittaker.
Final
Dec 3 v Chelsea (h) 4-1
Ward 2, Anderson, Court
McKechnie; Bacuzzi, Clarke, Smithson, Ferry, Groves, Anderson, Ward, Court, Bloomfield, Whittaker.

1963-64
Oct 7 v Wealdstone (a) 2-1
Court, B.Gould
R.Wilson; Bacuzzi, Smithson, Barnwell, Neill, Snedden, Anderson, Court, B.Gould, Sammels, Skirton.
Round 2
Oct 21 v Chelsea (a) 0-3
R.Wilson; Bacuzzi, F.Clarke, Smithson, Neill, Ferry, Anderson, B.Gould, Radford, Simpson, Whittaker.

1964-65
Round 1
Oct 8 v Hendon (h) 3-4
Radford 3
Wilson; Magill, Storey, Simpson, Ure, Court, Anderson, Baldwin, Radford, Sammels, Tawse.

1965-66
Round 1
Oct 4 v Millwall (a) 2-1
D.Baker, Baldwin
Burns; Pack, Storey, Boot, Wilkinson, Simpson, Skirton, D.Baker, Baldwin, Tyrer, Tawse.
Round 2
Oct 18 v Crystal Palace (a) 3-3
Boot, D.Baker, Tyrer
Burns; Magill, Storey, Boot, Ure, Walley, Skirton, D.Baker, Baldwin, Tyrer, Tawse.
Replay
Oct 25 v Crystal Palace (h) 0-0 (after extra-time)
Wilson; Pack, Storey, Boot, Neill, Walley, Skirton, D.Baker, Baldwin, Tyrer, Tawse.

Second Replay
Nov 1 v Crystal Palace (a) 4-3
Baldwin 2, Tawse 2
Wilson; Pack, McCullough, Simpson, Neill, Walley, Skirton, Radford, Baldwin, Tyrer, Tawse.
Semi-final
Nov 8 v Tottenham Hotspur (h) 3-0
Simpson, Tyrer, Radford
Wilson; Pack, McCullough, Simpson, Ure, Walley, Skirton, Radford, Baldwin, Tyrer, Tawse.
Final
May 10 v Queen's Park Rangers (h) 0-4
Burns; Pack, McCullough, Jenkins, Wilkinson, Walley, Neilson, Tyrer, Baldwin, Sammels, Corr.

1966-67
Round 1
Oct 3 v Wealdstone (a) 4-1
Jenkins 2, Neilson, Corr
Wilson; Rice, Stanton, McGill, Howe, Davidson, Neilson, Jenkins, Milne, Cumming, Corr.
Round 2
Oct 19 v Brentford (h) 0-1
Wilson; Rice, Stanton, McGill, Howe, Woodward, Neilson, Jenkins, Radford, Cumming, Corr.

1967-68
Round 1
Oct 2 v Millwall (a) 0-2
Wilson; Rice, McNab, Woodward, Carmichael, Gillibrand, Coakley, Howe, Jenkins, Johnston, Neilson.

1968-69
Round 1
Sep 30 v Barnet (a) 1-4
Opponent (og)
J.Detnam; Rice, Nelson, Kelly, Carmichael, Ure, Cumming, Woodward, Simmons, Graham, Armstrong.

1969-70
Round 1
Sep 29 v Charlton Athletic (a) 1-1
Burton
Cernis; Batson, Nelson, Roberts, Carmichael, Kelly, Cumming, Ritchie, Davies, Woodward, Burton.
Replay
Oct 8 v Charlton Athletic (h) 6-2
Kennedy 2, Cumming 2, de Garis, Carmichael
Webster; Rice, Nelson, Woodward, Carmichael, Kelly, Cumming, Court, Davies, Kennedy, de Garis.
Round 2
Oct 13 v Queen's Park Rangers (h) 3-1
Kennedy, Kelly, George
Johnson; Rice, Nelson, Woodward, Carmichael, Kelly, Cumming, Court, George, Kennedy, Armstrong.
Semi-final
Oct 27 v West Ham United (a) 2-0
George, Davies
Johnson; Rice, Nelson, Roberts, Carmichael, Ritchie, Cumming(Burton), George, Kennedy, Woodward, Davies.

Final
Nov 17 v Wimbledon (a) 2-1
Gould 2
Johnson; Rice, Nelson, Roberts, Carmichael, Kelly, George, McLintock, Gould, Kennedy, Davies.

1970-71
Round 1
Sep 30 v Queen's Park Rangers (h) 0-0
Barnett; Batson, Nelson, Woodward, Carmichael, Simpson, Marinello, Davies, Pearce, Metchick(de Garis), Harding.
Replay
Oct 7 v Queen's Park Rangers (a) 1-0 (after extra-time)
Marinello
Barnett; Batson, Shovelar, Woodward, Simpson, de Garis, Marinello, Metchick, Davies(Pearce), Nelson, Harding.
Round 2
Oct 12 v Tottenham Hotspur (h) 0-1
Barnett; Batson(Pearce), Shovelar, Carmichael, Simpson, de Garis, Marinello, Woodward, Davies, Nelson, Harding.

1971-72
Round 1
Sep 27 v Wealdstone (a) 3-0
Hornsby 2, Kennerley
Horn; Powling, Rixon, Price(Newton), Batson, Donaldson, Hornsby, Metchick, P.Davies, Kennerley, Shovelar.
Round 2
Oct 11 v Orient (a) 2-4
Davies, Metchick (pen)
Barnett; Donaldson, Rixon, Shovelar, Price, Batson, Hornsby, Newton, P.Davies, Metchick, Kennerley.

1972-73
Round 1
Sep 27 v Enfield Town (h) 0-2
Tilsed; Rixon, Nelson, Simpson, Batson, Matthews, Armstrong, Cruse, Ritchie, Brady, Harding.

1973-74
Round 1
Sep 24 v Bexley United (a) 1-1
Ritchie
Barnett; O'Brien, Rixon, Vassallo, Batson, Matthews, Brady, Chambers, Ritchie, Stapleton, Price.
Replay
Oct 11 v Bexley United (h) 2-0
Price, Ritchie
Barnett; O'Brien, Rixon, Vassallo, Davis, Powling, Rostron, Matthews, Stapleton, Ritchie, Price.
Round 2
Oct 22 v West Ham United (h) 2-1
Ritchie, Tones
Barnett; O'Brien, Nelson, Powling, Tones, Matthews, Rostron, Chambers, Stapleton, Ritchie, Brady(Winston).
Semi-final
Nov 12 v Tottenham Hotspur (a) 0-3
Barnett; Rixon, Nelson, Powling, Tones, Matthews, Chambers, Hornsby, Ritchie, Price, Brady.

Arsenal in Other Competitions

Southern Floodlight Challenge Cup

1956-57
Round 1
Oct 2 v Crystal Palace (h) 4-0
Tapscott 2, Tiddy, Bloomfield
Kelsey; Charlton, Evans, Goring, Dodgin, Bowen, Clapton, Tapscott, Groves, Bloomfield, Tiddy.
Round 2
Nov 12 v West Ham United (a) 1-1
Holton
Sullivan; Charlton, Evans, Wills, Fotheringham, Bowen, Nutt, Herd, Holton, Bloomfield, Haverty.
Att: 14,000
Replay
Dec 4 v West Ham United (h) 3-2
Herd 2, Haverty
Sullivan; Charlton, Evans, Wills, Fotheringham, Bowen, Clapton, Barnwell, Herd, Bloomfield, Haverty.
Att: 14,156
Semi-final
Apr 3 v Reading (a) 1-2
Clapton
Sullivan; Wills, D.Bennett, Goring, Dodgin, Petts, Clapton, Tapscott, Herd, Swallow, Haverty.

1957-58
Round 1
Oct 30 v Brentford (a) 1-4
Holton
Standen; Charlton, D.Bennett, Ward, Dodgin, Goring, Clapton, Barnwell, Holton, Bloomfield, Tiddy.
Att: 13,000

1958-59
Round 1
Oct 15 v Aldershot (a) 3-2
Bloomfield, Evans, Groves
Sullivan; Wills, Evans, Ward, Dodgin, Goring, Clapton, Groves, Holton, Bloomfield, Nutt.

Round 2
Dec 8 v Brentford (a) 2-1
Nutt, Clapton
Kelsey; Wills, Evans, Ward, Fotheringham, Docherty, Clapton, Goulden, Henderson, Bloomfield, Nutt.
Semi-final
Apr 6 v West Ham United (a) 2-0
Charles 2
Standen; Evans, McCullough, Docherty, Dodgin, Bowen, Groves, Barnwell, Charles, Julians, Haverty.
Att: 15,681
Final
Apr 27 v Crystal Palace (a) 2-1
Clapton, Charles
Coe; Wills, McCullough, Docherty, Dodgin, Bowen, Clapton, Groves, Charles, Barnwell, Henderson.

1959-60
Round 2
Oct 27 v Portsmouth (h) 2-1
Julians, Bloomfield
Kelsey; Wills, McCullough, Ward, Dodgin, Groves, Henderson, Bloomfield, Herd, Julians, Nutt.
Round 3
Nov 23 v Leicester City (h) 4-2
Bloomfield, Haverty, Henderson, Wills
Kelsey; Wills, McCullough, R.Sleap, Dodgin, Petts, D.R.Clapton, Henderson, Groves, Bloomfield, Haverty.
Semi-final
Apr 5 v West Ham United (h) 1-3
Docherty
Standen; Magill, McCullough, Ward, Docherty, Groves, Henderson, Herd, Julians, Bloomfield, Haverty.

Chatham Charity Cup

1898-99
Jan 18 v Chatham (a) 1-1
Anderson
Ord; McPhee, McAvoy, Moir, Dick, Davis, Hunt, Haywood, Anderson, Dailly, Mitchell.
Feb 20 v Chatham (h) 3-3
Hunt, Dick, Cottrell
Ord; McAvoy, Anderson, Moir, Dick, Davis, Hunt, Cottrell, McGeoch, Hannah, Shaw.
Att: 1,500

Mar 6 v Chatham (at Gravesend) 1-2
White (pen)
Ord; McAvoy, McConnell, Moir, Dick, Hannah, Hunt, White, McGeoch, Haywood, Shaw.
Att: 3,000

Arsenal also entered this competition in 1902-03 and 1909-10, but fielded reserve teams.

Southern Professional Charity Cup

1901-02
Round 1
Apr 7 v Portsmouth (a) 2-1
Foxall, Gooing
Ashcroft; McNichol, Cross, Theobald, Dick, J.Anderson, Briercliffe, Main, Gooing, W.Anderson, Foxall.
Att: 3,000

Semi-final
Apr 23 v Tottenham Hotspur (h) 0-0
Ashcroft; McNichol, Jackson, Coales, Dick, J.Anderson, Edgar, Main, Gooing, W.Anderson, Foxall.
Att: 2,500

Replay
Apr 29 v Tottenham Hotspur (a) 1-2
W.Anderson
Ashcroft; McNichol, Jackson, Coles, Dick, J.Anderson,
Edgar, Main, Gooing, W.Anderson, Foxall.
Att: 2,000

1902-03
Round 1
Feb 9 v Millwall (h) 2-3
Keena, J.Bradshaw
Ashcroft; Wolfe, J.Anderson, Coles, Theobald, Ransom,
Hunt, J.Bradshaw, Keena, W.Bradshaw, Vaughan.
Att: 3,000

1903-04
Round 1
Oct 12 v West Ham United (h) 1-0
Pratt
Ashcroft; Cross, Thorpe, Dick, Bannister, Ransom,
Tomlinson, Coleman, Pratt, Shanks, Busby.
Att: 3,000
Semi-final
Jan 18 v Reading (at Tottenham) 3-1
Tomlinson, Pratt 2
Ashcroft; Cross, Thorpe, Theobald, Bannister,
McEachrane, Tomlinson, Watson, Pratt, Fitchie, Busby.
Att: 4,000
Final
Apr 28 v Millwall (a) 1-2
Gooing
Ashcroft; Cross, Jackson, Dick, Bannister, McEachrane,
Watson, Coleman, Gooing, Shanks, Neave.
Att: 10,000

1904-05
Round 1
Oct 10 v Tottenham Hotspur (h) 1-3
Coleman
Ashcroft; Cross, Jackson, Dick, Buchan, McEachrane,
Briercliffe, Coleman, Gooing, Hunter, Satterthwaite.
Att: 8,000

1905-06
Round 1
Oct 9 v West Ham United (h) 3-2
Coleman 2, Fitchie
Ashcroft; Gray, Sharp, Dick, Theobald, McEachrane,
Bellamy, Fitchie, Coleman, Blair, Templeton.
Att: 5,000
Semi-final
Apr 9 v Tottenham Hotspur (a) 0-0
Ashcroft; Sharp, Sutherland, Bigden, Theobald, Dick,
Garbutt, Coleman, Freeman, Satterthwaite,
Templeton.
Att: 7,000
Replay
Apr 28 v Tottenham Hotspur (h) 5-0
Coleman 2, Sands, Satterthwaite, Ducat
Ashcroft; Cross, Sharp, Bigden, Sands, McEachrane,
Garbutt, Coleman, Ducat, Satterthwaite, Neave.
Att: 12,000
Final
Apr 30 v Reading (at Fulham) 1-0
Sands
Ashcroft; Cross, Sharp, Bigden, Sands, Theobald,
Bellamy, Coleman, Ducat, Satterthwaite, Neave.
Att: 3,500

1906-07
Round 1
Dec 10 v Millwall (h) 1-2
Sharp (pen)
Ashcroft; Gray, Sharp, Bigden, Dick, McEachrane,
Garbutt, Coleman, Kyle, Satterthwaite, Neave.
Att: 4,000

1907-08
Round 1
Sep 23 v Reading (h) 0-1
Bateup; Shaw, Sharp, Dick, Theobald, Low, Lee,
Coleman, Ducat, Kyle, Mordue.
Att: 2,000

London Professional Footballers Association Charity Fund

1908-09
Dec 7 v Chelsea (a) 1-0
Lewis
McDonald; Shaw, Gray, Ducat, Theobald, McKinnon,
Greenaway, Lewis, Raybould, Satterthwaite, Curle.
Att: 6,000

1909-10
Nov 1 v Tottenham Hotspur (a) 0-3
H.McDonald; Shaw, D.McDonald, Dick, Bassett,
McEachrane, Greenaway, Lawrence, Thomson, Lewis,
Neave.
Att: 4,500

1910-11
Sep 26 v Fulham (a) 3-2
Thomson, Common, Rippon
Bateup; Ducat, Shaw, McKinnon, Thomson,
McEachrane, Lewis, Common, Rippon, Logan, Neave.
Att: 2,500

1911-12
Sep 4 v Chelsea (a) 2-2
Lewis, Chalmers
Burdett; Shaw, Gray, McKinnon, Grant, Thomson,
Greenaway, Common, Chalmers, Flanagan, Lewis.
Att: 6,000
Replay
Oct 30 v Chelsea (h) 1-0
Flanagan
Burdett; Shaw, Gray, Thomson, Grant, McKinnon,
Greenaway, G.Hoare, McLaughlan, Flanagan,
Winship.
Att: 1,500

1912-13
Sep 30 v Chelsea (a) 3-1
McLaughlan 2, Flanagan
Crawford; Shaw, Peart, King, Thomson, McKinnon,
Greenaway, Common, McLaughlan, Flanagan, Lewis.
Att: 5,000

1913-14
Oct 27 v West Ham United (a) 2-3
Stonley, Flanagan
Lievesley; Shaw, Fidler, Thomson, Jobey, McKinnon, Lewis, Flanagan, Stonley, Hardinge, Burrell.
Att: 4,000

1914-15
Nov 2 v West Ham United (h) 1-0
Rutherford
Lievesley; Shaw, Benson, Grant, Liddell, Graham, Rutherford, Flanagan, Groves, Bradshaw, Norman.
Att: 2,000

1919-20
Sep 29 v Tottenham Hotspur (h) 0-1
Williamson; Shaw, Bradshaw, Graham, Butler, McKinnon, Groves, Burgess, White, Blyth, Baker.
Att: 10,000

1920-21
Oct 25 v Tottenham Hotspur (a) 0-2
Williamson; Shaw, Bradshaw, Baker, Pattison, McKinnon, Rutherford, White, Walden, Hardinge, Blyth.
Att: 17,436

Foord Flood Relief Fund

1909-10
Nov 25 v **Shorncliffe Garrison & District XI (at Folkestone) 5-2**
Lewis 2, Dick, Thomson, Oliver
Cannon; Gray, Cross, Dick, Thomson, McKinnon, Ayre, Lewis, Oliver, Satterthwaite, Heppinstall.

Titanic Disaster Fund

1911-12
Apr 29 v Tottenham Hotspur (at White City) 3-0
Hanks, Greenaway, Thomson
Crawford; Shaw, Peart, McKinnon, Thomson, McEachrane, Greenaway, Common, Hanks, Flanagan, Lewis.
Att: 5,000

Kent Senior Shield

1912-13
Oct 16 v Crystal Palace (a) 0-1
Crawford; G.Ford, Peart, King, Thomson, Graham, Lewis, Flanagan, McLaughlan, Spittle, Winship.

Prince of Wales National Relief Fund

1914-15
Aug 22 v Tottenham Hotspur (a) 5-1
King 2, Flanagan 2, Rutherford
Lievesley; Shaw, Benson, Grant, Buckley, Graham, Rutherford, Flanagan, King, Bradshaw, Lewis.
Att: 13,564

Norfolk & Norwich Hospital Cup

1913-14
Apr 30 v Norwich City (a) 3-0
King 3
Lievesley; Shaw, Benson, Grant, Graham, McKinnon, Lewis, Flanagan, King, Spittle, Winship.
Att: 6,683

1934-35
May 6 v Norwich City (a) 1-0
Parkin
Wilson; L.Compton, Hapgood, Hill, Roberts, Cartwright, Kirchen, Parkin, Cox, Dougall, John.
Att: 15,550

Southend Hospital Cup

1920-21
May 9 v Southend United (a) 4-0
White 2, Blyth, Toner
Dunn; Peart, Hutchins, Whittaker, Pattison, McKinnon, Rutherford, Blyth, White, Hopkins, Toner.
Att: 5,000

1921-22
May 9 v Southend United (h) 2-1
McKenzie, White
Williamson; Bradshaw, Hutchins, Milne, Voysey, John, Creegan, McKenzie, White, Hopkins, Blyth.

1922-23
Oct 11 v Southend United (a) 0-1
Dunn; Elvey, Turnbull, Baker, Jewett, Graham, Henderson, White, Young, Boreham, Paterson.

Metropolitan Hospital Cup

1920-21
May 11 v Clapton Orient (h) 2-0
White, Blyth
Dunn; Shaw, Hutchins, Whittaker, Graham, McKinnon, Rutherford, Blyth, White, North, Toner.
Att: 6,000

1922-23
Apr 16 v Clapton Orient (a) 1-2
Toner
Robson; Mackie, Kennedy, Milne, Butler, John, Voysey, Blyth, Turnbull, Baker, Toner.

Northampton Charity Shield

1929-30
May 5 v Northampton Town (a) 7-0
Bastin 3, Hulme, Lambert, Jack, Opp og
Preedy; Parker, Hapgood, Baker, Seddon, John, Hulme, Jack, Lambert, James, Bastin.
Att: 9,132

1930-31
May 4 v Northampton Town (a) 1-0
Lambert
Harper; Parker, Hapgood, Diaper, Roberts, John,
Hulme, Jack, Lambert, Bastin, C.Jones.

1931-32
May 10 v Northampton Town (a) 3-2
Lambert 2, Beasley
Moss; L.Compton, Hapgood, Male, Haynes, John,
Beasley, Stockill, Lambert, C.Jones, Bastin.

Sheriff of London Shield

1930-31
Apr 22 v Corinthians (h) 5-3
Hulme 2, Lambert 2, John
Harper; Parker, Hapgood, C.Jones, Haynes, John,
Hulme, Jack, Lambert, James, Bastin.
Att: 12,000

1932-33
Oct 26 v Corinthians (h) 9-2
Coleman 5, Jack, Hulme, Bastin, John (pen)
Moss; Male, Hapgood, Parkin, Haynes, John,
Hulme, Jack, Coleman, Hill, Bastin.
Att: 9,493

1964-65
Oct 14 v Corinthian Casuals (at Crystal Palace
Recreation Centre) 7-0
Anderson 3, Strong 2, Baker, Armstrong
Burns; Howe, F.Clarke, McLintock, Ferry,
Simpson, Anderson, Strong, Baker, Eastham,
Armstrong.

1965-66
Sep 21 v Corinthian Casuals (h) 5-2
Baldwin 2, Skirton, Radford, Sammels
Wilson; Magill, Storey, Simpson, Ure, Walley,
Skirton, Radford, Baldwin, Sammels, Tawse.

Bath Coronation Cup

1936-37
Apr 19 v Portsmouth (at Bath) 2-0
D.Compton, Bowden
Boulton; L.Compton, Hapgood, Crayston, Atter,
Copping, Nelson, James, Bowden, Davidson,
D.Compton.

Mayor of Colchester's Cup

1937-38
Apr 25 v Wolverhampton Wanderers (at Colchester)
0-1
Swindin; Scott, L.Compton, Crayston, Fields,
Collett, Nelson, L.Jones, Carr, Drury, D.Compton.
Att: 17,584

1938-39
Apr 17 v Tottenham Hotspur (at Colchester) 2-1
Drury 2
Marks; Male, L.Compton, L.Jones, Fields, Collett,
Drake, Drury, Lewis, B.Jones, Cumner.

Football League Jubilee Fund

1938-39
Aug 20 v Tottenham Hotspur (h) 0-2
Swindin; Male, Hapgood, Crayston, Joy, Copping,
Griffiths, L.Jones, Drake, B.Jones, Bastin.
Att: 41,997

1939-40
Aug 19 v Tottenham Hotspur (a) 1-0
Drury
Marks; Male, Hapgood, Crayston, Joy, L.Jones,
Kirchen, Drury, Lewis, B.Jones, Nelson.
Att: 32,702

Coronation Cup

1952-53
May 11 v Glasgow Celtic (a) 0-1
Swindin; Wade, Chenhall, Forbes, Dodgin, Mercer,
Roper, Goring, Holton, Lishman, Marden.
Att: 59,000

Wembley International Tournament

1988-89
Aug 13 v Tottenham Hotspur 4-0
Marwood 2, Merson, Smith
Lukic; Dixon, Winterburn, Thomas, O'Leary(Bould),
Adams, Rocastle, Davis, Smith, Merson(Hayes),
Marwood.
Att: 30,104

Aug 14 v Bayern Munich 3-0
Smith 2, Dixon
Lukic; Dixon, Winterburn, Thomas, Bould, Adams,
Rocastle(Richardson), Davis, Smith, Merson(Hayes),
Marwood.
Att: 27,364

Merchantile Credit Centenary Trophy

1988-89
Quarter-final
Aug 31 v Queen's Park Rangers (a) 2-0
Adams, Marwood
Lukic; Richardson, Winterburn, Thomas, O'Leary,
Adams, Rocastle, Davis, Smith, Merson(Hayes),
Marwood.
Att: 10,019

Semi-final
Sep 20 v Liverpool (h) 2-1
Groves, Marwood
Lukic; Dixon, Winterburn, Thomas, O'Leary, Adams,
Rocastle(Hayes), Richardson, Smith, Groves, Marwood.
Att: 29,135
Final
Oct 9 v Manchester United (at Villa Park) 2-1
Davis, Thomas
Lukic; Dixon, Winterburn, Thomas, Bould, Adams,
Rocastle, Davis, Smith, Groves(Merson), Marwood.
Att: 22,182

Makita International Tournament
(Played at Wembley)

1989-90
Jul 29 v FC Porto 1-0
Demol (og)
Lukic; Dixon, Winterburn, Thomas, O'Leary, Adams,
Rocastle(Hayes), Richardson, Smith(Campbell),
Bould, Merson.
Att: 20,374

Jul 30 v Liverpool 1-0
Bould
Lukic; Dixon, Winterburn(Caesar), Thomas, O'Leary,
Adams, Rocastle, Richardson, Smith, Bould(Hayes),
Merson.
Att: 23,026

1990-91
Aug 10 v Aston Villa 2-0
Limpar, Campbell
Seaman; Dixon, Winterburn, Thomas, Linighan,
Adams, Rocastle(Groves), Davis, Smith, Merson
(Campbell), Limpar.
Att: 20,063
Aug 11 v Sampdoria (Italy) 0-1
Seaman; Dixon, Winterburn, Thomas, Linighan
(Bould), Adams, Rocastle, Davis, Smith, Merson
(Campbell), Limpar.
Att: 21,542

1991-92 (Played at Highbury)
Aug 3 v Panathinaikos (Greece) 1-0
Rocastle
Seaman; Dixon, Winterburn, Hillier, Bould, Adams,
Rocastle(Thomas), Davis, Groves, Merson, Limpar
(Cole).
Att: 19,983
Aug 4 v Sampdoria (Italy) 1-1 (Lost 3-2 on penalties)
Merson
Seaman; Dixon, Winterburn, Hillier, Bould, Adams,
Rocastle(Groves), Davis, Cole, Merson(Thomas),
Limpar.
Att: 18,267

Zenith Data Systems Challenge Trophy

1989-90
**Aug 6 v Independiente of Argentina (in Miami,
Florida) 2-1**
Rocastle 2 (1 pen)
Lukic; Dixon, Morrow, Thomas, O'Leary, Adams,
Rocastle, Richardson, Smith, Caesar, Merson.
Att: 5,000

Caltex Cup
(Played in Singapore)

1989-90
May 9 v South Korea 2-1
Smith, Dixon (pen)
Lukic; Dixon, Winterburn, Thomas, O'Leary, Adams,
Rocastle, Davis, Smith, Campbell, Groves.

1990-91
May 17 v Liverpool 1-1 aet (Won 4-3 on penalties)
Winterburn
Seaman; Dixon, Winterburn, Hillier(Thomas), Bould,
Adams(Rocastle), O'Leary, Davis, Smith(Groves),
Campbell, Limpar(Merson).
Att: 45,000

FA Youth Cup

1954-55
Round 1
Oct 23 v Leiston (h) 9-1
Kingsland 3, Saxby 3, Goulden 2, Jarrold
P.Goy; Dooler, K.Nicholas, D.Barrett, B.Kirby,
J.Petts, B.Jarrold, R.Saxby, R.Kingsland, Goulden,
Ward.
Round 2
Nov 6 v Leyton Orient (h) 1-3
Barrett
P.Goy; Dooler, K.Nicholas, D.Barrett, B.Kirby,
J.Petts, B.Jarrold, Saxby, R.Kingsland, Goulden,
Ward.

1955-56
Round 2
Nov 5 v Gorleston (h) 3-0
Dennis, Pearce, Opponent (og)
Goy; G.De'Ath, G.Cox, R.Feist, W.Turner, D.Barrett,
W.Pearce, Goulden, W.Dennis, D.Bennett, D.Dodson.
Round 3
Dec 10 v Fulham (a) 2-0
Bennett 2
Goy; G.De'Ath, Nicholas, G.Cox, W.Turner, J.Petts,
W.Dennis, Saxby, D.Barrett, Goulden, D.Bennett.
Round 4
Jan 21 v Luton Town (h) 2-1
Barnwell, Saxby
Goy; G.De'Ath, Nicholas, G.Cox, W.Turner, J.Petts,
Saxby, J.Barnwell, D.Barrett, Goulden, D.Bennett.
Round 5
Mar 14 v Bristol City (a) 3-4
Dennis, Cox, Barrett
Goy; R.Feist, Nicholas, G.Cox, W.Turner, Saxby,
W.Dennis, J.Barnwell, D.Barrett, D.Bennett,
D.Dodson.

1956-57
Round 1
Sep 20 v Aveley (h) 6-1
Dodson 4, Bennett, Barrett
M.Leigh; R.Feist, J.Sanchez, M.Everitt, R.Kingsland,
D.M.Bennett, W.Pearce, W.Dennis, Barrett,
J.Barnwell, D.Dodson.
Round 2
Oct 31 v Leyton Orient (h) 3-0
Dennis, Barnwell, Dodson
B.Lilley; G.De'Ath, J.Sanchez, Petts, R.Kingsland,
D.M.Bennett, W.Pearce, W.Dennis, Barrett,
J.Barnwell, D.Dodson.
Round 3
Nov 27 v Charlton Athletic (h) 4-1
Dodson 2, Pearce, Barnwell
N.Coe; G.De'Ath, J.Sanchez, R.Feist, R.Kingsland,
Petts, N.Rowe, M.Everitt, W.Pearce, J.Barnwell,
D.Dodson.
Round 4
Jan 15 v Chelsea (h) 3-0
Pearce, Barnwell, Opponent (og)
N.Coe; R.Feist, J.Sanchez, M.Everitt, R.Kingsland,
Petts, W.Pearce, Barnwell, Barrett, D.M.Bennett,
Dodson.
Round 5
Mar 4 v West Ham United (a) 1-3
Opponent (og)
N.Coe; R.Feist, J.Sanchez, M.Everitt, R.Kingsland,
Petts, W.Pearce, Barnwell, Barrett, D.M.Bennett,
Dodson.

1957-58
Round 1
Nov 6 v Briggs Sports (h) 7-0
Clapton 2, Dodson 2, Barber, King, Opponent (og)
N.Coe; M.Male, J.Harris, C.Winship, A.Young,
Sanchez, M.Everitt, D.P.Clapton, M.Barber, F.King,
Dodson.
Round 2
Nov 30 v Brentwood & Warley (a) 8-0
Clapton 2, Dodson 3, King 2, Everitt
N.Coe; M.Male, J.Harris, A.Durrant, J.Read,
Sanchez, Dodson, D.Nash, D.P.Clapton, F.King,
M.Everitt.
Round 3
Jan 4 v Watford (a) 0-0
N.Coe; M.Male, J.Harris, A.Durrant, A.Young,
Sanchez, M.Everitt, J.Read, D.P.Clapton, P.Kelly,
Dodson.
Replay
Jan 27 v Watford (h) 1-0
Nash
N.Coe; D.Robson, J.Harris, P.Kelly, J.Read, Sanchez,
M.Everitt, D.P.Clapton, M.Barber, D.Nash, Dodson.
Round 4
Feb 8 v Charlton Athletic (a) 1-1
Clapton
N.Coe; D.Robson, J.Harris, A.Durrant, A.Young,
Sanchez, D.Nash, J.Read, D.P.Clapton, P.Kelly,
Everitt.
Replay
Mar 5 v Charlton Athletic (h) 5-2
Clapton 2, Dodson 2, Everitt
N.Coe; D.Robson, J.Harris, J.Read, D.P.Clapton, P.Kelly,
Sanchez, Everitt, J.Read, D.P.Clapton, P.Kelly,
Dodson.
Round 5
Mar 19 v Icknield (h) 5-0
Clapton 3, Howson, Durrant
N.Coe; D.Robson, J.Harris, A.Durrant, A.Young,
Sanchez, Everitt, P.Kelly, D.P.Clapton, R.Howson,
Dodson.
Semi-final (1st leg)
Apr 15 v Chelsea (a) 1-3
Dodson
N.Coe; D.Robson, Sanchez, Everitt, A.Young,
W.West, M.Barber, P.Kelly, D.P.Clapton, R.Howson,
Dodson.
Semi-final (2nd leg)
Apr 17 v Chelsea (h) 1-3
Everitt
N.Coe; D.Robson, Sanchez, Everitt, A.Young,
W.West, M.Barber, P.Kelly, D.P.Clapton, R.Howson,
Dodson.

1958-59
Round 1
Oct 14 v Tottenham Hotspur (h) 2-0
Heard, Read
Coe; D.Bacuzzi, J.Harris, Sanchez, A.Young,
C.Meldrum, M.Barber, Everitt, J.Read, W.Meadows,
D.Heard.
Round 2
Nov 10 v Dagenham (a) 3-1
Read, Meldrum, Meadows
Coe; D.Robson, J.Harris, Sanchez, A.Young,
C.Meldrum, M.Barber, Everitt, J.Read, W.Meadows,
I.McKechnie.

Round 3
Dec 22 v Queen's Park Rangers (h) 5-0
Barber 2, Everitt, Hinton, Meldrum
Coe; D.Bacuzzi, J.Harris, Sanchez, J.Snedden, Meldrum, T.Hinton, Everitt, M.Barber, W.Meadows, D.Heard.
Round 4
Jan 20 v Bristol City (h) 2-1
Heard, Reynolds
Coe; D.Bacuzzi, A.Young, Sanchez, J.Snedden, Meldrum, T.Hinton, Everitt, R.Reynolds, W.Meadows, D.Heard.
Round 5
Mar 10 v Reading (h) 5-0
Callaghan 2, Hinton, Meadows, Heard
Coe; D.Bacuzzi, A.Young, Snedden, Meldrum, Sanchez, T.Hinton, W.Callaghan, W.Meadows, Everitt, D.Heard.
Semi-final (1st leg)
Apr 14 v West Ham United (a) 1-1
Everitt
Coe; D.Bacuzzi, Sanchez, Snedden, Young, Meldrum, T.Hinton, W.Callaghan, J.Read, Everitt, W.Meadows.
Semi-final (2nd leg)
Apr 23 v West Ham United (h) 0-1
Coe; D.Bacuzzi, Sanchez, Snedden, Young, Meldrum, T.Hinton, W.Callaghan, W.Meadows, Everitt, D.Heard.

1959-60
Round 1
Oct 20 v Leyton Orient (h) 1-1
Morton
McKechnie; J.Read, J.Harris, Snedden, Meldrum, J.Watson, B.Smithson, Morton, W.Meadows, R.Piper, M.Broad.
Replay
Nov 7 v Leyton Orient (a) 4-2
Morton, Court, Read, Snedden
J.Green; J.Read, R.Griffith, Snedden, Meldrum, W.Belger, B.Smithson, Morton, D.Court, W.Meadows, T.Anderson.
Round 2
Dec 15 v Norwich City (h) 4-0
Piper 2, Court, Morton
McKechnie; Read, J.Harris, W.Belger, Meldrum, W.Meadows, R.Piper, Snedden, D.Court, Morton, T.Anderson.
Round 3
Jan 11 v Brentford (a) 2-0
Meadows 2
McKechnie; Read, J.Harris, Neill, Snedden, Meldrum, R.Piper, Morton, D.Court, W.Meadows, T.Anderson.
Round 4
Feb 2 v West Ham United (h) 0-3
McKechnie; Read, J.Harris, Neill, Snedden, Meldrum, T.Anderson, Morton, D.Court, W.Meadows, W.Belger.

1960-61
Round 1
Oct 10 v Chelmsford (a) 8-1
Anderson 2, Court 2, Smithson, Simpson, Whittaker, Muir
Whitson; Smithson, Parkes, W.Belger, Ferry, P.Simpson, T.Anderson, R.Bloomfield, Court, Muir, R.Whittaker.
Round 2
Nov 8 v Norwich City (h) 3-0
Tapping, Court, Muir
Whitson; Smithson, Tapping, Gould, Ferry, W.Belger, T.Anderson, Court, J.O'Rourke, Muir, R.Whittaker.

Round 3
Dec 12 v Millwall (a) 8-0
Anderson 3, O'Rourke 2, Gould 2, Court
Whitson; Smithson, Tapping, Turner, Ferry, P.Simpson, R.Whittaker, Gould, J.O'Rourke, Court, T.Anderson.
Round 4
Jan 25 v Oxford City (h) 9-0
Gould 5, Anderson 2, Whittaker, Court
Whitson; Smithson, Tapping, Turner, Ferry, P.Simpson, R.Whittaker, R.Bloomfield, Court, Gould, T.Anderson.
Round 5
Mar 7 v West Ham United (h) 3-0
Tapping 2, O'Rourke
Whitson; Smithson, Tapping, Gould, Ferry, P.Simpson, Muir, R.Bloomfield, J.O'Rourke, Court, T.Anderson.
Semi-final (1st leg)
Mar 21 v Chelsea (a) 0-2
Whitson; Smithson, Tapping, Gould, Ferry, P.Simpson, T.Anderson, R.Bloomfield, J.O'Rourke, Court, Muir.
Semi-final (2nd leg)
Apr 11 v Chelsea (h) 0-2
Whitson; Smithson, Tapping, Gould, Ferry, P.Simpson, Muir, R.Bloomfield, J.O'Rourke, Court, T.Anderson.

1961-62
Preliminary Round
Sep 19 v Norwich City (h) 6-1
O'Rourke 3, Gould, Armstrong, Sammels
Black; Smithson, Tapping, Gould, Ferry, P.Simpson, Court, Sammels, J.O'Rourke, R.Bloomfield, Armstrong.
Round 1
Oct 24 v Queen's Park Rangers (h) 4-1
Gould 3, Opponent (og)
Black; Smithson, Tapping, Turner, Ferry, P.Simpson, Court, R.Bloomfield, Gould, Sammels, Armstrong.
Round 2
Nov 28 v Ford United (h) 12-0
Bloomfield 5, Court 3, Gould, Sammels, Armstrong, Whittaker
C.Lemon; Smithson, Tapping, Gould, Ferry, P.Simpson, Armstrong, R.Bloomfield, Court, Sammels, R.Whittaker.
Round 3
Jan 17 v Chelsea (h) 1-2
Whittaker
C.Lemon; Smithson, Tapping, Turner, Ferry, P.Simpson, Court, R.Bloomfield, Gould, Sammels, R.Whittaker.

1962-63
Round 2
Dec 10 v Leyton Orient (h) 4-1
Sammels 2, Bell, Radford
Black; Storey, Hunt, Simpson, D.Milne, Adams, Dunlop, Sammels, J.Radford, Bell, Whittaker.
Round 3
Apr 2 v Fulham (h) 2-1
Jenkins, Radford
Black; Storey, Hunt, Adams, D.Milne, Simpson, B.Tawse, Jenkins, J.Radford, Bell, Whittaker.
Round 4
Apr 30 v Exeter City (h) 3-0
Bloomfield, Radford 2
Burns; Storey, Hepplewhite, Adams, D.Milne, Simpson, B.Tawse, Bloomfield, J.Radford, Sammels, Whittaker.

Round 5
May 6 v Wolverhampton Wanderers (a) 1-1
Simpson
Burns; Storey, Hepplewhite, Adams, D.Milne,
Simpson, B.Tawse, T.Baldwin, J.Radford, Bloomfield,
Whittaker.
Replay
May 15 v Wolverhampton Wanderers (h) 0-4
Black; Storey, Hepplewhite, Adams, Simpson,
Bloomfield, B.Tawse, T.Baldwin, J.Radford, Sammels,
Whittaker.

1963-64
Round 2
Dec 28 v Bexley United (a) 5-1
Radford 2, Adams, Boot, Jenkins
Black; Pack, Hinton, V.Adams, Milne, Wilkinson, Ley,
Boot, Radford, Jenkins, N.Leven.
Round 3
Jan 20 v Chelsea (h) 3-1
Radford, Adams, Jenkins
Black; Pack, Storey, V.Adams,, Wilkinson, C.Clarke,
Ley, Jenkins, Radford, Boot, N.Leven.
Round 4
Feb 10 v West Ham United (h) 2-1
Clarke, Jenkins
Black; Pack, Storey, Wilkinson, Milne, C.Clarke, Ley,
Jenkins, Radford, Boot, N.Leven.
Round 5
Mar 10 v Swindon Town (a) 0-2
Black; Pack, Storey, V.Adams, Wilkinson, C.Clarke,
Ley, Jenkins, Radford, Boot, N.Leven.

1964-65
Round 2
Nov 30 v West Ham United (a) 7-0
Baker 5, Leven, Jenkins
E.Adams; Pack, Hinton, V.Adams, Wilkinson, Boot,
N.Leven, Jenkins, Radford, D.Baker, Bristow.
Round 3
Jan 5 v Tottenham Hotspur (h) 0-0
E.Adams; Pack, Hinton, V.Adams, Wilkinson,
Rhodes, N.Leven, Boot, Thear, D.Baker, Bristow.
Replay
Feb 1 v Tottenham Hotspur (a) 3-1 (after extra-time)
Baker, Radford, Jenkins
E.Adams; Pack, Hinton, V.Adams, Wilkinson, Boot,
N.Leven, Jenkins, Radford, D.Baker, Bristow.
Round 4
Feb 17 v Portsmouth (a) 2-0
Baker, Jenkins
E.Adams; Pack, Youlden, V.Adams, Wilkinson, Boot,
N.Leven, Jenkins, Radford, D.Baker, Bristow.
Round 5
Mar 3 v Watford (h) 0-0
E.Adams; Pack, Hinton, V.Adams, Wilkinson,
Jenkins, N.Leven, Cumming, Radford, D.Baker,
Bristow.
Replay
Mar 18 v Watford (a) 5-2
Baker 4, Radford
E.Adams; Pack, Hinton, V.Adams, Wilkinson,
Jenkins, Neilson, Cumming, Radford, D.Baker,
N.Leven.
Semi-final (1st leg)
Apr 7 v Chelsea (h) 4-1
Baker 2, Boot, Jenkins
E.Adams; Hinton, Youlden, V.Adams, Wilkinson,
Jenkins, N.Leven, Boot, Thear, D.Baker, Bristow.

Semi-final (2nd leg)
Apr 10 v Chelsea (a) 0-2
E.Adams; Hinton, Youlden, V.Adams, Wilkinson,
Jenkins, Neilson, Boot, Thear, D.Baker, N.Leven.
Final (1st leg)
Apr 28 v Everton (h) 1-0
Jenkins
E.Adams; Pack, Hinton, V.Adams, Wilkinson,
Jenkins, Neilson, Boot, Radford, D.Baker, N.Leven.
Att: 5,348
Final (2nd leg)
May 3 v Everton (a) 1-3 (after extra-time)
Radford
E.Adams; Pack, Hinton, V.Adams, Wilkinson,
Jenkins, Neilson, Boot, Radford, D.Baker, N.Leven.

1965-66
Round 2
Dec 13 v Brentford (h) 5-0
Cumming 2, Leven, Rhodes, Opponent (og)
E.Adams; Hinton, Youlden, O'Rourke, Thear, Boot,
Leven, Cumming, Davidson, Rhodes, Bristow.
Round 3
Jan 4 v Fulham (h) 8-3
Davidson 3, Leven 2, Cumming 2, Rhodes
E.Adams; O'Rourke, Youlden, Boot, Thear,
Gillibrand, Leven, Cumming, Davidson, Rhodes,
Bristow.
Round 4
Feb 1 v Wolverhampton Wanderers (h) 1-0
Davidson
E.Adams; O'Rourke, Youlden, Boot, Woodward,
Gillibrand, Neville, Cumming, Davidson, Rhodes,
Leven.
Round 5
Mar 1 v Bristol City (h) 3-2
Simmons, Cumming, Bristow
E.Adams; O'Rourke, Youlden, Boot, Woodward,
Gillibrand, Leven, Cumming, Davidson, Simmons,
Bristow.
Semi-final (1st leg)
Apr 4 v Queen's Park Rangers (a) 1-1
Woodward
E.Adams; Rice, Youlden, Davidson, Woodward, Boot,
Leven, Rhodes, Thear, Simmons, Bristow.
Semi-final (2nd leg)
Apr 27 v Queen's Park Rangers (h) 3-2
Cumming 2, Simmons
E.Adams: Rice, Youlden, Gillibrand, Woodward,
Davidson, Leven, Cumming, Milne, Simmons,
Bristow.
Final (1st leg)
Apr 29 v Sunderland (a) 1-2
Simmons
E.Adams; Rice, Youlden, Gillibrand, Woodward,
Rhodes, Leven, Cumming, Milne, Simmons, Bristow.
Final (2nd leg)
May 9 v Sunderland (h) 4-1
Milne, Boot, Simmons, Leven
E.Adams; Rice, Youlden, Boot, Woodward,
Gillibrand, Leven, Cumming, Milne, Simmons,
Nelson.
Att: 5,123

1966-67
Round 2
Dec 5 v Watford (a) 5-0
Simmons 2, Gillibrand, Jones, McCall
Humphreys; Rice, Youlden, Gillibrand, Davidson,
J.O'Rourke, D.Jones, Mackenzie, Simmons, McCall,
Nelson.

Round 3
Jan 4 v Charlton Athletic (h) 4-0
Simmons 2, Davidson, Nelson
Humphreys; Rice, Youlden, J.O'Rourke, Woodward, Mackenzie, D.Jones, Gillibrand, Simmons, Davidson, Nelson.
Round 4
Jan 30 v Millwall (a) 3-1
Simmons 2, Davidson
Humphreys; Rice, Woodward, Mackenzie, Youlden, Gillibrand, Dixon, Davidson, Simmons, R.Griffiths, Nelson.
Round 5
Mar 7 v Southampton (h) 0-0
Humphreys; J.O'Rourke, Woodward, Mackenzie, Youlden, Davidson, Gillibrand, D.Jones, K.O'Rourke, Simmons, Nelson.
Replay
Mar 20 v Southampton (a) 0-2
Humphreys; Rice, Youlden, Mackenzie, Woodward, Dixon, George, Gillibrand, K.O'Rourke, Davidson, Nelson.

1967-68
Round 2
Dec 5 v Orient (a) 3-0
O'Rourke 2, Dixon
Webster; Dixon, Arber, Kelly, Mackenzie, D.Jones, R.Griffiths, O'Rourke, George, L.Redmile, T.Thomson.
Round 3
Dec 27 v Chelsea (a) 1-3
George
Webster; Dixon, Arber, L.Redmile, Mackenzie, Kelly, R.Griffiths, O'Rourke, George, D.Jones, T.Thomson.

1968-69
Round 2
Dec 3 v Charlton Athletic (h) 4-0
Ritchie 2, Kennedy, de Garis
Webster; J.Williams, G.English, T.Burton, L.Redmile, Kelly, J.de Garis, R.Ritchie, P.Addo, Kennedy, G.Simmonds.
Round 3
Jan 7 v Gillingham (a) 5-1
Kennedy 3, Simmonds 2
Webster; J.Williams, J.Reilly, T.Burton, L.Redmile, J.de Garis, R.Ritchie, George, Kennedy, Kelly, G.Simmonds.
Round 4
Jan 22 v Chelsea (a) 1-2
George
Webster; J.Reilly, G.English, T.Burton, L.Redmile, J.de Garis, R.Ritchie, George, Kennedy, Kelly, G.Simmonds.

1969-70
Round 2
Nov 25 v Watford (a) 2-0
Shovelar, Ritchie
Johnson; Metcalfe, Coombes, Burton, Breach, de Garis, Wareing, Rutherford, Ritchie, Shovelar, Davies.
Round 3
Jan 5 v Tottenham Hotspur (a) 0-1
Johnson; Metcalfe, Moore, Burton, Breach, de Garis, Harding, Ritchie, Allen, Davies, Shovelar.

1970-71
Round 2
Dec 1 v Queen's Park Rangers (a) 6-0
Davies 3, Harding 2, Hornsby
Horn; Donaldson, Shovelar, Burton, Price, de Garis, Hornsby, Newton, P.Davies, Allen, Harding.

Round 3
Jan 5 v Leicester City (a) 1-0
Hornsby
Horn; Donaldson, Blanchard, de Garis, Price, Metcalfe, Hornsby, P.Davies, Allen, Newton, Harding.
Round 4
Jan 28 v Coventry City (h) 1-0
Hornsby
Horn; Donaldson, Shovelar, Metcalfe, Price, de Garis, Hornsby, Burton, P.Davies, Allen, Harding.
Round 5
Feb 23 v Birmingham City (h) 2-1
Hornsby, Davies
Horn; Donaldson, Shovelar, Burton, Price, P.Davies, Hornsby, Newton, Wareing, Allen, Harding(Metcalfe).
Semi-final (1st leg)
Mar 24 v Wolverhampton Wanderers (h) 2-0
Allen, Opponent (og)
Horn; Donaldson, Shovelar, Burton, Batson, de Garis, Hornsby, Newton, P.Davies, Allen, Wareing.
Semi-final (2nd leg)
Apr 5 v Wolverhampton Wanderers (a) 1-0
Davies
Horn; Donaldson, Shovelar, Burton, Batson, de Garis, Hornsby, Newton, P.Davies, Allen, Wareing.
Final (1st leg)
Apr 28 v Cardiff City (h) 0-0
Horn; Donaldson, Shovelar, Price, Batson, de Garis, Hornsby, Newton, P.Davies, Burton, Wareing.
Final (2nd leg)
May 5 v Cardiff City (a) 2-0
Kennerley, Burton
Horn; Donaldson, Shovelar, Price, Batson, de Garis, Hornsby, Newton, P.Davies, Burton, Kennerley.

1971-72
Round 2
Nov 16 v Charlton Athletic (h) 3-1
Hornsby 2, Powling
Horn; Powling, Matthews, Vassallo, Rixon, Newton, L.Brady, Shovelar, Hornsby, Kennerley, Wareing (Winston).
Round 3
Dec 20 v Luton Town (h) 4-0
Kennerley 2, Hornsby, Shovelar
Horn; Donaldson, Matthews, Price, Rixon, Powling, Williams, Newton, Hornsby, Kennerley, Shovelar.
Round 4
Jan 25 v Queen's Park Rangers (h) 2-0
Donaldson, Shovelar
Horn; Donaldson, Powling, Price, Rixon, Newton, Brady, Williams, Hornsby, Kennerley, Shovelar.
Round 5
Feb 26 v Bolton Wanderers (a) 1-0
Hornsby
Horn; Donaldson, Powling, Price, Rixon, Newton, Brady (Matthews), Williams, Hornsby, Kennerley, Shovelar.
Semi-final (1st leg)
Mar 23 v Aston Villa (h) 0-0
Horn; Donaldson, Powling, Price, Rixon, Newton, Brady, Williams, Hornsby, Kennerley, Shovelar.
Semi-final (2nd leg)
Mar 27 v Aston Villa (a) 0-1
Horn; Donaldson, Powling, Price, Rixon, Newton, Williams, Shovelar, Hornsby, Kennerley, Winston (Brady).

1972-73
Round 2
Nov 28 v Brighton & Hove Albion (h) 5-0
Stapleton 2, Brady 2, Vassallo
Freeman; Donaldson, Powling(Vassallo), Price, Rixon, Matthews, Hornsby, Brady, Ross, Stapleton, Winston.
Round 3
Jan 9 v Norwich City (h) 1-0
Stapleton
Freeman; Donaldson, Matthews, Powling, Rixon, Hornsby, Price, Brady, Winston, Stapleton, W.Rostron.
Round 4
Jan 31 v Manchester United (a) 2-2
Vassallo, Rostron
G.Williams; Rixon, Donaldson, Powling, Price, Brady, W.Rostron, Vassallo, Stapleton, Hornsby, Matthews.
Replay
Feb 6 v Manchester United (h) 2-0
Matthews, Hornsby
G.Williams; Donaldson, Powling, Price, Rixon, Vassallo, Matthews, Brady, Hornsby, Stapleton, W.Rostron.
Round 5
Feb 20 v Bristol City (a) 0-2
G.Williams; Donaldson, Powling, Price, Rixon, Vassallo, Matthews, Brady, Hornsby, Stapleton, W.Rostron(Winston).

1973-74
Round 2
Nov 27 v Crystal Palace (h) 3-0
Stapleton 2, Brady
K.Millard; MacKinnon, Powling, L.Madden, O'Brien, M.Connell, Vassallo, Brady, Winston, Stapleton, Rostron.
Round 3
Dec 19 v Bristol City (a) 4-1
Brady 2, Winston, Vassallo
Gould; MacKinnon, Powling, Matthews, L.Madden, Vassallo, O'Brien, Brady, Winston, Stapleton, Rostron.
Round 4
Jan 22 v Sheffield Wednesday (h) 3-1
Brady 2, Vassallo
Gould; MacKinnon, Matthews, L.Madden, J.Davis, Vassallo, O'Brien, Brady, Rostron, Stapleton, Winston(Ambrose).
Round 5
Mar 4 v Middlesbrough (a) 3-0
Stapleton 2, Winston
Gould; O'Brien, Matthews, Powling, L.Madden, Vassallo, Ross, Brady, Winston, Stapleton, Rostron.
Semi-final (1st leg)
Apr 9 v Tottenham Hotspur (a) 0-1
Gould; MacKinnon, Powling, Matthews, L.Madden, O'Brien, Davis, Brady, Winston, Vassallo, Rostron.
Semi-final (2nd leg)
Apr 23 v Tottenham Hotspur (h) 0-1
Gould; MacKinnon, Powling, O'Leary, Davis, O'Brien, Vassallo, Matthews, Winston, Ross, Rostron.

1974-75
Round 2
Dec 3 v Soham Town Rangers (a) 5-1
Rostron 3, Ross, Goodchild
Gould; Twidell, O'Leary, Noon, J.Devine, Ross, Rix, Bean, Goodchild, Stapleton, Rostron.

Round 3
Dec 23 v Oxford United (h) 3-0
Williams; Goodchild, O'Brien
Gould; Twidell, Noon, O'Leary, Devine, O'Brien, Ross, Rix, Williams, Goodchild, Rostron.
Round 4
Jan 14 v West Bromwich Albion (h) 3-1
Stapleton 2, Walker (pen)
Gould; Twidell, O'Leary, O'Brien, Devine, Walker, Ross, Rix, Goodchild, Stapleton, Rostron.
Round 5
Mar 4 v Ipswich Town (a) 0-1
Gould; Twidell, O'Leary, O'Brien, Devine, Williams, Ross, Rix, Goodchild, Stapleton, Rostron.

1975-76
Round 2
Nov 17 v Luton Town (h) 7-0
Rix 3, Goodchild 2, Duffy 2
Gould; Twidell, P.Armstrong, Gatting, Devine, Brinkman(Dutton), Brooks, Rix, Goodchild, Bean, Duffy.
Round 3
Dec 17 v Wigston Fields (h) 4-1
Goodchild 2, Rix, Cant
Gould; Wright, Gatting, P.Armstrong, Devine, Twidell, Brinkman, Rix, Goodchild, Dutton, A.Chapman(C.Cant).
Round 4
Jan 1 v Crystal Palace (h) 0-2
Gould; Wright, P.Armstrong, Gatting, Devine, Twidell, Brooks(A.Chapman), Rix, Goodchild, Dutton, Brinkman.

1976-77
Round 2
Dec 6 v Luton Town (a) 0-0
New; Tyler, Gatting, P.Armstrong, Devine, Cant, Townsend, D.Drummy, McLeod, G.Crane, Chapman.
Replay
Dec 15 v Luton Town (h) 1-0
Armstrong
New; Tyler, P.Armstrong, Gatting, Devine, D.Drummy, Townsend, Cant, Chapman, G.Crane (Brignall), McLeod.
Round 3
Feb 1 v Crystal Palace (a) 2-2
Armstrong, Townsend
N.Sullivan; Flight, Tyler, P.Armstrong, Devine, Cant, Brignall, Townsend, Gatting, Chapman, McLeod (D.Drummy).
Replay
Feb 12 v Crystal Palace (h) 0-0
N.Sullivan; Tyler, P.Happe, Gatting, Devine, Townsend, Cant, Brignall, Chapman, D.Drummy, P.Armstrong.
Second Replay
Feb 15 v Crystal Palace (a) 0-4
N.Sullivan; L.Hudson, Tyler, Gatting, Devine, D.Drummy(G.Crane), Cant, Brignall, Townsend, Chapman, P.Armstrong.

1977-78
Round 2
Dec 6 v West Ham United (a) 0-0
Sullivan; Johnson, Pittaway, P.Armstrong, Flight, Drummy, Brignall, Cant, Heeley, Chapman, McDermott.

Replay
Dec 13 v West Ham United (h) 1-0
McDermott
Sullivan; Johnson, Pittaway, P.Armstrong, Flight, Townsend, Brignall, Cant(Drummy), Heeley, Chapman, McDermott.
Round 3
Jan 9 v West Bromwich Albion (a) 0-2
Sullivan; Johnson, Pittaway, P.Armstrong, Flight, Drummy, Brignall, Townsend, Heeley, Chapman, McDermott.

1978-79
Round 2
Dec 4 v Peterborough United (a) 0-0
Wilmot; Cansick, Law, Pittaway, Johnson, Drummy, Davis, Sparrow, Meade, Emencheta(Whyte), McDermott.
Replay
Dec 11 v Peterborough United (h) 4-2
Meade, Davis, Smith, Law
Wilmot; Cansick, Johnson, Whyte, Law, Drummy, Davis, Sparrow, Meade(Armatrudo), Smith, McDermott.
Round 3
Jan 6 v Luton Town (a) 0-1
Wilmot; Cansick, Law, Pittaway, Johnson, Drummy, Davis, Armatrudo(Meade), Sparrow, McDermott, Vaessen.

1979-80
Round 2
Nov 26 v Charlton Athletic (a) 3-0
Meade, Vaessen, Opponent (og)
Wilmot; O'Shea, Whyte, Pittaway, Johnson, Cork, Gorman, Sparrow, Meade, Vaessen, Williams (Armatrudo).
Round 3
Jan 5 v Tottenham Hotspur (h) 0-1
Wilmot; O'Shea, Law, Pittaway, Johnson, Armatrudo(Evans), Cork, Gorman, Sparrow, Vaessen, Meade.

1980-81
Round 2
Dec 2 v Wimbledon (h) 6-0
Kay, Cork, O'Shea, Meade, Gorman, Harrison
Lewin; Evans, Sweeney, Watt, Robson, O'Shea, Kay, Cork, Meade(Harrison), Gorman, Hill.
Round 3
Dec 16 v Queen's Park Rangers (h) 1-1
Hill
Lewin; Evans, Smith, Watt, Robson, O'Shea, Cork(Harrison), Gorman, Meade, Kay, Hill.
Replay
Jan 6 v Queen's Park Rangers (a) 2-2 (after extra-time)
O'Shea, Meade
Lewin; Evans, Robson, Watt, Smith, Kay, Cork, O'Shea, Hill(Harrison), Meade, Gorman.
Second Replay
Jan 12 v Queen's Park Rangers (h) 0-1
Lewin; Evans, Smith, Watt, Robson, Gorman, Kay, Cork, Hill, Meade, O'Shea.

1981-82
Round 2
Dec 3 v Gillingham (h) 3-0
Robson 2, Lee
Lewin; Beaumont, Ridley, Robson, Keown, Murtagh, Gorman, Lee, Harrison, Gerbaldi, Hill.

Round 3
Jan 6 v Southampton (h) 0-1
Lewin; Beaumont, Ridley, Watt, Keown, Hill, Kay, Gorman, Gerbaldi, Lee, Harrison.

1982-83
Round 2
Dec 2 v Norwich City (h) 2-2
Gerbaldi 2
Adamson; Woollard, Ridley, Adams, Keown, Rees, Driscoll, Campbell, Gerbaldi, Lee, Hayes.
Replay
Dec 9 v Norwich City (a) 2-4
Rees, Campbell
Adamson; Woollard, Ridley, Keown, Adams, Rees, Gymer(Beaumont), Campbell, Gerbaldi, Lee, Hayes.

1983-84
Round 2
Dec 1 v Carshalton (a) 2-0
Isaacs, Caesar
Veysey; Thomas, Caesar, Adams, Keown, Rocastle, Isaacs, Campbell, Woods, Hayes, Purdie.
Round 3
Dec 31 v Bristol Rovers (a) 4-4
Hayes 2, Rocastle, Campbell
Hammond; Caesar, Thomas, Keown, Adams, Rees, Rocastle, Campbell, Isaacs, Hayes, Purdie(Woods).
Replay
Jan 2 Bristol Rovers (h) 3-1
Rocastle, Purdie, Woods
Hammond; Caesar, Thomas, Keown, Adams, Rees, Rocastle, Campbell, Isaacs(Woods), Hayes, Purdie.
Round 4
Jan 17 v Cambridge United (h) 1-0
Campbell
Veysey; Thomas, Caesar, Keown, Adams, Rocastle, Rees, Campbell, Woods, Hayes, Purdie.
Round 5
Feb 21 v Aston Villa (h) 2-1
Hayes 2
Veysey; Caesar, Thomas, Keown, Adams, Rocastle, Hayes, Rees, Quinn, Campbell, Purdie.
Semi-final (1st leg)
Mar 26 v Stoke City (a) 2-3
Rees, Hayes
Hammond; Caesar, Thomas, Keown, Adams, Rees, Hayes, Rocastle, Quinn(Woods), Campbell, Purdie.
Semi-final (2nd leg)
Apr 3 v Stoke City (h) 0-3
Hammond; Russo, Thomas, Keown, Adams, Rocastle, Hayes, Rees, Quinn(Woods), Campbell, Purdie.

1984-85
Round 2
Dec 12 v Wimbledon (a) 0-2
Hammond; Thomas, Solomon, Rocastle, Quinn, Pennington, Smith, Osborne(Caven), Merson, Say, Allen.

1985-86
Round 2
Dec 3 v Plymouth Argyle (a) 5-0
Pennington, Osborne 3, Merson
Hammond; Rivero, Thomas, Reid, Dolan, Pennington, Smith, Osborne, Merson(Birch), Allen, Stanislaus.
Round 3
Jan 6 v Luton Town (a) 0-0
Hammond; Rivero, Thomas, Reid, Dolan, Pennington, J.Ball, Osborne, Merson, Allen, Stanislaus.

Replay
Jan 14 v Luton Town (h) 2-0
Merson 2
Hammond; Rivero(Smith), Thomas, Reid, Dolan, J.Ball, Turner, Osborne, Merson, Allen, Stanislaus.
Round 4
Feb 5 v Wimbledon (h) 1-0
Osborne
Hammond; Rivero, Thomas, Reid, Dolan, J.Ball, Smith, Osborne, Merson, Allen, Turner(Stanislaus).
Round 5
Apr 7 v Millwall (a) 1-1
Osborne
Hammond; Russo, Thomas, Turner, Dolan, J.Ball, Smith, Osborne, Merson, Allen, Milton.
Replay
Apr 14 v Millwall (h) 4-1
Merson 2, Smith, Thomas
Hammond; Russo, Thomas, J.Ball, Dolan, Stanislaus, Smith(Rebuck), Osborne, Birch, Allen, Merson.
Semi-final (1st leg)
Apr 16 v Manchester City (h) 1-0
Merson
Hammond; Russo, Thomas, Pennington, Dolan, Stanislaus, Smith, Merson, Osborne, Allen, Birch(Rebuck).
Semi-final (2nd leg)
Apr 22 v Manchester City (a) 1-2 (after extra-time - lost 4-5 on penalties)
Osborne
Hammond; Russo, Thomas, Turner, Dolan, Pennington(Birch), Smith, Osborne, Merson, Allen, Stanislaus.

1986-87
Round 2
Dec 1 v Southampton (h) 0-3
Miller; J.Ball, Stanislaus, Turner, Scully, Pennington, Rivero(Francis), Reid, Campbell, Esqulant(S.Ball), Milton.

1987-88
Round 2
Nov 23 v Millwall (a) 5-1
K.Campbell 3, Ball, Hillier
Miller; P.Campbell, Carstairs, Hillier(Donnelly), Scully, Morrow, Francis(McKeown), Cagigao, K.Campbell, Ball, Esqulant.
Round 3
Jan 12 v Wimbledon (a) 2-1
K.Campbell 2
Miller; Donnelly, Carstairs, Connelly, Scully, Morrow(McKeown), Hillier, Lee, K.Campbell, Ball, Esqulant.
Round 4
Feb 9 v Southampton (a) 2-1
K.Campbell, Ball
Miller; Donnelly, Carstairs, Hillier, Scully, Hannigan, Connelly, Cole, K.Campbell, Ball, Heaney.
Round 5
Mar 29 v Crewe Alexandra (a) 1-1
Campbell
Miller; Donnelly, Carstairs, Hillier, Scully, Morrow, Francis, Cagigao(Lee), K.Campbell, Connelly, Esqulant(Hannigan).
Replay
Apr 5 v Crewe Alexandra (h) 5-1
Esqulant 3, Connelly, Hillier
Miller; Francis, Morrow, Hillier(McKeown), Scully, Hannigan, Lee, Cagigao, K.Campbell, Connelly, Esqulant.

Semi-final (1st leg)
Apr 19 v Nottingham Forest (h) 1-1
Cagigao
Miller; Francis, Morrow, Hillier, Scully, Hannigan, Heaney, Cagigao, K.Campbell, Connelly, Esqulant.
Semi-final (2nd leg)
Apr 23 v Nottingham Forest (a) 3-0
K.Campbell 2, Cagigao
Miller; Francis, Carstairs, Hillier, Hannigan, Morrow, Heaney, Cagigao, K.Campbell, Ball, McKeown.
Final (1st leg)
Apr 29 v Doncaster Rovers (a) 5-0
K.Campbell 3, Ball (pen), Lee
Miller; Francis, Carstairs, Hillier, Hannigan, Morrow, Heaney, Cagigao, K.Campbell(Lee), Ball, McKeown.
Final (2nd leg)
May 3 v Doncaster Rovers (h) 1-1
McKeown
Miller; Francis, Carstairs, Hillier, Hannigan, Morrow, Heaney, Cagigao, K.Campbell(Lee), Ball, McKeown.

1988-89
Round 2
Dec 6 v Epsom & Ewell (a) 11-0
Cole 2, Hoyle 3, Ampadu, McKeown 2, Hannigan, Mockler 2
Marriott; Donnelly, Hartfield, Lee, Hannigan, Carstairs(Flanagan), Hoyle, Cole, Mockler(Heaney), Ampadu, McKeown.
Round 3
Jan 3 v Luton Town (h) 3-2
Cole 3
Marriott; Donnelly, Carstairs, McKeown(Mockler), Hannigan(Hartfield), Flanagan, Hoyle, Cole, Lee, Ampadu, Heaney.
Round 4
Jan 24 v West Bromwich Albion (h) 2-0
Cole, Ampadu
Marriott; Donnelly, Carstairs, McKeown, Hannigan, Flanagan, Hoyle, Cole, Parlour, Ampadu, Hartfield.
Round 5
Feb 27 v Newcastle United (a) 0-1
Marriott; Donnelly, Carstairs, McKeown, Hannigan, Flanagan, Hoyle(Parlour), Cole, Lee, Ampadu, Hartfield.

1989-90
Round 2
Nov 28 v Luton Town (h) 2-2
Cole, Bacon
Will; Hoyle(Joseph), Fowler, Parlour, Marshall, Hartfield, Heaney(Young), Clements, Bacon, Cole, Gooden.
Replay
Dec 6 v Luton Town (a) 4-2
Clements 2, Cole, Young
Will; Faulkner(Flatts), Fowler, Parlour, Webster, Hartfield, Warden, Clements, Bacon(Young), Cole, Joseph.
Round 3
Jan 8 v Oxford United (a) 5-1
Clements, Cole 2, Hoyle, Heaney
Will; Joseph, Hartfield(Bacon), Clements, Marshall, Webster, Hoyle, Flatts, Young, Cole, Heaney.
Round 4
Jan 29 v Portsmouth (h) 0-1
Will; Joseph, Hartfield, Parlour(Warden), Webster, Marshall, Flatts, Clements, Bacon(Dickov), Cole, Heaney.

386

1990-91
Round 2
Nov 26 v Notts County (a) 0-0
Brading; Webster, Fowler, Parlour, Gaunt, Marshall, Joseph, Flatts, Dickov(Warden), Shaw, Young.
Replay
Dec 3 v Notts County (h) 1-1 aet
Dickov
Brading; Webster, Fowler, Clements(Selley), Marshall, Gaunt, Warden, Flatts, Dickov, Young(Read), Joseph.
Second Replay
Dec 7 v Notts County (a) 1-2
Flatts
Brading; Webster, Fowler, Parlour, Marshall, Gaunt, Warden, Clements(Joseph), Read(Selley), Dickov, Flatts.

1991-92
Round 2
Nov 25 v Brighton & Hove Albion (a) 5-2
Read 2, Zumrutel 2, Brissett
Rust; Swain, Lee, Selley, Charlton, O'Brien(Kirby), Zumrutel, Shaw, Connolly(Brissett), Read, Clarke.
Round 3
Dec 9 v Watford (h) 4-0
Read 3 (1 pen), Lee
Rust; Kirby, S.Campbell, Selley(Brissett), Charlton, O'Brien, Zumrutel, Lee, Read, Shaw, Clarke(Harford).
Round 4
Jan 28 v Everton (h) 1-2
Read
Rust; Kirby, S.Campbell, Selley, Charlton, O'Brien, Zumrutel(Brissett), Shaw, Read, Lee, Clarke.

ARSENAL

1516 T. WHITTAKER

C. BUCKLEY

571 ARSENAL

J. R. ELVEY

122 ARSENAL

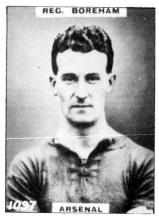

REG. BOREHAM

1097 ARSENAL

A. HUTCHINS

568 ARSENAL

A. YOUNG

ARSENAL

London Combination/Football Combination

When the Football League suspended its normal activities in 1915 for the duration of World War One, this competition was formed for the first teams of London clubs during the war period (see *Arsenal in Wartime*). After the war, on the resumption of the Football League's regular tournaments in 1919-20, the Combination became a competition for the clubs' reserve teams only and has remained so up to present date. Over the years it has taken on various forms with extensions (and reductions) to include clubs from the South, South West, Wales, and the Midlands as well as the London clubs and, on occasion, ran two Divisions. In 1939-40, at the outbreak of World War Two (it did not operate during the war), the title was changed to the Football Combination, and for a number of years after the war a cup competition was also run. Under sponsorship, it became known as the Sunday Mirror Combination and currently the Ovenden Papers Football Combination.

Arsenal's record in the competition from 1919-20 is as follows:

	P	W	D	L	F	A	Pts	Pos
1919-20	36	18	10	8	81	41	46	2nd
1920-21	36	12	4	20	57	63	28	9th
1921-22	40	21	13	6	67	47	55	2nd
1922-23	40	20	9	11	80	40	49	1st

Appearances: T.Adamson 5, A.Baker 2, W.N.Blyth 3, R.Boreham 4, F.Bradshaw 15, J.D.Butler 5, J.Clarke 6, G.Collin 4, W.E.Coopland 13, F.F.Cownley 7, W.W.Creegan 12, F.Currie 15, S.Dunn 13, S.J.C.Earle 1, J.R.Elvey 9, S.Gash 5, A.Graham 13, S.Haden 20, W.Henderson 14, J.Hopkins 12, A.V.Hutchins 15, A.W.Jewett 11, R.F.John 15, A.L.Kennedy 8, J.A.Mackie 8, A.McKenzie 14, W.Milne 11, A.G.Moody 15, E.J.Norris 1, Dr.J.A.Paterson 7, J.H.Robson 9, A.Roe 32, J.Rutherford 1, A.Sissons 4, J.Toner 14, F.A.Townrow 17, R.Turnbull 6, C.R.Voysey 7, H.A.White 7, T.J.Whittaker 20, E.C.Williamson 18, A.Young 22.
Goalscorers: Roe 19, Townrow 11, Haden 7, McKenzie 6, Graham 5, Henderson 5, Young 4, Coopland 3, Hutchins 3, White 3, Boreham 2, Creegan 2, Voysey 2, Clarke 1, Cownley 1, Hopkins 1, Moody 1, Norris 1, Sissons 1, Toner 1, Whittaker 1.

	P	W	D	L	F	A	Pts	Pos
1923-24	44	16	11	17	69	66	43	6th
1924-25	44	17	12	15	62	54	46	6th
1925-26	44	20	6	18	83	68	46	5th
1926-27	42	30	4	8	124	45	64	1st

Appearances: J.Bacon 1, A.Baker 4, J.C.Barley 40, W.N.Blyth 2, E.Bowen 29, H.W.Cope 3, S.Haden 12, W.Harper 16, S.Hoar 17, A.L.Kennedy 31, J.Lambert 27, J.Lawson 4, J.W.Lee 30, D.Lewis 16, J.A.Mackie 10, W.Milne 35, J.Moody 10, H.B.Peel 17, J.H.Ramsay 7, H.Roberts 8, R.Robinson 35, J.J.Rutherford 13, W.C.Seddon 26, J.Shaw 36, G.Smith 1, R.W.Tricker 6, R.Warnes 1, W.H.Warnes 1, T.C.Wells 4, A.Young 20.
Goalscorers: Shaw 30, Bowen 29, Lee 19, Lambert 13, Haden 8, Peel 7, Barley 3, Ramsay 3, Rutherford 3, Young 3, Baker 1, Lawson 1, Milne 1, Moody 1, Tricker 1, Opponents own-goal 1.

	P	W	D	L	F	A	Pts	Pos
1927-28	42	27	7	8	105	46	61	1st

Appearances: J.H.Ashcroft 1, J.C.Barley 32, E.Bowen 20, J.Brain 1, F.H.Cheesmur 17, A.Clark 41, A.S.Crowther 1, S.Haden 8, E.A.Hapgood 21, W.Hill 1, S.Hoar 1, A.L.Kennedy 11, J.Lambert 24, J.W.Lee 22, J.A.Mackie 13, W.J.Maycock 3, W.Milne 2, J.Moody 15, R.Parkin 12, W.Paterson 16, H.B.Peel 32, H.Roberts 33, R.Robinson 39, W.C.Seddon 33, J.Shaw 28, G.Smith 11, L.Thompson 1, R.W.Tricker 21, W.H.Warnes 2.
Goalscorers: Bowen 22, Lambert 13, Shaw 12, Clark 11, Cheesmur 10, Tricker 7, Peel 6, Barley 5, Haden 5, Lee 4, Hapgood 3, Brain 1, Maycock 1, Thompson 1, Warnes 1, Opponents own-goals 3.

	P	W	D	L	F	A	Pts	Pos
1928-29	42	26	7	9	108	42	59	1st

389

Appearances: A.Baker 1, J.C.Barley 30, W.Blyth 1, J.D.Butler 3, F.H.Cheesmur 1, A.Clark 15, H.W.Cope 17, S.A.Dobbin 3, B.G.Foster 3, J.Frost 1, E.A.Hapgood 23, A.E.Haynes 28, S.Hoar 11, C.Jones 1, J.Lambert 31, D.Lewis 1, W.J.Maycock 27, A.W.Meeson 7, R.Parkin 29, W.Paterson 31, H.B.Peel 14, H.Roberts 11, R.Robinson 42, W.C.Seddon 41, J.Shaw 15, L.Thompson 26, R.W.Tricker 13, W.H.Warnes 36.
Goalscorers: Lambert 26, Thompson 21, Warnes 15, Shaw 14, Maycock 9, Parkin 9, Barley 3, Peel 3, Clark 2, Tricker 2, Haynes 1, Hoar 1, Opponents own-goals 2.

	P	W	D	L	F	A	Pts	Pos
1929-30	42	30	5	7	132	55	65	1st

Appearances: W.M.L.Allison 13, A.Baker 4, C.S.Bastin 16, J.Brain 28, J.D.Butler 25, H.W.Cope 28, B.Diaper 1, S.A.Dobbin 13, J.Frost 8, D.Halliday 16, A.E.Haynes 30, J.H.A.Hulme 9, A.E.Humpish 17, A.James 1, R.F.John 2, W.Johnstone 22, C.Jones 4, J.Lambert 16, D.Lewis 5, W.J.Maycock 27, R.Parkin 15, H.B.Peel 13, C.J.F.Preedy 24, R.Robinson 42, W.C.Seddon 19, J.Shaw 11, L.Thompson 28, W.H.Warnes 5, J.J.Williams 22.
Goalscorers: Halliday 24, Brain 20, Lambert 18, Bastin 13, Johnstone 13, Maycock 10, Williams 8, Thompson 5, Warnes 4, Hulme 3, Jones 3, Parkin 3, Peel 3, Baker 1, Haynes 1, Opponents own-goals 3.

	P	W	D	L	F	A	Pts	Pos
1930-31	42	28	6	8	120	48	62	1st

Appearances: W.M.L.Allison 6, A.Baker 11, J.Brain 23, H.W.Cope 34, B.Diaper 9, D.Halliday 13, W.Harper 5, A.E.Haynes 39, J.H.A.Hulme 5, A.E.Humpish 4, D.B.N.Jack 1, W.Johnstone 18, C.Jones 13, G.P.Keyser 9, J.Lambert 6, D.Lewis 1, H.H.Lewis 6, C.G.Male 37, W.J.Maycock 22, R.Parkin 39, C.J.F.Preedy 27, R.Robinson 42, W.C.Seddon 17, N.W.Sidey 8, L.Thompson 41, W.H.Warnes 5, J.J.Williams 2.
Goalscorers: Thompson 33, Parkin 18, Halliday 15, Johnstone 8, Williams 8, Lambert 7, Maycock 7, Sidey 7, Brain 5, Jones 4, Cope 3, Baker 1, Haynes 1, Hulme 1, Male 1, Opponents own-goal 1.

	P	W	D	L	F	A	Pts	Pos
1931-32	42	27	8	7	111	43	62	2nd
1932-33	46	31	5	10	145	57	67	3rd
1933-34	46	32	5	9	129	44	69	1st

Appearances: A.E.Beasley 20, A.G.Biggs 6, R.J.Birkett 21, E.R.Bowden 2, J.P.Carr 1, S.Cartwright 20, E.Coleman 14, E.Collett 31, L.H.Compton 44, G.Cox 18, P.Dougall 32, J.Dunne 5, A.C.Godding 3, R.C.G.Green 35, A.E.Haynes 12, F.R.Hill 10, J.H.A.Hulme 13, D.B.N.Jack 2, A.James 4, C.Jones 2, S.Kirkwood 2, J.Lambert 4, F.Moss 3, R.Parkin 30, H.Roberts 9, N.W.Sidey 28, R.Stockill 33, R.F.Trim 42, E.W.Tuckett 9, C.E.Walker 12, A.Wilson 39.
Goalscorers: Green 22, Stockill 19, Cox 18, Beasley 17, Birkett 12, Hulme 8, Coleman 7, Dougall 5, Dunne 5, Compton 4, Lambert 3, Jack 2, Sidey 2, Hill 1, James 1, Parkin 1, Opponents own-goals 2.

	P	W	D	L	F	A	Pts	Pos
1934-35	46	33	5	8	131	50	71	1st

Appearances: A.E.Beasley 8, A.G.Biggs 17, R.J.Birkett 21, E.R.Bowden 5, G.F.Bradshaw 10, S.Cartwright 25, J.Clare 8, E.Collett 22, D.C.S.Compton 7, L.H.Compton 42, G.Cox 31, W.J.Crayston 2, R.T.Davidson 1, P.Dougall 32, J.Dunne 16, J.L.Evans 6, R.C.G.Green 28, F.R.Hill 12, G.L.Holden 3, J.H.A.Hulme 6, R.F.John 5, A.J.Kirchen 6, J.Marshall 26, R.Parkin 30, E.Rogers 7, N.W.Sidey 39, R.Stockill 2, R.F.Trim 44, C.E.Walker 8, W.H.Webster 1, A.Wilson 36.
Goalscorers: Cox 23, Dunne 17, Birkett 14, L.Compton 11, Green 11, Dougall 8, Marshall 7, Biggs 5, Beasley 3, Collett 3, D.Compton 3, Hulme 3, Kirchen 3, Rogers 3, Stockill 3, Clare 2, Hill 2, Holden 2, Parkin 2, Bowden 1, Webster 1, Opponents own-goals 4.

	P	W	D	L	F	A	Pts	Pos
1935-36	46	29	5	12	117	55	63	3rd
1936-37	46	30	8	8	139	39	68	1st

Appearances: A.M.Atter 3, A.E.Beasley 1, A.G.Biggs 44, P.L.Bosse 4, F.P.Boulton 3, A.Bowden 1, E.R.Bowden 3, G.H.Bremner 1, S.Cartwright 34, J.Cocker 3, E.Collett 37, D.C.S.Compton 32, L.H.Compton 25, W.J.Crayston 3, G.F.Curtis 12, R.T.Davidson 10, E.J.Drake 2, J.L.Evans 15, W.M.Griffiths 11, E.A.Hapgood 4, J.H.A.Hulme 8, R.F.John 19, B.Joy 13, A.J.Kirchen 3, R.Lewis 9, R.MacFarlane 29, J.V.Milne 10, D.Nelson 29, L.W.Reader 1, L.Scott 5, N.W.Sidey 24, G.A.Strasser 1, G.H.Swindin 19, R.F.Trim 42, E.W.Tuckett 19, W.H.Webster 3, A.Wilson 24.
Goalscorers: Biggs 41, D.Compton 32, Kirchen 9, Tuckett 8, Lewis 7, Nelson 6, Hulme 5, MacFarlane 4, Davidson 3, Milne 3, Webster 3, E.Bowden 2, Collett 2, L.Compton 2, Crayston 2, Drake 2, Evans 2, Griffiths 2, Cocker 1, Curtis 1, Reader 1, Opponents own-goal 1.

	P	W	D	L	F	A	Pts	Pos
1937-38	46	28	15	3	116	42	71	1st

Appearances: A.M.Atter 18, A.G.Biggs 14, P.L.Bosse 4, F.P.Boulton 9, A.Bowden 2, G.H.Bremner 21, E.M.Carr 25, S.Cartwright 28, E.Collett 35, D.C.S.Compton 32, L.H.Compton 34, G.F.Curtis 14, R.T.Davidson 3, A.M.Farr 21, A.G.Field 2, D.J.Ford 2, W.M.Griffiths 23, L.N.Hockaday 2, J.H.A.Hulme 1, G.S.Hunt 1, R.F.John 1, B.Joy 8, A.J.Kirchen 2, R.Lewis 34, C.G.Male 2, D.Nelson 35, D.Pryde 30, L.Scott 43, N.W.Sidey 25, G.H.Swindin 18, A.Wilson 17.
Goalscorers: D.Compton 22, Lewis 22, Griffiths 16, Farr 11, Nelson 10, Carr 8, Bremner 7, Biggs 5, L.Compton 5, Davidson 3, Cartwright 1, Curtis 1, Hunt 1, Kirchen 1, Opponents own-goals 3.

	P	W	D	L	F	A	Pts	Pos
1938-39	46	30	7	9	139	57	67	1st

Appearances: C.S.Bastin 3, J.Blakeney 6, G.H.Bremner 21, E.M.Carr 13, S.Cartwright 24, E.Collett 35, D.C.S.Compton 23, L.H.Compton 20, W.J.Crayston 2, R.H.Cumner 13, G.F.Curtis 28, G.B.Drury 16, C.C.Fairchild 7, A.M.Farr 10, A.G.Fields 34, D.J.Ford 2, W.M.Griffiths 4, G.L.Holden 4, B.Jones 1, L.J.Jones 9, A.J.Kirchen 3, R.Lewis 31, C.G.Male 6, G.W.Marks 16, A.S.Morgan 3, D.Nelson 28, D.Pryde 18, S.J.Pugh 11, L.Scott 33, N.W.Sidey 12, E.F.Smith 3, G.H.Swindin 8, C.E.Tooze 10, W.Walsh 15, A.Wilson 18, A.H.Woolcock 2, A.E.Young 14.
Goalscorers: Lewis 43, D.Compton 15, Drury 13, Bremner 8, Nelson 8, Blakeney 7, Carr 7, Cumner 7, L.Compton 6, L.Jones 6, Farr 4, Walsh 4, Kirchen 3, Curtis 3, Bastin 1, Collett 1, Griffiths 1, B.Jones 1, Opponent own-goal 1.

	P	W	D	L	F	A	Pts	Pos
				(Section 'A')				
1946-47	30	23	3	4	83	29	49	1st

In the championship play-off, Arsenal beat Portsmouth (Section 'B' winners) 3-0 at home.

Appearances (including play-off): C.H.Barnard 5, W.Barnes 1, C.S.Bastin 4, N.Bowden 3, J.C.Chenhall 8, D.Clelland 13, E.Collett 14, G.F.Curtis 16, R.W.Daniel 4, L.Delaney 13, A.Dingley 4, G.B.Drury 6, J.Edington 9, D.M.Farquhar 15, A.G.Fields 19, C.Grant 9, A.Gudmundsson 10, L.Henley 9, C.L.Hodges 7, E.J.Holland 3, A.Horsfield 6, S.Jones 19, C.G.Male 1, C.A.Milton 1, A.S.Morgan 18, D.Nelson 3, E.I.Newman 3, D.J.Oakes 2, E.H.Platt 24, J.Ollerenshaw 3, D.Pryde 18, T.W.Rudkin 3, J.A.Sherratt 7, J.W.Sloan 7, A.Smith 14, E.F.Smith 5, L.Smith 6, T.H.W.Vallance 6, J.S.Wade 13, H.Waller 15, T.Whalley 5.
Goalscorers: Clelland 8, Hodges 7, Morgan 7, Barnard 6, Grant 6, Curtis 5, Drury 5, Gudmundsson 5, Sherratt 5, Whalley 5, Henley 4, Sloan 4, Vallance 4, A.Smith 3, Farquhar 2, Nelson 2, Bastin 1, Bowden 1, Edington 1, Holland 1, Horsfield 1, Opponents own-goals 3.

Football Combination Cup
Arsenal won Qualifying Group 1, beating Coventry City (a) 1-0 in the semi-final, and lost 2-1 to Swansea Town (at Tottenham) in the final.

	P	W	D	L	F	A	Pts	Pos
				(Section 'B')				
1947-48	30	20	6	4	55	26	46	1st

In the championship play-off, Arsenal lost 2-0 to West Ham United (a).

Football Combination Cup
Arsenal won Group 4, and lost 1-0 to Leicester C (h) in the semi-final.

	P	W	D	L	F	A	Pts	Pos
			(Section 'B')					
1948-49	30	20	5	5	62	31	45	1st

In the championship play-off, Arsenal lost 3-1 to Chelsea (a).

Football Combination Cup
Arsenal failed to qualify for the semi-finals.

	P	W	D	L	F	A	Pts	Pos
			(Section 'A')					
1949-50	30	15	4	11	59	33	34	3rd

Football Combination Cup
Arsenal failed to qualify.

	P	W	D	L	F	A	Pts	Pos
			(Section 'A')					
1950-51	30	21	5	4	73	25	47	1st

In the championship play-off, Arsenal beat Chelsea (a) 5-0.

Appearances (including play off): P.K.Atkinson 2, D.L.Bowen 26, J.C.Chenhall 29, F.J.A.Cox 4, R.W.Daniel 18, G.Dunkley 2, D.M.Farquhar 1, A.G.Fields 4, C.G.Grimshaw 9, P.Hancock 10, W.R.Healey 10, E.J.Holland 3, C.C.Holton 30, A.Horsfield 14, A.J.Kelsey 23, R.J.Marden 18, I.B.McPherson 1, C.A.Milton 17, D.J.Oakes 21, E.H.Platt 5, J.W.Robertson 7, D.P.Rossiter 1, M.J.Ryan 10, A.Shaw 2, N.Smith 10, G.H.Swindin 1, D.S.Tilley 4, J.S.Wade 31, L.E.Wills 28.
Goalscorers: Holton 26, Oakes 12, Marden 11, Milton 9, Horsfield 5, Grimshaw 4, Bowen 3, Ryan 2, Tilley 3, Wade 2, Robertson 1.

Football Combination Cup
Arsenal won Section 2, beating Ipswich Town (a) 3-2 in the semi-final, and lost at home to Charlton Athletic 2-0 in the final.

	P	W	D	L	F	A	Pts	Pos
			(Section 'B')					
1951-52	30	18	7	5	70	32	43	2nd

Football Combination Cup
Arsenal won Section 2, and in the semi-final drew with Fulham (h) 1-1 and 1-1 at Fulham. The second replay was held over to 1952-53, when Arsenal lost 1-0 at home.

	P	W	D	L	F	A	Pts	Pos
			(Division 1)					
1952-53	30	12	4	14	47	46	28	9th

Football Combination Cup
Arsenal won Section 2, beating West Ham United (h) 2-0 in the semi-final, and won at home in the final against Southampton 1-0 (Ward)
Team: Kelsey; Chenhall, Evans, Wills, Dodgin, Bowen, Walsh, Oakes, F.Cox, P.Tilley, G.Ward.

	P	W	D	L	F	A	Pts	Pos
			(Section 1)					
1953-54	30	13	8	9	56	36	34	6th

Football Combination Cup
Arsenal failed to qualify for the semi-finals.

	P	W	D	L	F	A	Pts	Pos
			(Section 1)					
1954-55	30	15	6	9	73	43	36	4th

Football Combination Cup
Arsenal failed to qualify

	P	W	D	L	F	A	Pts	Pos
1955-56	42	19	8	15	96	76	46	9th
1956-57	42	22	9	11	105	65	53	7th
1957-58	42	22	7	13	103	64	51	6th

			(Division 1)					
1958-59	34	15	10	9	86	60	40	4th
1959-60	34	15	6	13	62	45	36	7th
1960-61	34	12	11	11	76	62	35	6th
1961-62	34	21	5	8	97	46	47	2nd

			(Saturday Section)					
1962-63	34	25	5	4	105	40	55	1st

Appearances: T.K.Anderson 17, G.Armstrong 15, D.R.Bacuzzi 29, J.Barnwell 5, J.Black 14, R.Bloomfield 10, L.Brown 4, E.Clamp 1, D.R.Clapton 2, F.R.G.Clarke 26, D.J.Court 22, G.E.Eastham 4, G.Ferry 25, J.B.Gould 11, A.T.Griffiths 2, V.G.Groves 20, P.Kane 18, T.Kinsella 12, R.Massey 2, J.McClelland 5, I.H.McKechnie 15, W.J.T.Neill 11, J.W.F.J.Petts 4, J.C.Sammels 10, P.F.Simpson 2, A.F.G.Skirton 6, R.G.Smithson 24, R.Still 10, T.Tapping 2, B.Tawse 1, G.Ward 29, R.Whittaker 15. P.E.Storey 1.
Goalscorers: Court 18, Kane 15, Anderson 13, Ward 13, Armstrong 9, Whittaker 5, Eastham 4, B.Gould 4, Groves 3, Kinsella 3, Sammels 3, Bloomfield 2, Massey 2, Skirton 2, Bacuzzi 1, Griffiths 1, Neill 1, Petts 1, Opponents own-goals 5.
The championship play-off was held over to 1963-64, when Arsenal beat Chelsea (Midweek Section winners) at Chelsea 2-0 (Sammels, Anderson). **Team:** R.Wilson, Bacuzzi, F.Clarke, Smithson, Neill, Snedden, Anderson, Sammels, J.B.Gould, Bloomfield, Whittaker.

	P	W	D	L	F	A	Pts	Pos
			(Division 1)					
1963-64	34	19	3	12	87	48	41	6th
1964-65	34	17	5	12	73	54	39	6th
1965-66	34	21	7	6	90	37	49	2nd
1966-67	32	18	4	10	60	41	40	2nd

Football Combination Cup
Arsenal won their qualifying group, and lost to Tottenham Hotspur (a) 2-1 in the semi-final.

	P	W	D	L	F	A	Pts	Pos
			(Division 1)					
1967-68	28	11	6	11	33	28	28	7th

Football Combination Cup
Arsenal won their qualifying group, beating Walsall in the quarter-final, and Ipswich Town (h) 3-1 in the semi-final. In a two-legged final they beat Tottenham Hotspur 4-3 on aggregate.

1st leg (h) 2-2
Simmons, Davidson
Furnell; Rice, Nelson, Woodward, Carmichael, Davidson, Cumming, Jenkins, Simmons, George, Johnston.

2nd leg (a) 2-1
Jenkins, Simmons
Furnell; Rice, Dixon, Woodward, Carmichael, Davidson, Kelly(George), Cumming, Johnston, Simmons, Jenkins.

	P	W	D	L	F	A	Pts	Pos
			(Division 1)					
1968-69	25	20	4	1	71	18	44	1st

Appearances (substitutes in brackets): G.Armstrong 1, S.Burtenshaw 0(1), J.Carmichael 25, G.Cumming 25, R.Davidson 19(1), P.Davies 0(1), W.E.Dixon 4(1), F.C.George 19, R.A.Gould 1, G.Graham 2, G.W.Johnson 5, G.Johnston 25, E.P.Kelly 18, R.Kennedy 20(1), F.McLintock 1, W.J.T.Neill 5, S.Nelson 24, J.Radford 1, P.J.Rice 23, J.G.Robertson 3, J.C.Sammels 1, D.Simmons 7(1), P.F.Simpson 1, I.F.Ure 1, M.W.Webster 20, J.Woodward 24.
Goalscorers: Johnston 21, Cumming 15, George 9, Kennedy 8, Simmons 6, Davidson 3, Graham 2, Kelly 2, Dixon 1, Rice 1, Simpson 1, Woodward 1, Opponents own-goal 1.

393

Football Combination Cup
Arsenal failed to qualify in Group B

	P	W	D	L	F	A	Pts	Pos
1969-70	25	18	5	2	66	23	41	1st

Appearances: G.Armstrong 10, G.C.Barnett 9, B.M.Batson, T.Burton 2(3), J.Carmichael 24, D.J.Court 10, G.Cumming 9, P.Davies 14(2), J.de Garis 18, F.C.George 6, R.A.Gould 14, R.Harding 3, G.W.Johnson 8, E.P.Kelly 12, R.Kennedy 19, F.McLintock 1, W.J.T.Neill 6, S.Nelson 22, T.Pearce 4, J.Radford 1, P.J.Rice 19, R.Ritchie 6(1), J.G.Roberts 14, J.G.Robertson 5, J.C.Sammels 3, M.Shovelar 1, I.F.Ure 1, M.W.Webster 6, R.P.Wilson 2, J.Woodward 23.
Goalscorers: Gould 16, Kennedy 12, Davies 9, Cumming 7, George 7, Armstrong 3, Harding 2, Court 1, de Garis 1, Kelly 1, Nelson 1, Rice 1, Robertson 1, Sammels 1, Woodward 1, Opponents own-goals 2.

Football Combination Cup
Arsenal won their qualifying group and in a two-legged semi-final beat Tottenham Hotspur 5-2 on aggregate. In the final, held over to 1970-71, they beat West Ham United 6-1 on aggregate.

1st leg (a) 0-1
Barnett; Batson, Nelson, Woodwarde, Carmichael, de Garis, Harding, Burton, Allen(Pearce), P.Davies, Marinello.

2nd leg (h) 6-0
Marinello 2, George, Batson, Woodward, Pearce
Barnett; Batson, Woodward, Carmichael, Simpson, de Garis, Marinello, Sammels, George, Pearce, Harding.

	P	W	D	L	F	A	Pts	Pos
1970-71	42	23	12	7	83	32	58	2nd
1971-72	40	14	11	15	59	52	39	13th
1972-73	40	23	11	6	79	37	57	3rd
1973-74	42	16	13	13	51	38	45	9th
1974-75	40	21	8	11	50	32	50	5th
1975-76	42	16	14	12	54	42	46	8th
1976-77	42	19	10	13	54	41	48	6th
1977-78	42	15	14	13	61	45	44	10th
1978-79	42	13	18	11	56	44	44	10th
1979-80	42	26	7	9	96	48	59	2nd
1980-81	42	20	13	9	68	48	53	6th
1981-82	38	10	12	16	47	51	32	11th
1982-83	42	17	13	12	65	46	47	6th
1983-84	42	29	8	5	96	30	66	1st

Appearances: I.J.R.Allinson 29, T.A.Adams 28, G.C.Caesar 10(1), G.Campbell 13(1), L.R.Chapman 11, R.Coleville 2, D.Cork 22, P.V.Davis 2, P.A.Gorman 31(4), M.Hayes 16(3), C.F.Hill 2, A.L.Isaacs 1(1), J.Kay 23(1), M.R.Keown 30(1), T.D.Lee 32 (4), J.Lukic 27, D.J.Madden 22(3), B.J.McDermott 18, R.J.Meade 26, P.Nicholas 6, D.E.O'Shea 21, J.Purdie 0(2), N.J.Quinn 1, G.Rix 1, S.I.Robson 3, D.Rocastle 2(4), B.E.Sparrow 24, A.Sunderland 5, B.E.Talbot 2, M.L.Thomas 13(1), C.A.Whyte 23, R.J.Wilmot 5, J.Woods 1.
Goalscorers: Meade 24, Allinson 14, Chapman 13, Lee 10, McDermott 7, Hayes 4, Adams 3, Madden 3, Sunderland 3, Cork 2, Gorman 2, Rocastle 2, Sparrow 2, Caesar 1, Coleville 1, Kay 1, Keown 1, Rix 1, Whyte 1, Opponent own-goal 1.

	P	W	D	L	F	A	Pts	Pos	
1984-85	42	27	8	7	117	46	62	2nd	
1985-86	*41	26	10	5	124	41	62	2nd	*One fixture not played
1986-87	38	23	7	8	77	42	53	3rd	
1987-88	38	19	5	14	77	48	43	8th	
1988-89	38	20	12	6	83	44	52	2nd	
1989-90	38	26	6	6	84	51	84	1st	
1990-91	38	19	8	11	65	54	65	7th	
1991-92	38	22	6	10	80	49	72	3rd	

Appearances: K.Ampadu 32(2), J.Bacon 1(2), G.C.Caesar 23, K.J.Campbell 20, J.Carstairs 33(1), S.Clements 4(3), A.A.Cole 8(2), D.Connelly 26(4), P.V.Davis 10, P.Dickov 0(1), L.Francis 24, P.Groves 8, A.J.Hannigan 11(2), C.J.Hartfield 2, M.Hayes 21, N.A.Heaney 13(1), D.Hillier 11(4), C.R.Hoyle 1, S.Jonsson 7, M.Joseph 2, R.Lee 16(4), B.Marwood 7, G.McKeown 23(5), C.A.McKernon 10, P.C.Merson 2, A.J.Miller 35, A.Mockler 2(2), S.Morrow 15(1), D.A.O'Leary 2, C..G.Pates 7, N.J.Quinn 18, D.Rocastle 2, P.Scully 16(1), M.L.Thomas 1, J.Will 3, N.Winterburn 1, S.Young 1.
Goalscorers: Campbell 20, Hayes 10, Ampadu 9, McKeown 6, Marwood 6, Quinn 5, Heaney 4, Connelly 3, Caesar 3, Groves 3, Cole 3, Lee 2, Hoyle 1, Carstairs 1, Jonsson 1, Davis 1, Bacon 1, Merson 1, Young 1, Opponents own-goals 3.

ARSENAL FRIENDLY MATCHES
1893-94 to 1991-92

Due to the large content in this section and the space available, it is only possible to include the *full* details for those matches which it is considered had particular interest.

1893-94
Sep 4 v Doncaster Rovers (h) 4-1
Shaw 2, Elliott, Booth
Att: 4,000
Sep 16 v Chatham (h) 5-0
Heath 3, Shaw, Elliott
Att: 11,000
Sep 23 v Middlesbrough (h) 4-1
Gemmell, Elliott, Booth, Shaw
Att: 7,000
Oct 7 v Casuals (h) 5-1
Elliott 4, Heath
Att: 7,000
Oct 9 v Sunderland (h) 1-4
Henderson
Att: 10,000
Oct 12 v London Caledonians (h) 10-3
Heath 3, Henderson 4, Elliott, Shaw 2
Att: 1,000
Oct 23 v Mr Roston Bourke's XI (h) 4-3
Heath, Shaw 2, Cooper
Att: 4,000
Oct 30 v Wolverhampton Wanderers (h) 1-0
Crawford
Att: 5,000
Nov 30 v London Caledonians (a) 1-1
Buist
Att: 2,000
Dec 2 v West Bromwich Albion (h) 5-0
Boyle, Shaw 3, Elliott
Att: 5,000
Dec 11 v Preston North End (h) 1-1*
Henderson
Att: 6,000
*Abandoned after 80 minutes — bad light
Dec 23 v Crusaders (h) 7-0
Heath 3, Shaw 2, Crawford 2
Att: 3,000
Jan 13 v Accrington Stanley (h) 2-0
Elliott 2
Att: 4,000
Jan 15 v Aston Villa (h) 1-3
Henderson
Att: 6,000
Jan 20 v Chatham (a) 4-0
Shaw 2, Elliott 2
Att: 6,000
Jan 29 v Blackpool (h) 5-2
Crawford, W.Williams, Booth 2, Worrall
Att: 2,000
Mar 1 v London Caledonians (h) 1-0
Henderson
Att: 1,000
Mar 5 v Luton Town (h) 2-0
Bryan, Elliott
Att: 4,000
Mar 12 v Sheffield United (a) 2-0
Shaw, Henderson
Att: 1,000
Mar 17 v Millwall Athletic (h) 2-2
Henderson, Powell (pen)
Att: 12,000

Mar 26 v St Mirren (h) 1-3
Henderson
Att: 8,000
Apr 2 v Nottingham Forest (h) 1-3
Crawford
Att: 4,000
Apr 7 v Millwall Athletic (a) 4-1
Mortimer, Henderson 2, Worrall
Att: 10,000
Apr 9 v Sheffield United (h) 0-1
Att: 2,000
Apr 12 v Westerham & District XI (a) 6-3
Bryan, McNab 2, Elliott 2, Mortimer
Att: 700
Apr 16 v Luton Town (a) 3-3
Crawford, Worrall, Mortimer
Att: 'Good'
Apr 18 v New Brompton (a) 4-2*
McNab, Powell (pen), Worrall, Mortimer
Att: 6,000
*Only 85 minutes played — bad light
Apr 21 v Burnley (h) 2-0
Crawford, Mortimer
Att: 5,000
Apr 25 v Corinthians (at Leyton) 2-3
O'Brien 2
Williams; Powell, Jeffrey, Davis, Heath, Boyle, Crawford, Henderson, Worrall, O'Brien, Mortimer.
Att: 5,000
Apr 28 v Stoke (h) 3-3
O'Brien, Mortimer, Crawford
Att: 3,000

1894-95
Sep 3 v Nottingham Forest (h) 3-2
Henderson 2, Stevenson
Att: 4,000
Sep 8 v Fleetwood Rangers (h) 4-0
Boyd, Crawford, O'Brien 2
Att: 2,000
Sep 17 v West Bromwich Albion (h) 0-1
Att: 2,000
Sep 24 v Renton (h) 6-1
Boyd 4, Crawford, Buchanan
Att: 2,500
Oct 4 v Casuals (at Leyton) 8-0
Shaw 3, Mortimer 4, Henderson
Att: 3,000
Oct 15 v Sunderland (h) 2-1
Buchanan, Davis
Att: 12,000
Oct 29 v Luton Town (h) 5-0
Meade 2, Caldwell, O'Brien, Boyle
Att: 3,000
Nov 12 v Roston Bourke's XI (h) 6-2
Henderson 2, Buchanan, O'Brien 2, Boyle
Att: 1,000
Nov 17 v Casuals (h) 4-1
Henderson, Buchanan 2, Crawford
Att: 3,000

395

Nov 21 v Marlow (a) 4-2
Buchanan 2, Stevenson, O'Brien
Att: 'Large'
Dec 1 v Stoke (h) 3-1
Crawford, Boyle, O'Brien
Att: 6,000
Dec 3 v St Bernards (h) 1-2
Henderson
Att: 3,000
Dec 24 v New Brompton (a) 0-5
Att: 4,000
Dec 29 v Dresden United (Staffs) (h) 1-0
Mortimer
Att: 2,500
Jan 5 v Sheppey United (a) 6-1
Mortimer, O'Brien 2, Meade, Boyle 2
Att: 800
Feb 11 v Luton Town (a) 2-1
Meade 2
Att: 'Good'
Feb 16 v Chatham (a) 6-0
Boyle, Mortimer 2, O'Brien 2, Buchanan
Att: 4,000
Feb 25 v Liverpool (at Hornsey) 4-3
O'Brien 2, Buchanan 2
Att: 1,200
Mar 6 v Eastbourne (a) 5-1
O'Brien 2, Mortimer 3
Att: 'Large'
Mar 13 v Bromley & District (a) 4-1
Boyle, Crawford, Mortimer, Bayman (og)
Att: 2,000
Mar 16 v Gainsborough Trinity (at Gravesend) 2-0
Sharpe, Mortimer
Att: 2,000
Mar 20 v Home Park FC (Plymouth) (a) 2-1
O'Brien 2
Mar 21 v Weymouth Athletic (a) 5-0
Davis, Howat, Mortimer, O'Brien 2
Att: 1,000
Mar 25 v Millwall Athletic (h) 1-1
O'Brien
Att: 10,000
Apr 1 v Blackburn Rovers (h) 2-2
Mortimer 2
Att: 5,000
Apr 8 v Millwall Athletic (a) 0-0 *
Att: 7,000
*Abandoned after 85 minutes — bad light
Apr 13 v Dumbarton (h) 5-1
Mortimer, Caldwell 2, Boyle, Howat
Att: 5,000
Apr 15 v Small Heath (h) 3-4
Mortimer 2, Buchanan
Att: 8,000
Apr 25 v Royal Ordnance (a) 0-1
Att: 2,000
Apr 27 v Millwall Athletic (h) 3-1
Mortimer 2, Powell (pen)
Att: 7,000
Apr 29 v Grimsby Town (h) 1-2
Hare
Att: 1,200

1895-96
Sep 9 v Millwall (a) 3-1
Mills, Hare, Buchanan
Att: 6,000
Sep 23 v Sheffield Wednesday (h) 2-1
Mortimer, Buchanan
Att: 3,000

Oct 14 v Everton (h) 0-2
Att: 4,000
Nov 4 v Royal Ordnance (h) 3-1
Mortimer, McAvoy 2
Att: 2,000
Nov 21 v Casuals (a) 3-0
Boyd 2, Hare
Att: 2,000
Nov 23 v Barnsley St Peter's (h) 4-1
Mortimer, Boyd 2, Powell (pen)
Att: 2,000
Dec 9 v Sunderland (h) 1-2
Boyd
Att: 4,000
Dec 26 v Cliftonville (h) 10-1
Mills 2, Buchanan 3, Boyd 4, McAvoy
Att: 500
Dec 28 v Darlington (h) 6-2
Mills, Boyd, McAvoy 2, Mortimer, Jenkyns
Att: 4,000
Jan 1 v Hastings (a) 12-0
Boyd 6, Mortimer 2, McAvoy 2, Mills, O'Brien
Att: 'Large'
Jan 20 v Cambridge University (h) 7-1
O'Brien 4, Boyd, Haywood, McAvoy
Att: 2,500
Feb 8 v Royal Ordnance (h) 6-0
Boyd 2, Haywood 3, Mortimer
Att: 4,000
Feb 22 v East Stirlingshire (h) 5-0
Haywood 3, Chalmers, Mortimer
Att: 3,500
Feb 24 v Newton Heath (h) 6-1
Mortimer, Boyd 2, O'Brien, Chalmers
Att: 1,000
Mar 2 v Casuals (h) 4-1
Boyd 3, Haywood
Att: 3,000
Mar 16 v Tottenham Hotspur (h) 1-3
Boyd (pen)
Att: 'Numerous'
Mar 23 v Sheffield United (h) 3-1
Boyd 2, O'Brien
Att: 2,000
Mar 26 v Tottenham Hotspur (a) 3-1
O'Brien, Haywood 2
Att: 3,000
Mar 28 v Millwall (a) 3-1
Boyd, Haywood 2
Att: 6,000
Apr 2 v Stockton (h) 2-0
Boyd 2
Att: 1,000
Apr 3 v Dundee (h) 3-1
Boyd 2, O'Brien
Att: 9,000
Apr 8 v Gravesend (a) 4-0
McAvoy, Mortimer, Hare, Jenkyns
Att: 2,000
Apr 11 v Millwall (h) 2-2
Buchanan, O'Brien
Att: 11,000
Apr 13 v Everton (h) 2-0
Gordon, Hare
Att: 2,000
Apr 20 v Mr Nat. Whittaker's XI (h) 3-2
McAvoy, Hare, Davis
Att: 1,000
Apr 25 v Luton Town (h) 5-2
Crawford, Hare, Powell (pen), Johnson, O'Brien
Att: 'Poor'

Apr 27 v Luton Town (a) 0-2
Att: 'Large'
Apr 29 v Chatham (a) 1-0
O'Brien
Att: 1,500
Apr 30 v Tottenham Hotspur (a) 2-3
Hare, Jenkyns
Att: 1,500
1896-97
Sep 1 v Rossendale (h) 4-0
Johnson, Boyd, McAvoy 2
Att: 3,000
Sep 10 v Millwall (a) 2-1
Boyd, O'Brien
Att: 3,500
Oct 10 v Millwall (h) 1-5
McAvoy
Att: 13,000
Oct 26 v Luton Town (a) 1-3
Boyd
Att: 'Good'
Oct 31 v Clyde (h) 2-3
Haywood, Boyd
Fairclough; Ferguson, Sinclair, Crawford, Steel,
Davis, Brodie, Haywood, Boyd, O'Brien, Russell.
Att: 4,000
Nov 21 v Millwall (a) 2-2
Boyd, Russell
Att: 8,500
Dec 7 v Aston Villa (h) 1-3
Haywood
Att: 6,000
Jan 30 v Ilkeston (h) 7-0
Meade 2 (1 pen), O'Brien, McAvoy 3, Anderson
Att: 'Small'
Feb 8 v Luton Town (h) 5-1
Brock, O'Brien, Haywood, Russell 2
Att: 2,000
Feb 15 v Glasgow Celtic (h) 4-5
Russell 2, Caie, O'Brien
Talbot; Cassidy, Sinclair, Crawford, Boyle, McAvoy,
Brock, Haywood, Caie, O'Brien, Russell.
Att: 2,000
Mar 1 v Reading (h) 6-2
Russell 2, O'Brien, Caie, Haywood 2
Att: 1,350
Mar 6 v Casuals (a) 3-5
Caie, O'Brien, Russell
Att: 7,000
Mar 10 v Reading (a) 2-0
Brock, McFarlane
Att: 1,000
Mar 15 v Southampton St Mary's (h) 2-1
McFarlane, Caldwell
Att: 1,000
Mar 27 v Nottingham Forest (h) 1-0
Haywood
Att: 6,000
Apr 1 v Kent Association (at Tonbridge) 3-0
McAvoy, Russell, Haywood
Att: 2,500
Apr 20 v Norfolk County (a) 3-4
McAvoy, Crawford, Russell
Att: 3,000
Apr 26 v Sheffield United (h) 1-1
Haywood
Att: 1,000
Apr 29 v Southampton St Mary's (a) 5-1
McAvoy, Caie 2, O'Brien 2
Att: 'Small'
On April 10, to fill a gap in the fixture list, the first
team played the Reserves and lost 2-1.

1897-98
Sep 15 v Gravesend (a) 3-1
McGeoch 2, Haywood
Att: 1,000
Nov 1 v Reading (h) 3-1
Brock, Hannah 2
Att: 'Good'
Nov 8 v Blackburn Rovers (h) 3-0
McAvoy, Haywood, McGeoch
Att: 1,500
Nov 15 v Bristol City (a) 2-4
Crawford, Hannah
Att: 3,000
Feb 9 v Maidstone (a) 3-0
Hannah, McGeoch, Duff
Mar 21 v Bristol City (h) 3-1
McGeoch, White, Hunt
Att: 5,000
Apr 26 v Thames Ironworks (a) 2-2
Brock, McGeoch
Att: Moderate
Apr 28 v Tottenham Hotspur (h) 5-0
Brock 2, White 2, Murphy
Att: 'Large'
Apr 30 v Millwall (a) 0-2
Att: 4,500

1898-99
Sep 1 v Gravesend (h) 0-1
Att: 3,000
Sep 19 v Thames Ironworks (h) 4-0
Dailly 2, McGeoch, Hunt
Att: 'Poor'
Nov 23 v Corinthians (at Kensington) 1-4
Hunt
Att: 'Fair'
Nov 28 v Chatham (a) 1-3
McGeoch
Dec 8 v Thames Ironworks (a) 2-1
McGeoch, Dailly
Jan 25 v Sevenoaks (a) 7-1
Shaw 2, Haywood, Hunt, Ord, McGeoch 2
Jan 30 v Millwall (h) 2-4
Mitchell, Hunt
Att: 'Limited'
Feb 15 v Gravesend (a) 2-3
Haywood, Hannah
Att: 1,000
Feb 27 v Clapton (a) 3-0
McGeoch, White, Hunt
Att: 2,000
Mar 9 v Casuals (at Tufnell Park) 3-1
Haywood 2, McGeoch
Att: 1,500
Mar 23 v Past v Present 1-3 (A.Haywood's Benefit)
Past-Buchanan, Present-Cottrell 3
Att: 1,000
Apr 4 v Millwall (a) 0-0
Att: 2,500
Apr 24 v Notts County (h) 2-1
Haywood 2
Att: 'Poor'
Apr 26 v Woolwich League () 3-0
Hunt, Haywood, Mitchell

1899-1900
Sep 4 v Stoke (h) 5-3
Aston, Logan, McCowie, Sanders, Tennant
Att: 4,000
Oct 2 v Aston Villa (h) 1-0
Hunt
Att: 4,000

397

Nov 29 v Eastbourne (a) 2-1
Dick, McCowie
Dec 9 v Southampton (h) 1-1
Gaudie
Att: 1,000
Dec 23 v Swindon Town (h) 2-1
Tennant, McCowie
Att: 3,000
Jan 27 v Bedminster (h) 3-0
Gaudie, Logan 2
Feb 19 v Derby County (h) 0-1
Att: 1,500
Apr 13 v Burnley (h) 2-0
Cottrell, Tennant
Att: 6,000

1900-01
Oct 1 v Aston Villa (h) 3-0
Low, Blackwood 2
Att: 3,000
Nov 21 v Southampton (a) 1-4
Place
Att: 1,000
Dec 25 v West Ham United (h) 1-0
Gaudie
Att: 4,000
Dec 26 v Newcastle United (h) 1-1
Turner
Jan 1 v Newcastle United (a) 1-5
Main
Att: 6,000
Mar 4 v Southern League XI (h) 2-1
Blackwood 2
Att: 1,500
Apr 1 v Millwall (h) 1-1
Place
Att: 2,000
Apr 5 v Nottingham Forest (h) 1-1
Blackwood
Att: 'Capital'
Apr 20 v Notts County (h) 3-0
Childs, Turner, Anderson
Att: 'Fair'
Apr 25 v West Ham United (a) 0-0
Att: 300

1901-02
Nov 2 v Reading (h) 1-0
Briercliffe
Att: 4,000
Nov 18 v Southampton (h) 0-1
Att: 1,500
Apr 1 v Blackburn Rovers (h) 2-0
Gooing 2
Att: 3,000

Devon Tour
Apr 25 v Plymouth Argyle (a) 4-1
Main 2, W.Anderson, Gooing
Apr 26 v West Bromwich Albion (at Exeter) 0-1
Att: 5,500

1902-03
Sep 8 v New Brompton (a) 3-2
Connor 2, Lawrence
Mar 18 v Brighton & HA (a) 3-1
Coleman 2, Lawrence
Apr 14 v Northampton Town (a) 1-1
Dick
Att: 2,000

Apr 22 v Bristol City (a) 2-1
Coles, Shanks
Att: 500
Apr 25 v Chesterfield (h) 1-0
Shanks
Att: 4,000

1903-04
Oct 7 v Luton Town (h) 2-2
Gooing, Linward
Att: 6,000
Nov 30 v The Army (h) 4-0
Watson, Tomlinson 2, Pratt
Att: 2,000

1904-05
Sep 1 v Bristol City (h) 3-2
Satterthwaite 2, Coleman
Att: 6,000
Sep 12 v West Ham United (a) 1-1
Crowe
Att: 2,000
Oct 31 v Cambridge University (h) 3-0
Crowe, Satterthwaite, Bellamy
Att: 1,000
Nov 22 v Cambridge University (a) 4-3
Gooing 2, Satterthwaite 2
Att: 'Handful'
Dec 5 v A Parisian XI (h) 26-1
(French international team)
Watson 7, Ransom, Coleman 4, Briercliffe 4, Buchan 2, Linward 2, Hunter 5, Blackman
Ashcroft; Cross, Blackman, Bigden, Buchan, Ransom, Briercliffe, Hunter, Watson, Coleman, Linward.
Att: 3,000
Feb 18 v Corinthians (at Leyton) 1-2
Ducat
Att: 600
Feb 27 v Queen's Park (Glasgow) (h) 6-1
Satterthwaite 2, Ducat 2, Neave, Coleman
Att: 3,000
Mar 25 v Burnley (h) 3-0
Badger 2, Ducat
Att: 7,000
Apr 12 v West Norwood (a) 7-0
Coleman 3, Crowe 2, Linward 2
Att: 2,000
Apr 21 v New Brompton (h) 3-1
Ducat 2, Bellamy
Att: 6,000
Apr 24 v Dundee (h) 3-0
Crowe, Bellamy, Jeffrey (og)
Att: 6,000
Apr 26 v Ipswich Town (a) 3-1
Hunter 2, Theobald
Apr 27 v Norwich City (a) 1-2
Satterthwaite
Att: 4,000
Apr 29 v Sheffield United (h) 2-3
Fitchie, Coleman
Att: 5,000

1905-06
Sep 21 v Faversham Rangers (a) 9-0
Satterthwaite 2, Coleman 2, Chaplin, Crowe 2, Badger, Neale (og)
Att: 850
Oct 18 v Corinthians (at Fulham) 1-2
Coleman
Att: 6,500

Oct 30 v Oxford University (h) 3-1
Minter 2, Bigden
Att: 1,500
Dec 26 v Corinthians (h) 1-1
Badger
Jan 15 v Cambridge University (h) 4-2
Minter 3, Badger
Att: 800
Jan 22 v Oxford University (a) 4-0
Badger 2, Bellamy, Crowe
Apr 18 v West Hartlepool (a) 4-0
Freeman 3, G.Blair
Att: 2,000

1906-07
Sep 12 v Reading (a) 1-0
Minter
Att: 2,000
Sep 19 v West Norwood (at Herne Hill) 1-0
Theobald
Att: 1,000
Nov 5 v Oxford University (h) 7-1
Minter 2, Freeman 3, Ducat, Dick
Att: 1,500
Nov 19 v Leyton (a) 3-1
Freeman 2, Neave
Dec 3 v Cambridge University (a) 3-1
J.Satterthwaite 3
Dec 25 v Glasgow Celtic (h) 0-2
Ashcroft, Cross, Gray, Bigden, Theobald, Low,
Bellamy, Ducat, Freeman, Minter, T.Lee
Att: 15,000
Jan 14 v Cambridge University (h) 6-3
Freeman 4, Ducat, Tudor-Owen (og)

1907-08
Sep 16 v Barnsley (h) 1-0
Neave
Att: 1,000
Oct 14 v Rest of Kent (at Maidstone) 3-1
Dick, Mordue, Brearley (og)
Att: 800
Dec 26 v Liverpool (h) 2-2
Coleman, Neave
Att: 3,000
Feb 1 v Tottenham Hotspur (a) 1-0
C.Satterthwaite
Att: 10,000
Scottish Tour
Apr 21 v Heart of Midlothian 1-3
C.Satterthwaite
Att: 3,000
Apr 22 v Raith Rovers 0-1
Apr 23 v Aberdeen 1-4
Lewis
Att: 4,000
Apr 25 v Dundee 1-2
Lewis
Apr 27 v Motherwell 1-1
C.Satterthwaite
Att: 1,500
Apr 28 v Glasgow Rangers 1-1
Lee
Ashcroft; Gray, Chisholm, Bigden, Theobald, Low,
Stirling(of Clydebank), Lewis, Lee, Hastie(of Ashfield),
Neave.
Att: 2,000
Apr 29 v Greenock Morton 0-1
Att: 3,000
Apr 30 v Kilmarnock 2-1
Lee 2
Att: 2,000

1908-09
Oct 7 v Rest of Kent (a) 3-0
Greenaway 2, Hoare
Oct 22 v Ryde (Isle of Wight) 2-0
C.Satterthwaite 2
Mar 10 v Hastings (a) 3-1
Fitchie, Hoare, Beney
Att: 3,000
Apr 9 v Exeter City (h) 2-3
Beney, Raybould

1909-10
Sep 22 v Rest of Kent (a) 3-2
Lawrence, Neave, D.Wood
Att: 1,000
Oct 28 v Barnsley (a) 2-3
Thomson, Lewis
Att: 1,000
Feb 19 v Fulham (h) 2-2
Lewis, Beney
Mar 5 v Millwall (a) 3-3
McKellar, Beney, Greenaway
Att: 3,000
Apr 28 v Colchester (a) 3-2
Greenaway, Lewis 2
Apr 30 v Ilford (a) 2-3
Lewis, Beney

1910-11
No senior friendly matches played

1911-12
Mar 30 v West Ham United (h) 3-0
Common, McLaughlan 2
Att: 2,000
Apr 20 v Glasgow Rangers (a) 0-0
Crawford; Shaw, Peart, Grant, Thomson, McKinnon,
Greenaway, Common, E.Hanks, Flanagan, Lewis.
Att: 8,000

1912-13
No senior friendly matches played

1913-14
Sep 11 v Queen's Park Rangers (a) 2-0
Bell, Graham (pen)
Jan 31 v Everton (h) 1-2
Hardinge
Att: 10,000

1914-15
Dec 19 v Swindon Town (h) 1-2
Thompson
Att: 2,000

1919-20
Apr 2 v Bolton Wanderers (a) 2-4
Hardinge 2
Att: 14,700
Apr 12 v Clapton Orient (a) 1-5
Whittaker

1920-21
Sep 27 v Clapton Orient (a) 1-2
Groves
Mar 5 v Nottingham Forest (h) 2-1
Hopkins, White
Att: 10,000
May 4 v Wigan (a) 1-2
Burgess

399

1921-22
Sep 21 v Gillingham (a) 2-3
Graham (pen), Baker
Att: 6,000

1922-23
Oct 16 v Southampton (a) 5-3
Rutherford 2, White 2, Hopkins
Att: 3,982
Feb 24 v Athenian League (a) 11-1
White 7, Creegan 2, Sissons 2

1923-24
No senior friendly matches played

1924-25
Oct 9 v Clapton Orient (a) 2-2
Blyth 2
Jan 31 v Chelsea (h) 0-1
Apr 20 v Luton Town (h) 4-1
Hughes 3, Ramsay

1925-26
Oct 14 v Lincoln City (a) 0-3
Att: 4,000
Apr 26 v Hibernian (h) 5-0
Ramsay, Brain 2, Hulme, Buchan
Lewis; Mackie, John, Milne, Seddon, Young, Hoar,
Buchan, Brain, Ramsay, Hulme.

1926-27
Oct 11 v Clapton Orient (a) 4-0
Buchan, Shaw, Parker (pen), Haden

1927-28
Sep 21 v Corinthians (h) 0-4
Att: 4,500

1928-29
Oct 24 v Corinthians (at Aldershot) 4-1
Thompson 3, Parkin
Nov 14 v Nottingham Forest (h) 0-1

1929-30
Sep 19 v Nottingham Forest (h) 4-0
Bastin 2, Peel, Lambert
Att: 3,340

1930-31
See *Arsenal Overseas*

1931-32
May 4 v Plymouth Argyle (a) 2-1
Parkin 2

1932-33
Sep 26 v St Johnstone (at Perth) 0-0
Att: 15,000
Nov 30 v Racing Club de Paris (h) 3-0
Stockill 2, Hulme
Moss; Male, Hapgood, Hill, Haynes, Sidey, Hulme,
Parkin, Lambert, Stockill, Bastin.
May 3 v Cliftonville (Belfast) (a) 4-0
Bowden, Parkin 3

1933-34
Sep 20 v Glasgow Rangers (a) 0-2
Moss; L.Compton, Hapgood, Hill, Roberts, John,
Jack, Bowden, Coleman, James, Bastin.
Att: 37,000

Sep 27 v Glasgow Rangers (h) 1-3
Lambert
Moss; Male, Hapgood, Hill, Roberts, John, Birkett,
Bowden, Lambert, James, Bastin.
Att: 45,000
Dec 4 v Vienna XI (h) 4-2
Bastin 2, Hulme, Jack
Moss; Male, Hapgood, C.Jones, Sidey, John, Hulme,
Jack, Coleman, James, Bastin.

1934-35
Sep 12 v Glasgow Rangers (h) 1-1
Bastin
Moss; Male, Hapgood, Crayston, Sidey, Copping,
Hulme, Marshall, Dunne, Dougall, Bastin.
Att: 53,000
Sep 24 v St Johnstone (a) 3-0
Drake 2, Bastin
Att: 12,000

1935-36
Sep 25 v Glasgow Rangers (a) 2-2
Davidson, Dunne
Wilson; L.Compton, Hapgood, Hill, Joy, John, Milne,
Davidson, Dunne, Bastin, Beasley.
Att: 25,000

1936-37
Sep 23 v Glasgow Rangers (h) 2-1
Davidson, Drake
Swindin; Male, L.Compton, Crayston, Joy, Copping,
Milne, Davidson, Drake, Bastin, D.Compton.
Att: 35,000

1937-38
May 2 v Southampton (a) 3-2
Bremner 2, Drury

1938-39
Aug 29 v Glasgow Rangers (a) 0-1
Swindin; Male, L.Compton, L.Jones, Joy, Collett,
B.Jones, Bremner, Carr, Drury, Cumner.
Sep 21 v Swiss Wanderers (h) 3-2
Drake 2, Kirchen

1946-47
Oct 2 v Sparta (Prague) (h) 2-2
Male, Senecky (og)
Swindin; Scott, Joy, Male, L.Compton, Logie,
McPherson, Gudmundsson, O'Flanagan, Curtis,
Nelson.
Jan 25 v Tottenham Hotspur (a) 0-2
Att: 27,000
Mar 29 v Leicester City (h) 3-1
Logie, Lewis, Rooke

1947-48
Jan 24 v Nottingham Forest (a) 3-2
Lewis 2, Roper
Att: 25,479
Apr 28 v Colchester United (h) 3-0
Rooke 2, Roper
Att: 35,000

1948-49
Sep 29 v Bexhill Town (a) 8-1
Lewis 4, Logie, McPherson, Lishman, Forbes
Oct 17 v Bohemians (Dublin) (a) 6-0
Rooke 3, Roper 2, McPherson
Att: 27,000

400

Feb 12 v Swindon Town (a) 4-1
Lishman 2, Lewis, McPherson
Att: 23,000

1949-50
Sep 28 v Portsmouth (at Brighton) 1-2
Roper
Att: 12,000
Dec 8 v AIK (Solna, Sweden) (h) 8-0
Lewis 4, Goring, McPherson, Roper, Forbes (pen)
Platt; Scott, L.Smith, Forbes, L.Compton, Shaw,
McPherson, Logie, Goring, Lewis, Roper.
Att: 24,000
May 1 v Hendon Town (a) 2-1 (Will Mather Cup)
Lishman, Opponent (og)
May 17 v Bohemians Select (Dublin) 5-2
Lishman 3, Goring 2
Att: 28,000
May 19 v Glentoran (Belfast) 4-2
Goring 3, Lishman

1950-51
See *Arsenal Overseas*

1951-52
Sep 3 v Horsham (a) 4-2
Milton 3, Roper
Sep 19 v Hapoel Tel-Aviv (h) 6-1
Holton 3, Lewis 2, Milton
Swindin; Barnes, L.Smith, Forbes, Daniel, Bowen,
Milton, Logie, Holton, Lishman(Lewis), Cox(Roper).
Att: 44,385
Oct 17 v Glasgow Rangers (h) 3-2
Lishman 2, Barnes (pen)
Swindin; Barnes, L.Smith, Forbes, Daniel, Mercer,
Milton, Logie, Holton, Lishman, Roper.
Att: 62,012

1952-53
Sep 29 v All Stars (at Brighton) 2-4
(Alex Wilson Benefit)
Lishman, Logie (pen)
Oct 22 v Hibernian (h) 7-1
Roper 5, Lishman 2
Kelsey, Wade, L.Smith, Forbes, Daniel, Mercer,
Milton, Logie, Goring, Lishman, Roper.
Att: 55,001
May 4 v Tottenham Hotspur (h) 0-2
**(Lord Mayor of London's National Flood Disaster
Fund)**

1953-54
Sep 23 v South Africa (h) 2-2
Lishman, Holton
Att: 19,482
Oct 1 v Preston North End (h) 2-1
Roper 2
Att: 25,039
Oct 5 v Queen's Park Rangers (a) 3-1
Oakes 2, Roper
Att: 16,028
Oct 21 v Anderlecht (Belgium) (h) 2-3
Roper, Logie
Dec 8 v Glasgow Rangers (a) 2-1
Roper, Holton
Kelsey; Wills, L.Smith, Forbes, Dodgin, Mercer,
Milton, Logie, Holton, Lawton, Roper.
Att: 75,000
Feb 20 v Portuguesa de Desportos (Brazil) (h) 7-1
Holton 5, Walsh, Lishman
Kelsey; Wills, Barnes, Forbes, Dodgin, Dickson,
Walsh, Logie, Holton, Lishman, Roper.
Att: 44,491

Mar 23 v Hull City (a) 3-1
Roper 2, Lawton
Att: 27,000
Mar 30 v Bristol City (a) 1-3
Wills
Att: 28,991
Apr 27 v Racing Club de Paris (h) 4-0
Holton 2, Roper, Tapscott
Kelsey; Barnes, Wade, Goring, Dickson, Bowen,
Clapton(Milton), Tapscott, Holton, Lishman, Roper.
Att: 19,822

1954-55
Sep 21 v Grasshopper Zürich (h) 4-5
Herd 2, Lishman 2
Att: 20,000
Oct 26 v Maccabi Tel-Aviv (h) 4-1
Holton 3, Tapscott
Att: 13,058
Nov 9 v Spartak Moscow (USSR) (h) 1-2
Logie
Kelsey; Barnes, Wade, Goring, Fotheringham, Forbes,
Milton, Logie, Holton, Lishman, Roper.
Att: 65,838
Mar 2 v Tottenham Hotspur (a) 4-1
Roper, Tapscott 2, Marden
Att: 14,000
Mar 15 v Glasgow Rangers (h) 3-3
Lawton, Goring, Evans (pen)
Kelsey; Barnes, Evans, Goring, Fotheringham, Forbes,
Clapton, Lishman, Lawton, Bloomfield, Marden
(Bennett).
Att: 28,123
Mar 21 v Hibernian (a) 2-2
Lishman, Bloomfield
Att: 24,000
May 2 v Hendon (a) 3-2 (Will Mather Cup)
Clapton, Roper, Marden

1955-56
Sep 13 v England Amateur XI (h) 2-1
D.Flanagan, Roper
Att: 4,420
Sep 20 v Clyde (h) 1-2
D.Flanagan
Att: 16,241
Oct 4 v Brentford (a) 3-2
Roper 2, Nutt
Att: 11,300
Nov 7 v Leeds United (a) 3-0
Tapscott 2, Lishman
Att: 19,000
Nov 21 v Glasgow Rangers (a) 0-2
Sullivan; Wills(Charlton), Evans, Goring, Fother-
ingham, Holton, Clapton, Bloomfield, Lawton, Roper,
Tiddy.
Att: 40,000
Apr 25 v Nottingham Forest (a) 1-1
Herd
Att: 7,650

1956-57
Sep 25 v Leyton Orient (h) 4-0
Tapscott 2, Tiddy, Charlton
Att: 14,441
Oct 16 v CCA Bucharest (h) 1-1
Holton
Kelsey; Charlton, Evans, Goring, Dodgin, Bowen,
Clapton, Tapscott, Holton, Bloomfield, Haverty
Att: 20,773

401

Nov 5 v British Olympic XI (h) 3-2
Tapscott 2, Holton
Att: 4,154
Apr 24 v Hereford Town (a) 4-0
Tapscott 2, Herd 2
Att: 6,923
Apr 29 v Hendon (a) 2-2
Swallow, Clapton

1957-58
Sep 24 v Hapoel Tel-Aviv 10-2
Holton 2, Clapton 2, Bloomfield 2, Herd, Tiddy, Groves 2
Att: 8,754
Jan 25 v Swansea Town (a) 3-2
Herd, Tapscott 2
Att: 16,000
Feb 15 v Eintracht Frankfurt (h) 1-0
Groves
Att: 18,110
Feb 15 v Barnsley (a) 6-0
Tapscott 2, Herd 2, Barnwell 2
Att: 8,424
Apr 30 v Hendon (a) 4-1
Swallow 3, Biggs

1958-59
Nov 10 v Southampton (a) 1-1
Henderson
Att: 11,853
Nov 26 v Juventus (Italy) (h) 3-1
Barnwell, Goulden, Bloomfield
Kelsey; Wills, Evans, Docherty, Dodgin, Petts, Nutt (Clapton), Barnwell, Henderson (Goulden), Bloomfield, Haverty.
Att: 51,107
Dec 1 v Reading (a) 3-0
Nutt, Henderson, Haverty
Att: 8,034
Apr 21 v Glasgow Rangers (h) 0-3
Standen; Evans, McCullough, Ward, Dodgin, Docherty, D.R.Clapton, Groves, Charles, Barnwell, Haverty.
Att: 34,503
Apr 30 v Bath City (a) 3-4
Docherty, Julians, Henderson
May 8 v Bristol XI (a) 4-5
Clapton, Groves 2, Henderson

1959-60
Oct 13 v Grasshopper Zürich (h) 8-2
Julians 5, Barnwell 2, Opponent (og)
Standen; Wills, McCullough, Docherty, Snedden, Groves, Henderson, Bloomfield, Julians, Barnwell, Nutt.
Att: 18,006
Nov 4 v Aberdeen (a) 2-1
Henderson, Bloomfield
Att: 10,000
Jan 25 v Great Britain Olympic XI (h) 4-0
Barnwell 2, Julians, Nutt
Jan 29 v West Ham United (h) 0-1
Att: 11,538
Feb 8 v Peterborough United (a) 1-1
Bloomfield
Att: 17,665
Feb 16 v Ipswich Town (a) 0-4
Att: 15,835
Mar 12 v Leyton Orient (h) 0-2
Att: 18,059

1960-61
Oct 10 v Northampton Town (a) 3-2
Barnwell, Docherty, Herd
Att: 9,702
Oct 19 v Norwich City (a) 2-3
Henderson, Herd
Dec 13 v Glasgow Rangers (a) 2-4
Herd, Henderson
Kelsey; Wills, McCullough, Docherty, Snedden, Groves, Clapton, Barnwell, Herd, Eastham, Henderson.
Jan 28 v Charlton Athletic (a) 2-4
Eastham, Henderson
Att: 14,196
Feb 21 v Wiener Sport-Club (h) 1-0
Eastham
McClelland; Bacuzzi, McCullough, Neill, Charles, Groves, Skirton, Barnwell, Herd, Eastham, Haverty.
Att: 12,389

1961-62
Aug 5 v Middlesbrough (a) 1-2
Griffiths
Att: 8,865
Aug 11 v Ipswich Town (h) 3-3
Barnwell, Skirton, Eastham
Att: 6,166
Sep 6 v Stamford FC (a) 9-0
Henderson 3, Armstrong 2, Eastham, Skirton 2, Brown
Nov 20 v Dinamo Kiev (USSR) (h) 1-1
Eastham
Kelsey; Bacuzzi, McCullough, Clamp, Brown, Groves, MacLeod, Eastham, Strong, Henderson, Skirton.
Att: 17,599
Feb 17 v Dundee (h) 2-2
Eastham (pen), Skirton
Att: 16,341
Mar 7 v Bohemians (Dublin) 8-3
Eastham 3, Skirton 3, Kinsella, Strong
Att: 12,000
Mar 10 v Dundee (a) 1-0
Strong
Att: 10,000

1962-63
Aug 8 v Bristol Select XI (a) 2-1
Barnwell 2
Sep 13 v Real Madrid (Spain) (h) 0-4
McKechnie; Magill, McCullough, Neill, Brown, Snedden, MacLeod, Court, Baker, Barnwell, Skirton.
Att: 32,574
Oct 2 v Barnet (a) 5-2
Court 2, Skirton 2, MacLeod
Att: 5,113
Jan 23 v Brighton & HA (a) 1-2
Strong
Jan 26 v Tottenham Hotspur (a) 1-3
Strong
Att: 19,893
May 20 v Glasgow Rangers (h) 2-2 (Jack Kelsey Testimonial)
Skirton 2
McKechnie; Magill, McCullough, Barnwell, Brown, Groves, MacLeod, Court, Baker, Eastham, Skirton.
Att: 33,007

1963-64
Apr 14 v Watford (a) 0-1
Apr 22 v Dublin Select (a) 2-0
MacLeod, Skirton
Att: 25,000

402

1964-65
Aug 15 v Portsmouth (a) 5-1
Armstrong, Strong 2, Baker, Eastham
Oct 27 v Kettering Town (a) 6-2
Radford 3, Sammels, McLintock, Armstrong
Nov 2 v Dundee (a) 7-2
Sammels 2, Eastham, McLintock, Radford, Anderson,
Armstrong
Att: 12,000
Dec 2 v Exeter City (a) 4-1
McLintock 3, Skirton
Att: 11,507
Dec 16 v Bath City (a) 4-2
Eastham 2, Skirton, Sammels

1965-66
Oct 26 v Bournemouth & BA (a) 6-2
Radford 3, Baker 2, Howe
Nov 16 v Brazil XI (h) 2-0
Sammels 2
Burns (Furnell); Howe, Storey, McLintock, Neill,
Court, Skirton, Sammels, Baker, Eastham, Armstrong.
Att: 17,789
Nov 30 v Dinamo Moscow (USSR) (h) 3-0
Skirton, Radford, Storey
Burns; Howe, Storey, McLintock, Neill, Court,
Skirton, Radford, Baldwin, Eastham, Armstrong.
Att: 21,912
Feb 12 v Southampton (a) 3-1
Skirton, Radford, McLintock
Att: 12,292
Mar 29 v Ipswich Town (a) 2-3
Skirton, Radford
Att: 7,614
May 3 v Swansea Town (a) 3-1
Skirton, Baldwin, Armstrong
May 10 v Torquay/Plymouth XI (a) 4-5
Eastham, Radford 3

1966-67
Aug 6 v Glasgow Rangers (a) 0-2
Att: 40,000
Aug 8 v Dunfermline (a) 0-0
Att: 8,000
Aug 13 v Huddersfield Town (a) 1-0
Sammels
Nov 15 v Cardiff City (h) 4-2 (Aberfan Disaster Fund)
Radford 2, Addison, McLintock
Att: 4,543
Apr 7 v Charlton Athlteic (a) 0-0
Att: 7,821
Apr 14 v Dunfermline (h) 2-1
Neill (pen), McNab
Att: 7,755
May 3 v Apoel FC (Cyprus) 1-1
Sammels
Att: 8,480
May 15 v Romford (a) 3-1
Addison 2, Johnston

1967-68
Aug 5 v Glasgow Rangers (h) 3-0
Sammels 2, Armstrong
Furnell; Simpson, Storey, McLintock, Neill, Ure,
Johnston(Jenkins), Court, Graham, Sammels,
Armstrong.
Att: 34,586
Aug 9 v Maccabi Select (Israel) 1-0
Johnston
Nov 21 v Portsmouth (a) 0-2

1968-69
Aug 3 v Glasgow Rangers (a) 2-2
Jenkins, Johnston
Att: 40,000
May 8 v Watford (a) 2-1
George 2

1969-70
Aug 2 v Swindon Town (h) 3-0
Robertson, Radford, Gould
Att: 21,498
May 5 v Folkestone (a) 4-0
Kennedy 2, Rice, Graham

1970-71
Aug 7 v Crystal Palace (a) 2-0
Radford 2

1971-72
Aug 4 v Benfica (Portugal) (h) 6-2
Graham 2, Roberts, Armstrong, Radford, Storey (pen)
Wilson(Barnett); Storey, Nelson(McNab), Kelly,
McLintock, Roberts(George), Armstrong(Marinello),
Graham, Radford, Kennedy, Simpson.
Att: 44,135

1972-73
Oct 17 v Plymouth Argyle (a) 1-1 (W.Harper
Kennedy   **Testimonial)**
Att: 18,093

1973-74
Aug 20 v Glasgow Rangers (a) 2-1
George, Radford
Wilson; Rice, McNab, Storey, Blockley, Simpson,
George, Ball, Radford, Kennedy, Price.
Att: 65,000
Nov 5 v Portsmouth (a) 1-2
Radford
Att: 8,859
Mar 12 v Barcelona (h) 1-3 (G.Armstrong Testimonial)
Ball (pen)
Wilson(Barnett); Rice, McNab, Storey, Simpson,
Nelson, Ball, Brady, Chambers(Price), Kennedy,
Armstrong.
Att: 36,099
May 6 v Kettering Town (a) 3-0
George, Hornsby, Radford
Att: 6,270

1974-75
Jul 31 v Cardiff City (a) 2-1 (F.Keenor Testimonial)
Kidd, Rice
Oct 2 v Reading (a) 2-0 (F.May Testimonial)
Kidd, Radford
Att: 6,987
Nov 6 v Chelsea (a) 1-1 (J.Hollins Testimonial)
Radford
Rimmer; Rice(Powling), McNab, Kelly, Mancini,
Simpson, Storey, Ball, George, Brady(Radford),
Kidd(Armstrong).

1975-76
Jul 30 v Heart of Midlothian (a) 2-0
Hornsby, Mancini
Att: 12,000
Aug 2 v Dundee (a) 1-2
Cropley
Att: 6,950
Aug 4 v Aberdeen (a) 1-0
Brady
Att: 10,500

403

Aug 9 v Crewe Alexandra (a) 3-1
Kidd 3
Att: 2,644
Oct 22 v Tottenham Hotspur (a) 2-2 (C.Knowles
Testimonial)
Nelson, Kidd
Att: 17,346
Oct 28 v Charlton Athletic (a) 4-1
Ball, Kidd, Stapleton, Hornsby
Dec 9 v Feyenoord (Holland) (h) 2-1 (P.Storey
Testimonial)
Ball (pen), Brady
Parker; Rice, Nelson(Simpson), Storey, Mancini,
Powling, Armstrong(Rostron), Ball, Radford, Kidd
(Stapleton), Brady.
Att: 18,813

1976-77
Oct 9 v Tottenham Hotspur (h) 1-2 (P.Simpson
Testimonial)
Macdonald
Rimmer(Parker); Storey, Radford(Rostron),
Matthews, O'Leary(Howard), Simpson, Ball, Brady,
Macdonald, Stapleton, Armstrong(Gatting).
Att: 19,456
Nov 23 v Tottenham Hotspur (a) 2-3 (P.Jennings
Testimonial)
Nelson, Macdonald
Att: 28,582
Mar 26 v Chelsea (a) 0-3
Att: 4,495
May 10 v Hajduk Split (Yugoslavia) (h) 5-0 (J.Radford
Testimonial)
Stapleton 3, George, Ross
Wilson(Rimmer); Rice, Nelson, McLintock
(Matthews), O'Leary, George(Ross), Brady, Hudson
(Rix), Radford, Stapleton(Macdonald), Armstrong.
Att: 14,152

1977-78
Aug 8 v Aldershot (a) 1-0
Stapleton
Aug 12 v Luton Town (a) 1-1
Ross
Sep 20 v Northampton Town (a) 3-2
Ross 2, Rix
Att: 3,558
Nov 22 v Tottenham Hotspur(h) 1-3 (P.Rice Testimonial)
Stapleton
Jennings; Rice, Nelson, Walford(Simpson), O'Leary,
Young, Brady, Sunderland(Heeley), Macdonald,
Stapleton, Rix.
Att: 17,154
May 12 v Tottenham Hotspur(a) 5-3 (J.Pratt Testimonial)
Fuccillo (Luton) 3, Radford, Sunderland
Att: 23,044

1978-79
Aug 8 v Glasgow Celtic (a) 3-0
Stapleton, Lynch (og), MacDonald (og)
Jennings; Rice, Nelson, O'Leary, Young, Brady,
Sunderland, Macdonald(Kosmina), Stapleton
(Walford), Rix.
Aug 12 v Crystal Palace (h) 1-1
Stapleton
Att: 11,494

1979-80
Sep 11 v Fulham (a) 2-2 (Ted Drake Testimonial)
Vaessen, Gatting
Jennings(Barron); Rice, Nelson, Talbot(Davis),

Hollins, Young, Heeley(McDermott), Sunderland,
Vaessen, Price, Gatting.
Att: 3,350

1980-81
Aug 1 v Glasgow Rangers (a) 0-2
Att: 27,000
Aug 3 v Aberdeen (a) 1-2
Stapleton
Nov 25 v Glasgow Celtic (h) 0-0 (S.Nelson Testimonial)
Jennings; Devine(Price), Nelson(Davis), Talbot,
Whyte, Walford, McDermott(Vaessen), Sunderland,
Stapleton(Meade), Gatting, Rix.
Att: 20,149
Jan 27 v 1.FC Cologne (h) 1-0
O'Leary
Jennings; Hollins, Sansom, Talbot, O'Leary(Walford),
Young, McDermott, Sunderland, Stapleton, Gatting,
Rix.
Att: 10,540
Feb 15 v St Mirren (a) 3-2
O'Leary, Stapleton, Davis
Att: 10,000
Mar 17 v Orient (a) 1-0
Young
Att: 3,623
Apr 8 v Kent County FA XI (at Gillingham) 2-2
Sunderland 2
Att: 3,778

1981-82
Aug 22 v Portsmouth (a) 1-0
P.Nicholas
Att: 6,706
Dec 29 v Glentoran (a) 2-0
Davis 2
Att: 7,000

1982-83
Aug 20 v Chelsea (a) 3-1
Talbot 2, Chapman
Att: 8,261
Oct 11 v Barnet (a) 3-0
Chapman, Sunderland, Lee
Att: 804
Nov 1 v Barnet (a) 4-2 (R.Powling Testimonial)
Talbot 3, Kay
Att: 1,504
May 17 v Gillingham (a) 3-1
McDermott 2, Sunderland

1983-84
Aug 13 v Aberdeen (a) 1-0 (Boys Brigade Centenary
Talbot **Match)**
Jennings; Robson, Sansom, Talbot, Whyte, Hill,
McDermott, Davis, Woodcock, C.Nicholas, Rix.
Aug 20 v Portsmouth (a) 1-2
C.Nicholas
Att: 9,125
Oct 18 v Aldershot (a) 3-3
Sunderland, Chapman, C.Nicholas
Nov 1 v Chelsea (a) 1-2 (M.Droy Testimonial)
C.Nicholas
Att: 7,555
Mar 20 v Windsor & Eton (a) 3-0
Woodcock 2, McDermott
Apr 15 v Heart of Midlothian (a) 2-3
Mariner 2
Att: 10,500
May 16 v Charlton Athletic (a) 4-3
Davis 2, Meade, Talbot

404

1984-85
Aug 4 v Glasgow Celtic (a) 2-3
Meade, Nicholas
Att: 23,000
Aug 17 v Brighton & HA (a) 1-1
Allinson
Nov 27 v Australian National Team (h) 3-2
Allinson 2, Meade
Lukic; Anderson, Sansom, Talbot, Whyte, Caton,
Cork(Meade), Allinson, Mariner, Woodcock(Hayes),
Nicholas.
Att: 4,090
May 8 v Tottenham Hotspur (h) 2-3 (P.Jennings
Testimonial)
Brady, Hayes
Jennings(Still); Anderson(Hill), Sansom, Talbot,
Mariner, Brady, Williams, Allinson(Hayes),
Woodcock, Rix, Nicholas.
Att: 25,252

1985-86
Jul 30 v Windsor & Eton (a) 1-0
Woodcock
Aug 2 v Brighton & HA (a) 2-1
Robson, Mariner
Aug 4 v Tottenham Hotspur (a) 1-1 (G.Hoddle
Testimonial)
Robson
Lukic; Anderson, Sansom, Williams, O'Leary, Caton,
Allinson, Robson, Mariner(Nicholas), Woodcock,
Rix.
Aug 7 v Reading (a) 3-0
Rix, Robson, Woodcock
Att: 2,261
Aug 10 v Portsmouth (a) 1-0
Allinson
Dec 9 v Colchester United (a) 2-1
Allinson, Woodcock
Feb 25 v Shamrock Rovers (a) 0-1
Att: 8,000

1986-87
Aug 5 v Glasgow Celtic (h) 0-2 (D.O'Leary Testimonial)
Lukic; Anderson, Sansom, Robson, O'Leary, Adams
(Caton), Rocastle, Davis(Williams), Quinn(Allinson),
Nicholas, Rix.
Att: 29,376
Aug 10 v Shamrock Rovers (a) 2-0
Davis, Rix
Aug 13 v Waterford (a) 1-1
Allinson
Aug 15 v Southend United (a) 1-0
Allinson

1987-88
Jul 21 v Gloucester City (a) 6-0
Hayes 3, Adams, Smith, Nicholas
Att: 3,170
Jul 25 v Morton (a) 1-0
Groves
Att: 4,000
Jul 28 v Ayr United (a) 6-0
Smith 3, Davis, Quinn, Nicholas
Aug 1 v Glasgow Celtic (a) 5-1
Sansom, Nicholas, Hayes 2, Groves
Att: 26,195
Aug 5 v Brighton & HA (a) 7-2
Nicholas 3, Hayes 2, Adams, Smith
Att: 4,314
Aug 10 v Tottenham Hotspur (a) 1-3
Adams   *Att: 17,826*

Sep 5 v Derry City (a) 2-0
Smith, Merson
Att: 8,500
Oct 20 v Barnet (a) 2-2
Merson 2
Att: 5,000
May 11 v Millwall (a) 2-2
Hayes, Smith

1988-89
Jul 23 v Yeovil Town (a) 5-0 (Alan Skirton Testimonial)
Davis, Marwood, Merson, Hayes, Richardson
Att: 5,480
Aug 16 v Birmingham City (a) 4-0
Marwood 2, Merson, Smith
Att: 2,200
Aug 19 v Leicester City (a) 4-1
Thomas, Adams, Smith, Opponent (og)
Dec 13 v Shrewsbury Town (a) 2-1 (Bernard McNally
Testimonial)
Davis, Ampadu
Att: 3,612
Feb 14 v France (h) 2-0
Hayes, Smith
Lukic; Dixon, Winterburn, Thomas, O'Leary(Bould),
Adams, Rocastle(Groves), Richardson, Smith(Quinn),
Merson, Marwood(Hayes).
Att: 21,785

1989-90
Aug 30 v Bohemians (Dublin) 2-1
Richardson, Campbell
Att: 8,000
Dec 19 v Glasgow Rangers (a) 2-1 (Zenith Data Systems
British Challenge)
Davis, Quinn
Lukic; Dixon, Winterburn, Davis, O'Leary(Caesar),
Adams, Rocastle(Hayes), Richardson, Quinn, Merson,
Marwood(Groves).
Att: 31,118
Feb 21 v Southend United (a) 4-2 (Paul Clark
Testimonial)
Davis, Campbell, Merson, Connelly
Att: 5,548

1990-91
Aug 3 v Wolverhampton Wanderers (a) 1-0
Smith
Att: 10,000
Aug 17 v Brighton & HA (a) 2-2 (Steve Gatting
Testimonial)
Rocastle, Smith
Oct 13 v Tottenham Hotspur (h) 2-5 (Graham Rix
Testimonial)
Smith, Merson
Att: 14,806
Apr 27 v Liverpool (h) 1-3 (Ray Kennedy Testimonial)
Campbell
Leighton(Man Utd); Thomas, Winterburn(Lee), Hillier
(Rice), Linighan, Adams, Rocastle, Davis(McKernon),
Campbell(Sammels), Groves(Lewin), Limpar
(Armstrong).
Att: 18,224
May 18 v Barnet (a) 4-2
Groves, Adams, Merson, Campbell
Att: 7,724

1991-92
Jul 26 v Plymouth Argyle (a) 2-0 (Graham Little
Testimonial)
Campbell, Smith

Jul 30 v Glasgow Celtic (h) 2-2 (Paul Davis Testimonial)
Smith, Dixon
Seaman; Dixon, Winterburn, Hillier, Bould, Adams, Campbell, Davis(Thomas), Smith, Merson, Limpar (Rocastle).
Att: 28,639
Aug 7 v Watford (a) 3-1 (Watford Centenary Celebration)
Campbell, Dixon, Ashby (og)
Att: 10,108

Feb 29 v Barnet (a) 6-0 (Barry Fry Testimonial)
Campbell 2, Limpar, Parlour, Wright, Smith
Att: 4,484
Mar 5 v Shelbourne (Dublin) 1-1
Smith
Att: 6,000

Arsenal players line up before the start of their friendly match against Racing Club de Paris in the French capital in 1946.

Opposite: German newspaper advertisement for the visit of Woolwich Arsenal in May 1912.

Arsenal Overseas

For the purpose of this section, Ireland and Northern Ireland have not been considered as 'overseas' and the record of matches against teams in these countries can be found in the section on friendly matches.

1906-07
May 5 v Belgian XI (Brussels) 2-1
Garbutt, Kyle
Bateup; Cross, Dick, Bigden, Theobald, McEachrane, Garbutt, Coleman, Kyle, Satterthwaite, Mordue.
Att: 4,000
May 7 v The Hague (Holland) 6-3
Scorers and team not known
May 9 v Preussen (Berlin) 9-1
Freeman 5, Satterthwaite 2, Bateup (pen), Mordue
Ashcroft; Cross, Dick, Bateup, Bigden, Theobald, Coleman, Kyle, Freeman, Satterthwaite, Mordue.
May 12 v SK Slavia IPS (Czechoslovakia) 7-5
Coleman 4, plus 3 others
Team not known
May 16 v SK Slavia IPS (Czechoslovakia) 4-2
Coleman 2, Satterthwaite, plus 1 other
Team not known
May 18 v Vienna (Austria) 4-2
Scorers and team not known
May 19 v Budapest (Hungary) 9-0
Scorers not known
Bateup; Cross, Dick, Bigden, Theobald, McEachrane, Freeman, Coleman, Kyle, Satterthwaite, Mordue.
May 20 v Budapest (Hungary) 2-2
Scorers and team not known

1911-12
May 11 v Hertha BSC (Berlin) 5-0
Calder 2, Flanagan, Graham 2
Crawford; Shaw, Peart, Grant, Thomson, McKinnon, Lewis, Flanagan, Calder, Graham, Winship.
Att: 2,500
May 12 v Viktoria 89 (Berlin) 2-2
Winship, plus one other
Crawford; Rogers, Peart, Grant, Thomson, McKinnon, Greenaway, Calder, McLaughlin, Flanagan, Winship.
Att: 5,000
May 16 v Deutscher FC (Prague) 4-1
Opponent own-goal – other scorers not known
May 19 v Ferencvárosi Torna (Budapest) 2-1
Scorers not known
Att: 23,000
May 22 v Grazer AK (Austria) 6-0
Scorers not known
Att: 2,000
May 24 v Tottenham Hotspur (in Vienna) 4-0
Calder 3, Winship
May 26 v Rapid Vienna (Austria) 8-2
Winship, plus 4 others
May 27 v Wiener Sport-Club (Austria) 5-0
Calder 3, Lewis, Shaw
May 29 v Sp Vgg Fürth (Germany) 6-0
McLaughlan 4, Lewis, Winship
Att: 3,000
Tour Goalscorers: Calder 9, Winship 9, McLaughlan 8, Flanagan 4, Graham 3, Lewis 2, Shaw, Grant, Peart (pen), Thomson, Greenaway, McKinnon, Opponent own-goal.

1921-22
May 14 v IFK Gothenburg (Sweden) 3-2
Hutchins, Hopkins, Turnbull
Williamson; Bradshaw, Hutchins, Milne, Butler, Whittaker, Creegan, Townrow, Turnbull, Hopkins, Blyth.
Att: 11,000

May 16 v GAIS (Gothenburg) 4-1
Voysey 2, Bradshaw, Baker
Williamson; Turnbull, Hutchins, Milne, Voysey, Whittaker, Creegan, Bradshaw, Young, Baker, Blyth.
Att: 7,000
May 19 v Örgryte IS (Gothenburg) 2-0
Baker 2
Att: 7,033
May 21 v Helsingborgs IF (Sweden) 1-0
Baker
Att: 3,500

1922-23
May 10 v BK Frem (Copenhagen) 4-2
Turnbull 4
Dunn; Mackie, Kennedy, Baker, Butler, John, Moffat, Cockle, Turnbull, Haden, Blyth.
Att: 10,000
May 12 v B 93 Copenhagen 1-0
Turnbull
Dunn; Mackie, Kennedy, Baker, Butler, John, Moffat, Cockle, Turnbull, Haden, Blyth.
Att: 9,724
May 13 v Danish XI (Copenhagen) 2-1
Turnbull, Haden
Dunn; Mackie, Kennedy, Baker, Butler, John, Moffat, Cockle, Turnbull, Haden, Blyth.
Att: 14,000
May 16 v Gothenburg Alliance 3-2
Moffat, Blyth, Turnbull
Dunn; Mackie, Collin, Milne, Butler, John, Moffat, Blyth, Turnbull, Cockle, Haden.
Att: 9,000
May 18 v Combined XI (Gothenburg) 2-1
Turnbull, Moffat
Dunn; Mackie, Collin, Milne, Butler, John, Moffat, Blyth, Turnbull, Cockle, Haden.
May 23 v SFK Lyn (Norway) 0-0
Dunn; Mackie, Shaw, Whittaker, Butler, John, Moffatt, Voysey, Turnbull, Haden, Blyth.
Att: 12,000
May 25 v Norwegian XI (Christiana) 9-2
Turnbull 6, Blyth 2, Haden
Dunn; Mackie, Collin, Milne, Butler, John, Moffat, Blyth, Turnbull, Haden, Voysey.
Att: 12,000

1923-24
May 10 v TSC 99 (Düsseldorf) 6-3
Baker 2, Townrow, Collin, Turnbull, Milne
May 11 v FC Preussen (Berlin) 6-1
Scorers and team not known   *Att: 8,000*
May 14 v Hamburg XI 2-2
Scorers not known
Dunn; Baker, Kennedy, Milne, Butler, Young, Rutherford, Neil, Woods, Ramsay, Haden.
Att: 10,000
May 18 v Sp Vgg Fürth 1-0
Woods
Dunn; Baker, Kennedy, Milne, Butler, Blyth, Rutherford, Neil, Woods, Ramsay, Haden.
Att: 12,000
May 22 v Stuttgart Kickers 2-0
Woods 2
Dunn; Baker, Kennedy, Milne, Butler, Young, Rutherford, Neil, Woods, Ramsay, Blyth.
Att: 6,000

407

May 26 v Cologne Sportklub 99 9-0
Scorers and team not known

1925-26
May 13 v MTK/VM (Budapest) 2-2
Scorers and team not known
Att: 28,000
May 15 v SK Slavia IPS (Prague) 5-1
Buchan, Brain 2, Ramsay, Lee
Lewis; Parker, John, Seddon, Butler, Blyth, Hoar,
Buchan, Brain, Ramsay, Lee.
May 18 v Rapid Vienna 3-3
Seddon, Buchan, Bowen
Lewis; Kennedy, John, Milne, Seddon, Young, Lawson,
Buchan, Bowen, Brain, Lee.
Att: 11,000
May 20 v Amateure FK Austria 5-3
Parker, Butler, Buchan, Brain, Ramsay
Lewis; Parker, John, Seddon, Butler, Blyth, Hoar,
Buchan, Brain, Ramsay, Lee.
May 26 v Rapid/Amateure All Stars (Vienna) 0-1
Lewis; Parker, John, Seddon, Butler, Blyth, Hoar,
Buchan, Brain, Ramsay, Lee.
Att: 15,000
May 27 v Innsbruck Select XI 4-2
Scorers and team not known

1927-28
May 17 v Danish FA XI (Copenhagen) 3-2
Hoar, Shaw, Peel
Lewis; Parker, John, Baker, Butler, Blyth, Hulme, Shaw,
Brain, Peel, Hoar.
Att: 12,000
May 20 v Danish FA XI (Copenhagen) 1-0
Hulme
Att: 11,000
May 22 v Danish International XI 5-3
Lambert 3, Brain, Hulme
Lewis; Parker, Hapgood, Blyth, Hulme, Parkin, Brain,
Lambert, Jones.
Att: 8,000
May 25 v Helsingborgs IF (Sweden) 3-2
Hulme 2, Clark
Lewis; Parker, John, Clark, Roberts, Seddon, Hulme,
Shaw, Lambert, Peel, Hoar.
Att: 6,990
May 28 v IFK Gothenburg (Sweden) 3-1
Brain 2, Parkin
Lewis; Parker, Hapgood, Baker, Butler, Blyth, Hulme,
Parkin, Brain, Peel, John.
Att: 10,142
May 30 v Staevnet Combined XI (Copenhagen) 3-1
John, Jones, Lambert
Att: 20,000

1930-31
Nov 11 v Racing Club de Paris (France) 7-2
Lambert 4, Jack, James, Parkin
Preedy; Parker, Hapgood, Parkin, Roberts, John,
Hulme, Jack, Lambert, James, Bastin.
Att: 35,000
May 14 v Danish XI (Copenhagen) 2-0
Bastin, Jack
Harper; Parker, Hapgood, Jones, Roberts, John,
Williams, Jack, Lambert, Thompson, Bastin.
Att: 15,000
May 17 v Danish XI (Copenhagen) 5-1
Brain, Parkin, Thompson, Bastin, Havn (og)
Harper; Parker, Hapgood, Seddon, Haynes, John,
Williams, Brain, Parkin, Thompson, Bastin.
Att: 10,000

May 19 v Copenhagen Combination 1-1
Lambert
Harper; Parker, Hapgood, Seddon, Roberts, John,
Williams, Jack, Lambert, Thompson, Bastin.
Att: 20,000
May 22 v Stockholm Combined XI (Stockholm) 5-1
Bastin, Williams, Parkin 2, Sidey
Harper; Robinson, Hapgood, Seddon, Haynes, John,
Williams, Brain, Parkin, Sidey, Bastin.
Att: 6,000
May 27 v Swedish Combination XI (Stockholm) 6-1
Lambert 4, Jones, Williams
Harper; Parker, Hapgood, Seddon, Roberts, John,
Williams, Jack, Lambert, C.Jones, Bastin.
Att: 12,000
May 29 v AIK (Stockholm) 5-0
Jack 3, Brain, Lambert
Harper; Parker, Hapgood, Seddon, Roberts,
Thompson, Williams, Jack, Lambert, Brain, Bastin.
Att: 21,000
Jun 3 v Gothenburg Combination (Gothenburg) 3-2
Jack, Lambert, Bastin
Harper; Parker, Hapgood, Seddon (Roberts), John,
Williams, Jack, Lambert, Brain, Bastin.

1931-32
Nov 11 v Racing Club de Paris (France) 3-2
Male, Parkin, Jack
Preedy; Parker, Hapgood, C.Jones, Haynes, Male,
Hulme, Jack, Parkin, James, Bastin.

1932-33
Oct 31 v Racing Club de Paris (France) 5-2
Bastin 4, Lambert
Moss; Male, Hapgood, Hill, Haynes, Parkin, Hulme,
Jack, Lambert, James, Bastin.
Att: 30,000

1933-34
Nov 19 v Racing Club de Paris (France) 1-0
Bowden
Moss; Male, Hapgood, C.Jones, Sidey, John,
Hulme(Beasley), Hill, Bowden, Dougall, Bastin.
Att: 25,000

1934-35
Nov 18 v Racing Club de Paris (France) 3-0
Hill 2, Marshall
Moss; Male, L.Compton, Crayston (Bastin), Sidey,
Copping, Hulme, Marshall, Drake, John, Hill.
Att: 40,000

1935-36
Nov 11 v Racing Club de Paris (France) 2-2
Dougall, Drake
Wilson; Male, John, Crayston(L.Compton), Sidey,
Copping, Kirchen(Dunne), Davidson, Drake, Dougall,
Hill.

1936-37
Nov 1 v Racing Club de Paris (France) 5-0
Milne 3, Drake, Kirchen
Swindin; Male, Hapgood, Drake, Bastin, Sidey, Copping,
Kirchen, Bowden, Drake, Davidson, Milne.
May 25 v IFK Gothenburg (Sweden) 1-1
Milne
Boulton; L.Compton, Hapgood, Crayston, Sidey,
Copping(Cartwright), Griffiths, James, Kirchen,
Davidson, Milne.
Att: 27,398
May 28 v Copenhagen 4-1
Lewis 2, Davidson, James
Boulton; Male, Hapgood, Crayston, Sidey, Copping,
Nelson, James, Lewis, Davidson, Milne.
Att: 20,000

May 31 v Copenhagen 5-1
Lewis, Davidson, Crayston, Biggs, Nelson
Boulton; Scott, L.Compton, Crayston, Atter, Cartwright, Griffiths, Davidson, Lewis, Biggs, Nelson.
Jun 2 v Copenhagen 3-0
Lewis, Nelson, Atter
Boulton; Male, Hapgood, Crayston, Sidey, Copping, Nelson, James, Lewis(Atter), Davidson, Milne.
Att: 22,000
Jun 6 v Feyenoord (Rotterdam) 3-0
Milne, Biggs 2
Boulton; Male, Hapgood, Crayston, Sidey, Copping, Nelson, James, Biggs, Davidson, Milne.
Att: 55,000

1937-38
Nov 28 v Racing Club de Paris (France) 2-0
Hunt, Lewis
Boulton; Male, Hapgood, Collett, Joy, Cartwright, Kirchen, Hunt(Briggs), Lewis(L.Compton), L.Jones, Milne.
May 8 v Feyenoord (Rotterdam) 0-1
Swindin; Male, L.Compton, L.Jones, Joy, Copping (Collett), Crayston, Bremner, Carr, Drury, Nelson.

1938-39
Nov 27 v Racing Club de Paris (France) 1-1
Drury
Swindin; Male, Hapgood, Crayston, Joy, Copping (Collett), Kirchen, Drury, Drake(Lewis), Curtis, Bastin.
Att: 30,000
May 10 v Sweden (Stockholm) 4-0
Kirchen 2, Crayston, Drury
Marks; Scott, L.Compton, Crayston, Fields, L.Jones, Kirchen, Drury, Drake, B.Jones, Nelson.
Att: 40,000
May 12 v Swedish Combined XI (Norrköping) 8-2
Nelson 3, Drake 2, Lewis 2, L.Compton (pen)
Marks; L.Compton, Young, Cartwright, Sidey, Collett, Drake, Bremner, Lewis, Drury, Nelson.
May 16 v Gothenburg Alliance (Gothenburg) 3-0
Drake 2, Drury
Marks; Scott, L.Compton, Crayston, Fields, L.Jones, Kirchen, Drury, Drake, B.Jones, Nelson.
Att: 26,00
May 22 v Danish Combined XI (Copenhagen) 3-0
Lewis 2, Drury
Marks; Scott, L.Compton, Pryde, Fields, Collett, Drake, Drury, Lewis, B.Jones, Kirchen.
Att: 30,000
May 24 v Danish Combined XI (Copenhagen) 4-1
Lewis 3, Bremner
Marks; Cartwright, Young, Pryde, Sidey, Collett, Walsh, Bremner, Lewis, Curtis, Nelson.
Att: 4,500
May 26 v Danish Combined XI (Copenhagen) 6-0
Kirchen 2, Crayston 2, Drury, Lewis
Marks; Scott, L.Compton, Crayston, Fields, L.Jones, Kirchen, Drury, Lewis, B.Jones, Nelson.
Att: 21,000
Jun 4 v Diables Rouges (Brussels) 5-1
Nelson 2, Drury 2, Lewis
Marks; Male, L.Compton, Crayston, Fields, L.Jones, Kirchen, Drury, Lewis, B.Jones, Nelson.
Att: 25,000

1947-48
Nov 11 v Racing Club de Paris (France) 1-2
Lewis
Swindin; Joy, Wade, Sloan, L.Compton, Waller, McPherson, Gudmundsson, Lewis, Curtis, Nelson.

1947-48
Nov 11 v Racing Club de Paris (France) 3-4
Rooke 2, Compton
Swindin; Scott, Wade, Sloan(Male), L.Compton, Mercer, Roper, Lewis, Rooke, Logie, McPherson.
Att: 40,000
May 3 v Benfica (Lisbon) 4-0
Rooke 2, Roper, Forbes
Swindin; Male, Scott, Macaulay, L.Smith, Mercer, Roper, Logie, Rooke, Forbes, McPherson.
Att: 50,000
May 6 v FC Porto (Portugal) 2-3
Rooke (pen), B.Jones
Swindon; Scott, Barnes, Macaulay, L.Smith, Mercer, Roper, Logie, Lewis(Rooke), Forbes(B.Jones), McPherson.
May 11 v Liege Select (Belgium) 2-1
Logie, Rooke
Swindin; Male, Barnes, Macaulay, L.Smith, B.Jones, Roper, Logie, Rooke, Forbes, McPherson.
1948-49
Nov 1 v Racing Club de Paris (France) 3-3
Logie, Roper, Rooke
Swindin; Scott, Barnes, Macaulay, L.Smith, Mercer, Roper, Logie, Rooke, Forbes, B.Jones.
Att: 50,000
May 15 v Fluminense (in Rio de Janeiro) 5-1
Lishman 4, Roper
Swindin; Barnes, L.Smith, Macaulay, Daniel, Forbes, McPherson, Logie, Roper, Lishman, Vallance.
Att: 60,000
May 18 v Palmeiras (in São Paulo) 1-1
Logie
Swindin; Barnes, L.Smith, Macaulay, Daniel, Forbes, McPherson, Logie, Roper, Lishman, Vallance.
May 22 v Corinthians (in São Paulo) 2-0
Lishman, Vallance
Swindin; Barnes, L.Smith, Macaulay, Daniel, Forbes, Roper(Rooke), Logie(B.Jones), Lewis(McPherson), Lishman, Vallance.
May 25 v Vasco da Gama (in Rio de Janeiro) 0-1
Swindon; Barnes, L.Smith, Macaulay, Daniel(Fields), Forbes, McPherson, Logie, Rooke, Lishman, Vallance.
May 29 v Flamengo (in Rio de Janeiro) 1-3
Goring
Swindin; Barnes, L.Smith(Wade), Macaulay (B.Jones[Grimshaw]), Fields, Forbes, McPherson (Rooke), Logie, Goring, Lishman, Vallance(Lewis).
Jun 1 v Botafogo (in Rio de Janeiro) 2-2
Lewis 2
Swindin; Scott, Barnes, Macaulay, Fields, Forbes, McPherson(B.Jones), Lewis, Roper, Lishman, Vallance.
Jun 4 v São Paulo (in São Paulo) 0-1
Swindin(Platt); Wade, Barnes, Forbes, Fields, Grimshaw, Goring, Lewis, Roper, Macauley, B.Jones (Lishman).

1949-50
Nov 1 v Racing Club de Paris (France) 2-1
Mercer, Logie
Platt; Barnes, L.Smith, Macaulay, L.Compton, Mercer, Cox(Goring), Logie, Roper, Lewis, McPherson.
Att: 35,000
May 29 v Servette (Geneva, Switzerland) 3-1
Logie, Goring, Lishman
Swindin; Barnes, L.Smith, Macaulay, Daniel, Shaw, Cox(McPherson), Logie, Goring, Lewis(Lishman), Roper.
Att: 20,000
May 30 v A Swiss National XI (Zürich) 4-2
Lishman 2, Macaulay, Goring
Swindin; Barnes, L.Smith, Macaulay, Daniel, Shaw, McPherson, Logie, Goring, Lishman, Roper.

1950-51
Nov 13 v Racing Club de Paris (France) 5-1
Roper 3, Lewis 2
Swindin(Platt), Scott, Wade, Forbes, Fields, Mercer, McPherson, Logie(Shaw), Goring(Cox), Lishman (Lewis), Roper.
Att: 35,000
Apr 25 v Royal Anderlecht (Brussels) 3-2
Holton, Marden, Roper
Swindin; Scott, Barnes, Mercer, L.Compton, Bowen, Roper, Logie, Holton, Lishman(Forbes), Marden (McPherson).
May 20 v Fluminense (in Rio de Janeiro) 0-2
Swindin; Scott, Barnes, Forbes, Daniel, Bowen, Roper, Logie, Holton(Goring), Lishman(Gudmundsson), McPherson(Marden).
May 24 v Botafogo (in Rio de Janeiro) 0-2
Swindin(Platt), Scott, Barnes, Forbes, Daniel, Bowen (Shaw), Roper, Logie, Goring(Lewis), Gudmundsson, Marden(Cox).
May 27 v América (in Rio de Janeiro) 1-2
Gudmundsson
Swindin; Scott, Barnes, Forbes, Daniel, Bowen, Cox (McPherson), Logie, Goring(Lishman), Gudmundsson, Marden.
May 30 v São Paulo (in São Paulo) 1-0
Roper
Swindin; Scott, Barnes, Forbes, Daniel, Bowen, McPherson, Logie, Gudmundsson, Lishman, Marden (Roper).
Jun 6 v Palmeiras (in São Paulo) 1-3
Logie
Swindon; Scott, Barnes, Forbes, Daniel, Bowen, McPherson, Logie(Lewis), Gudmundsson, Lishman, Roper.
Jun 12 v Vasco da Gama (in Rio de Janeiro) 0-4
Swindin; Scott, Barnes, Forbes, Daniel, Bowen(Shaw), McPherson, Logie(Lishman), Goring, Gudmundsson, Marden(Roper).

1951-52
Nov 7 v Racing Club de Paris (France) 5-0
Goring 4, Mercer
Swindin; Barnes, Wade, Forbes, Daniel, Mercer, Milton, Logie, Goring, Lishman, Roper.
Att: 30,000
May 14 v RSC Anderlecht (Brussels) 0-1
Swindin; Chenhall, Wade, Forbes, Fields, Mercer, Roper, Logie, Holton(Lewis), Lishman, Marden.
May 15 v Grasshopper Zürich (Switzerland) 5-2
Roper 2, Lishman 2, Forbes
Swindin; Chenhall, Wade, N.Smith, Fields, Bowen, Forbes, Logie, Goring, Lishman, Roper.
May 20 v FC Basel (Switzerland) 1-0
Lishman
Swindin; Chenhall, Wade, N.Smith, Fields, Bowen, Forbes(Cox), Logie, Goring, Lishman, Roper.
May 22 v Lausanne-Sports (Switzerland) 2-2
Lishman, Marden
Swindin; Chenhall, Wade, Bowen, Fields, Mercer (Grimshaw), Cox, Logie, Lewis(Goring), Lishman, Roper(Marden).

1952-53
Oct 1 v Racing Club de Paris (France) 0-2
Kelsey; Chenhall, Wade, Mercer(Shaw), Daniel, Forbes, Milton, Logie, Goring, Lishman(Lewis), Roper.
May 24 v Rapid Vienna (in Bruges, Belgium) 1-6
Lishman
Kelsey; Wade, L.Smith, Forbes, Daniel, Shaw, Roper, Logie, Holton, Lishman(Bowen), Marden.

May 27 v Grasshopper Zürich (Switzerland) 2-1
Holton 2
Swindin; Wade, Chenhall(Evans), Forbes, Dodgin, Shaw, Cox(Bowen), Logie, Holton, Lishman, Roper.

1953-54
Oct 28 v Racing Club de Paris (France) 4-2
Holton 3, Roper
Kelsey; Wills, Barnes, Dickson, Dodgin, Forbes, Roper, Logie(L.Smith), Holton, Lishman, Marden.
Att: 30,000
May 5 v Grasshopper Zürich (Switzerland) 3-2
Bowen, Lishman, Logie
Sullivan; Wills(Wade), L.Smith, Goring, Dickson, Bowen, Forbes(Walsh), Logie, Lawton(Holton), Lishman, Roper.
Att: 15,000
May 6 v BSC Young Boys (Berne) 1-3
Holton
Sullivan; Wade, Evans, Goring, Dickson, Bowen, Walsh, Logie, Holton, Lishman, Roper.

1954-55
Oct 5 v Dinamo Moscow (Russia) 0-5
Kelsey; Barnes, Wade, Goring, Dickson, Forbes, Tapscott, Logie, Lawton, Lishman, Roper.
Att: 90,000
Oct 20 v Racing Club de Paris (France) 3-1
Bloomfield, Lawton, Forbes
Kelsey; Barnes, Wade, Goring, Dodgin, Forbes, Walsh, Logie, Lawton, Bloomfield, Roper.
May 11 v Grasshopper Zürich (Switzerland) 5-5
Roper 3, Forbes 2
Kelsey; Wills, Evans, Smailes, Fotheringham, Forbes, Clapton, Herd, Roper, Tapscott, Bloomfield.
May 15 v BSC Young Boys (Berne) 3-0
Wills, Forbes, Lawton
Kelsey; Wills, Evans, Smailes(Wade), Fotheringham, Forbes, Clapton, Holton(Tapscott), Lawton, Roper, Bloomfield.
May 19 v München 1860 (Munich) 2-1
Tapscott 2
Kelsey; Wade, Evans, Wills, Fotheringham, Forbes, Clapton, Tapscott, Lawton, Roper, Bloomfield.
Att: 45,000

1955-56
Apr 18 v Racing Club de Paris (France) 4-3
Holton 2, Bloomfield, Groves
Kelsey; Charlton, Evans, Goring, Dodgin, Forbes, Clapton, Tapscott, Holton, Groves(Bloomfield), Haverty.

1956-57
Aug 4 v VfB Stuttgart (West Germany) 1-1
Tapscott
Kelsey; Charlton, Evans, Wills, Dodgin, Bowen, Clapton(Nutt), Tapscott, Holton, Bloomfield, Tiddy.
Att: 41,500
Oct 10 v Racing Club de Paris (France) 4-3
Tapscott 4
Kelsey; Charlton, Evans, Goring, Dodgin, Bowen, Clapton, Tapscott, Holton, Bloomfield, Haverty.
Att: 13,000
May 5 v Eintracht Frankfurt (West Germany) 2-0
Bloomfield, Holton
Kelsey; Charlton, Evans, Holton, Dodgin, Bowen, Clapton, Tapscott, Herd, Bloomfield, Nutt.
Att: 12,000

May 8 v Grasshopper Zürich (Switzerland) 4-2
Tapscott, Groves, Clapton, Bowen
Kelsey(Sullivan); Charlton, Evans, Holton, Dodgin,
Bowen, Clapton, Tapscott(Herd), Groves, Bloomfield,
Tiddy.
May 10 v Fortuna/Rot-Weiss Combined 2-2
Groves 2
Kelsey; Charlton, Evans, Holton, Dodgin, Bowen,
Clapton, Herd, Groves, Bloomfield, Tiddy.

1957-58
Aug 4 v AIK (Solna, Sweden) 2-1
Tapscott 2
Kelsey; Charlton, Evans, Holton, Dodgin, Bowen,
Clapton, Tapscott, Groves, Bloomfield, Haverty.
Att: 40,000
Nov 11 v Racing Club de Paris (France) 1-1
Herd
Standen; Charlton, Evans, Holton, Dodgin, Goring,
Clapton, Groves, Herd, Bloomfield, Haverty(Nutt).
Att: 20,000

1958-59
Aug 9 v FC Schalke 04 (Gelsenkirchen) 1-3
Herd
Kelsey; Charlton, Evans, Ward, Dodgin, Bowen, Nutt,
Groves, Herd(Biggs), Bloomfield, Haverty.
Att: 25,000
Aug 13 v Enschede Sportsclub (Holland) 2-1
Groves, Bloomfield
Kelsey; Wills, Evans(Charlton), Ward, Dodgin,
Bowen, Clapton, Groves, Biggs(Bloomfield), Goulden,
Haverty.
Att: 20,000
Aug 16 v Young Fellows Club (Zürich) 5-0
Clapton 2, Groves 2, Evans (pen)
Kelsey; Charlton(Wills), Evans, Ward, Dodgin
(Fotheringham), Bowen, Clapton, Groves(Goulden),
Herd, Bloomfield, Haverty.
Nov 19 v Racing Club de Paris (France) 1-0
Henderson
Kelsey; Wills, Evans, Ward, Dodgin, Docherty,
Clapton, Groves, Henderson, Bloomfield, Haverty.
Att: 40,000
May 14 v Juventus (Turin, Italy) 1-3
Charles
Sims (Aston Villa); Wills, Evans, Docherty, Charles,
Bowen, Clapton, Groves, Henderson, Bloomfield,
Haverty(Julians).
May 20 v Fiorentina (Italy) 2-1
Henderson, Bloomfield
Sims; Wills, Evans, Docherty, Charles, Bowen,
Clapton, Groves, Henderson, Bloomfield, Haverty.
May 24 v FC Lugano (Switzerland) 4-1
Henderson, Charles, Bloomfield, Opponent (og)
Standen; Wills, Evans, McCullough(Everitt), Charles,
Dodgin, Docherty, Groves, Henderson, Bloomfield
(D.R.Clapton), Haverty.

1959-60
Aug 8 v Sparta Rotterdam 2-2
Clapton, Ward
Standen(Kelsey); Wills, Evans, Ward, Charles,
Docherty, Clapton, Groves, Herd, Bloomfield,
Henderson.
Aug 12 v ADO (The Hague) 7-0
Herd 3, Clapton, Barnwell, Haverty, Opponent (og)
Standen; Wills, Evans, Ward(Barnwell), Charles,
Docherty, Clapton, Groves, Herd, Bloomfield,
Henderson(Haverty).
Att: 16,000

Sep 23 v PSV Eindhoven (Holland) 4-1
Herd 2, Groves, Bloomfield
Standen(Kelsey); Wills, McCullough, Groves, Dodgin,
Docherty, Clapton, Barnwell, Herd, Bloomfield,
Haverty.
Att: 19,000
May 7 v Grasshopper Zürich (Switzerland) 4-2
Herd 2, Henderson, Bloomfield
Kelsey; Wills, McCullough, Docherty(Ward), Dodgin,
Petts, Clapton, Herd, Groves, Bloomfield, Henderson.
May 11 v Racing Club de Paris (France) 3-4
Herd, Bloomfield, Henderson
Kelsey; Wills, McCullough, Docherty, Snedden, Petts,
Clapton, Herd, Groves, Bloomfield, Henderson.
May 14 v RSC Anderlecht (Brussels) 4-1
Herd, Wills, Clapton, Henderson
Kelsey; Wills, McCullough, Docherty, Snedden
(Dodgin), Petts, Clapton, Barnwell(Magill), Herd,
Bloomfield, Henderson.
May 19 v Fortuna Geleen 54 (Holland) 5-5
Herd 2, Groves, Bloomfield, Henderson
Kelsey; Wills, McCullough, Docherty, Snedden, Petts,
Clapton, Herd, Groves, Bloomfield, Henderson.

1960-61
Nov 1 v Entente Royale Anversoise (Antwerp) 2-2
Charles 2
Kelsey; Wills, McCullough, Docherty, Snedden,
Groves, Strong, Barnwell, Charles, Herd, Henderson.
Att: 15,000
May 1 v DOS Utrecht (Holland) 2-2
Griffiths, Barnwell
Kelsey; Bacuzzi, McCullough, Ward, Charles, Groves,
Skirton, Griffiths, Strong(Magill), Barnwell,
Henderson.
May 5 v Racing Club de Paris (France) 4-1
Henderson 2, Skirton, Petts
Kelsey; Bacuzzi, McCullough, Ward, Charles, Petts,
Clapton, Griffiths, Groves, Henderson, Skirton.
May 16 v Staevnet (Copenhagen) 1-0
Groves
McKechnie; Bacuzzi, McCullough, Ward, Neill, Petts,
Clapton, Griffiths, Groves, Henderson, Skirton.
Att: 12,500
May 18 v Swedish National XI (Gothenburg) 3-2
Groves, Henderson, Skirton
McKechnie; Bacuzzi, McCullough, Ward, Neill, Petts,
Clapton(Haverty), Griffiths, Groves, Henderson,
Skirton.
Att: 42,056
May 21 v Vejle Boldklub (Denmark) 3-0
Henderson 2, Skirton
McKechnie; Bacuzzi, McCullough, Ward, Neill, Petts,
Skirton, Griffiths, Groves, Henderson, Haverty
(Clapton).
Att: 7,800

1961-62
May 4 v Berlin City Select XI 5-0
Strong, Skirton, MacLeod
McClelland; Magill, McCullough, Clamp, Neill,
Snedden(Brown), MacLeod, Griffiths, Strong, Ward,
Skirton(Clapton).
Att: 8,000
May 8 v Gothenburg Alliance XI (Sweden) 5-1
Ward 3, Barnwell, Skirton
McKechnie; Magill, McCullough, Petts, Neill,
Snedden(Clamp), MacLeod, Barnwell, Strong, Ward,
Skirton.
Att: 11,000

May 10 v Skeid Oslo (Norway) 3-0
Brown, McCullough, Groves
McClelland; Bacuzzi, McCullough, Brown, Neill,
Clamp, Clapton, Griffiths, Groves, Barnwell(Ward),
MacLeod(Skirton).
Att: 9,378
May 15 v Staevnet (Copenhagen) 1-1
Ward
McClelland; Magill, McCullough, Petts, Neill, Clamp,
MacLeod, Griffiths, Barnwell, Ward, Skirton.
May 17 v Skane-Alliansen (Helsingborg) 4-0
Skirton 2, Barnwell, Groves
McClelland; Magill, McCullough, Brown, Neill,
Clamp, MacLeod, Barnwell, Groves, Ward, Skirton.
Att: 8,514

1962-63
Aug 11 v FK Austria Vienna (in Vienna) 0-2
McKechnie; Magill, McCullough, Clamp, Neill,
Snedden, Armstrong, Barnwell, Strong, Eastham,
Skirton.
Att: 27,000
Sep 25 v Racing Club de Paris (France) 3-0
Strong 3
McKechnie; Magill, McCullough(Bacuzzi), Neill,
Brown, Ward, MacLeod, Strong, Baker, Barnwell,
Skirton.

1963-64
Aug 14 v Enschede Sportsclub (Holland) 2-2
Skirton 2
Burns(Wilson); Magill, McCullough, Barnwell, Brown,
Snedden, MacLeod, Strong, Court, Eastham, Skirton.
Aug 17 v Hamburger SV (West Germany) 2-2
Strong, Skirton
Wilson; Magill, McCullough, Barnwell, Brown, Neill,
Skirton, Strong, Baker, Eastham, Armstrong.
Att: 30,000
**May 14 v Transvaal-Orange Free State XI 2-0 (in
Johannesburg)**
Sammels, Court
Furnell; Howe, McCullough, Neill, Ure, Snedden,
MacLeod, Strong, Baker(Court), Sammels, Skirton.
Att: 24,000
May 17 v Natal XI (in Durban) 8-2
Baker 2, Strong 2, Sammels 2, Skirton, Court
Furnell; Howe, McCullough, Neill, Ure, Snedden,
MacLeod, Strong, Baker(Court), Sammels, Skirton.
Att: 22,000
May 20 v Western Province (in Cape Town) 5-1
Baker 2, Armstrong 2, Court
Burns; Magill, McCullough, Neill, Ure, Simpson,
MacLeod, Strong, Baker, Court, Armstrong.
Att: 19,000
May 22 v Eastern Province (Port Elizabeth) 6-0
Baker 2, Howe, MacLeod, Armstrong, Strong
Burns; Magill, Howe, Snedden, Ure, Simpson,
MacLeod, Strong, Baker, Court, Armstrong.
Att: 11,000
May 30 v South Africa XI (in Johannesburg) 5-0
Baker 3, Sammels, MacLeod
Furnell(Burns); Howe, McCullough, Neill, Ure,
Snedden, MacLeod, Strong, Baker, Sammels,
Armstrong.
Att: 32,000

1964-65
Aug 8 v Eintracht Frankfurt 2-2
Eastham, Baker
Furnell; Howe, McCullough, Neill, Ure, Snedden,
MacLeod, Strong, Baker, Eastham, Anderson.
Att: 13,000

Aug 11 v VfB Stuttgart (West Germany) 1-1
Strong
Furnell; Howe, McCullough, Snedden, Ure, Simpson,
Skirton, Strong, Court, Eastham, Armstrong.
Att: 32,000
Sep 30 v Odense Select XI (Denmark) 6-3
Eastham 2, Armstrong 2, Baker, Strong
Furnell; Magill, McCullough, Snedden, Ferry(Court),
Neill, Skirton, Strong, Baker, Eastham, Armstrong.
Att: 4,400
Apr 30 v Torino (Italy) 2-2
Baldwin, Sammels
Furnell; Howe, McCullough, McLintock, Ure, Neill,
Tawse, Sammels, Baldwin, Court, Skirton.
Att: 5,000
May 2 v Lazio SS (Italy) 2-0
Baldwin, Armstrong
Furnell; Howe, McCullough, Neill, Ure, McLintock,
Skirton, Sammels, Baldwin, Court, Armstrong.
May 5 v AC Brescia (Italy) 1-1
Skirton
Furnell; Howe, McCullough, McLintock, Ure, Court,
Skirton, Baldwin(Simpson), Radford, Sammels,
Armstrong.
Att: 2,000
May 9 v AC Latina (Italy) 3-0
Sammels, Baldwin, Tawse
Wilson(Burns); Howe, Storey, Court, Neill(Ure),
McLintock(Skirton), Tawse, Simpson, Radford
(Baldwin), Sammels, Armstrong.
May 11 v Grasshopper Zürich (Switzerland) 3-0
Sammels, Court, Howe (pen)
Burns; Howe, McCullough, Neill, Ure, McLintock,
Skirton, Sammels, Baldwin, Court, Armstrong.

1965-66
Aug 3 v Trinidad XI 3-1
Eastham, Baker, Sammels
Furnell; Howe, McCullough, Neill, Ure, McLintock,
Sammels, Eastham, Baker, Court(Storey), Armstrong.
Aug 4 v Jamaica Sugar Estates XI 12-0
Baker 6, Shannon 4, Armstrong 2
Wilson; Howe, McCullough, McLintock, Wright
(manager), Neill, Sammels, Eastham, Baker, Shannon
(coach), Armstrong.
Aug 7 v Jamaica XI 2-0*
Skirton 2
Furnell; Howe, McCullough, McLintock, Ure, Neill,
Skirton, Eastham, Baker, Court, Armstrong.
**Abandoned after 50 minutes, when spectators began
a bottle-throwing riot.*
Aug 10 v Curaçao XI 3-1
Neill, McLintock, Armstrong
Wilson; Howe, McCullough, McLintock, Ure, Neill,
Sammels, Eastham, Baker, Court, Armstrong.
Aug 11 v Aruba XI 2-2
Eastham, Court
Furnell; Howe, McCullough, McLintock, Ure, Neill,
Eastham, Sammels, Baker, Court, Armstrong.
Aug 15 v Trinidad XI 6-2
Eastham 3, Armstrong 2, McLintock
Wilson; Howe, Storey, Neill, Ure, McLintock, Skirton,
Eastham, Sammels, Court, Armstrong.
Oct 12 v Israel Select XI (Tel Aviv) 2-2
Baker, Simpson
Furnell; Howe, McCullough, McLintock, Neill, Ure,
Armstrong, Radford, Baker, Sammels, Eastham
(Simpson)
Att: 35,000

Mar 9 v Valencia (Spain) 0-0 (lost 12-13 on penalties)
(Valencia Fairs Trophy)
Furnell; Storey, Simpson, McLintock, Ure, Neill,
Armstrong, Tyrer, Radford, Court, Walley.
Att: 30,000
May 21 v Beşiktaş (in Istanbul, Turkey) 0-2
Furnell(Wilson); Court, Storey, McLintock, Ure,
Wright(Neill), Coakley, Sammels, Radford, McGill,
Neilson.
May 25 v Beşiktaş (in Ankara) 0-0
Wilson; Court, Storey, McLintock(Walley), Ure, Neill,
Neilson, Simpson, Radford, Sammels, Coakley(Tyrer).

1966-67
May 20 v Omonia FC (in Nicosia) 4-1
Armstrong, Jenkins, Coakley, Johnston
Furnell(Wilson); Howe, Simpson, Radford, Neill,
Court, Coakley, Addison(Johnston), Graham, Jenkins,
Armstrong.
May 24 v Apollon/AEL Select (Limassol) 7-0
Addison 2, Radford, Graham, Sammels, Neill, McNab
Furnell(Wilson); Howe, McNab, Radford, Neill,
Simpson, Coakley, Addison(Jenkins), Graham
(Johnston), Sammels, Armstrong.
May 27 v Apoel FC (in Nicosia) 1-1
Radford
Wilson(Furnell); McNab, Storey, Radford, Neill,
Simpson, Coakley, Addison(Howe), Graham,
Sammels, Armstrong.
May 31 v NEA Salamis (in Famagusta) 2-0
Neill, Howe
Furnell(Wilson); McNab, Storey, Radford, Neill,
Simpson, Coakley, Addison(Johnston), Graham
(Jenkins), Howe, Armstrong.

1967-68
Aug 12 v Hertha BSC (Berlin) 1-2
Johnston
Furnell; McNab, Storey, McLintock, Neill, Ure,
Jenkins(Johnston), Simpson, Graham, Sammels,
Armstrong.
Att: 7,682
Nov 14 v Feyenoord (Rotterdam) 2-3
Sammels 2
Furnell; Storey, McNab, McLintock, Neill, Simpson,
Radford, Johnston, Graham, Sammels, Armstrong.
Att: 60,000
May 23 v All Japan XI (in Tokyo) 3-1
Gould, Radford, Neill (pen)
Wilson; Rice, Storey, McLintock, Neill, Simpson,
Radford, Court, Graham, Gould, Armstrong.
Att: 50,000
May 26 v All Japan XI (Fukuoka, Kyushu) 1-0
Simmons
Wilson(Furnell); Rice, Storey, McLintock
(Woodward), Simpson, Court, Radford, Jenkins,
Graham(Simmons), Gould, Armstrong.
Att: 10,000
May 29 v All Japan XI (in Tokyo) 4-0
McLintock 2, Jenkins, Radford
Wilson(Furnell); McNab, Storey(Rice[Nelson]),
McLintock(Woodward), Neill, Simpson, Radford,
Court, Jenkins, Gould(Simmons), Armstrong.
Att: 70,000 (Record for soccer in Japan)
Jun 2 v President's XI (Kuala Lumpur, Malaya) 6-2
Jenkins 3, Gould, Court, Simmons
Furnell; McNab, Storey(Rice), McLintock, Neill,
Simpson, Radford, Court, Graham(Simmons), Gould
(Jenkins), Armstrong.
Att: 20,000

1968-69
Jul 27 v Allemmania Aachen (West Germany) 2-3
Jenkins 2
Wilson; Storey, McNab, McLintock, Neill, Simpson,
Radford, Sammels, Graham, Gould, Jenkins
(Simmons).
Att: 20,000
Jul 30 v Borussia Mönchengladbach 0-0
Wilson; Storey, McNab, McLintock, Neill, Simpson,
Radford, Sammels, Graham, Gould(Jenkins), Court.
Att: 18,000
May 4 v Reykjavik Select XI (Iceland) 3-1
Robertson, Gould, Radford
Wilson(Webster); Rice, Storey(Nelson), Court,
McLintock, Graham(Kelly), Robertson, Sammels,
Radford, Gould(George), Armstrong.
May 18 v Floriana FC (Valletta, Malta) 4-0
Gould, Robertson, Roberts, Court
Wilson; Storey(Nelson), McNab(Rice), McLintock,
Neill(Roberts), Graham, Robertson, Sammels, Court,
Gould, Armstrong.
Att: 9,000
May 20 v Hibernians FC (Malta) 0-0
Wilson; Storey(Nelson), McNab(Rice), McLintock,
Neill, Graham(Roberts), Robertson, Sammels, Court,
Gould, Armstrong.
Att: 14,000

1969-70
Jul 26 v Borussia Dortmund (West Germany) 2-2
Radford, Gould
Wilson; Rice(Storey), McNab, McLintock(George),
Neill, Simpson(Ure), Robertson, Court, Graham
(Sammels), Gould, Radford.
Att: 9,500
Jul 30 v 1.FC Kaiserslautern (West Germany) 2-2
Radford, George
Wilson; Rice(Storey), McNab, McLintock(George),
Neill(Ure), Simpson, Robertson, Gould, Sammels,
Graham(Court), Radford.
Att: 15,000
May 10 v Omonia FC (Cyprus) 4-3
George 3, Armstrong
Wilson(Barnett); Storey(Rice), Nelson, Kelly, Roberts,
Simpson, Armstrong, Sammels(Marinello), Kennedy,
George, Graham.
Att: 6,000
May 13 v Apollon FC (Cyprus) 2-0
Marinello, George
Wilson; Storey, Nelson, Kelly, Roberts, Simpson,
Armstrong, Marinello, Kennedy, George, Graham.

1970-71
Jul 28 v Gothenburg Alliance (Sweden) 4-2
George 2, McNab, Graham
Wilson; Storey, McNab, Kelly, McLintock, Simpson,
Armstrong, Sammels, Radford, George, Graham.
Att: 5,069
Jul 31 v Kungsbacka BI (Sweden) 5-0
George 2 (1 pen), Sammels 2, Kennedy
Barnett; Rice, McNab(Storey), Kelly, Roberts,
McLintock(Simpson), Marinello, Sammels, Kennedy,
George, Graham(Armstrong).
Aug 4 v Copenhagen Alliance XI (Denmark) 1-1
George
Wilson; Storey, McNab, McLintock, Simpson
(Roberts), Armstrong, Sammels(Marinello), Radford,
George, Graham.
Att: 5,700

413

1971-72
Jul 31 v Benfica (Portugal) 0-2
Wilson(Barnett); Rice, Nelson, Simpson(Roberts), McLintock, Kelly, Storey, Graham, Radford, Kennedy, Armstrong(Marinello).
Att: 35,000
Aug 7 v Feyenoord (Rotterdam) 0-1
Wilson; Storey, McNab, Roberts(Nelson[Marinello]), McLintock, Kelly, Armstrong, Graham, Radford, Kennedy, Simpson.
Att: 60,000
May 31 v Miami Gatos FC (America) 3-2
George, Kennedy, Radford
Barnett; Rice, Nelson, Storey, McLintock, Simpson(Roberts), Armstrong, Ball(Kelly), George, Radford, Kennedy.

1972-73
Jul 29 v Lausanne-Sports (Switzerland) 6-0
George 2, Kennedy 2, Radford, Opponent (og)
Barnett; Rice, McNab, Storey, McLintock, Simpson, Marinello, George, Radford, Kennedy, Graham.
Substitutes used: Nelson, Roberts, Armstrong.
Aug 2 v Grasshopper Zürich (Switzerland) 2-1
George 2 (1 pen)
Barnett; Rice, McNab, Storey, McLintock, Simpson, Armstrong, Ball, Radford, Kennedy, George.
Substitutes used: Nelson, Roberts, Marinello, Graham.
Aug 4 v Hamburger SV (West Germany) 0-4
Barnett; Rice, McNab, George, McLintock, Simpson, Armstrong, Ball, Radford, Kennedy, Graham.
Substitutes used: Nelson, Roberts.
Nov 14 v Paris XI (Paris) 1-0
Rice
Wilson; Rice(Batson), McNab, Kelly, Blockley, Simpson, Marinello(Armstrong), George(Hornsby), Radford, Kennedy, Nelson.
Att: 19,526
May 23 v Toronto Select (Canada) 1-0
George
Wilson; Rice, McNab, Kelly, Simpson, Powling, Marinello, Chambers, Radford, George, Armstrong.
May 27 v Devonshire Colts (Bermuda) 4-0
Radford 2, Marinello, George
Wilson(Barnett); Rice, McNab, Kelly, Simpson, Powling, Marinello, Chambers, Radford, George, Armstrong.

1973-74
Aug 11 v SK Brann (Norway) 2-0
Ball, Radford
Wilson(Barnett); Rice, McNab, Storey, Blockley, Simpson, Armstrong, Ball, Radford, Kennedy, George.
Att: 9,000
Aug 14 v Frigg FK (Norway) 0-1
Wilson(Barnett); Rice, McNab, Batson, Blockley, Storey, Armstrong(Chambers), Ball, Radford, Kennedy, Hornsby.
Att: 8,829
Oct 16 v Barcelona (Spain) 0-1
Wilson(Barnett); Rice, McNab, Batson, Simpson, Kelly, Armstrong, Chambers, Ritchie, Price, Nelson(Powling).
Nov 20 v KV Mechelen (Belgium) 2-2
Hornsby 2
Wilson(Barnett); Rice, McNab(Nelson), Storey, Simpson, Price, Brady, George, Hornsby, Kennedy, Armstrong.

1974-75
Aug 3 v Rapid JC Haarlem (Holland) 0-3
Rimmer; McNab(Rice), Nelson, Kelly, Simpson, Storey, Ball(Hornsby), Brady, Radford, George, Kidd.
Att: 5,000

Aug 5 v FC Dordrecht (Holland) 1-1
Brady
Rimmer(Barnett); Rice, Nelson, Kelly, Simpson, Storey, Hornsby, Brady, George(Price), Kidd, Armstrong.
Att: 6,000
Aug 7 v AZ '67 Alkmaar (Holland) 2-0
Kidd, Opponent (og)
Rimmer(Barnett); Rice, Nelson, Kelly, Matthews, Storey, Armstrong, Brady, Radford(Hornsby), Kidd, Price.
Att: 10,000
Aug 10 v FC Partizan (Belgrade) 0-1
Rimmer(Barnett); Rice, Nelson, Kelly, Sim;son, Storey, Armstrong, Brady, Radford, Kidd, Price.
Att: 6,000
May 10 v A Malaysian XI (Kuala Lumpur) 0-2
Barnett; Storey, Nelson, Kelly, Mancini, Simpson (Matthews), Armstrong, Cropley, Hornsby, Kidd, Rostron(Radford).
May 14 v A Malaysian Select XI (Penang) 1-1
Kidd
Barnett; Powling, Nelson, Storey, Mancini, Simpson, Kelly(Matthews), Cropley, Radford, Kidd, Armstrong.
May 17 v Singapore National XI (Singapore) 3-2
Kidd, Cropley, Radford
Barnett; Powling, Nelson, Matthews(Hornsby), Mancini, Simpson, Kelly, Cropley, Radford, Kidd, Armstrong.
Att: 40,000
May 20 v Thailand National XI (Bangkok) 3-0
Cropley, Kidd 2
Barnett; Powling, Nelson, Kelly, Matthews, Simpson, Hornsby, Cropley, Radford(Rostron), Kidd, Armstrong.

1975-76
Aug 11 v Hajduk Split (Yugoslavia) 0-2
Rimmer; Rice, Nelson, Kelly, O'Leary, Simpson (Mancini), Armstrong, Cropley, Hornsby, Kidd, Brady.
Nov 4 v Fenerbahçe (Istanbul, Turkey) 2-0
Ball, Powling
Rimmer(Parker); Rice, Nelson, Storey, O'Leary, Powling, Ball, Armstrong, Kelly, Kidd(Mancini), Hornsby.

1976-77
Aug 10 v Grasshopper Zürich (Switzerland) 3-0
Macdonald 2, Brady
Rimmer; Rice, Nelson, Armstrong(Ross), O'Leary (Matthews), Simpson, Ball, Brady, Macdonald, Stapleton, Cropley.
Aug 13 v NK Rijeka (Yugoslavia) 2-2
Brady, Ross
Rimmer; Powling, Storey(Nelson), Ross(Cropley), Matthews, Simpson, Ball, Brady, Macdonald, Stapleton, Armstrong.
Aug 15 v FK Željezničar (Yugoslavia) 1-1
O'Leary
Rimmer; Rice, Nelson, Storey(Armstrong), O'Leary (Matthews), Simpson, Ball, Brady, Macdonald, Stapleton, Cropley.
Nov 2 v Al-Nasr (Dubai) 3-1
Macdonald, Matthews, Radford
Rimmer; Storey(Powling), Nelson, Ross, Howard, Simpson, Armstrong, Matthews, Macdonald, Radford, Rostron.
Nov 15 v National Civil Service XI (Dubai) 3-0
Matthews, Rostron 2
Rimmer; Storey, Powling, Ross, Simpson, Howard, Armstrong, Matthews(Price), Macdonald, Radford, Rostron.

May 17 v Rosenborg BK (Norway) 4-0
Macdonald 3, Stapleton
Rimmer; Rice, Nelson, Matthews(Rostron), O'Leary,
Howard, Brady, Hudson, Macdonald, Stapleton,
Armstrong.
Att: 7,500
May 18 v Nessegoten (Norway) 3-0
Macdonald 2, Armstrong
Rimmer(New); Powling, Nelson(Price), Matthews
(Rice), Brady, Howard, Rostron, Hudson,
Macdonald(Stapleton), Rix, Armstrong(O'Leary).
Att: 2,500
May 20 v Roros (Norway) 6-0
Macdonald 3, Price, Stapleton, Rix
New(Rimmer): Rice, Powling, Matthews, O'Leary,
Howard(Nelson), Rix, Hudson(Stapleton), Mac-
donald(Armstrong), Price(Brady), Rostron.
Att: 2,135

1977-78
Jul 12 v Red Star Belgrade (in Singapore) 1-3
Macdonald
Rimmer; Rice, Nelson(Matthews), Powling, O'Leary,
Young, Brady(Rix), Hudson, Macdonald, Stapleton,
Armstrong.
Jul 16 v Singapore 5-1
Macdonald 3, Stapleton, Brady
Rimmer(New); Rice, Nelson, Powling, Price,
Matthews, Hudson, Macdonald, Stapleton, Armstrong
(Brady), Rix.
Jul 20 v Australia National XI (in Sydney) 1-3
Armstrong
Rimmer; Rice, Nelson, Powling(Matthews[O'Leary]),
Price, Young, Brady, Hudson, Macdonald, Stapleton,
Armstrong.
Jul 24 v Glasgow Celtic (in Sydney, Australia) 2-3
Macdonald (pen), Rice
Rimmer; Rice, Nelson, Price, O'Leary, Young, Rix
(Brady), Hudson, Macdonald, Stapleton, Armstrong.
Jul 26 v Red Star Belgrade(in Adelaide,Australia) 1-0
Brady
Rimmer; Rice, Nelson, Powling, O'Leary, Young,
Brady(Matthews), Price, Stapleton, Rix, Armstrong.
Dec 12 v Qadsia (Kuwait) 1-1
Stapleton
Jennings; Rice(Matthews), Nelson, Price, O'Leary,
Young, Brady, Sunderland, Macdonald, Stapleton,
Rix.

1978-79
Jul 26 v 1.FC Kaiserslautern (West Germany) 0-3
Jennings; Rice, Nelson, Price, O'Leary, Young, Rix,
Brady, Sunderland, Matthews, Stapleton.
Jul 28 v Borussia Dortmund (West Germany) 1-0
Rix
Jennings(Barron); Rice, Nelson, Price, O'Leary, Young
(Walford), Rix, Brady, Sunderland, Matthews
(Harvey), Kosmina.
Att: 10,500
Aug 5 v PSV Eindhoven (Holland) 0-2
Jennings; Rice, Nelson, Price, O'Leary, Young, Rix,
Brady, Sunderland, Stapleton, Kosmina(Matthews).
Att: 11,000
May 15 v Lyngby Boldklub (Copenhagen) 4-2
Brady, Price, Gatting, Rice
Jennings(Sullivan); Rice, Nelson, Gatting, O'Leary,
Walford, Brady(Neill), McDermott, Macdonald
(Vaessen), Price(Devine[Young]), Rix.
Att: 9,800

1979-80
Jul 28 v München 1860 (in Duisburg) 1-1
Stapleton
Jennings; Rice, Nelson, Talbot, O'Leary, Young
(Walford), Brady, Sunderland(Vaessen), Stapleton,
Price(Hollins), Rix.
Att: 8,000
Jul 31 v MSV Duisburg (West Germany) 1-1
Opponent (og)
Barron; Devine(Rice), Nelson(Walford), Talbot,
O'Leary, Young, Brady, Sunderland(Vaessen),
Stapleton, Hollins, Rix.
Att: 5,000
Amsterdam Tournament (Holland)
Aug 3 v Ajax 0-0 (lost 3-4 on penalties)
Jennings; Rice, Nelson, Talbot, O'Leary, Young
(Walford), Brady, Sunderland, Stapleton, Price, Rix.
Att: 40,000
Aug 5 v Hamburger SV 3-0
Sunderland, Stapleton, Rice
Jennings; Rice, Nelson, Talbot(Hollins), O'Leary,
Walford, Price(Gatting), Sunderland, Stapleton,
Brady, Rix.
Att: 35,000
Arsenal finished third out of four

1980-81
International Tournament (Belgrade, Yugoslavia)
Aug 9 v Vasco da Gama (Brazil) 1-2
Rix
Jennings; Rice(Devine), Nelson, Talbot, Walford,
Young, Allen(Sunderland), Hollins, Stapleton, Price,
Rix.
Aug 10 v FC Partizan (Belgrade) 0-0 (lost 3-4 on pens)
Penalty scorers – Hollins, Devine, Sunderland
Barron; Devine, Nelson, Talbot(Rice), Young,
Walford, Hollins, Sunderland, Stapleton, Price, Rix.
Arsenal finished last out of four
May 9 v Eastern Ath Association(in Hong Kong) 3-0
Stapleton, Davis, Sunderland
Jennings(Wood); Hollins(Devine), Sansom, Talbot,
O'Leary, Young, McDermott, Sunderland(Rix),
Stapleton, Nicholas, Davis.
Att: 16,210
*Arsenal players Nelson, Gatting and Meade played for
Eastern.*

1981-82
Aug 5 v AIK (Solna, Sweden) 0-0
Jennings(Wood); Devine, Sansom, Talbot, Whyte,
Young, Hollins(Nelson), Sunderland, McDermott,
P.Nicholas, Davis(Gatting).
Att: 12,766
Aug 16 v Olympiakos (Greece) 3-2
Devine, Sunderland, Davis
Jennings; Devine, Sansom, Talbot, O'Leary, Young,
Hollins, Sunderland, McDermott(Vaessen), Nicholas
(Gatting), Davis.
Aug 20 v Juventus (Italy) 2-2
Talbot 2
Jennings; Devine, Sansom, Talbot, O'Leary, Young,
Hollins(Davis), Sunderland, McDermott, P.Nicholas,
Rix.
May 18 v ASL Club (Trinidad) 2-3
Hollins (pen), Davis
Jennings; Hollins, Sparrow, Talbot, O'Leary, Whyte,
Davis, Sunderland, Hawley, Robson, McDermott
(Meade).

415

May 20 v Trinidad Representative XI 2-0
Talbot, Hawley
Jennings; Hollins, Sparrow, Talbot, O'Leary, Whyte, Davis, Sunderland, Hawley(McDermott), O'Shea, Meade.

1982-83
Aug 6 v Feyenoord (Rotterdam) 0-2
Wood(Jennings); Hollins(Devine), Sansom, Talbot, O'Leary, Whyte, Robson, Sunderland, Woodcock, Davis(Hawley), Rix.
Att: 29,000
Aug 8 v FK Austria (in Rotterdam) 0-4
Wood; Hollins, Sansom, Talbot, O'Leary, Whyte, Robson, Hawley, Woodcock(Devine), Davis, Rix.
Att: 30,000
Aug 14 v Alexandria Select (Alexandria) 0-0
Wood(Jennings); Hollins, Sansom, Talbot, O'Leary, Whyte, Davis, Hawley(Chapman), Woodcock, Devine, Rix.
Aug 16 v Egypt (in Alexandria) 1-0
Robson
Wood; Hollins, Sansom, Talbot, O'Leary(Devine), Whyte, Sunderland, Chapman, Woodcock, Robson, Rix.
Jun 9 v VSP (Medan) 3-0
McDermott, Meade, Lee
Jennings; Hill, Sansom, Talbot, O'Leary, Whyte, McDermott, P.Nicholas, Chapman(Meade), Sunderland(Lee), Davis.
Jun 12 v VSPSSI (Djakarta, Indonesia) 5-0
Sunderland, Meade, Chapman, McDermott, Sansom
Jennings(Wilmot); Hill, Sansom, Talbot(Robson), O'Leary, Whyte, Lee, Sunderland, Meade(Chapman), Davis, McDermott(Rix).
Jun 15 v VSNIAC Mitra (Surabaja, Indonesia) 0-2
Jennings; Hill(Robson), Sansom, Talbot, O'Leary, Whyte(Lee), McDermott, Sunderland, Meade (Chapman), Davis, Rix.

1983-84
Jul 31 v Meppen (West Germany) 4-1
C.Nicholas 2, Woodcock, Chapman
Jennings(Lukic); Hill, Sansom, P.Nicholas, O'Leary, Whyte, McDermott, Robson, Woodcock(Chapman), C.Nicholas, Rix.
Att: 3,500
Aug 5 v VfL Bochum (West Germany) 1-1
Chapman
Jennings(Lukic); Whyte(Davis), Sansom, Talbot, O'Leary, Hill, McDermott(P.Nicholas), Robson, Woodcock, C.Nicholas(Chapman), Rix.
Att: 7,500
Aug 9 v SV Werder Bremen (West Germany) 0-2
Jennings(Lukic); Whyte, Sansom, Talbot, O'Leary (McDermott), Hill, Robson, Davis, Woodcock (Chapman), C.Nicholas(Meade), Rix.
Att: 13,000

1984-85
Bielefeld Tournament (West Germany)
Aug 10 v Heraklis (Salonika, Greece) 3-1
Allinson, Anderson, Davis
Jennings; Anderson, Sansom, Talbot(Cork), O'Leary, Caton, Robson, C.Nicholas, Mariner, Davis, Allinson (Meade).
Att: 5,000

Aug 12 v Arminia Bielefeld (West Germany) 1-0
Mariner
Jennings; Anderson, Sansom, Talbot, O'Leary, Caton, Robson, C.Nicholas, Mariner, Davis(Cork), Allinson.
Att: 11,000
Arsenal won the tournament
Aug 15 v FC Twente Enschede (Holland) 0-1
Jennings; Anderson, Sansom, Talbot, O'Leary, Caton, Robson, C.Nicholas, Mariner, Woodcock, Davis.
Att: 8,500
Oct 2 v Saudi Arabia National Team (Dhahran) 1-1
Talbot
Jennings(Lukic); Anderson, Sansom, Talbot, O'Leary, Caton(Hill), Robson, Rix(Davis), Mariner(Allinson), Woodcock, C.Nicholas.

1985-86
Dec 4 v Trinidad & Tobago (Port of Spain, Trinidad) 3-0
C.Nicholas (pen), Allinson, Opponent (og)
Wilmot; Keown(Anderson), Sansom, Rix, O'Leary, Caton, Williams, Robson, C.Nicholas, Woodcock (Allinson), Hayes.

1986-87
Aug 3 v Sporting Clube de Portugal (Portugal) 0-0
Lukic(Wilmot); Caesar, Anderson, Rocastle(Davis), O'Leary, Adams(Caton), Robson, Davis(Williams), C.Nicholas, Quinn(Allinson), Rix.
Att: 35,000
May 11 v Apoel (Cyprus) 2-2 (won 5-4 on penalties)
Davis, Hayes
Lukic(Wilmot); Thomas, Rix, Williams, Caesar (Quinn), Adams, Rocastle, Davis, Groves, C.Nicholas, Hayes.
On May 14 a combined Arsenal/Luton Town team beat a combined Apoel/Omonia XI 3-2. Arsenal players who appeared were Adams, Thomas, Smith, C.Nicholas, Wilmot and Groves. Thomas scored one goal.

1987-88
Arsenal's only overseas competition this season was in a Soccer-Six tournament in Australia.

1988-89
Aug 2 v Örebro (Sweden) 1-1
Smith
Lukic; Dixon, Winterburn, Thomas(Richardson), O'Leary, Adams(Caesar), Rocastle(Groves), Davis, Smith(Quinn), Hayes(Merson), Marwood.
Att: 2,400
Aug 4 v Anundsjo (Sweden) 3-1
Rocastle 2, O'Leary
Wilmot; Dixon, Winterburn(Thomas), Richardson, O'Leary, Caesar, Rocastle, Davis, Quinn(Smith), Groves(Merson), Marwood(Hayes).
Att: 2,700
Aug 9 v Enköping (Sweden) 6-0
Merson 3, Rocastle 2, Groves
Lukic(Wilmot); Dixon, Winterburn, Thomas, O'Leary(Bould), Adams(Caesar), Rocastle, Davis(Richardson), Smith(Quinn), Merson(Groves), Marwood(Hayes).
Jan 25 v Somerset Cricket Club (Bermuda) 1-0
Hayes
Lukic(Wilmot); Dixon, Winterburn, Davis, O'Leary, Caesar, Hayes, Richardson(Thomas), Smith(Groves), Merson, Marwood(Quinn).

Jan 27 v Bermuda National XI (a) 4-2
Lukic(Wilmot); Dixon, Winterburn, Davis, O'Leary,
Caesar(Adams), Hayes(Thomas), Richardson,
Smith(Quinn), Merson, Marwood(Groves).

1989-90
Jul 22 v Skelleftea AIK (Sweden) 3-2
Smith, Merson, Campbell
Lukic(Miller); Dixon, Winterburn, Thomas(Davis),
Bould(O'Leary), Adams(Caesar), Rocastle(Groves),
Richardson, Smith(Quinn), Merson(Campbell),
Hayes(Marwood).
Jul 24 v FK Mjolner, Narvik (Norway) 4-0
Merson, Adams, Campbell, Quinn
Lukic; Dixon(Caesar), Winterburn, Thomas, O'Leary,
Bould (Adams), Groves(Rocastle), Richardson(Davis),
Smith(Quinn), Merson (Campbell), Marwood(Hayes).
Att: 4,000
Jul 26 v Lulea (Sweden) 2-2
Campbell, Adams
Lukic; Caesar, Winterburn(Hayes), Thomas(Davis),
O'Leary, Adams, Campbell, Richardson, Smith
(Quinn), Bould(Merson), Marwood(Rocastle).

1990-91
Jul 22 v Varbergs BoIS (Sweden) 2-0
Merson, Rocastle
Seaman(Miller); Caesar(Dixon), Winterburn,
Jonsson(Thomas), Bould(Pates), Adams(Linighan),
Rocastle, Davis, Smith, Merson(Campbell), Groves
(Marwood).

Jul 24 v Västra Frölunda IF (Gothenburg) 4-0
Linighan, Smith, Merson 2
Seaman(Miller); Dixon, Winterburn(Caesar), Thomas,
Linighan(Adams), Pates(Bould), Rocastle(Groves),
Davis(Jonsson), Smith, Campbell(Merson), Limpar
(Marwood).
Jul 26 v IFK Värnamo (Sweden) 2-2
Limpar, Merson
Seaman; Dixon, Winterburn, Thomas(Jonsson),
Linighan, Adams, Rocastle, Davis, Smith(Campbell),
Merson, Limpar(Groves).
Att: 2,000

1991-92
Jul 17 v Stockholm Select (Malarvik) 4-1
Smith 2, Groves, Campbell
Seaman(Will); Dixon, Winterburn(Pates), Thomas
(Rocastle), Linighan(Bould), Adams(O'Leary),
Campbell, Davis(Hillier), Smith, Merson, Limpar
(Groves).
Att: 3,217
Jul 20 v Trollhattan Select (Sweden) 1-0
Hillier
Seaman; Dixon, Winterburn(Pates), Hillier, O'Leary
(Linighan), Adams(Bould), Groves(Rocastle), Davis
(Thomas), Smith, Campbell, Limpar(Merson).
Att: 3,504
Jul 22 v IFK Eskilstuna (Sweden) 6-1
Dixon, Campbell, Davis, Hillier, Limpar, Smith
Seaman; Dixon, Winterburn, Hillier, Bould, Adams,
Campbell(Rocastle), Davis, Smith, Merson(Groves),
Limpar.
Att: 6,015

*Dennis Clapton scores with a header against London University at Motspur Park in January 1960. The Gunners
beat the University 7-0.*

417

Arsenal Against Other League Clubs

Arsenal have played 75 clubs in the Football League since 1893-94. Below is the Gunners' record against each club. Some clubs changed their names (eg Small Heath became Birmingham then Birmingham City) and some clubs modified their titles (eg Leicester Fosse became Leicester City). In all cases the last name used by each club cover all games under previous names.

		HOME					AWAY				
	P	W	D	L	F	A	W	D	L	F	A
ASTON VILLA	126	33	12	18	108	75	15	13	35	87	131
BARNSLEY	16	7	0	1	20	4	0	1	7	5	15
BIRMINGHAM C	110	35	16	4	109	37	13	13	29	66	108
BLACKBURN R	72	21	10	5	80	32	12	12	12	56	69
BLACKPOOL	72	26	8	2	85	34	12	13	11	57	50
BOLTON W	92	26	13	7	104	45	10	13	23	60	86
BRADFORD	6	3	0	0	7	1	2	1	0	4	2
BRADFORD C	18	4	2	3	11	7	3	2	4	11	15
BRENTFORD	10	1	3	1	6	6	1	0	4	2	8
BRIGHTON & HA	8	3	1	0	8	1	2	0	2	6	3
BRISTOL C	28	7	4	3	23	13	9	2	3	23	10
BURNLEY	86	25	9	9	94	46	12	10	21	50	67
BURSLEM PORT V	18	8	1	0	24	3	3	2	4	9	11
BURTON U	22	8	1	2	31	6	3	0	8	12	25
BURTON W	6	2	1	0	7	1	1	0	2	5	6
BURY	32	12	2	2	41	12	1	5	10	16	35
CARDIFF C	30	7	5	3	26	14	4	6	5	19	24
CARLISLE U	2	1	0	0	2	1	0	0	1	1	2
CHARLTON A	36	10	4	4	43	28	10	5	3	40	21
CHELSEA	110	25	14	16	88	71	18	19	18	72	68
CHESTERFIELD	10	5	0	0	15	2	2	1	2	7	7
COVENTRY C	50	14	7	4	44	19	13	6	6	33	24
CREWE A	6	3	0	0	17	2	1	2	0	1	0
CRYSTAL P	18	7	2	0	22	7	4	4	1	19	10
DARWEN	10	4	0	1	15	4	2	1	2	11	10
DERBY C	84	22	8	12	77	48	9	9	24	48	83
DONCASTER R	4	2	0	0	4	0	1	0	1	1	1
EVERTON	142	45	11	15	134	75	19	18	34	86	114
FULHAM	28	13	1	0	38	13	5	4	5	24	28
GAINSBOROUGH T	16	8	0	0	36	5	3	2	3	8	9
GLOSSOP	14	6	1	0	16	1	6	0	1	13	4
GRIMSBY T	42	16	4	1	76	18	4	6	11	26	31
HUDDERSFIELD T	64	15	9	8	47	37	10	14	8	39	47
HULL C	4	1	1	0	2	1	1	0	1	2	2
IPSWICH T	42	10	5	6	33	25	9	3	9	24	28
LEEDS C	4	2	0	0	3	0	0	2	0	2	2
LEEDS U	76	19	9	10	68	41	7	11	20	43	72
LEICESTER C	100	29	15	6	115	53	15	15	20	78	88
LEYTON O	6	2	1	0	6	3	1	0	2	2	3
LINCOLN C	26	10	3	0	39	11	3	4	6	18	31
LIVERPOOL	136	31	22	15	107	63	18	11	39	74	132
LOUGHBOROUGH T	10	5	0	0	26	1	2	1	2	7	13
LUTON T	38	16	1	2	46	19	6	7	6	21	28
MANCHESTER C	138	41	15	13	132	68	23	19	27	93	103

		HOME					AWAY				
	P	W	D	L	F	A	W	D	L	F	A
MANCHESTER U	146	44	11	18	151	84	12	20	41	70	143
MIDDLESBROUGH	90	29	11	5	111	43	13	13	19	55	68
MIDDLESBROUGH I	2	1	0	0	1	0	1	0	0	6	3
MILLWALL	4	1	1	0	2	0	2	0	0	4	2
NEW BRIGHTON T	6	3	0	0	11	1	1	0	2	3	4
NEWCASTLE U	120	27	15	18	93	68	14	11	35	71	123
NORTHAMPTON T	2	0	1	0	1	1	0	1	0	1	1
NORTHWICH V	2	1	0	0	6	0	0	1	0	2	2
NORWICH C	34	11	5	1	33	11	4	7	6	24	22
NOTTINGHAM F	82	23	12	6	76	38	16	7	18	52	57
NOTTS C	44	11	5	6	30	19	6	2	14	36	48
OLDHAM A	16	3	4	1	10	7	0	5	3	3	10
OXFORD U	6	2	1	0	4	1	0	2	1	0	3
PORTSMOUTH	52	13	7	6	55	29	8	10	8	41	39
PRESTON NE	72	20	10	6	65	37	11	7	18	37	56
QUEEN'S PARK R	32	11	4	1	31	13	5	3	8	14	18
ROTHERHAM T	6	2	1	0	9	1	1	1	1	3	5
SHEFFIELD U	88	28	7	9	106	49	8	12	24	60	97
SHEFFIELD W	92	25	13	8	97	52	14	13	19	70	82
SOUTHAMPTON	44	12	8	2	36	18	8	4	10	30	31
STOCKPORT C	12	6	0	0	20	4	1	3	2	3	6
STOKE C	74	27	5	5	74	21	9	13	15	38	47
SUNDERLAND	108	27	12	15	103	60	10	18	26	65	110
SWANSEA C	4	1	0	1	2	3	1	0	1	2	3
TOTTENHAM H	110	27	12	16	85	65	19	12	24	83	93
WALSALL TS	14	4	3	0	19	4	1	0	6	9	20
WATFORD	12	2	1	3	9	10	1	0	5	6	14
WEST BROMWICH A	104	30	13	9	112	63	19	12	21	65	76
WEST HAM U	76	17	12	9	66	47	13	13	12	57	57
WIMBLEDON	12	2	4	0	11	6	4	0	2	14	7
WOLVERH'TON W	90	24	13	8	108	65	16	11	18	67	81

Consolidated Competitive Record 1889-1992

		HOME					AWAY				
	P	W	D	L	F	A	W	D	L	F	A
First Division	3096	862	386	300	2994	1610	459	411	678	2026	2567
Second Division	428	162	26	26	578	163	54	47	113	246	387
FA Cup (Proper)	316	86	27	22	282	121	73	45	63	243	230
FA Cup (Qual Rounds)	31	15	3	1	89	17	4	6	2	16	13
League Cup	126	48	10	10	132	46	20	20	18	82	72
European Competitions	55	20	3	4	67	21	7	9	12	32	28
FA Charity Shield	12	4	0	1	13	6	3	1	3	8	7
United League	50	17	5	3	63	34	7	7	11	40	54
Southern District Com	16	5	1	2	16	6	3	0	5	11	16
London League (Prem)	30	8	2	5	29	18	6	2	7	18	24
Totals	4160	1227	463	374	4263	2042	636	548	912	2722	3398

Notes:
1. The three League matches of the 1939-40 season and abandoned matches are not included.
2. All matches played on neutral venues have been taken as 'away' matches with the exception of two League matches played at New Brompton and Leyton in 1894-5, when the Arsenal ground was closed.
3. European Competitions covers European Cup, European Cup-winners' Cup, Fairs Cup and UEFA Cup.
4. The Southern District Combination includes one uncompleted match where the score has been counted a result.

Arsenal Internationals

Many players won additional caps with other clubs but the totals given here are for appearances made whilst Arsenal players. Before 1924 there was only one 'Ireland' team, then the Republic began separate matches and that position is reflected here. Unofficial and wartime international matches are not included. The date given is the year in which the match was played.

ENGLAND

Adams TA (19) 1987 v Spain, Turkey (twice), Brazil, West Germany, Yugoslavia; 1988 v Holland (twice), Hungary, Scotland, Colombia, Switzerland, Republic of Ireland, USSR; 1989 v Denmark, Sweden, Saudi Arabia; 1990 v Republic of Ireland; 1991 v Republic of Ireland.

Anderson VA (16) 1984 v Turkey; 1985 v Northern Ireland, Republic of Ireland, Romania, Finland, Scotland, USA, Mexico; 1986 v USSR, Mexico, Sweden, Northern Ireland, Yugoslavia; 1987 v Spain, Northern Ireland, Turkey.

Ashcroft J (3) 1906 v Northern Ireland, Wales, Scotland.

Baker A (1) 1906 v Northern Ireland, Wales, Scotland.

Baker JH (3) 1965 v Northern Ireland, Spain; 1966 v Poland.

Ball AJ (19) 1972 v West Germany (twice), Scotland, Yugoslavia, Wales; 1973 v Wales (twice), Scotland (twice), Northern Ireland, Czechoslovakia, Poland; 1974 v Portugal (sub); 1975 v West Germany, Cyprus (twice), Northern Ireland, Wales, Scotland.

Bastin CS (21) 1931 v Wales; 1933 v Italy, Switzerland, Northern Ireland, Wales; 1934 v Scotland, Hungary, Czechoslovakia, Italy; 1935 v Northern Ireland, Scotland, Germany; 1936 v Wales (twice), Scotland, Austria, Northern Ireland; 1938 v Scotland, Germany, Switzerland, France.

Blockley JP (1) 1972 v Yugoslavia.

Bowden ER (6) 1934 v Wales, Italy; 1935 v Northern Ireland; 1936 v Wales, Austria, Hungary.

Butler JD (1) 1924 v Belgium.

Clapton DR (1) 1958 v Wales.

Coleman JG (1) 1907 v Northern Ireland.

Compton LH (2) 1950 v Wales, Yugoslavia.

Copping W (13) 1934 v Italy, Northern Ireland; 1936 v Austria, Belgium; 1937 v Norway, Sweden, Finland, Northern Ireland, Wales, Czechoslovakia; 1938 v Scotland, Wales, Rest of Europe.

Crayston WJ (8) 1935 v Germany; 1936 v Wales, Scotland, Austria, Belgium; 1937 v Northern Ireland, Wales, Czechoslovakia.

Dixon LM (12) 1990 v Czechoslovakia, Hungary, Poland, Republic of Ireland; 1991 v Cameroon, Republic of Ireland, Turkey (twice), Argentina, Germany, Poland; 1992 v Czechoslovakia (sub).

Drake EJ (5) 1934 v Italy; 1935 v Northern Ireland; 1936 v Wales, Hungary; 1938 v France.

Ducat A (3) 1910 v Northern Ireland, Wales, Scotland.

Eastham GE (19) 1963 v Brazil, Czechoslovakia, East Germany, Wales, Rest of World, Northern Ireland; 1964 v Scotland, Uruguay, Portugal, Republic of Ireland, USA, Brazil, Argentina; 1965 v Hungary, West Germany, Sweden, Spain; 1966 v Poland, Denmark.

Hapgood EA (30) 1933 v Italy, Switzerland, Northern Ireland, Wales; 1934 v Scotland, Hungary, Czechoslovakia, Wales, Italy; 1935 v Northern Ireland (twice), Scotland, Holland, Germany; 1936 v Wales, Scotland, Austria, Belgium; 1937 v Finland; 1938 v Scotland, Germany, Switzerland, France, Wales, Rest of Europe, Norway, Northern Ireland; 1939 v Scotland, Italy, Yugoslavia.

Hulme JHA (9) 1927 v Scotland, Belgium, France, Northern Ireland, Wales; 1928 v Scotland, Northern Ireland, Wales; 1933 v Scotland.

Jack DBN (5) 1930 v Scotland, Germany, Austria; 1932 v Wales, Austria.

Joy B (also Casuals) (1) 1936 v Belgium.

Kirchen AJ (3) 1937 v Norway, Sweden, Finland.

McNab R (4) 1968 v Romania (sub), Bulgaria; 1969 v Romania, Northern Ireland.

Male CG (19) 1934 v Italy; 1935 v Northern Ireland (twice), Scotland, Holland, Germany; 1936 v Wales, Scotland, Austria, Belgium, Northern Ireland, Hungary; 1937 v Scotland, Norway, Sweden, Finland; 1939 v Italy, Yugoslavia, Romania.
Mariner P (2) 1984 v East Germany; 1985 v Romania.
Marwood B (1) 1988 v Saudi Arabia (sub).
Merson PC (2) 1991 v Germany (sub); 1992 v Czechoslovakia.
Milton CA (1) 1951 v Austria.
Moss F (4) 1934 v Scotland, Hungary, Czechoslovakia, Italy.
Radford J (2) 1969 v Romania; 1971 v Switzerland (sub).
Rimmer JJ (1) 1976 v Italy.
Rix G (17) 1980 v Norway, Romania, Switzerland (sub); 1981 v Brazil, Wales, Scotland; 1982 v Holland (sub), Finland (sub), France, Czechoslovakia, Kuwait, West Germany (twice, plus 1 sub), Spain, Denmark; 1983 v Greece (sub); 1984 v Northern Ireland.
Roberts H (1) 1931 v Scotland.
Rocastle D (13) 1988 v Denmark, Saudi Arabia; 1989 v Greece, Albania (twice), Poland (twice, including 1 sub), Denmark, Sweden (sub), Yugoslavia; 1990 v Denmark (sub); 1991 v Poland; 1992 v Czechoslovakia.
Sansom KG (77) 1980 v Norway, Romania, Switzerland; 1981 v Spain, Romania, Brazil, Wales, Scotland, Switzerland; 1982 v Northern Ireland, Wales, Holland, Scotland, Finland, France, Czechoslovakia, West Germany (twice), Spain, Denmark, Greece, Luxembourg; 1983 v Greece, Holland (twice), Northern Ireland, Scotland, Denmark, Luxembourg; 1984 v France, Scotland, USSR, Brazil, Uruguay, Chile, East Germany, Finland, Turkey; 1985 v Northern Ireland (twice), Republic of Ireland, Romania (twice), Finland, Scotland, Italy, Mexico, West Germany, USA, Turkey; 1986 v Egypt, Israel, USSR, Spain, Mexico, Canada, Portugal, Morocco, Poland, Paraguay, Argentina, Sweden, Northern Ireland, Yugoslavia; 1987 v Spain, Northern Ireland, Turkey (twice), West Germany, Yugoslavia; 1988 v Holland (twice), Scotland, Colombia, Switzerland, Republic of Ireland, USSR.
Scott L (17) 1946 v Northern Ireland, Republic of Ireland, Wales, Holland; 1947 v Scotland, France, Switzerland, Portugal, Belgium, Wales, Northern Ireland, Sweden; 1948 v Scotland, Italy, Denmark, Northern Ireland, Wales.

George Allison with the six Arsenal men who played for England against Wales in 1936. Left to right: Male, Drake, Bastin, Allison, Hapgood, Bowden and Crayston.

421

Seaman DA (5) 1991 v Cameroon, Republic of Ireland, Turkey, Argentina; 1992 v Czechoslovakia.
Smith AM (10) 1988 v Saudi Arabia (sub); 1989 v Greece, Albania (sub), Poland (sub); 1991 v Turkey (twice); USSR, Argentina, Germany, Poland (sub).
Smith L (6) 1950 v Wales; 1951 v Wales, Northern Ireland; 1952 v Wales, Belgium; 1953 v Scotland.
Storey PE (19) 1971 v Greece, Northern Ireland, Scotland, Switzerland; 1972 v West Germany Wales (twice), Northern Ireland, Scotland, Yugoslavia; 1973 v Wales (twice), Scotland (twice), Northern Ireland, Czechoslovakia, Poland, USSR, Italy.
Sunderland A (1) 1980 v Australia.
Talbot BE (1) 1980 v Australia.
Thomas ML (2) 1988 v Saudi Arabia; 1989 v Yugoslavia.
Williamson EC (2) 1923 v Sweden (twice).
Winterburn N (1) 1989 v Italy (sub).
Woodcock AS (18) 1982 v West Germany (sub), Greece, Luxembourg; 1983 v Greece, Luxembourg; 1984 v France (sub), Northern Ireland, Wales, Scotland, Brazil, Uruguay (sub), East Germany, Finland, Turkey; 1985 v Northern Ireland, Romania (sub), Turkey (sub); 1986 v Israel (sub).

SCOTLAND

Docherty TH (3) 1958 v Wales, Northern Ireland; 1959 v England.
Fitchie TT (3) 1905 v Wales; 1906 v Wales, Northern Ireland.
Forbes AR (9) 1950 v England, Portugal, France, Wales, Northern Ireland, Austria; 1951 v Wales; 1952 v Denmark, Sweden.
Graham A (1) 1921 v Northern Ireland.
Graham G (8) 1971 v Portugal, Holland; 1972 v Northern Ireland, Yugoslavia, Czechoslovakia, Brazil, Denmark (twice).
Harper W (2) 1926 v Northern Ireland, England.
Henderson JG (2) 1958 v Wales, Northern Ireland.
Herd DG (5) 1958 v Wales, Northern Ireland; 1959 v England; 1961 v Republic of Ireland, Czechoslovakia.
James A (4) 1929 v Wales; 1930 v Northern Ireland, England; 1932 v Wales.
Logie JT (1) 1952 v Northern Ireland.
Macaulay AR (6) 1947 v Northern Ireland, Wales; 1948 v England, Belgium, Switzerland, France.
McLintock F (6) 1964 v Northern Ireland; 1967 v USSR; 1970 v Northern Ireland; 1971 v Wales, Northern Ireland, England.
Nicholas C (13) 1983 v Belgium; 1984 v France (sub), Yugoslavia (sub), Iceland (sub); 1985 v Spain (sub), Wales (sub); 1986 v Israel, Romania (sub), England, Denmark, Uruguay (sub), Bulgaria; 1987 v England (sub).
Sharp J (3) 1907 v Wales, England; 1908 v England.
Templeton RB (1) 1905 v Wales.
Ure JF (3) 1963 v Northern Ireland, Norway; 1967 v Northern Ireland.
Wilson RP (2) 1971 v Portugal, Holland.
Wood G (1) 1982 v Northern Ireland.

WALES

Barnes W (22) 1947 v England, Scotland; 1948 v Northern Ireland, Scotland, England; 1949 v Northern Ireland, England, Scotland, Belgium; 1950 v Northern Ireland, Scotland, England; 1951 v Northern Ireland, Portugal, England, Scotland, United Kingdom; 1952 v Northern Ireland; 1953 v England, Scotland; 1954 v Yugoslavia, Scotland.
Bowen DL (19) 1954 v Yugoslavia, Scotland; 1957 v Northern Ireland, Czechoslovakia, East Germany (twice), England, Scotland; 1958 v Israel (twice), Northern Ireland, Hungary (twice), Mexico, Sweden, Brazil, Scotland, England; 1959 v Northern Ireland.
Charles M (6) 1961 v Northern Ireland, Spain (twice), Hungary, England, Scotland.
Cumner RH (3) 1938 v England, Scotland; 1939 v Northern Ireland.
Daniel RW (12) 1950 v England, Northern Ireland, Portugal; 1951 v England, Scotland, United

Kingdom; 1952 v Northern Ireland, Scotland, England; 1953 v Northern Ireland, France, Yugoslavia.
Jenkyns CAL (1) 1896 v Scotland.
John RF (15) 1923 v Scotland, Northern Ireland; 1925 v Northern Ireland; 1926 v England; 1927 v England (twice); 1928 v Northern Ireland; 1929 v Scotland, England; 1931 v England; 1932 v Northern Ireland; 1933 v France; 1935 v Northern Ireland, Scotland; 1936 v England.
Jones B (7) 1938 v England, Scotland; 1939 v Northern Ireland; 1946 v Scotland; 1947 v Northern Ireland, England; 1948 v Scotland.
Jones C (4) 1929 v Scotland, England; 1931 v England; 1933 v France.
Jones LJ (4) 1937 v England; 1938 v Northern Ireland, England, Scotland.
Kelsey AJ (41) 1954 v Northern Ireland, Austria, Yugoslavia, Scotland; 1955 v Northern Ireland, England, Scotland, Austria; 1956 v Northern Ireland, Scotland, England; 1957 v Northern Ireland, Czechoslovakia (twice), East Germany, England, Scotland; 1958 v Israel (twice), Northern Ireland, Hungary (twice), Mexico, Sweden, Brazil, Scotland, England; 1959 v England, Scotland; 1960 v Northern Ireland, Scotland, England; 1961 v Northern Ireland, Spain (twice), Hungary, England, Scotland, 1962 v Northern Ireland, Brazil (twice).
Lewis D (3) 1927 v England; 1928 v Northern Ireland; 1929 v England.
Nicholas P (17) 1981 v Turkey, Scotland, England, USSR (twice), Czechoslovakia, Iceland; 1982 v Spain, England, Scotland, Northern Ireland, France, Yugoslavia; 1983 v Bulgaria, Scotland, Northern Ireland, Norway.
Roberts JG (7) 1971 v Scotland, England, Northern Ireland, Finland (twice); 1972 v England, Northern Ireland.
Tapscott DR (12) 1954 v Austria, Yugoslavia, Scotland, England; 1955 v Northern Ireland, England, Scotland, Austria; 1956 v Northern Ireland; 1957 v Northern Ireland, Czechoslovakia, East Germany.

NORTHERN IRELAND (and Ireland before 1924)

Dickson W (3) 1953 v England; 1954 v Wales, England.
Jennings PA (42) 1977 v Iceland, Holland, Belgium; 1978 v Republic of Ireland, Denmark; 1979 v Bulgaria (twice), England (thrice), Scotland, Wales, Denmark, Republic of Ireland; 1980 v Israel; 1981 v Scotland (thrice), Portugal, Sweden, Israel; 1982 v England, Wales, Yugoslavia, Honduras, Spain, France; 1983 v Albania, Scotland (twice), England, Wales, Austria, Turkey, West Germany; 1984 v Wales, Finland (twice), Romania; 1985 v England, Spain, Turkey.
Kennedy AL (2) 1923 Wales; 1924 v England.
McClelland J (5) 1960 v West Germany; 1961 v Wales, Italy, Greece, West Germany.
McCullough WJ (9) 1961 v Italy; 1963 v Spain (twice), Scotland, England; 1964 v Wales, Uruguay, England, Switzerland.
Mackie JA (1) 1923 v Wales.
Magill EJ (21) 1961 v Scotland, Greece, England; 1962 v Poland (twice), England, Scotland; 1963 v Wales, Spain (twice), Scotland, England; 1964 v Wales, Uruguay, England, Switzerland (twice), Scotland; 1965 v Holland, Albania, Scotland.
Morrow SJ (6) 1990 v Uruguay (sub), Austria (sub); 1991 v Poland, Yugoslavia, Faroe Islands; 1992 Scotland (sub).
Neill WJT (44) 1961 v Italy, Greece (twice), West Germany, Scotland, England; 1962 v Wales, England, Poland; 1963 v Wales, Spain (twice), Scotland, England; 1964 v Wales, Uruguay, England, Switzerland, Scotland; 1965 v Holland (twice), Wales, Albania (twice), Scotland, England; 1966 v Wales, West Germany, Mexico, Scotland; 1967 v Wales, Scotland, England; 1968 v Israel, Turkey (twice); 1969 v England (twice), Scotland (twice), Wales (twice), USSR (twice).
Nelson S (48) 1970 v England (sub), Wales, Spain; 1971 v Cyprus, England, Scotland, Wales, USSR (twice); 1972 v Spain, Scotland, England, Wales; 1973 v Bulgaria, Cyprus, Portugal; 1974 v Scotland, England, Sweden; 1975 v Yugoslavia, Sweden, Norway; 1976 v Israel, England, Belgium (sub); 1977 v West Germany, Wales, Iceland (twice), Holland, Belgium; 1978 v Wales (sub), Republic of Ireland, Denmark; 1979 v Bulgaria (twice), England (thrice), Scotland, Wales, Denmark, Republic of Ireland, 1980 v Israel; 1981 v Scotland (twice), Portugal, Sweden.
Rice PJ (49) 1968 v Israel; 1969 v USSR; 1971 v England, Scotland, Wales, USSR; 1972 v Spain, Scotland, England, Wales; 1973 v Bulgaria (twice), Cyprus, England, Scotland, Wales,

Portugal; 1974 v Scotland, England, Wales, Norway; 1975 v Yugoslavia (twice), England, Wales, Scotland, Sweden, Norway; 1976 v Israel, Scotland, England, Wales, Holland, Belgium; 1977 v West Germany, England, Scotland, Iceland (twice), Holland, Belgium; 1978 v Republic of Ireland, Denmark; 1979 v England (thrice), Scotland, Wales, Denmark.
Shanks T (2) 1903 v Scotland; 1904 v Wales.
Sloan JW (1) 1947 v Wales.
Toner J (6) 1922 v Wales; 1923 v Wales, England; 1924 v Wales, England; 1925 v Scotland.

REPUBLIC OF IRELAND

Brady WL (26) 1974 v USSR, Turkey; 1975 v Switzerland (twice), USSR, Turkey; 1976 v Norway, Poland, England, Turkey, France; 1977 v France, Spain, Bulgaria (twice); 1978 v Norway, Northern Ireland, England; 1979 v Denmark, Bulgaria (twice), West Germany, Argentina, Wales; 1980 v England, Cyprus.
Devine JA (7) 1979 v Czechoslovakia, Northern Ireland; 1981 v Czechoslovakia, Holland; 1982 v Algeria, Spain; 1983 v Malta.
Dunne J (3) 1936 v Switzerland, Hungary, Luxembourg.
Haverty J(15) 1956 v Holland, Denmark, West Germany; 1957 v Denmark, England (twice); 1958 v Poland (twice), Austria; 1959 v Sweden; 1960 v Chile, Wales, Norway; 1961 v Scotland (twice).
Mancini TJ (1) 1974 v USSR.
O'Flanagan KP (3) 1946 v England; 1947 v Spain, Portugal.
O'Leary DA (64) 1976 v England, France; 1977 v France, Spain, Bulgaria (twice); 1978 v Norway, Denmark, England; 1979 v Bulgaria (twice), West Germany, Argentina, Wales, Northern Ireland; 1980 v England, Cyprus, Holland; 1981 v Czechoslovakia, Poland, Holland, France; 1982 v Holland, Iceland; 1983 v Spain; 1984 v Poland, Israel, China, USSR, Norway, Denmark; 1985 v Israel, England (sub), Norway, Spain, Switzerland (twice), USSR, Denmark; 1986 v Wales; 1988 v Spain; 1989 v Malta (twice), Hungary, West Germany, Northern Ireland (sub); 1990 v Wales (sub), USSR, Finland, Romania (sub), Turkey (twice), Malta, Morocco, England; 1991 v England, Poland (twice), Chile, Hungary, Turkey; 1992 v Wales, Switzerland, USA.
Quinn NJ (13) 1986 v Iceland (sub), Czechoslovakia; 1987 v Bulgaria (2 sub), Luxembourg (sub), Israel, 1988 v Romania (sub), Poland (sub), Norway (sub), England (sub), Tunisia (sub), Spain (sub); 1989 v Hungary (sub).
Scully PJ (1) 1988 v Tunisia (sub).
Sloan JW (2) 1946 v Portugal, Spain.
Stapleton FA (24) 1976 v Turkey, France; 1977 v Spain, Bulgaria (twice); 1978 v Norway, Denmark, Northern Ireland, England (sub); 1979 v Denmark, West Germany, Argentina, Wales, Bulgaria, Northern Ireland; 1980 v England, Cyprus (twice), Holland, Belgium, France; 1981 v Belgium, Czechoslovakia, Poland.

OTHERS

S.Jonsson (Iceland) and **A.E.Limpar (Sweden)** have also represented their countries in international matches whilst with Arsenal.

ENGLAND 'B'

Adams TA (4) 1989 v Italy, Yugoslavia; 1990 v Republic of Ireland, Czechoslovakia.
Campbell KJ (1) 1991 v Spain.
Davis PV (1) 1991 v Wales.
Dixon LM (4) 1989 v Italy, Yugoslavia; 1990 v Republic of Ireland; 1992 v CIS.
Lewis R (2) 1950 v Italy, Luxembourg.
Lishman DJ (1) 1953 v Scotland.
Merson PC (2) 1991 v Spain; 1992 v France.
Rix G (3) 1979 v Austria, New Zealand; 1981 v Spain.
Rocastle D (2) 1991 v Spain; 1992 v CIS.
Roper DGB (1) 1953 v Scotland.

Scott L (4) 1950 v Switzerland, Italy, Holland, Luxembourg.
Seaman DA (3) 1991 v Spain; 1992 v France, CIS.
Smith AM (4) 1990 v Czechoslovakia, Algeria; 1992 v Czechoslovakia, CIS.
Sunderland A (7) 1978 v West Germany (sub), Czechoslovakia; 1979 v New Zealand; 1980 v Spain, USA; Australia; 1981 v Spain.
Talbot BE (2) 1979 v New Zealand; 1980 v USA.
Thomas ML (4) 1989 v Italy; 1990 v Czechoslovakia (sub), Algeria (sub); 1991 v Wales.
Winterburn N (3) 1990 v Republic of Ireland, Czechoslovakia; 1991 v Spain.
Wright IE (1) 1992 v France.

NORTHERN IRELAND 'B'

McCullough WJ (1) 1959 v France.
Morrow SJ Details not to hand.

REPUBLIC OF IRELAND 'B'

Scully PJ (1) 1990 v England.

UNDER-23

ENGLAND
Armstrong G (5) 1965 v Czechoslovakia, West Germany, Austria, Yugoslavia; 1966 v Turkey.
Baker JH (1) 1963 v Yugoslavia.
Barnwell J (1) 1961 v West Germany.
Blockley JP (4) 1973 v Scotland, Denmark, Holland, Czechoslovakia.
Bloomfield JH (2) 1956 v Denmark; 1957 v Bulgaria.
Dodgin W (1) 1954 v Italy.
George FC (5) 1972 v Wales; 1973 v Holland, Czechoslovakia, Poland, Denmark.
Groves VG (1) 1956 v France.
Kennedy R (6) 1972 v Wales; 1973 v Holland (twice, plus 1 sub), Denmark, Czechoslovakia (sub), Poland.
Radford J (4) 1968 v Wales, Holland; 1969 v Holland, Portugal.
Sammels JC (9) 1966 v Wales; 1967 v Austria, Greece, Bulgaria, Turkey, Italy; 1968 v Italy, Hungary, West Germany.

SCOTLAND
Kelly EP (3) 1971 v England, Wales; 1974 v Wales.
Marinello P (1) 1970 v England (sub).

WALES
Griffiths AT (2) 1961 v England (sub); 1962 v Northern Ireland.
Roberts JG (1) 1969 v England.
Walley JT (2) 1966 v England; 1967 v Northern Ireland.

NORTHERN IRELAND
Clarke FRG (4) 1962, 1963, 1964, 1965 v Wales.
Magill EJ (1) 1962 v Wales.
Neill WJT (4) 1962, 1963, 1964, 1965 v Wales.
Nelson S (1) 1969 v Italy.
Rice PJ (2) 1968 v Wales; 1969 v Italy.

UNDER-21

ENGLAND
Adams TA (5) 1985 v Republic of Ireland, Finland; 1986 v Denmark, Sweden, Yugoslavia.

Caesar GC (3) 1987 v Morocco, USSR (sub), France.
Campbell KJ (4) 1990 v Hungary; 1991 v Turkey (twice, 1 sub), Germany.
Coton TS (4) 1984 v France (twice), Italy (twice).
Davis PV (11) 1982 v Poland, Scotland, Denmark, Greece; 1983 v Greece (sub), Hungary (sub); 1987 v Turkey (twice), West Germany, Yugoslavia; 1988 v France.
Hayes M (3) 1987 v Spain, Turkey; 1988 v France (sub).
Hillier D (1) 1991 v Turkey.
Merson PC (4) 1988 v Denmark; 1989 v Greece, Poland (twice, including 1 sub).
Miller AJ (4) 1988 v Morocco (sub); 1989 v Senegal; 1990 v Hungary, Poland.
Rix G (7) 1977 v Finland (sub); 1978 v Yugoslavia, Denmark; 1979 v Sweden, Denmark (sub); 1980 v Bulgaria; 1980 v Scotland.
Robson SI (6) 1984 v Italy, Finland; 1985 v Israel, Finland, Romania; 1986 v Italy.
Rocastle D (14) 1986 v Sweden, Yugoslavia; 1987 v Spain, Turkey (twice), West Germany, Yugoslavia; 1988 v Scotland (twice), France (twice), Mexico, USSR, Morocco.
Thomas ML (12) 1987 v Yugoslavia; 1988 v Scotland, France (twice), Mexico, USSR, Morocco; 1989 v Greece, Albania (twice), Poland, Sweden.
Whyte CA (4) 1982 v Scotland (plus 1 sub), Denmark, Greece.

SCOTLAND
Nicholas C (1) 1984 v Yugoslavia.
Ross TW (1) 1977 v Wales.
Will JA (1) 1992 v Denmark (sub).

WALES
Nicholas P (1) 1982 v France.
Wilmot RJ (6) 1981 v France; 1982 v France, Norway, Yugoslavia, Holland; 1983 v Yugoslavia.

NORTHERN IRELAND
Morrow SJ Details not to hand.

REPUBLIC OF IRELAND
Ampadu K (2) 1990 v Malta, Turkey.
Scully PJ (5) 1989 v England; 1990 v Malta, England, Turkey; 1991 v England.

YOUTH INTERNATIONALS
ENGLAND
T.A.Adams, T.K.Anderson, G.Armstrong, D.R.Bacuzzi, J.Barnwell, D.Bennett, D.M.Bennett, R.Bloomfield, D.P.Clapton, A.A.Cole, D.A.Dodson, D.J.Donaldson, D.Esqulant, R.Feist, M.M.Flatts, K.A.Fowler, C.J.Hartfield, N.A.Heaney, D.Heard, B.G.Hornsby, C.R.Hoyle, G.W.Johnson, M.N.A.Joseph, M.R.Keown, T.Lee, A.Marriott, B.J.McDermott, G.McKeown, P.C.Merson, K.W.Nicholas, J.O'Rourke, N.C.I.Rust, J.W.F.J.Petts, R.F.Powling, D.J.Price, D.Ridley, S.I.Robson, J.C.Sammels, J.Sanchez, R.E.Saxby, R.G.Smithson, M.L.Thomas, K.D.Webster, M.W.Webster, R.H.Whittaker.

SCOTLAND
D.Connelly, G.R.R.Cumming, P.Dickov, E.P.Kelly, N.Leven, S.Marshall, J.A.Will, J.Woodward.

WALES
P.Davies, C.Evans, C.H.Newton, B.Vassallo, R.J.Wilmot.

REPUBLIC OF IRELAND
K.Ampadu, J.P.G.Bacon, W.L.Brady, G.Campbell, J.A.Devine, P.Dolan, D.Drummy, R.Duffy, P.A.Gorman, P.J.Scully, F.A.Stapleton.

NORTHERN IRELAND
A.J.Hannigan, S.Morrow.

TOP APPEARANCES

LEAGUE

1. D.O'Leary 517/30
2. G.Armstrong 490/10
3. R.John 421
4. P.Rice 391/6
5. E.Hapgood 393
6. P.Storey 387/4
7. J.Radford 375/4
8. P.Simpson 353/17
9. G.Rix 338/13
10. C.Bastin 350
11. J.Hulme 333
12. J.Kelsey 327
13. P.Sands 327
14. P.Davis 301/18
15. W.Blyth 314
16. K.Sansom 314
17. F.McLintock 312/2
18. R.McEachrane 313
19. A.Baker 310
20. Joe Shaw 309

FA CUP

P.Rice 67
D.O'Leary 65/1
G.Armstrong 58/2
P.Simpson 53
P.Storey 49/2
R.John 46
J.Radford 42/2
G.Rix 42/2
C.Bastin 42
A.Baker 41
E.Hapgood 41
J.Hulme 39
R.McNab 39
P.Jennings 38
F.McLintock 36
H.Roberts 36
S.Nelson 33/2
L.Brady 31/4
T.Parker 34
A.Sunderland 34

LEAGUE CUP

1. D.O'Leary 66/2
2. K.Sansom 48
3. G.Rix 45/2
4. P.Davis 41/3
5. P.Storey 36/1
6. P.Rice 36
7. G.Armstrong 35
8. F.McLintock 34
9. J.Radford 34
10. T.Adams 33/1
11. D.Rocastle 32/1
12. P.Simpson 32/1
13. P.Jennings 32
14. J.Lukic 32
15. G.Graham 27/2
16. S.Nelson 27
17. R.McNab 26/1
18. F.Stapleton 26/1
19. B.Talbot 26/1
20. A.Sunderland 26
    P.Groves 18/8

EUROPE

P.Rice 26/1
G.Armstrong 24/2
G.Graham 23/2
J.Radford 24
R.Wilson 24
P.Storey 22
D.O'Leary 21
G.Rix 21
R.McNab 20/1
P.Simpson 20/1
S.Nelson 19/2
P.Jennings 19
F.McLintock 19
W.Young 18
C.George 15/1
R.Kennedy 14/2
J.Sammels 15
F.Stapleton 15
B.Talbot 15
E.Kelly 13/2

TOTAL

1. D.O'Leary 669/33
2. G.Armstrong 607/14
3. P.Rice 520/7
4. P.Storey 494/7
5. J.Radford 475/6
6. P.Simpson 458/19
7. R.John 467
8. G.Rix 446/17
9. E.Hapgood 434
10. F.McLintock 401/2
11. P.Davis 394
12. K.Sansom 394
13. C.Bastin 392
14. J.Hulme 372
15. R.McNab 362/3
16. J.Kelsey 351
17. A.Baker 350
18. P.Sands 350
19. R.McEachrane 346
20. W.Blyth 343

David O'Leary

TOP GOALSCORERS

LEAGUE
1. C.Bastin 150
2. J.Brain.............................125
3. D.Lishman 125
4. E.Drake 124
5. D.Jack..............................113
6. J.Radford 111
7. J.Hulme 107
8. R.Lewis.............................103
9. J.Lambert............................98
10. D.Herd 97
11. J.Baker 93
12. D.Roper 88
13. C.Holton.............................83
14. J.Coleman 79
15. A.M.Smith 78
16. F.Stapleton 75
17. G.Strong.............................69
18. J.Logie 68
19. R.Rooke 68
20. D.Tapscott...........................62

FA CUP
C.Bastin 26
J.Hulme 17
A.Sunderland...........................16
J.Radford 15
F.Stapleton 15
J.Brain................................14
R.Lewis................................13
E.Drake................................12
Jas Henderson 12
C.George...............................11
J.Lambert..............................11
G.Armstrong 10
D.Herd 10
D.Jack 10
D.Lishman 10
M.Macdonald 10
C.Nicholas 10
A.Elliott...............................9
C.Booth.................................8
J.Logie.................................8

LEAGUE CUP
1. F.Stapleton 14
2. A.Sunderland..........................13
3. J.Radford............................12
4. A.M.Smith 12
5. L.Brady..............................10
6. C.Nicholas 10
7. G.Graham 9
8. P.Groves 6
9. D.Rocastle 6
10. M.Hayes 5
11. D.Jenkins 5
12. M.Macdonald..........................5
13. P.Merson 5
14. M.Thomas 5
15. A.Woodcock 5
16. T.Baldwin 4
17. P.Davis 4
18. R.Kennedy 4
19. F.McLintock 4
20. N.Quinn..............................4

EUROPE
J.Radford..............................11
R.Kennedy...............................8
G.Graham 7
J.Sammels 7
A.Sunderland 7
C.George................................5
L.Brady.................................4
A.M.Smith...............................4
F.Stapleton 4
W.Young.................................4
J.Baker.................................3
G.Armstrong.............................2
L.Chapman 2
E.Kelly.................................2
D.Price.................................2
P.Storey................................2

TOTAL
1. C.Bastin 176
2. J.Radford 149
3. J.Brain.............................139
4. E.Drake 136
5. D.Lishman 135
6. J.Hulme 124
7. D.Jack..............................123
8. R.Lewis.............................116
9. J.Lambert 109
10. F.Stapleton 108
11. D.Herd 107
12. J.Baker 100
13. A.M.Smith 98
14. D.Roper 95
15. A.Sunderland 91
16. C.Holton............................88
17. J.Coleman 84
18. G.Graham 77
19. G.Strong............................77
20. J.Logie.............................76

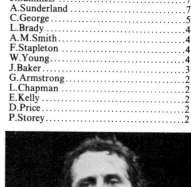

John Radford

Cliff Bastin

Alex James

Frank McLintock shows off the Fairs Cup in May 1970, accompanied by the Mayor of Islington.

Charlie Buchan (left) shakes hands with Tottenham's Arthur Grimsdell before the opening game of the 1925-6 season between the two North London rivals.